THE PRACTICAL ENCYCLOPEDIA OF

WATERCOLOUR

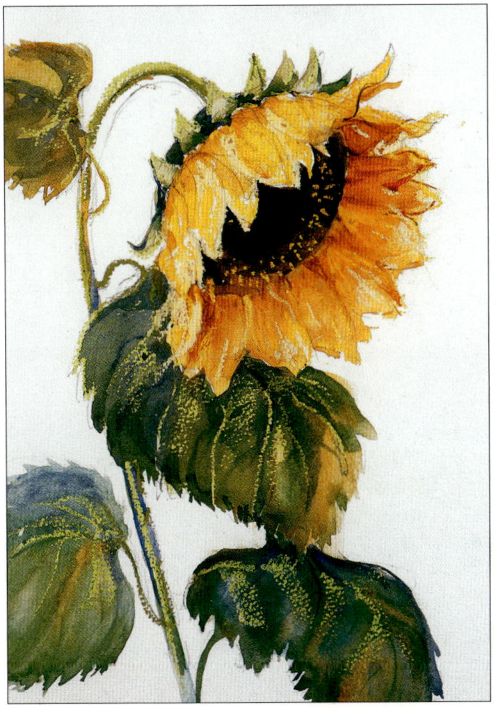

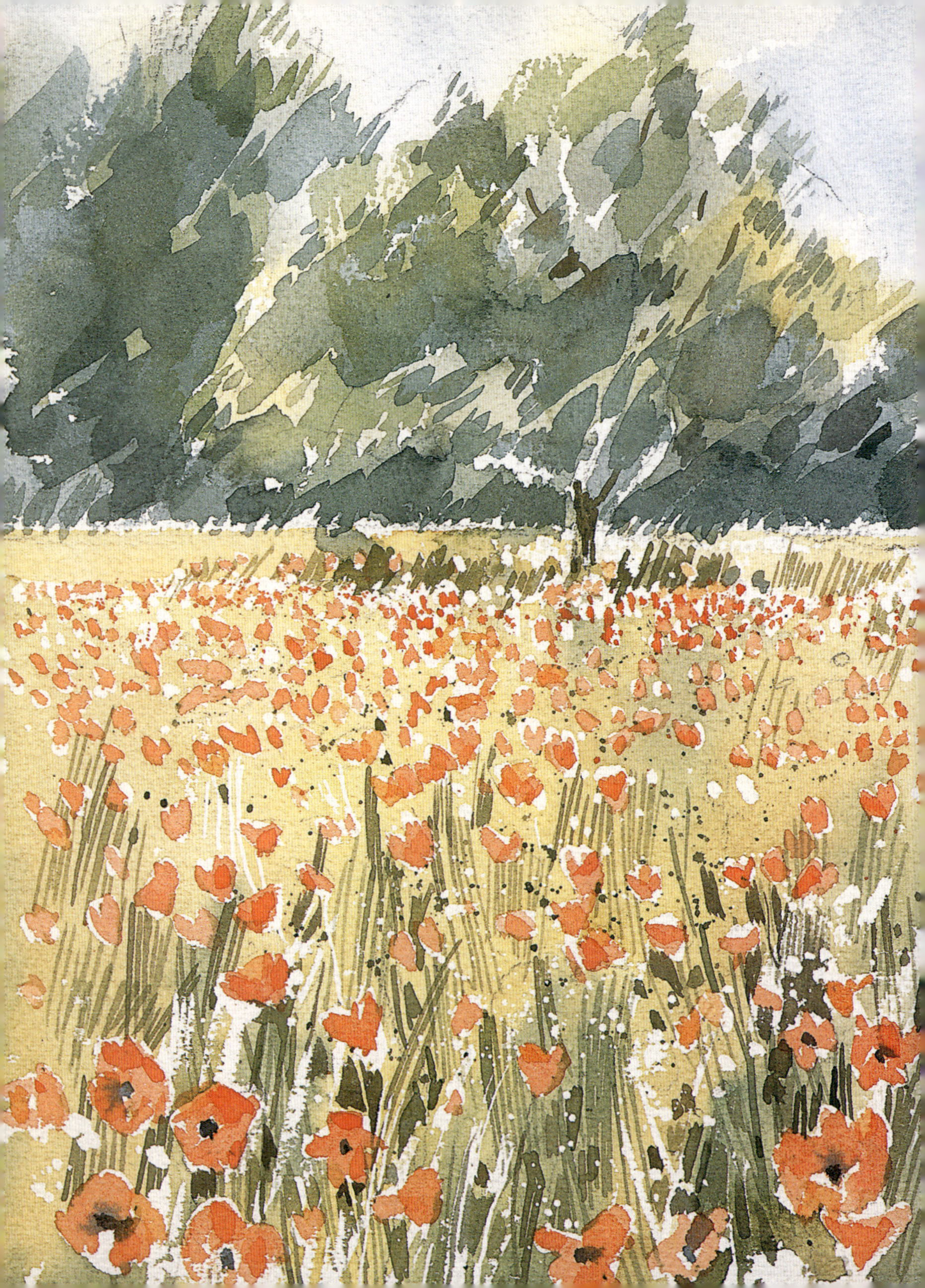

THE PRACTICAL ENCYCLOPEDIA OF WATERCOLOUR

mixing paint • brush strokes • gouache • masking out • glazing • wet into wet drybrush painting • washes • using resists • sponging • light to dark • sgraffito

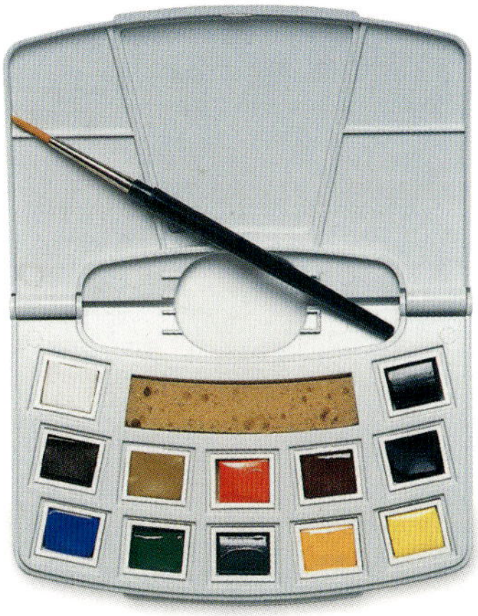

WENDY JELBERT & IAN SIDAWAY

HERMES HOUSE

This edition is published by Hermes House

Hermes House is an imprint of
Anness Publishing Ltd
Hermes House,
88–89 Blackfriars Road,
London SE1 8HA
tel. 020 7401 2077;
fax 020 7633 9499
www.hermeshouse.com;
www.annesspublishing.com

A CIP catalogue record for this book is available from the British Library.

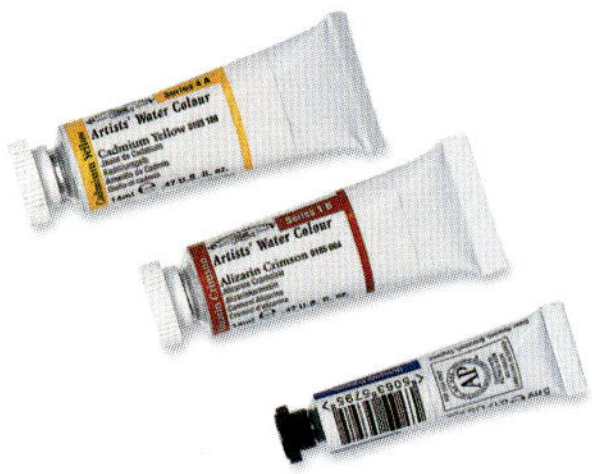

Publisher: Joanna Lorenz
Managing Editor: Judith Simons
Senior Editor: Sarah Ainley
Consultant Editor: Sarah Hoggett
Photographers: George Taylor and Nigel Cheffers-Heard
Designer: Nigel Partridge
Illustrator: Ian Sidaway
Project contributors: Ray Balkwill, Diana Constance, Joe Francis Dowden, Paul Dyson, Abigail Edgar, Wendy Jelbert, Melvyn Petterson, Paul Robinson, Ian Sidaway, Albany Wiseman
Editorial Reader: Jay Thundercliffe
Production Controller: Don Campaiello

1 3 5 7 9 10 8 6 4 2

Contents

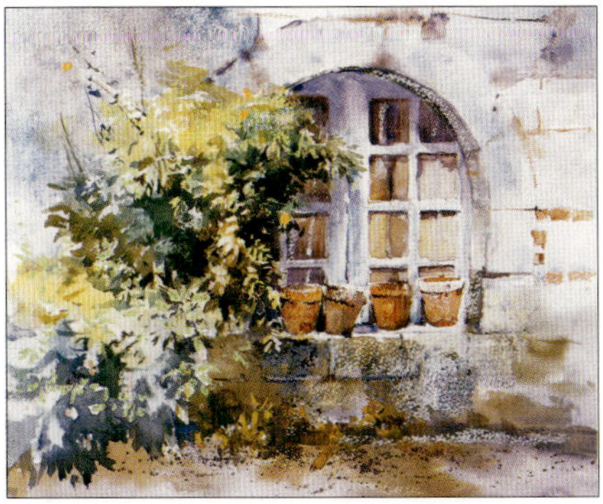

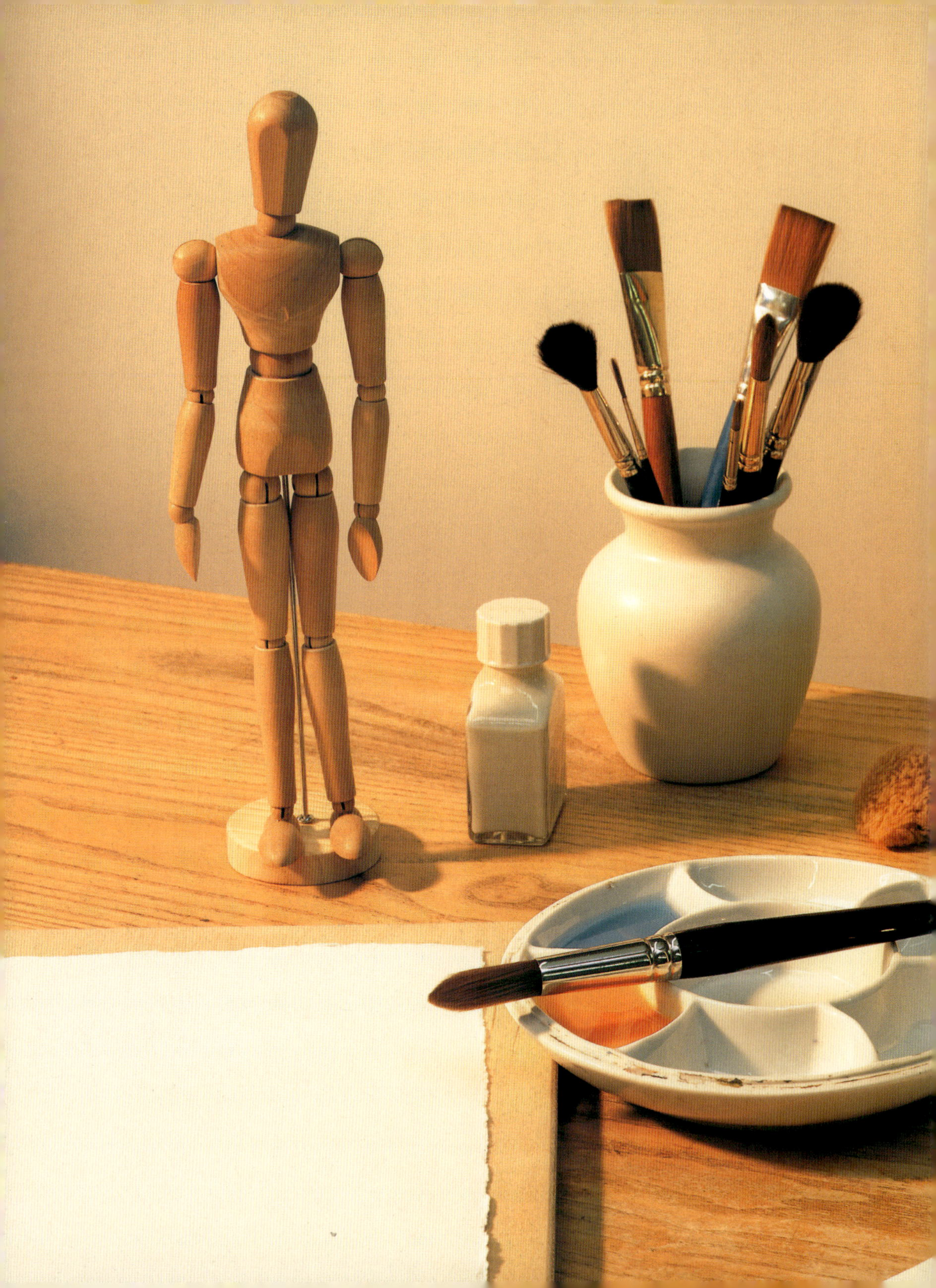

Getting Started in Watercolour

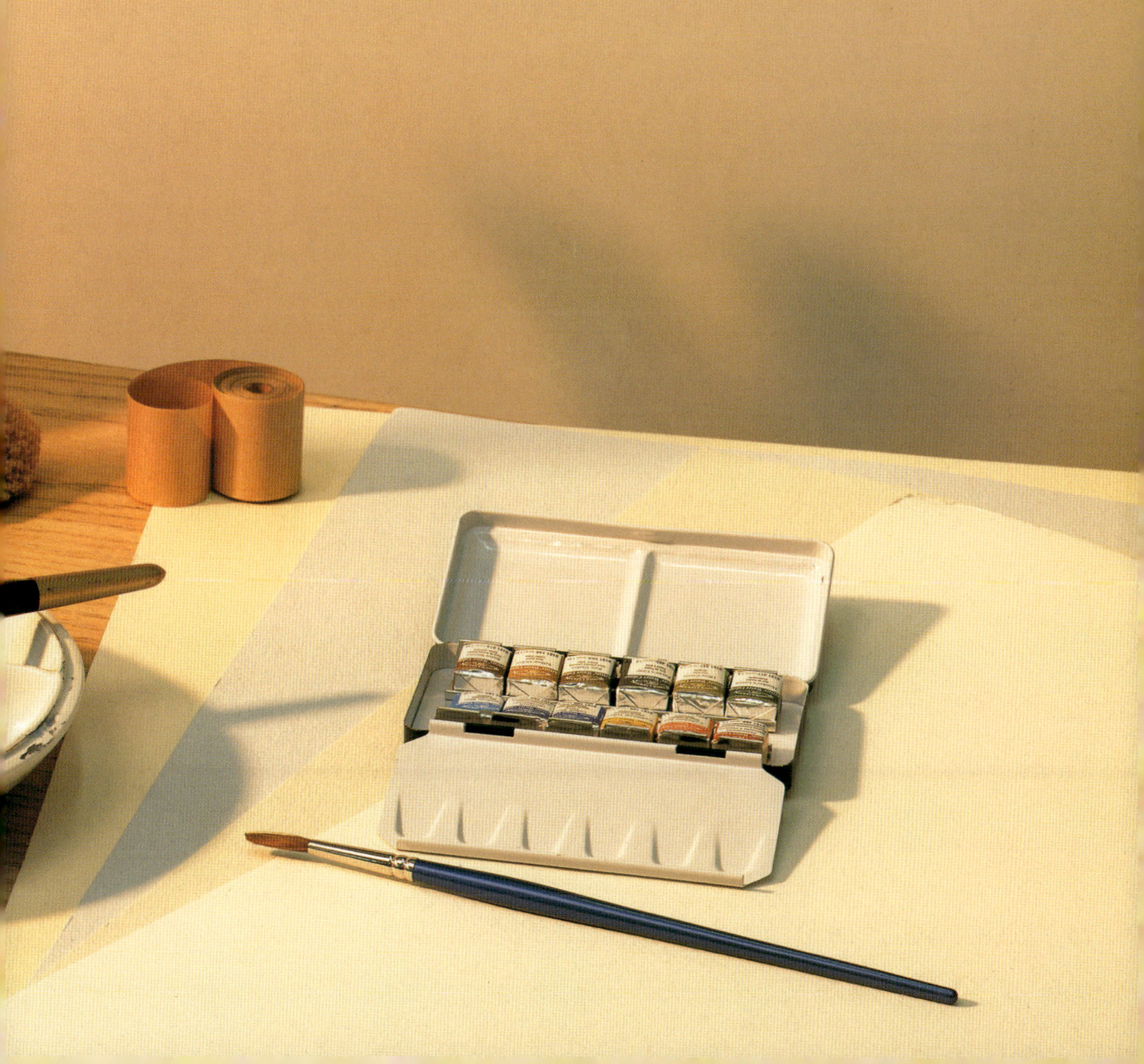

Paints

Watercolour paints are available in two main forms: pans, which are compressed blocks of colour that need to be brushed with water in order to release the colour, and tubes of moist paint. The same finely powdered pigments bound with gum-arabic solution are used to make both types. The pigments provide the colour, while the gum arabic allows the paint to adhere to the paper surface, even when highly diluted with water.

Both pans and tubes can be bought in sets or singly. Pans are available as full pans and half pans, the only difference is size. If there are certain colours that you use only infrequently, buy half pans. Tubes range in size from 5–20ml (0.17–0.66 fl oz).

It is a matter of personal preference whether you use pans or tubes. The advantage of pans is that they can be slotted into a paintbox, making them easily portable, and this is something to consider if you often paint on location. Tubes, on the other hand, are often better if you need to make a large amount of colour for a wash, although it is easy to squeeze out more paint than you need, which is wasteful. You also need to remember to replace the caps of tube colours immediately, otherwise the paint will harden and become unuseable.

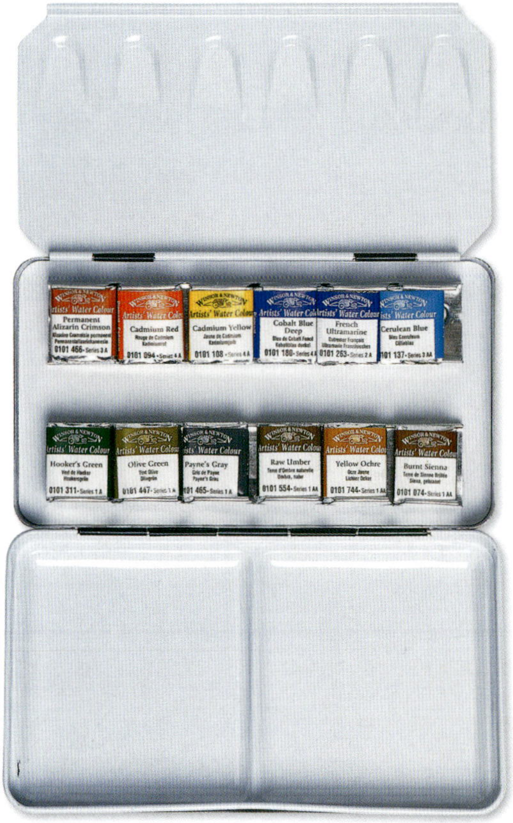

◄ Paintbox
You can buy paintboxes that are already filled with a selection of colours, or empty boxes that you then fill with colours of your own choice. The model shown here is for pans of paint, but you can also buy ones with spaces for tube colours.

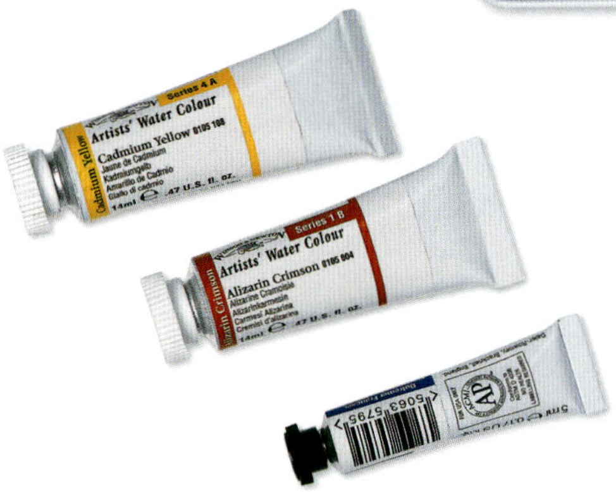

Tubes ▲
Tubes of watercolour paint are available in different sizes. It is worth buying the larger sizes for colours that you think you will use frequently.

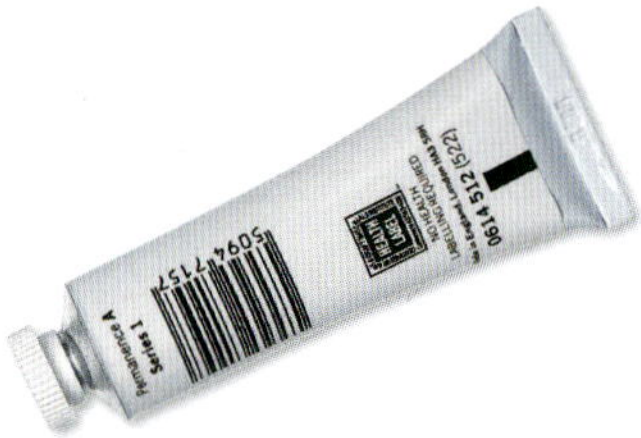

Gouache paint ▲
This is a kind of water-based paint. Unlike pure watercolour, it is opaque, although the techniques and equipment used for gouache are similar to those used for watercolour. White gouache, in particular, is often used in conjunction with pure watercolour, both to add small highlights and to mix with watercolour to make pale, opaque colours.

Palettes

Even if you usually mix colours in the lid of your paintbox, it is useful to have one or two separate palettes as well, particularly when you want to mix a large quantity of a wash. There are several shapes and sizes available, but two of the most common are the segmented round palette and the slanted-well tile.

Palettes are made from white ceramic or plastic. Although plastic is lightweight, which is an advantage when you need to carry your materials for painting on location, it is also slightly porous and will become stained over time.

For an inexpensive alternative, look out for white china saucers and plates in charity shops or jumble (rummage) sales. They must be white, as you would be able to see any other colour through the transparent paint, which would make it difficult to judge the colour or tone being mixed. Old teacups and bowls are good if you need to mix large quantities.

Pigment does settle, so remember to stir the wash in your palette from time to time to ensure that it is evenly dispersed. Always wash your palette thoroughly after use to prevent dried paint residue from muddying subsequent mixes.

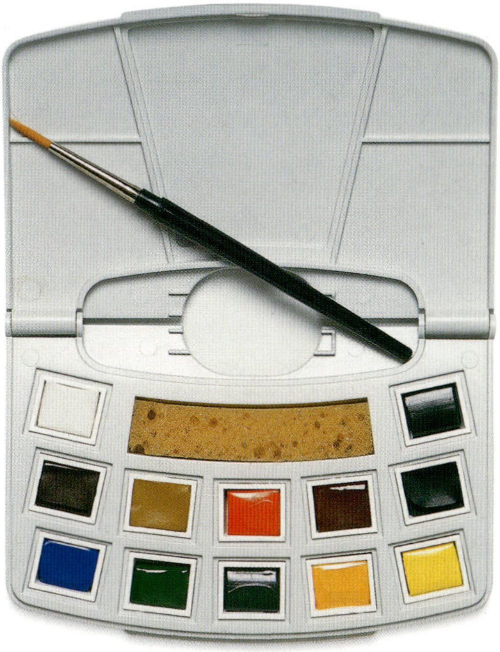

Field box ▲
Most of the major manufacturers sell field boxes specifically for use on location, which include a small brush and perhaps a sponge as well as a selection of paints.

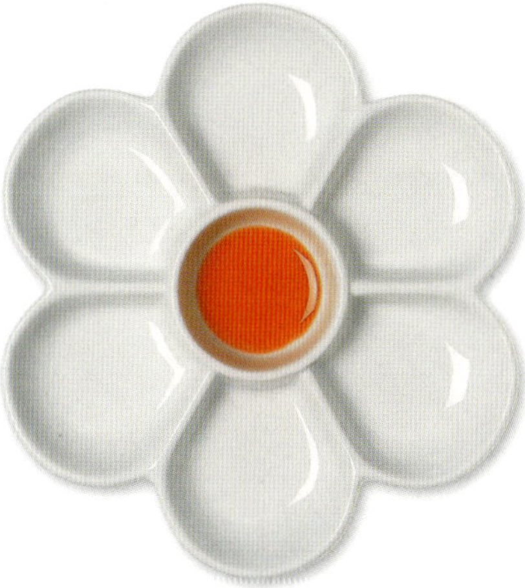

◄ Segmented round palette
This kind of palette, which is sometimes referred to as a chrysanthemum palette because of its flower-like shape, has deep wells that are perfect for mixing large washes.

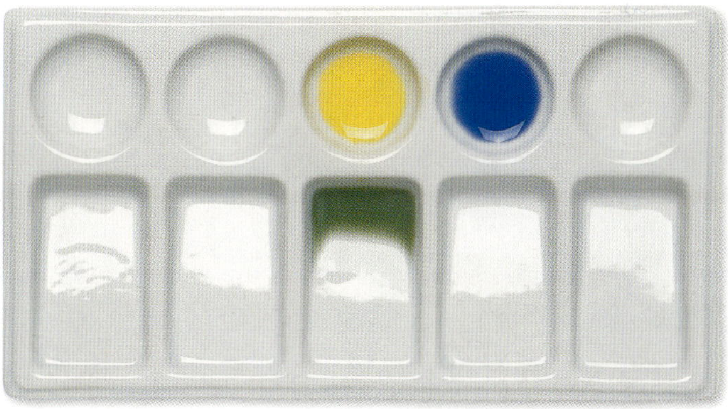

◄ Slanted-well tile palette
This type of palette is useful for mixing two or more colours together: place each colour in one of the round wells at one end of the palette and transfer a little on your brush to one of the flat, slightly sloping sections.

Grades of paint

There are two grades of watercolour paint: artists' and students' quality. Artists' quality paints are the more expensive, because they contain a high proportion of good-quality pigments. Students' quality paints contain less pure pigment and more fillers, and are usually available in a smaller range of colours than artists' quality paints.

If you come across the word "hue" in a paint name, it indicates that the paint contains cheaper alternatives to the real pigment. Generally speaking, you get what you pay for: artists' quality paints tend to produce more subtle mixtures of colours.

The other thing that you need to think about when buying paints is their permanence. The label or the manufacturer's catalogue should give you the permanency rating. In the United Kingdom, the permanency ratings are class AA (extremely permanent), class A (durable), class B (moderate) and class C (fugitive). The ASTM (American Society for Testing and Materials) codes for lightfastness are ASTM I (excellent), ASTM II (very good), and ASTM III (not sufficiently lightfast).

Some pigments, such as alizarin crimson and viridian, stain more than others: they penetrate the fibres of the paper and cannot be removed.

Finally, although we always think of watercolour as being transparent, you should be aware that some pigments are actually slightly opaque and will impart a degree of opacity to any colours with which they are mixed. These so-called opaque pigments include all the cadmium colours and cerulean blue.

Characteristics of paint ▼
Different pigments have different characteristics. The only way to learn about them is to use them and see how they behave, both singly and in combination with other colours. The chart below shows the characteristics of some of the most popular watercolour paints.

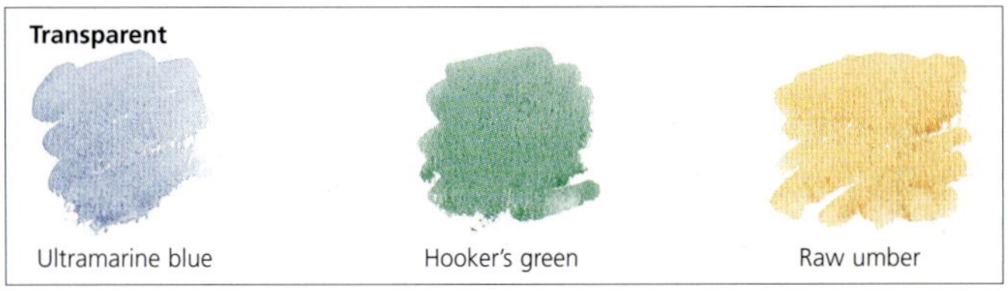

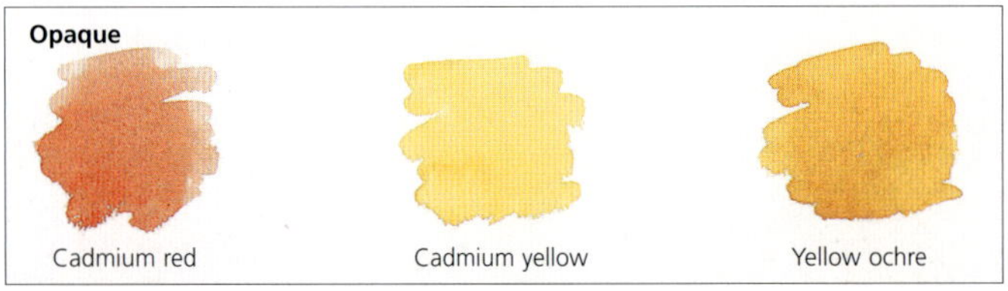

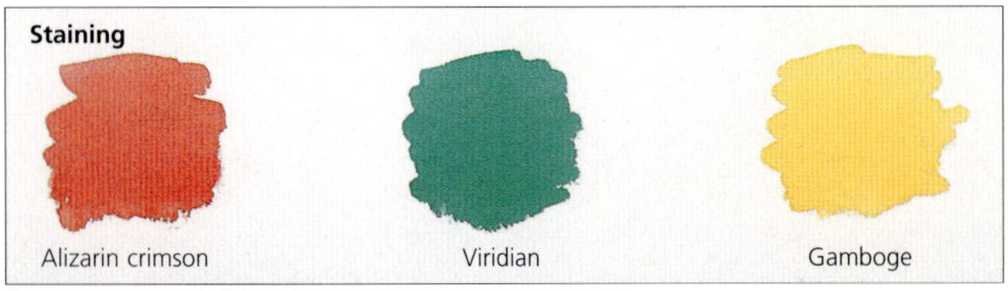

Judging colours

It is not always possible to judge the colour of paints simply by looking at the pans in your palette, as they often look dark. In fact, it is very easy to dip your brush into the wrong pan by mistake, so always check before you apply the brush to the paper.

Even when you have mixed a wash in your palette, appearances can be deceptive, as watercolour paint always looks lighter when it is dry. The only way to be sure what colour or tone you have mixed is to apply it to paper and let it dry. It is always best to build up tones gradually until you get the effect you want. The more you practise, the better you will get at anticipating results.

Appearances can be deceptive ▼
These two pans look very dark, almost black. In fact, one is Payne's grey and the other a bright ultramarine blue.

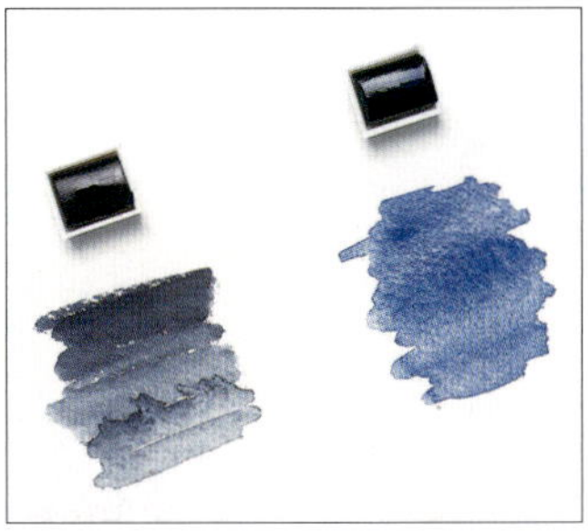

Test your colours ▼
Keep a piece of scrap paper next to you as you work so that you can test your colour mixes before you apply them to your painting.

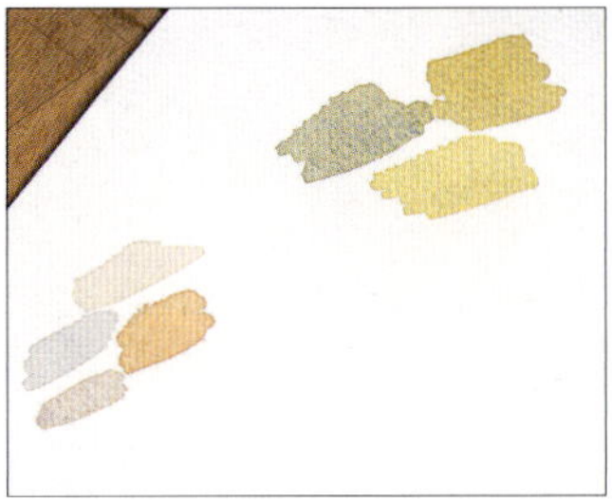

What colours to choose?

With so many colours to choose from (some manufacturers offer as many as 100 artists' quality paints and up to 50 students' quality), how do you decide which ones to buy?

Although art supply stores and catalogues contain rainbow-like selections of every colour imaginable, the most important thing to realize is that you don't need to buy a huge range. You might choose to produce a painting entirely from ready-made colours, but learning how to mix your own will give you far more scope and is far more economical.

Some artists choose to work with a very limited palette of as few as five or six colours, creating astonishingly subtle variations in hue and tone in the process. Start with a few colours and learn as much as you can about them before you add to your range. In practice, most people find that a range of 12–20 colours enables them to mix pretty much anything that they could wish for.

As you gain more experience, you will probably find that you discard certain colours in favour of others: this is all part of the learning process. Set aside some time to experiment and see how many colours and tones you can create by mixing two, or even three, colours together.

Above all, keep a note of any mixes that you particularly like, or find useful for certain subjects (such as trees, skies or water) so that you can recreate them in the future. Remember, however, that the more colours you combine, the more risk there is that the resultant mixes will look muddy and dull: one of the received wisdoms in pure watercolour painting is that you should not mix more than three colours together at any one time.

As always, your exact choice of colours is largely a matter of personal preference, but a good "starter palette" should contain at least one of each of the three primary colours (red, yellow and blue); in fact, it's helpful to have one blue with a warm bias, such as ultramarine blue, and one that is slightly cooler, such as cerulean. Earth pigments such as raw and burnt umber and raw and burnt sienna are useful for mixing neutral browns and greys. Although you can mix your own greens, versatile ready-mixed greens include viridian, Hooker's green and sap green. Payne's grey is a good colour to mix with other colours for cast shadows.

Suggested starter palette ▼
The palette shown below is a versatile selection of colours that will enable you to create a wide range of mixes.

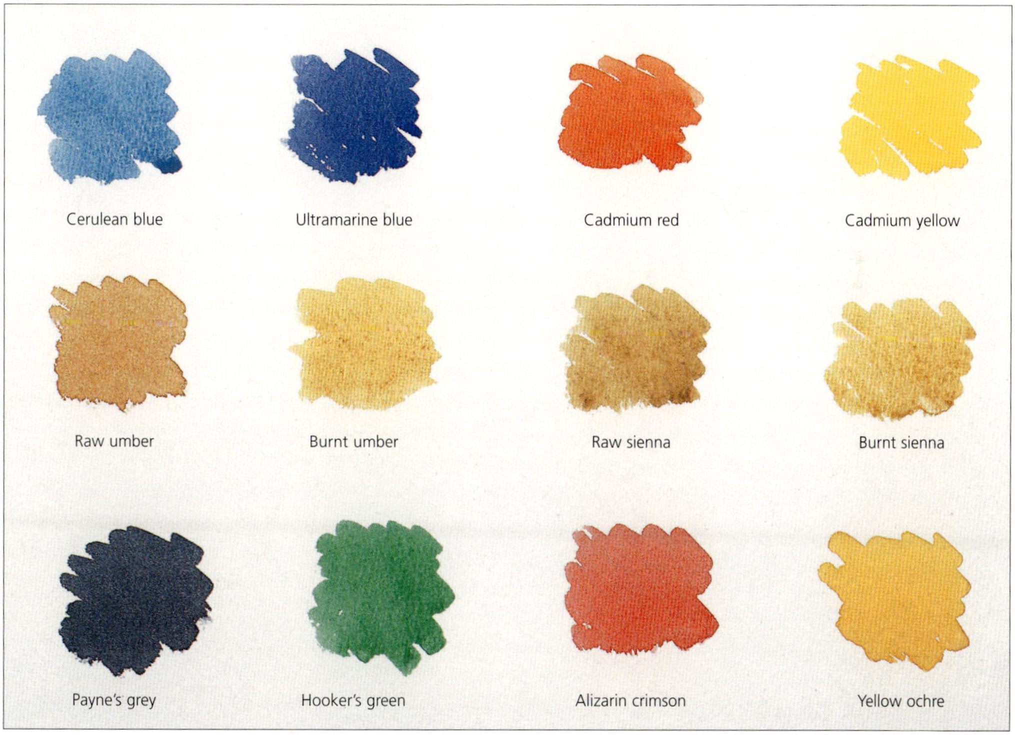

Papers

There are three main types of watercolour paper: hot-pressed (HP), NOT, and rough. Hot-pressed paper is best for drawing and detailed work; it is very smooth to the touch. NOT surface, meaning not hot-pressed (cold-pressed), has a slight texture. Rough paper has a prominent "tooth"; when a wash is laid over it, some of the deep cavities are left unfilled, giving a sparkle to the painting. The best papers are handmade from pure linen rag and the quality is reflected in the price.

Good-quality paper has a right and a wrong side. The right side is coated with size, which is receptive to watercolour applications. To find out which side to use, hold the paper up to the light and look for the water mark on the right side.

Watercolour paper is available in rolls, sheets, and pads and blocks of various sizes. Pads are either spiral bound or glued; blocks are glued on all sides to keep the paper flat until you need to remove a sheet. Pads and blocks are more practical for location work and quick sketches.

Tinted papers ▼

Tinted papers are sometimes frowned upon by purists, but there are times when you want to establish an overall colour key; these ready-made tinted papers are a good alternative to laying an initial flat wash.

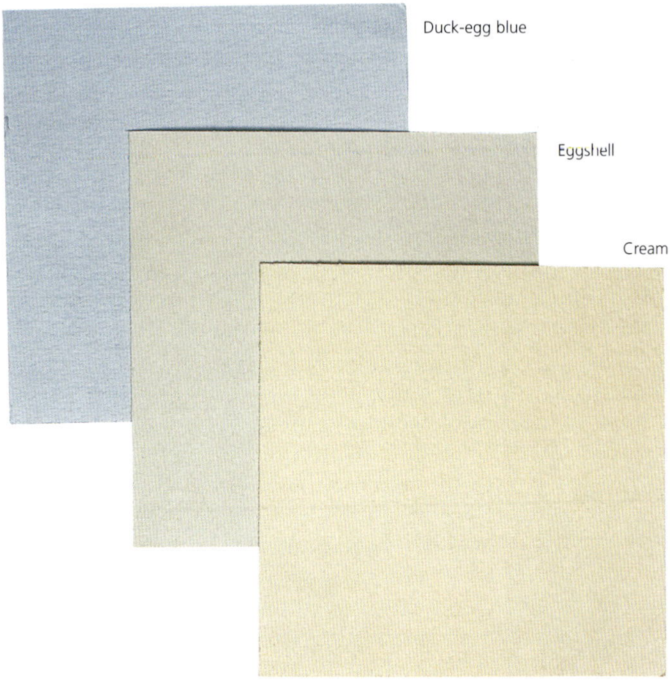

Duck-egg blue

Eggshell

Cream

Types of paper ▼

From left to right: hot-pressed (HP), NOT and rough watercolour papers. Hot-pressed paper has a very smooth surface, while the other two are progressively more textured.

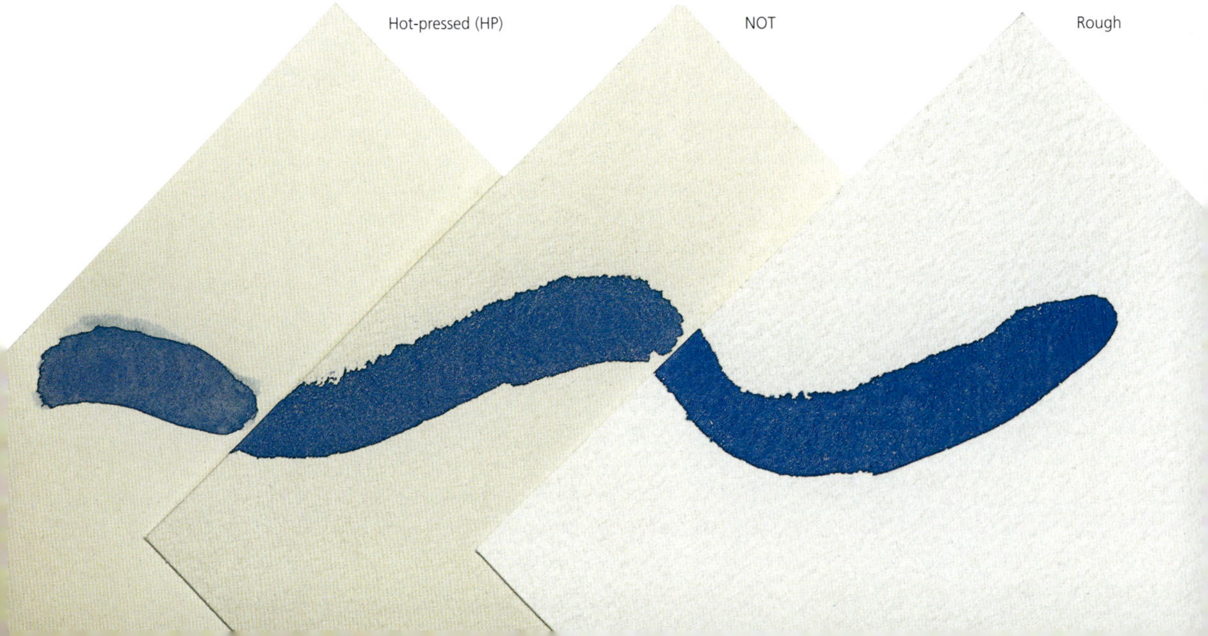

Hot-pressed (HP)

NOT

Rough

Stretching paper

Papers come in different weights. The weight refers to the weight of a ream (500 sheets) and can vary from 90lb (185 grams per square metre or gsm) for lightweight papers to 300lb (640gsm) or more. The heavier the paper, the more readily it will take the water. Papers that are less than 140lb (300gsm) in weight need to be stretched before use, otherwise they will cockle when water is applied. First, the paper is soaked in water so that it expands; it is then taped or stapled to a board. As it dries it contracts, giving a taut surface that will not buckle when subsequent washes are applied.

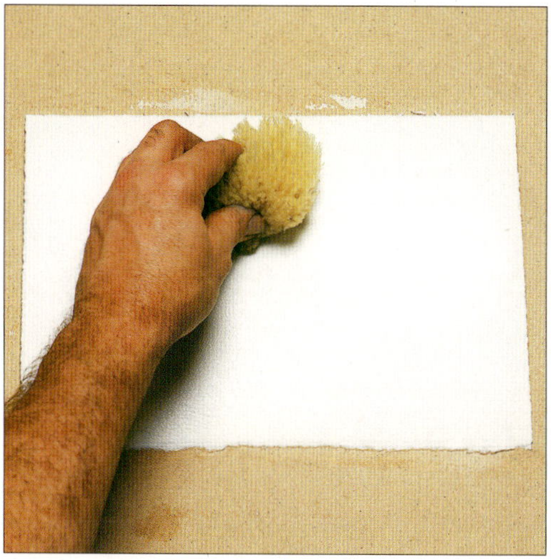

1 Dip a sponge in clean water and wipe it over the paper, making sure you leave no part untouched.

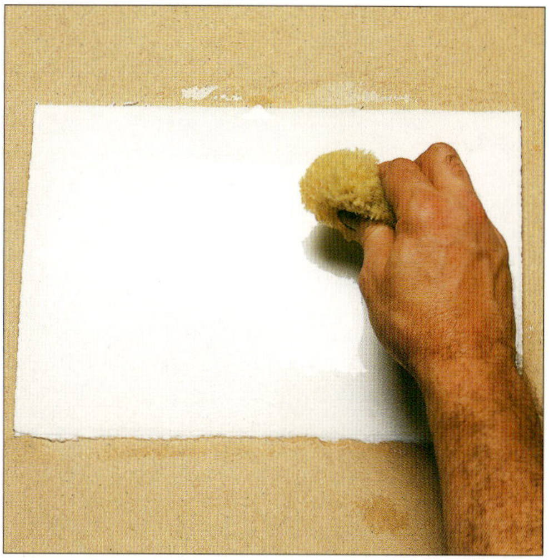

2 Make sure a generous amount of water has been applied over the whole surface and that the paper is perfectly flat.

3 Moisten four lengths of gum strip and place one along each long side of the paper. (Only gummed brown-paper tape is suitable; masking tape will not adhere to damp paper.)

4 Repeat for the short edge of the paper. Leave to dry. (In order to be certain that the paper will not lift, some artists also staple it to the board.)

Brushes

A quick glance through any art supplier's catalogue will reveal a bewildering range of brushes, from outrageously expensive sable brushes to budget-range synthetics. Although you might be tempted to invest heavily and stock up on a vast selection, in all shapes and sizes, in practice you can get away with a small number: a large brush for laying a wash, a medium-sized brush for moderate washes and larger details, and a smaller brush for fine detail should be enough to begin with.

The two main shapes of brush are flat and round. Round brushes are perhaps the most useful general-purpose brushes. They hold a lot of paint, allowing you to lay down broad strokes of colour and washes, but they also come to a fine point for more precise marks. Flat brushes have a square, chisel-shaped end. These, too, can be used for broad washes, while the flat end is used for making clean-edged, linear marks.

Many artists use Chinese-style brushes similar to those used by calligraphers: like good-quality round brushes, they hold a lot of paint but also come to a fine point. You may also come across rigger brushes (round brushes with long hairs and a fine point), which are useful for fine lines and details, and spotter brushes (less common, with very short hairs), which tend to be used by miniaturists and other artists whose work involves painting fine, very precise details.

Brushes can be made from natural hair. Sable, which is obtained from the tail of the sable marten, a relative of the mink, is the best, and the best sables come from the Kolinsky region of northern Siberia. Camel, ox and squirrel hair are common, as are synthetic materials. Buy the best quality you can afford. Cheaper brushes may shed hairs or wear out more quickly, and they may not hold as much colour or come to a point. Look for seamless, corrosion-resistant ferrules: they hold the hairs tightly and will not tarnish. Also check whether they hold their shape well. Unfortunately, you can't always tell this when you buy brushes as they are often "dressed" with some kind of adhesive, which needs to be washed out before you use them, so that they hold their points.

Round brushes ▼

Most art stores stock round brushes ranging in size from the ultra-fine 000 right up to the rather fat size 12, although you will also find brushes that lie outside this range. To begin with, however, three brushes – one small, one medium and one large – will provide you with a versatile selection that should cover most eventualities. It is good practice to use the largest brush that you can for any given painting situation, so that you get into the habit of making broad, sweeping marks rather than tight, fussy ones.

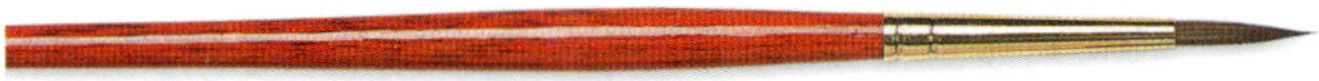

Small round brush

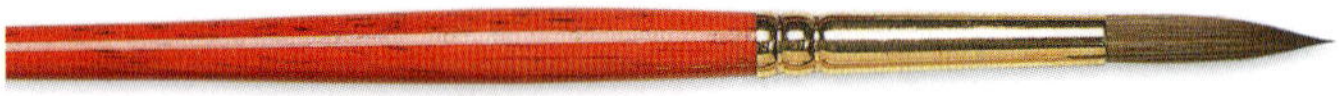

Medium round brush

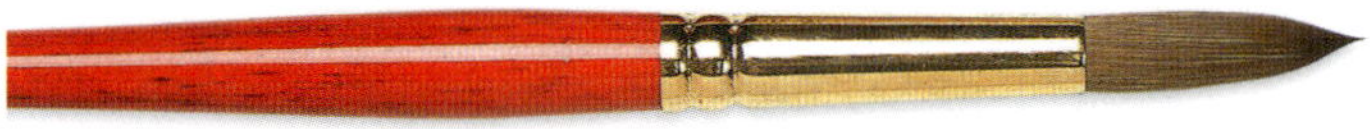

Large round brush

Large brushes ▼

Both flat brushes and mop brushes can be used to lay a wash over the paper ground. Flat brushes are wide and straight-edged, while mop brushes have large, round heads.

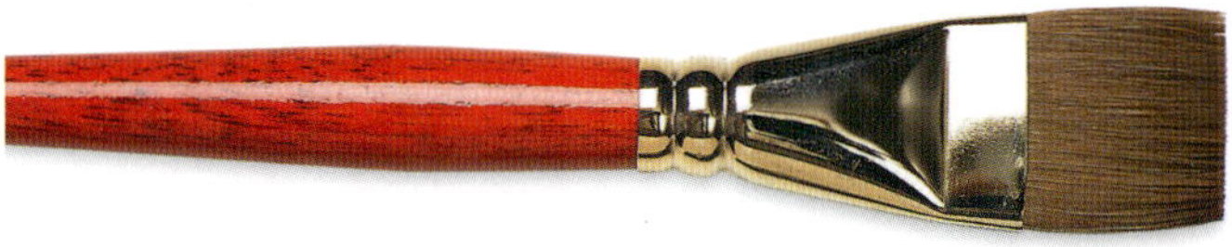

Flat brush

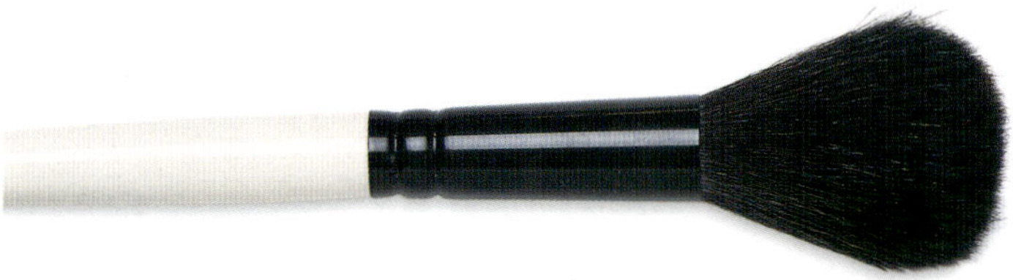

Mop brush

Other types of brush ►

Your choice of brush is very much a matter of personal taste, so experiment to find out which ones you enjoy using. You will find that some suit your style of painting better than others. Shown here are some of the other types of brush that you might come across.

A rigger brush has long hairs and a very fine point, and is good for painting fine lines and details. A Chinese-style brush is good for flowing, calligraphic marks; it holds a lot of paint and keeps its shape well, making it a versatile brush. The flat edge of a chisel brush makes it a good choice for painting straight-edged shapes – when painting up to the edge of a building, for example. In a fan brush, the bristles are splayed out, and this makes it useful for drybrush work.

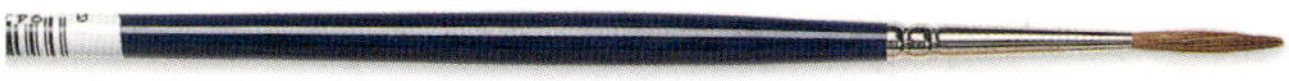

Rigger

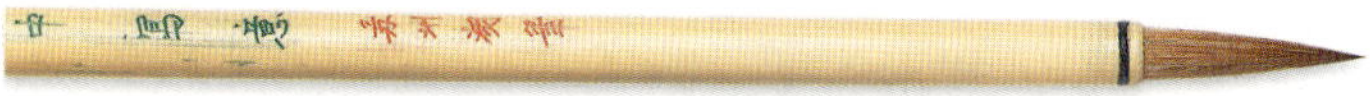

Chinese

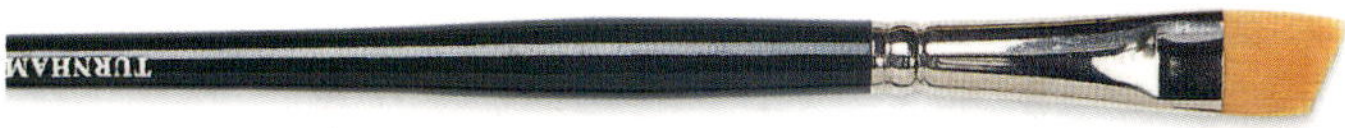

Chisel

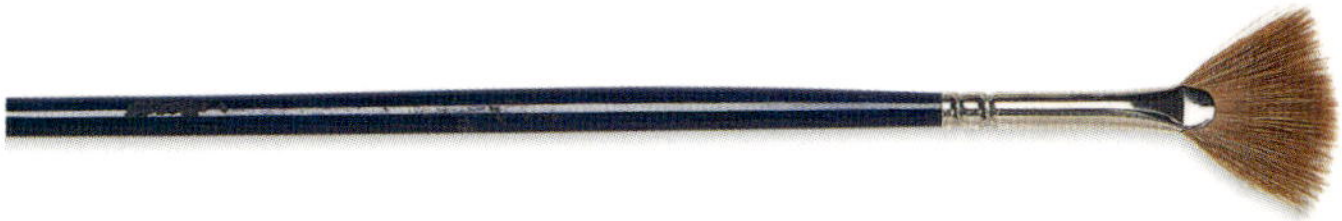

Fan

Caring for brushes

Given the cost of good-quality brushes, it is worth taking the time and trouble to look after them properly in order to prolong their life.

You should always clean your brushes immediately after use. Gently rub a little liquid detergent into the hairs, working it in with your fingertips and working right up to the ferrule. Rinse in clean running water until all the paint has been removed.

Cleaning brushes ▼

No matter how carefully you rinse your brushes, liquid detergent is the only way to be sure that you have got rid of all paint residue.

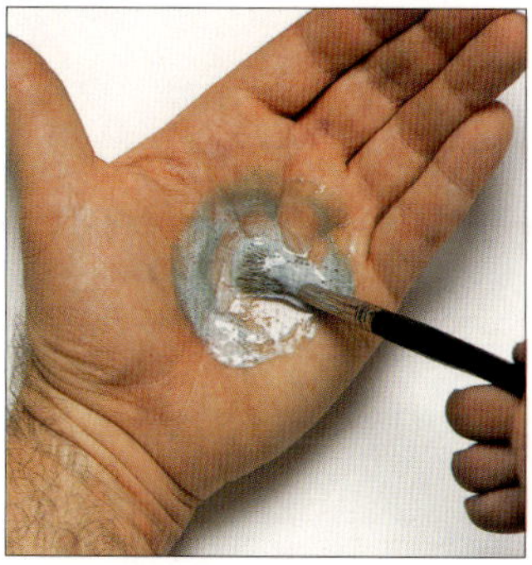

Storing brushes ►

After cleaning your brushes, squeeze the hairs to remove any excess water and then gently reshape the brush with your fingertips. Leave to dry. Store brushes upright in a jar to prevent the hairs from becoming bent as they dry.

Tips: • When you are painting, try not to leave brushes standing in water as this can ruin both the hairs and the wooden handles.

• When cleaning brushes, keep rinsing the brush under running water until the water runs clear. Make sure that any paint near the metal ferrule has been completely removed.

• Do not be tempted to store newly cleaned and still-wet brushes in an airtight container as mildew can develop.

• Moths are very keen on sable brushes, so if you need to store your brushes for any length of time, it is a good idea to use mothballs to act as a deterrant.

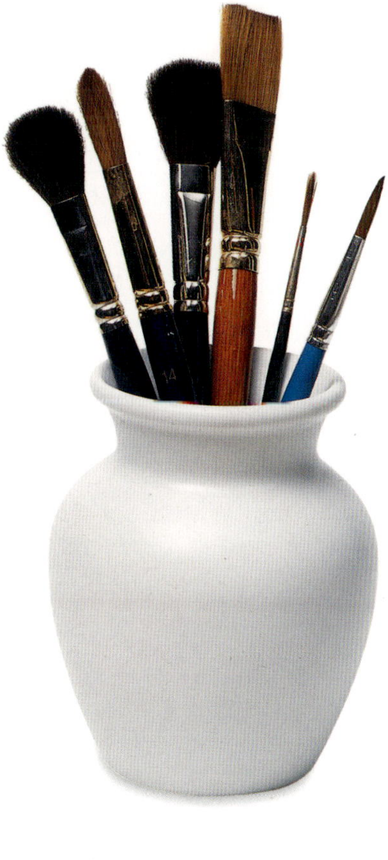

Pencils and pens

While there is no need to have more than a small selection, pencils and pens are valuable accessories in the artist's tool kit.

Pencils

The most common use of pencils in watercolour paintings is to make an initial underdrawing to map out the composition and put in the main lines of your subject as a guideline for when you come to apply the paint. It is very useful to keep a small selection of pencils to hand for this purpose.

Although graphite pencils range from 9B (very soft) to 9H (very hard), the more extreme choices are actually less useful: very soft pencils can smear while very hard ones make light, unimpressive marks. A more average HB and a 2B or 4B should be adequate for most underdrawings, depending on how strong you want the marks to be. It is also worth having a few very soft pencils in your collection to make quick tonal studies. Charcoal pencils and sticks are ideal.

Coloured pencils, too, are useful, and are particularly good for making colour notes when you are sketching on location. They are available in many colours but, unlike graphite pencils, only one degree of hardness.

You can also buy water-soluble pencils and crayons, both of which allow you to combine linear marks with the fluidity of watercolour washes. Easily portable, they are useful for location work. The range of colours is extensive, but many artists feel that they lack the subtlety of watercolour paints. Some brands seem to blend better than others, so experiment to find out which kinds you enjoy using.

Tip: If you wish to use water soluble pencils on location but do not want to carry the pencils, make heavy scribbles on paper in a range of colours: when you brush the scribbles with clean water you can pick up enough colour on the brush to use them as watercolour paints.

Pencils ▼

It is useful to keep a small range of pencils to hand for making tonal studies and underdrawings. For general usage, choose a medium hard pencil such as HB or 2B.

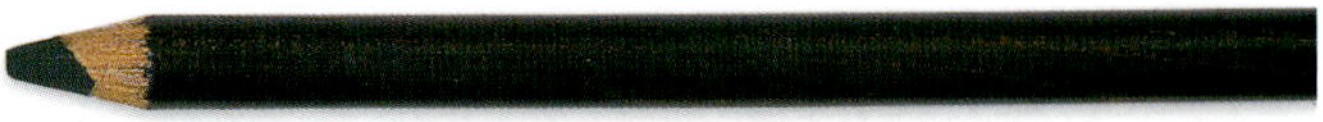

Charcoal pencil

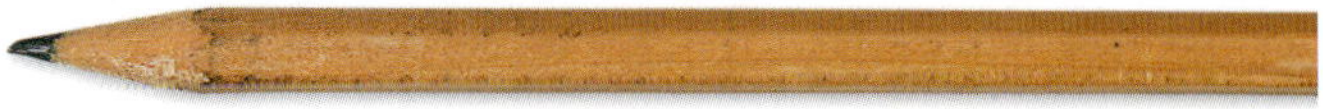

HB graphite pencil

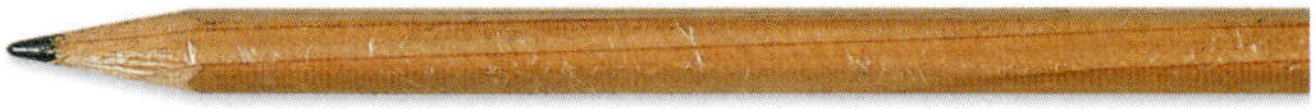

2B graphite pencil

Water-soluble pencils ▼

Water-soluble pencils can be used dry, to make clearly defined marks, or wet to create soft blends and colour mixes. To use a water-soluble pencil wet, either dip the tip in clean water or apply the pencil to the paper in the normal way and brush over the marks with a wet brush.

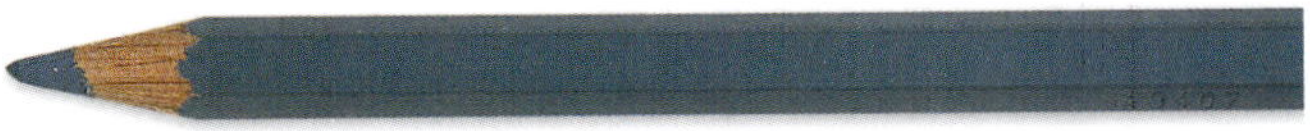

Blue

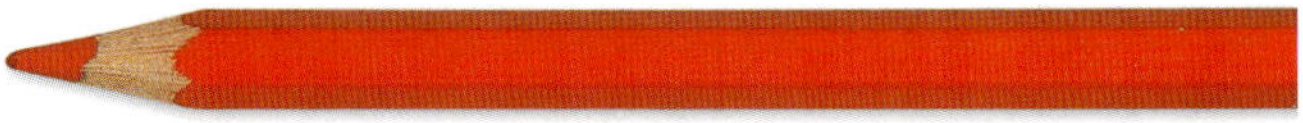

Red

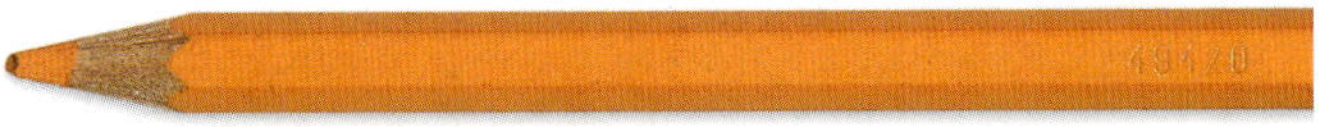

Orange

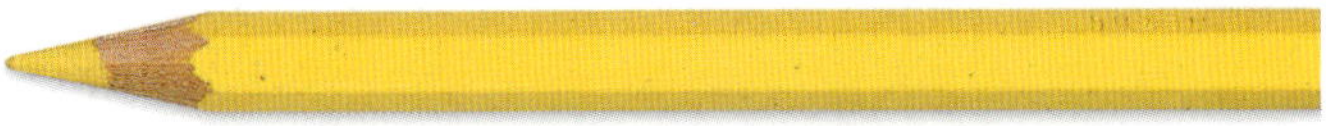

Yellow

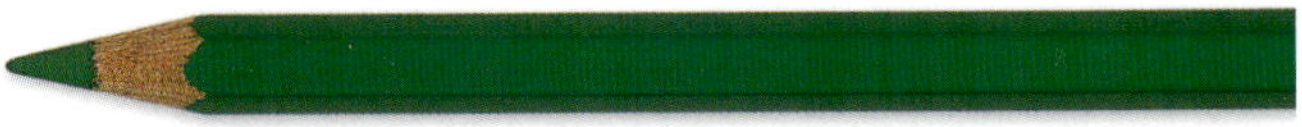

Green

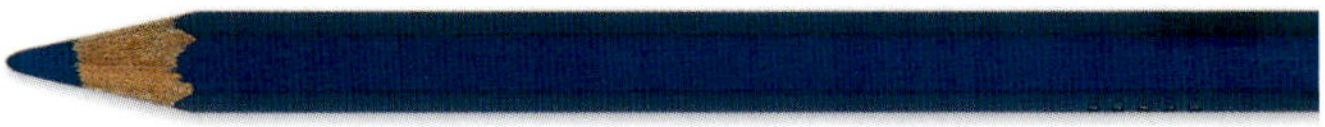

Purple

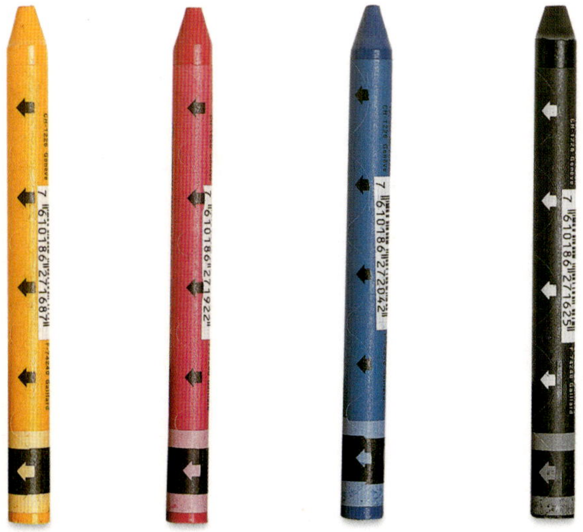

◄ Crayons
These colour sticks are similar in consistency to hard pastels. Crayons are capable of much bolder effects than pencil, and are excellent for crisp, decisive lines and for areas of solid dark tone, as they can be sharpened to a point or broken into short lengths and used sideways. Bear in mind that crayons cannot be erased easily.

Pens

Pens are most frequently used in watercolour in the line-and-wash technique, in which linear detail is put in in ink on top of (or under) loose watercolour washes.

There are various kinds of pen suitable for this technique. Fountain pens have the advantage of having a reservoir to hold the ink (or are loaded with a cartridge of ink), which means that you don't have to keep stopping to reload, but many artists prefer the spontaneity and rougher lines of dip pens. Both have interchangeable nibs, allowing you to vary the width and character of the lines you make. You can also create different widths of line by turning the pen over and using the back of the nib. Technical drawing pens of the type used by architects and graphic designers deliver a line of uniform width. These are available in a range of sizes.

As far as inks are concerned, your choice is between waterproof and water-soluble. Once dry, waterproof ink marks will remain permanent even when watercolour paint is applied over the top. Water-soluble inks, on the other hand, will blur and spread.

Inks can be used at full strength or diluted with water to create different tones; you may want to use several dilutions of ink in the same painting. Black is the colour traditionally used in line and wash, but there are many other colours available; they do not, however, possess the lightfastness of watercolour pigments.

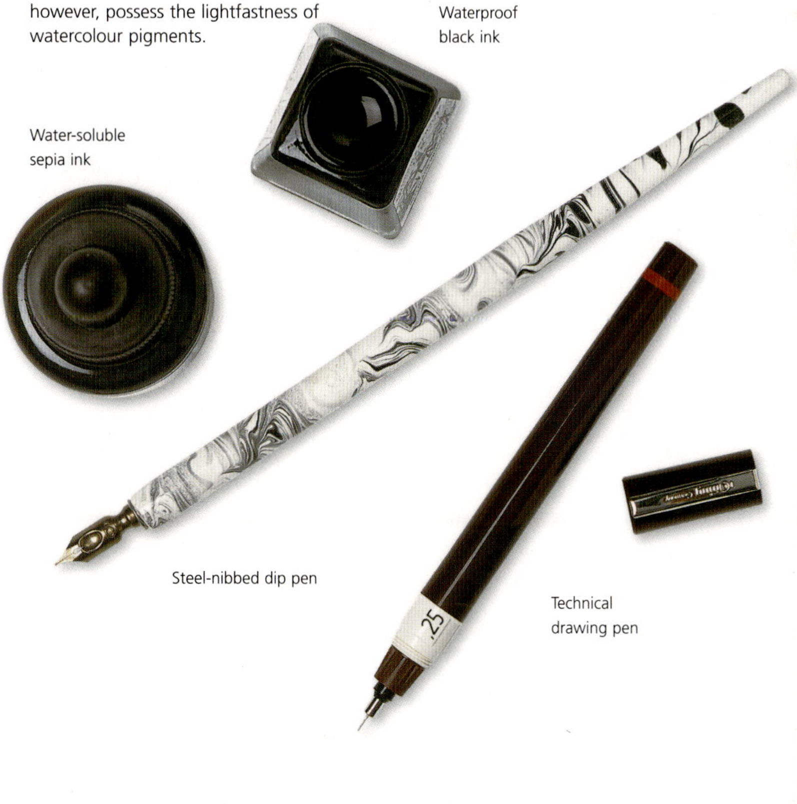

Waterproof black ink

Water-soluble sepia ink

Steel-nibbed dip pen

Technical drawing pen

Additional equipment

There are a few other pieces of equipment that you will probably find useful in your watercolour painting, ranging from things to secure your work to the drawing board and easels to support your painting to aids to specific painting techniques.

The most important thing is that the surface on which you are working must be completely flat and unable to wobble around as you work. If you use blocks of watercolour paper, then the block itself will provide enough support; you can simply rest it on a table or your knee. If you use sheets of watercolour paper, then they need to be firmly secured to a board. Buy firm boards that will not warp and buckle (45 x 60cm/18 x 24in is a useful size), and attach the paper to the board by means of gum strip or staples.

It is entirely a matter of personal preference as to whether or not you use an easel. There are several types on the market, but remember that watercolour paint is a very fluid liquid and can easily flow down the paper into areas that you don't want it to touch. Choose an easel that can be used flat and propped at only a slight angle. The upright easels used by oil painters are not really suitable for watercolour painting.

Other useful pieces of equipment include a scalpel or craft (utility) knife: the fine tip allows you to prise up pieces of masking tape that have become stuck down too firmly without damaging the paper. You can also use a scalpel to scratch off fine lines of paint – a technique known as sgrafitto. Absorbent kitchen paper is invaluable for cleaning out paint palettes and lifting off or softening the colour before it dries.

As you develop your painting style and techniques, you may want to add other equipment to the basic items shown here. You will probably assemble a selection of props, from bowls, vases and other objects for still lifes, to pieces of fabric and papers to use as backgrounds. Similarly, you may want to set aside pictures or photographs that appeal to you for use as reference material. The only real limit to what you can use is your imagination.

Box easel ▼

This easel includes a handy side drawer in which you can store brushes and other paraphernalia, as well as adjustable bars so that it can hold various sizes of drawing board firmly in place. Some easels can only be set at very steep angles, which is unsuitable for watercolour, so do check before you buy.

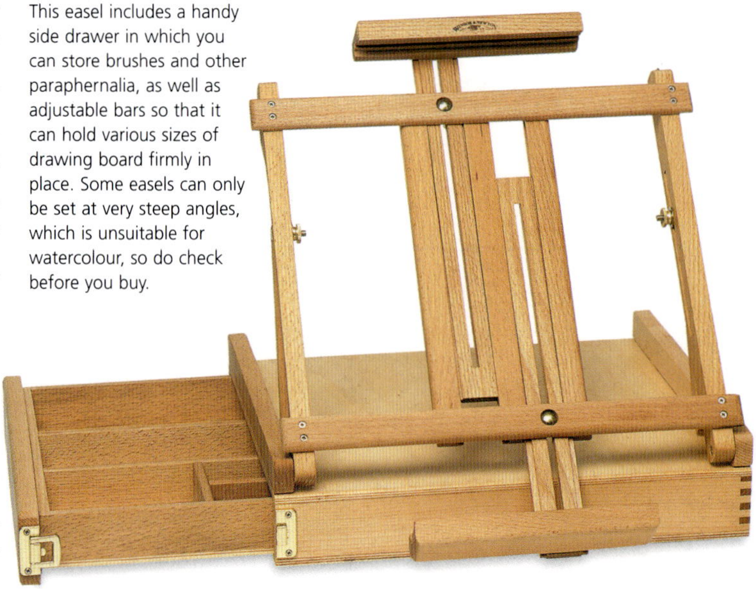

Table easel ▼

This inexpensive table easel is more than adequate for most watercolourists' needs. Like the box easel it can be adjusted to a number of different angles, allowing you to alter the angle to suit the technique you are using. It can also be folded flat so that it can be stored neatly when it is not in use.

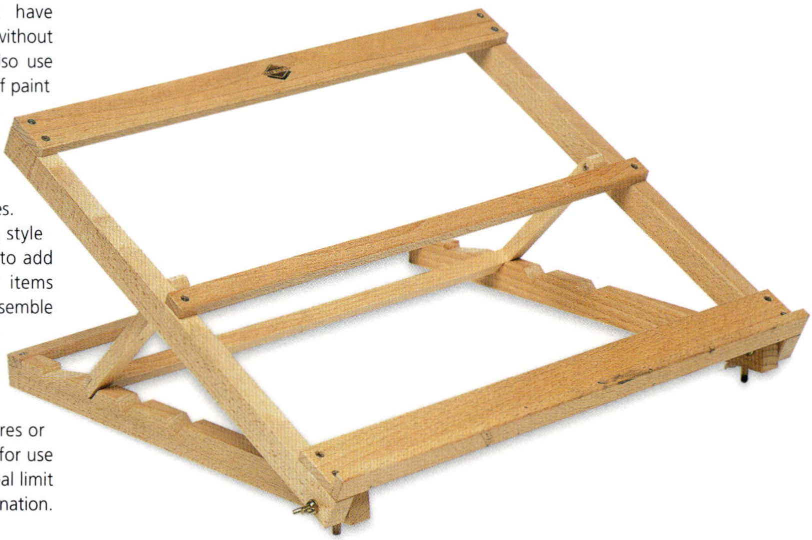

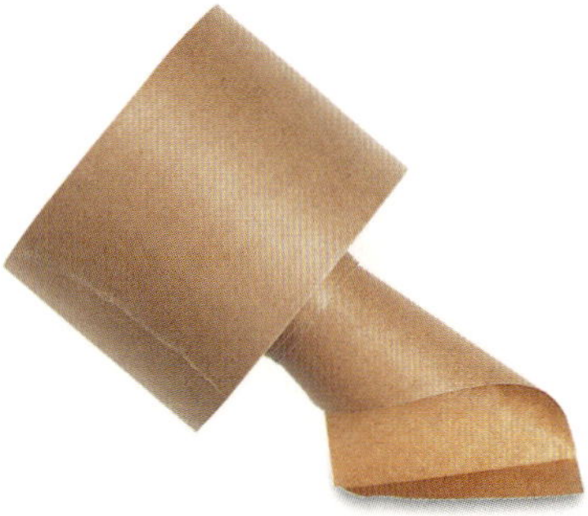

Gum strip ▲
Gummed brown-paper strip is essential for taping stretched lightweight watercolour paper to a board, to ensure that it does not buckle when the water is applied. Leave the paper stretched on the drawing board until you have finished your painting and the paint has dried, then simply cut it off, using a scalpel or craft (utility) knife and a metal ruler, and discard. Masking tape cannot be used in place of gum strip for the purpose of taping stretched watercolour paper.

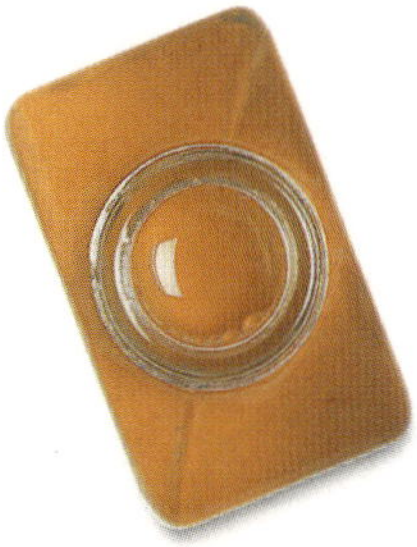

Gum arabic ▲
Adding gum arabic to watercolour paint increases the viscosity of the paint and slows down the drying time. This gives you longer to work, which is often what you need when painting detail or referring to a reference photo while you are painting. Add a few drops of the gum arabic to your paint and stir to blend. Gum arabic also imparts a slight sheen on the paper, which can be useful for certain subjects, and it increases the intensity of the paint colour.

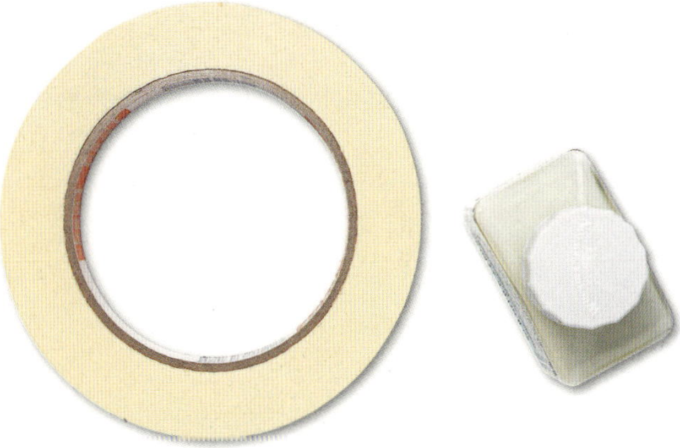

Masking fluid and masking tape ▲
Masking is one of the most basic techniques in watercolour. It is used to protect white areas of the paper so that they do not get splashed with paint, or when you want the white of the paper to represent the lighter areas of your subject. Depending on the size and shape of the area you want to protect, masking fluid and masking tape are the most commonly used materials. Masking tape can also be used to secure heavy watercolour paper, which doesn't need to be stretched, to the drawing board.

Eraser ▲
A kneaded eraser is useful for correcting the pencil lines of your underdrawing, and for removing the lines so that they do not show through the paint on the finished painting.

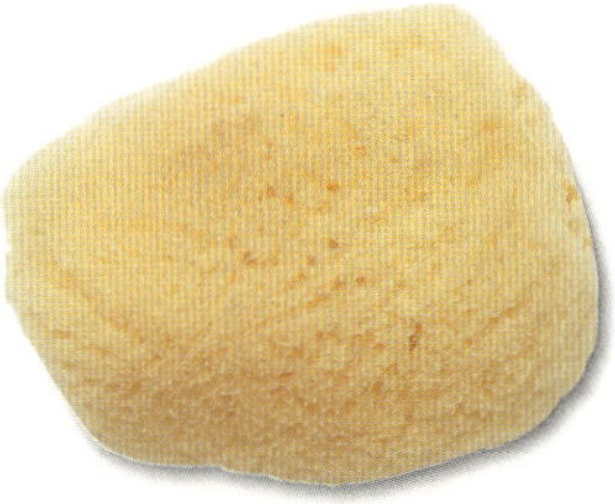

Sponge ▲
Natural or synthetic sponges are useful for mopping up excess water. Small pieces of sponge can be used to lift off colour from wet paint. Sponges are also commonly used to apply paint, with the pitted surface of the sponge creating interesting textures on the paper.

Tips: • Store small painting accessories such as sponges and rolls of tape in lidded boxes to keep things neat and tidy; plastic food storage boxes are ideal.
• Store bottles upright and always put the lids back on immediately after use to prevent spillage.
• Wash sponges immediately after use.

From light to dark

One of the things that attracts people to watercolour painting, and the one characteristic for which watercolour is most renowned, is its translucency. Good watercolours glow with a light that seems to come from within the painting itself. The reason for this is that pure watercolour paints are transparent: when a wash of watercolour paint is applied to paper, the white of the paper shines through. This is what makes watercolour the perfect choice for capturing subtle nuances of light and shade and creating a feeling of airiness that is unrivalled by any other painting medium.

However, the transparency of the paint imposes a technical constraint that you need to be aware of. When one colour is laid on top of another, particles of the first colour will still show through.

In opaque media such as oils, you can obliterate a dark colour by placing a light one on top of it. In pure watercolour, however, if you try to paint a pale yellow on top of a dark blue, some of the blue will remain visible – so instead of yellow, the two colours will appear to merge to form a green.

In practical terms, this means that you have to work from light to dark, putting down the lightest tones first and working around them as you develop the painting. You have plan ahead and work out where the light tones and colours are going to be before you pick up a brush and begin the actual painting.

One other important consideration is that in pure (transparent) watercolour there is no such thing as white paint. If you want certain areas of your painting to be white, the only white available to you is the white of the paper, and so you leave those areas free of paint, protecting them if necessary by applying some kind of mask. Alternatively, you can use white gouache, but gouache is opaque, and so you have to be very careful not to lose the feeling of luminosity.

Osprey ▼
The artist has combined watercolour with white gouache to great effect. The billowing clouds were created by leaving areas of the sky free of paint and by blotting off paint with a paper towel to soften the colour around the edges of the clouds. The ripples and spray in the water were painted using very dilute white gouache so as not to lose the wonderful feeling of light.

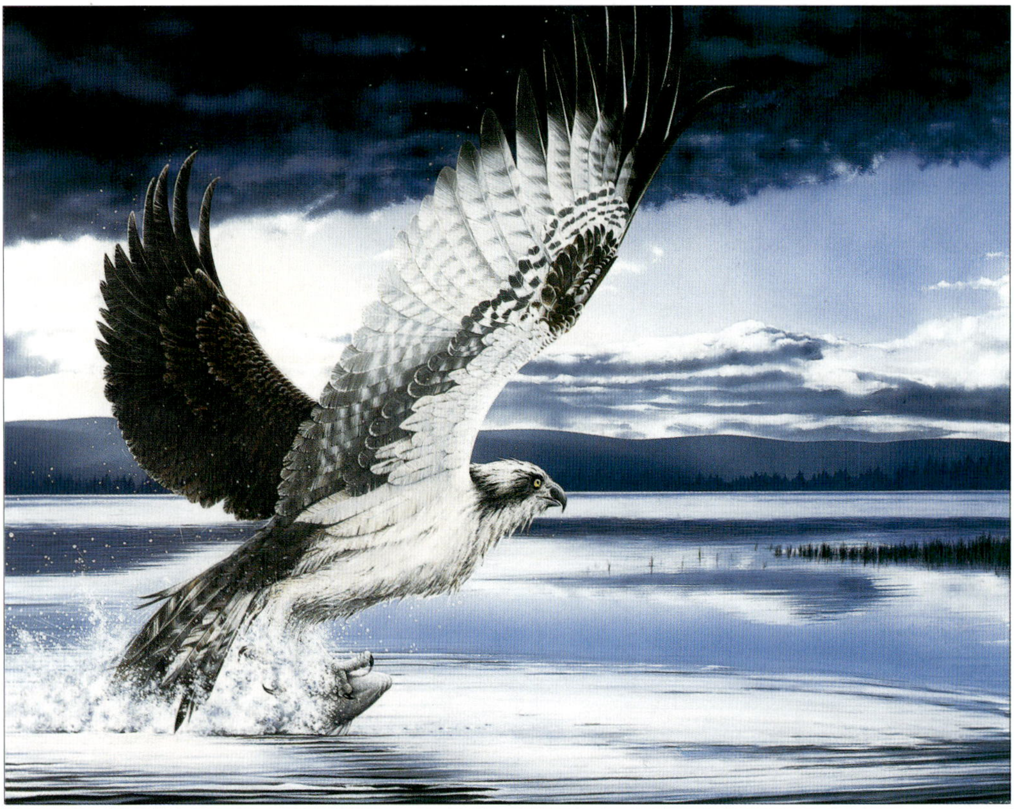

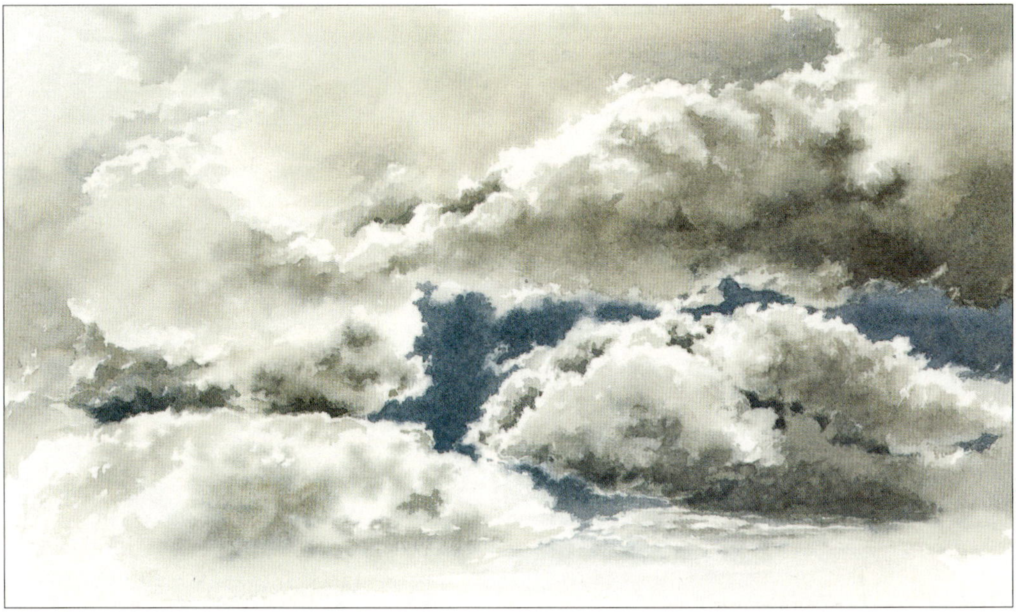

Stormy sky ▲

The artist began this study of a stormy sky by dampening the paper with clean water and dropping in a very pale grey colour, allowing it to spread of its own accord. She then blotted off paint in some areas with a paper towel to reveal the white of the paper before adding the mid- and dark greys and the deep blue of the sky, wet into wet.

Poppies ►

Watercolour is a wonderful medium for painting translucent subjects such as flower petals. Following the light to dark rule, the artist began by putting down the very pale yellowy green colour that is visible in the background and around the edges of the flowers. She then gradually applied more layers of colour to build up the density of tone on the petals and make the flowers look three-dimensional, taking care to allow some of the first very pale washes to show through in places. Note how paint has been scraped off to create the striations in the petals and delineate the petal edges: using the white of the paper in this way adds "sparkle" to the image. Tiny touches of opaque yellow gouache give the flower centres and stems solidity, without destroying the translucency of the painting as a whole or the balance between the two media. Careful planning and observation of the light and dark tones have resulted in a fresh and spontaneous-looking study of a perennially popular subject.

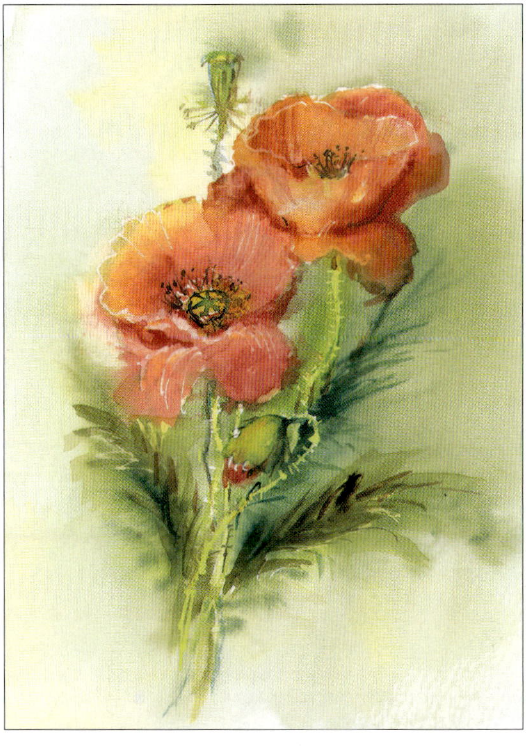

Making marks

Although artists are, by definition, inventive and apply watercolour paint with a variety of tools in order to create as wide a range of marks as possible, a brush is still the most basic and the best tool for the job. There are so many different brushes on the market that it seems as if there is a shape and a size to cover every eventuality, and it is easy to get carried away and buy a lot of brushes that you will rarely, if ever, use. With a little practice, however, you will find that you can get a remarkable range and variety of marks from a single, carefully chosen brush simply by altering the way you hold it and apply it to the paper.

A good first brush is a round, soft-haired (preferably sable) watercolour brush. This is probably the most widely used and versatile type. A medium round brush (say, no.8 or no.10) is a good, general-purpose brush, as it holds sufficient paint to make washes but also comes to a good point for fine detail work.

The conventional, and perhaps the most obvious, way to hold a brush is to hold it in the same way as you would a pen or a pencil, but that is by no means the only option.

Holding the brush with four fingers on one side of the barrel and your thumb on the other and pushing or pulling it quickly sideways will leave a broken smear of paint that is perfect for depicting texture and is totally unlike the mark made when using the point of the brush. These marks can be long or short; the density and spread of paint depends on the speed of the stroke.

Holding the brush vertically allows you to make a stabbing action, which results in a series of individual marks. You can vary the size of the marks by altering the amount of pressure you apply and the speed at which you apply it. The amount of pressure that you apply also has a marked effect. Increasing the amount of pressure that you apply, so that more of the sable hair comes into contact with the support, increases the width of the stroke.

A flat or a mop-shaped brush will result in a completely different range of marks. Experiment with different brushes to find out what you can achieve.

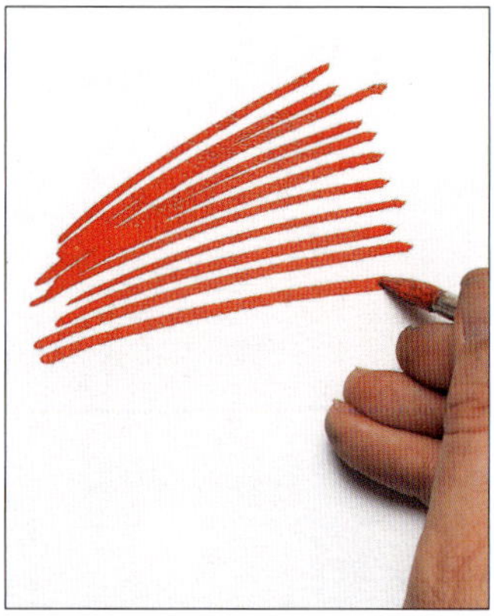

Strokes of an even width
To create strokes of an even width, use the tip of the brush and apply a steady pressure. Apply more pressure to increase the width of the line. For short strokes, you may find it helpful to rest your little finger on the paper surface as a balance, but take care not to smudge any wet paint if you do this.

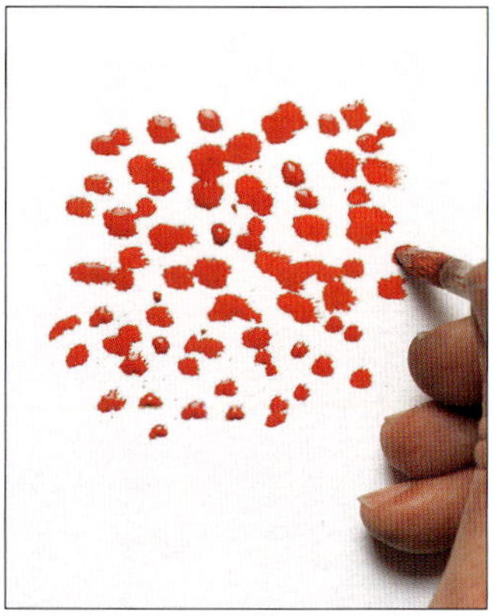

Dots
A stabbing or stippling creates a series of dots or blob-shaped marks. Holding the brush in an upright position helps to speed up the process and make it more controllable.

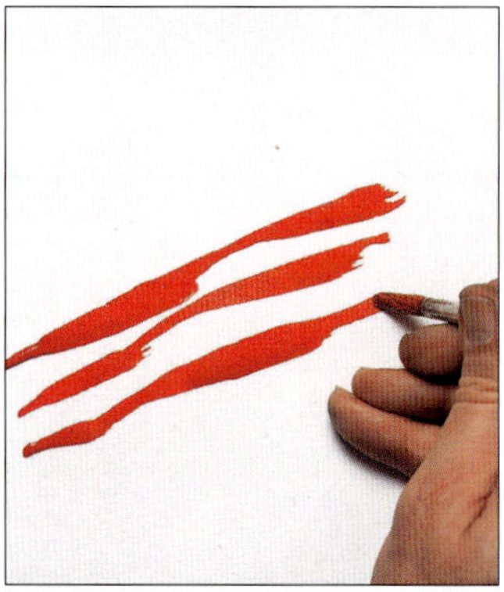

Strokes of varying widths
Varying the amount of pressure you apply also varies the width of the brushstroke, resulting in expressive calligraphic marks.

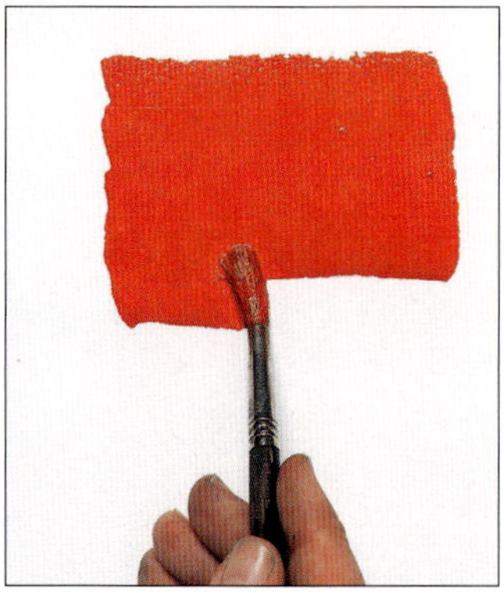

Broad washes
To make a wash that covers a wide area, use the side of the brush, rather than the point, and apply even pressure as you make the stroke.

Tip: Load your brush with plenty of paint. Using too little paint will mean that you run out quickly, often in mid mark. The amount of paint delivered to the support should come as much from the pressure applied as from the amount of liquid held within the brush fibres.

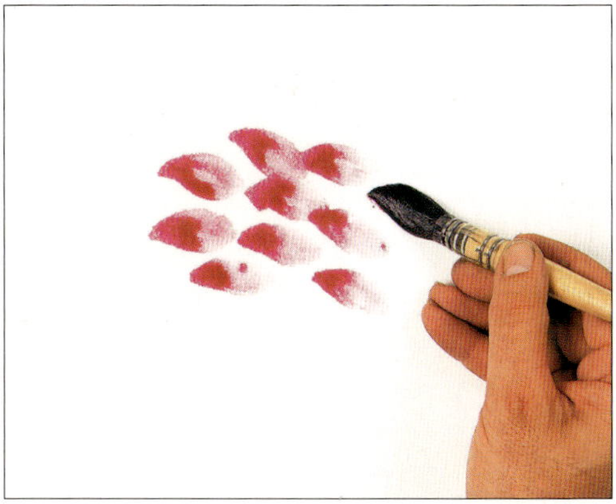

Brush shape
Pressing the brush to the paper surface without moving it results in marks that reflect the shapes of the brush.

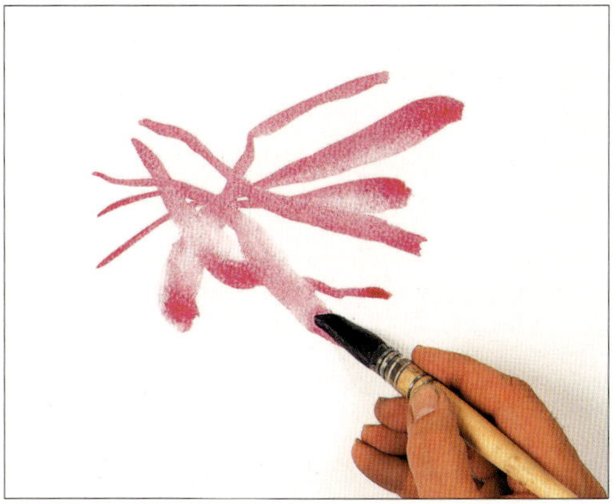

Thick and thin
Provided your brush holds a point well, you can create marks that vary greatly in thickness by applying more or less pressure.

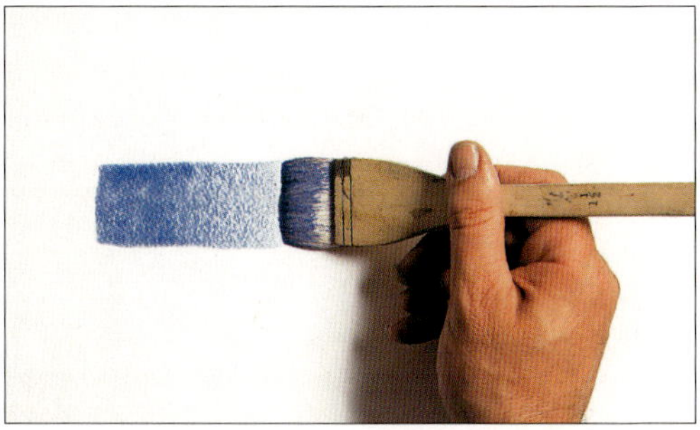

Quick washes
A Japanese-style hake brush holds a large amount of paint, and this makes it easy to lay flat washes. This is a good choice of brush if you need to cover a large area with paint.

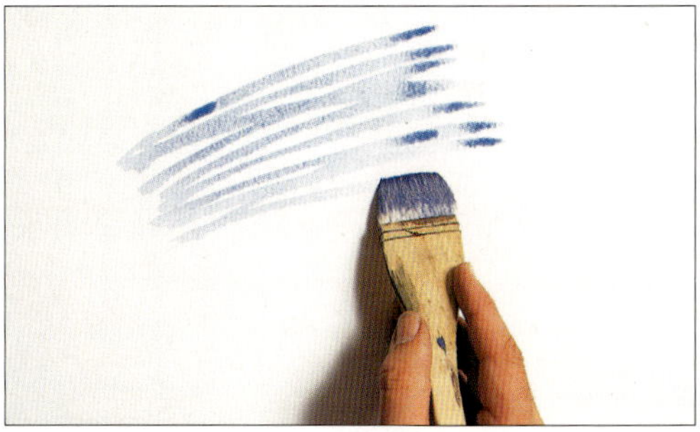

Thin lines
Used on its edge and with a light touch, even a large flat brush can be made to make delicate brush marks. Practise until you get a feel for the amount of pressure needed.

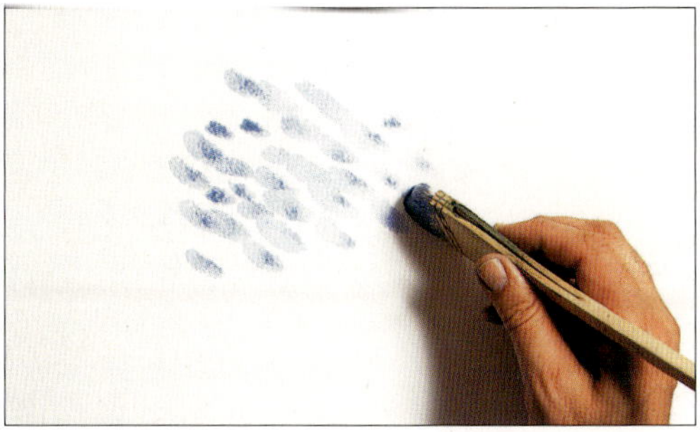

Uniform pattern
Using even pressure and the corner of the brush to dab or stipple paint on to the support will result in a series of uniformly shaped marks.

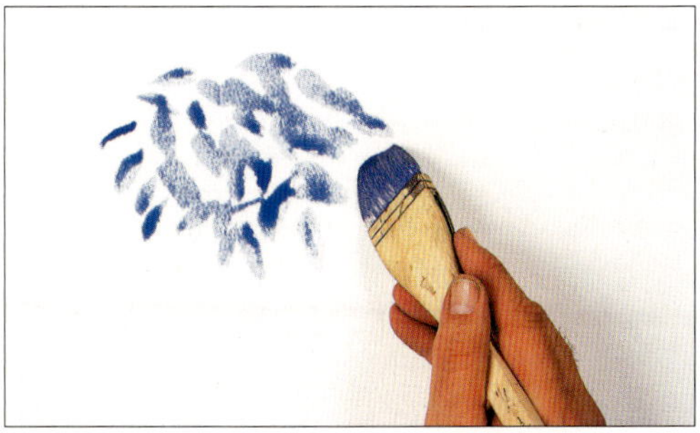

Varying the texture
Using a similar stippling action while varying the pressure and the angle at which the brush is held will create a loosely textured area, made up of marks of different shapes.

Washes

A wash is the term used to describe the process of applying watercolour paint in a single layer. There are three kinds of washes – flat, gradated and variegated (which is really a variation on a gradated wash). Although the technique is broadly the same way in all three cases, the results look very different.

Washes are among the most fundamental of all watercolour techniques. Sometimes washes are applied over the whole of the paper, and sometimes they are used over only selected areas. It is very rare for a painting to be composed entirely of washes, but as a wash of one kind or another is very often the first stage in producing a watercolour, it is well worth taking the time and trouble to master the technique. It will stand you in good stead for all your subsequent work and is an essential first step in getting used to manipulating paint on paper.

A flat wash is, as the name implies, a wash that is completely even in tone. All pictures need some blank and uncluttered areas, so flat washes are necessary on occasions, either to provide a base for the rest of the painting or as "breathing spaces" that allow the viewer's eye to rest. Flat washes can be particularly useful in abstract, or semi-abstract, work. In representational work, however, too many flat washes will lead to a dull and uninteresting painting. A flat wash contrasts well with many of the techniques used to introduce texture into watercolour paintings, such as spattering and stippling, as well as with other media, such as pastels, inks and coloured pencils.

Gradated and variegated washes are both designed to give some variety of tone. Like the flat wash, both are normally used in conjunction with other techniques. Both gradated and variegated washes are particularly useful in landscape painting.

Tip: It is difficult to mix two washes that are identical in tone, so always mix more wash than you think you will need, so that you don't have to stop halfway through a painting to mix more, then find that you cannot match the tone.

Flat wash

A well laid flat wash should show no variation in tone. Having said that, however, the kind of paper you use does have an effect and it is worth experimenting so that you know what results you can expect.

Work smoothly and confidently, without hesitation. Never go back over an area that you have already painted or the tones will be uneven. Work with your drawing board flat, or angle it slightly to help the paint flow down the paper. Use a large round-headed brush that holds a lot of paint, so that you can work quickly without having to re-load the brush.

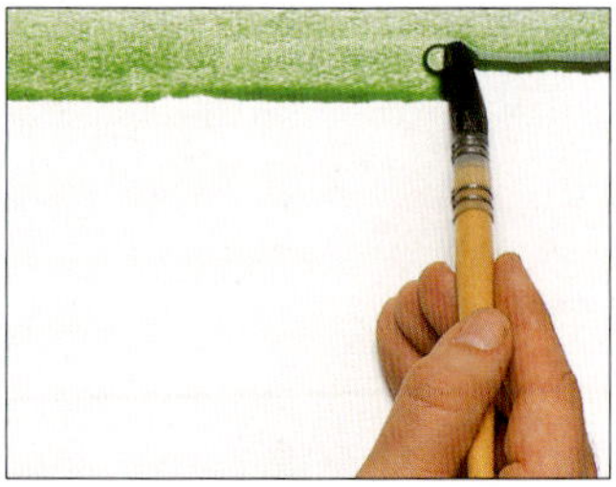

1 Using a large wash brush, mix a generous amount of wash (here, sap green was used). Working from left to right, lay a smooth stroke of colour across the paper.

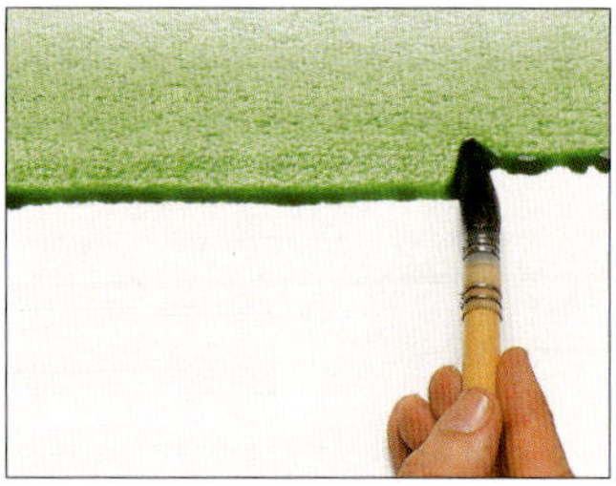

2 Quickly re-load your brush with more paint. Pick up the pool of paint at the base of the first stroke with your brush and continue across the paper, again working from left to right.

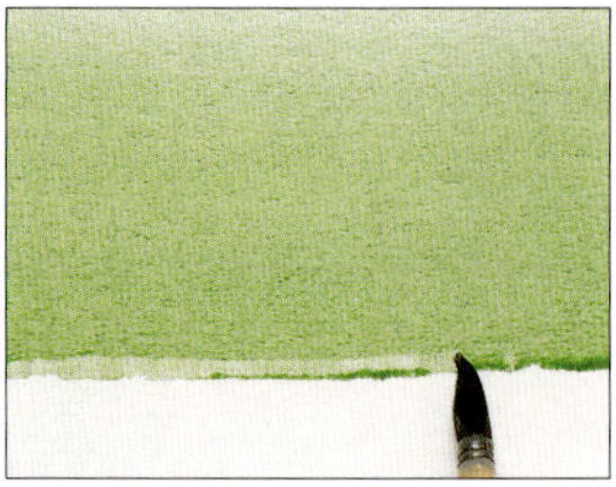

3 If you find you've got too much paint at the base of the wash, dry your brush on tissue paper and run it along the base of the wash to pick up the uneven streaks.

The finished flat wash
The wash has dried to a flat, even tone with no variation or visible brushstrokes. The fewer strokes you use, the flatter the wash will be – so use a large brush if you want to cover the whole paper.

Gradated wash

A gradated wash is painted in a similar way to a flat wash, using a large brush and brushstrokes that dry evenly without leaving any streaks, but it shows a variation in tone. More water is added to the wash as you work down the paper so that the colour gradually gets lighter. Alternatively, you can add more pigment to the wash so that it gradually becomes darker in tone.

A gradated wash is often used to paint skies which, because of the effects of aerial perspective, are usually darkest at the top of the painting and paler towards the horizon.

You can also use a gradated wash to make one side of your subject darker in tone than another; the dark side looks as if it is in shadow, and this helps to make your subject look three-dimensional. Transitional gradations such as this are excellent for painting curved surfaces, such as glass bottles, oranges and domed roofs.

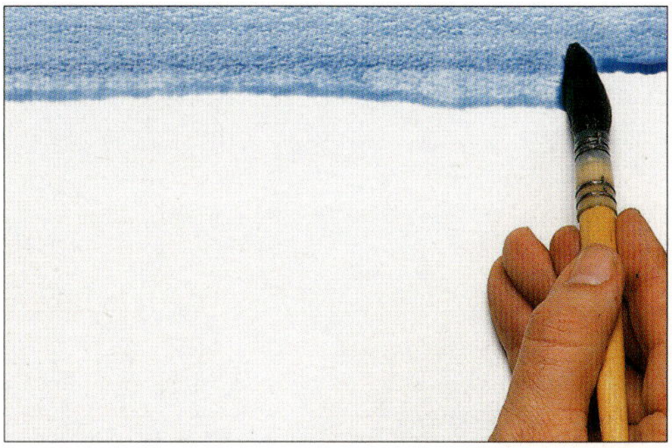

1 Lay the first stroke of colour as for a flat wash, working from left to right with smooth, even strokes.

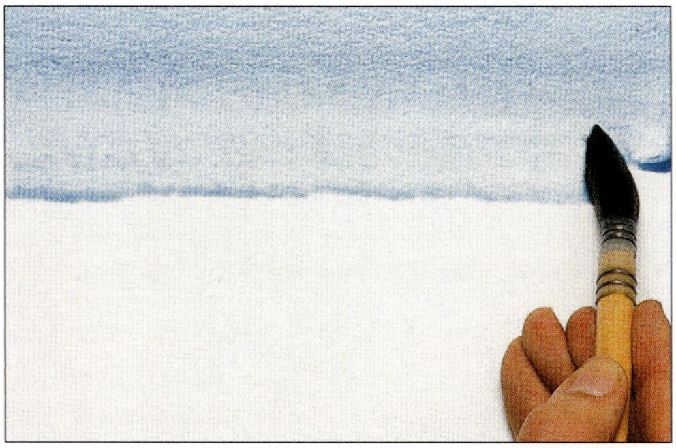

2 Add more water to the wash to make a paler tone and continue to work across the page from left to right.

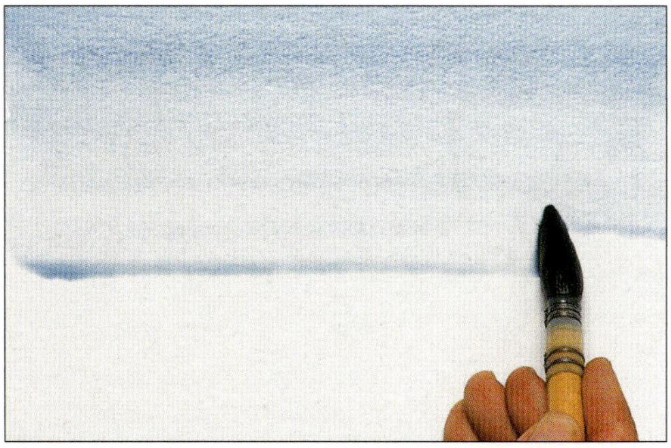

3 Continue as before, adding more water to the wash with each stroke so that it gets lighter as you move down.

4 As more water is added to the paint mixture, the colour virtually disappears.

The finished gradated wash
In the final wash, the colour has paled from a strong tone at the top to almost nothing at the base.

Practice exercise: **Landscape using flat and gradated washes**

Although washes are among the most fundamental of watercolour techniques, they can be used as the basis for simple little studies that you can be proud to hang on your wall.

This exercise is based around using flat and gradated washes to establish the planes of an imaginary landscape scene. The simple detailing that is added on top of the washes – the trees and the distant farmhouse – create texture and add visual interest to the painting.

You could easily adapt this exercise to create an imaginary landscape of your own. Choose colours for the underlying washes that are appropriate to the main subject of the painting – perhaps warm yellows and greens for a woodland scene, or blues for a seascape.

Materials

- *2B pencil*
- *140lb (300gsm) rough watercolour paper, pre-stretched*
- *Watercolour paints: cerulean blue, yellow ochre, cadmium lemon, cobalt blue, viridian, raw sienna, Payne's grey, ultramarine violet, neutral tint, light red, cadmium red, burnt umber*
- *Brushes: large mop, medium round, fine round*

Reference sketch

A quick sketch made in situ outdoors, when standing in front of your chosen scene, is a useful way of trying out compositions and colour combinations to see what works best. Use it as reference material to produce a more detailed painting when you get home.

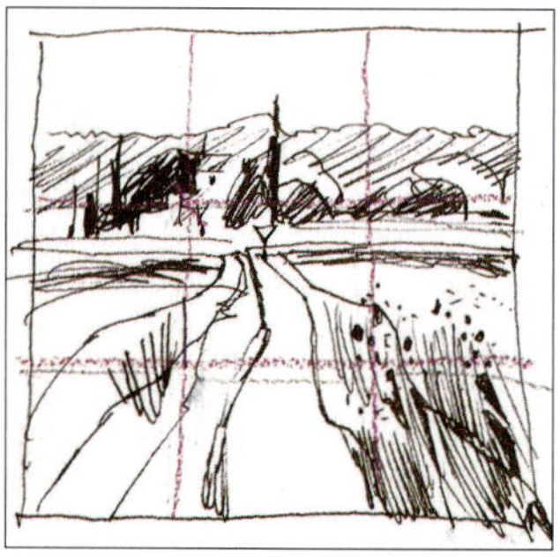

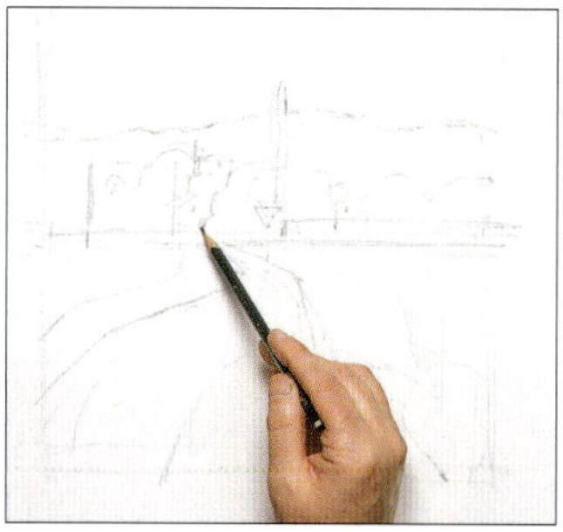

1 Using a 2B pencil, sketch the main shapes of the subject – in this case, the foreground path, the house and trees in the middle distance, and the tree-covered hills in the background.

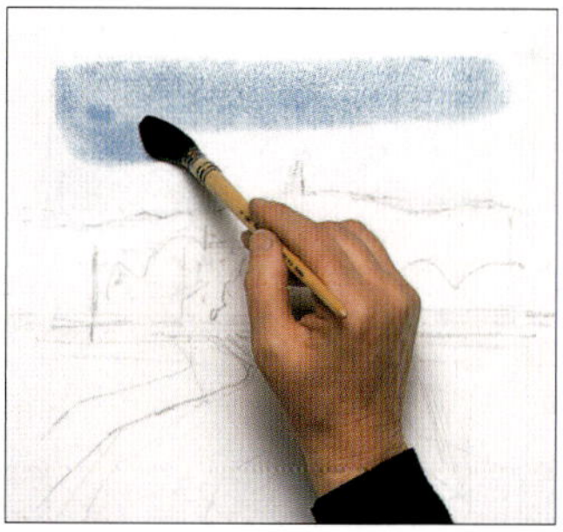

2 Using a large mop brush, dampen the whole of the sky area with clean water. As soon as you have finished, lay a gradated wash of cerulean blue across the top of the sky.

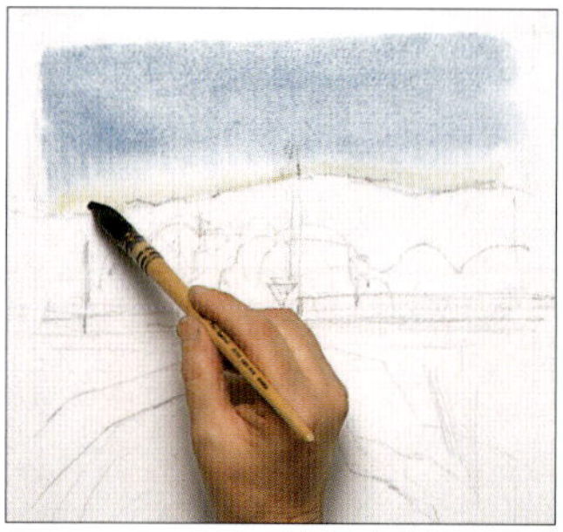

3 At the bottom of the gradated wash, where the colour has paled to almost nothing, put down a broad stroke of very pale yellow ochre. You may need to tilt the drawing board backwards slightly to prevent paint from flowing into the dry part of the paper, below the sky area.

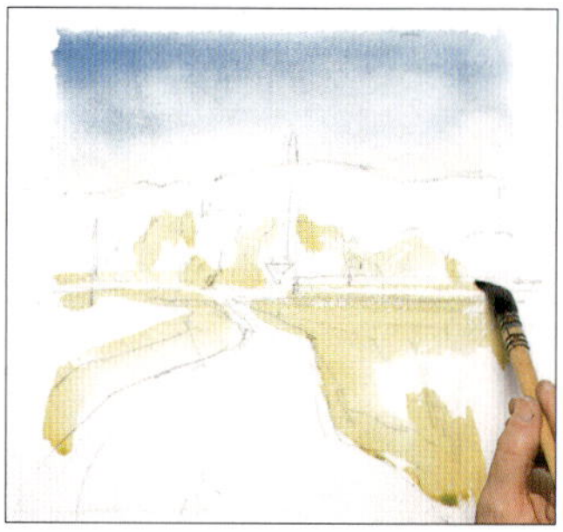

4 While the first wash is still damp, lay a stroke of cerulean blue across the top of the sky to intensify the colour. Leave to dry. Mix a pale green from cadmium lemon and cerulean blue and wash it over the foreground grass on either side of the road and the trees in the middle distance. Leave to dry.

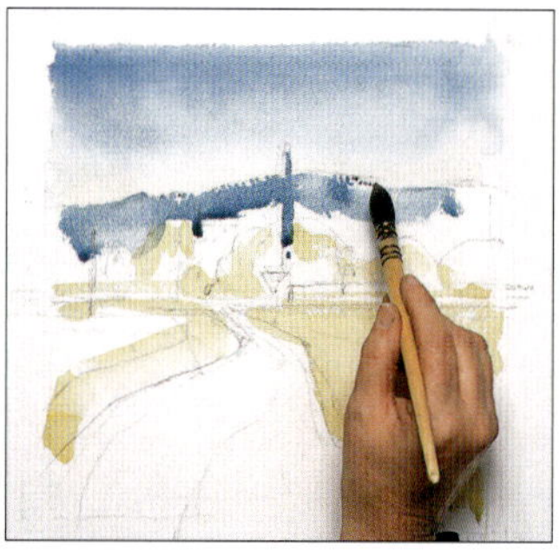

5 Mix a bluish green from cobalt blue and a little viridian. Using a large mop brush, wash the paint over the tree-covered hill in the distance, taking care to leave the house untouched. You may need to use a finer brush to go around the outline of the house. Dot in the shapes of trees along the horizon and leave to dry.

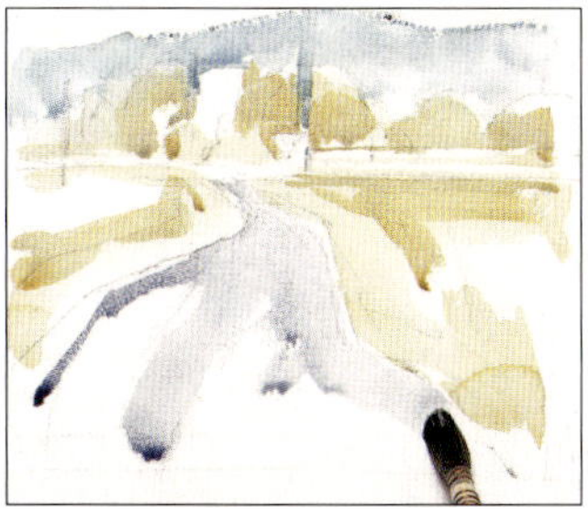

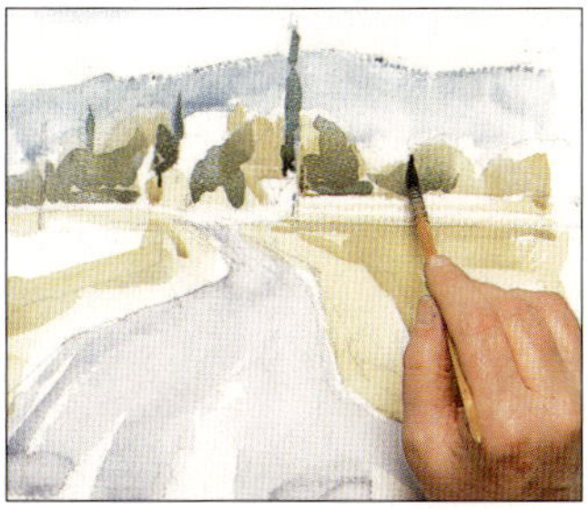

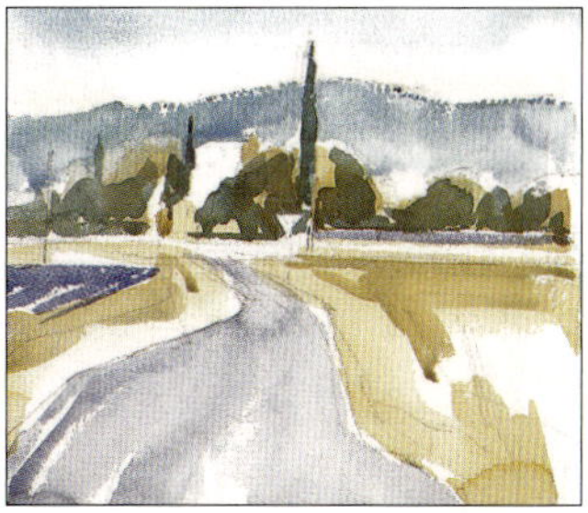

6 Mix an olive green from raw sienna, cobalt blue and a little cadmium lemon. Brush the mixture over the trees and the foreground. Mix a pale mauve from Payne's grey and ultramarine violet and paint the road. Leave to dry.

7 Mix a dark green from neutral tint and viridian. Using a medium round brush, paint in the dark shapes of the trees. Don't worry too much about making the shapes accurate, just go for the overall effect. Leave to dry.

8 Mix a strong wash of ultramarine violet and paint a broad stroke of colour below the trees, to the right of the farmhouse. Paint another to the left of the road to indicate the brightly coloured fields of lavender.

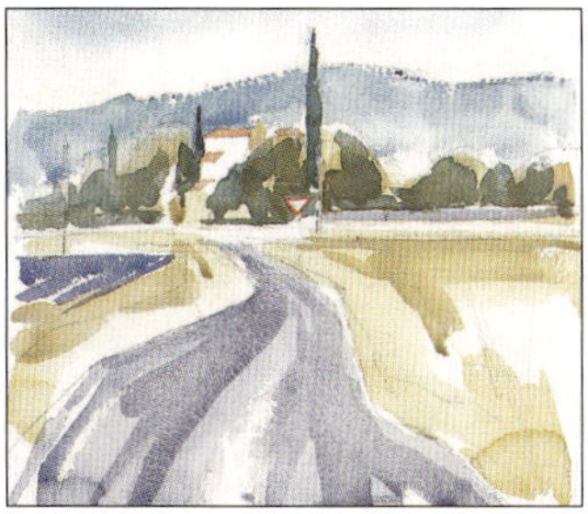

9 Paint the roofs in light red and the outline of the road sign in cadmium red. Note how these small touches of hot colour stand out against the cool blues and greens used elsewhere in the painting. Mix a wash of ultramarine violet and burnt umber, and paint over the foreground road.

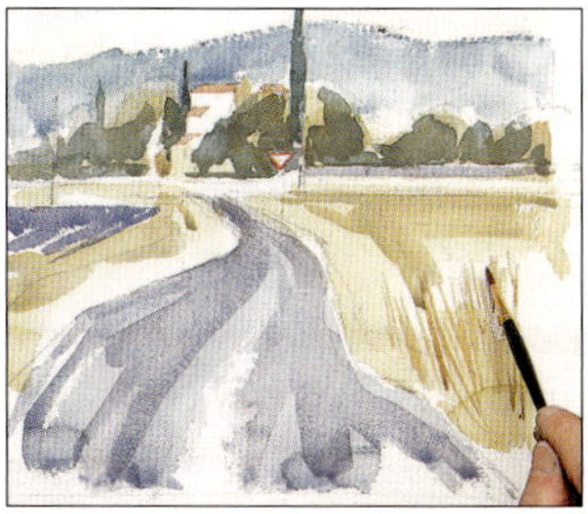

10 Mix a warm brown from cadmium lemon, raw sienna and a little cobalt blue. Paint in the fine foreground grasses, using a fine round brush.

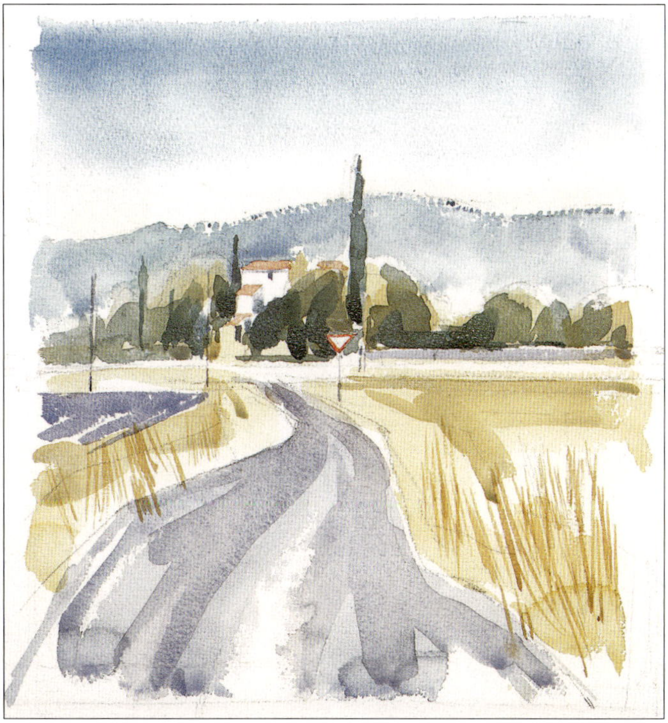

The finished painting

This painting effectively combines flat and gradated washes in a charming landscape that is full of character. Flat washes of colour on the hillside and winding foreground road, and a gradated wash of cerulean blue on the sky, establish the basis of the scene, while a few simple details – the broad strokes of colour for the trees in the distance, the sharp lines of the foreground grasses and the small touches of red on the roof in the middle distance – help to bring the scene to life.

Variegated wash on damp paper

A variegated wash is a variation on the gradated wash, but instead of adding more water, you gradually introduce another colour. When properly done, the transition from one colour to the next should be almost imperceptible.

Some artists find it easier to dampen the paper first, using either a sponge or a lmop brush dipped in clean water. This allows the colours to blend and merge in a much more subtle way, without any risk of hard lines appearing between one colour and the next. You may need to allow the paper to dry slightly before you apply any paint: this is something you will learn with practice. However, if you prefer, you can work on dry paper.

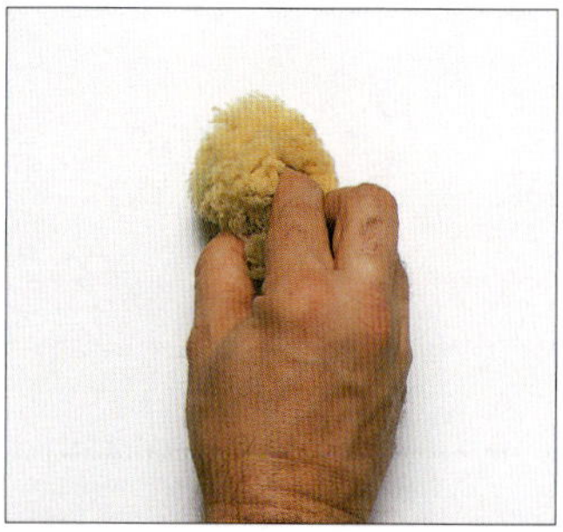

1 Dampen the paper with a sponge dipped in clean water. Use plenty of water: you can let the paper dry a little before applying the paint, if necessary.

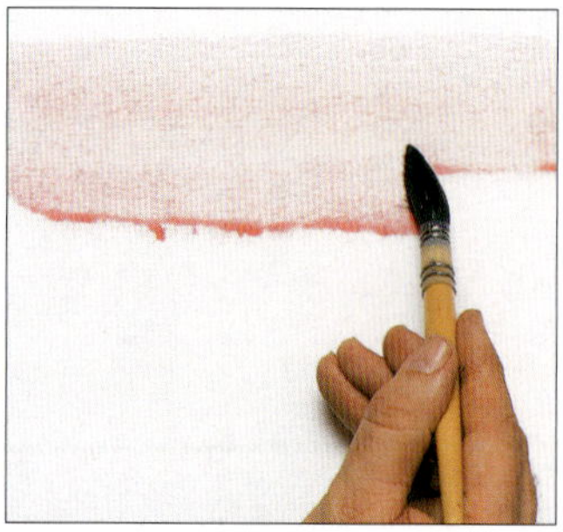

2 Using a large wash brush, lay a stroke of colour over the paper, working from left to right. The paint spreads more evenly on damp paper.

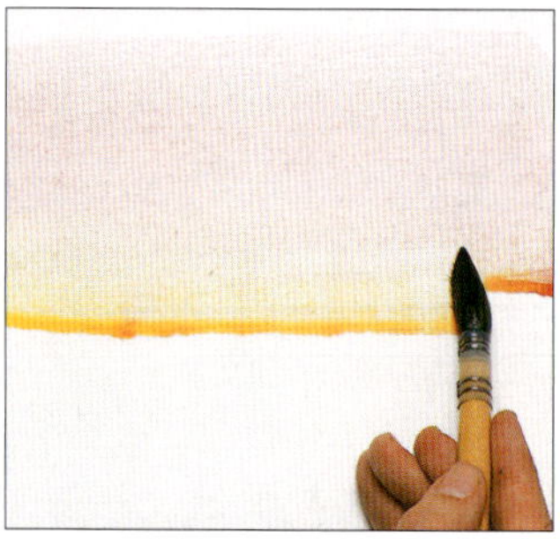

3 Clean your brush thoroughly and load it with a second colour. Start laying this colour over the first. Continue until the wash is complete.

Variegated wash on damp paper
In the finished wash, the colours merge together almost imperceptibly, with no obvious division between the two.

Variegated wash on dry paper
Here, the division between the two colours is slightly more obvious.

Practice exercise: **Sunset using a variegated wash**

A variegated wash is one of the most useful techniques for painting a sunset in watercolour. This simple exercise also shows you how to create a silhouette to turn the variegated wash into an attractive landscape painting.

Materials
- *2B pencil*
- *140lb (300gsm) rough watercolour paper, pre-stretched*
- *Watercolour paints: ultramarine blue, cadmium orange, cadmium red, ultramarine violet, alizarin crimson, sepia*
- *Brushes: large round, small round*

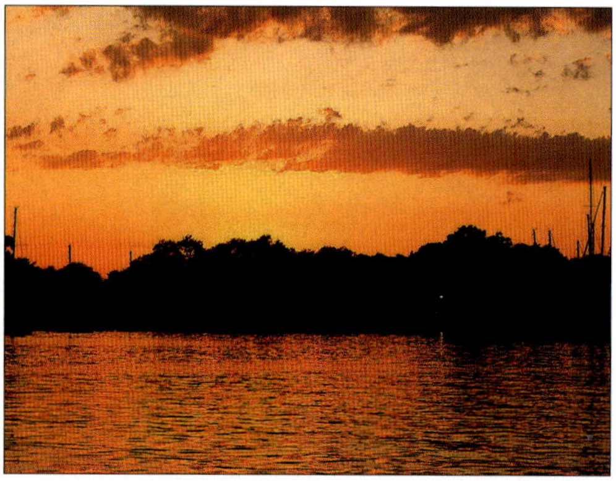

The original scene
Striking colours, shimmering reflections and a bold silhouette – all the ingredients for a sunset with impact.

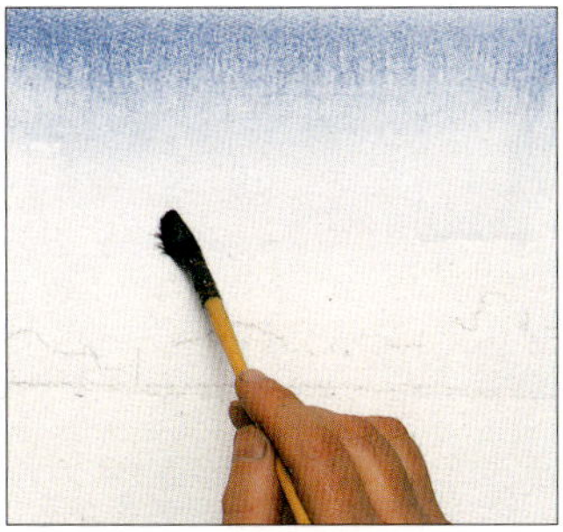

1 Using a 2B pencil, lightly sketch the outline of the silhouetted trees on the skyline. Using a large round brush, dampen the paper with clean water. Mix a wash of ultramarine blue and, again using the large round brush, lay a gradated wash over the top half of the paper, adding more water with each brushstroke so that the blue colour pales to almost nothing just above the horizon.

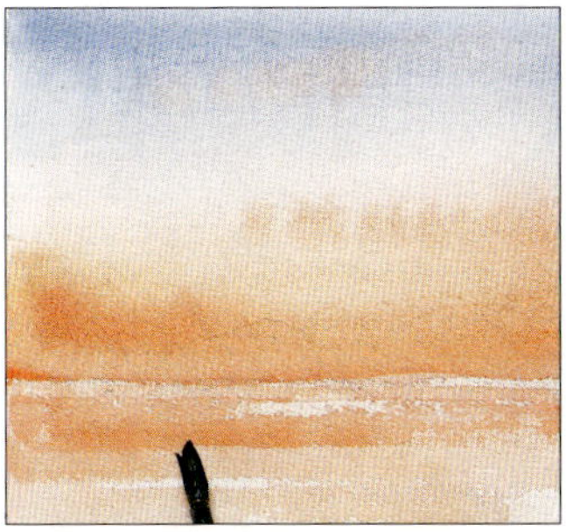

2 Mix an orangey red from cadmium orange and cadmium red. While the paper is still damp lay this colour over the lower half of the paper, allowing it to merge wet into wet into the very pale blue around the horizon line. Leave to dry. Dampen the paper again very slightly. Brush a broad stroke of the same orangey red mix across the middle of the painting (this will form the basis of the silhouetted land area) and dot it into the sky. Leave to dry.

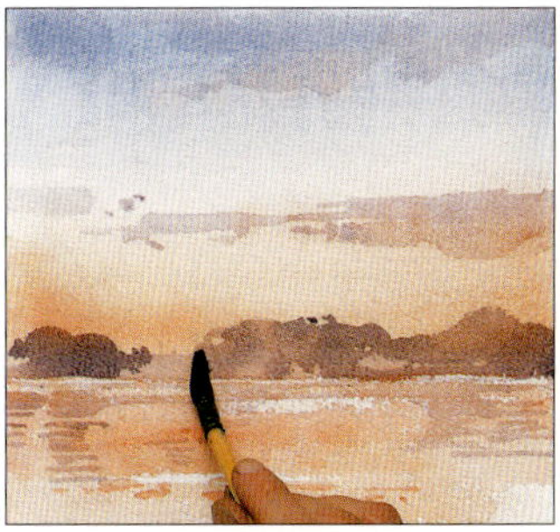

3 Mix a warm purple from ultramarine violet and a little alizarin crimson. Using a large round brush, brush this mixture on to the sky to represent the dark cloud shapes. Add a little more pigment to the mixture to make a darker tone and paint the outline of the silhouetted trees. Using the same mixture, paint a few broken brushstrokes on the water for the dark reflections of both the trees and the land area.

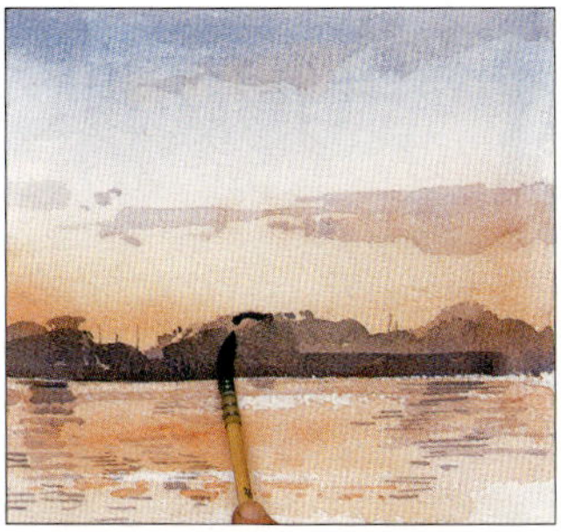

4 Mix a dark violet from ultramarine violet and sepia and darken the silhouetted area, adding a few fine vertical lines for the boat masts that stick up into the sky.

The finished painting

A two-colour variegated wash forms the basis of this colourful sunset, while a bold silhouette gives the viewer a strong shape on which to focus. Although the painting itself is very simple, the choice of rich colours and the careful placing of both the silhouetted land form and the reflections in the water combine to make an atmospheric little study.

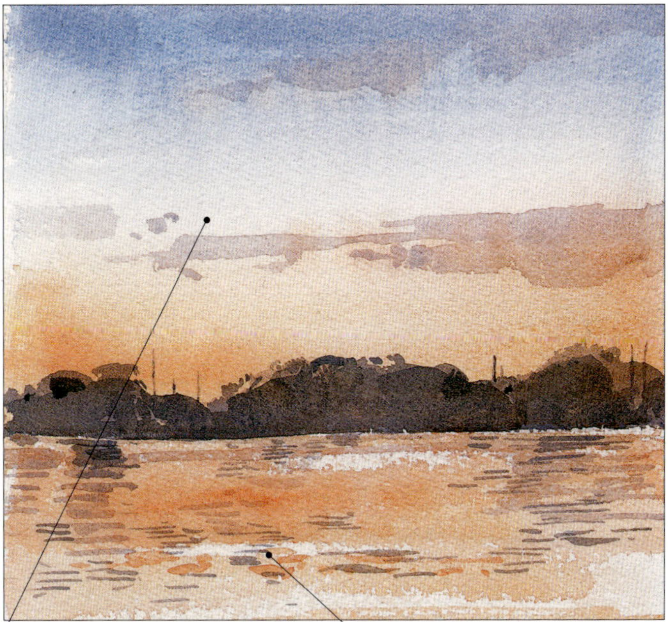

The initial blue wash merges almost imperceptibly with the rich, warm colours of the sunset.

The white of the paper shows through in places – a simple but effective way of implying water sparkling in the last rays of the setting sun.

Understanding tone

"Tone" is a word that you will often come across in art books: it simply means the relative lightness or darkness of a colour. The exact tone depends on the degree and quality of light falling on a particular object: if one side of an object is in shadow, it will be darker in tone than a side that is in direct sunlight. You can often see this clearly by looking at two adjacent sides of a building, where the front of the building is illuminated by the sun and the other forms one side of a narrow, shaded alleyway. Both sides of the building are made from the same materials, and we know they are the same colour, but the side that is in shade looks considerably darker.

But why is tone important in painting? The answer is that it enables you to create a convincing impression of light and shade, and this is one of the things that helps to make your subjects look three-dimensional.

This means that you have to analyse your subject and decide at the outset where the lightest areas of your painting are going to be. Because watercolour paint is transparent and you cannot lay a light colour on top of a dark one without the underlying colour showing through, you usually start with the lightest tones and build up to the darkest. Before you begin painting, therefore, it is often helpful to make a quick tonal sketch to work out where the light, medium and dark tones should be placed. Get the tonal structure right and much of the rest of your work will fall into place.

Single-colour subject ▼
Even a single-colour subject, such as this strongly lit orange, consists of hundreds of slightly different tones. The human eye, however, can only make out the difference between a fraction of this number.

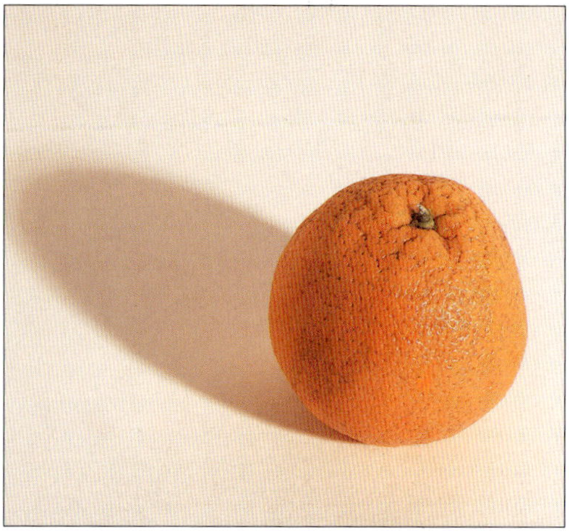

Tonal sketch ▼
When you sketch a single-colour subject, you need to show some differences in tone in order for it to look convincing. However, most images will still read convincingly when broken into only a handful of tones, as here. The side of the orange that faces away from the light, looks dark. The side that is directly illuminated by the light is a much lighter tone. In very strong light, the best way to convey this may be to leave highlight areas completely white and untouched by paint.

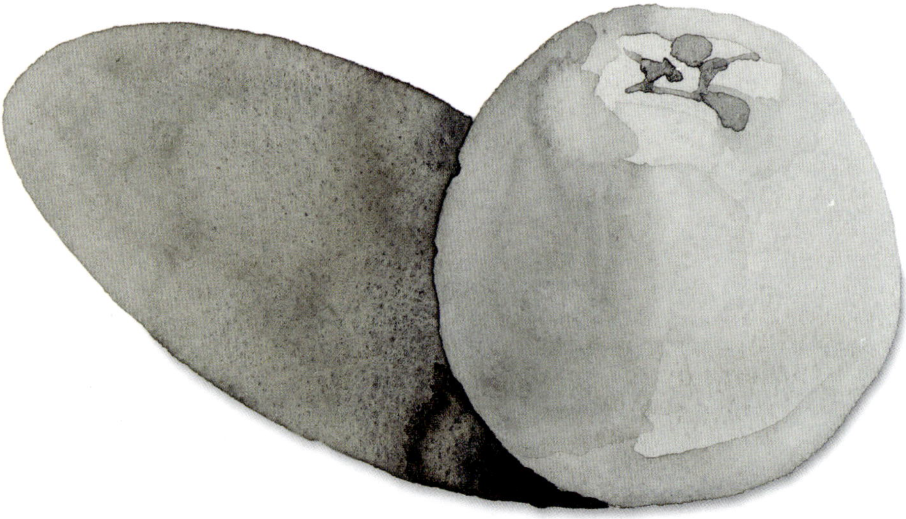

Translating colours to tones

But just how do you analyse the tones in your subject? We're used to describing things by their colour – red, blue, green and so on – but assessing tones is a different matter. One of the best ways to grasp the concept is try to imagine what a black-and-white photograph of your subject would look like.

Confusingly, colours that look very different (say, red and green) may turn out to be very similar in tone, while colours that you might expect to be light in tone (such as yellow) may actually be fairly dark, depending on how the light hits them. In addition, of course, you will find infinitely subtle gradations of tone across an object.

To make it simple, break down what you see into a few tones only – say, four or five – varying from white to black in stages. To get yourself more attuned to tones, set up some contrasting objects and, using numbers, place them in the correct order from light to dark. Time yourself. You will gradually train yourself to recognize tones more quickly. Start with objects that are strongly lit from one side, as this makes it easier to discern different tones, and gradually move on to more evenly lit objects as you develop your ability to assess tonal values. Another useful exercise is to make black-and-white photocopies of colour photographs.

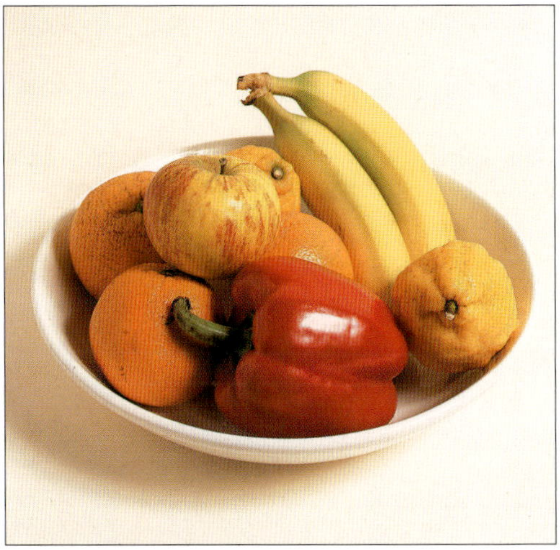

Multi-coloured subject ▲
When you're dealing with a subject that contains many colours, it can be difficult to work out which tones are light and which ones are dark. Try to imagine your subject as if it was a black-and-white photograph.

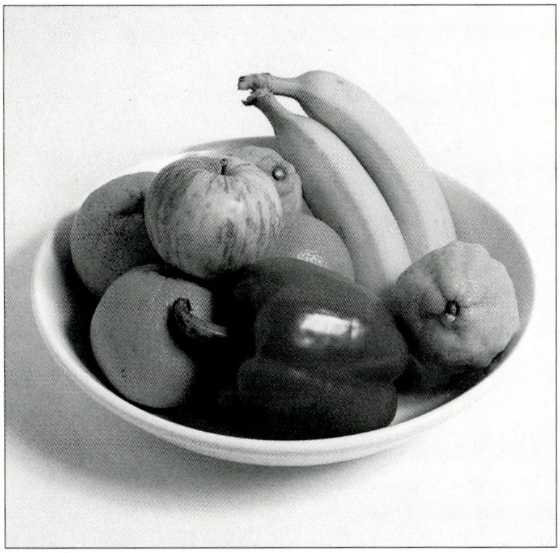

Colour converted to tone ▲
Note that different colours – for example, the oranges and the foreground lemon – are very similar in tone. The shaded sides of the bananas, which we know to be a lighter yellow than the lemon, look darker than one might expect.

Mixing tones

Once you've trained yourself to analyse tones, you need to apply this knowledge in your paintings. In pure watercolour, you make tones darker by adding more pigment (or black) and lighter by adding more water. Practise doing this with a range of different colours so that you get better at judging how much more pigment or water to add.

Tonal strip ▼
Here, alizarin crimson watercolour paint (shown in the centre of the strip) has been progressively darkened by adding black and lightened by adding water.

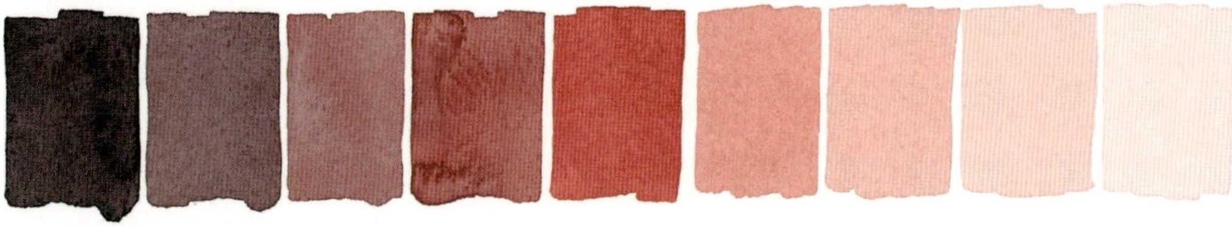

▶

Practice exercise: **Tonal study in monochrome**

This exercise trains you to assess tone by using five tones of the same colour to create a three-dimensional impression of blue and green children's play bricks. The image is painted in layers, working from light to dark, with each layer being allowed to dry before the next one is applied.

Note that the tone of the mixed washes always looks darker when it is wet than it does when it is dry. With practice you will learn to compensate for this by mixing your tones so that, when you first apply them, they appear to be a little darker or more intense than necessary.

Once you have done this exercise, try your own versions of it using other objects that you might have lying around the home. Books and plastic food containers are good choices as they are straight sided, so you can concentrate on the tones without having to worry too much about getting the shapes right.

Materials

- *200lb (425gsm) NOT watercolour paper, pre-stretched*
- *2B pencil*
- *Watercolour pigment: burnt umber*
- *Brush: medium round*

The set-up

Set up your subject on a plain white background (a large sheet of paper will do), with a table lamp in front and slightly to the left of it. Spend some time looking at it in order to decide which tone each area is going to be. If it helps, make a quick pencil sketch and number each area from one to five, with one being the lightest tone and five the darkest.

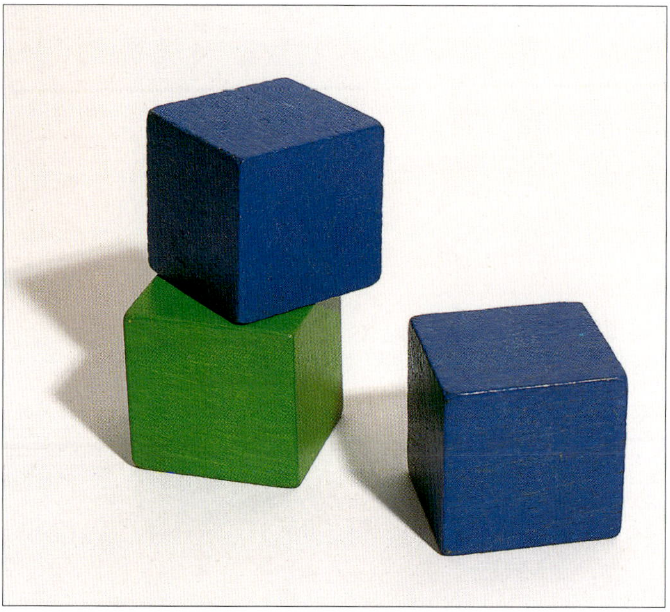

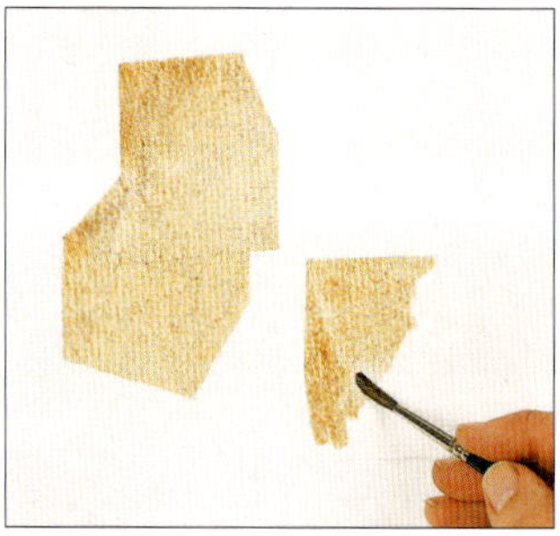

1 Using a 2B pencil, lightly sketch the bricks, taking careful note of where they overlap. Mix a thin wash of burnt umber (tone 1) and, using a medium round brush, paint all the brick shapes in this tone. This is the lightest tone.

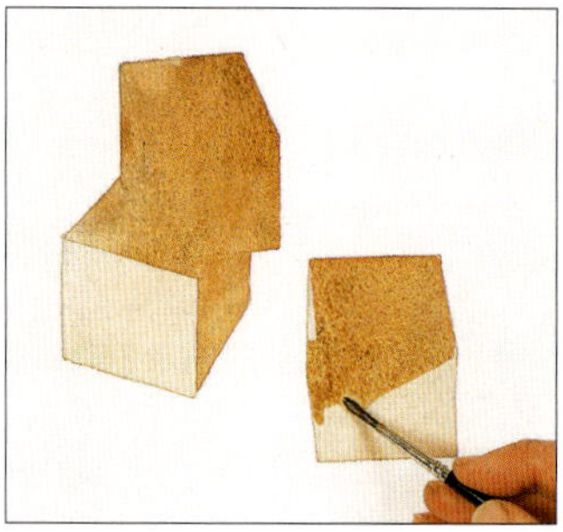

2 Strengthen the wash slightly by adding a little more burnt umber pigment (tone 2). Leaving the lightest area (the side of the green brick) untouched, apply tone 2 over all the remaining areas. Even though only two tones have been used so far, the image instantly begins to have form.

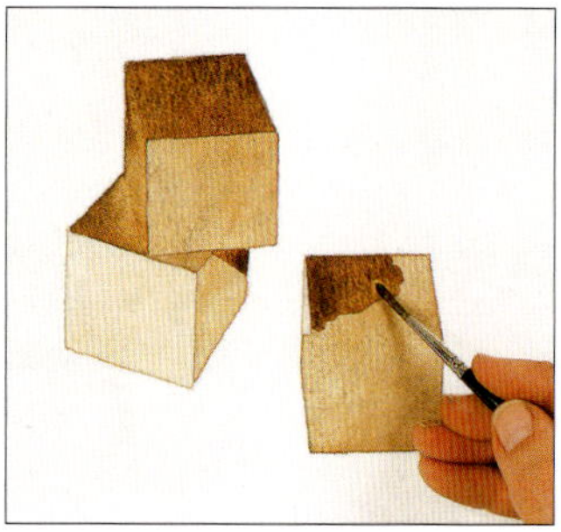

3 Add a little more pigment to the wash to darken it further and brush it over those areas that are in deeper shadow (tone 3). The shape of the three bricks is becoming ever more apparent. The tone is deepened both by adding more pigment and by overlaying successive layers of colour.

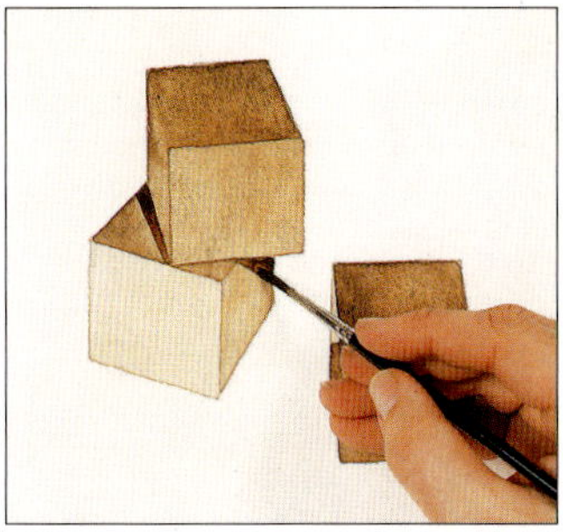

4 Now mix up tone 4. As before, do not by make a new mix, but instead, add more burnt umber pigment to the previous one to make it darker. Carefully apply this tone along the lower edge of, and below, the topmost blue brick, where a small shadow is cast across the green brick.

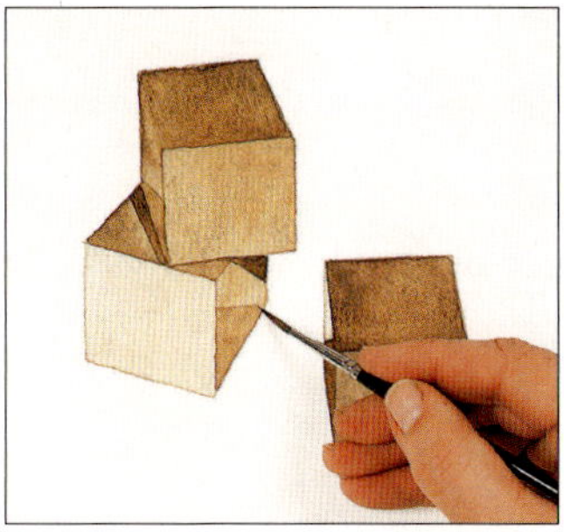

5 Tone 5, the darkest tone (created by the deep shadow reflected in the slightly shiny surface), is evident on the left-hand side of the topmost brick. A similar dark tone can be seen on the right-hand side of the brick below. This is created by the reflection of the shadow from the right-hand brick.

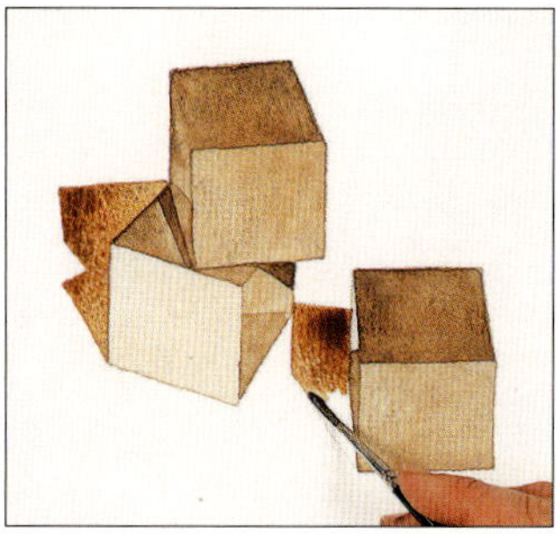

6 Put the finishing touches to the study by adding the cast shadow of all three bricks. Leave to dry.

The finished painting

Although this is nothing more than a technical exercise, the bricks look convincingly three-dimensional. This is entirely due to the fact that the artist paid very careful attention to the relative tones and built up the density by overlaying several layers where necessary, even though he used only five tones of the same colour to make the painting.

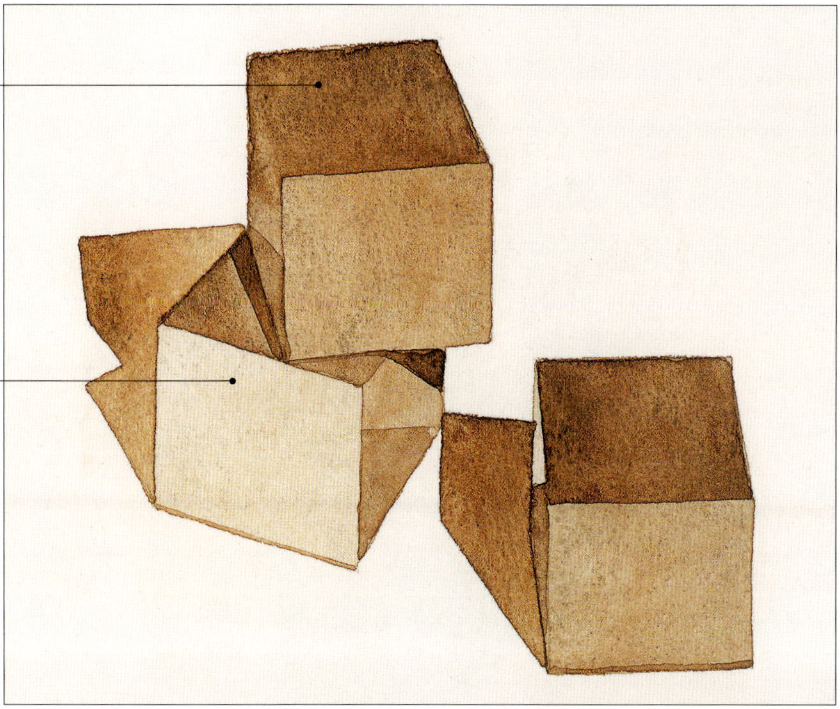

The darker tones are created by adding more pigment to the wash and also by applying several layers so that the tone is darkened gradually.

The lightest tone is created by means of a single wash of tone 1.

Understanding colour

Colour is an important element in most artistic endeavours, but in order to capture the subtle and elusive qualities of light seen in the best watercolours, a basic knowledge of colour theory is especially valuable. It will help you to understand why some colour mixes work better than others, and how to use the emotional effect of colours in your paintings.

Primary, secondary and tertiary colours

It was the Englishman Isaac Newton who first proved that white light is made by the mixing together of the seven spectrum colours of red, orange, yellow, green, blue, indigo (or blue/violet), and violet. This is known as additive colour mixing, because the "adding" together of the seven spectrum colours results in white light.

Pigment colours, however, behave in a different way. Mix together a similar range of pigment colours and the result is an almost black, mud-coloured mess. This is because every time you mix one pigment colour with another, the resulting colour is always duller and less pure than the parent colours. The more colours that are mixed together, the less pure the resulting colour will be, and the darker the resulting mix. If the three primary colours are mixed together, all the light waves are absorbed from white light, ultimately resulting in black. In other words, you subtract light and so this is known as subtractive colour mixing.

The classic diagram for explaining colour theory is the colour wheel, which illustrates the relationships between the different colours. Red, yellow and blue are the three primary pigment colours. These can only be manufactured: they cannot be mixed by combining any other colours. They are also sometimes known as the "first" or "principal" colours.

Mixing equal amounts of red with yellow creates a mid-orange; mixing yellow with blue creates a mid-green; and mixing blue with red creates a mid-violet. These are known as the secondary colours.

Mixing a primary colour with an equal amount of the secondary colour next to it results in six more colours, which are known as tertiary colours. These are red-orange, orange-yellow, yellow-green, green-blue, blue-violet, and violet-red. The quality and intensity of these tertiary colours can be extended almost indefinitely, not only by varying the proportion of the primary and secondary colours used in the mix, but also by varying the amount of water added to lighten them.

However, it is important to remember that there are many different versions of the three primary colours, and your choice of primaries therefore dictates the kind of secondary and tertiary colours that you can mix.

Warm colour wheel ► This colour wheel shows the secondary and tertiary mixes that are made using the classic warm primaries of cadmium red, cadmium yellow and ultramarine blue.

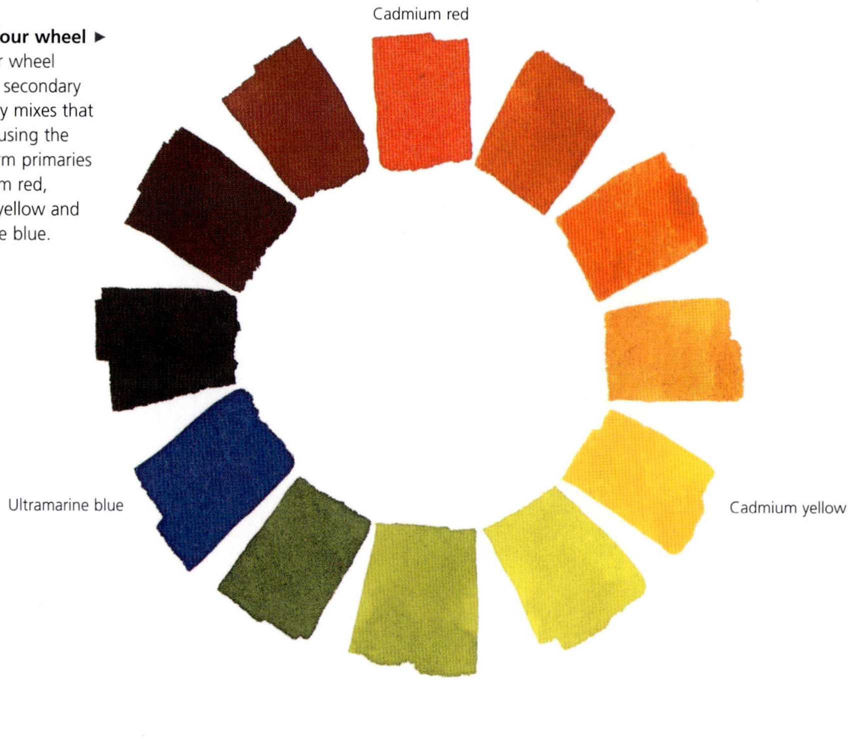

Cool colour wheel ►
This colour wheel shows the secondary and tertiary colour mixes that are made using the classic "cool" primaries of alizarin crimson, cadmium lemon and cerulean blue.

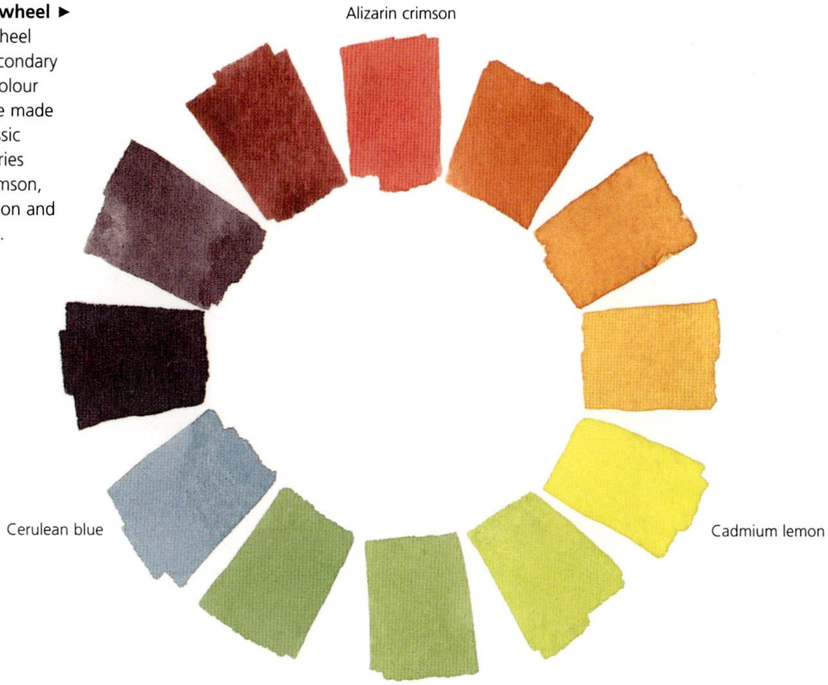

The language of colour

There are several terms relating to colour that you may come across in art books and magazines. It is important to be clear about the meaning of each.

A hue is simply another name for a colour. Red, purple and yellow are all hues. Two different reds might be described as being close in hue, while yellow and blue are different hues. There are many different versions (or hues) of the primary reds, yellows and blues, and the quality of the secondary and tertiary colour mixes depends very much on which of the primary versions you use.

A tint is made when white is added to a colour, or, in the case of pure watercolour, clean water. The opposite of a tint is a shade. This is made by making the colour darker, either by adding black or a little of its complementary colour. When you make a shade, the colour should not change dramatically in hue.

Mixing from different primaries ►
The primary phthalocyanine blue is mixed with two versions of primary red, cadmium red (left) and alizarin crimson (right), to create two different violets.

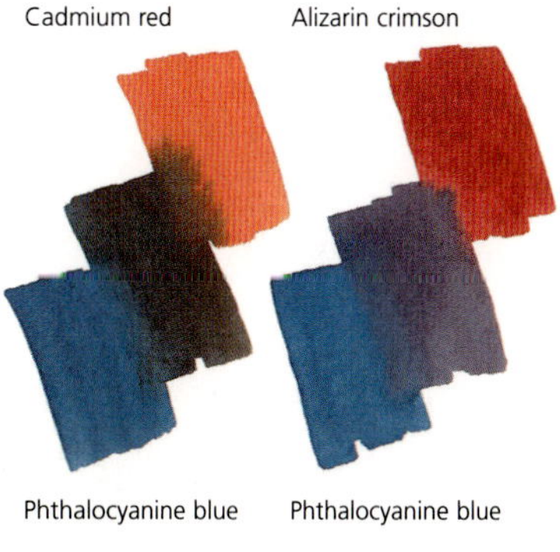

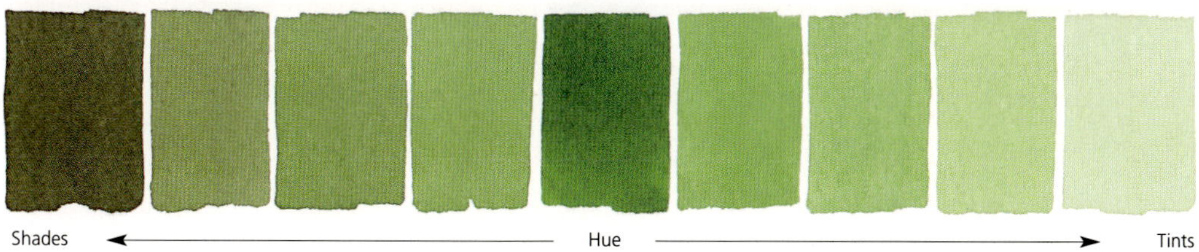

Colour temperature

All colours are described as being either warm or cool. We think of red, orange and yellow as being warm colours; these are found on one side of the colour wheel, opposite the so-called cool colours of violet, blue and green. However all colours, regardless of their position on the colour wheel, have either a warm or a cool bias. For example, blue is a cool colour and red is a warm colour, but you can have a warm blue or a cool red. If a red has a blue bias, it is described as cool; if a red has a yellow bias, it is described as warm.

In order to be able to mix a full range of colours, you need to include both warm and cool variants of at least the three primaries in your chosen palette.

Warm and cool primaries ►
This illustration shows the classic warm primaries (top row) and the classic cool primaries (bottom row).

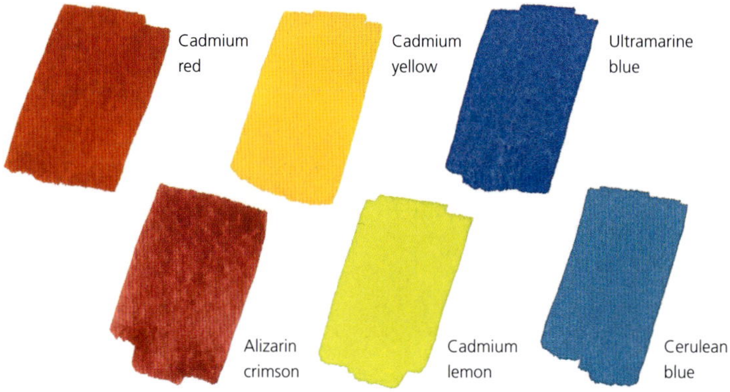

Modern paint technology, however, has meant that paint manufacturers now have primary reds, blues, and yellows that display very little or no warm or cool bias. These are the perfect primaries which, in theory, make it possible to mix a full range of colours from just three.

Colour temperature is an important part of colour mixing. Those primary colours that have a bias towards one another on the colour wheel invariably make more intense secondaries when mixed. Primaries that lean away from each other result in muted secondaries.

Colour temperature is especially important when you are trying to create the illusion of depth. Warm colours are perceived to advance while cool ones recede, so objects painted in a warm colour seem to be closer to the viewer.

Intense and subdued secondary mixes ►
Secondary and tertiary mixes are either intense or subdued, depending on the primary hues used to create them.

Here, ultramarine blue, which has a red bias, is mixed with cadmium yellow, which also has a red bias. This places them further apart on the colour wheel and results in a subdued secondary.

Phthalocyanine blue, on the other hand, has a yellow bias, and this results in an intense secondary when mixed with cadmium lemon.

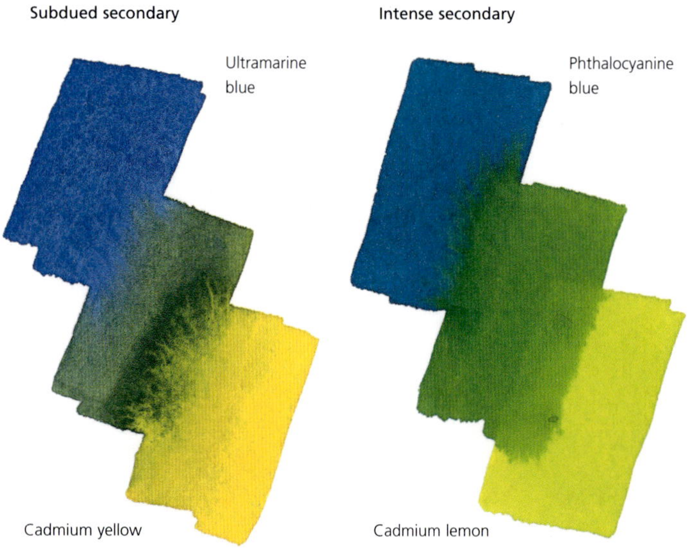

Colour contrast

Colours that fall opposite each other across the colour wheel – such as orange/blue, yellow/violet and red/green – have a special relationship and are known as complementary pairs. When they are placed next to each other in a painting, complementary colours create vibrant colour contrasts and have the effect of making each other appear more intense than they really are.

This is due to an effect known as "simultaneous contrast". If you stare at an area of green and then look away to a white surface, you will see a red after-image – red being the complementary of green. If red is placed next to a green area, it will be visually intensified by this red after-image. Likewise, the green would be intensified by the green after-image from the red. This effect can be used to add intensity to your work.

Complementary pairs ►
These special colour pairings seem more intense when placed next to each other, but they neutralize each other when the paints are physically mixed together.

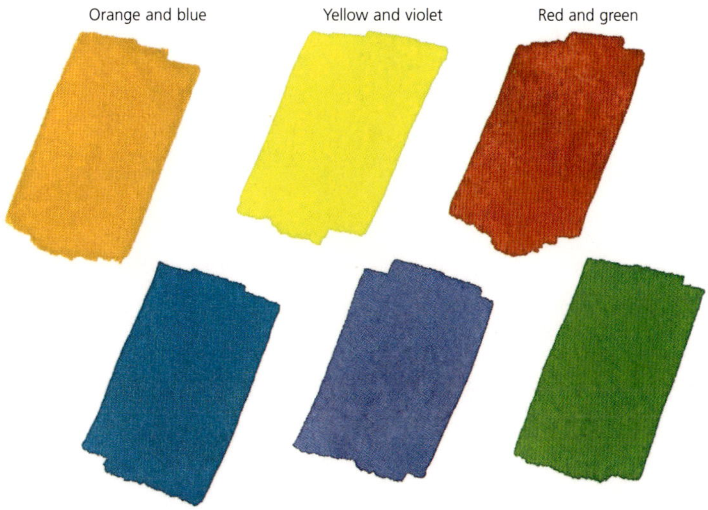

Mixing complementaries

If a little of one complementary colour is added to another, it subdues the recipient colour, knocking it back but without dulling it in the way that adding black would. If more of the colour's complementary is added, the result (depending on which complementaries are used) is a range of browns and greys, known as neutral colours. The advantage of mixing neutral colours in this way, rather than by adding black, is that the mixes look much fresher.

If you look at a colour wheel, you will see that regardless of their position all complementary pairs are, to a greater or lesser extent, composed of all three primary colours. When you mix equal amounts of all three primaries together, the result is a dark grey – almost black. However, by carefully managing the relative amounts of the three primaries that enter the mix, you can create a wonderful range of subtle, neutral mixes that echo those found in the natural world.

Mixing neutral greys ▼
Neutral greys and browns are made by mixing together two complementary colours. Here, progressively larger amounts of viridian green are added to alizarin crimson, resulting in a dark grey. A range of grey tints is then made by adding increasing amounts of water.

Colour harmony

Using harmonious colours that work well together creates a distinct feel or mood, and this adds immeasurably to the success of a work. This is especially true if you are trying to depict a specific season of the year or time of day, or if you are trying to show how a subject has been lit, for example, a still life bathed in candlelight or a figure lit with harsh mid-day light.

As the colour wheel below shows, there are many different ways of achieving colour harmony. With practice you will find that your instinct is the best guide: if something looks right, then it is right. However, a little basic theory about colour harmony will set you on the right path.

Different types of colour harmony ▼
Complementary harmony is created by using those colours that fall opposite each other on the colour wheel. Triad harmony is achieved by using the colours found at the angles of an equilateral triangle, superimposed at any position over the colour wheel. Using an isosceles triangle will point to the colours to form a split complementary, while using a square or a rectangle will produce tetrad harmonies. Alternatively, you can create harmony by using those colours that have one primary in common or are close to each other on the colour wheel. These are known as analogous colours.

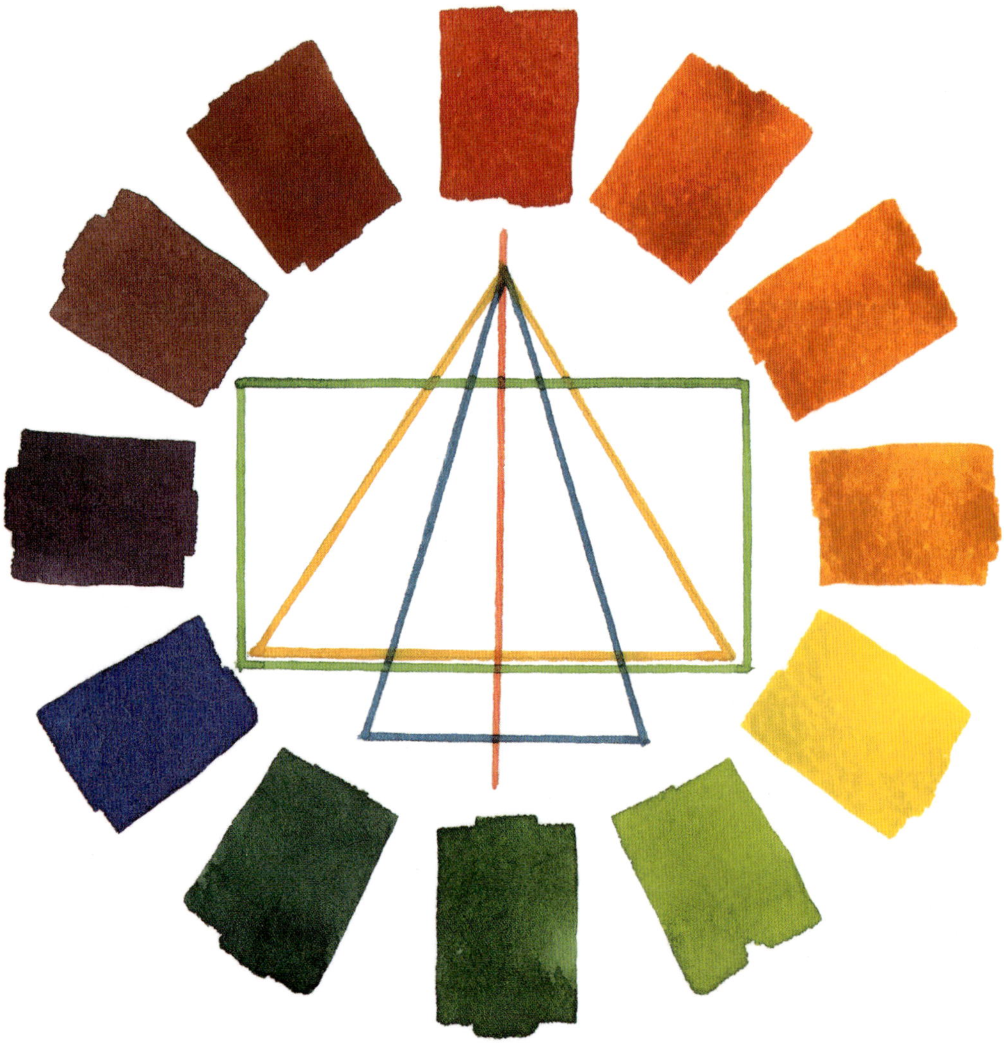

Tone and optical mixing

Traditional watercolour technique relies on one transparent wash being laid over another in such a way as to modify or consolidate the initial wash without necessarily obliterating it. It is, however, easy to overdo these wash layers so that the image and the colours look dull, lacking the sparkle and elusive inner light for which good watercolour is renowned.

Try to think ahead when planning your work, and aim to use no more than three layers of wash at the most. Working on the light to dark principle, the first washes would include the lightest tones and colours, the second layer the mid-tones and colours, and the final layer the darkest ones. As with all best laid plans, of course, this is not always possible, but it is a useful discipline to keep in mind. This is one of the reasons why the ability to assess tonal values is such an important part of watercolour painting.

Building up colour density ▼
Colour density can be built up by overlaying washes. This illustration shows three layers of the same colour, though the same principle holds true when you apply different colours on top of each other.

This layering technique can also create colour mixes that are impossible when certain colours are mixed together physically. Physically mixing any two complementary colours together will result in the chosen colours being neutralized and, depending on the amounts used, being turned into a brown or a grey. However, you can mix these colours optically by applying a transparent wash of one colour over a dry wash of the other. This retains the integrity of both washes; a certain amount of the lower wash colour will show through the upper wash, modifying it. Another name for this type of colour application is broken colour. It can provide both texture and interest to those areas of a work where the colour is intrinsically flat and featureless, as well as being used to depict difficult subjects consisting of complex colour variations, such as foliage, water or extreme weather conditions.

Optical mixes ▼
When one wash is applied over another, wet on dry, the two colours mix optically to produce a third colour. These optical mixes look crisp and clean, as the colours retain their integrity.

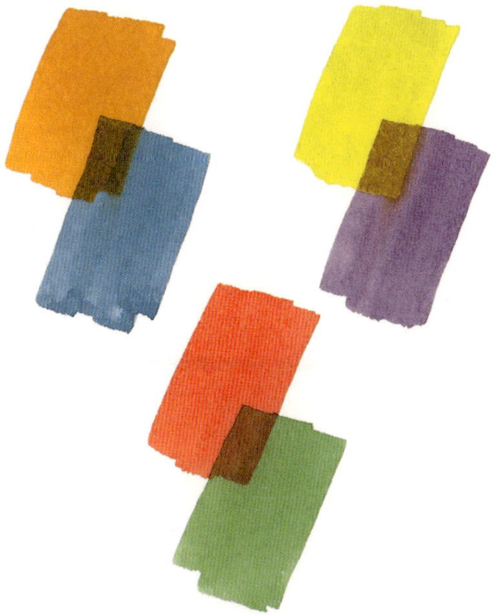

Physical mixes ▼
When colours are mixed physically, the resulting colours look duller than their optical counterparts. This is true regardless of whether the colours are mixed wet into wet (left) or wet on dry.

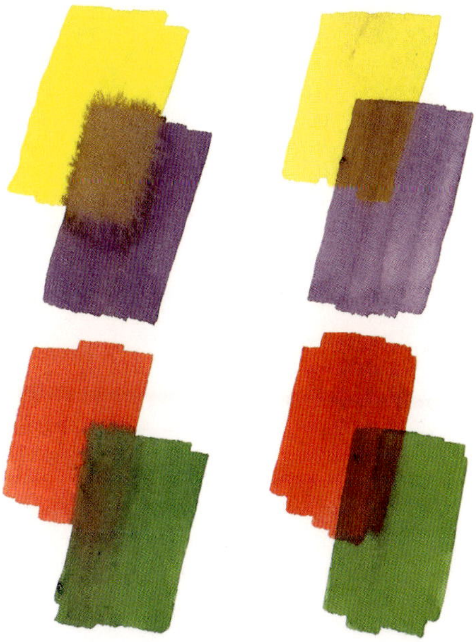

Practice exercise: **Overlaying colours**

In this exercise, colours are overlaid both to build up density of tone and to optically "mix" colours on the paper. Because watercolour paint is transparent, some of the colour of your initial wash will show through any subsequent washes, modifying their appearance. The only way you can be sure of the effect is to practise on a piece of scrap paper in advance. Remember that watercolour always looks lighter when it is dry, so you must wait until your practice piece is completely dry before deciding whether you've got the colour you want.

Materials

- *140lb (300gsm) NOT watercolour paper, pre-stretched*
- *2B pencil*
- *Watercolour paints: cerulean blue, lemon yellow, yellow ochre, burnt umber, mauve, alizarin crimson, cadmium yellow*
- *Brushes: large round, fine round, mop*
- *Sponge*

The set-up

When setting up a still life, choose objects of different shapes and sizes. The elongated shape of the pear and the rounded swede (rutabaga) used here give interesting visual contrasts. In terms of their colour, the same underlying green occurs on both, giving unity to the still life, while the red coloration on the swede complements the green, making it more exciting.

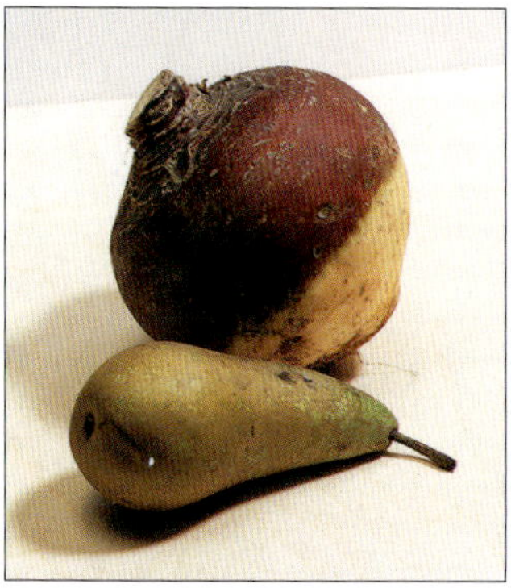

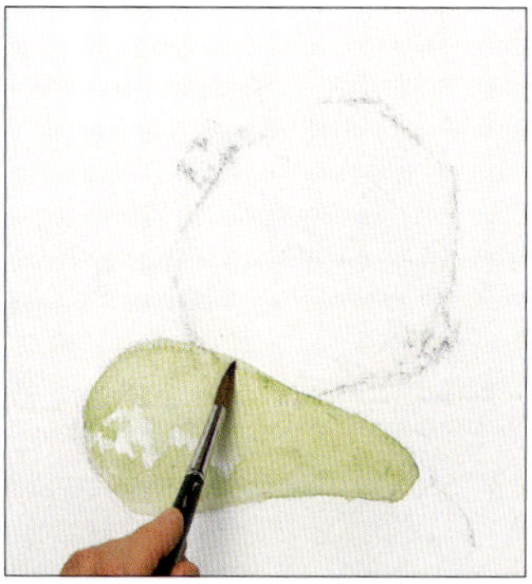

1 Lightly sketch the pear and swede. Mix a bright green from cerulean blue and lemon yellow, and brush over the pear, leaving highlights untouched. Dot paint on to give an uneven texture.

Tip: When drawing fruit, work out the position of the stem and the base and draw a line between them to help get the angle of the fruit right.

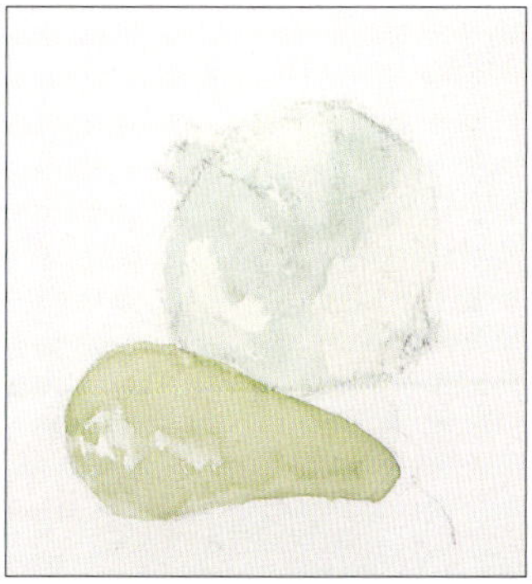

2 Add more cerulean blue to the mixture and more water to make it very dilute, and brush it unevenly over the top half of the swede, again leaving some gaps. You have now established the underlying colours of both the pear and the swede. These colours will be allowed to show through in parts of the finished painting, but they will also influence any colours that are laid down on top of them, creating mixes that could not be achieved in the palette.

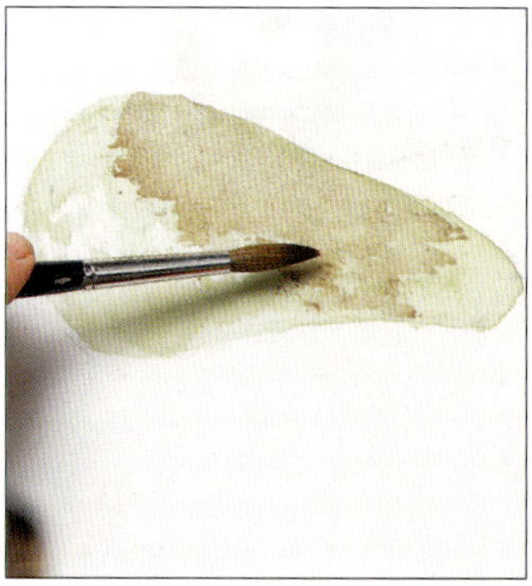

3 Mix a dark brown from yellow ochre, a little burnt umber and a touch of mauve. Using the side of the brush, brush this mixture unevenly over the pear, leaving gaps in places so that some of the first green wash is visible. The brown mixture is transparent, hence its appearance is modified by the underlying bright green. The two colours on top of each other look like a dull, mottled green.

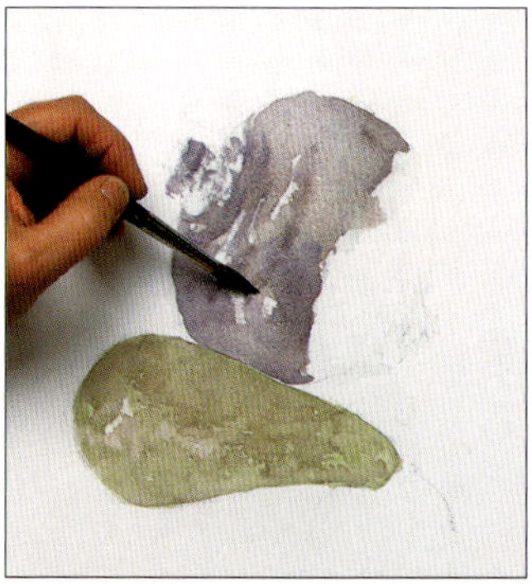

4 Mix a dull purple from mauve with a little burnt umber and brush it over the swede, making the top lighter than the bottom by adding more water. As on the pear, keep the texture and density of tone uneven by dotting more paint on in places. While the paint is still wet, build up the colour by touching more paint into selected areas so that it spreads wet into wet and you do not get any hard-edged shapes.

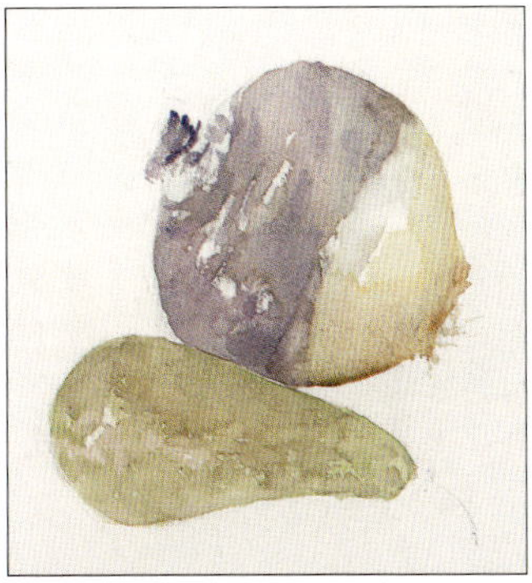

5 Mix a dilute wash of yellow ochre and brush it over the lower half of the swede, adding more pigment as you work down so that the base is darker. While the paint is still wet, brush a line of the green used in Step 1 between the two halves of the swede.

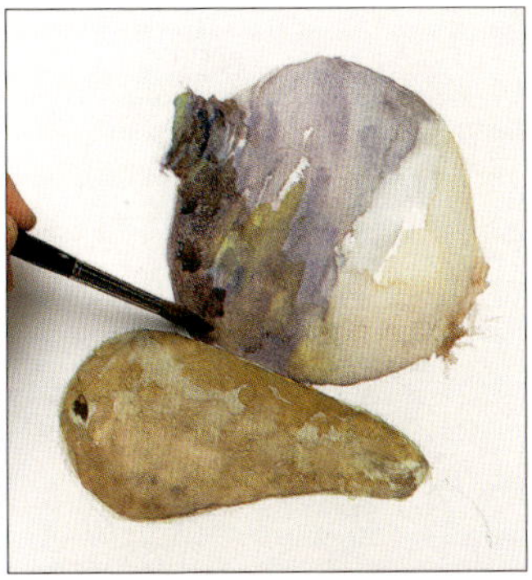

6 Using the same mixture as before, continue building up tone and depth on the purple half of the swede, applying the paint unevenly to create interesting textures. Using the same dark brown mixture as in Step 3, put a few spots and blemishes on the pear.

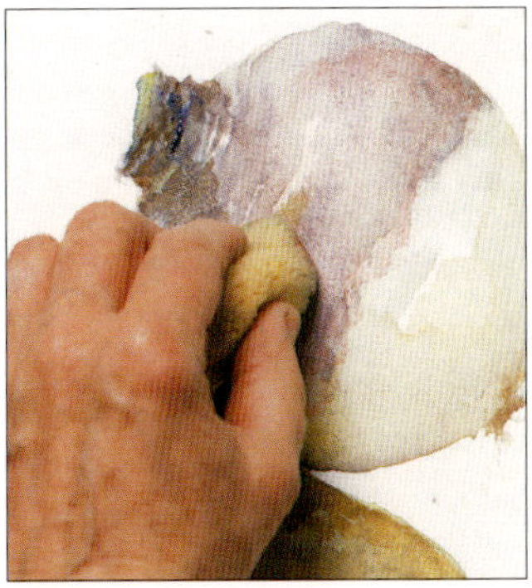

7 Mix up a very dilute wash of alizarin crimson. Using a small sponge, dab it on to the purple half of the swede. Crimson and green are complementary colours, so using the two together in the picture immediately gives it a lift. Leave to dry.

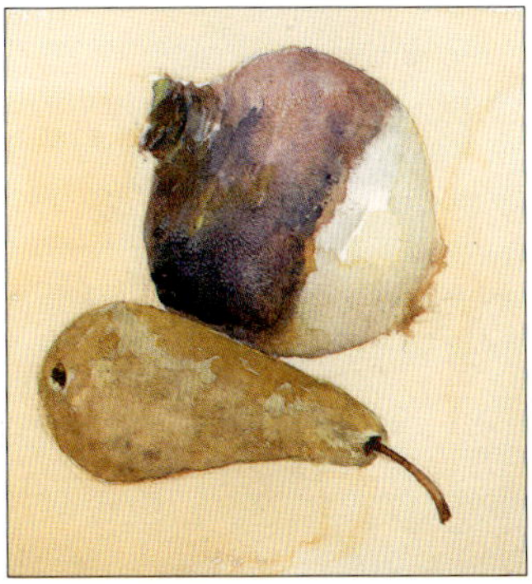

8 Mix a warm orange from alizarin crimson and cadmium yellow. Using a large mop brush, brush this mixture carefully on to the background; you may need to tilt the board to prevent paint from running over the pear or swede. Mix a dark brown from burnt umber and mauve and, using a fine round brush, paint the pear stem.

The finished painting

The initial green washes have modified the colour of subsequent layers, creating subtle optical mixes that are more effective than a single, solid wash could ever be. Applying several layers of the same colour (as on the swede) allows you to build up the tone gradually.

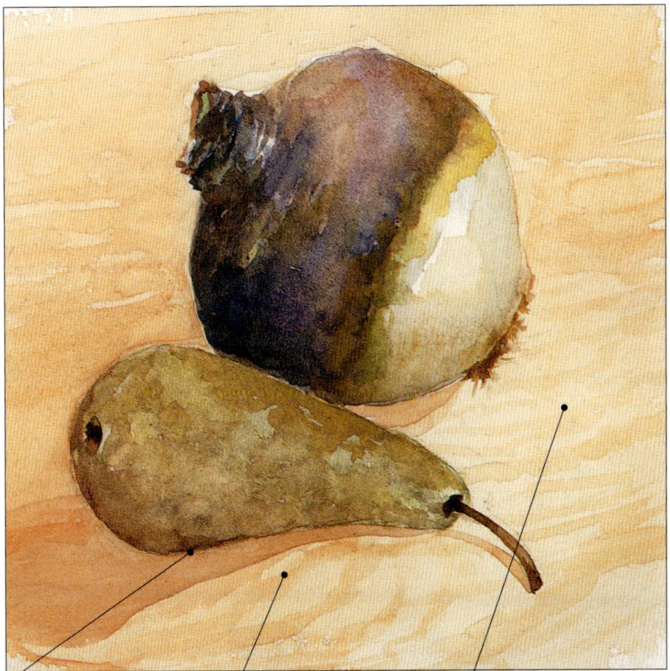

The shadows under the pear and swede anchor them to the surface and make the still life look more three-dimensional.

The "woodgrain" is painted using a more pigmented version of the background colour plus a little mauve.

The background colour harmonizes with the pear and swede but is sufficiently different to allow them to stand out.

Wet into wet

Working wet into wet means exactly what it says – applying wet paint to wetted paper. When you do this, the paint spreads outwards in soft-edged blurs, and the wetter the paper, the further the paint spreads. You can apply paint either to paper that has been dampened with clean water or on top of a wash that has not yet dried, creating interesting colour mixes. Paint will not spread into any areas that are completely dry.

Dropping gorgeous, rich colours on to wetted paper is an exhilarating experience, as you can never predict exactly what will happen or how far the paint will spread on the paper. For many people, that unpredictability is part of the charm of watercolour painting.

Colours that have been applied wet into wet always look lighter when they dry than they do when they are first put on. With experience you will learn to compensate for this by using stronger, more pigmented washes.

The wet-into-wet technique is excellent for cloudy skies, distant trees and woods, and atmospheric effects, such as fogs or storms. However, a picture painted entirely wet into wet would look very blurred and indistinct. Try to keep a balance between wet-into-wet areas and sharper, more clearly defined sections. It is particularly important not to make the foreground too blurred. The soft-focus effect of wet into wet is normally best reserved for distant parts of a scene where you do not want a lot of sharp detail. When you apply paint on top of wet-into-wet washes that have dried, make sure you allow the underlying, diffuse effect of wet into wet to be seen in places, otherwise you will lose the character of the technique.

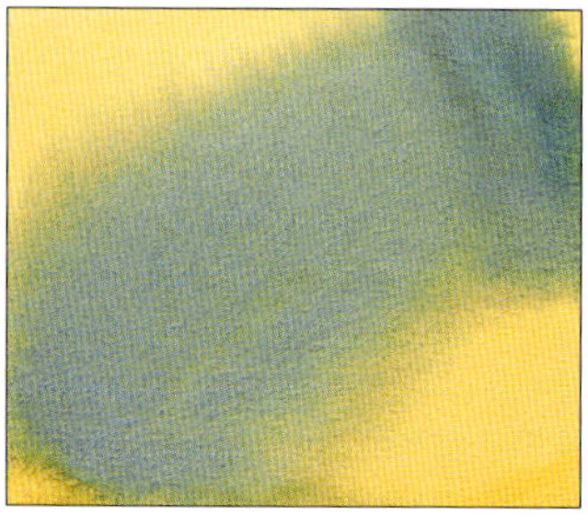

On very damp paper ▲
The paint spreads far beyond the line of the brushstroke.

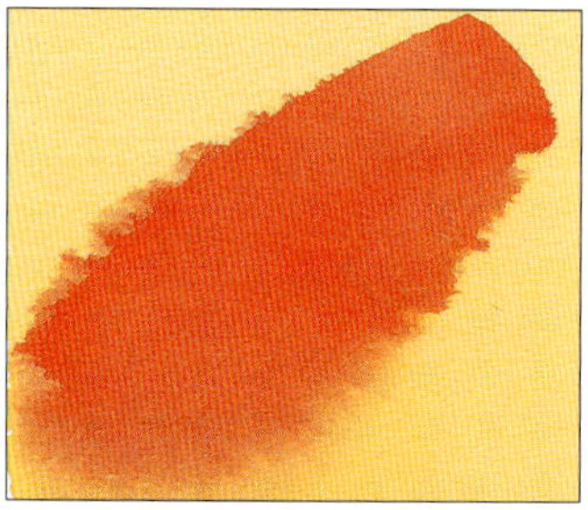

On moderately damp paper ▲
The paint still blurs but it does not spread so far.

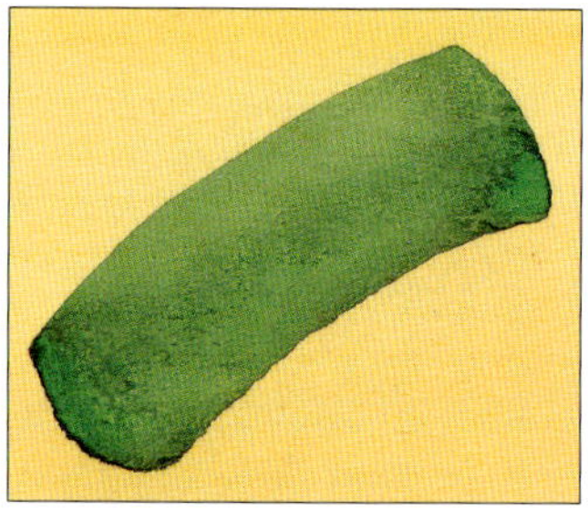

On almost dry paper ▲
The paint barely spreads beyond the brushstroke.

Practice exercise: **Still life painted wet into wet**

With their wonderful markings and silvery undersides, mackerel are beautiful fish to paint. This exercise allows you to practise controlling the degree of wetness on the paper. On the background and undersides of the fish, paint is applied to very damp paper so that it spreads freely. For the markings, the paint is applied to paper that is only very slightly damp. The paint blurs a little but the markings remain distinct.

Materials

- *2B pencil*
- *140lb (300gsm) rough watercolour paper, pre-stretched*
- *Watercolour paints: Payne's grey, Delft blue, alizarin crimson, aureolin, viridian, raw sienna, light red, sap green, cadmium lemon*
- *Brushes: large round*

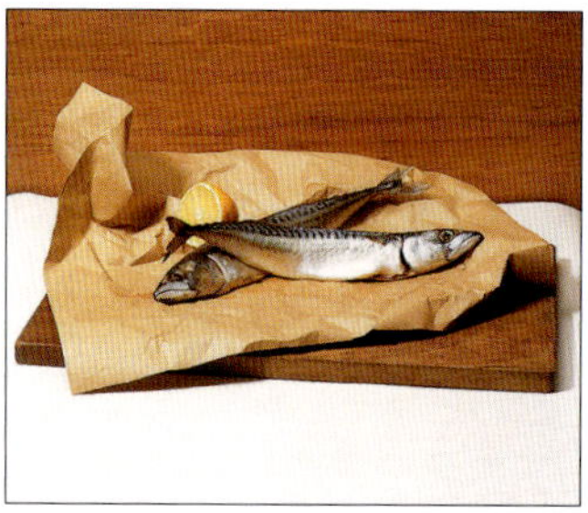

The set-up
Crumpled brown parcel paper provides a textured but simple background to this still life. Arrange the fish so that you can see both the markings and the silvery belly, and add a lemon for a touch of extra colour. Position a lamp to one side of your subject, so that it casts definite shadows.

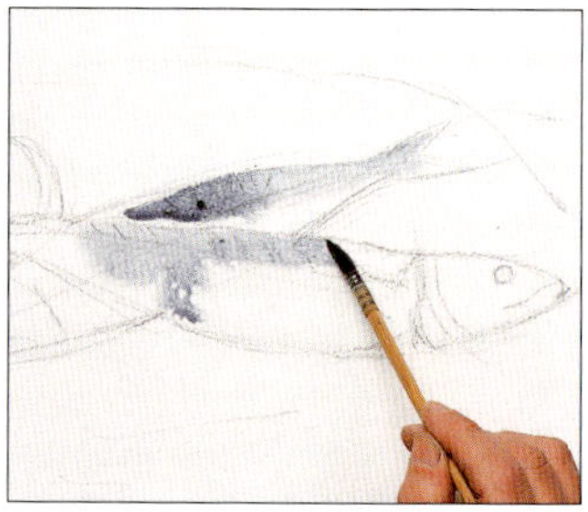

1 Using a 2B pencil, lightly sketch the still life. Using a large round brush, dampen the fish with clean water, leaving the highlights around the eyes and on the belly untouched and keeping within the outline of the fish. Mix a greyish blue from Payne's grey and Delft blue. Brush this mixture on to the damp areas so that it spreads.

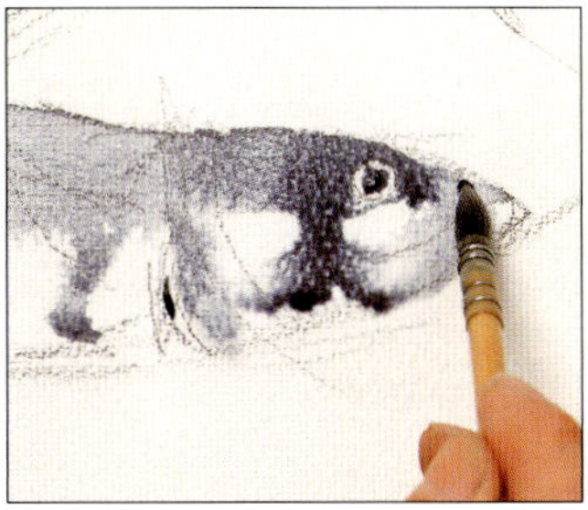

2 Add a little more Delft blue to the mixture and, using the tip of the brush, touch in the dark details around the head, again working carefully around the highlight areas.

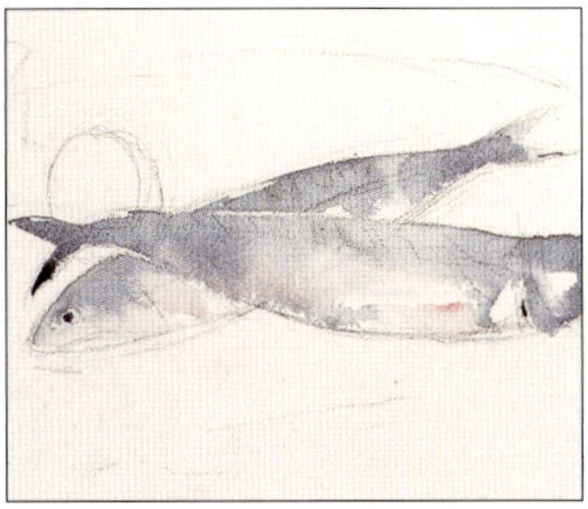

3 While the first wash is still damp, brush alizarin crimson on to the belly of the foreground fish and the head of the background fish. It will merge with the underlying wash. Leave to dry.

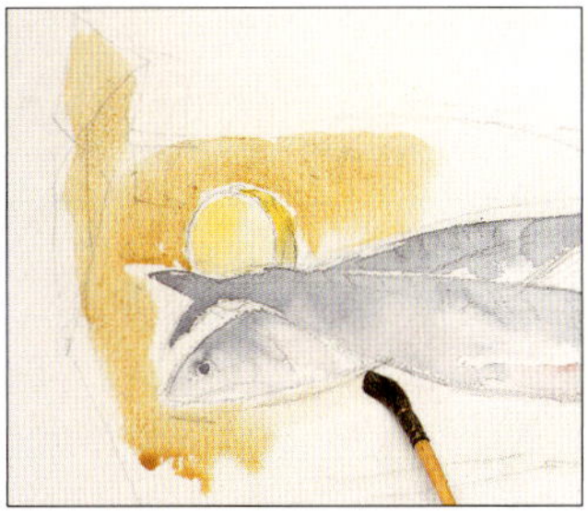

4 Dampen the lemon and brush on a pale mix of aureolin. Mix a pale green and brush on to the shaded side of the lemon. Leave to dry. Dampen the background and brush on raw sienna.

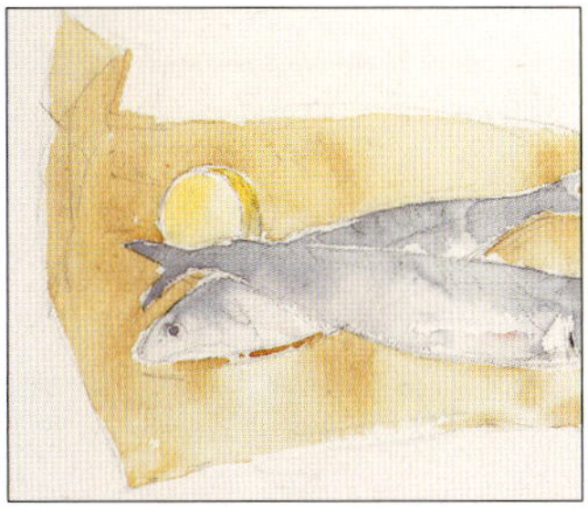

5 While the background wash is still damp, add a little light red to the raw sienna and touch it into those areas of the background that you want to appear darkest in order to build up the tone and imply the creases in the paper. Leave to dry.

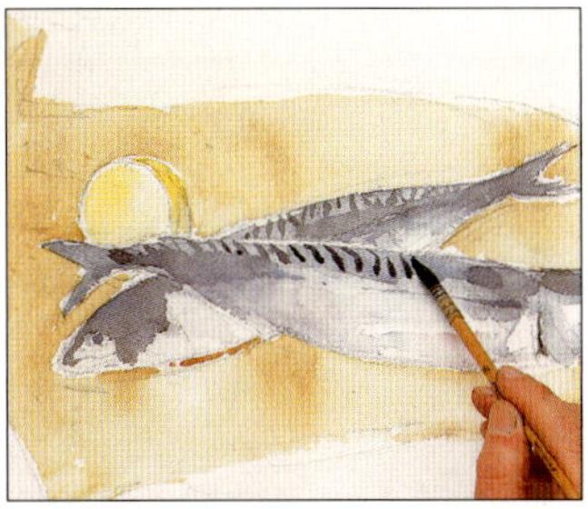

6 Mix a dark blue-grey from Delft blue, Payne's grey and a little alizarin crimson. Dampen the backs of the fish with clean water and brush the paint on to the darkest areas. Add more Delft blue to the mixture and, when the paper is nearly dry, paint the markings.

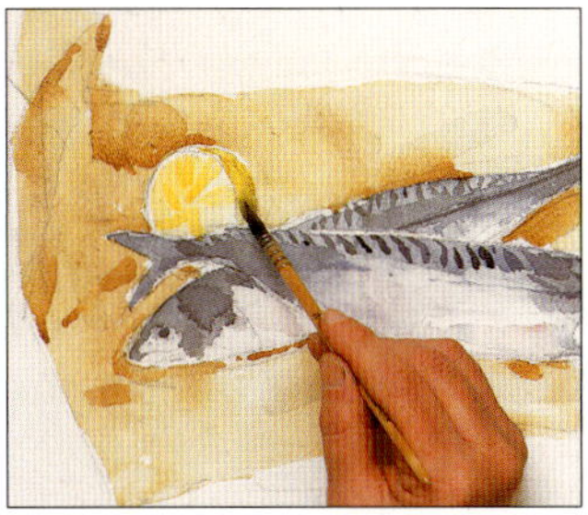

7 Dampen the darkest areas of the background and touch in more of the mixture used in Step 5. Paint the lemon segments in aureolin. Dampen the rest of the lemon and brush a mixture of sap green and cadmium lemon on to the right-hand side.

The finished painting
The subtle transitions of colour on the bellies of the fish and the background paper could only be achieved using the wet-into-wet technique. These areas contrast well with the dry applications of colour on the lemon and around the fish head.

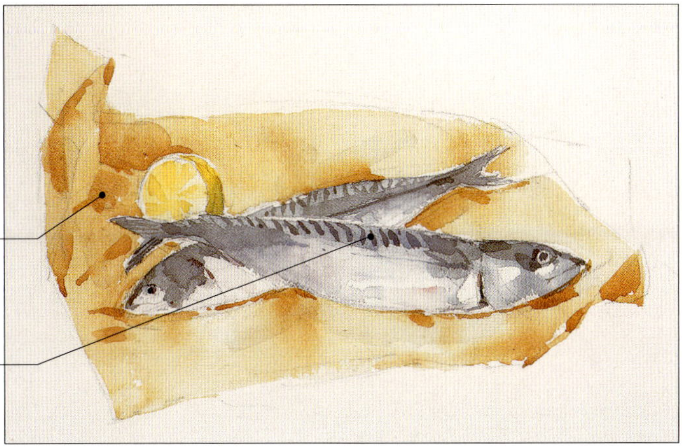

Several layers of colour are applied to the background while the paper is still very damp. The paint spreads, creating soft-edged blocks of colour.

For the markings, the paint is applied to paper that is only slightly damp. It spreads enough to soften the markings, but not so far that they become blurred and indistinct.

Masking

Often in watercolour, you want the white of the paper to represent the lightest areas of your subject. Sometimes you will need to protect the white areas so that they don't get splashed with paint accidentally. Masking is the way to do this. The masking technique can also be applied over a coloured wash. When a second wash is applied over the mask, the mask can then be removed to reveal the underlying base colour. This technique is used to give an aged and weathered look to paths, walls and painted timber.

There are many subjects that might benefit from masking, from whitewashed buildings and structural objects, such as ladders, to water foam splashing against a rock, tiny flowers, and even the delicate tracery of lace and spiders' webs.

There are three methods of applying masking. The one you choose will depend largely on whether you need to mask straight lines, delicate lines or curved shapes, or larger areas.

Masking tape

Masking tape is useful for masking straight-edged shapes, such as buildings, although it can also be cut or even torn to create more random effects. Make sure you use the low-tack variety of masking tape, otherwise you may find that you damage the surface of your watercolour paper when you attempt to remove it.

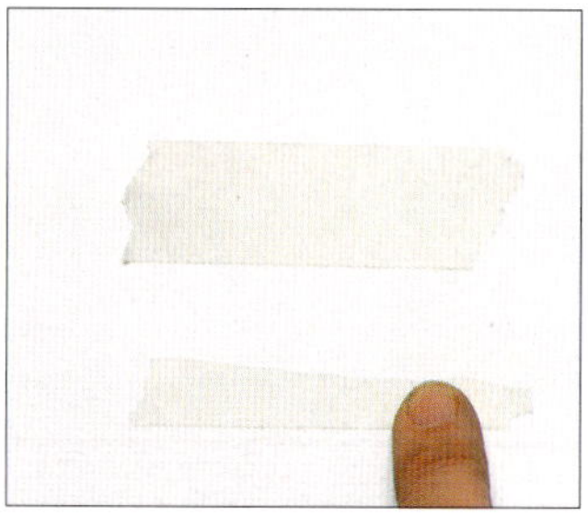

1 Place the masking tape on the watercolour paper, smoothing it down at the edges so that no paint can get underneath.

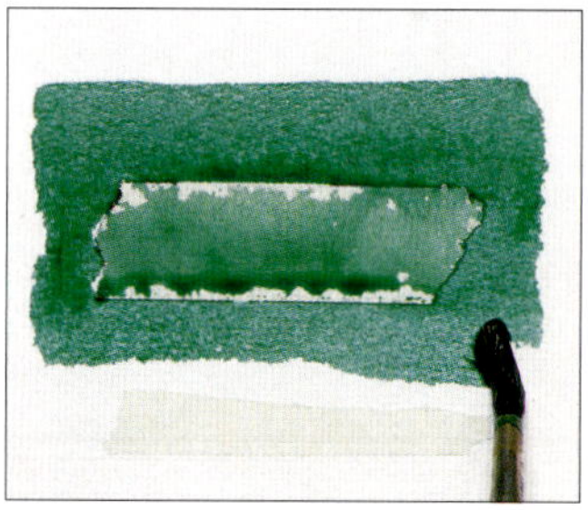

2 Apply a wash over the top of the masking tape and then leave it to dry completely.

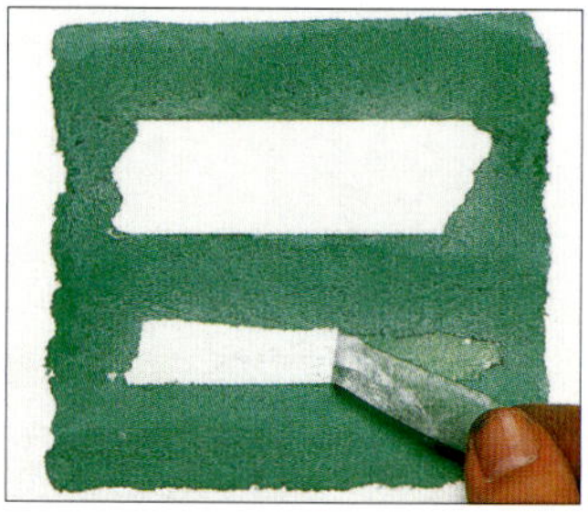

3 Carefully peel off the tape (you may need to use the tip of a scalpel or craft or utility knife to lift the edge). The area underneath remains white.

Masking fluid

Masking fluid is useful when you want to mask out thin lines, such as grasses in the foreground of a landscape. You can also spatter it on to the paper for subjects such as white daisies in a meadow or the white foam of a waterfall. Always wash the brush thoroughly with liquid detergent immediately after use, as it is almost impossible to remove the fluid from the bristles once it has dried; better still, keep old brushes specifically for use with masking fluid.

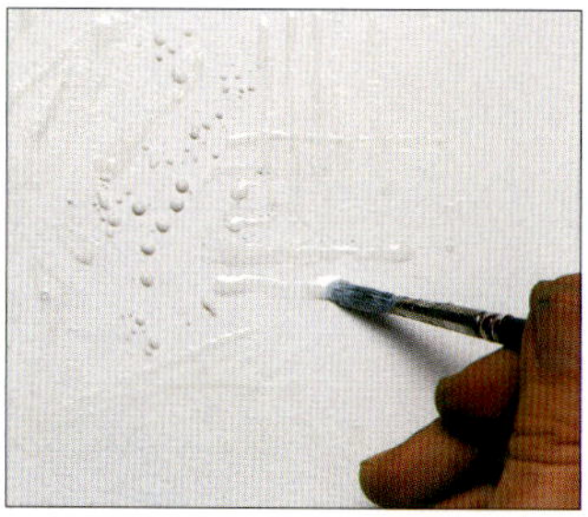

1 Using an old brush, paint masking fluid over the areas you want to protect. Leave it to dry completely.

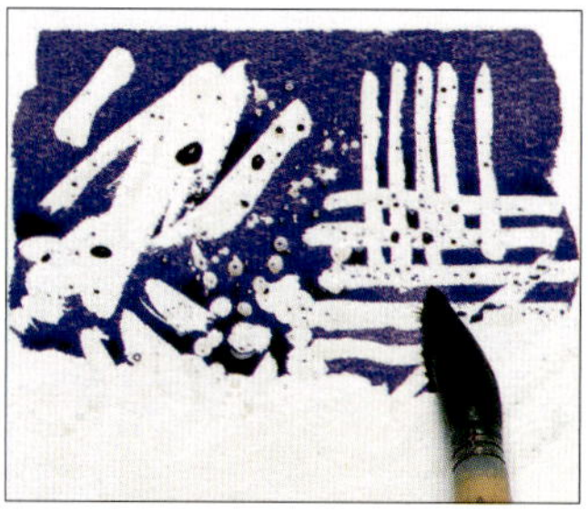

2 Apply a wash over the paper and leave it to dry completely.

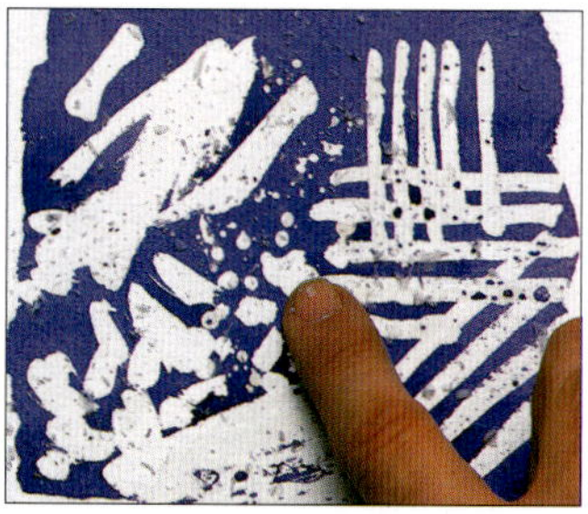

3 Using your fingertips, gently rub off the fluid. (You will find that it can be rubbed off quite easily.)

Masking film

Masking film (frisket paper) is used by draughtsmen and is available from most good art supply stores. It works best with large, clearly defined areas that you can easily cut around, such as hills or a pale-coloured building.

You need to use a very smooth watercolour paper or board so that the film has a perfectly flat surface to adhere to, otherwise paint may seep under the edges and ruin the effect.

Alternatively, you could cut a paper mask and either hold it in position with one hand while you paint with the other, or fix it to your painting surface with low-tack masking tape. This is not advisable for fiddly, intricate details where you need the mask to be stuck down firmly, but if you need to protect, say, the sky area of a landscape while you spatter paint on to the land, then a paper mask is a good, low-cost option.

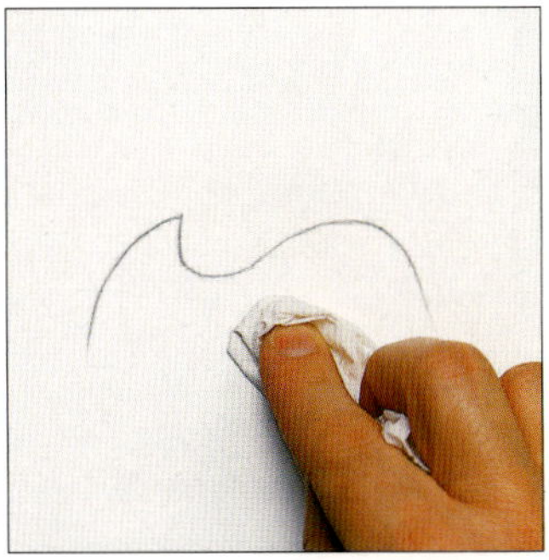

1 Cut a piece of masking film (frisket paper) to roughly the same size as your painting. Peel the film from its backing paper, position it on your underdrawing, and smooth it down with a soft cloth or piece of tissue paper to make sure it is stuck down firmly and smoothly.

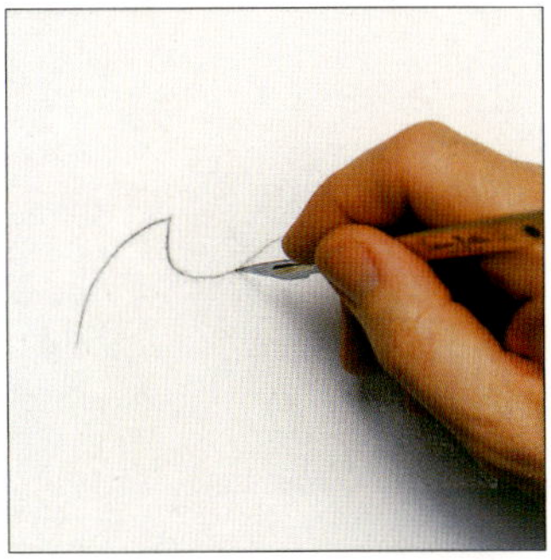

2 Using a scalpel or craft (utility) knife, carefully cut around the outer line of your subject, taking care not to cut into the paper or board.

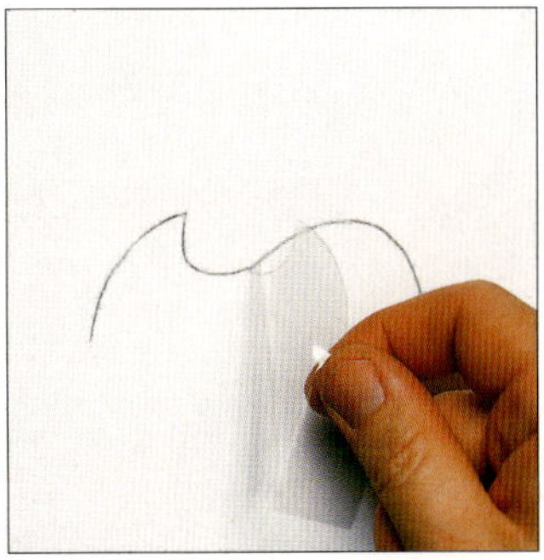

3 Slowly peel back the masking film from the area that you do not want to protect from paint (ie. the area that you want to paint with colour).

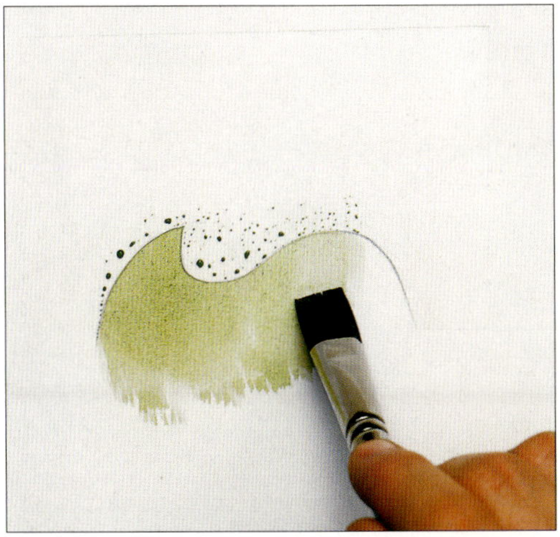

4 Apply a colour wash to the exposed paper, using a large round brush. Leave the wash to dry completely before you attempt to remove the masking film.

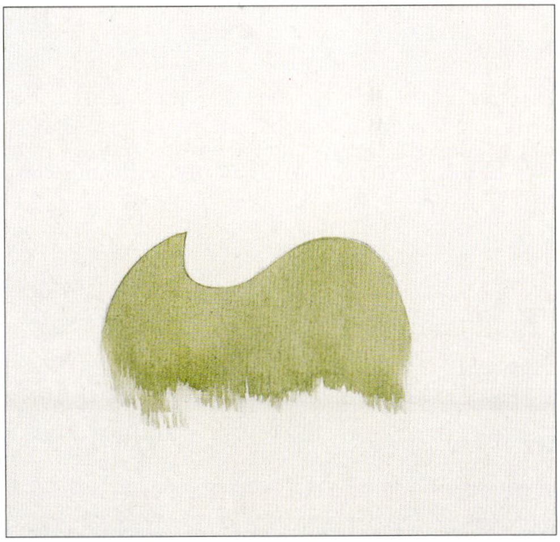

5 Check that the wash is dry, then slowly peel back the masking film from the unpainted area. Remove it in a smooth movement, so as not to tear the paper.

Practice exercise: **Masking a white-patterned jar**

This short exercise allows you to experiment with using both masking fluid (to mask out the sweeping curved lines and fine detail of the decorative jar) and low-tack masking tape (to mask out the straight-edged rectangle of paper on which the jar is placed). Painting around the pattern on the jar in order to leave the paper white would be a painstakingly slow and laborious process, and it would be very difficult to create such fine lines. Protecting the pattern with masking fluid allows you to work in a much more free and spontaneous manner.

Materials

- *2B pencil*
- *200lb (425gsm) NOT watercolour paper, pre-stretched*
- *Watercolour paints: cobalt blue, ultramarine blue, Payne's grey, raw umber, dioxazine purple*
- *Brushes: old brush for masking, medium round, fine round*
- *Masking fluid*
- *Low-tack masking tape*

The set-up

Arrange your subject on a piece of coloured paper that harmonizes with it, and position a table lamp in front of and slightly to the right of the subject so that you get an interesting shadow.

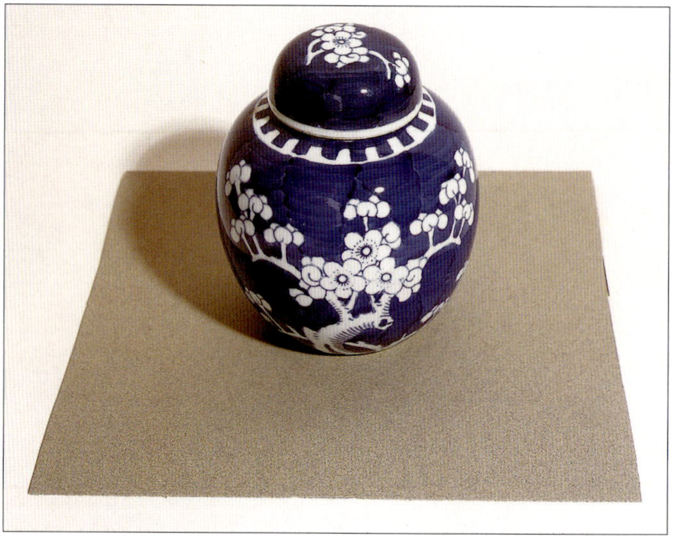

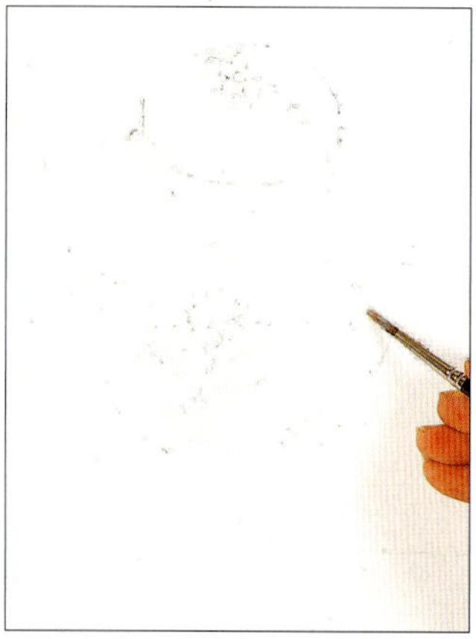

1 Using a 2B pencil, lightly sketch the jar and its decorative pattern. Using an old brush and liquid rubber masking fluid, mask out any areas that you want to keep white and clear of paint. Rinse the brush thoroughly and allow the masking fluid to dry completely before moving on to the next stage.

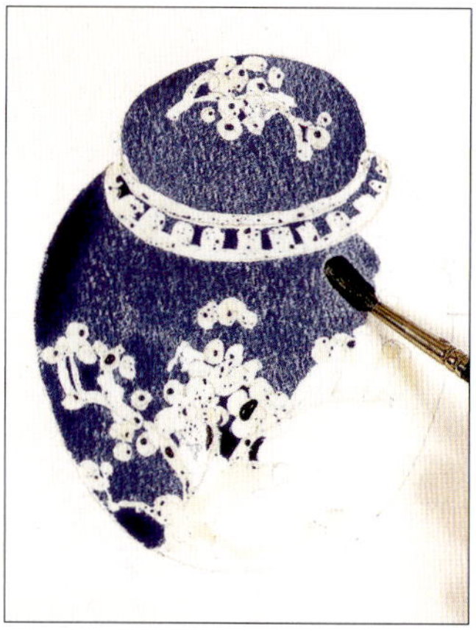

2 With the design protected by the masking fluid, there is no risk of accidentally painting over the white areas. Mix a vivid blue from cobalt blue, ultramarine blue and a little Payne's grey. Using a medium round brush, wash this mixture evenly over the jar. Leave to dry.

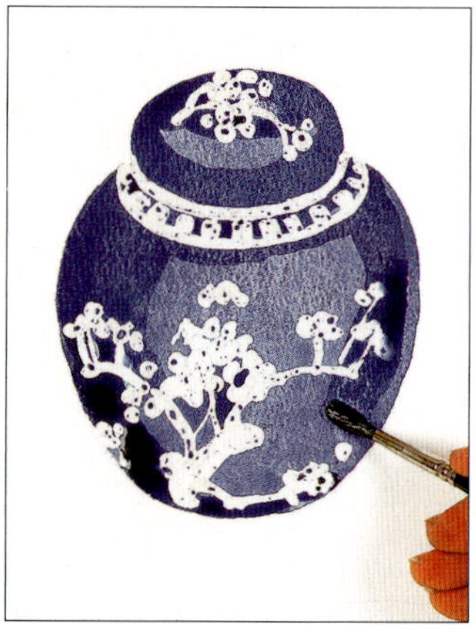

3 Using the same blue paint mixture, work over the jar once again to strengthen the tone. Add more Payne's grey to the mixture when you paint the right-hand side of the jar, which is slightly in shadow. This darker tone helps to make the jar look realistically three-dimensional. Leave to dry.

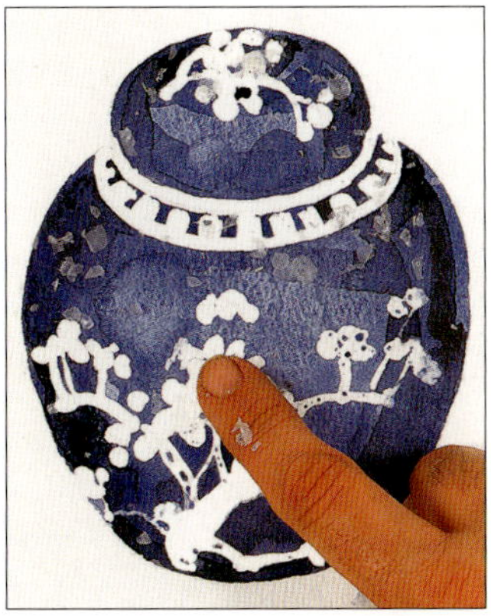

4 Using your fingertip, gently rub off the masking fluid. It should come off easily, but if any of the masking fluid is hard to remove, use a soft kneaded eraser. Blow or brush any bits of loose masking fluid off the paper before continuing.

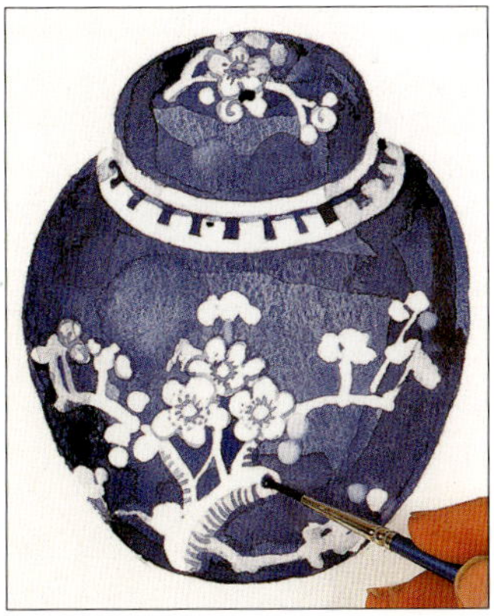

5 Using the same blue mixture used in Step 2, carefully paint in the detailing on the pattern – the outline of the flowers, the flower centres, and tiny brushmarks to indicate the bark of the branches. Leave to dry. Mix a mid-toned Payne's grey and brush over those parts of the white patterns that are in shadow. This helps to integrate the stark design into the painting and reinforces the three-dimensional feel.

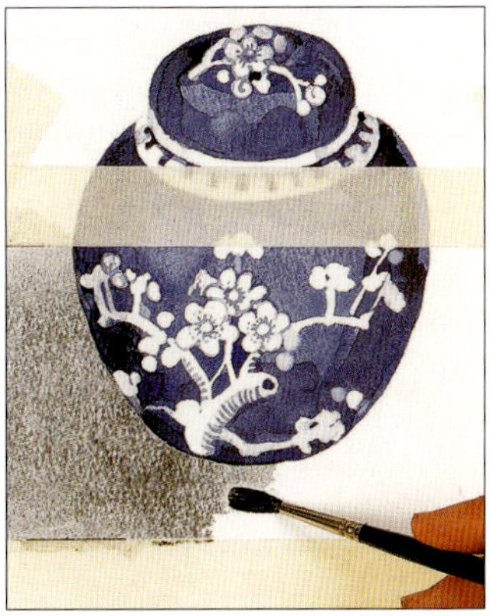

6 Using low-tack masking tape, mask out the square of dark grey paper on which the jar is standing. Mix a warm grey from Payne's grey and raw umber and, using a medium round brush, paint in the rectangular shape. Do not flood on too much paint, as there is always a risk that some may seep under the tape and ruin the clean edge. Leave to dry.

The finished painting

Once the tape has been removed, complete the painting by adding the dark shadow cast by the jar using a pale mauve mixed from Payne's grey and dioxazine purple. The result is an attractive little study that preserves the flowing lines and brilliant white pattern on the jar, without looking tight or laboured in its execution.

The brilliant white of the paper is preserved to the last.

The shadow anchors the jar on the surface.

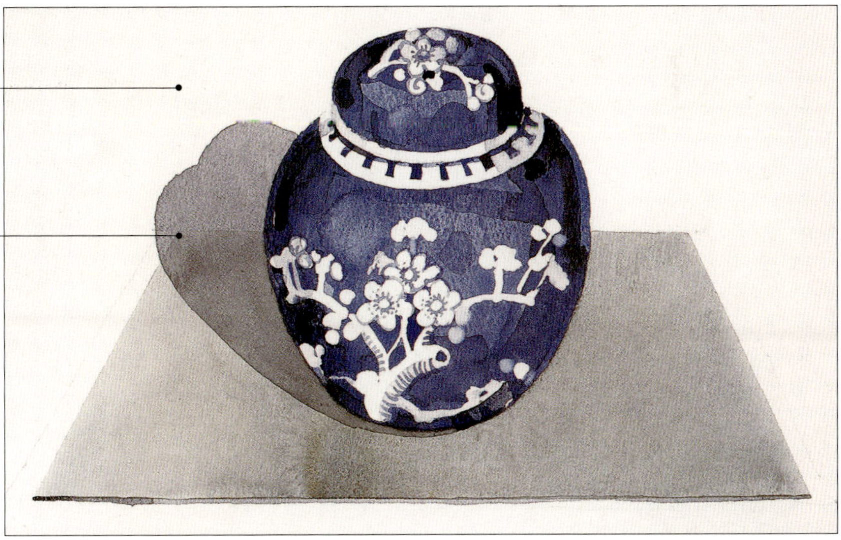

Resists

Resist techniques are based on the principle that wax and water do not mix. Wax repels water, so if there is wax on your watercolour paper, any watercolour paint that is subsequently applied to those areas will not adhere to the surface.

Wax can be applied in several ways. You can use a clear wax candle, coloured wax crayons or oil pastels to draw on to the support. Interesting results can also be obtained by brushing on furniture wax using a stiff bristle brush.The technique is similar to using masking fluid but, unlike masking fluid, a resist cannot be removed.

Since the wax remains on the support and will continue to repel any subsequent washes, you need to plan where and at what point you introduce the resist. It does not have to be applied to the paper at the beginning of the work; you can introduce it at any point by working over existing dry washes.

The technique is difficult to use in confined, detailed areas and is more commonly used to create broader areas of texture. The success of the technique depends on how much pressure you apply and on the type of surface on which you are working. On a smooth, hot-pressed paper, the wax takes to the surface in a uniform way, resulting in a more subtle, flatter effect. On a rough paper, the wax is picked up only on the "peaks" of the paper surface, resulting in the wash lying in the "troughs", producing a highly textured, speckled effect.

An interesting variation can be made by combining it with frottage. Frottage allows you to incorporate textures other than that of the watercolour paper into your painting. Place smooth, lightweight paper on a textured surface, such as a plank of wood, and rub on the wax. The wax will pick up the texture of the underlying surface and, once a wash has been applied, the pattern will be revealed.

Resist techniques are ideal for light sea waves and for broken textural effects for sand and shingle. These patterns can be applied as a drawing or as a fragmented layer of light colour. Try drawing the white petals of a daisy with a wax resist and then covering them with deep blue – the contrasting tones are quite startling.

Household candle

Using an uncoloured household candle as a resist is an effective and inexpensive way of creating large areas of texture on a painting. Be aware that you cannot remove the wax once it has been applied, so don't get too carried away!

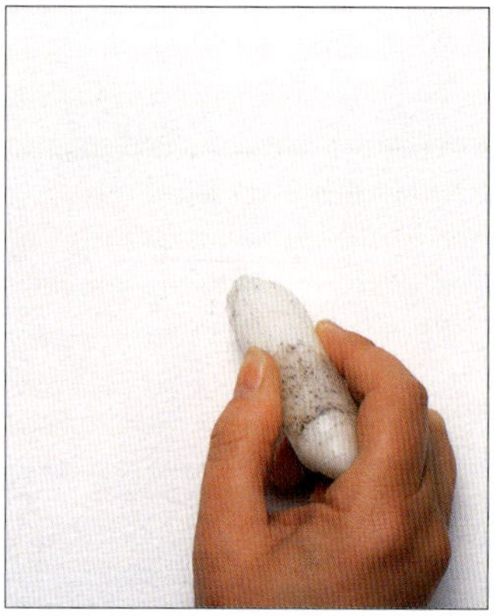

1 Rub a household candle over the paper, presssing quite hard to ensure that enough wax is deposited on the surface of the paper.

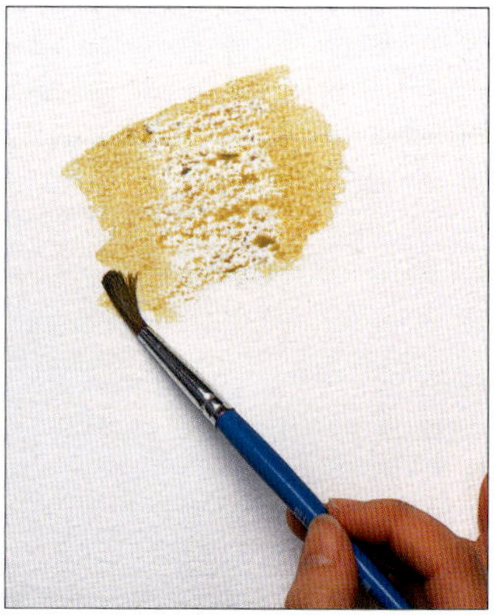

2 Apply a watercolour wash. Note how the wax repels the water in the paint. Here a rough paper was used, creating a broken texture.

On smooth, hot-pressed paper

On smooth, hot-pressed paper, the wax can be applied more smoothly. As a result, when the watercolour wash has been applied, the effect is much more subtle.

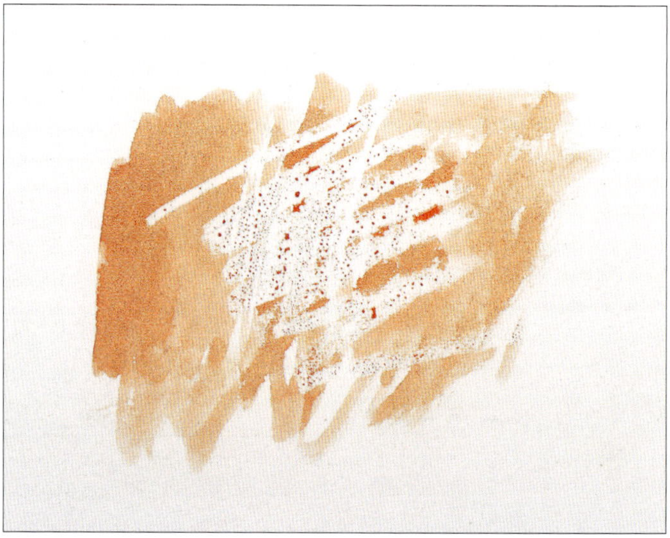

Coloured wax crayon or oil pastel

With a coloured wax crayon or oil pastel, not only can you make finer, more linear marks which will remain visible in the finished painting, but it is also easier to see exactly where the wax has been applied. This makes it less likely that you will apply too much of the resist that cannot then be removed, and it is a useful way to practise the resist technique.

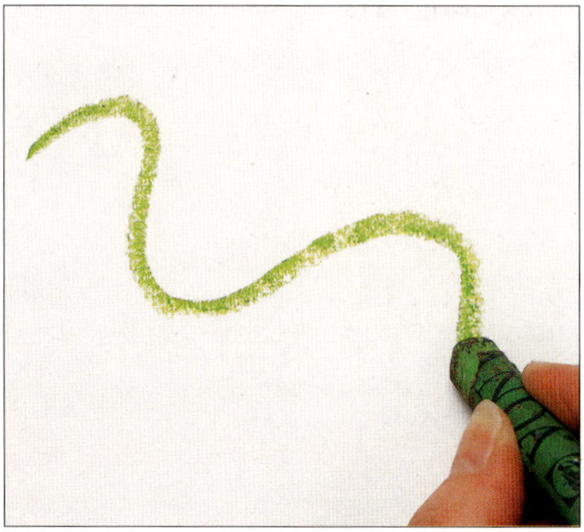

1 Use the tip of the coloured wax crayon or oil pastel to draw in the areas where you want to apply the resist. Work slowly and in one smooth, continuous movement.

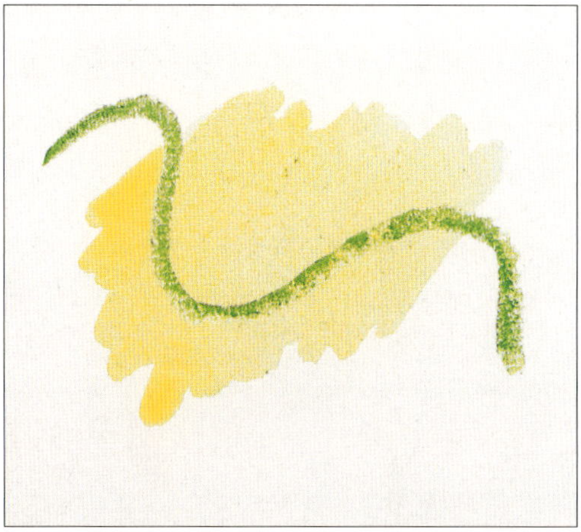

2 Apply a watercolour wash over the top of the resist. The fine coloured lines of the wax remain visible, even though the wash was applied over the whole surface.

Practice exercise: **Using resists to create texture**

In this exercise, a combination of oil pastels and watercolour is used to give tiny variations in tone across the surface of the fruits, revealing the dimpled texture. Resists are used both to add colour and to reserve the white of the paper. The colour of the oil pastels is rich and vibrant, and it shows through the lighter watercolour washes because the oil in the pastels acts as a resist and repels the watercolour paint. Candle wax is used to reserve the white of the paper for the brightest highlights.

Materials

- *200lb (425gsm) NOT watercolour paper, pre-stretched*
- *2B pencil*
- *Watercolour paints: cadmium lemon, cadmium orange, burnt umber, sap green, Payne's grey, dioxazine purple*
- *Oil pastels: cadmium yellow, yellow ochre, deep orange*
- *Brushes: medium round*
- *Household candle*

The set-up

Odd numbers of objects always seem to work better in a still-life composition than even numbers. Arrange the fruit to form a composition that is roughly triangular in shape, with the lemon angled to "point" towards the oranges.

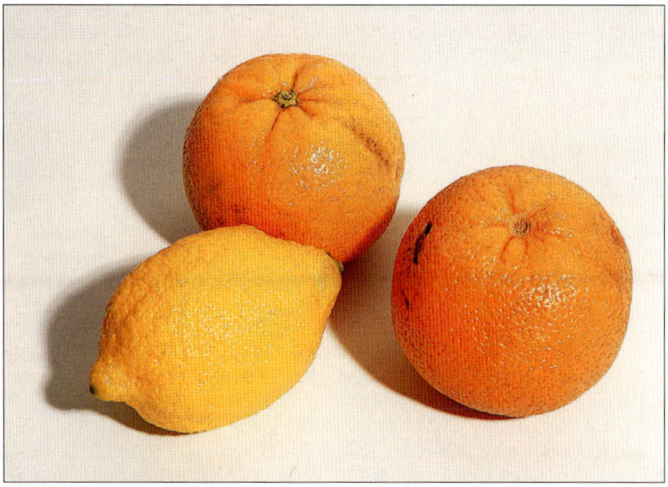

▶

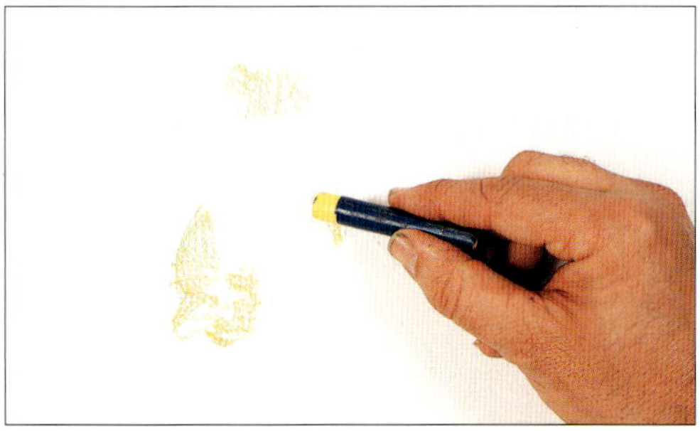

1 Using a 2B pencil, lightly sketch the outline of the fruits, looking carefully at their positions in relation to one another and at where they overlap. Scribble in the lighter yellow areas using a cadmium yellow oil pastel. Take care not to press too heavily, or the pastel will build up in the tooth of the paper to such an extent that there will be nowhere for the watercolour wash to adhere to the paper.

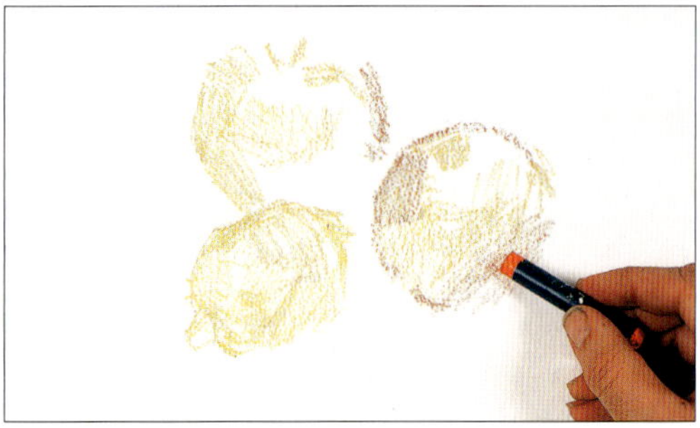

2 Using a clear wax candle, draw the white highlight on each orange and on the lemon; the wax will repel the watercolour paint, with the result that these areas will remain white in the finished painting. Develop the colours on the oranges and lemon using yellow ochre and deep orange oil pastels. As before, keep the pastel marks light and open so that they help describe and follow the contours of the fruit.

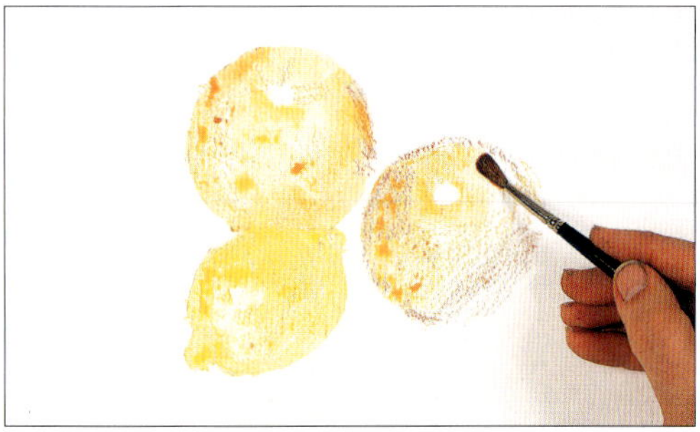

3 Brush on the lightest washes – cadmium lemon on the lemon and cadmium orange on the oranges. The paint gathers and puddles on those areas of the paper that are free of oil pastel and candle wax. Leave to dry.

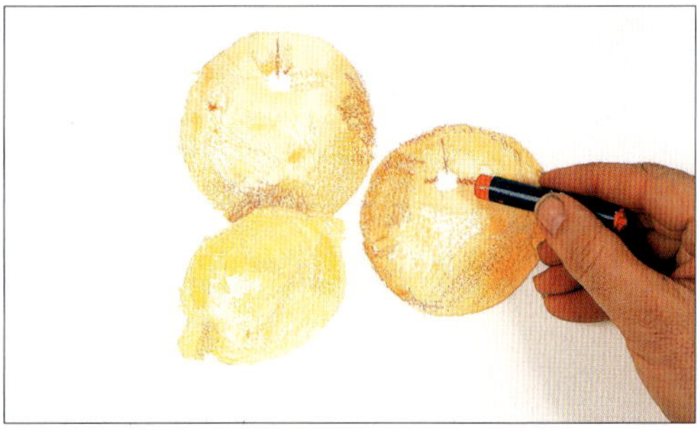

4 When dry, go back to the oil pastels to redraw areas and add colour and detail. Now that some paint has been applied, you can make this subsequent pastel work heavier, as it will not affect the washes that have been put down.

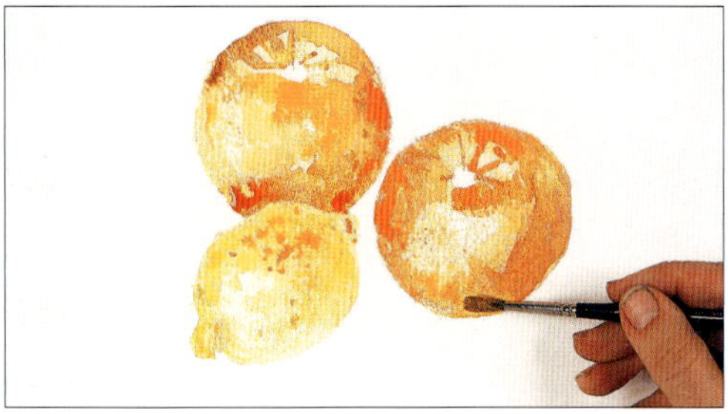

5 Using concentrated mixes of cadmium orange, cadmium lemon and burnt umber, paint the shaded sides of the fruits, and the areas where the stalks are attached, in order to make them look more rounded and three-dimensional. Allow the paint to puddle as before and leave to dry.

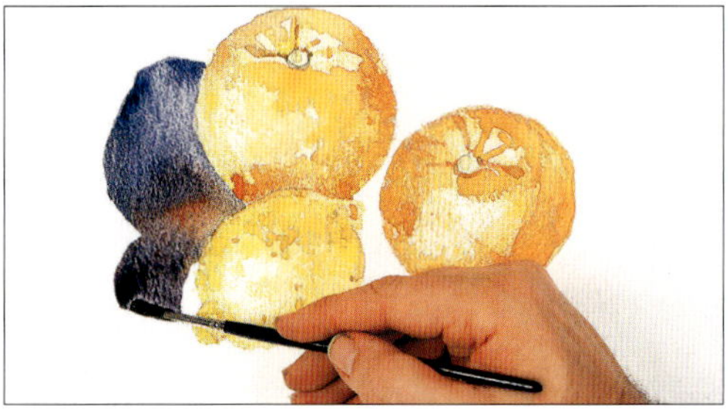

6 Mix a brownish green from sap green, cadmium orange and burnt umber and paint the point where the stalk is attached. Paint the shadow in Payne's grey and drop cadmium orange and dioxazine purple into the grey to hint at the colours reflected from the underside of the fruit.

The finished painting

This is a lively and spontaneous painting of a very simple still life. The oil pastel resists add both depth of colour and texture to the image, while the watercolour washes provide smoother, calmer areas that act as an effective contrast. Even the white highlight areas have gained some texture from the candlewax resist.

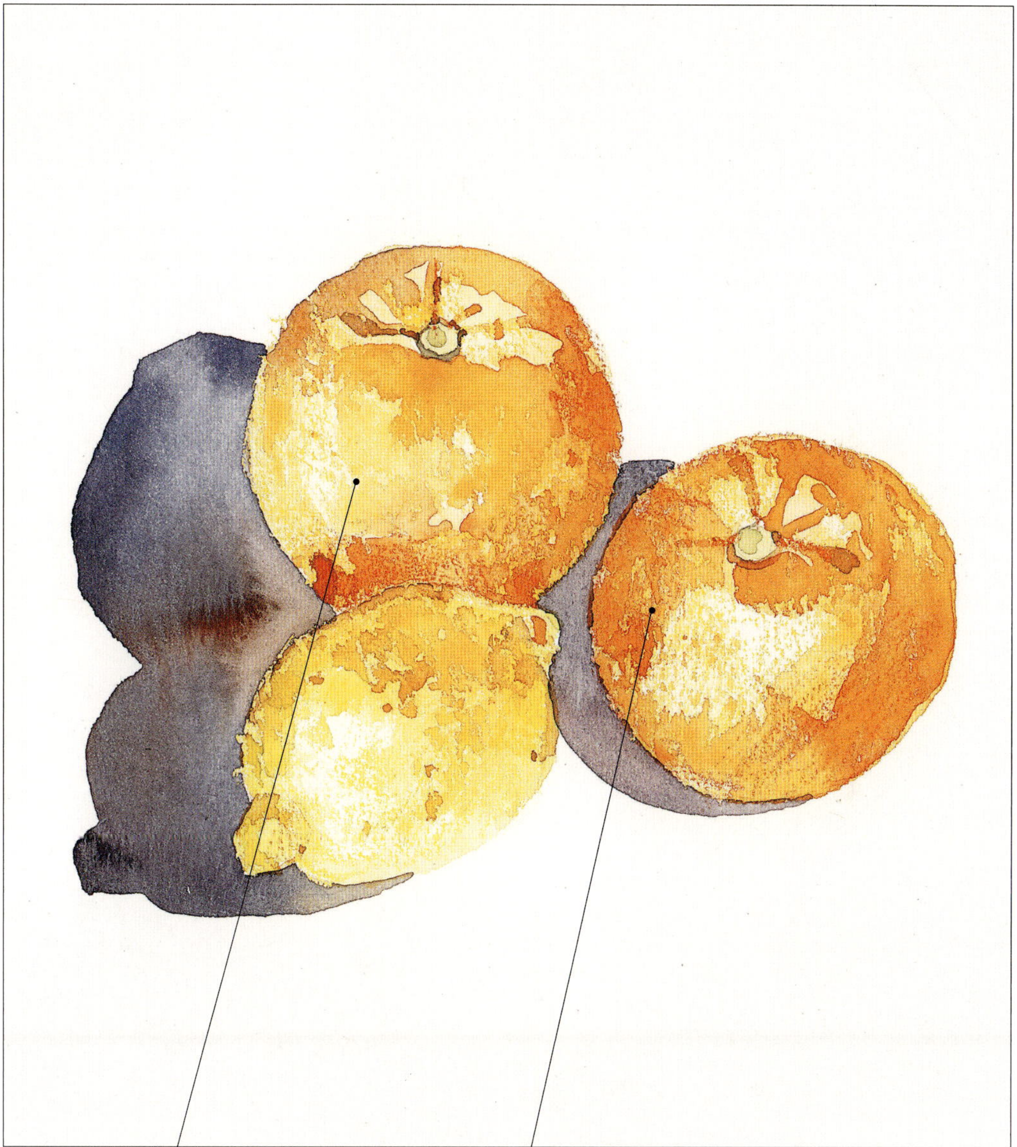

The bright highlighted areas of the fruits are reserved by using clear candle wax.

Yellow ochre and deep orange oil pastels convey the colours of the oranges and also repel the paint to create interesting textures.

Spattering

Spattering is an effective technique for creating texture in paintings. It consists of flicking paint on to the paper to create a random series of dots or flecks. It is done either by tapping a brush loaded with paint, so that drops of paint fall on the paper beneath, or by pulling back the bristles of a loaded brush with your fingers, so that paint droplets fly off.

You can apply spatter to either dry or wet paper, or even combine the two approaches in a single painting. They give very different effects. On a dry ground, the spatter doesn't blur, so this is a good technique for subjects such as old stone walls and pebbly garden paths, where you want the dots and flecks of paint to be crisp and sharp. On a wet surface, the spatter blurs and spreads, which can be useful for snow or foam-crested waves lapping against the shore.

The amount of water in the paint mixture affects the size of the spatter marks: the wetter the mixture, the larger the marks. Distance also plays a part: the further away you hold the brush, the smaller the marks and the wider the area that will be covered. Practise on scrap paper to find out how much pressure you need to apply and how far away from the paper you need to hold the brush in order to create the effect you want.

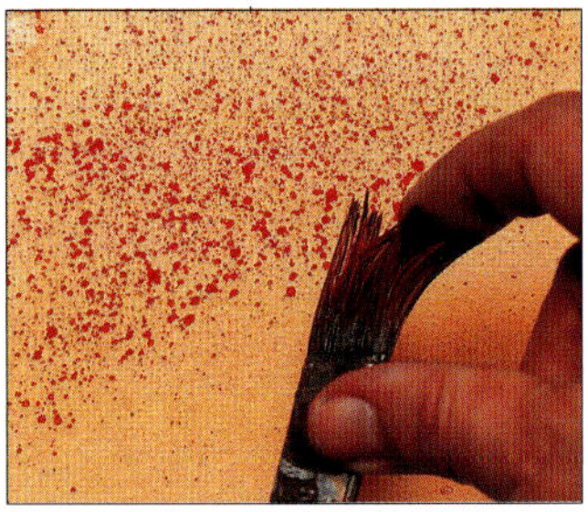

Pulling back the bristles
Load a stiff-bristled brush with paint and gently pull the bristles back towards you.

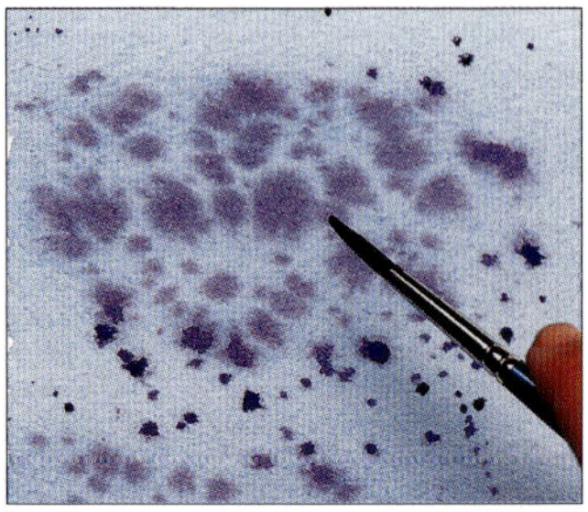

Tapping the brush
Load the brush with paint, hold it horizontally over the area that you want to spatter, and gently tap the handle.

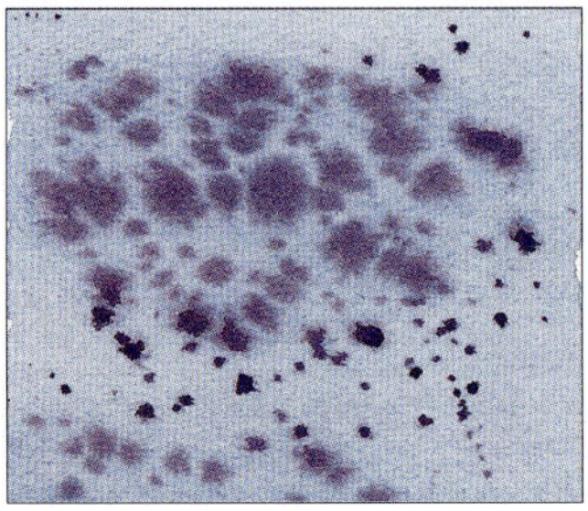

Spatter on a damp wash
Applied to a wet surface, the paint droplets blur and spread.

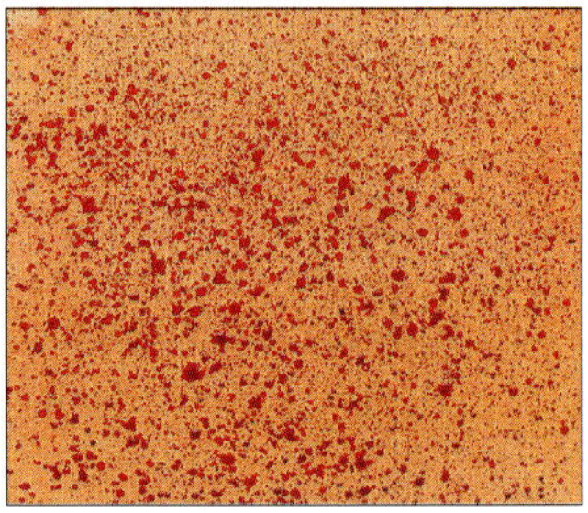

Spatter on a dry wash
Applied to a dry surface, the paint droplets remain crisp and well defined.

Practice exercise: **Beach with spattered pebbles**

Spattering is the perfect technique for this pebbly beach scene. Make the foreground spatters slightly larger than those in the distance. The foreground pebbles appear larger because they are closer to the viewer, so this will help to create an impression of distance.

Materials

- *2B pencil*
- *140lb (300gsm) rough watercolour paper, pre-stretched*
- *Watercolour paints: cobalt blue, raw sienna, light red, sepia, ultramarine violet, cadmium red, cadmium orange, Payne's grey*
- *Brushes: old brush for masking, large round, fine round*
- *Masking fluid*

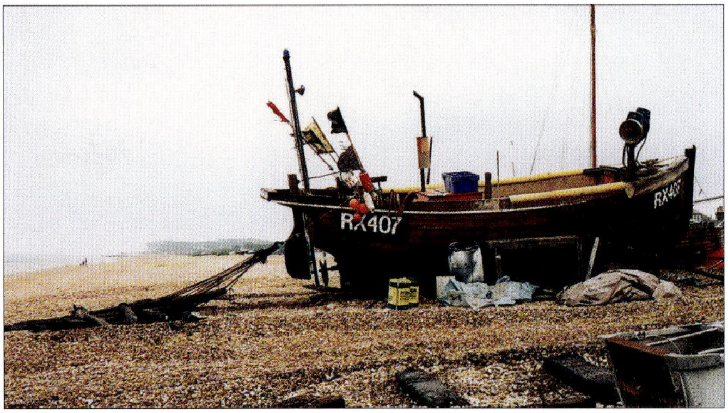

The original scene
You can almost feel the hard, crunchy texture of this shingle beach. Spattering the paint on to dry paper will create crisp dots of texture.

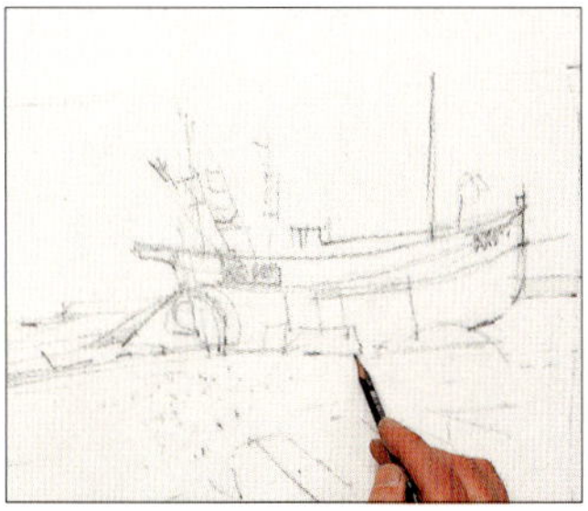

1 Using a 2B pencil, lightly sketch the outline of the boat and flags and the planks of wood that lie in the foreground of the beach scene.

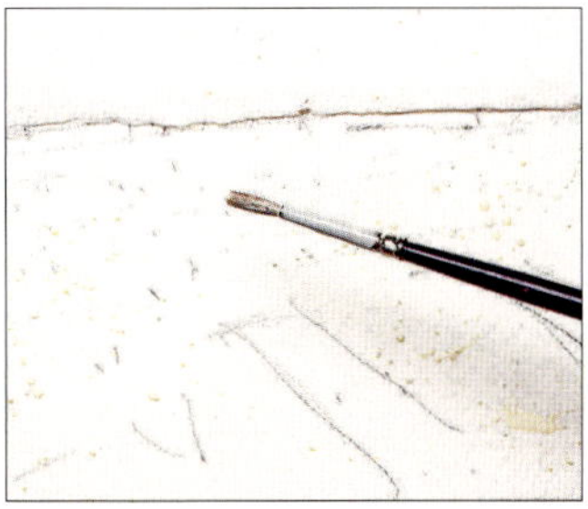

2 Hold a piece of scrap paper over the boat to protect it and, using an old brush, spatter masking fluid over the beach. Leave to dry.

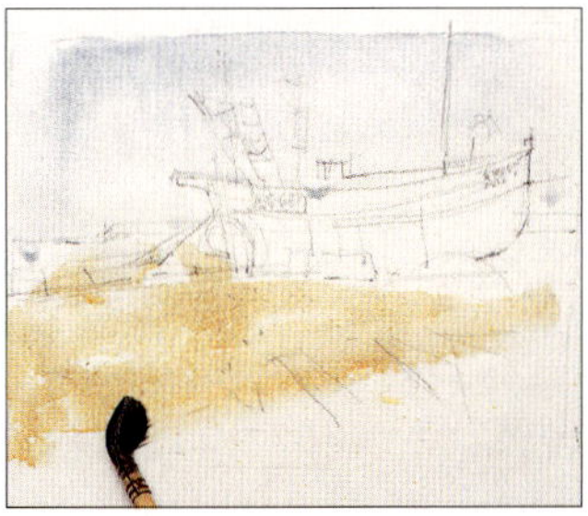

3 Dampen everything except the boat with water. Brush pale cobalt blue over the sky. Brush a mixture of raw sienna and light red over the beach.

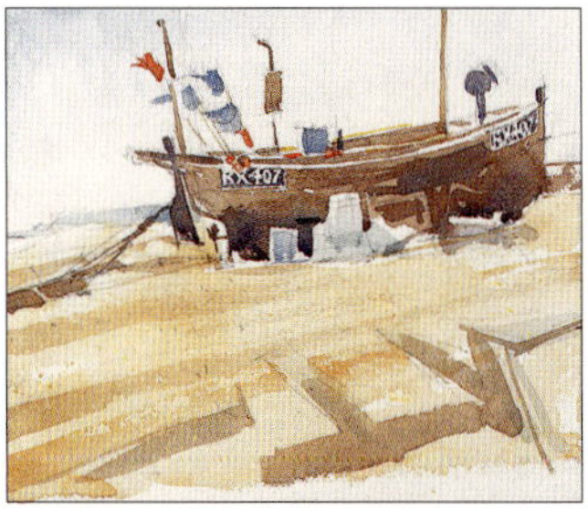

4 When the previous stage is dry, mix a dark brown from sepia, ultramarine violet and a little light red and paint the boat, adding more ultramarine violet for the stern. Use a pale version of the mixture for the planks and brush broad strokes of the same colour across the beach. Paint the flags in cobalt blue and the floats in a mixture of cadmium red and cadmium orange. Using a fine brush, paint around the lettering in Payne's grey.

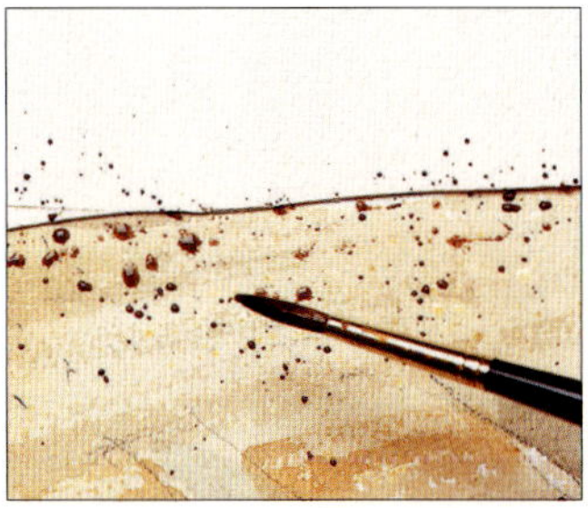

5 Mix a warm brown from raw sienna and sepia. Hold a piece of scrap paper over the boat to protect it and, using a fine brush, spatter the paint mixture over the foreground.

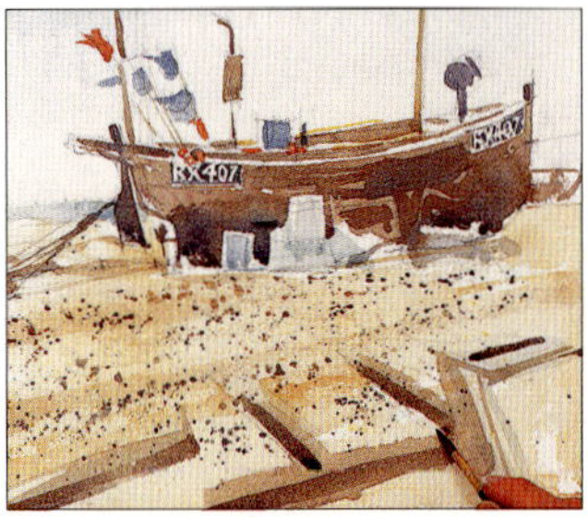

6 Add ultramarine violet to the mixture to darken it and continue spattering as before. Using the same mixture, darken the ropes tethering the boat and the planks. Leave to dry.

The finished painting

Complete the picture by rubbing off the masking fluid. This is a delightful little scene of a beach at low tide. The spattering is subtle and does not detract from the painting of the boat, but it captures the texture of the hard, shingly beach very effectively.

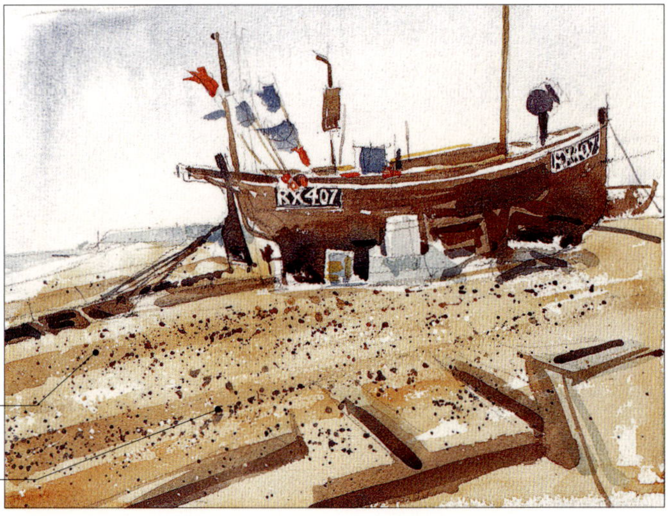

These stripes of colour help to imply the ripples in the sand.

The spattering in the foreground contrasts well with the flat colour of the sky.

Stippling

Stippling consists of placing dots or blobs of colour on the paper. The techique is often used to create texture in a painting, but it can also be used to optically mix colours on the paper, as it was by the French Pointillist School, whose most famous exponent was Georges Seurat (1859–91).

The dots can be placed close together or further apart, depending on the effect you want to create. You can use either a specialist stippling brush, which is a short, stubby brush with hard bristles, or the tip of your normal painting brush. To create even stipples, dip an almost dry brush into a thick mix of watercolour paint. A wetter mix of paint will produce dots that are less sharply defined.

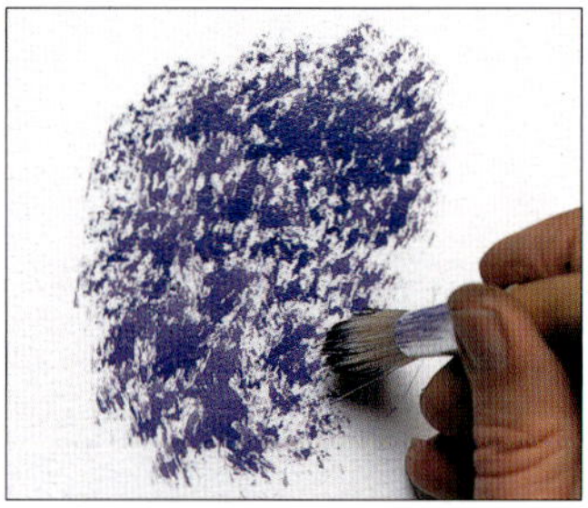

The technique
Load a stippling brush with paint and, holding the brush almost vertically, dab it on to the paper with short, sharp movements. Vary the amount of pressure to create dots of different weights.

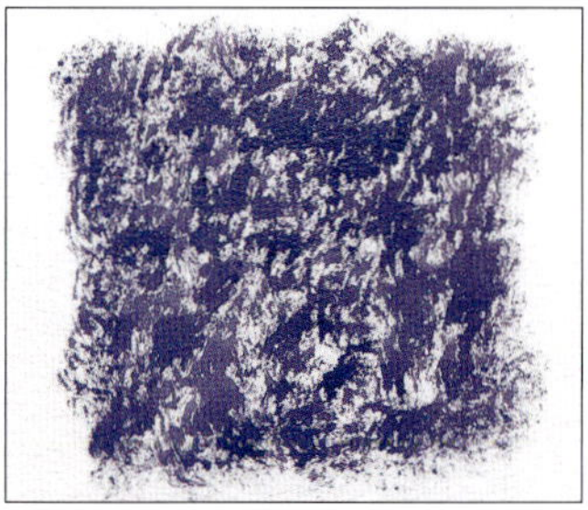

The effect
A stippling brush creates areas of random texture that are perfect for subjects such as lichen-covered pebbles and stones.

Practice exercise: **Fruits with stippled texture**

Stippling is a great way of painting fruits with dimpled surfaces, such as the citrus fruits and avocado shown here. Use a fine brush and stipple darker tones on to the base colours of the fruits to convey the pitted hollows in the skin.

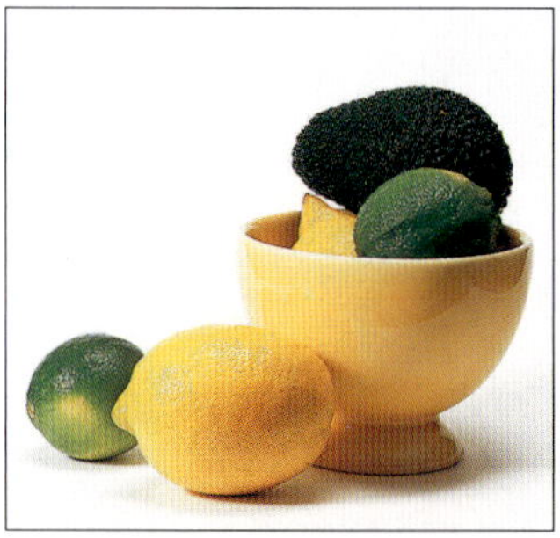

The set-up
When you set up a still-life exercise like this, position a table or anglepoise lamp to one side. The raking light will pick out the dimples on the fruit, making it easier for you to see where to apply the stippling, and will cast interesting shadows that make the subject look three-dimensional.

Materials

- *2B pencil*
- *140lb (300gsm) rough watercolour paper, pre-stretched*
- *Watercolour paints: aureolin, yellow ochre, raw sienna, sap green, Payne's grey, ultramarine blue, burnt umber, ultramarine violet*
- *Brushes: fine-pointed old brush for masking, medium round, fine round*
- *Masking fluid*

Tip: As you make your initial drawing, turn it upside down every now and then to check that you've drawn the ellipses of the bowl and the fruits correctly. Looking at the drawing upside down makes it much easier for you to see what you've drawn as simple geometric shapes, without being distracted by the subject matter.

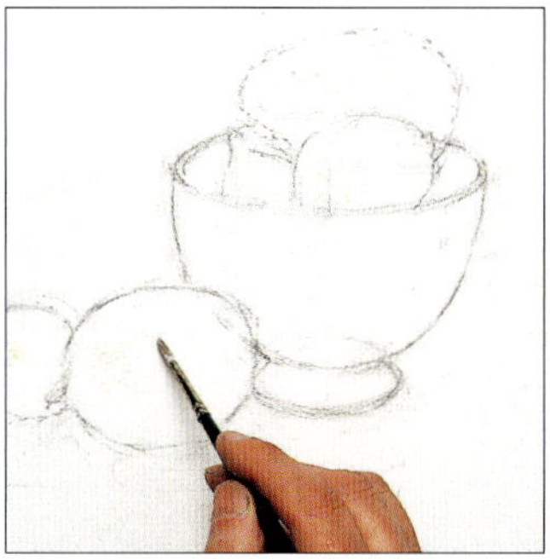

1 Using a 2B pencil, lightly sketch the outline of your subject. Using an old, fine brush, stipple masking fluid on any highlight areas on the left-hand side, where light hits the fruit. Leave to dry completely.

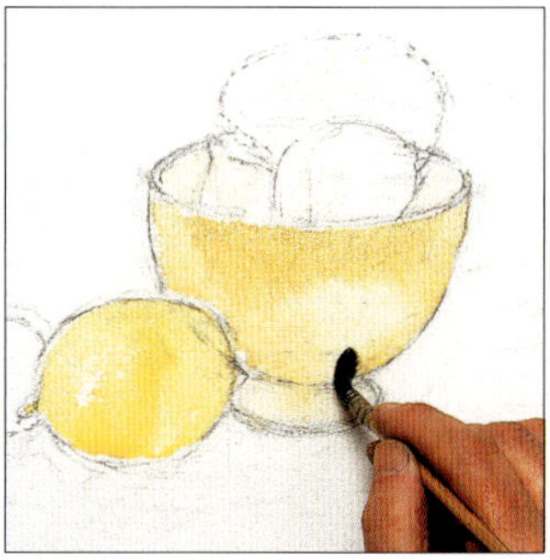

2 Mix two washes, one from aureolin with a little yellow ochre and the other from yellow ochre alone. Dampen the foreground lemon and bowl with clean water. Paint the lemon with the aureolin and yellow ochre mixture and the bowl in the plain yellow ochre.

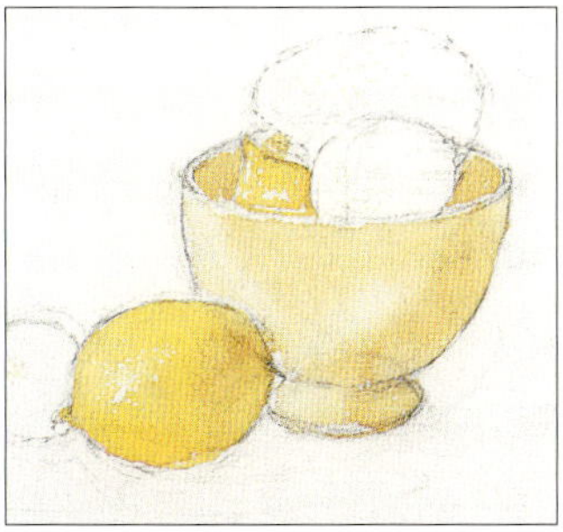

3 Mix raw sienna with a little yellow ochre and, while the paper is still damp, touch this mixture on to the right-hand side of the bowl, which is in shadow. Add a little sap green to the mixture and brush it on to the shadowed side of the foreground lemon. Paint the lemon in the bowl with the aureolin and yellow ochre mixture used in Step 2. Leave to dry.

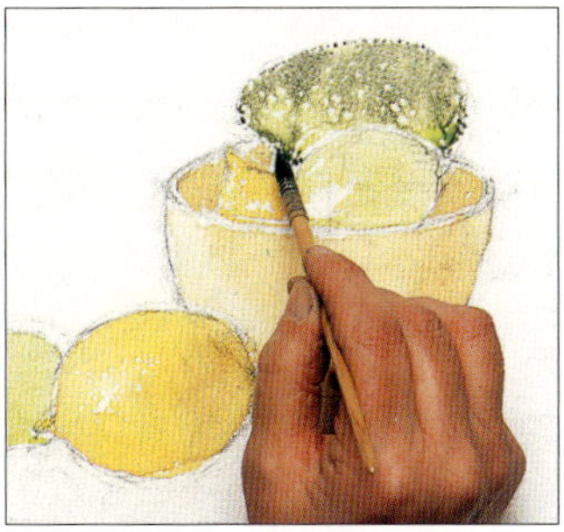

4 Mix a pale green colour from sap green and aureolin. Wet the limes and the avocado with clean water. While the paper is still damp, using a medium round brush, brush this mixture over the limes, leaving some white areas untouched where the light hits the fruits. Add some Payne's grey to the mixture and stipple it over the avocado. Leave to dry.

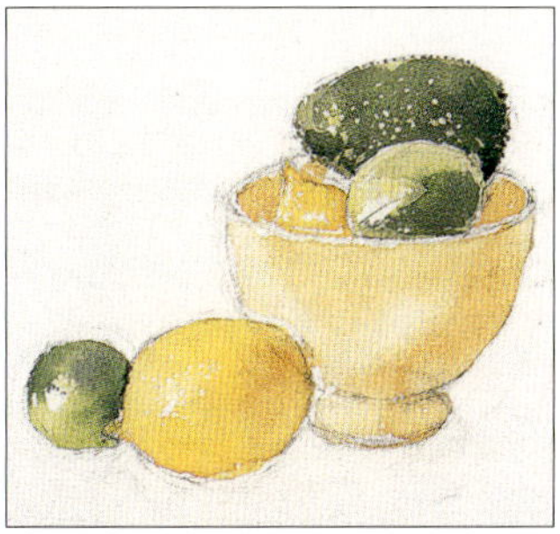

5 Mix a dark green from ultramarine blue and sap green. Using a fine round brush, stipple the mixture over the darker areas of the limes and leave to dry. Mix sap green with a little Payne's grey and wash this mixture over the right-hand side of the avocado and the shadowed underside of the lime in the bowl. Leave to dry.

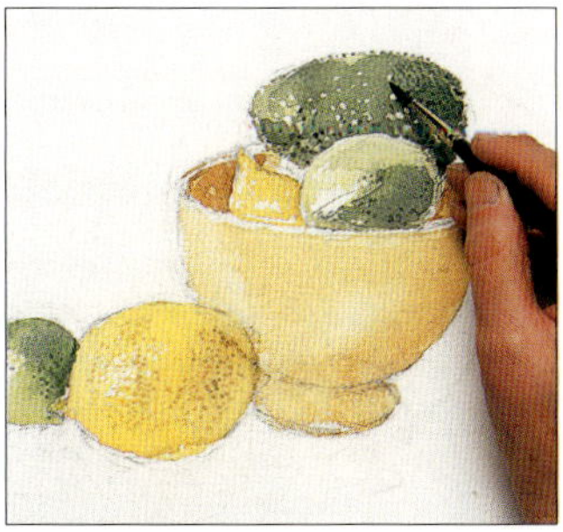

6 Strengthen the tone on the bowl by applying another wash of yellow ochre, leaving a white edge on the rim. Add a touch of burnt umber to the inside of the bowl. Leave to dry. Stipple a mixture of aureolin and yellow ochre on to the foreground lemon, adding burnt umber for the side that is in shadow. Stipple a mixture of sap green and Payne's grey on to the dark side of the avocado and the foreground lime. Leave to dry.

The finished painting

To complete the painting, rub off the masking fluid to reveal the brightest highlights. Next, paint the shadows by dropping a very pale wash of ultramarine violet and burnt umber wet into wet on to dampened paper. Random stippling conveys the texture of the fruits and contrasts well with the wet-into-wet washes used on the smooth china bowl.

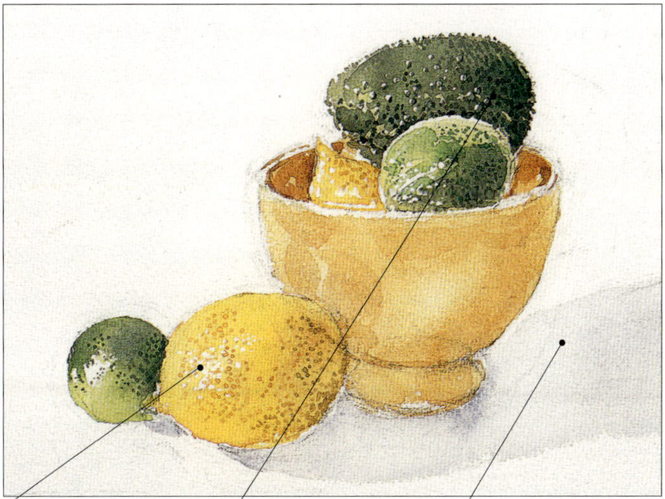

The brightest highlights are left unpainted, protected by masking fluid until the final stages.

Random stippling conveys the pitted surface of the fruits perfectly.

The shadows help to anchor the painting and show that the subject is not floating in mid-air.

Drybrush

In the drybrush technique, paint is put on with a brush that is quickly skimmed over the paper, leaving the colour on the ridges of the surface but not in the troughs. As you might expect, the brush should be fairly dry. If either the paper or the brush is too wet, the indentations of the paper will quickly fill with colour. Keep a piece of kitchen paper close to hand so that you can dab off any paint that is too wet.

The drybrush technique is useful for subjects such as wood bark or ageing stonework, and for foreground grasses. Because drybrush work is often used in the final stages of a painting, to add texture and visual interest, it is a good idea to test your loaded brush on a piece of scrap paper before you use the technique in your almost completed work.

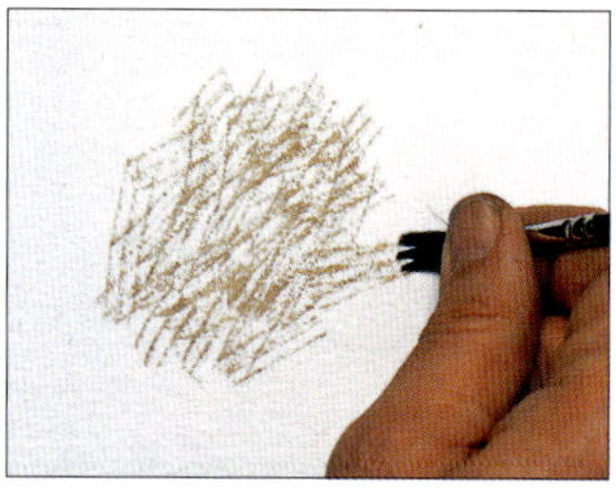

Using a round brush
Dip the brush in your chosen paint colour and, using your fingertips, squeeze out any excess paint so that the brush is almost dry and splay out the bristles. Drag the brush over the surface of the paper. It will make broken, textured marks.

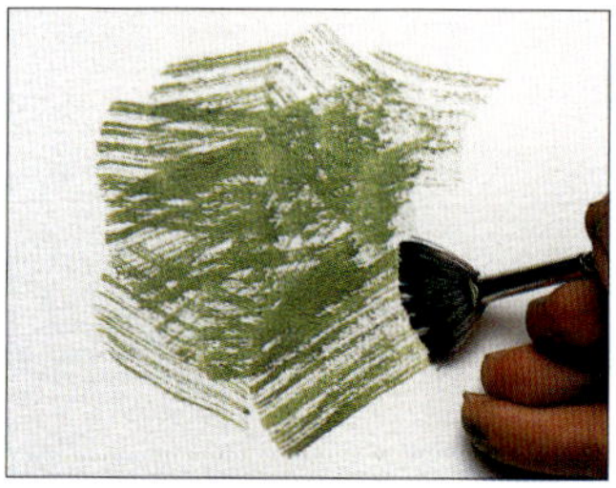

Using a fan brush
A fan brush, in which the bristles are naturally splayed, allows you to cover a wider area of the paper.

Practice exercise: **Lily with drybrushed leaves and buds**

The drybrush technique is perfect for subjects with slightly broken textures, such as leaf forms. On rough paper, dragging an almost dry brush across these areas will give an immediacy and freshness to the painting.

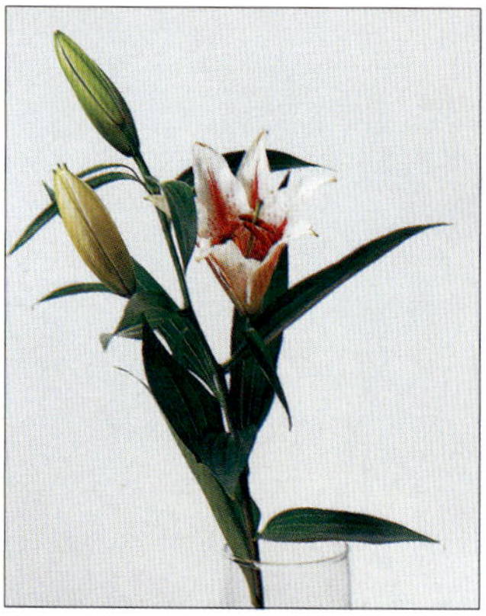

The set-up
Position your subject on a large sheet of white paper: this is a good way of practising the technique, without having to worry about painting a complicated background. Turn the lily around until you find an angle that allows you to see the inside of the half-opened flower.

Materials

- *2B pencil*
- *140lb (300gsm) rough watercolour paper, pre-stretched*
- *Watercolour paints: aureolin, sap green, yellow ochre, rose madder deep, ultramarine blue, cadmium orange*
- *Brushes: medium round, fine round*
- *Kneaded eraser*
- *Kitchen paper*

Tip: If you find it hard to get the shape of the half-open lily flower right, try to think of it as a simple geometric shape – such as an inverted cone – on top of which you superimpose an ellipse and the triangular shapes of the individual petals. Taking an objective approach to your subject can be helpful when dealing with irregular shapes.

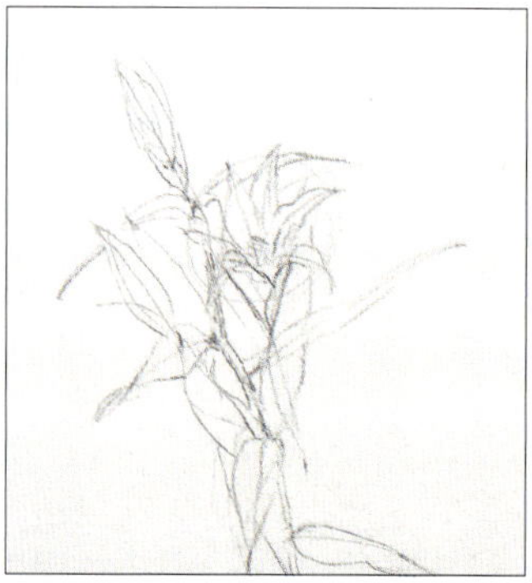

1 Using a 2B pencil, make a light sketch of the lily. It is important to count the number of petals and leaves beforehand, and to work out the position of each one carefully.

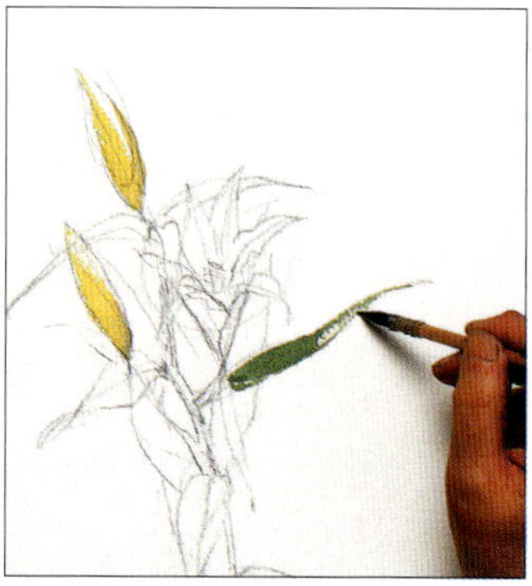

2 Mix a yellowish green from aureolin, sap green and a little yellow ochre. Holding an almost dry brush vertically, paint the buds. Add more sap green and paint the leaves in the same way.

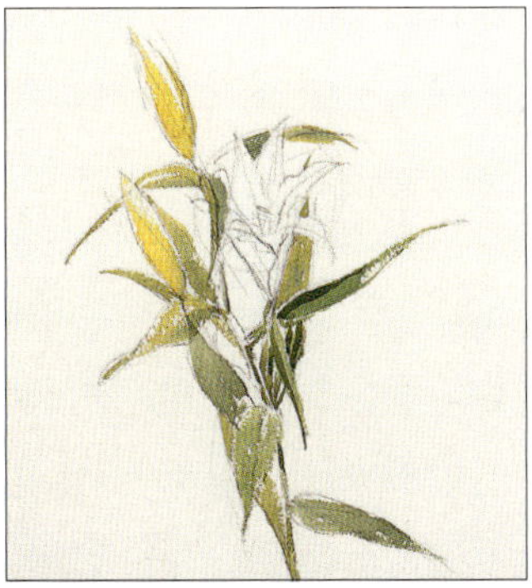

3 Continue putting in the leaves in the same way. Use a slightly darker version of the same mixture for the stalks and one edge of some of the main leaves, so that the painting starts to take on a three-dimensional quality.

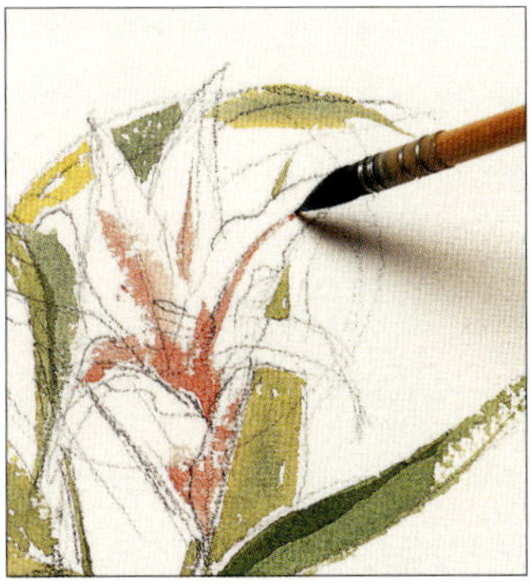

4 Mix a dark pink colour from rose madder deep and drybrush it on to the petals of the open lily flower.

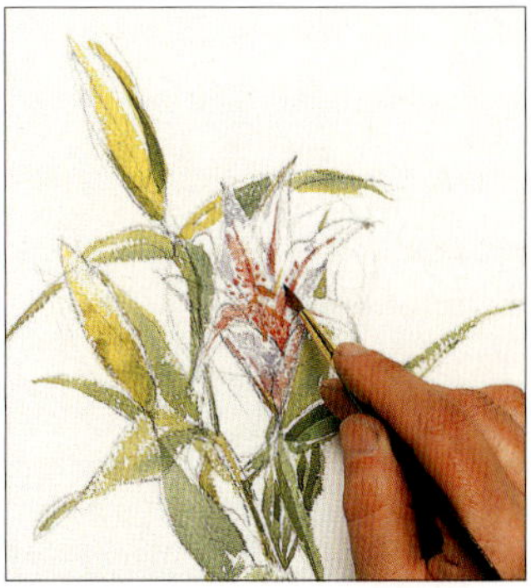

5 Mix a very pale ultramarine blue and paint the shadow on the underside of the petals. Paint the stamens in cadmium orange. Using a fine round brush, stipple tiny dots of the dark pink colour inside the petals.

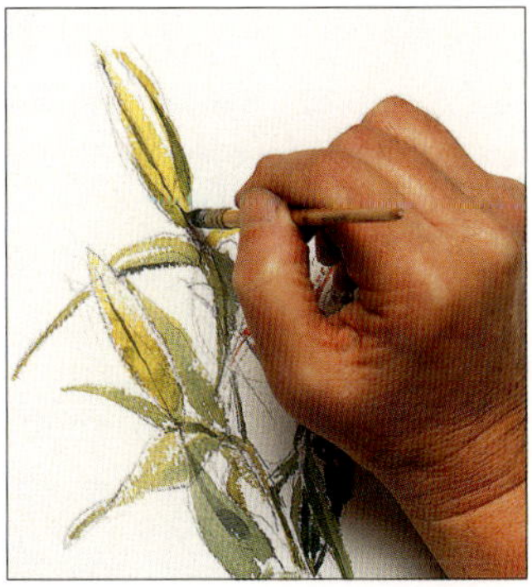

6 Mix a dark green from ultramarine blue and sap green and, using a fine round brush, drybrush this mixture over the leaves to paint the veins. Paint the same colour on the unopened buds to delineate the individual petals.

The finished painting

Rub out some of the superfluous pencil markings with a kneaded eraser and the painting is complete. Working on dry paper, with an almost dry brush, is the perfect way to delineate the fine leaf forms and the lines that separate the petals of this lily. The technique has also allowed the texture of the paper to show through, creating a painting that is full of visual interest.

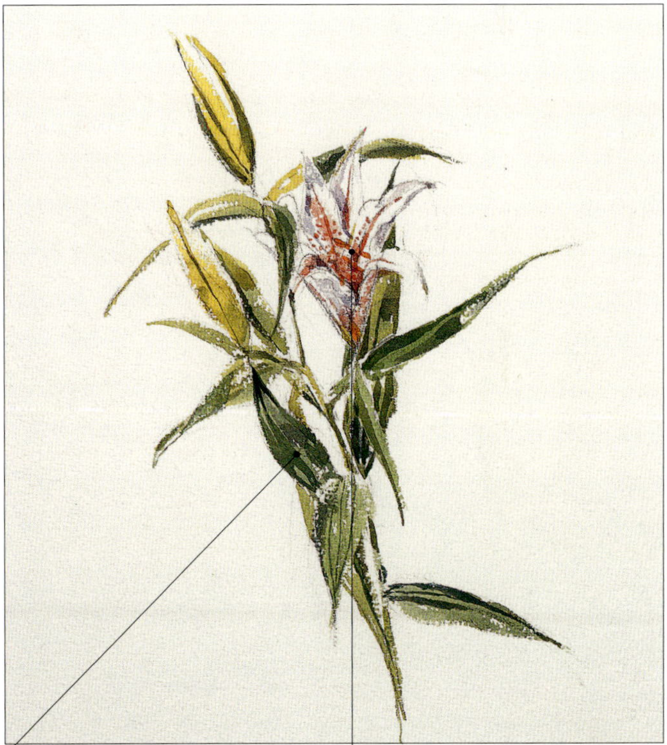

The drybrush work on the leaves has created an interesting texture.

Warm and cool colours help to make the lily look three-dimensional: the warm rose advances, while the cooler purple recedes.

Sponging

Sponges can be used to lift off unwanted colour while the paper is still damp (for example, to wipe out clouds in a dark sky) and instead of a brush to dampen paper. However, the main purpose of sponging is to produce texture.

Natural sponges are more randomly textured than synthetic ones, which have a very regular pattern. Experiment with different kinds to find out what kind of marks they make. You can sponge on to dry or damp paper. On damp paper, the marks will merge together, while on dry paper they will be more crisply defined.

Sponging is a useful technique for painting stone walls and pebbled paths and beaches. It is also excellent for misty trees and anything that needs a soft edging, and for creating the effect of lichen on walls and wooden gates.

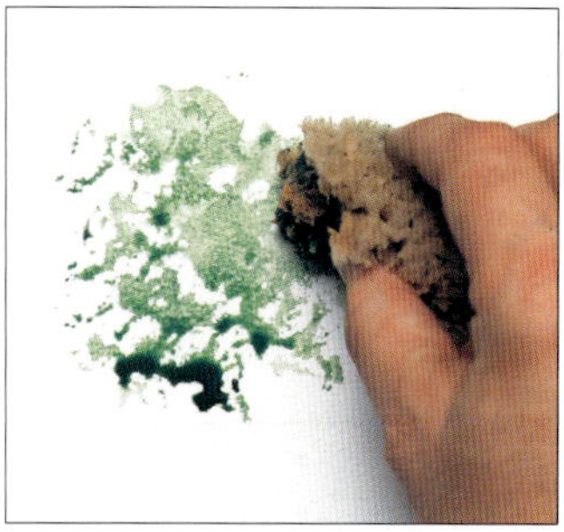

The technique
Wet the sponge so that it is soft and pliable and squeeze out any excess water. Dip the sponge in your chosen paint (you will need to mix a large wash, as the sponge is very absorbent). Gently dab it on to the paper.

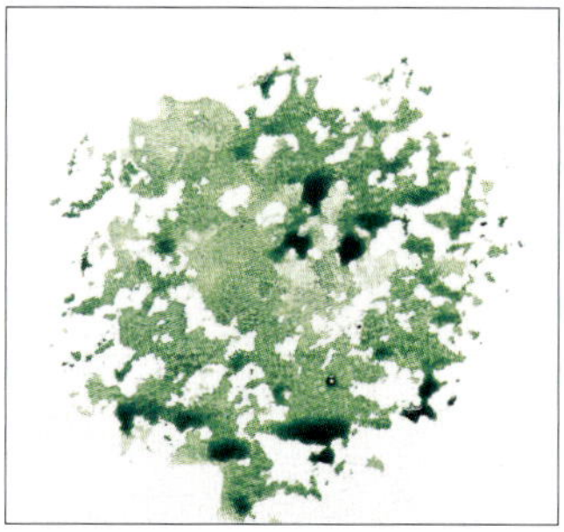

The effect
The sponge leaves a series of pitted marks that are ideal for conveying texture. This technique is particularly useful for painting clumps of foliage.

Practice exercise: **Removing and adding colour with a sponge**

In this exercise, sponging is used both to remove paint, softening colours applied with a brush, and to add it, creating small areas of soft texture.

Materials

- *300lb (640gsm) rough watercolour paper*
- *Watercolour paints: alizarin crimson, Prussian blue, cadmium lemon, ultramarine blue, cadmium yellow*
- *Brushes: medium round*
- *Small sponge*

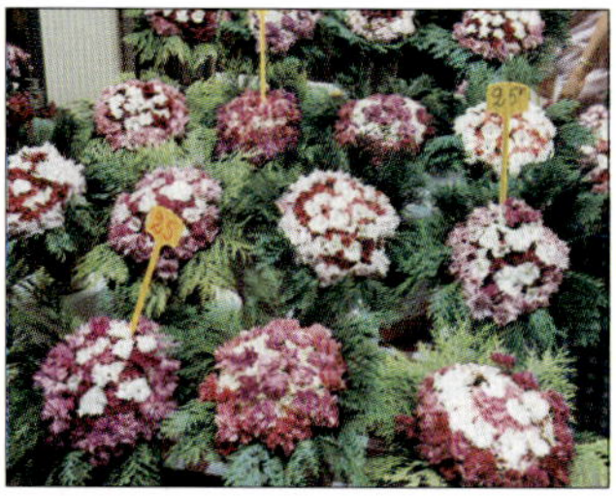

The original scene
This array of bouquets on a market stall is almost overpoweringly colourful. The artist decided to paint a single bouquet in order to concentrate on the effects created from the sponging technique.

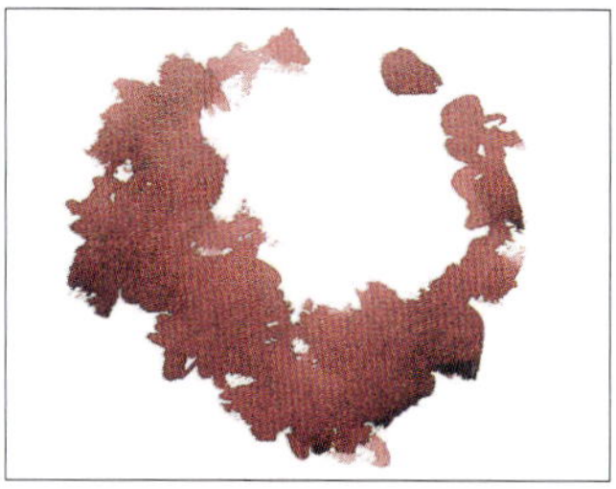

1 Mix a deep pink from alizarin crimson with a tiny amount of Prussian blue. Using a medium round brush, loosely paint the shapes of the outer ring of flowers in the bouquet.

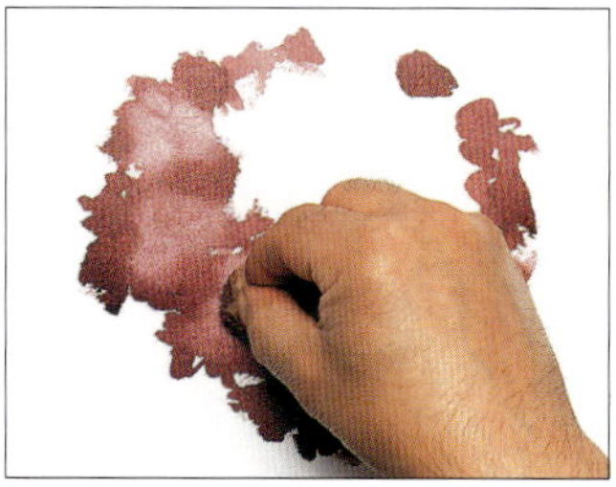

2 While this paint is still wet, dampen a small sponge in clean water and squeeze out any excess moisture. Wipe the sponge over the paint around the inner edge of the ring of flowers, removing colour and softening the brush marks. This creates the basis for a ring of lighter-coloured flowers.

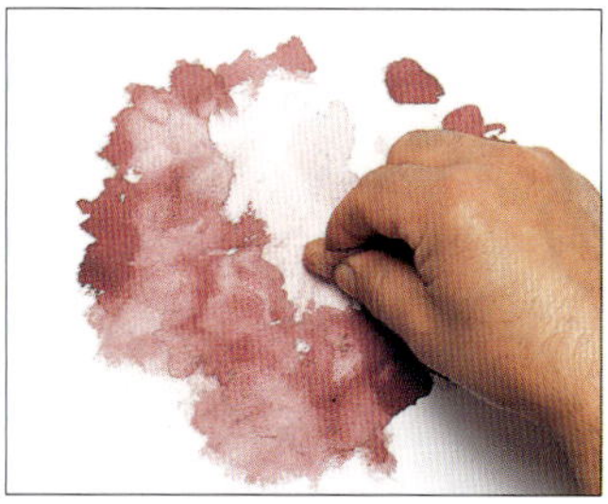

3 Dilute the pink mixture used in Step 1 by adding more water. Dip the sponge into the mixture and gently dab it into the empty centre of the bouquet to reduce the starkness of the white.

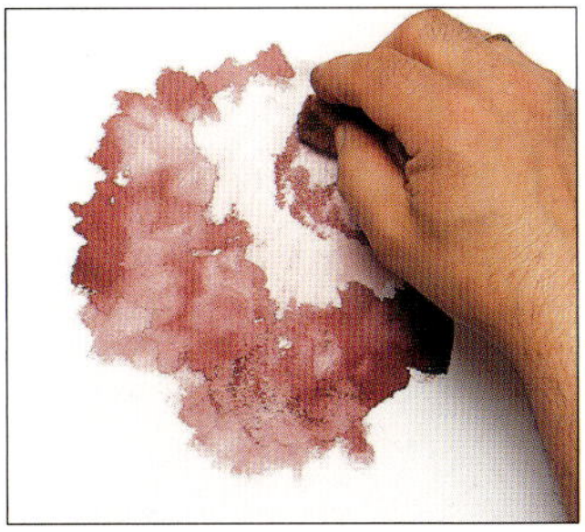

4 You may find that the centre now looks too dark. If so, rinse the sponge in clear water and squeeze out any excess moisture. Gently wipe the sponge over the centre of the bouquet to remove some of the colour you have just applied and soften any hard edges.

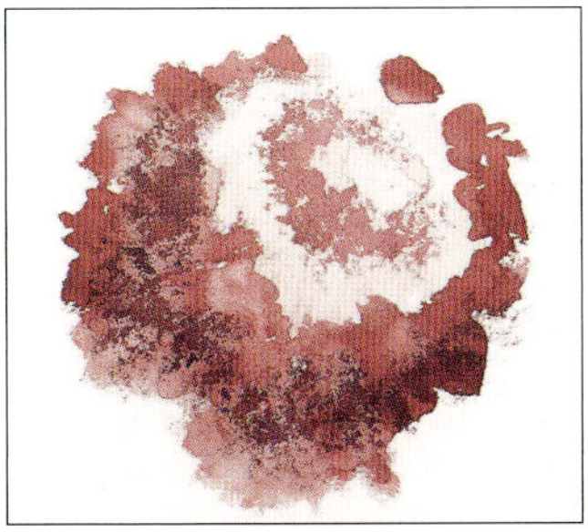

5 Load the sponge with a more highly pigmented version of the mixture used in Step 3 and gently dab it into the centre of the bouquet, to create an inner ring of flowers, and around the outer ring to create some texture and more depth of colour in this area.

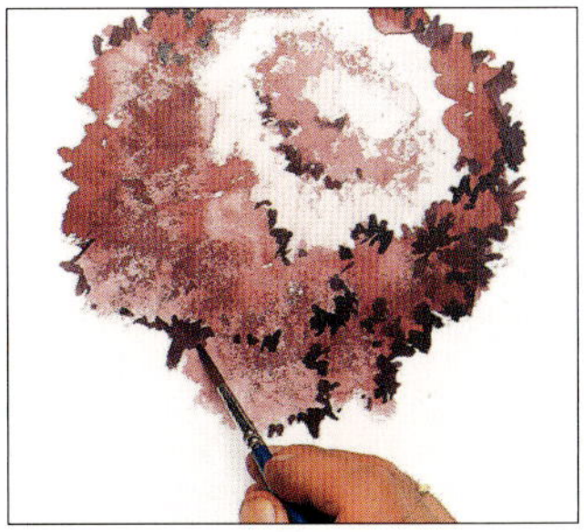

6 Using a slightly bluer version of the mixture and a medium round brush, loosely delineate the edges of individual flowers within the bouquet and around the outer rim.

The finished painting

Complete the painting by lightly brushing in the foliage around the outside of the bouquet, using a light green mixed from cadmium lemon and a little ultramarine blue and a darker green mixed from cadmium yellow and ultramarine blue and paint the darkest outer leaves in the same way. This is a loose, but lively, interpretation which owes much of its success to the random sponging technique, used here both to add colour and to remove it.

Light, calligraphic brushstrokes for the leaves complement the loose textures created with the sponge.

Sponging on the outer ring of flowers has created tonal variety and a sense of depth.

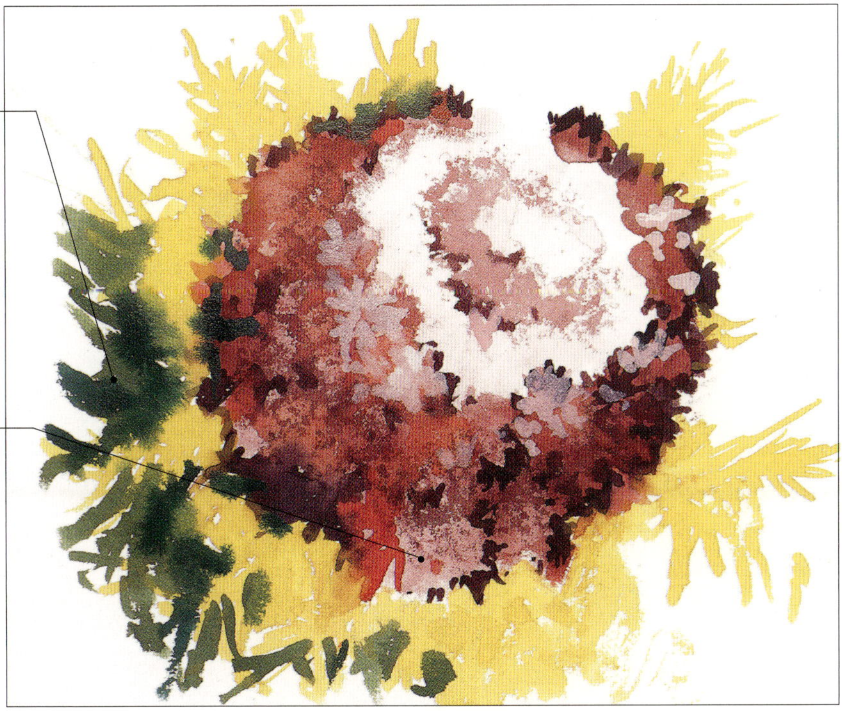

Additives

There are all kinds of materials that can be added to the brush or mixed into watercolour paint. Some materials alter the characteristics of the paint, while others create textures that could not be achieved using a brush alone. These additives should be used in moderation and only in carefully selected areas of the painting, as they can easily become too dominant and detract from the effect of the work as a whole, but they are useful additional tools in your armoury.

Additives that alter the characteristics of the paint

One of the most useful additives in this category is gum arabic. Adding a few drops to your paint mixture has two effects. First, it slows down the drying time, giving you more time to work. Second, it gives the paint a slight sheen, which is particularly useful when you are painting shiny or varnished surfaces such as a wooden table in a still life. Gum arabic also makes colours appear stronger and more saturated. Glycerin will also slow down the drying time and makes the paint slightly sticky and easier to control on the paper.

Another additive that changes the characteristics of the paint is granulation medium. Some colours, such as French ultramarine, granulate naturally, but this medium allows you to exploit that characteristic with any colour, although it works better with darker colours and ones that have a natural tendency to granulate.

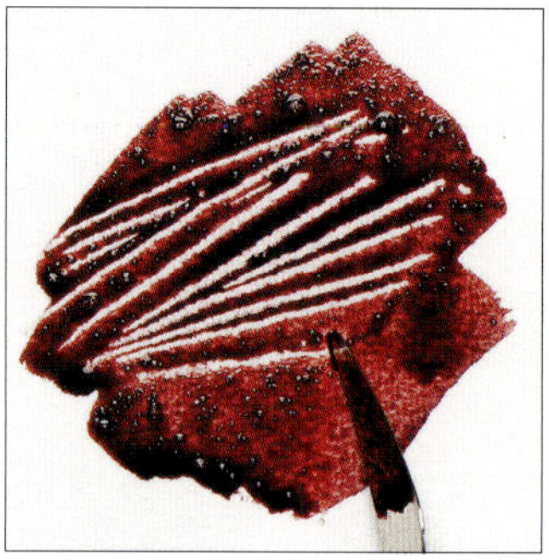

Gum arabic
Pour a few drops of gum arabic into pre-mixed watercolour paint and mix thoroughly. Apply the paint to the paper with a brush. Because the gum arabic retards the paint's drying time, you can then work into it with a palette knife or the tip of a brush handle.

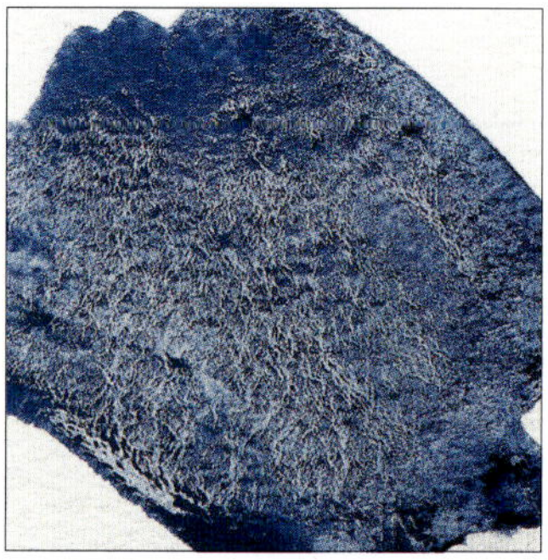

Granulation medium
Add a few drops of granulation medium to pre-mixed watercolour paint and mix thoroughly. Apply the paint to the paper as normal. When the paint dries, it will have a slightly speckled, granular appearance. This is an effective way of painting old, worn stonework.

Additives for texture

Texture pastes and gels can be applied directly to the paper with a palette knife or mixed with watercolour paint first and brushed on. When they dry, the surface is slightly raised. Paint applied on top of the raised surface will settle in intriguing ways.

Sand, grit, tissue paper and other textured materials can be added to glue. Apply the glue to your painting, stir or press the required material into the glue, and allow to dry thoroughly before painting on top.

Finally, common household salt can create some exciting effects. Drop salt into a wet watercolour wash and leave to dry before brushing off the crystals. The salt leaches the colour out of the watercolour. The result depends on how wet the wash is: if it is too wet, the effect will not be so pronounced, and if it is too dry the salt will have no effect.

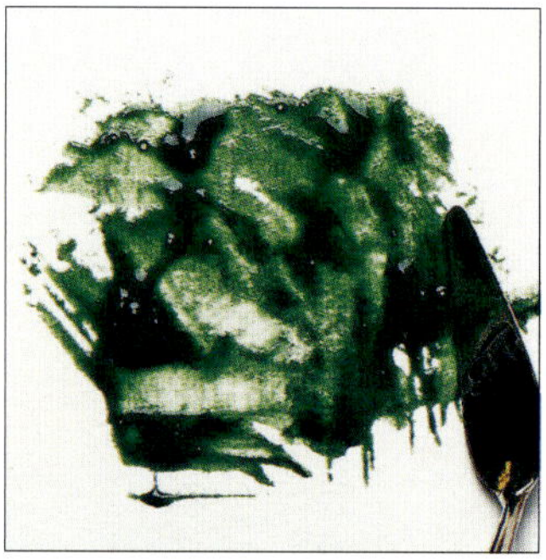

Texture medium
This is a viscous, white-coloured fluid. Mix it thoroughly into the pre-mixed watercolour paint, or apply it directly to the paper, and stipple it on to the painting surface with a palette knife. When the paint dries, the surface will be slightly raised.

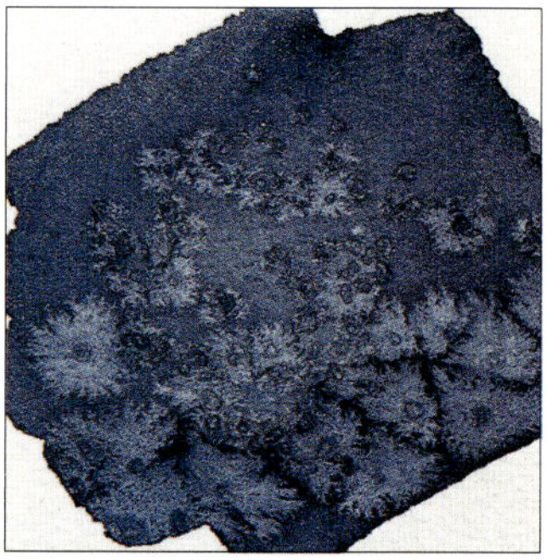

Salt
Sprinkle common household salt on to a wet wash. When it is completely dry, gently brush off the salt crystals. The salt will leach the colour out of the paint, leaving mottled marks. This is a useful technique for painting snow or textured subjects, such as lichen.

Practice exercise: **Textured stone and iron**

In this study of a rusty chain on a worn, lichen-encrusted harbour wall, the artist has indulged in a little lateral thinking: if salt can create interesting textures, why not see what you can achieve with other items from the kitchen? Here, olive oil and plain white flour have been used as inexpensive alternatives to oil-pastel or candlewax resists and texture medium. Don't feel constrained by convention: painting should be all about experimenting and having fun.

Materials

- *HB pencil*
- *220lb (450gsm) rough watercolour paper, unstretched*
- *Watercolour paints: yellow ochre, burnt umber, cadmium red, alizarin crimson, ultramarine blue, Naples yellow, burnt sienna*
- *Gouache paints: Chinese white*
- *Brushes: medium flat, medium round, fine round, large wash*
- *Olive oil*
- *Salt: fine-grained, coarse-grained*
- *Flour*

The original scene

The lovely, subtle colours on this old stone wall give you the opportunity to work wet into wet, allowing the colours to merge on the paper. The speckled textures in the wall provide additional visual interest, while the chain forms a diagonal line across the frame, giving a dynamic composition.

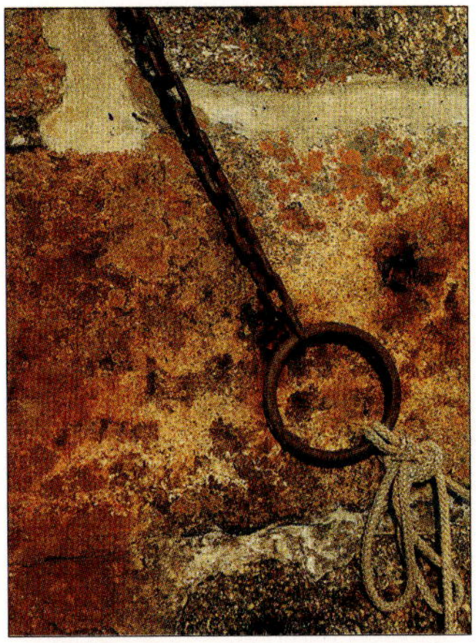

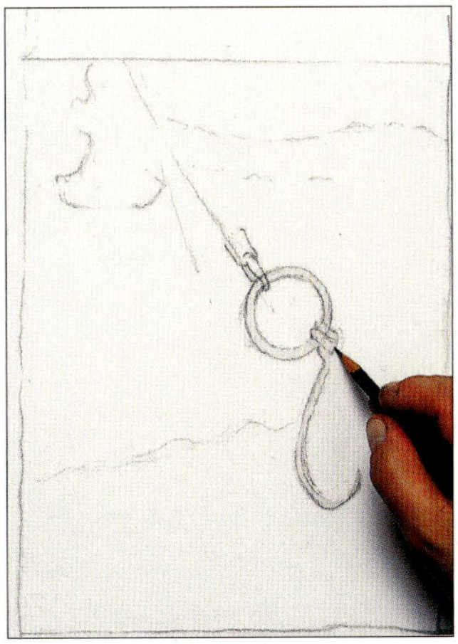

1 Using an HB pencil, sketch the subject, indicating the position of the chain and rope and the main bands of colour on the wall behind. Look at how the links of the chain are joined and at how the rope loops twist and fall over each other: the composition is very simple, but elements such as this are key to making it look realistic.

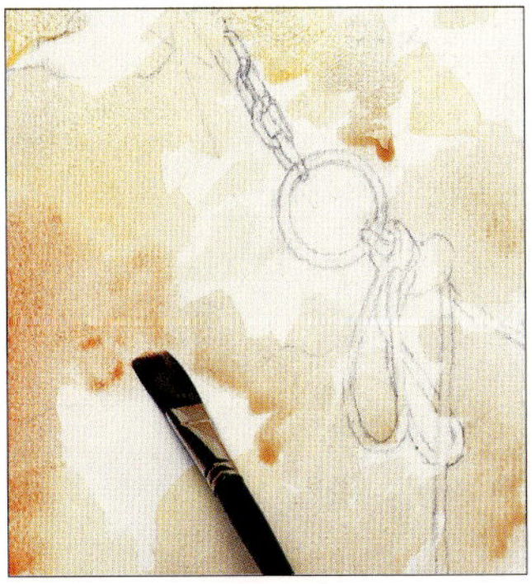

2 Mix three very pale washes for the background colours: yellow ochre, burnt umber, and a pinkish mixture of yellow ochre, cadmium red and alizarin crimson. Using a medium flat brush, dab yellow ochre on at the top of the paper, burnt umber at the base, and the pink mixture on the left-hand side. Dampen any unpainted areas with clean water so that the whole paper is wet.

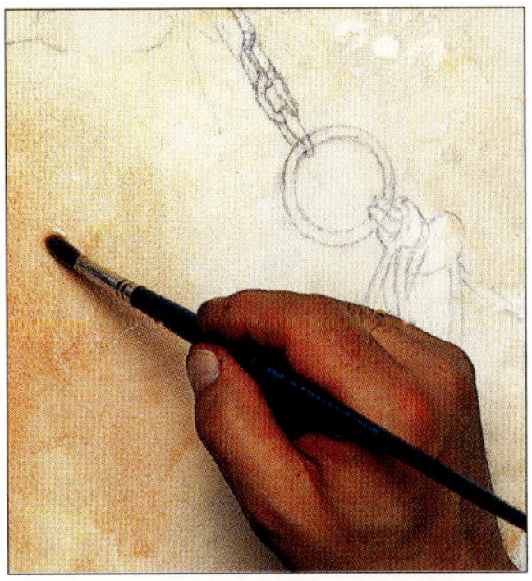

3 While the first washes are still wet, dip a medium round brush in olive oil and dab large and small marks into the washes. The oil acts as a resist and repels watercolour paint, and will give a mottled appearance when dry – although, because the oil is applied on top of the watercolour, rather than the other way round, the effect is subtle and understated.

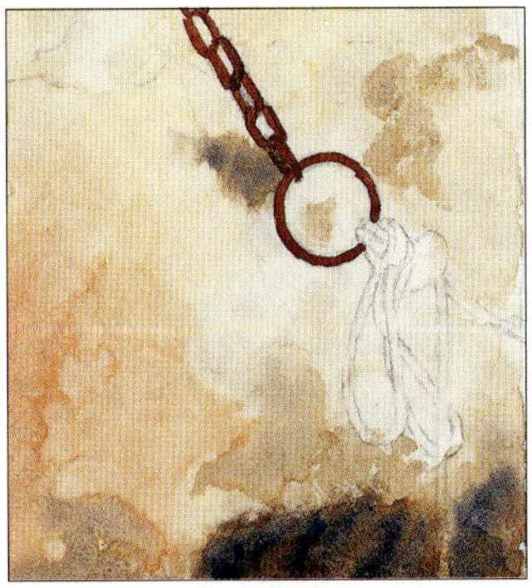

4 Mix a dark brown from burnt umber and ultramarine blue and dab it on to the darker areas at the base of the picture. While it is still wet, dab on more olive oil. Leave to dry. Mix a pale, rusty brown colour from burnt umber, alizarin crimson, Naples yellow and ultramarine blue. Using a fine round brush, paint the iron chain and ring.

▶

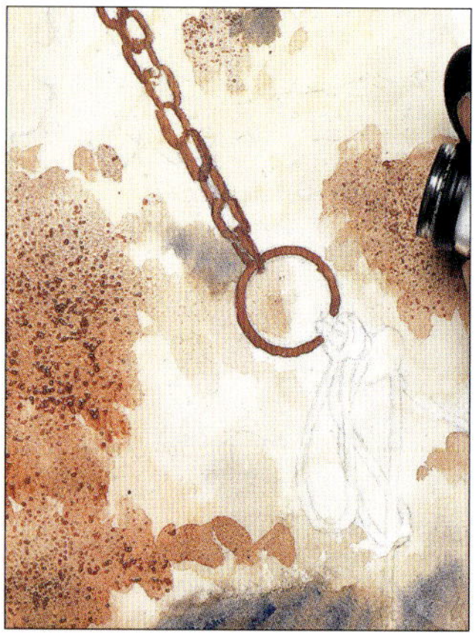

5 Add a little ultramarine blue to the pinkish mixture used in Step 2 to make an orangey brown. Using a large wash brush, dab the mixture over the left-hand side of the wall. While this is still wet, sprinkle a little fine-grained salt over it.

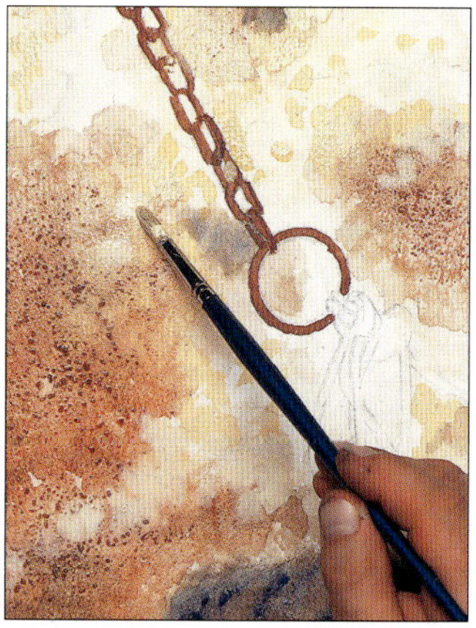

6 Mix an opaque, creamy yellow from yellow ochre and Chinese white gouache. Using a medium round brush, dot it on to the chain and the salted area on the left of the picture. This area is still damp, so the paint spreads a little and looks like small patches of lichen.

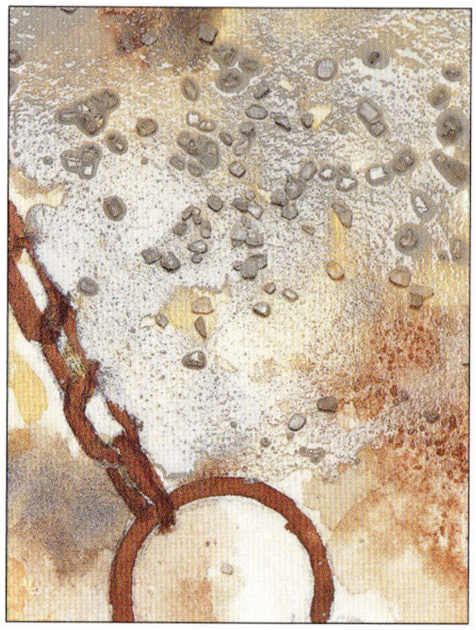

7 Add burnt sienna and ultramarine blue to the opaque yellow mixture used in Step 6 to make a pale, bluish grey. Using a medium round brush, dab the mixture over the light area at the top of the wall. Sprinkle on some coarse-grained salt.

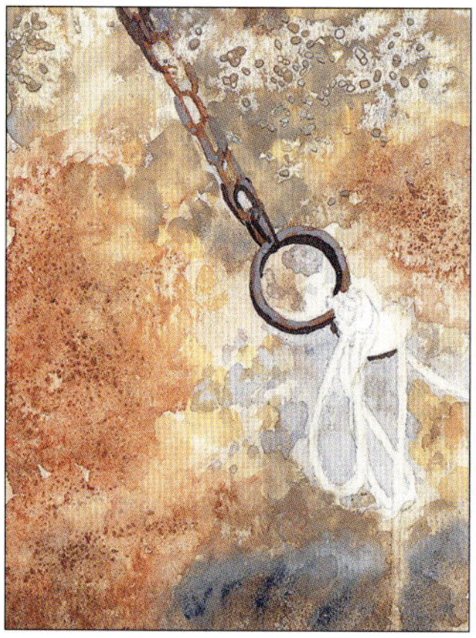

8 Mix an opaque pinkish grey from yellow ochre, alizarin crimson, Naples yellow, a little ultramarine blue and Chinese white gouache. Brush it over the shaded parts of the chain and ring; suddenly they look three-dimensional. Add more ultramarine blue to the mixture and paint inside the rope loops and around the chain. Mix a dark brown from burnt umber, ultramarine blue and a little alizarin crimson and paint inside the ring.

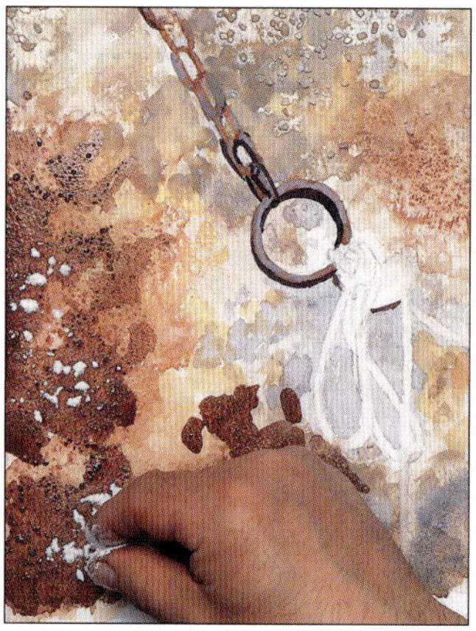

9 Using a medium round brush, dab the same dark brown mixture on to the left-hand side of the wall. Sprinkle flour into the wet areas; it will sink into the wet paint in clumps, leaving a slightly raised surface when it dries.

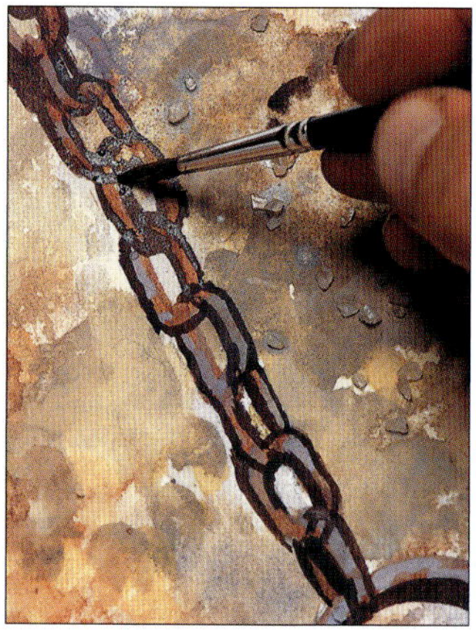

10 Outline the links of the chain in pure burnt sienna, taking care to break the line where the links overlap to give a three-dimensional effect.

Tip: Take plenty of time over this stage and study your reference photo carefully: these dark lines indicate how the links of the chain are joined together, so it's important to get them right.

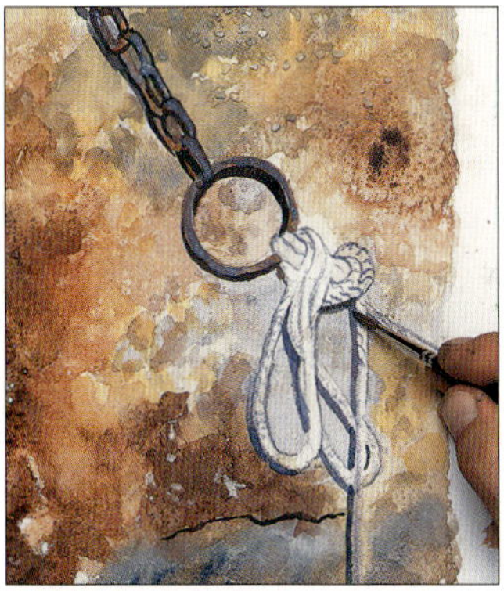

11 Mix a pale blue from ultramarine blue, burnt sienna and Chinese white gouache. Paint the rope strands and the shadows underneath the rope.

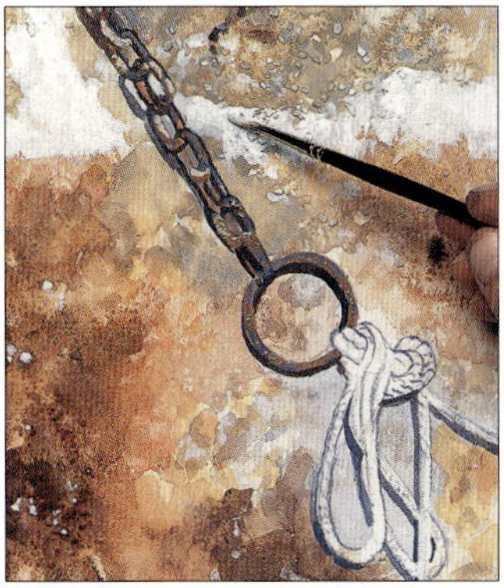

12 Mix Chinese white gouache with a tiny amount of ultramarine blue and paint the mortar lines in the brickwork of the wall.

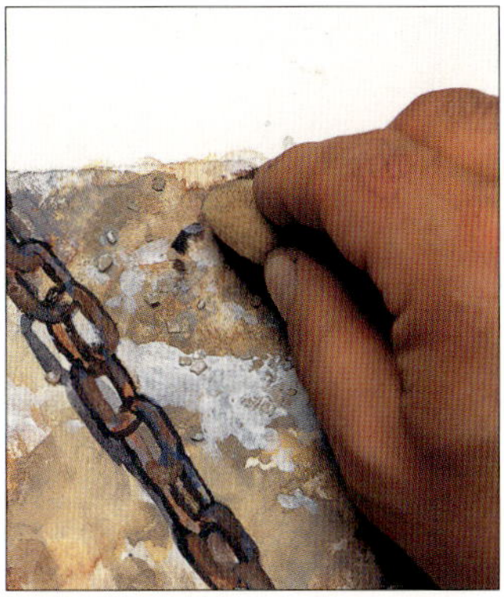

13 Gently brush off the dry salt crystals to reveal mottled, bleached-out marks that look like lichen growing on the harbour wall.

The finished painting

Often, insignificant details can make intriguing paintings: there is nothing exceptional about this subject, but the soft colours and contrasts of texture make it very appealing. The artist has applied a number of additives – some more unusual and unorthodox than others – to the wet watercolour washes, thereby creating interesting textures that could not have been achieved by brushwork alone.

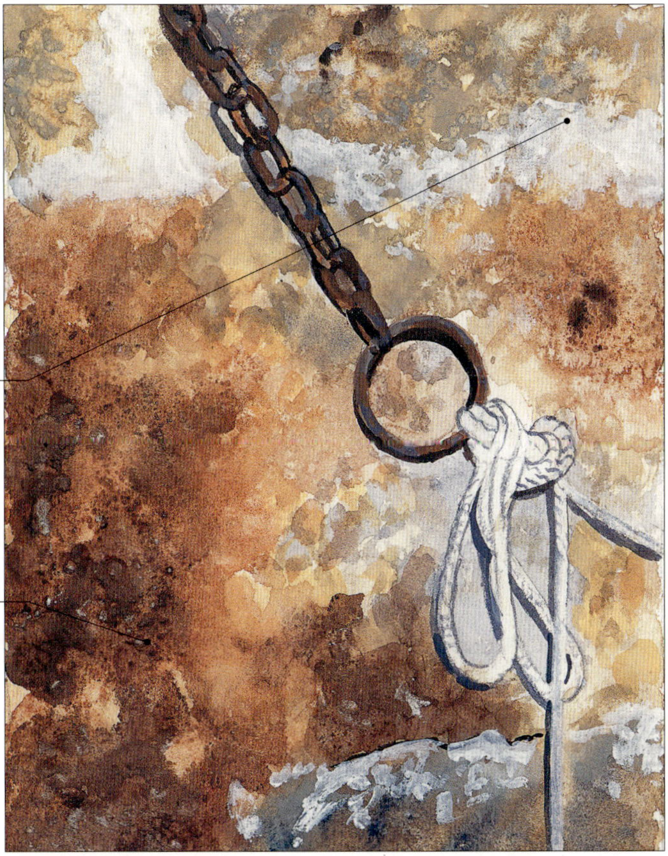

Salt leaches colour out of the paint, creating a mottled effect like lichen.

The flour has dried on to the paint in lumps, creating a slightly raised surface that looks like worn, uneven stonework.

Line and wash

Combining inks with watercolours – a technique that is commonly known as line and wash – is one of the most challenging and exciting of all watercolour techniques. It enables you to combine the precise detail of pen-and-ink work with the fluidity and transparency of watercolour washes.

It doesn't matter whether you do the ink drawing or the watercolour washes first, that really depends on what you want to say about your subject. The real danger, especially for beginners, is putting in too much linear detail and consequently overworking the picture. Make a conscious effort to simplify your subject and put down only the essentials.

The key to a successful line-and-wash painting is to maintain a balance between the two media. Although there are no hard-and-fast rules, a useful guideline is that if your subject contains relatively little colour you can afford to do a lot of pen work, while a very colourful subject will probably require less. (Lots of pen work in a painting of a colourful flower border, for example, would detract from the colours of the subject; with an action subject such as a dancer or sporting scene, you might choose to make the pen work tell most of the story, applying just a little colour for atmosphere.) It takes a certain amount of practice and skill to get the balance right.

Experiment with different inks, as there are both waterproof and water-soluble kinds. If you want the pen marks to be permanent, use waterproof inks. Water-soluble ink marks will blur and run when you apply watercolour washes on top of them, but you can create some exciting effects in this way.

Try different kinds of pen, too, to find out which ones you like using, and use the back of the nib, as well as the tip, to create different widths of line. Steel-nibbed dip pens make lovely lines, but they hold relatively little ink and you may find it frustrating to have to keep stopping to re-load the pen. Fountain pens and technical drawing pens have an ink reservoir, but the quality of line that they make may be a little too neat and regular for some people's tastes.

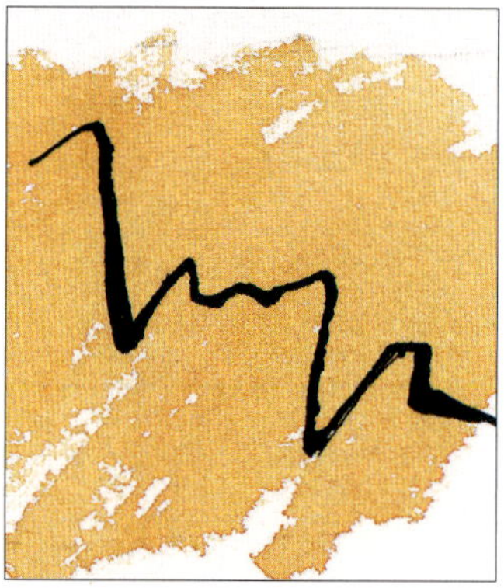

Watercolour wash over ink
Provided you use waterproof ink, as here, and allow it to dry completely, the lines will remain permanent and unsmudged even when you apply a watercolour wash over the top.

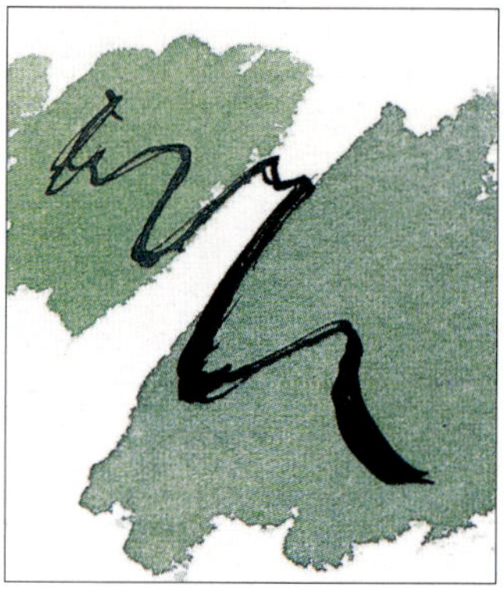

Semi-opaque paint over ink
The top half of the image shows a mixture of watercolour paint and permanent gouache applied over ink: the semi-opaque paint partially covers the ink, making the lines more muted. Compare this with the deep lines of the ink covered by pure watercolour in the bottom half of the image.

Practice exercise: **Church spire in line and wash**

Line and wash is the perfect technique for architectural subjects such as this picturesque church steeple and spire. Details can be held sharply in ink while watercolour washes provide colour and tonal variety. The dip pen used here provides a less regular and mechanical quality of line than a technical drawing pen, which helps to make the study of the building more lively.

Materials

- *2B pencil*
- *300lb (640gsm) rough watercolour paper*
- *Watercolour paints: yellow ochre, raw umber, ultramarine blue, cadmium red, burnt sienna, ultramarine blue, cadmium yellow*
- *Brushes: medium round*
- *Medium-nibbed steel dip pen*
- *Black waterproof ink*

The original scene
There is a lot of interesting detail in this scene. The arched bell-tower windows and a rounded turret cry out to be depicted in a crisp, linear way, while the soft transitions from light to dark tones in the stonework require soft-edged wet-into-wet washes.

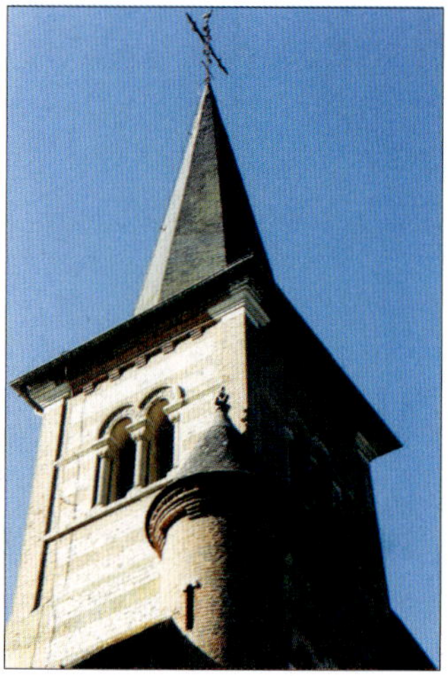

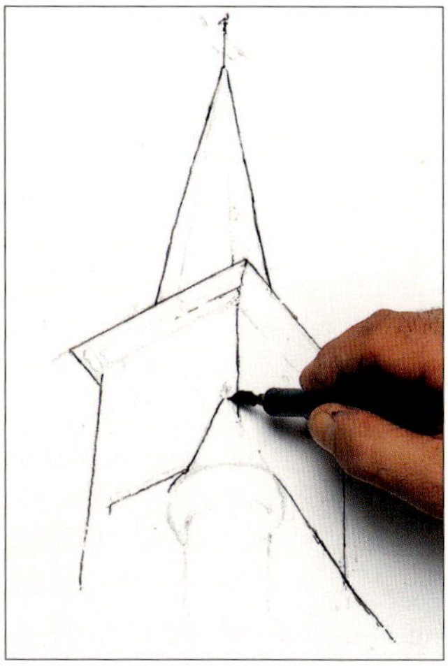

1 Using a 2B pencil, sketch the building. (If you are confident, start working in pen and ink straight away – but you cannot erase mistakes.) Using a medium dip pen and waterproof black ink, ink over the pencil lines.

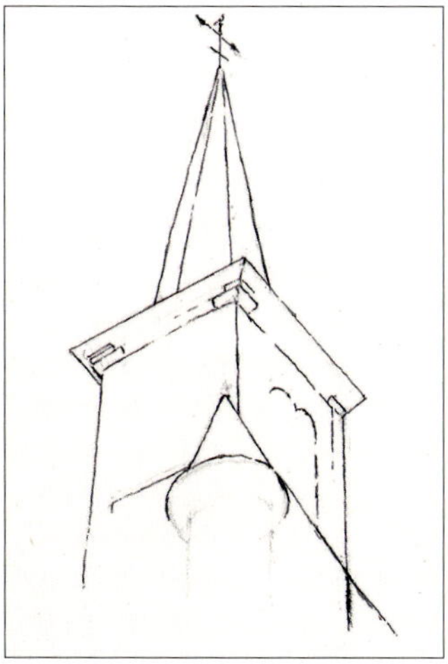

2 Continue with the pen-and-ink work until you have put in all the main lines of the spire, steeple and rounded turret. Leave to dry completely before going on to the next stage of the painting.

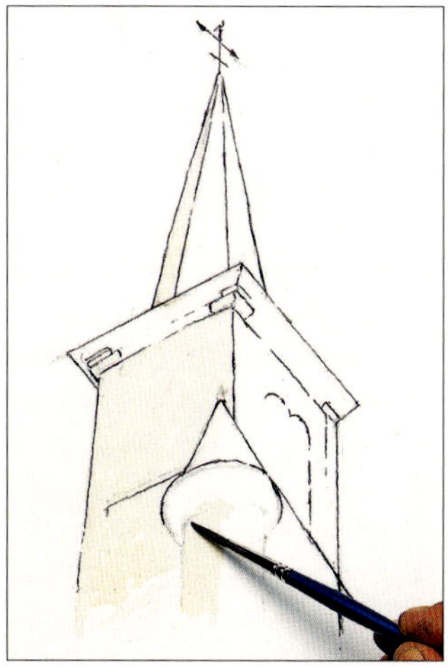

3 Mix a pale wash of yellow ochre. Using a medium round brush put in the lightest tone, which is on the left-hand side of the steeple and spire. This establishes the underlying colour of the honey-coloured stonework.

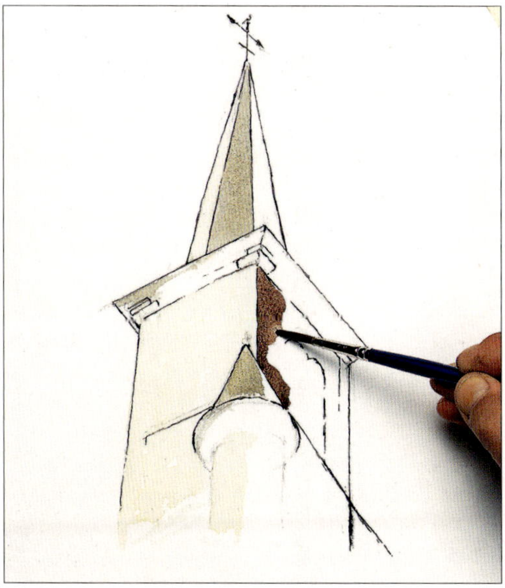

4 Mix a mid-toned grey from raw umber with a little ultramarine blue. Put in the second facet of the spire, the shadow under the eave on the left, and the roof of the rounded turret. Add a little cadmium red and paint the right-hand side of the steeple, painting around the arched window.

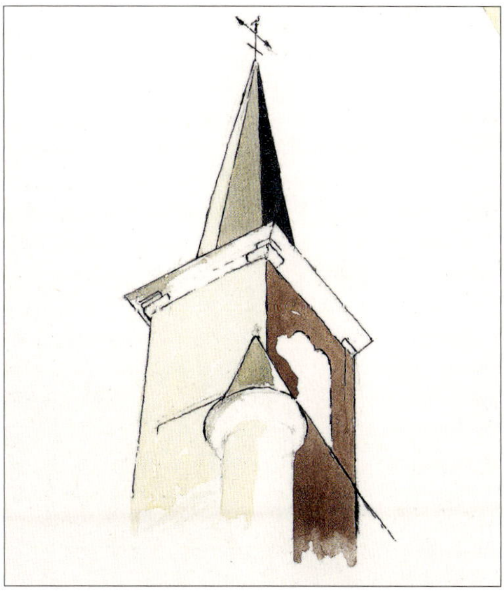

5 Mix a dark brown from burnt sienna and ultramarine blue and put in the darkest facet of the steeple, the side that is in shade. The building is now starting to look three-dimensional, and this will be reinforced in the later stages of the painting.

▶

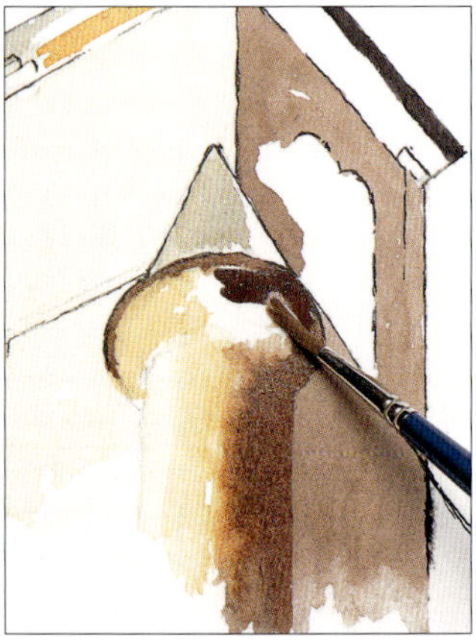

6 Mix a rich, orangey-brown from cadmium yellow, cadmium red and a little ultramarine blue and paint the rounded turret. Use the dark brown mixture from Step 5 to paint the shaded right-hand side of the turret and the eaves under the right-hand side of both the steeple and turret.

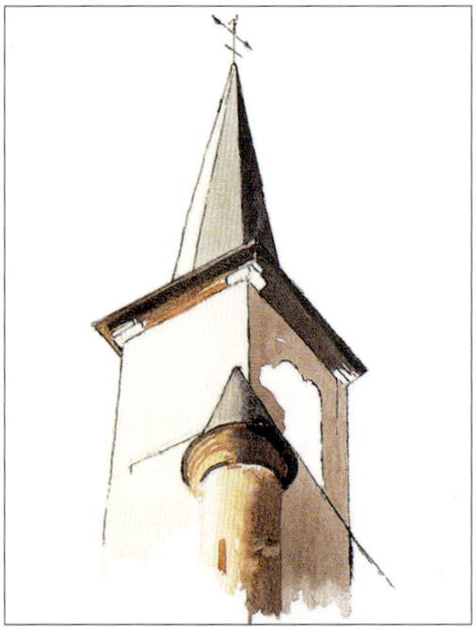

7 Using the orangey-brown mixture from Step 6, "draw" concentric lines underneath the conical roof of the turret so that you begin to establish the form of this structure. Paint the window in the turret in the same colour. Darken the mixture and paint under the eave on the right-hand side of the steeple.

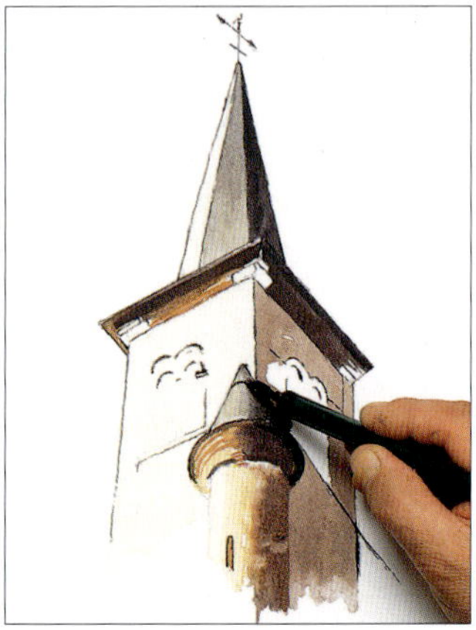

8 Darken the middle facet of the spire using the dark brown mixture from Step 5. Using the steel-nibbed dip pen and waterproof black ink, reinforce some of the structural lines of the building and put in the curves of the arched window on the left-hand side of the steeple.

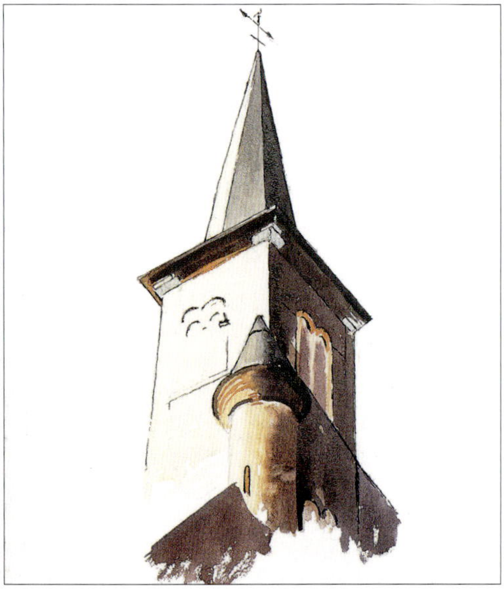

9 The right-hand side of the steeple looks too light, so mix a warm brown from ultramarine blue and cadmium red and darken it. Mix a neutral mauve from yellow ochre and ultramarine blue and paint the window on the right-hand side of the steeple.

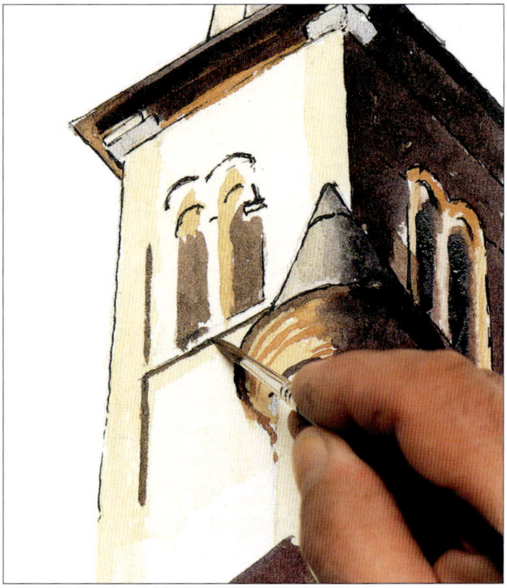

10 Brush pale yellow ochre over the left-hand side to warm up the colour of the stone. Use the dark brown mixture from Step 5 to paint the recessed window on the left. Paint horizontal and vertical lines to the left of and below the window, indicating that the façade is not completely flush.

The finished painting

The artist has achieved a good balance between linear pen work and watercolour washes, with the ink establishing the structure and some of the fine detail of the building and the watercolour the subtle tonal transitions from light to dark. On its own the pen work could have looked rather tight and mechanical, but successive layers of watercolour washes have helped to enliven the study and provide it with some depth and colour.

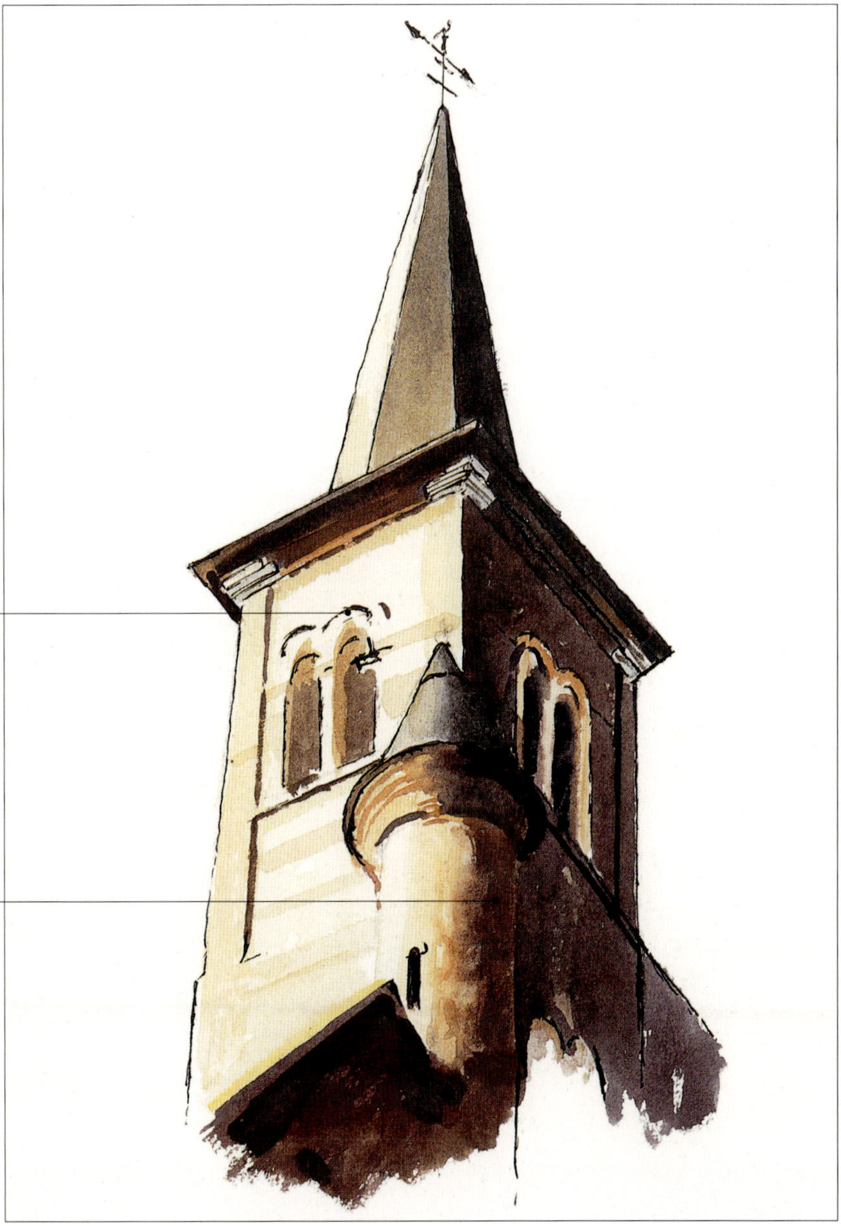

Pen lines establish the structure of the building.

Wet-into-wet washes convey the variety of colour in the stonework and the form of the building.

Water-soluble pencils

The advantage of water-soluble pencils is that they combine the linear appeal of pencil work with the fluidity of transparent watercolour washes. They are incredibly versatile: you can use them wet or dry, on their own or in conjunction with other media, and the colours do not go muddy. Easily portable, water-soluble pencils are a real boon when it comes to making sketches on location, but they are equally useful in the studio.

Water-soluble pencils are available in a breathtaking range of colours – there are far more shades available than you will find in any range of paints. You can also blend several colours together on the paper to produce subtler shades. However, some brands of water-soluble pencil seem to blend better than others, so it is worth experimenting with different brands in order to find one that you like.

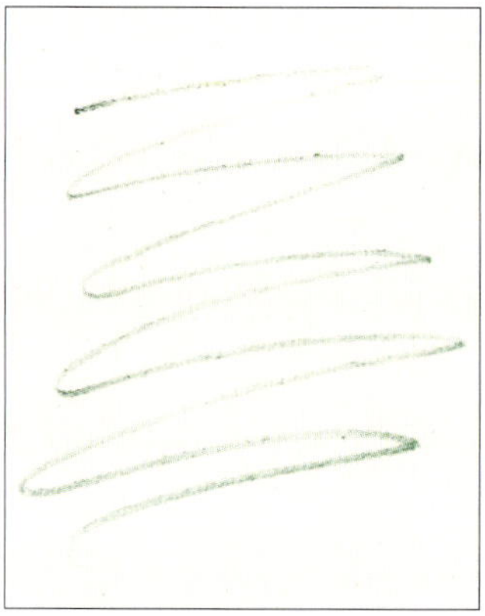

Dry on dry
Applied dry on top of dry paper or watercolour washes, water-soluble pencils can be used to draw fine lines and details, such as veins in flower petals and leaves, feathers, mortar lines in brickwork, wood-grain effects, and highlighting on objects such as bottles.

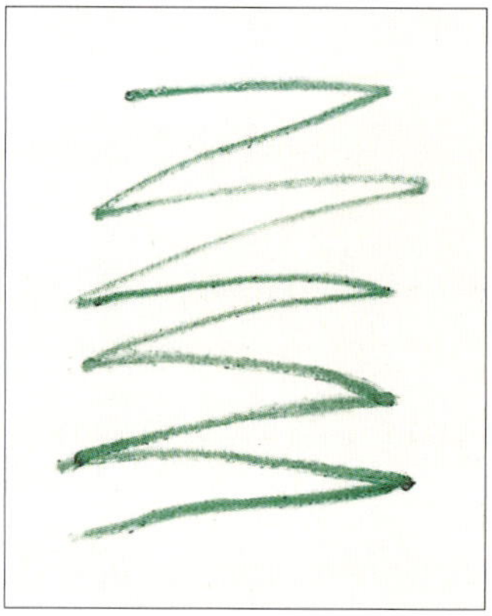

Wet on dry
Dipping the tip of the pencil in water before you apply it to the dry paper has two effects: it intensifies the colour and it also fixes the pencil marks, so that they do not blur (or do not blur as much) when a watercolour wash is applied on top.

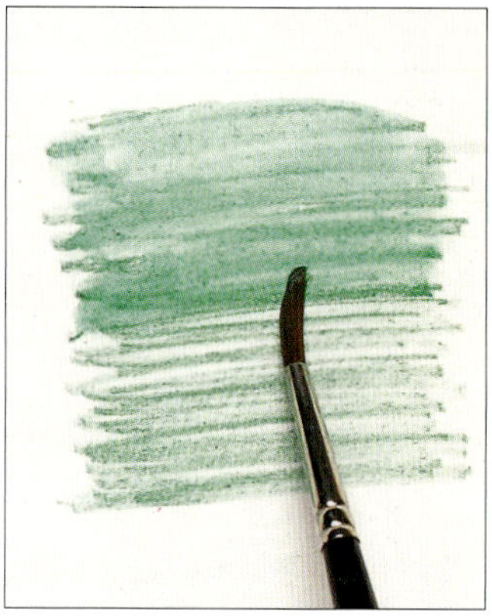

Dry marks brushed with water
If water or a watercolour wash is brushed over dry water-soluble pencil marks, they will blur and spread a little – a useful technique for implying that objects are far away, such as a distant woodland. (Foreground details should always be crisp and sharp.)

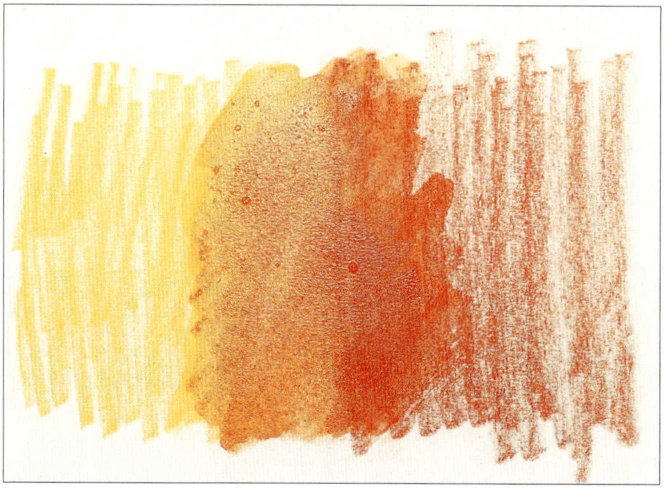

Blending water-soluble pencil marks
Brushing clean water over water-soluble pencil marks will allow you to blend colours together easily.

Tip: Make heavy scribbles in a range of colours and use them as easily portable "palettes": when you brush the scribbles with clean water, you can pick up enough colour on the brush to work with them in the same way as watercolour paints. However, the "paints" thus produced are generally less intense in colour than real watercolour paints.

Practice exercise: **Peacock feathers**

This exercise demonstrates the linear characteristics of using water-soluble pencils dry, and it gives you the chance to practise mixing colours optically by overlaying one colour on top of another. It also shows how the colour intensifies into a smooth, velvety finish when the tips of the pencils are dipped in water and used wet. For the best effect, use a smooth, HP paper.

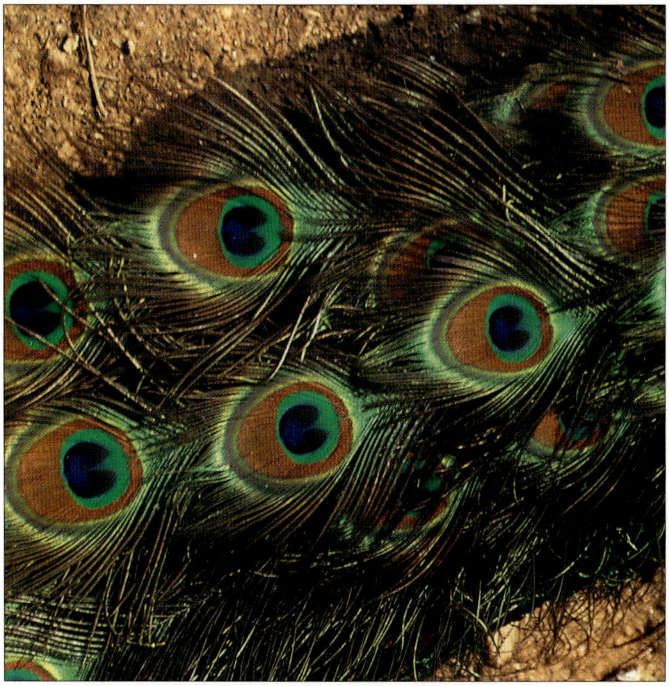

Materials

- *HP paper, unstretched*
- *Water-soluble pencils: yellow-green, jade green, orange, light violet, light green, dark green, emerald green, turquoise, light blue, ultramarine blue, ivory black*

The display

When a male peacock displays, his tail feathers fan out into a shimmering mass of iridescent colours. Although you won't find true iridescent colours in your range of water-soluble pencils, you can come close to recreating the effect by carefully overlaying colours on the paper, so that they mix optically.

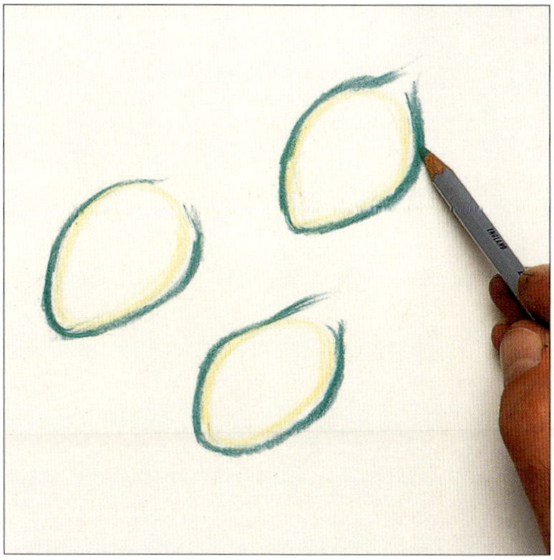

1 Outline the "eyes" of the peacock feathers with a pale, yellow-green line. Draw around the outside of the yellow lines with a jade green pencil.

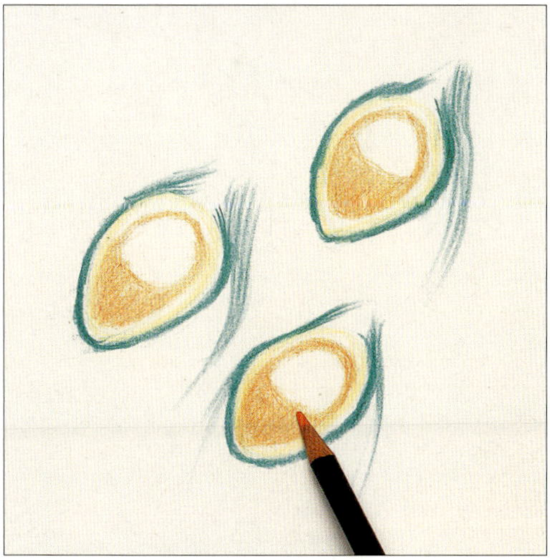

2 Using the jade green pencil again, draw long, feathery strokes on the outer edges of the eyes. Draw an orange line inside the first yellow-green lines and fill in the lower half of the eyes in orange.

▶

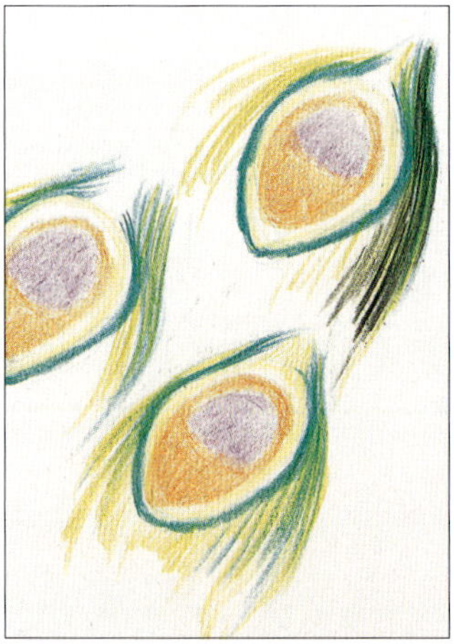

3 Fill in the upper half of the eyes with light violet. Following the direction of the peacock feathers, draw light green marks over the straggly jade green feathers, so that the two greens blend optically. Then repeat the process using a dark green pencil.

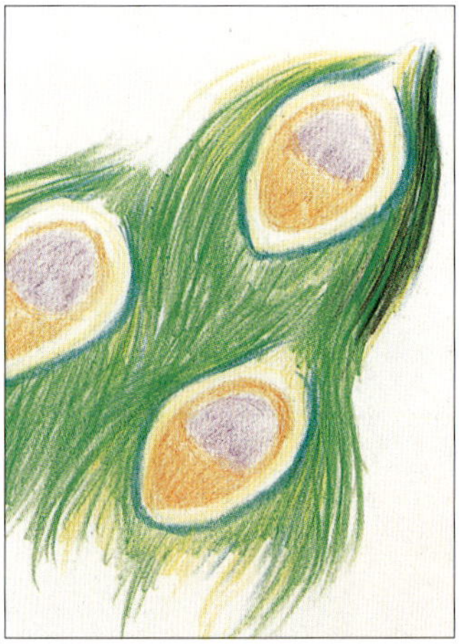

4 Go over the other greens again, and the large spaces between the eyes, with an emerald green pencil – again, making sure that your pencil marks follow the direction in which the feathers grow. Take care not to block in the colour too heavily.

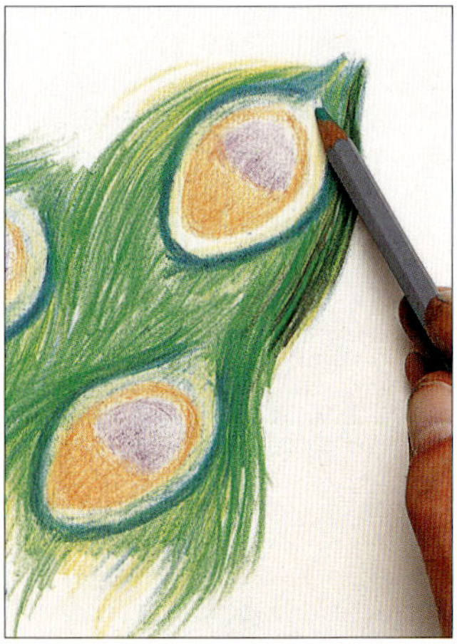

5 Draw around the outside of the eyes with a turquoise pencil and draw over the initial yellow-green lines with jade green. Note how you are beginning to build up the depth of colour while still maintaining the linear quality of the pencil work.

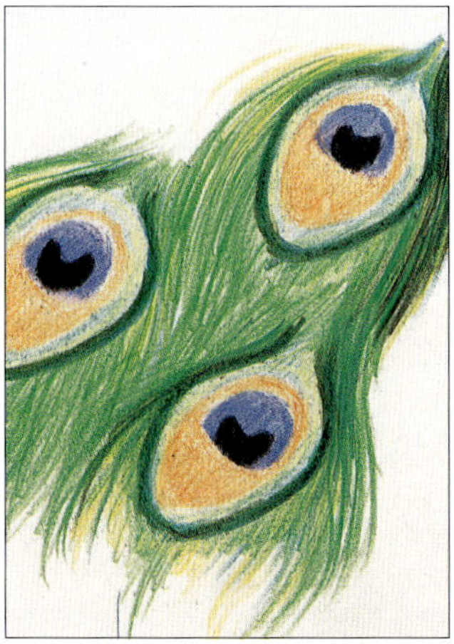

6 Go over the light violet of the eyes with a light blue pencil. Although you can't really see the underlying violet any more, the colours merge on the paper to create a purplish blue that you could not have created by using just one pencil on its own. Draw the "pupils" of the eyes in ivory black. (Note the irregular shape: they are not a neat circle or semi-circle.).

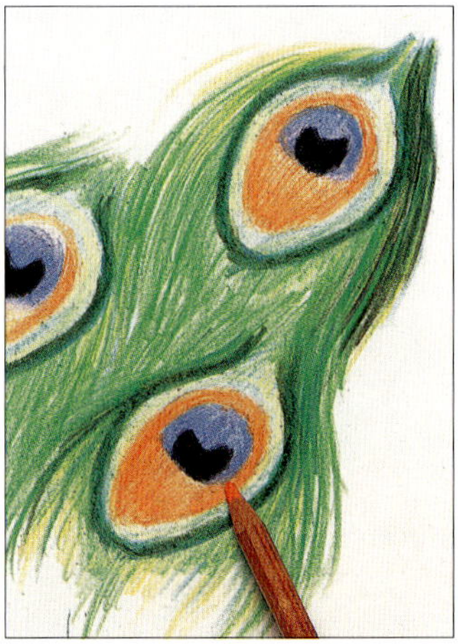

7 Dip the tip of an orange pencil in water and go over the orange colour again. Note how using the pencil wet intensifies the colour and creates a smooth, velvety block of colour in which the individual pencil strokes can no longer be clearly differentiated.

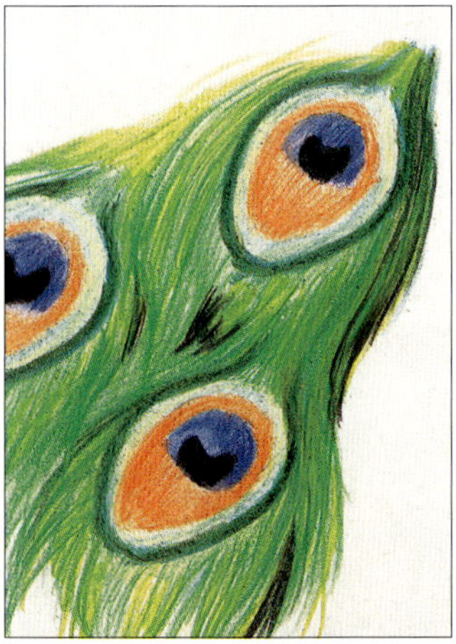

8 Strengthen the green feathers further by applying layers of emerald green and light green pencil. As before, follow the direction of the feathers and take care not to block in the colours completely, otherwise the feathers will look like a solid mass rather than individual strands. Draw in small touches of ivory black between the feathers: this adds drama.

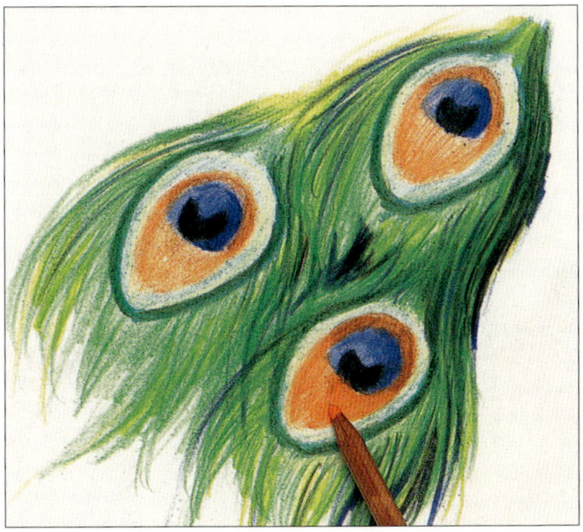

9 The green markings look a little too green at this stage; you need to relieve the intensity and also hint at the iridescence of the feathers. Go over the green markings in places with an ultramarine blue pencil. Dip the ultramarine blue pencil in water and intensify the blue of the eye. Strengthen the orange of the eye in the same way.

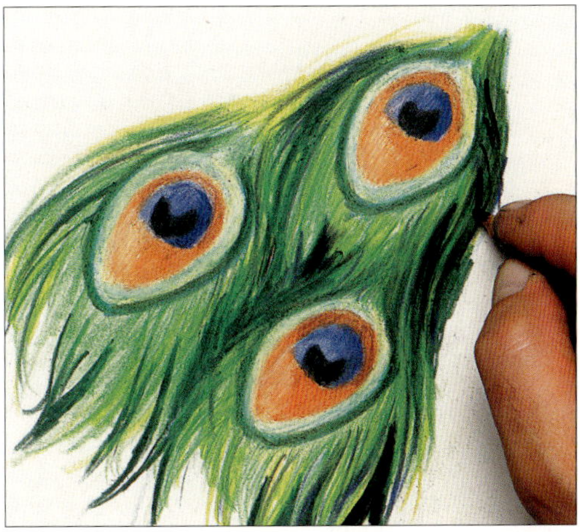

10 Dip a dark green pencil in water and go over any areas that you want to be very dark. Because the pencil is used wet, the resulting marks are very smooth and intense in colour. Dip an ivory black pencil in water and build up more of the base feathers. This provides a background against which the colours will stand out more strongly.

The finished work

More a drawing than a painting, this little detail sketch nonetheless shows the range of marks and intensity of colour that can be produced with water-soluble pencils. It is also a lovely example of optical colour mixing.

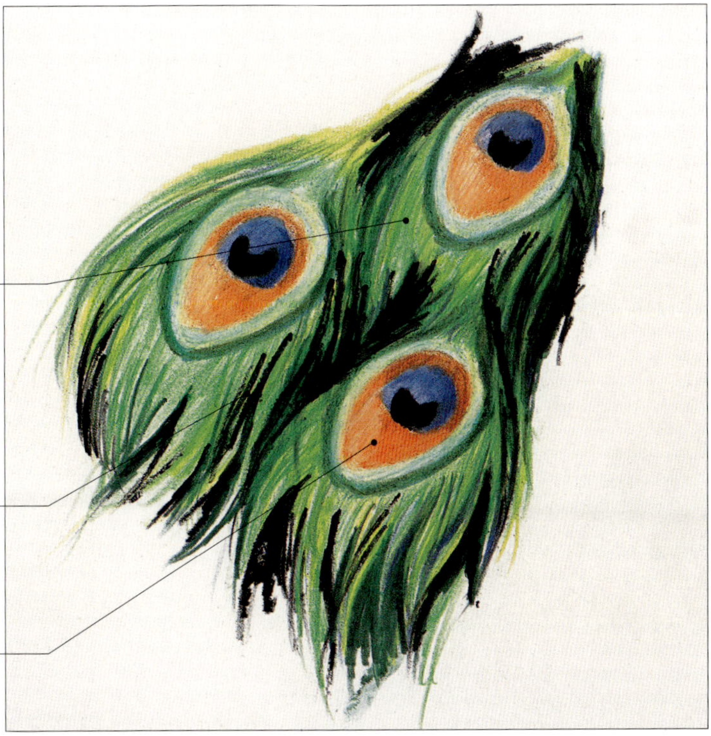

Greens and blues intermingle to create subtle optical mixes that hint at the iridescence of the feathers.

The individual pencil strokes can clearly be seen.

More solid blocks of colour are achieved by dipping the tip of the pencil in water.

Using a toned ground

Although it is more usual for traditional transparent watercolour to be painted on white paper, it is possible – and, in some cases, even preferable – to work on a coloured or toned ground or paper.

Using a toned ground can create a colour harmony as, to a greater or lesser extent, the colour of the ground influences the colour of the washes that are applied over the top. It establishes a colour key that can help create a mood. A toned ground can also simplify and cut down considerably on the amount of time it takes to paint the picture: applying a wash over the whole paper in order to establish a colour key is often the first stage in making a watercolour painting.

Ready-prepared watercolour papers are available from art stores in shades of cream, oatmeal, grey, light blue and light green. If you require another colour, you will need to prepare the paper yourself by applying a wash of the desired hue in either watercolour or acrylic paint. Acrylic paint has the additional advantage of being permanent: there is no risk of the colour being disturbed by subsequent layers of watercolour washes. However, it does leave a slight residue and seals the surface, and this can affect the way the watercolour lies on the paper.

The toned ground need not be flat and uniform. If appropriate to the subject, you could create a textured ground using sponges or rough brush work.

The colour you choose for the ground should reflect the mood and atmosphere of the piece and complement the colours to be used. This is particularly important when using transparent watercolour. If you are using opaque watercolour (that is, watercolour to which body colour has been added), the opacity and covering power of the paint make the colour of the ground less noticeable.

If you are using opaque watercolour, the colour of the toned ground can lean towards the complementary colour of the main colours in the painting – for example, a predominantly green landscape on a pale red ground. Because of the effect of simultaneous contrast, a ground in a contrasting colour can make the colours used in the painting seem brighter.

Practice exercise: **Log and axe on toned ground**

This exercise shows how to create an overall colour harmony by using a toned ground. When you first start experimenting with toned grounds, keep the subject very simple, with a limited colour range, and think carefully about what colour will work best. Here, the overall colour of the wooden log and axe is a warm brown and so a pale, warm ground is the obvious choice.

Materials
- *2B pencil*
- *Soft graphite pencil*
- *200lb (425gsm) NOT watercolour paper, pre-stretched*
- *Watercolour paints: yellow ochre, burnt umber, Payne's grey, raw umber, ivory black, burnt sienna*
- *Brushes: large wash, medium round*

The set-up

The plain cream paper on which the log is set is helpful in some ways, because it allows you to see the cast shadow very clearly, but it is also very stark and bright and detracts from the subject.

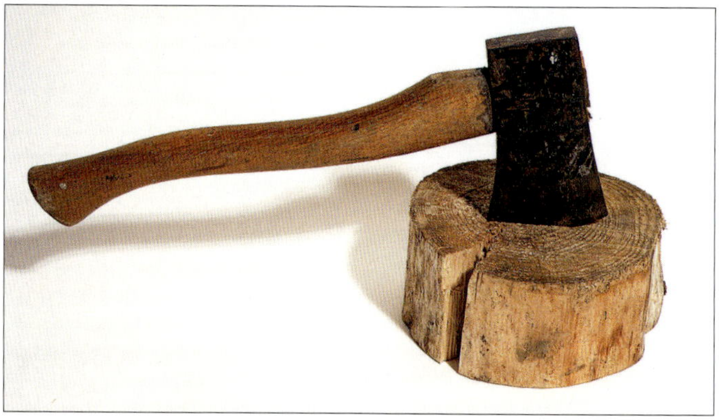

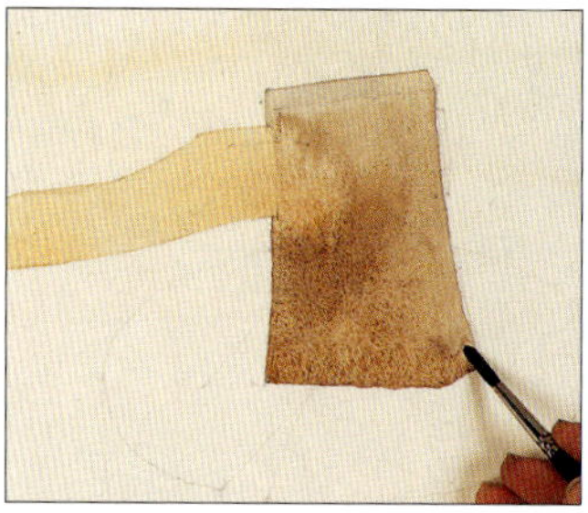

1 Tone the paper with a pale wash of yellow ochre. Leave to dry. Using a 2B pencil, sketch the outline of the axe and log. Paint the axe handle in a dilute wash of raw umber. Mix a light brown from burnt umber and Payne's grey and paint the axe head. Leave to dry.

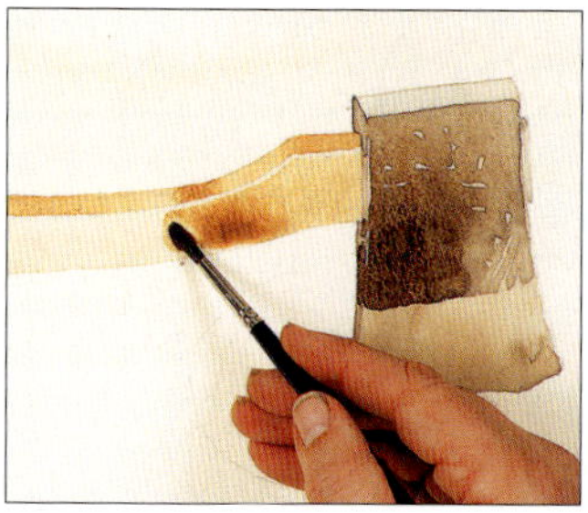

2 Mix a dark brown from burnt umber and ivory black and paint the dark on the side and bottom of the axe head. Add raw umber and burnt sienna to the mixture and paint the handle, leaving the underlying colour where the light hits the handle. Leave to dry.

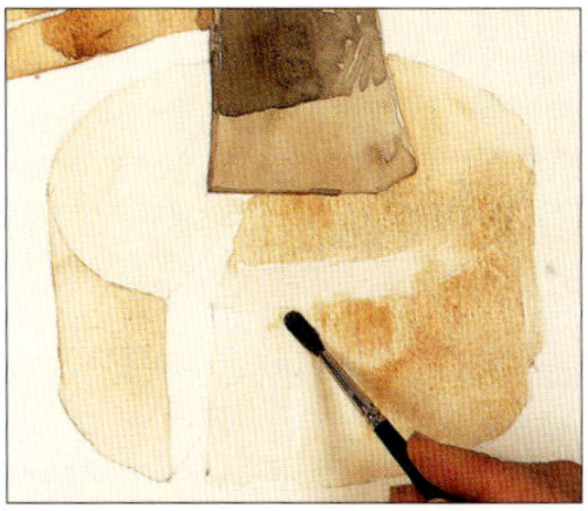

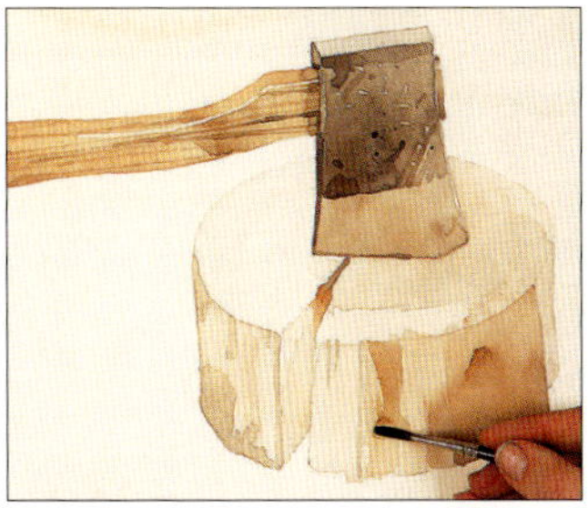

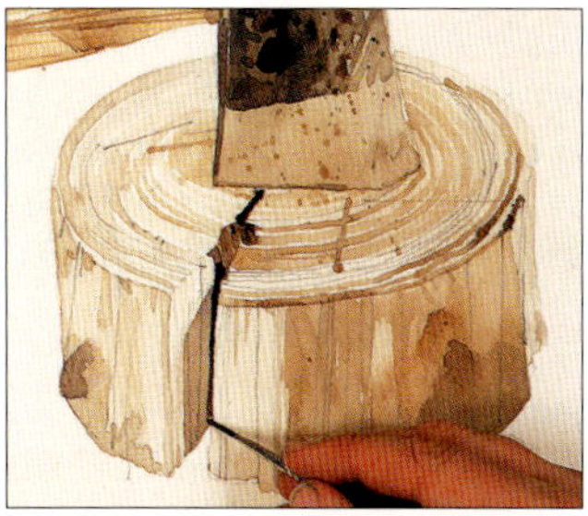

3 Add a little Payne's grey and plenty of water to the mixture to lighten the colour, then paint the side and top of the log. Using a slightly darker version of the same mixture, begin to paint some of the growth rings on the top of the log, but leave the split in the wood unpainted as parts of it are considerably lighter in tone than the surrounding wood.

4 Paint a series of fine burnt umber lines along the length of the axe handle to suggest the grain and pattern in the polished wood. Mix a warm brown from burnt umber and raw umber and paint the side of the log, using the side of the brush and a slight scrubbing action in order to create a broken, uneven texture.

5 Using the same raw umber and burnt umber mixture, paint the growth rings on the top of the log. Add burnt umber and Payne's grey to the mixture and paint the shadow inside the split. Using a soft graphite pencil, indicate the grain and growth rings on the side and top of the log. Once dry, rework the dark shadows deep within the split.

The finished painting

Crisp shadows painted in a warm grey mixed from Payne's grey and a little burnt umber complete the image and make it look three-dimensional. The yellow ochre ground harmonizes well with the colours used to paint the axe and log, whereas a white ground would have looked too stark and would have competed for the viewer's attention. It makes a subtle but important contribution to the overall warm tone of the image.

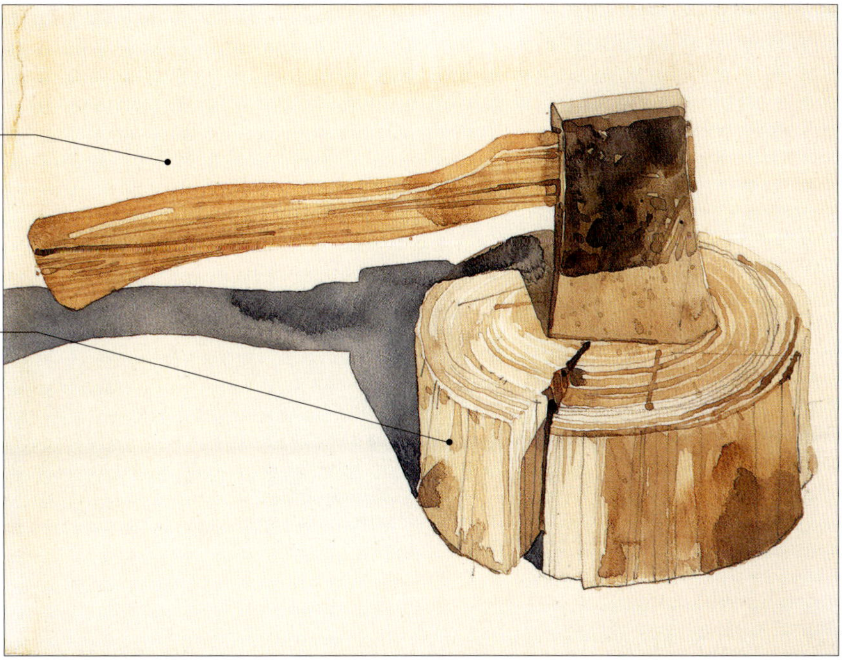

The yellow ochre ground is similar in colour to the axe and log.

The texture of the log is convincingly portrayed.

Working into wet paint

Watercolour washes can be manipulated in several ways when they are wet. They can be moved around, removed or worked into using various tools. The only restriction is the amount of time available before the paint dries to such an extent that it is no longer movable.

Certain papers facilitate working into wet paint better than others. The fibres in highly absorbent papers soak up the washes and make any manipulation impossible, even immediately after they have been applied. Even better are papers that have been sized to such a degree that washes sit on the surface and dry slowly, rather than soak in.

Some techniques work better when the paint is very wet, while others are more effective when the paint has dried a little. Adding gum arabic to your washes can facilitate certain techniques, as it thickens the paint, increasing its viscosity so that it is less fluid. Thickening the paint prevents it from flowing freely and allows you to work into it more readily.

You can work into wet paint to depict any type of textured surface. You can remove paint by using textured fabrics, absorbent paper, man-made and natural sponges, to name but a few.

You can also make marks in wet paint by using a variety of tools that you might not normally associate with painting, such as combs, palette knives, pieces of stiff card, or the wooden end of your brushes. These are all excellent for this purpose, as is the relatively new range of rubber paint-shaping tools. Pressing fabrics, paper, and even aluminium kitchen foil or clear film (plastic wrap) all create interesting textures that you could not achieve using an ordinary brush.

When a wash is partially dry, dropping water or paint into it results in an effect known as a back-run (sometimes called the cauliflower effect). This can be put to good use when painting cloudy skies or flowers, as it creates a crinkled, often highly pigmented edge as the wetter paint pushes into the drier paint. A similar effect can be seen when paint that has collected in a puddle on buckled paper dries at a much slower rate than paint on the surrounding area.

Lifting off colour

There will be many occasions during your painting when you find that you need to remove some colour from your work – either to make minor corrections or simply to soften tones and edges. The methods shown below are particularly useful for lifting out clouds from a blue sky – but remember to turn the paper or sponge around in your hand each time you use it in order to find a clean area, otherwise you run the risk of dabbing paint back on.

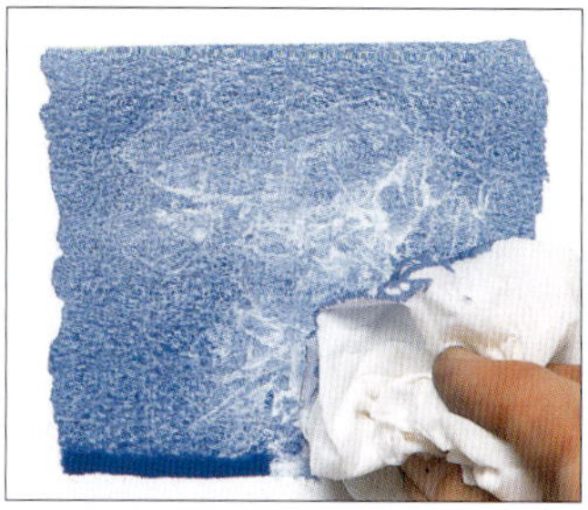

Absorbent paper
First, lay a wash. While it is still wet, blot off any excess paint with a scrunched-up piece of clean, absorbent tissue or a paper towel.

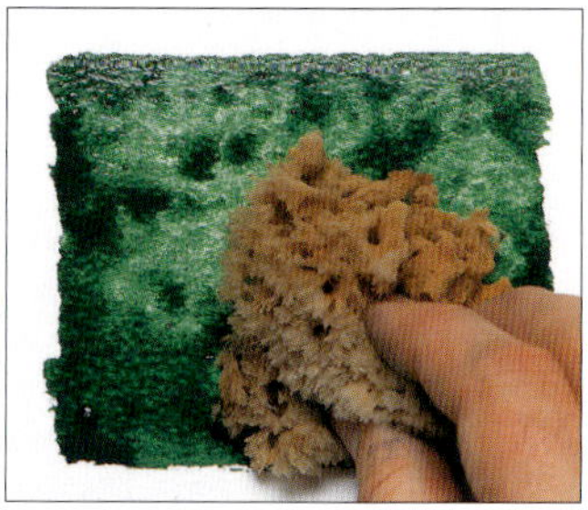

Sponge
You can also lift off colour from a wet wash using a sponge. This gives more texture, as the texture of the sponge is impressed into the wet wash.

Pressing materials into wet paint

You can create interesting textures by pressing things into wet paint and removing them once the paint is dry. The results are a little unpredictable, but well worth experimenting with. Two possible materials are shown below, but you can easily come up with others from readily available household items. Lace, soft absorbent fabrics, such as cotton and felt, thick wool: experiment to see how many different effects you can create with whatever you have to hand.

Clear film

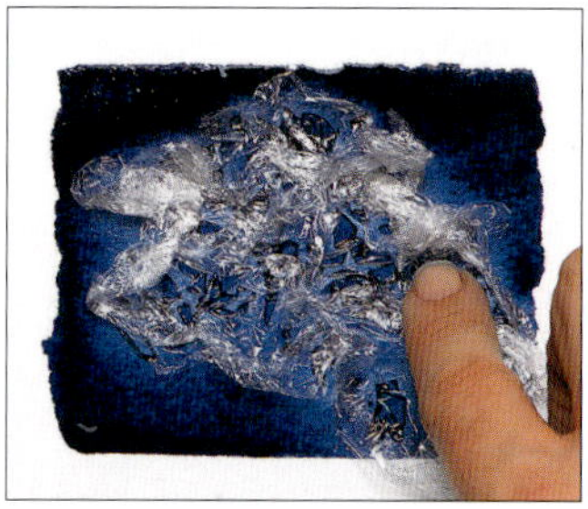

1 Scrunch up a piece of clear film (plastic wrap) in your fingers and gently press it into a wet watercolour wash. Leave it to dry.

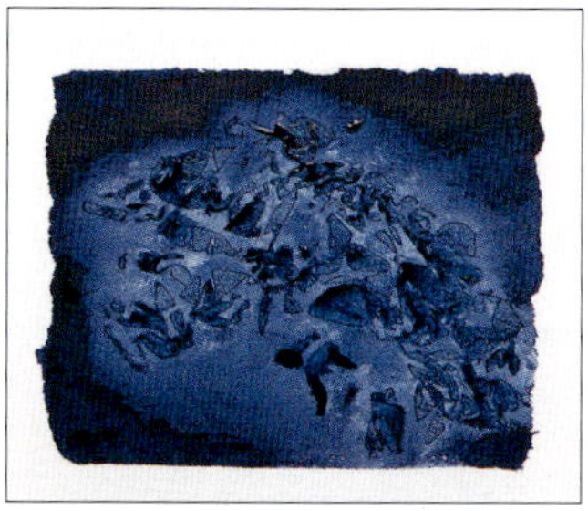

2 When the paint is dry, carefully remove the clear film. The lines of the scrunched-up food wrap are clearly visible in the dry paint.

Aluminium kitchen foil

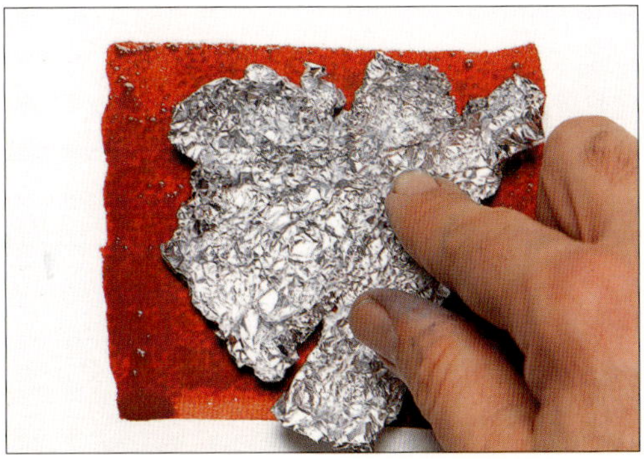

1 Scrunch up a piece of cooking foil and press it into a wet wash. Leave to dry.

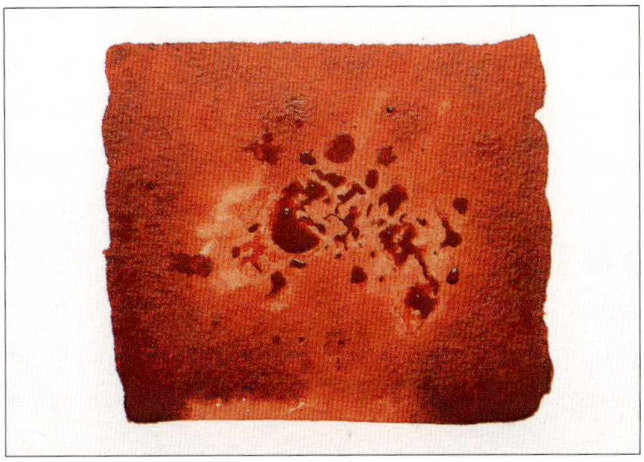

2 When the paint is dry, carefully remove the foil. This creates crisper, sharper lines than the food wrap.

Practice exercise: **Graffiti-style abstract**

Remember how much fun you had as a child, messing around with poster paints and coming home with your fingers stained with bright, primary colours? This exercise is all about recapturing that sense of fun and excitement and getting a feel for how wet watercolour paint behaves. The result is an abstract mass of colour and texture, rather like graffiti sprayed on to a wall.

Feel free to experiment with materials other than the ones shown here: there are no limits to what you can use. Work quickly while the paint is still wet. Above all, don't try to plan ahead, simply react to the way the paint flows and puddles on the paper.

Materials

- *300lb (640gsm) rough watercolour paper*
- *Watercolour paints: alizarin crimson, cobalt blue, burnt sienna, ultramarine blue, cadmium yellow*
- *Watercolour pigments: alizarin crimson*
- *Brushes: old brush for masking, medium round*
- *Masking fluid and tape*
- *Paper towels*
- *Toothbrush*
- *Card*
- *Cotton bud*

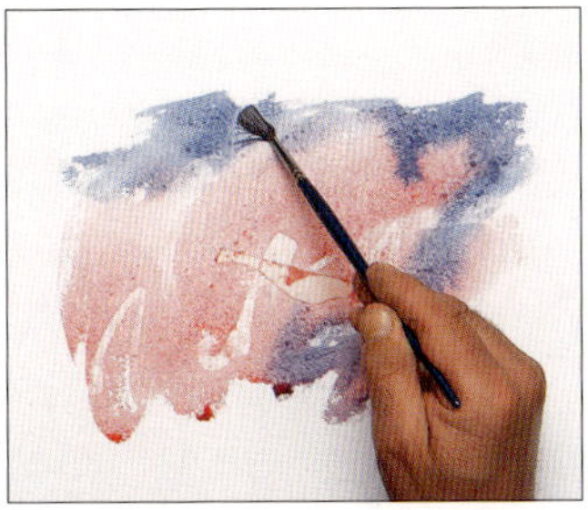

1 Brush on random swirls of masking fluid and leave to dry. Cut abstract shapes from masking tape and press them on to the paper. Wash alizarin crimson and cobalt blue on to the paper, allowing the colours to merge.

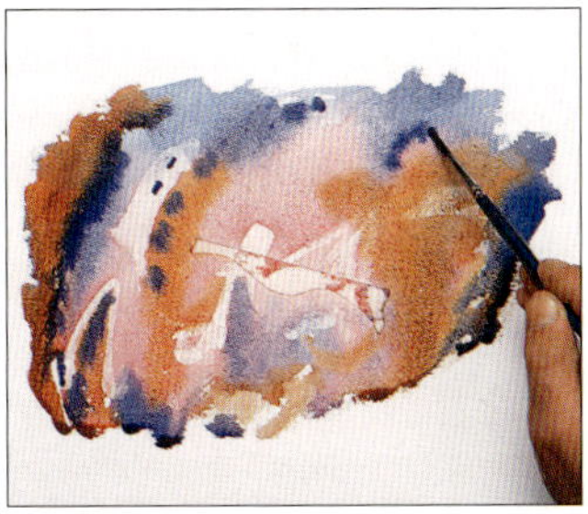

2 While the first washes are still wet, brush on burnt sienna and ultramarine blue, again allowing the colours to run together and merge on the paper in a completely random way. Tilt the board to facilitate this.

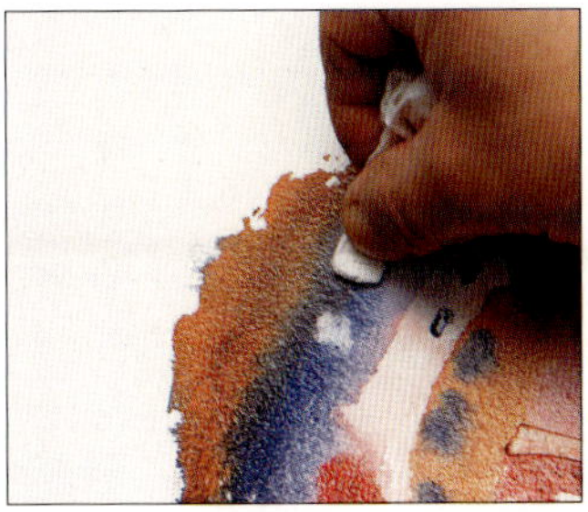

3 Brush on more alizarin crimson and dab a piece of kitchen paper onto the paper to lift off and soften colour.

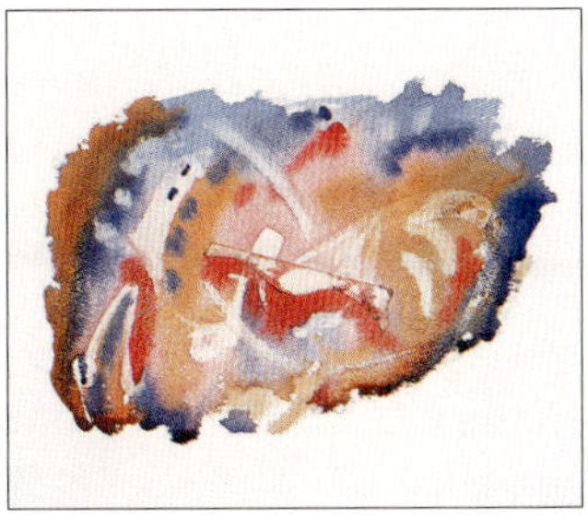

4 You have now established a mass of abstract wet colours into which you can work.

▶

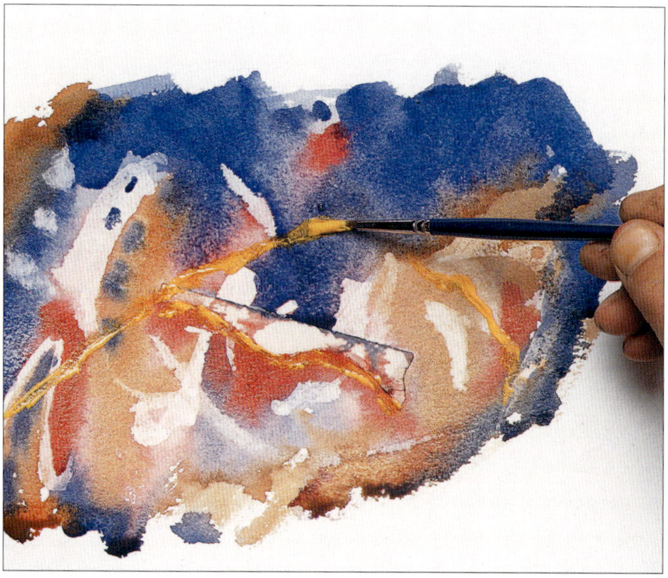

5 Using thick paint straight from the tube, brush on a few long strokes of cadmium yellow. This gives an impasto-like texture similar to oil paint.

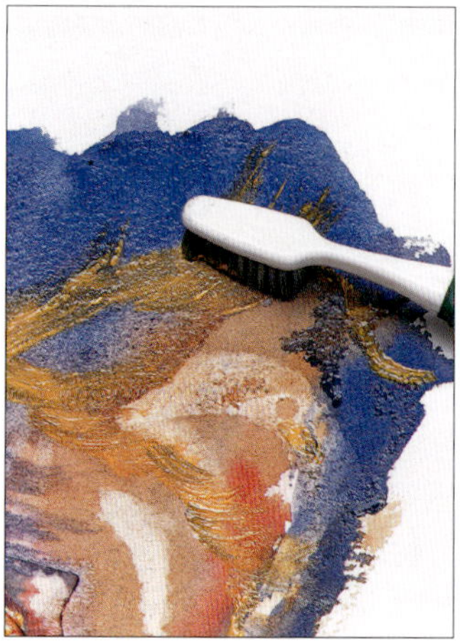

6 Drag an old toothbrush over the yellow lines to spread and diffuse them. Because the bristles of the toothbrush are stiff and the paint is relatively thick, you can clearly see the marks that are left behind – an unusual way of adding texture to a watercolour.

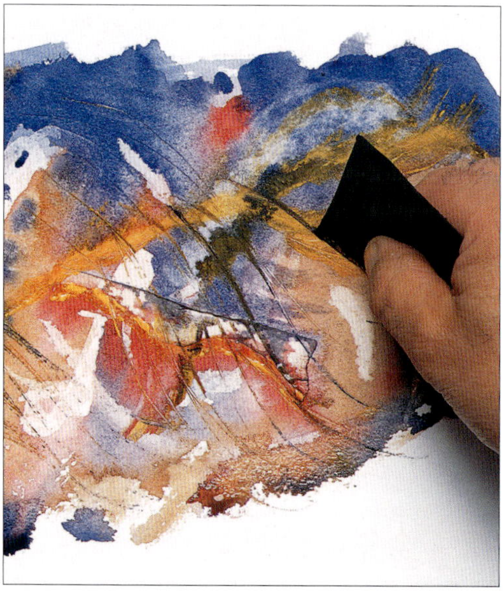

7 Take a small piece of card and scrape into the wet paint, dragging it from one colour into the next. The card is flexible, so you can make curved lines, while its thin edge allows you to create lines that are clearly defined. An old, cut-up credit card would have the same effect.

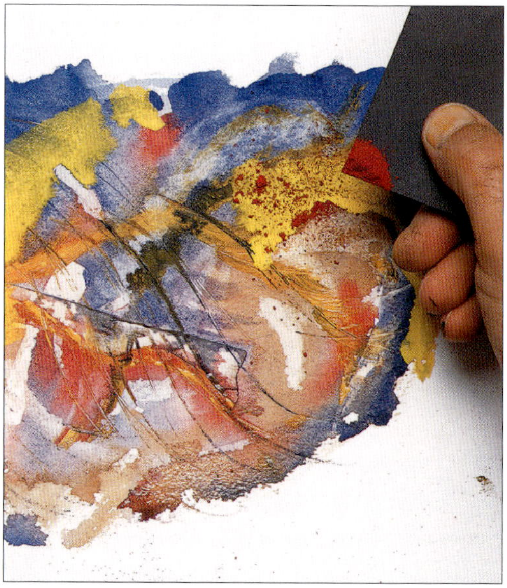

8 Pick up a little powder pigment on a piece of card and, gently tapping it with your finger, lightly sprinkle the pigment on to the paper. Note how the pigment colour spreads and blurs in damp areas but remains on the surface, creating an impasto-like texture, in dry parts.

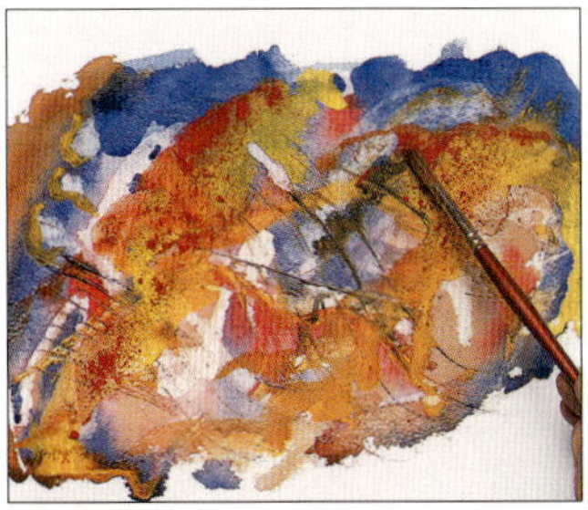

9 Dip a brush in clean water and brush over the pigment particles to blur and spread them. The more water you have on the brush, the further the powder will spread and the paler the colour will become.

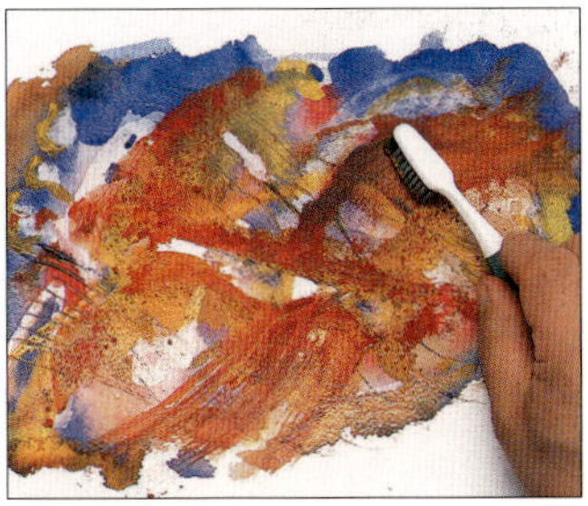

10 Pull off the masking tape and rub off the fluid to reveal small areas of bright white. Brush more alizarin crimson on to selected areas of the paper and, while it is still wet, drag a toothbrush through it as before.

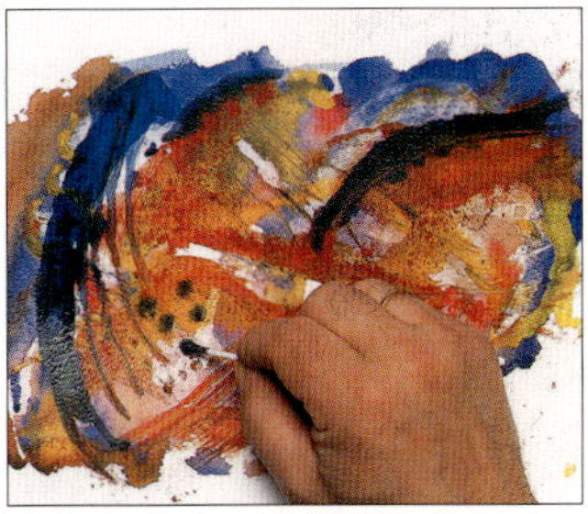

11 Dip a cotton bud in ultramarine blue paint and dot it on to the paper to make more clearly defined marks in selected areas.

The finished painting

This is a completely abstract, explosive riot of colour and texture. It was not pre-planned in any way, but was created by the artist responding to the way the wet paint behaved on the paper. Exercises like this will teach you a lot about manipulating paint and free you from any hang-ups about having to paint lifelike subjects.

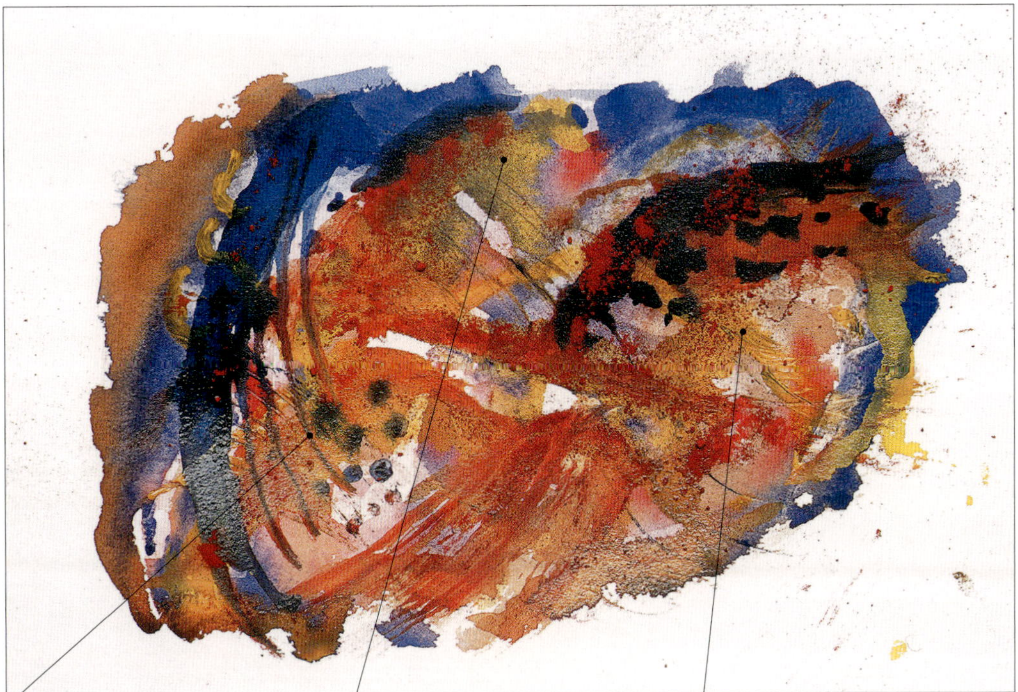

Clear lines and dots are created by scraping into the paint with card and dotting on colour with a cotton bud.

Allowing the paint to merge wet into wet creates soft background colour.

Using thick cadmium yellow paint straight from the tube creates an impasto-like effect.

Sgraffito

The technical name for scratching into dry paint comes from the Italian, *graffiare*, which means to scratch. Sgraffito can be used to reveal white paper beneath a wash, and is a good way to create highlights, such as sunlight on water. It can also be used to scratch through one layer of colour to reveal the layer beneath.

Paint can be scratched into using a variety of sharp implements. A scalpel or craft (utility) knife is useful for scratching fine lines, as are sharpened brush handles, paper clips and even your fingernails. For larger areas, sandpaper is very effective; experiment with fine and harsh grades of sandpaper for different results.

You can also use sgraffito to remove small areas of paint to correct minor mistakes – for example, if you want to neaten an edge or the outline of an object. To do this, scrape gently, using the edge of the scalpel blade rather than the point, so that the paper is not torn and the scraped area remains flat.

All these techniques work better if the paint sits on the paper surface, rather than soaking into it to any depth, so try to avoid using sgraffito with staining colours such as alizarin crimson, viridian or phthalocyanine blue. Needless to say, it is best to use sgraffito on heavy paper (say, 300lb/640gsm) as it is less likely to tear, and on top of dry washes.

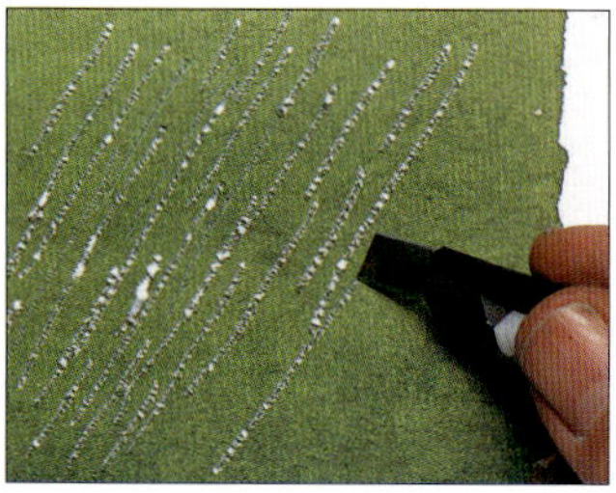

Scalpel or craft knife
To scratch fine lines, such as highlights on water, use the tip of a scalpel or craft (utility) knife, pulling the blade sideways to avoid slicing into the paper and damaging it.

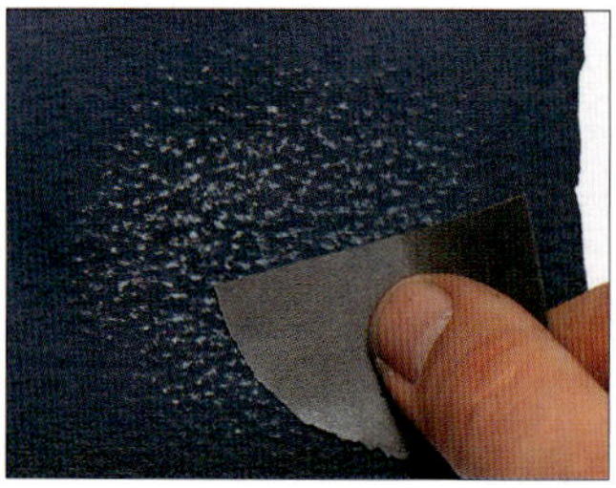

Fine sandpaper
Stroke the sandpaper over the surface of the dry paint. This is particularly effective on rough watercolour paper, as the paint remains in the troughs but is removed from the higher ridges.

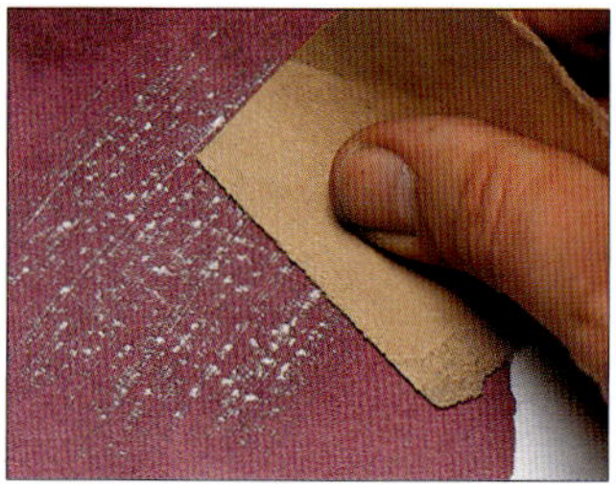

Coarse sandpaper
Because the sand particles on course paper are bigger, the sgraffito lines are further apart. You can also fold the sandpaper to create a crisp edge, enabling you to scratch off sharp lines.

Practice exercise: **Conch shell**

This conch shell contains a number of different textures, from hard, raised ridges and points to the mottled surface of some of the flatter areas and the porcelain smoothness of the inside. The following exercise gives you the chance to practise two methods of sgraffito, using sandpaper for general areas of texture and a scalpel or craft (utility) knife for the crisp, sharp ridges on the outer side of the shell.

Materials
- *2B pencil*
- *300lb (640gsm) NOT watercolour paper*
- *Watercolour paints: yellow ochre, Payne's grey, alizarin crimson, raw umber*
- *Brushes: medium round*
- *Medium-grade sandpaper*
- *Scalpel or craft (utility) knife*

The set-up
Arrange the shell at an interesting angle, so that you can see both the hard, spiky outer shell and the smooth, slightly shiny interior. This provides an attractive contrast of textures and makes it easier to appreciate the form of the object.

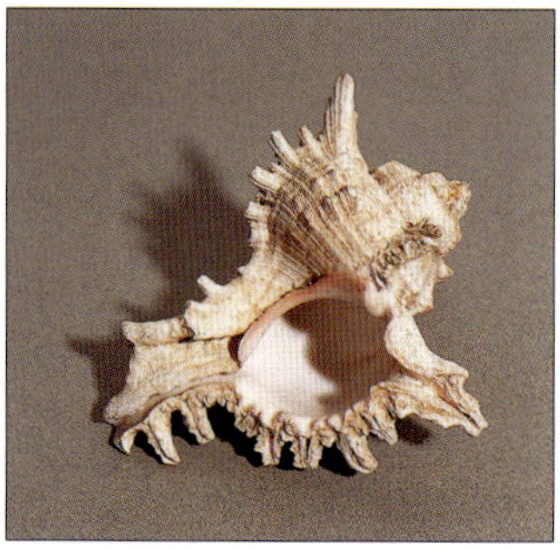

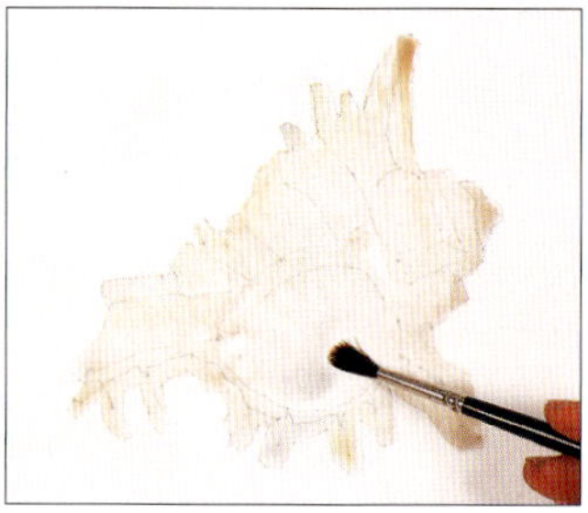

1 Using a 2B pencil, lightly sketch the shell to establish the general outline shape and the main ridges. Using a medium round brush, establish the overall colour with pale washes of yellow ochre, Payne's grey and a little alizarin crimson, allowing the colours to blend together on the paper and create a surface with subtle variations in colour. Leave to dry.

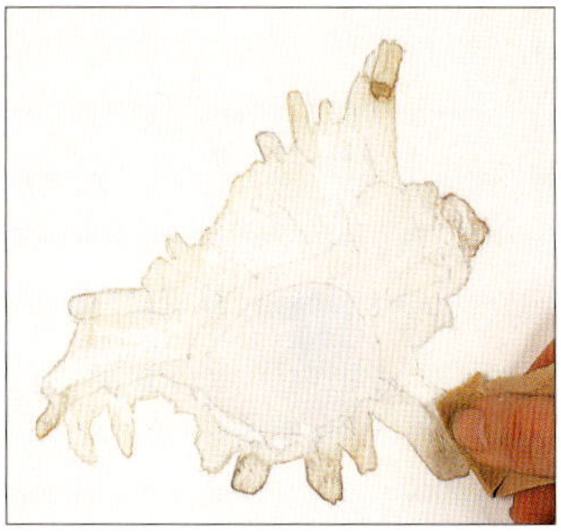

2 Take a small piece of medium-grade sandpaper and stroke it over the paper to recreate the rough, pitted surface of the shell. (Leave the areas of smooth shell that lie deep within the interior untouched.) To scratch into small or tight areas of the image, fold the sandpaper to make a crisp, sharp edge.

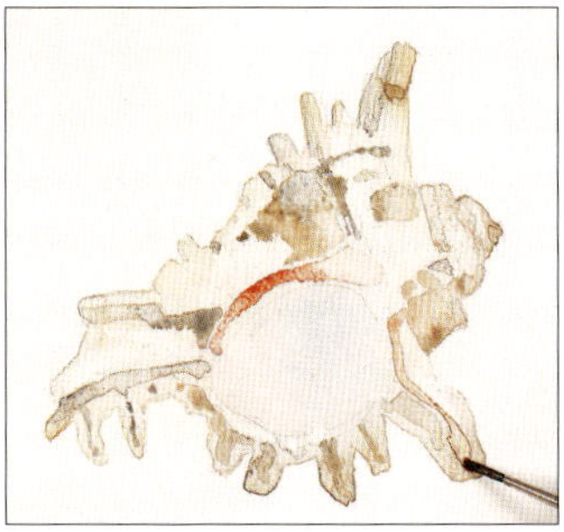

3 Mix a cool brown from yellow ochre and Payne's grey and paint the areas in shadow and some of the linear detail. When the paint dries, it will leave a rough texture on areas of the paper that have been rubbed with sandpaper. Mix a dull pink from alizarin crimson and yellow ochre and paint the warm colours on the shell "lip". Leave to dry.

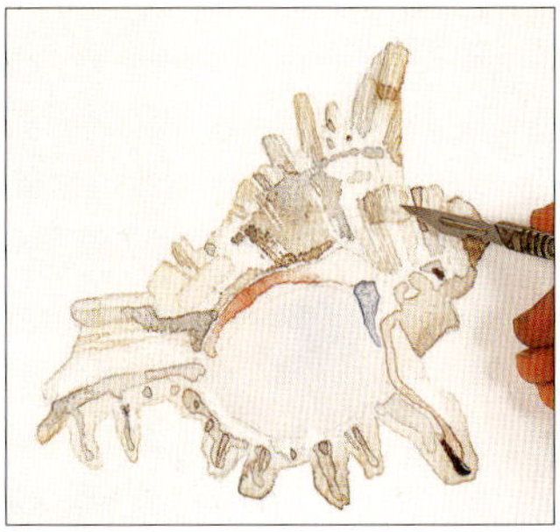

4 Using a sharp scalpel or craft (utility) knife, gently scratch into the dark paint until clean paper fibres are revealed, creating the ridges on the outer side of the shell.

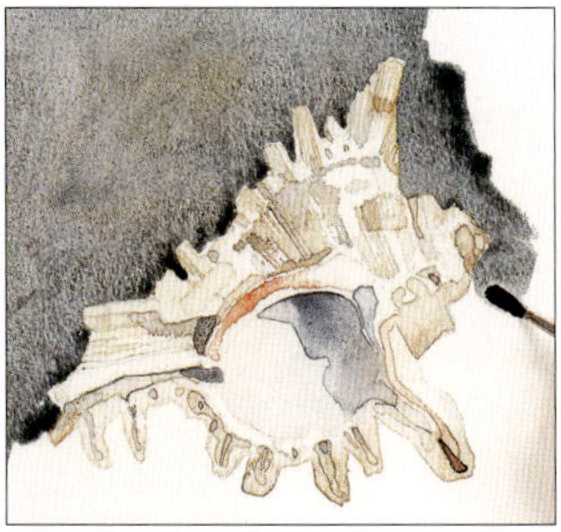

5 Mix a mid-toned grey from Payne's grey and a little yellow ochre and paint the shadow inside the shell. Mix a darker grey from Payne's grey and raw umber and wash in the background, painting very carefully around the shell.

The finished painting

The dense, cast shadow is painted in a darker, more pigmented mixture, which anchors the shell to the surface on which it rests, and also has the effect of throwing it into sharp relief. When painted over, the rough texture made by the sandpaper creates a broken effect that contrasts well with the fine, crisp lines made with the point of the scalpel or craft (utility) knife blade.

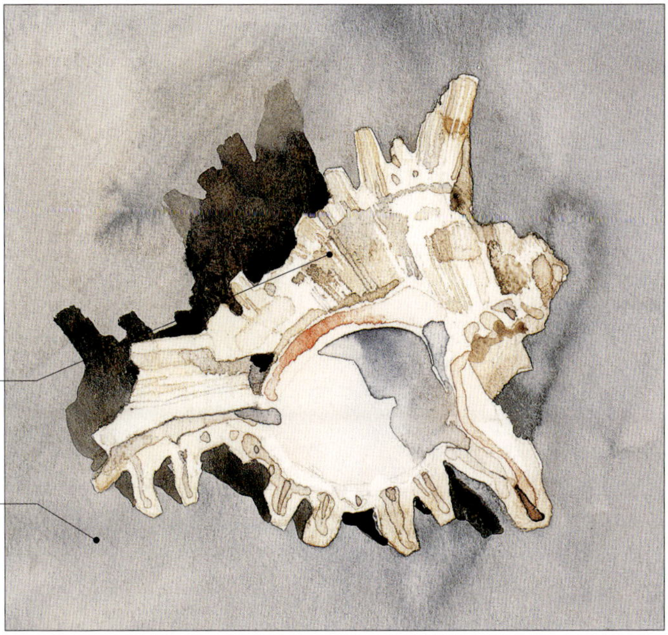

A scalpel or craft (utility) knife is used to scratch off these crisp lines on the outside of the conch shell.

General areas of rough texture are created using medium-grade sandpaper.

Body colour

Traditional transparent watercolour uses no white paint. Instead, you have to leave any areas of the painting that you want to be white, such as clouds or highlights sparkling on water, free of paint. Colours are made paler by adding more water.

The white of the paper also serves to reflect light back through transparent coloured washes. Depending on the depth of the colour, this can make them appear lighter or darker. Because the washes are transparent, when one colour is painted on top of another the underlying colour will always show through. This makes it impossible in pure watercolour to paint a light colour on top of a dark one.

Body colour is somewhat different. White and pale shades are obtained by adding white pigment, which adds "body" to the paint and renders it opaque. Chinese white, which is made from zinc oxide and gum arabic, was traditionally used as body colour. It is a dense white with a very high tinting strength. A good alternative, which many artists use, is white gouache.

You can use body colour straight from the tube to create highlights and details that would normally have been made by preserving the white of the paper – catchlights in people's eyes, for example, or white whiskers on a cat. You can also mix it with transparent watercolour paint to produce light, opaque pastel tints that can then be painted on top of dark colours. This is particularly useful when you want to add subtle pale details or textures – for example, by spattering white paint on to the support to represent falling snow in a snow scene.

Body colour comes into its own when you are working on a coloured or tinted ground because it enables you to use light tones and colours without them being influenced by the underlying ground colour, which can completely overpower pale, transparent washes.

Body colour can also be used to correct mistakes – perhaps highlights that you have forgotten to leave white, or even entire passages that you want to cover up and repaint. Use it cautiously, however, as too much can look heavy and deaden the lovely translucent quality for which pure watercolour is renowned.

You need a degree of competence and flair to mix the two techniques of body colour and transparent washes. It is easy for the two techniques to jar and work at odds with one another, but if used carefully, body colour can extend the creative possibilites of watercolour as a medium, and will bring another dimension to your watercolours.

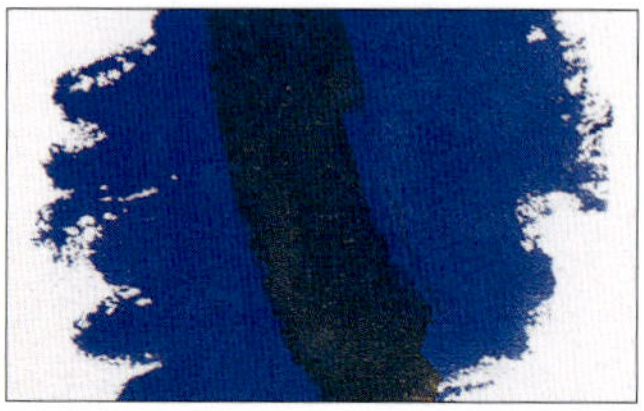

Light watercolour over dark watercolour
When a paler or lighter transparent watercolour paint is applied over the top of a darker paint, the underlying dark wash will show through.

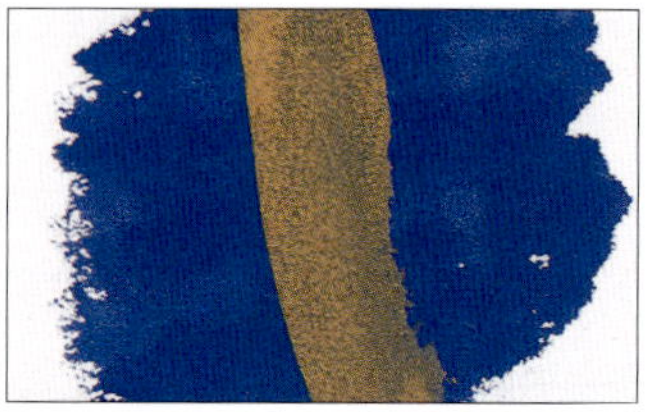

Light gouache over dark watercolour
When a paler or lighter watercolour paint is combined with Chinese white gouache, the mixture becomes opaque. It then becomes possible to apply a lighter colour on top of a darker one.

Practice exercise: **Painting light on dark**

A lighter blue pattern on a rich, dark blue background: in pure watercolour, the only ways to paint the pattern on this little embossed vase would be either to mask the light areas, which might look too bright when the masking is removed, or to paint the light areas first, and then carefully paint the darker blue around them, which is quite a fiddly process.

With body colour, however, things are much simpler. By mixing Chinese white gouache with transparent watercolour paints, you can create pale, opaque mixtures that can be painted on top of the dark, underlying colours. The opaque pattern also contrasts well with the translucent watercolour used to paint the blue of the vase.

The set-up
Tiny orange flowers were chosen to contrast with the rich blue of the vase – orange and blue are complementary colours and they work well together. Positioning a table lamp to one side of the vase helps to pick up the texture of the embossed pattern.

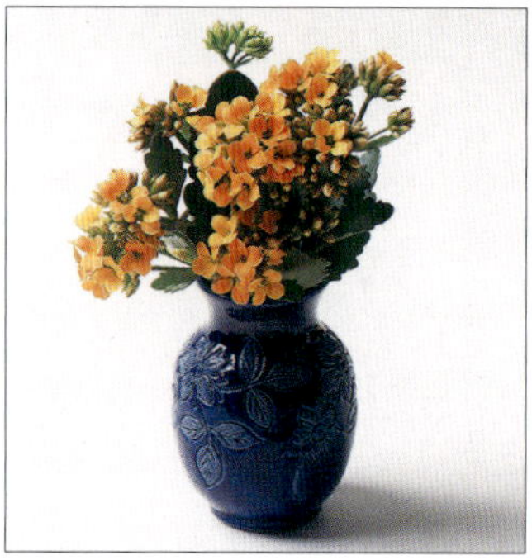

Materials
- *B pencil*
- *140lb (300gsm) rough watercolour paper, unstretched*
- *Watercolour paints: ultramarine blue, burnt sienna, cadmium lemon, cadmium red, cadmium yellow*
- *Gouache paints: Chinese white*
- *Brushes: medium round, large wash*

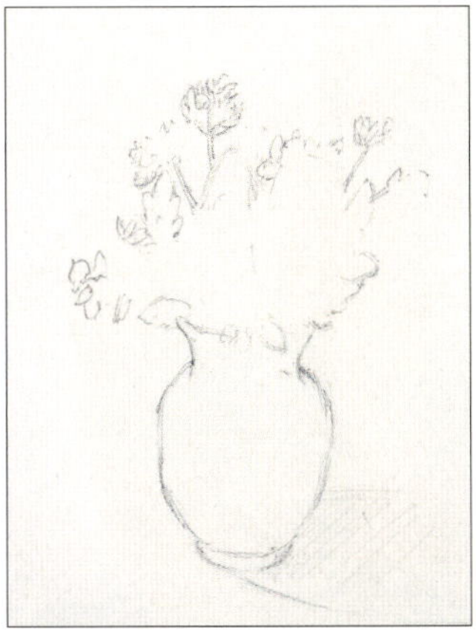

1 Using a B pencil, sketch the subject. Don't attempt to draw every single leaf and flower: a light indication of the general areas is sufficient.

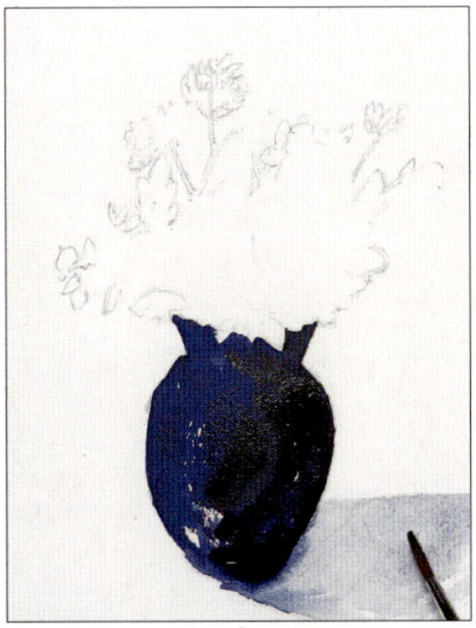

2 Mix a rich blue from ultramarine blue with a little burnt sienna. Using a medium round brush, paint the vase, adding a little more burnt sienna for the right-hand side of the vase, which is in shade. Dilute the mixture for the shadow cast by the vase.

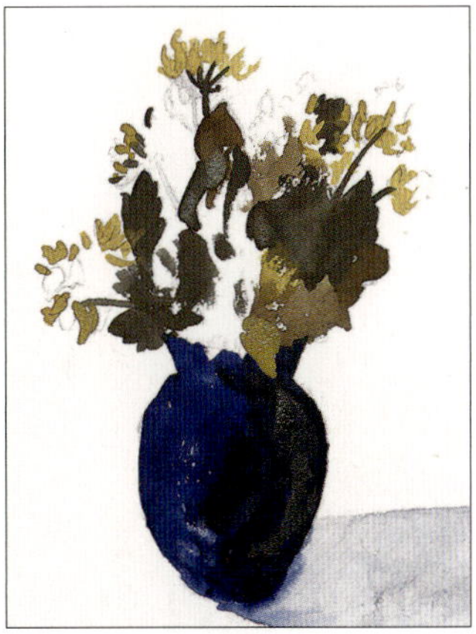

3 Mix a dull green from cadmium lemon, ultramarine blue and a little cadmium red and brush in the broad shapes of the leaves. Add more cadmium lemon to the mixture and paint the lighter leaves. Dot the same mixture over the unopened buds.

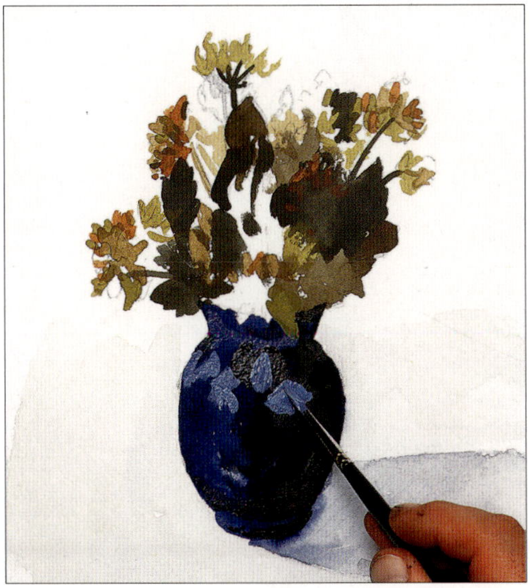

4 Add a little cadmium yellow to the dilute shadow mixture used in Step 2 and, using a medium round brush, brush it over the background to relieve the whiteness. Mix an orangey green from cadmium lemon, ultramarine blue and cadmium red and start to put in the flower buds that are just starting to open. Mix a pale, opaque blue from ultramarine blue and Chinese white gouache and paint the pattern on the vase.

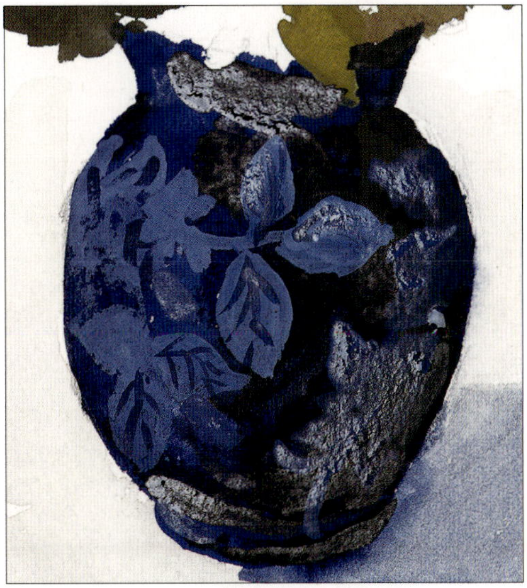

5 Add a tiny amount of burnt sienna to the opaque blue mixture and continue painting the pattern on the right-hand side of the vase. These subtle changes in tone help to establish which areas are in shade, as a result of which the vase begins to take on a more three-dimensional quality. Burnt sienna is also slightly orange in tone: shadow colours often contain a hint of a complementary colour.

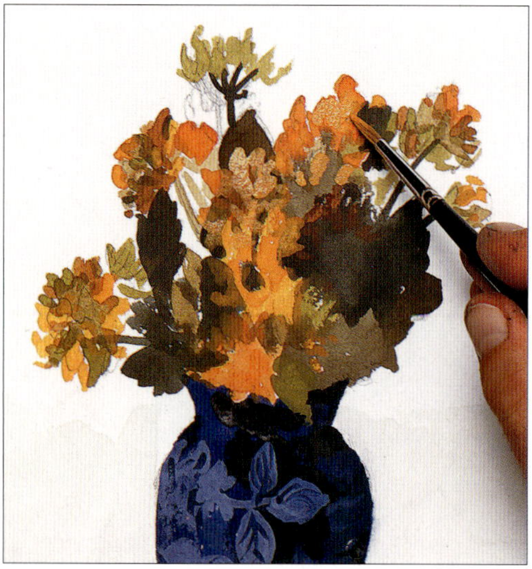

6 Mix a bright orange from cadmium red and cadmium yellow, and paint the tiny open flowers. Note how this use of complementary colours (the orange flowers against the blue of the vase) immediately makes the painting look more lively and dynamic.

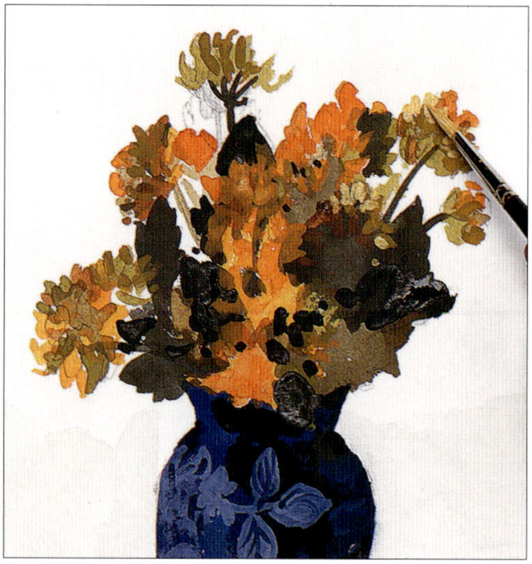

7 Mix a dark green from ultramarine blue, burnt sienna and cadmium yellow and paint the darkest leaves. Mix a light green from cadmium yellow and ultramarine blue and paint the unopened buds. Mix orange from cadmium lemon, cadmium red and Chinese white gouache and paint the opening buds.

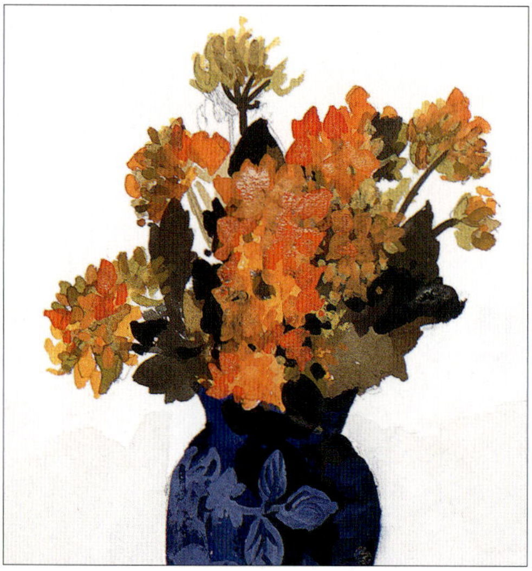

8 Add Chinese white gouache to the bright orange used in Step 6 to make it opaque. Use the mixture to paint the flowers that overhang the deep green leaves.

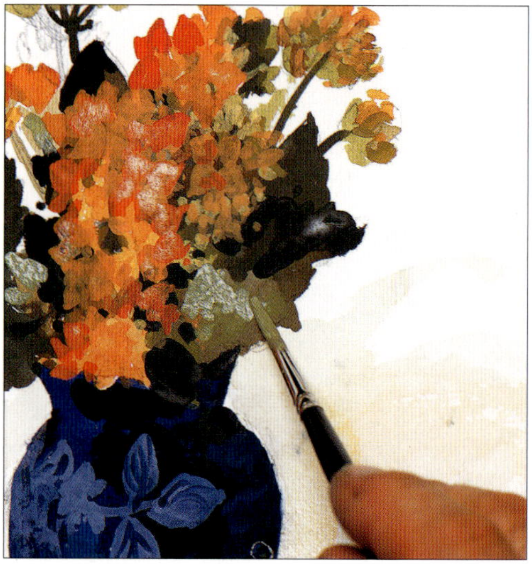

9 Mix a pale orange from cadmium yellow and cadmium red and brush it over the surface on which the vase sits. This will tone down the brightness and will provide a visual link to the colour of the flowers. Mix an opaque light green from cadmium lemon, ultramarine blue and Chinese white gouache and paint some light leaves over the dark ones.

The finished painting

Combining pure watercolour paint with Chinese white gouache makes it possible to paint light colours on top of dark ones. Because of its opacity, the body colour is also very effective in suggesting the embossed texture of the vase. Note also the effective use of the complementary colours blue and orange for the flowers.

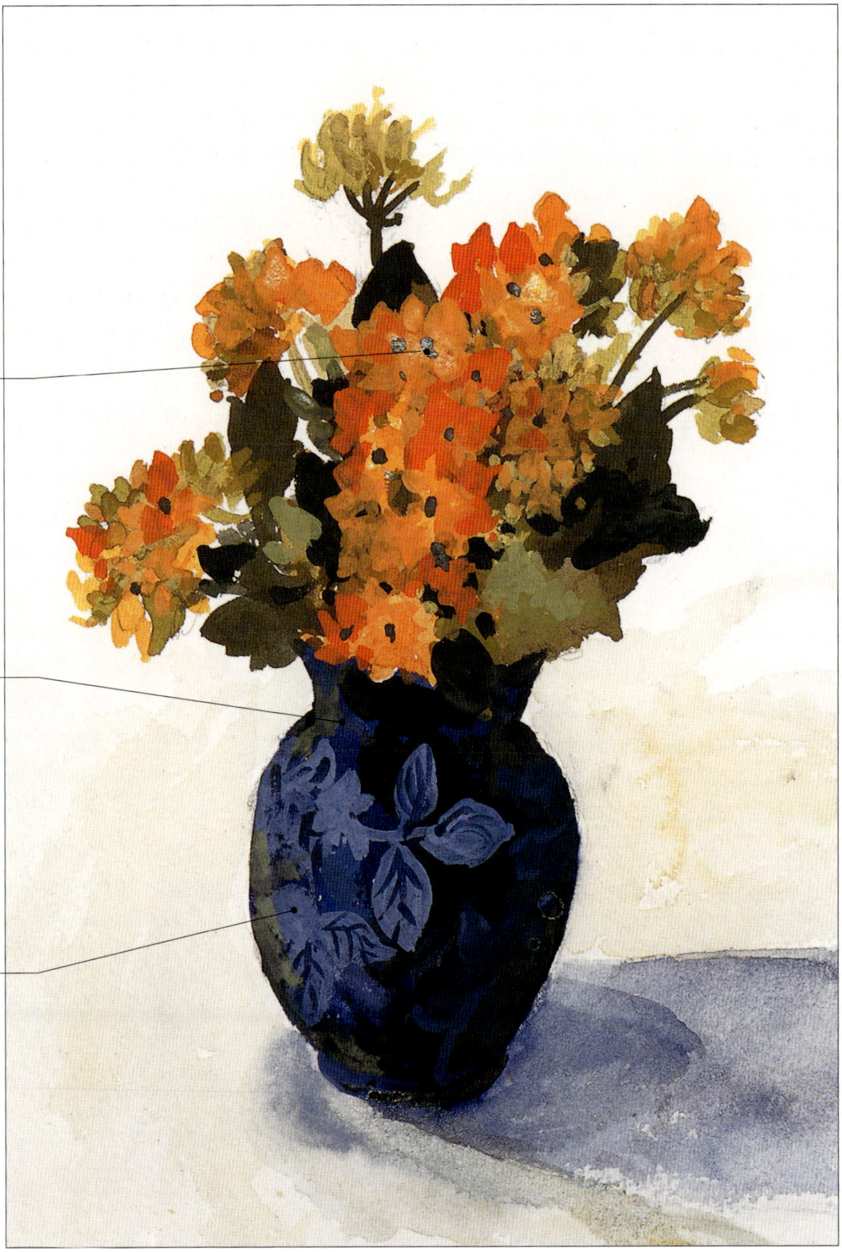

Chinese white gouache has been used to tone down the bright orange of the flowers.

Pure watercolour paint is used for most of the vase. The translucency of the paint conveys the shiny glaze very effectively.

The opaque, pale blue mixture completely covers the underlying dark blue wash.

Scale and perspective

The further away something is from you, the smaller and less distinct it seems with the naked eye. In order to convincingly depict depth and recession, and so add a sense of realism to your work, you need to depict this shift in scale accurately. This is done by using a technique known as perspective.

At first sight, perspective may seem complex and confusing, but the basics are easy to understand and even a rudimentary grasp of the fundamentals will enable you to position elements in your work so that they appear to occupy their correct "space" in the composition.

As with any endeavour, planning is the key to success. You need to consider any perspective issues from the moment you begin a work and incorporate them from the outset. If you are unsure, make a sketch or a working drawing before you begin work on the painting. This will allow you to work out any problems in advance.

Aerial perspective

Sometimes known as atmospheric perspective, aerial perspective refers to the way the atmosphere combined with distance influences and affects what you see. Being able to identify and utilize these effects will enable you to paint realistic and convincing three-dimensional landscapes.

Four things are directly influenced by distance: these are texture, colour, tone and size. The most obvious of these is size. Objects gradually become smaller the further away from you they are. You can see this most clearly by looking along a row of identically sized telegraph poles, fence posts or trees.

Second, detail and textures become less evident with distance. Close-up texture and detail are often large and in sharp focus, while texture and detail that is further away is vague and less clearly defined.

Third, colours seen in the foreground and near distance appear bright and vibrant because the warm colours – reds, oranges and yellows – are in evidence. Colours in the far distance appear much less bright. They are also cooler and contain more blue and violet.

Finally, tonal contrast is dramatically reduced with distance, and sometimes it disappears completely, so that distant hills, for example, might appear as one pale mass.

These effects on size, detail and colour are caused by our own visual limitations. They are also caused by the gases, dust and moisture present in our atmosphere, which create a veil through which light has to filter. In addition, all these effects are directly influenced not only by the time of day, but also by the season of the year, the location, and the inherent local weather conditions.

The principles of aerial perspective apply not only to terra firma but also to the sky. Clouds appear larger when they are viewed immediately overhead. The sky alters colour too, being a warmer, deeper blue immediately overhead, gradually becoming paler and often with a cool yellow tinge as it falls towards the horizon and the far distance.

The effects of aerial perspective ▼
This simple landscape clearly illustrates the effects of aerial perspective and shows how atmosphere combined with distance influence the way we see things.

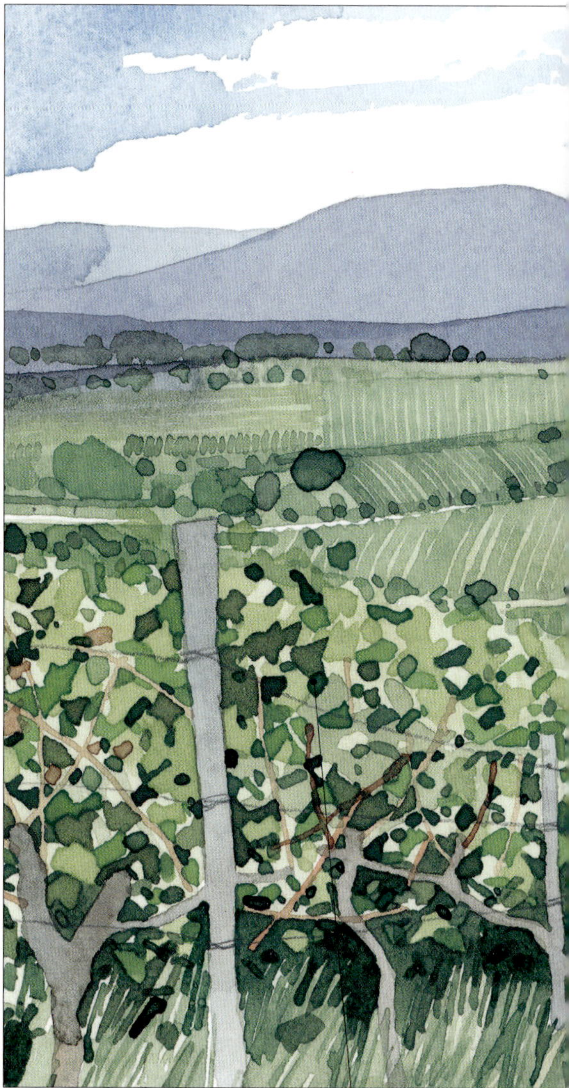

Colours in the foreground look warmer and brighter.

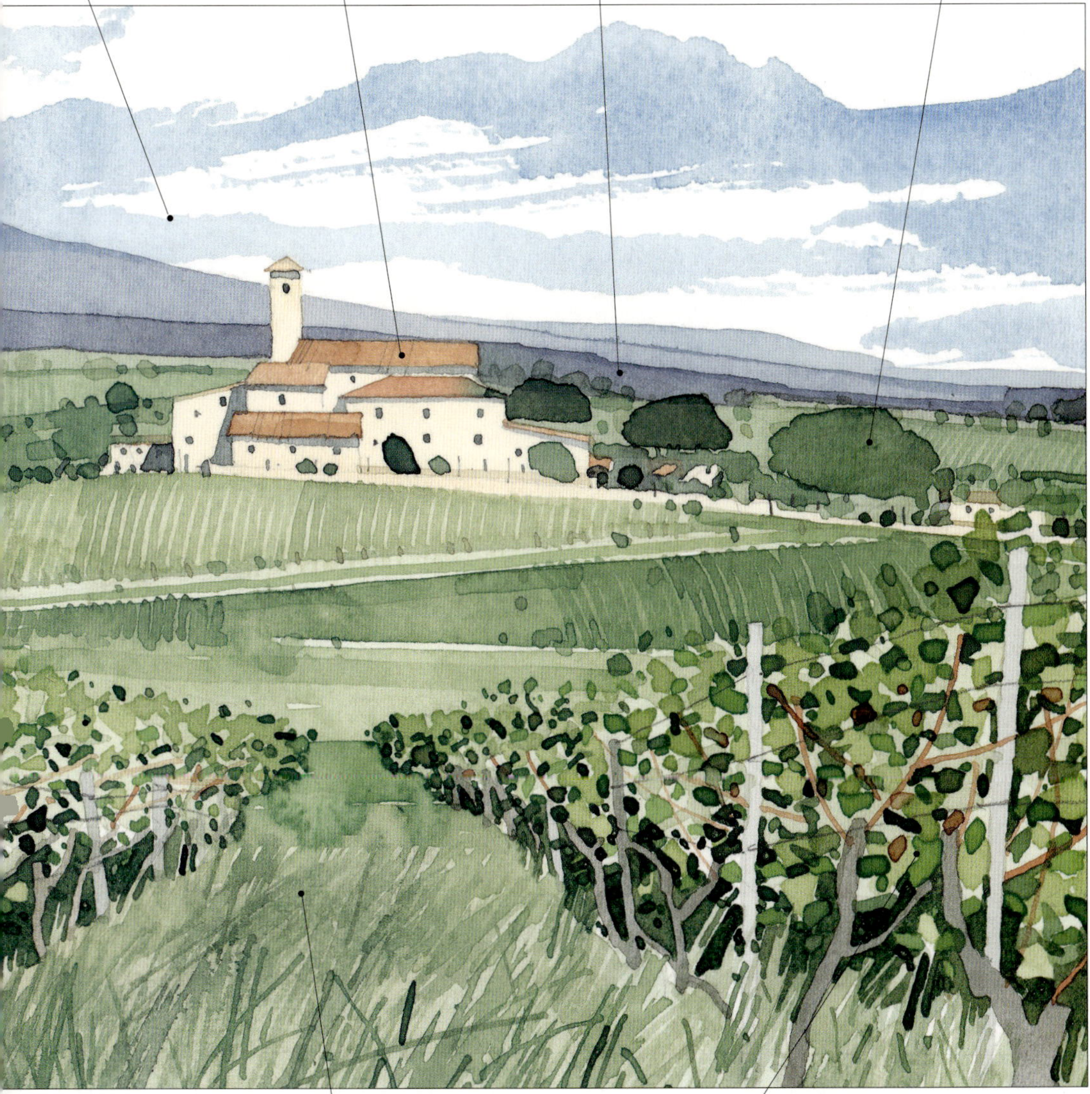
Clouds appear smaller the closer they are to the horizon.
Colours in the distance are cooler and less intense.
Detail is less apparent in the distance.
Tonal contrast is reduced in the background.
Detail is more apparent in the foreground.
A full range of tones can be seen in the foreground.

Linear perspective

Linear perspective is a system or device that allows you to create the illusion of three-dimensional space on a two-dimensional flat surface. The system is based on the principle that all parallel lines, known as perspective lines, when extended from any receding surface meet at a point in space known as the vanishing point.

The vanishing point is on what is known as the horizon line, which runs horizontally across the field of vision. The horizon line is also known as the eye level, because it always runs horizontally across the field of view at eye level, regardless of whether you are sitting or standing. All perspective lines that originate above the eye level run down to meet the vanishing point and all perspective lines that originate below the eye level run up to meet it. All vertical lines remain vertical.

The simplest form of perspective is single, or one-point, perspective. This occurs when all the receding perspective lines meet at one single point. The vanishing point in single-point perspective always coincides with your centre of vision, which is directly in front of you.

You can see the effect of single-point perspective by looking along a train track that runs straight away from you into the distance. The two rails are, in reality, consistently spaced the same distance apart, but because they are resting on the ground plane, which is receding away from you, the rails appear to converge the further away they get, eventually meeting when they reach the vanishing point.

A similar effect can be seen when you are standing in a straight road and looking into the distance along a row of identical houses. Using straight perspective lines to extend the roof line, the gutters, the top and bottom of the windows and doors, you will see that they all meet at the same vanishing point.

Parallel lines receding away from the viewer ▼
In this simple illustration of one-point perspective the trees – which, in reality, are all of similar size – appear to get smaller the further away they are. All perspective lines above eye level run down to the vanishing point (VP) and all perspective lines below eye level run up to the vanishing point.

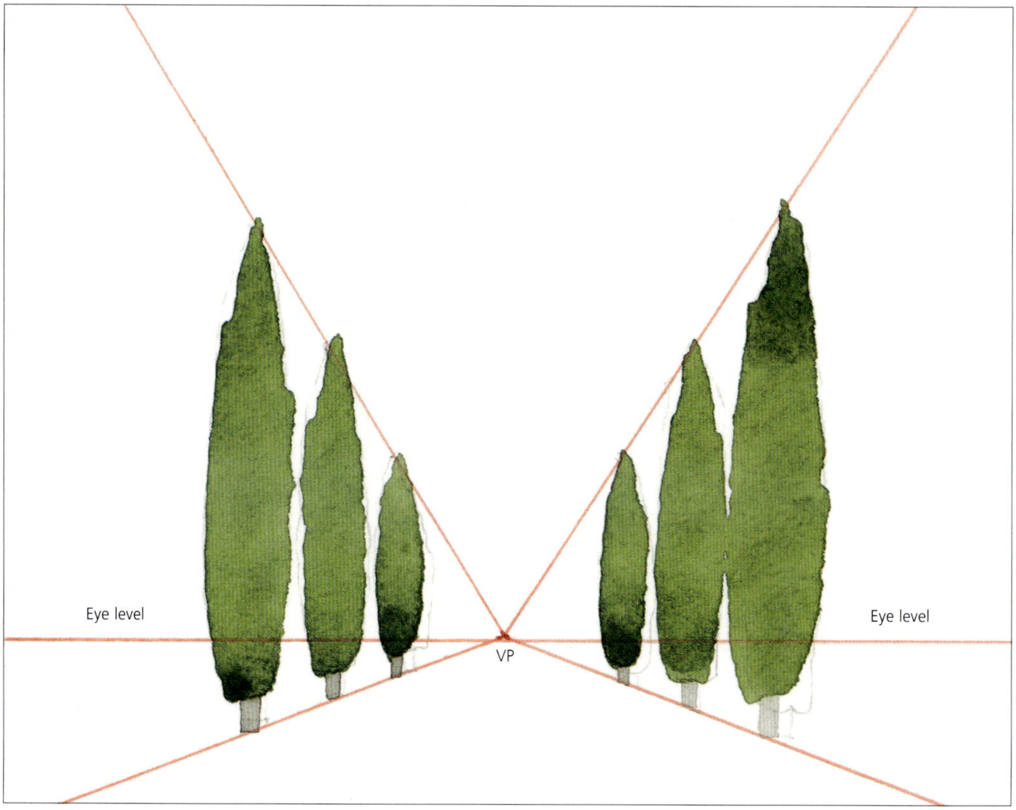

Parallel lines receding to one side ▼
Here, all the elements on the front of the house are on the same plane and so they all meet at the same vanishing point.

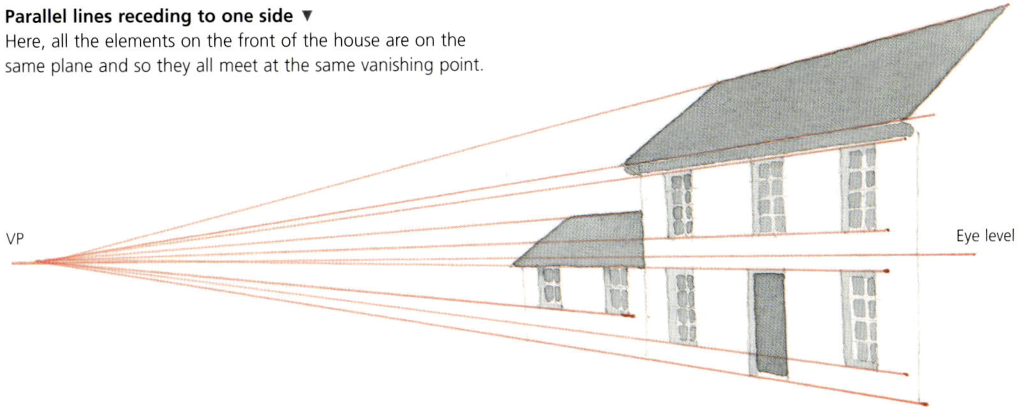

Subject below eye level ▼
As in the other examples shown on these two pages, a single vanishing point is all that is required in this view of a chess board, because the chess board is orientated with one side square to the viewer.

All the receding parallel lines on the board extend to the vanishing point. Because the board is below eye level, the perspective lines run up to meet the vanishing point. The width of each row of squares is arrived at by measurement; the depth of the board is also measured. Drawing a diagonal line from corner to corner of the board will help you to work out the depth of each row of squares, as the corners of these squares have to fall on the diagonal line.

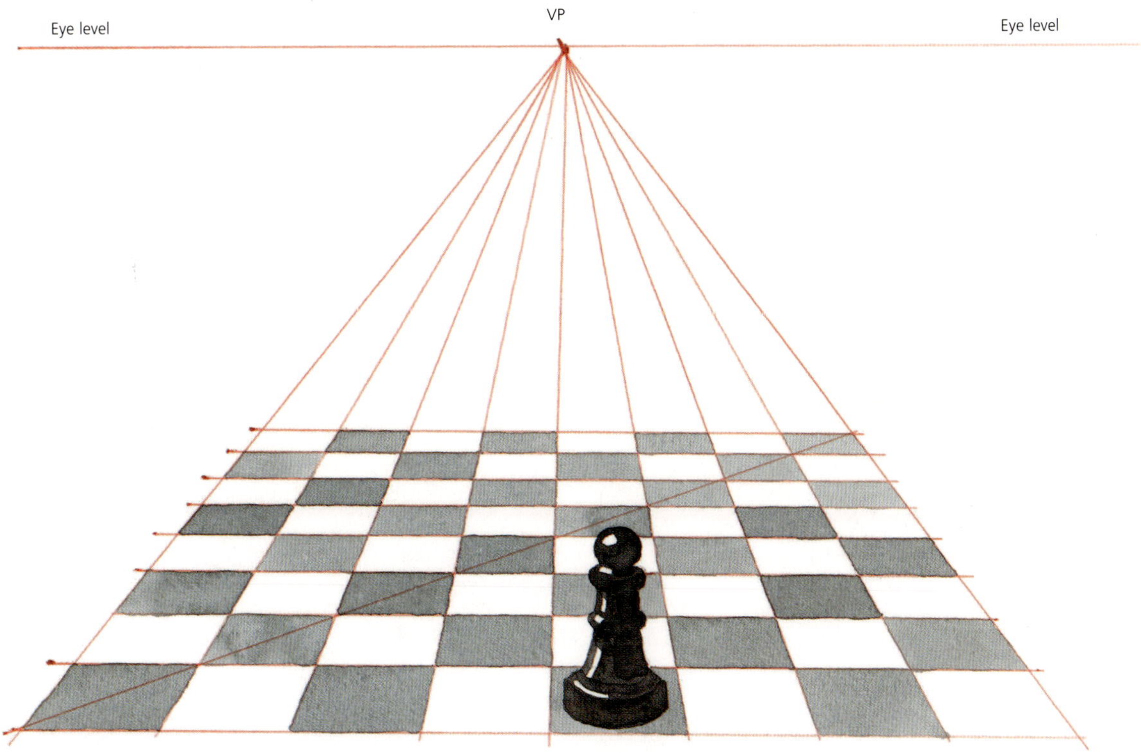

Two-point perspective

If any two sides of an object can be seen at the same time, then two-point perspective comes into play. The principle remains the same as that discussed in one-point perspective, but because two surfaces are visible and both surfaces are at different angles, any parallel lines on those surfaces will eventually meet at their own vanishing point.

In two-point perspective, neither vanishing point falls at your centre of vision. Perspective lines on the right-hand side will converge at a vanishing point off to the right and perspective lines on the left-hand side will converge at a vanishing point off to the left. Even if you move to a position that is higher than your subject, the horizon line on which any vanishing points are situated will still run across your field of vision at eye level, so all perspective lines will run at an upwards angle to meet it. Similarly, if you move to a position below your subject, so that you are looking up at it, all perspective lines will run at a downwards angle to meet the horizon line.

Two planes visible – two-point perspective ▼
Two-point perspective needs to be taken into consideration when you can see two or three sides (planes) of a rectangular object at the same time. Here, we see two sides of a row of coloured boxes, all of which are orientated the same way. The perspective lines of each side of each box extend to the same vanishing point.

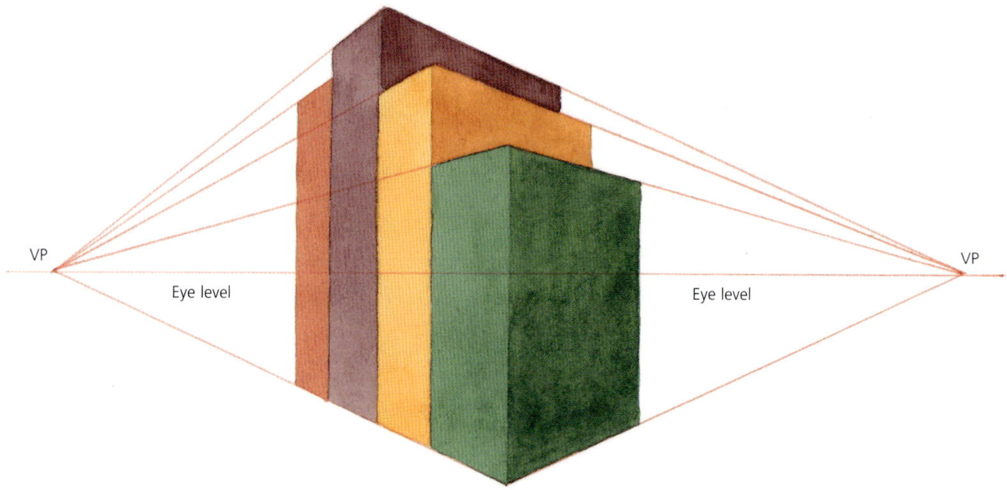

Multiple-point perspective

When several objects are arranged at different heights and angles, then multiple-point perspective comes into play. It looks a little more complicated, but the rules remain the same. Each object needs to be treated as a separate entity and its vanishing points and perspective lines should be plotted accordingly.

Objects at different angles – multiple-point perspective ►
Here, three box-like shapes are resting on what might be a table top. Each box is facing in a slightly different direction, so each one needs to have separate vanishing points – as does the table top, which is orientated differently to the boxes.

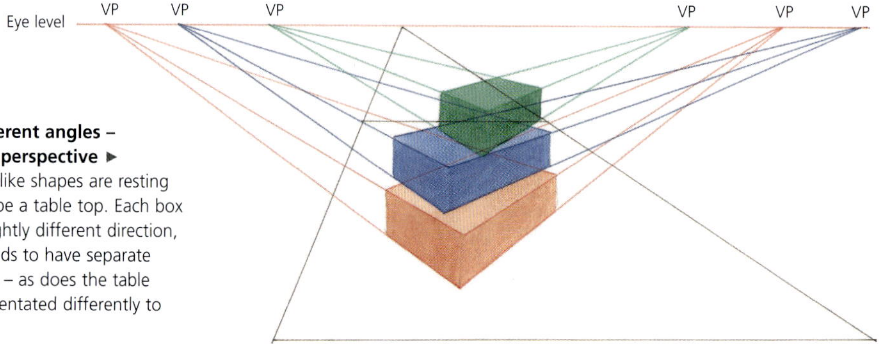

Drawing curved and circular objects in perspective

Understanding the principles of perspective enables you to represent not only simple box-like structures, as in the examples that we've looked at so far, but also highly complex-shaped objects that possess curved, as well as flat, surfaces.

Curved and circular objects become ellipses when they are seen in perspective. To draw them accurately, first work out the area they occupy using squares and rectangles, which are also in perspective.

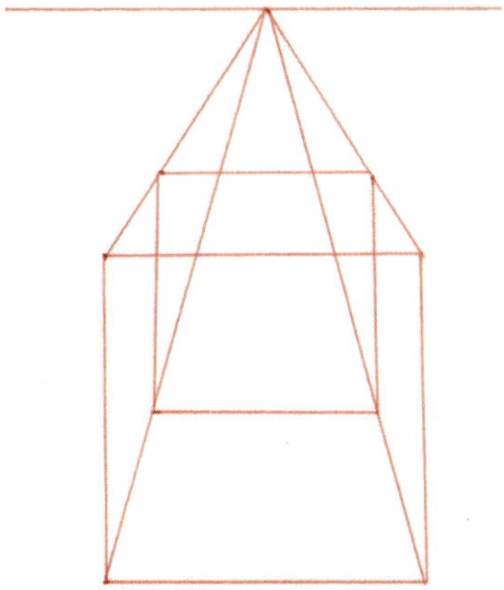

1 First work out the area that the object (in this case, a cylinder) occupies, using simple squares or rectangles seen in perspective. Here the cylinder is viewed from directly in front and slightly above. A simple cube seen in single-point perspective indicates the position and approximate size of the cylinder.

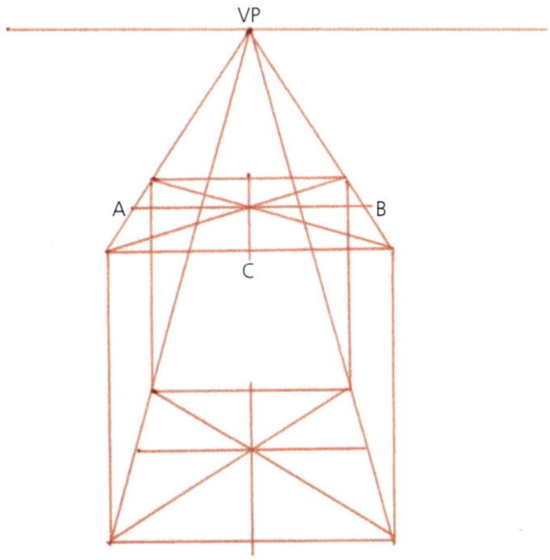

2 Find the centre of the top of the cube by drawing lines from corner to corner. Further divide the top of the cube into quarters by drawing a line (A–B) parallel to the front of the cube through the centre point and by drawing another line (C) through the centre point to line up with the vanishing point (VP). Do the same to the base of the cube.

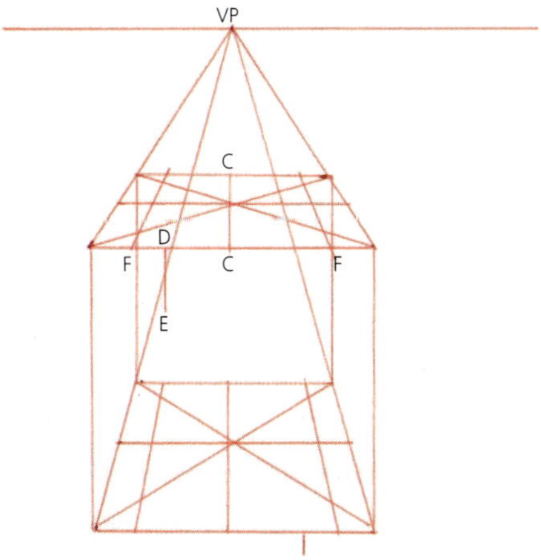

3 From point C on the front edge of the top of the cube, measure halfway to the corner (D). Drop a line at right angles to E, the same length as the measurement C–D. Position a compass point at C, with the radius set to E. Swing the compass from here to find points F. Draw a line from F to line up with the vanishing point (VP). Repeat on the base.

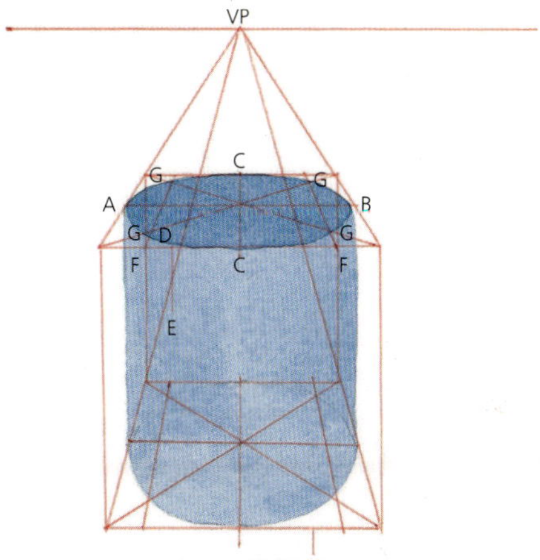

4 The exact curvature of the top of the cylinder is established by drawing a curved line to connect points A, B and C at point G – through the points where the line F–VP intersects the lines that run from corner to corner. Follow the same procedure to find the curvature at the bottom of the cylinder.

Composition

The way in which all the visual elements within a painting are put together is known as composition. The factors that govern composition include shape, scale, perspective, colour and texture. The purpose of composition is to manipulate and lead the eye while finding a pleasing visual balance of all these elements. Balance does not mean visual symmetry: shape can be offset with texture or colour with scale.

Composition can also be used to create mood. A composition can evoke feelings of heaviness and oppression, or be airy, light and uplifting. There are certain rules to composition, but breaking these rules often gives a work a certain edge that can lift it from the mundane and pedestrian into something much more eyecatching.

Formats

The first thing you need to consider is what shape (or format) to make your painting. The three main formats are vertical (also know as portrait), horizontal (also known as landscape) and square. Needless to say, portraits can be painted on landscape-format supports and landscapes on portrait ones. Two other formats that are often used are round (or oval) and a wider horizontal format known as panoramic.

Catching the light ▼
The roughly square format suits the subject perfectly: the neck and head curve around, balancing the bulk detail of the body.

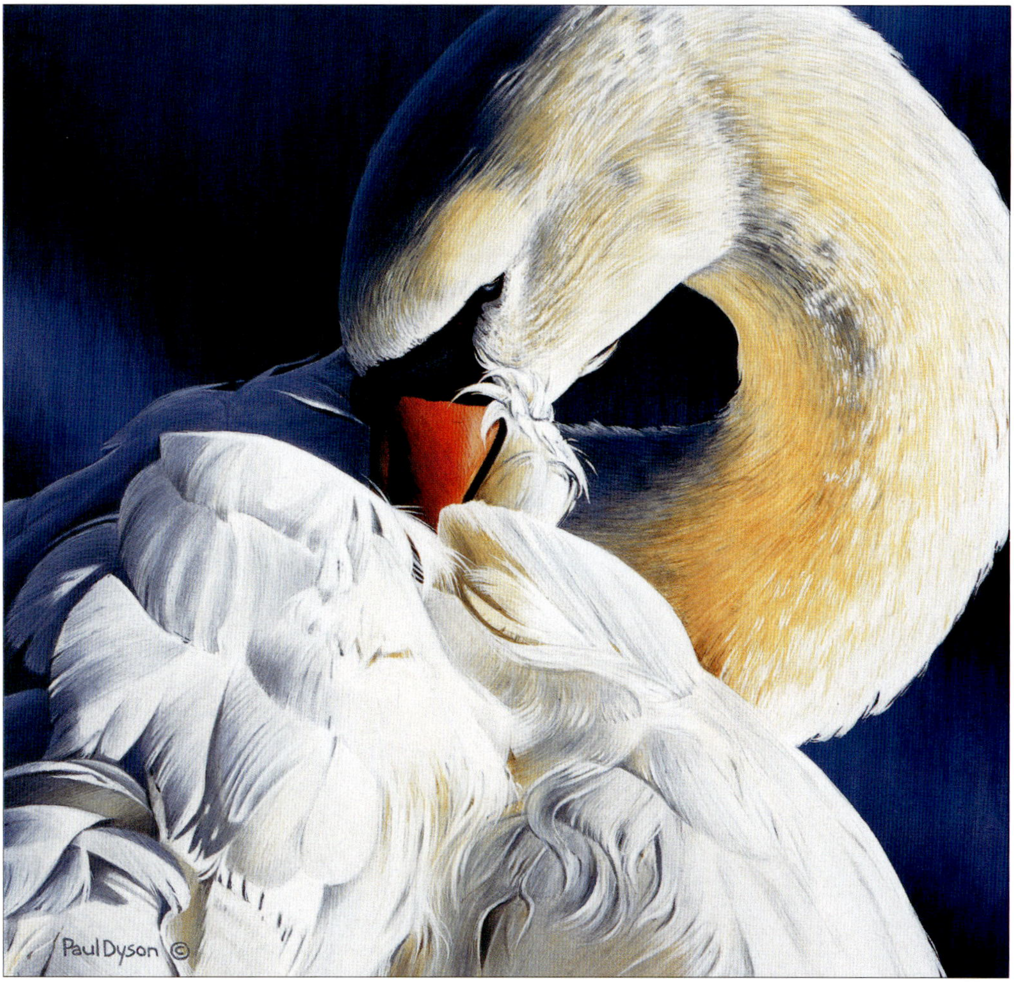

Robin ▼

A wide, panoramic format has been chosen for this painting of a robin on a branch. At first glance, it might seem that the subject is quite insignificant and does not warrant such an extreme format, but exaggerating the width of the painting has introduced a tension that would be lacking if the more usual landscape format had been used. The clever device of the arching branch, which runs the entire width of the image, prevents the picture from appearing one-sided: the eye wanders along it and across the picture, but always returns to the brilliant flash of red on the bird's breast.

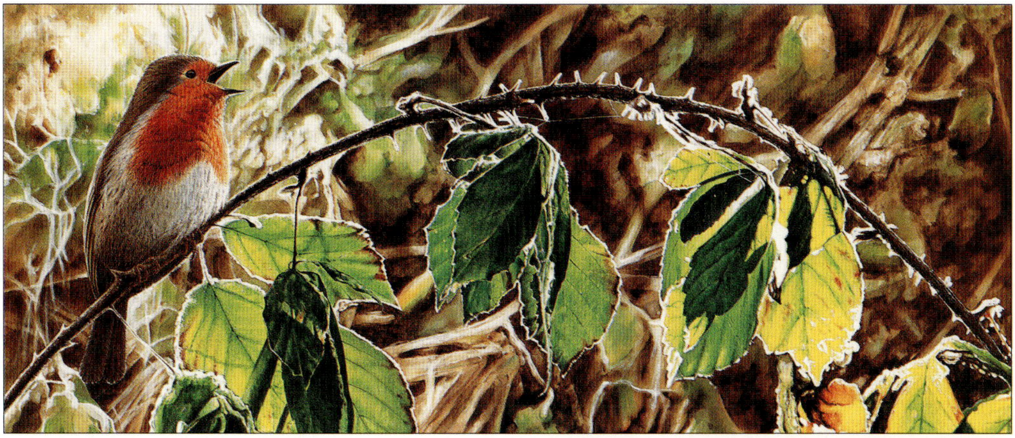

Seaside steps ►

The vertical format of this work again suits the subject. The eye is pulled along the length of the craft and up the steps towards the building. The golden yellow stonework pulls the eye down to the bottom of the picture and the circular journey begins again.

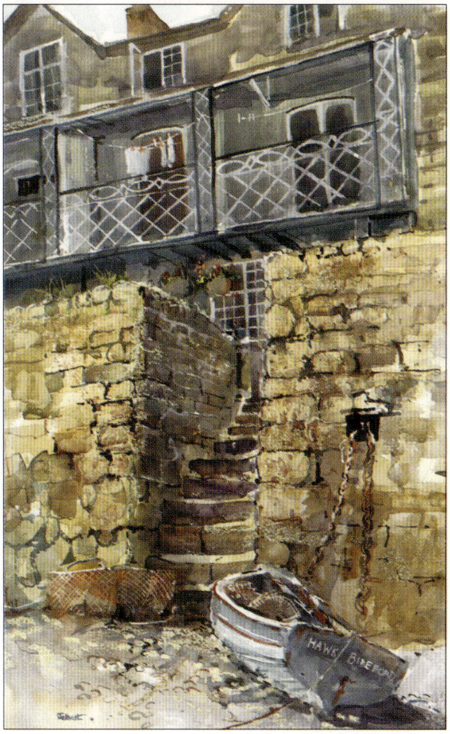

Etretat, Normandy ▼

The image of these cliffs in northern France sits comfortably in the horizontal format. The curve of the waterline sweeps the eye around to the cliffs and into the painting. At the base of the cliffs, the viewer's attention is caught by the dark ripples and reflection in the water; these in turn bring the eye down to the breaking waves and round again.

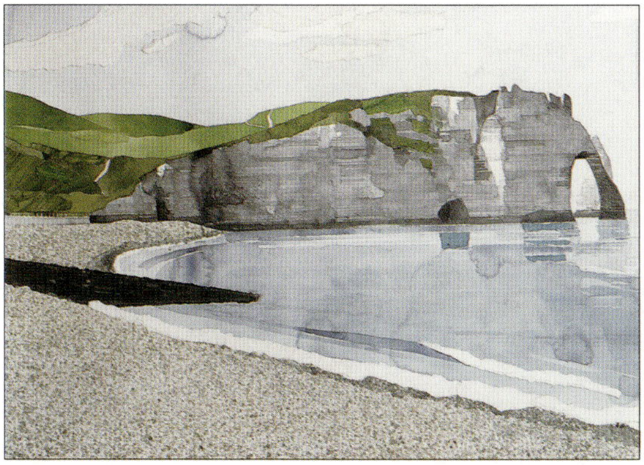

Dividing the picture area

The principle of good composition is that nothing should dominate to such an extent that it holds the viewer's attention completely and exclusively – although, of course, there are occasions when artists deliberately choose to do precisely that. Dividing the picture area up and deciding exactly what should go where can be difficult, but there are some general guidelines that will help you.

Over the centuries, artists have devised ways of positioning the main pictorial elements and focal points on an invisible grid around specific positions within the picture area. The classic compositional device, and the one that is considered to be the ideal division of an area and aesthetically superior to others, is based on the golden section – the term used for a mathematical formula devised by Euclid and developed by Plato. Also known as divine proportion, it states that a line or area can be divided so that the "smaller part is to the larger as the larger part is to the whole".

A simpler and less rigid grid, which is easier to follow and use, is made by splitting the picture area into thirds, regardless of the format chosen. This is done by simply dividing the image area into three, both horizontally and vertically, which gives a grid consisting of nine sections, with lines crossing at four points. The theory is that positioning major elements of the image near these lines or at their intersections will result in a pleasing image. As with the golden section, the formula is a good starting point on which to base your compositions.

It is generally considered inadvisable to position your subject in the very centre of the picture area, as it makes for a rather static image. However, a feeling of calmness and inactivity are sometimes exactly what the subject requires. Be guided by your instincts, even if they sometimes appear to be going against the rules.

Beach, early morning ▼
This simple painting of a beach umbrella and sun loungers silhouetted in the early morning sun is firmly based on the rule of thirds. The umbrella provides a strong vertical element approximately a third of the way in from the right-hand side, while the shoreline and sun loungers provide a horizontal element approximately one third of the way up from the bottom of the picture. These dark shapes are balanced by the empty area of water.

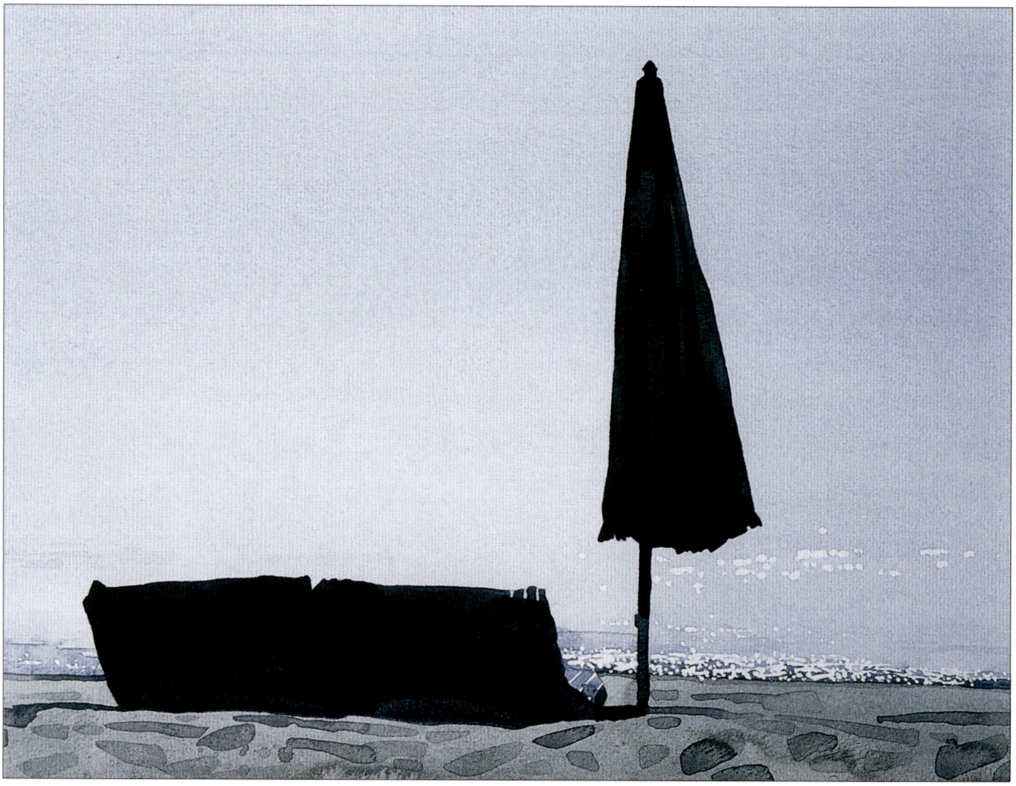

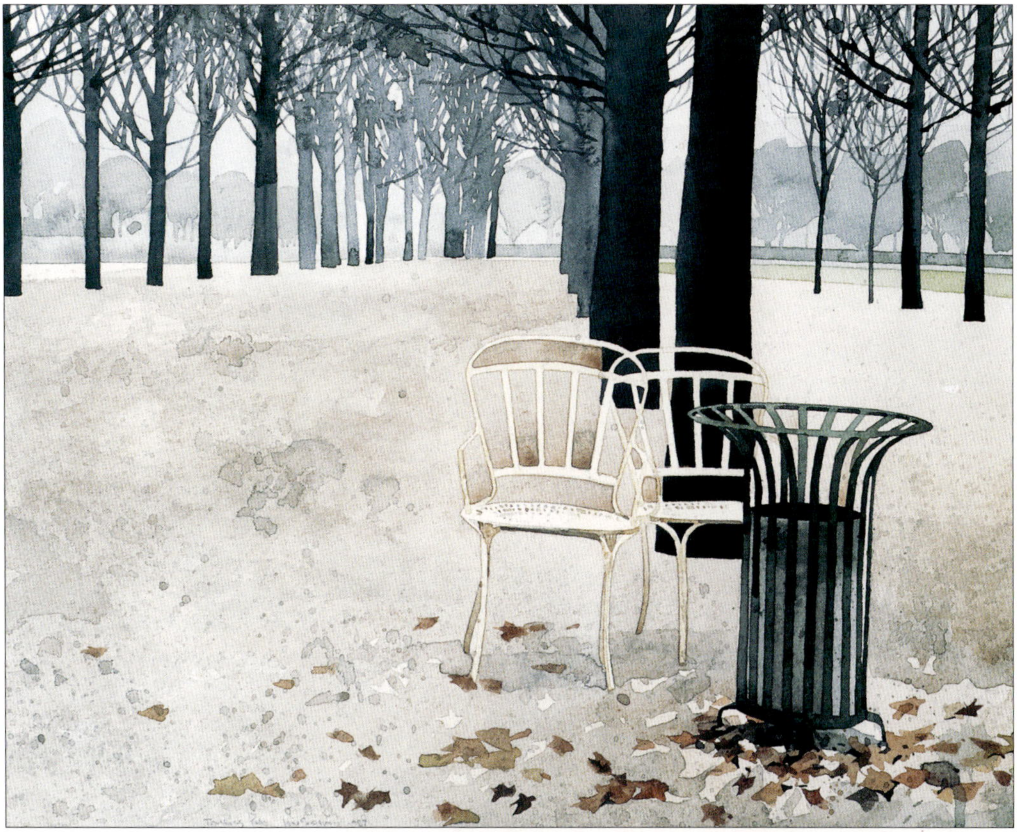

The Tuileries, Paris ▲
The chairs and litter bin are the centre of interest and are loosely positioned on the intersecting grid lines to the right of the image while the top third of the painting is filled with row upon row of leafless trees. Together, they balance the empty space in the bottom left of the image.

Flamenco guitarist ►
Although it is perhaps not immediately apparent, this portrait is also based around the rule of thirds. The head of the guitarist, the bulk of the guitar body, and the tuning head are all positioned at points where the grid lines intersect, while the figure's torso and the ornate pillar are placed a third of the way in from the left- and right-hand sides respectively.

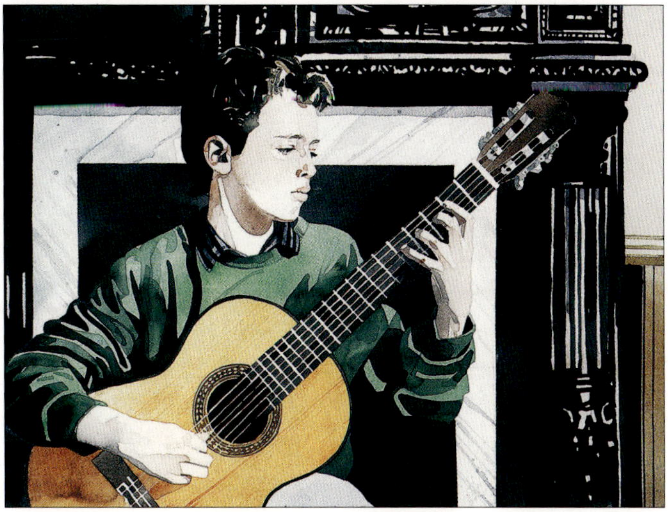

Leading the eye

In a successful composition, the viewer's eye should be directed towards the image's centre of interest and encouraged to linger on the picture. Introducing curves and lines within the picture, either real or implied, are one way of doing this. Obvious examples of this might be a road leading up to a building, a river snaking its way through a landscape, or a line of trees receding into the distance.

All compositions are either "open" or "closed". A closed composition is one in which the eye is held within the picture area. It may be induced to move around from object to object, but essentially its focus is firmly held. An example of a closed composition might be a view from a dark interior through a window, with the window surround acting as a frame within a frame. An open gateway or tree trunks and branches might serve the same purpose. An open composition encourages the eye to move around the image, but also seems to suggest that the image continues well beyond the boundaries of the picture area. Many landscapes are perfect examples of open compositions.

Another strong compositional device, especially when painting landscapes, is the positioning of the horizon. This can have a profound effect on the mood of the image. Landscapes can be given extra impact by making the horizon very high within the picture area or even eliminating it altogether. Clouds can also be an important compositional consideration, providing large, eye-catching shapes in what might otherwise be an empty space.

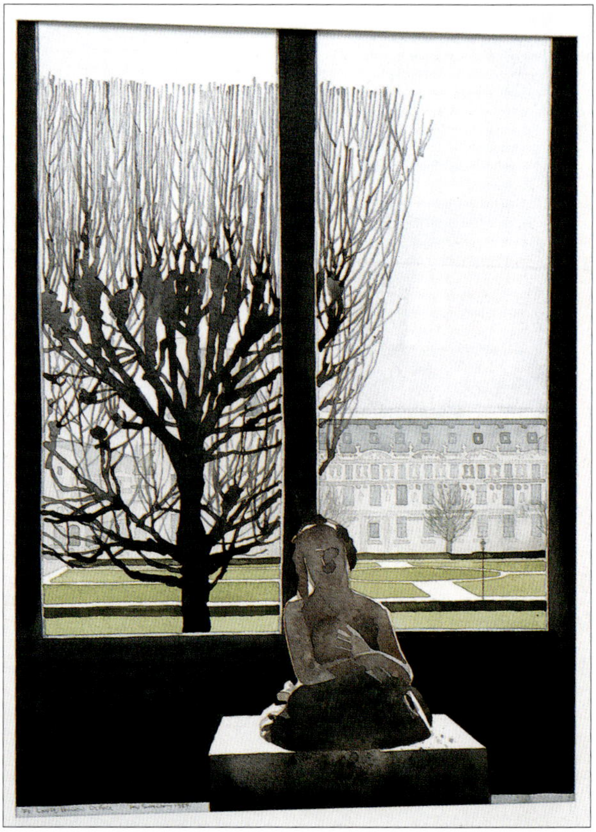

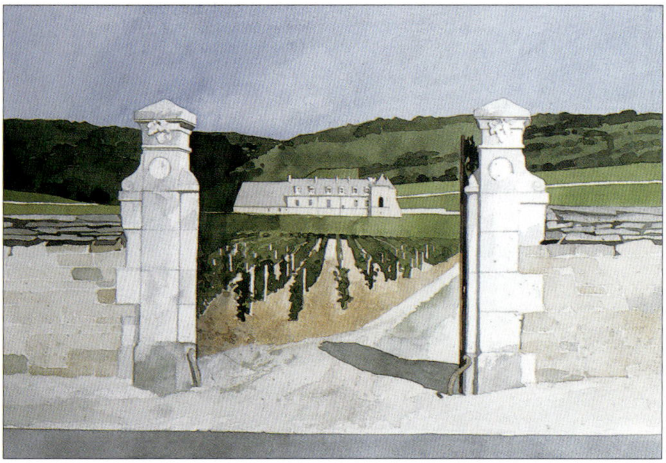

Louvre Museum, Paris ▲
This is a good example of a closed composition. The eye is unavoidably pulled into the work past the sculpture and out the window into the centre of the image. The dark window surround acts as a visual barrier and encourages the eye to linger in the central area.

◄ Clos de Vosges
These weathered gate pillars act as a frame within a frame, drawing the eye through to the vineyard and buildings beyond. Because the pillars are placed centrally, the eye can move around within the rest of the painting. If they were placed closer to the edge of the image, the composition would seem more closed and confined.

Springs ▼

Rules are made to be broken. Placing the horizon line across the centre of an image is generally considered bad practice, but it can be made to work. Here, the strong sense of perspective leads the eye into the centre of the image. The visual activity on the horizon line acts as a buffer, pushing the eyes out to either side. The bottom part of the image is roughly divided into thirds. The wide expanse of sky is broken by the row of telegraph poles.

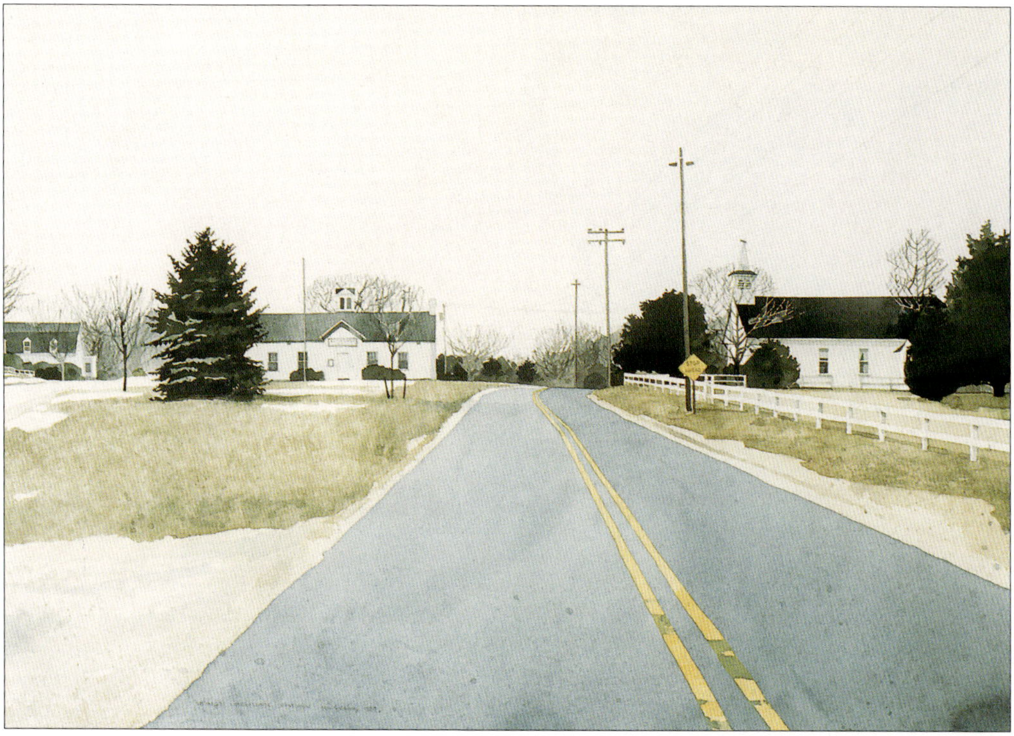

Mont St Michel ►

This is an example of both an open composition and breaking the so-called rules about where to position the horizon. The landscape and building are placed low in the picture area, with the horizon running across the image about a quarter of the way up. This has the effect of drawing attention to the sky, which is a featureless pale blue. One would not normally expect so much emphasis to be given to seemingly empty space, but in this instance the sheer size and weight of the sky provide a counterbalance to the visual activity in the lower part of the painting. The result is a powerful, atmospheric image that is possessed of a perfect spirit of place.

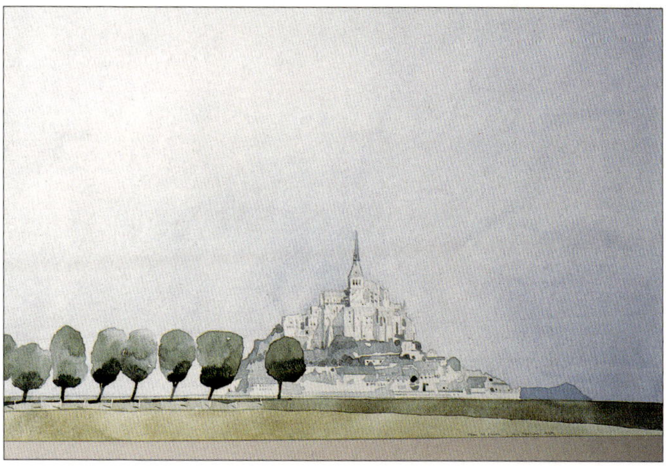

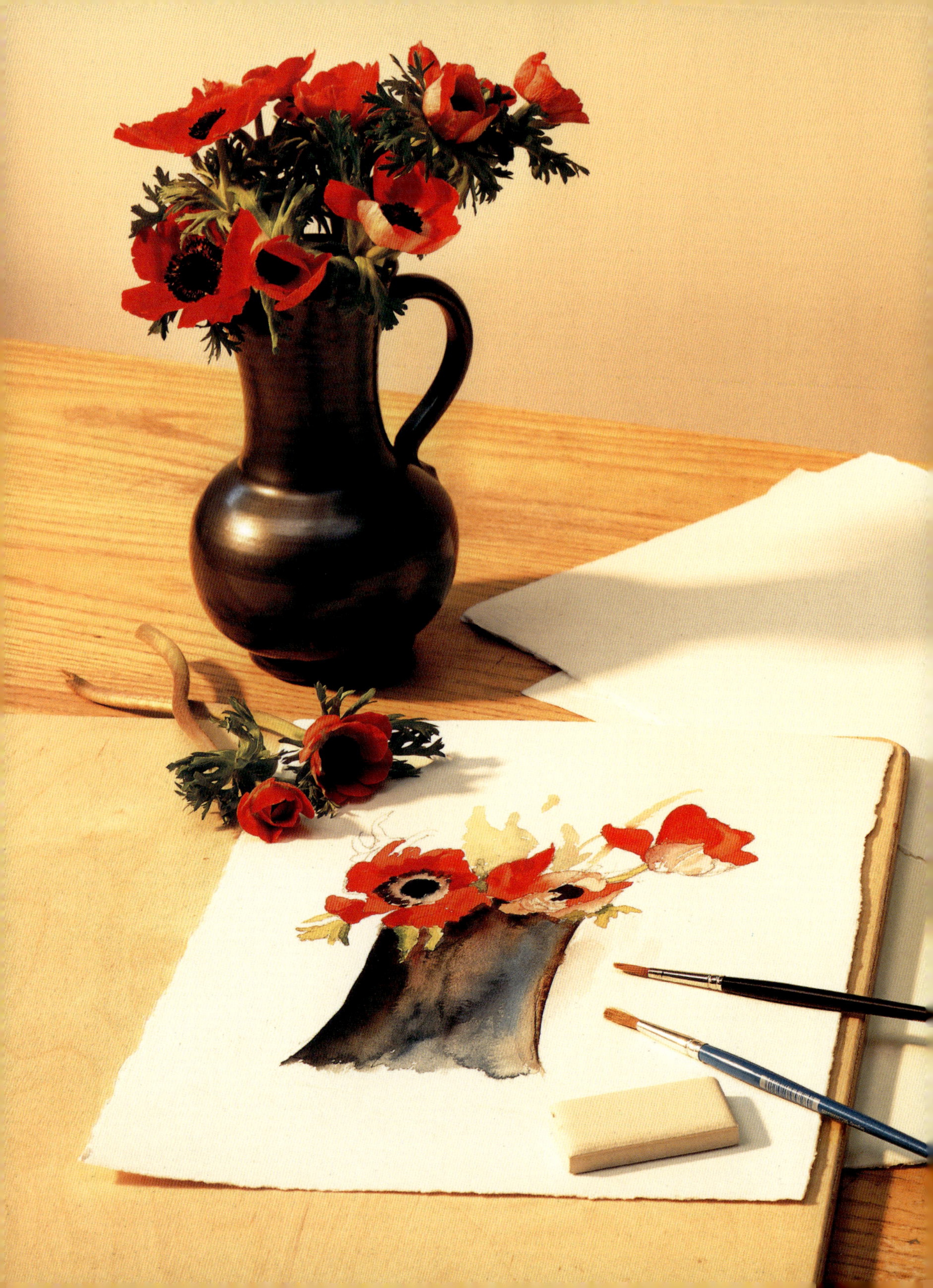

Watercolour Projects

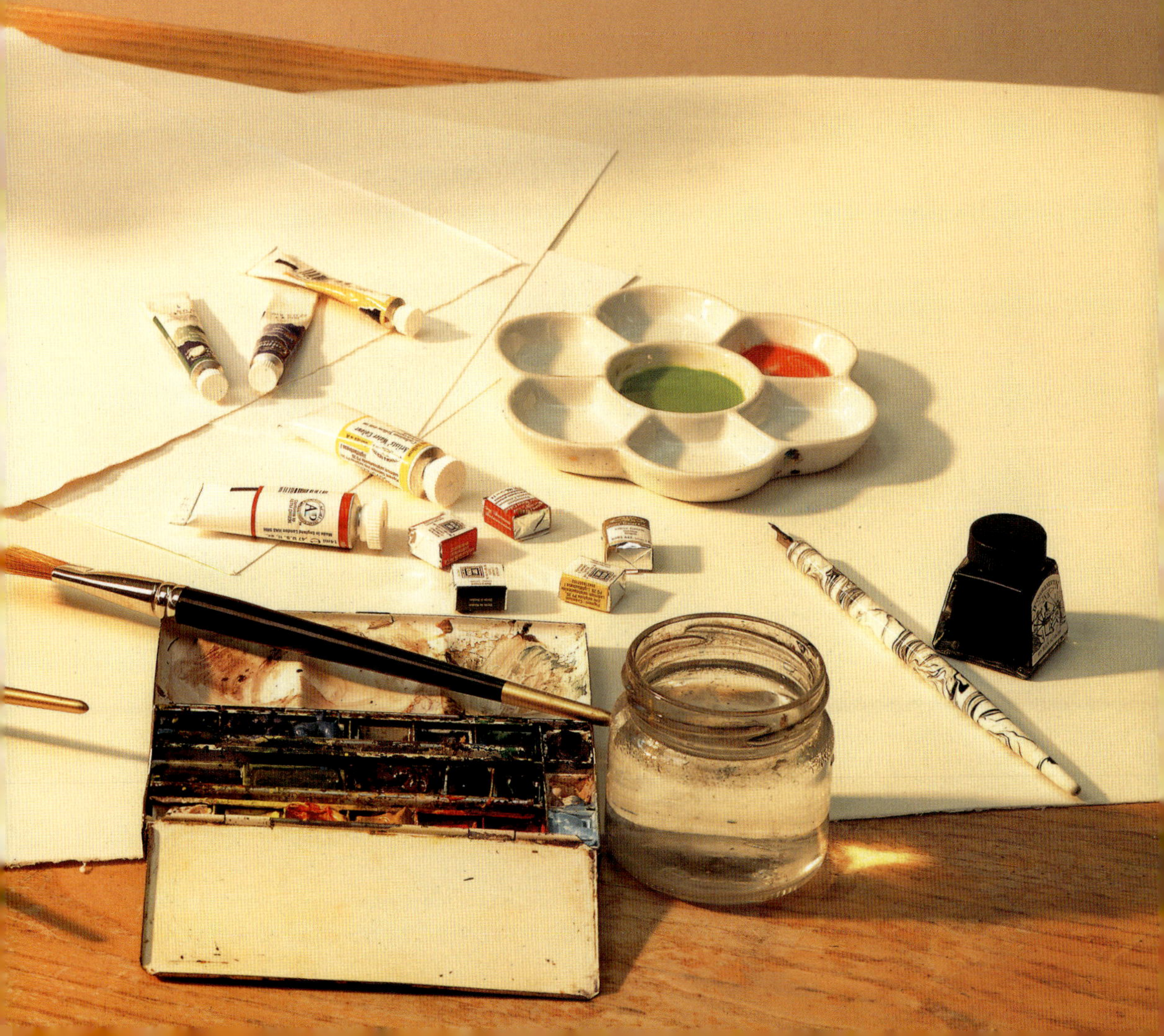

Painting Skies

Skies have always both fascinated and frustrated artists. The fascination comes from the infinite combinations of cloud formations and colours, which can change minute by minute depending on the weather conditions and the time of day, and the frustration from trying to decide on the most appropriate way in which to represent them.

Although skies can be painted as a subject in themselves, they are more commonly viewed as part of a landscape – and an important part, at that. It is from the sky that light comes to illuminate the landscape below, and the colour and mood of all landscapes are directly influenced by the sky above.

When you are painting a sky as part of a landscape, you must make sure that each looks connected and related to the other. The best way to achieve this is to make the sky an integral and important part of the overall composition. As with all things, however, you can exercise a degree of artistic licence. A dramatic and powerful sky can very easily overpower a less interesting landscape, so don't be afraid to alter the balance from what you can actually see in reality.

Although the use of colour is important, particularly when you are painting sunsets, the most critical elements in any sky scene are the cloud formations. Getting to know cloud formations is a useful step towards painting skies well. Artists who paint skies frequently tend to make practice studies of the clouds before they begin.

Beginners often make the mistake of depicting clouds as flat objects against a background of blue, but the reality is very different. Clouds have a top (which the light hits), sides, and a bottom (which is often in deep shadow). They also conform to the laws of perspective, and appear smaller with less distinct colours as they stretch to the horizon. Applying the rules of aerial perspective to clouds can throw up an anomaly, however, for while skies are usually more intense and warmer in colour immediately overhead, becoming cooler and paler nearer the horizon, the exact reverse can be seen on occasions – particularly when looking out to sea, or in large cities with atmospheric pollution.

There are several techniques that you can use to paint clouds successfully. The sky colour and cloud positions might be made using wet-into-wet washes. Cloud shapes can be left as white paper or lifted out using a paper towel or a dry brush. As these washes dry, darker washes can be flooded on to create the parts of the clouds that are in shadow, with more washes being painted over the top to strengthen colour or redefine shapes when the first washes are dry.

Alternatively, you could paint the sky using only wet on dry washes, assessing the colour and tone of each so that the shape and colour of the clouds are built up in layers. Avoid hard edges, which look out of place in a sky scene. Cloud edges can be softened periodically by using clean water and a brush or by blotting with a natural sponge or paper towel.

The Thames at Richmond ▼
In this expansive view, the landscape and the sky are of equal importance. Placing the horizon on the halfway mark is risky, but the image works because the carefully arranged cloud formations balance the intricate landscape. The clouds were created by means of carefully planned wet on dry washes. The blue colour in the sky was painted last, with the cloud shapes being "cut out" as it was applied.

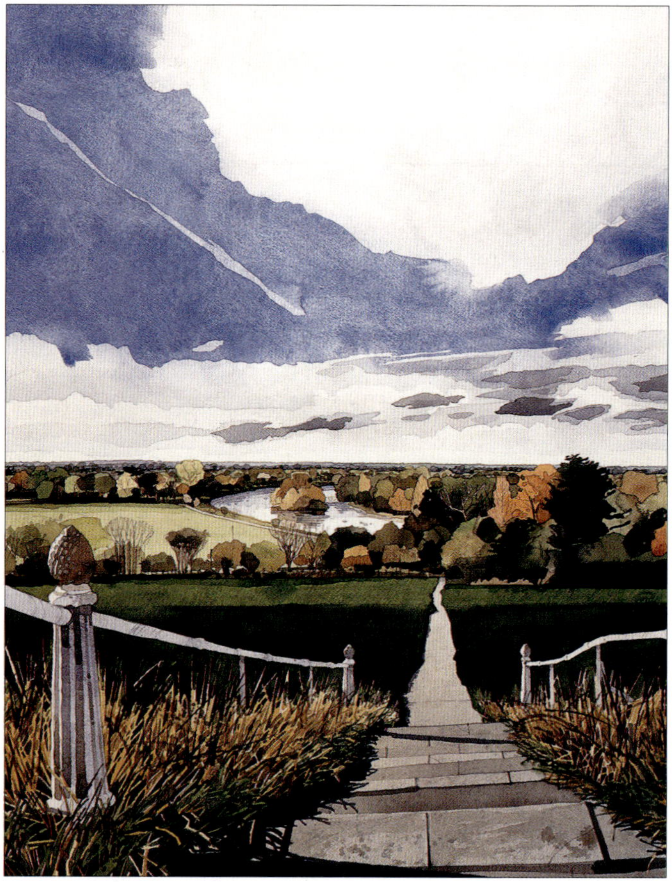

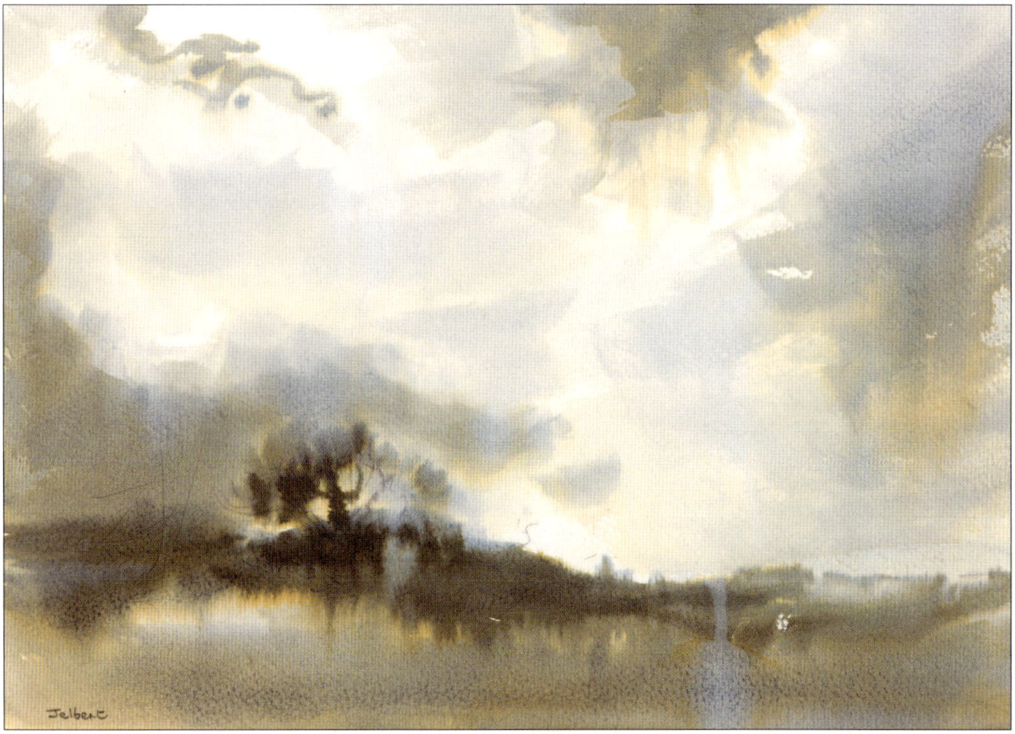

Storm clouds ▲
This loose impression of storm clouds gathering in a pale grey sky uses the same colours as the dark, wet landscape below. Washes were applied wet into wet in order to give a feeling of indistinct focus, which is often apparent in falling rain.

Sunset ▼
A gradated pale blue wash provided the foundation for this sunset. The pale orange strip of light on the horizon takes on an added brilliance seen against the dark landscape and the deep grey clouds above.

Tips: • Use clouds to balance dominant elements in the landscape.
• Take care not to make clear blue skies dominate your landscapes as, without clouds to add interest, such skies tend to look flat and boring.
• Remember that skies and clouds conform to the same laws of perspective as the land. As a general rule, colours get paler the nearer they are to the horizon, with clouds becoming smaller and less distinct.
• Practise painting various wash and cloud combinations. Only by knowing what your materials can do and how they behave will you be free to concentrate on creating the effects you want.

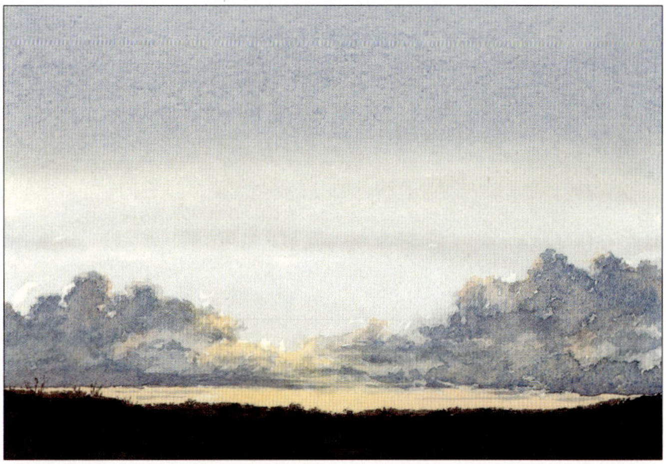

Clouds at sunset

The presence of a few clouds in the sky almost always adds to the drama of a sunset, as the clouds pick up reflected light and add textural interest that might otherwise be lacking.

This project is an excuse to have fun and to play around with wet-into-wet washes to see what effects you can create. Although the wet-into-wet technique is perfect for depicting the gradual transitions of colour that you find in a sunset, it is also notoriously unpredictable. Different papers give different effects, and the degree of wetness also plays an important part. Knowing how wet the paper should be to create a particular effect is something that comes with practice, so don't despair if things initially turn out very differently from what you'd expected. Instead of aiming for a photo-realistic rendition, with every cloud and subtle tonal change in exactly the "right" place, use the scene as a starting point for your explorations: let the flowing paint do the work and adapt your ideas as you go, responding to the shapes and colours that emerge.

Include a hint of the land beneath in a sunset painting, even if it's just a tiny sliver at the very base of the picture. This anchors the image and provides a context for the visual feast above.

Materials

- *140lb (300gsm) rough watercolour paper, pre-stretched*
- *Watercolour paints: cobalt blue, cerulean blue, cadmium yellow, cadmium red, alizarin crimson, ultramarine violet*
- *Brushes: large round*
- *Sponge*

The original scene

Pinks, oranges and violets; glowering clouds fringed with a pure and intense light: a sunset guaranteed to take away the breath of even the most hardened cynic! Clouds like these, with dramatic contrasts of light and dark, are generally much more interesting than fluffy white clouds in a brilliant blue sky.

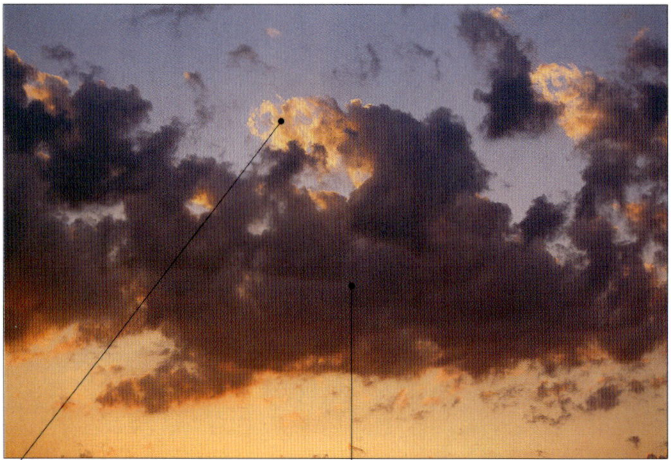

Reflected light on these clouds provides a much-needed "lift" of colour.

These brooding clouds dominate the scene and add textural interest.

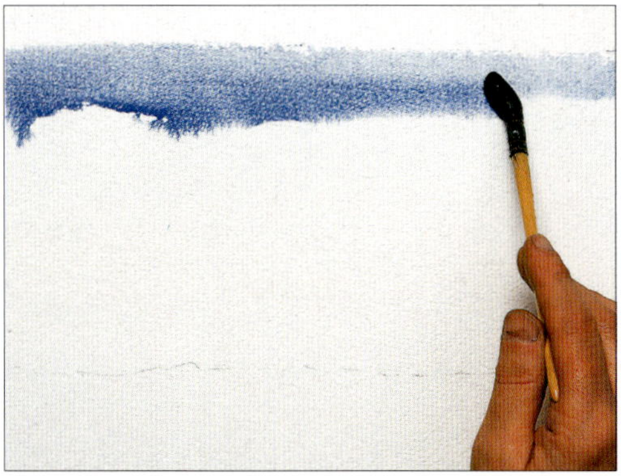

1 Using a large round brush, dampen the paper with clean water, leaving a few areas untouched. Mix a deep blue from cobalt blue and a little cerulean blue and lay a gradated wash, fading to almost nothing and stopping about halfway down the paper.

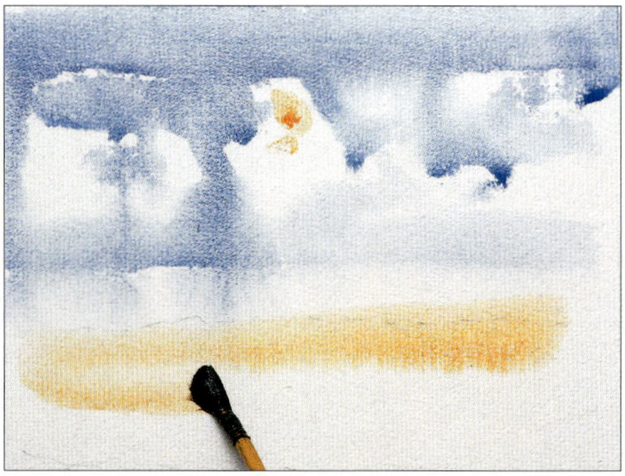

2 Mix a pale orange from cadmium yellow and a little cadmium red. Using a large round brush, wash this mixture over the lower half of the painting and dot it into the sky, where the setting sun catches the top of some of the cloud formations.

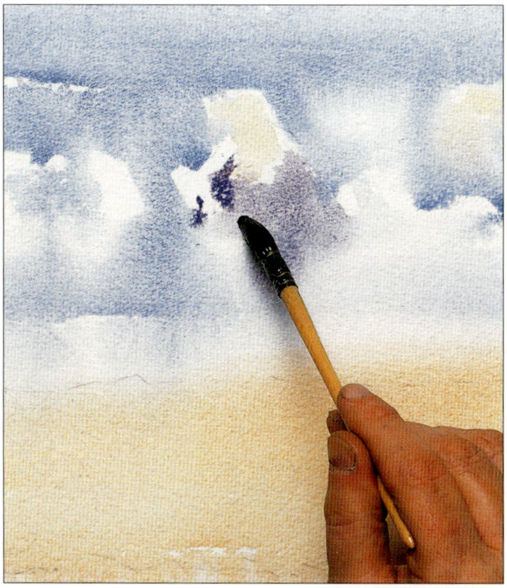

3 Touch the orange mixture into the dry cloud shapes left in Step 1. Working quickly, while the paper is still damp, deepen the orange colour on the lower half of the painting. Mix a dark purple from cobalt blue, alizarin crimson and ultramarine violet and drop this mixture into the centre of the painting, so that the colours blur.

4 Add more purple across the middle of the painting, going into both the blue and the orange areas, to establish the dark bank of cloud that runs across the centre of the image. Leave to dry completely before moving on to the next stage.

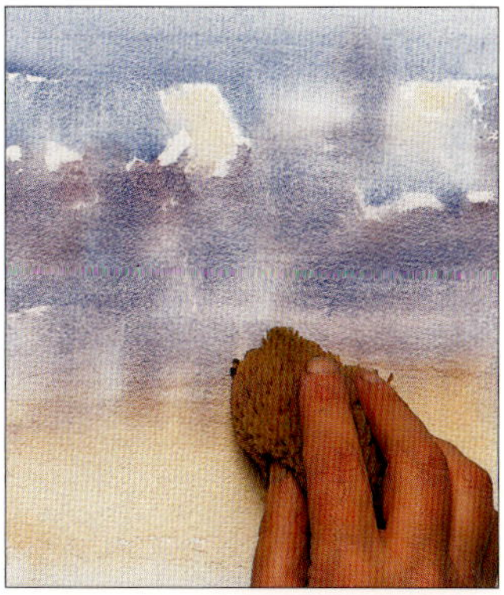

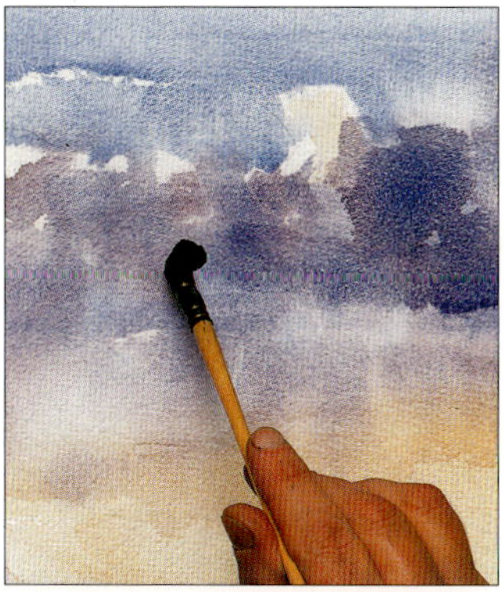

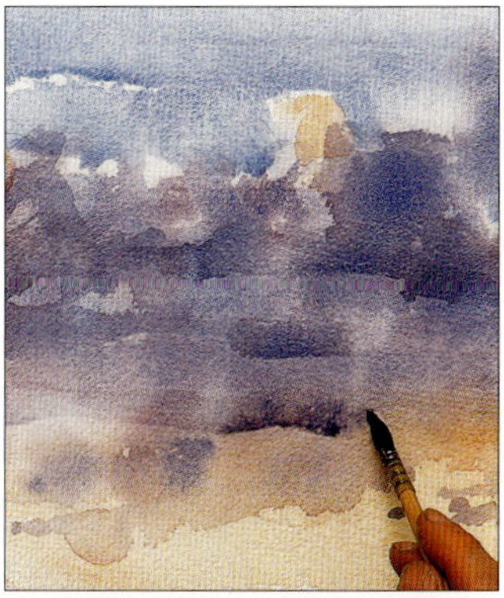

5 Dip a sponge in water, squeeze out any excess water and stroke it across the top half of the paper.

6 Using a large round brush, touch the purple mixture used in Step 3 into the dark clouds at the top.

7 Using the same paint mixtures as before, continue touching colour into damp areas, allowing it to spread and find its own way. Watch what happens rather than starting out with preconceived ideas: you will find that the paint suggests shapes that you can then strengthen and make an integral part of the painting.

Tip: With the paper used in this demonstration, the colours laid down earlier will not lift if the underlying washes are completely dry before you re-dampen the paper. Not all papers behave in this way, however, so it pays to experiment in advance.

Clouds at sunset

This is an expressive painting, with subtle shifts from one colour to another, which demonstrates one of the main attributes of watercolour – its translucency – to the full. Although it is not a painstaking copy of the original scene, it nonetheless captures the quality of the light and the sense of rapidly changing lighting conditions very well.

The artist has exploited the unpredictability of the wet-into-wet technique by responding to changes as they occur on the paper, and so the painting has a lovely sense of freshness and spontaneity. At the same time he has paid careful attention to the light and dark areas so that the clouds really do look three-dimensional.

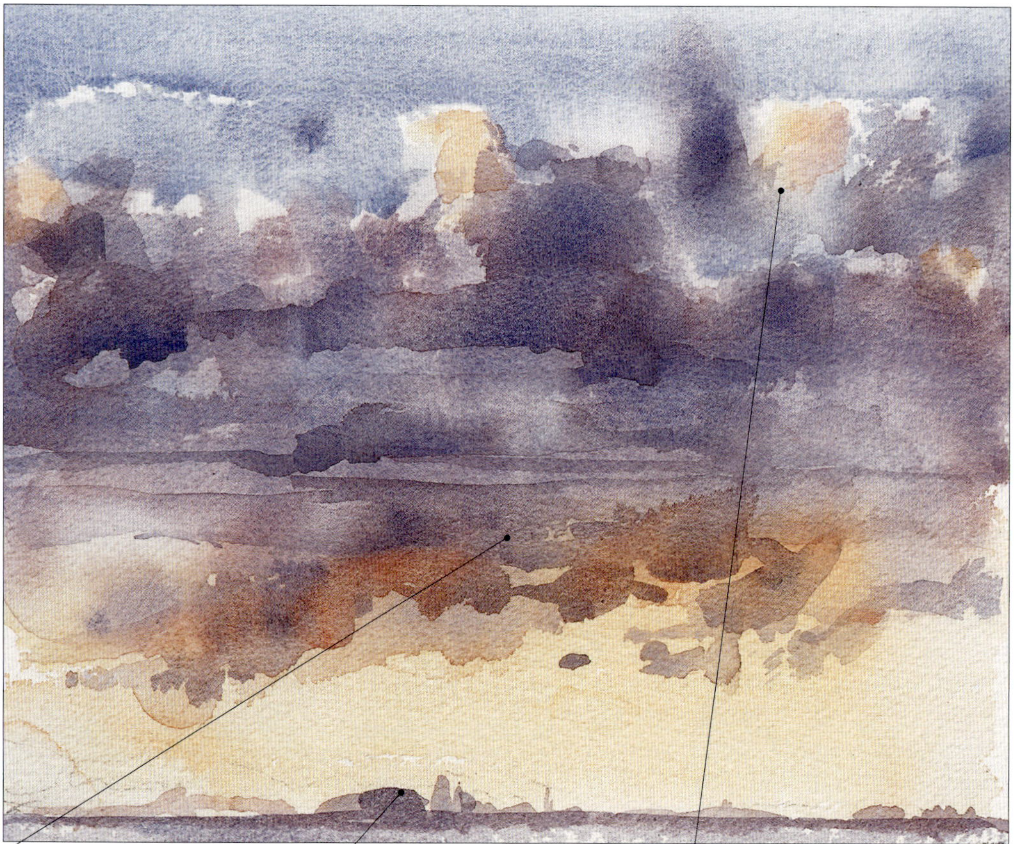

Successive wet-into-wet applications build up depth of tone.

Silhouetted shapes on the horizon anchor the scene.

The rough surface of the paper also helps to add textural interest.

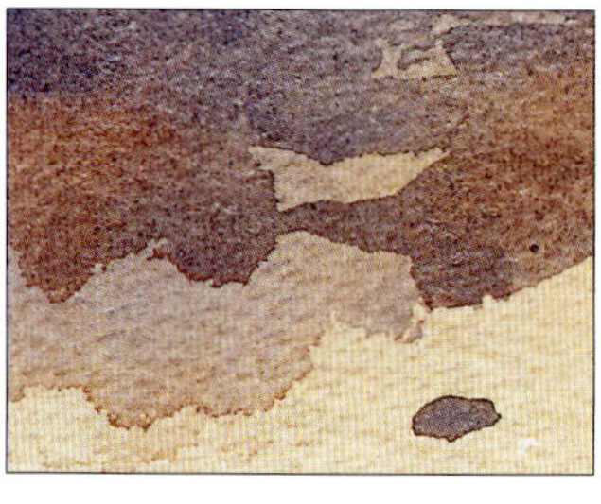

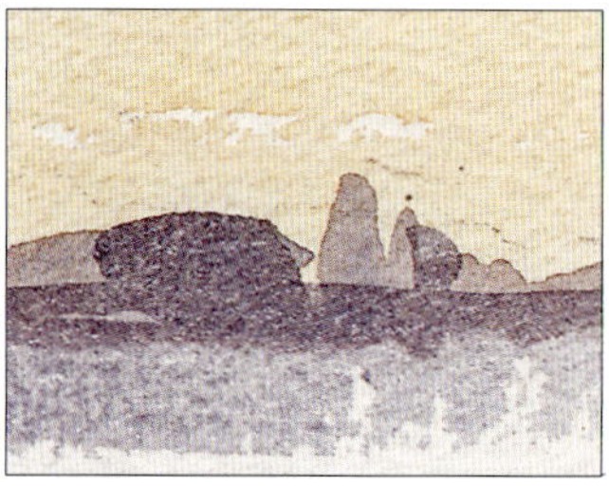

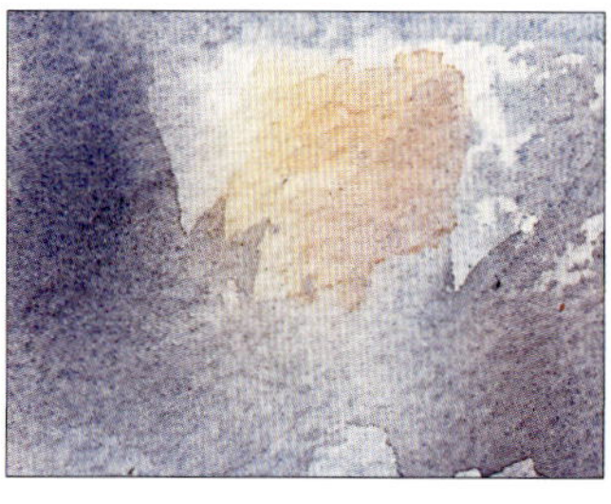

Variation: **Clouds at sunset painted on smooth paper**

The same scene painted on smooth paper gives a rather different result. In the previous painting, the rough texture of the paper played an important role. In this painting, however, the smooth surface means that there is a more uniform band of colour across the top of the image. The paint also behaves differently on smooth paper: although this scene was also painted by dropping colour wet into wet, there are a number of hard-edged rings. It is impossible to say that one type of surface is better than the other for this type of work: it is entirely down to personal preference.

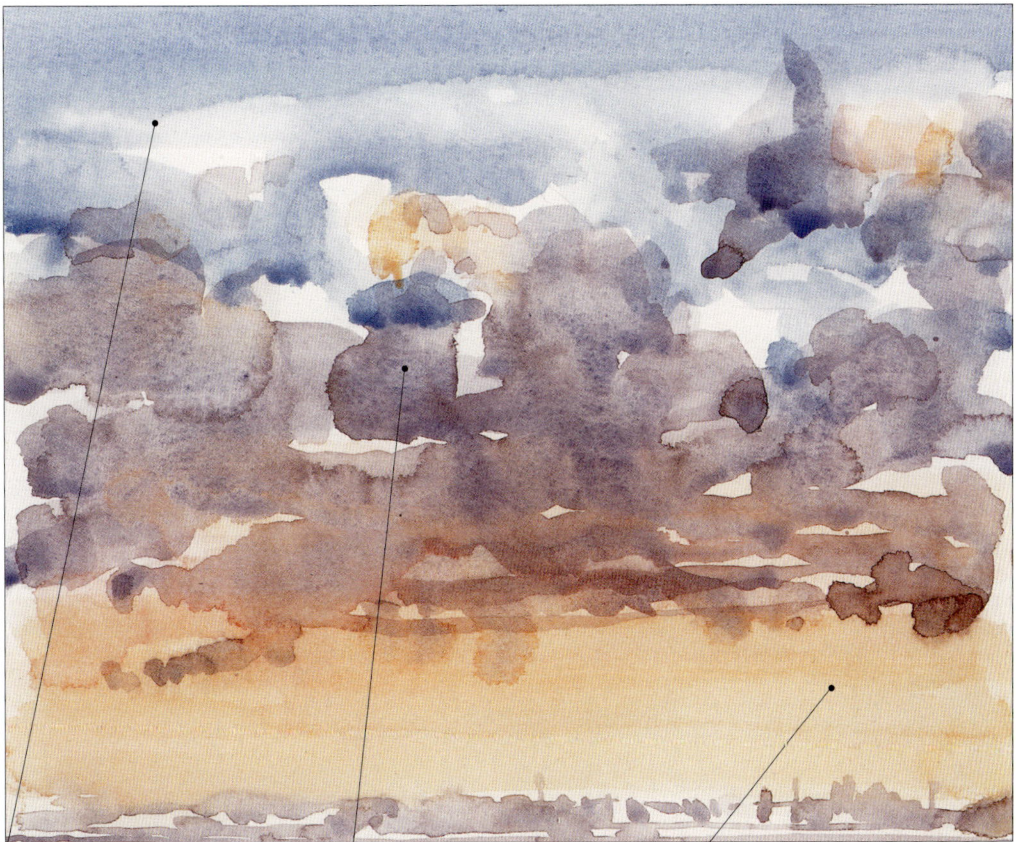

Allowing some of the initial wash to show through is an effective technique for skies.

On smooth paper, hard-edged rings of colour sometimes appear.

The paint goes on smoothly, and the paper texture is less evident.

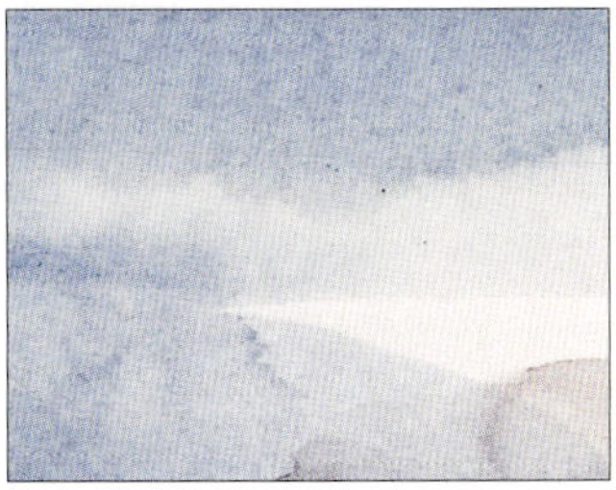

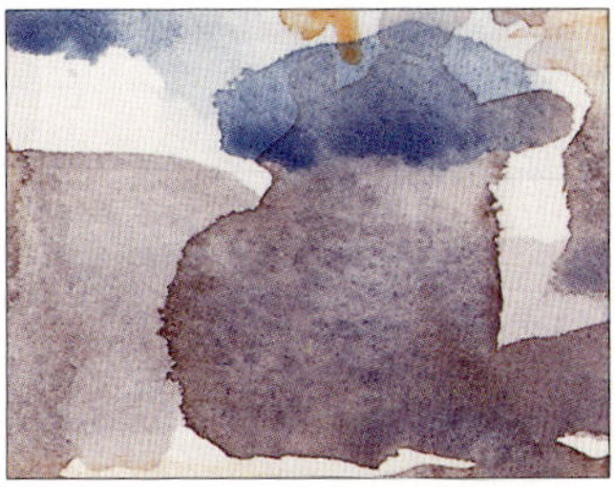

Storm clouds and rainbow

Watercolour is a wonderful medium for painting clouds. The translucency of the paint enables you to create a feeling of light and air, while wet-into-wet washes are perfect for creating subtle transitions from one colour to another.

One of the most important things to remember is that you need to make your clouds look like solid, three-dimensional forms, not just wispy trails of vapour in the sky. Clouds have a top, a bottom and a side. The top usually faces the sun and is therefore lighter than the side and the bottom. Before you start painting, work out which direction the light is coming from so that you can decide which areas of cloud are in shadow and need to be darker in tone.

Make sure that any changes in tone are very gradual. You can soften colours where necessary by lifting off paint with a piece of kitchen paper or a sponge, but try to avoid hard edges at all costs.

The rules of perspective that apply to painting land also apply to painting the sky, and clouds that are further away will appear smaller than those that are immediately overhead. They will also be lighter in tone.

In this project, dramatic banks of cumulus cloud before an evening storm are the focus of interest and the land below is almost an irrelevance. Although the land is so dark that relatively little detail is visible, it is an important part of the picture, as it provides a context for the scene and an anchor for the painting as a whole. In any landscape, the sky must relate to the land beneath and so you need to continually assess the tonal balance between the two.

Materials

- *2B pencil*
- *140lb (300gsm) rough watercolour paper*
- *Watercolour paints: yellow ochre, cadmium lemon, sap green, raw umber, ultramarine blue, cadmium yellow, Prussian blue, cadmium red, burnt sienna, alizarin crimson, viridian*
- *Brushes: medium round, fine round, large wash*
- *Kitchen paper*

The original scene

This is a dramatic and unusual sky. Although the clouds and rainbow provide the main focus of interest, the low-angled early evening sunlight picks out enough detail on the land to relieve the monotony of the dark foreground.

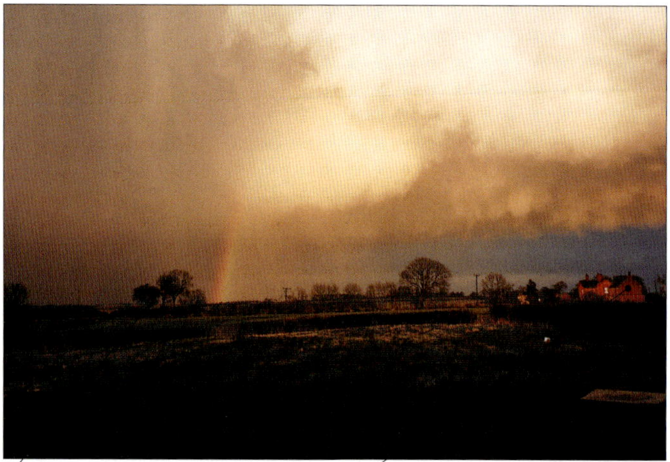

Silhouetted tree shapes provide a visual link between sky and ground.

Low-angled sunlight picks out the house and a patch of the foreground field.

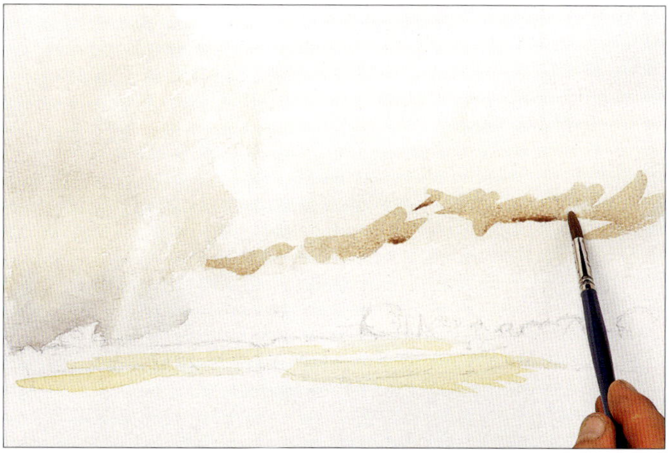

1 Using a 2B pencil, outline the tree shapes on the horizon. Mix a very pale wash of yellow ochre and, using a medium round brush, loosely brush it over the sky, leaving gaps for the lightest areas. Mix cadmium lemon and sap green and brush the mixture over the lightest areas of the fields. Mix a dilute wash of dark brown from raw umber and a touch of ultramarine blue and brush it on to the clouds in the top left of the picture. Add more ultramarine blue to the brown mixture and brush loose strokes over the base of the clouds on the right.

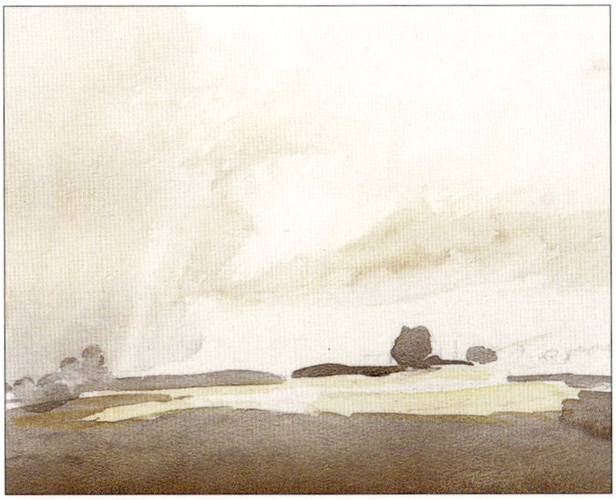

2 While the sky is still damp, add more raw umber to the mixture and brush short calligraphic strokes over the clouds to delineate the lower edges, dabbing some of the paint off with kitchen paper to soften the edges. Mix a dark olive green from cadmium yellow and ultramarine blue and block in the dark areas of the foreground and the silhouetted shapes on the horizon.

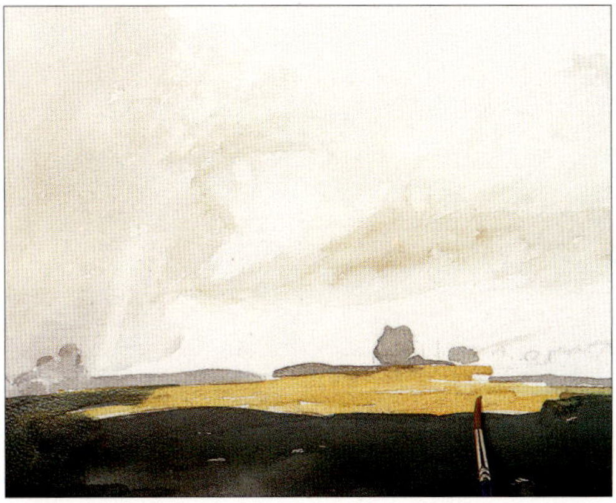

3 While the foreground is still damp, mix a bluish green from cadmium yellow, ultramarine blue and Prussian blue and brush it over the foreground to darken it. Mix a warm yellowish green from cadmium lemon and cadmium red with a little ultramarine and brush the mixture over the brightest areas of the fields, which are illuminated by shafts of low-angled evening sunlight.

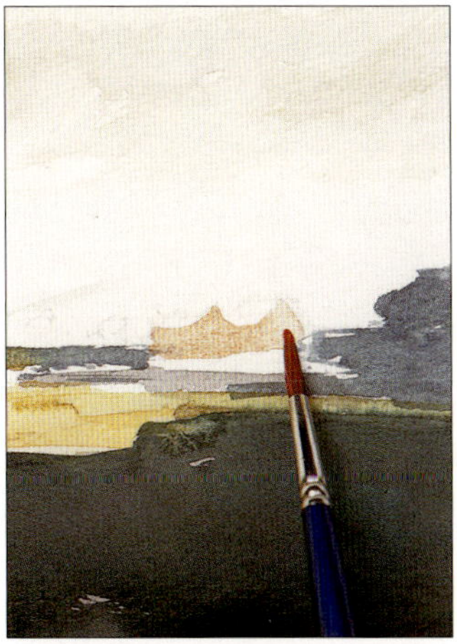

4 Finish blocking in the silhouettes on the skyline. Mix an orangey red from cadmium red and yellow ochre and, using a medium round brush, block in the shape of the distant house.

Tip: The only details you need on the house are the roof and walls. The rules of perspective make further detail, such as windows, unncessary.

Assessment time

With the addition of a hint of blue sky and the dark hedge that marks the boundary between the house and the field, the painting is really starting to take shape. The foreground is very dark, and so the next stage is to work on the sky so that the picture has a better overall balance.

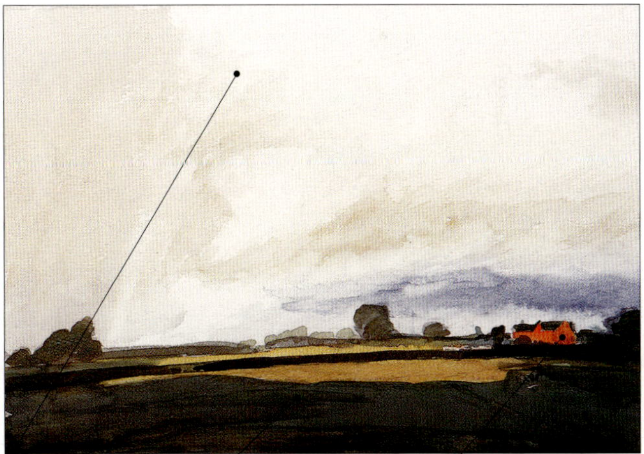

The sky is too pale to hold any interest.

The foreground is oppressively dark; the sky needs to be much stronger to balance it.

Note how the red house immediately attracts the eye, even though it occupies only a small area.

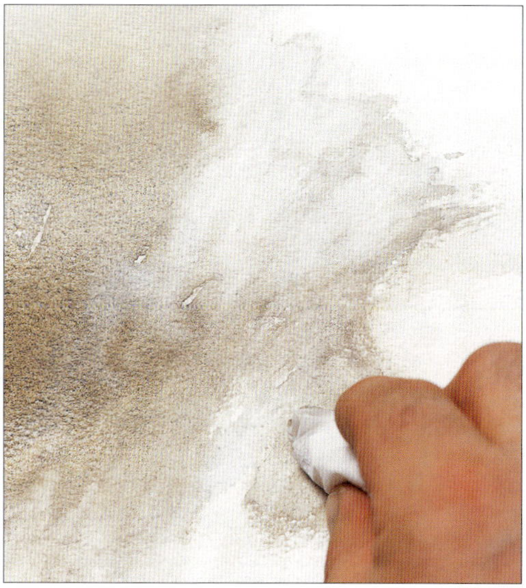

5 Mix a rich, dark brown from ultramarine blue and burnt sienna. Using a large wash brush, loosely scrub it into the left-hand side of the sky, leaving a gap for the rainbow and dabbing off paint with kitchen paper to soften the edges. Note how this creates interesting streaks in the sky.

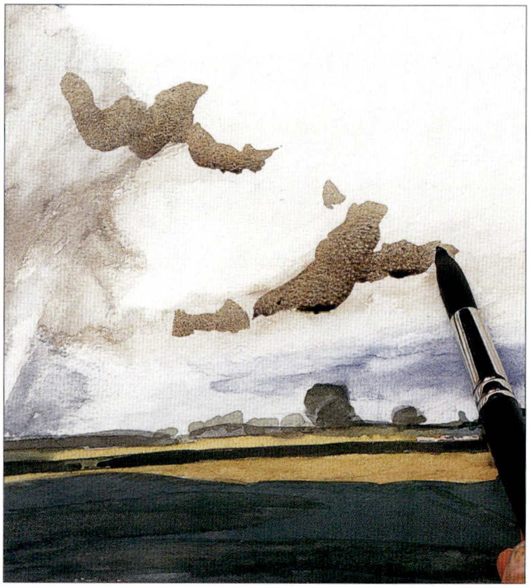

6 Using the same colour, make a series of short calligraphic strokes on the sky at the base of the clouds. The clouds are lit from above, so giving them dark bases helps to establish a sense of form. Brush yellow ochre on to the sky above the dark clouds.

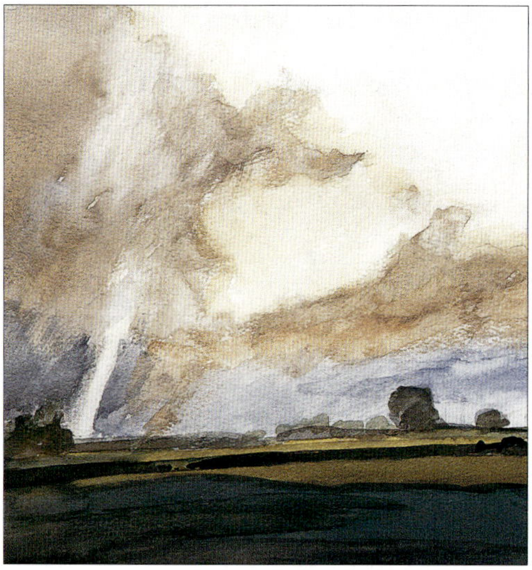

7 Again, dab off paint with kitchen paper to get rid of any obvious brushstrokes and create interesting streaks and wispy textures in the clouds. The clouds should look as if they are swirling overhead, their brooding presence dominating the entire scene.

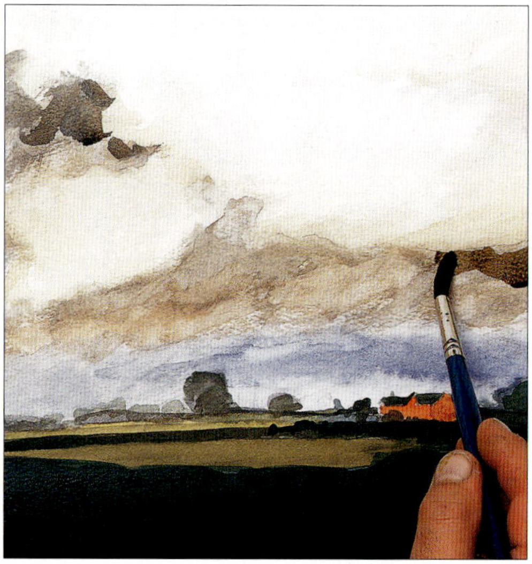

8 Using a darker version of the mixture, darken the clouds again so that the sky has more impact. You need to continually assess the tones in a painting like this, as an alteration to one area can disrupt the tonal balance of the painting as a whole.

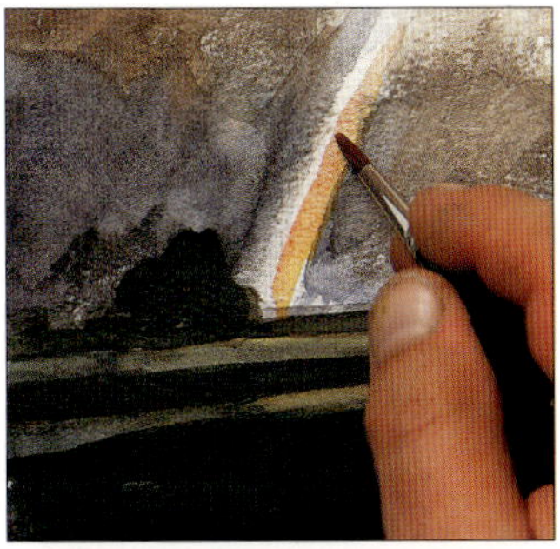

9 Finally, paint the rainbow, using a very fine round brush and long, confident strokes. There is no distinct demarcation between one colour and the next, so it doesn't matter if the colours merge. If you do want to boost any of the colours, allow the paint to dry and then strengthen the colours with a second application.

Storm clouds and rainbow
This is a bold and dramatic interpretation of glowering storm clouds. In the sky, the paint is applied in thin, transparent layers, softened in places by dabbing off paint with kitchen paper, and the white of the paper is allowed to show through, creating a wonderful feeling of luminosity. The land below, in contrast, is solid and dark and forms a complete counterpoint to the rapidly moving clouds above.

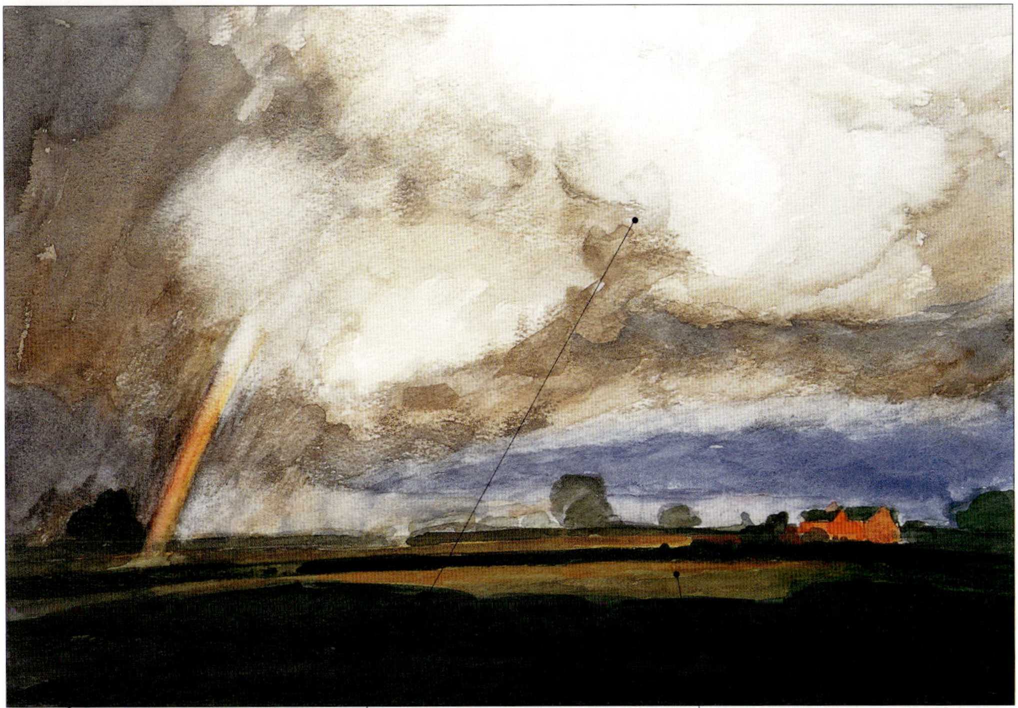

Successive layers of colour applied quite thickly in the foreground create a feeling of solidity.

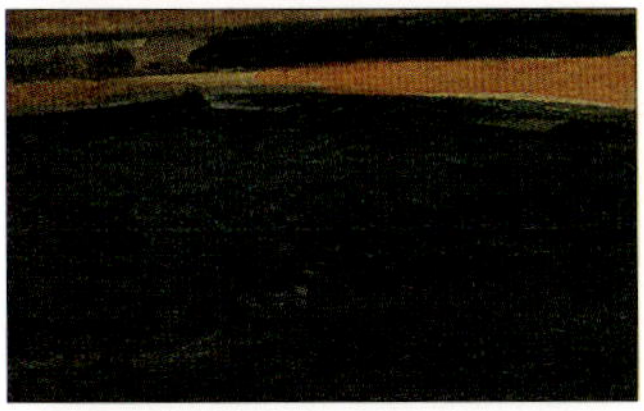

The clouds have an airy texture, achieved by applying the paint wet into wet and then dabbing it off with kitchen paper.

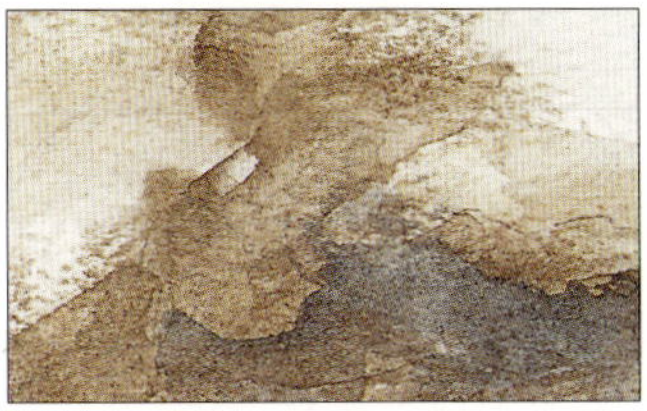

A shaft of warm, evening sunlight leads the viewer's eye across the painting.

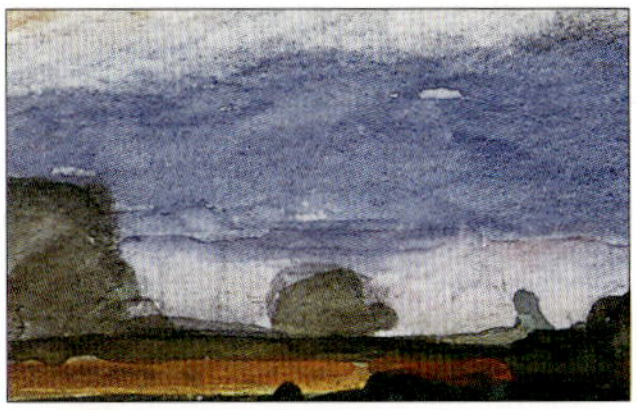

Painting Water

Watercolour is, by its very nature, the perfect material for painting water. Its fluidity and transparency, and its habit of puddling, pooling and generally behaving in an unpredictable way, are characteristics that can be used to great effect.

The colour and appearance of water are heavily influenced by the predominant weather conditions, the reflected colours and shapes in the environment, and the colours of any rocks, sand or vegetation seen beneath the surface. The sea is blue because it reflects the sky, for example, while a pond deep in the woods looks deep and foreboding because it reflects the dark foliage of the surrounding trees.

Several watercolour techniques are particularly suited to painting water. Broad wash techniques, using as large a brush as possible, should be used to paint large expanses of water. Washes can be worked wet on wet to suggest subtle colour changes, or wet on dry to suggest wave or ripple shapes or reflected objects and colours.

Broken colour techniques using a dry brush dragged across rough paper give the impression of ripples or dappled sunlight. Scraping back into wet paint, using a cut-off piece of card or one of the purpose-made rubber paint shapers, is a particularly good way of representing ripples, especially on smooth, hot-pressed paper. Highlights in the water can be created by scratching back to reveal white paper or by applying masking fluid prior to making any washes.

Tips: • Always follow the rules of perspective. Waves of equal size will appear smaller the further away from you they are, while colour becomes less intense and cooler and detail is less evident.

• Note how objects in the water are slightly distorted due to the way light waves are refracted. The colours of objects reflected in water are generally less intense and more subdued than the colours of the objects themselves.

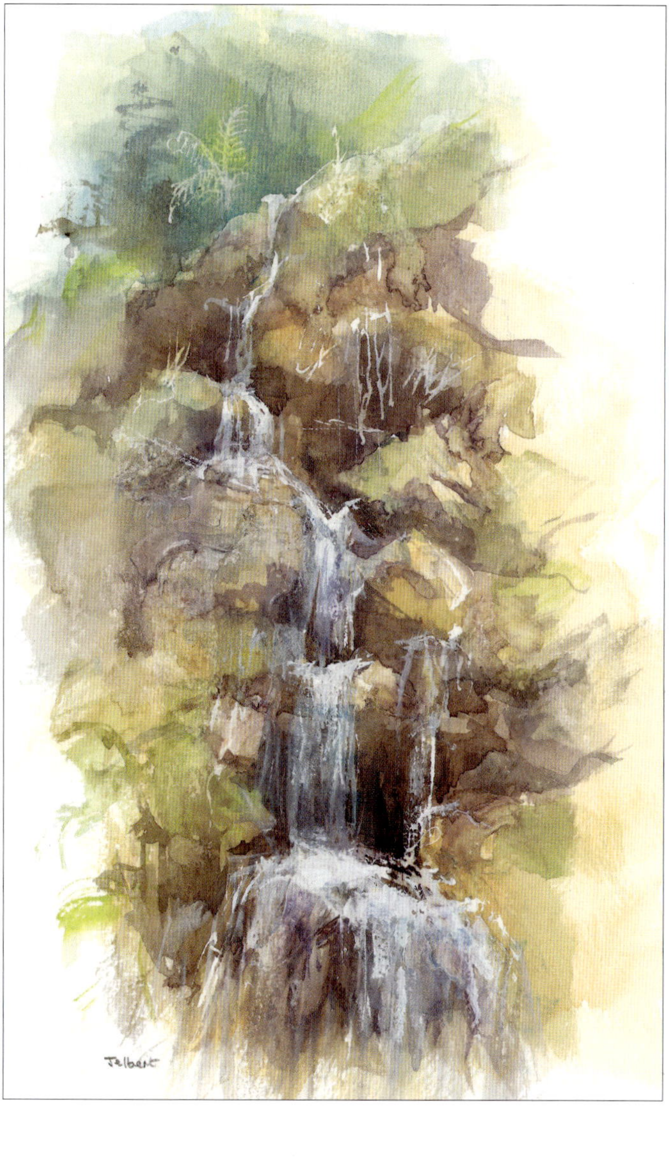

◄ **Waterfall**
White body colour was applied using a mixture of fluid wash and drybrush techniques to capture the light catching on the falling water as it tumbles over rocks and boulders. The stones and boulders were painted using a texture paste to give them added form.

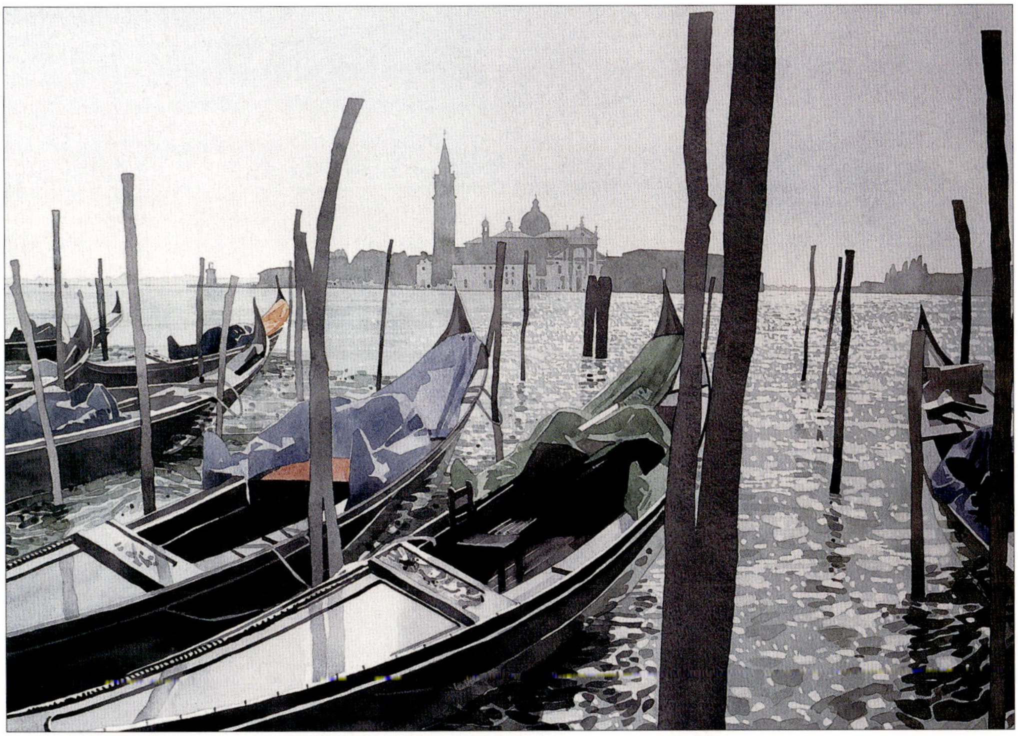

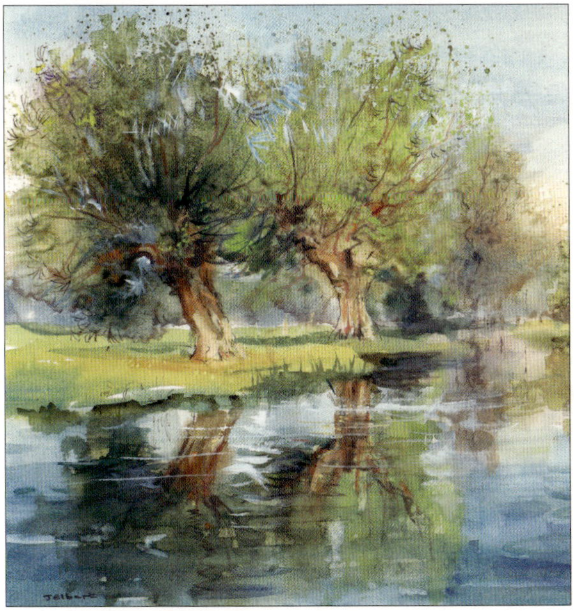

8 a.m, Venice Lagoon ▲

This painting, made as the early-morning light highlighted the ripples on the water, uses carefully applied wet-on-dry washes. The dappled sunlight on the water surface was created by applying masking fluid prior to making any washes. Colours were kept crisp and clean by using no more than three overlapping washes. Note how the ripples conform to the laws of perspective by getting smaller as they get closer to the horizon.

◄ Willows

Wet-into-wet washes lay the foundation and general shape of the reflections of these riverside trees. Wet-on-dry washes define the shapes further, while a little linear brush and coloured pencil work hint at a slight breeze rippling the almost still surface.

Tip: Choose a surface to complement the subject. A rough sea will look rougher if painted on a rough-surface paper, while a smooth, hot-pressed paper is ideal for a painting of a tranquil, mirror-like pond.

Woodland waterfall

Waterfalls offer particular challenges to watercolour artists. Not only do you have to paint a liquid that lacks any real colour of its own but takes its colour from its surroundings, but you also need to make that liquid look wet and convey a sense of how quickly it is moving.

As always, the key is to try to convey an overall impression, rather than get caught up in attempting to recreate life, and paint every single water droplet and leaf. Before you start painting, and even before you make your first preliminary sketch, stop and think about what it is that appeals to you in the scene. Is it the intensity of the rushing water or the sunlight sparkling on the water surface? Is the waterfall itself the most important feature or are the surroundings just as interesting? This will help you to decide on the main focus of interest in your painting – and armed with this knowledge, you can decide how best to tackle the painting as a whole.

In real life, all your senses come into play: you can hear the water cascading down and feel the dappled sunlight on your face. In a painting, however, you have to convey these qualities through visual means alone. Sometimes this means you need to exaggerate certain aspects in order to get the message across – making the spray more dramatic, perhaps, or altering the composition to remove distracting features or make interesting ones more prominent.

Materials

- *B pencil*
- *Tracing paper*
- *140lb (300gsm) NOT watercolour paper, pre-stretched*
- *Watercolour paints: cadmium lemon, phthalocyanine green, Payne's grey, burnt sienna, phthalocyanine blue, alizarin crimson*
- *Brushes: large round, fine round, medium wash, old brush for masking fluid*
- *Masking fluid*
- *Low-tack masking tape*
- *Drawing paper to make mask*
- *Household candle*
- *Gum arabic*

The original scene

Although the scene is attractive, the lighting is flat and the colours dull. Here, the artist decided he needed to increase the contrast between light and shade. To do this, you need to carefully work out which areas will be hit by light from above and which will be in shadow. He also increased the size of the pool below the waterfall: paradoxically, the waterfall itself has more impact if it is surrounded by calmer areas.

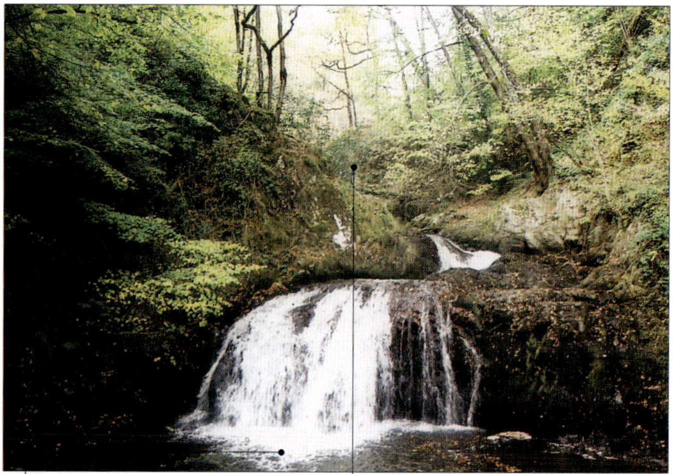

The waterfall ends too near the bottom of the frame.

The colours are very subdued. Increasing the contrast between light and shade will make the painting more interesting.

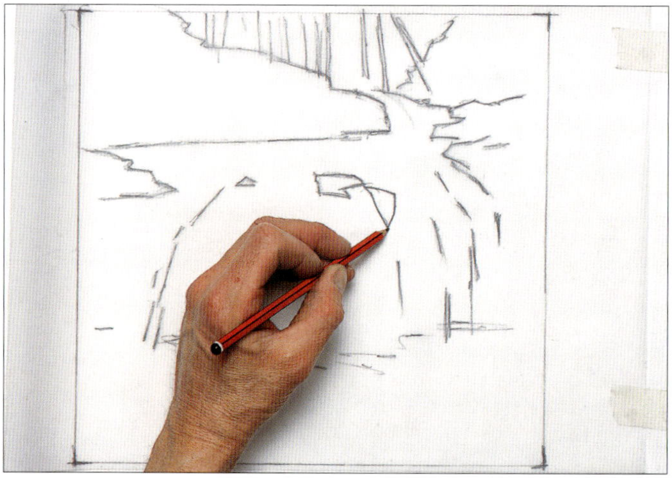

1 Using a B pencil, make a sketch on tracing paper to establish the main lines of your subject and work out the size and shape of your painting. When you are happy with the result, transfer your tracing on to pre-stretched watercolour paper.

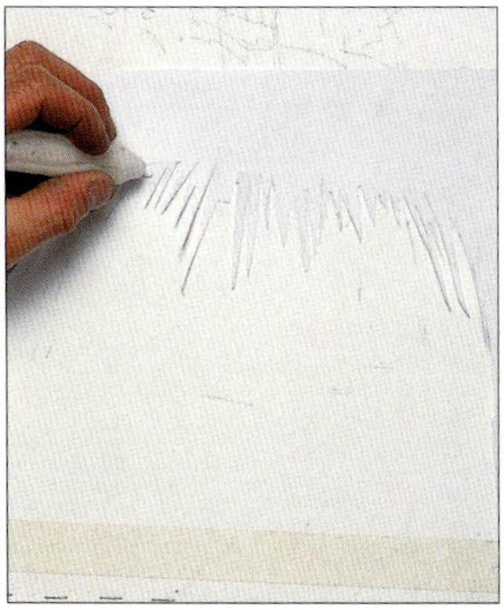

2 Place a sheet of white drawing paper between the watercolour paper and the tracing paper and draw around the waterfall area. Cut out the shape of the waterfall and place it in position on the watercolour paper as a mask, fixing it in place with low-tack masking tape. Gently rub a household candle over the area of water below the waterfall, keeping the strokes very loose. This will preserve some of the white of the paper and add an interesting texture.

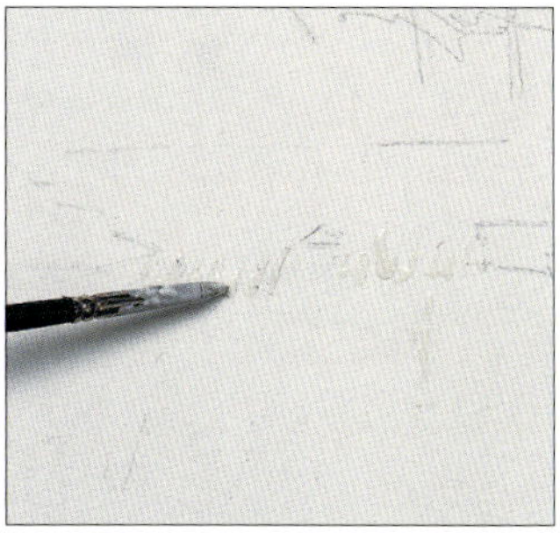

3 Using an old brush, apply masking fluid over the white lines of the waterfall. Leave to dry.

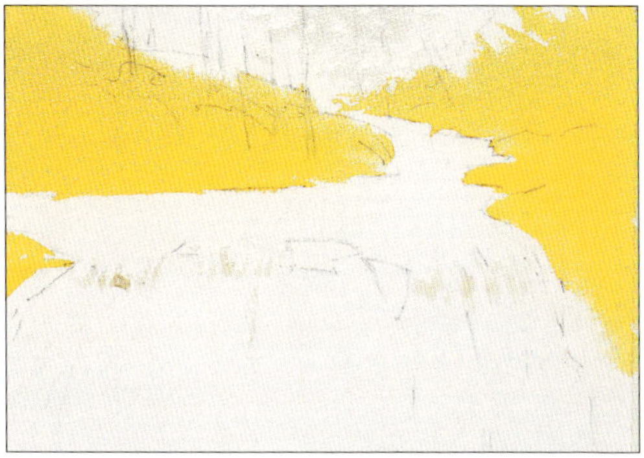

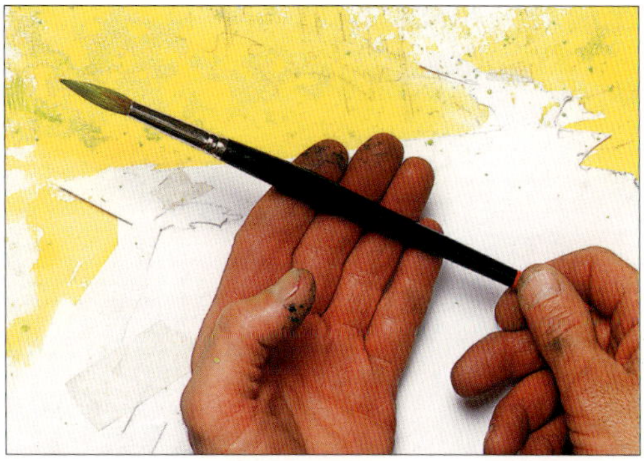

4 Apply masking fluid to the bright highlight area of sky at the top of the picture area and leave to dry. Using a large round brush, brush clean water over the trees. Mix a strong wash of cadmium lemon and brush it over all the damp areas. Leave to dry.

5 Mask off the water area with paper. Mix a mid-toned green from cadmium lemon and a little phthalocyanine green. Holding a fine round brush at the same angle at which the branches grow, spatter water across the top of the picture. Spatter the damp area with green paint. Leave to dry.

6 Continue spattering first with water and then with the green mixture of phthalocyanine green and cadmium lemon, as in Step 5, until you achieve the right density of tone in the trees. Leave each application of spattering to dry completely before you apply the next one.

> **Tip**: Spattering clean water on to the paper first, before you spatter on the paint mixture, means that the paint will spread and blur on the wet paper. If you spatter the paint on to dry paper, you will create crisply defined blobs of colour – a very different effect.

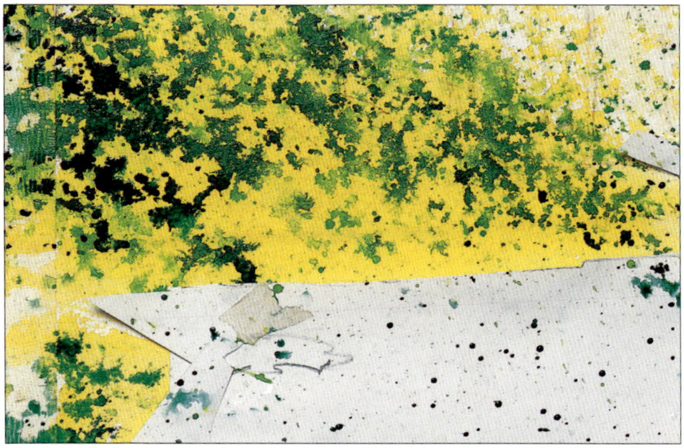

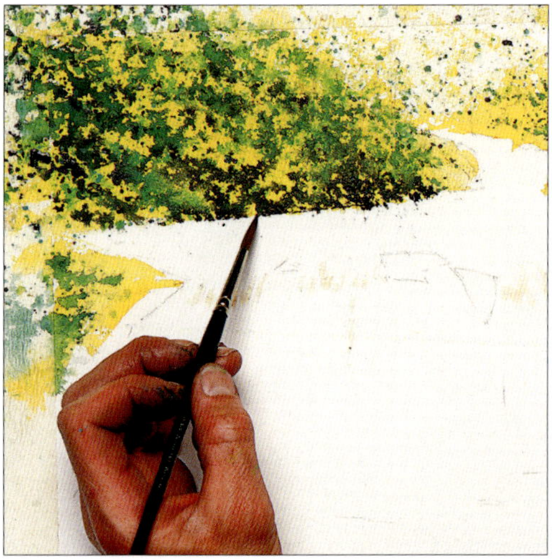

7 Add Payne's grey to the phthalocyanine green and cadmium lemon mixture and, using a fine brush, put in the very dark tones along the water's edge in order to define the edge of the river bank.

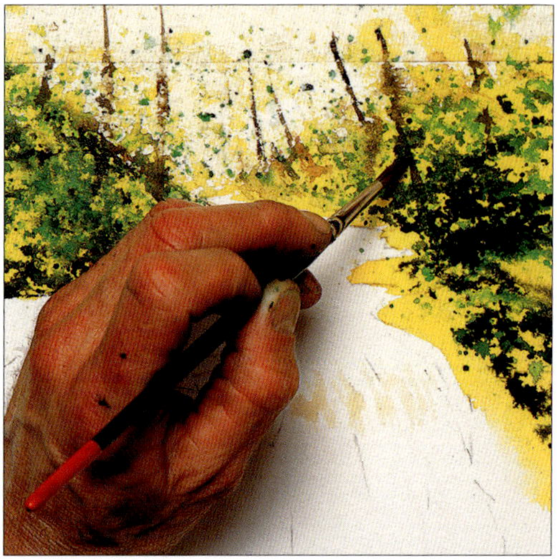

8 Using a fine brush, brush burnt sienna between the leaves adjoining the dark spattered areas. Mix a rich brown from burnt sienna and Payne's grey and paint the tree trunks and branches. Leave to dry.

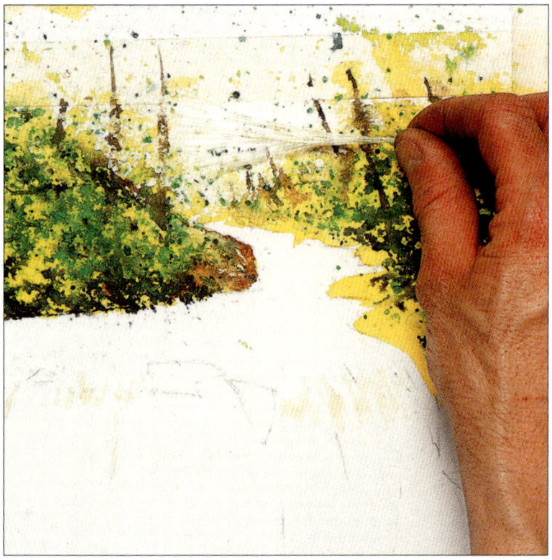

9 Using your fingertips, gently rub and peel the masking fluid off the sky area. The sky area is very bright in comparison with the rest of the scene, and so it is important to reserve these light areas in the early part of the painting – even though they will be toned down very slightly in the later stages.

Assessment time

The surrounding woodland is now almost complete. Before you go any further, make sure you've put in as much detail as you want here. The water takes its colour from what's reflected in it. Because of this it is essential that you establish the scenery around the waterfall before you begin to put in any of the water detail.

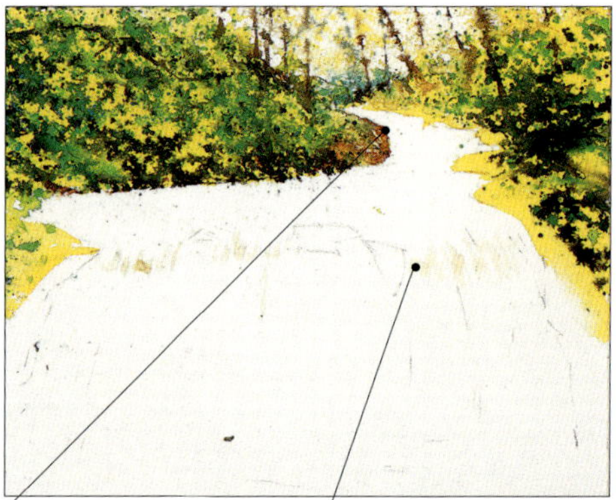

The line of the riverbank is crisply painted, establishing the course of the river.

The rocks in the waterfall have been marked in pencil, providing an underlying structure for the scene.

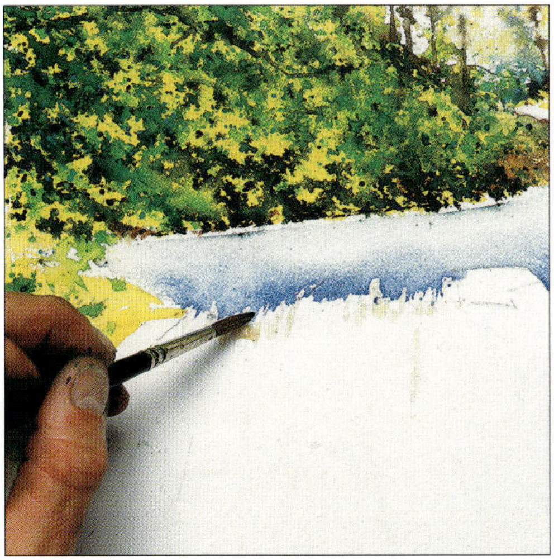

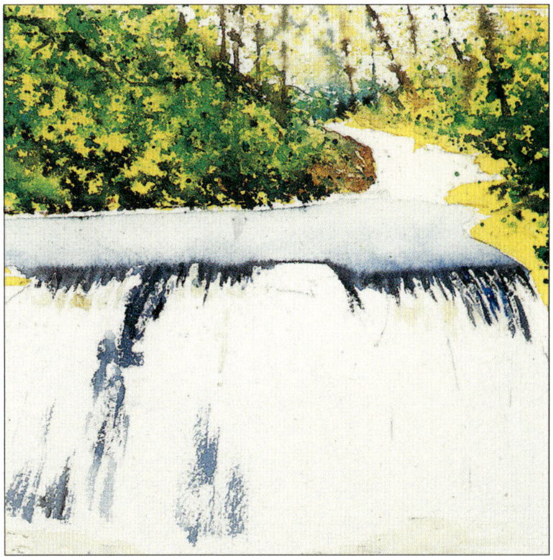

10 Using masking fluid, mask the long strokes of white that cascade down from the waterfall into the pool below. Leave to dry. Using a medium wash brush, brush clean water horizontally across the top of the water above the waterfall. Brush a little gum arabic on to the damp area. Keeping the brush fairly dry in order to control the colour, brush vertical strokes of phthalocyanine blue mixed with a little alizarin crimson and burnt sienna on to the damp area.

11 Brush straight lines of Payne's grey across the top of the waterfall to denote the edge over which the water topples. Mix Payne's grey with phthalocyanine blue and brush on to the waterfall itself, using a drybrush technique. On the lower part of the fall, make the marks longer and rougher to indicate the increased speed of the water. Leave to dry.

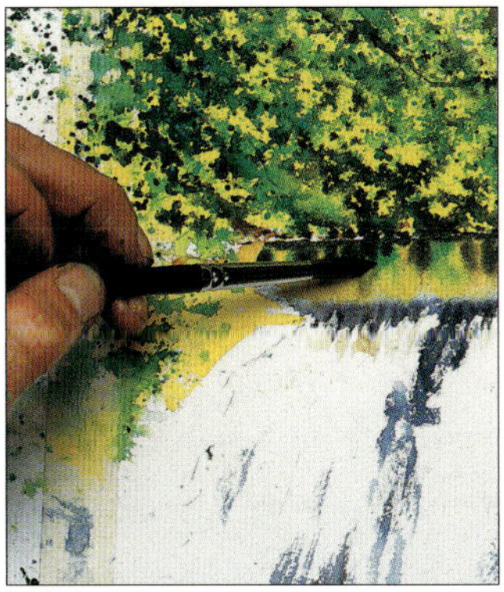

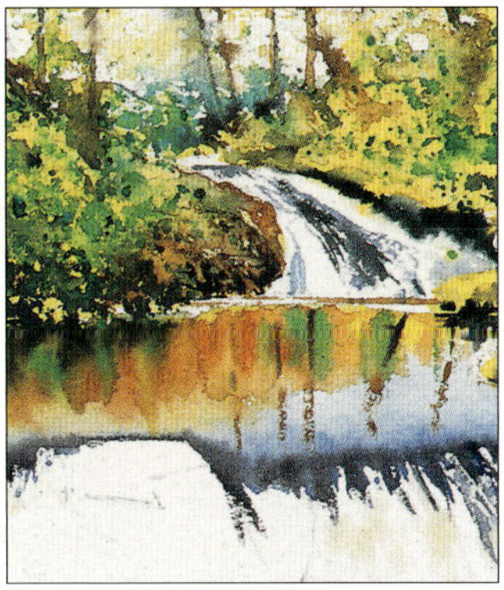

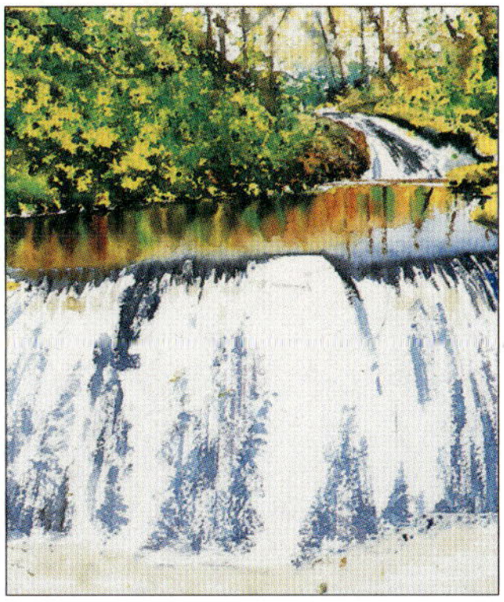

12 Re-wet the pool above the fall. Using a fine, round brush, touch cadmium lemon into the damp area. Dab on vertical strokes of cadmium lemon, burnt sienna, and phthalocyanine green for the tree trunk reflections. The colours will merge together and the fact that they are blurred helps to convey the wetness of the water.

13 Brush burnt sienna mixed with Payne's grey on to the cascade of water than runs into the pool.

> **Tip**: By applying clean water to the surface before you paint, the strokes diffuse and blur, giving soft blends rather than hard-edged streaks of colour.

14 Working from the bottom of the waterfall upwards, brush a mixture of Payne's grey and phthalocyanine blue into the waterfall. Note how the texture of the candle wax shows through. Keep the brush quite dry, dabbing off excess paint on kitchen paper, if necessary. Add a little alizarin crimson to the mixture for the darker water at the base of the fall.

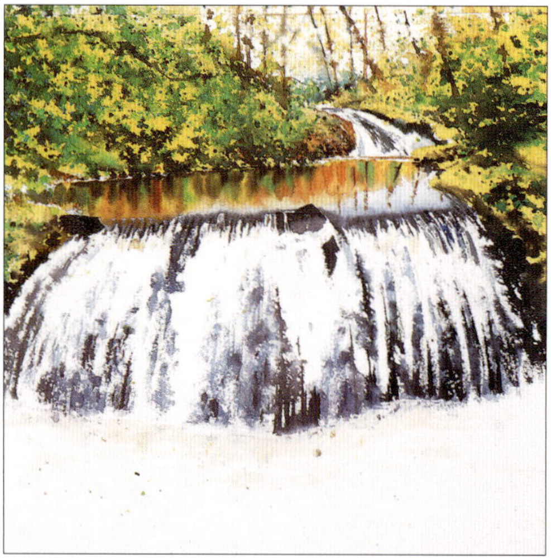

15 Paint the rocks under the waterfall in a mixture of Payne's grey, phthalocyanine blue and a little alizarin crimson. Use the same mixture to paint more rocks poking up through the foam of the water. Drybrush water along the left and right edges of the painting and apply the rock colour – again with an almost dry brush. The paint will spread down into the damp area.

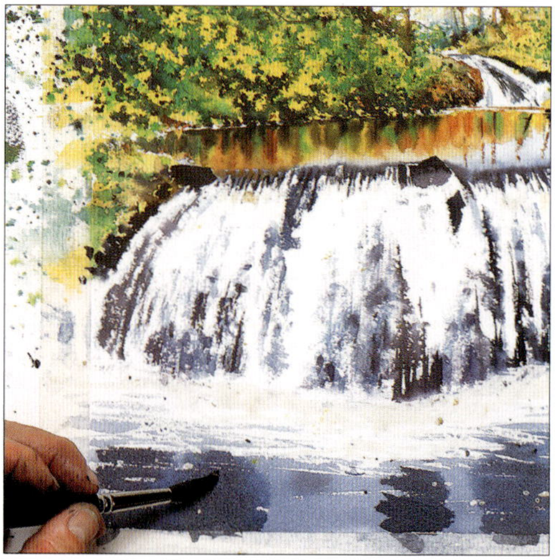

16 Stipple little dots of masking fluid on to the base of the pool below the waterfall for the white bubbles of foam. Leave to dry. Apply a light wash of phthalocyanine blue mixed with a little Payne's grey over the pool below the waterfall, brushing the paint on with loose, horizontal strokes. While the paint is still damp, run in a few darker vertical lines of the same mixture. Leave to dry.

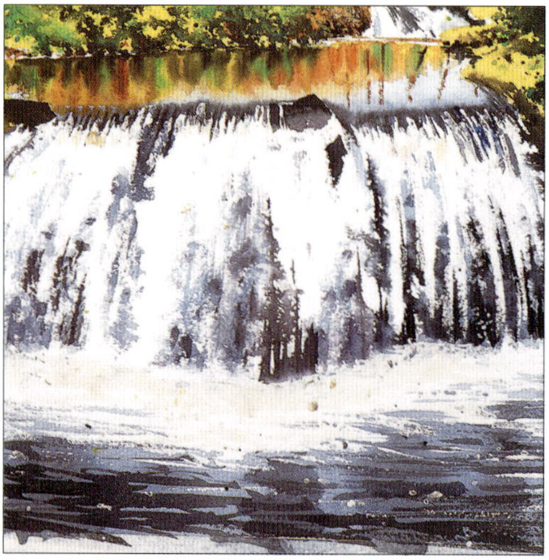

17 Using a large brush and a darker version of the phthalocyanine blue and Payne's grey mixture, paint the dark area at the base of the pool with bold, zigzag-shaped brushstrokes. Leave to dry.

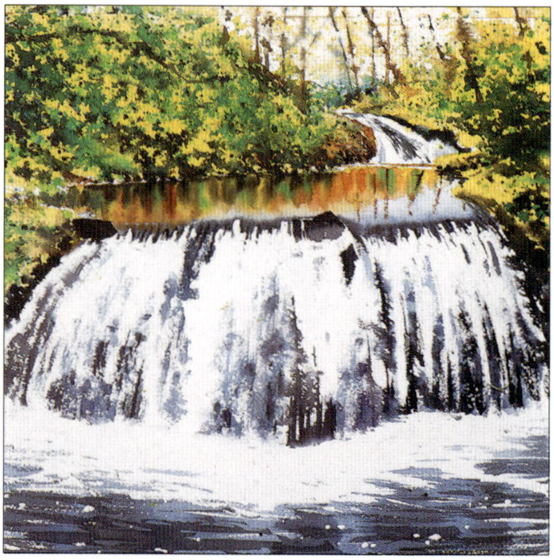

18 Using your fingertips, gently rub off the masking fluid on the lower half of the painting. Stand back and assess the tonal values of the painting as a whole. If the exposed area looks too white and stark, you may need to touch in some colour in the water areas to redress the overall balance of the scene.

Woodland waterfall

This is a very lively rendition of a waterfall in full spate, which conveys the mood and atmosphere of the scene rather than capturing every leaf and twig in painstaking detail. Much of the paper is left white, in order to convey the full force of the rushing water. The painting has a stronger feeling of light and shade than the original photo, and hence more impact.

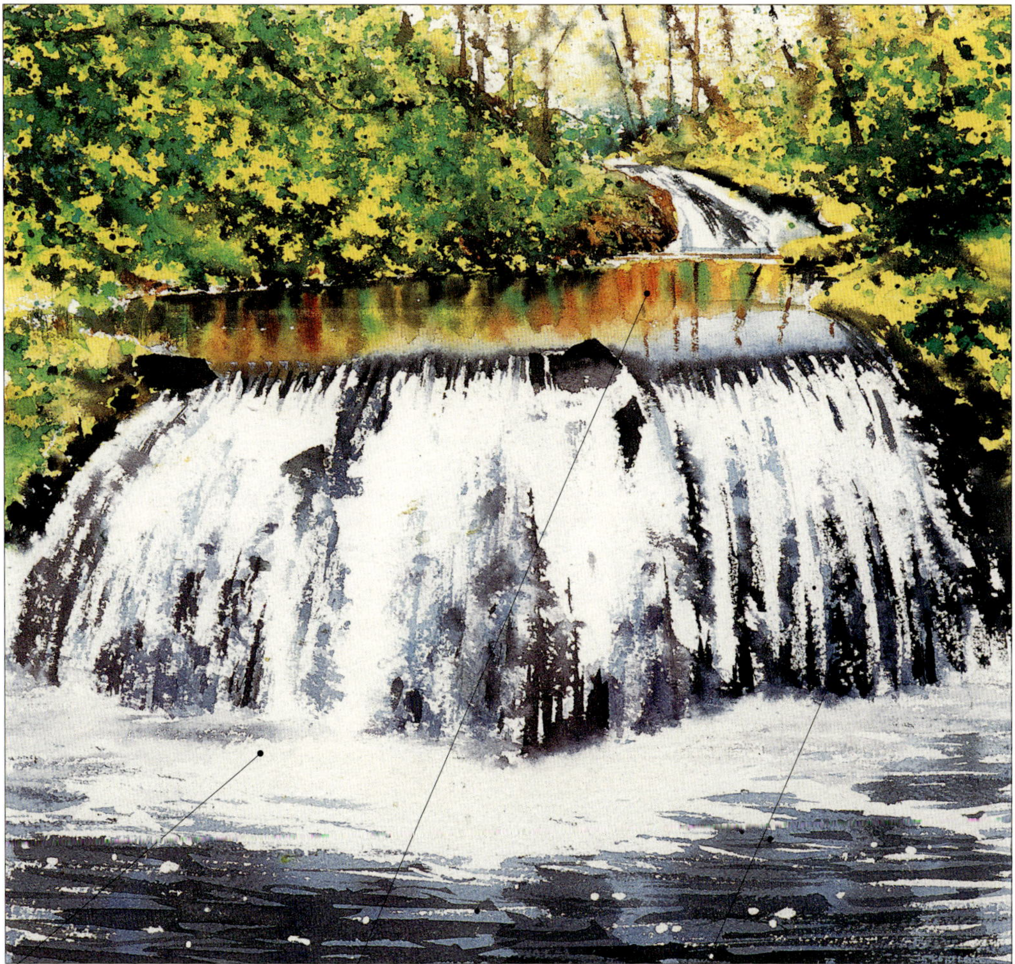

The white of the paper conveys the cascading, foaming water.

Skilful use of the wet-into-wet technique has allowed colours to merge on the paper, creating realistic-looking reflections.

Longer brushstrokes in the lower part of the waterfall help to create an impression of movement in the water.

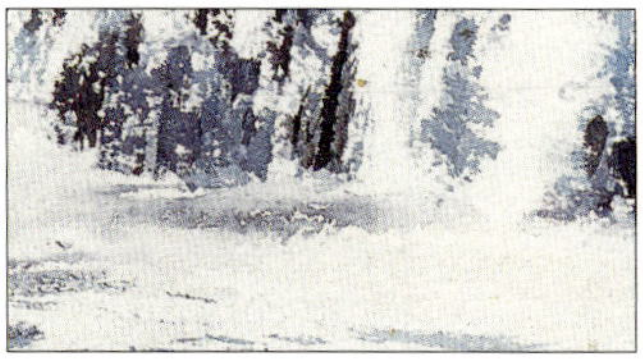

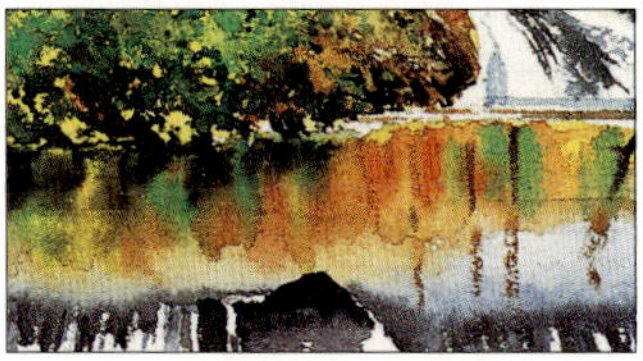

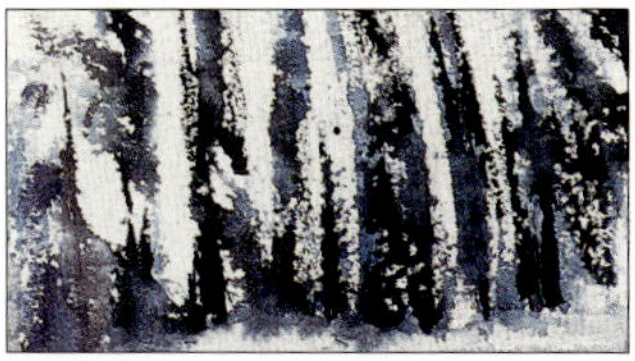

Crashing waves

This project depicts a massive sea wave just as it is about to break over craggy rocks. Your challenge is to capture the energy and power of the scene.

Few people would go as far in their search for realism as the great landscape artist J.M.W. Turner, who is reputed to have tied himself to a ship's mast in order to experience the full force of a storm at sea. Fortunately, there are easier and less perilous ways of adding drama to your seascapes.

The first thing to think about is your viewpoint. Construct your painting as if you are viewing the scene from a low viewpoint, so that the waves seem to tower above you.

For maximum drama, capture the waves while they are building or when they are at their peak, just before they break and come crashing down. You can gauge the height of the waves by comparing them with nearby rocks or clifftops, while including such features in your painting will provide you with both a focal point and a sense of scale.

Try to attune yourself to the sea's natural rhythms. Watch the ebb and flow of the waves and concentrate on holding the memory of this rhythm in your mind as you are painting. This will help you to capture the energy of the scene.

Finally, remember that water takes its colour from objects in and around it. You may be surprised at how many different colours there are in a scene like this.

Materials

- *4B pencil*
- *140lb (300gsm) NOT watercolour paper, pre-stretched*
- *Watercolour paints: Payne's grey, phthalocyanine blue, cadmium yellow, lemon yellow, Hooker's green, cerulean blue, yellow ochre, raw sienna, sepia, violet, burnt sienna, cobalt blue*
- *Gouache paints: permanent white*
- *Brushes: medium round, fine round*
- *Mixing or palette knife*
- *Fine texture paste*
- *Ruling drawing pen*
- *Masking fluid*
- *Sponge*

The original scene

It is notoriously difficult to photograph a breaking wave at exactly the right moment, and so the artist used this photograph merely to remind herself of the energy of the scene and the shapes and colours.

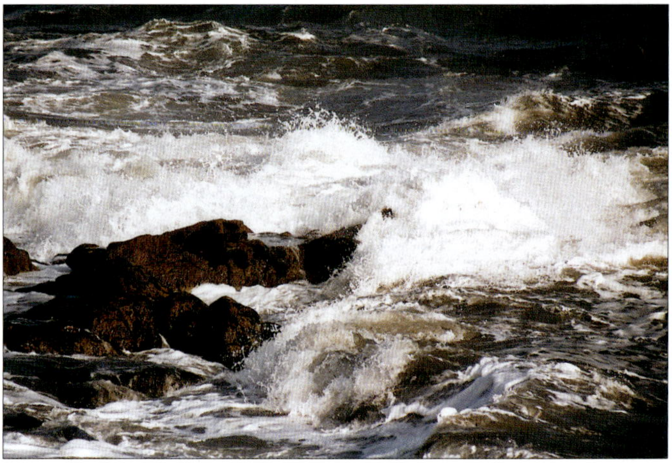

Reference sketches

Tonal sketches are a very good way of working out the light and dark areas of the scene. You will find that it helps to think of the waves as solid, three-dimensional objects, with a light and a shaded side. Try several versions so that you get used to the way the waves break over the rocks.

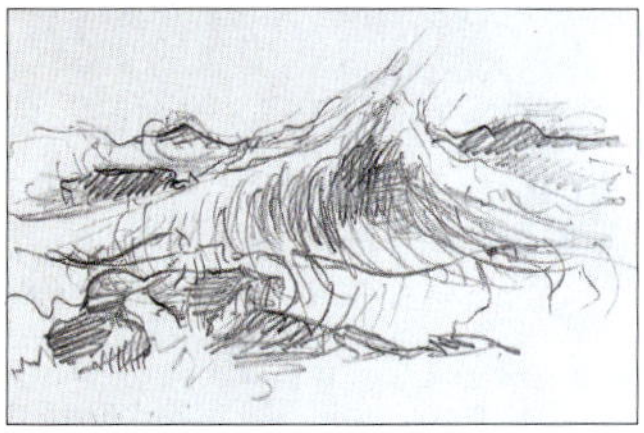

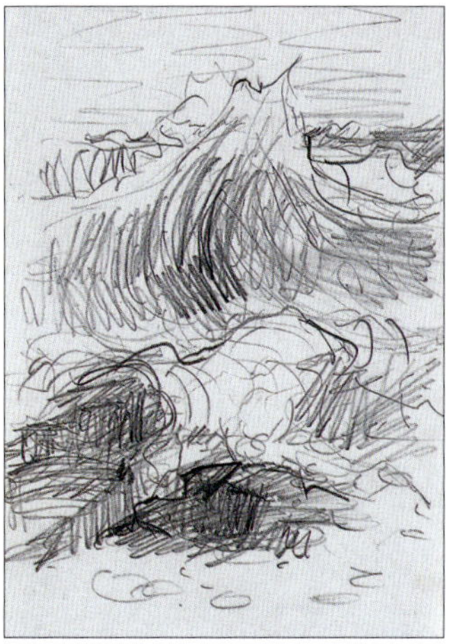

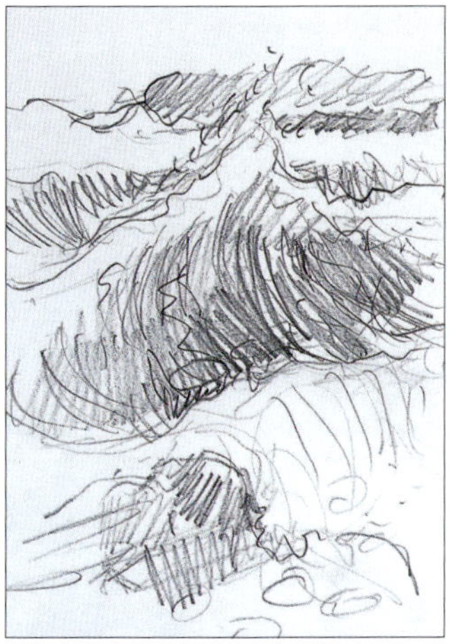

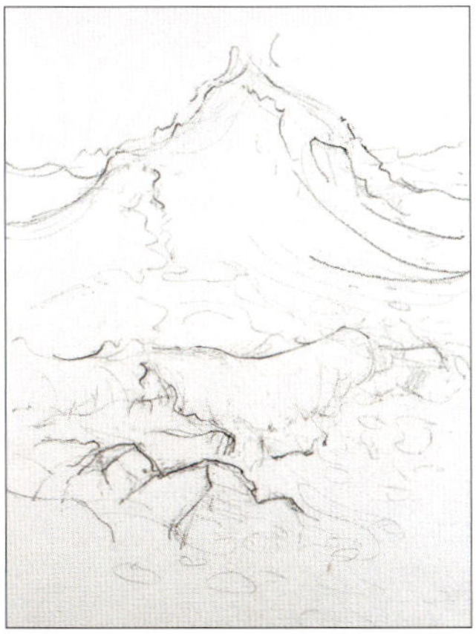

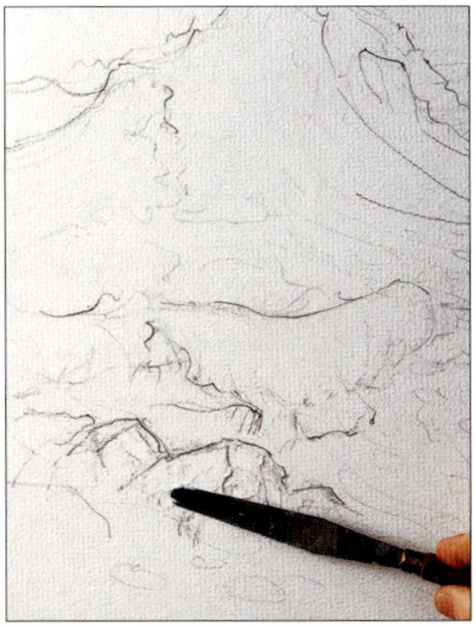

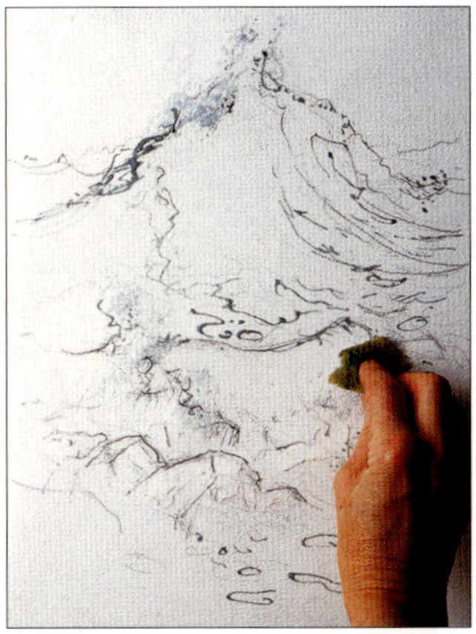

1 Using a 4B pencil, lightly sketch the scene, putting in the foreground rocks and the main waves. Take time to get the angles of the waves right: it is vital that they look as if they are travelling at speed and are just about to come crashing down.

2 Using a palette knife, apply fine texture paste over the rocks. Leave to dry. (Texture paste is available in several grades; the coarser it is, the more pronounced the effect. Here, the wave is more important than the rocks, so fine texture paste is sufficient).

3 Using a ruling drawing pen, apply masking fluid over the crest of the main wave and dot in flecks and swirls of foam in the water. Using a small sponge, dab masking fluid on to selected areas of the sea to create softer foamy areas. Leave to dry.

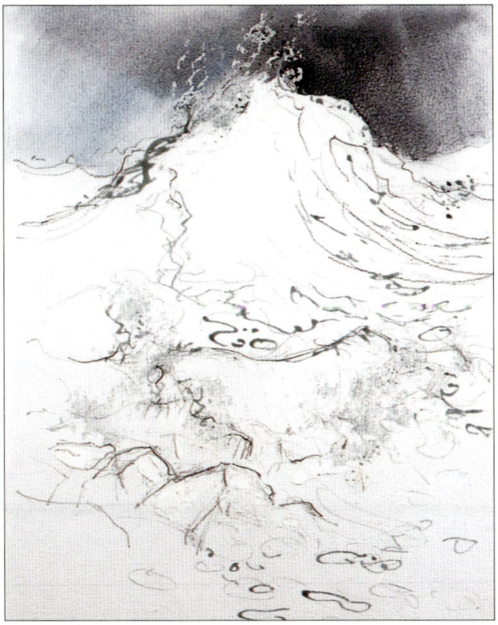

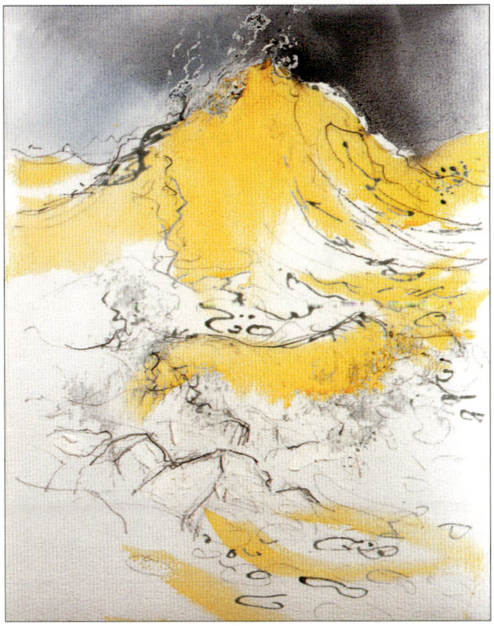

4 Mix a mid-toned wash of Payne's grey and another of phthalocyanine blue. Dampen the sky area with clean water and brush Payne's grey on to the right-hand side and phthalocyanine blue on to the left-hand side. Leave to dry.

5 Mix a strong wash of cadmium yellow with a touch of lemon yellow. Dampen the waves with clean water and lightly brush the bright yellow paint mixture over the tops of the waves.

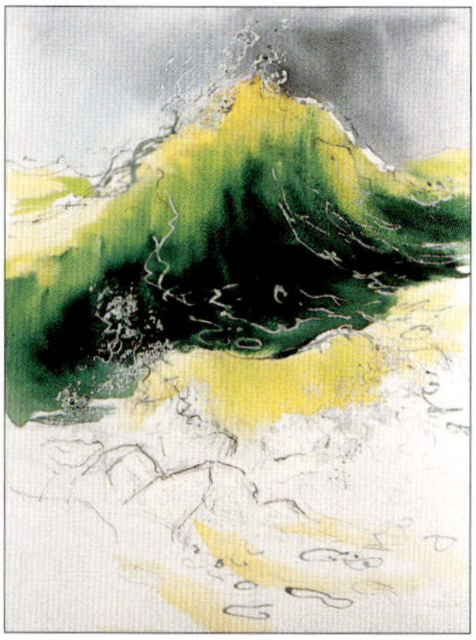

6 While the first wash is still wet, brush Hooker's green into the yellow so that the colours merge together. Mix a darker green from Hooker's green, phthalocyanine blue and a little cadmium yellow and brush this mixture into the lower part of the waves, feathering the mixture up into the yellow so that the colours blend imperceptibly on the paper. Brush over this darker green several times to build up the necessary density of tone.

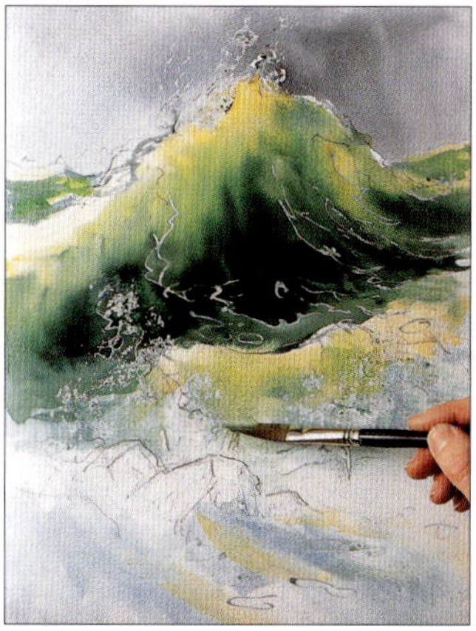

7 Mix a dark blue from phthalocyanine blue and cerulean blue and brush this mixture into the lower part of the large wave, feathering the colour upwards. Because the previous washes are still wet the colours spread and merge together on the paper, building up darker tones without completely blocking out the underlying colours. Use loose, swift brushstrokes and try to capture the energy and power of the sea.

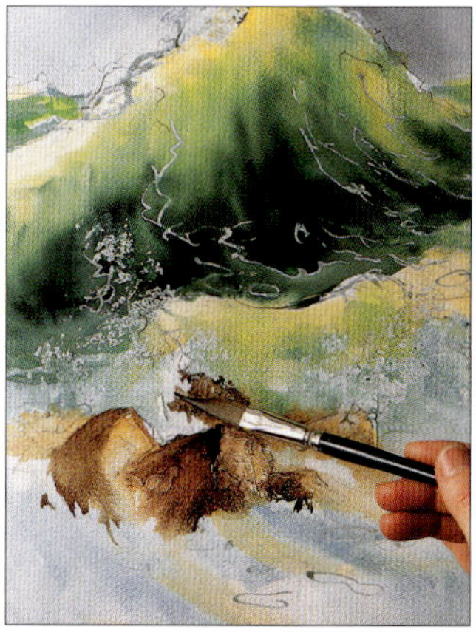

8 Mix a mid-toned wash of yellow ochre and brush it over the texture paste on the rocks, adding raw sienna and sepia for the dark foreground.

Tip: Allow the colour to "drift" into the sea so that it looks as if the sea is washing over the rocks. Unless you do this the rocks will simply look as if they are floating on the water.

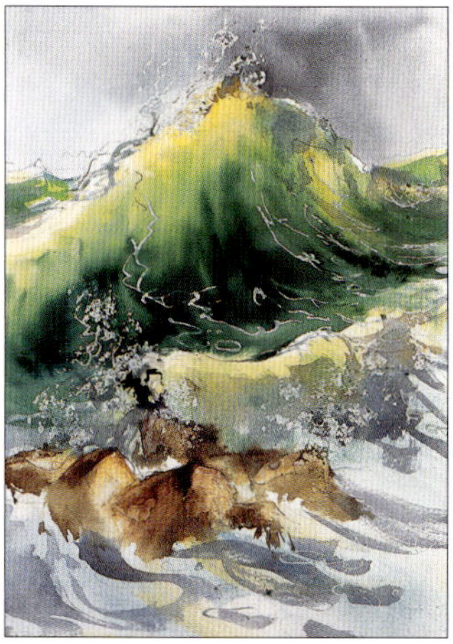

9 Mix a greyish blue from violet and Hooker's green. Brush little touches of this colour into the waves and into the pools at the base of the rocks, making swirling brushstrokes to help convey the movement of the water.

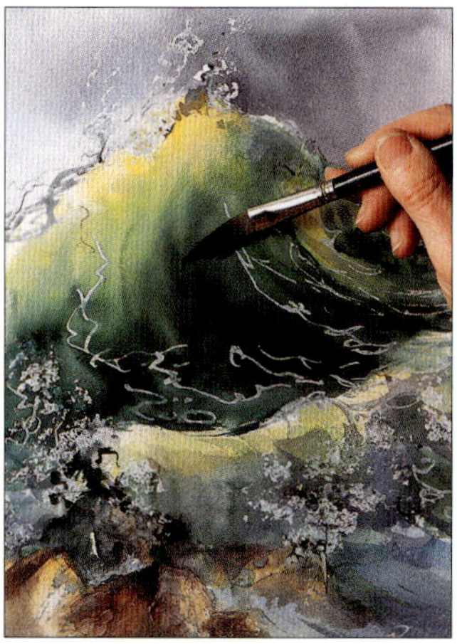

10 Using the dark green mixture from Step 6 and the brown used on the rocks, put a few dark accents into the waves. Soften the brushstrokes by brushing them with clean water to blend them into the other wave colours.

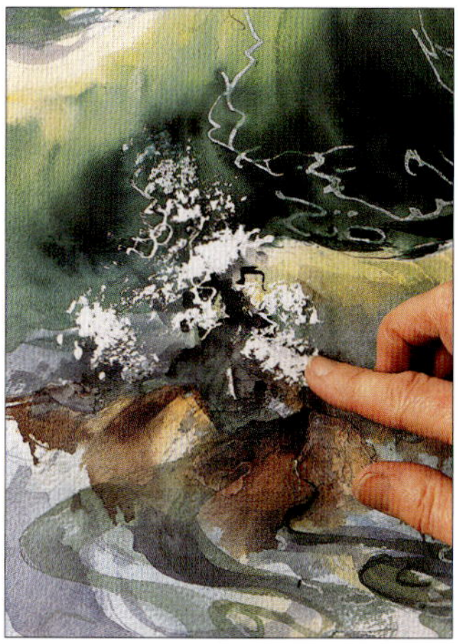

11 When you are sure that the paint is completely dry, gently rub off the masking fluid with your fingertips to reveal the foaming crests of the waves and the spattered highlights on the water.

Assessment time

Now that all the masking fluid has been removed, you can see how effectively the white of the paper has been reserved for the swirls and flecks of foam in the sea. However, these areas now look glaringly white and stark: they need to be toned down so that they become an integral part of the scene. However, you will need to take great care not to lose the very free, spontaneous nature of the swirling lines or the water will start to look too static and overworked. The contrast between the light and the very dark areas also needs to be strengthened a little in order to give a better feeling of the volume of the waves.

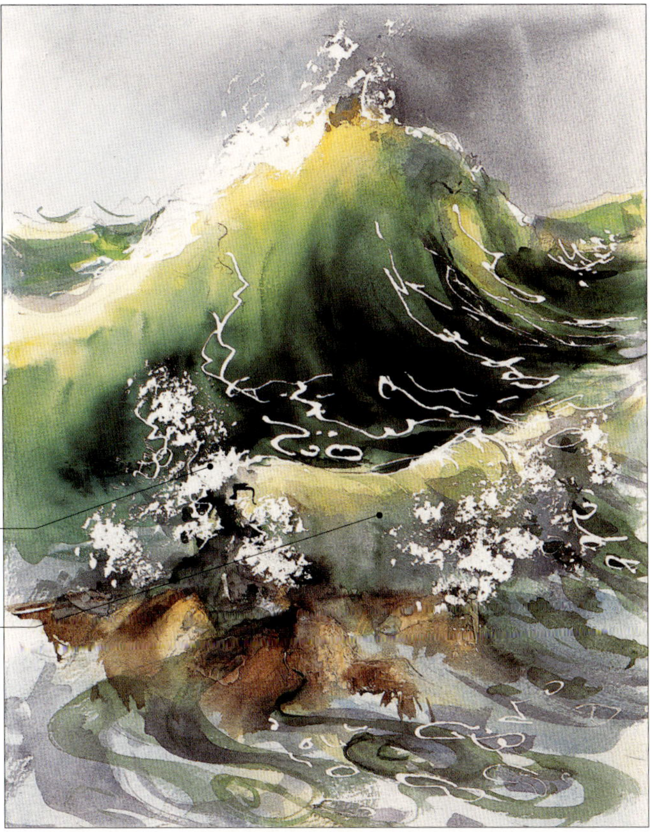

The exposed areas are much too bright.

The colours work well in this area, but there is not enough of a sense of the direction in which the water is moving.

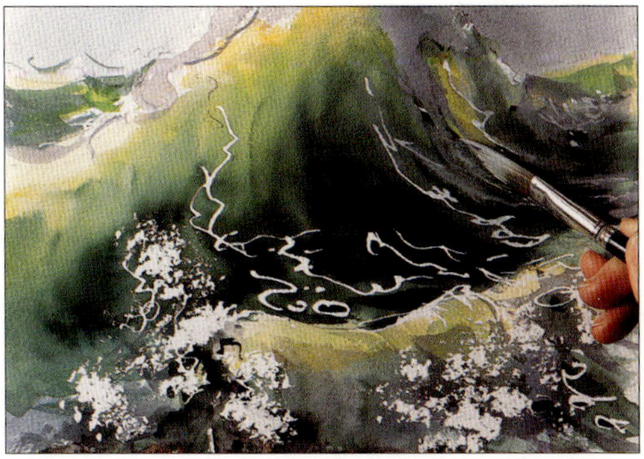

12 Mix an opaque mauve from permanent white gouache, violet and a tiny touch of burnt sienna. Brush this mixture under the crest of the main wave, so that it looks like shadows under the very bright, white foam.

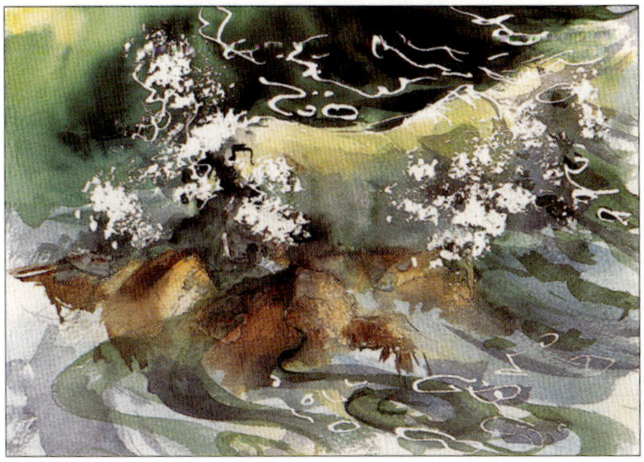

13 The exposed white areas look too stark against the dark colours of the water and rocks. Mix a very pale opaque blue from cobalt blue and permanent white gouache and cover up the exposed swirls of white in the water.

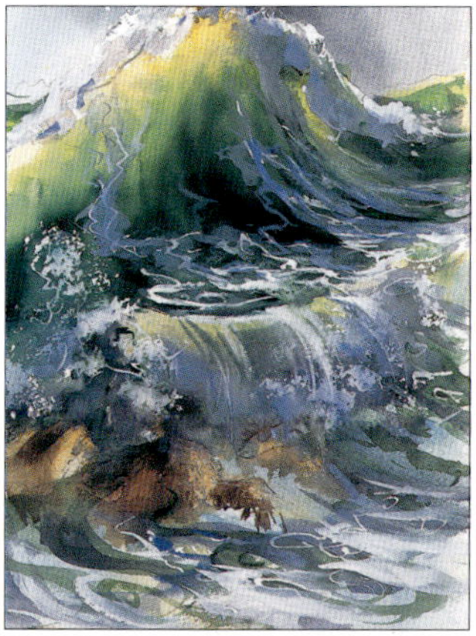

14 Soften the harsh markings by brushing over more of the cobalt blue and gouache mixture. Paint some swirls of white gouache at the base of the main wave. Putting a little opaque colour into the water helps to give it some solidity.

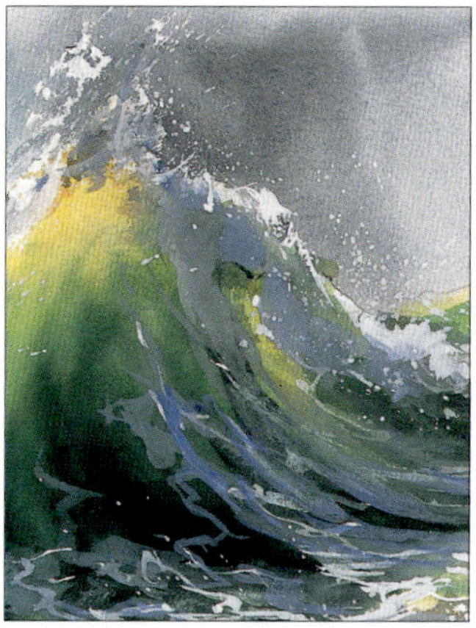

15 Spatter a few specks of white gouache above the crest of the wave for the flecks of foam that fly into the air. Don't overdo it: too much gouache could easily overpower the light, translucent watercolour washes that you've worked so hard to create.

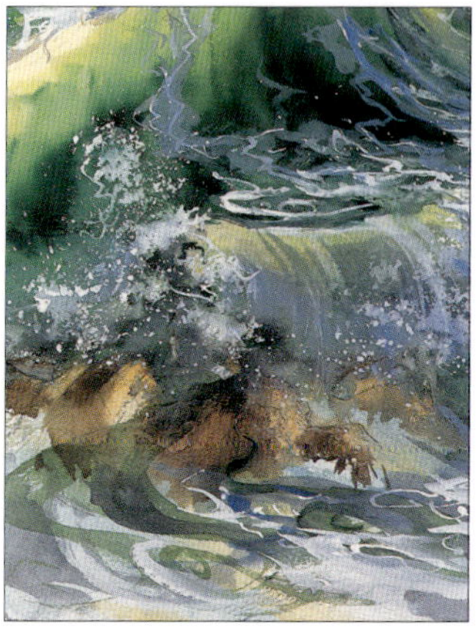

16 Spatter a few specks of the cobalt blue and white gouache mixture above the rocks. (This area is very dark and pure white gouache would look too stark.)

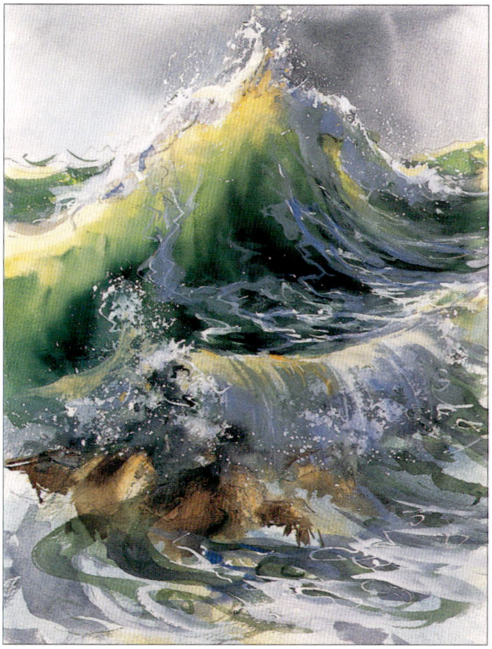

17 Stand back from the painting and assess the tonal values. You may find that you need to darken some of the colours in the centre of the painting.

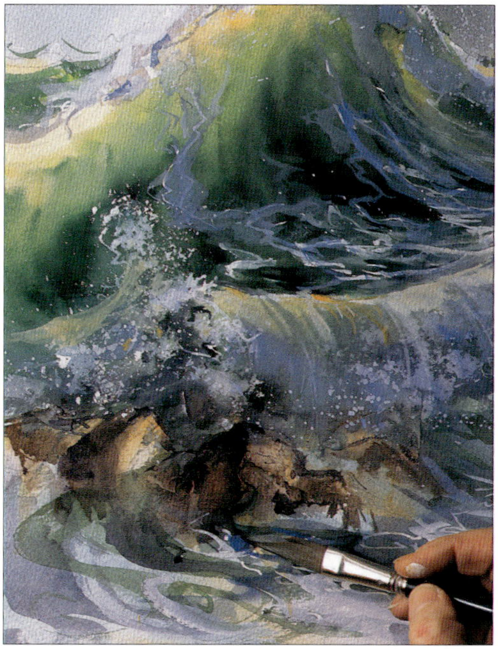

18 Using the same dark brown mixture as before, build up the tones on the rocks. They need to stand out from the water that surrounds them.

Crashing waves

This is a dramatic and carefully observed painting that captures the energy of the scene to perfection. Note the many different tones in the water and the way the brushstrokes echo the motion of the waves. The rocks provide solidity and a sense of scale, but do not detract from the large wave that is hurtling forwards.

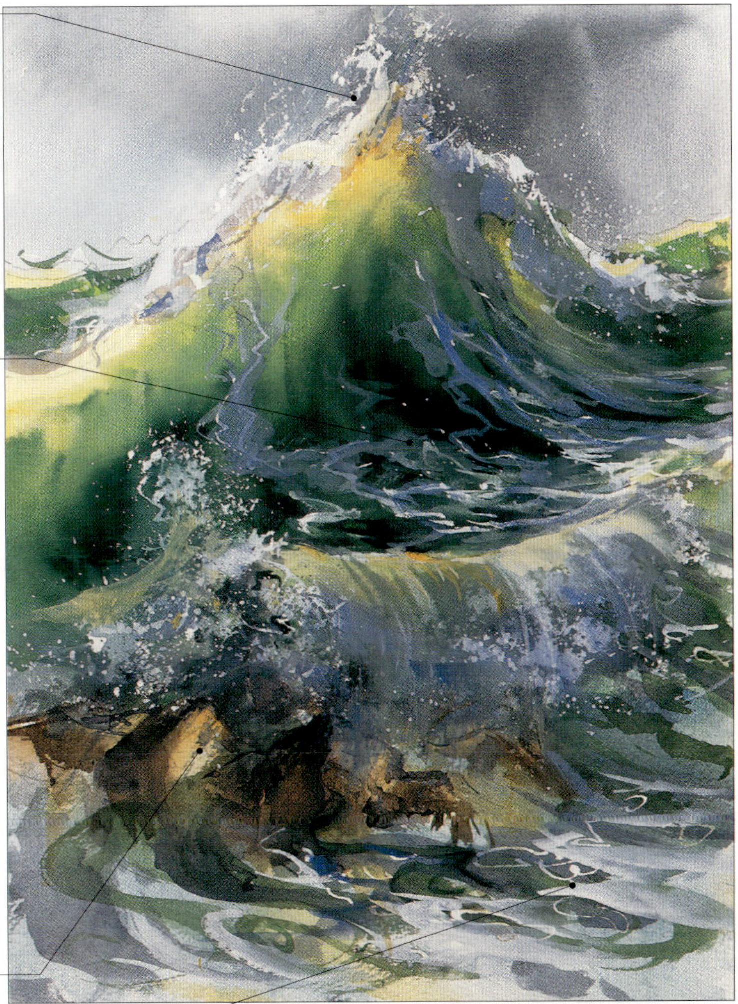

Spattering is the perfect technique for depicting foam-flecked waves.

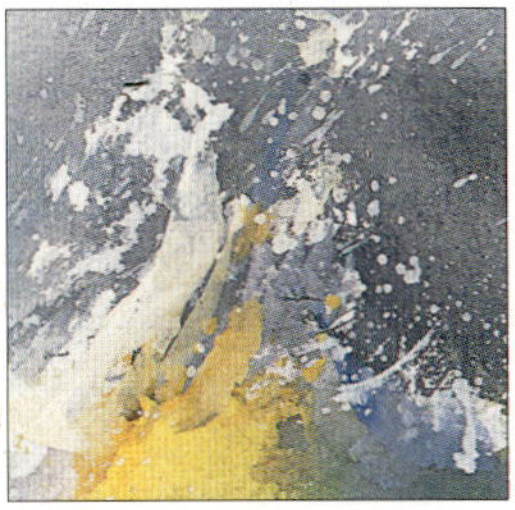

Dark tones in this area contrast with the light edge of the breaking wave and help to give it volume.

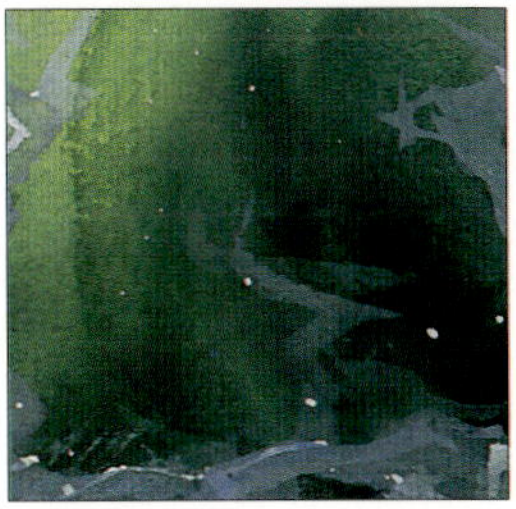

The rocks provide a necessary point of solidity in the scene.

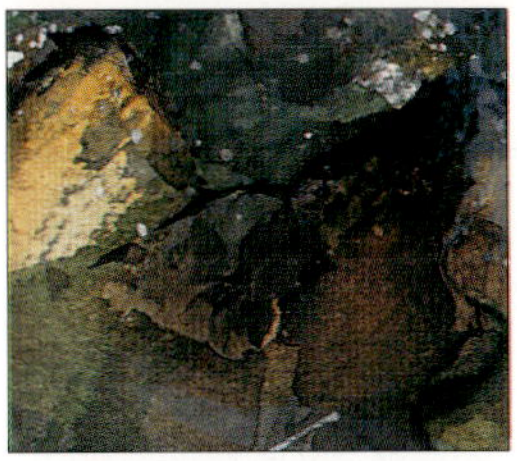

Loose, swirling brushstrokes capture the motion of the sea.

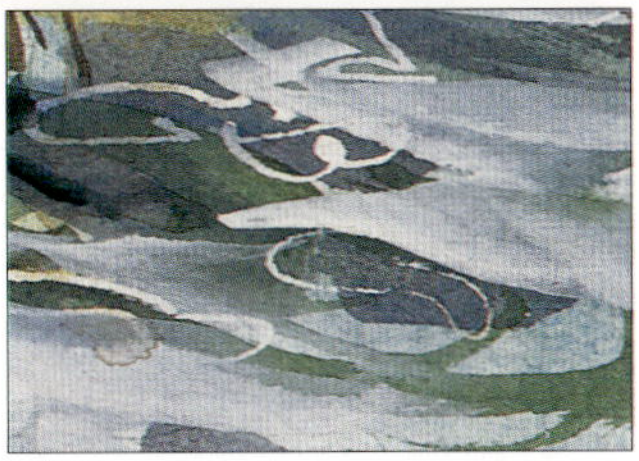

Lake with reflections

Who could resist the bright, sunny colours of this lakeside scene in the heat of the summer, with its reflections of hillsides covered in trees? Any artist would be happy to while away a few hours sketching and painting in such a tranquil setting.

However, straightforward symmetrical reflections can sometimes look a little boring and predictable, so look out for other things that will add interest to your paintings. Sweeping curves, such as the foreshore on the right in this scene, help to lead the viewer's eye through the picture, while interesting textures are always a bonus.

This project also provides you with the challenge of painting partially submerged objects. Here you need to think about the rules of perspective: remember that things look paler and smaller the further away they are. As an added complication, the way that water refracts lights also distorts the shape of submerged objects. Trust your eyes and paint what you see, rather than assuming you know what shape things actually are.

Materials

- *B pencil*
- *Tracing paper*
- *140lb (300gsm) NOT watercolour paper, pre-stretched*
- *Watercolour paints: alizarin crimson, Naples yellow, phthalocyanine blue, phthalocyanine green, burnt sienna, French ultramarine, Payne's grey, quinacridone magenta*
- *Brushes: medium round, fine round, old brush for masking fluid*
- *Masking fluid*
- *Gum arabic*
- *Kitchen paper*

Tip: Leave the tracing paper attached to one side of the watercolour paper, so that you can flip it back over if necessary during the painting process and reaffirm any lines and shapes that have been covered by paint.

The original scene

You can almost feel the heat of the sun when you look at this photograph of a lake in southern Spain. The foreshore and hillside are dry and dusty, while the lake itself appears to be slowly evaporating, exposing rocks in the shallows. Because of the angle at which the photograph was taken, the colours are actually less intense than they were in real life. The artist decided to exaggerate the colours slightly to emphasize the feeling of heat.

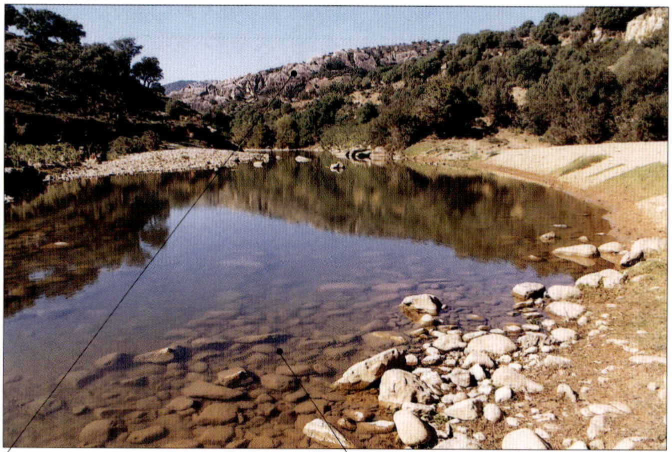

The distant mountains are muted in colour and will benefit from being made more intense in the painting.

Much of the foreground is made up of submerged stones. You could put some exposed stones in this area to add interest.

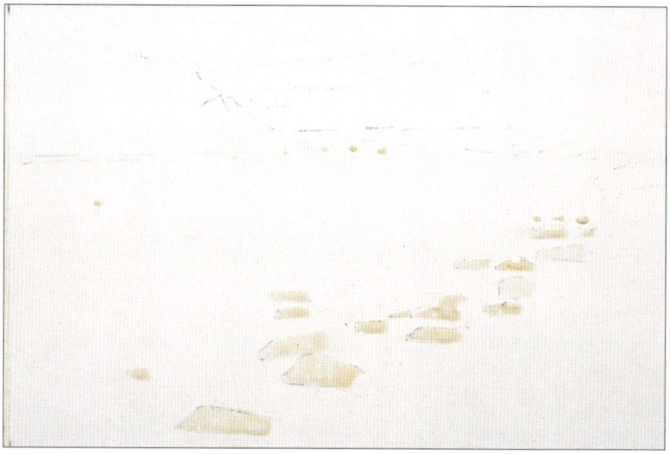

1 Using a B pencil, make an initial sketch on tracing paper to establish the main lines of your subject. When you are happy with the result, trace your sketch on to pre-stretched watercolour paper. Using an old brush, apply masking fluid to some of the large foreground stones. Leave to dry.

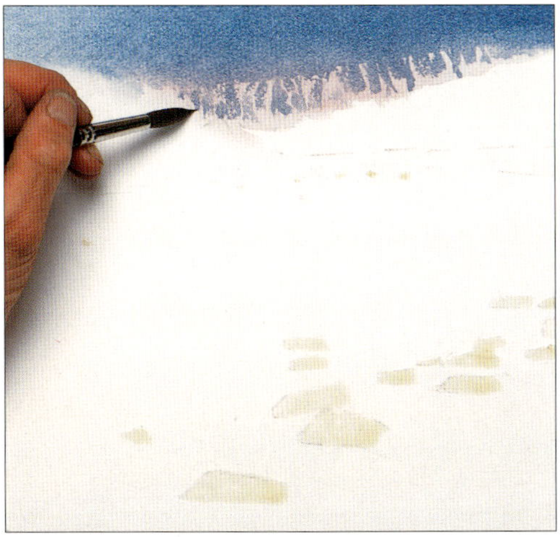

2 Mix alizarin crimson with a little Naples yellow and, using a medium round brush, brush the mixture over the mountains and up into the sky. Leave to dry. Mix a bright blue from phthalocyanine blue and a little phthalocyanine green. Dampen the sky with clear water and, while the paper is still wet, brush on the blue mixture, stopping along the ridge and drawing the colour down into the mountains. Leave to dry.

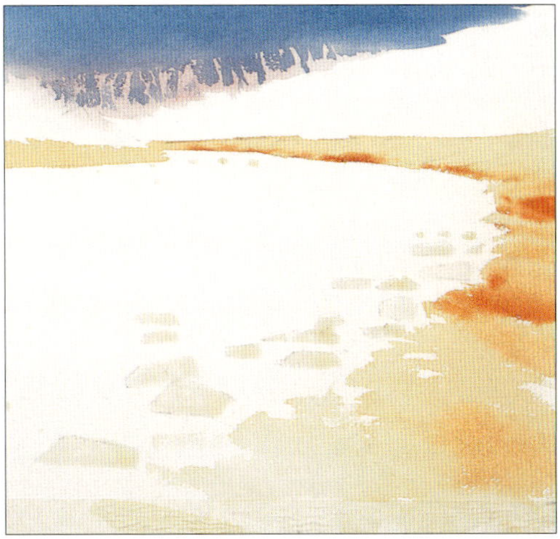

3 Mix a mid-toned orangey brown from Naples yellow and burnt sienna, and paint the dry and dusty foreshore of the lake, dropping in more burnt sienna for the darker areas. Leave to dry.

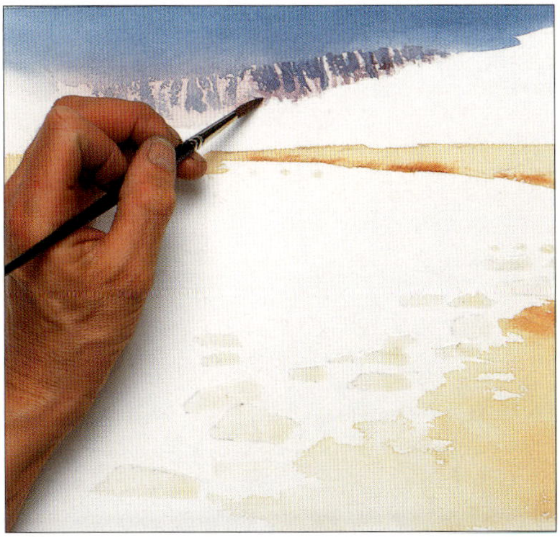

4 Mix a purplish grey from burnt sienna, French ultramarine and alizarin crimson. Using a fine round brush, brush clean water across the mountains and then brush on marks of the grey mixture. Leave to dry.

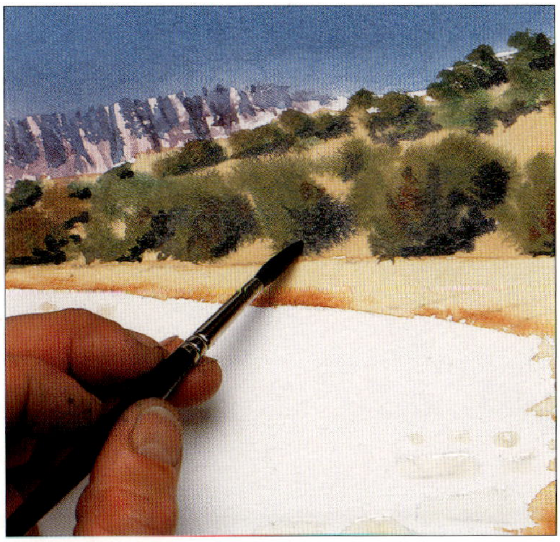

5 Make up more of the burnt sienna and Naples yellow mixture and, using a medium round brush, paint the arid, sandy background on the top right of the painting. While this area is still wet, mix an olive green from phthalocyanine green, burnt sienna and a little Naples yellow and, using a medium round brush, paint in the loose shapes of trees and bushes. Paint the shadow areas in the trees in the same purplish grey mix used in Step 4. Leave to dry.

▶

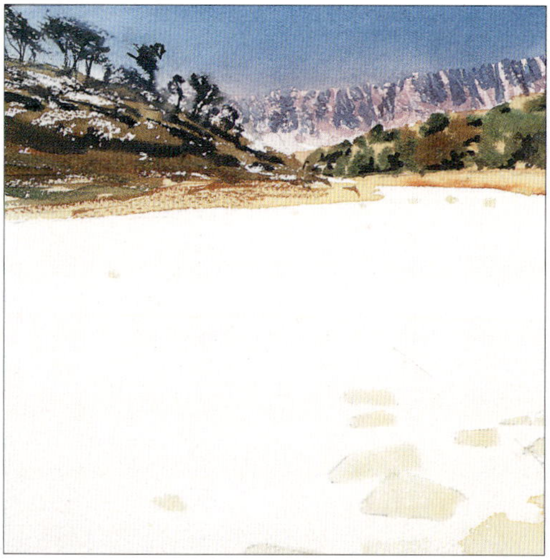

6 Paint more trees on the left-hand side of the painting in the same way. Brush clean water across the sky. Mix Payne's grey with a little phthalocyanine green and, using the tip of the brush, dot this mixture into the damp sky area to denote the trees that stand out above the skyline. The colour will blur slightly. Leave to dry.

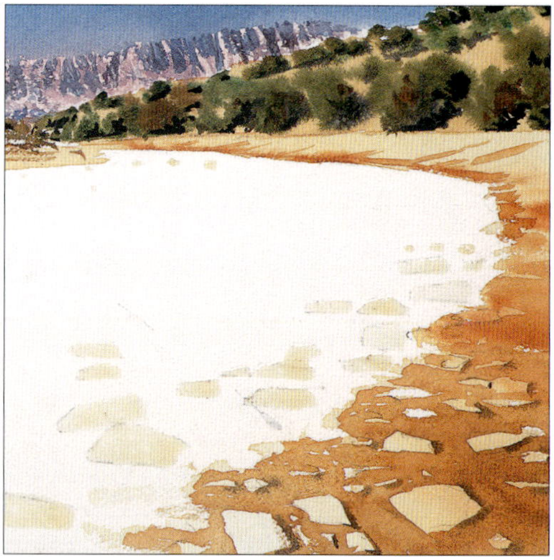

7 Using a B pencil, map out a few more stones on the shoreline. Mix a warm brown from burnt sienna and French ultramarine and brush in on to the foreground, working around the stones. Add more French ultramarine to the mixture and paint shadows around the edges of the stones to establish a three-dimensional effect. Leave to dry.

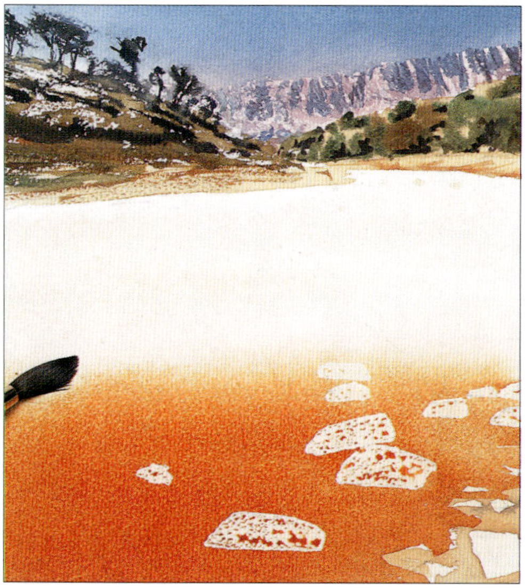

8 Brush clean water over the lake area. Mix burnt sienna with a little quinacridone magenta and, using a medium round brush, wash this mixture loosely over the shallow foreground of the lake, where partially submerged stones are clearly visible.

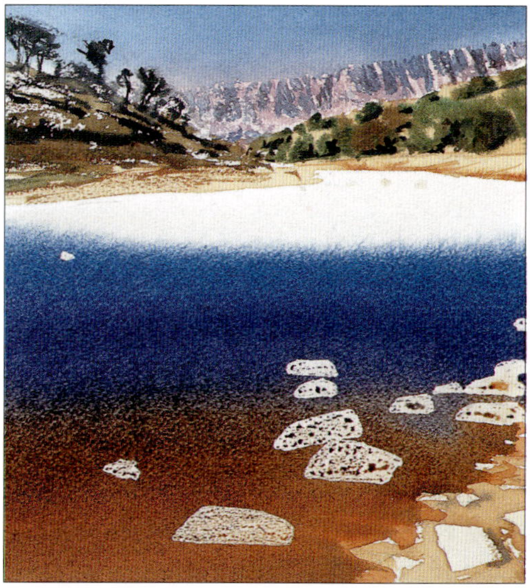

9 While the lake is still damp, brush phthalocyanine blue over the centre of the lake, adding a little quinacridone magenta as you work down over the stones in the foreground. Apply a second layer of the same colours over the same area and leave to dry.

Assessment time
Wet the blank area at the top of the lake and brush gum arabic on to the damp area. Using a fine brush, brush on vertical strokes of Naples yellow, burnt sienna, quinacridone magenta mixed with French ultramarine, and the olive green mixture used in Step 5. Leave to dry.

With the reflections in place, the painting is nearing its final stages. All that remains to be done is to put in some of the fine detail. Step back and think carefully about how you are going to do this. Far from making the painting look more realistic, too much detail would actually detract from the fresh, spontaneous quality of the overall scene.

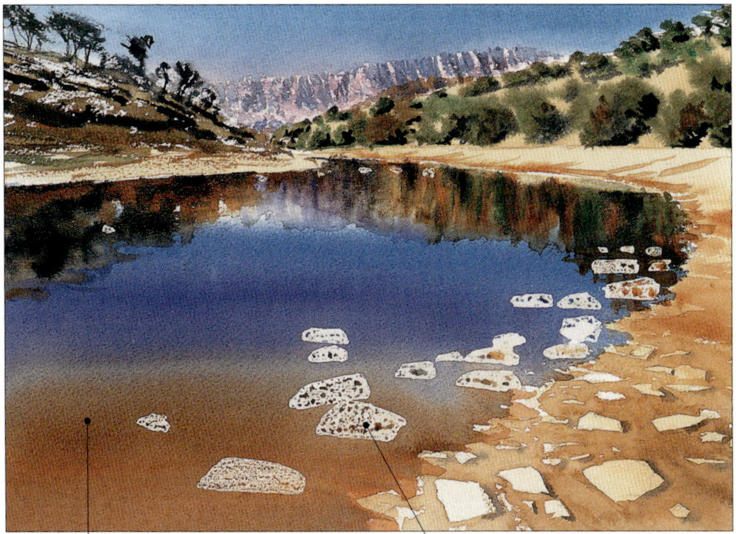

This area lacks visual interest. Adding submerged stones here will indicate both the clarity of the water and how shallow it is at this point.

These stones look as if they're floating on the surface of the water.

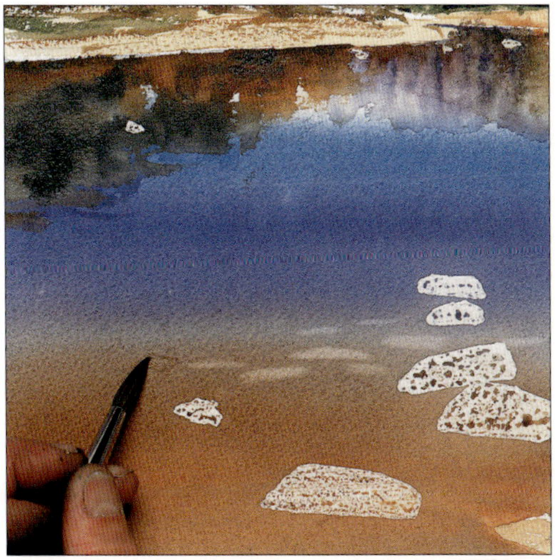

10 Dip a medium round brush in clean water and gently lift off the flattened, elongated shapes of underwater stones, varying the sizes. You may need to stroke the brush backwards and forwards several times on the paper in order to loosen the paint.

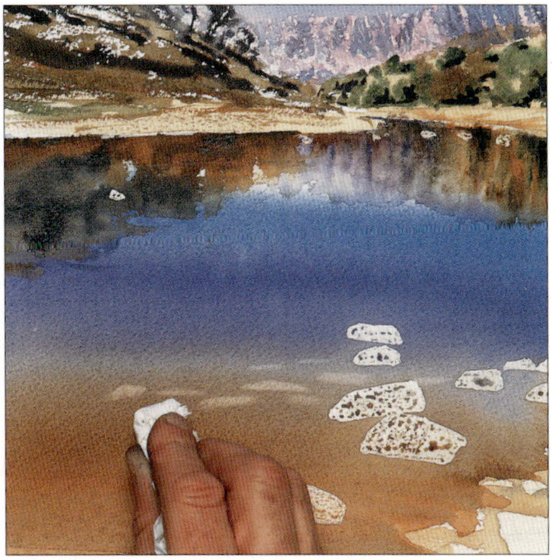

11 As you lift off each shape, dab the area firmly with clean kitchen paper to remove any excess water. Turn and re-fold the kitchen paper each time you use it, to prevent the risk of dabbing paint back on.

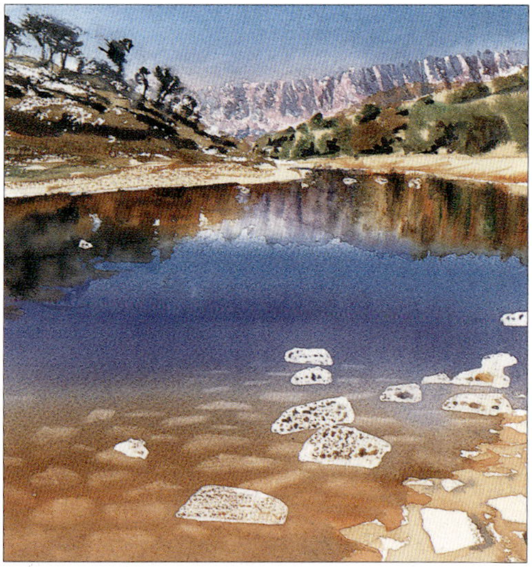

12 The submerged stones in the foreground of the lake add visual interest to what would otherwise be a dull, blank area of the scene, but as yet they do not look three-dimensional. The large stones above the surface of the water and on the shoreline also need more texture if they are to look convincing.

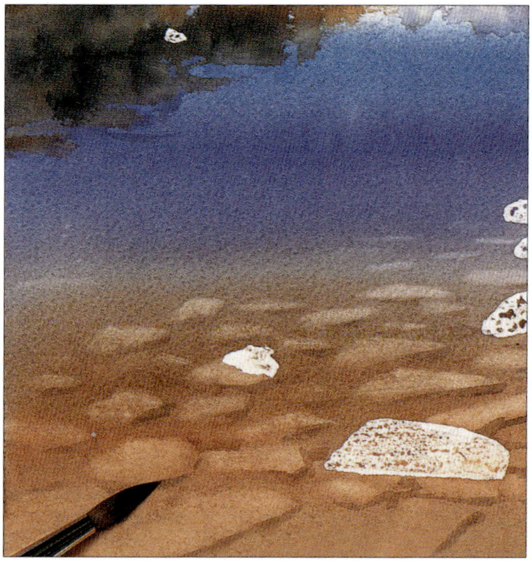

13 Mix a dark brown shadow colour from burnt sienna and French ultramarine and, using a medium round brush, use this mixture to loosely paint the shadows underneath the submerged stones. This makes the stones look three-dimensional and allows them to stand out more clearly from the base of the lake. It also adds texture to the base of the lake. Leave to dry.

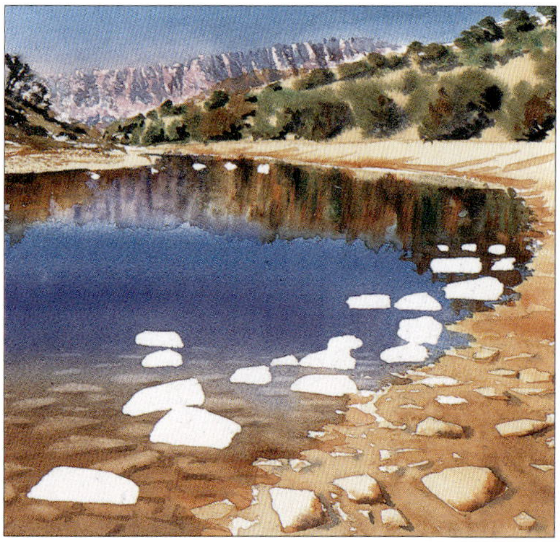

14 Using a fine brush, wet the area at the base of the reflection and touch in a mixture of French ultramarine and alizarin crimson to soften the edges. Mix burnt sienna with a little French ultramarine and use it to touch in the shadows under the largest rocks on the shoreline. Leave to dry. Using your fingertips, gently rub off the masking fluid.

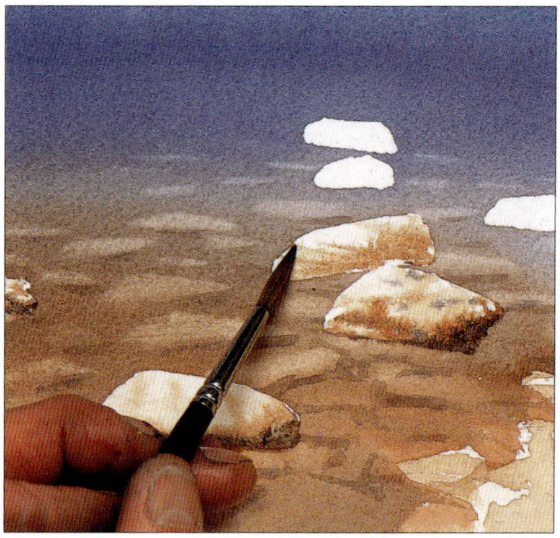

15 Using a fine, almost dry brush, brush water over the exposed rocks and then drop in a very pale wash of burnt sienna. Leave to dry. Drybrush a darker mixture of burnt sienna on to the rocks in places, for dark accents. To make the rocks look more three-dimensional, stroke on a little French ultramarine for the shadow areas.

Lake with reflections

This is a truly inviting image. The lake looks so realistic that you want to dabble your toes in it, while the feeling of heat is almost tangible.

The artist's skilful use of complementary colours (the bright blue of the sky set against the rich orangey brown of the stones and earth) has helped to create a really vibrant painting.

Textural details, such as the dry brushwork on the rocks and the distant trees painted wet into wet, are subtle but effective, while the careful blending of colours in the reflections conveys the stillness of the water perfectly. The composition is simple, but the foreshore leads the eye in a sweeping curve right through the painting.

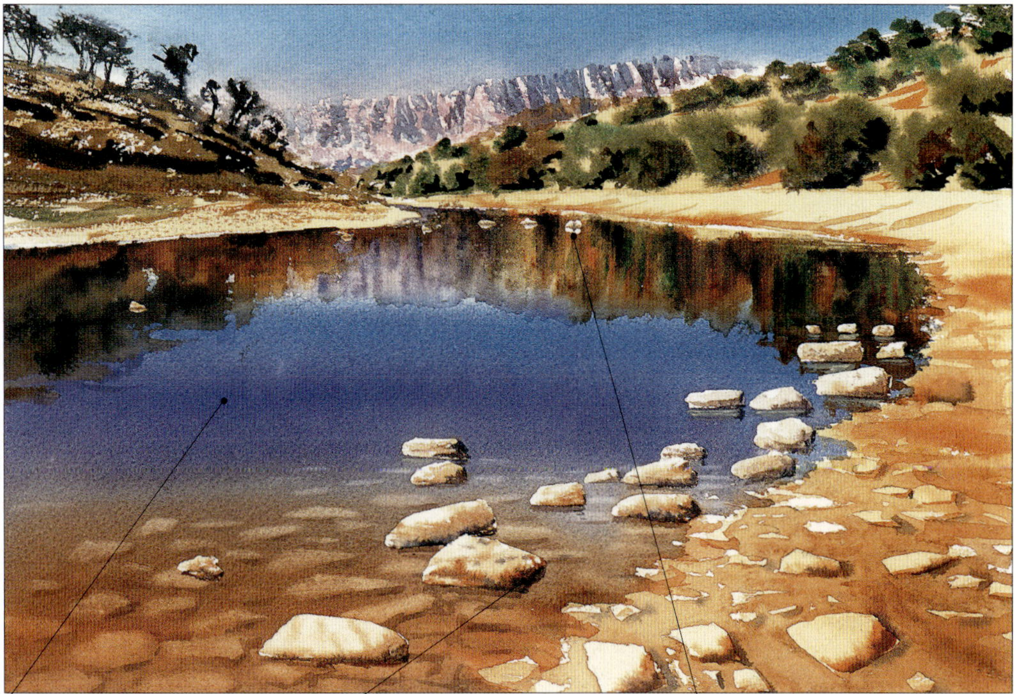

The lake is not a uniform blue throughout, but takes its colour from the objects that are reflected in it, as well as from the visible shallow areas.

A judiciously placed shadow under one edge of the stones helps to make them look three-dimensional.

The easiest way to paint the reflection of the small rocks in the distance is simply to paint a thin line of burnt sienna right through the middle.

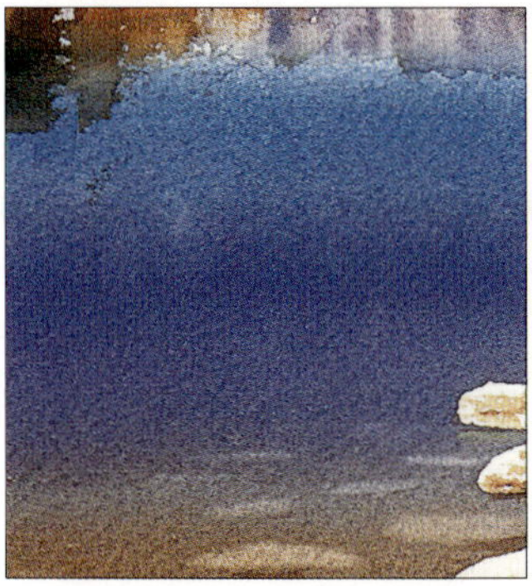

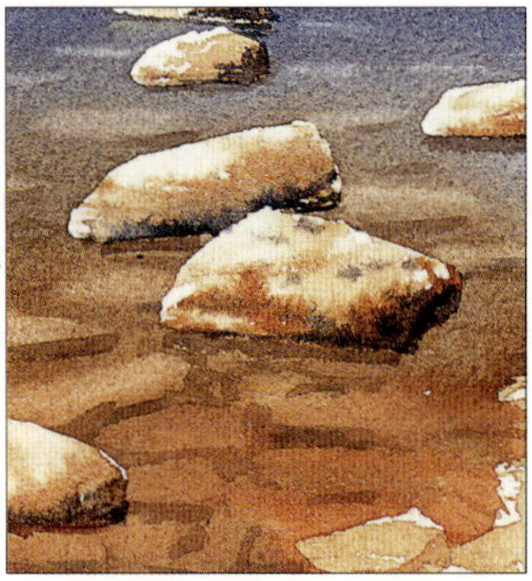

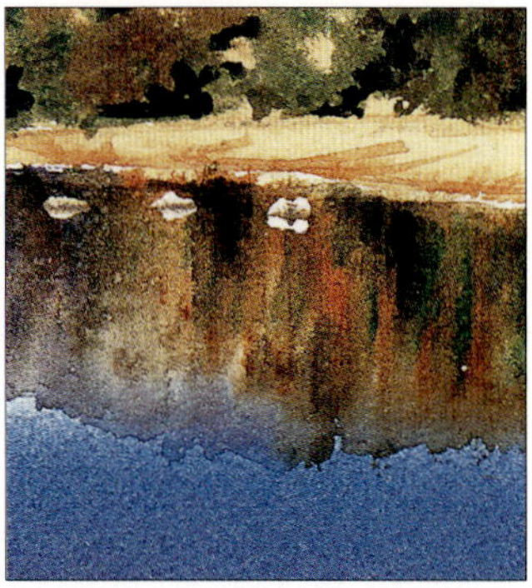

Harbour moorings

Ports and harbours are a never-ending source of inspiration for artists. The scene is constantly moving as the tide ebbs and flows, and the changing seasons bring different weather and lighting conditions. Reflections in the water, patterns in the sand, and countless details from boat masts to barnacles: there are thousands of things to stir the imagination. It's not just a visual feast: the sound of lapping water and squawking gulls, and the smell of seaweed combine to make this one of the most satisfying of all subjects to paint.

The key is to plan ahead and think about what you want to convey. Harbours are busy places, with lots of things going on and a host of fascinating details and textures to distract the eye, and you will almost invariably need to simplify things when you're painting. Decide on your main focus of interest and construct your painting around it. You may find that you need to alter the position of certain elements within the picture space, or to subdue some details that draw attention away from the main subject and place more emphasis on others.

This particular project uses a wide range of classic watercolour techniques to create a timeless scene of a working harbour at low tide. Pay attention to the reflections and the way the light catches the water: these are what will make the painted scene come to life, and there is no better medium for these transient effects of the light than watercolour.

Materials

- *4B graphite pencil*
- *140lb (300gsm) NOT watercolour paper, pre-stretched*
- *Watercolour paints: cadmium orange, Naples yellow, phthalocyanine blue, cerulean blue, permanent rose, raw sienna, ultramarine blue, burnt umber, cadmium red, burnt sienna, light red*
- *Gouache paints: permanent white*
- *Brushes: old brush for masking, 1in (2.5cm) hake, small round, medium filbert, fine filbert, fine rigger*
- *Masking fluid*
- *Masking tape*
- *Plastic ruler or straightedge*

The original scene

The tilted boats, wet sand and textures on the harbour wall all have the potential to make an interesting painting, but the sky and water are a little bland and there is no real focus of interest.

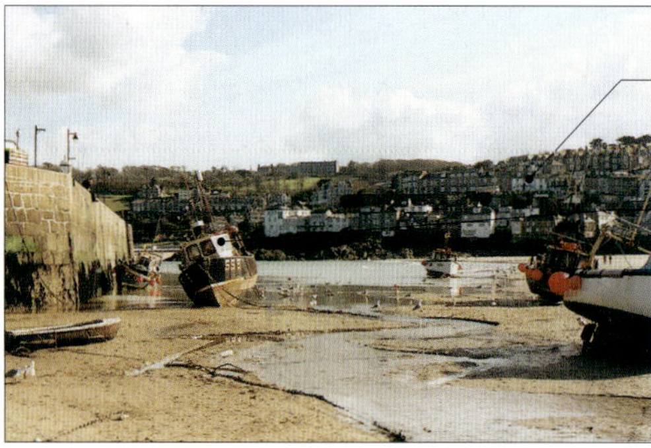

The town on the far side of the estuary is a little distracting.

The boats form a straight line across the image; it is unclear where the main focus of interest lies.

Preliminary sketch

The artist decided to make more of the water in his painting, introducing reflections that were not there in real life. He made this preliminary charcoal sketch to work out the tonal values of the scene. He then decided that the boats were too close together and that the scene was too cramped. In his final version, therefore, he widened the image so that the right-hand boat was further away; he also introduced two figures walking across the sand to provide a sense of scale.

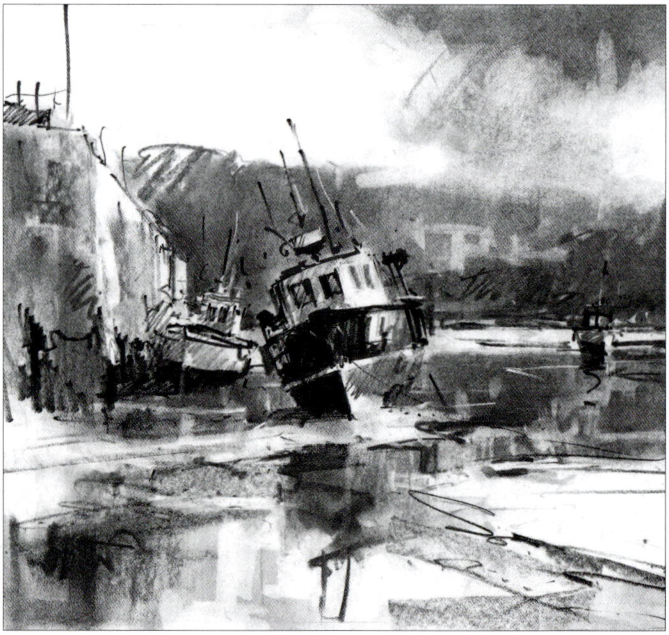

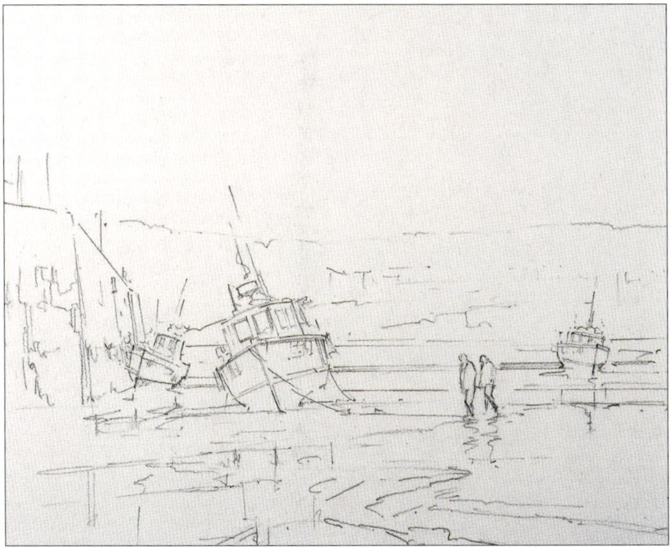

1 Using a 4B graphite pencil, sketch the scene, putting in the outlines of the harbour wall, distant hill, boats and figures and indicating the different bands of sand and water in the foreground.

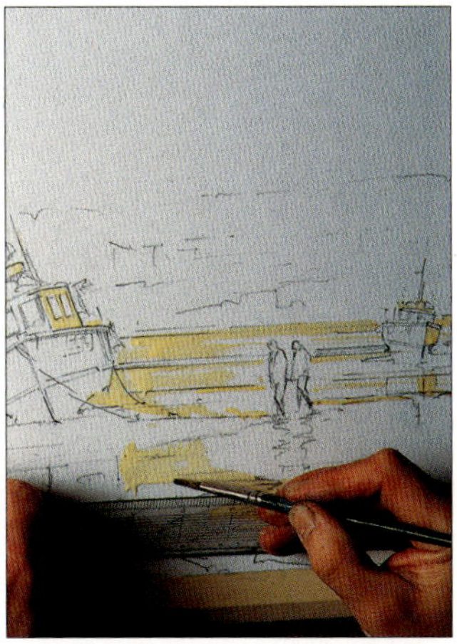

2 Using an old brush, apply masking fluid over the foreground water and the brightly lit right-hand side of the main boat to protect the highlight areas that you want to remain white in the finished painting. To get fine, straight lines, place a plastic ruler or straightedge on its side, rest the ferrule of the brush on top and gently glide the brush along.

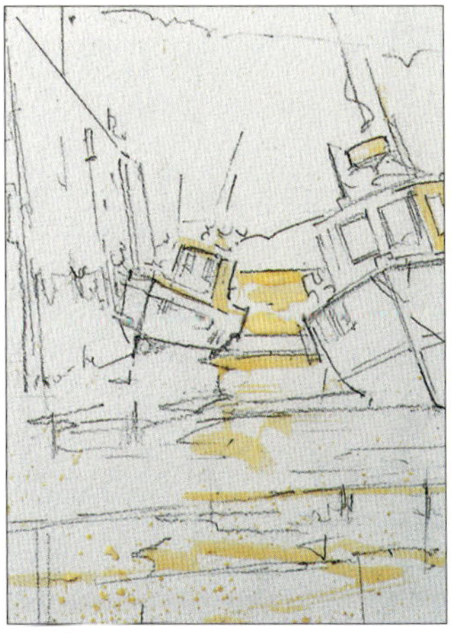

3 Spatter a little masking fluid over the foreground of the scene to suggest some random texture and highlights in the sand and water. Be careful not to overdo it as you need no more than a hint of the sun glinting on these areas.

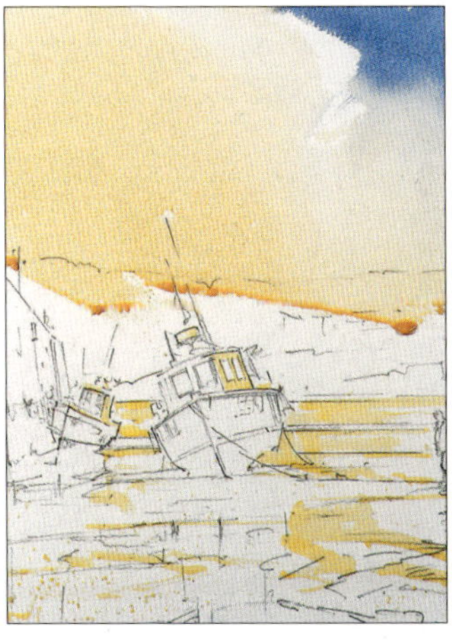

4 Mix a pale orange from cadmium orange and Naples yellow. Wet the sky in places with clean water. Using a hake brush, wash the orange mixture over the left-hand side of the sky and phthalocyanine blue over the right-hand side, leaving some gaps for clouds.

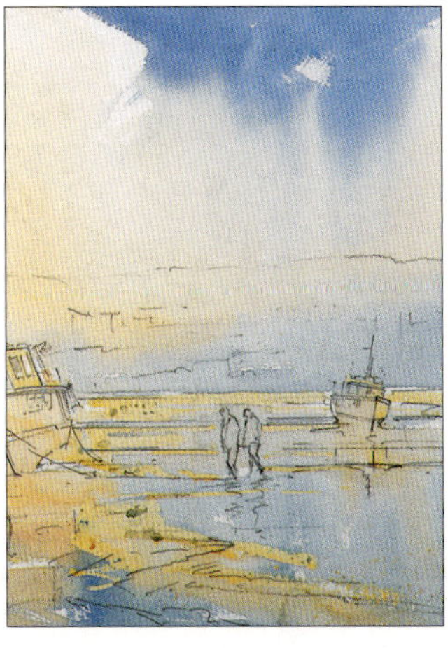

5 Using the same mixtures, carry the sky colours down into the water and sand, paying careful attention to the colours of the reflections in these areas. The warm colours used in the sky and sand set the mood for the rest of the painting.

▶

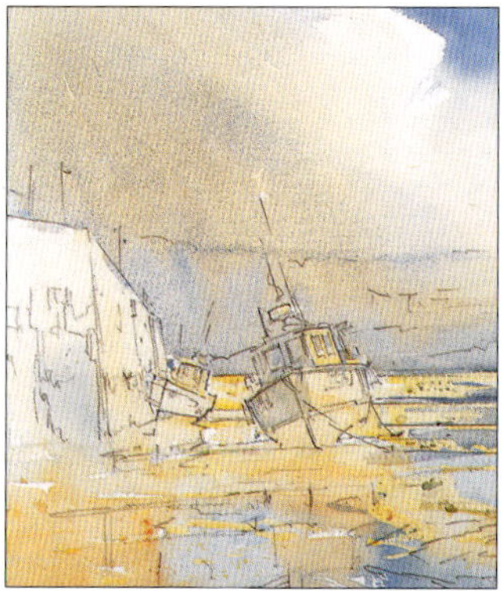

6 Mix a dilute wash of pale greyish purple from cerulean blue and a little permanent rose. Wet selected areas of the sky with clean water so that the colours will merge on the paper. Using the hake brush, wash the mixture over the darkest areas of cloud on the left-hand side of the sky and bring the colour down into the background hills and water. Darken this greyish purple mixture by adding more pigment to it and start putting a little colour on the shaded side of the largest boat in the scene.

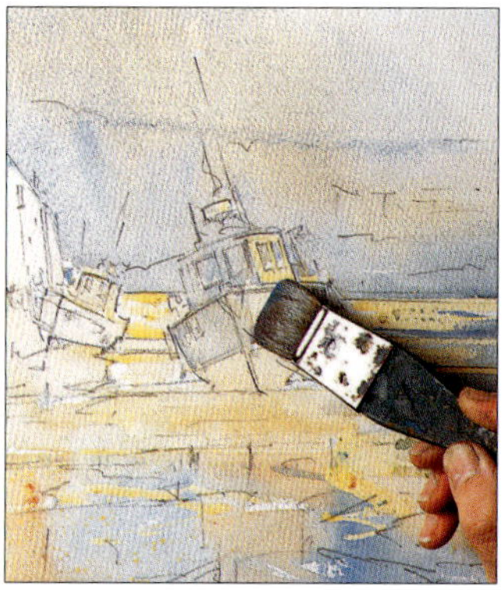

7 Using the same mixture of cerulean blue and permanent rose, continue building up washes on the sides of the largest boat.

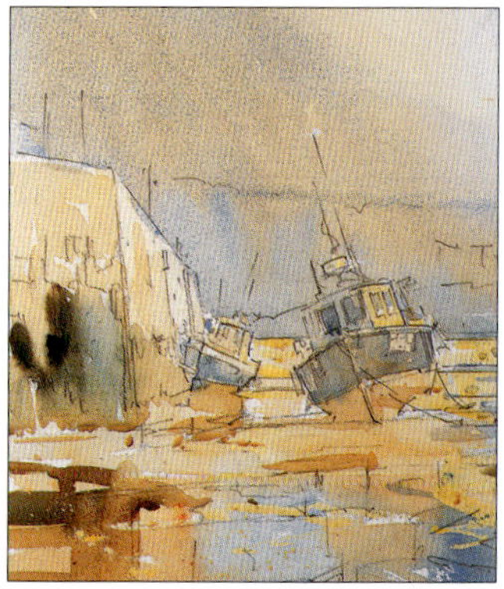

8 Darken the harbour wall with a wash of cadmium orange mixed with Naples yellow. While still wet, drop in a mixture of phthalocyanine blue and a little raw sienna. Paint the reflections of the harbour wall in the wet sand. Apply a little cerulean blue to the main boat and the one behind it.

Tip: Do not make the wall too dark at this stage: assess how strong it should be in relation to the background.

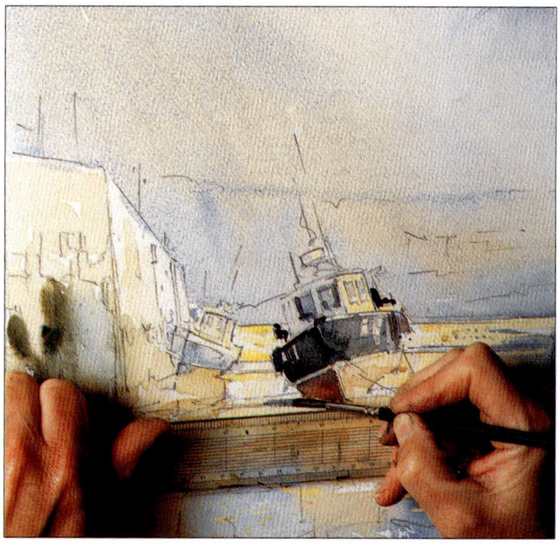

9 Using a small round brush, apply a dark mixture of ultramarine blue, burnt umber and a little cadmium red to the main boat. Mix a purplish grey from cerulean blue and permanent rose and, using a ruler or straightedge as in Step 2, paint the shadow under the main boat. Leave to dry.

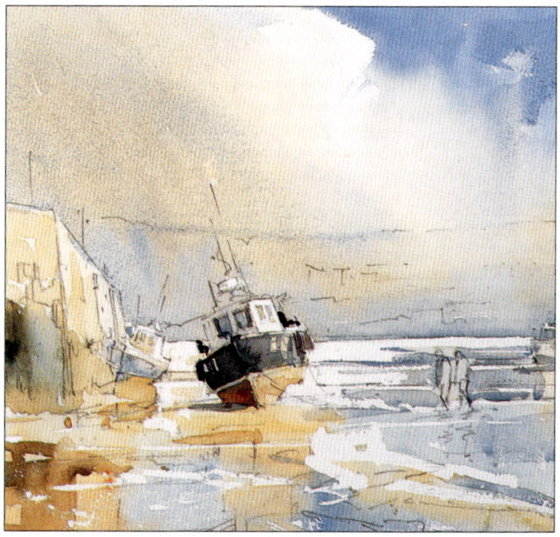

10 Using your fingertips, gently rub off the masking fluid to reveal the highlights on the water and sand.

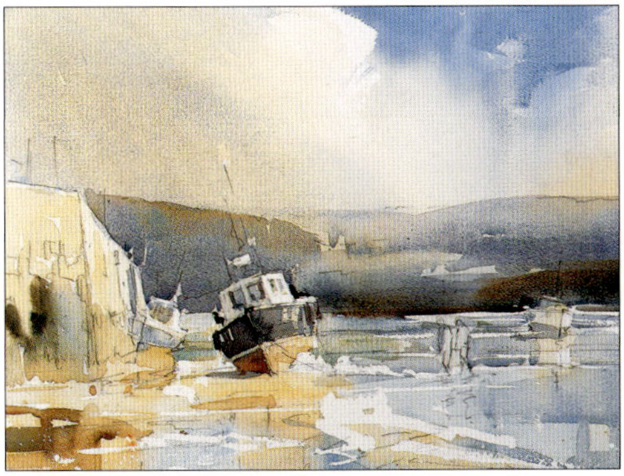

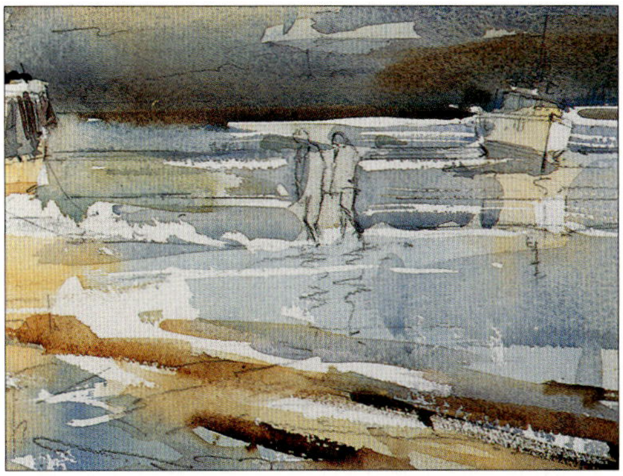

11 Apply further washes, wet into wet, over the hill in the background of the scene so that the colours fuse together on the paper, using ultramarine blue and light red, with a touch of raw sienna for the dark areas in the middle distance. Continue building up the tones of the reflections and intensify the colour of the water by adding a little cerulean blue with a touch of Naples yellow.

12 To add more texture to the ridges of sand in the foreground, apply strokes of burnt sienna straight from the tube, lightly stroking an almost dry medium filbert brush over the dry painting surface. This allows the paint to catch on the raised tooth of the paper, creating expressive broken marks that are equally suitable for depicting the sparkle of light on the water.

Assessment time

The basic structure of the painting is now in place. There are four principal planes – the sky, the landscape on the far side of the river which has put some solidity into the centre of the picture, the boat and harbour wall (the principal centre of interest in the painting), and the immediate foreground, which is structured to lead the eye up to the boat. Now you need to tie everything together in terms of tones and colours.

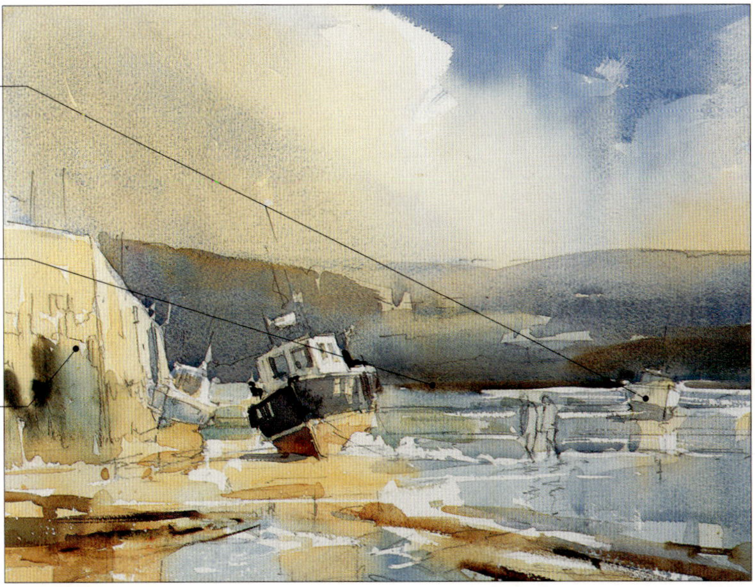

All the boats need to be strengthened, as they are the main interest in the painting.

The land is not sufficiently well separated from the estuary area.

More texture and depth of tone are needed on the harbour wall to hold the viewer's eye within the picture area.

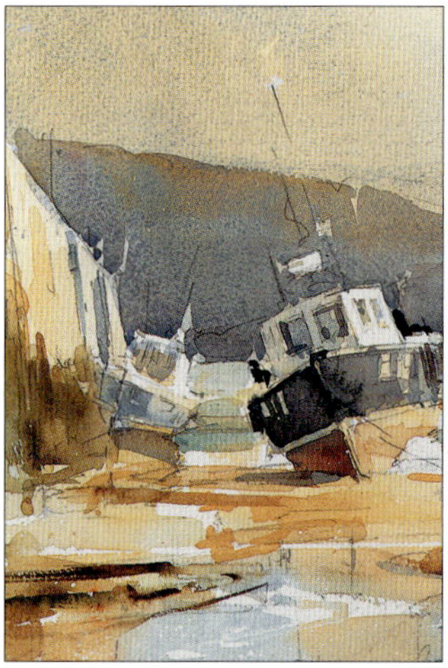

13 Now you can begin gradually to build up the washes to achieve the correct tonal values. Darken the harbour wall, using the original mixture of cadmium orange and a touch of raw sienna and build up the sandy area immediately in front of the main boat with the same mixture.

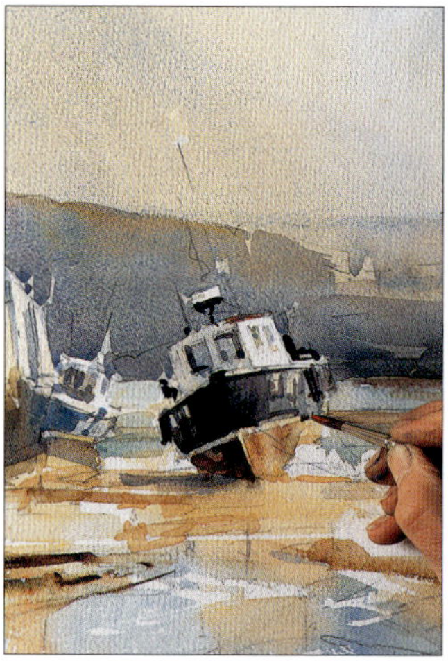

14 Using a small round brush and a dark mixture of ultramarine blue and light red, put in some of the detail on the boats.

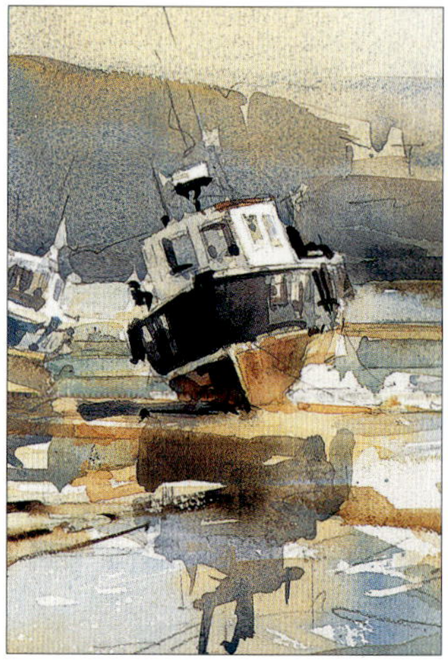

15 Now concentrate on the reflections of the boats, using colours similar to those used in the original washes. Do not to make the reflections too opaque. Keep these washes watery and as simple as possible. Use vertical brushstrokes so that they look more like reflections.

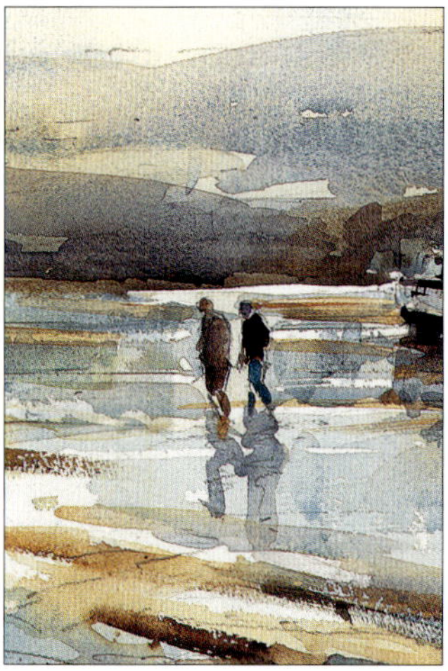

16 Mix a warm blue from cerulean blue, permanent rose and a touch of burnt umber and put in the two figures and their reflections.

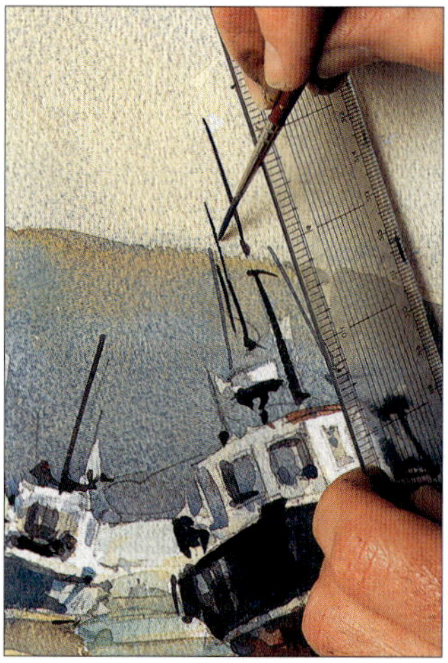

17 Using a fine rigger brush and resting the ferrule on a plastic ruler or straightedge, as in Step 2, put in the masts on the main boat in a mixture of ultramarine blue and light red and the rigging in a paler mixture of cerulean blue and permanent rose.

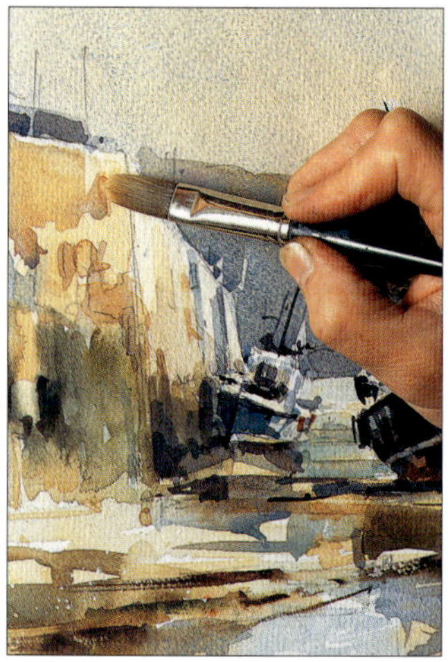

18 Using a filbert brush and the original mixture of cadmium orange and a little permanent rose, darken the stonework on the harbour wall. These uneven applications of colour give the wall texture and make it look more realistic.

Harbour moorings

This project brings together a range of classic watercolour techniques – wet into wet, building up layers of colour, using masking fluid to preserve the highlights, drybrush work – to create a lively painting that captures the atmosphere of the scene beautifully. The background is deliberately subdued in order to focus attention on the moorings. The main subject (the largest boat) is positioned at the intersection of the thirds, with the diagonal line of the sand directing the viewer's eye towards it. The different elements of the scene are perfectly balanced in terms of tone and composition.

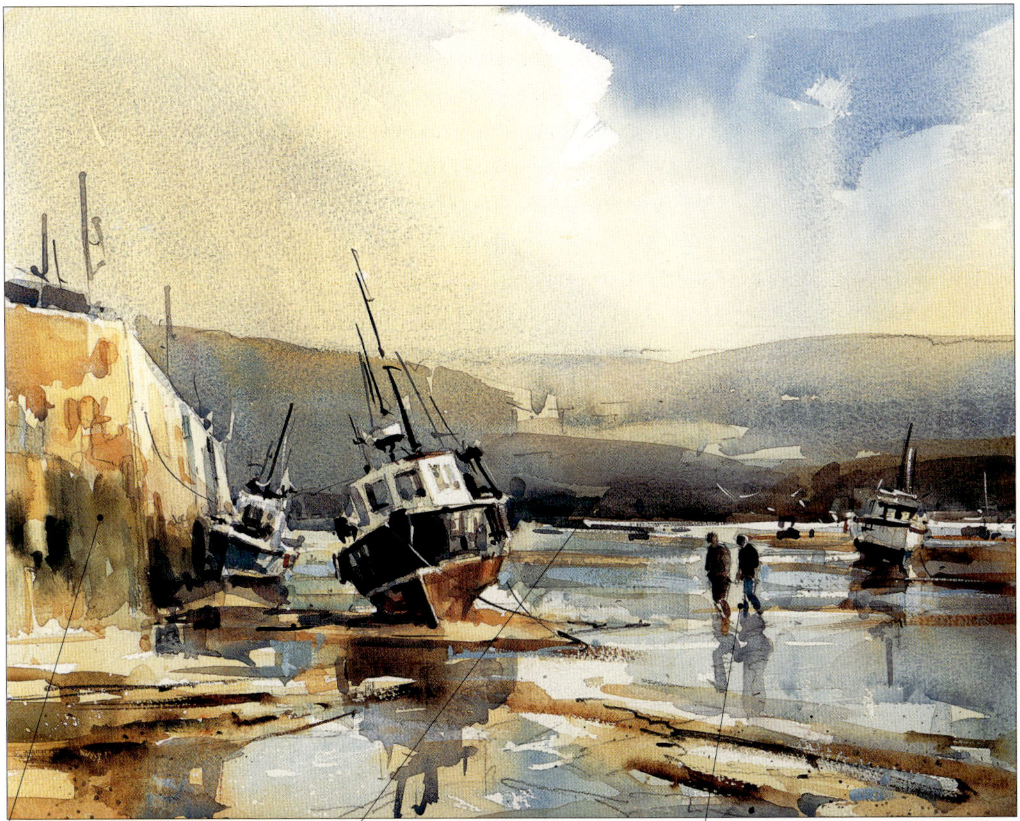

The harbour wall is painted wet into wet to create muted but interesting colours and textures.

The town in the original scene has been replaced by an atmospheric blend of colours that suggests wooded hills.

The two walking figures introduce human interest to the scene and provide a sense of scale.

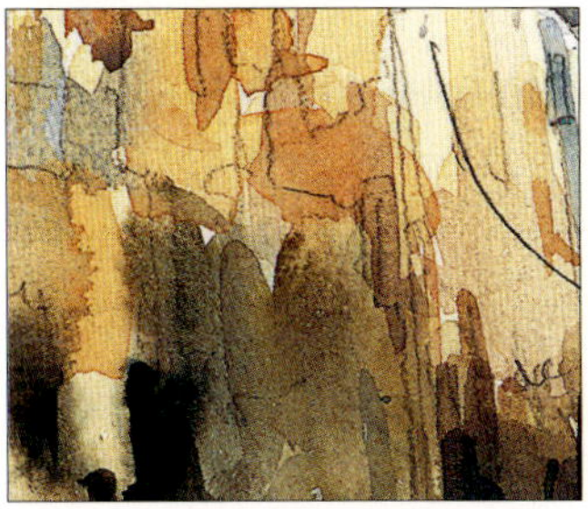

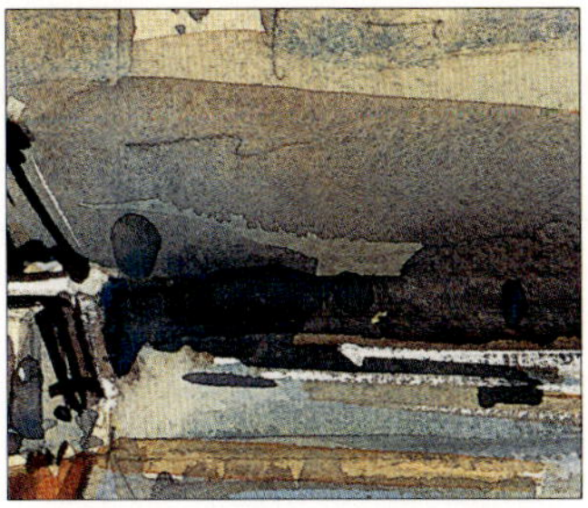

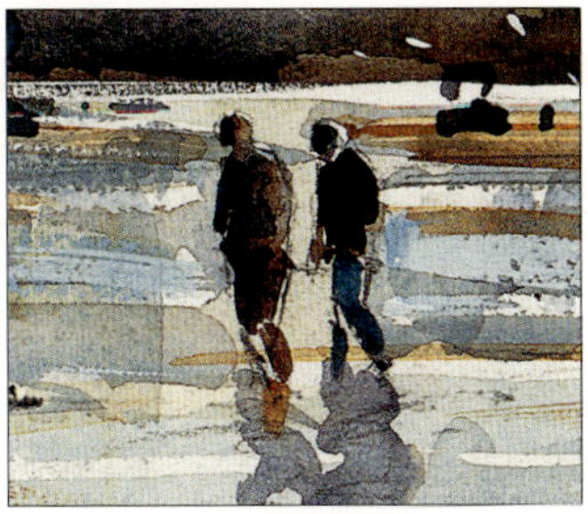

Painting Trees

It is virtually impossible to paint landscapes without painting trees as they feature heavily, even in many urban views. Trees add texture, colour and pattern, and they provide an important vertical element that often cuts startlingly across or through a work, dividing the picture area and drastically affecting the composition.

The most common mistake when painting trees is to make them all look the same. Even trees of the same species can look surprisingly different to each other, with no two trees growing in exactly the same way.

Trees are complex objects and not the easiest of things to draw or paint well. The best way to approach the subject is to simplify it, so that you paint the underlying structure and general shape of the tree before adding any detail. All trees can be seen as simple shapes which are either rounded, rectangular, columnar or pointed in their overall shape. The underlying structure is best seen in winter, when trees are devoid of leaves. The skeletal network of limbs, branches and twigs shows how the trees grow upwards and outwards from the roots and central trunk.

Although you can paint foliage as blocks of colour, you should remember that trees are composed of thousands upon thousands of delicately shaped individul leaves. Do not attempt to paint every leaf, but pay attention to the broken edge quality of the tree shape and carefully depict any spaces that you see between the leaves and branches, where the sky becomes visible.

Colour is another very important consideration. Foliage is not always green, nor are tree trunks always brown. Silver, yellow, orange, red and even purple foliage can be found, and the colour of trunks and stems can vary just as much.

A number of watercolour techniques are especially useful when painting trees. Drybrush is perfect for painting the texture on bark, as are sgraffito and linear marks made using a pencil or a fine brush. Broken colour techniques are particularly successful for foliage: try using natural sponges to gently dab a second colour over dry washes.

Winter trees ▼

The initial scene was established using wet-into-wet washes. Once these had dried, further washes were applied to bring out the intricate forms and pattern of the crossing jumble of gnarled branches and the shadows they cast across the trunk. The shadow of the tree seen coming in from the bottom of the picture is a compositional device, indicating that things do not end at the picture edge.

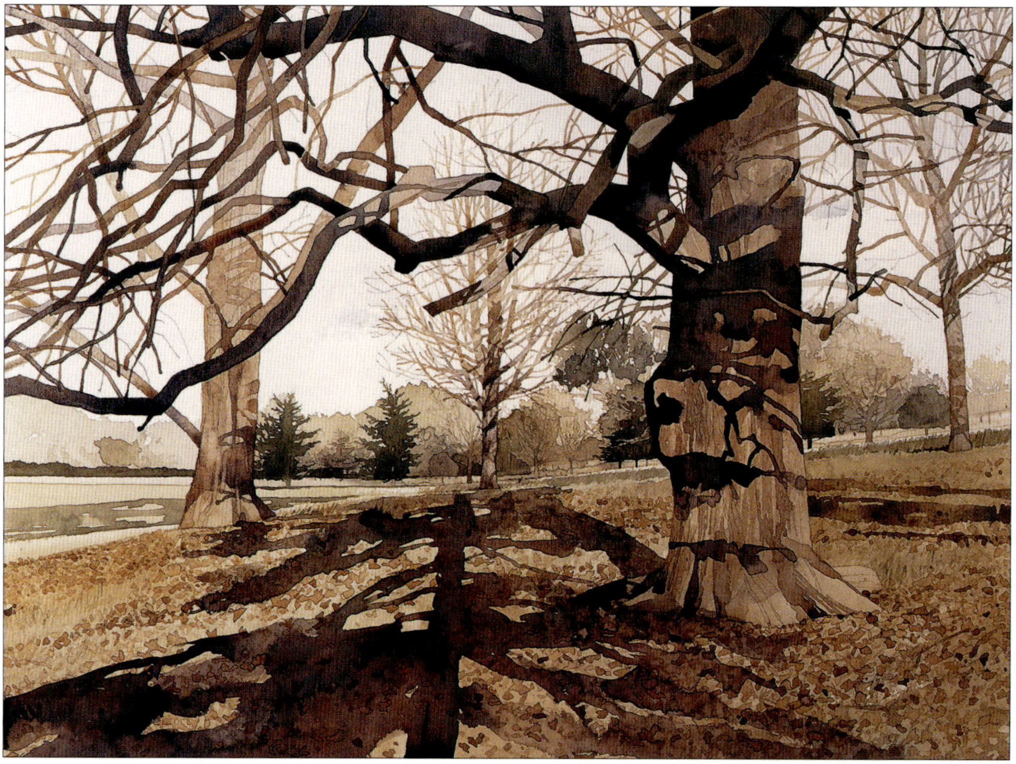

Autumn beech tree ▼

The fine linear textures on the trunk of this beech tree were made by applying masking fluid with a pen. The same technique was used for some of the fine branches. The foliage colour was flooded on using orange, yellows and browns applied wet into wet, while the foliage texture was achieved by sprinkling rock salt onto the wet paint.

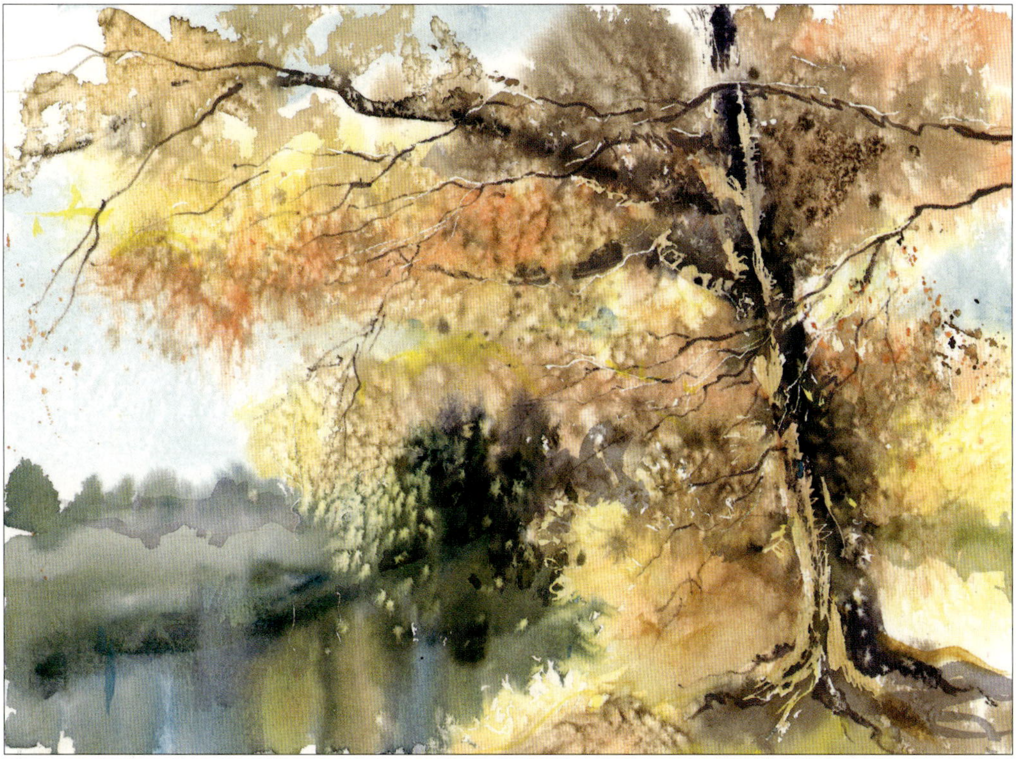

Cedar tree ►

This delicate painting carefully observes the way the branches spread and fall in layers around the thick central trunk. Painted using a fine brush and wet-on-dry washes, the foliage colours consist of only three tones of the same silver-green colour.

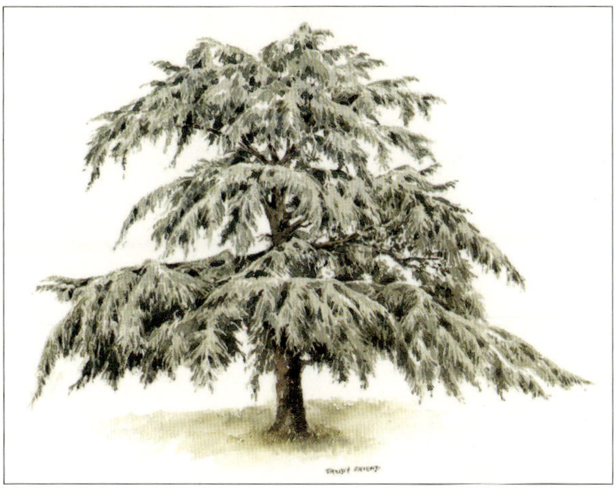

Tips: • Study the tree's growth habit and break it down into a simple basic shape. Establish the overall shape of the tree before adding surface detail.
• Use drying marks where paint has puddled and dried at different speeds to suggest clumps of foliage.
• Experiment with textural techniques like wax resists, sponging, and using rock salt.
• Instead of using colours straight from the paint box, mix greens and other tree colours: the results will look far more natural and subtle.

Woodland in spring

Green is, without any doubt, the most important colour in the landscape artist's paint palette. Once you start to look, it is astonishing how many different shades there are, from the bright, almost acidic greens of fresh spring growth through to muted tones of olive and sage.

Although a quick glance through any paint manufacturer's catalogue will reveal a wide range of ready-made greens, it is quite unusual to find one that suits your needs exactly, and you almost always have to modify commercial colours or mix your own. This project, of a spring woodland in the late-afternoon sunlight, gives you the opportunity to do precisely that.

So that you build on what you learn here, make a point of painting different types of woodland: a coniferous forest, for example, tends to contain darker greens than the deciduous woodland shown here. It is a good idea to keep a note of the paint colours used in successful colour mixes so that you can easily recreate them at a later date.

The time of year makes a difference, too. At the height of summer, you will find that leaves are larger and darker than they are in spring, and the tree canopy is more dense, making it harder for light to penetrate through to the woodland floor. In a deciduous woodland in winter, on the other hand, the trees will have lost their leaves and so it will be much easier to see the underlying shapes and structure of different tree types.

The direction and angle of the light also affects the shade of green: the same leaves can look completely different in colour depending on whether the sun is to one side or behind. A single back-lit leaf, with the veins clearly visible, can make an interesting watercolour study in its own right.

Materials

- *2B pencil*
- *90lb (185gsm) rough watercolour paper, pre-stretched*
- *Watercolour paints: cadmium red, yellow ochre, lemon yellow, alizarin crimson, phthalocyanine blue, cobalt blue, raw umber*
- *Brushes: Chinese*

The original scene

This photograph captures the essence of the scene – the slender trees and dappled light – but there is no real focus of interest. The artist decided to make one tree more prominent by bringing it forwards. This breaks the straight line across the centre of the image and allows the viewer's eye to weave in and out of the trees.

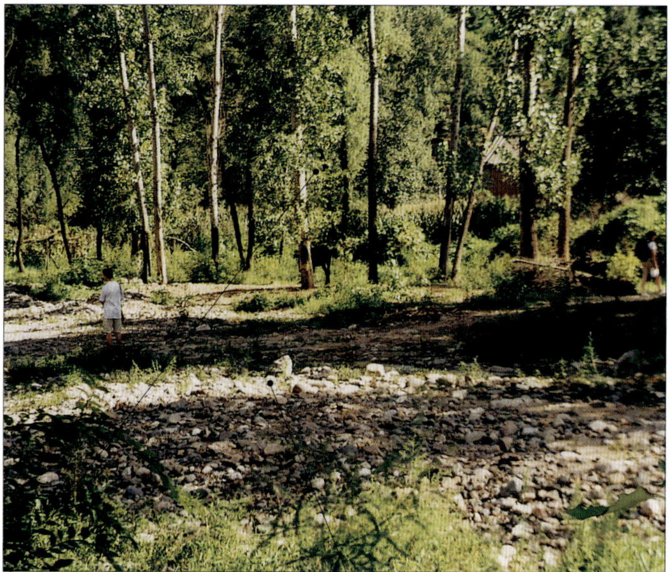

The trees form a straight line across the picture and appear to merge together.

Bright, wide shafts of sunlight indicate that the tree canopy is not very dense.

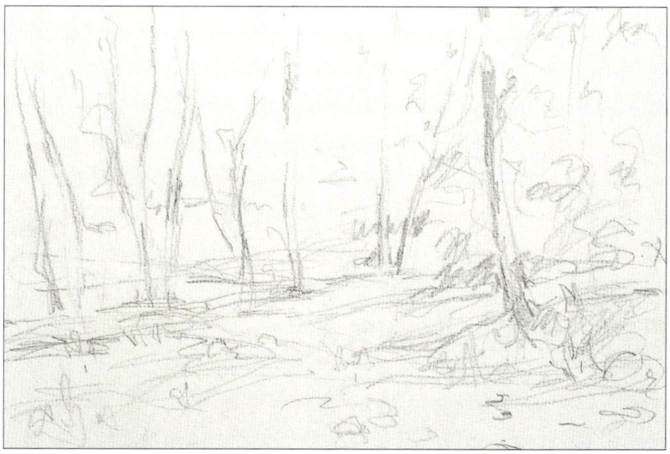

1 Using a 2B pencil, lightly sketch the scene, putting in the trunks of the main trees and indicating some of the clumps of grass alongside the track.

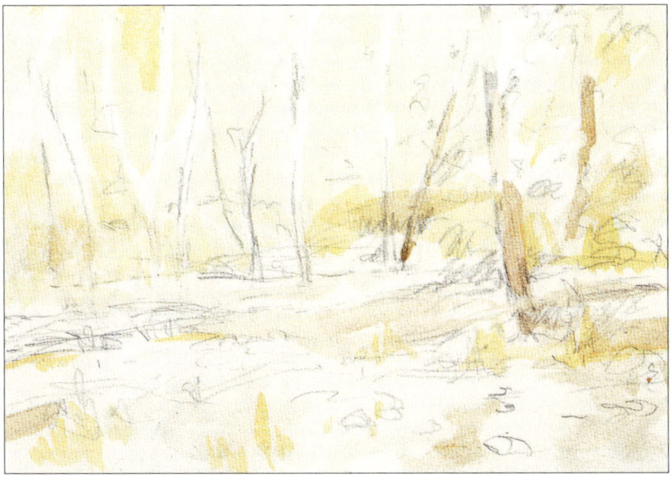

2 Mix a pale golden brown from cadmium red and yellow ochre. Using a Chinese brush, loosely brush the mixture on to the trunks of the main foreground trees and the pebbly track to establish the warm undertones of the painting. Mix a pale wash of lemon yellow and brush it over the foliage area as a base colour, leaving some gaps for where the brightest patches of sky show through. Add a little more pigment to the wash as you get closer to ground level, as not as much light reaches this area. Brush the same lemon yellow wash loosely over the clumps of grasses in the foreground. Leave to dry.

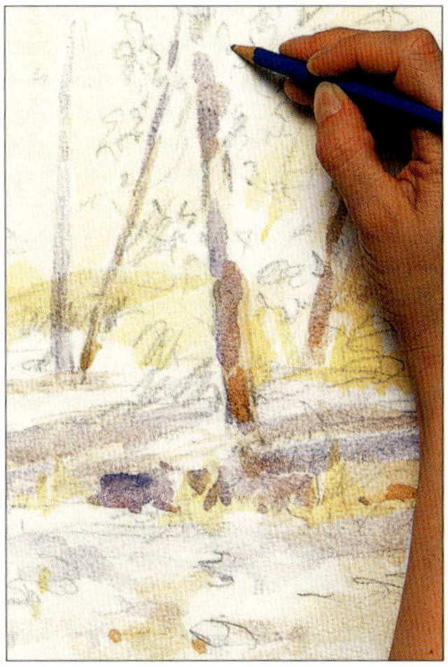

3 Mix a warm purplish grey from alizarin crimson and phthalocyanine blue and brush it over the shaded areas of the track. Paint the tree trunks with the same mixture. Mix a warm brown from yellow ochre and cadmium red and paint the larger stones on the track. Using a 2B pencil, lightly sketch in the leaf masses on the trees.

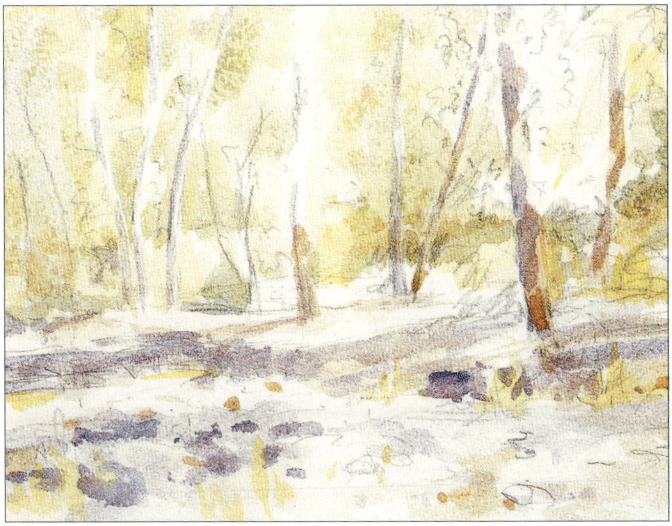

4 Mix a cool green from lemon yellow and cobalt blue and brush in the mid-tone foliage areas. Take care not to obliterate all the very lightest foliage areas that you applied in Step 2, otherwise you will lose the feeling of dappled light and fresh spring growth in the image.

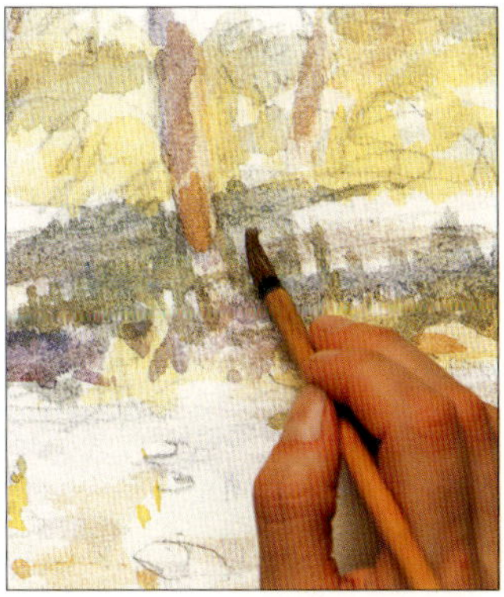

5 Mix a dark green from lemon yellow and phthalocyanine blue and paint the grasses growing under the trees, using short vertical strokes.

Tip: When painting foliage and grasses, try to make your strokes follow the direction of growth.

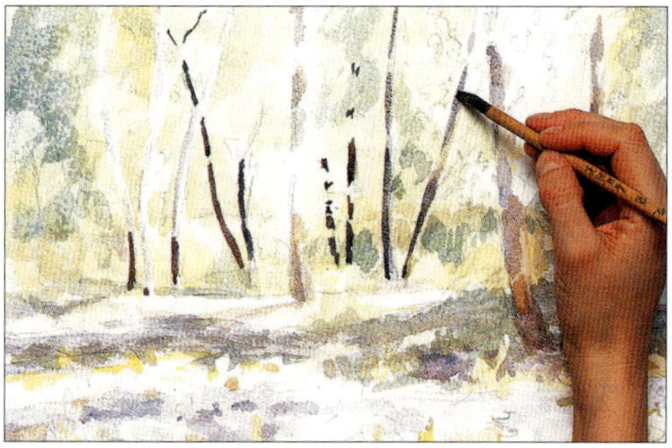

6 Add more phthalocyanine blue to the mixture and dab it over the foliage for the darkest greens. Strengthen the tree trunks, using the same grey mixture as in Step 3. Mix a dark brown from phthalocyanine blue, alizarin crimson and raw umber, and paint the shaded sides of the tree trunks, cutting in and out of the foliage masses.

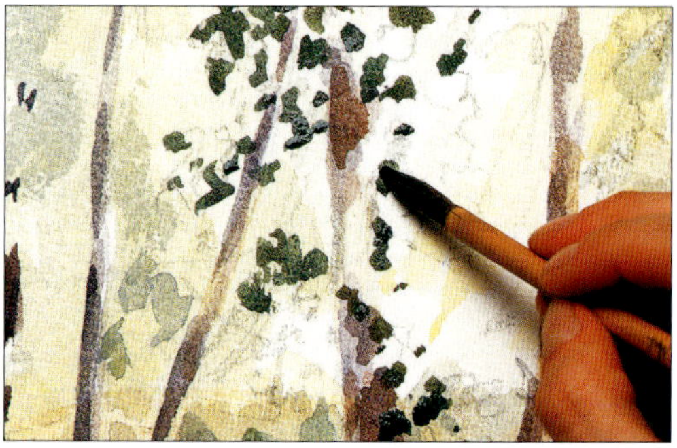

7 Put in the darker tones of the main foreground tree, using the same mixture. Mix a bright, dark green from phthalocyanine blue and raw umber and dot in the darker foliage tones on the foreground trees. It is important to have more detail in the foreground, as it is closer to the viewer, while impressionistic blurs will suffice in the background.

Assessment time

The woodland scene is beginning to take shape but the details are still relatively indistinct and much more needs to be done to separate the foreground elements from the background. When you move on to the next stage, make sure you don't concentrate on one area at the expense of the rest. Work across the painting as a whole, standing back every now and then to assess the tonal values and compositional balance.

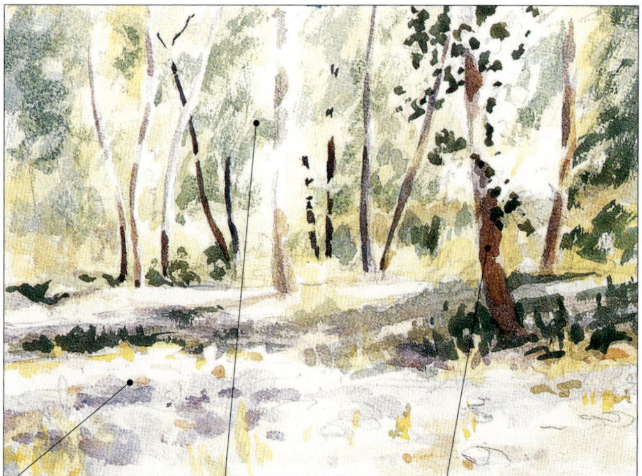

The foreground shadows need to be strengthened to enhance the feeling of dappled light coming through the trees.

The background is all of a similar tone. As a result, there is not a strong enough sense of depth in the image.

The main tree is beginning to stand out from the background, but more detail is still needed here.

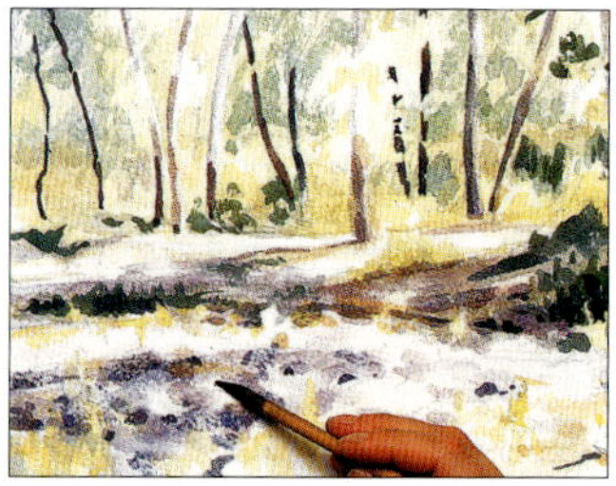

8 Strengthen the shadow colour on the track, using the same alizarin crimson and phthalocyanine blue mixture as before. Add more alizarin crimson and put in some thin trunks on the left of the painting. Using a blue-biased mixture of alizarin crimson and phthalocyanine blue, start dotting in some dark pebbles on the track.

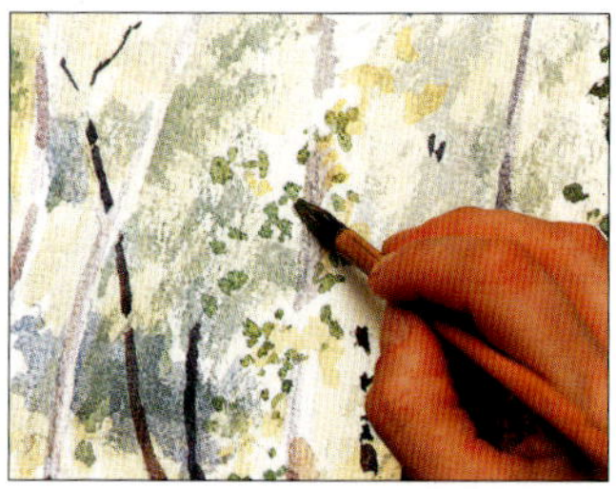

9 Some of the foliage areas look very light. Dot in a mid-toned green to tone down the brightness a little.

Woodland in spring

With its bright, fresh greens and dappled light, this painting is suffused with a wonderful feeling of spring sunlight. The painter has used a little artistic licence to make the composition more dynamic than it was in real life: one tree has been placed at the intersection of the thirds to provide a focus of interest, and the straight line of trees has been staggered in order to encourage the viewer's eye to move around the whole picture.

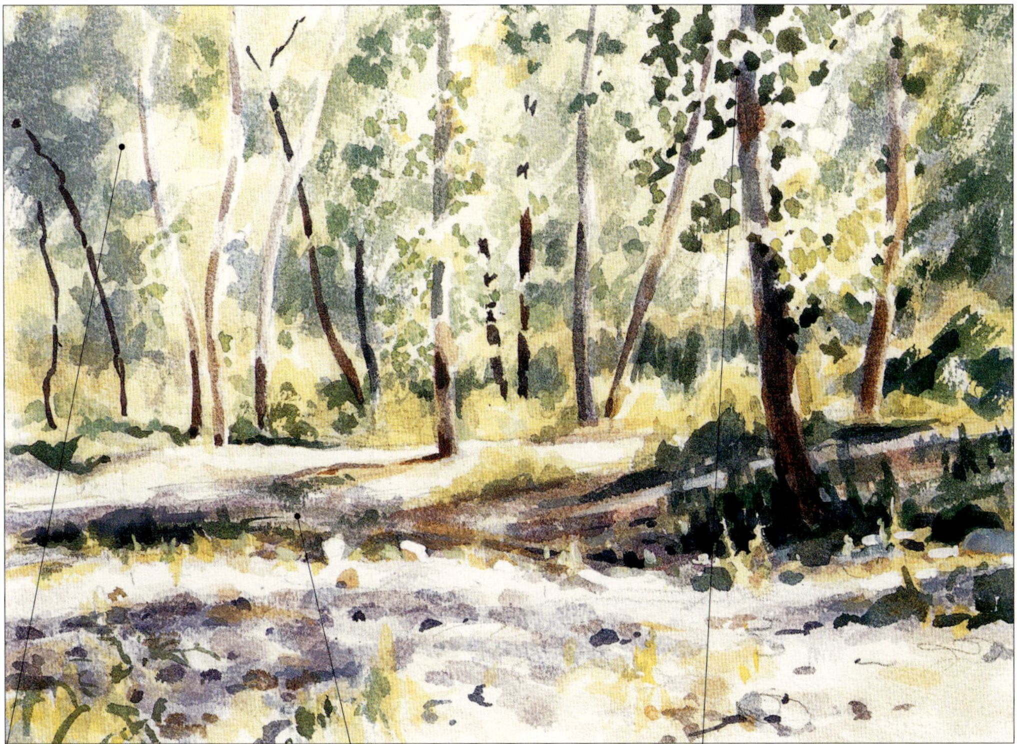

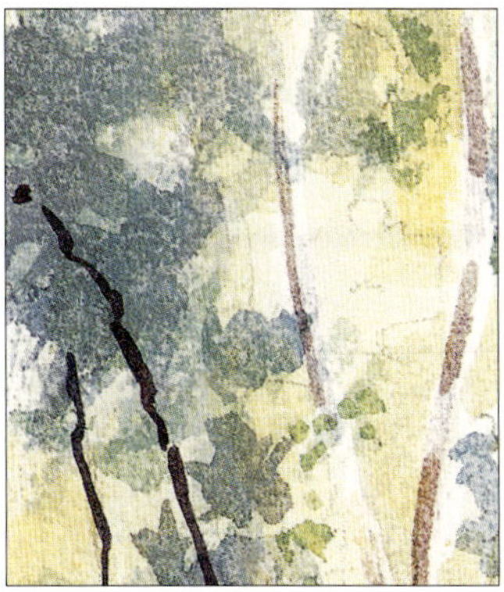

Soft, pale colours and a lack of detail imply that this area of the scene is further away from the viewer.

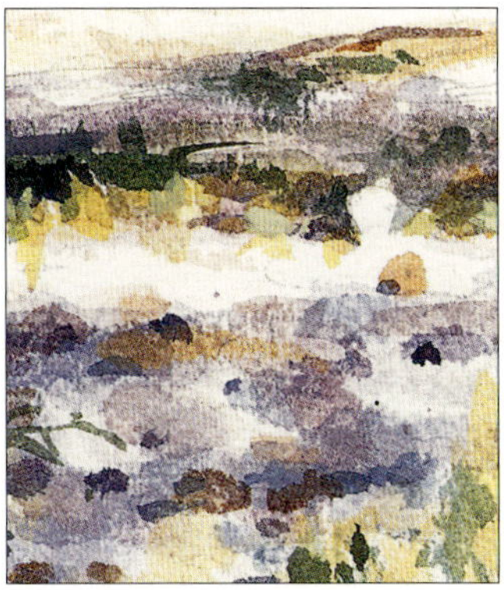

Long shadows lead the viewer's eye through the scene and indicate low-angled afternoon sunlight.

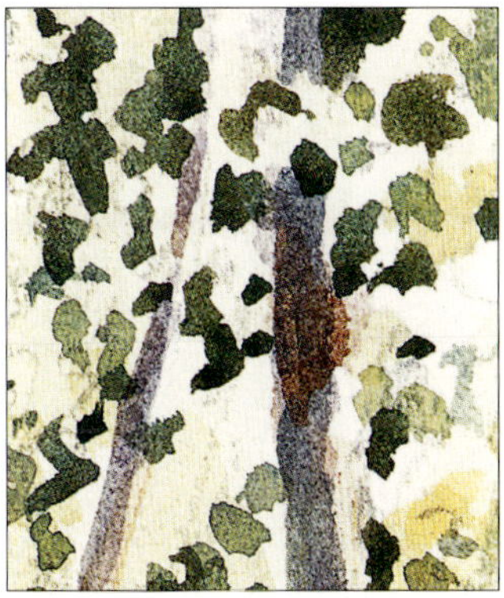

Crisp leaf detail helps to separate this tree from those in the background, where the foliage is much less distinct.

Autumn tree

Many trees are at their most dramatic in the autumn, when the leaves change from green to dazzling displays of reds, russets and golds. Combine those colours with early-morning mists, as in this scene, and you will have the makings of a very atmospheric painting.

When you are painting trees, always start by establishing the overall shape. The oak tree in this project has a spreading habit: the branches radiate outwards from the main trunk, while the crown is rounded and reasonably symmetrical. When trees are in leaf the underlying "skeleton" can sometimes be hidden from view, but you need to be aware of it. The leaves do not simply sit on top of the branches in clumps; they are attached to branches and twigs, and you must convey a sense of the shapes underneath and the directions in which the branches and twigs grow, even if you cannot see them clearly, in order for your painting to look convincing.

Because the sunlight in this scene is coming from behind the tree, the tree itself is in semi-silhouette. However, the light does catch the edge of the tree branches in places, creating warm wisps of colour against the dark branches and trunk. Pay careful attention to these highlights and look for areas where shafts of sunlight break through.

Textures, too, are important. Although you cannot see much detail because the tree is in semi-silhouette, the gnarled trunk is an essential part of the tree's character. Here, water-soluble pencils were used to establish a base texture that was then overlaid with watercolour washes.

Materials

- *4B pencil*
- *140lb (300gsm) NOT watercolour paper, pre-stretched*
- *Water-soluble pencils: sepia*
- *Watercolour paints: cadmium yellow, burnt sienna, alizarin crimson, cobalt blue, sepia, violet*
- *Gouache paints: neutral grey, permanent white*
- *Brushes: medium round, small round*
- *Ruling drawing pen*
- *Masking fluid*

Preliminary sketch

The artist made a quick colour sketch in situ to work out the overall shape of the tree and which colours to use for the vibrant autumn leaves.

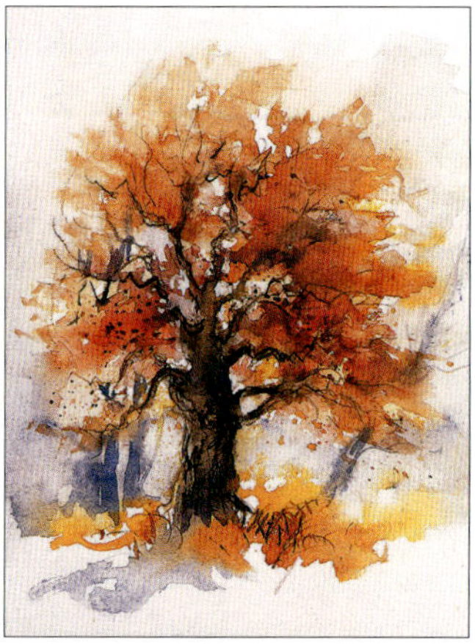

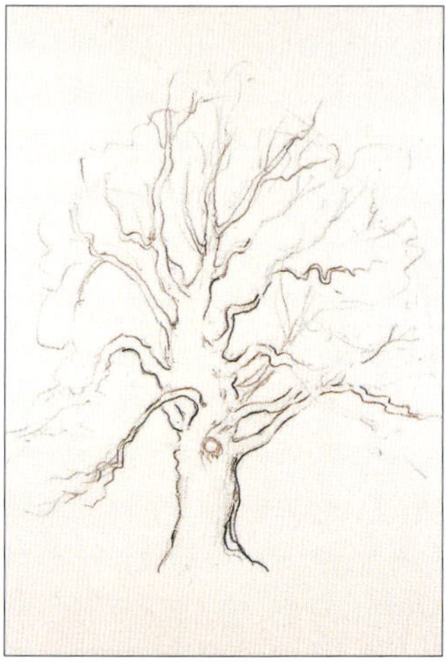

1 Using a 4B pencil, lightly sketch the scene, putting in the main branches of the tree. Look carefully at how they twist and overlap.

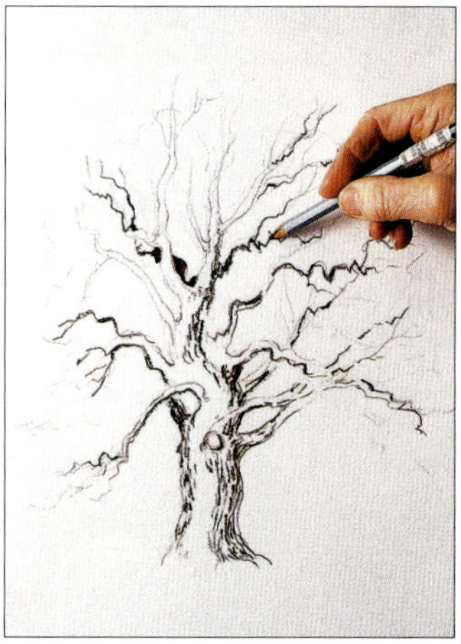

2 Dip the tip of a sepia water-soluble pencil in water and put in the dark textural markings of the gnarled trunk and the main branches. (Dipping the pencil in water intensifies the colour and makes the marks more permanent, so that this linear pencil work is still visible when the watercolour washes are applied to the tree in the later stages of the painting.)

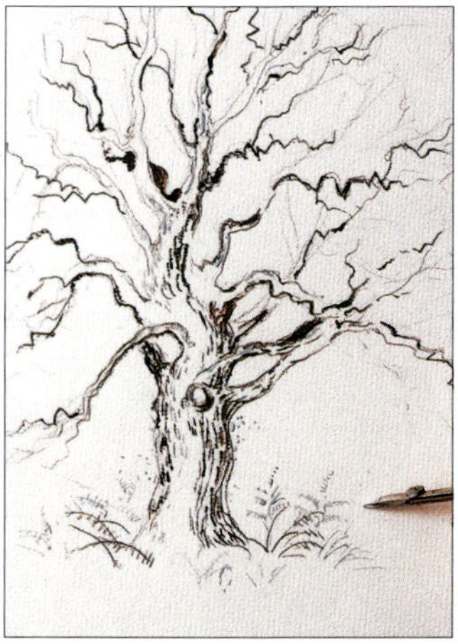

3 Using a ruling drawing pen, apply masking fluid to the highlighted edges of the branches and the foreground grasses. Leave to dry completely. The masking is subtle, but it plays an important role in establishing a sense of light and shade.

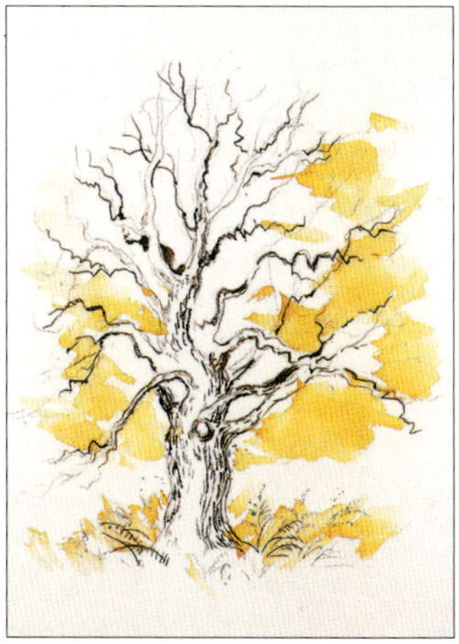

4 Mix a pale wash of cadmium yellow and wash it over the background behind the tree and the foreground grasses. Dot some of the same cadmium yellow mixture into the branches to establish the lightest-coloured foliage areas.

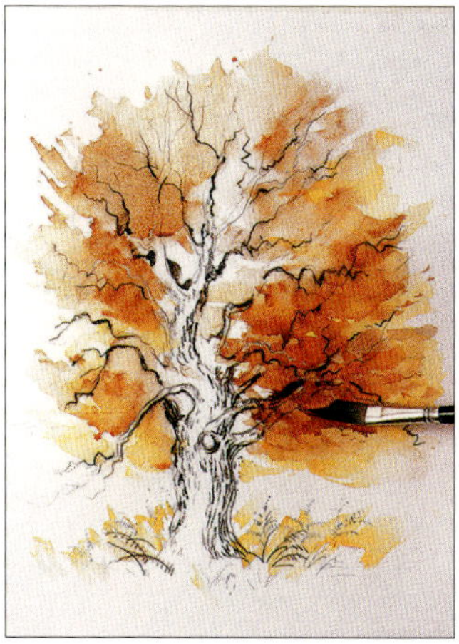

5 Wet the tree with clean water and touch in burnt sienna, dabbing it on with the side of the brush. The colour will spread over the damp paper and merge with the yellow applied in Step 4. Apply several layers wet into wet, in some places, to deepen the tones.

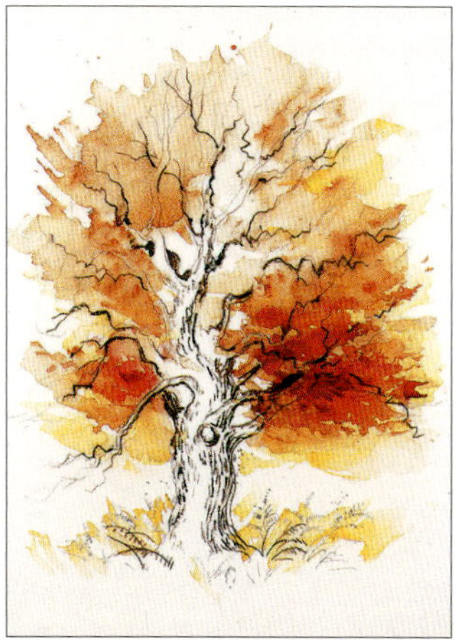

6 While the burnt sienna washes are still wet, drop alizarin crimson into the lower branches, angling your brushstrokes in the direction in which the branches and leaves naturally grow. The richness of the autumnal colours is now starting to develop. Leave to dry.

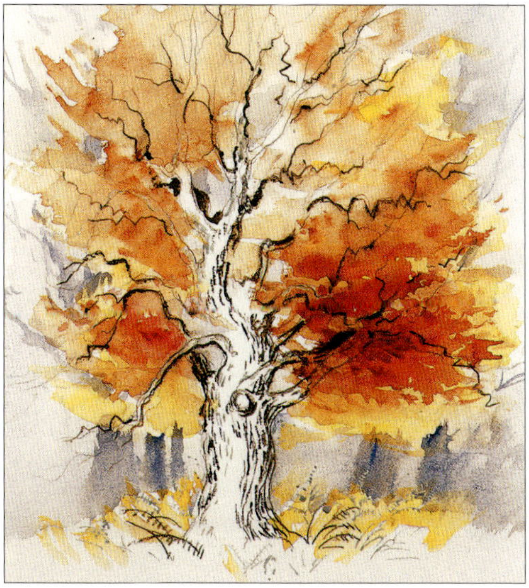

7 Wash around the edges of the tree and into the negative spaces with clean water. Mix a very pale, dilute grey from neutral grey gouache and cobalt blue watercolour and touch this mixture on to the damp paper. Add a tiny amount of burnt sienna to the mixture and paint the misty tree trunks in the background, wet into wet.

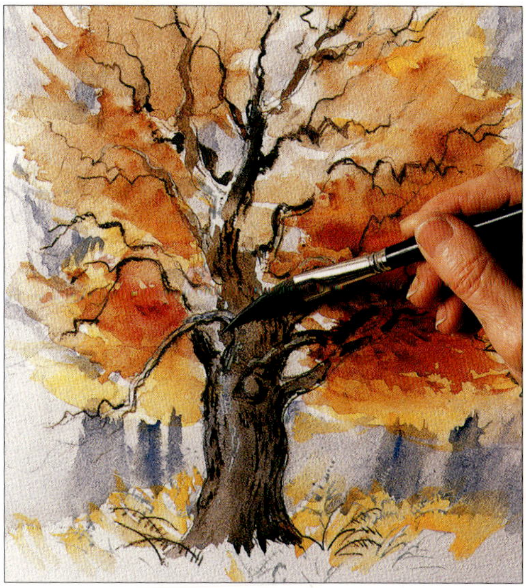

8 Mix a greyish brown from burnt sienna, sepia and a tiny amount of cobalt blue. Paint the branches of the main tree, looking carefully to see which branches go behind others. Even though you are brushing over the water-soluble pencil marks made in Step 2, they will show through again once the watercolour wash is dry.

Assessment time

The main colours have been established but it is hard to tell which direction the light is coming from, and without any strong indication of light and shade, the tree looks rather flat and one-dimensional. For the remainder of the painting, concentrate on improving the tonal contrast and creating a feeling of sunlight streaming through the tree branches.

There needs to be more tonal contrast on the trunk, in particular, to make the tree look natural and rounded.

Foreground detail is essential in order to make the tree look as if it is standing on solid earth.

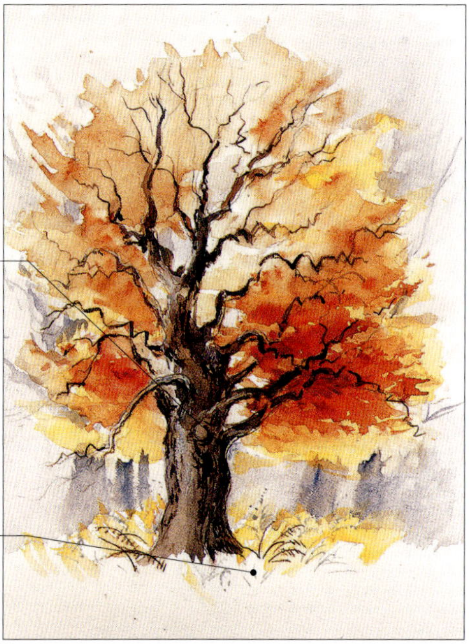

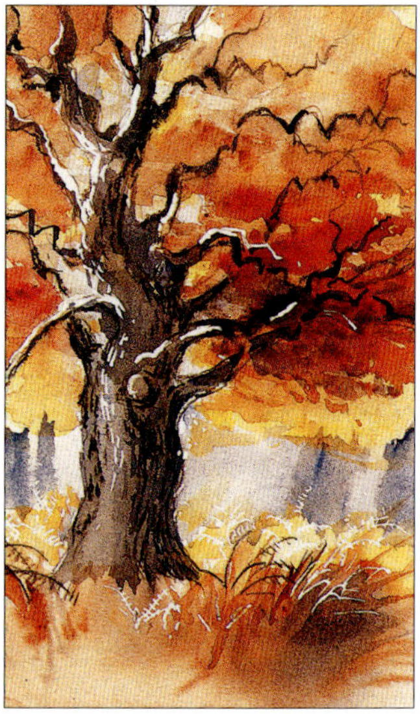

9 Brush loose strokes of burnt sienna into the foreground, bringing some of your strokes up over the yellow grasses. The warm colour and foreground texture help to bring this area of the painting forward. Leave to dry completely. Using your fingertips, gently rub off the masking fluid to reveal the highlighted edges of the branches and the foreground grasses. The feeling of light and shade in the painting is now much stronger.

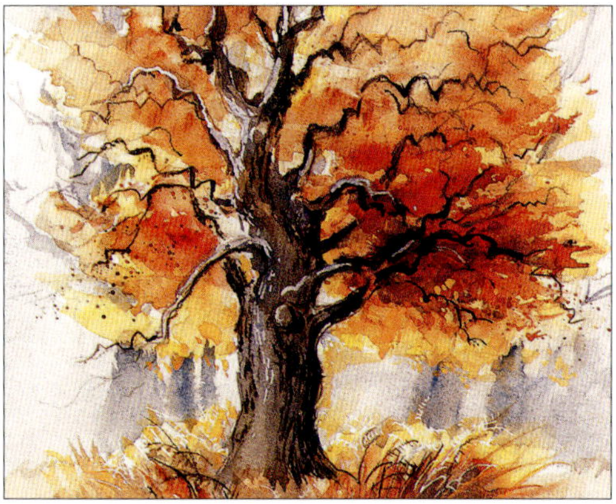

10 Mix a pale grey from white gouache, cobalt blue and violet and paint the exposed areas of the branches and trunk. Spatter alizarin crimson on to the leaves. Leave to dry.

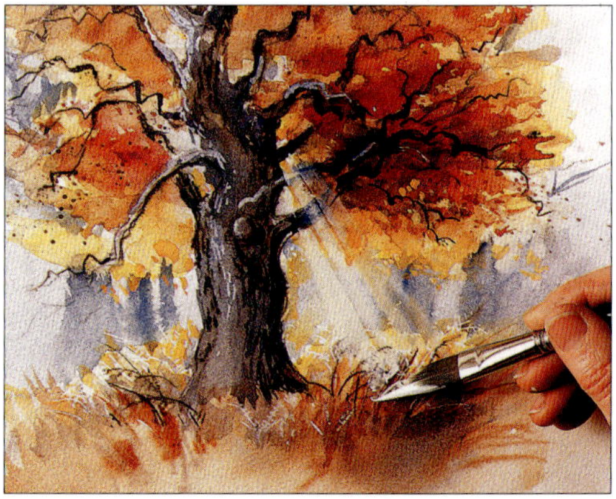

11 Mix a very pale yellow from permanent white gouache with a little cadmium yellow. Brush in very thin shafts of misty early-morning sunlight.

Autumn tree

Painted in a free and spontaneous manner, this little study exploits the richness of autumn colours to the full. In any subject that is viewed against the light, the detail is subdued: here, the dense browns of the trunk and branches provide the necessary structure for the painting, while virtually everything else is reduced to an impressionistic mass of colour. The semi-opaque yellow mixture used to create the shafts of sunlight mutes the underlying colours but does not obscure them completely. This is a very effective way of creating the effect of early-morning mist.

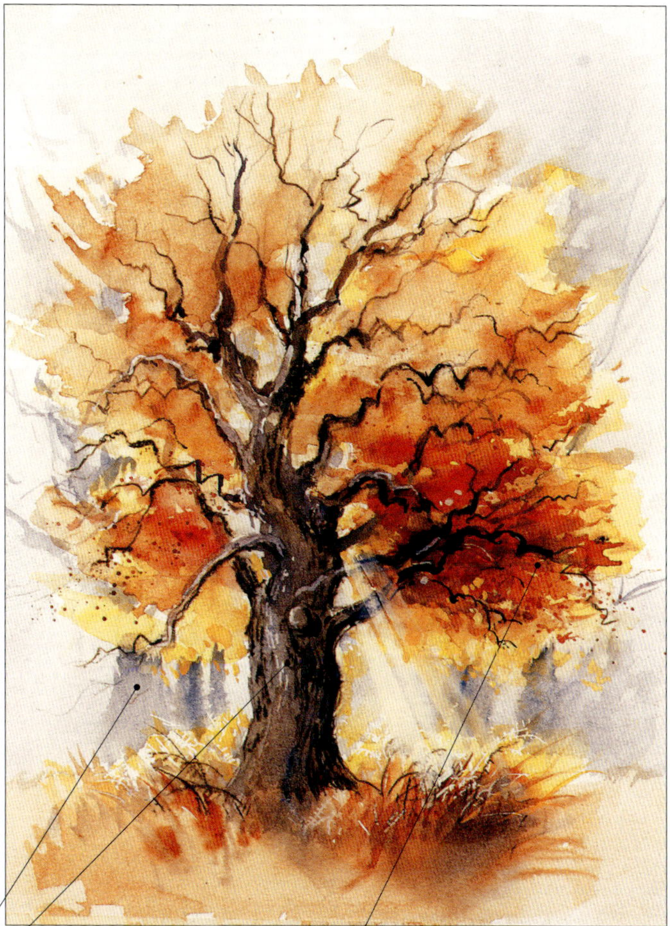

The misty trees in the background provide a hint of the landscape beyond.

Water-soluble pencil marks convey the texture of the tree bark beautifully.

Spattering provides the merest hint of leaf texture: too much would be distracting.

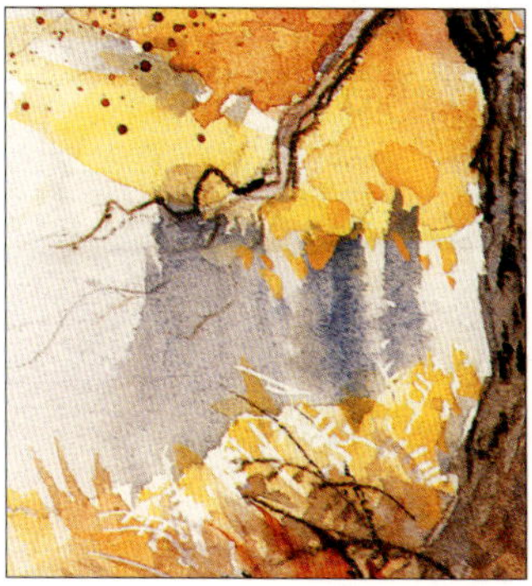

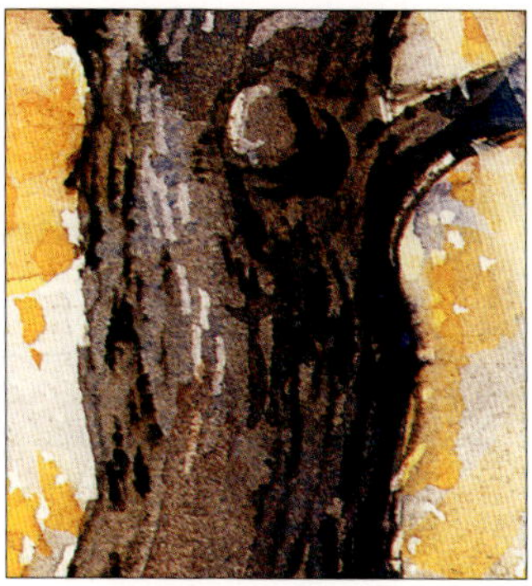

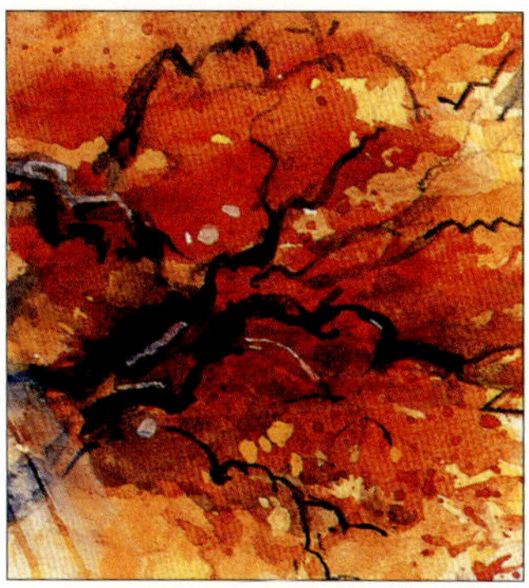

Poppy field

Lush expanses of wild flowers are always attractive, and when those flowers are a rich and vibrant red, like this stunning array of poppies, the subject simply cries out to be painted.

This project presents you with several challenges. First and foremost, it is an exercise in painting spontaneously and in creating an impression of the scene, rather than trying to capture each individual flower. Work quickly and freely, and concentrate more on the overall tones than on specific details. Make sure you don't make the poppies look as if they have been planted in neat, straight rows. It is surprisingly difficult to position dots of colour randomly, but unpredictable techniques, such as spattering, can help.

Second, remember that this is not a botanical study: what you are trying to create is an overall impression of the scene, not an accurate record of how the flowers are constructed. You really don't want a lot of crisp detail in a scene like this, otherwise it will look stilted and lifeless. This is where watercolour really comes into its own. Wet-into-wet washes that merge on the paper create a natural-looking blur that is perfect for depicting a mass of flowers and trees gently blowing in the breeze.

Finally, take some time considering the tonal balance of the painting. Red and green are complementary colours and they almost always work well together, but if the greens are too dark they could easily overpower the rest of the painting. On the other hand, if they are too light they will not provide a strong enough backdrop for the flowers.

Materials

- *2B pencil*
- *140lb (300gsm) rough watercolour paper, pre-stretched*
- *Watercolour paints: cobalt blue, alizarin crimson, gamboge, raw sienna, sap green, Delft or Prussian blue, burnt umber, viridian, cadmium orange, cadmium red, Payne's grey*
- *Brushes: large mop, medium mop, fine rigger, old brush for masking fluid, medium round, fine round*
- *Masking fluid*

The original scene
This field is a blaze of red poppies as far as the eye can see, counter-balanced by a dark green background of trees. Although the horizon is very near the middle of the picture, which can sometimes makes an image look static, this is offset by the fact that the top half of the image is divided more or less equally into trees and sky. However, the sky is very bright, and this detracts from the poppies; adding colour here will improve the overall effect.

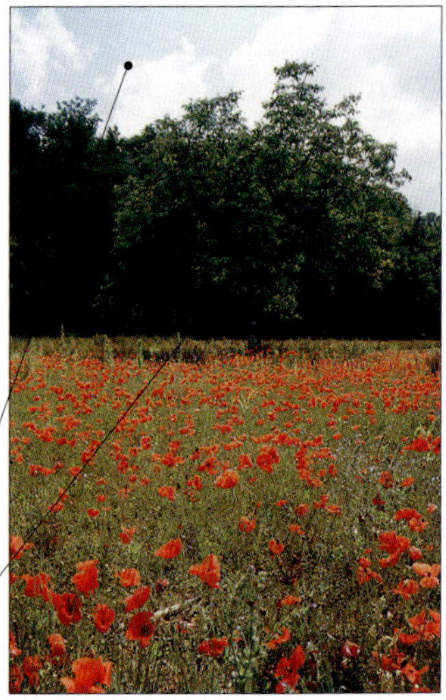

The sky lacks colour and needs to be made less dominant.

The dark trees provide a neutral background that makes the red of the poppies all the more vibrant.

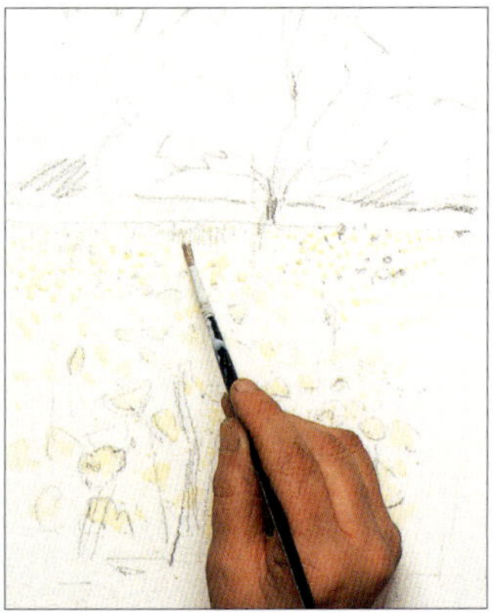

1 Using a 2B pencil, lightly sketch the outline of the trees and some of the larger foreground poppies. Don't attempt to put in every single flower – a few of the more prominent ones are all you need as a guide at this stage. Using an old brush, apply masking fluid over the poppies in the foreground. In the middle ground and distance, dot and spatter masking fluid to create a more random, spontaneous effect. Draw some thin lines of masking fluid for the long grasses in the foreground. Clean your brush thoroughly and leave the painting to dry.

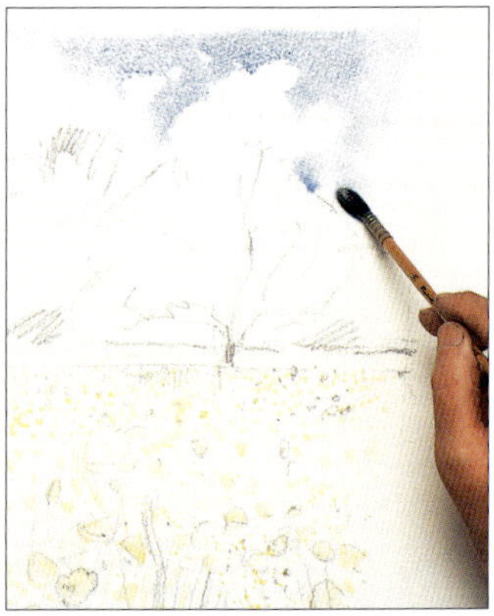

2 Using a medium round brush, dampen the sky area with clean water, leaving a few strategically placed gaps for clouds. Mix up a strong wash of cobalt blue and drop this on to the damp sky area, so that it spreads up to the gaps left for the cloud shapes. The colour is more intense than it was in reality, but the sky needs to look dramatic. Leave to dry.

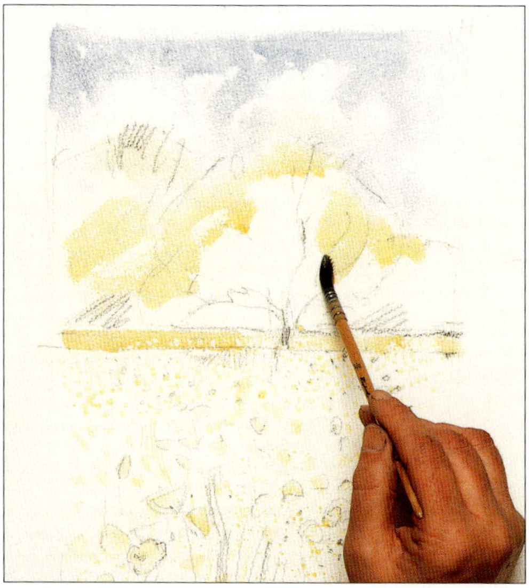

3 Apply a strong wash of gamboge to the tree tops. Add raw sienna and brush over the base of the trees and the horizon. Touch raw sienna into the clouds. While this is still damp, touch a purplish-blue mixture of cobalt blue and alizarin crimson on to the underside of the clouds. Leave to dry.

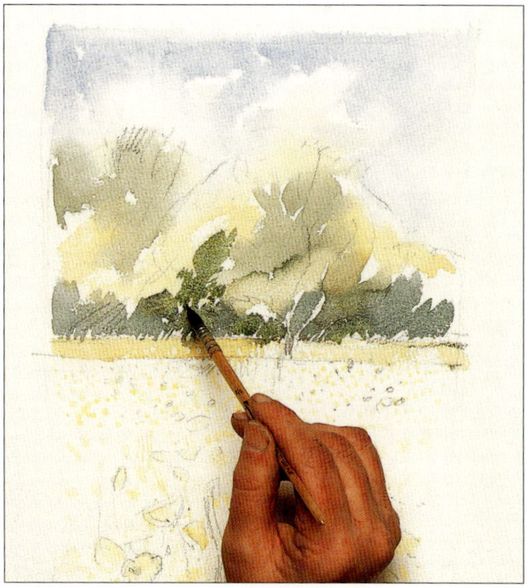

4 Mix a dark green from sap green, raw sienna and a little Delft or Prussian blue. Using a medium round brush, brush this mixture over the trees to create dark foliage areas, allowing some of the underlying gamboge to show through in places.

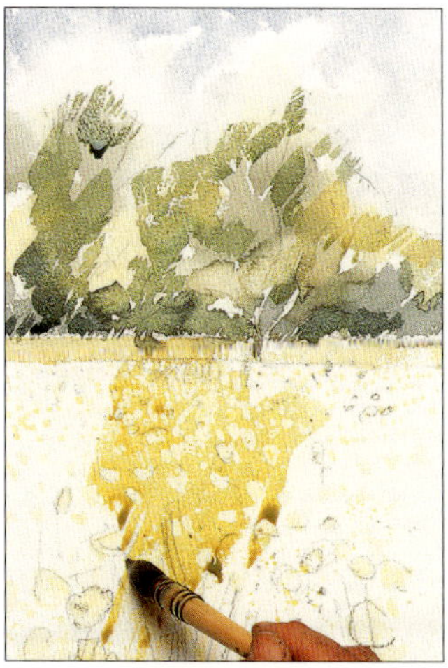

5 Continue building up the foliage on the trees, leaving a few gaps. Mix a mid-toned green from gamboge and sap green and, using a large mop brush, brush this mixture over the lower part of the painting – the poppy field. Leave to dry.

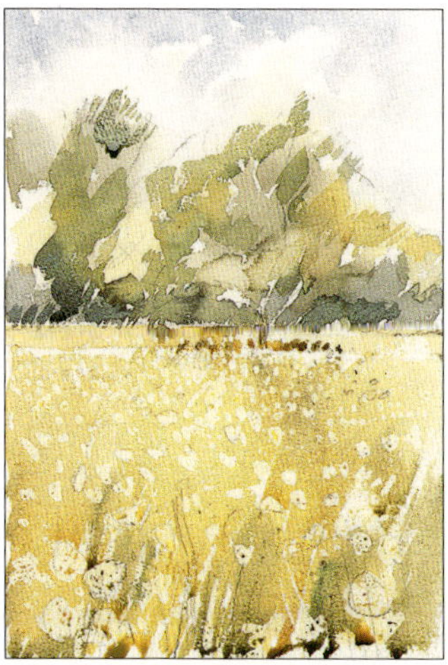

6 Mix a darker green from viridian and cobalt blue and apply this mixture to the foreground, using a large mop brush. Use the same colour to touch in some dark lines for the long shadows under the main tree. Leave to dry.

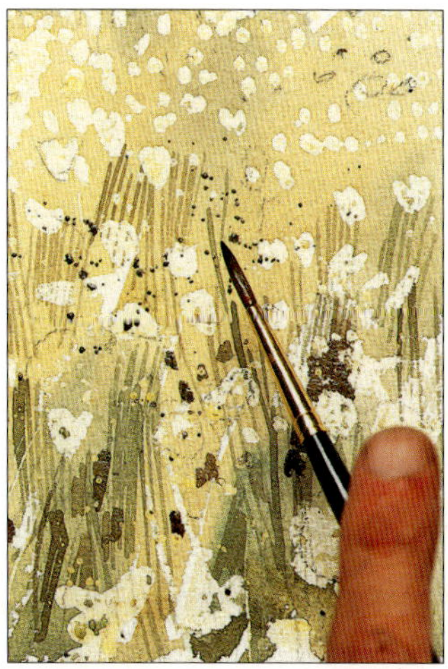

7 Mix a dark green from sap green, raw sienna and burnt umber and, using a fine rigger brush, brush thin lines on to the foreground. Leave to dry. Spatter the same mixture over the foreground to represent the grass seed heads and add texture. Leave to dry.

Assessment time

Cool greens and yellows have been put in across the whole painting, establishing the general tones of the scene. As you continue to work, you will probably find that you need to darken some of the background colours to maintain a balance between them and the foreground. This kind of tonal assessment should be an on-going part of all your paintings. Now it is almost time to start putting in the bright red poppies in the foreground, the finishing touches that will bring the scene to life. Try above all else to maintain a feeling of spontaneity in the painting as you work: the poppies must look as if they are randomly distributed over the scene.

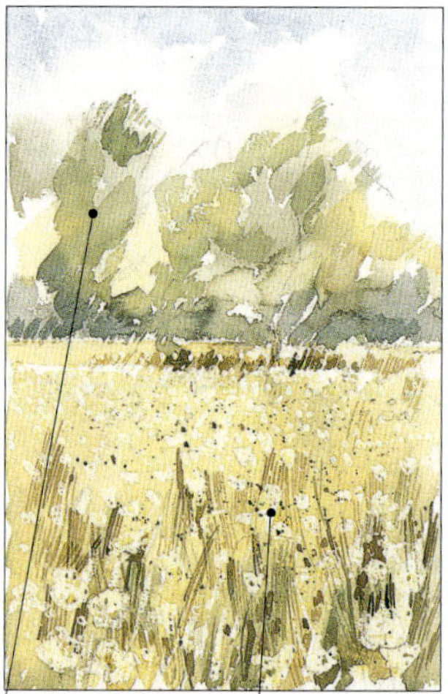

The dark tonal masses of the background have been established.

Spattering in the foreground gives interesting random texture.

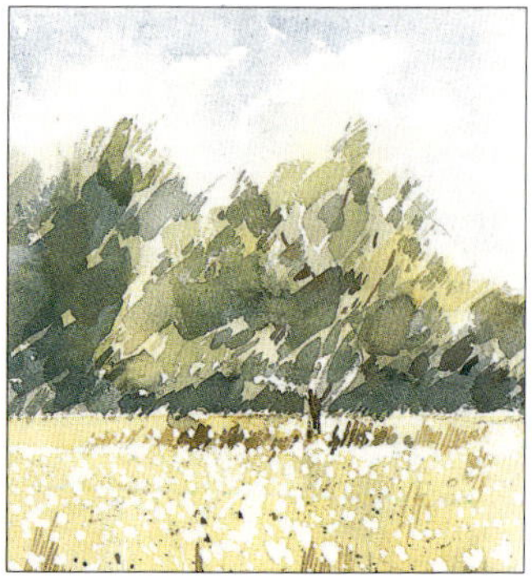

8 Mix a dark green from Delft or Prussian blue, viridian and burnt umber and, using a medium mop brush, darken the trees, leaving some areas untouched to create a sense of form. Add a little more burnt umber to the mixture and, using a fine rigger brush, paint the tree trunks and some fine lines for the main branches. Leave to dry. Using your fingertips, gently rub off the masking fluid.

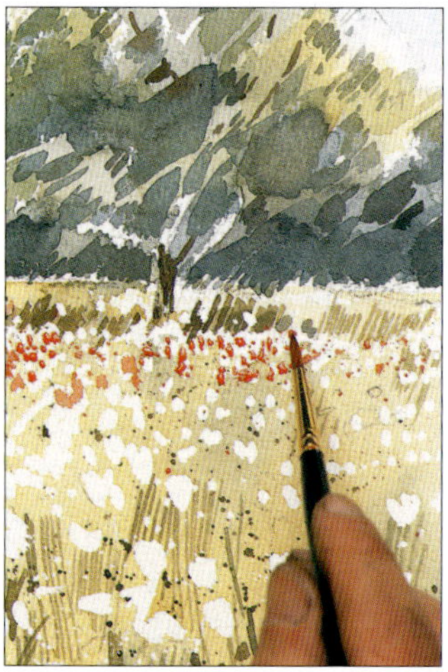

9 Mix an orangey red from cadmium orange and cadmium red. Using a fine round brush, start painting the poppies in the background.

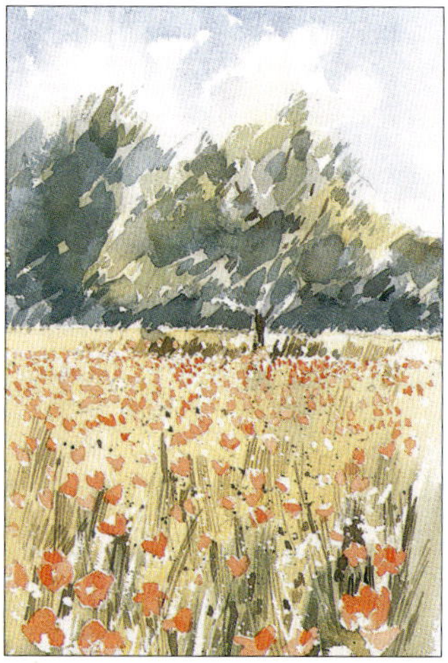

10 Continue painting the white spaces with the red mixture used in Step 11, leaving a few specks of white to give life and sparkle to the painting. Apply a second layer of colour to some poppies while the first layer is still wet; the paint will blur, giving the impression of poppies blowing in the wind, and the tone will deepen.

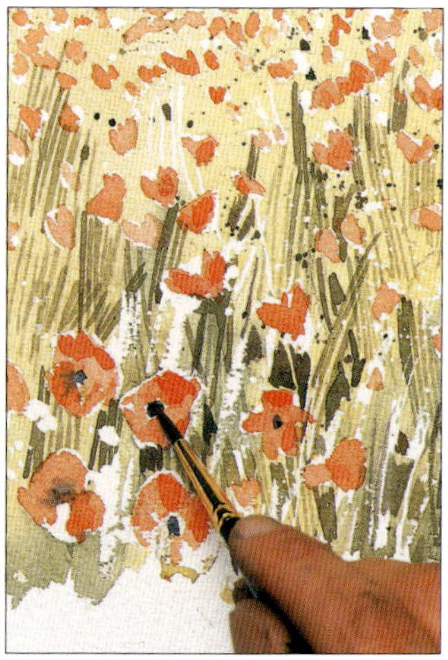

11 Using a fine, almost dry brush and the same dark green mixture used in Step 7, paint in the exposed foreground stalks and grasses. Finally, using a fine rigger brush, touch in the black centres of the poppies with a strong mixture of Payne's grey.

Poppy field

This is a loose and impressionistic painting that nonetheless captures the mood of the scene very well. It exploits the strong effect of using complementary colours (red and green), but the density of colour has been carefully controlled so that the whole painting looks balanced, with no one part dominating the rest.

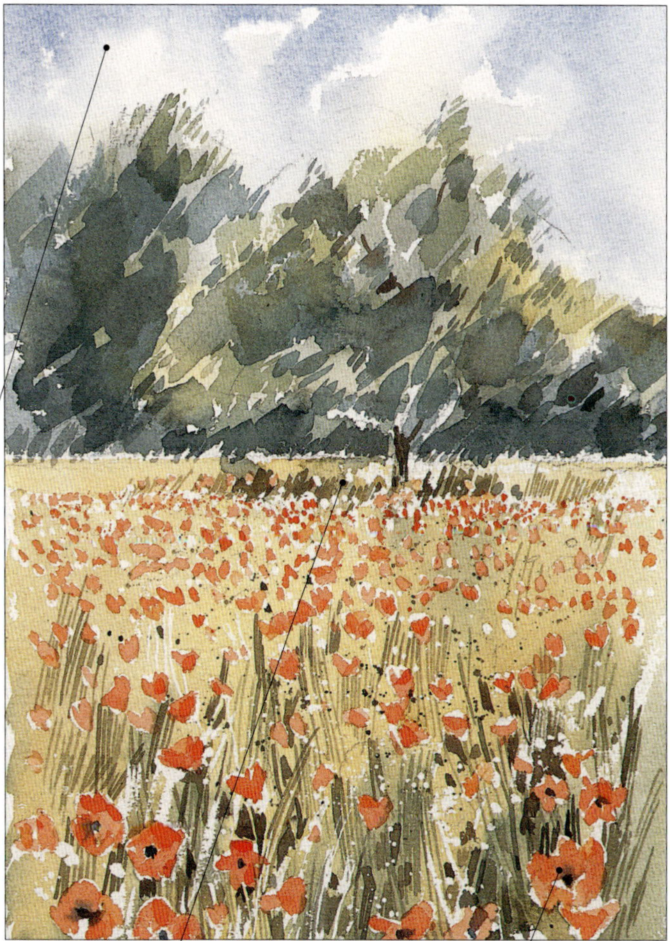

The sky is darker than in the original photograph, which helps to maintain the tonal balance of the scene.

The shadow under the tree is painted with short brushstrokes that echo the direction in which the grasses and flowers grow.

Only the foreground poppies have painted centres. Those in the background are so far away that a blur of colour suffices.

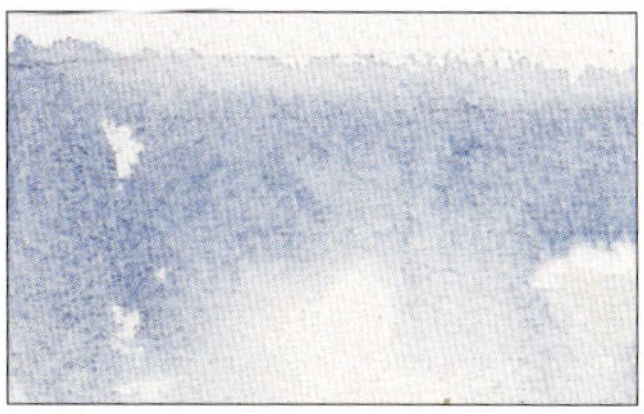

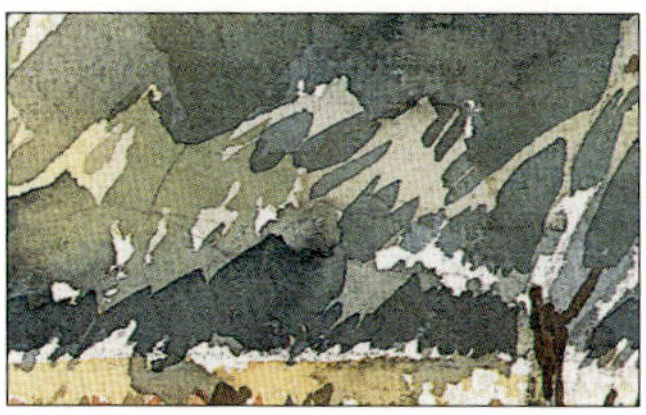

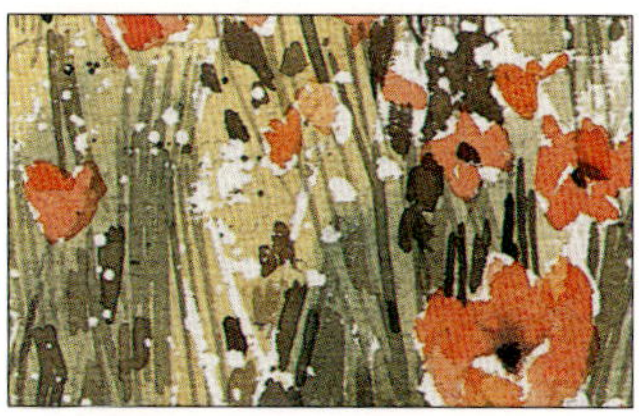

Painting Flowers

The aim of botanical artists is to record for scientific purposes. They need to create as faithful a representation of the flower or plant as possible, with every detail in evidence. The so-called fine artists usually paint flowers for decorative and symbolic reasons, and, of course, because flowers and plants make such terrific subjects.

Like other subjects, you should start by looking at and understanding the basic shape of the flowers you are painting. Look at how they grow and at how the leaves are attached to the stem and radiate out from it. Remember that the flower or flowers are an extension of the stem and not simply something that is stuck on the end of it. The flower head is made up of several different parts: note how each is connected to the others.

Analysing and reducing these often complex elements into simple geometric shapes is a good way to start. Look closely and you will see that flower heads can resemble saucer-like discs, simple spheres, upright or inverted cones, bell or goblet shapes, to name but a few. Learning to look at flowers in this way will not only allow you to draw and paint them well, but it will also let you approach the subject in a looser, more impressionistic or expressionistic way, secure in the knowledge that you are capturing the character of your subject correctly.

You can use every watercolour technique in your repertoire when painting flowers, but planning the sequence in which you are going to work is essential. Unless you are using body colour, you will be working from light to dark, and this often raises the question of how to paint small, complex-shaped flowers against a dark background without painstakingly painting around each flower. (The answer is, of course, masking fluid.)

The colour of certain flowers can seem particularly elusive, as can the way in which colours often bleed into each other, or are distributed on the petals. Make your colour mixes a little stronger and more intense that you think they should be, as watercolour always looks paler when it is dry. Use wet-into-wet techniques, as these will allow the colours to run and mix together by themselves.

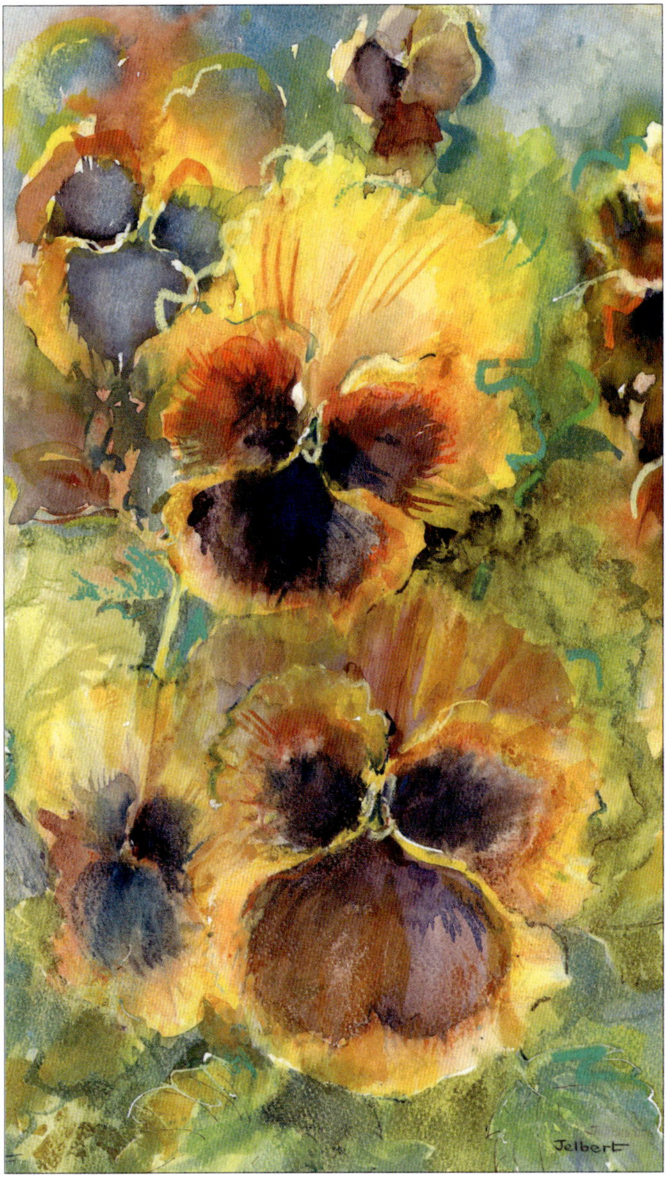

◄ Pansies
This colourful painting uses several watercolour techniques. The image was blocked in using wet-into-wet washes of transparent watercolour. Body colour was then added, some of which was removed by carefully blotting with a paper towel. Detail was added using more body colour and soft pastel.

Parrot tulips ▼
Wet-into-wet and wet-on-dry wash techniques were used to paint these parrot tulips. Chance back-runs and drying marks add to the pattern and interest on the leaves and flower heads, while the characteristic curve of the stems under the weight of the flower heads has been perfectly captured.

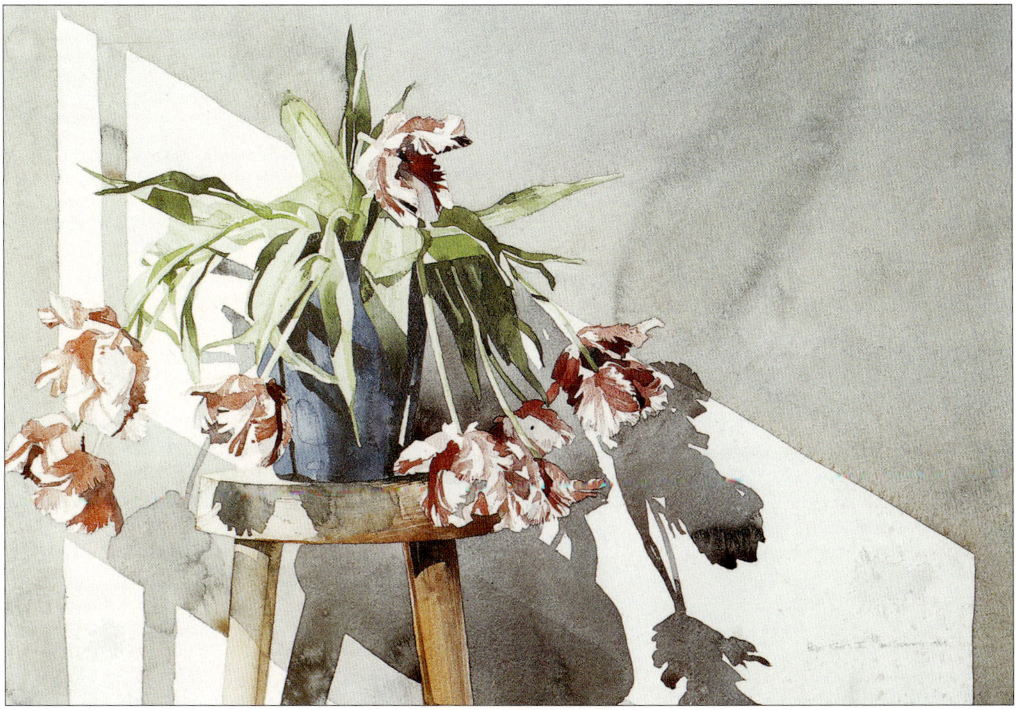

Spring bouquet ►
Here, irises, tulips, anemones and small yellow narcissi have been painted in their wrapping paper. Although the arrangement looks casual, it was very carefully arranged. Wet-on-dry washes were used exclusively. The colours were kept bright by using no more than three layers of wash in any one place.

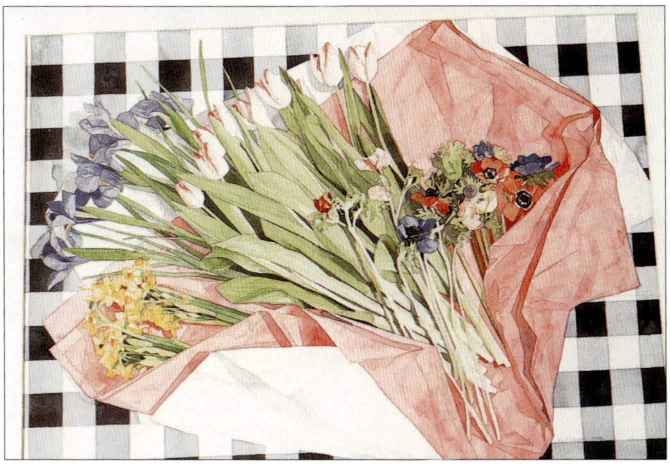

Tips: • Look at the underlying structure and simplify what you see into basic geometric shapes.
• Make several studies of your subject before you begin painting, to increase not only your technical skills, but also your familiarity with the subject.

Sunflower

Bold and bright, their faces turning to follow the sun as it travels through the sky, sunflowers are an artist's dream.

Although the aim of this project is not to produce a botanical illustration, with every last detail precisely rendered, a good flower "portrait" should show something of how the flower is constructed. Is the stem straight or twisted? Are the leaves grouped together at the base of the stem or spread out evenly? Does the flower consist of a single large bloom or lots of little florets? A side view will often tell you more than a face-on viewpoint and can make it easier to make the flower look three-dimensional, particularly when you are painting a relatively flat, symmetrical flower, such as a sunflower.

Materials

- *4B pencil*
- *140lb (300gsm) NOT watercolour paper, pre-stretched*
- *Oil pastels: orange, lemon yellow, bright yellow, sage green, light green, burnt sienna*
- *Watercolour paints: burnt sienna, violet, cadmium yellow, yellow ochre, Hooker's green, cobalt blue, cerulean blue*
- *Gouache paints: permanent white*
- *Brushes: medium round*

The set-up

Because sunflowers were not in bloom when this painting was done, an artificial sunflower was used for the composition. The stem and flowerhead have been twisted slightly to make the image more interesting.

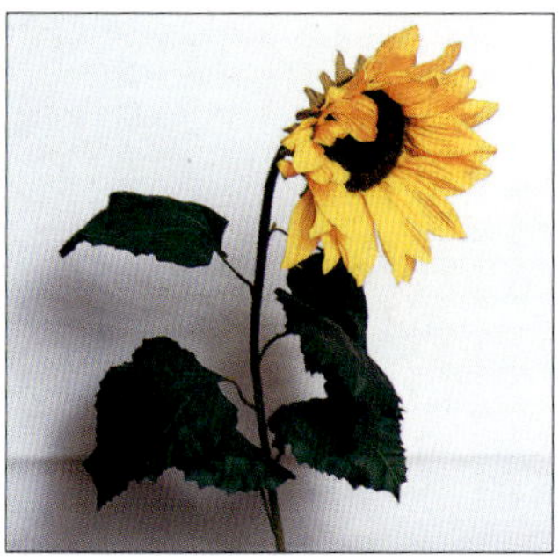

Reference photograph

The artist used a photograph as reference for the colours and the texture in the flower centre. However, the head-on viewpoint and frontal lighting do not make a very interesting composition as there are virtually no shadows or changes of tone in the petals.

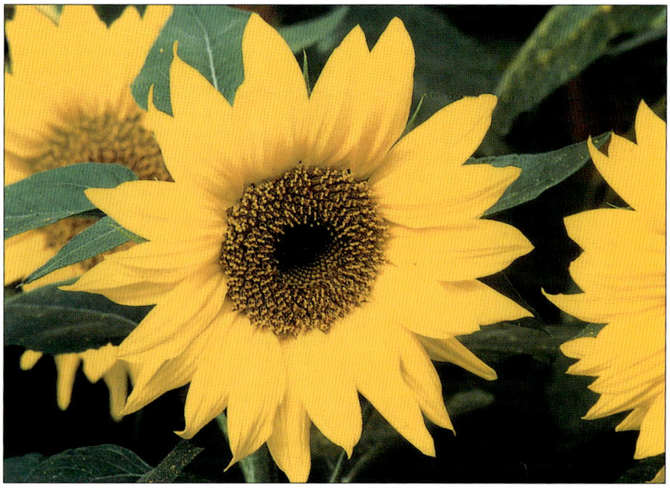

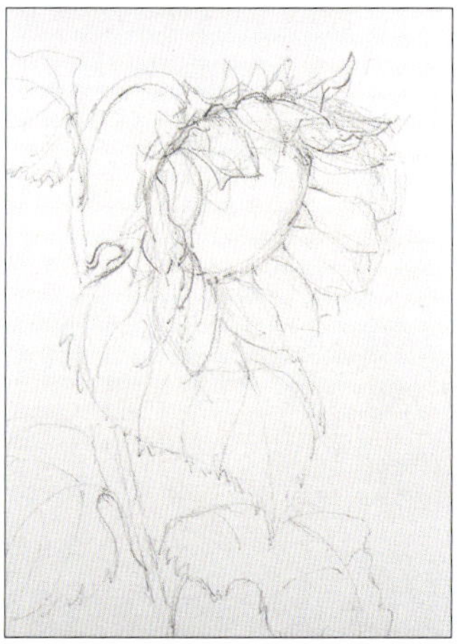

1 Angle the sunflower so that you can see both the interior of the flower and the backs of some of the petals. Using a 4B pencil, lightly sketch the sunflower, paying careful attention to the way the leaves are twisted.

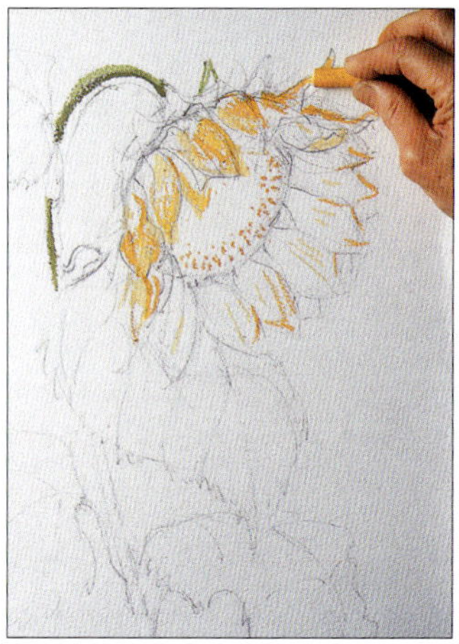

2 Begin putting in some detail with oil pastels, which will act as a resist and allow you to make short, textural marks that would be difficult to achieve using a brush alone. Use orange in the flower centre, lemon yellow and bright yellow on the lightest parts of the petals, and sage and light green on the stalk.

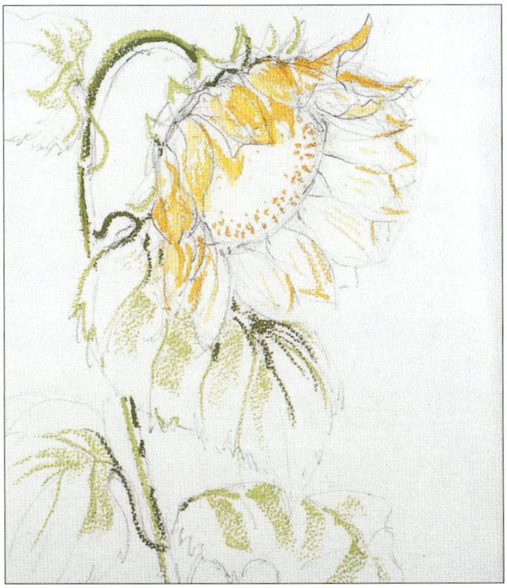

3 Continue using the oil pastels on the stalk and leaves, using sage for the shadowed side of the stalk and the deepest creases in the leaves and light green for the other leaf markings and highlights.

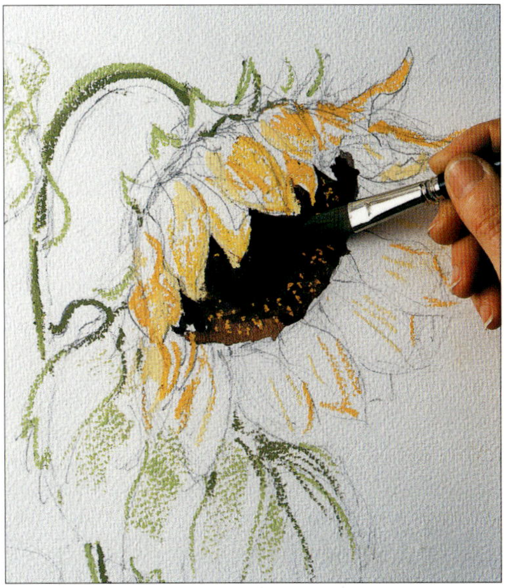

4 Mix a mid-toned wash of burnt sienna watercolour paint and brush it over the centre of the flower. Mix a dark brown from burnt sienna and violet and paint the darkest part of the flower centre.

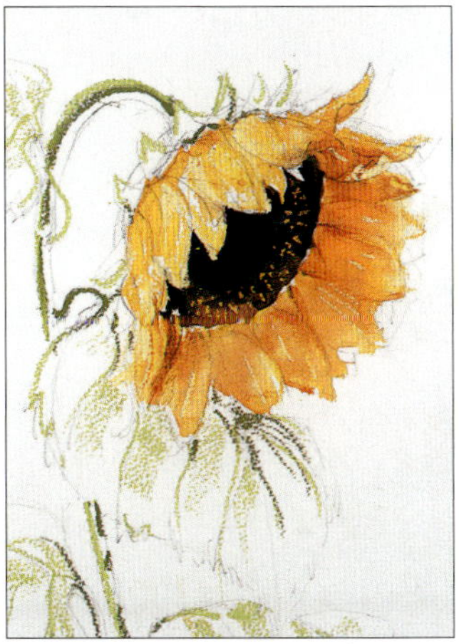

5 Mix a mid-toned wash of cadmium yellow and brush it all over the flower. While this first wash is still wet, mix a light brown from yellow ochre and burnt sienna and drop it wet into wet on to the inner petals, allowing some of the underlying yellow to show through as striations in the petals.

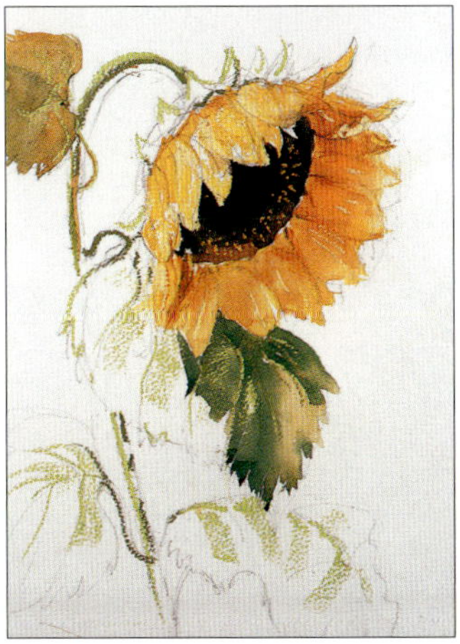

6 Mix a mid-toned green from Hooker's green with a little yellow ochre and begin brushing in the colour for the leaves. Add more yellow ochre to the mixture for the top leaf, which is slightly withered. Note how the oil pastel markings show through from beneath the watercolour.

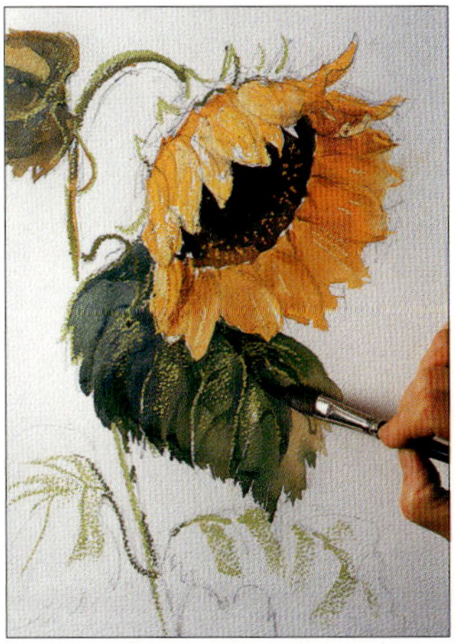

7 While this first green wash is still wet, continue painting the leaves. Sunflower leaves are very textured, so paint the deep crinkles in the main leaf, wet into wet, in cobalt blue, using the tip of the brush. This foreground texture helps to imply that the leaf is closer to the viewer than the others.

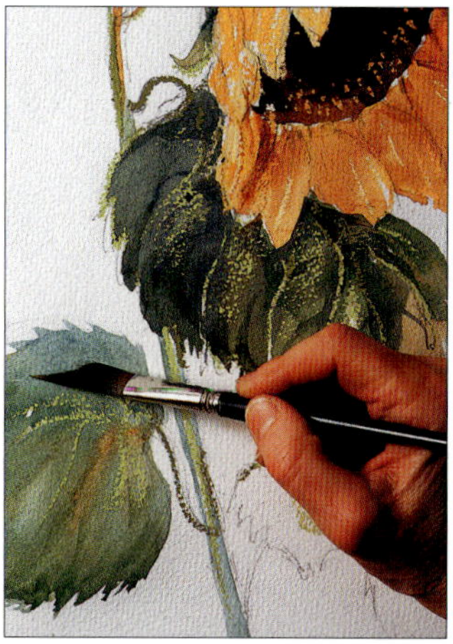

8 Paint the base petals around the outer edge of the flower in a light green mixture of Hooker's green and cadmium yellow. Paint the lowest leaf on the left in the same green mixture used in Step 6, adding cerulean blue to the mixture for the top edge. This cool colour helps to make the leaf recede. Brush yellow ochre, wet into wet, on to the outer edge of this leaf.

Assessment time

The use of warm and cool tones in the leaves is beginning to make the spatial relationships clearer. The cool blue-green of the leaf to the left of the stalk makes it recede, while the warmer greens and yellow ochre of the leaf immediately below the flower make it advance, implying that it is closer to the viewer. Although the painting is nearing completion, some subtle adjustments need to be made in order to create more texture and build up the tones.

More variety of tone is needed on the petals.

The two lowest leaves are too similar in tone: the one at the base needs to be very slightly darker, so that it comes forward more.

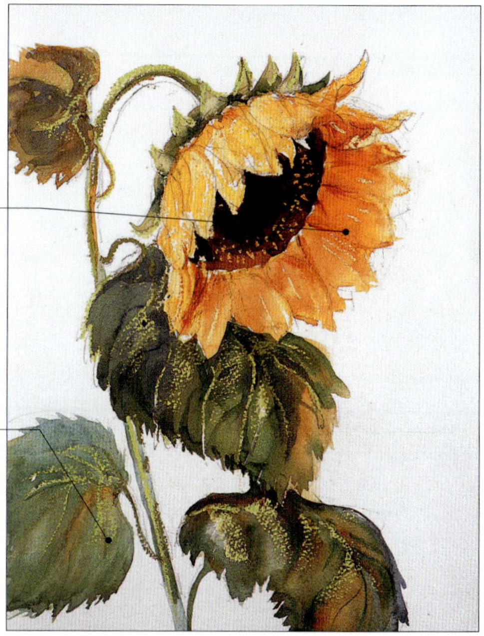

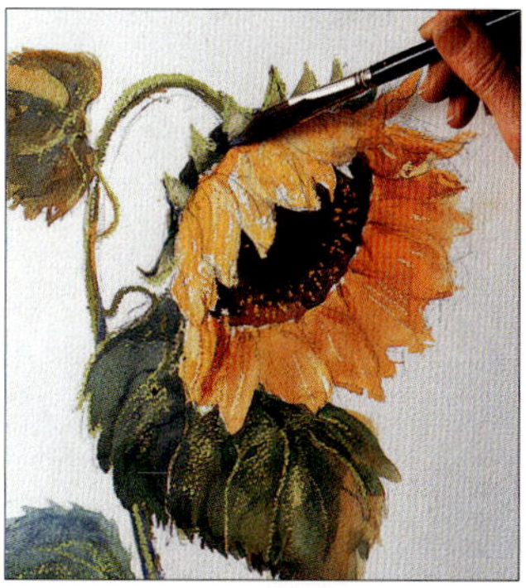

9 Enhance the feeling of light and shade by painting the shadowed side of the stalk in cobalt blue. Dot more blue in behind the base petals.

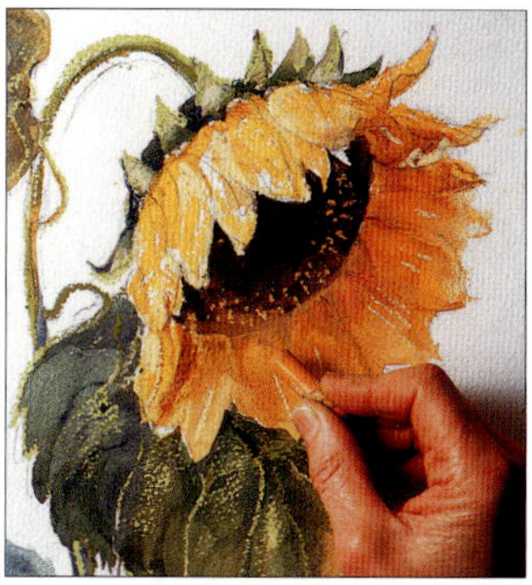

10 Darken the petals and add texture to the inside of the flower, which is shaded from the light, by dotting in orange oil pastel.

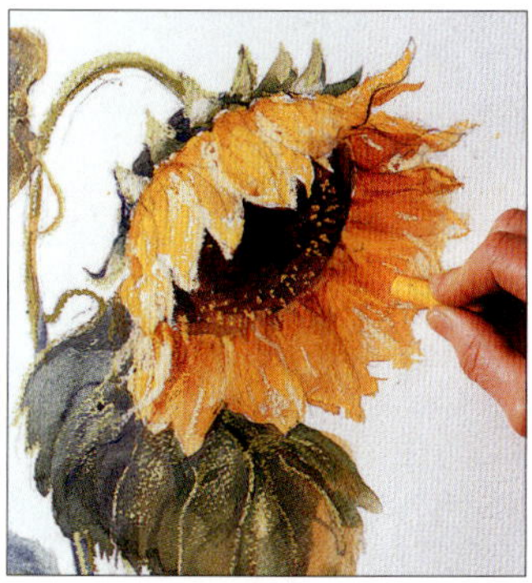

11 Dash short strokes of burnt sienna and yellow oil pastel on to the inner petals in order to darken the tones still further.

Sunflower

This is a colourful and lively flower study that captures the essence of the plant. Note how wet-into-wet washes create subtle variations in tone on both the flower and the leaves, while the use of oil resists provides interesting textures and highlights. Angling the head of the sunflower and positioning the stalk on a slight diagonal have also helped to create a dynamic composition.

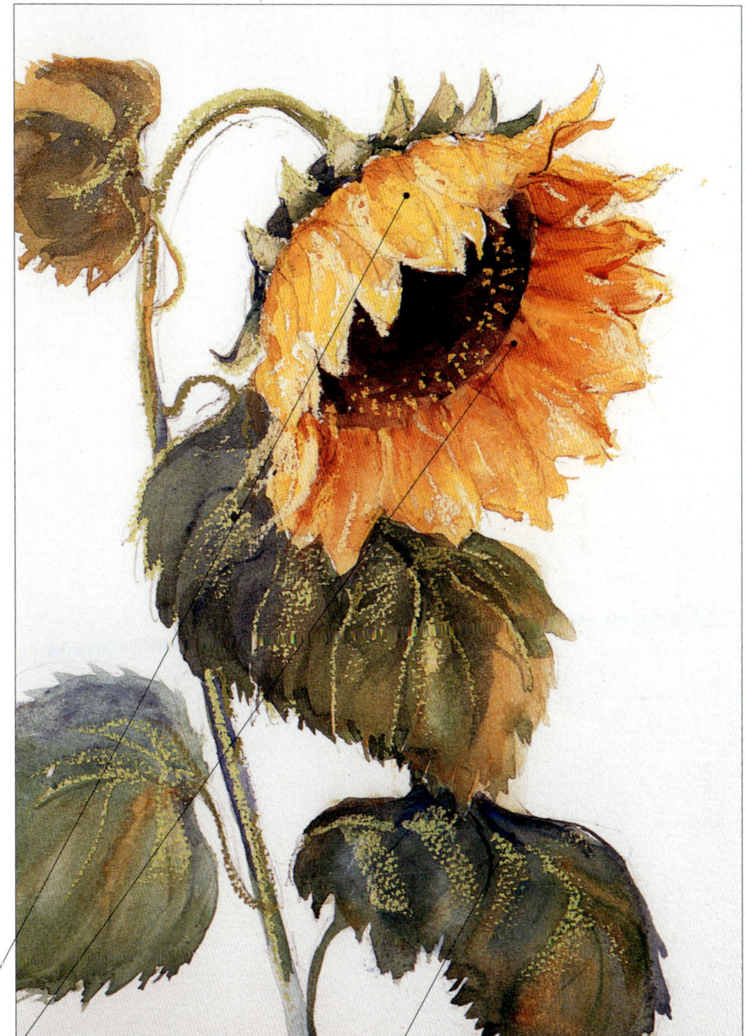

Using pale tones and leaving some of the white paper still visible indicate that this area receives the most direct light.

Oil pastel markings create important tonal and textural contrasts in the centre of the flower.

The shadow cast by the leaf above helps to define the spatial relationships of the leaves.

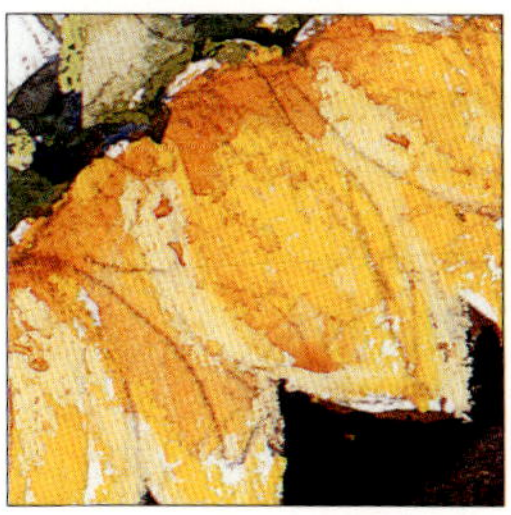

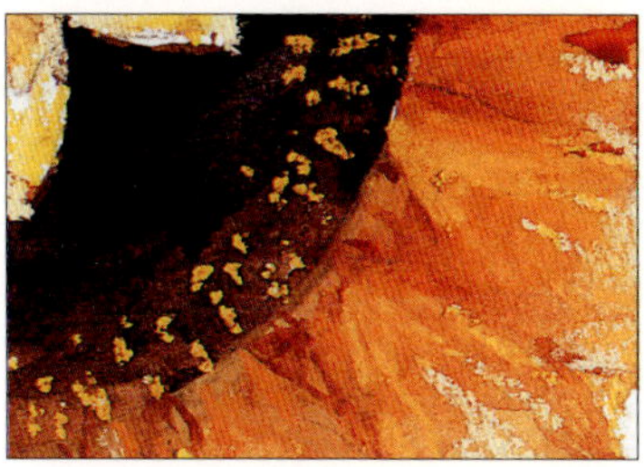

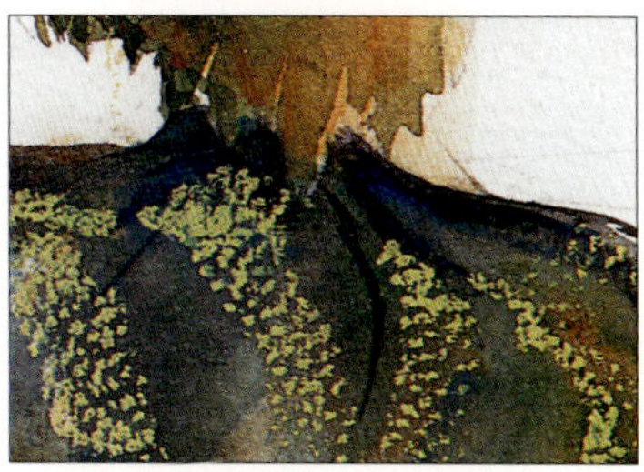

Summer flower garden

This scene was invented entirely from the artist's imagination, using quick sketches of flowers in her own garden and photographs from a garden centre catalogue as reference. When you are combining material from several sources, take the trouble to check a few basic facts. Make sure that the flowers you've selected really do bloom at the same time, and check the relative sizes, so that you don't make a ground-hugging plant appear taller than a small tree.

The project gives you the chance to combine classic watercolour techniques with the relatively modern medium of water-soluble pencils. The characteristics of water-soluble pencils are exploited to the full here. The pencil marks are used dry, to create fine linear detail, particularly in the foreground. They are also covered with watercolour washes, so that the colours merge. You can control the amount of blur to a certain extent: if you wet the tip of the pencil before you apply it, the pencil marks will blur less, allowing you to hold some of the detail and texture in these areas.

Materials

- *140lb (300gsm) NOT watercolour paper, pre-stretched*
- *Water-soluble pencils: dark blue, light brown, cerulean blue, light violet, dark violet, blue-green, olive green, red, yellow, orange, deep red, green*
- *Watercolour paints: cerulean blue, rose doré, Linden green, dark olive, olive green, cobalt blue, cadmium yellow, Naples yellow, burnt sienna, vermilion, alizarin crimson, Payne's grey*
- *Brushes: medium round, fine round*
- *Ruling drawing pen*
- *Masking fluid*

Tip: Changing from a horizontal to a vertical format may alter other elements as well. In the final composition, the path still runs from the bottom right to the top left but the artist made the foreground flower border more prominent.

Reference sketches

Look closely at detailed sketches, illustrations or photographs of individual flowers before you embark on your full-scale painting. Although a massed clump of foliage and flowers may look like an indistinct jumble, knowing the shape and colour of an individual bloom will help you capture the essential features of the plant.

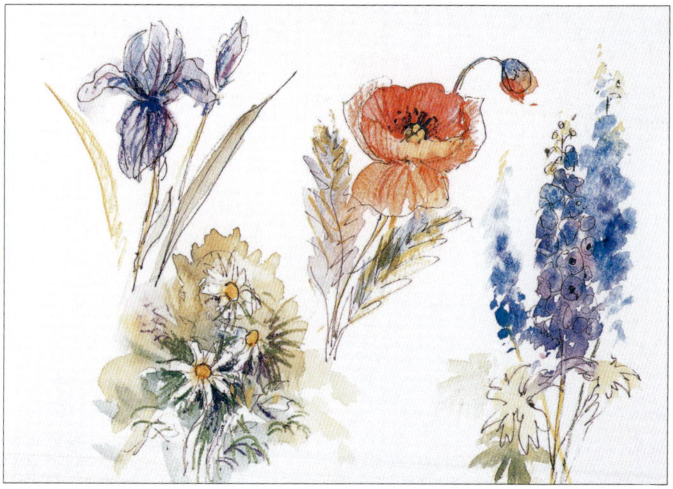

Preliminary sketch

The artist invented a garden scene and made a small sketch to try out the colours and the composition. To begin with, she opted for a horizontal format. Then she decided that this placed too much emphasis on the pathway and that a vertical format, with the rose arch as the main feature, would have more impact.

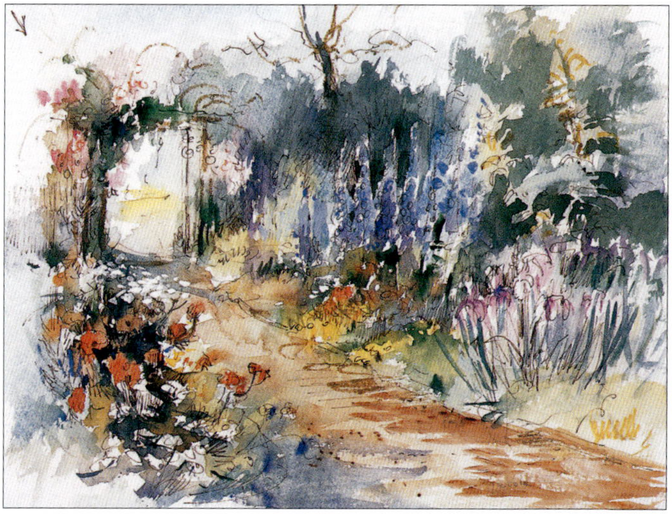

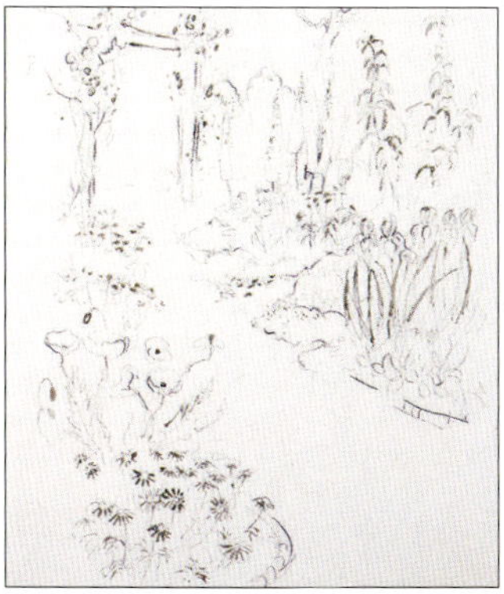

1 Using a dark blue water-soluble pencil, sketch the main shapes of your subject. Dip a ruling drawing pen in masking fluid and mask the lightest parts of the flowers.

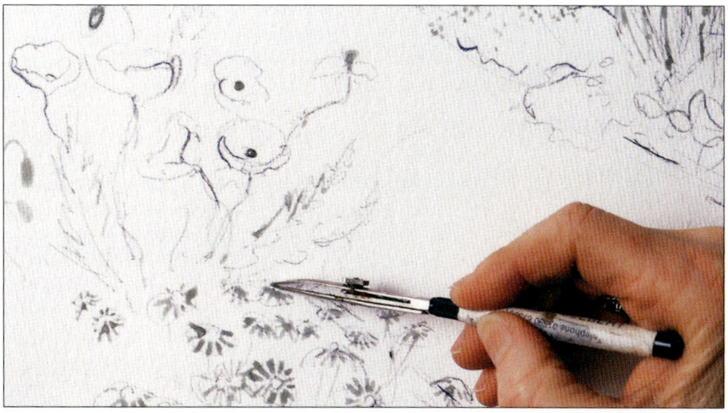

2 One of the advantages of using a ruling drawing pen is that it holds the masking fluid in a reservoir. A range of marks is used to convey the different textures of each of the massed clumps – flowing lines for the poppy heads and little dashes for the daisy petal in the foreground. It would be more difficult to achieve this with a dip pen as the nib would block up, leaving blobs and blots on the paper.

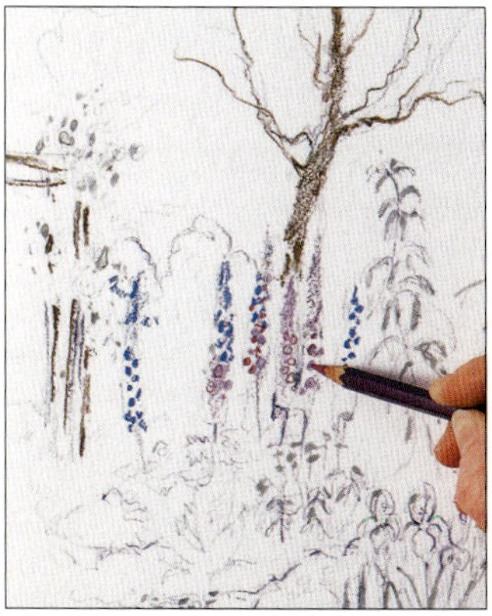

3 Shade in the trunk of the tree with loose pencil strokes, using a light brown water-soluble pencil. (This makes the marks more permanent.) Dip the tip of the pencil in clean water and draw the branches. Draw the wooden rose arch in the same colour. Colour in the individual delphinium blooms with small dots of cerulean blue, changing to light and dark violet for the stems that are in deeper shade. Dip the pencil tip in water to make some of the marks.

Tip: Take care not to rub off any of the masking fluid as you work.

Assessment time

Continue with these dots and dashes of pencil work until you have established the general colour scheme of the garden. Don't be tempted to do too much or the pencil work might begin to overpower the picture: this is a painting, not a drawing, and it is the watercolour paint applied in the subsequent stages that will give the work its character.

Blue-green for the foliage.

Olive green and light violet for the iris leaves.

Yellow, red and orange for the poppies.

The negative spaces between the clumps of flowers are as important as the flowers themselves.

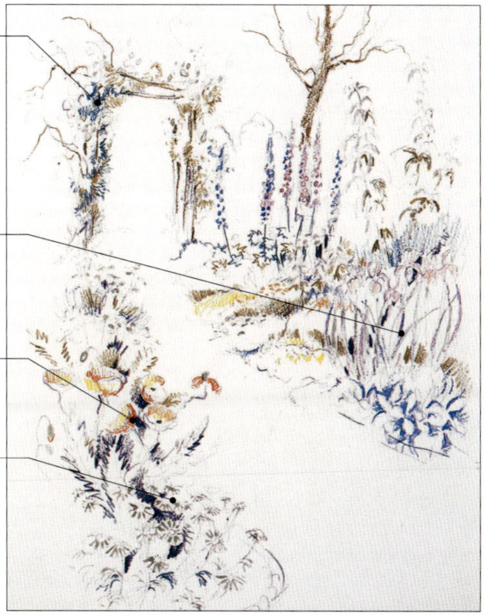

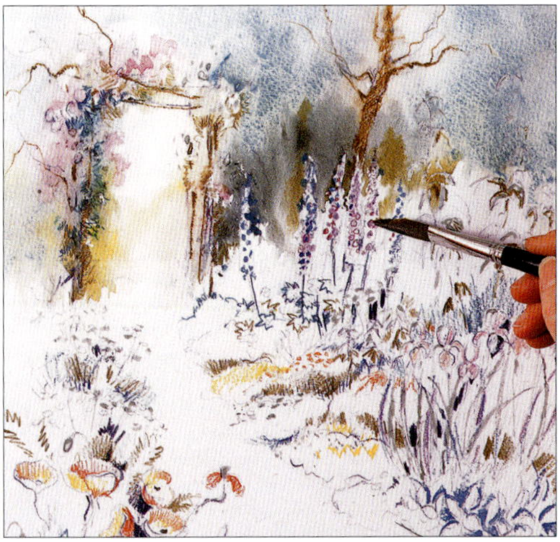

4 Dampen the background with water. Wash a pale mix of cerulean blue watercolour paint over the sky, brushing around the branches. Dot rose doré over the rose arch: the paint will blur, suggesting full-blown blooms. Brush Linden green under the arch and dot a mixture of dark olive and cerulean blue into the background and between the delphiniums. While the paint is still damp, add bright olive green with cerulean blue and brush over the first blue wash.

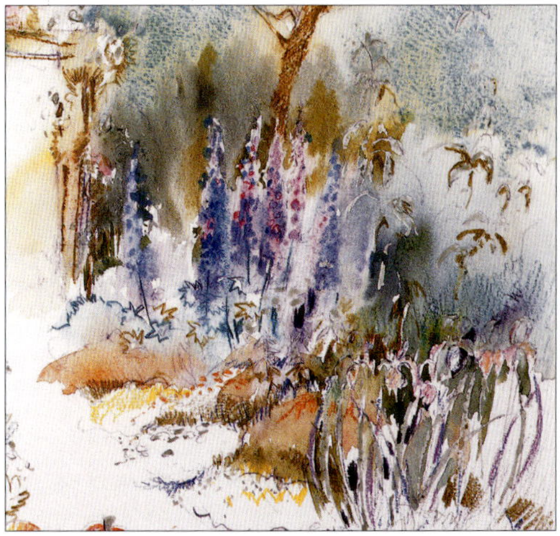

5 Dampen the middle distance with clean water. Dot cerulean blue, rose doré and cobalt blue on to the delphiniums. Both the paint and the initial water-soluble pencil marks will blur and spread, causing the flowers to look slightly out of focus. Mix a neutral brown from olive green and rose doré and brush it into the negative spaces between the iris stems. The flowers will begin to stand out more against this dark background.

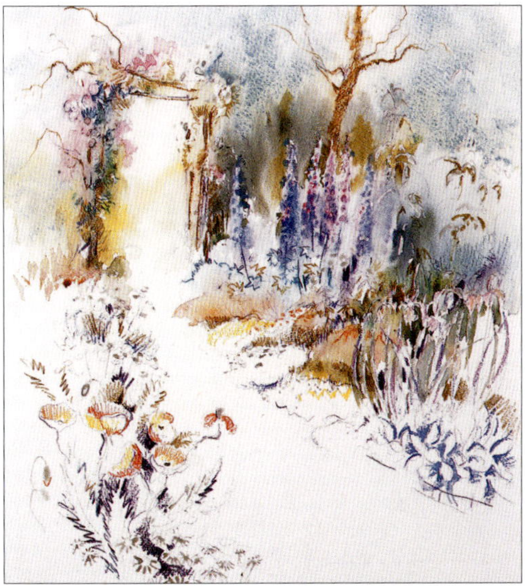

6 The distance and middle ground have now been established. Note how the soft tones and lack of clear detail help to imply that these areas are further away from the viewer.

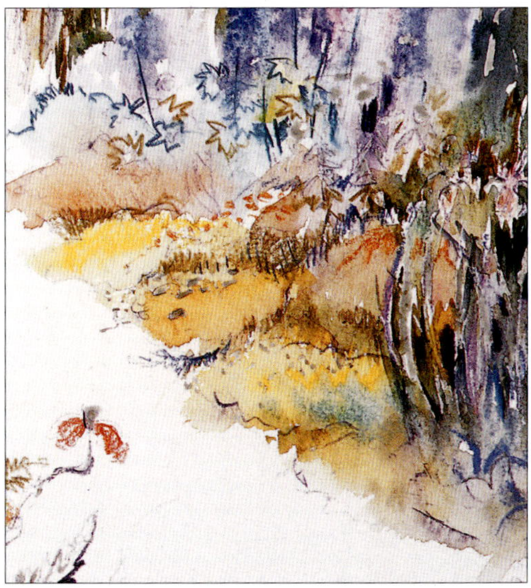

7 Mix a bright green from cerulean blue and cadmium yellow and dot it loosely into the pathside area for the hummocks of low-growing ground-cover plants that spill over on to the path.

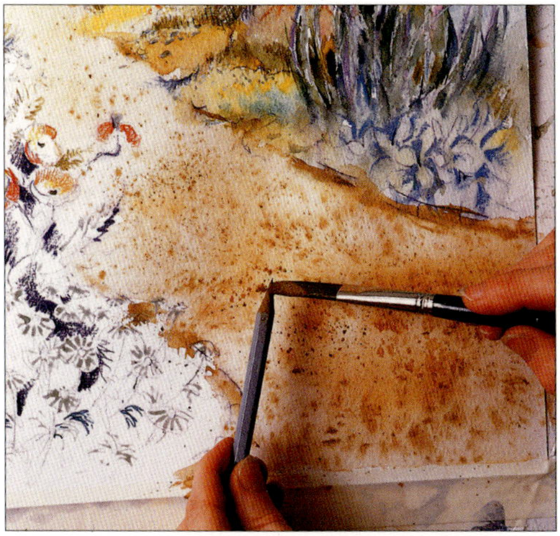

8 Dampen the path. Starting near the arch, brush pale Naples yellow over the path, adding burnt sienna towards the foreground. Brush clean water over the tip of a brown water-soluble pencil and spatter colour on to the path, using the brush. Start spattering in the foreground and work towards the rose arch. As the brush dries, the drops of water – and the dots of colour – get smaller, and this will help to create a sense of recession.

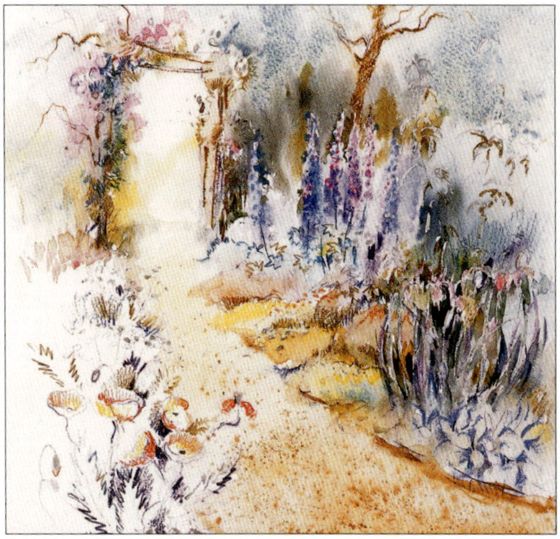

9 Note how effectively the curved path leads the eye to the focal point of the painting – the rose-covered arch. The spattered drops of colour provide important texture in what would otherwise be a large expanse of flat brown.

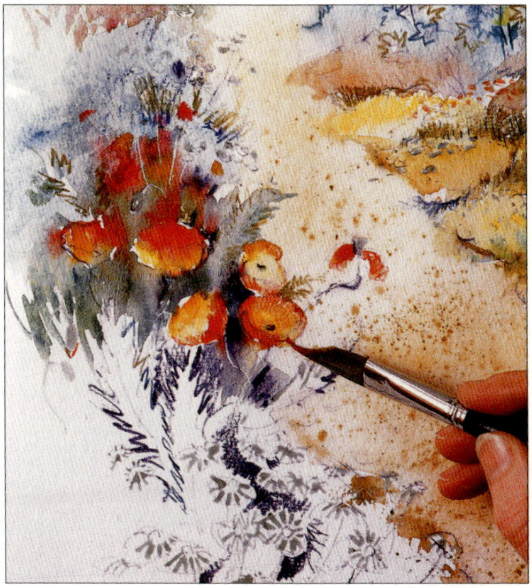

10 Brush cadmium yellow and then vermilion over the red poppy heads, allowing the colours to blend on the paper, and brush a tiny bit of alizarin crimson over parts of the foreground poppies to give added depth of tone.

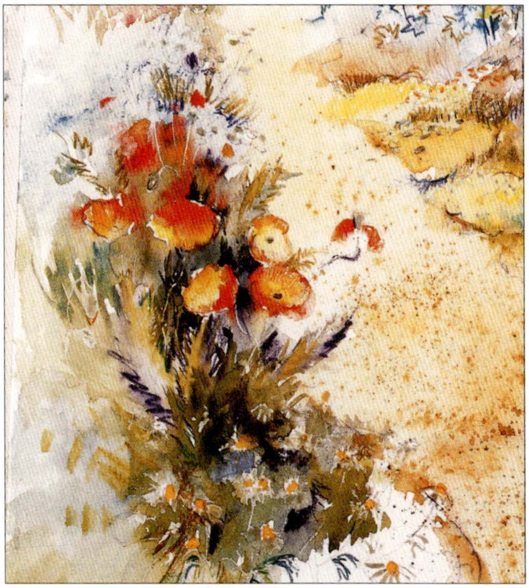

11 Mix Payne's grey with olive green for some of the background poppy leaves and stems. Add a little cobalt blue to the mixture for the foreground poppy leaves. Dot cadmium yellow in the centre of the daisy flowers.

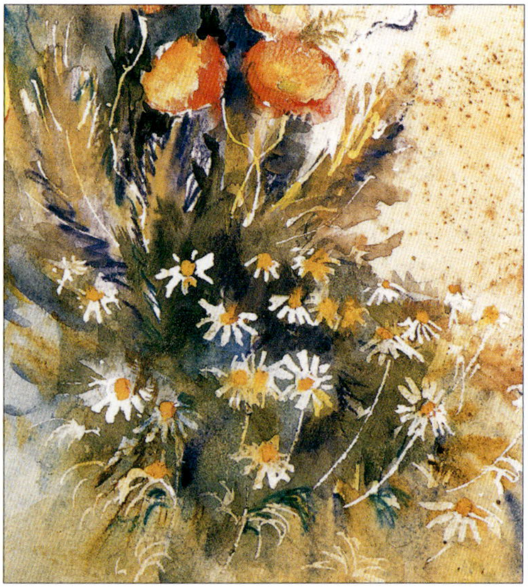

12 Finish the bottom left-hand corner, using the same green mixture as before.

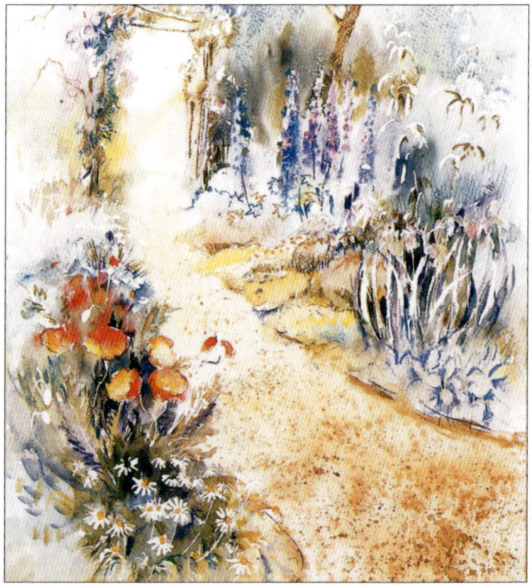

13 Using your fingertips, gently rub off the masking fluid to reveal the white parts of the flowers.

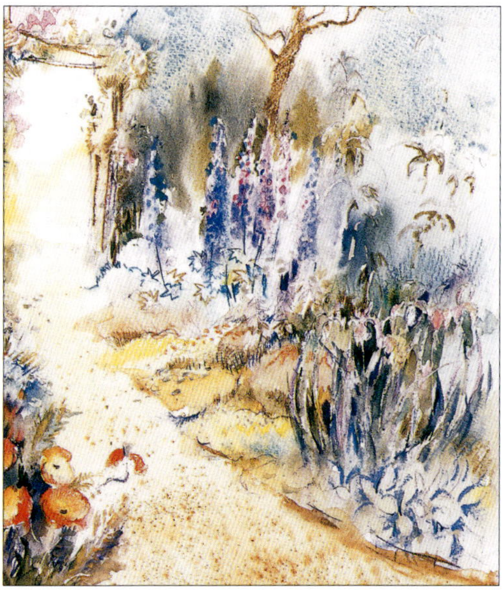

14 Some of the exposed white areas now look too stark – particularly in the background. Mix a very pale wash of cerulean blue and brush it over some of the iris stems to tone down the brightness – otherwise the viewer's eye will be drawn to these areas, which are not the most important parts of the scene.

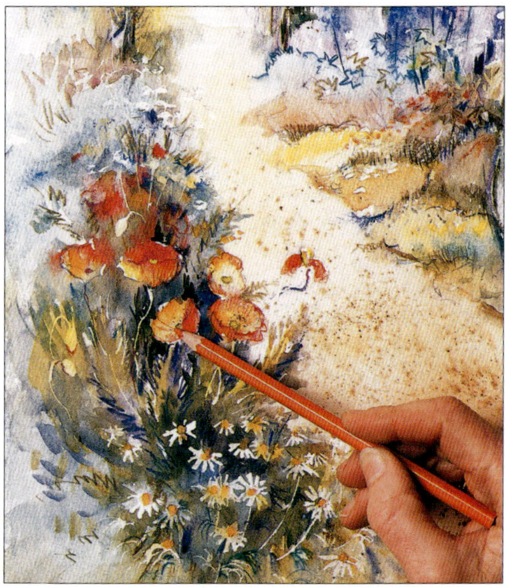

15 Now go back to the water-soluble pencils to add sharper details in the foreground. Use a deep red pencil to delineate the petals and frilly edges of some of the larger poppies, and draw a green pencil circle around the yellow centres of the poppies. Darken the spaces between the daisy petals with a dark blue pencil.

Summer flower garden

This painting is a romantic, impressionistic portrayal of a traditional flower garden. Softly coloured poppies, irises, daisies and delphiniums line the winding path, which leads to the focal point of the image – the rose arch. There is a hint of mystery in the painting, too: what lies on the other side of the archway?

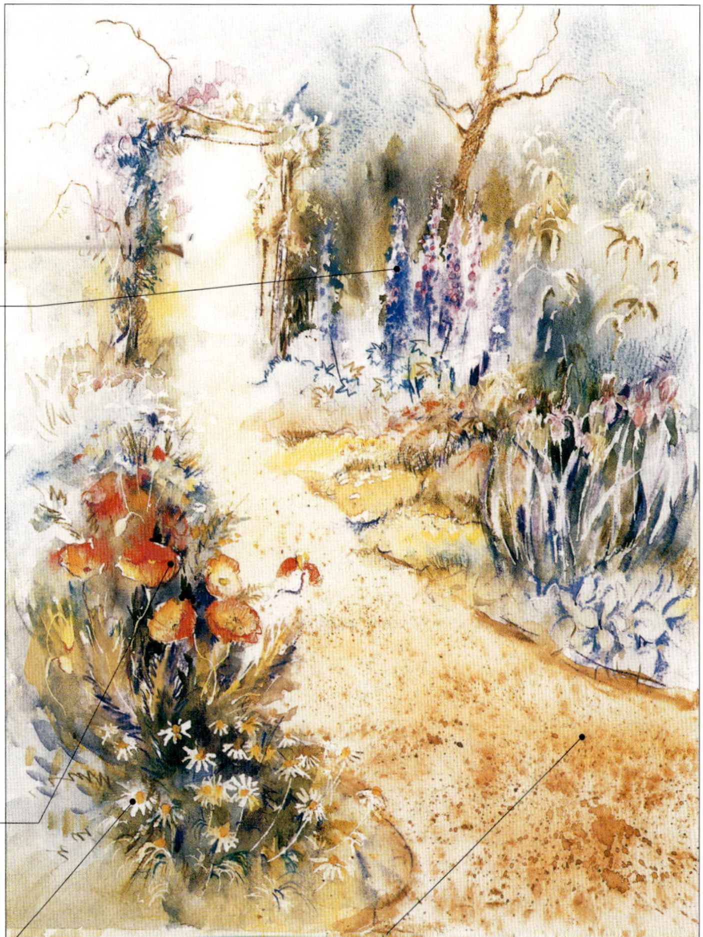

Flowers in the background are more blurred than those in the foreground, but some linear detail is still visible.

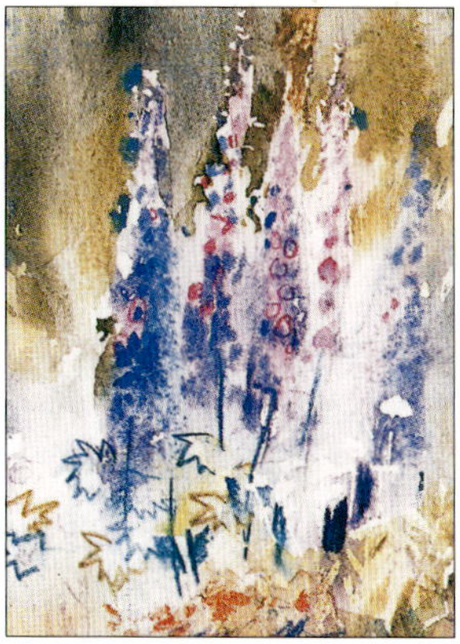

The poppies are painted with a number of different techniques – masking for the twisting stems, wet-into-wet washes for subtle colour blends, and fine pencil detail.

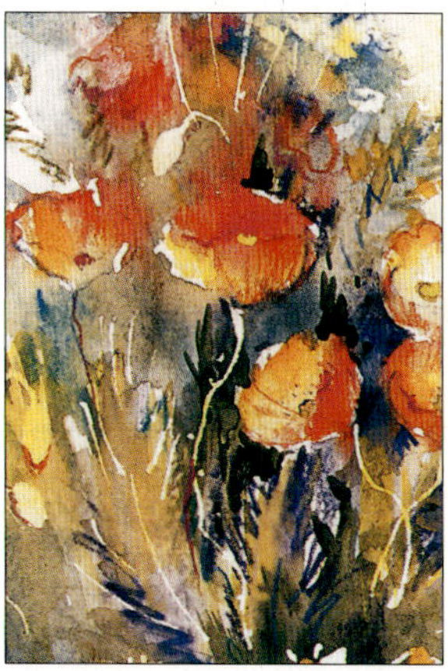

Reserving the white of the paper for the daisy petals adds sparkle to the image.

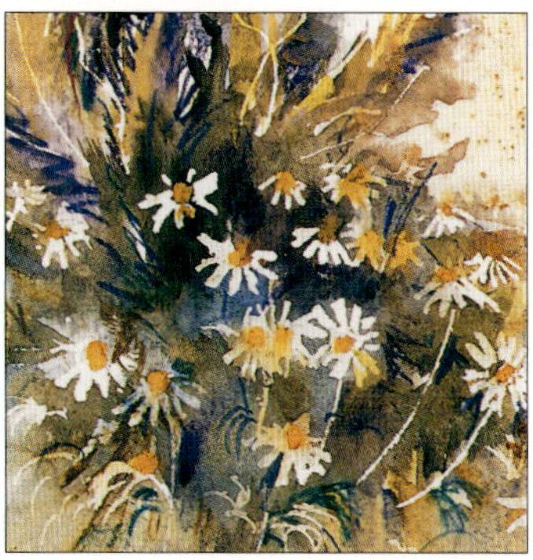

The textured path provides subtly coloured but necessary foreground interest.

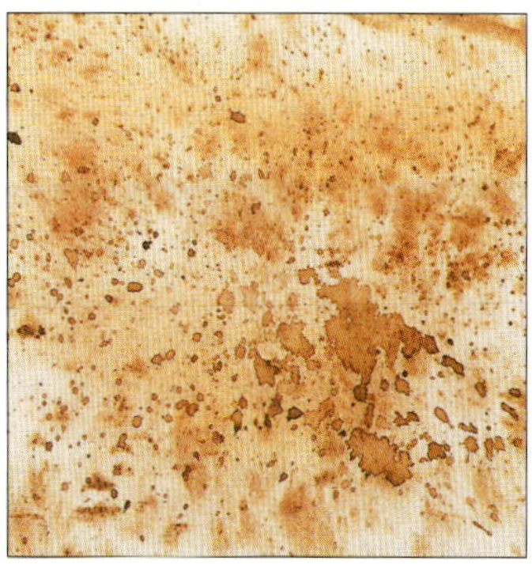

French vineyard

This deceptively simple-looking scene is a useful exercise in both linear and aerial perspective. Take care over your underdrawing, as it underpins all the rest of the painting: if the rows of vines appear to be going in the wrong direction it will look very strange. It is worth taking plenty of time over this stage.

You also need to mix tones carefully. Note how the dark green vine leaves in the foreground give way to a much paler, yellower green in the distance – and then see how these pale greens gradually darken again above the horizon line, shifting from a mid green to a very bluish green on the distant hills. Remember to test out each tone on a scrap piece of paper before you apply it to the painting.

Materials

- *2B pencil*
- *140lb (300gsm) rough watercolour paper, pre-stretched*
- *Watercolour paints: cerulean blue, Naples yellow, gamboge, light red, sap green, ultramarine violet, cobalt blue, viridian, Payne's grey, burnt umber*
- *Brushes: large mop, medium mop, fine round*

Reference photographs

Sometimes one reference image simply doesn't give you enough information to create the painting you want. Don't be afraid to combine elements from several photos or sketches to create the desired effect. Here, the artist referred to the long panoramic-format photograph for the close-up detail of the vine leaves and the farm buildings, but based his composition on the larger photograph, in which the rows of vines are angled in a more interesting way.

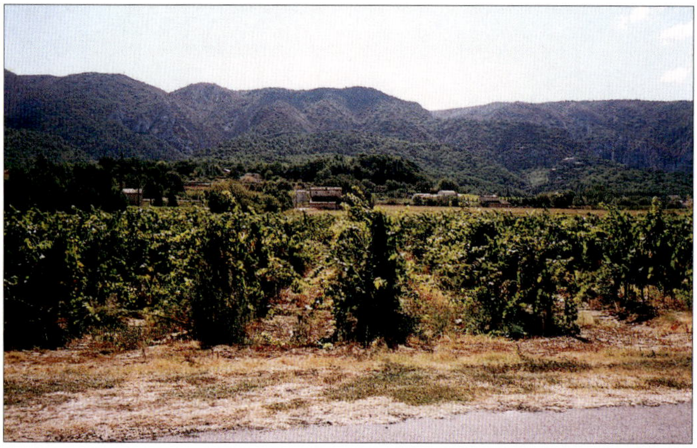

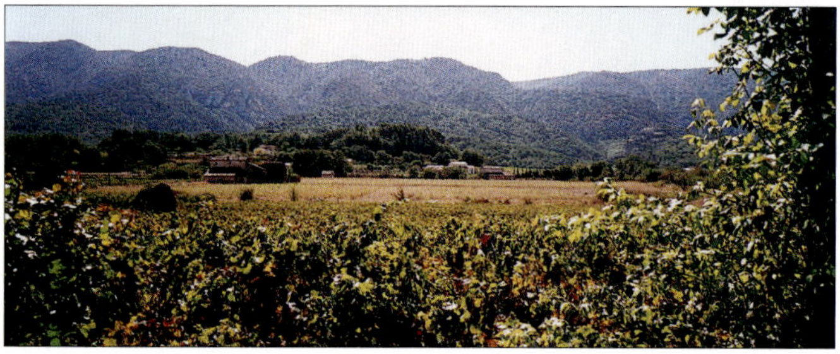

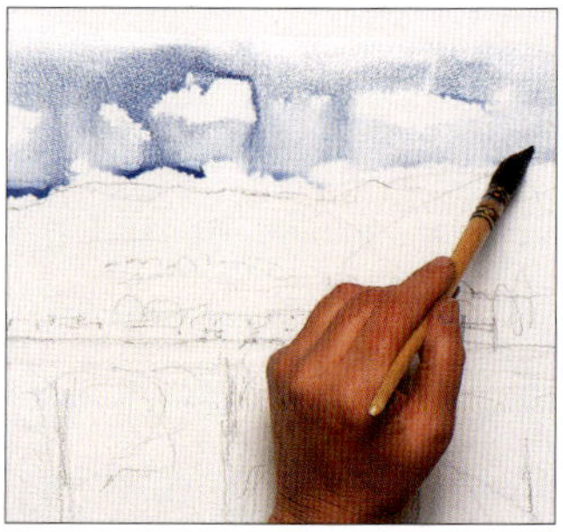

1 Sketch the outline of the hills and vines, then dampen the sky with clean water, leaving some gaps. Mix a wash of cerulean blue and drop it on to the damp areas. Leave to dry.

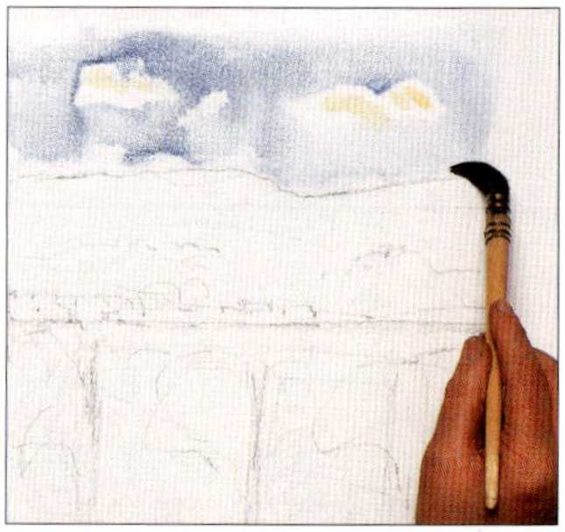

2 Mix a pale wash of Naples yellow and touch it into the dry cloud shapes and along the horizon line. Leave to dry.

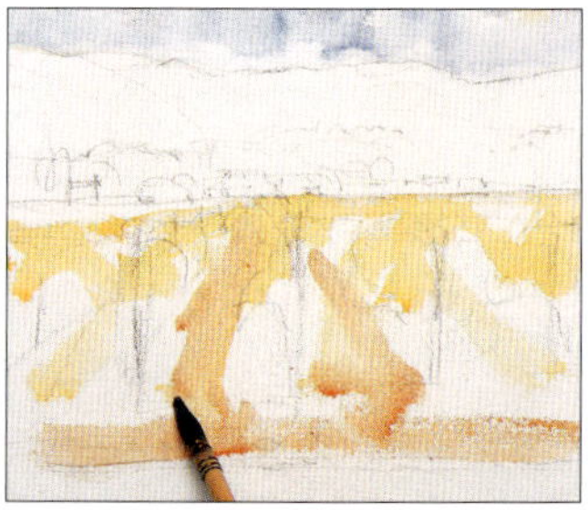

3 Darken the top of the sky with cerulean blue and leave to dry. Mix gamboge with light red and brush over the vines. Paint light red on the foreground and in between the vines.

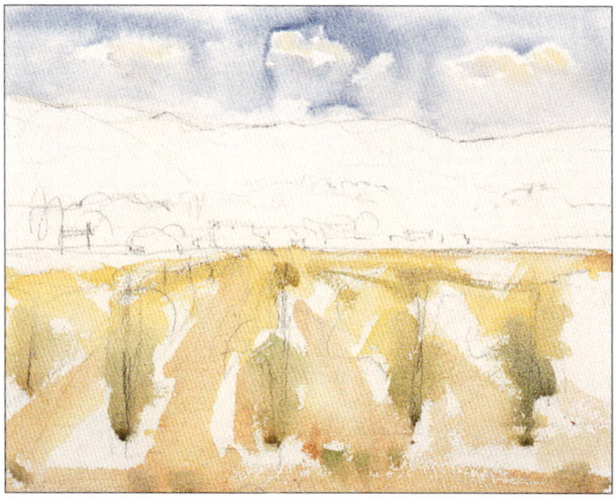

4 Using a medium mop brush, loosely paint sap green into the foreground to indicate the rows of vines. Leave to dry.

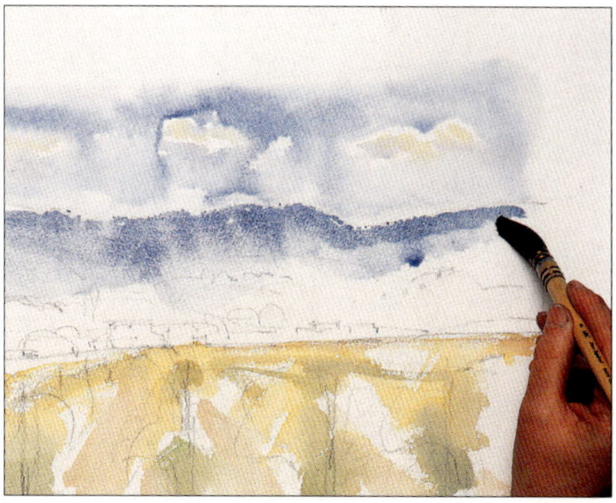

5 Mix a deep blue from ultramarine violet, cobalt blue and viridian and wash it over the hills. Put a few dots along the top edge to break up the harsh outline and imply trees.

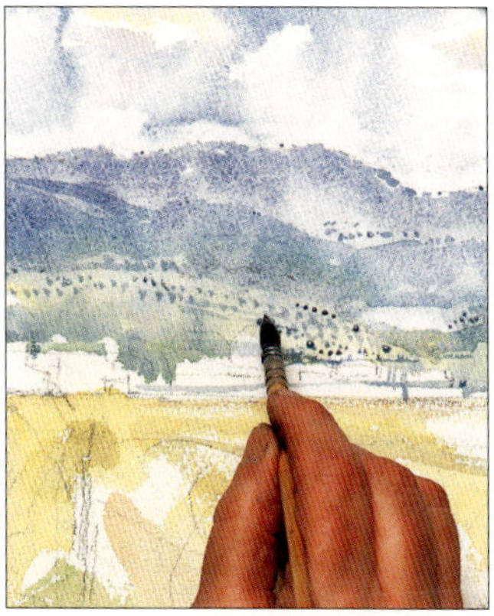

6 Mix a mid-toned green from viridian with a little cobalt blue. Using a medium mop brush, brush this mixture over the lower part of the hills. Mix a dark blue from cobalt blue, ultramarine violet and viridian. Using a large mop brush, darken the shadows on the distant hills. Use the same colour to stipple a few dots on the green hills to imply trees on the horizon.

Tip: It is often easier to assess colours if you turn your reference photo upside down. This allows you to concentrate on the tones without being distracted by the actual subject matter.

Assessment time

Once you are happy with the general lines and colours of the scene, you can start thinking about adding those all-important touches of detail and texture. Don't be tempted to do this too early: once you have painted the detail, it will be much harder to go back and make any tonal corrections to the background or the spaces between the rows of vines.

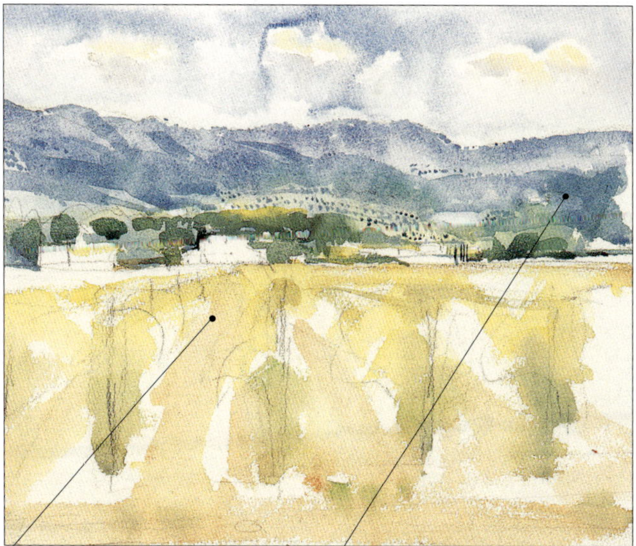

The perspective of the foregound has been established, leaving you free to add detail and texture.

The background is virtually complete, with darker shadows on the hills providing a sense of light and shade.

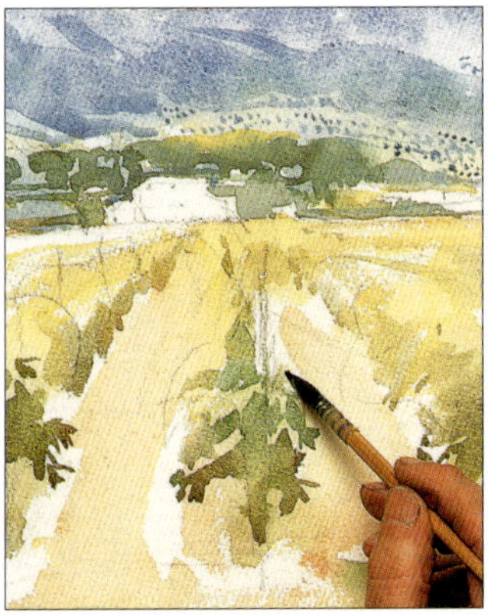

7 Mix a dark green from sap green, Payne's grey, and a little burnt umber. Using a large mop brush, wet the foreground with clean water, leaving gaps for the vines. Using a medium mop brush, brush the dark green mixture on to the damp areas and let it flow on the paper to define the general green masses of the vines and their leaves. Paint the dark shapes of the foreground vine leaves.

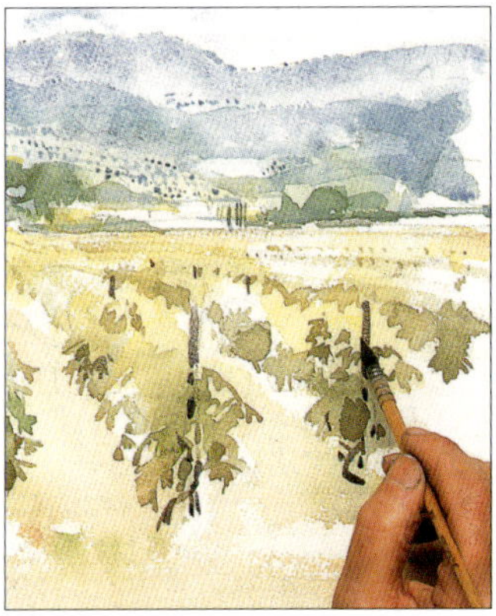

8 Continue painting the vine leaves, as in Step 7. Don't try to be too precise or the painting may easily start to look overworked: generalized shapes will suffice. Mix a warm but neutral grey from ultramarine violet and burnt umber and, using a fine round brush, paint in the stems of the vines and the posts that support them, taking care to make the posts smaller as they recede into the distance.

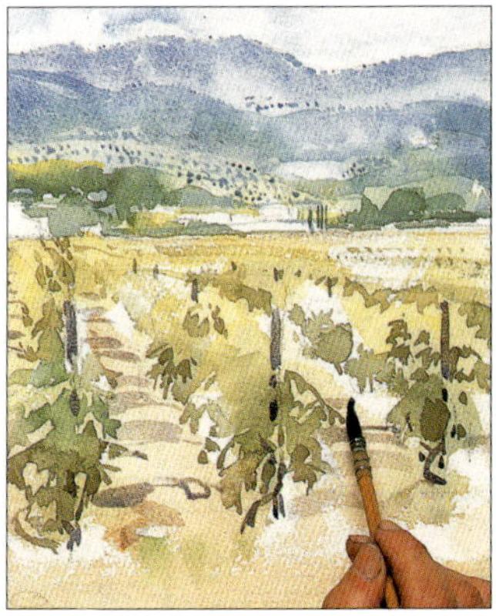

9 Mix a dark shadow colour from ultramarine violet and a little burnt umber and brush this mixture across the ground in between the rows of vines. Again, take care over the perspective and make the shadows narrower as the vines recede into the distance.

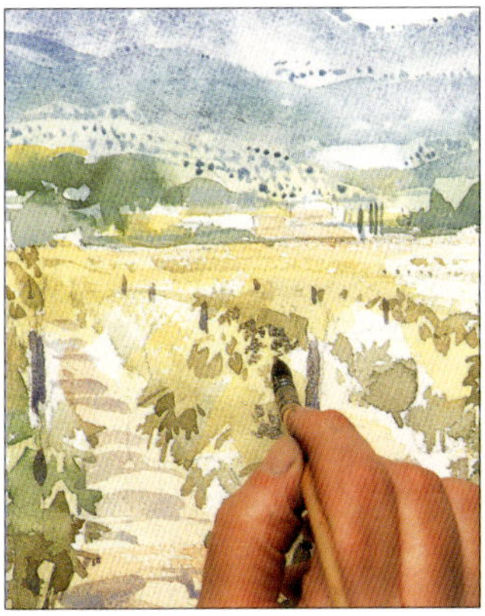

10 Mix a warm, reddish brown from light red and a touch of Naples yellow and use this to paint the buildings in the background. This warm colour causes the buildings to advance, even though they occupy only a small part of the picture area. Using a fine brush and the same dark green mixture that you used in Step 7, touch in some of the detail on the vines.

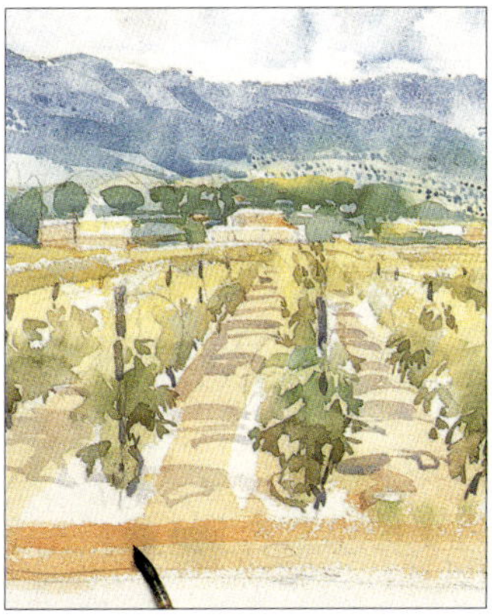

11 Using an almost dry brush held on its side, brush strokes of light red in between the rows of vines. This strengthens the foreground colour but still allows the texture of the paper to show through, implying the pebbly, dusty texture of the earth in which the vines are planted.

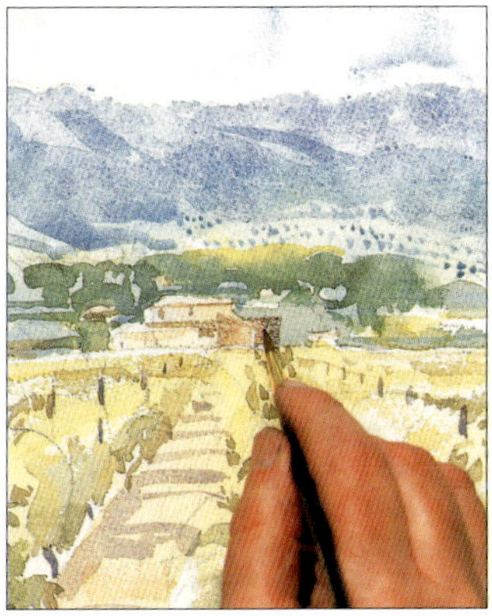

12 Using a fine brush, brush a little light red on the top of the roofs. This helps the roofs to stand out and also provides a visual link with the colour of the earth in the foreground. Add a little burnt umber to the light red mixture to darken it, and paint the window recesses and the shaded side of the buildings to make them look three-dimensional.

French vineyard

Fresh and airy, this painting is full of rich greens and warm earth colours, providing a welcome dose of Mediterranean sunshine. Note how most of the detail and texture are in the foreground, while the background consists largely of loose washes with a few little dots and stipples to imply the tree-covered mountains beyond. This contrast is a useful device in landscape painting when you want to establish a sense of scale and distance.

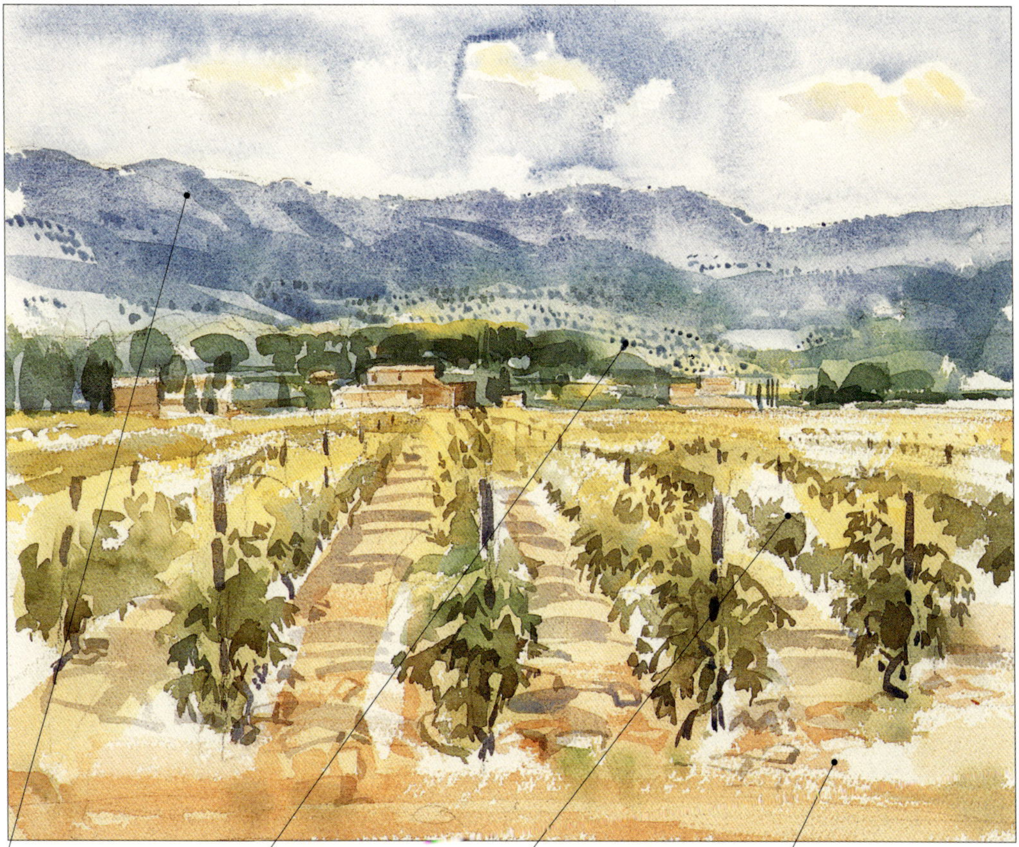

Cool colours in the background recede.

Simple dots and stipples are enough to give the impression of distant trees.

Note how the rows of vines slant inwards and converge towards the vanishing point.

Warm colours in the foreground advance.

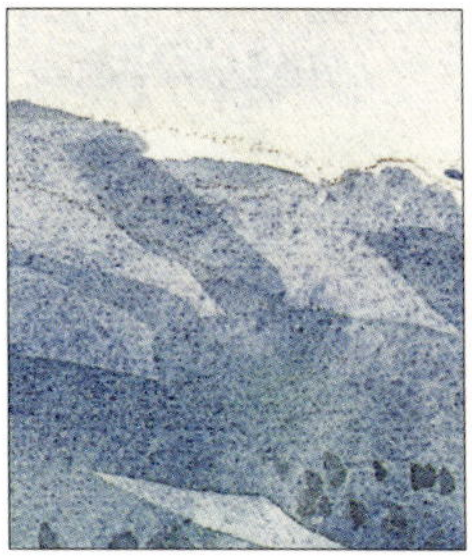

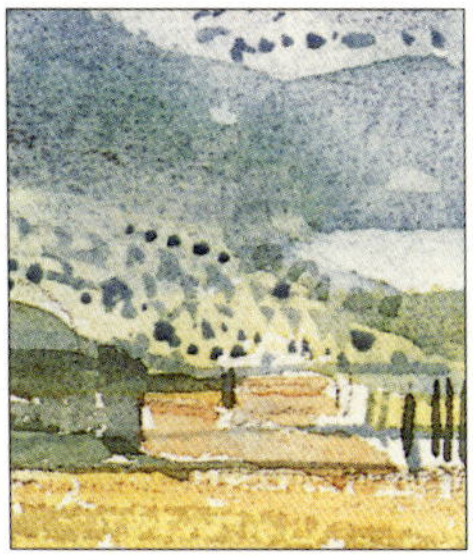

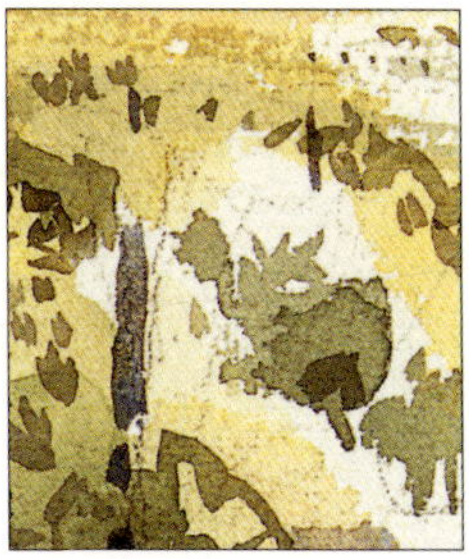

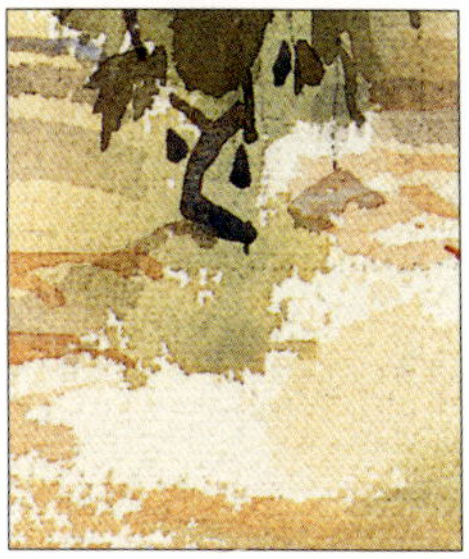

Craggy mountains

This project is a good exercise in aerial perspective. Although the scene itself is very simple, you must convey a sense of the distances involved in order for it to look convincing. Tonal contrast is one way of achieving this: remember that colours are generally paler towards the horizon, and so the mountains in the far distance look paler than those in the immediate foreground. Textural contrast is another way to give a sense of distance: details such as jagged rocks and clumps of snow need to be more pronounced in the foreground than in the background.

The use of warm and cool colours to convey a sense of light and shade is important, too. Cool colours, such as blue, appear to recede and so painting crevices in the rocks in a cool shade makes them look deeper and further away from the viewer. Warm colours, on the other hand, appear to advance and seem closer to the viewer. These should be used for the areas of rock that jut upwards into the sunlight.

Although you want the painting to look realistic, don't worry too much about capturing the exact shapes of individual rocks: it is more important to convey an overall impression. Use short, jagged strokes that follow the general direction of the rock formations. This will help to convey the mountains' craggy texture.

The original scene

These craggy peaks, stretching far into the distance, make a dramatic image in their own right. In the late spring, when this photograph was taken, the drama is enhanced by the billowing white clouds, set against a brilliant blue sky, and the last vestiges of snow clinging to the rocks.

Materials

- *2B pencil*
- *Rough watercolour board*
- *Watercolour paints: ultramarine blue, burnt sienna, cobalt blue, phthalocyanine blue, alizarin crimson, raw umber*
- *Brushes: large round, old brush for masking*
- *Sponge*
- *Tissue paper*
- *Masking fluid*
- *Scalpel or craft (utility) knife*

Tip: The sponge is used in this project to lift off paint colour applied to the sky area, and to apply paint. The surface of the sponge leaves a soft, textured effect.

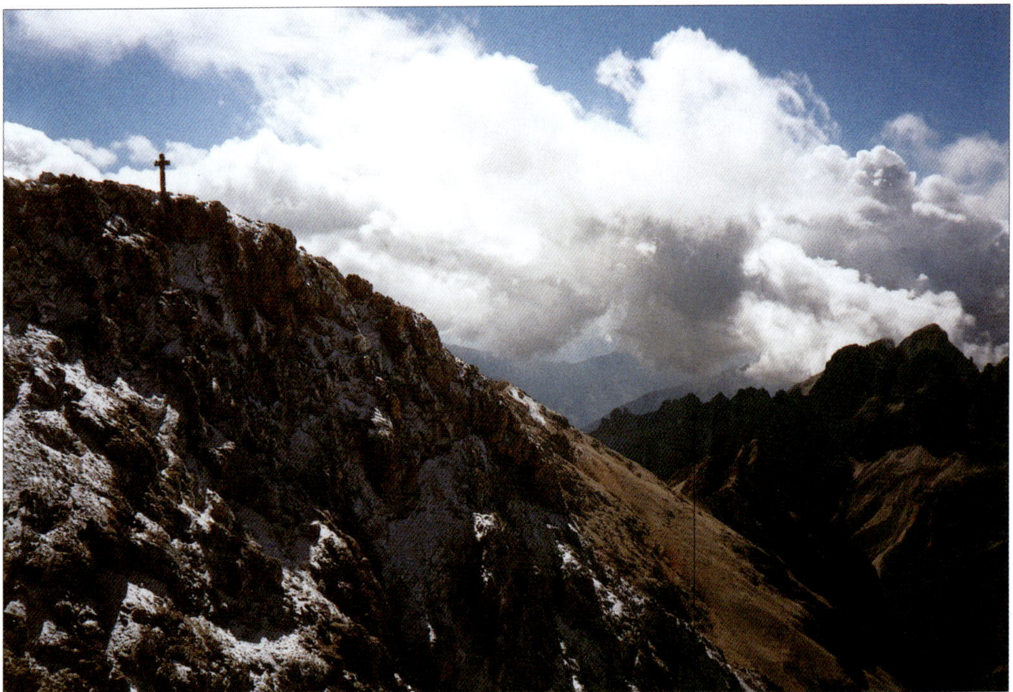

Textural detail is most evident in the foreground; this also helps to create a sense of distance.

Note how the colours look paler in the distance, due to the effect of aerial perspective.

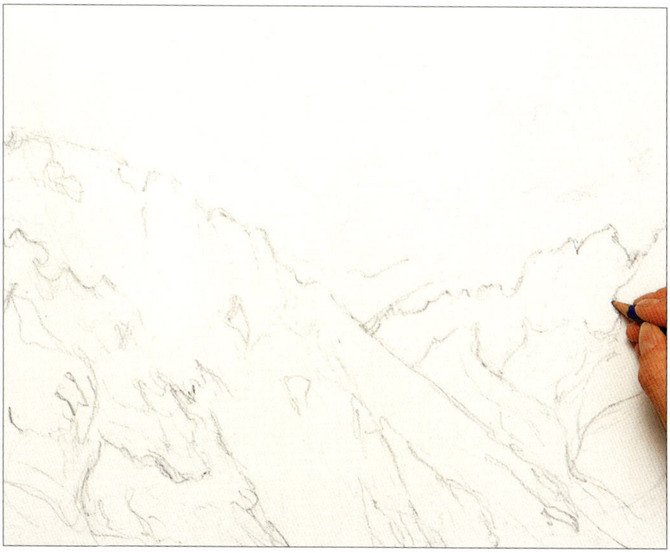

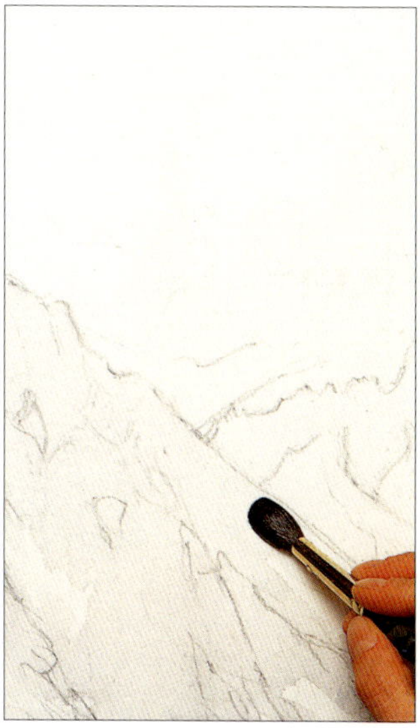

1 Using a 2B pencil, lightly sketch the scene, indicating the main gulleys and crevices and the bulk of the clouds in the sky. Keep your pencil lines loose and fluid: try to capture the essence of the scene and to feel the "rhythm" of the jagged rock formations.

2 Mix a pale, neutral grey from ultramarine blue and burnt sienna. Using a large round brush, wash this mixture over the foreground mountain.

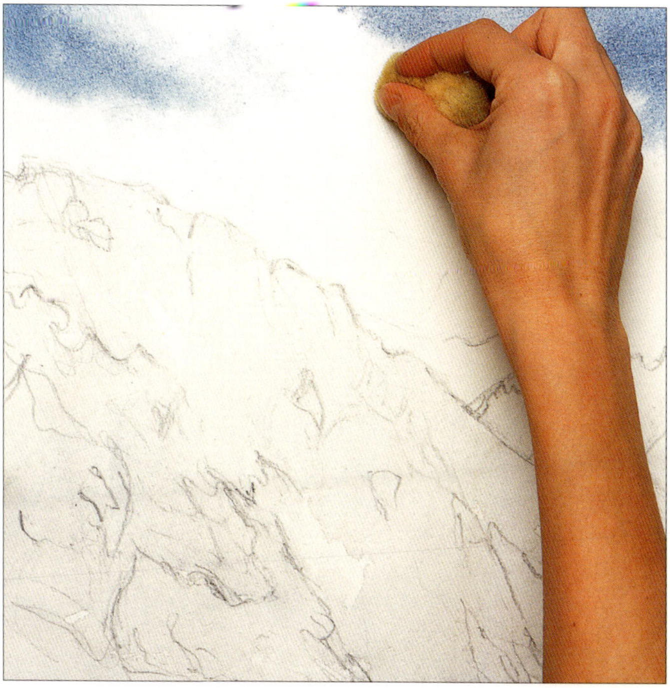

3 Mix a bright blue from cobalt blue and a little phthalocyanine blue. Using a large round brush, wash it over the top of the sky. While this is still wet, dampen a small sponge in clean water, squeeze out the excess moisture, and dab it on the sky area to lift off some of the colour. This reveals white cloud shapes with softer edges than you could achieve using any other technique.

Tip: Each time you apply the sponge, turn it around in your hand to find a clean area, and rinse it regularly in clean water so that you don't accidentally dab colour back on to the paper.

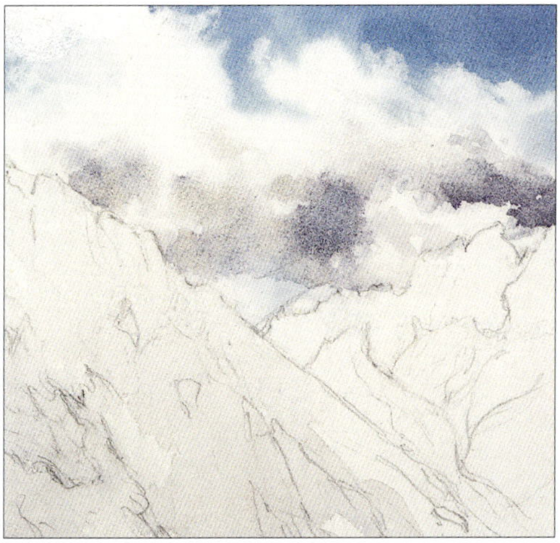

4 Mix a neutral purple from alizarin crimson, ultramarine blue and a little raw umber. Using a large round brush, dampen the dark undersides of the clouds and touch in the neutral purple mixture. While this is still damp, touch in a second application of the same mixture in places to build up the tone. If necessary, soften the edges and adjust the shapes of the dark areas by dabbing them with a piece of sponge or clean kitchen paper to lift off colour.

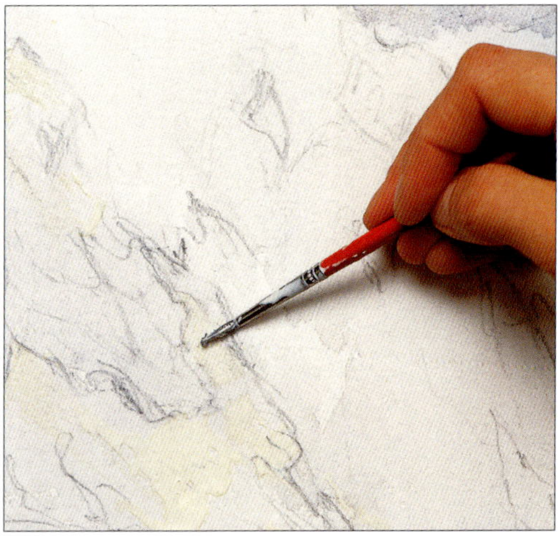

5 Study your reference photograph to see exactly where the little patches of snow lie on the foreground mountain. Using an old brush, apply masking fluid to these areas to protect them from subsequent applications of paint. Use thin lines of fluid for snow that clings to the ridges and block in larger areas with the side of the brush. Wash the brush in liquid detergent and warm water. Leave the masking fluid to dry completely before moving on to the next stage.

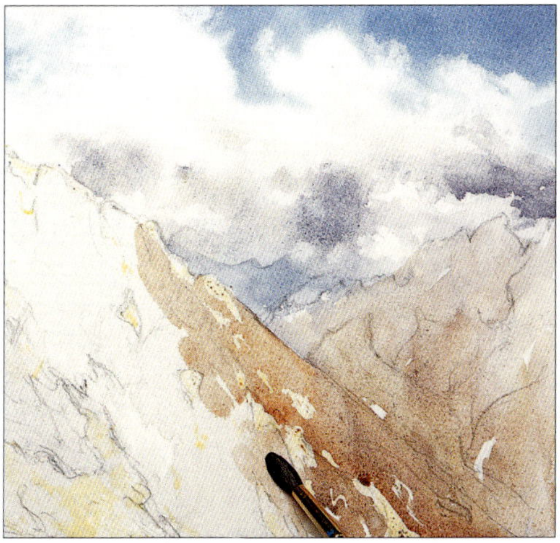

6 Mix a dark blue from cobalt blue and phthalocyanine blue and paint the distant hills between the two mountains. Dilute the mixture and brush it over the background mountain. Leave to dry. Mix a dark brown from burnt sienna with a little alizarin crimson and ultramarine blue, and wash this mixture over the background mountain. Add a little alizarin crimson and begin painting the foreground mountain.

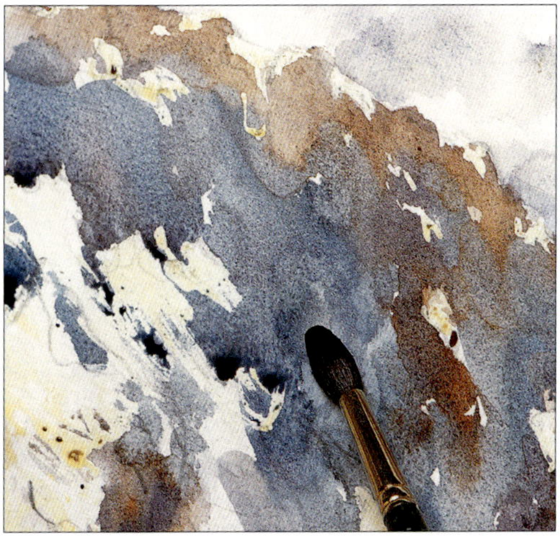

7 Using a large round brush, continue to paint the foreground mountain. Use the same dark brown mixture that you used in Step 6 for the areas that catch the sun, and phthalocyanine blue for the areas that are in the shade. Paint with relatively short and slightly jagged vertical brushstrokes that echo the direction of the rock formations. This helps to convey the texture of the rocks.

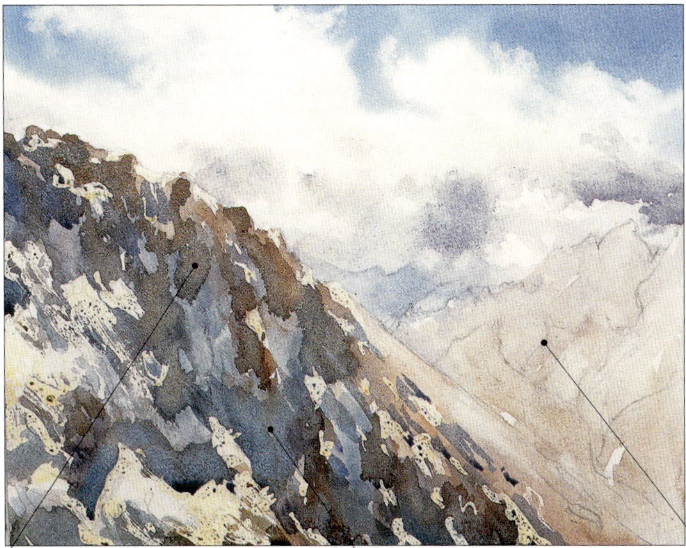

Assessment time

Because of the careful use of warm and cool colours, the painting is already beginning to take on some form. Much of the rest of the painting will consist of building up the tones you have already applied to enhance the three-dimensional effect and the texture of the rocks. At this stage, it is important that you take the time to assess whether or not the areas of light and shade are correctly placed. Note, too, the contrast between the foreground and the background: the foreground is more textured and is darker in tone, and this helps to convey an impression of distance.

The rocks that jut out into the sunlight are painted in a warm brown so that they appear to advance.

The crevices are in deep shade and are painted in a cool blue so that they appear to recede.

The background mountain is painted in a flat colour, which helps to convey the impression that it is further away.

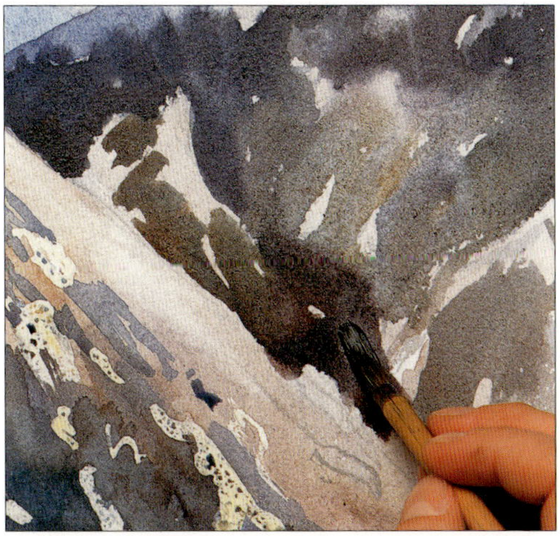

8 Mix a deep, purplish blue from alizarin crimson, phthalocyanine blue and raw umber. Brush this mixture along the top of the background peak, leaving some gaps so that the underlying brown colour shows through. Using the dark brown mixture used in Step 6, build up tone on the rest of the background mountain, applying several brushstrokes wet into wet to the darker areas.

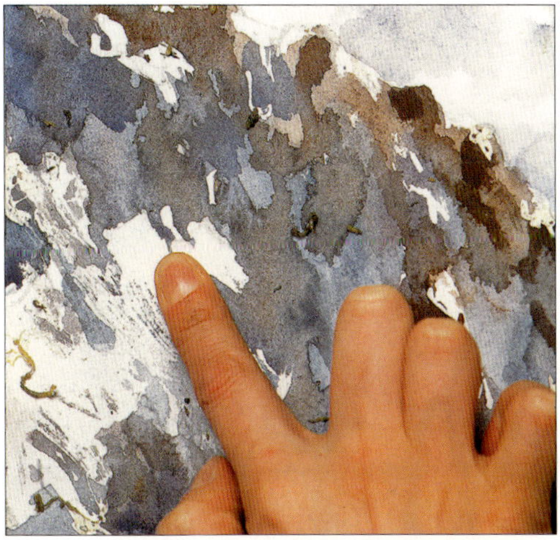

9 Continue building up the tones on both mountains, using the same paint mixtures as before. Leave to dry. Using your fingertips, gently rub off the masking fluid to reveal the patches of white snow. (It is sometimes hard to see if you've rubbed off all the fluid, so run your fingers over the whole painting to check that you haven't missed any.) Dust or blow all dried fluid off the surface of the painting.

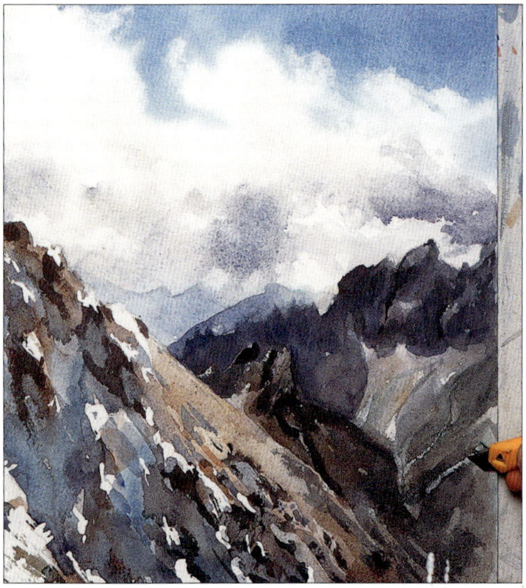

10 Using the tip of a scalpel or craft (utility) knife and pulling the blade sideways, so as not to cut through the paper, scratch off thin lines of paint to reveal snow in gulleys on the background mountain.

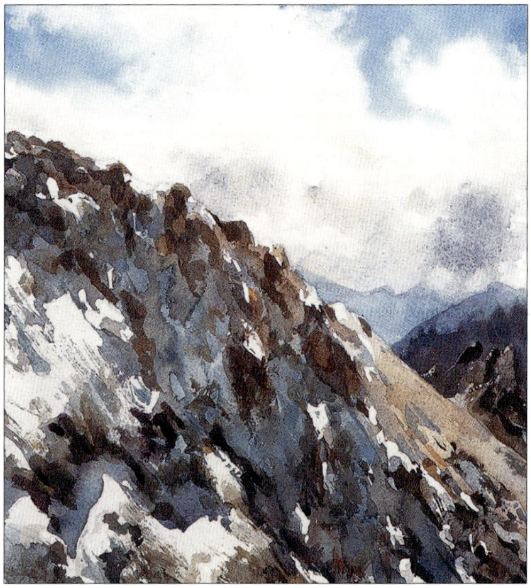

11 Apply tiny dots of colour around the edges of some of the unmasked areas to tone down the brightness a little. Continue the tonal build-up, making sure your brushstrokes follow the contours of the rocks.

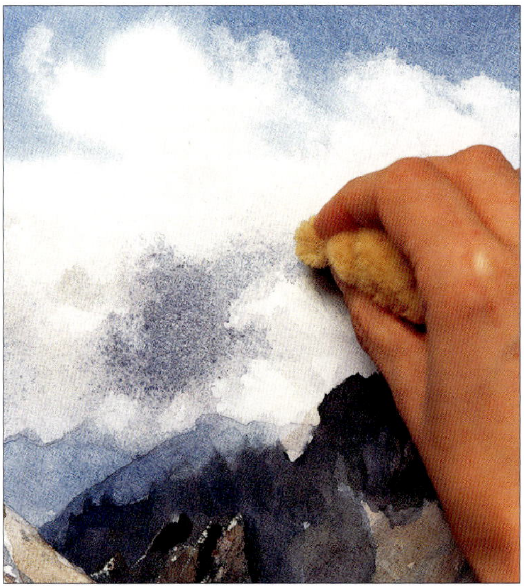

12 Dip a sponge in clean water, squeeze out any excess moisture and dampen the dark clouds. Dip the sponge in the neutral purple mixture used in Step 4 and dab it lightly on to the clouds to darken them and make them look a little more dramatic.

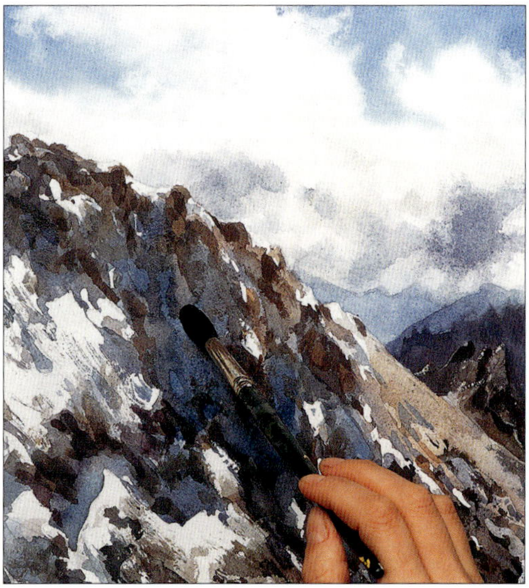

13 The final stage of the painting is to assess the tonal values once more to make sure that the contrast between the light and dark areas is strong enough. If necessary, brush on more of the purplish blue mixture used in Step 8 to deepen the shadows.

Craggy mountains

This is a beautiful and dramatic example of how contrasting warm colours with cool colours can create a sense of three dimensions. Although the colour palette is restricted, the artist has managed to create an impressively wide range of tones.

Jagged brushstrokes that follow the direction of the rock formations create realistic-looking textures on the foreground mountain and the white of the paper shines through in places, giving life and sparkle to the image.

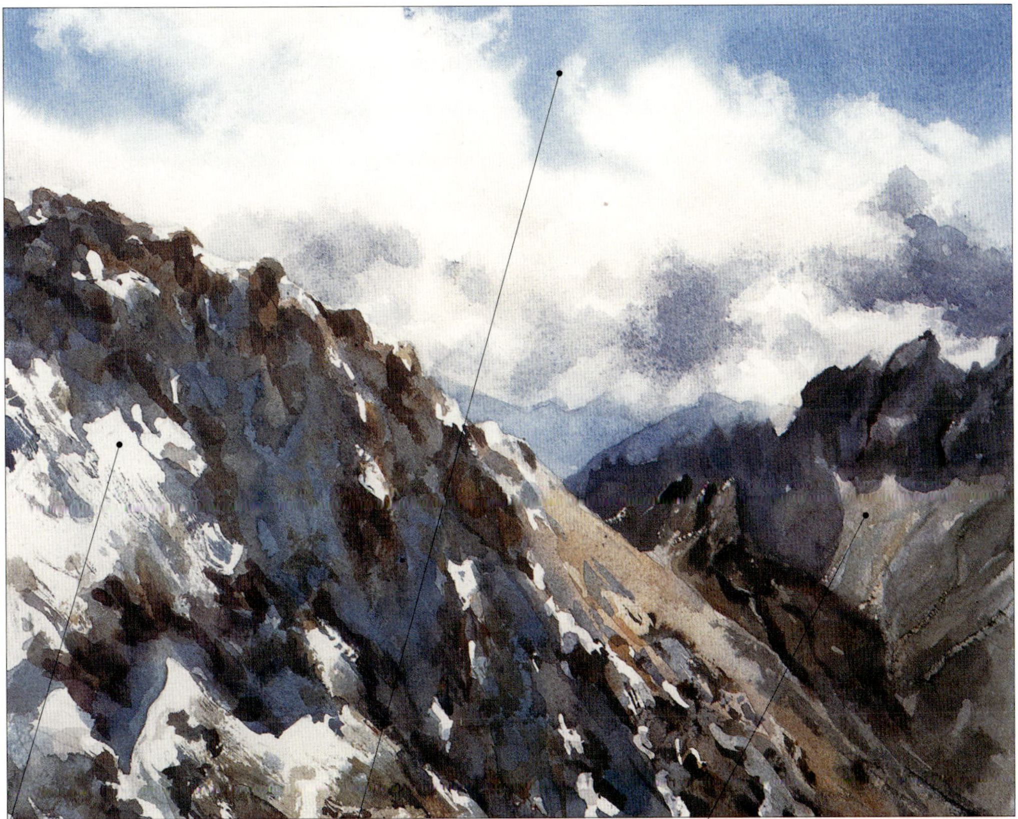

The white of the paper is used to good effect to imply patches of snow clinging to the rocks.

The soft-edged clouds and brilliant blue sky provide a perfect counter-balance to the harshness of the rocks below.

The background mountain is painted in flat washes, with far less textural detail than the foreground.

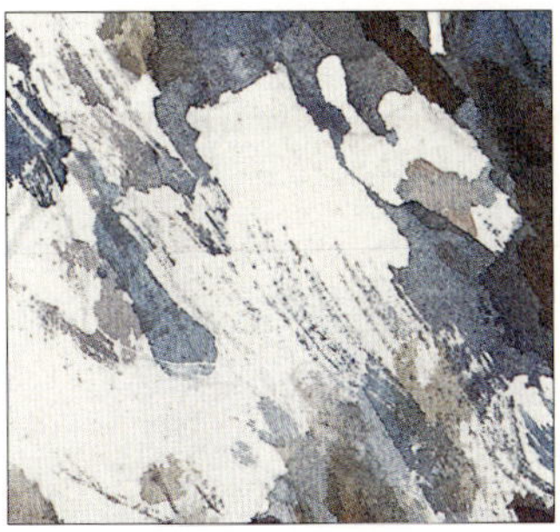

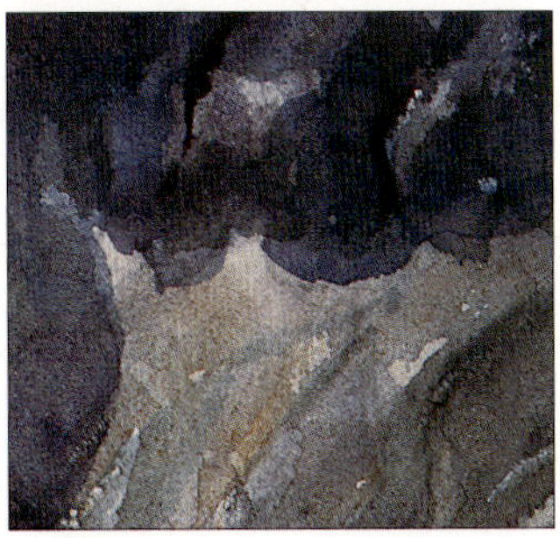

Painting Still Lifes

Of all the subjects to draw and paint, still lifes are unique as all the elements are under your control – not only the objects being used, but also their position and the quality and direction of the light used to illuminate them. This gives you the chance to work at your leisure, with no pressure, and to experiment with composition, colour and technique.

Still-life subjects are found everywhere. The obvious ones include the numerous and ever-increasing varieties of fruit, vegetables and flowers available all year round. Kitchen and gardening equipment, children's toys, ceramics and glassware, patterned fabrics, found natural objects and the numerous objets d'art that litter most homes: the list is endless.

Traditionally, the objects used in a still life have some kind of association with each other, but you can also make interesting images by grouping together a range of objects that have little, or no, common ground.

There are also what are known as "found" still lifes, which are arrangements that you simply come across by chance. By definition, these are usually less contrived and more natural-looking than an arranged grouping. Found groupings might include fruit and vegetables falling out of a shopping basket, or a group of terracotta flower pots and garden tools in the corner of a shed or outbuilding.

Perhaps the most important point to consider with still lifes is the quality or type of light that you use to illuminate your subject. Although natural light is ideal, it can prove problematic. Arranging still-life groups directly in the sun can make for dramatic, strong images, but the sun will move and the light will constantly change. You can use lamps of various kinds to light your subject. It is important to remember that low-voltage bulbs can give an orange cast, so it is better to invest in a few daylight bulbs, as these will make colours look cleaner and brighter.

Tips: • Invest in a couple of anglepoise lamps and daylight bulbs, so that you can control the direction and quality of the light.

• Make a series of thumbnail sketches of the composition before you begin. Often, you will find that a better composition suggests itself.

• Take risks with your groupings and compositions in order to give your images an edge.

• Look out for "found" groupings that may give rise to an image. If you do not have painting materials to hand, capture the moment with a photograph.

Tulips ▼
Natural sunlight pours through a window and falls on a bunch of tulips. The intensity of the light is exaggerated by making the shadow on the wall much darker than it was in reality.

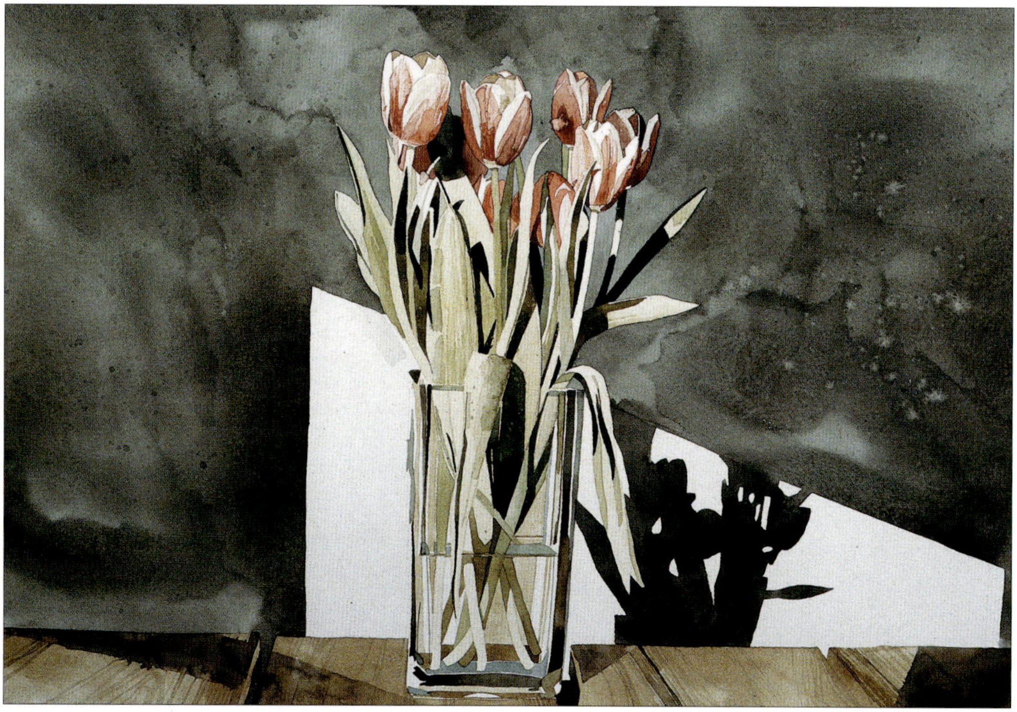

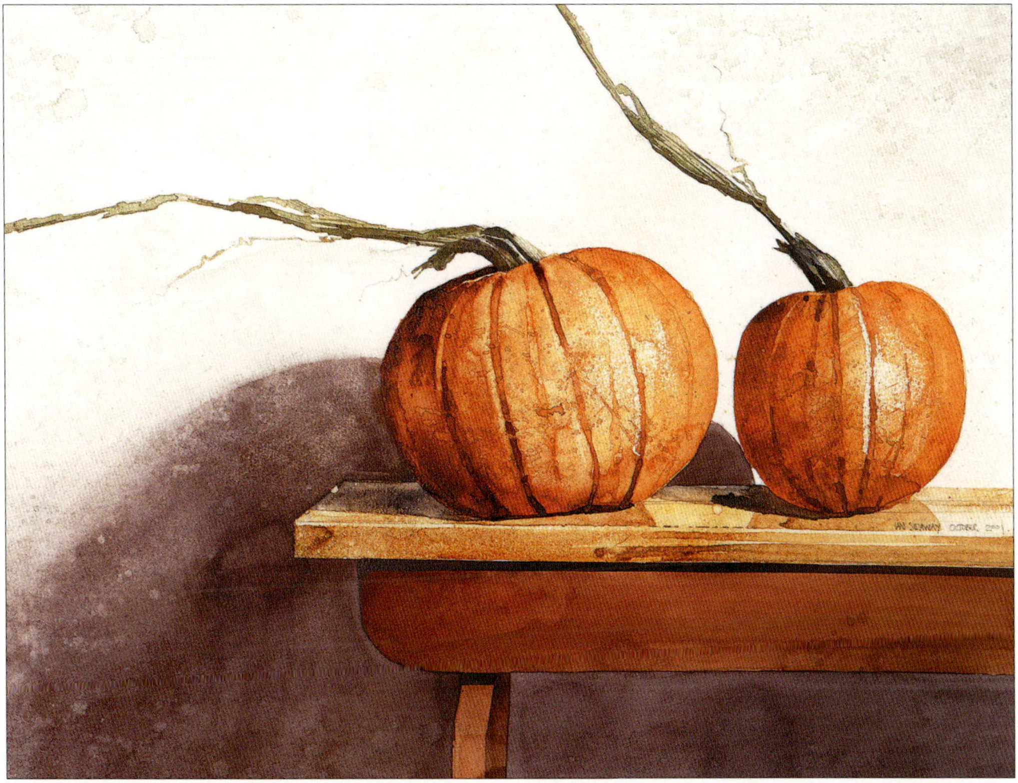

Pumpkins ▲
This painting was made on a heavy, rough paper that did not require stretching. Gum arabic was used in the mixes to increase the intensity and transparency of the paint. The paint was applied wet into wet and wet on dry, with areas of paint removed and distressed using sandpaper.

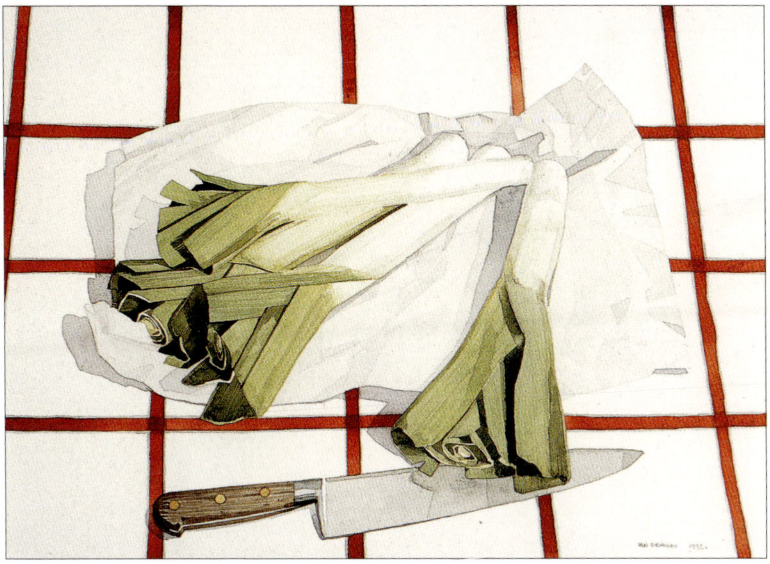

Leeks ►
This is a contrived and carefully arranged still life. The leeks and knife are viewed from above, and an illusion of depth is achieved by painting the linear pattern on the cloth at a slight angle.

Strawberries and cherries in a bowl

Still lifes don't have to be complicated, and with a few colourful fruit and a china bowl, you can set up a simple but very attractive study on a corner of your kitchen table. However, you do need to spend time thinking about your composition: with relatively few elements, the position of each one is critical.

When you have chosen your subject, move the fruit and bowl around until you get an arrangement that you are happy with. Look at the shadows and the spaces between the objects, as well as at the objects themselves: they are just as important in the overall composition.

Above all, this is an exercise in colour. Choose fruit that have some variation in colour, to provide visual interest. Also look for complementary colours – ones that are opposite each other on the colour wheel – such as red and green, or yellow and violet. Here, touches of green on the leaves and stems offset the vibrant reds of the fruit, while shadows on the yellow ochre background are painted in a complementary shade of violet.

Remember that even things that you know are a brilliant white, such as the doily on which the bowl stands, should rarely (if ever) be painted as such. Shadows and reflected light imbue them with a subtle but definite hue of another colour. Half close your eyes to help you assess what colours and tones to use, and keep any washes in these areas very pale to begin with. You can build them up later if necessary, but if you make them too strong there's no going back.

Materials

- *2B pencil*
- *140lb (300gsm) NOT watercolour paper, pre-stretched*
- *Watercolour paints: yellow ochre, dioxazine violet, cobalt blue, Hooker's green, vermilion, cadmium orange, cadmium red, cerulean blue, cadmium yellow, Naples yellow, alizarin crimson, leaf green, olive green, phthalocyanine blue*
- *Brushes: medium chisel*
- *Ruling drawing pen*
- *Masking fluid*

The set-up

Set up your still life on a plain white piece of paper, so that you can concentrate on the subject, and position a table lamp to one side to cast interesting shadows. Experiment by placing the fruit in different positions and at different angles: you need to create a balanced composition so that you don't end up with too large an area of empty background.

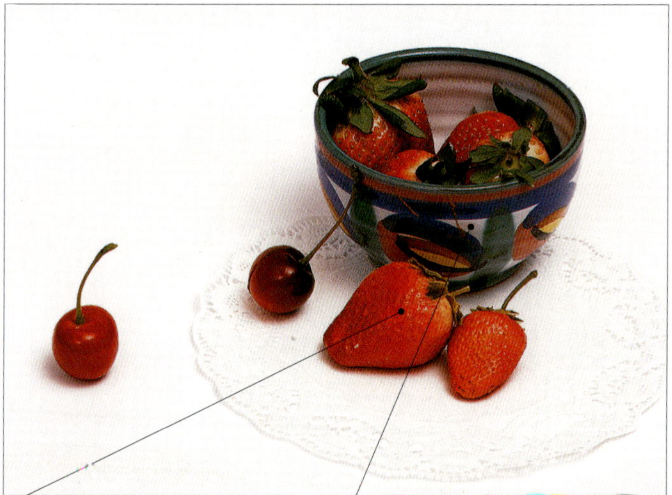

The strawberries shade gradually from deep red to a pale yellow.

The bowl is painted in strong colours that detract from the fruits.

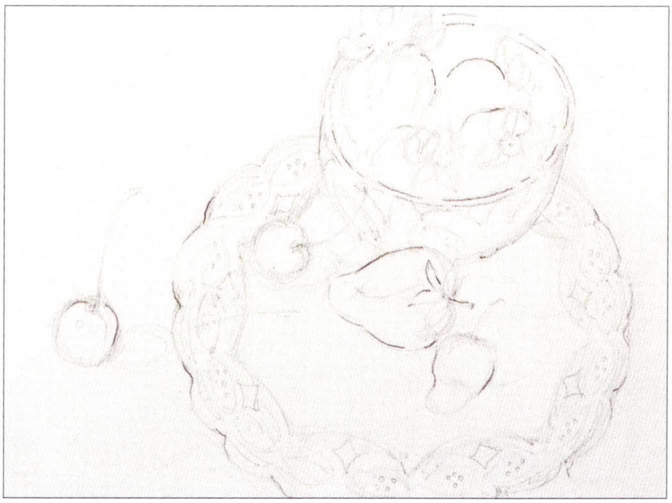

1 Using a 2B pencil, lightly sketch the fruit and the bowl and roughly indicate the cut-paper pattern on the doily.

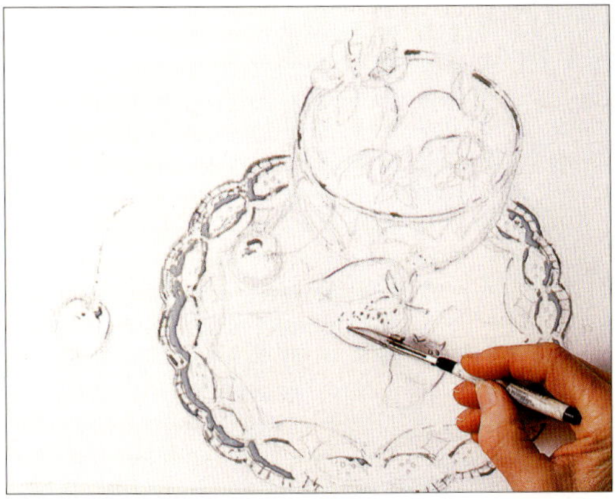

2 Dip a ruling drawing pen in masking fluid and mask out the areas that will be left white in the final painting – the bright highlights on the fruit and the rim of the bowl and the pattern on the doily.

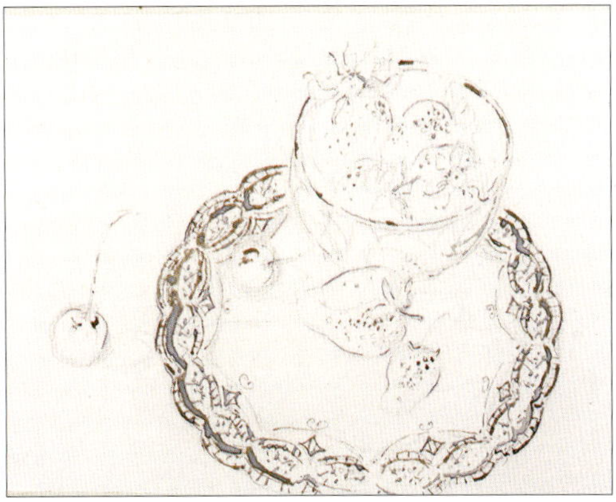

3 Finish off the masking. You must leave it to dry completely before you start to apply any paint, otherwise you run the risk of smudging it and destroying the crisp, clean lines that you want to keep.

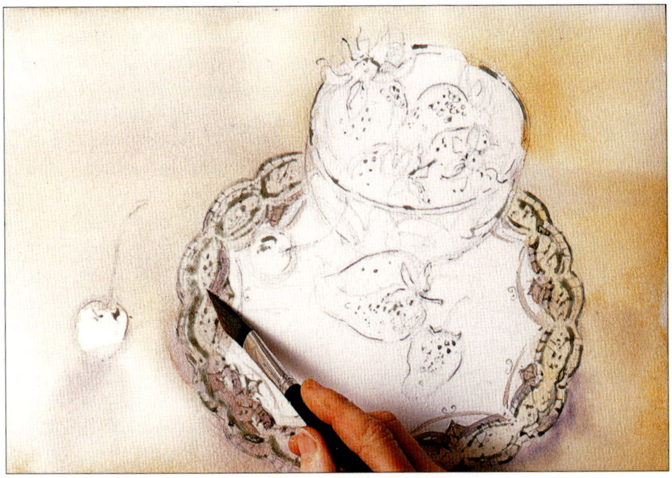

4 The white background is very stark, so start by mixing yellow ochre with a little dioxazine violet to make a dull yellow as a background colour. Dampen the background and the patterned edge of the doily with clean water, taking care to brush around the cherry, and brush the mixture over this area, adding a little more violet to the mixture on the left-hand side. Brush a slightly darker violet under the edge of the doily to create a slight shadow. The background and shadow colours are virtually complementary colours, which work well together.

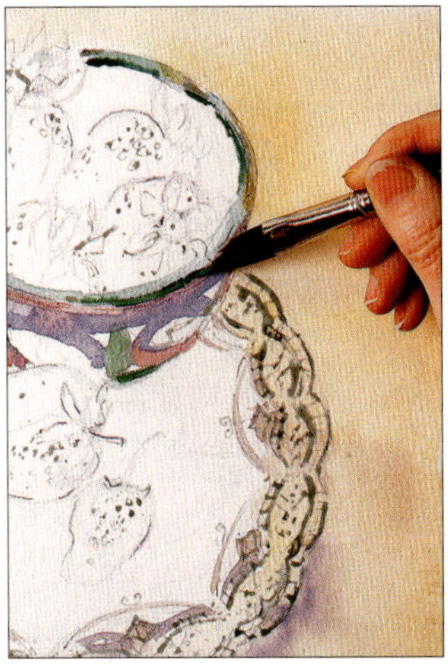

5 Mix a dull blue from cobalt blue and a little dioxazine violet. Using the tip of the brush, start to paint the blue of the pattern on the bowl. Continue to build up the pattern, using Hooker's green and a pale mixture of vermilion and a little dioxazine violet.

Tip: Make the colours on the bowl more subdued than they are in real life, so that they do not detract from the vibrant reds of the fruit.

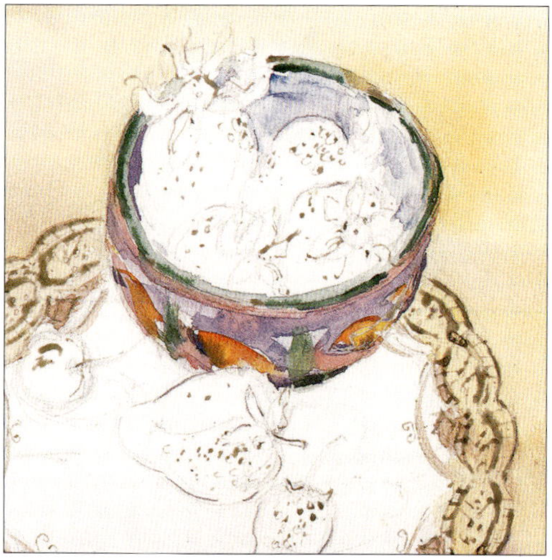

6 Mix a rich orange from cadmium orange and cadmium red and finish painting the pattern on the bowl. Mix a very pale blue from cobalt blue and cerulean blue and paint the inside of the bowl, taking care not to touch any of the fruit. Brush a little dioxazine violet into the most deeply shaded part of the inside of the bowl. Leave to dry.

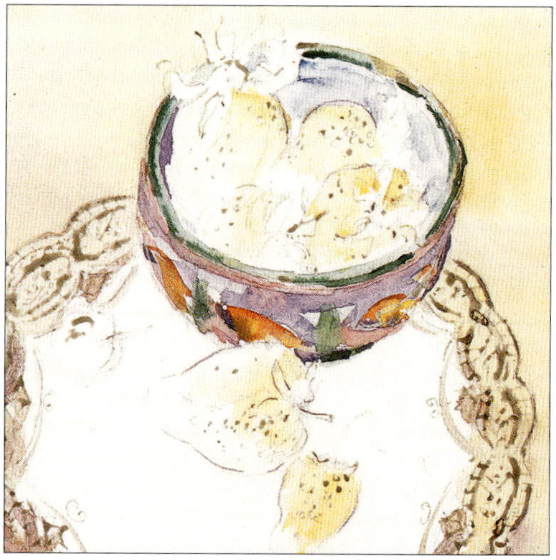

7 You need to work quickly for the next two stages, which are painted wet into wet so that the colours merge on the paper. Mix a very pale yellow from cadmium yellow and a hint of Naples yellow. Wet the strawberries with clean water and carefully brush this yellow mixture on to the palest areas, taking care not to allow any paint to spill over on to the doily.

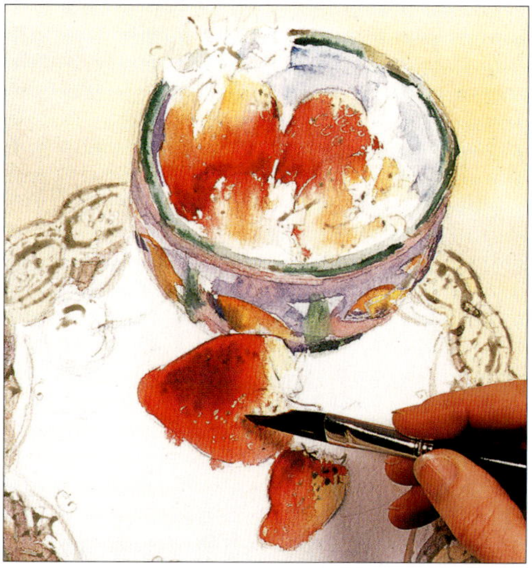

8 While this is still damp, mix cadmium red with a little cadmium orange and brush this mixture over the red parts of the strawberries. Mix vermilion with alizarin crimson and drop this mixture wet into wet on to the very darkest parts of the strawberries. (You may need several applications to build up the necessary density of tone.)

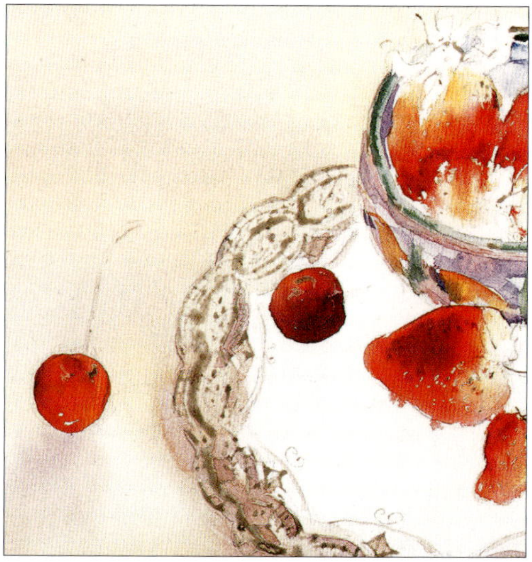

9 Paint the cherry on the background in vermilion. Apply another layer of vermilion while the first one is still wet, brushing a little cadmium yellow on to the right-hand side to give some variety of tone. Mix alizarin crimson with a hint of dioxazine violet and paint the cherry on the doily, which is a darker tone than the one on the background. Leave to dry.

10 Brush clean water over the strawberry leaves. Paint the lightest leaf areas in cadmium yellow, the mid tones in leaf green, and the darkest tones in olive green, adding a little phthalocyanine blue to the olive green for the very shaded parts.

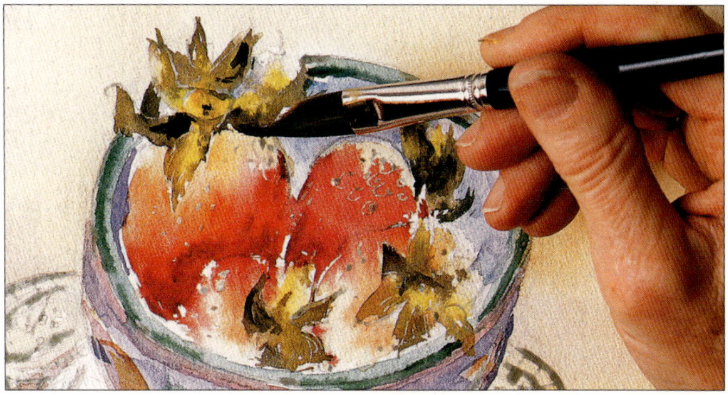

Assessment time

Paint the cherry stalks in olive green and darken the tone of the leaves overall, if necessary. The painting is very nearly complete, but you need to build up the shadows to make the still life look more realistic. Study your subject carefully to work out where the shadows fall and how dark they need to be in relation to the rest of the painting.

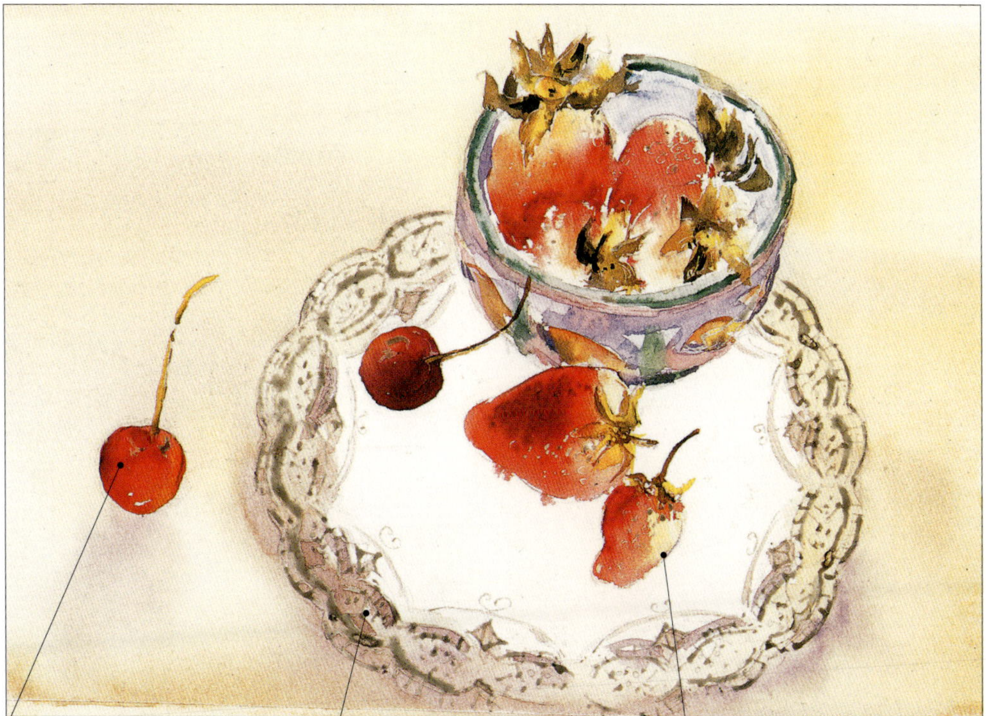

Subtle variations in tone across the surface of the fruit help to make them look lifelike.

Even though the doily is very thin, the lighting is so strong that it should cast a definite shadow.

With no shadows to anchor them, the cherries and strawberries look as if they are suspended in mid-air.

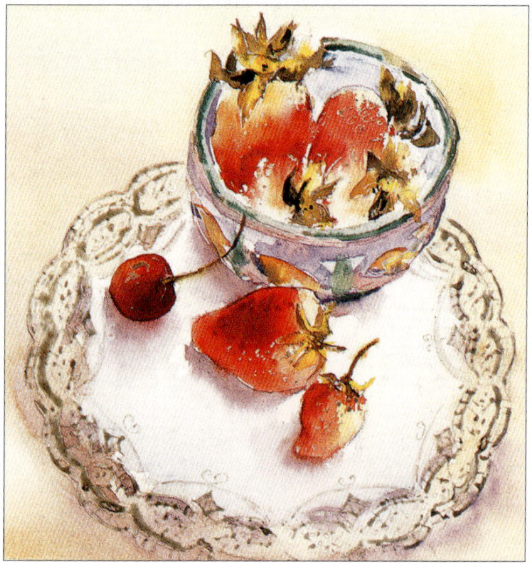

11 Brush clean water over the doily, carefully brushing around the fruit and bowl. Mix a very pale wash of cerulean blue and brush it over the doily; the paint will blur and spread softly, without leaving any harsh edges. While this wash is still damp, mix a very pale purple from dioxazine violet with a tiny amount of Hooker's green and paint the shadows under the fruit and bowl, wet into wet. Use the same paint mixture to brush in the shadow under the background cherry, this time wet on dry.

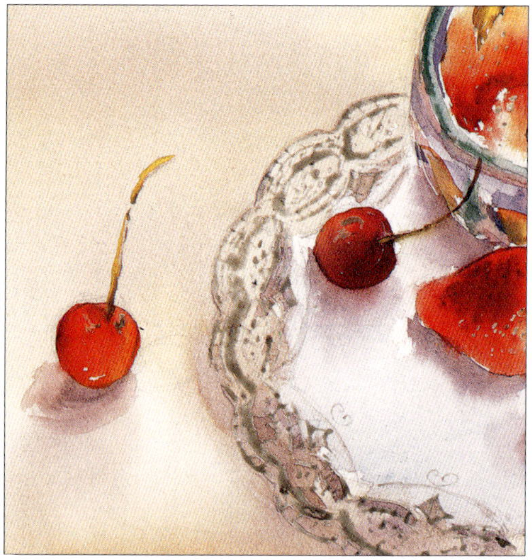

12 Although one is painted wet into wet and one wet on dry with harsher edges, the shadows under the two cherries look equally effective.

Tip: Using a very pale wash of colour over the doily prevents it from looking too stark and bright, and helps to highlight the intricate patterning.

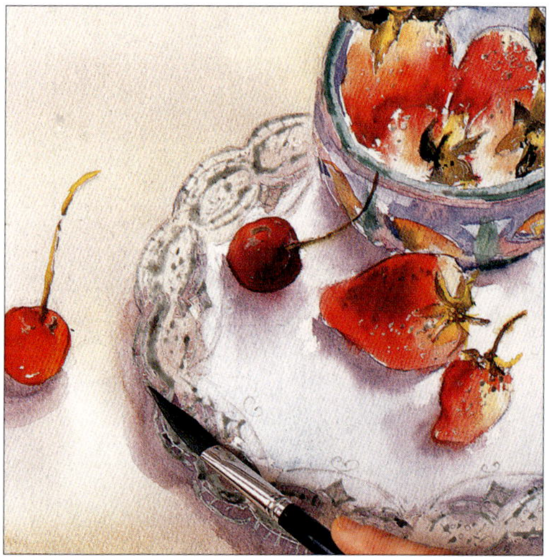

13 Deepen the shadow under the doily, using the same purple mixture of dioxazine violet and Hooker's green as used in Step 11. Leave to dry.

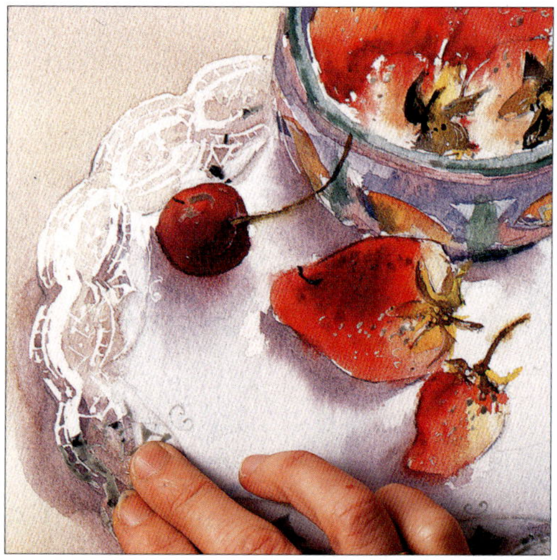

14 Using your fingertips, gently rub off the masking fluid, revealing the brilliant white of the doily and the highlights on the fruit and bowl.

Strawberries and cherries in a bowl

This is a simple, yet carefully thought out, still life in which rich colours and textures abound. Note, in particular, the effective use of complementary colours. The artist has put together an attractive arrangement in which the shadows and the spaces between the objects play as important a role in the overall composition as the objects themselves.

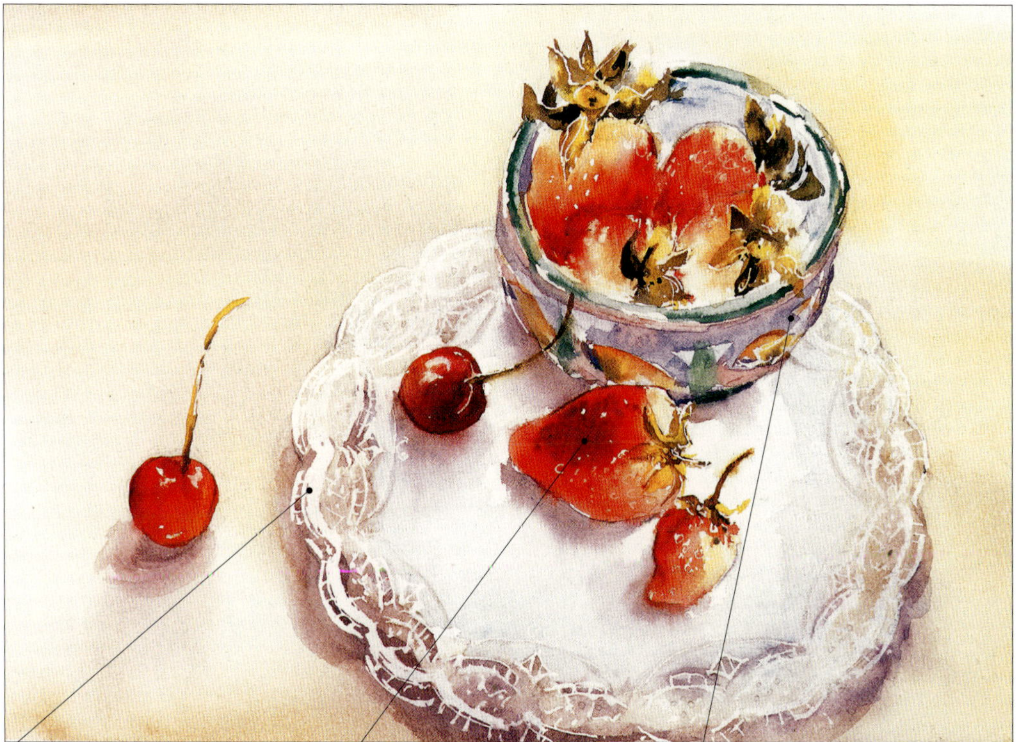

The intricate pattern and brilliant white of the doily are preserved through the careful application of masking fluid.

The reds are achieved by carefully building up a number of different tones – cadmium red, vermilion and alizarin crimson.

The colours of the bowl are deliberately subdued, so as not to detract from the richly coloured fruit.

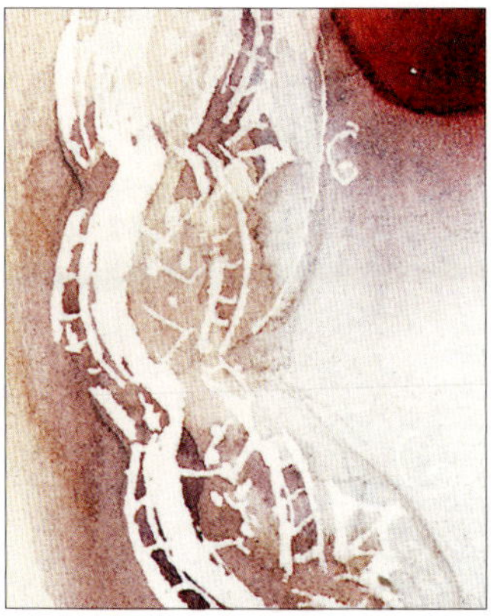

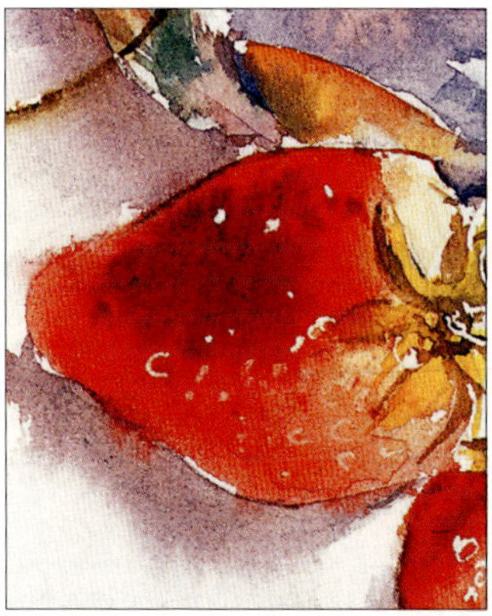

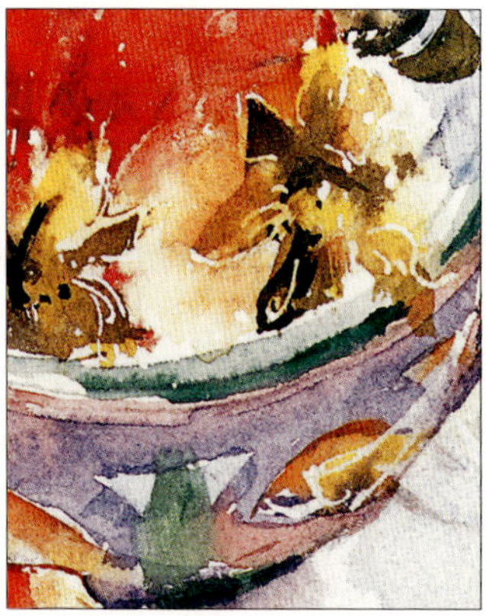

Still life with stainless steel

This kind of still life project is easy to set up at home. The trick is not to make the composition too complicated: a few colourful objects, strategically placed to exploit the way they are reflected in the metallic surfaces, will suffice.

Although this looks, at first glance, like a relatively simple still life, it requires very careful assessment of tone. Metal objects and other reflective surfaces take a lot of their colour from the objects that are reflected in them, so in this project you will need to look carefully at the reflections in order to assess what colours and tones you need to apply. However, the reflections tend to be a little more subdued in tone and less crisply defined than the objects being reflected. Bear this in mind while you are working and adjust your paint mixtures accordingly.

It is a common mistake to paint reflective surfaces too light, with the result that they lack substance. Remember to assess the tones of your painting at regular intervals and build up the tones gradually until the density is right.

Another aspect of tone that you need to consider here is how to make your subject look three-dimensional. To give form to a subject, you need to put darker tones on the shadowed side, but when you are dealing with curved or spherical shapes, like the stainless steel olive oil pourers in this project, the curves are so smooth that it can be hard to decide where the darker colours should begin. Work wet into wet for these areas, so that the colours merge naturally on the paper without any hard edges.

Materials

- *2B pencil*
- *200lb (425gsm) NOT watercolour paper, pre-stretched*
- *Watercolour paints: cerulean blue, Payne's grey, cadmium lemon, ivory black, raw umber, burnt umber, lamp black, yellow ochre, burnt sienna, dioxazine purple, cadmium orange, alizarin crimson*
- *Brushes: fine round, medium round*
- *2B graphite stick*

The set-up

When you are setting up a still-life that contains shiny, reflective surfaces, make sure that the light source (which, indoors, is invariably some kind of lamp) does not reflect too prominently in the subject. The best way to do this is to place the light source to one side and at a reasonable distance from your subject.

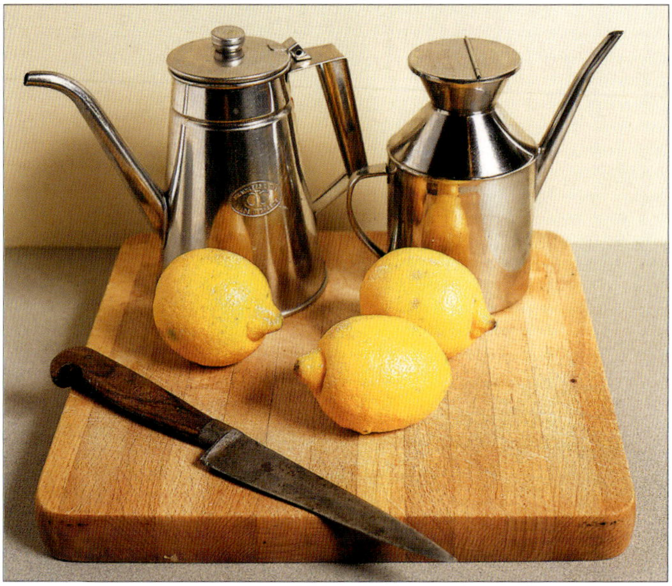

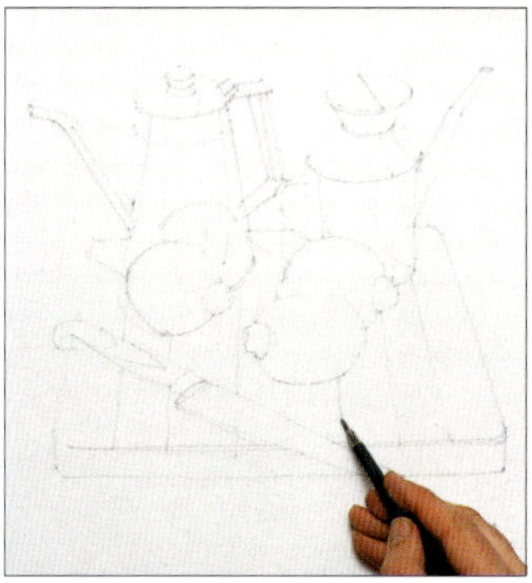

1 Using a 2B pencil, lightly sketch the outline of your subject, making sure the shapes are accurate. You may find it easier to assess the shapes objectively if you turn your drawing upside down.

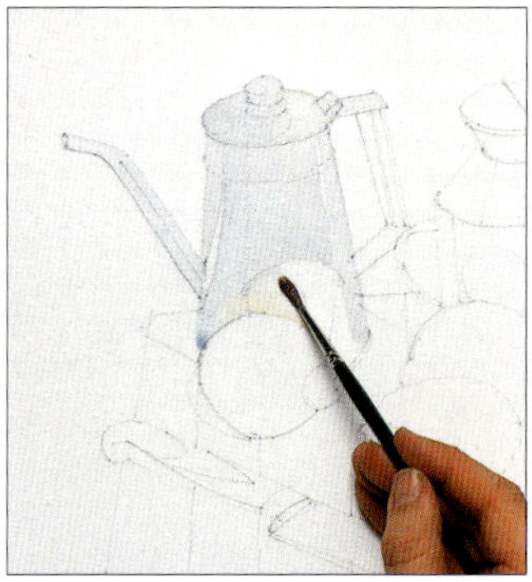

2 Mix pale washes of cerulean blue, Payne's grey, cadmium lemon and ivory black. Using a fine round brush, start to paint the lightest tones on the stainless-steel olive oil pourers, leaving any highlights as white paper. Judge which colour to use where by looking carefully at the reflections.

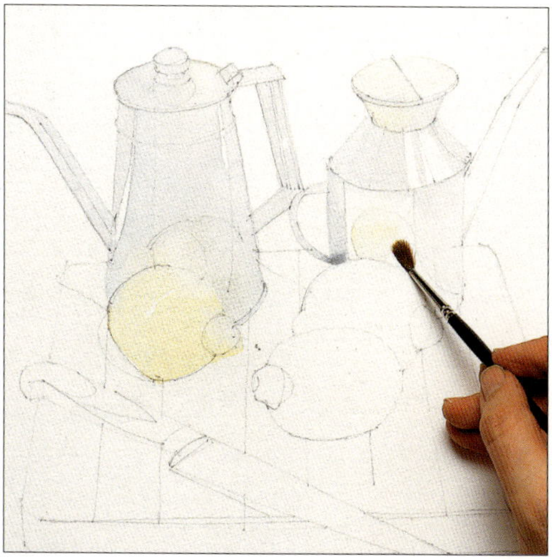

3 Paint the left-hand lemon and the reflected yellow highlights in the right-hand olive oil pourer in the same cadmium lemon wash used in Step 2. Leave some white highlights on both the lemon and the olive oil pourer. Note that the reflected yellows are duller in tone than those used to paint the actual lemon.

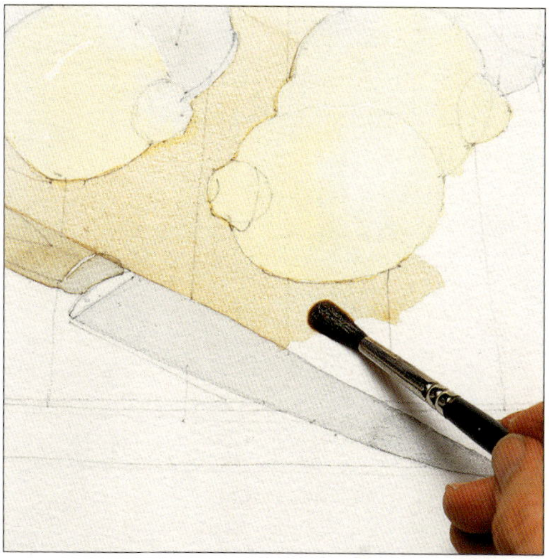

4 Paint the two right-hand lemons in the same pale cadmium lemon wash. Mix a mid-toned brown from raw umber with a touch of burnt umber and paint the handle of the knife. Paint the blade of the knife in a very dilute wash of lamp black, leaving a highlight near the handle. Leave to dry. Mix a pale brown from yellow ochre and a little burnt sienna and, using a medium round brush, paint the wooden chopping board.

Assessment time

The initial, lightest washes have now been laid down and the base colours of the whole still life established. You can now begin to elaborate on this, building up tones to the correct density and putting in the details. Work slowly, building up the tones gradually to avoid the risk of laying down a tone that is too dark.

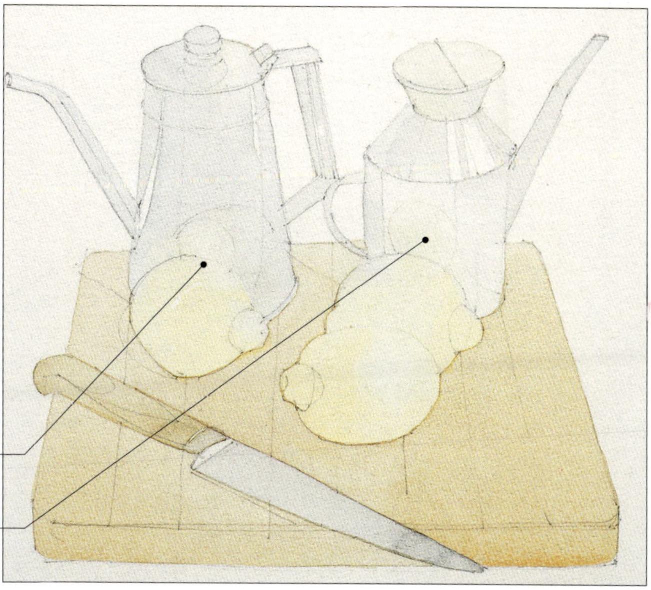

The very brightest highlights have been left as white paper.

The reflections are muted in colour and worked wet into wet so that the colours blur a little.

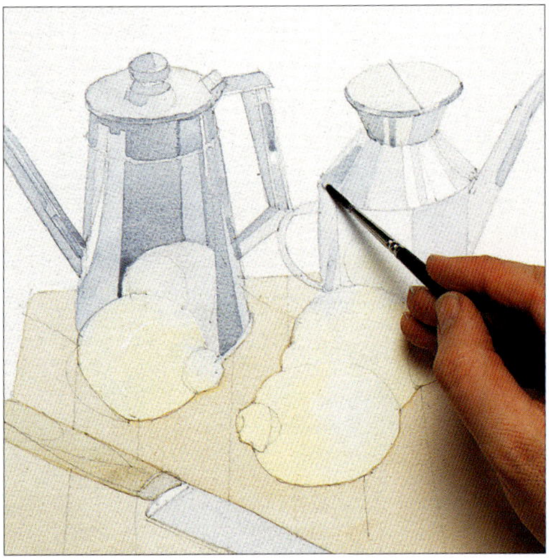

5 Mix slightly darker versions of the greys and blues used in Step 2, adding a touch of dioxazine purple to the cerulean blue, and start to paint in the mid tones on the olive oil pourers, gradually defining the individual facets more clearly. Leave to dry.

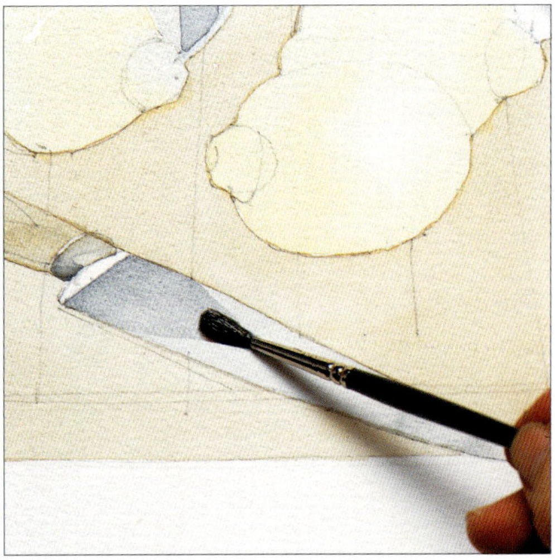

6 Mix a mid-toned grey from Payne's grey and ivory black and darken the blade of the knife, leaving an area of lighter tone near the handle. Make sure you don't go outside the pencil lines: the outline of the knife must be crisply defined. Leave to dry.

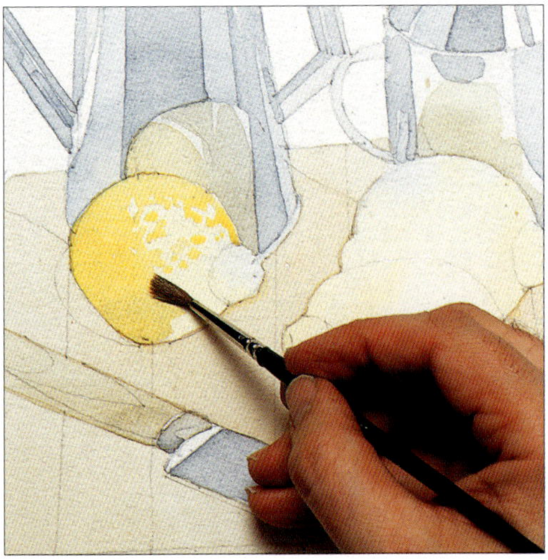

7 Add cadmium lemon to the mixture used to paint the chopping board in Step 4 and paint the reflections of the lemon in the pots. Begin to intensify the colour on the lemons themselves with a wash of cadmium lemon, working around the highlights. As you work down the lemons, gradually add cadmium lemon and then a hint of cerulean blue to the mixture, so that the colour is darker on the shadowed underside and the rounded shape of the fruit is clearer.

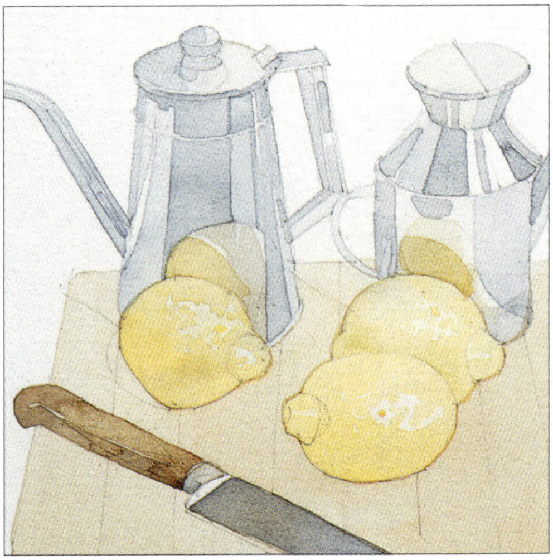

8 Touch a little more greenish yellow into the reflections of the lemons. Paint the handle of the knife again with the same mixture of raw umber and burnt umber used in Step 4, leaving a slight gap in the middle, where light hits the edge, to indicate the change of plane between the side and top of the handle. Leave to dry. All the mid tones of the painting have now been established.

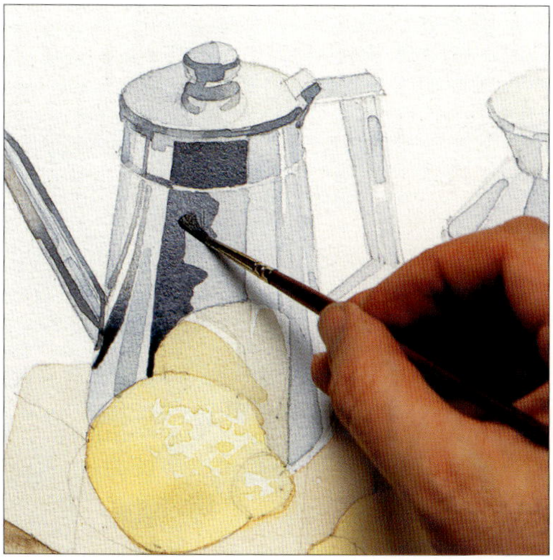

9 Mix slightly darker versions of the greys and blues used in Step 5 and continue reinforcing the tones on the olive oil pourers. As you darken these tones, the reflections (which are considerably lighter in colour) will begin to stand out even more clearly.

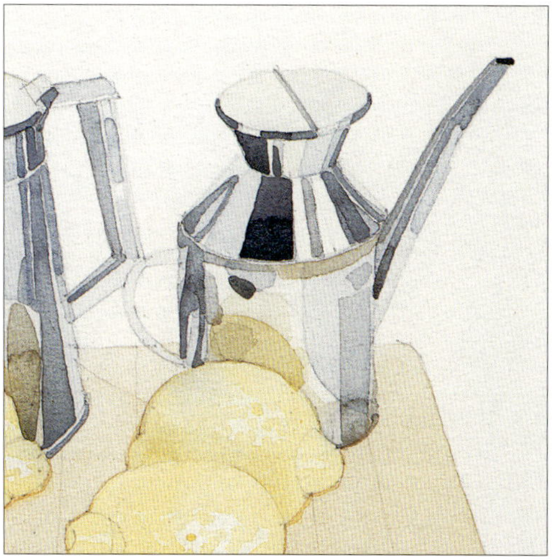

10 Strengthen the tones of the right-hand olive oil pourer in the same way, paying careful attention to the different facets of the two pourers. Add a touch of cadmium orange to paint the reflection of the chopping board.

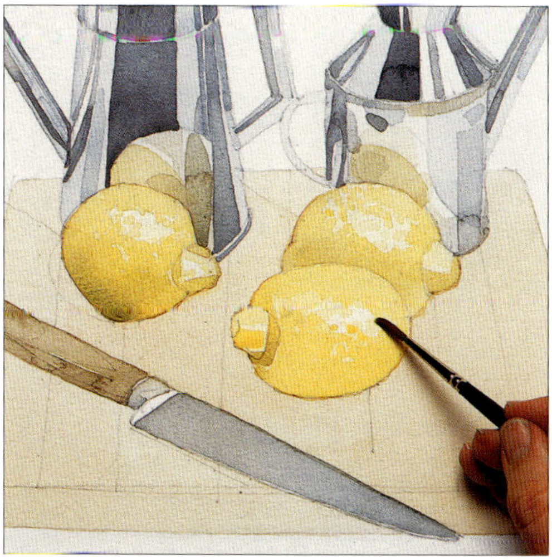

11 Using the same yellow mixtures as used in Step 7, build up the density of tone on the lemons. Again, remember to work carefully around the highlights that you left white in Step 3. Leave to dry.

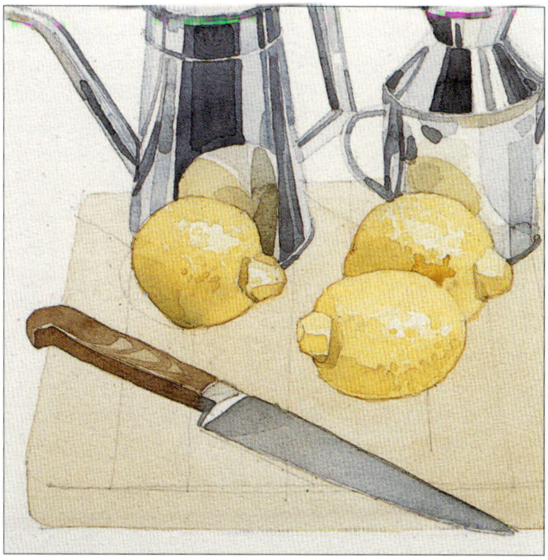

12 Mix a dark brown from burnt umber and burnt sienna and, using a fine round brush, carefully paint the shaded side of the knife handle under the highlight line, making sure you retain the crisp, sharp lines. The knife immediately looks much more three-dimensional. Leave to dry. Using the same fine round brush, stipple a little of the greenish yellow mixture on to the dark undersides of the lemons to create the pitted surface texture of the fruit.

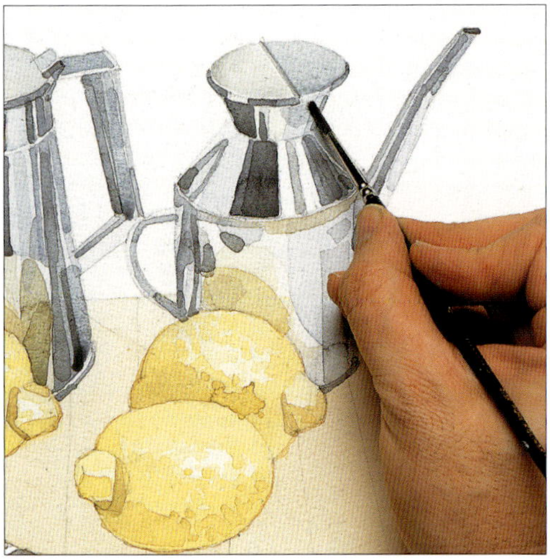

13 In these final stages of the painting, put in the very darkest tones. Work across the painting as a whole, assessing the tones in relation to each other rather than concentrating on one specific area.

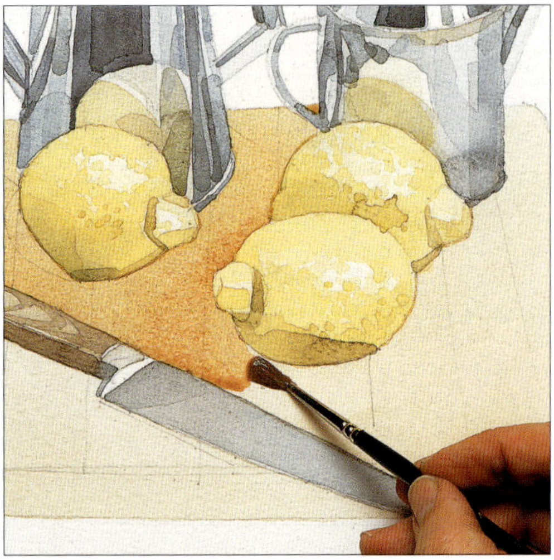

14 Brush a little more of the greenish yellow mixture on to the underside of the foreground lemon. Leave to dry. Using the dark brown mixture of burnt umber and burnt sienna, and a medium round brush, paint the top of the chopping board. Leave to dry.

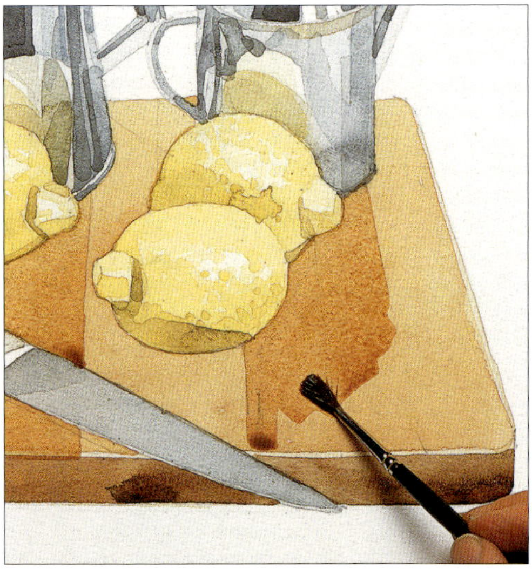

15 Darken the burnt umber and burnt sienna mixture by adding a little more burnt sienna and a hint of alizarin crimson. Paint the front of the chopping board, which is in shadow, leaving a tiny highlight along the edge between the top and front of the board. Leave to dry. Paint alternate panels on the top of the board in a mixture of burnt umber and burnt sienna. Leave to dry.

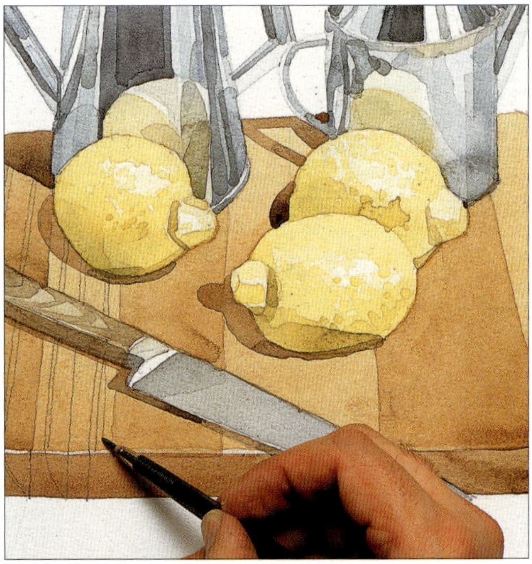

16 Add a little dioxazine purple to the dark brown mixture that you used to paint the front of the chopping board and paint the shadows behind the olive oil pourers and under the lemons and the knife. Leave to dry. Using a 2B graphite stick, draw vertical lines on the chopping board to indicate the grain of the wood.

Still life with stainless steel

This is a contemporary-looking still life with bold shapes and shadows. All the elements are contained within a triangle formed between the tip of the knife and the spouts of the olive oil pourers. Placing the knife on the diagonal also makes the composition more dynamic. Several layers of colour are applied to build up the tones to the right density.

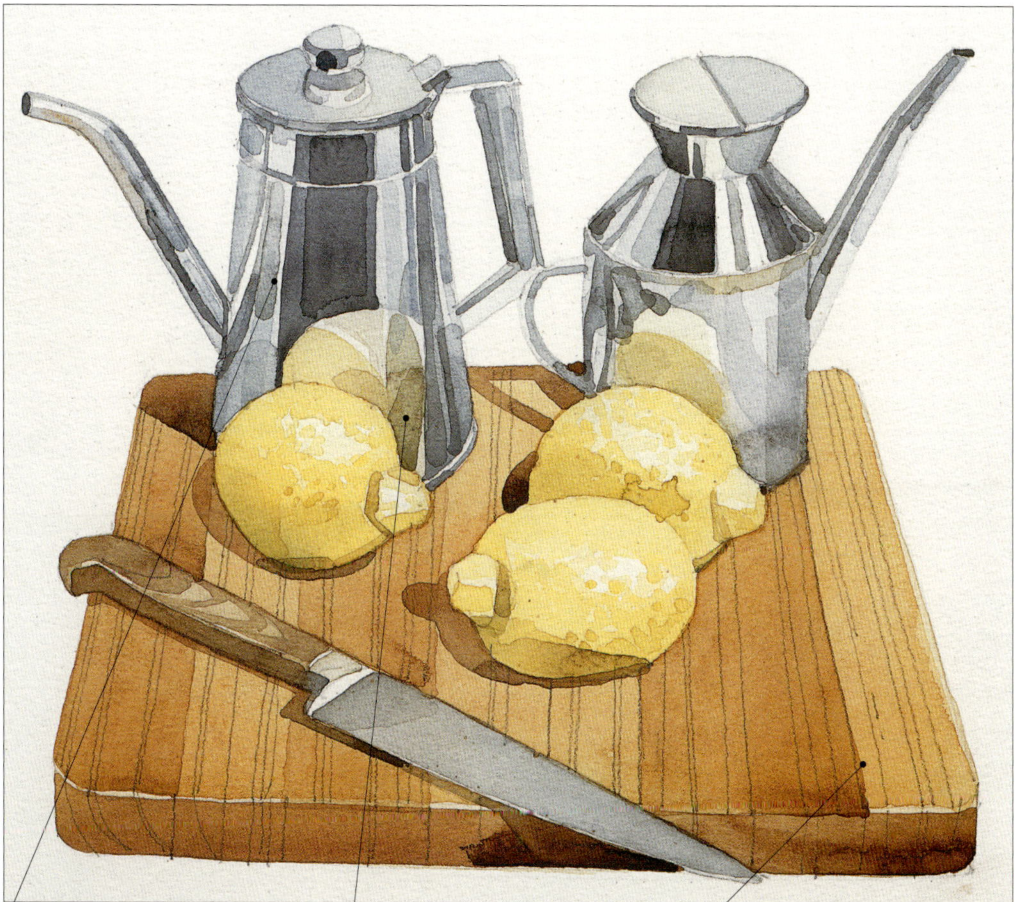

Variations in tone convey the shape of the olive oil pourers.

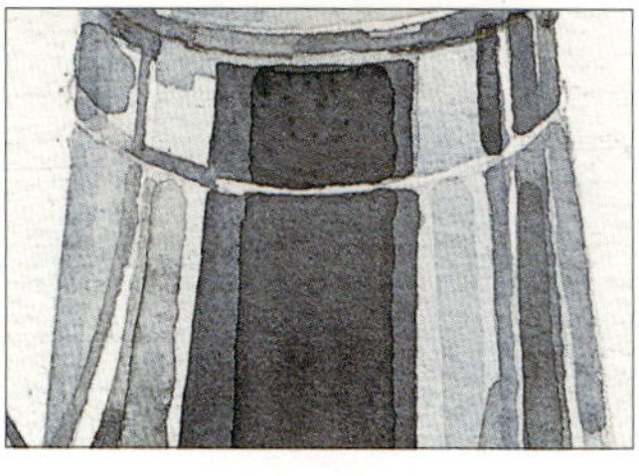

The reflections are slightly blurred and more subdued in tone that the objects being reflected.

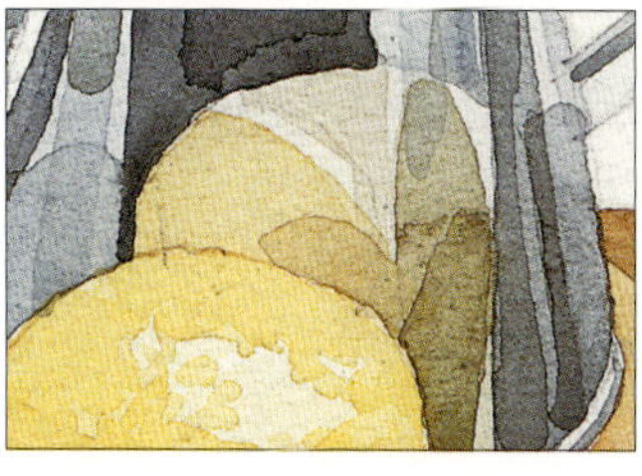

Simple pencil lines effectively convey the grain of the wooden board without detracting from the main subjects.

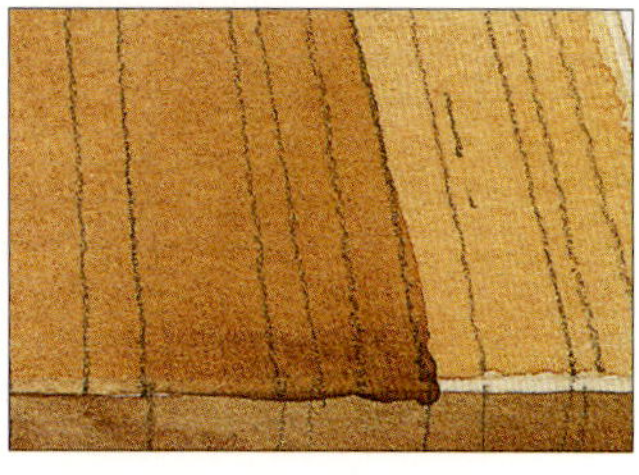

Eye of the tiger

People sometimes say that the eyes are the windows of the soul and, regardless of whether you are painting humans or animals, they certainly tell you a lot about the character and mood of your subject. All too often, eyes are drawn and painted as circles or ovals, which looks very unnatural. The eyeball is spherical even though, of course, only a small part of it is visible. This spherical shape is particularly obvious if you look at an eye from the side, but regardless of your viewpoint it helps to think of the eye as a three-dimensional form.

Subtle blends of colour are essential when it comes to painting the iris of the eye, while the "white" of the eye is often shadowed and not white at all. Finally, you must capture that all-important sparkle, which makes your subject look alive. Look at the position and shape of bright highlights in the eyes.

The artist chose a tiger's eye for this demonstration, because he also wanted to explore the markings on the surrounding fur, but the same principles apply to all subjects. An original painting of a tiger was used as reference material.

Materials

- *HB pencil*
- *Hot-pressed watercolour board or paper*
- *Watercolour paints: cadmium yellow, cadmium red, burnt sienna, Payne's grey, viridian, French ultramarine, Vandyke brown, ivory black*
- *Gouache paints: permanent white*
- *Brushes: fine round, ultra-fine round*

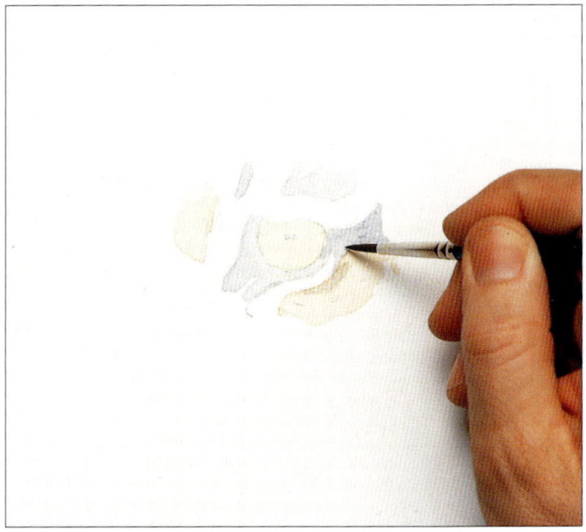

1 Using an HB pencil, lightly sketch the tiger's eye on smooth watercolour board or paper. Mix cadmium yellow with cadmium red for the gold of the eye and apply it carefully, using a fine round brush. Leave to dry. Mix burnt sienna with a little cadmium yellow and brush it over the tiger's fur, leaving the highlight area under the eye untouched. Paint the black facial markings around the eye in a dark mixture of Payne's grey. Leave to dry.

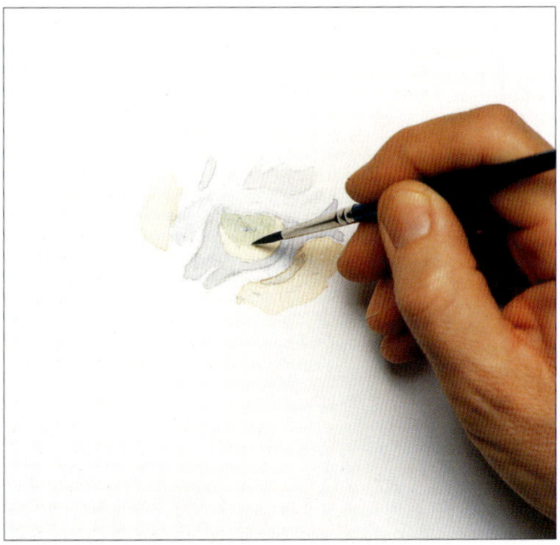

2 Mix a cool green from viridian and a little French ultramarine and, using a fine round brush, brush it over the top half of the iris, covering the pupil. Leave to dry. The basic colours and shapes have now been established. The next stage is to make the eye look three-dimensional by showing how the lids curve over the eyeball.

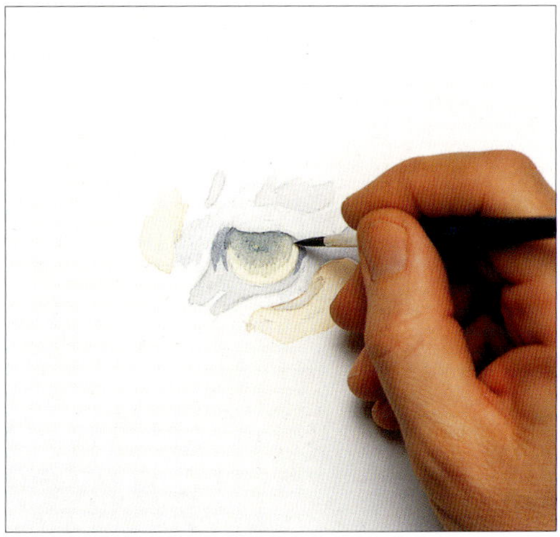

3 Using an ultra-fine round brush, paint the upper part of the iris in Payne's grey, gently feathering the colour down on to the green. This softens the transition in colour from one part of the eye to the next and looks much more natural than hard-edged, concentric circles of colour. Darken the upper rim of the eye with Payne's grey. Leave to dry.

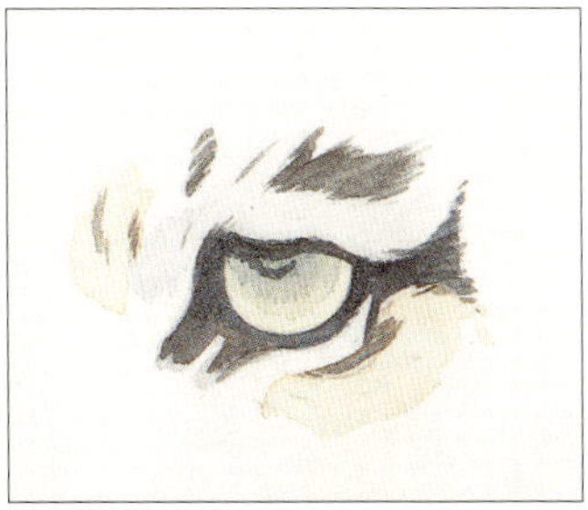

4 Darken the markings around the eye with a mixture of Vandyke brown and Payne's grey. Paint the pupil in the same colour.

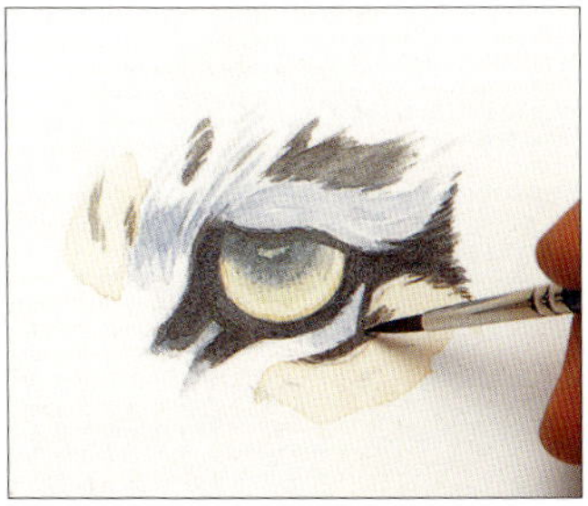

5 While the pupil is still damp, feather the colour down on to the iris, so that there is a very subtle transition of colour. Mix French ultramarine with a touch of permanent white gouache and, using a fine round brush, brush in the shaded areas of the fur, making sure your brushstrokes follow the direction of the fur growth. Build up the dark markings around the eye with ivory black. Leave to dry.

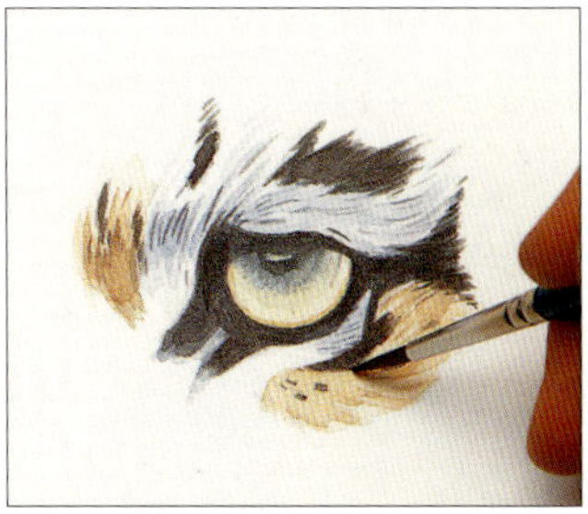

6 Continue to build up the dark markings around the eye with ivory black. Darken the brown fur colour with burnt sienna and Vandyke brown, alternating between the two. Add tiny strokes of permanent white gouache on the eyeball and the lower eyelid to create highlights.

Eye of the tiger

The dramatic colouring and fine detail make this a very attractive study. Subtle feathering of colour and the careful positioning of the highlights on both the eyeball and the lower lid combine to depict a rounded and very life-like eye. Tiny details like this can have as much impact as a full-scale painting and are a good way of practising difficult subjects.

Tiny touches of permanent white gouache on the pupil reflect the light, while subtle feathering softens the transition from one colour to the next.

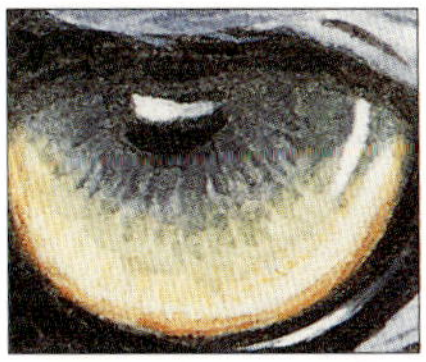

Although the fur is white, it is in shade here and is painted in pale French ultramarine.

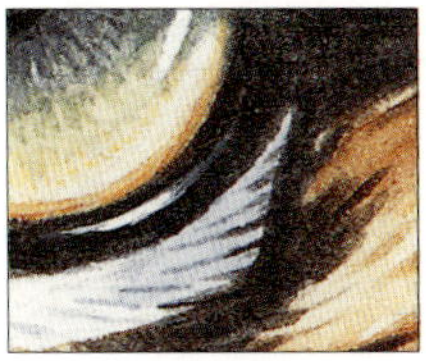

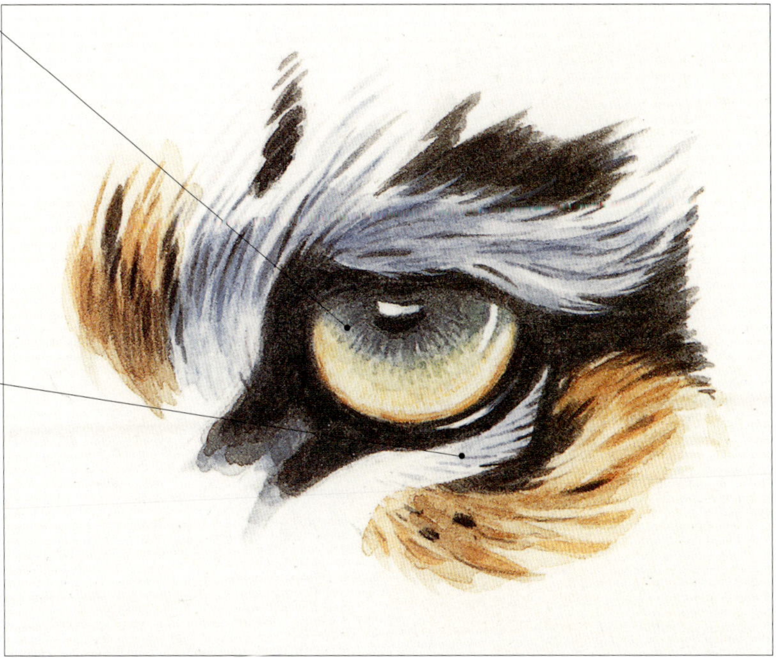

Tabby cat

Cat fur is fascinating to paint and you will find a huge variety of markings, from tortoiseshell and tabby cats with their bold stripes to sleek, chocolate-point Siamese and long-haired Maine Coons. One of the keys to painting fur is being able to blend colours in a very subtle way, without harsh edges. Even pure white or black cats, with no obvious markings, have their own "patterns": because of reflected light and shadows, the fur of a pure white cat will exhibit clear differences in tone which you need to convey in your paintings.

Fur markings also reveal a lot about the shape of the animal. You need to look at an animal's fur in much the same way as a portrait painter looks at how fabrics drape over the body of a model: changes in tone and in the direction of the fur markings indicate the shape and contours of the body underneath. Always think about the basic anatomy of your subject, otherwise the painting will not look convincing. If you concentrate on the outline shape when you are painting a long-haired cat, for example, you could end up with something that looks like a ball of fluff with eyes, rather than a living animal. The cat in this project has relatively short hair, which makes it easier to see the underlying shape.

Cats seem to spend a lot of their time sleeping or simply sprawled out, soaking up the sunlight and, if you are lucky, you might have time to make a quick watercolour sketch. For "action" pictures – kittens batting their paws at a favourite toy or adult cats jumping from a wall or stalking a bird in the garden – you will almost certainly have to work from a photographic reference. You will be amazed at the number of ways cats can contort their bodies.

Materials

- *HB pencil*
- *140lb (300gsm) rough watercolour paper, pre-stretched*
- *Watercolour paints: yellow ochre, raw umber, alizarin crimson, ultramarine blue, cadmium red, Prussian blue, burnt sienna*
- *Gouache paints: Chinese white*
- *Brushes: medium round, fine round*

Reference photograph

This is a typical cat pose – the animal is relaxed and sprawled out, but at the same time very alert to whatever is happening around it. The markings on the fur are subtly coloured but attractive. The face is full of character, and this is what you need to concentrate on in your painting. If you can get the facial features to look right, you are well on the way to creating a successful portrait.

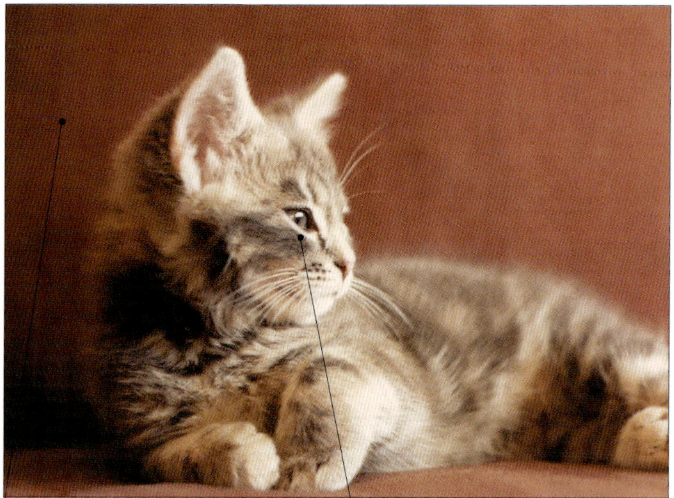

A plain background allows you to concentrate on the subject.

The eyes, the most important part of the portrait, are wide open and alert.

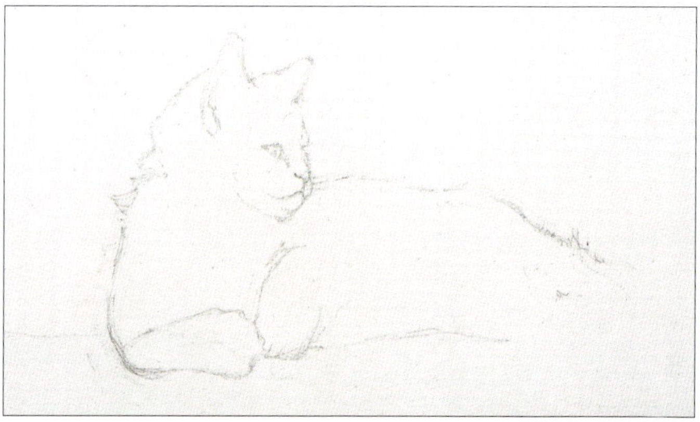

1 Using an HB pencil sketch the cat, making sure you get the angle of the head right in relation to the rest of the body. Start with the facial features, sketching the triangle formed by the eyes and nose, then work outwards. This makes it easier to position the features in relation to each other. If you draw the outline of the head first, and then try to fit in the facial features, the chances are that you will make the head too small.

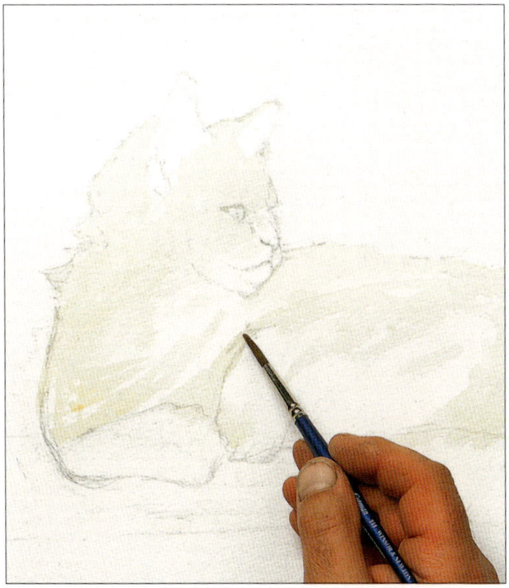

2 Mix a pale wash of a warm brown from yellow ochre and raw umber. Using a medium round brush, wash the mixture over the cat leaving the palest areas, such as the insides of the ears and the very light markings, untouched.

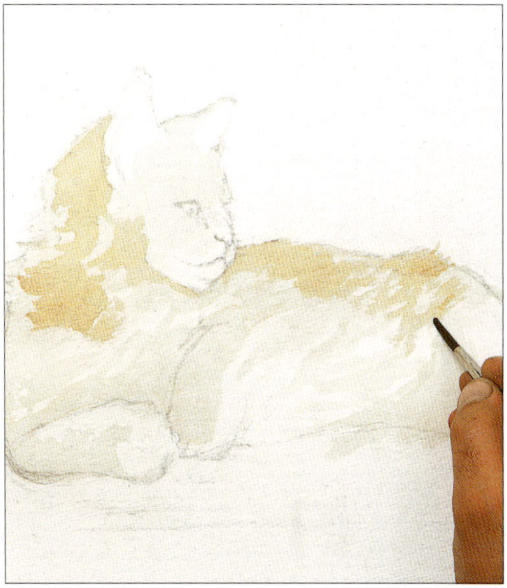

3 Add a little more raw umber to the mixture to make a darker brown and paint the darker areas on the back of the head and back.

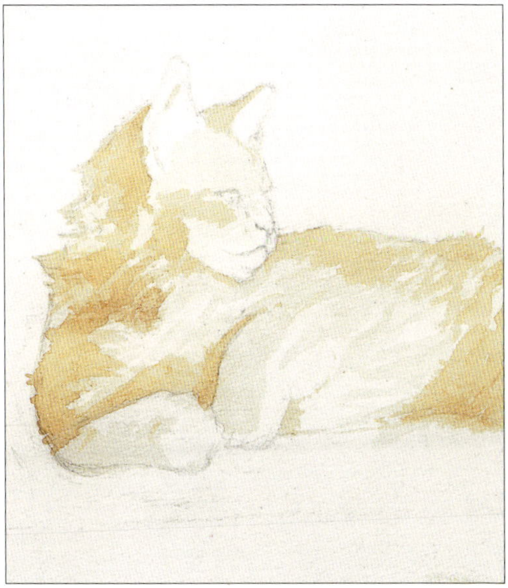

4 Continue applying the darker brown mixture, which gives the second tone. You are now beginning to establish a sense of form in the portrait.

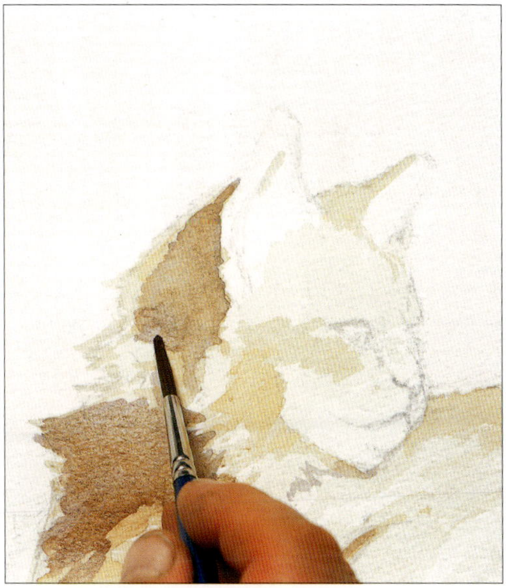

5 Add a little alizarin crimson and ultramarine blue to the mixture to make a dark, neutral grey. Begin brushing in some of the darker areas around the head.

▶

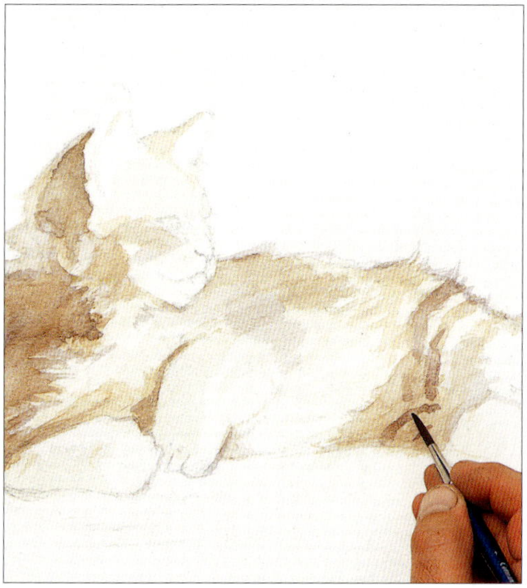

6 Add more water to the mixture and paint the cat's back, which is less shaded. Start painting some of the markings on the hind quarters, using short, spiky brushstrokes along the top of the cat's back. This indicates that the fur does not lie completely flat.

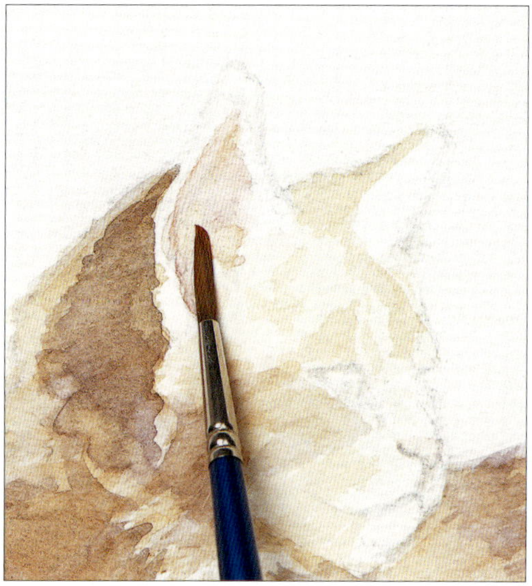

7 Mix a warm brown from yellow ochre and raw umber and brush it loosely over the mid-toned areas. Mix a warm pink from alizarin crimson and a little yellow ochre and, using a fine round brush, paint the insides of the ears, the pads of the paws, and the tip of the nose.

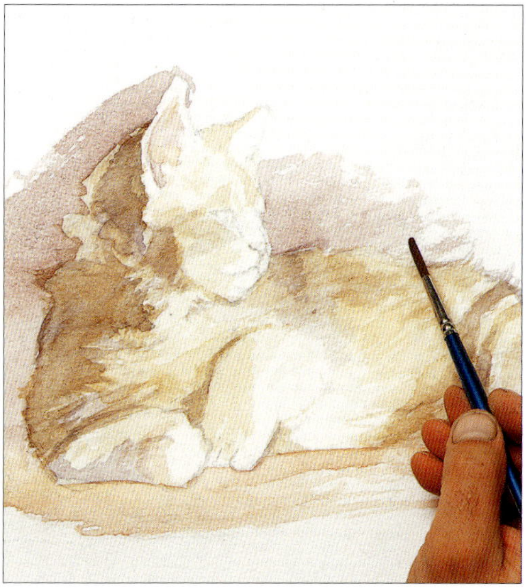

8 Mix a warm maroon colour from cadmium red, yellow ochre and alizarin crimson and paint the surface on which the cat is lying. Add ultramarine blue to darken the mixture and paint the background, carefully brushing around the cat.

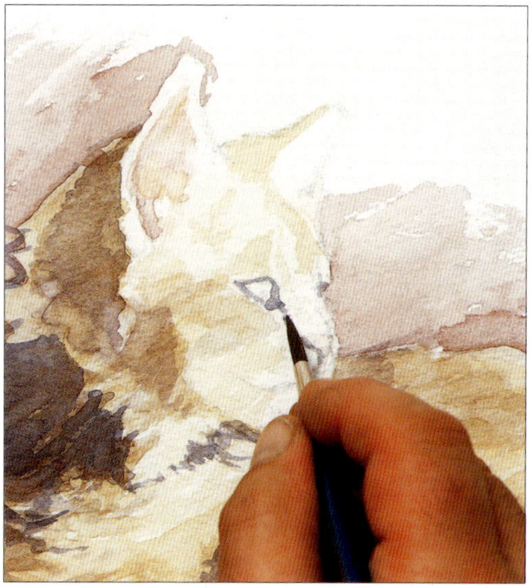

9 Mix a purplish blue from ultramarine blue and cadmium red. Using a fine round brush, paint the dark fur on the side of the cat's head, the nostril, the area under the chin and the outline of the eye.

Assessment time

Although the broad outline of the cat is there, along with some indication of the markings on the fur, the painting does not yet look convincing because the body looks flat rather than rounded. In addition, the cat's head is merging into the warm colour of the background, when it needs to stand out much more clearly.

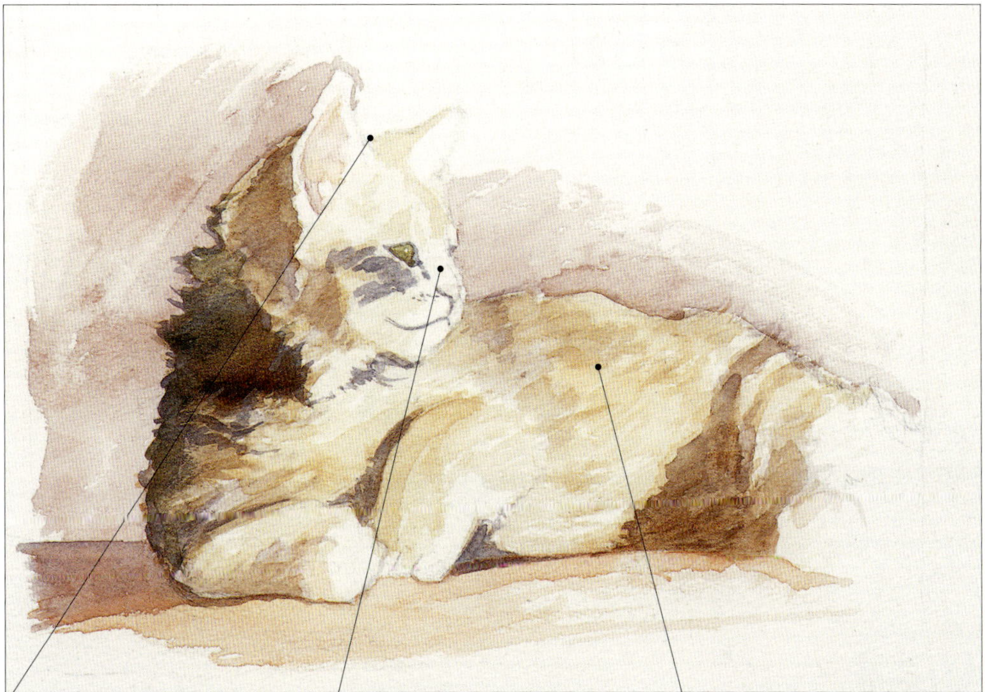

The head merges into the background.

The facial features need to be strengthened further.

At this stage, much of the body is a relatively flat expanse of colour.

10 Mix a greenish black from Prussian blue, burnt sienna and cadmium red and paint the pupil of the eye, leaving a white highlight. Brush more of the purplish-blue mixture used in Step 9 on to the shaded left-hand side of the cat and strengthen the shadow under the chin and on the back of the cat's head.

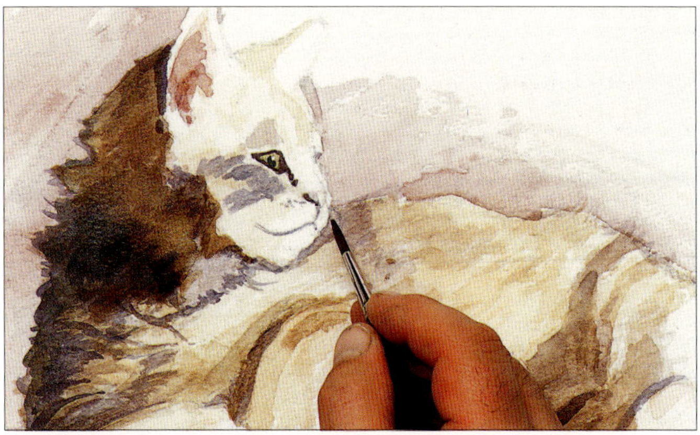

Tip: Pay careful attention to the highlight in the cat's eye. The shape and size of the white area must be accurate in order to look lifelike.

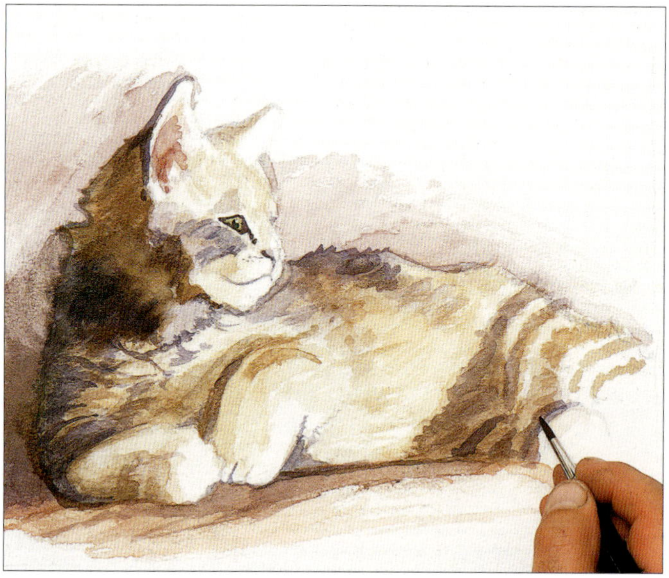

11 Using the same purplish-blue mixture, put in some of the stripes on the hind quarters and darken the tones on the back, paying careful attention to the direction of the brushstrokes so that the markings follow the contours of the body.

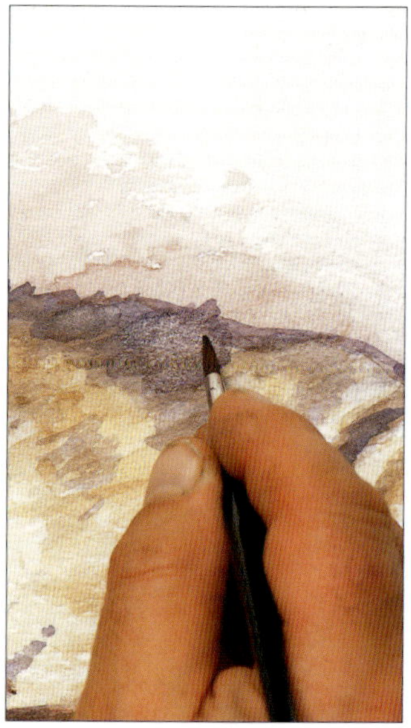

12 Using the same mixture, continue darkening the tones on the back to give a better sense of form.

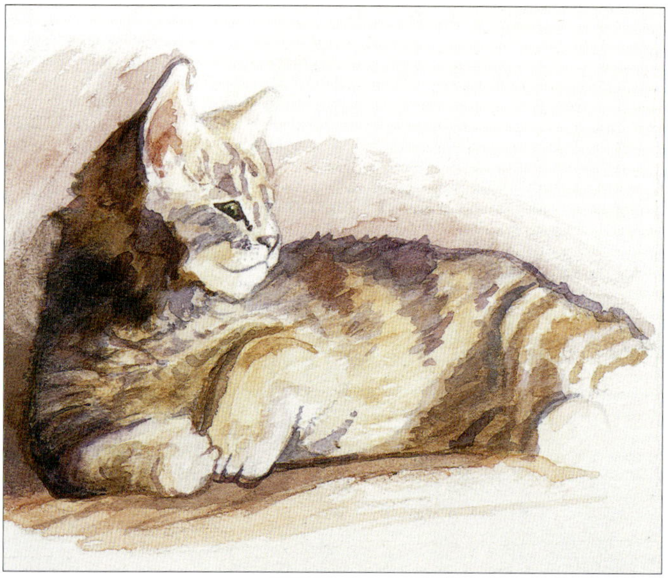

13 Adjust the tones where necessary. Now that you have put in lots of darks, you may need to tone down some of the bright areas that have been left unpainted by applying a very dilute wash of the first pale brown tone.

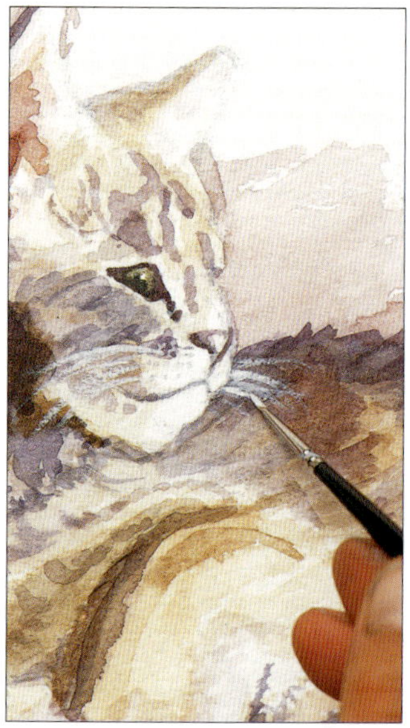

14 Darken the insides of the ears with alizarin crimson. Using a very fine brush and Chinese white gouache, paint the whiskers.

Tabby cat

This is a lively and engaging study of a favourite family pet. All portraits, whether they are of humans or animals, need to convey the character of the subject. The artist has achieved this here by placing the main focus of interest on the cat's face and its alert expression. The fur is softly painted, with careful blends of colour, but the markings are clearly depicted.

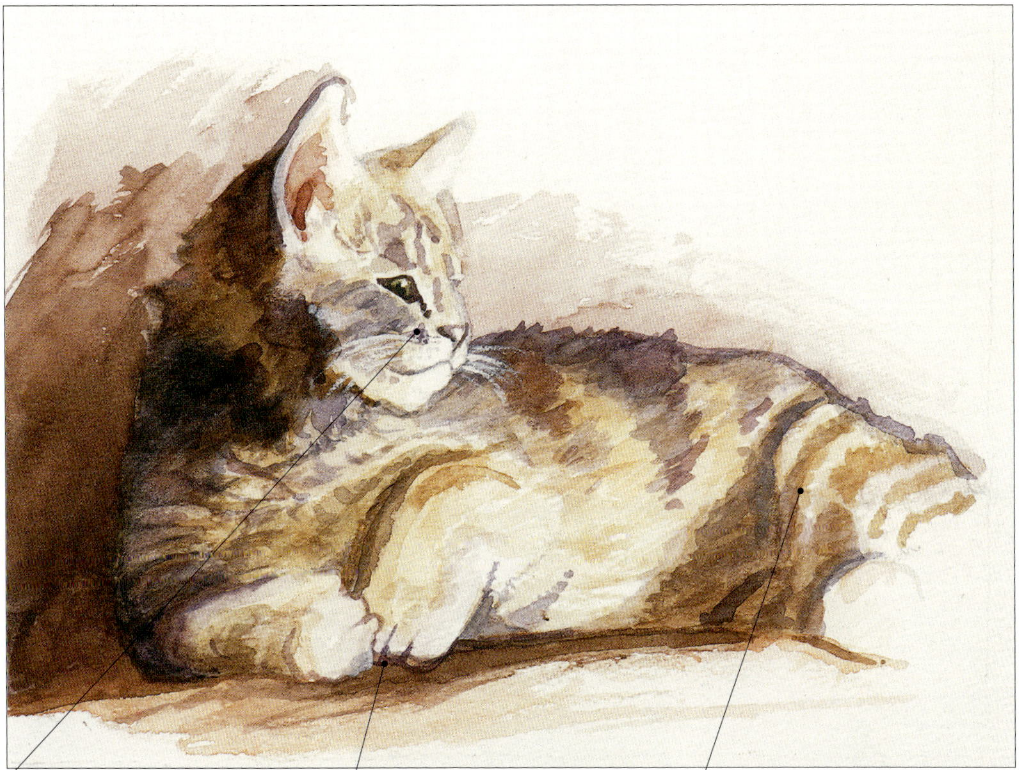

The facial features are crisply painted.

Deep shadow between the paws helps to create a sense of depth in the painting.

The markings change direction, following the contours of the body beneath.

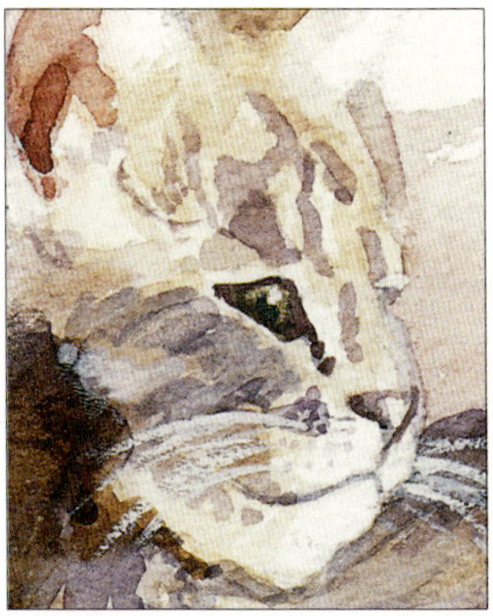

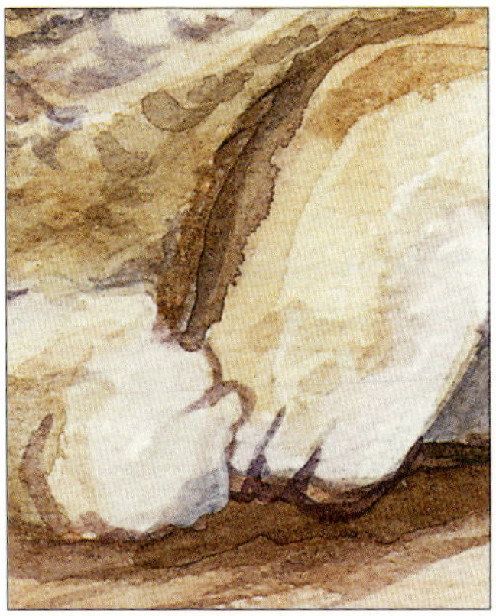

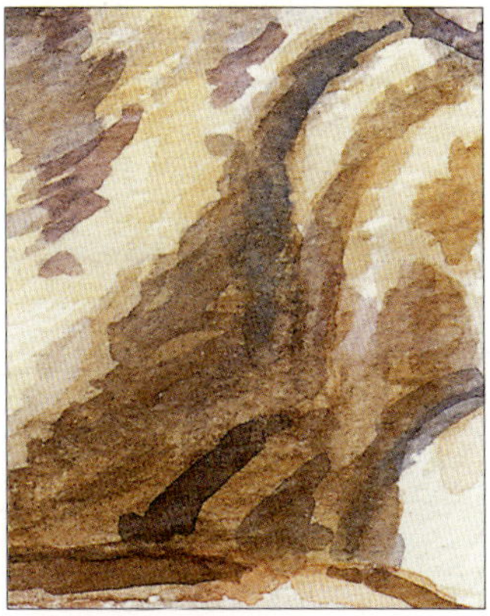

Otter

This delightful study of an otter, peering inquisitively out to sea, is an exercise in building up textures. You can put in as much or as little detail as you wish, but don't try to finish one small area completely before you move on to the next. Go over the whole painting once, putting in the first detailed brushmarks, and then repeat the process as necessary.

Remember to work on a smooth, hot-pressed watercolour paper or board when using masking film (frisket paper). If you use masking film on a rough-surfaced paper there is a risk that the film will not adhere to the surface properly, allowing paint to slip underneath and on to the area that you want to protect. Smooth paper also enables you to make the fine, crisp lines that are essential in a detailed study such as this.

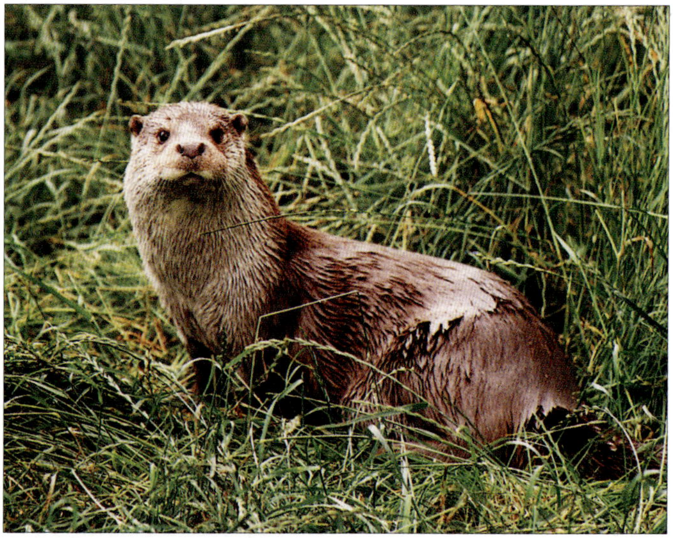

Materials

- *HB pencil*
- *Hot-pressed watercolour board or smooth paper*
- *Watercolour paints: ultramarine blue, cadmium yellow, burnt sienna, Vandyke brown, Payne's grey, cadmium red*
- *Gouache paints: permanent white*
- *Brushes: medium flat, medium round, fine round, very fine round*
- *Masking film (frisket paper)*
- *Scalpel or craft (utility) knife*
- *Tracing paper*

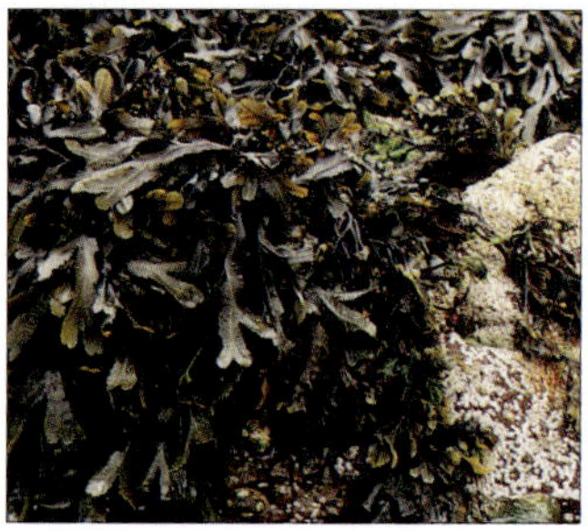

Reference photographs
Here the artist worked from two reference photographs – one for the otter's pose and fur detail, and one for the seaweed-covered rocks in the foreground. When you do this, you need to think carefully about the direction of the light. If you follow your references slavishly, you may find that sunlight appears to hit different areas of the picture at different angles, which will look very unnatural.

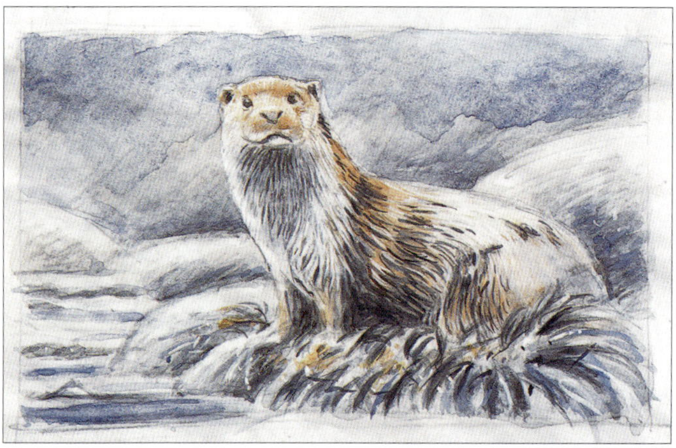

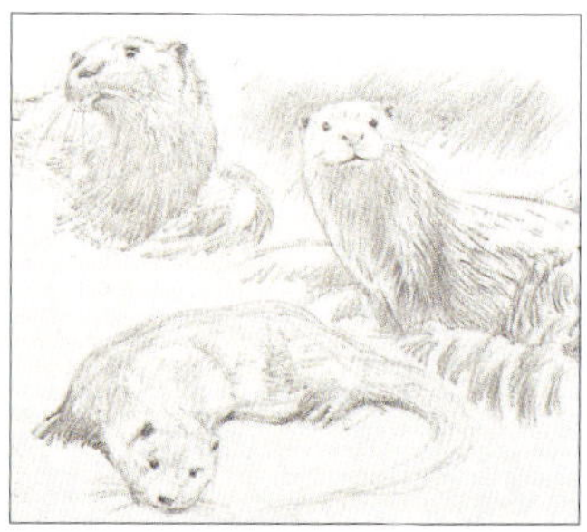

Preliminary sketches
Quick pencil sketches will help you to select the best composition, while a watercolour sketch is a good way of working out which colours to use.

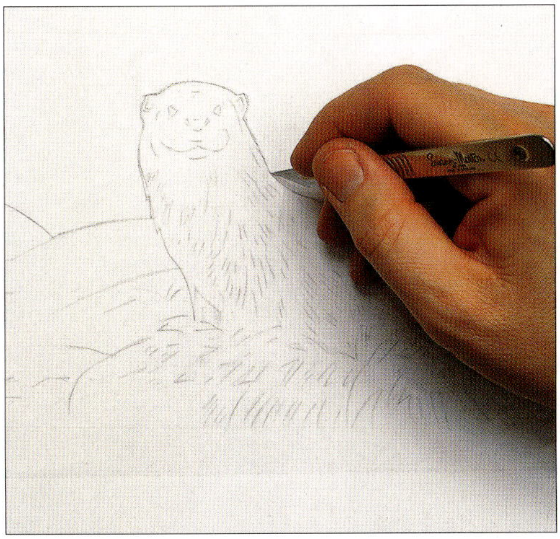

1 Using an HB pencil, copy your reference sketch on to watercolour board or smooth paper. Place masking film over the picture area. Using a sharp scalpel or craft (utility) knife, cut around the otter and rocks. To avoid damaging your painting surface, trace your pencil sketch, then place the masking film over the tracing paper, cut it out, and reposition the film on the painting surface.

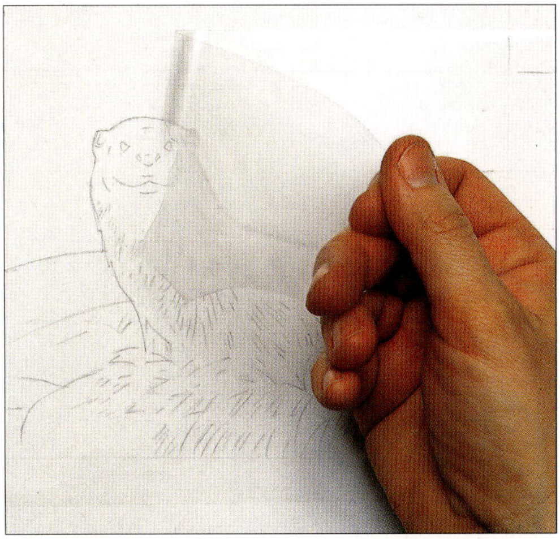

2 Carefully peel back the masking film from the top half of the painting. You may need use a scalpel or craft knife to lift up the edge. You can now work freely on the sky and background area, without worrying about paint accidentally spilling over on to the otter or foreground rocks – though it is worth rubbing over the stuck-down film with a soft cloth or piece of tissue paper to make sure it adheres firmly to the surface and that no paint can seep underneath.

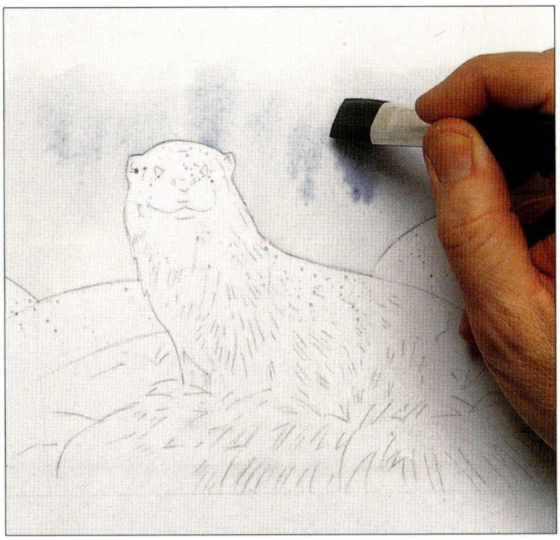

3 Mix a pale blue wash from ultramarine blue with a hint of cadmium yellow. Using a medium flat brush, dampen the board above the masking film with clean water and then brush in vertical strokes of the pale blue mixture. While the first wash is still damp, brush more vertical blue strokes along the top of the paint and allow the paint to drift down, forming a kind of gradated wash. Leave to dry.

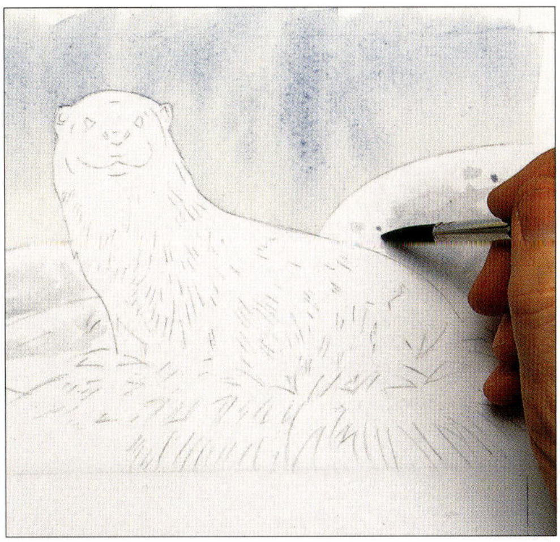

4 Carefully peel back the masking film from the bottom half of the painting, revealing the otter and rocks. Using a medium round brush, dampen the rocks with clean water and dot on the pale blue mixture used in Step 3.

▶

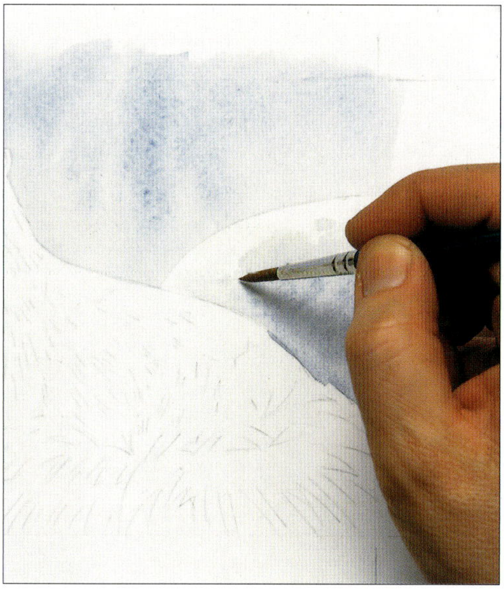

5 While the paint is still damp, use a fine round brush to dot in a darker mix of ultramarine blue and start building up tone on the rocks. Because you are working wet into wet, the colours will start to blur. Stipple a very pale cadmium yellow onto the rocks in places and leave to dry.

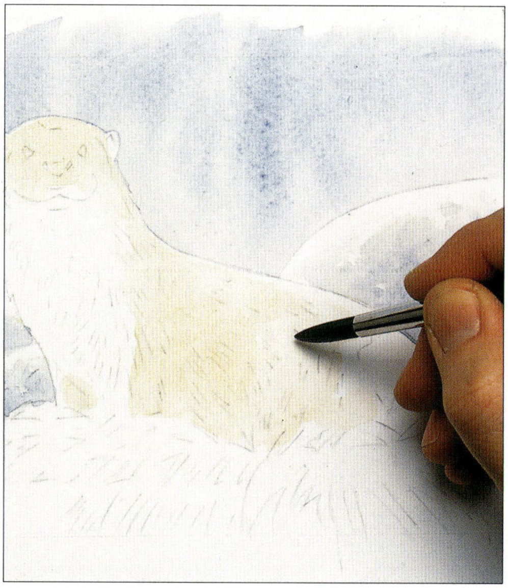

6 Mix a pale wash of burnt sienna and brush it over the otter's head and body. Brush over the chest area with the pale blue wash used in step 3. Leave to dry. Mix a darker brown wash from Vandyke brown and Payne's grey, and brush from shoulder to abdomen. Add a line around the back legs.

Assessment time

The base colours have now been established across the whole scene. Using the same colour (here, ultramarine blue) on both the background and the main subject creates a colour harmony that provides a visual link between the background and the foreground. You can now start to put in detail and build up the fur. In the later stages of this painting, you will want lots of crisp detail, so it's important to let each stage dry completely before you move on to the next – otherwise the paint will blur and spread.

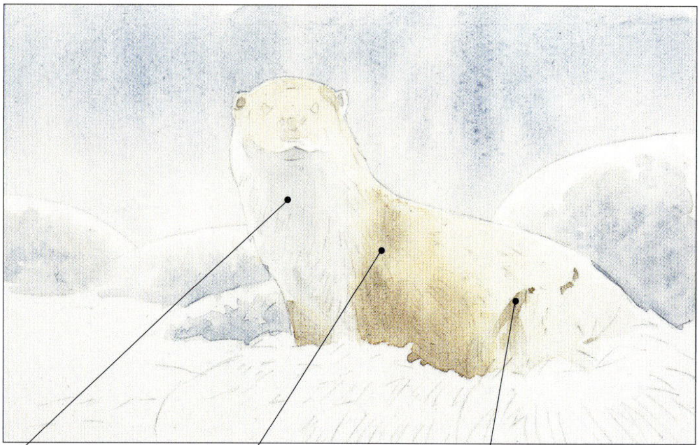

The chest, which is in shadow, is painted in a cool, pale mixture of ultramarine blue.

This darker brown helps to show the direction in which the fur is growing.

This dark line around the otter's back legs starts to establish the rounded form of the body.

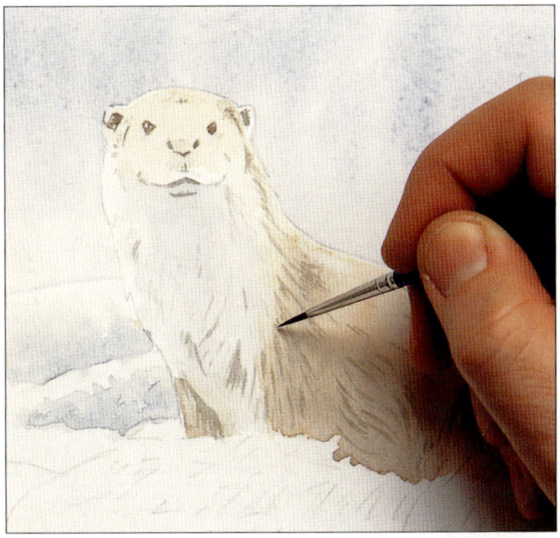

7 Mix a very dark brown from Vandyke brown and Payne's grey and, using a very fine round brush, put in the dark detail on the head – the inside of the ears, the eyes and the nose. Using the same colour, start to put in short brush marks that indicate the different directions in which the fur grows.

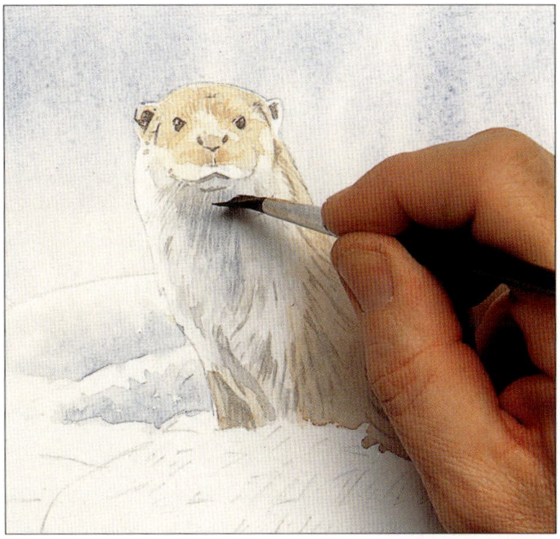

8 Mix a warm grey from Payne's grey and a little Vandyke brown. Using a fine round brush with the bristles splayed out in a fan shape, drybrush this mixture on to the otter's chest, taking care to follow the direction of the fur.

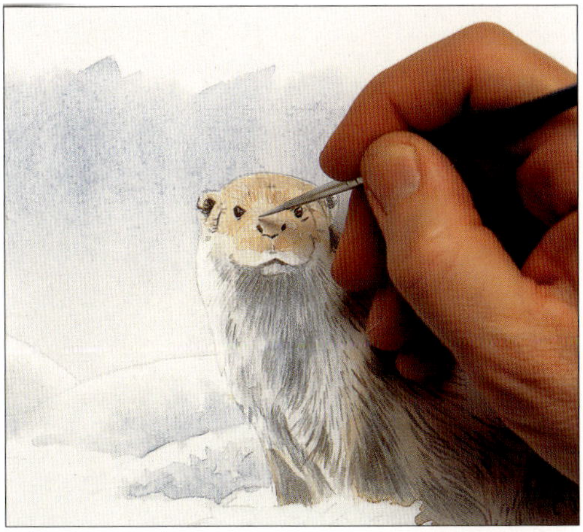

9 Continue building up tones and textures on the otter's chest and body. Paint the lightest areas on the otter's face with permanent white gouache. Mix a light, warm brown from burnt sienna and Vandyke brown and build up tones and textures on the otter's body. Darken the facial features.

Tip: The facial features help to establish the animal's character. If you can get these right, it will make it easier to overlook slight mistakes elsewhere. Spend plenty of time on this stage.

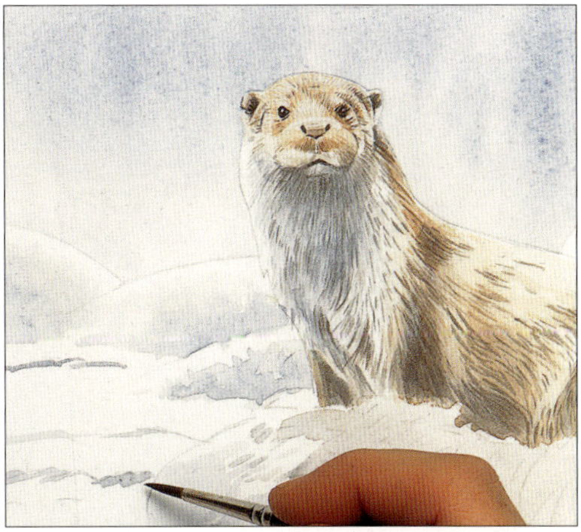

10 Mix a bright but pale blue from ultramarine blue with a hint of cadmium yellow and, using a fine round brush, brush thin horizontal lines on to the rocks on the left-hand side of the painting. This blue shadow colour helps to establish some of the crevices and the uneven surface of the rocks.

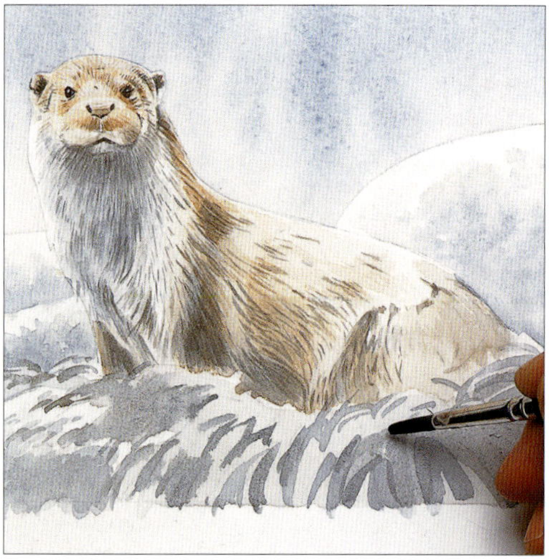

11 Mix a dark, bluish grey from Payne's grey and Vandyke brown and, using a medium round brush, paint the strands of seaweed on the rocks on the right of painting with loose, broad brushstrokes of this mixture. Leave to dry.

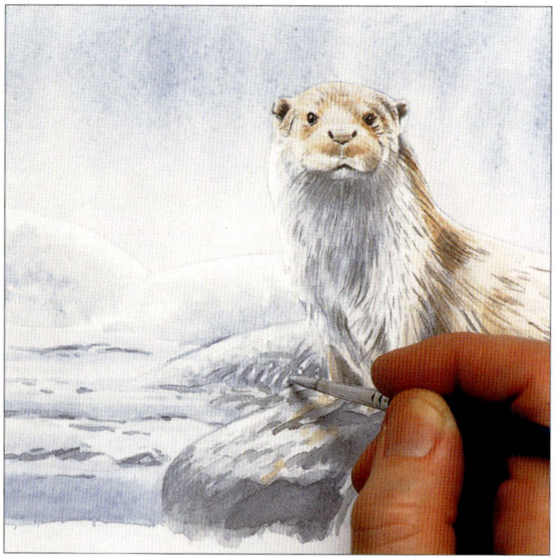

12 Brush a little ultramarine blue into the bottom left corner. Mix a warm brown from cadmium yellow and cadmium red and brush this mixture on to the rocks. Leave to dry. Paint lines of sea foam in permanent white gouache.

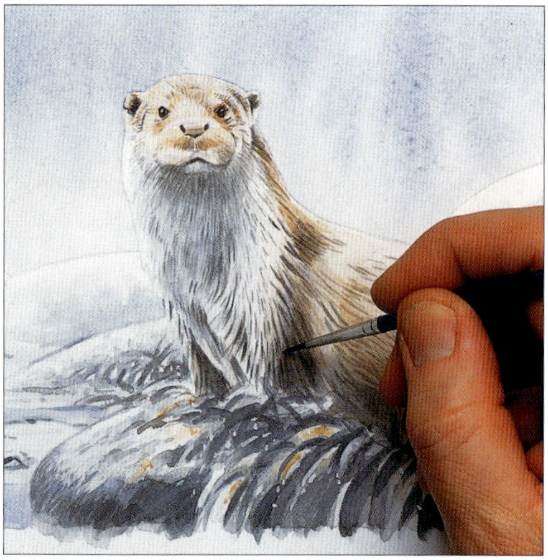

13 Now add more texture to the rock on the right, behind the otter, by stippling on a dark mixture of ultramarine blue. Note that the top of the rock, which is hit by the sunlight, is very light while the base is much darker. Using the drybrush technique, continue to add tone and form to the body of the otter, using a warm mixture of burnt sienna and ultramarine blue. Build up tone and texture on the otter's chest in the same way, using a mid-toned mixture of ultramarine blue.

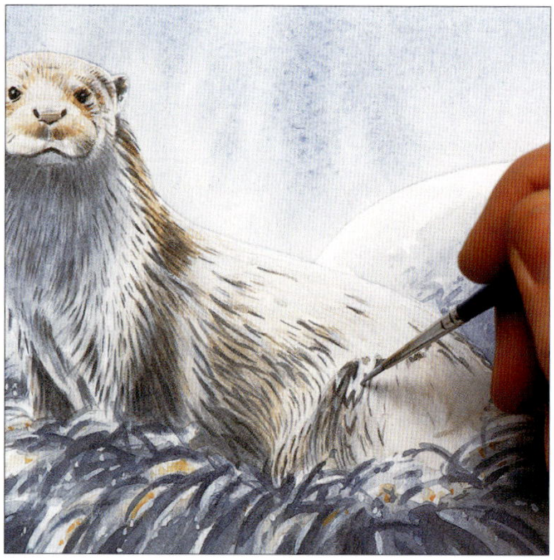

14 Using a fine round brush and very short brushstrokes, paint white gouache to form the highlights along the top of the otter's back and on the body, where water is glistening on the fur. Use white gouache to paint the otter's whiskers on either side of the muzzle.

Otter

This is a fresh and lively painting that captures the animal's pose and character beautifully. The background colours of blues and greys are echoed in the shadow areas on the otter's fur, creating a colour harmony that gives the picture unity.

By including a lot of crisp detail on the otter itself and allowing the background colours of the sky and rocks to blur and merge on the paper, the artist has made the main subject stand out in sharp relief.

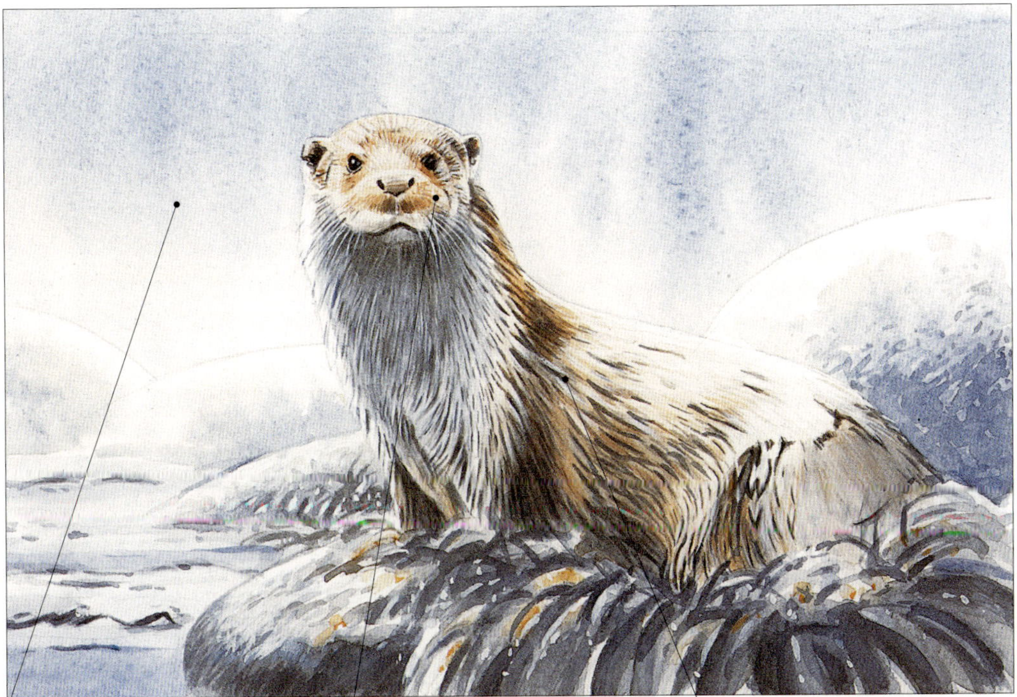

The background is painted in translucent, wet-into-wet washes that blur into indistinct shapes.

White gouache is used for very fine details such as the whiskers, which it would be very difficult to achieve simply by leaving the paper white.

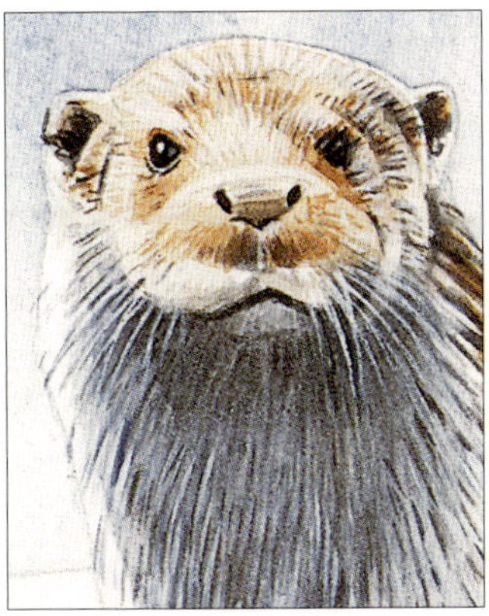

The crisp fur detail on the otter is made up of several layers of tiny brushstrokes, worked wet on dry – a painstaking technique but one that is well worth the effort.

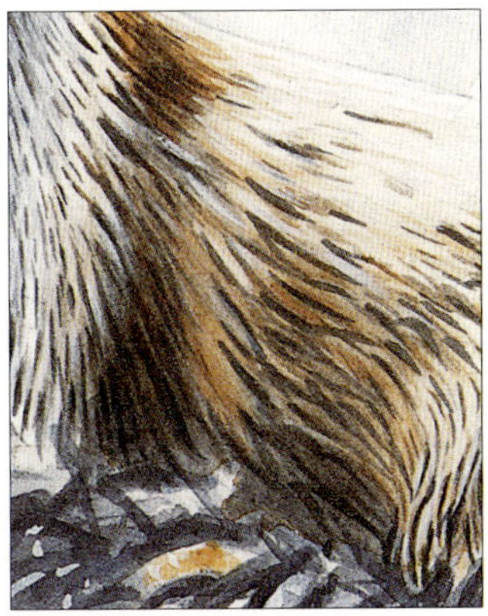

Flamingo

This project offers you the opportunity to practise building up layers of colour and to use your brush in a very controlled way. You need to assess the tones quite carefully when you are painting a subject that is mostly just one colour. You may find that it helps to half close your eyes, as this makes it easier to work out where the lightest and darkest areas are.

It is often a good idea to keep the background soft and blurred by using wet-into-wet washes when you are painting a textured subject like this, as the details stand out more clearly and the subject is separated from its surroundings.

Materials

- *HB pencil*
- *Hot-pressed watercolour board or smooth paper*
- *Watercolour paints: viridian, Payne's grey, cadmium red, ultramarine blue, ivory black, cadmium yellow*
- *Gouache paints: permanent white*
- *Brushes: large round, medium round, fine round, small flat, very fine*
- *Masking film (frisket paper)*
- *Scalpel or craft (utility) knife*

Preliminary sketches

Try out several compositions to decide which one works best before you make your initial underdrawing.

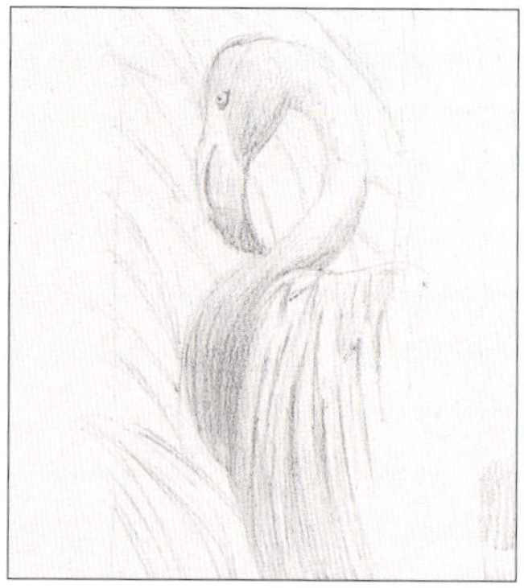

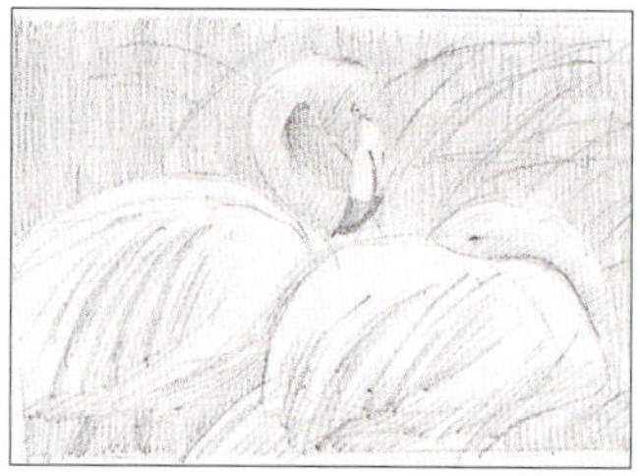

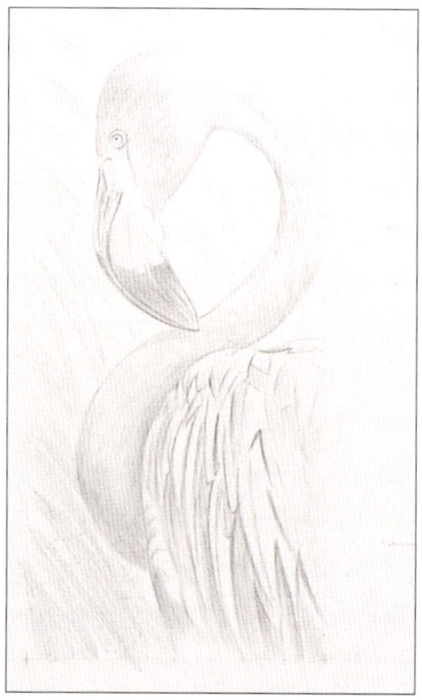

Reference photograph

This shot was taken in a nature reserve as reference for the feather colours. Wildlife parks and nature reserves are good places to take photos of animals and birds that you might not be able to get close to in the wild.

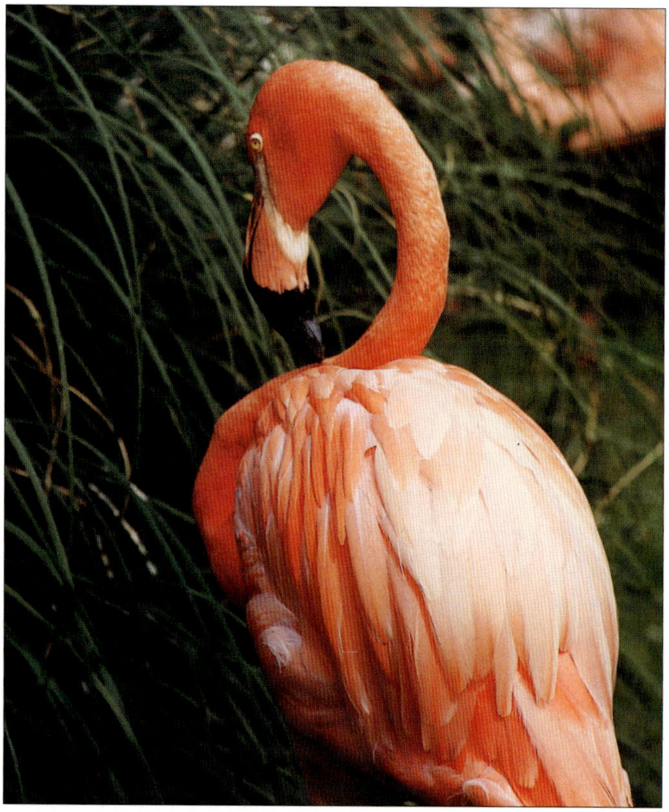

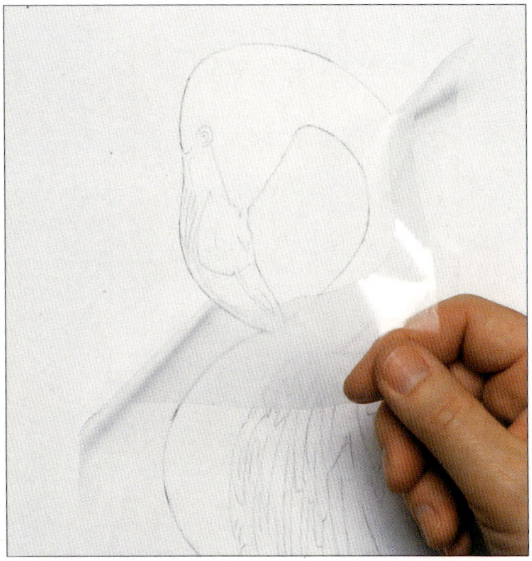

1 Using an HB pencil, trace your reference sketch on to hot-pressed watercolour board or smooth paper. Place masking film (frisket paper) over the whole picture area. Using a sharp scalpel or craft (utility) knife, carefully cut around the outline of the flamingo and the oval shape formed by the curve of the bird's neck. Peel back the masking film from the background, leaving the flamingo covered.

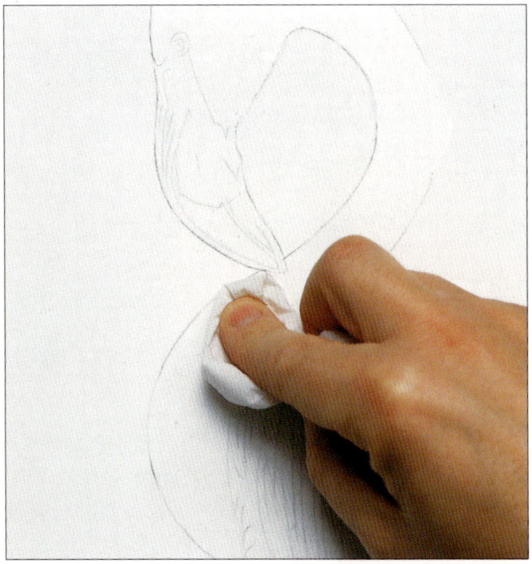

2 Take a piece of tissue paper and gently rub it over the film to make sure it is stuck down firmly and smoothly. It is essential that the background wash can't slip under the mask and on to the flamingo's body.

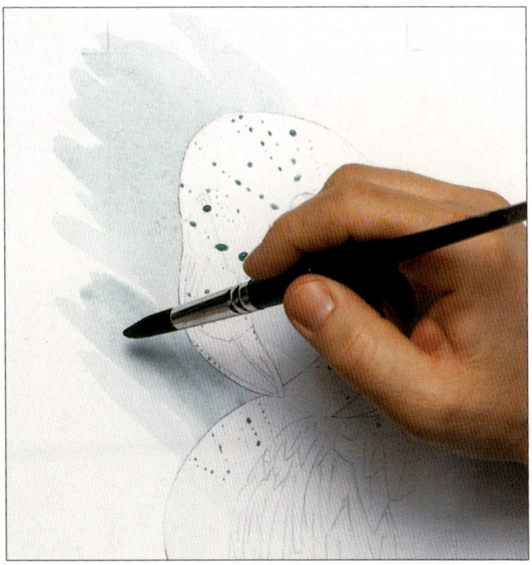

3 Mix a pale, watery wash of viridian. Using a large round brush, brush it over the background in long diagonal strokes, stopping about halfway down the paper.

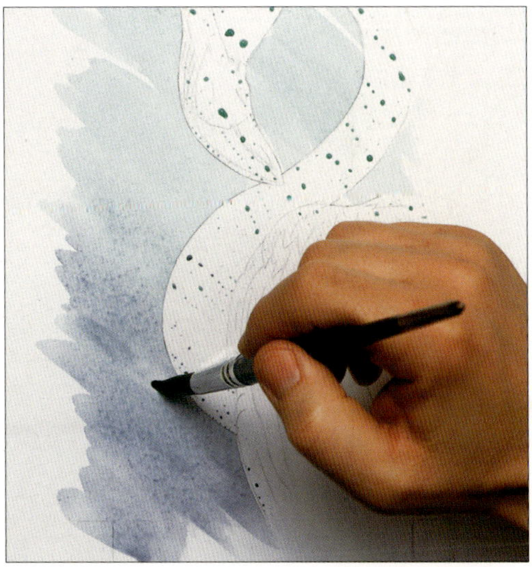

4 Mix a pale wash of Payne's grey. While the first wash is still damp, working from the bottom of the painting upwards, brush the Payne's grey over the background, stopping at the point where it overlaps the viridian a little.

▶

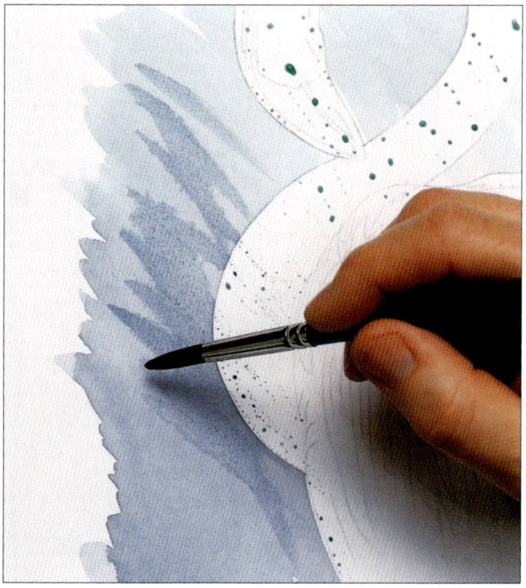

5 Using a medium round brush and holding the brush almost vertically, brush long strokes of Payne's grey over the damp wash to imply the foreground grasses. The paint will blur slightly, creating the effect of an out-of-focus background. Leave to dry.

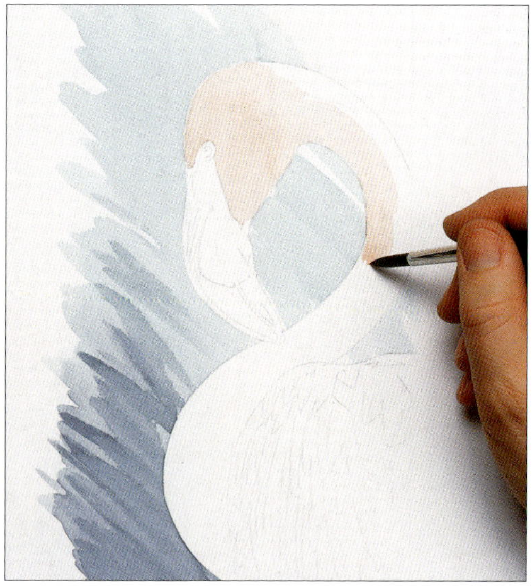

6 Remove the masking film from the flamingo. Mix a pale, watery wash of cadmium red. Using a medium round brush with a fine point, carefully brush the mixture over the flamingo's head and neck, leaving the bill and a small highlight area on the top of the head unpainted. Make sure none of the paint spills over on to the background.

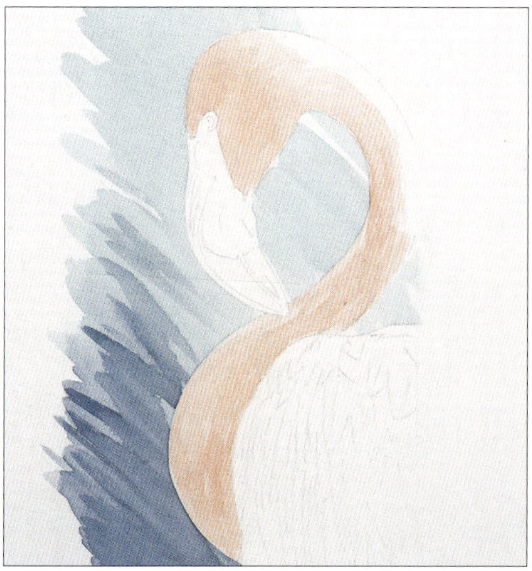

7 Strengthen the colour on the bird's head and neck by applying a second layer of cadmium red. Paint the pale pink wash on to the central part of the face.

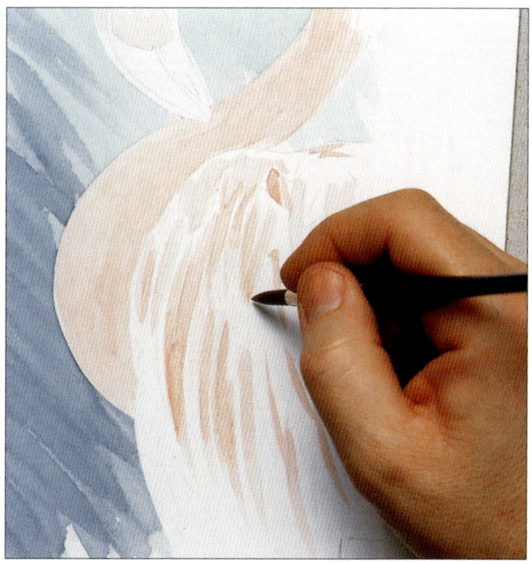

8 Using the first wash of pale cadmium red, move on to the body, making broad strokes that follow the direction of the wing feathers. Leave the highlight areas unpainted. Add a wash of Payne's grey to the bill. Leave to dry.

Assessment time

The overall base colours of the painting have been established and we are beginning to see a contrast between the blurred, wet-into-wet background and the sharper, wet-on-dry brushstrokes used on the bird, which will be reinforced as the painting progresses. Much of the rest of the painting will be devoted to building up tones and feather texture on the flamingo.

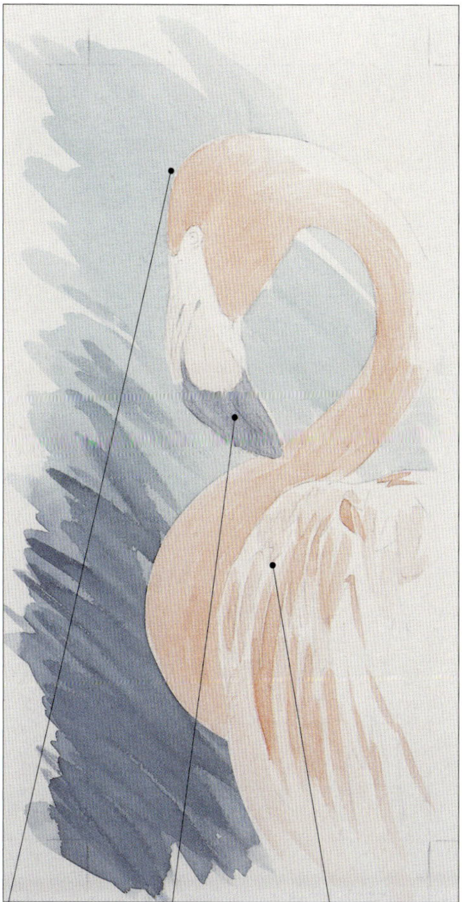

Note the use of complementary colours – red on the bird and green on the background.

The bill has been given a pale wash of Payne's grey.

The strokes follow the direction of the feathers.

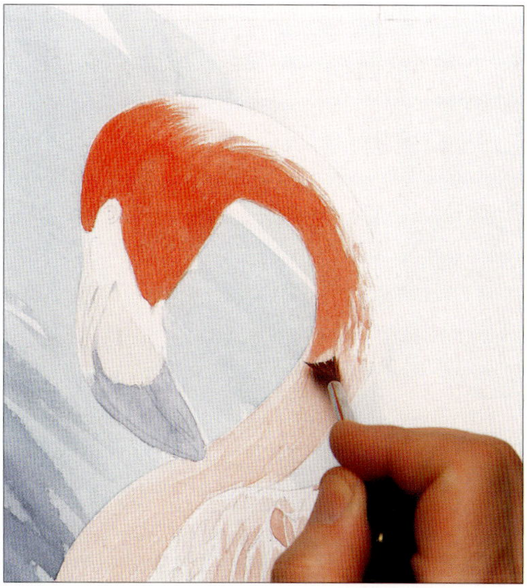

9 Mix a stronger wash of cadmium red and, using a very small, almost dry, round brush, start building up the colour on the head, making tiny, evenly spaced brushstrokes to create the feeling of individual feathers. Using a small flat brush with the bristles splayed out, start working down the neck, again making tiny brushstrokes.

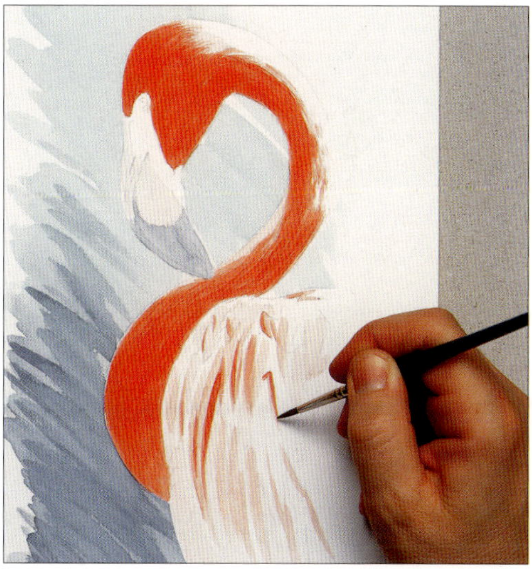

10 Continue painting the flamingo's neck, making sure that your strokes follow the direction in which the feathers grow. Using a fine round brush, paint over the main wing feathers again. Leave to dry.

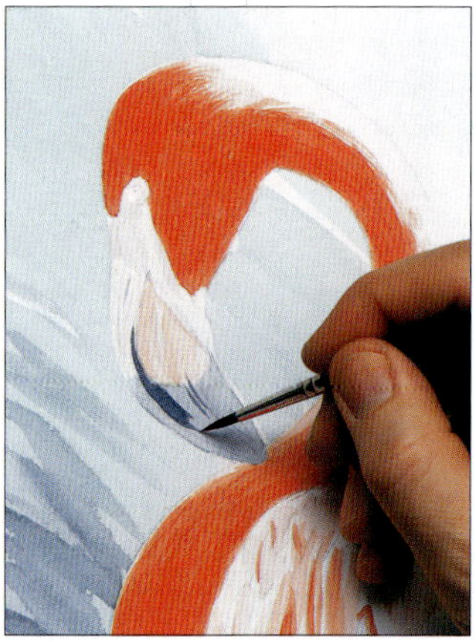

11 Mix a very pale pink from pale cadmium red with a little permanent white gouache and, using a fine round brush, carefully paint the area around the eye. Mix a mid-toned wash of Payne's grey and, using a fine round brush, paint the detailing on the bird's bill. Leave to dry.

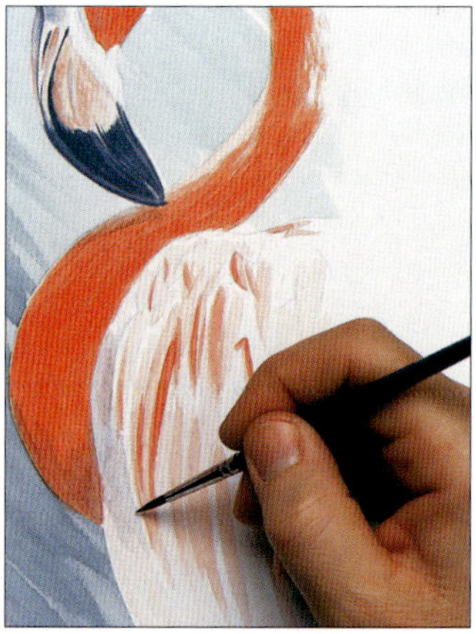

12 Continue building up detail on the bill. Add a little ultramarine blue to the Payne's grey mixture and paint the shadow cast by the beak and the shadowed area on the outer edge of the bird's body. Leave to dry.

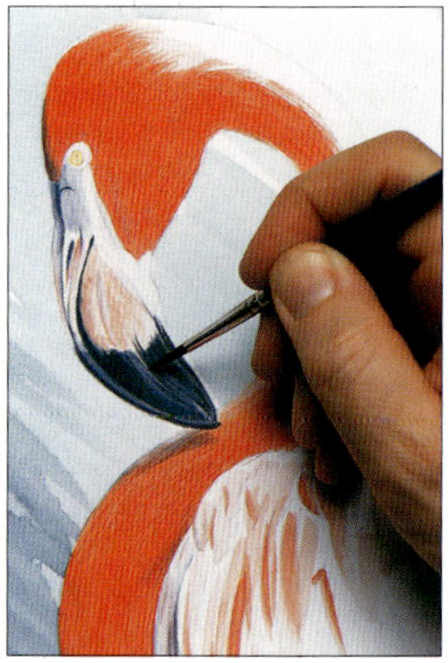

13 Mix a wash of ivory black and paint the bill, leaving spaces between your brushstrokes in order to give some texture and show how light reflects off the shiny bill. Add a dot of pale cadmium yellow for the eye.

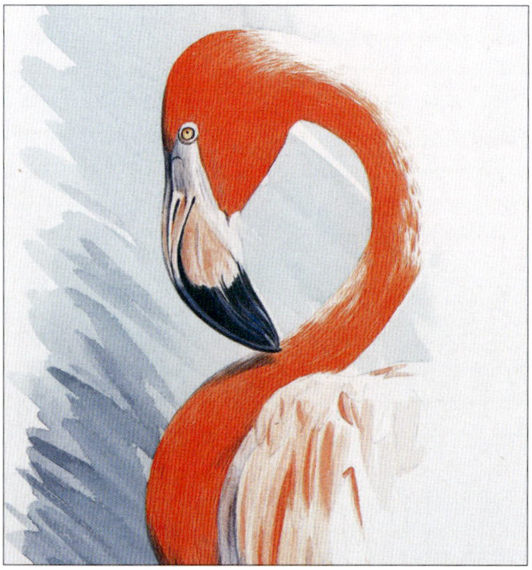

14 Mix cadmium red with a little cadmium yellow and, using a very fine round brush, dot this mixture on to the bird's neck, just beyond the point where the initial cadmium red washes end, so that there isn't such a sharp transition from red to white. Use a fine round brush to add detail in ivory black to the eye.

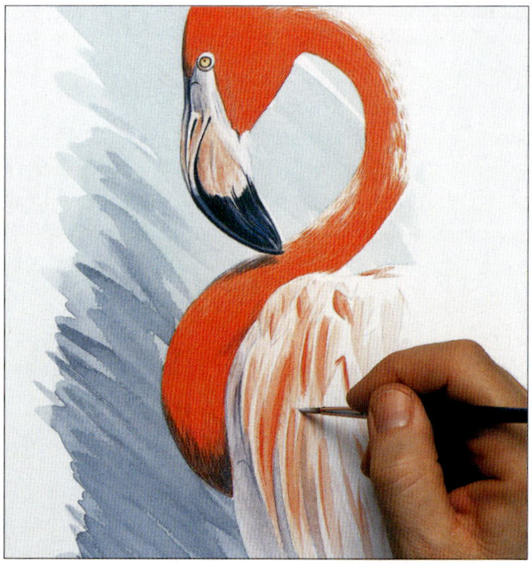

15 The body looks very pale compared to the head and neck so, using a fine round brush and cadmium red, continue to build up tone on the body with tiny brushstrokes that follow the direction of the feathers. Touch permanent white gouache into the white spaces on the bird's body, leaving white paper on the right-hand side so that the image appears to fade out on the lightest side.

Flamingo

This is a beautiful example of the effectiveness of building up layers of the same colour to achieve the desired density of tone. The lovely soft texture is achieved through countless tiny brushstrokes that follow the direction of the feathers.

The composition is very effective, too. The tall, thin shape of the painting echoes the shape of the flamingo, and the viewer's eye is led in a sweeping curve from the bottom right-hand corner to the focal point – the bird's head.

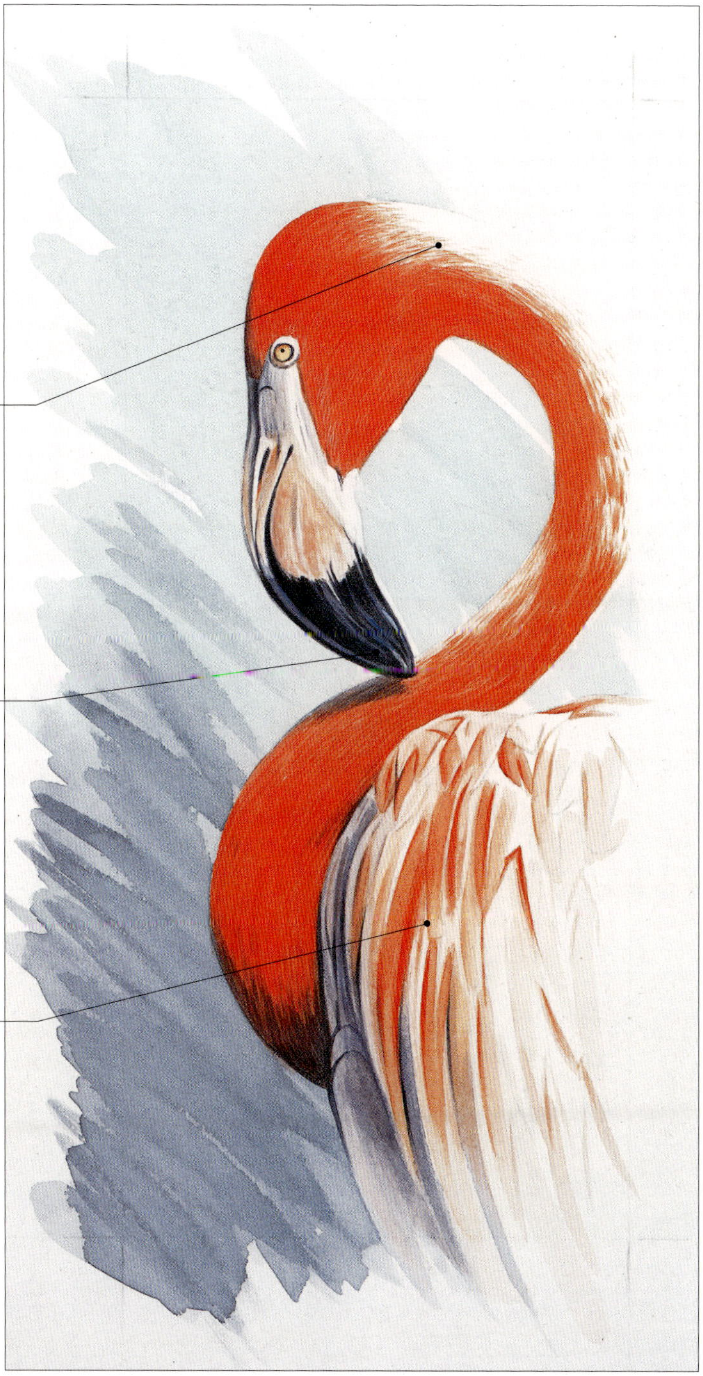

Softly feathered brushstrokes soften the transition from red to white.

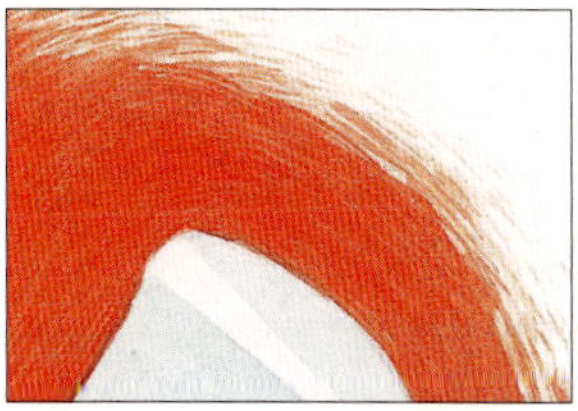

Paying careful attention to where the highlights fall has helped to make the bill look three-dimensional.

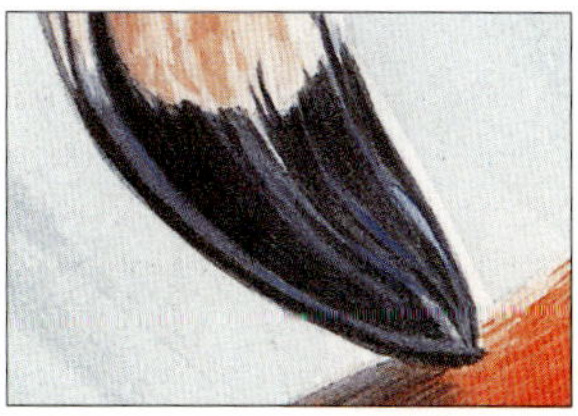

Note how gouache gives you much more control over the exact placement and size of highlights than simply leaving the paper unpainted, as you can paint over underlying colour with a very fine brush.

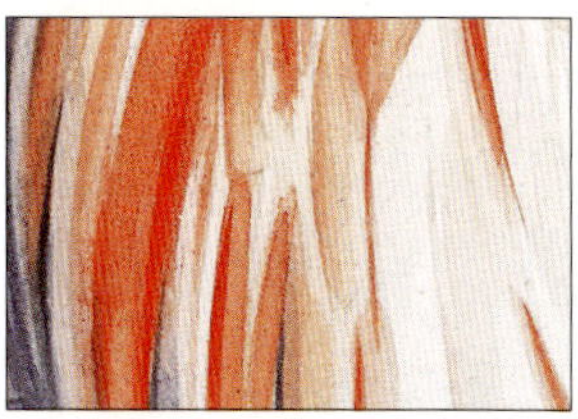

Painting Buildings

We spend our lives living and working inside buildings, but often pay them scant regard for, as long as they serve the purpose for which they were constructed, our attentions are focused elsewhere.

Buildings not only reflect function and purpose, but also the people for whom they were built. Styles can vary greatly, depending on location and the prevailing weather conditions and climate. Often, buildings can be immediately identified as belonging to a certain place – think of the palazzos of Venice or the art deco skyscrapers of New York or Chicago. They also reflect the age in which they were built and may also often give clues to the surrounding landscape and geology, as many buildings are constructed using materials that are obtained locally.

Building materials vary enormously in colour and texture. Honey-coloured dressed stone, red brick, grey concrete, flint, weathered and painted wood, steel and glass, terracotta tiles, blue-grey slate, mud and straw: the wide range makes demands on any artist and will require the use of several different techniques to successfully represent them.

Inevitably, when you are drawing and painting buildings, you will need to use both aerial and linear perspective. The idea of having to use perspective alarms some people, but once you have mastered the basic principles, the rest is relatively straightforward. Simplicity is the key, and even highly complex buildings consist, when all the intricate architectural and decorative detail has been stripped away, of a few simple geometric shapes. Try to analyse your subject in these terms before you set pencil to paper.

Draw your building in the same way and sequence in which it was constructed. First, the basic structure, then the doors and windows. Only in the very final stages should you attempt to add any decorative embellishment.

Although you do not need to become an architectural authority, it does help if you have some knowledge, no matter how rudimentary, of how buildings are constructed. It is all too easy to draw or paint a building that does not appear solid and looks as if it will fall over at any minute. This is a common mistake, particularly for novice painters.

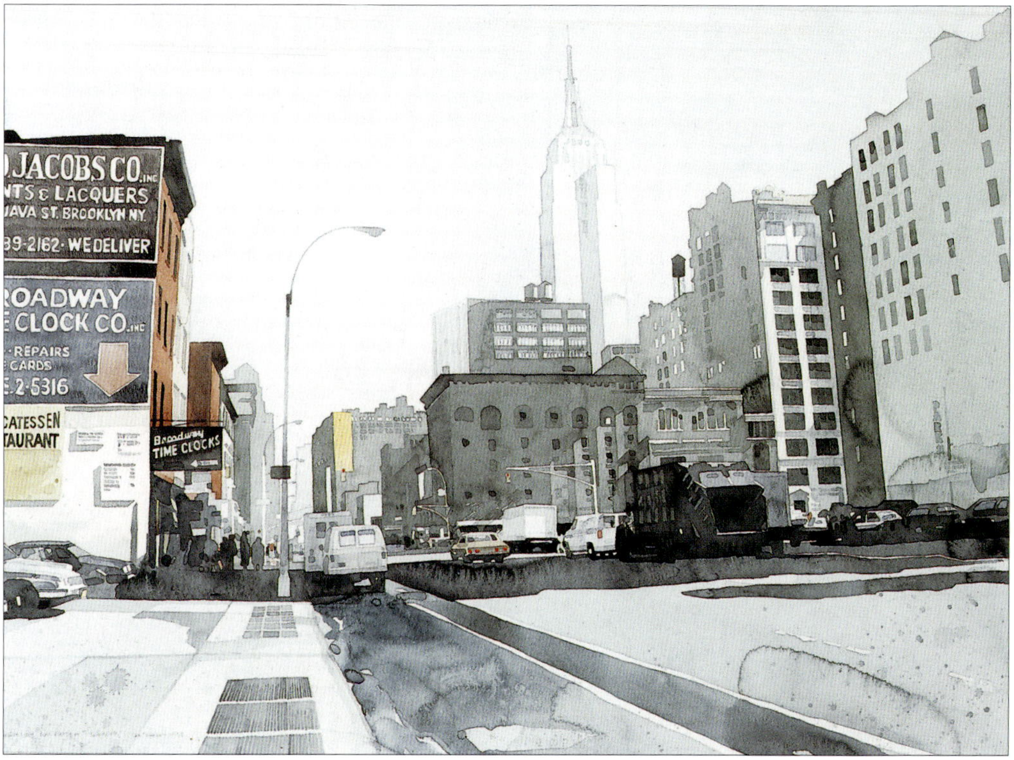

Broadway, New York ▼
This complex painting used both aerial and linear perspective. Linear perspective creates a sense of depth, leading the eye along the avenue and into the distance. Aerial perspective enhances the effect of distance, as the colour and the detail become less pronounced the further away they are.

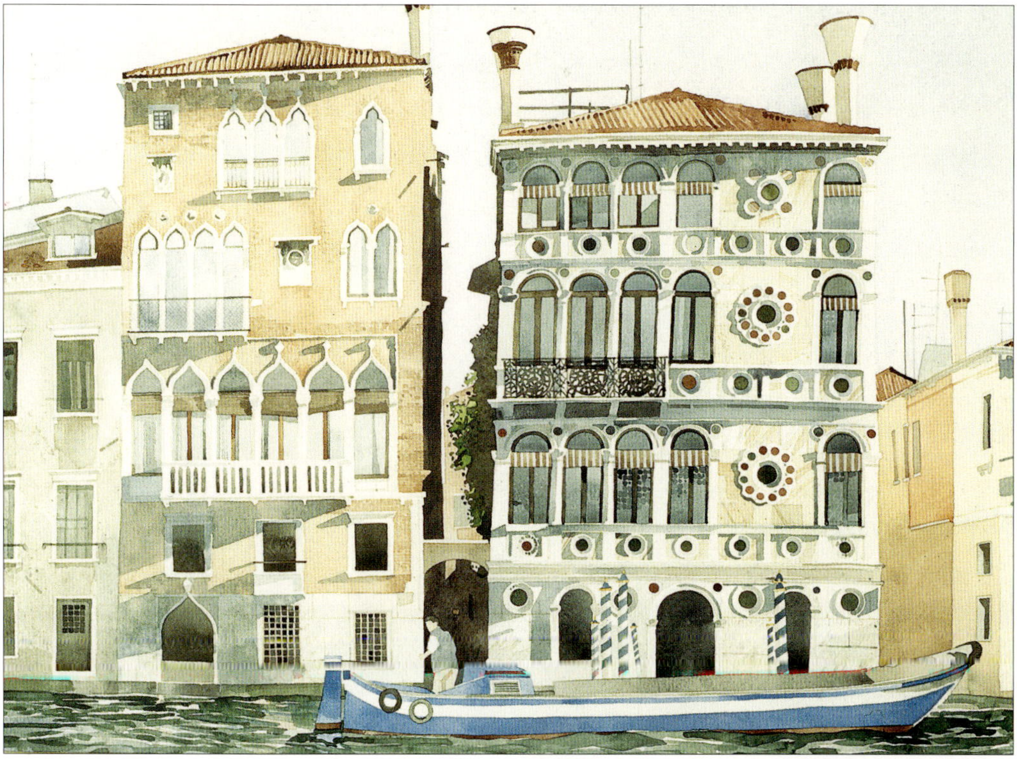

Grand Canal, Venice ▲
This painting of canalside buildings in Venice was made using wet-on-dry washes after a careful and detailed preliminary drawing.

Tips: • Unless you are particularly confident, begin by making a light underdrawing to work out any problems regarding perspective and proportion.
• Use both linear and aerial perspective. Both will help to create an illusion of depth, and the correct use of linear perspective will ensure that your building does not look as if it is about to fall over.
• Pay attention to shadows: they contribute to the composition and will help to establish a sense of depth.
• Use a range of watercolour techniques to capture the texture and character of the building and the materials used in its construction.

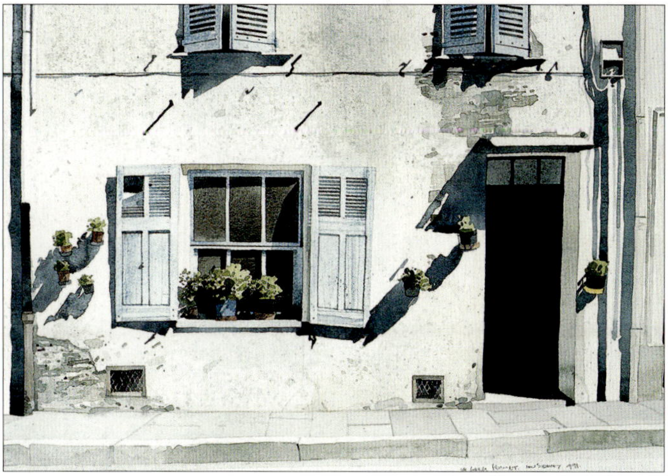

Le Garde Freinet ▲
This painting of a house in a small French village uses wet-on-dry and wet-into-wet techniques, along with careful spattering and drybrush work, to show the crumbling plaster and weathered paint on the pale blue shutters.

Hillside town in line and wash

Line and wash is the perfect technique for this brightly coloured lakeside town, where you need fine detailing in the buildings and soft wet-into-wet washes in the surrounding landscape.

This project uses both waterproof and soluble inks, as they bring very different qualities to the image. Waterproof ink must be used in areas where you want the pen lines to remain permanent, such as the skyline and the wrought-iron balconies. Soluble ink, on the other hand, blurs and runs in unpredictable and exciting ways when you brush water or watercolour paint over it. Before you embark on any pen work, therefore, you need to think carefully about what kind of ink to use where.

In this scene, the tree-covered background is darker than the foreground. (Often in landscape paintings, you find that things in the background appear paler because of the effect of aerial perspective.) This helps to hold the image together, as it provides a natural frame around the focal point – the colourful buildings and their reflections.

Materials

- *HB pencil*
- *120lb (220gsm) good-quality drawing paper*
- *Art pen loaded with waterproof sepia ink*
- *Art pen loaded with water-soluble sepia ink*
- *Watercolour paints: ultramarine blue, cobalt blue, sap green, yellow ochre, phthalocyanine green, cadmium orange, cadmium red, burnt sienna, cadmium yellow, alizarin crimson, deep violet*
- *Brushes: medium round*

Tip: If you are working from a reference photograph in which the light is very flat and bland, imagine how the light would fall on the scene on a bright sunny day. Where and how long would the shadows be? Make sure you keep your imaginary lighting consistent over the whole scene.

The original scene

This photograph was taken on a very overcast day, simply as a reference shot for the architectural details. As a consequence of the weather, the colours are dull and the light is flat and uninteresting. In situations like this, feel free to improve on what you saw at the time by making the colours brighter in your painting.

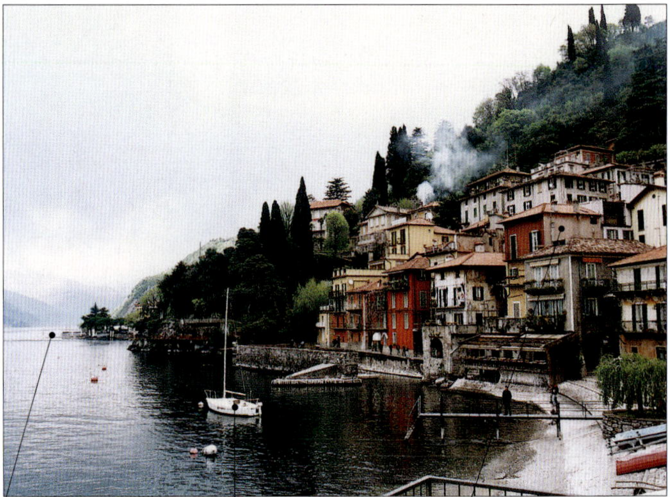

The composition pulls your eye to the edge of the picture, out into the centre of the lake.

The boat is a very stark white and detracts from the bright colours of the buildings.

The light is very flat: more contrast is needed to make the buildings look three-dimensional.

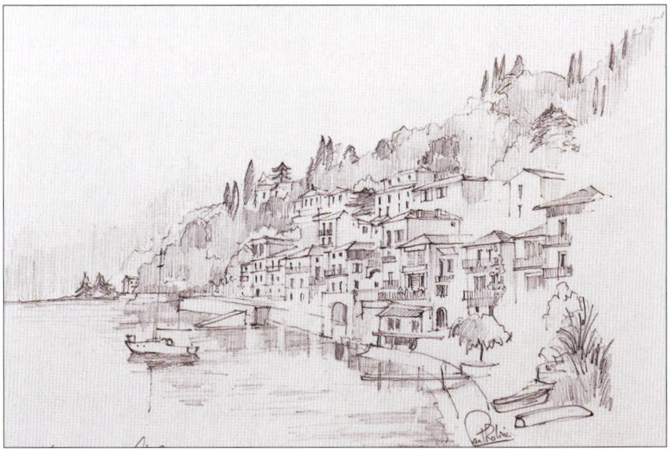

Preliminary sketch

Here the artist decided to crop in to make the composition tighter than it was in the original photograph. He also moved the boat further into the picture.

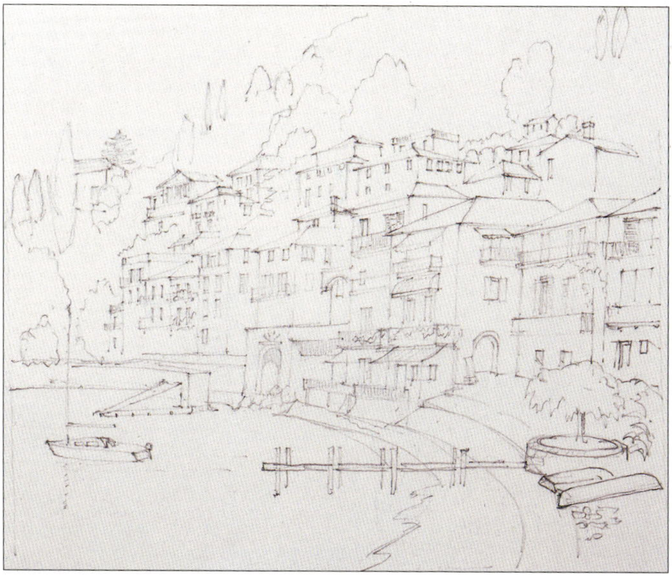

1 Using an HB pencil lightly sketch your subject, taking plenty of time to measure the relative heights and angles of the buildings carefully and making sure that you keep all the many vertical lines truly vertical. You can work much more loosely for the background hillside and trees, which will form a much softer, impressionistic backdrop to the scene.

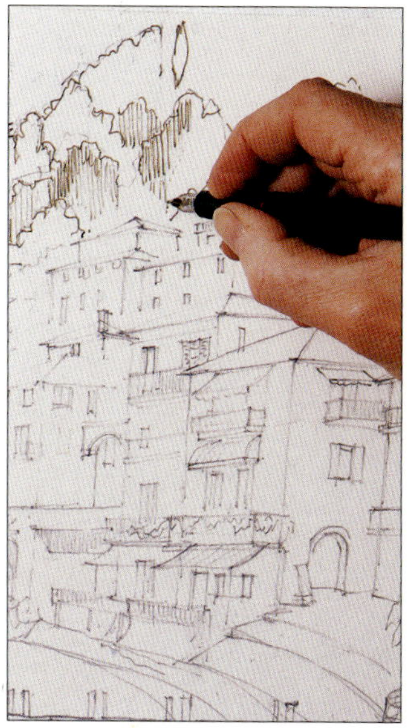

2 Using waterproof sepia ink, put in the skyline. Using water-soluble sepia ink, put in the roofs and background trees, loosely hatching the trees to indicate the tones.

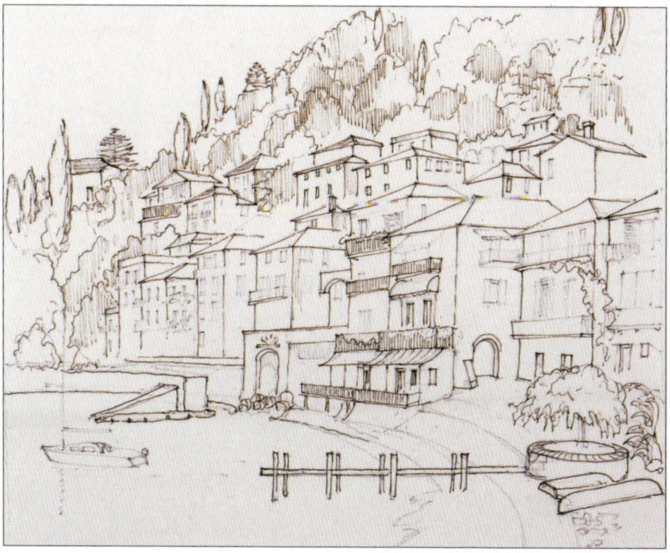

3 Continue with the line work, hatching the darkest areas of the trees in water-soluble ink, which you want to blend with paint in the later stages, and drawing the railings on the balconies in waterproof ink, so that the lines are permanent.

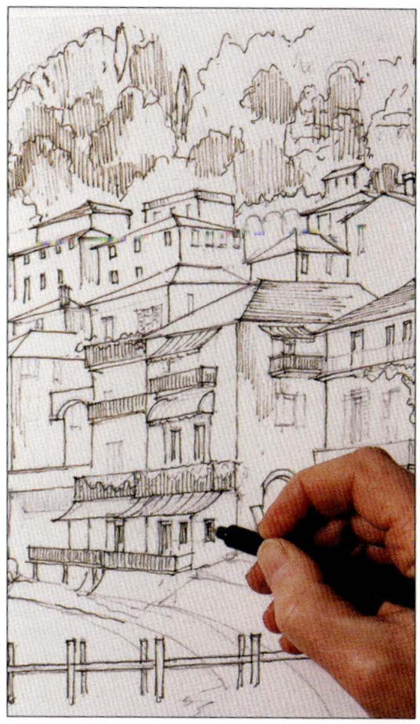

4 Using waterproof sepia ink, block in the windows on the shaded sides of the buildings.

▶

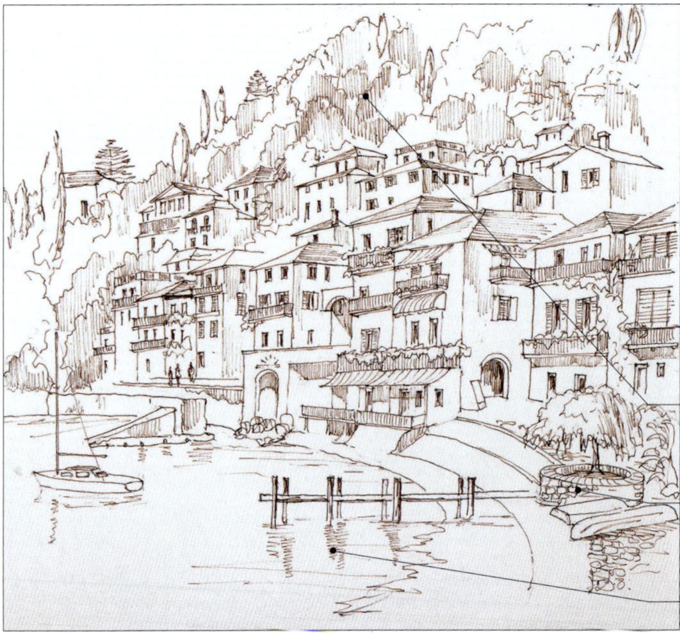

Assessment time
The pen work is now complete and will underpin the whole of the painting. If you have planned it properly, the lines drawn in waterproof sepia ink will be permanent, while those drawn in water-soluble ink will blur and run when washed over with watercolour paint. You cannot predict exactly how the lines will run, but this unpredictability is part of the fun and will impart great liveliness and spontaneity to the finished work.

Hatching in water-soluble ink indicates the areas of light and dark on the trees.

Waterproof ink is used for all the lines that need to be retained in the final painting.

Loose scribbles indicate the ripples in the water.

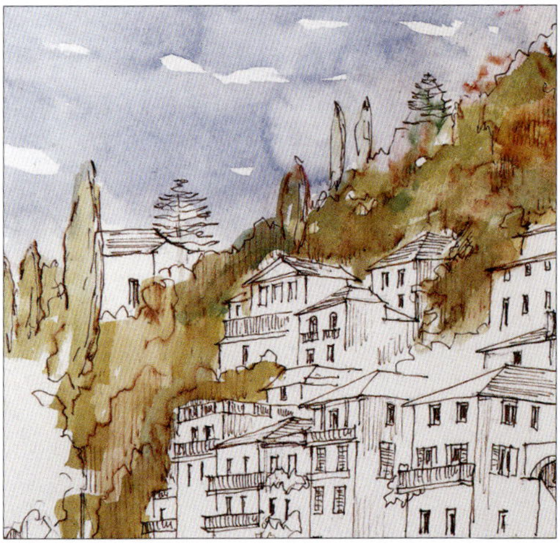

5 Mix a bright blue from ultramarine blue and cobalt blue watercolour paints. Using a medium round brush, wash this mixture over the sky, leaving some gaps for clouds. Mix a pale wash of sap green and brush it over the trees. Note how the soluble sepia ink blurs, giving the impression of the tree branches. Add a little yellow ochre to the mixture for the trees on the right-hand edge of the painting. Leave to dry.

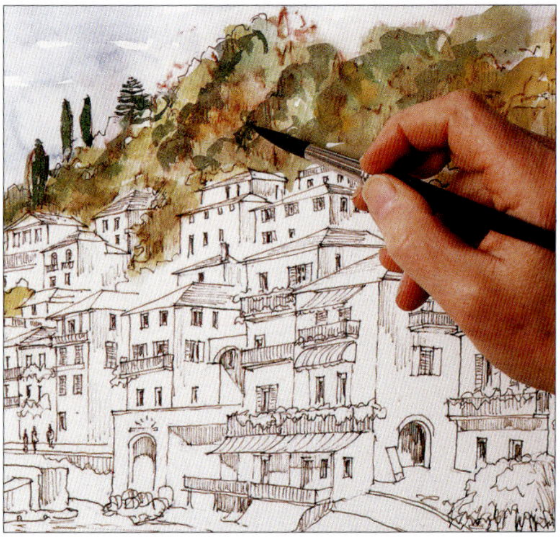

6 Mix a dark green from ultramarine blue and phthalocyanine green and paint the tall cypress trees that stand along the skyline. The vertical lines of the trees break up the horizon and add interest to the scene. Use the same dark green mixture to loosely brush in some dark foliage tones on the trees, taking care not to allow any of the paint to spill over on to the buildings below.

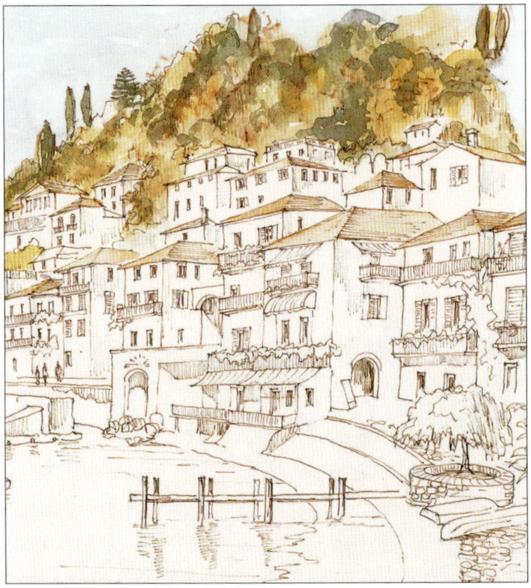

7 Mix a terracotta colour from cadmium orange, cadmium red and burnt sienna. Using the tip of the brush, paint the roofs, adding more burnt sienna for the shaded sides of the roofs. Note how the whole picture begins to take on more form and depth as soon as you put in some shading.

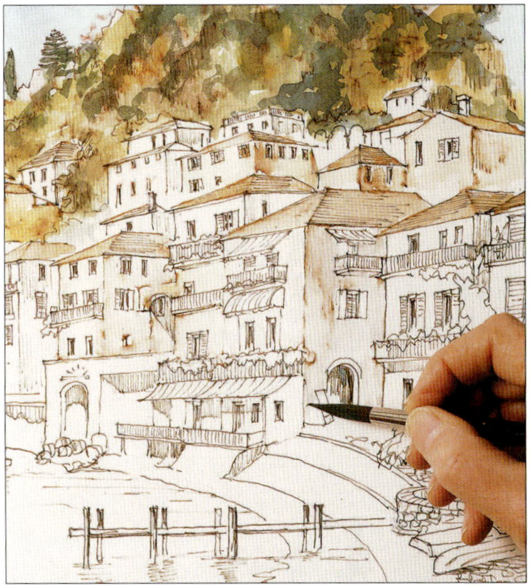

8 Use a slightly paler version of the mixture used for the roofs to paint the shaded sides of some of the buildings. Work carefully so that you retain the sharp vertical lines of the buildings. This is an important aspect of making the buildings look three-dimensional.

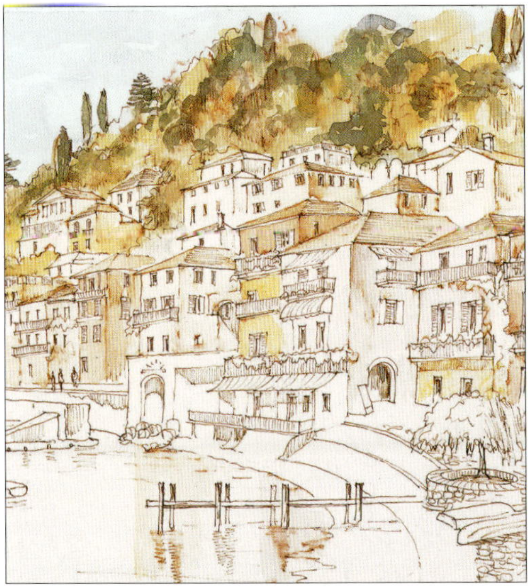

9 Mix a very pale wash of yellow ochre and brush it on to the front of some of the houses. Paint the shaded sides of the terracotta-coloured houses in a mixture of yellow ochre and burnt sienna.

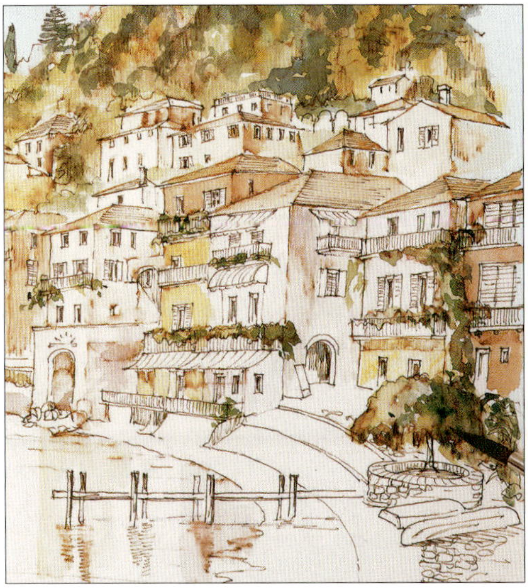

10 Finish painting the façades of the buildings. Mix a light green from sap green and cadmium yellow and dot in the foliage on the balconies. While this is still damp, dot on dark phthalocyanine green to build up some tone and depth.

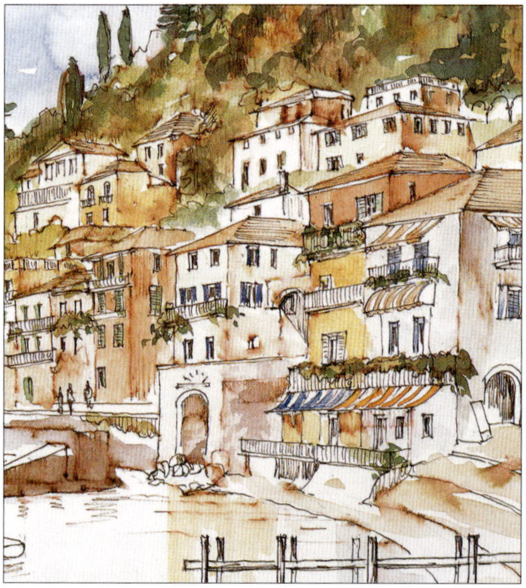

11 Paint the striped awnings in dilute washes of alizarin crimson and cobalt blue (but don't try to make the stripes on the awnings too precise and even, or the work will start to look stilted). Paint the window shutters in cobalt blue and phthalocyanine green.

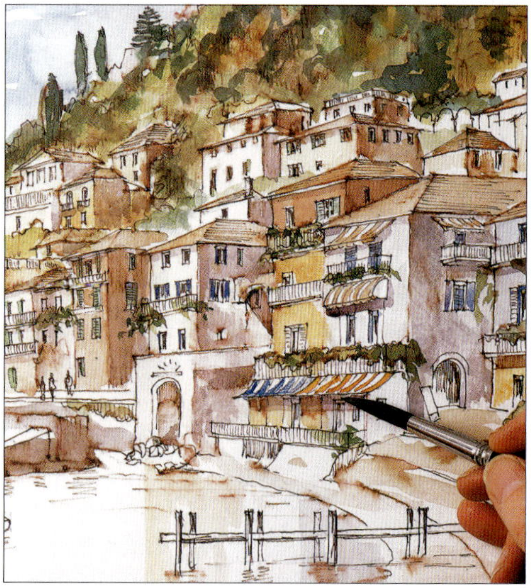

12 Mix a pale but warm purple from ultramarine blue, deep violet and burnt sienna and paint the shadowed sides of the buildings and a narrow strip under the awnings. This reinforces the three-dimensional effect and separates the houses from each other and from the background.

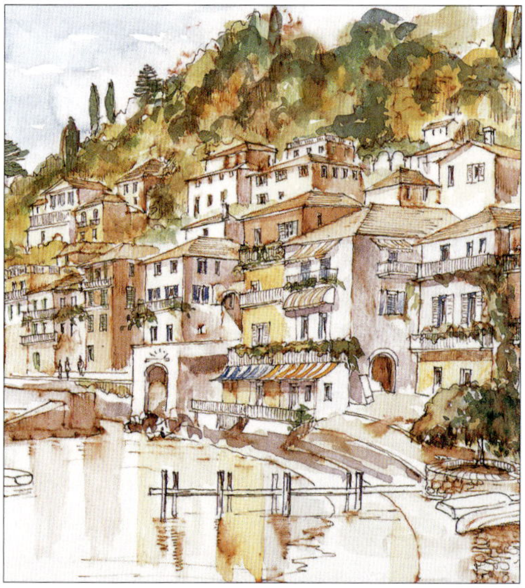

13 Using the same colour, continue putting in the shadows on the houses and on the shoreline promenade and jetty. Paint the reflections in the water, using watered-down versions of the colours used on the buildings. Leave to dry.

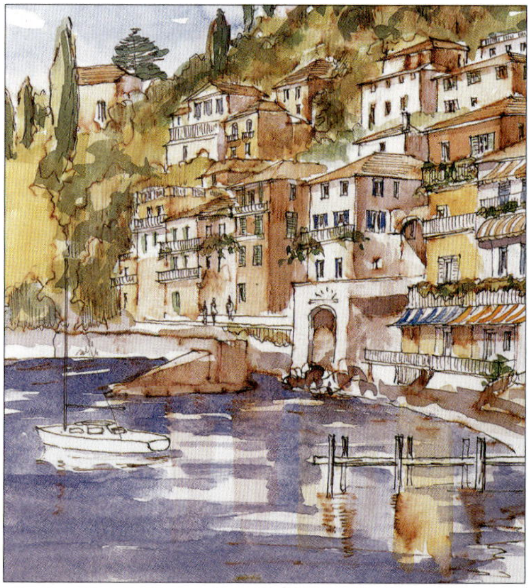

14 Mix a deep blue from ultramarine blue, cobalt blue and a little deep violet. Carefully brush this over the water area, working around the boat and the posts of the jetty and leaving some gaps for broken ripples and highlights.

Hillside town in line and wash

With the addition of a few final details (the jetty, painted in a mixture of burnt sienna and ultramarine blue; the upturned boats in very pale washes of alizarin crimson and ultramarine blue, and the boat on the lake in alizarin crimson), the painting is complete. Precise pen work in both water-soluble and waterproof ink has combined with loose brushstrokes and wet-into-wet washes to create a lively rendering of this charming lakeside town.

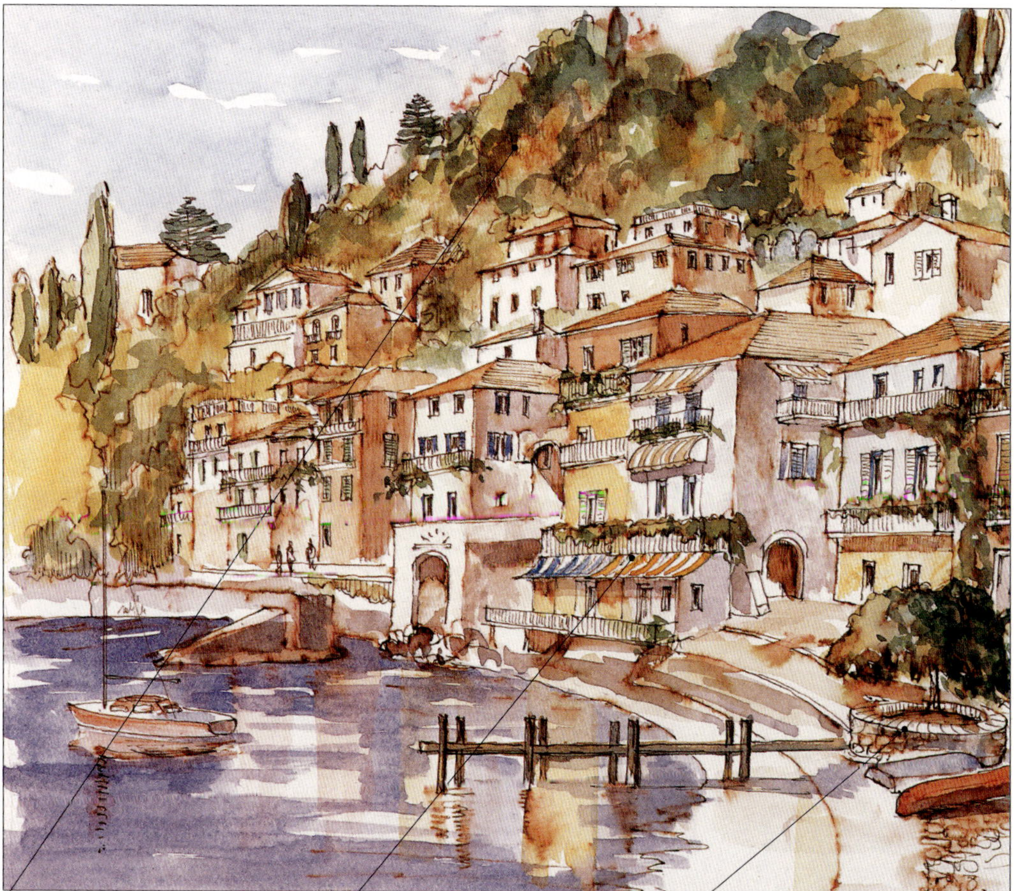

The blurred, wet-into-wet trees focus attention on the sharply defined buildings.

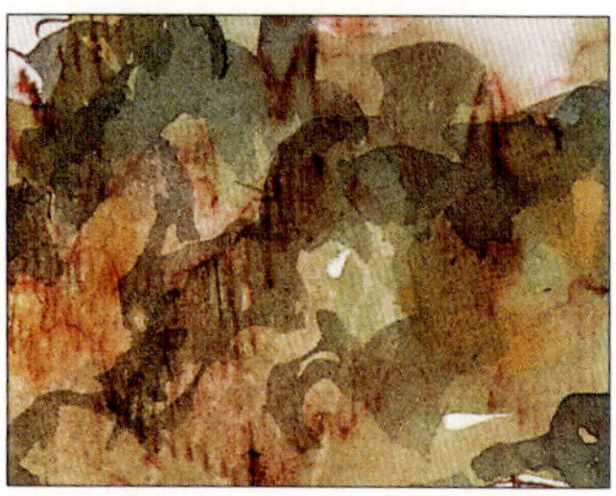

Loose strokes of colour are used to depict the awnings.

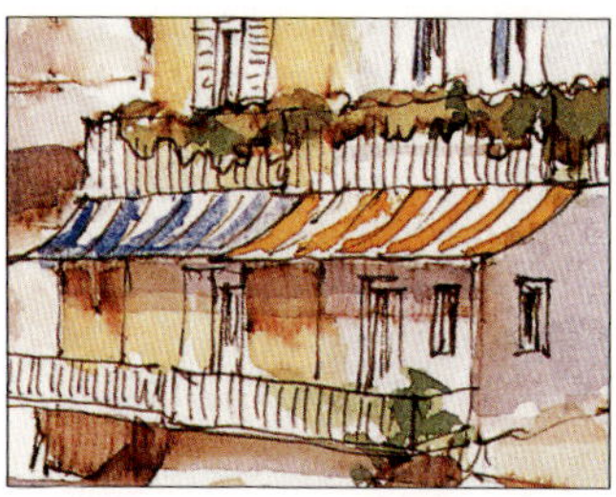

Precise pen lines set down in the very earliest stages remain in the finished work.

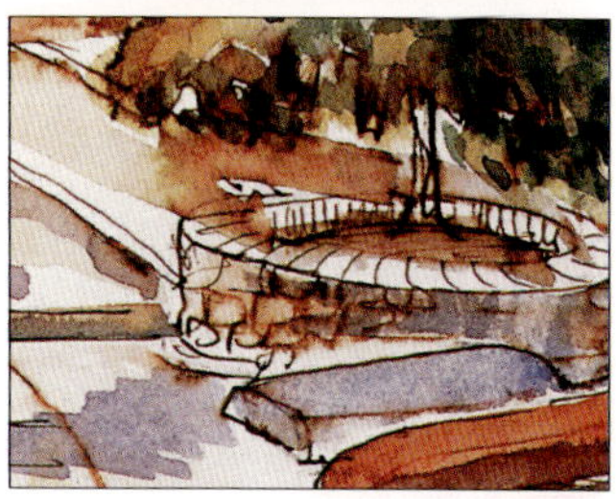

Moroccan kasbah

The location for this striking and unusual project is the World Heritage site of Ait-Ben-Haddhou, in southern Morocco. It is a traditional-style village made up of several earthen fortresses, each one some 10 metres (30 feet) high.

With its straight-edged buildings and clean lines, the scene looks deceptively simple, but it demonstrates well how important it is to train yourself to assess tones. The earthen buildings are all very similar in colour (predominantly ochre and terracotta), so without strong contrasts of tone you will never succeed in making them look three-dimensional.

If you are painting on location, you may find that the light and, consequently, the direction and length of any shadows changes as you work. It is a good idea to make light pencil marks on your paper, just outside the margins of your painting, indicating the angle of the sun. This makes it easier to keep the lighting consistent when you are painting over a period of several hours.

Materials

- *2B pencil*
- *140lb (300gsm) NOT watercolour paper, pre-stretched*
- *Watercolour paints: cerulean blue, yellow ochre, light red, vermilion, mauve, white, alizarin crimson, Hooker's green, Winsor yellow, Payne's grey, ultramarine blue, burnt umber*
- *Brushes: large wash, medium round, medium flat, fine filbert*

Tip: Use a pencil to measure the relative heights of the buildings. Hold the pencil out in front of you and align the tip with part of your subject (say, the top of the tallest building), then run your thumb down the pencil until it aligns with the base of the building. You can transfer this measurement to your watercolour paper, again holding the pencil at arm's length. It is important to keep your arm straight and the pencil vertical, so that the pencil remains a constant distance from the subject.

The original scene

The artist took this photograph around midday, when the sun was almost directly overhead. Consequently, the colours looked somewhat bleached out and there were no strong shadows to bring the scene to life. She decided to use a little artistic licence and enhance what she saw by intensifying the colours in order to make her painting more dramatic.

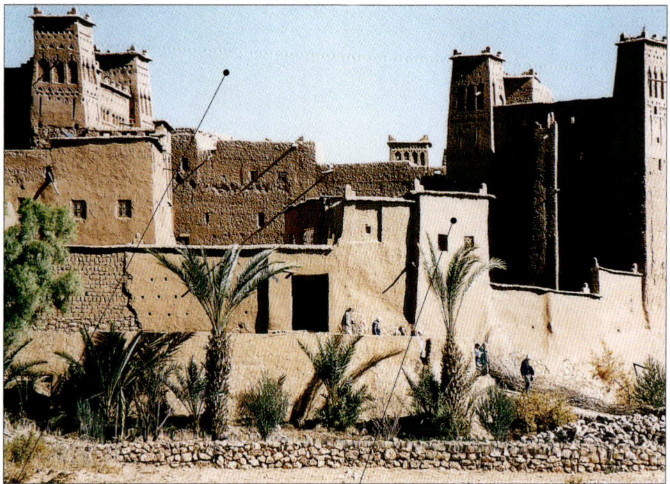

The sky looks pale and doesn't have the warmth that one associates with hot African countries.

Here, the mud-brick buildings look pale and bleached out; in the right light, however, they glow a warm orangey-red.

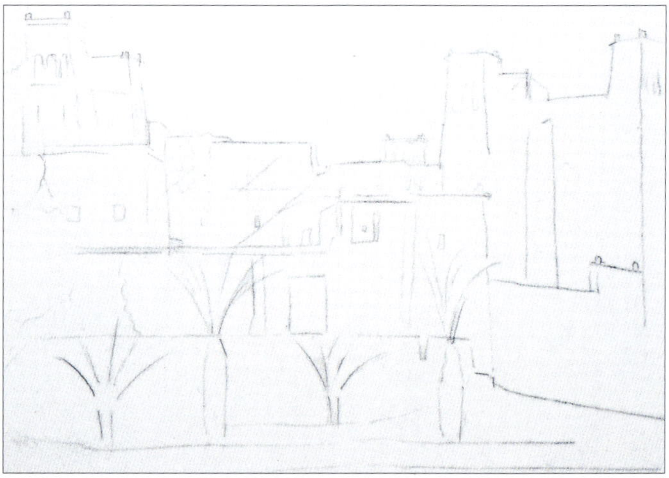

1 Using a 2B pencil, lightly sketch the scene, taking careful note of the relative heights of the buildings and their angles in relation to one another.

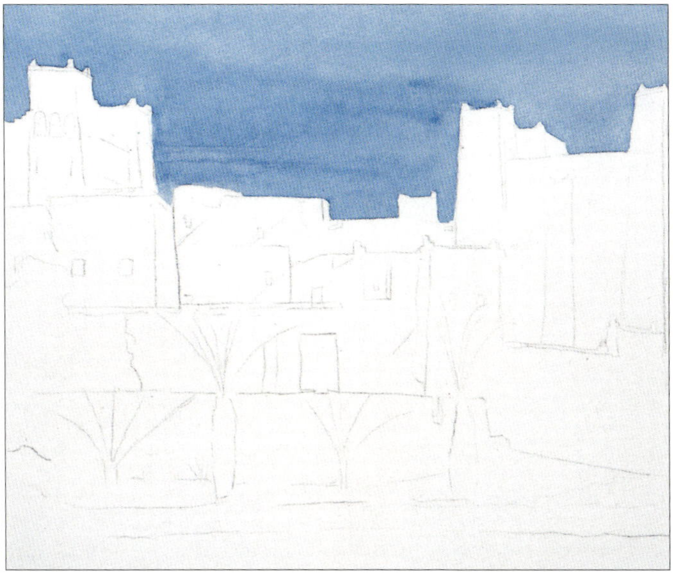

2 Using a large wash brush, dampen the sky area with clean water, brushing carefully around the outlines of the buildings to get a neat, clean edge. Mix a wash of cerulean blue. After about a minute, when the water has sunk in but the paper is still damp, quickly brush on the colour. (You may want to switch to a smaller brush to paint up to the edge of the buildings. Use the side of the brush and brush the paint upwards, to avoid accidentally getting any of the blue colour on the buildings.)

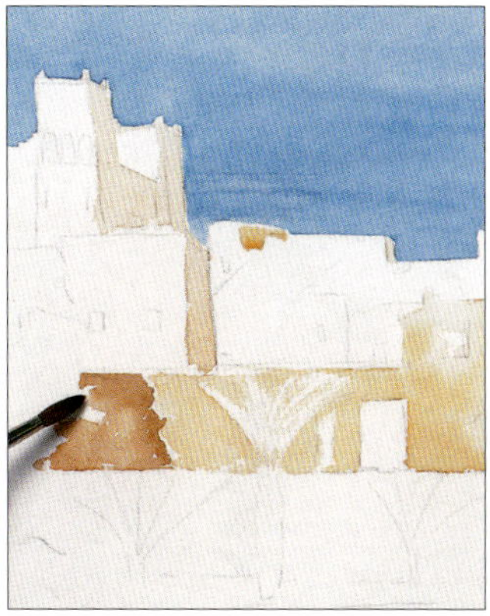

3 Mix a pale but warm terracotta colour from yellow ochre, light red and a tiny amount of vermilion. Using a medium round brush, wash this mixture over the buildings, working around the fronds of the foreground palm trees and adding a little more yellow ochre as you work across from right to left.

Tip: Vary the tone of the buildings. If they are too uniform in tone they will look newly built and mass produced.

4 Add a little mauve to the mixture to make a deeper tone. Paint the wall at the base of the picture, painting around the trunks of the palm trees. Hold the brush at an angle as you do this and make jagged marks, as this helps to convey the texture of the trunks and shows that they are not straight-edged.

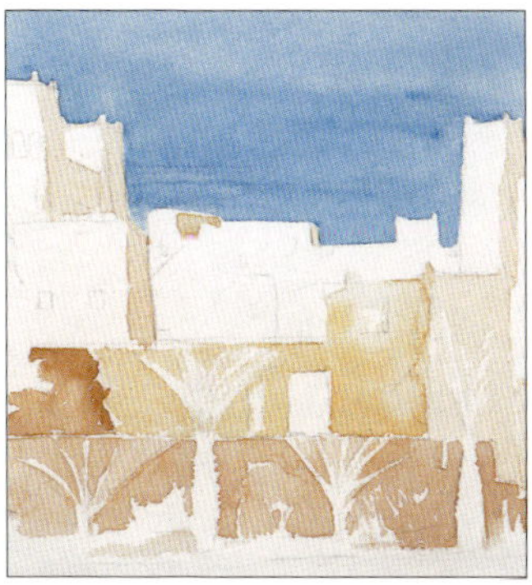

5 Continue working across the painting until you have put in all of the lightest tones of the buildings.

6 Mix a mid tone from yellow ochre and a tiny amount of mauve and, using a medium flat brush, stipple this mixture on to the buildings in the centre of the painting to give them some texture as well as tone. Add more mauve to the mixture for the darker left-hand side.

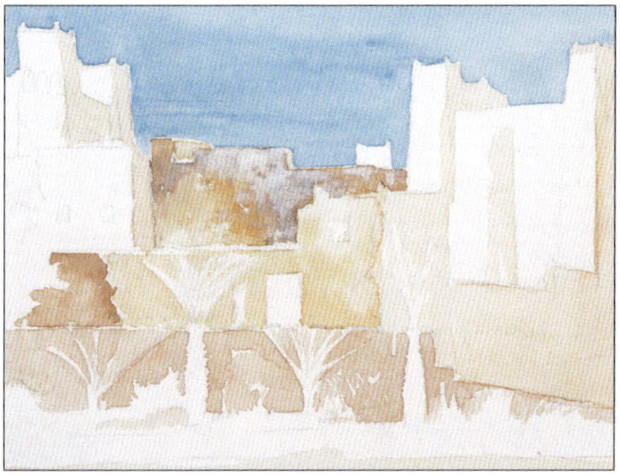

7 Brush white watercolour over the top edge of the building in the centre. This reduces the intensity of the yellow and makes it look as if it has been bleached by the sun.

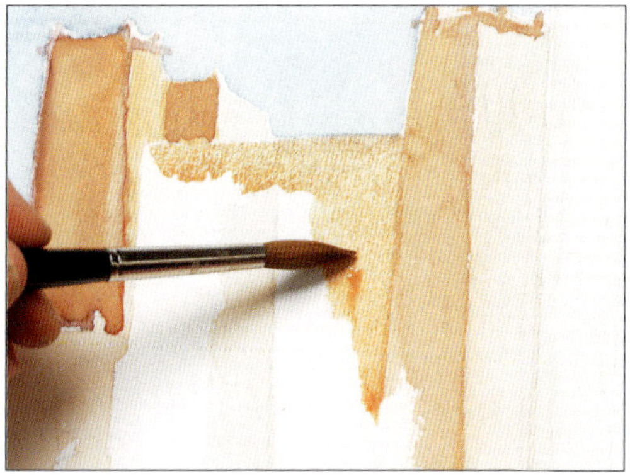

8 Mix a dark terracotta from light red, yellow ochre and a touch of alizarin crimson and start painting the darkest tones – the sides of the buildings that are in deepest shade.

Assessment time

The light, mid- and dark tones are now in place across the picture and, although the tones have not yet reached their final density, we are beginning to get a clear sense of which facets of the buildings are in bright sunlight and which are in shade. From this stage onwards, you need to continually assess the tonal values as you work, because even slight changes in one area will affect the balance of the painting as a whole. Take regular breaks, propping your painting up against a wall and looking at it from a distance to see how it is developing.

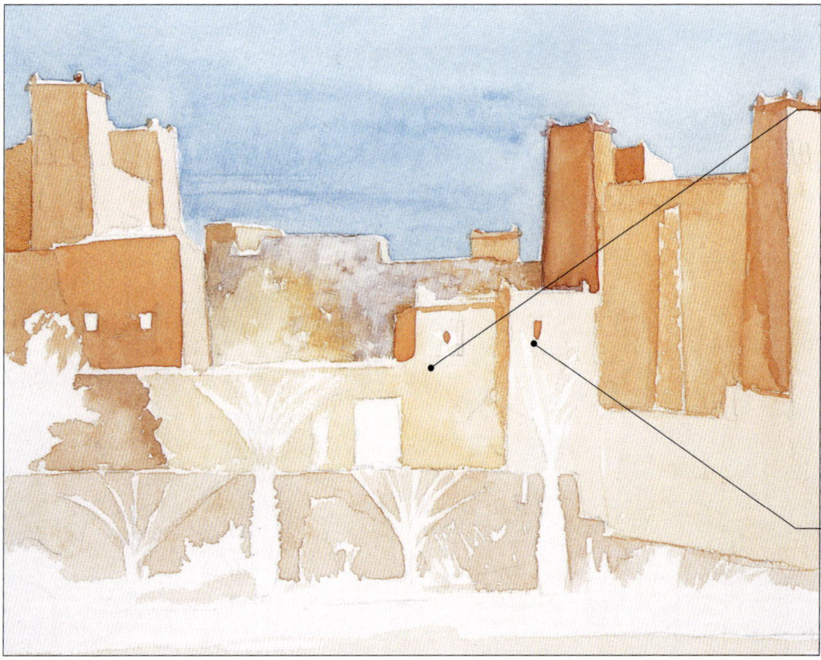

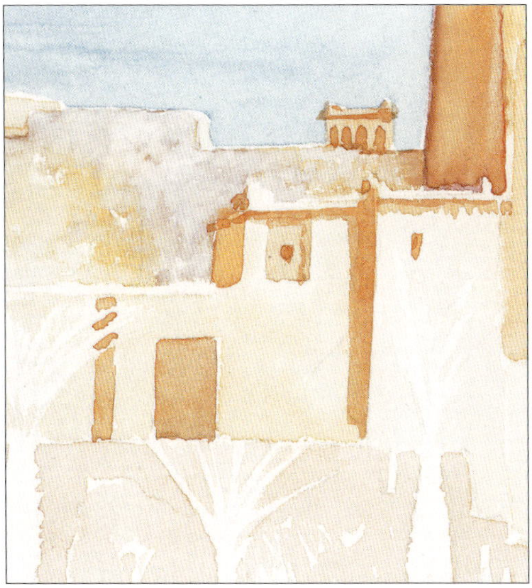

9 Mix a very dark terracotta colour from light red, yellow ochre and a touch of alizarin crimson, and begin putting in some of the fine details, such as the door in the exterior wall and some of the small windows. You are now beginning to establish a feeling of light and shade in the painting.

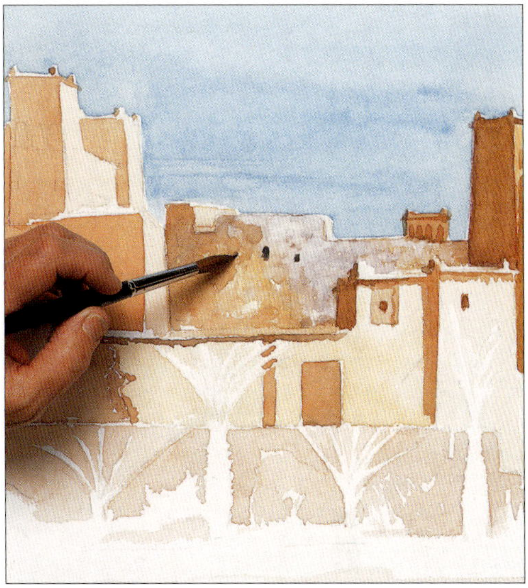

10 The right-hand buildings, which are in the deepest area of shade, look too light. Darken them as necessary by overlaying more washes of the colours used previously. Also darken the mid-toned wall in the centre of the picture and put some dark windows on the light side.

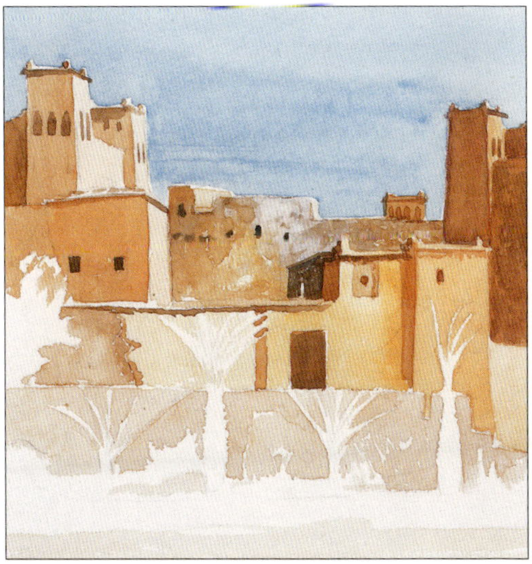

11 The lightest walls now look too light in relation to the rest of the painting, so darken them with another wash of the pale terracotta mixture used in Step 3. Build up the tone gradually. You can apply more washes if necessary, but if you make things too dark there is no going back.

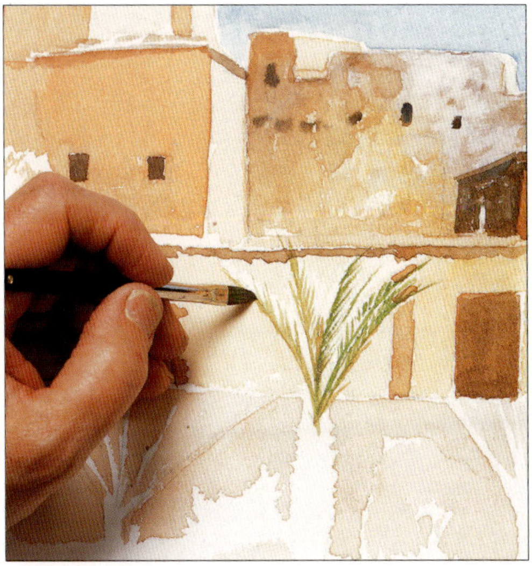

12 Mix a yellowy green from Hooker's green and a little yellow ochre and, using a fine filbert brush, start putting in the green palm fronds in the foreground. Make short upward flicks with the brush, following the direction in which the palm fronds grow.

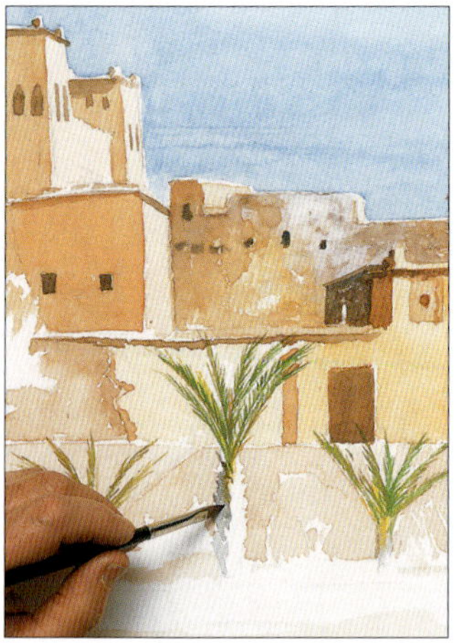

13 Continue painting the palm fronds, adding a little Winsor yellow at the point where the fronds spring out from the trunk. Paint the shaded sides of the palm trunks in Payne's grey, using short, broken strokes to indicate the knobbly surface texture of the trunks.

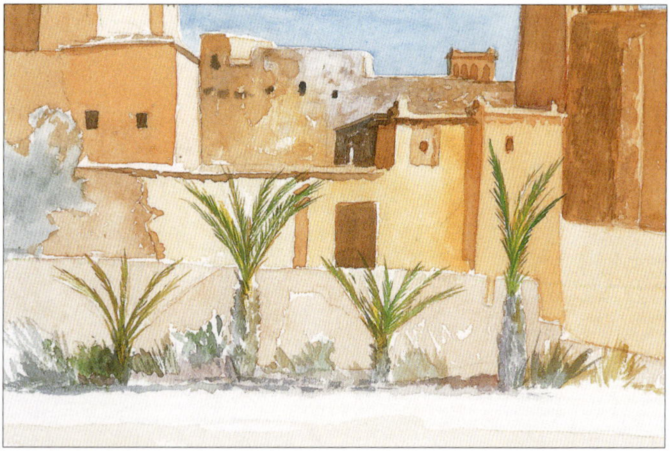

14 Lighten the grey by adding a little yellow ochre. Using the side of the brush, dab this mixture on to the left-hand side of the painting to indicate the scrubby texture of the bushes that grow in this area. Mix a very pale green from Payne's grey, yellow ochre and Hooker's green and dot in the side of the palm trunks that catches the light. Mix a grey-green from Payne's grey and Hooker's green and dot this mixture into the foreground shrubs. Mix a pale purple from alizarin crimson and ultramarine blue and paint the dry earth and the shadows around the base of the palm trees.

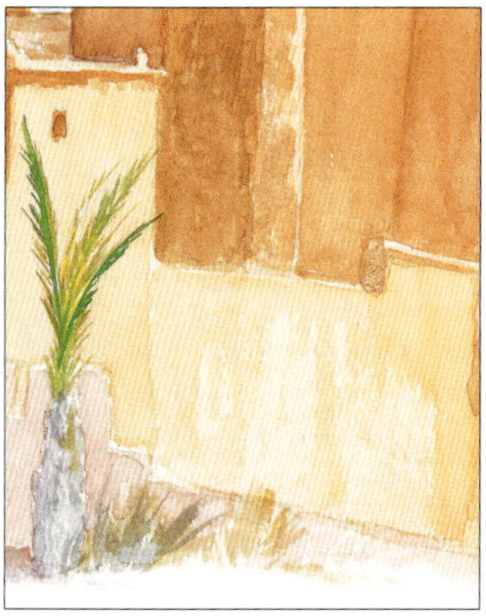

15 Mix a pale wash of alizarin crimson and darken the wall in the foreground. Feel free to use some artistic licence in your choice of colours. Although the wall is, in reality, more terracotta than pink, you are trying to put colour into a subject that doesn't have much in order to create some drama and variety in your image. Adjust the tones over the painting as a whole if you feel that it is necessary.

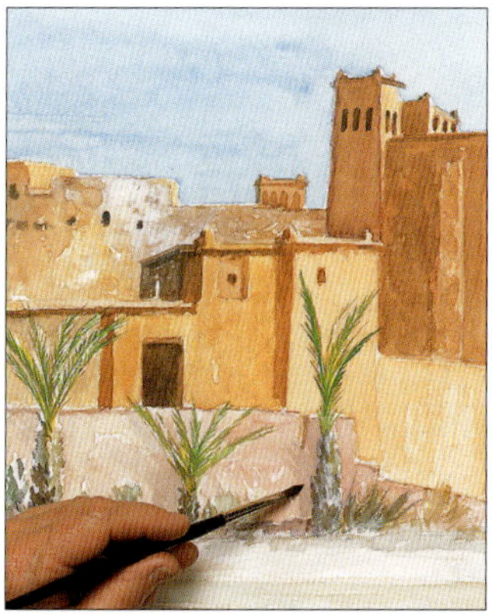

16 Mix a dark brown from light red and Payne's grey and put in the dark details, such as the windows. Drybrush a pale mixture of Hooker's green over the foreground to give it some tone. Mix a dark brown from burnt umber and Payne's grey and dab it on to the palm trunks to give them more tone and texture. Paint the shadows of the palm trees on the wall in a pale mixture of Payne's grey.

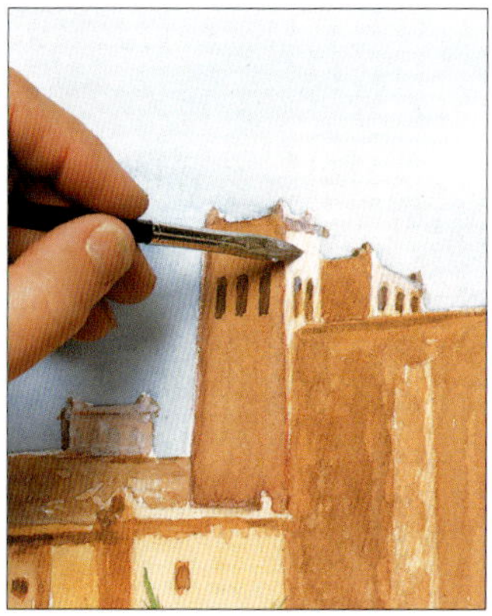

17 Mix a dilute wash of white watercolour paint and brush it over the tops of the highest buildings. Because the paint is transparent the underlying colour shows through, creating the effect of strong sunlight shining on the buildings and bleaching out the colour. Don't worry if the white looks too strong when you first apply it to the paper as it will quickly sink in and look natural.

Moroccan kasbah

The artist has managed to create a surprisingly wide range of tones in this painting, and this is one of the keys to its success, as the variety helps to convey not only the weathered textures of the mud bricks but also that all-important sense of light and shade. Rich, warm colours – far warmer than in the original reference photograph – help to evoke the feeling of being in a hot country. The foreground trees and bushes contrast well with the buildings in both colour and shape.

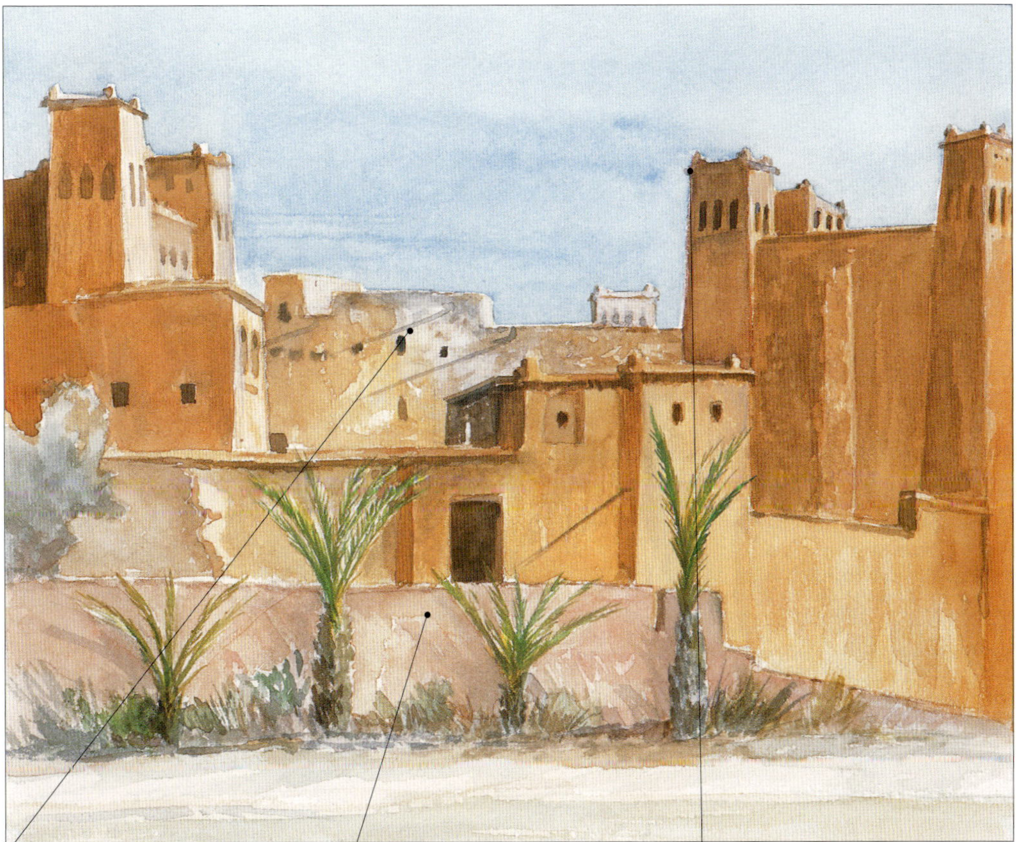

Transparent white watercolour paint allows some of the underlying colour to show through, and this creates the impression of sun-bleached brick.

In reality, this wall is the same colour as those behind. Painting it a warm pink brings it forward in the picture and helps to create an impression of distance.

Note the use of complementary colours – the orangey ochres and terracottas of the buildings against the rich cerulean blue of the sky.

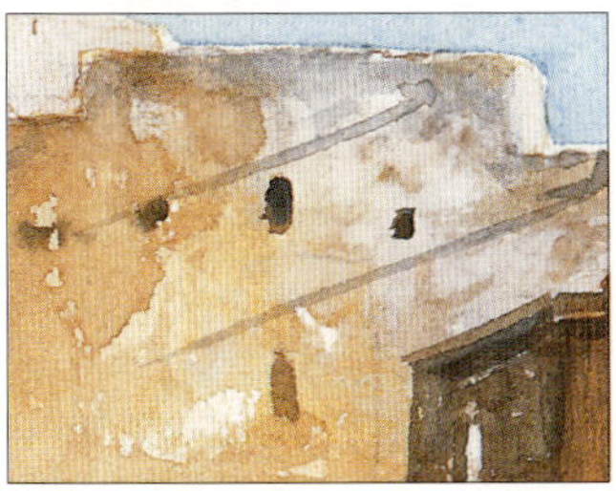

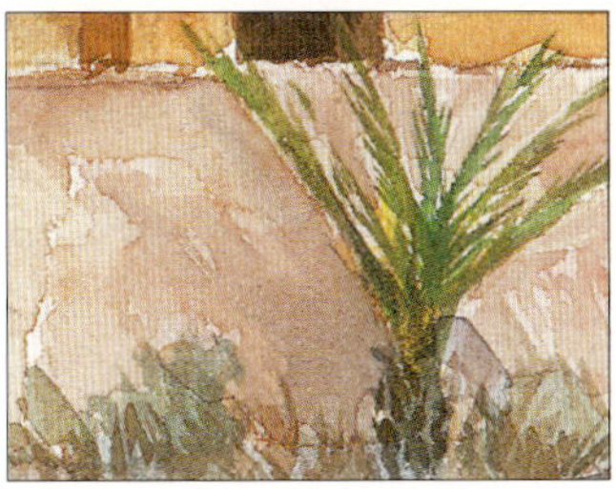

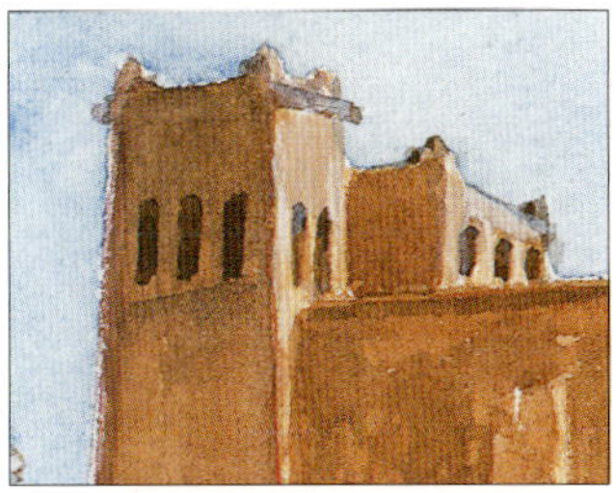

Arched window

Many people would have passed by this little window in favour of something with more obvious appeal, such as brightly painted shutters or a courtyard filled with colourful blooms. The beautiful proportions of this old window, however, with its worn stonework and row of empty terracotta pots, struck an instant chord with the artist. It is proof, if proof were needed, that you can find a subject to paint wherever you go.

Why not try this approach for yourself? Instead of looking for the picturesque, deliberately set out to find a subject that most people would consider to be unsuitable for a painting – the contents of a builder's skip, perhaps, or battered tin cans in the street. Even graffiti on a brick wall or a rusting padlock on a rickety old wooden gate can be turned into intriguing, semi-abstract studies.

From a pictorial point of view, one of the most fascinating things about old, worn subjects like this is that they have wonderfully subtle colours and textures, which makes them ideal candidates for the whole spectrum of watercolour textural techniques. Spattering, sponging, stippling and a whole range of additives can all be incorporated to good effect.

This project starts by using oil pastels as resists, revealing both the texture of the paper and underlying colours. Remember to press quite hard on the oil pastels, otherwise there won't be enough oil on the paper to resist the watercolour paint applied in subsequent stages.

Materials

- *2B pencil*
- *140lb (300gsm) NOT watercolour paper, pre-stretched*
- *Soft oil pastels: light green, dark green, pale yellow, terracotta, bright orange, pink, light grey, mid-toned grey, olive green*
- *Watercolour paints: cerulean blue, dioxazine violet, Payne's grey, olive green, burnt sienna, cadmium orange, leaf green, phthalocyanine blue, cobalt blue*
- *Brushes: medium round, fine round*
- *Ruling drawing pen*
- *Masking fluid*

Preliminary sketch

This scene contains relatively few colours and lots of dense shadows. The only way to make it look realistic is to work out in advance where the darkest and lightest tones are going to be, as the artist has done in this quick tonal sketch.

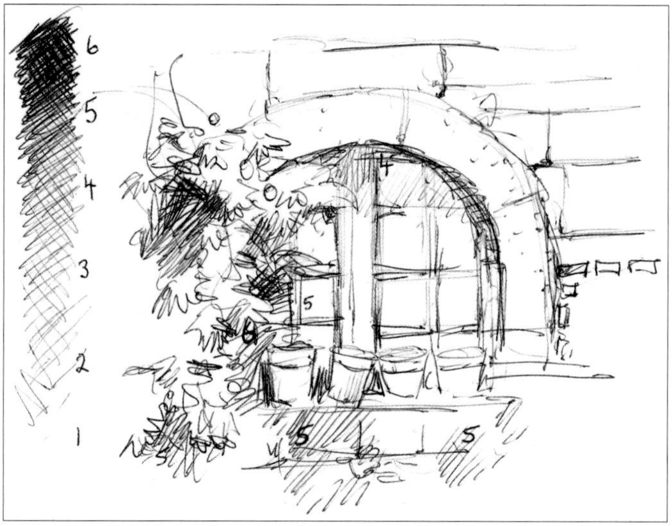

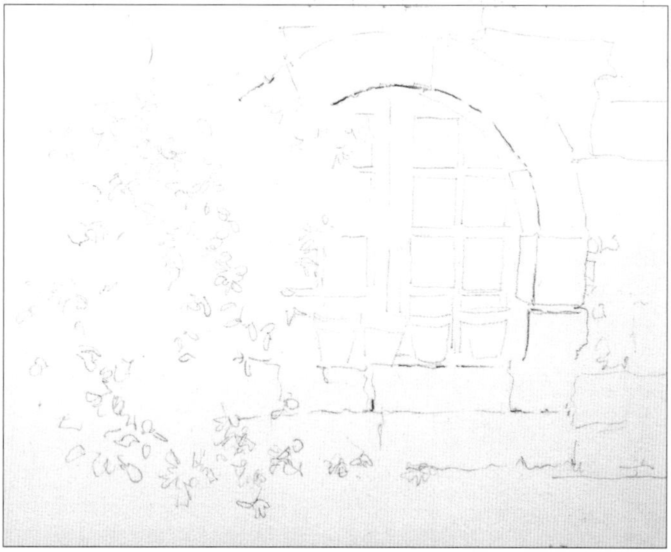

1 Using a 2B pencil, lightly sketch the outline of the window with its row of terracotta flowerpots, the main blocks of stone that surround it, and the mass of plants growing on the left-hand side.

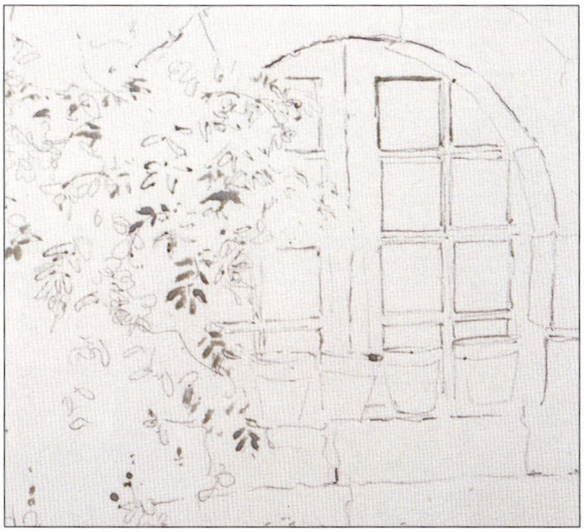

2 Dip a ruling drawing pen in masking fluid and mask the glazing bars on the window frame, the highlights on the rims of the terracotta flowerpots and the little yellow flowers on the bush on the left. Note the differing types of marks: thin straight lines for the highlights and short dots and dashes for the individual flower petals. Leave to dry.

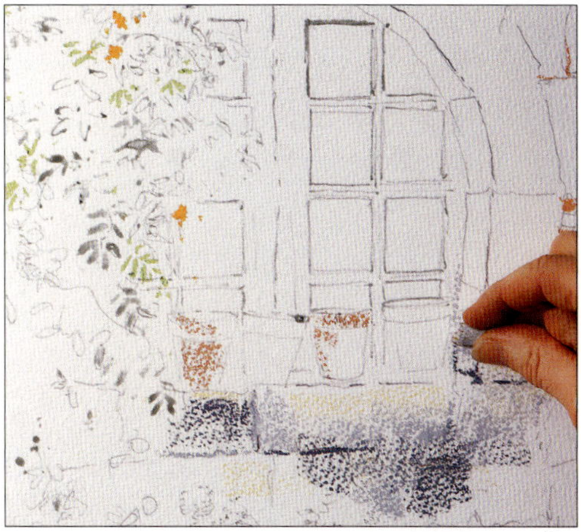

3 Now start to put in colour and texture with soft oil pastels, pressing quite hard to ensure that enough oil is deposited on the paper to act as a resist when the watercolour paint is applied. Roughly dash in the leaf shapes, using light green for the tallest bush and a darker green for the one in the foreground. Drag pale yellow streaks across the stonework under the window. Put in some terracotta pastel on some of the bricks and the flowerpots. Draw the orange and pink flowers on the bush. Put in some light- and mid-toned grey on the worn stonework under the window.

Assessment time

With the addition of a few more pastel marks – more green on the leaves, orange on the terracotta pots, and a dark olive green in the spaces between the pots – the oil pastel stage is now complete. Oil resists water, so these colours will show through any subsequent watercolour washes. Because you are using a rough paper, some of the oil pastel lines will be broken and the texture of the paper will also be visible. Take time to check that you have included all the areas where you want texture.

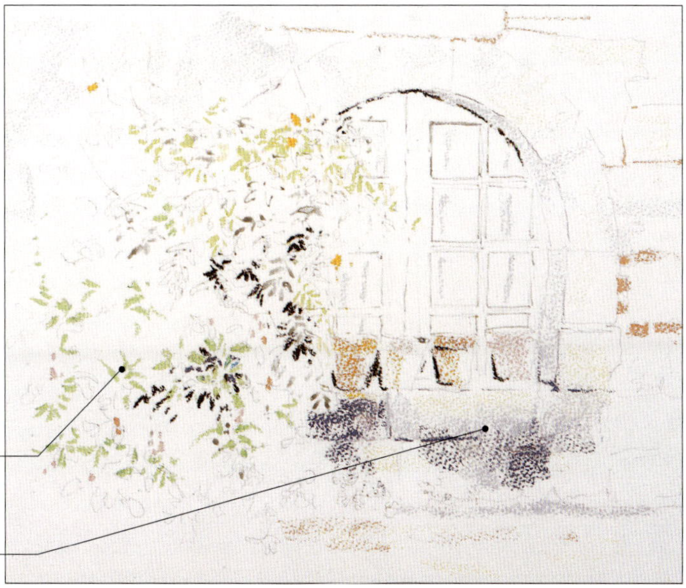

Short dots and dashes convey the shapes of the leaves and flowers.

Long, broken strokes are used for the worn stonework.

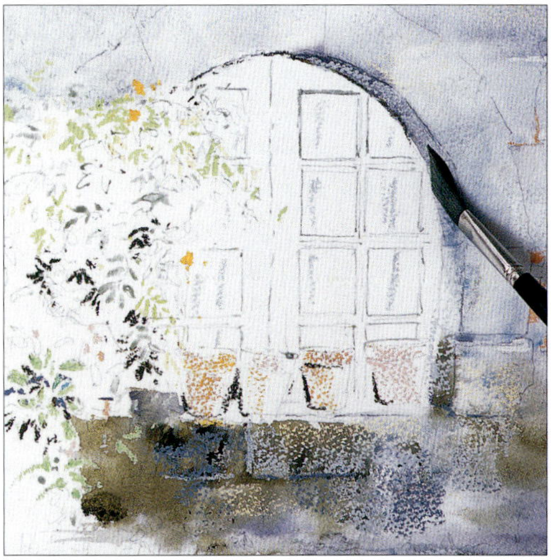

4 Now for the watercolour stages. Dampen the stonework with clean water. Mix a very pale greyish blue from cerulean blue and a little dioxazine violet watercolour paints and brush this mixture over the stonework, adding a little Payne's grey for the shadowed areas and a little more violet for the foreground. Brush very pale olive green over the shadowed stonework beneath the window ledge. Applied wet into wet, the colour blurs and looks like soft lichen.

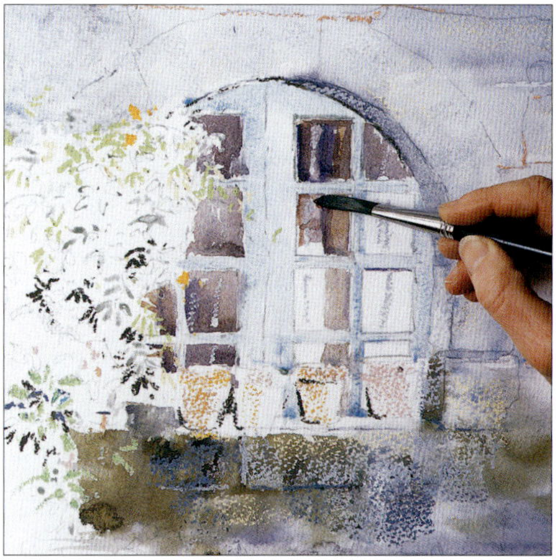

5 Mix a very pale wash of cerulean blue and paint the white woodwork of the right-hand window frame. (Leaving the frame as white paper would look too stark in relation to the rest of the image.) Mix a warm brown from burnt sienna and dioxazine violet and carefully paint the window panes, leaving some gaps for highlights reflected in the glass.

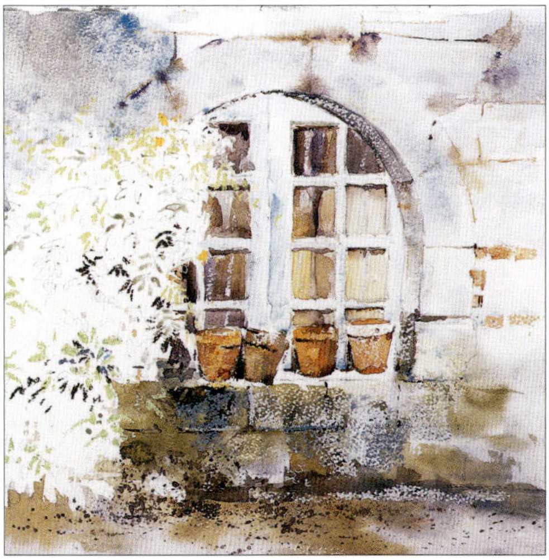

6 Mix an orangey brown from cadmium orange and dioxazine violet and paint the first terracotta flowerpot. Add Payne's grey to the mixture for the second pot in the row, which is in shadow, and burnt sienna for the third and fourth pots.

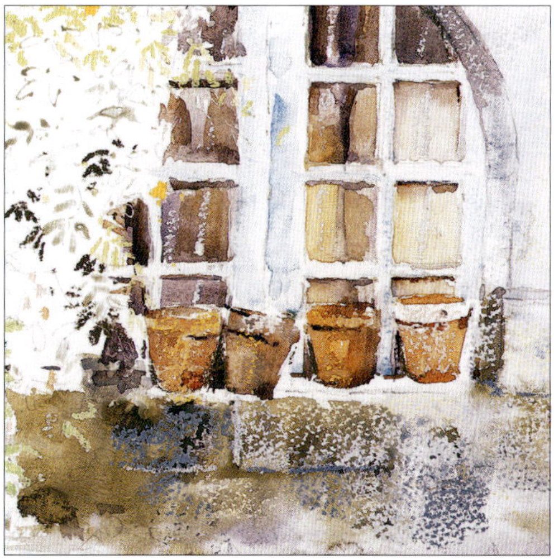

7 Note how the oil pastel marks that you applied in the early stages resist the watercolour paint, creating very realistic-looking but subtle texture in the stonework under the window and the flowerpots. The texture of the paper plays a part in this, too.

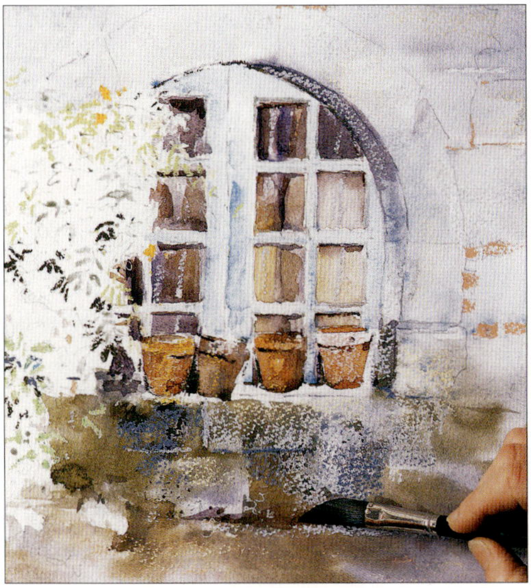

8 Mix a pale but warm grey from cerulean blue and a little dioxazine violet and wash this mixture over the stonework under the window. While the wash is still damp, brush burnt sienna over the terracotta pastel of the bricks. Allow the paper to dry slightly, add dioxazine violet to the burnt sienna wash and paint the cracks in the stonework.

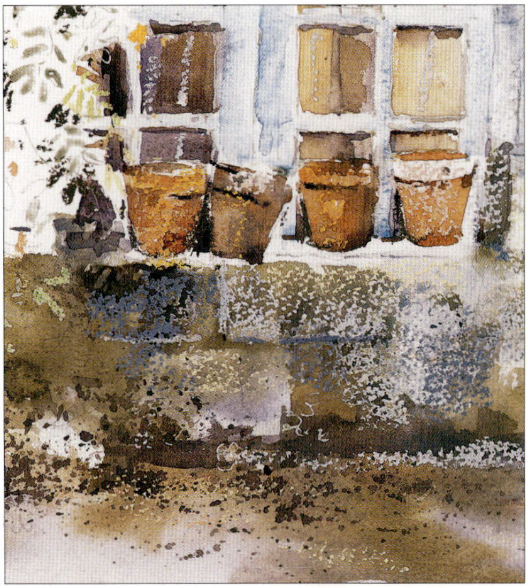

9 Mix dioxazine violet with a little olive green and spatter this mixture lightly over the foreground to create some texture on the path and wall. These spatters of dark colour look like clumps of moss or small pebbles – both of which are in keeping with the somewhat derelict and dilapidated nature of the subject.

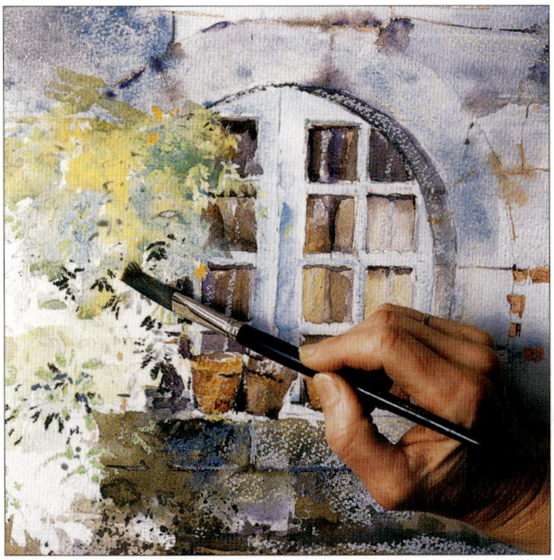

10 Mix a fairly strong wash of leaf green (which is a bright, yellowy green) and brush it over the lightest areas on the tops of the bushes. Add cerulean blue to the mixture and use this colour to paint the mid-toned leaves, taking care not to obliterate all of the light green.

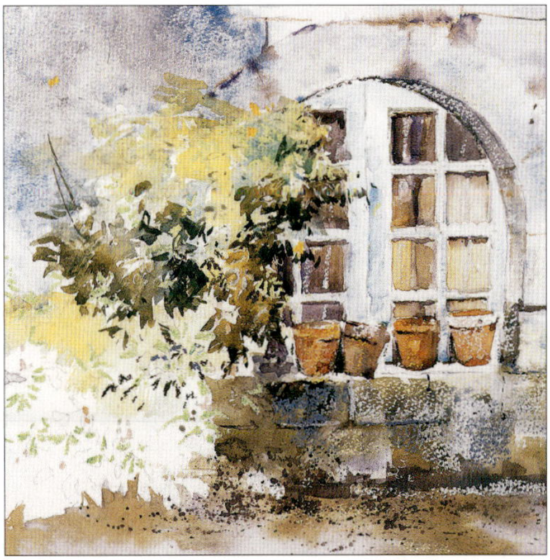

11 Mix a dark green from olive green and phthalocyanine blue and dot in the darkest tones of the leaves on the background bush, making sure your brushstrokes follow the direction in which the leaves grow. You are now beginning to establish the form of the bushes.

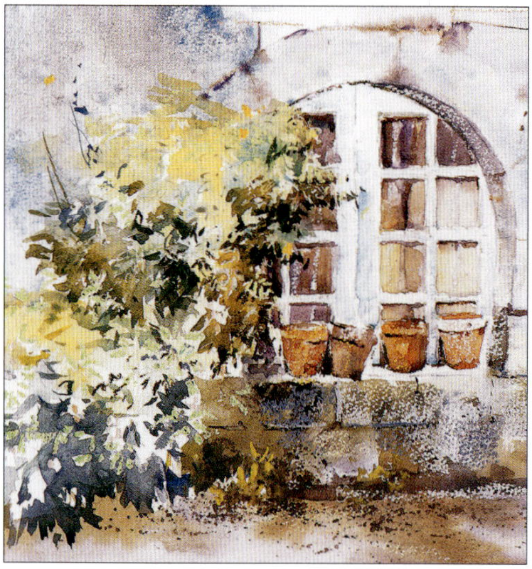

12 Add cobalt blue to the dark green used in Step 11. Paint the spaces between the leaves of the foreground bush.

Tip: Using a range of contrasting greens like this makes it clear that there are two very different bushes in this picture. You may find it easier to assess the tones if you half close your eyes.

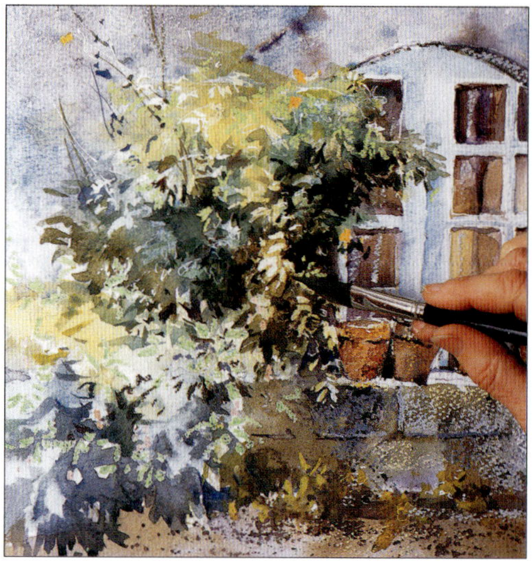

13 Mix a very pale wash of cerulean blue and brush it over the white spaces to the left of the bushes, which look very stark in relation to the rest of the image. Mix a very dark green from burnt sienna, olive green and a little phthalocyanine blue. Stroke this mixture on to the very darkest leaves on the foreground bush, taking the colour across the front of the window to imply overhanging leaves and branches. Leave to dry.

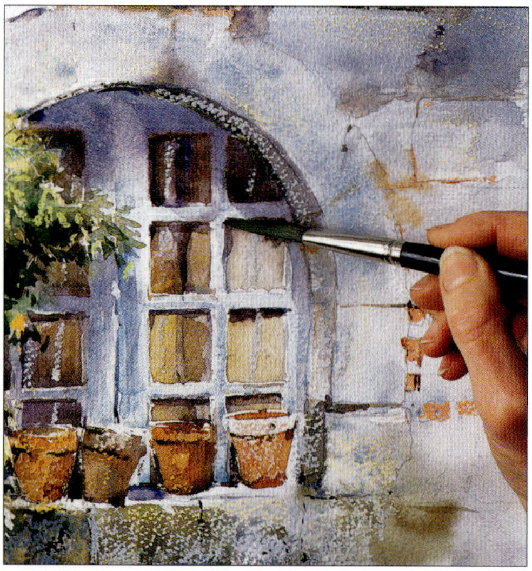

14 Gently rub off the masking fluid. Mix a dark purple from cobalt blue, violet and a little burnt sienna and darken some of the shadows around the window.

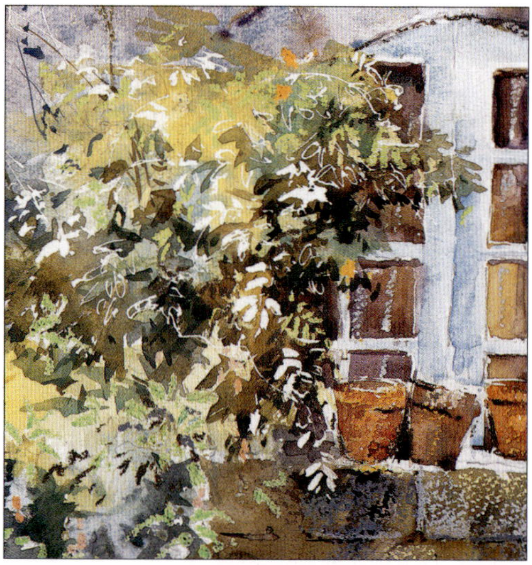

15 Mix a very pale wash of cerulean blue and tone down the starkness of some of the revealed whites.

Arched window

This is a beautifully controlled study in texture, painted using a relatively subdued and limited palette – proof that simplicity is often the most effective option. The empty flowerpots are what really make the picture: they provide visual interest in the foreground to hold the viewer's attention and also imply a human presence in the scene.

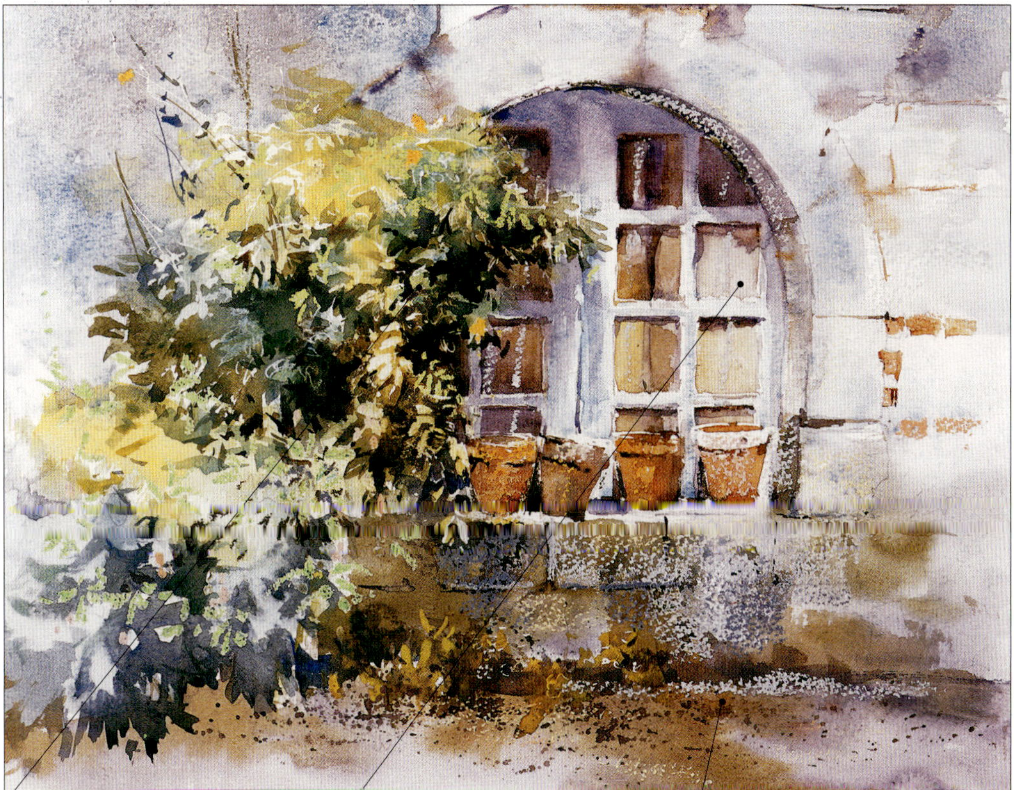

Using a range of greens both gives depth and indicates that there is more than one type of plant in this area.

Leaving tiny areas of window pane unpainted conveys the impression of light being reflected in the glass.

Two textural techniques, spattering and the use of resists, have been combined to good effect here.

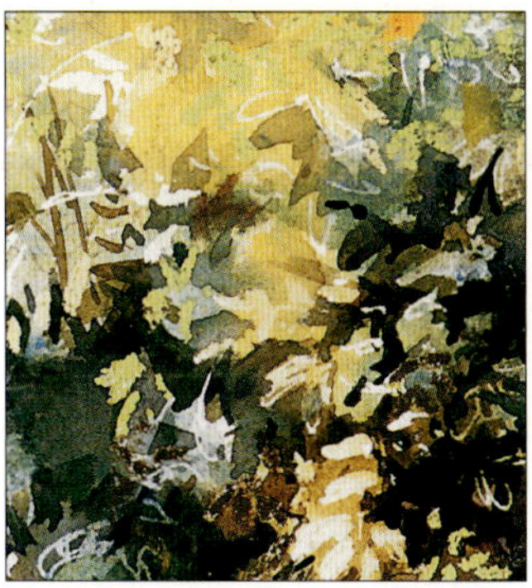

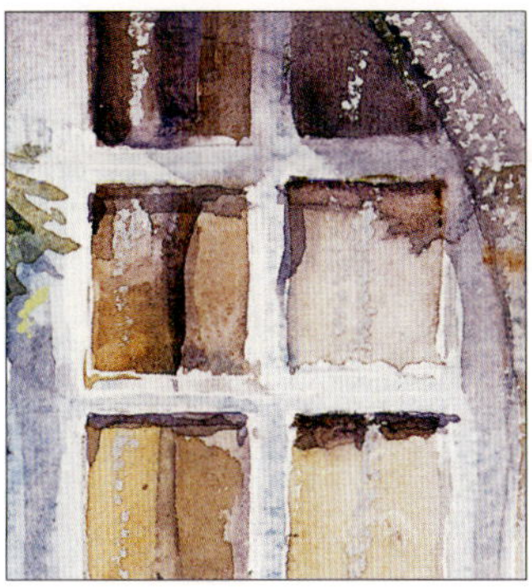

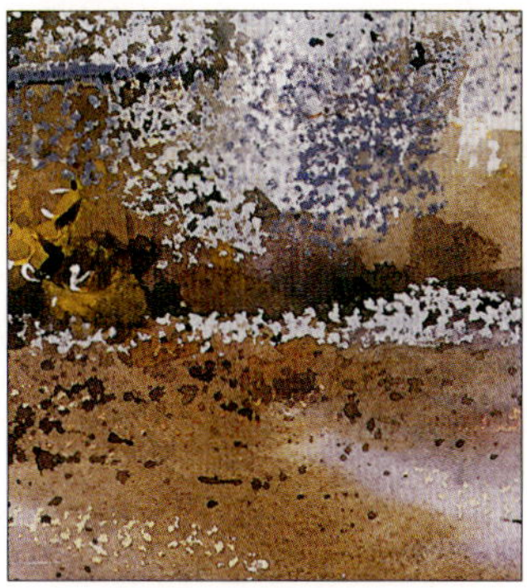

Painting People

Portraits are often considered difficult to paint, although in reality they are no more complicated than any other subject. Part of the perceived difficulty in painting portraits comes from the need to capture a true likeness of the sitter, as somehow we expect portraits to be more lifelike, and less subject to the artist's personal interpretation, than other subjects. If you approach the subject and construct your image in the same way as any other, taking measurements and observing proportions, then that likeness should – and will – follow. Take time over your underdrawing as this is important, and observe where each facial feature is positioned in relation to the others.

A little knowledge of what the human skull is like will make it easier to position the facial features correctly. Although facial features will differ, certain measurements and proportions are approximately the same on most people.

However, a really good portrait should achieve far more than a physical likeness of the subject, it should also reveal something of the sitter's character. Hair, make-up and clothes are all important in capturing an individual's personality, and should be subject to the same scrutiny as the sitter's features.

The main watercolour techniques that you will find yourself using are wet into wet and wet on dry. Techniques that are usually associated with making texture will, for obvious reasons, be used less often in portraiture, if at all, although drybrush can prove useful when painting hair. Watercolour is a good medium for portraits, but it requires a little forethought and planning. The traditional transparent watercolour technique of working light to dark is perfect for building up skin colours and tones, as new washes are applied over dry ones. Alternatively, flood paint colour into a wet area to create soft transitions, with one colour blending seamlessly into another. Wet-on-dry work, which creates a sharp, hard-edged focus, should be restricted to painting the features on the sitter's face.

Tips: • Spend time plotting the facial features. If your measurements and assessment of proportion are correct, a good likeness should follow.

• Limit yourself to one or two techniques. Use wet-into-wet washes initially, and then create sharper focus by using wet-on-dry washes as the work progresses.

• Use gum arabic in your washes, or work on a support that has been heavily sized: this makes it easier to make corrections by washing off paint.

• If you are painting someone in their environment, work on the background and setting at the same time as the figure per se to avoid the portrait looking as if it has simply been pasted in.

The red shirt ▼

The boy's mischievous and adventurous character is self-evident as he hangs from a tree branch with a considerable drop beneath. Carefully placed wet-on-dry washes were used over a drawing using very light wet-into-wet watercolour paints.

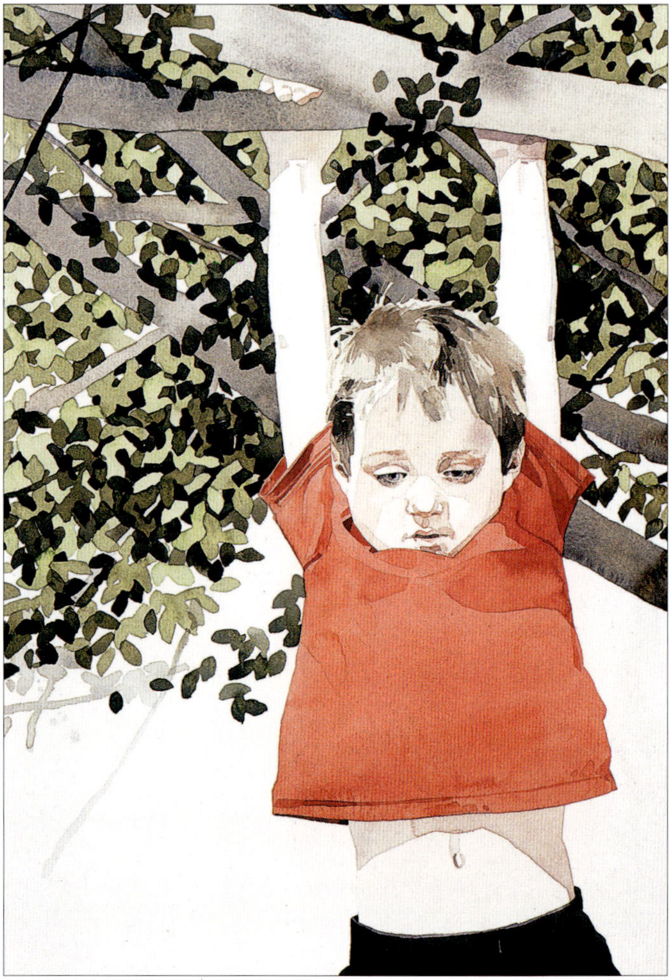

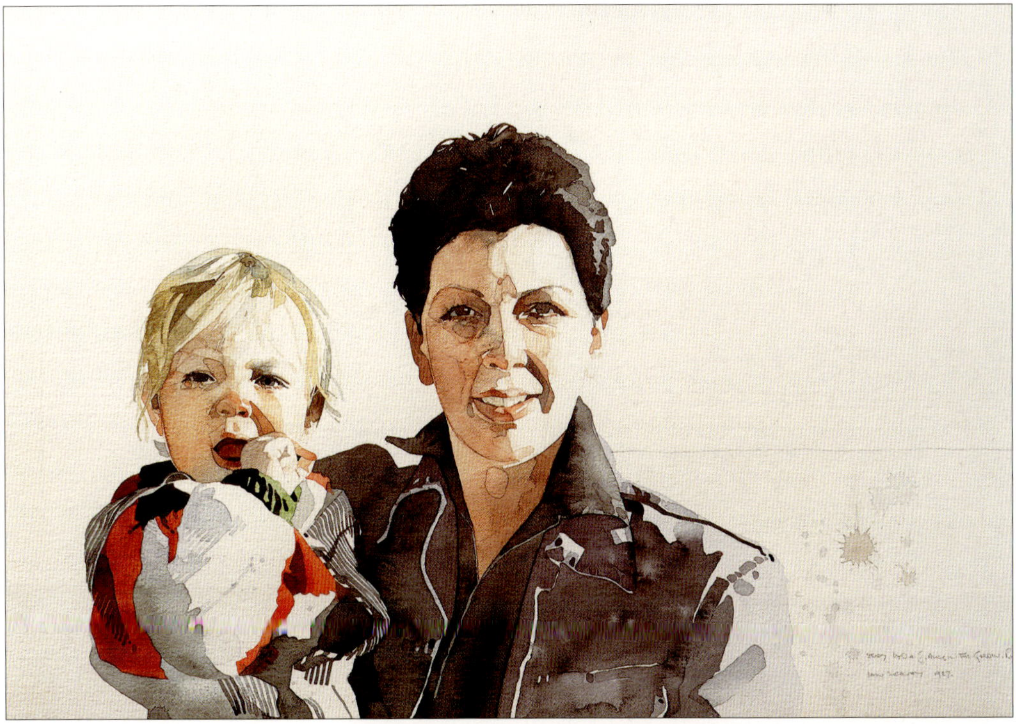

Lydia and Alice ▲
The initial work was made using wet-into-wet washes and the features were then sharpened using wet on dry. Gum arabic was used in many of the mixes. This has the effect not only of intensifying the colour but also of making the washes more transparent. Gum arabic also makes dry paint soluble if it is re-wet, so you can wash off dry paint and make any necessary corrections – this is a very useful facility when painting portraits.

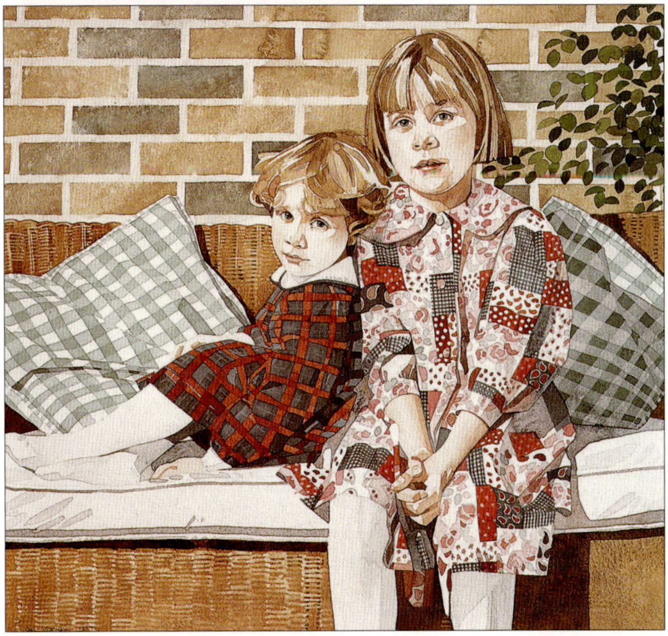

Sisters ►
Working over a careful pencil drawing using wet-on-dry washes, an overall colour harmony was achieved by using a limited range of colours. Interestingly, the two girls were painted at different times. The poses were carefully chosen so that the figures could be combined on the support.

Head-and-shoulders portrait

Painting a portrait from life for the first time can be a daunting prospect. Not only do you have the technical aspects to deal with, but you are working with a live model, who will almost certainly fidget and demand to see what you are doing. Before you embark on your first portrait session, practice drawing and painting from photographs to build up your skills and confidence.

You also have to consider your model's wellbeing. Make sure they are warm and comfortable and have adopted a pose that feels natural: they may have to hold the same pose for a long time. Ask them to fix their gaze on an object behind you (a picture on the wall, perhaps) so that, if they do move, they can easily regain their original position.

Put a lot of care into your underdrawing. If you can get the facial features in the right place and know where the main areas of light and shade are going to be, then you are well on the way to success.

Finally, don't try to do too much. Details like clothing are relatively unimportant in a head-and-shoulders portrait. Instead, try to capture your subject's mood and personality by concentrating on the eyes and expression.

Positioning the features

The sketches below are intended to provide some general guidelines to help position the facial features correctly. They are not infallible rules, however: everyone is different and you should train yourself to take objective measurements rather than relying on your preconceptions. Your viewpoint also makes a difference.

Resist the temptation to start by drawing an outline of the face. If you do this, the chances are that you will find you haven't allowed yourself enough space for the features. Start by working out the relative sizes and positions of the features and then worry about the overall outline.

It is always a good idea to put in faint pencil guidelines – a line down through the central axis of the face and lines across to mark the positions of the eyes, nose and mouth.

A large mass of hair can make things more complicated, as it is hard to work out exactly where the cranium ends and the hair begins. To begin with, try to work with a model whose hair sits close to the scalp or can be scraped back tight – or even a model with no hair at all.

Head-on view

The left and right sides of the face are not totally symmetrical, but drawing a central guideline is a good starting point.

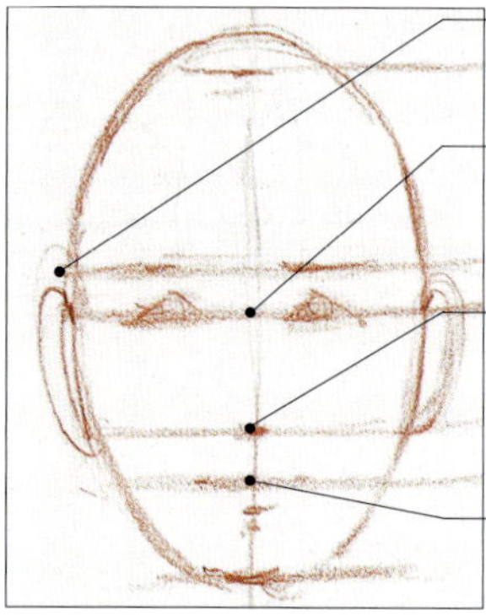

The eyes are level with the ear tips.

The eyes are approximately halfway down the facial area.

The nose is roughly halfway between the eyes and the base of the chin.

The mouth is less than halfway between the nose and chin.

Head tilted forwards

When the head is titled forward, you can see more of the cranium and less of the facial features.

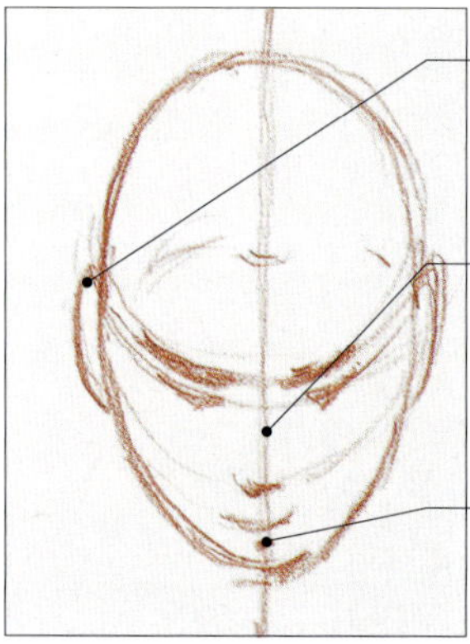

The ears become more prominent and protrude above the level of the eyes.

The distance between the eyes and nose appears to be greater here than in the head-on view.

The distance between the nose and mouth, and mouth and chin, is very small.

Head tilted backwards

When the head is tilted backwards, you can see very little of the cranium.

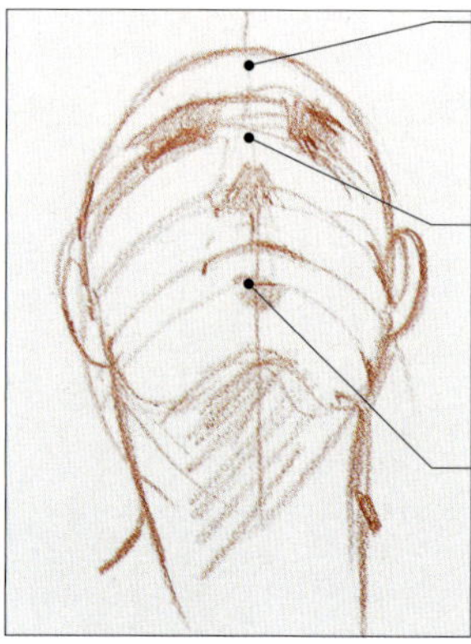

The distance between the eyes and the top of the cranium is very small from here.

The distance between the eyes and nose appears to be less here than in the head-on view.

The distance between the nose and mouth, and mouth and chin, is greater than in the head-on view.

Materials

- *HB pencil*
- *140lb (300gsm) HP watercolour paper, pre-stretched*
- *Watercolour paints: light red, yellow ochre, alizarin crimson, sap green, sepia tone, neutral tint, ultramarine blue, ultramarine violet, cobalt blue, burnt umber, cadmium orange, cadmium red*
- *Brushes: large round, medium round, fine round*

The pose

If you are new to portraiture, a simple pose, with the model looking directly at you, is probably the best way to begin. Place a strong light to one side of the model, as it will cast an obvious shadow and make it easier for you to assess areas of light and shade.

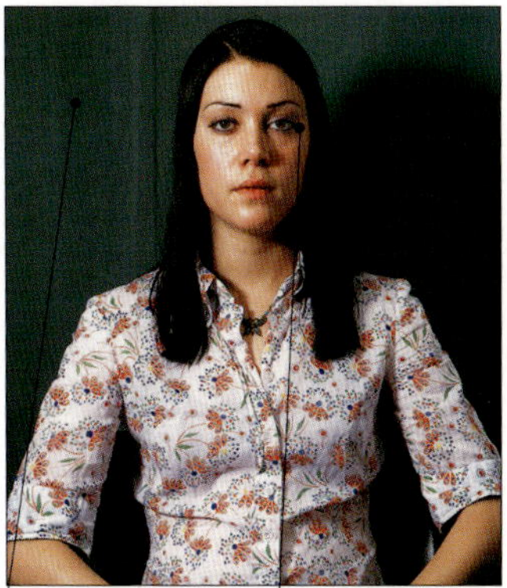

Select a plain background that does not draw attention away from your subject.

The eyes are the key to any portrait.

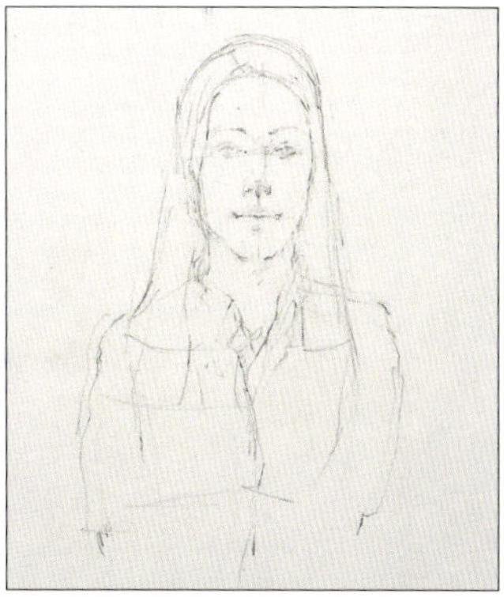

1 Using an HB pencil lightly sketch your subject, putting in faint construction lines as a guide to help you check that the features are accurately positioned.

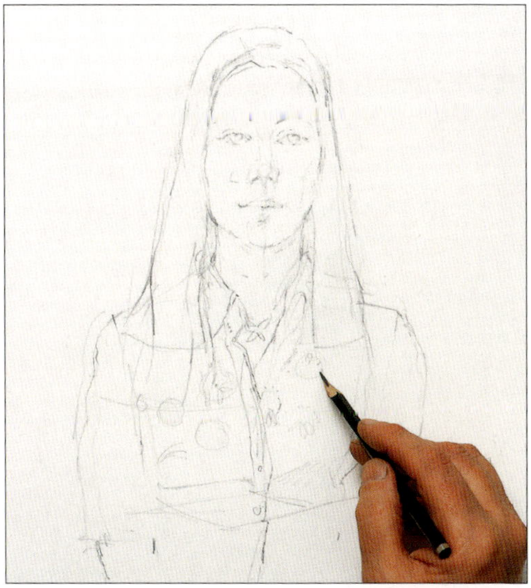

2 Begin to put in some indication of the pattern in the model's blouse. You do not need to make it detailed.

Tip: From time to time, look at your drawing in a mirror. This often makes it easier to assess if you have got the proportions and position of the features right. Also hold your drawing board at arm's length, with the drawing vertical, to check the perspective. When you work with the drawing board flat, the perspective sometimes becomes distorted.

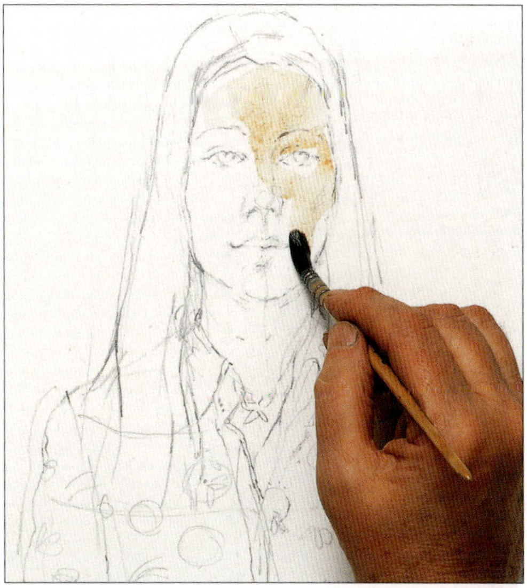

3 Mix light red and yellow ochre to make the first warm but pale flesh tone. Using a medium round brush, wash this mixture over the face, neck and forearms, avoiding the eyes and leaving a few gaps for highlights. This is just the base colour for the flesh. It will look a little strange at this stage, but you will add more tones and colours later on.

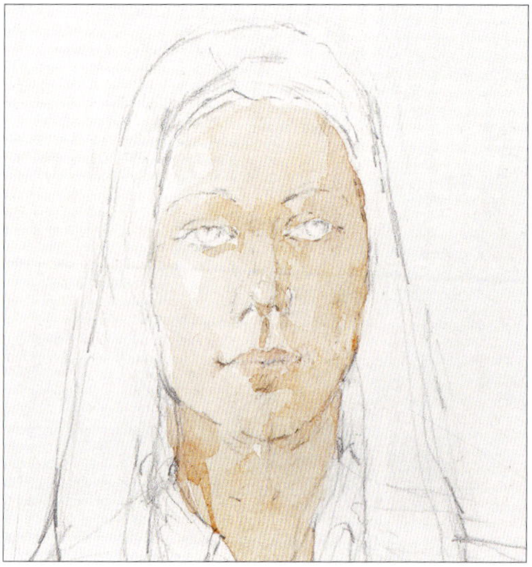

4 You have to work quickly at this stage to avoid the wash drying and forming hard edges. While the first wash is still damp, add more pigment and a little alizarin crimson to the first skin tone and paint the shadowed side of the face to give some modelling. Add more alizarin crimson to the mixture and paint the lips. Leave to dry.

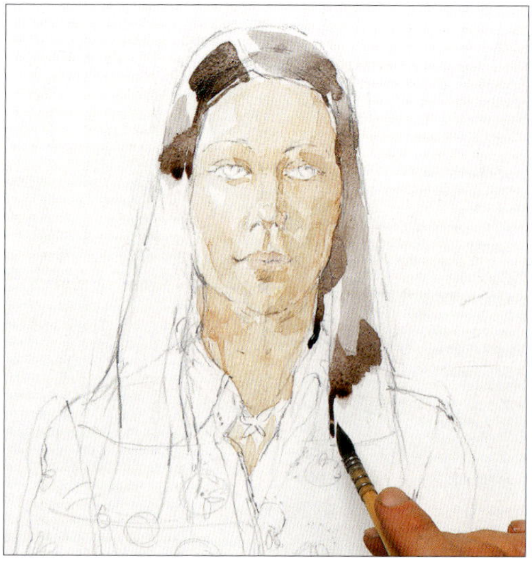

5 Touch a little very dilute alizarin crimson on to the cheeks and some very pale sap green into the dark, shaded side of the face. Mix a warm, rich brown from sepia tone and neutral tint and start to paint the hair, leaving some highlight areas and the parting line on the top of the head completely free of paint.

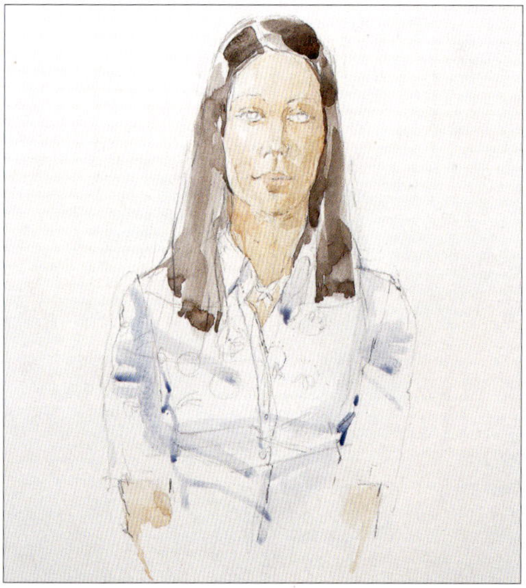

6 Mix a very pale blue from ultramarine blue and a hint of ultramarine violet. See where the fabric in the blouse creases, causing shadows. Using a fine round brush, paint these creases in the pale blue mixture.

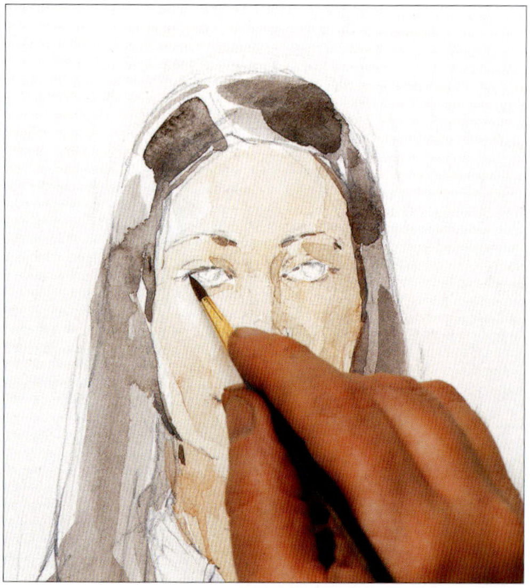

7 Go back to the hair colour mixture used in Step 5 and put a second layer of colour on the darker areas of hair. Paint the eyebrows and carefully outline the eyes in the same dark brown mixture.

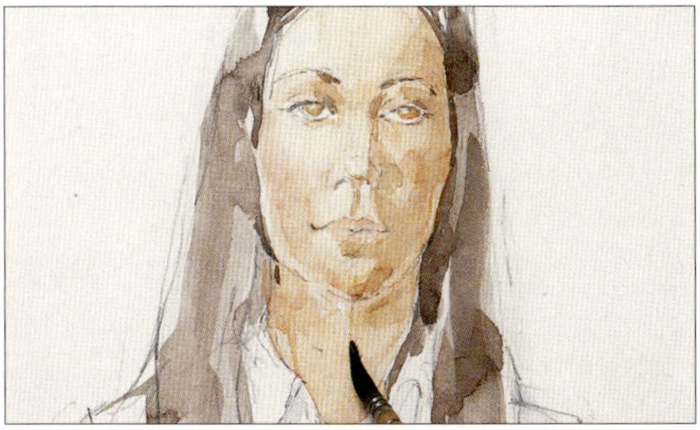

8 Mix a very light green from yellow ochre with a little sap green and, using a fine round brush, paint the irises, leaving a white space for the highlight where light is reflected in the eye. Strengthen the shadows on the side of the face and neck with a pale mixture of light red and a little sap green.

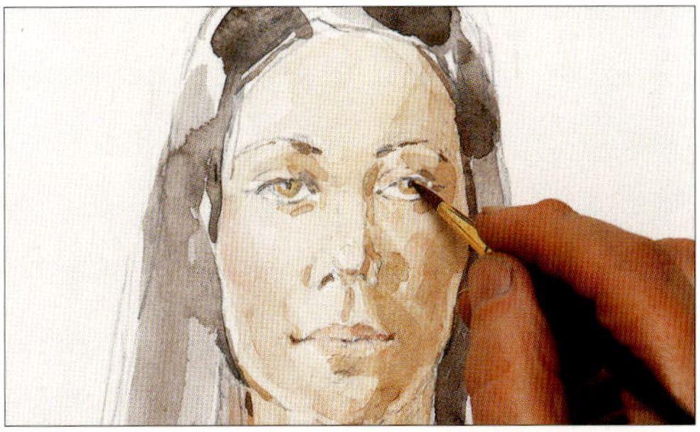

9 Use the same shadow colour to paint along the edge of the nose. This helps to separate the nose from the cheeks and make it look three-dimensional. Mix ultramarine violet with sepia tone and paint the pupils of the eyes, taking care not to go over on to the whites.

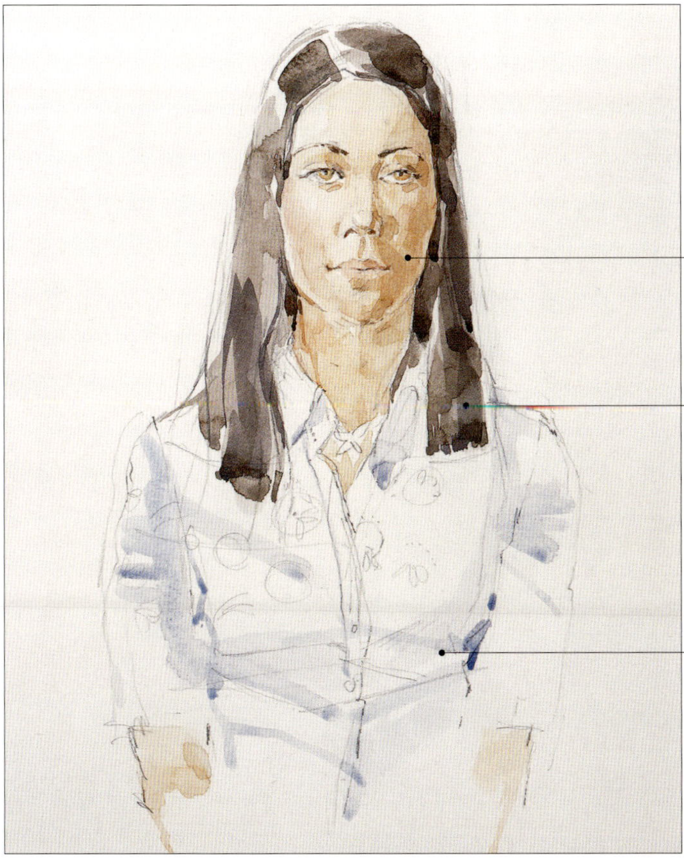

Assessment time

The portrait is nearing completion and it is time to stand back and decide what adjustments to make and what final details to add. Beware of overworking a portrait like this. The key to its success is its directness.

The model does not stand out clearly from the stark white background.

Successive washes of colour give the hair depth and sheen.

The creases and shadows in the blouse imply the contours of the body underneath the fabric.

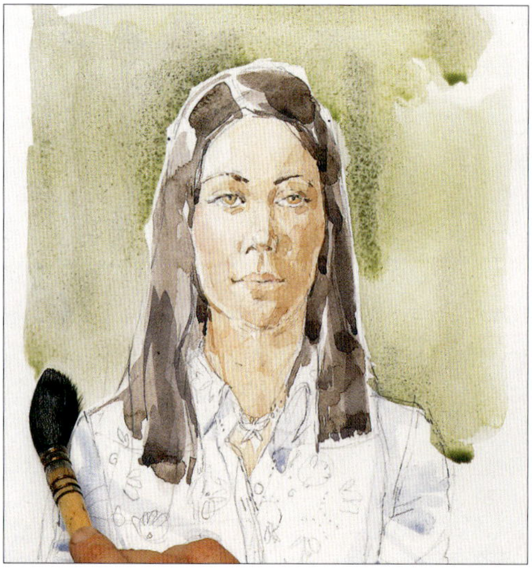

10 Mix a dark green from sap green, cobalt blue and burnt umber. Using a large round brush, carefully wash this mixture over the background, taking care not to allow any of the paint to spill over on to the figure. (You may find it easier to switch to a smaller brush to cut in around the figure.)

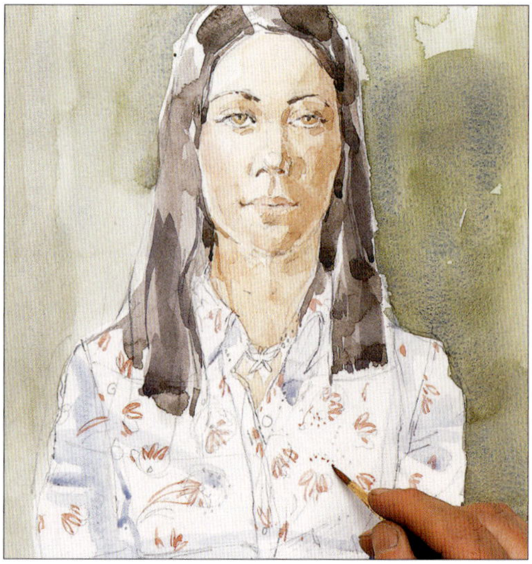

11 While the background wash is still damp, add a little more pigment to the green mixture and brush in the shadow of the girl's head. Mix an orangey-red from cadmium orange and cadmium red and, using a fine round brush, start putting in some of the detail on the girl's blouse.

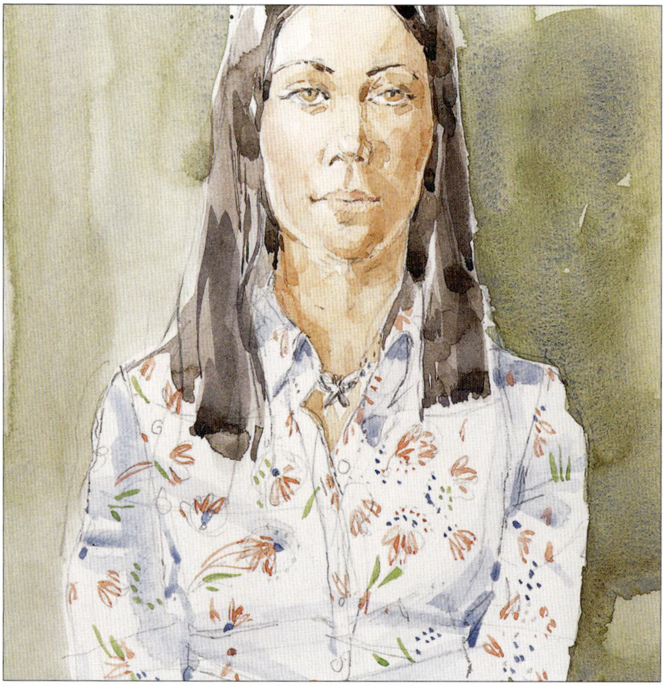

12 Continue building up some indication of the pattern on the girl's blouse, using the orangey red mixture from Step 11, along with ultramarine blue and sap green.

Tip: Don't try to replicate the pattern exactly: it will take far too long and will change the emphasis of the painting from the girl's face to her clothing.

Head-and-shoulders portrait

This is a sensitive, yet loosely painted portrait that captures the model's features and mood perfectly. It succeeds largely because its main focus, and the most detailed brushwork, is on the girl's eyes and pensive expression. Careful attention to the shadow areas has helped to give shape to the face and separate the model from the plain-coloured background.

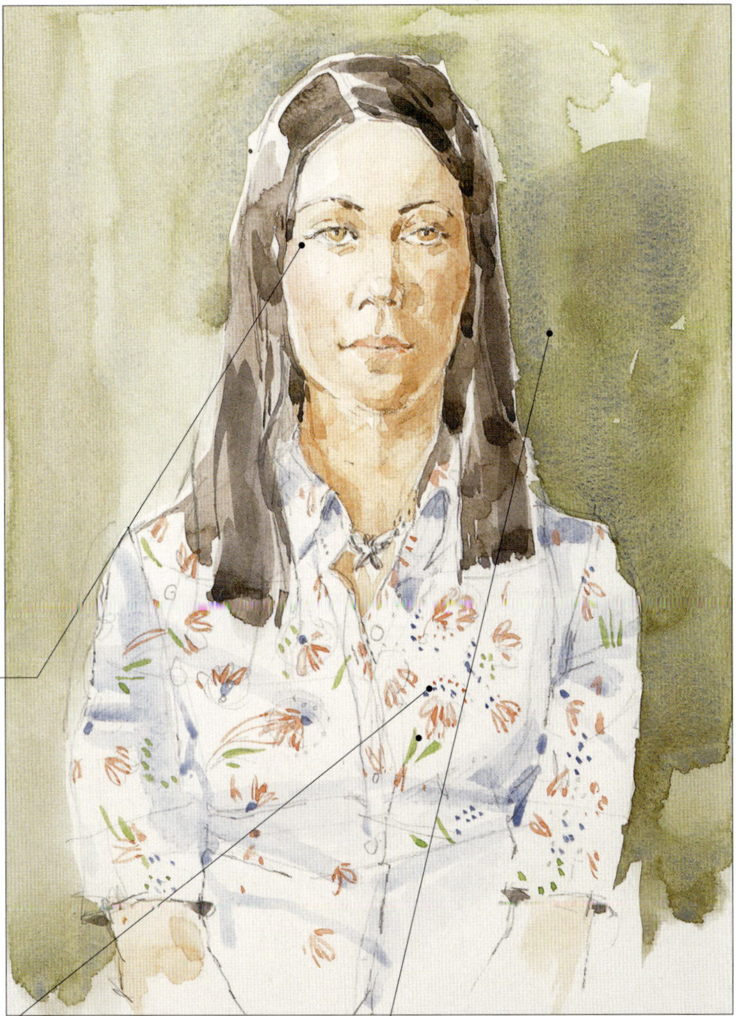

The detailed painting of the eyes and mouth helps to reveal the model's mood and character.

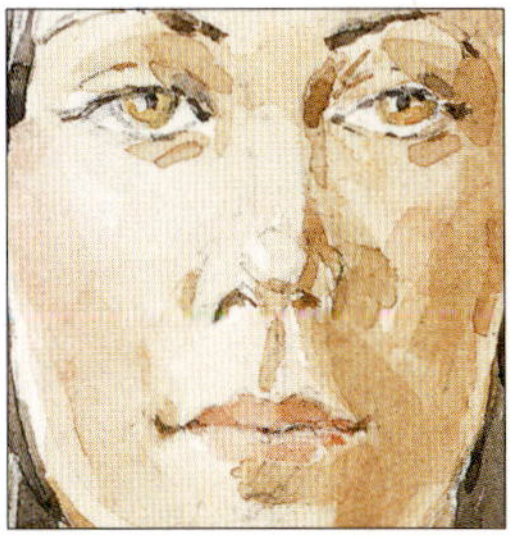

In reality, the pattern on the blouse is much more detailed than this, but a more accurate rendition would have drawn attention away from the girl's face.

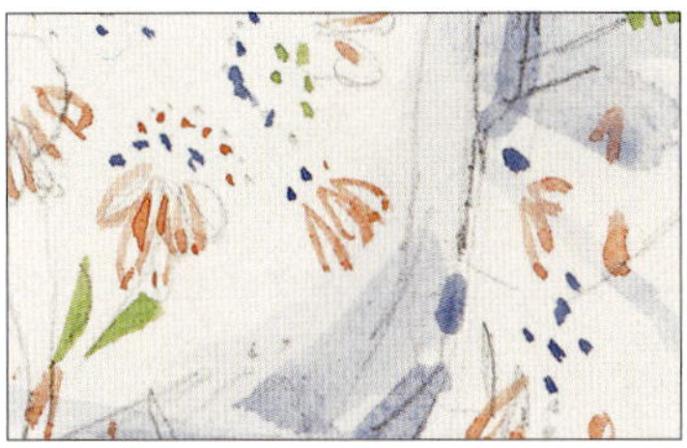

The shadow on the wall helps to separate the model from the background and gives the image more depth.

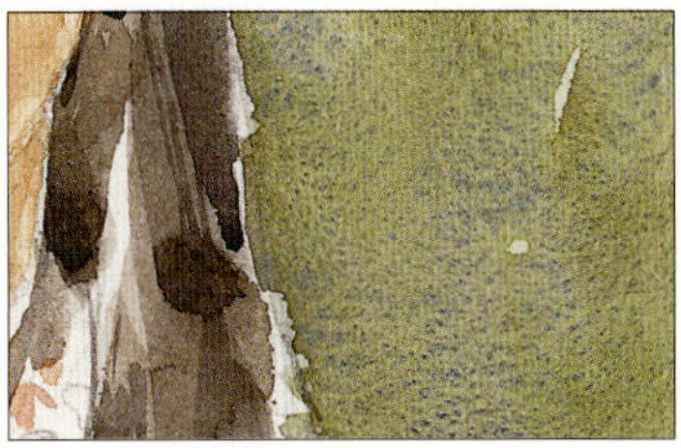

The swimmer

Although the subject of this project looks simple enough – a solitary figure swimming underwater, with relatively little discernible detail – the real interest lies in the play of light on the water and the way that shapes are slightly distorted, producing an image that tends towards abstraction. Your task is not only to capture the sleek form of the swimmer and to freeze a moment in time, but also to convey a sense of the dappled sunlight and the movement of the water.

As so often happens in painting, it helps to exaggerate certain elements in order to get across the mood that you want. Distorting the figure of the swimmer slightly in order to make it look more streamlined is one way to do this; making more of the dappled patches of sunlight on the water is another.

Adding a few drops of gum arabic to your paint mixes is a very useful technique when painting water, as it increases the gloss and transparency of watercolour paint. This, combined with the careful build-up of layers of colour, helps to make the water look as if it is shimmering in the sunlight.

Materials

- *2B pencil*
- *200lb (425gsm) NOT watercolour paper, pre-stretched*
- *Watercolour paints: cadmium lemon, alizarin crimson, cerulean blue, cobalt turquoise, cadmium red, cadmium yellow, Payne's grey, ivory black, burnt sienna, burnt umber*
- *Brushes: large round, medium round, small round*
- *Gum arabic*
- *3B graphite stick*

Reference photograph

Fascinated by the way the sunlight played on the water, the artist asked his daughter to dive repeatedly into this brightly tiled swimming pool, so that he could take reference photographs to work on at his leisure. When you are shooting a moving subject, it is hard to predict what you will actually capture on the film, so always take a lot more shots than you think you will need.

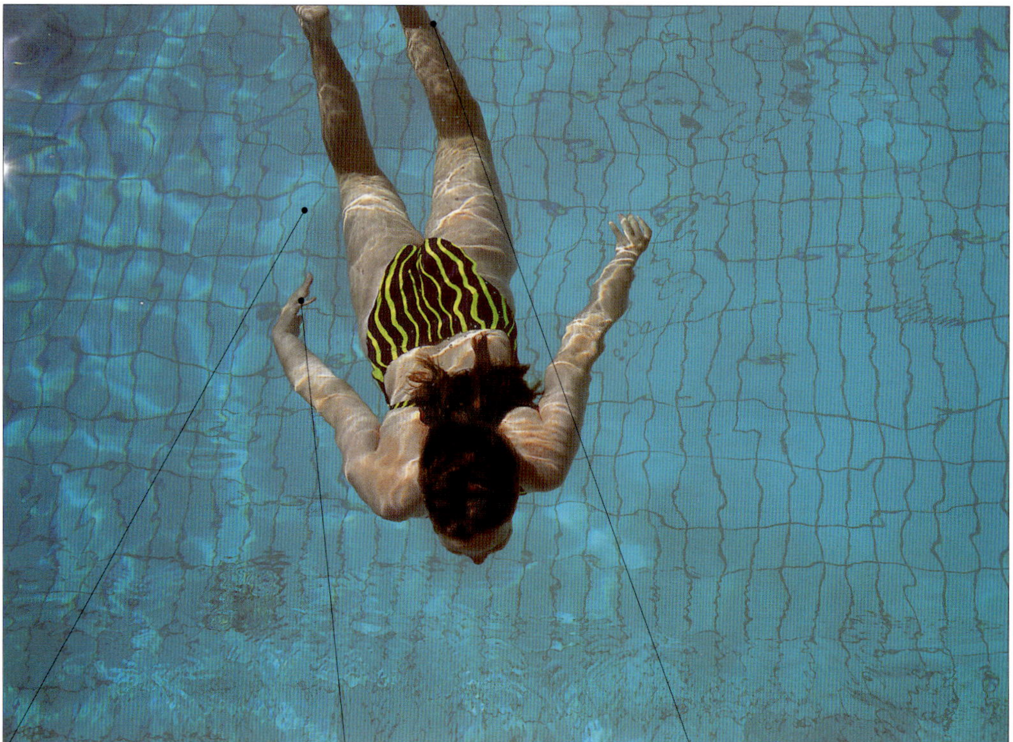

There is some dappled light on both the girl and the water, but this can be exaggerated in the painting to increase the feeling of sunlight.

Elongating the legs, arms and hands will increase the sense of movement.

Cutting off the legs at the top of the frame gives a more dynamic composition and allows the figure space into which to move.

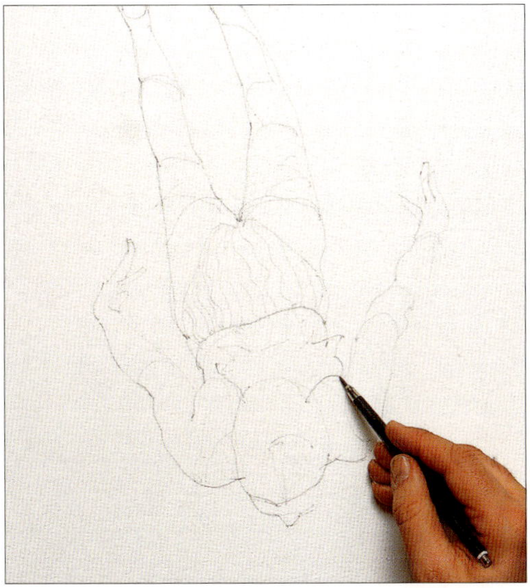

1 Using a 2B pencil, lightly sketch the figure. Note that it is slightly distorted because of the way the light is refracted through the water. In addition, the fingers and legs have been deliberately elongated a little to create a sense of the figure moving through the water at speed.

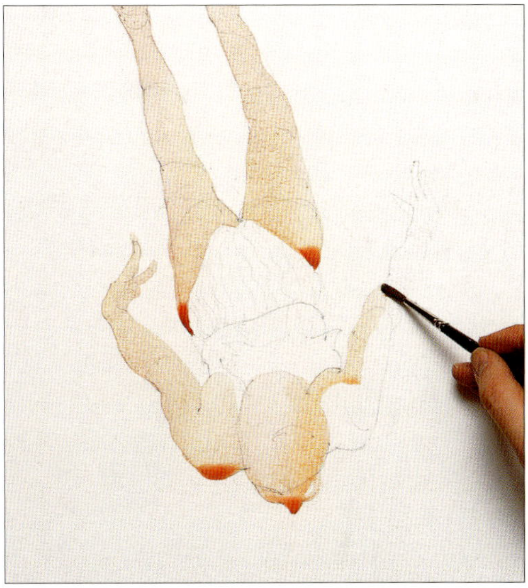

2 Mix a light pink wash from cadmium lemon and alizarin crimson, and a slightly redder version of the same mixture. Using a medium round brush, wash these colours over the whole of the body, alternating between the two mixtures to give some tonal variety. Leave to dry.

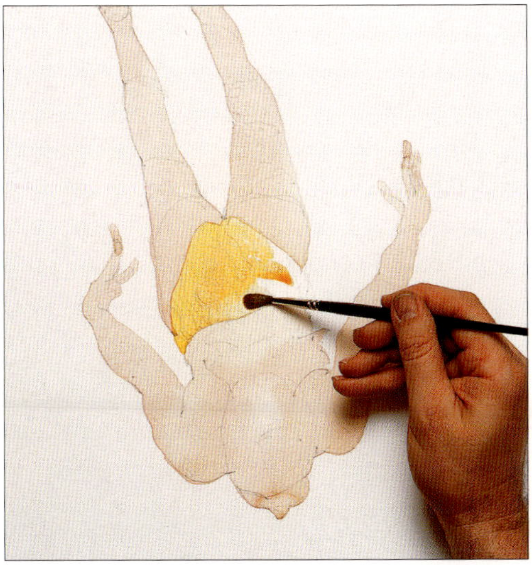

3 Mix a strong wash of cadmium lemon and add a little of the lighter pink wash used in Step 2. Using a medium round brush, paint the girl's bikini bottoms in this colour. Leave to dry.

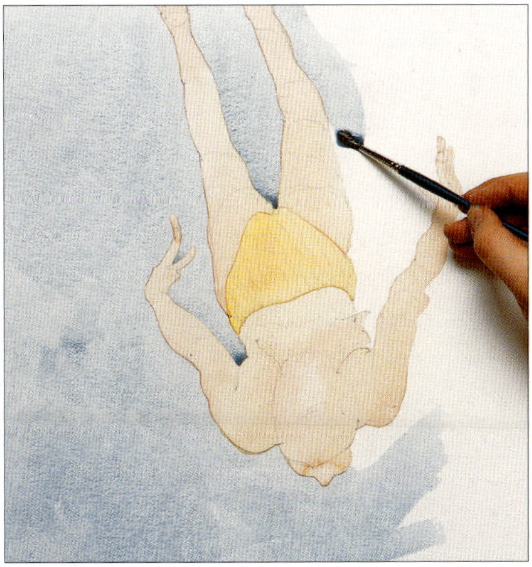

4 Mix a large quantity of a pale blue wash from cerulean blue and a little cobalt turquoise. Wash this mixture over the whole of the background, taking care not to allow any of the paint to go over the figure. (You may need to switch to a smaller brush to "cut in" around the edges of the figure.)

▶

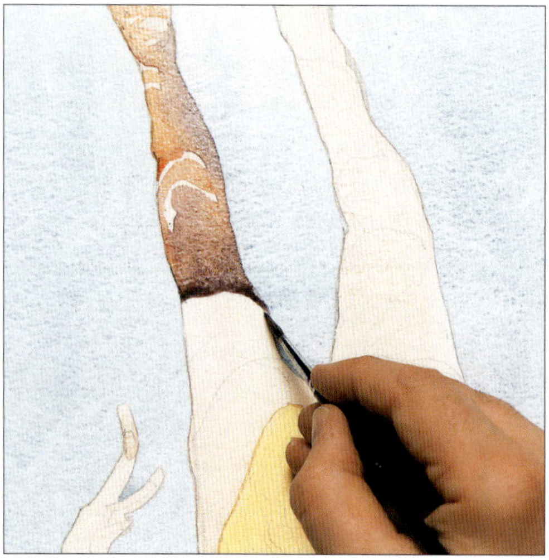

5 Mix three flesh tones from the following colours: alizarin crimson and cadmium lemon; alizarin crimson and a little cerulean blue; cadmium red and cadmium yellow. Dot a small amount of gum arabic into each mixture. Using a medium round brush and alternating between the three mixtures, start to paint over the girl's legs, leaving the base colour showing through in highlight areas. It doesn't matter too much which colour you use where, but try to reserve the darker mixtures for shadow areas.

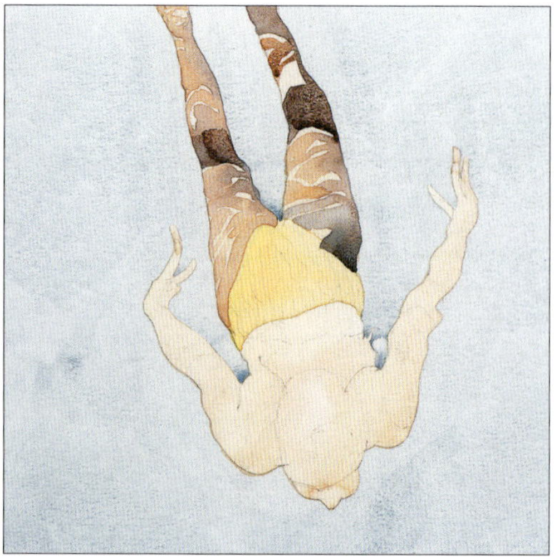

6 Continue in this way until you have finished painting the legs. Leave to dry.

Tip: Some of the washes may look very dark when you first apply them, but watercolour always dries to a slightly lighter tone. To be on the safe side, test your mixtures on a piece of scrap paper and leave to dry before applying them to the painting.

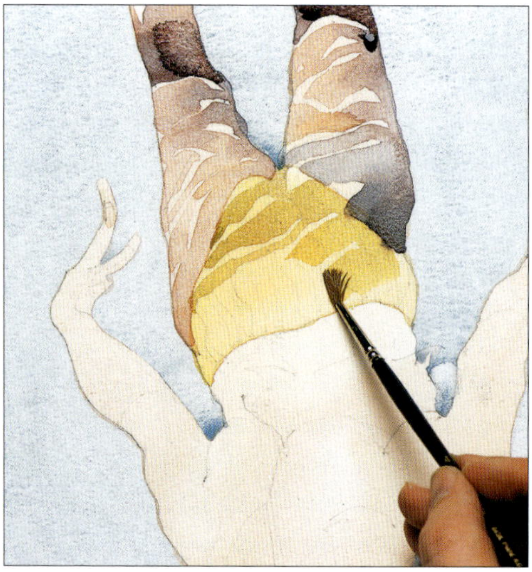

7 Mix a greenish yellow from cadmium lemon with a little Payne's grey. Using a small round brush, paint the ripples of light that run across the bikini bottoms.

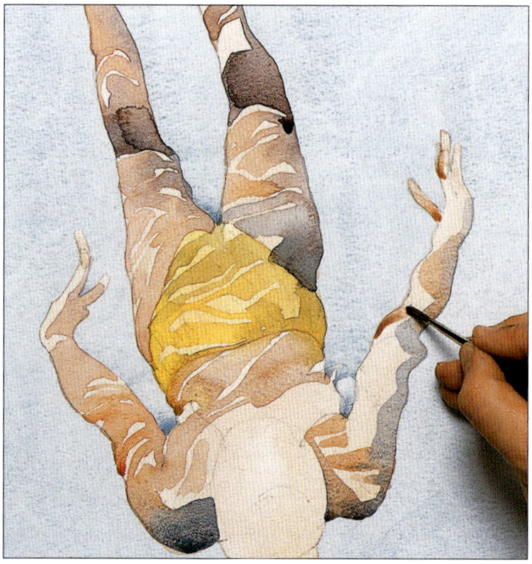

8 Using a small round brush and the same flesh tones that you mixed in Step 5, paint the girl's arms and back, leaving some of the underlying wash showing through.

Assessment time
The underpainting is almost complete. The figure stands out well against the pale blue background of the water and is starting to take on a three-dimensional quality. The next stage is to redefine the form by using slightly darker mixtures and to start to put in some of the details.

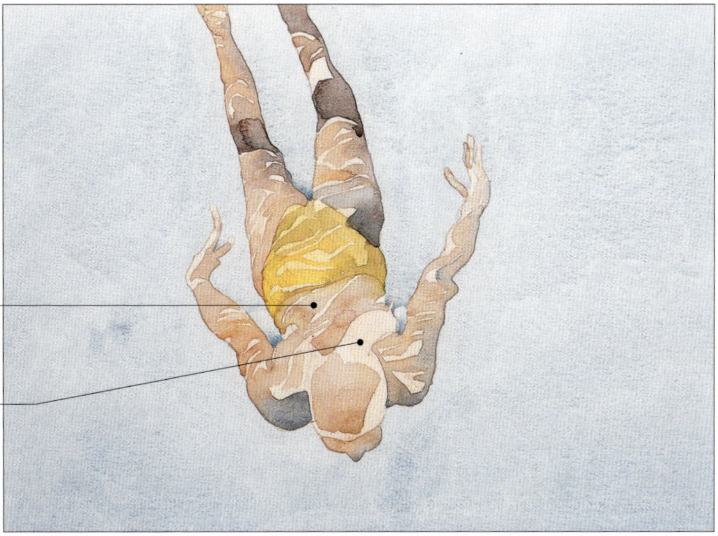

Varying the flesh tones gives the figure form.

The base colour alone is visible in the most strongly lit areas.

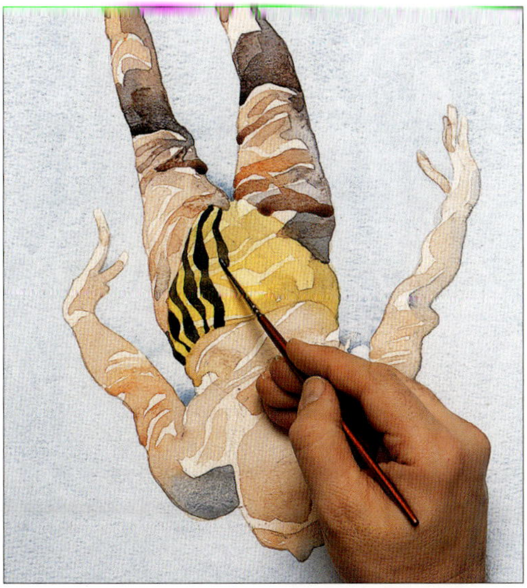

9 Mix slightly darker versions of the flesh tones used in Step 5 and work over the body again, in the same way as before. Mix a warm black from ivory black with a little Payne's grey and paint the stripes on the bikini bottoms. Note that the stripes are not straight lines. This is partly because the pattern is distorted by the way the light refracts from the water and partly because the fabric clings to the girl, helping to indicate the contours of her body.

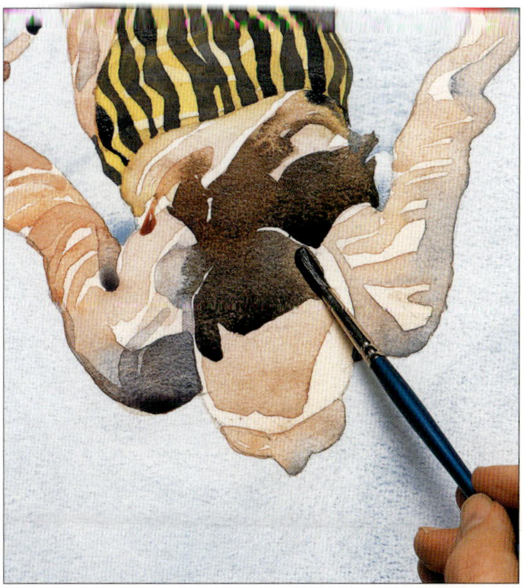

10 Mix a rich, dark brown from burnt sienna and burnt umber and, using a medium round brush, paint the girl's hair. Leave some areas unpainted and apply a second layer of colour in others so that the hair is not a solid mass of the same tone of brown.

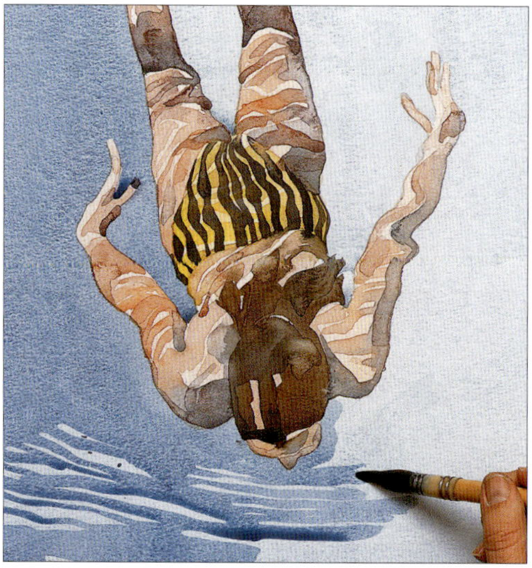

11 Mix a bright blue from cerulean blue and cobalt turquoise and, using a large round brush, begin to wash this mixture over the background. Leave some areas untouched in the top left-hand side, where sunlight dapples the water, and paint ripples in front of the girl's head to show how the water is displaced as she moves through it.

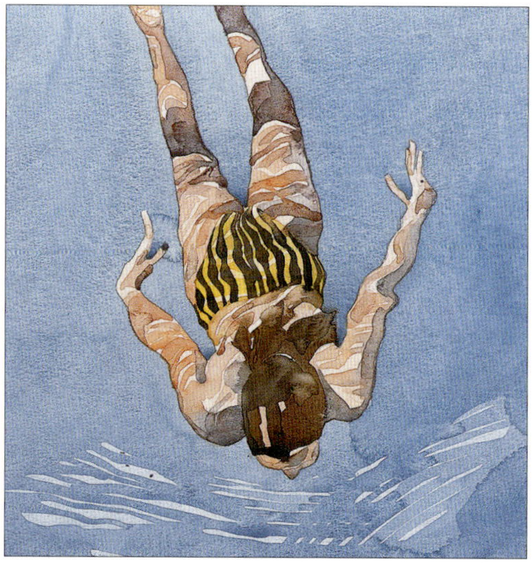

12 Continue working around the figure with the same blue mixture until you have been over the whole of the background. As in Step 4, you may find that you need to switch to a smaller brush in order to paint right up to the edge of the figure, as you must take care not to allow any of the blue mixture to spill over on to the figure. Leave to dry.

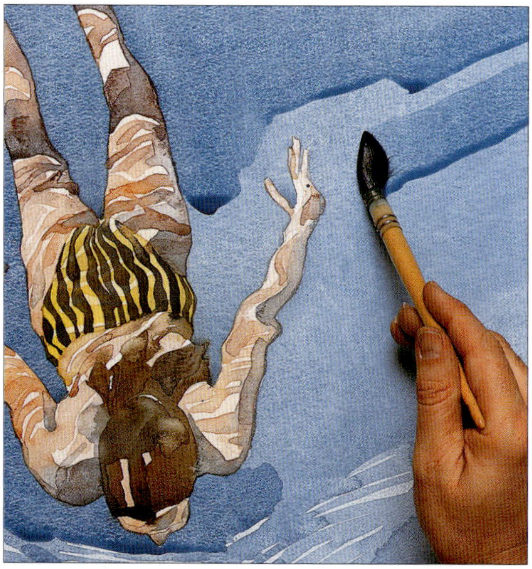

13 Mix a stronger version of the cerulean blue and cobalt turquoise mixture used in Step 11 and add a few drops of gum arabic. Paint over the background again, leaving a few spaces here and there to give the effect of dappled light. Leave to dry.

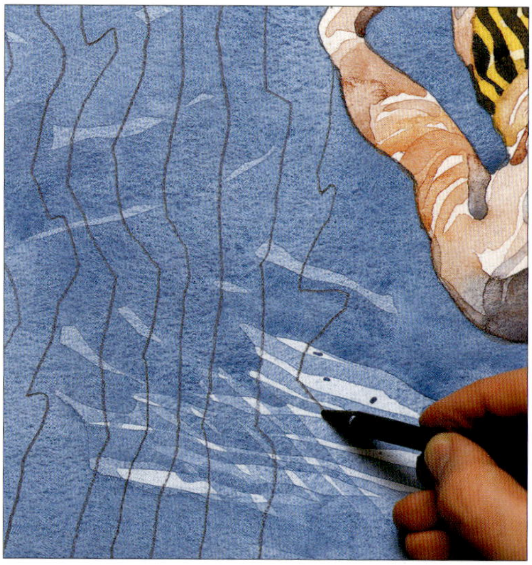

14 Using a 3B graphite stick, draw the lines of the tiles on the base of the pool. Note that, because of the way the light is refracted and the effects of perspective, the lines are not straight. The lines in the distance slope inwards because this area of the painting is further away from the viewer.

The swimmer

This is a graphic depiction of a swimmer slicing through water, the impression of speed reinforced by a deliberate distortion of her figure and the energetic ripples in front of her head. There is a wonderful feeling of light and warmth in this painting, achieved through the careful build-up of layers of colour.

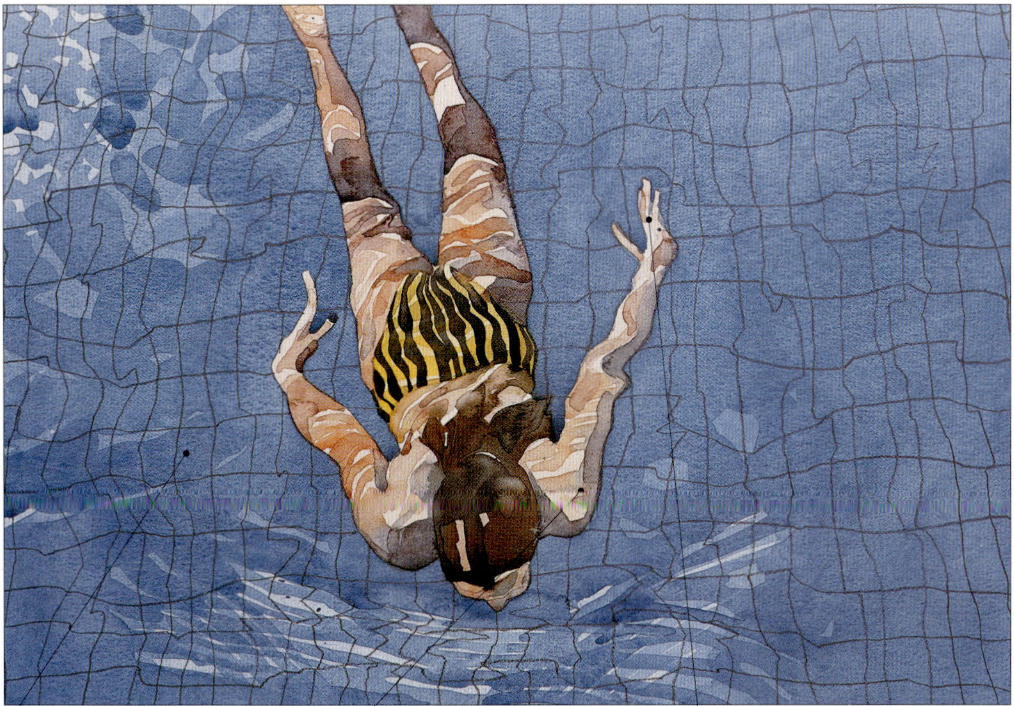

Because of the effects of perspective, the lines of the tiles slope inwards.

The effect of dappled sunlight is created by applying only one or two layers of colour to certain areas.

The swimmer's hands, arms and legs are slightly elongated, which helps to give the impression of movement.

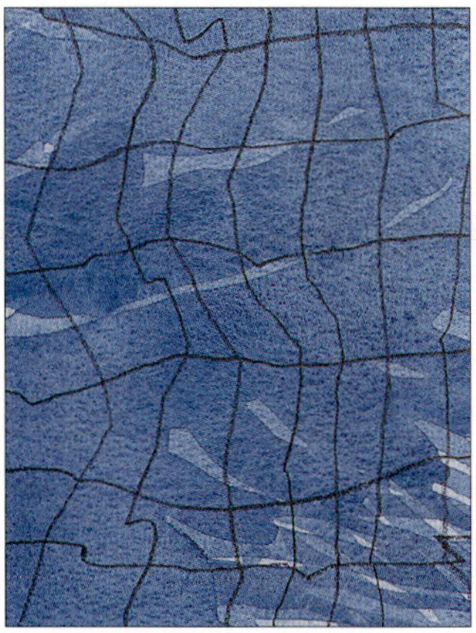

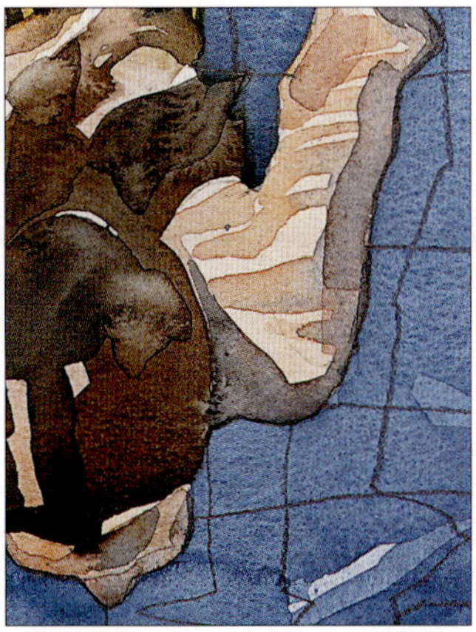

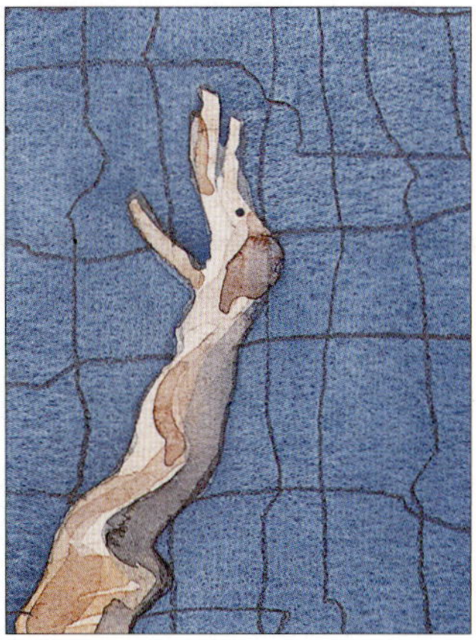

Seated figure in interior

Painting someone in a setting gives you the opportunity to say much more about them than you can in a straightforward head-and-shoulders portrait. For example, you might choose to include things that reveal something about your subject's interests – a keen musician with a guitar, perhaps, or an antiques collector surrounded by some of his or her most treasured possessions – or their work. In a domestic setting, the décor of the room itself is very often a reflection of your subject's tastes and personality.

The most important thing is not to allow the surroundings to dominate. The focus of the painting must remain on the person. This usually means that you have to deliberately subdue some of the detail around your subject, either by using muted or cool colours for the surroundings, so that your subject becomes more prominent, or, if the setting is very cluttered, by leaving some things out of your painting altogether.

Materials

- *3B pencil*
- *Rough watercolour board*
- *Watercolour paints: raw umber, alizarin crimson, cobalt blue, lemon yellow, phthalocyanine blue*
- *Brushes: medium flat, Chinese, fine round, old brush for masking*
- *Masking fluid*
- *Craft (utility) knife or scalpel*
- *Sponge*

Reference photographs

Here the artist used two photographs as reference – one for the seated, semi-silhouetted figure and one for the shaft of light that falls on the table top. Both photographs are dark and it is difficult to see much detail, but they show enough to set the general scene and give you scope to use your imagination. Instead of slavishly copying every last detail, you are free to invent certain aspects of the scene, or to embellish existing ones.

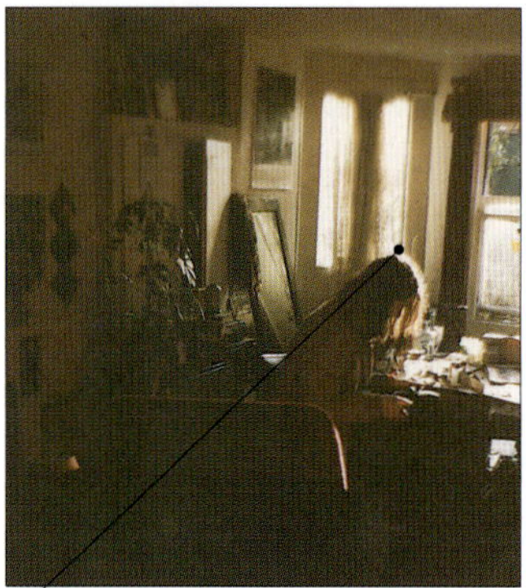

The highlight on the figure's hair is very atmospheric.

The shaft of bright sunlight illuminates part of the table top while almost everything else is in deep shade.

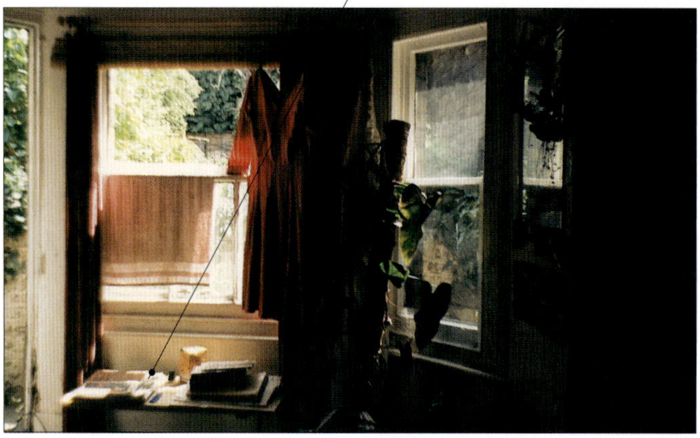

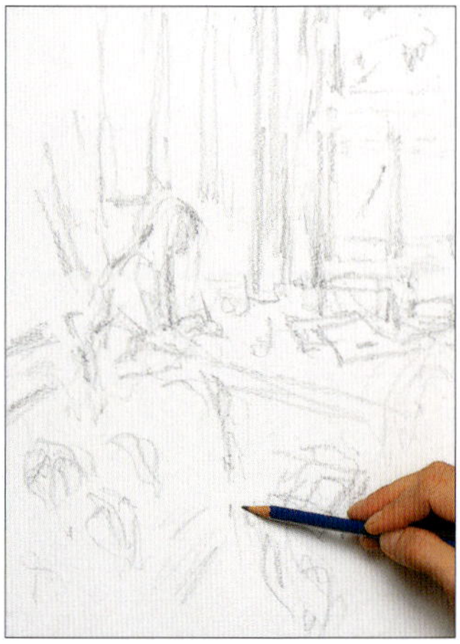

1 Using a 3B pencil, lightly sketch your subject, making sure you get the tilt of her head and the angles of the table, papers and books right.

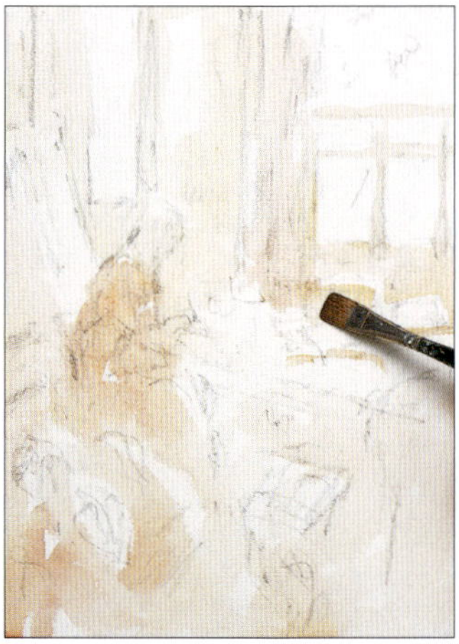

2 Mix a warm, pinky orange from raw umber and alizarin crimson. Using a medium flat brush, wash it over the background, avoiding the highlight areas on the window. Add more alizarin crimson to the mixture for the warmest areas, such as the girl's shirt and the left-hand side of the curtain, and more raw umber for the cooler areas, such as the wall behind the girl and the glazing bars on the window. Leave to dry.

3 Mix a very pale green from cobalt blue and lemon yellow and, using a Chinese brush, paint the lightest foliage shades outside the window, remembering to leave some white areas for the very bright sky beyond.

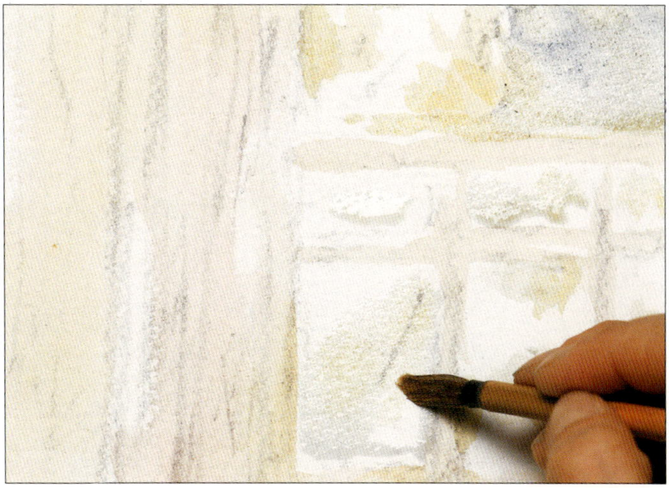

Tip: To enhance the impression of light coming through the window, take care not to paint foliage right up to the edge of the window frame.

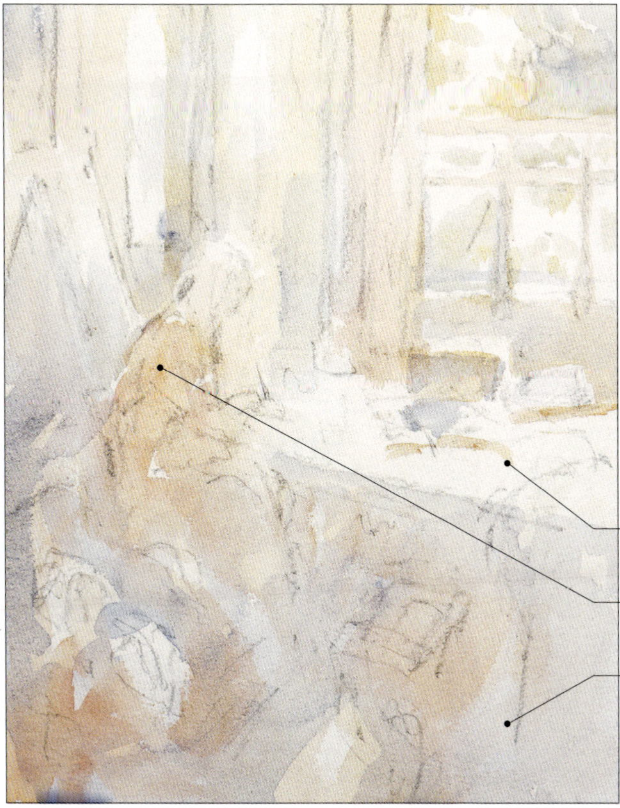

Assessment time

Mix a very pale blue from cobalt blue and a touch of raw umber and put in the cooler tones inside the room – the left-hand side, which the shaft of sunlight coming through the window doesn't reach, and the shadows under the table. Leave to dry.

You have now established the warm and cool areas of the painting, which you will build on in all the subsequent stages. Because of her position within the frame (roughly in the first third), the girl is the main focus of interest in the painting, even though she is largely in shadow. Keep this at the forefront of your mind as you begin to put in the detail and as you continually assess the compositional balance while painting.

This area is left unpainted, as it receives the most direct sunlight.

The warm colour of the girl's shirt helps to bring her forwards in the painting.

The shadow areas are the coolest in tone. They recede.

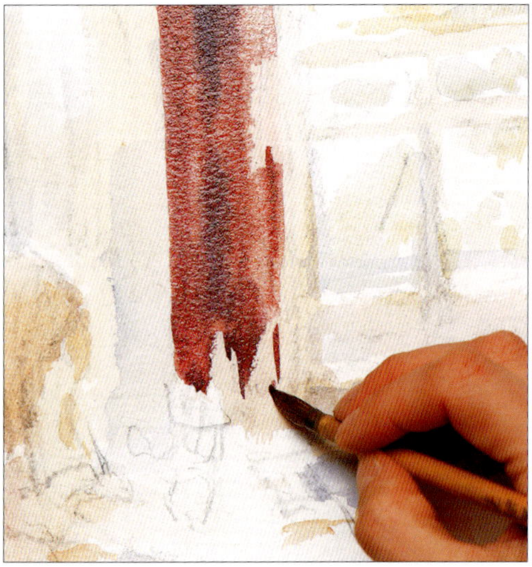

4 Mix a warm brown from alizarin crimson and raw umber and paint the girl's hair. Mix a rich red from alizarin crimson, cobalt blue and a little raw umber and, using a Chinese brush, paint the curtain. Apply several vertical brushstrokes to the curtain, wet into wet, to build up the tone and give the impression that it hangs in folds.

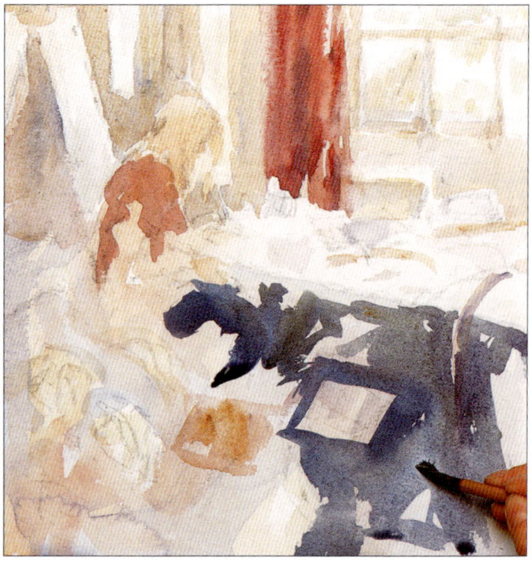

5 Using the same red mixture, paint the shoulders and back of the girl's shirt. Add more raw umber to the mixture and paint the shadow area between the wall and the mirror, immediately behind the girl. Mix a warm blue from phthalocyanine blue and a little alizarin crimson, and paint the dark area beneath the table using loose brushstrokes.

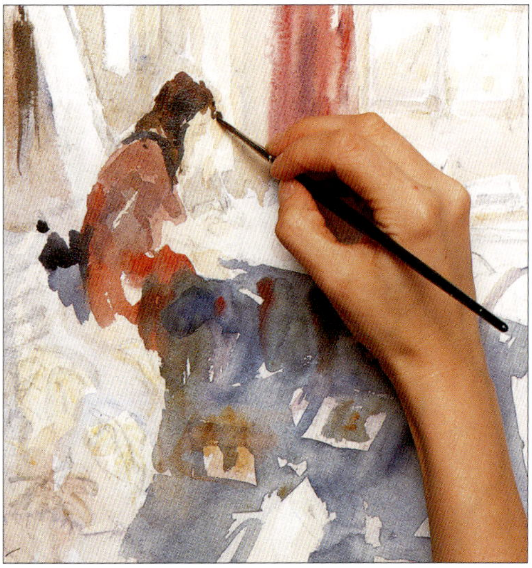

6 Using an old brush, "draw" the shapes of leaves in the bottom left-hand corner in masking fluid. Leave to dry. Mix a rich, dark brown from raw umber and a little alizarin crimson and, using a fine round brush, paint the darkest areas of the girl's hair.

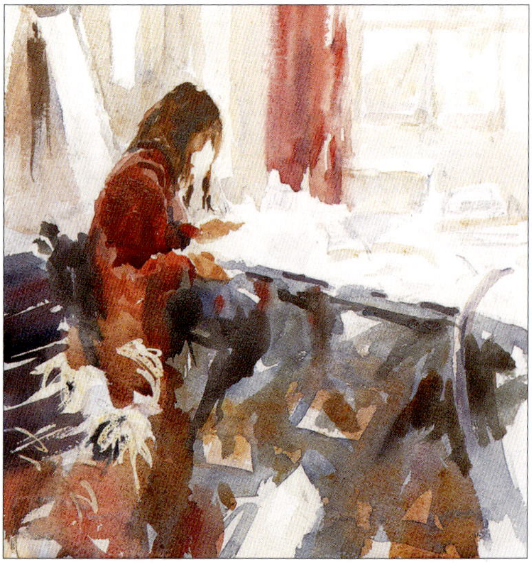

7 Add a little raw umber to the mixture for the lighter areas of hair around the face. Build up the shadow areas in the foreground of the scene, overlaying colours as before. Darken the girl's shirt in selected areas with the alizarin crimson, cobalt blue and raw umber mixture.

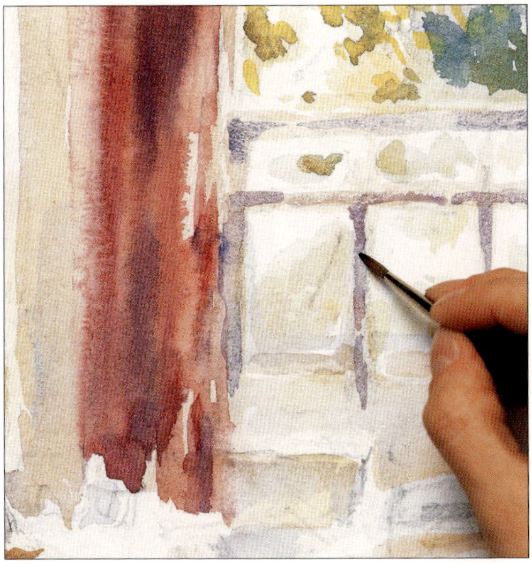

8 Mix a mid-toned green from phthalocyanine blue and lemon yellow and, using a fine round brush, dot this mixture into the foliage that can be seen through the right-hand side of the window. Mix a very pale purplish blue from pthalocyanine blue and a little alizarin crimson and darken the glazing bars of the window.

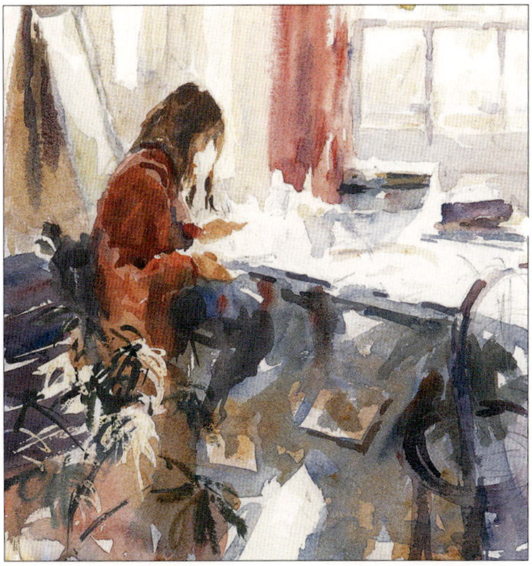

9 Paint the area under the window in a warm mixture of alizarin crimson and phthalocyanine blue. Mix a dark, olive green from raw umber and phthalocyanine blue and, making loose calligraphic strokes, paint the fronds of the foreground plant. Brush a very dilute version of the same mixture on to the lower part of the mirror. Build up the background tones.

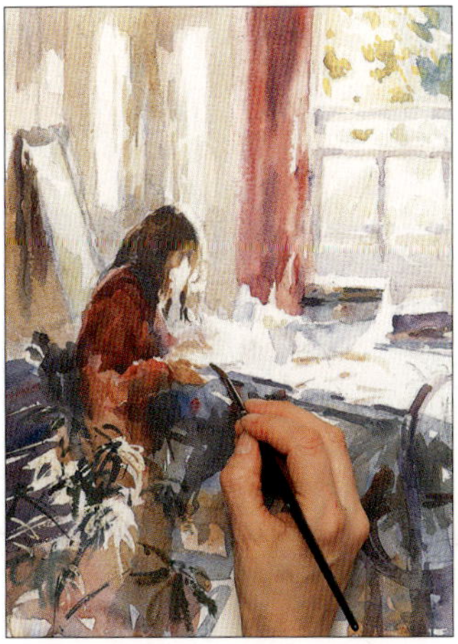

10 Mix a muted green from phthalocyanine blue and lemon yellow. Brush it over the background behind the girl. Because the green is relatively cool, it helps to separate the girl from the background. It also provides a visual link between this area and the foliage on the right.

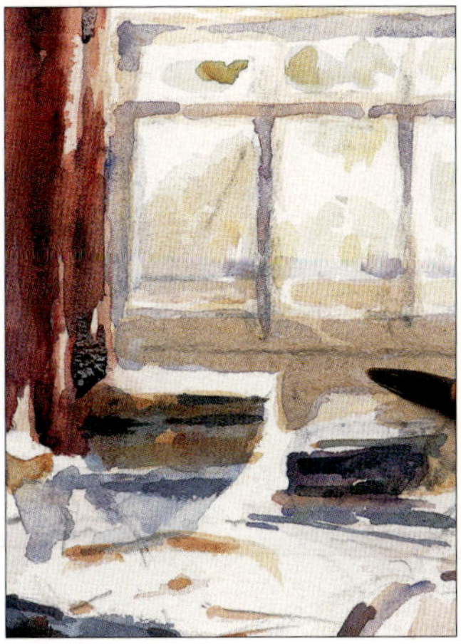

11 Paint a few vertical strokes on the curtain in a dark mixture of alizarin crimson and phthalocyanine blue. This helps to make the highlight on top of the pile of books stand out more clearly. Mix a warm brown from raw umber and phthalocyanine blue and paint under the window.

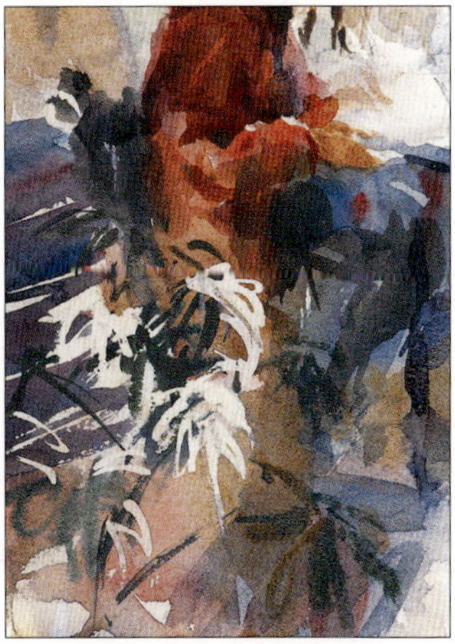

12 Rub off the masking fluid from the bottom left-hand corner. Continue building up the tones overall, using the same paint mixtures as before and loose, random brushstrokes to maintain a feeling of spontaneity.

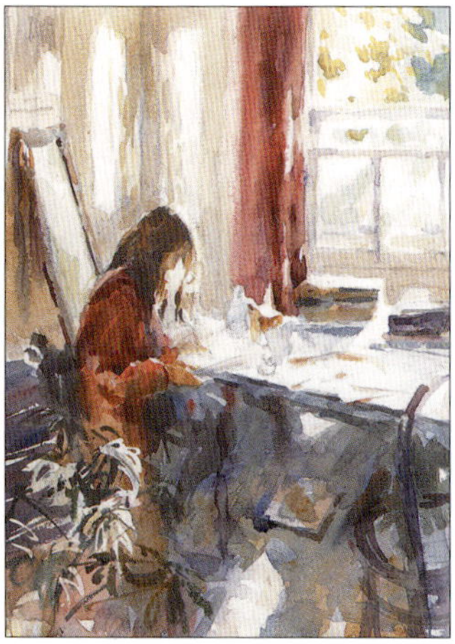

13 Mix a very pale wash of raw umber and lightly brush it on to some of the exposed areas in the bottom left-hand corner. Build up more dark tones in the foreground, using the same mixtures as before.

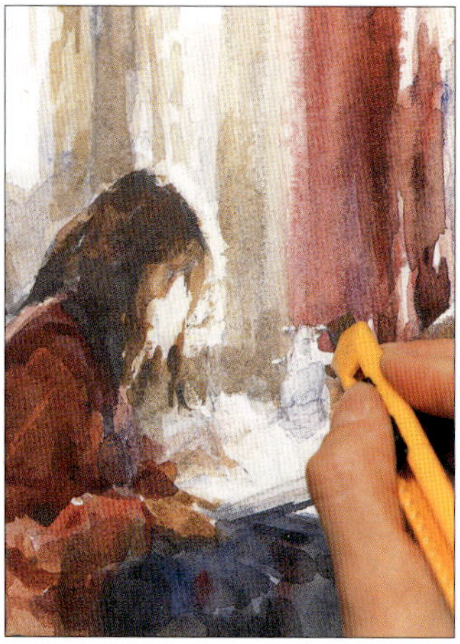

14 Using a craft (utility) knife or scalpel, carefully scratch off some of the highlights on the bottle on the table. Paint the wall behind the girl in a pale, olivey green mixture of raw umber and phthalocyanine blue.

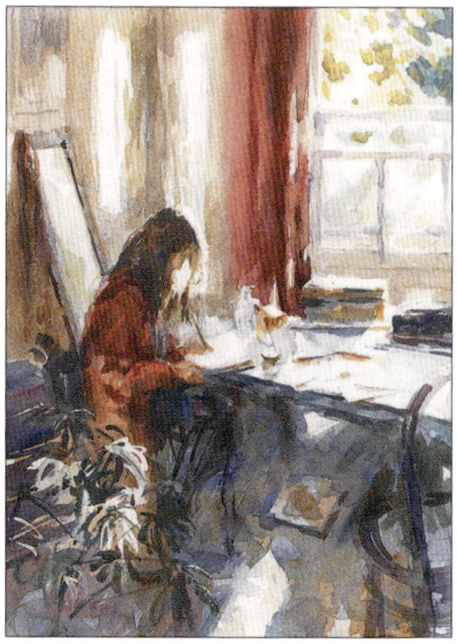

15 Brush a little very pale cobalt blue into the sky area so that this area does not look too stark and draw attention away from the main subject.

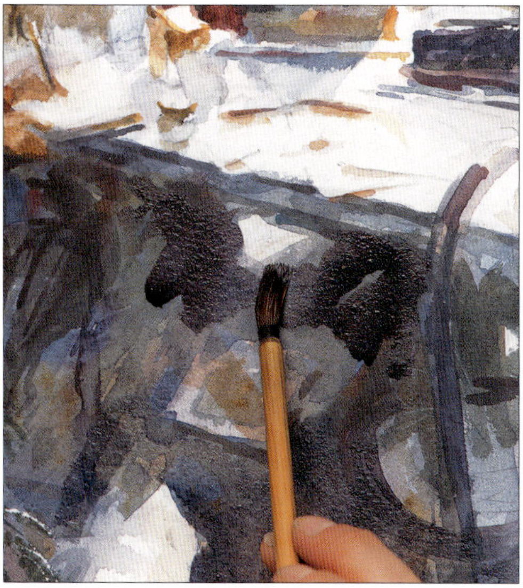

16 Continue building up tones by overlaying colours. Use very loose brushstrokes and change direction continually, as this helps to convey a feeling of the dappled light that comes through the window.

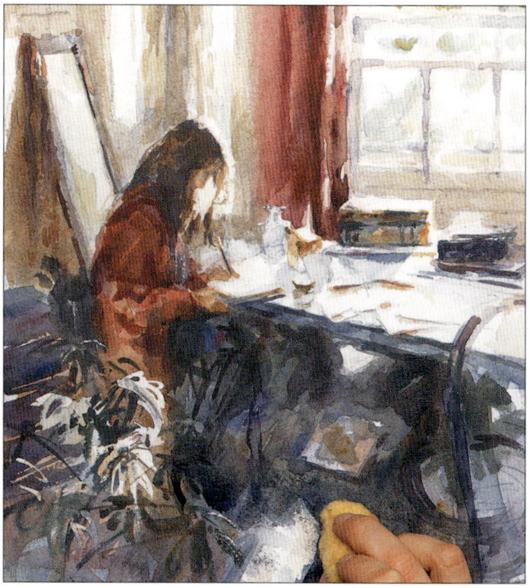

17 Using a 3B pencil, define the edges of the papers on the table. Mix a very pale wash of phthalocyanine blue and, using a fine round brush, carefully brush in shadows under the papers on the table to give them more definition. Dip a sponge in a blue-biased mixture of phthalocyanine blue and alizarin crimson and gently press it around the highlight area on the floor to suggest the texture of the carpet.

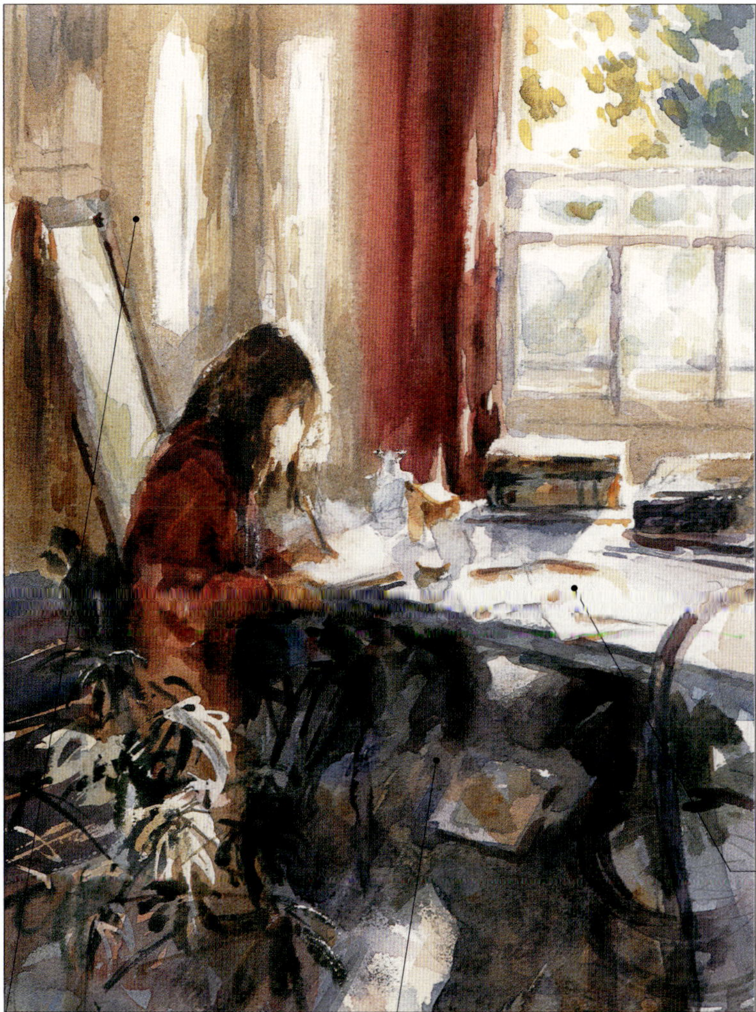

Seated figure in interior
There is a wonderful sense of light and shade in this painting, and the loose brushstrokes give a feeling of great freshness and spontaneity. The scene is beautifully balanced, both in terms of its distribution of colours and in the way that dark and light areas are counterposed.

Sunlight pours through the window, illuminating the books and papers. Much of this area is left unpainted.

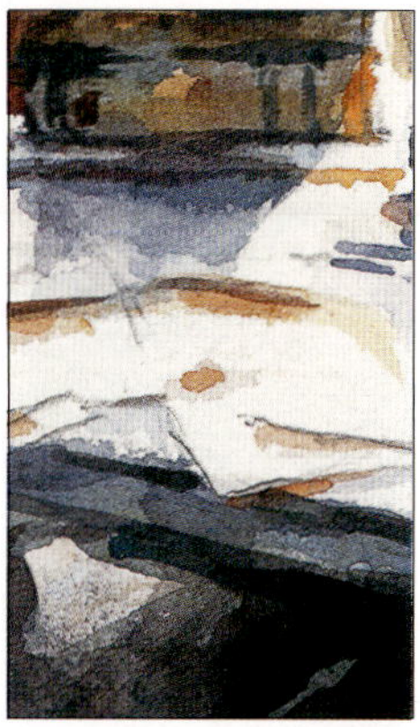

Pale, cool colours on the wall help to differentiate the girl from the background.

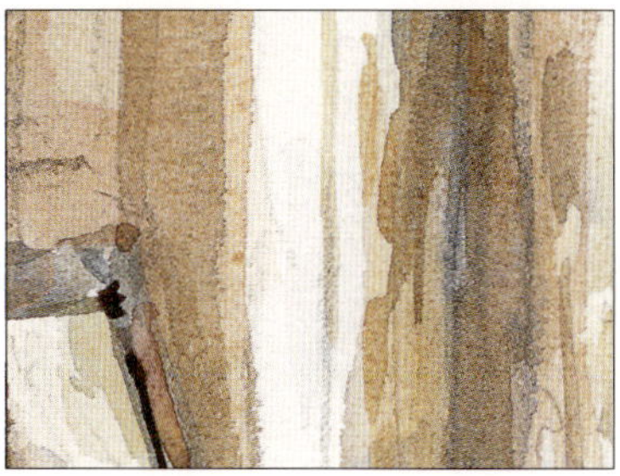

The foreground is loosely painted with overlayed colours, creating a feeling of spontaneity.

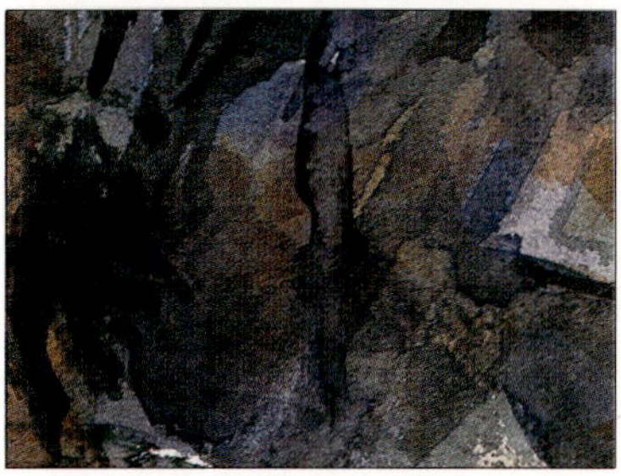

Indian market scene

Full of hustle and bustle, often packed with colourful displays of fruit, vegetables and other goods, street markets are a wonderful source of inspiration for artists – but with so much going on, it is often very difficult to work in situ. And even if you do manage to find a quiet spot to set up your easel, the chances are that you will soon find yourself surrounded by a crowd of curious onlookers, which can be somewhat intimidating.

This is one situation where it is useful to take reference photos, as you can work quickly and unobtrusively, and gather a whole wealth of material to paint from at a later date. Start with distant views and gradually move in closer to your chosen subject – and don't forget about things like advertisements, hand-written signs and unusual produce, all of which can add a lot of atmospheric local detail to your paintings.

If you want to take photographs of people, it is always best to ask their permission, although this does bring with it the risk that your subjects will start playing up to the camera. If this happens, take a few "posed" shots first and then, when they have turned back to their business, take a few more. Another good tip is to set your camera on its widest setting and point it slightly to one side of the person you are photographing. You will appear to be looking somewhere else, but the camera's field of view will be wide enough to include them in the frame, too. Above all, don't stint on the number of shots you take: film is inexpensive and if you've got a digital camera, there are no processing costs at all.

Materials

- *4B pencil*
- *90lb (185gsm) rough watercolour paper, pre-stretched*
- *Watercolour paints: indigo, alizarin crimson, raw umber, cobalt turquoise, cadmium red, Hooker's green, cadmium yellow, burnt umber, cobalt blue*
- *Gouache paints: Bengal rose, permanent white*
- *Brushes: Chinese, fine round*
- *Household candle*

Reference photographs

Here the artist used two photographs. The one on the right shows the corner of the stall and the stallholder selling his wares, and the one below shows the two ladies shopping and rows of colourful bowls of powdered dyes. In her compositional sketch, the artist angled the bowls to provide a more gentle lead-in to the picture.

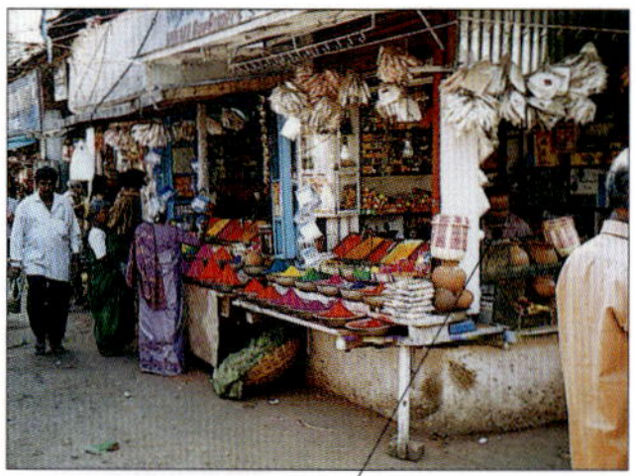

The stallholder is just visible. He will be more prominent in the painting.

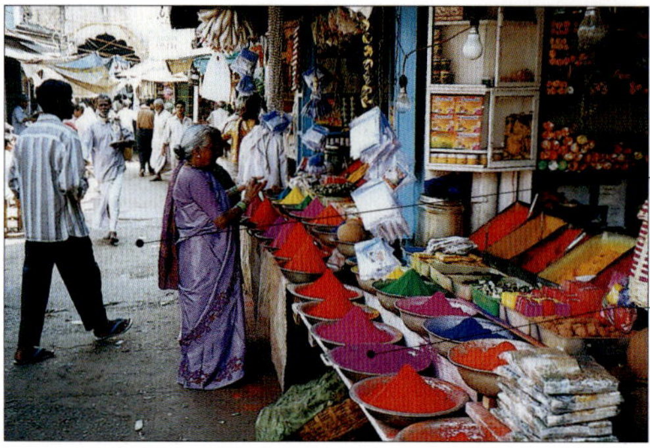

There is nothing of interest in this area.

A more gentle lead-in will be provided if the bowls start in the bottom right corner of the image.

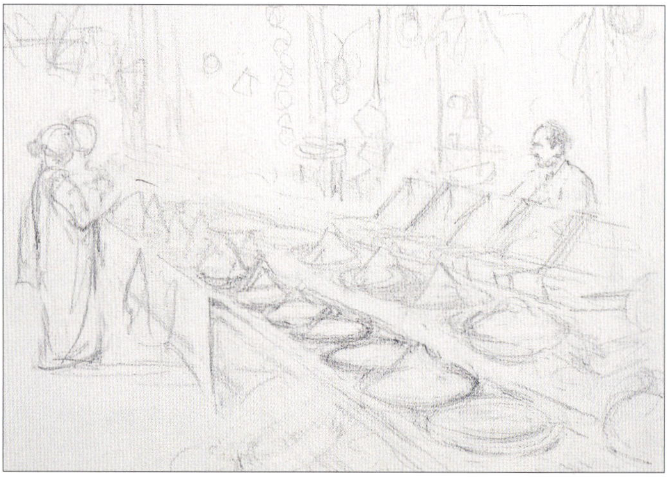

1 Using a 4B pencil, sketch the subject, taking care to get the perspective right. Note how the bowls of powder get smaller and closer together as they recede into the distance.

Tip: To make it easier to get the shapes of the bowls of powder right, think of them as simple geometric shapes – ovals with rough triangular shapes on top.

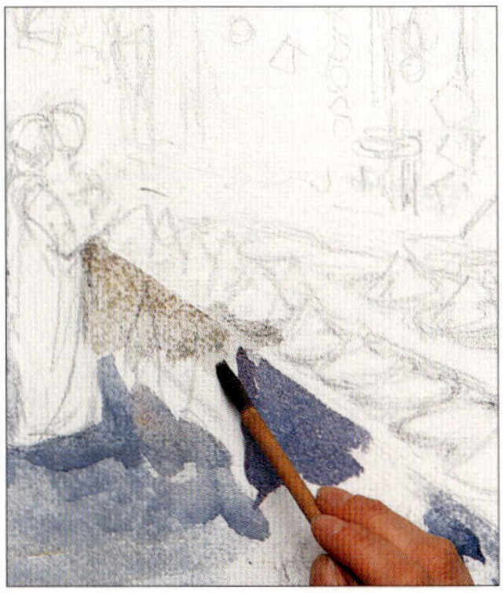

2 Mix a warm, greyish blue from indigo, alizarin crimson and a little raw umber and start putting in the cool background colours. Paint the area of deepest shade under the table, adding more raw umber to the mixture for the pavement area. This neutral background will help to unify the painting. With so many vibrant colours in the scene, the overall impact could easily be overwhelming.

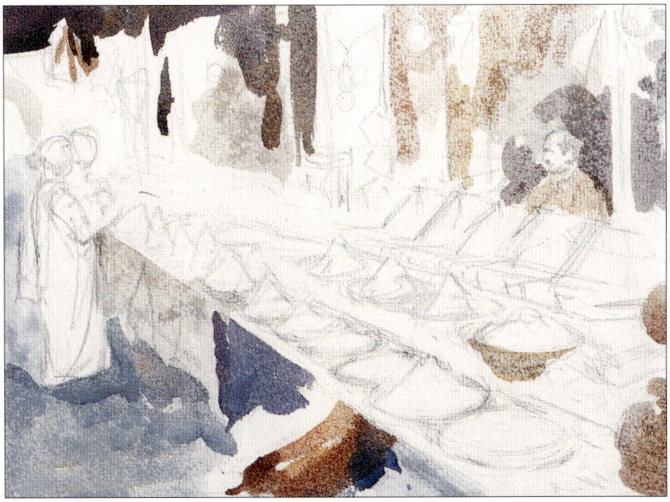

3 Add more alizarin crimson to the mixture to make a darker, brown colour and brush in the shadows under the bowls and the wooden vertical supports of the shelves in the background. Use a paler version of the mixture to paint the stallholder's shirt and a darker one to paint the background of the more distant stall and the area immediately behind the stallholder's head. Filling in the negative spaces in this way makes it easier to see what it is happening in such a complicated scene.

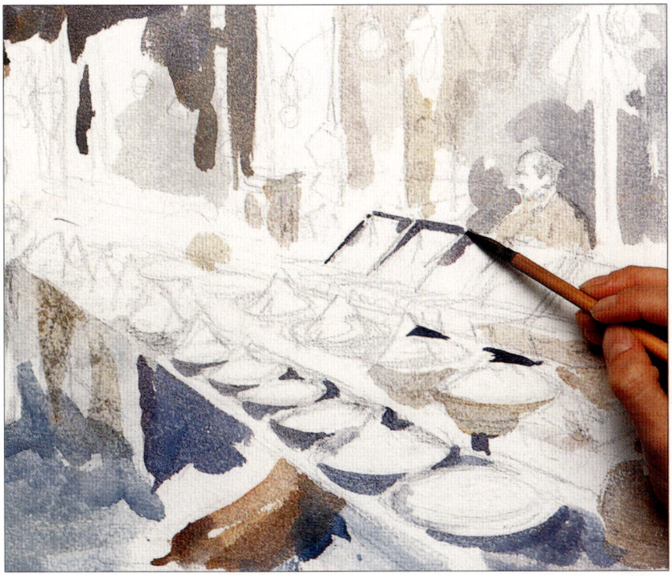

4 Mix a warm shadow colour from indigo with a tiny amount of alizarin crimson and paint the shadows under the steel bowls, taking care to leave highlights on the rims. Use the same mixture to paint lines in between the oblong dishes of powder in the background.

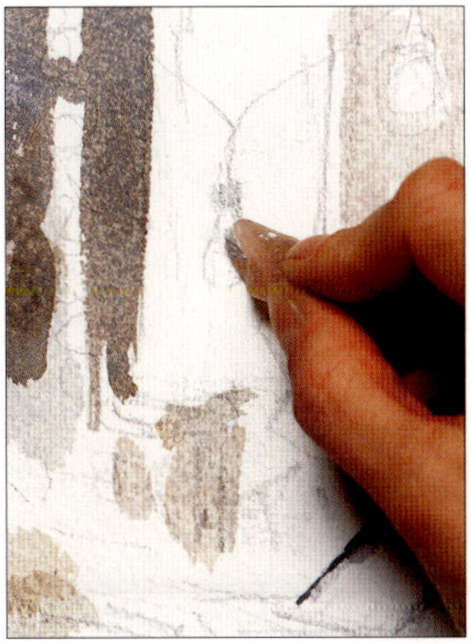

5 Using an ordinary household candle, stroke candle wax over the lightbulbs. Press firmly so that enough of the wax adheres to the paper. The wax will act as a resist. The white paper will show through in places, while other areas will take on the surrounding colour, as if that colour is reflected in the glass of the bulb.

Assessment time

Using the same basic mixtures as before, continue putting in some background colours and the shadows under the bowls. The basis of the background is now complete, both tonally and compositionally.

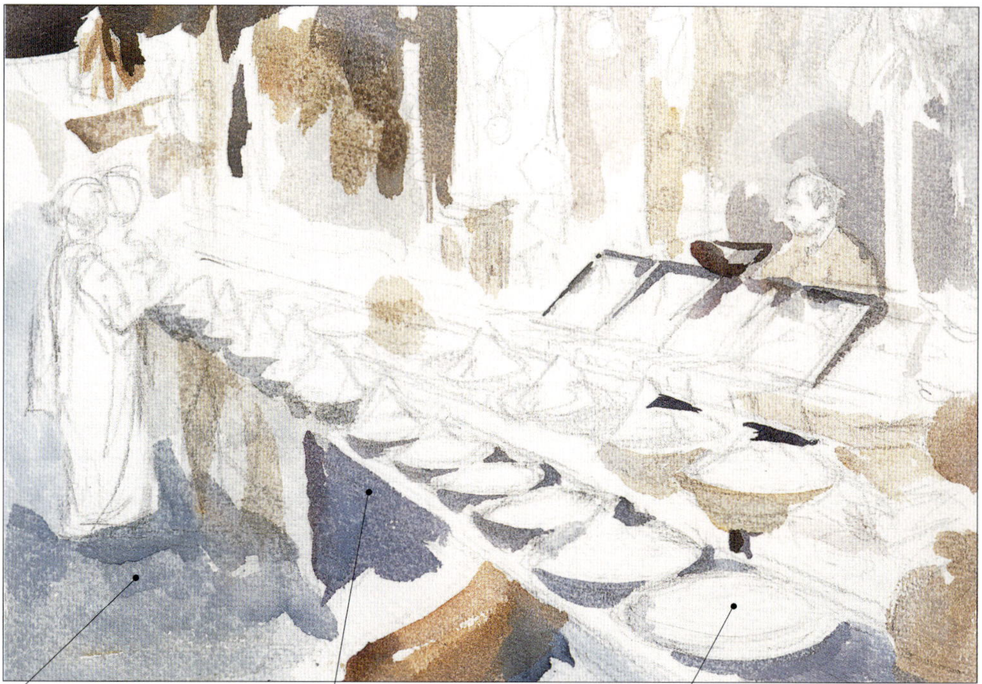

Blocking in the negative spaces makes it easier to see what is happening in the rest of the scene.

We "read" this shaded area as being on a different plane to the stall top, which is in bright sunlight.

Although the bowls are empty at this stage, their shapes and shadows are clearly established.

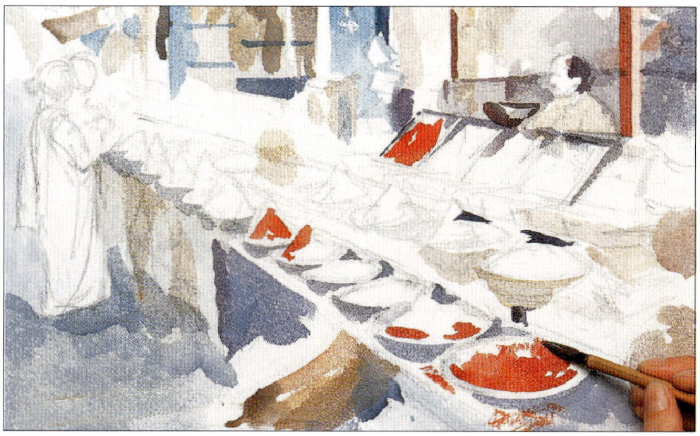

6 Mix a warm, purplish black from alizarin crimson and indigo and paint the stallholder's hair. Mix cadmium red with alizarin crimson and paint the wooden support on the right-hand edge of the foreground stall. Drybrush a little of the same colour on to the stall top, where powder has been spilt, and start putting the same colour into the bowls of powder. Paint cobalt turquoise on the walls at the far end.

Tip: While you have one colour mix on your palette, see where else you can use it in the painting.

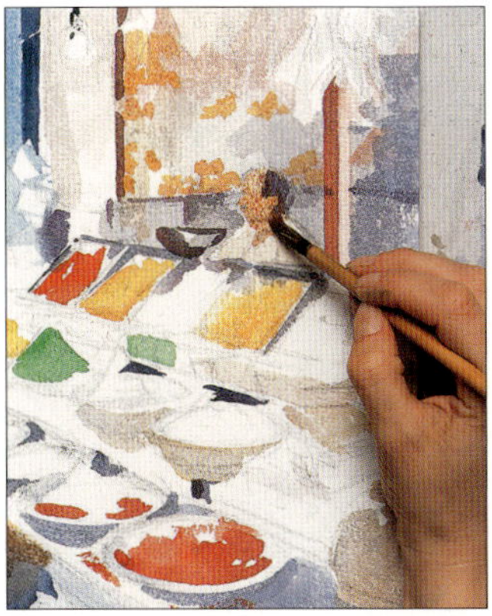

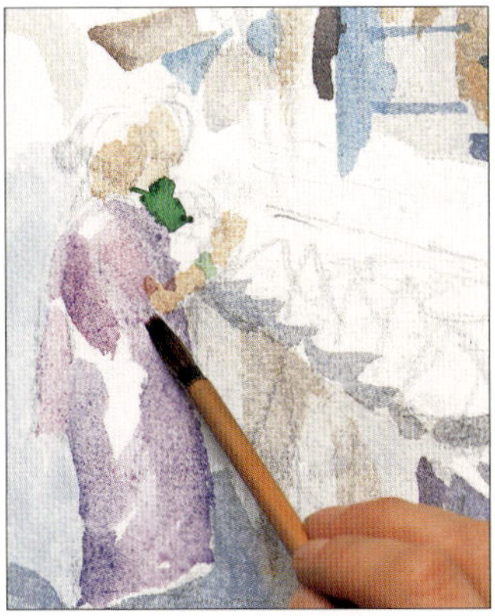

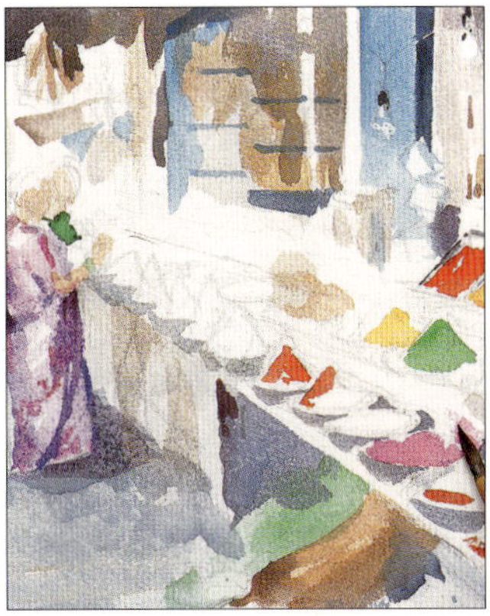

7 Mix a wash of Hooker's green and paint the green plastic that covers the basket on the ground and the mounds of green powder. Mix a warm orange from cadmium red and cadmium yellow and dot the mixture into the background immediately behind the stallholder to indicate the packages on sale. (A hint of the basic shape and colour is sufficient.) Add a little burnt umber to the orange mixture and paint the stallholder's face.

8 Paint the women's skin tones in the same orangey-brown mixture. Mix a strong purple from Bengal rose gouache and cobalt blue watercolour and paint the sari worn by the woman in the foreground, leaving a few highlight areas untouched.

9 Using the same mixture and a fine round brush, paint the creases in the sari, adding more cobalt blue to the mixture for the very darkest creases. By darkening the tones in this way, you will begin to imply the folds in the fabric. Mix a dark purple from Bengal rose, alizarin crimson and a little indigo and dot in the pattern on the sari. Mix Bengal rose with a tiny amount of cobalt blue and paint the mounds of very bright pink powder.

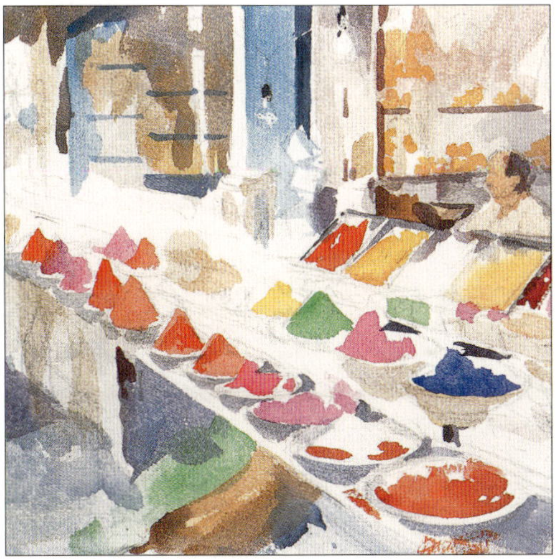

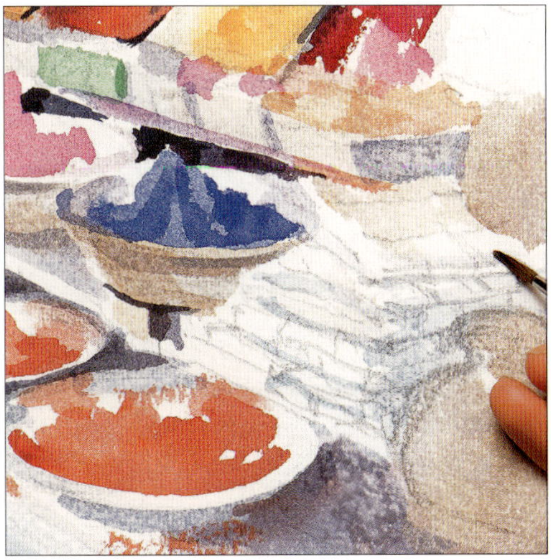

10 Continue painting the powders, mixing cadmium red with Bengal rose for the red powders and using cobalt blue for the blue ones. Don't worry too much about the shapes of the mounds at this stage. This will become clearer as you build up the tones later on.

11 Build up the tones on the powders, using the same mixtures as before. Using a 4B pencil, draw the lines of the plastic-wrapped packages on the corner of the stall. Mix a pale wash of cobalt turquoise and brush over the lines, using a fine round brush.

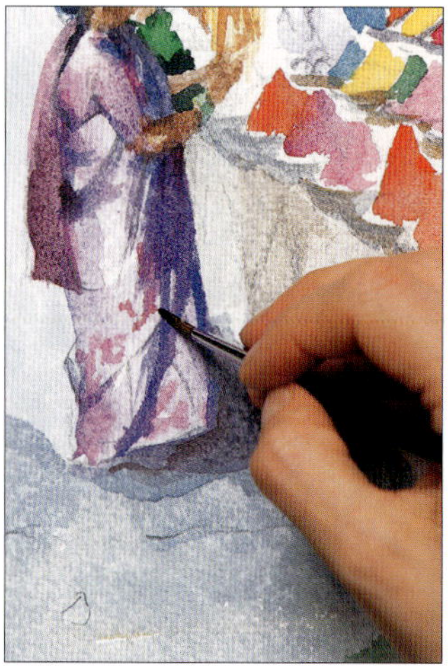

12 Mix a dark purple colour from Bengal rose, alizarin crimson and a little indigo. Using a fine round brush, accentuate the creases in the sari fabric in the same colour.

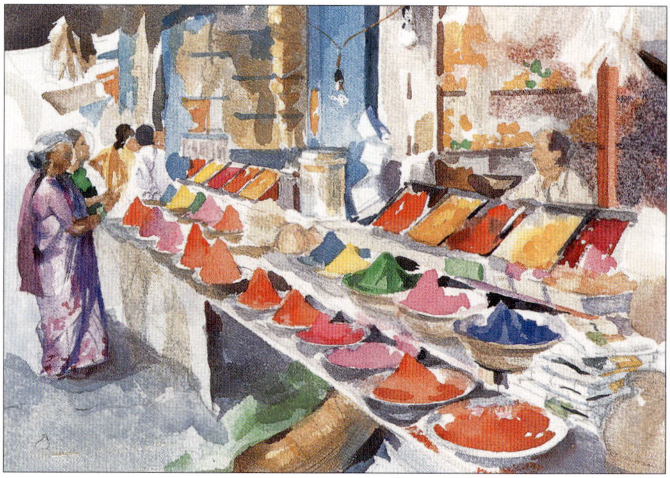

13 Using a mixture of alizarin crimson and indigo, paint around the stallholder. Darkening the background in this way helps to make him stand out from his surroundings. Use the same alizarin crimson and indigo mixture to strengthen the shadows on the right-hand side of the stall.

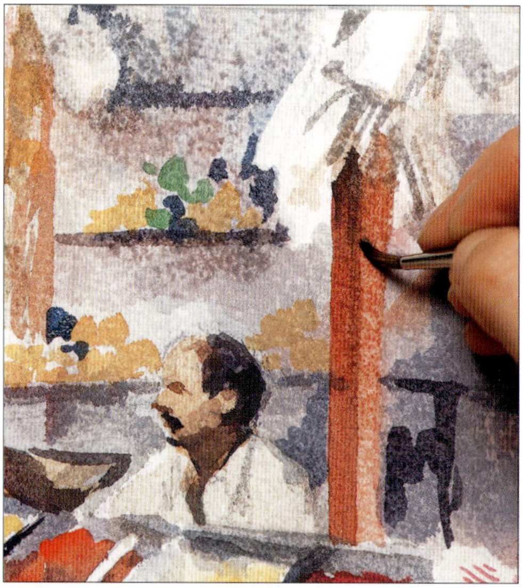

14 By this stage, all you need to do is refine some of the details. Mix a rich, brownish black from alizarin crimson, indigo and cadmium red and darken the stallholder's hair. Darken his skin tones with a more dilute version of the same mixture. Paint the stripes on the colourful woven basket in Bengal rose gouache and darken the tones on the wooden posts of the stall.

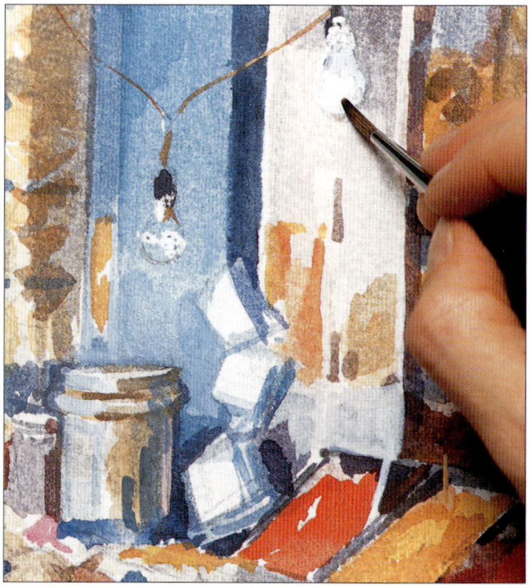

15 Tone down the brightness of the paper, where necessary, with very pale washes of the background colours. Paint the highlights on the lightbulbs in permanent white gouache.

Indian market scene

Here, the artist has created a lively interpretation of a busy market, packed with colourful sights and people going about their daily business. The composition is much more satisfactory than that of the original reference photographs. The line of bowls leads diagonally through the image to the two women, while the stallholder is positioned near enough to the intersection of the thirds to provide a secondary focus of interest for the painting.

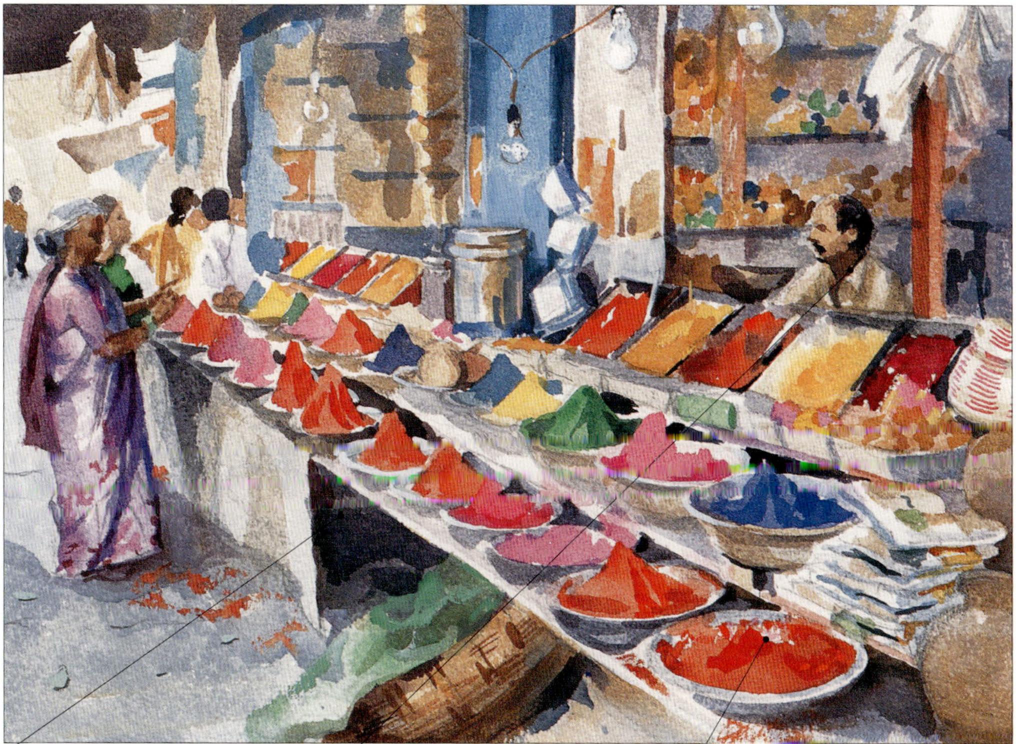

The contrast between light and dark areas establishes the different planes of the image.

The stallholder's direct gaze encourages us to follow his line of sight across the scene to the two women.

The indentations in the mounds of powder are skilfully conveyed by applying more layers of colour to the darker, shaded areas.

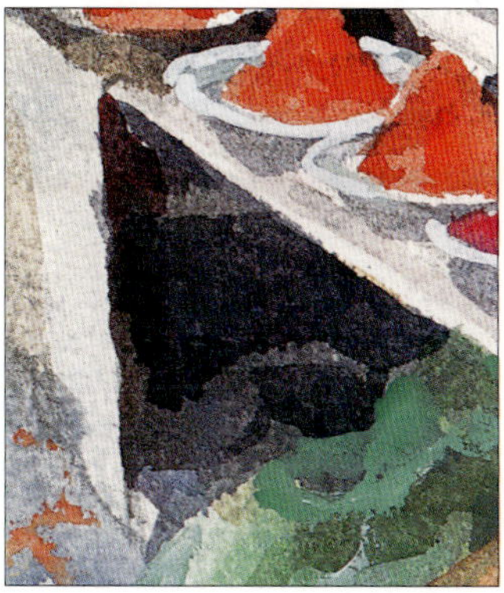

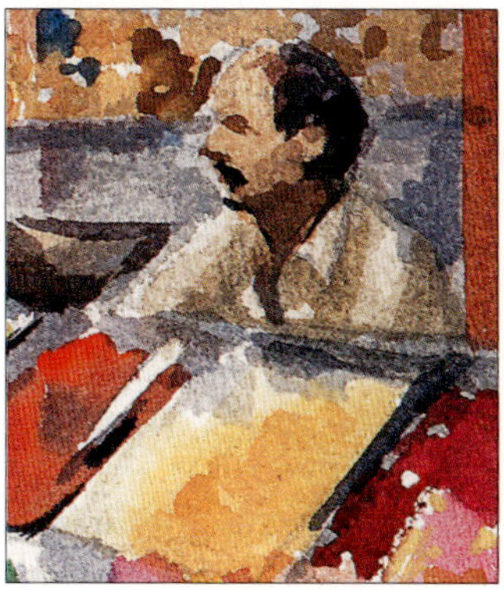

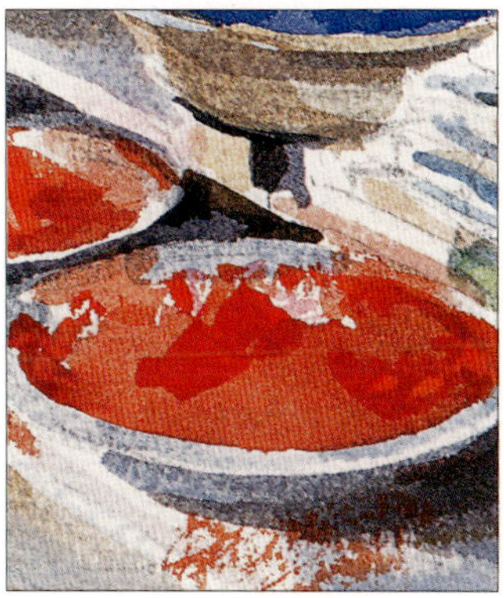

Glossary

Additive
A substance added to paint to alter characteristics such as the paint's drying time and viscosity. Gum arabic is a commonly used additive in watercolour painting.

Body colour
Opaque paint, such as gouache, which can obliterate underlying paint colour on the paper.

Colour
Complementary: colours that lie opposite one another on the colour wheel.
Primary: a colour that cannot be produced by mixing other colours, but can only be manufactured. Red, yellow and blue are the three primary colours.
Secondary: a colour produced by mixing equal amounts of two primary colours.
Tertiary: a colour produced by mixing equal amounts of a primary colour and the secondary colour next to it on the colour wheel.

Composition
The way in which the elements of a drawing or painting are arranged within the picture space. The composition does not need to be true to real life.

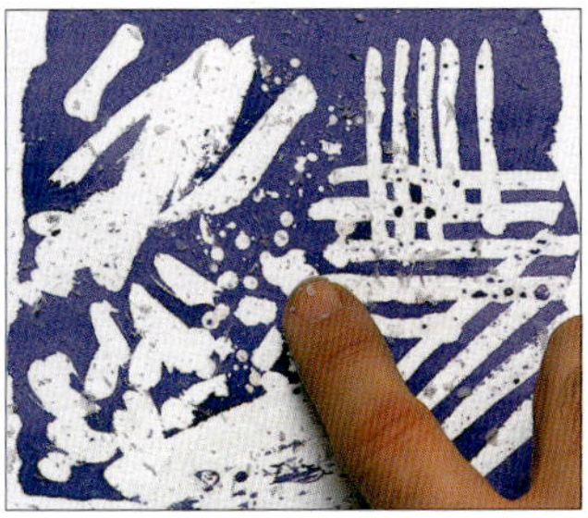

Closed composition: one in which the eye is held deliberately within the picture area.
Open composition: one that implies that the subject or scene continues beyond the confines of the picture area.

Drybrush
The technique of dragging an almost dry brush, loaded with very little paint, across the surface of the paper to make textured marks.

Format
The shape of a painting. The most usual formats are landscape (a painting that is wider than it is tall) and portrait (a painting that is taller than it is wide), but panoramic (long and thin) and square formats are also common.

Gouache
see also Body colour.

Ground
The prepared surface on which an artist works. *See also* Support.

Highlight
The point on an object where light strikes a reflective surface. In watercolour painting, highlights are often left as white paper.

Hue
A colour in its pure state, unmixed with any other.

Line and wash
The technique of combining watercolour washes with pen-and-ink work.

Mask
Any substance that is applied

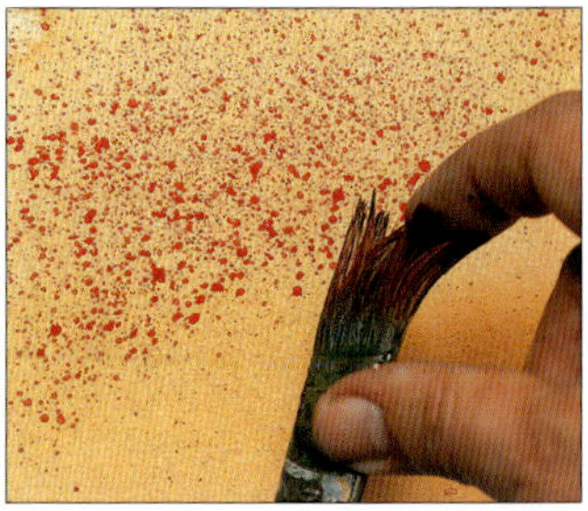

to paper to prevent paint from reaching specific areas. Unlike resists, masks can be removed when no longer required. There are three materials used for masking – masking tape, masking fluid and masking film – although, depending on the techniques you are using and the effect you want to create, you can simply cover up the relevant part of the painting by placing a piece of paper over it.

Overlaying
The technique of applying layers of watercolour paint over washes that have already dried in order to build up colour to the desired strength.

Palette
(1) In watercolour painting, a ceramic or plastic container in which paint colours are mixed.
(2) The range of colours used by an artist.

Pan
A small, rectangular container in which watercolour paint is sold.

Paper
The commonly used support for watercolour paintings.
HP (hot-pressed): The smoothest type of watercolour paper. HP paper is particularly good for fine brushwork.

NOT: This shortened name stands for "not hot-pressed". It is a slightly textured paper.
Rough: The most textured type of watercolour paper.
Tinted: Although watercolour paper is normally white, tinted watercolour paper is available in a small range of pale colours.
Weight: The weight of a paper is normally given in pounds per ream (a ream being 500 sheets) or grams per square metre. The heavier the watercolour paper, the more water it can absorb. Papers under 140lb (300gsm) need to be stretched before use to prevent them buckling when water is applied.

Perspective

A system whereby artists can create the illusion of three-dimensional space on the two-dimensional surface of the paper.
Aerial perspective: the way the atmosphere, combined with distance, influences the appearance of things. This is also known as atmospheric perspective.
Linear perspective: linear perspective exploits the fact that objects appear to be smaller the further away they are from the viewer. The system is based on the fact that all parallel lines, when extended from a receding surface, meet at a point in space known as the vanishing point. When such lines are plotted accurately on the paper, the relative sizes of objects will appear correct in the painting.

Resist

A substance that prevents one medium from touching the paper beneath it. Wax (in the form of candle wax or wax crayons) is the resist most commonly used in watercolour painting; it works on the principle that wax repels water.

Sgraffito

The technique of scratching off paint to reveal either an underlying paint colour or the white of the paper. The word comes from the Italian verb *graffiare*, which means "to scratch".

Shade

A colour that has been darkened by the addition of black or a little of its complementary colour.

Spattering

The technique of flicking paint on to the paper to create texture.

Sponging

The technique of applying colour to the paper with a sponge, rather than with a brush, in order to create a textured appearance.

Stippling

The technique of applying dots of colour to the paper, using just the tip of the brush.

Support

The surface on which a painting is made (normally paper in watercolour painting).

Tint

A colour that has been lightened. In pure watercolour, a colour is lightened by by adding water to the paint.

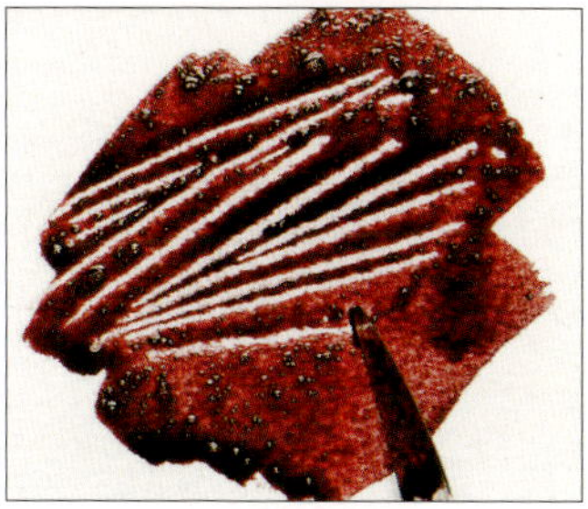

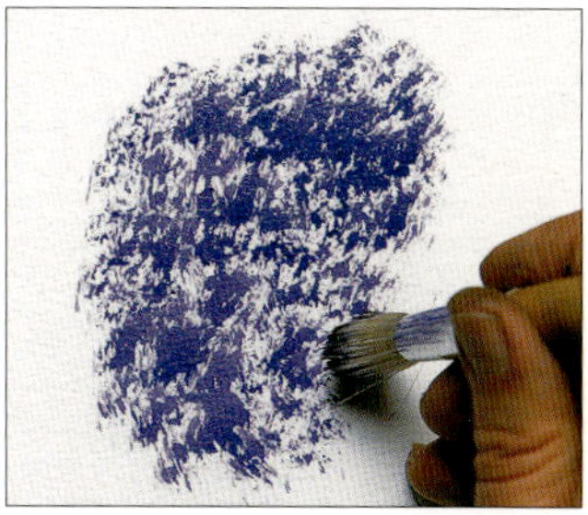

Tone

The relative lightness or darkness of a colour.

Underdrawing

A drawing made as a guide to where to apply the paint.

Wash

A thin layer of transparent paint that usually covers a large area of the painting.
Flat wash: an evenly laid wash that exhibits no variation in tone.
Gradated wash: a wash that gradually changes in intensity from dark to light or (less commonly) vice versa.
Variegated wash: a wash that changes from one paint colour to another.

Wet into wet

The technique of applying paint on to wet paper or on top of an earlier wash that is still damp.

Wet on dry

The technique of applying paint to dry paper or on top of an earlier wash that has dried completely.

Suppliers

Manufacturers

If you are unable to find what you want in your local art shop, the leading manufacturers of paints, papers and brushes should be able to supply you with details of stockists in your area.

Daler-Rowney UK Ltd
PO Box 10
Bracknell
Berkshire RG12 8ST
United Kingdom
Tel: (01344) 424621
Website: www.daler-rowney.com

Winsor & Newton
Whitefriars Avenue
Wealdstone
Harrow
Middlesex HA3 5RH
United Kingdom
Tel: (020) 8427 4343
Website: www.winsornewton.com

H. Schmincke & Co.
Otto-Hahn-Strasse 2
D-40699 Erkrath
Germany
Tel: (0211) 2509-0
Fax: (0211) 2509-461
Website: www.schmincke.de

Stockists

UNITED KINGDOM
ABS Brushes
Wetley Abbey, Wetley Rocks
Staffordshire ST9 0AS
Tel: (01782) 551551
Fax: (01782) 551661
Email: abs.brushes@btinternet.com
Website: www.absbrushes.com
(Brushes only)

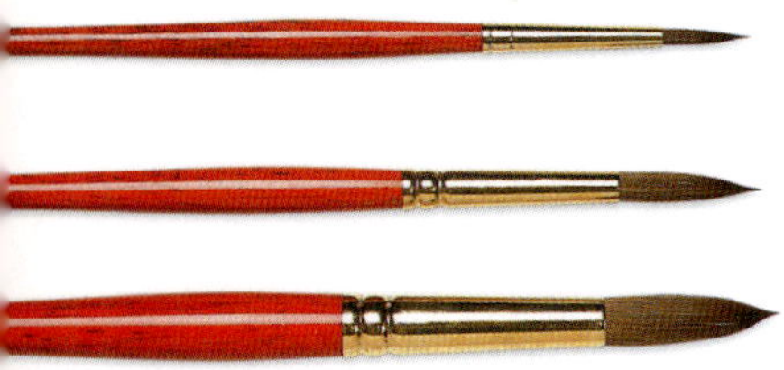

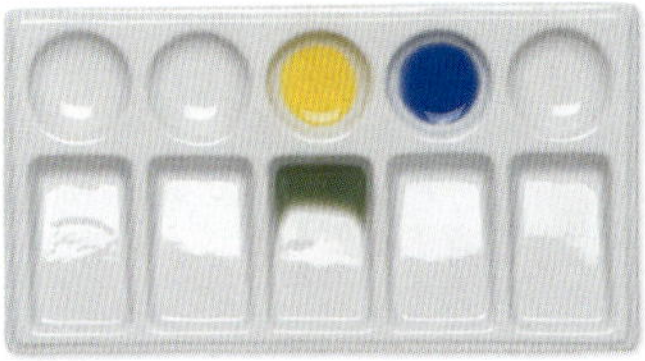

Art Express
Freepost NEA8739
Leeds LS1 1YY
Freephone: (0800) 731 4185
Fax: (0113) 243 6074
Website: www.artexpress.co.uk
(Postal address for overseas customers: Index House, 70 Burley Road, Leeds LS3 1JX, UK)

Dodgson Fine Arts Ltd
t/a Studio Arts
50 North Road
Lancaster LA1 1LT
Tel : (01524) 68014
Fax: (01524) 68013
Email: enquiries@studioarts.co.uk
Website: www.studioarts.co.uk
or www.studioartshop.com

Falkiner Fine Papers
76 Southampton Row
London WC1B 4AR
Tel: (020) 7831 1151
Fax: (020) 7430 1248
Email: falkiner@ic24.net

Hobbycraft
Hobbycraft specialize in arts and crafts materials and own 19 stores around the UK. For details of stores near you, phone freephone (0800) 027 2387 or check out the yellow pages or the company's website.
Website: www.hobbycraft.co.uk

Buy on-line from:
Jacksons Art Supplies
PO Box 29568
London N1 4WT
Tel: (0870) 241 1849
Fax: (020) 7354 3641
Email: sales@jacksonart.com
Website: www.jacksonart.com

SAA Home Shopping
PO Box 50
Newark
Notts NG23 5GY
Freephone: (0800) 980 1123
Tel: (01949) 844050 (overseas customers)
Email: homeshopping@saa.co.uk
Website: www.saa.co.uk

Stuart Stevenson
68 Clerkenwell Road
London EC1M 5QA
Tel: (020) 7253 1693

Turnham Arts & Crafts
2 Bedford Park Corner
Turnham Green Terrace
London W4 1LS
Tel: (020) 8995 2872
Fax: (020) 8995 2873

UNITED STATES
Many of the following companies operate retail outlets across the US. For details of stores in your area, check out the yellow pages or the relevant website.

Art & Frame of Sarasota
1055 South Tamiami Trail
Sarasota
FL 34236
Tel: (941) 366-2301
Toll Free: (800) 393-4278
Fax: 941-366-1352
Email: orders@in2art.com
Website: www.in2art.com

Dick Blick Art Materials
PO Box 1267
Galesburg
IL 61402-1267
Tel: (800) 828-4548
Fax: (800) 621-8293
Website: www.dickblick.com
(More than 30 stores in 12 states.)

Hobby Lobby
Website: www.hobbylobby.com
(More than 300 stores in 27 states.)

Michaels Stores
Michaels.com
8000 Bent Branch Dr.

Irving, TX 75063
Tel: (1-800) 642-4235
Website: www.michaels.com
(More than 750 stores in 48 states.)

Mister Art
913 Willard Street
Houston, TX 77006
Tel (toll-free): (866) 672-7811
Fax: (713) 332-0222
Website: www.misterart.com.

The Easel Studio
Tel (toll-free): (800) 916-2278
Fax (309) 273-0362
E-mail: bobbielarue@yahoo.com
Website: www.easelstudio.com

CANADA
Artists in Canada
803 Brightsand Terrace
Saskatoon
Saskatchewan
S7J 4X9
Website: www.artistsincanada.com

D. L. Stevenson & Son Ltd
1420 Warden Avenue
Scarborough
Ontario
M1R 5A3.
Tel: (416) 755-7795
E-mail (Canada): colourco@interlog.com
E-mail (US): customer service@
artpaintonline.com

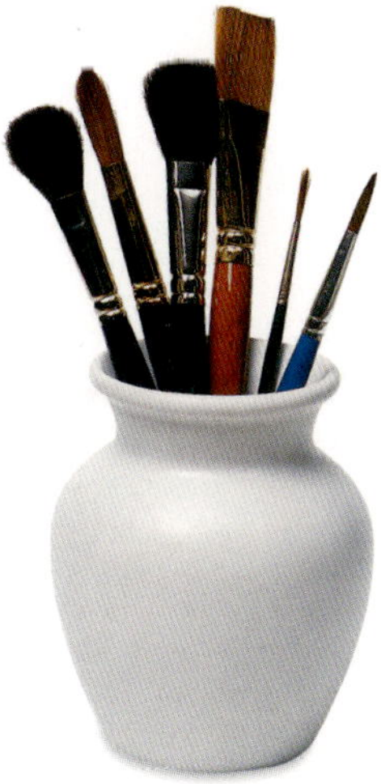

Buy customized paper and canvas stretchers from:
Upper Canada Stretchers Inc.
1750 16th Avenue East
Box 565 Owen Sound
Ontario
N4K 5R4
Tel: (1-800) 561-4944
Fax: (519) 371-7328
Email: donato@ucsart.com
Website: www.ucsart.com

The Paint Spot
Tel: (800) 363 0546
Website: www.paintspot.ca

Colours Artist Supplies
414 Graham Avenue
Winnipeg
Manitoba R3C 0L8
Tel: (204) 956-5364,
Fax: (204) 943-6989
Email: colours@mb.sympatico.ca
(6 stores across western Canada)

AUSTRALIA
Art Materials
Website: www.artmaterials.com.au

Dick Blick Art Materials
Customer Service: (800) 723-2787
Product Info: (800) 933-2542
International: (309) 343-6181
E-mail: info@dickblick.com
Website: www.dickblick.com

Madison Art Shop
Tel: (800) 961-1570
Website: www.MadisonArtShop.com

MasterGraphics Inc.
810 West Badger Road
Madison
WI 53713
Tel: (608) 256-4884
Toll Free: (800) 873-7238
Fax: (608) 210-2810
E-mail: mastergraphics@masterg.com
Website: www.masterg.com

North Shore Art Supplies
10 George Street
Hornsby
New South Wales
Tel: (02) 9476 0202
Fax: (02) 9476 0203

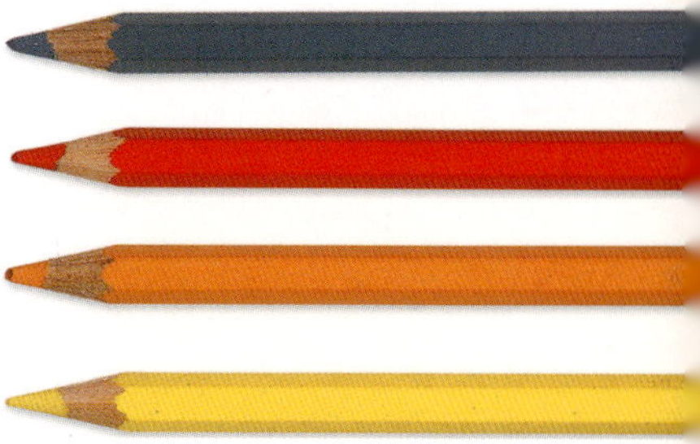

Oxford Art Supplies Pty Ltd
CITY
221–223 Oxford Street
Darlinghurst
NSW 2010
Tel: (02) 9360 4066
Fax: (02) 9360 3461
Email: orders@oxfordart.com.au
Website: www.oxfordart.com.au
or www.janetsart.com.au

Oxford Art Supplies and BOOKS Pty Ltd
Chatswood
145 Victoria Ave
Chatswood
NSW 2067.
Tel: (02) 9417 8572
Fax: (02) 9417 7617

NEW ZEALAND
Draw Art Supplies Ltd.
PO Box 24022
5 Mahunga Drive
Mangere Bridge
Auckland
Tel: (09) 636 4989
Fax: (09) 636 5162
Free Fax: (0800) 506 406
E-mail: enq@draw-art.co.nz
Website: www.draw-art.co.nz

Fine Art Supplies
PO Box 58 018,
38 Neil Park Dr.
Greenmount
Auckland
New Zealand
Tel: (64-9) 274 8896
Fax: (64-9) 274 1091
Website: www.fineart supplies.co.nz

Index

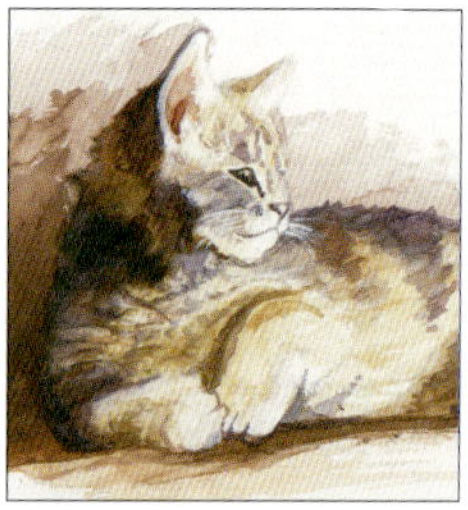

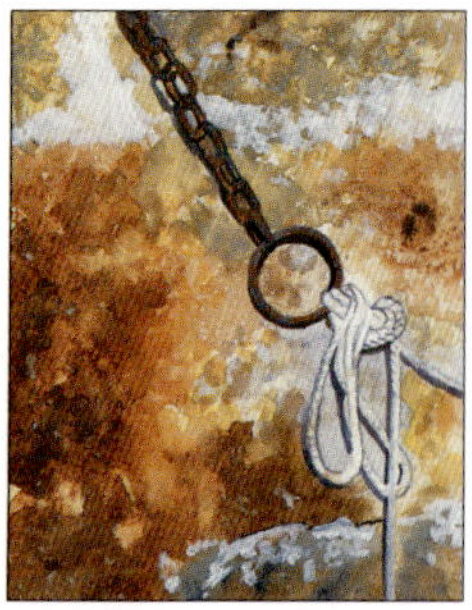

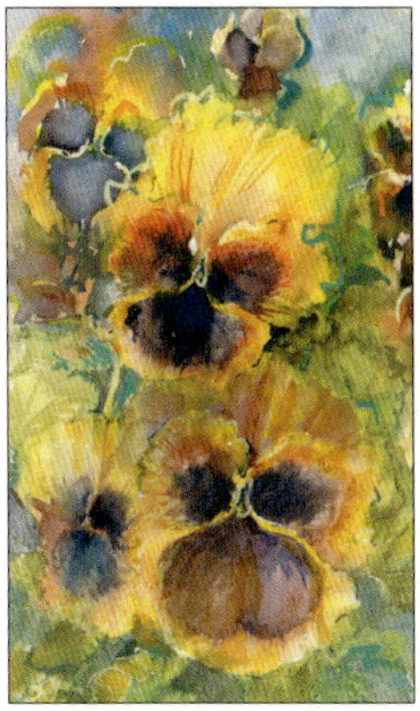

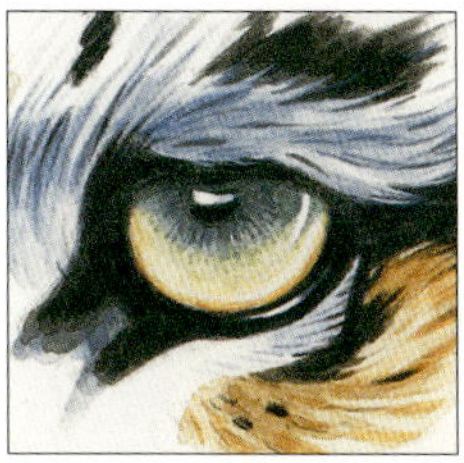

Acknowledgements

The publishers and authors are grateful to **Daler-Rowney UK** and **Turnham Arts and Crafts** for their generous loan of materials for the photography.

In addition, special thanks must go to the following watercolour artists for their step-by-step demonstrations:

t = top, b = bottom, l = left, r = right, c = centre.

Ray Balkwill: pages 128–133; **Diana Constance:** pages 40–41; 212–217; **Joe Francis Dowden:** pages 110–115; 122–127; **Paul Dyson:** pages 45, 184–185; 192–197; 198–203; **Abigail Edgar:** pages 136–139; 164–169; 238–243; 244–249; **Wendy Jelbert:** pages 116–121; 140–143; 150–153; 154–159; 172–177; 218–223; **Melvyn Petterson:** pages 58–59; 61–63; 64–67; 68–71; 75(b)–77; 80–83; 104–107; 186–191; **Paul Robinson:** pages 206–211; **Ian Sidaway:** pages 24–25; 28; 32–3; 44; 46–47; 50–51; 52 (tl, tr, cl, cr); 54 (tl, tr); 56 (tl, tr); 60; 72–73; 74–5 (t); 78–79; 178–183; 232–237; **Albany Wiseman:** pages 26–27; 29; 42–43; 52–53; 54–55; 56–57; 100–103; 144–147; 160–161; 226–231.

Copyright paintings and photographs are reproduced in this book by kind permission of the following:

t = top, b = bottom, l = left, r = right, c = centre.

Paul Dyson: pages 20, 90, 91 (t); **Trudy Friend:** pages 21 (t); 99 (b); 135 (b); **Jonathon Hibberd:** page 144 (t); **Sarah Hoggett:** pages 58 (bl); 61 (tl); 64 (b); **Wendy Jelbert:** pages 22 (b); 91 (br); 99 (t); 99 (t); 108; 109 (b); 135 (t); 148; **Ian Sidaway:** pages 91 (bl); 92–93; 94–95; 98; 109 (t); 134; 149; **George Taylor:** 28 (b); 100 (t).

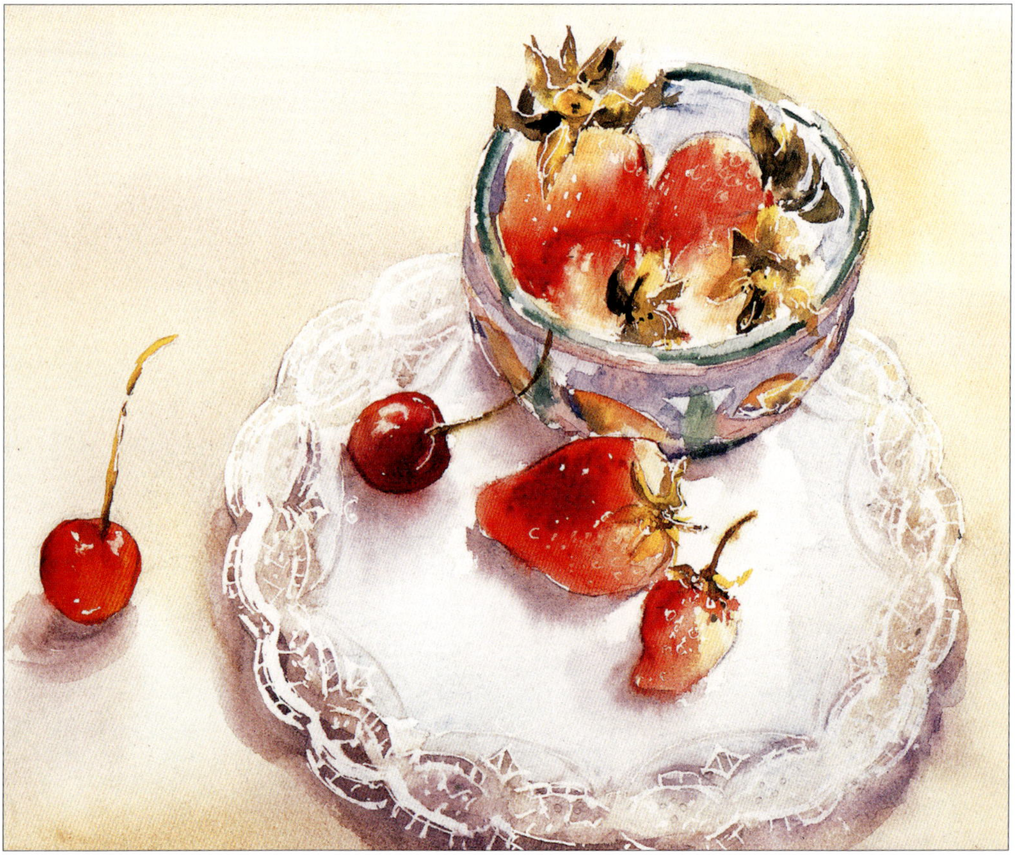

Notes

NOTES

NOTES

Notes

Notes

Notes

NOTES

Notes

The Woman

For Damian

The Woman Who Dared
A Biography of Amy Levy

Christine Pullen

KU
PRESS
KINGSTON UNIVERSITY
PRESS

Kingston University Press Ltd, Kingston University,
Penrhyn Road, Kingston upon Thames
Surrey KT1 2EE

British Library Cataloguing in Publication Data available.

ISBN 978-1-899999-43-9

Set in Palatino 9/15
Typeset by: July3rd Designs
Image layout by: July3rd Designs

Printed in the UK by Beamreach Printing
Cover designed by Gudrun Jobst

KU
PRESS
KINGSTON UNIVERSITY
PRESS

Acknowledgements

Firstly, I would like to pay tribute to my parents Violet and George Shaddock who, sadly, did not live to see this book published. After this, I would like to thank Gail Cunningham for her wise counsel and constant encouragement when supervising the doctoral thesis upon which the biography is based. But above all my heartfelt thanks must go to my husband Damian, who has been an unfailing source of love and support during the years that it has taken to research and write this book. His forbearance has been truly remarkable. Ready to dispense tea and sympathy at all times, willing to be dragged hither and thither (at home and abroad) in the quest for traces of Amy Levy, and able to cope with my bad moods when the going got tough, he has been a tower of strength throughout. I would never have completed the book without him, and it is my delight to be able to dedicate it to him now.

In addition I owe a huge debt of gratitude to Siobhan Campbell, Judith Watts, Laura Bottomley, Rosa Anderson and all at Kingston University Press. I am similarly indebted to David Bacon, Valerie Johnson and Lindsay Stainton of Camellia PLC. I must also thank the various Amy Levy scholars with whom I have exchanged ideas and information over the years. These include Linda Hunt Beckman, Susan David Bernstein, Naomi Hetherington, and Ana Parejo Vadillo. I am likewise grateful for the generous help given by Ann Thomson, College Archivist, Newnham College, Cambridge; Nancy S. Reinhardt, former Librarian, Special Collections Miller Library, Colby College, Maine, and her successor, Patricia Burdick; Gillian Furling and Steven Wright, Special Collections, University College, London; Carol Sommer, Head of Reader Services and Scott Jacobs, Senior Reader Services Assistant, William Andrews Clark Memorial Library, University of California, Los Angeles; Jeannette Cannon, former Administrator of the Jewish Historical Society of England and Martyn Woolf, Chairman of the Jewish Genealogical Society of Great Britain; David A. Thomas, Archivist, and Katrina Griffiths Archive Assistant, Cornwall County Council; Shirley Harris, General Secretary, Great Yarmouth and District Archaeological Society; Mark Beswick, Archive Information Officer, Met Office National Meteorological Archive; Gudren Muller, Tate Images; Tess Watts, Mary Evans Pictures; Iris Stehl, proprietor of the Hotel Ochsen, Saig, Christoph Näpflin, Seelisberg Tourismas, and the staff of the British Library at St. Pancras and Colindale; the British Library of Political and Economic Science, London School of Economics and Political Science; The Women's Library, London Metropolitan University; the Jewish Studies Library, University College, London; the London Metropolitan Archives; the National Archives, Kew, Surrey; the Boston Public Library, Boston, Massachusetts and the Maharishi Ayurveda Health Centre (formerly The Grand Hotel Sonnenberg).

In addition to those named above, there are numerous scholars, friends, acquaintances and colleagues who have offered advice and practical help along the way. As this book has taken a number of years to research and write I may have overlooked some, and for this I apologise, but they include Peter Prideaux Brune, Claire Burke, Norma Clarke, Marianne Colloms, Elizabeth Crawford, Eva David, Richard Garnett, Liselotte Glage, Mike Hawkins, Anthony Joseph, Elspeth MacDonald, the late Ann MacEwen and her daughters, Janet Machin, Kathy MacEwen and Sue Wheeler, Peter Morton, Liz Murley, Carol Seigal, Mary Shakeshaft, the late George A. Smith, Angela Thirlwell, and Sheila Watson. And last, but by no means least, my three dogs, Archie, Joey and Billy, who each in turn have occupied the space under my desk and with silent sympathy helped me through the hard times.

Picture Acknowledgments

1. Camellia PLC
2. Newnham College Archive (The Principal and Fellows, Newnham College, Cambridge)
3. Newnham College Archive (The Principal and Fellows, Newnham College, Cambridge)
4. The Pearson Papers, UCL Special Collections
5. British Library
6. Camellia PLC
7. The William Andrews Clark Memorial Library, University of California, Los Angeles
8. Seelisberg Tourismas
9. Seelisberg Tourismas
10. Camellia PLC
11. Family Stehl, Hotel Oschen, Saig
12. Image supplied by Cornwall Record Office. Copyright The Francis Frith Collection
13. Copyright Illustrated London News / Mary Evans
14. Copyright Tate London 2010
15. Camellia PLC

Contents

Preface

I took my power in my hand
And went against the world;
'Twas not so much as David had,
But I was twice as bold.

I aimed my pebble, but myself
Was all the one that fell.
Was it Goliath was too large,
Or was myself too small?

Emily Dickinson, 1830–1886: 'The Duel'

Described by Oscar Wilde as a 'girl of genius'[1] Amy Levy was a quintessential child of the *fin de siècle*. Like Wilde, she set out to challenge the status quo and ended up by destroying her life. Her story reflects the era in which she lived, taking us on a spellbinding journey through one of the most fascinating periods in recent British history, when Victorianism was in its death throes and modernism in its infancy. The closing decades of the nineteenth century were a time of contrast and a time of change. It was a time when men like Oscar Wilde were wearing their hair long, while New Women like Amy Levy cut theirs short.[2] A time when aesthetes like Wilde dithered over the exact shade of green for the carnation in their buttonhole and agonised over the precise tone of yellow to paint their drawing room, while ascetics like George Bernard Shaw and Edward Carpenter embraced the New Life, dining on root vegetables, encasing their feet in homemade sandals and clothing their bodies in ill-fitting garments made from undyed wool. In short, the *fin de siècle* was a time for unconventionality and boldness in thought and deed. And Amy Levy was one of the boldest spirits of her generation.

Tracing the course of a life is a similar process to that of tracing the course of a river. Although the primary objective is to track the path of the main stream, one must not ignore the tributaries that flow into it. For the biographer, these are not only the people and the places but also the ideologies that shape the destiny of any given individual. Amy Levy's destiny was shaped by two contrasting ideologies: Reform Judaism and Social Darwinism. Until now, critical analysis of her work has generally focused upon her Jewish family background, her depressive personality and the question of her sexual orientation.

The influence of Social Darwinism on both her life and her literature has been almost totally ignored. This has had the effect of creating an image of a marginalised, troubled individual who was a fringe figure in the literary world and a virtual outcast in society. But in reality, for a time at least, she was an active member of a circle of Darwinist inspired intellectuals and political activists who were responsible for the evolution of the ideas and ideologies which are the foundation stones of our present-day social and political system.

Although there is a considerable body of indirect information about Amy Levy's personal life in the short stories that were inspired by her travels, there is a surprisingly small amount of documentation that provides a direct record of her daily life. This is primarily the archive of letters, manuscripts and other papers that were originally in the possession of Beth Zion Abrahams (née Lask), who was the first twentieth-century scholar to take an interest in Amy Levy. Mrs. Abrahams was acquainted with Katherine (Katie) Solomon, Amy's surviving elder sister. Before her death, in 1952, Katie Solomon passed on her sister's papers to Mrs. Abrahams in order to further her research into Amy Levy's life and writing.[3] After Mrs. Abrahams' own death in the late 1980s, these family papers, together with other material which she had amassed during the course of her years of study, were auctioned and now form part of a private collection.[4] Other primary sources that I have drawn upon have been the handwritten family reminiscence given by Amy Levy's cousin, Lucy Marks, to Dr. Anthony Joseph[5] and the remaining portion of Amy Levy's correspondence which is not included in the Levy/Abrahams archive. Her letters to Vernon Lee are housed in the Special Collections Department of the Miller Library, Colby College, Maine, and the letters that she wrote to Dollie Radford are now in the possession of the legatees of the late Ann MacEwan, Dollie Radford's granddaughter. I am indebted to Ann MacEwan and Nancy Reinhardt (former curator of the Miller Library) for providing me with photocopies of the letters in their respective collections – and to Ann I owe a double debt of gratitude for the illuminating and delightful conversations that I had with her, plumbing the depths of her extensive knowledge about Dollie and Ernest Radford's friendship with Eleanor Marx, and various members of the first 'Men and Women's Club', which Amy Levy joined in 1882. At a later stage in my research I visited a number of the places mentioned in Amy Levy's correspondence and was also able to make contact with some of the surviving descendants of her family. As a result of this protracted and painstaking process I have not only been able to re-trace the course of her life, but also to reconnect her links with the group of intellectuals and social activists who were at the forefront of the campaigns that in the twentieth century resulted in women being given the vote and the creation of the welfare state.

As the collection of papers and letters that were passed to Beth Zion Lask by Katie Solomon has been the core source material that I have drawn upon when writing this biography, it is worth giving some consideration to both its content and its context. The letters and family papers that provide a record of Amy's childhood years are more numerous and comprehensive than those which document her later life. After her arrival at Newnham College, Cambridge in 1879, what survives of her correspondence contains large chronological gaps, and exhibits evidence of having been edited– one letter has had a section snipped out with scissors, and in other instances entire pages are missing. All that remains of two letters to Clementina Black are single-page fragments. I believe that these gaps in the correspondence are of great significance. It has previously been claimed that the Levy family 'hurt by [Amy's] suicide destroyed most of her personal effects.'[6] However, according to the terms of Amy's will, she left 'all I possess to be divided equally among my brothers and sisters except that I bequeath all books, papers, letters and documents of every kind … to Clementina Black.'[7] Clementina Black's biographer, Liselotte Glage, comments: 'Peculiarly enough, Clementina did not observe her friend's last wish so very faithfully. Most of Amy's books, papers, and manuscripts were left in possession of her family who destroyed some of them.'[8] This mysterious, and apparently deliberate, contravention of the terms of Amy's will cannot be attributed to any ill feeling on the part of the Levys towards Clementina Black, as there is ample evidence that both before and after Amy's death she was a close friend of the entire family. Indeed 'Clemmie', as she was known to them, was the first person to whom Amy's mother and sister Katie (by then Katie Solomon) turned for help following the distressing discovery of Amy's body on the morning after she died.[9]

The fact that Amy's remaining family correspondence has been interfered with suggests to me that the documents that were destroyed contained material that the family wished to suppress. Amy's specific instruction in her will that Clementina Black take charge of all her letters and personal papers suggests that she was aware of this possibility and wanted to forestall it. On 23rd September, two weeks after Amy's death, an unidentified correspondent at the *Star* claimed: 'Before Amy Levy died she made a careful collection of her papers, poems, magazine articles and short stories …'[10] The unnamed correspondent was probably Clement King Shorter, who at that time was writing a weekly column on 'Books and Bookmen' for the *Star*. Shorter knew many of Amy's friends, and may even have met her himself. He was to issue a limited edition pamphlet of her 'A Ballad of Religion and Marriage' in 1915. The manuscript of this poem was undoubtedly given to him by his friend Grant Allen, for whom 'A Ballad of Religion and Marriage' was originally written. Amy had been in close contact with Allen and his wife not long before she took her life. Given these circumstances, Shorter may well have known about Amy's 'careful collection of her papers' - an act which indicates how anxious she was that the instructions in her will would be carried out, by making sure that the specified documents were gathered together waiting for their transfer to Clementina Black. But the fact that Clementina was willing to allow the wishes of the Levy family to take precedence over those of her dead friend also implies that she must have agreed with their decision that the papers should not be preserved. The option of retaining the documents, but ensuring that they were kept from public scrutiny, was evidently not considered.[11] In a letter written to the *Athenaeum* not long after Amy died, Clementina openly acknowledged that Amy had suffered from 'fits of extreme depression'. It therefore seems unlikely that the letters were destroyed because they contained evidence of her psychological disturbance. In any case, a number of the letters that do survive contain ample testimony to the unstable state of her mind at the time that they were written. This leaves only one possible explanation for Clementina Black's action (or lack thereof), which is that the information contained in the missing sections of the letters was of such a sensitive nature that, should it have entered the public domain, it would have tarnished Amy's memory and possibly cast a slur upon others who survived her. The chapters that follow will reveal why parts of her correspondence may have been destroyed, and who it was that their destruction was intended to protect.

'On The Threshold' 1861-1881

– and I stood
At Life's great threshold with a beating heart,
And soul resolved to conquer and attain …

Amy Levy, 1861–1889: 'Xantippe'

The 9th September 1889 had been a lovely late summer day in London.[12] Towards nightfall, as the lamps were being lit in the streets and squares of the city, a young woman climbed the staircase of her parents' home in Endsleigh Gardens, Bloomsbury. When she reached the upper part of the house she opened a door to one of the bedrooms, stepped across the threshold, and after closing the door behind her began systematically to block all the sources of ventilation within the room. Once she was satisfied that the room was sufficiently airtight, she moved to the fireplace, where she lit a fire in the grate with a cache of charcoal that she had either hidden nearby or brought upstairs with her. And as soon as the fire was smouldering satisfactorily she lay down on the bed to wait for the deadly fumes to take their effect and carry her into oblivion.

On the face of it the young woman had everything to live for. Born into a prosperous middle-class Jewish home, she had apparently enjoyed all the benefits that life within a well-to-do, close-knit family had to offer. Against the custom of her class and the traditions of her community she had been given an excellent education, and had thereby achieved the distinction of becoming the first Jewish woman to be admitted to study at Newnham College Cambridge. After leaving the university she travelled widely on the Continent, but during the intervals when she was at home in London she continued to pursue her studies in the Reading Room of the British Museum. This gave her an entrée into the most avant-garde intellectual circle of her era, which meant that by the time she had reached her mid-twenties she was not only a seasoned traveller, but was also able to count amongst her friends Eleanor, the daughter of Karl Marx; the South African novelist, Olive Schreiner; Beatrice Potter, the social reformer who later became the wife of the founding Fabian, Sidney Webb; Karl Pearson, the statistician (and later eugenicist), the playwright George Bernard Shaw and last but by no means least, Oscar Wilde, who had only recently hailed her as 'a girl of genius'.[13]

A Londoner by birth and by inclination, she delighted in the life of the great city, wandering at will through the streets, and shocking her family by travelling on the open top of omnibuses – a mode of behaviour that was considered distinctly 'fast' by the standards of the time. This freedom of spirit was reflected in her writing which, if it had not brought her fortune, had brought her a degree of fame that meant she was now regarded as a successful author. Her most recent novel had caused a minor sensation and was selling well. Why then did she decide to kill herself at such a time of promise in this cruel way? Suicide can sometimes be an act of revenge. And it seems that the place, the time and the method that she used to put an end to her life were deliberately chosen to cause maximum pain to her family. According to one of her close friends, she had parted 'fondly' from both her unsuspecting parents and her sister not long before her final, fatal ascent of the staircase.[14] Most importantly, as she would have known only too well, by killing herself in her parents' house she would defile the sanctity of their 'hearth and home' – a concept of paramount importance to the Victorian psyche. But although she may have subliminally blamed her parents for her unhappiness, the specific cause of her suffering lay elsewhere. To find the answer to the enigma of her death it is necessary to make a journey back through her life, beginning with her earliest years which, like her final days, were played out against the backdrop of the city that she loved so much.

Amy Judith, the second child of Isabelle and Lewis Levy, was born on 10th November 1861 at 16 Percy Place, Clapham Road, South Lambeth. Although South Lambeth is now very much part of inner London, at that time it was located not far from the south-western fringe of the metropolis, where the once pretty countryside was rapidly disappearing under the relentless advance of bricks and mortar. Like its neighbours, Brixton and Stockwell, the borough owed its rapid expansion to the London & South Western Railway which, after its completion in 1841, had established the first direct link between the capital and the port of Southampton. The coming of the railway attracted speculative builders to the area, and within a few years vast tracts of the outer reaches of South London were transformed from semi-rural backwaters into thriving suburbs. South Lambeth, with its ranks of newly built villas, the more modest workers' dwellings that were sited cheek by jowl alongside commercial enterprises like Beaufoys Vinegar Works, the Anchor Brewery, and the railway line which cut a swathe through the market gardens that were a reminder of its rustic past, was a typical example of its kind. Within it Percy Place occupied a relatively eminent position, being one of the several terraces of larger houses fronting on to the Clapham Road that had been built to attract better-off families into the neighbourhood. In 1889 the social investigator Charles Booth classified Percy Place as 'Middle-class, well-to-do', and there is no reason to believe that the street had altered much in character since Amy Levy had been born there twenty-seven years earlier. [15]

In fact, the district's profile as an up-and-coming place to live may well have influenced the Levys' decision to set up home there, because at the time that Amy made her entrance into the world the family fortunes were in the ascendant. On his daughter's birth certificate Lewis entered his occupation as 'merchant'. As this indicates, like many within his community he was a self-made man who had gained his wealth through a combination of hard work and enterprise. Born into a family of second-generation immigrants that had fled to Britain from Europe at the end of the eighteenth century, he would have been acutely aware of the hardship that his ancestors had endured. Like so many refugees then and now, his parents had made their home in the East End of London, where his father, Solomon, set up in business as a furniture broker while his mother, Maria, applied her considerable energies to producing eight healthy children. Life in the overcrowded, poverty-stricken East End must have been particularly challenging for Maria, but despite the trials and tribulations that were her daily lot, she was apparently a cheerful soul - 'a tiny little woman, always singing and dancing.'[16] Her granddaughter Amy was destined to inherit her petite stature and her love of music – if not her carefree disposition.[17]

Perhaps because of the travails of their forebears, Solomon and Maria's sons were determined to rise in the world, and set about their task shrewdly. Amy's cousin Lucy Marks left a hand written family memoir in which she described how her father, Lewis' brother Nathaniel, 'emigrated to Australia then at the height of the gold digging fever' and 'prudently established a small store in Melbourne.' Nathaniel was later joined by his elder brothers, Goodman and Lewis. While Nathaniel and Lewis looked after the shop, Goodman drove 'a wagon stocked with shirts, pants, socks, etc., to the gold digging in Bendigo and Geelong.' This proved to be a particularly profitable exercise, as 'the miners who had no cash paid with gold nuggets, thus laying the foundation of a fortune.'[18] In consequence the three brothers came home to England rich men, whereupon, having established himself on a firm financial footing, Lewis returned to London and married his second cousin, Isabelle Levin.[19]

Isabelle and Lewis' great-grandparents in common were Lyon and Judith Joseph, members of the thriving Jewish community that had settled in the port of Falmouth, Cornwall. It seems that Lewis' decision to marry a kinswoman was not unusual within his family circle. Lyon Joseph had been a prominent figure within the town, having instigated the campaign to build the Falmouth synagogue, which was consecrated in 1808. But like his future great-grandsons he was as much concerned with the affairs of this world as the next, and appears to have taken every opportunity to advance his commercial interests. He owned a small fleet of trading vessels, and the site chosen for the erection of the synagogue overlooked the harbour. The expeditious siting of the building thus ensured that he could keep an eye on the comings and goings of his ships whilst paying homage to his maker.[20] Although she may not have inherited his business acumen, his great-granddaughter Isabelle evidently shared his dedication to the Jewish faith, as any references that Amy made to her religion in her childhood generally related to her mother's concern that the children should follow Jewish family tradition. For example, she refused to allow Amy's eldest sister Katie to attend a social event on a Friday evening, the start of the Jewish Sabbath. Lewis, on the other hand, perhaps because of his wider experience of the world, seems to have adopted a less doctrinaire approach to his religion. He socialised within radical Jewish circles and took an interest in progressive ideas, recording in a family Confessions Album that, of all people in the world, he would most have liked to have been Charles Darwin.[21] Amy's ideological development was to reflect both these strands of familial influence.

The census for the year in which Amy was born records Lewis Levy's age as 25 and Isabelle's as 21. Their first child Katherine (familiarly known as Katie) was registered as being one year old. This meant that no sooner had Isabelle had recovered from the birth of her first child than she became pregnant with her second. Given the traditions of their community, it is likely that the Levys hoped that this second child would be a son. However, any disappointment at Amy's arrival was destined to be short lived, as four of the five children subsequently born into the family were boys. A photograph showing Isabelle surrounded by her children reveals that she was probably in her early thirties by the time that her last child, Edmund, was aged about three.[22] Although a family of this size was not unusual in the nineteenth century, ten years of continuous childbearing would have inevitably taken its toll upon her, a fact that could have been noted by a perceptive and sensitive child - as Amy was. In a letter written to her mother when she was about 16 years old, she commented sarcastically: 'I must congratulate you on your new nephew. Poor Aunt Bessie with ten children!'[23] Although it is now impossible to determine how regularly the family attended religious services, when they did so they worshiped at the West London Synagogue in Upper Berkeley Street, which was the centre of Reform Judaism in England at that time.[24] Amy and her siblings were therefore familiar with the prayers and rituals of the Jewish faith, one of which is the daily offering of thanks by the male Jew for not having been born a woman. Amy was to cite this invocation in her novel *Reuben Sachs*, adding the comment: 'no prayer goes up from the synagogue with greater fervour than this'. [25]

In other respects, there is plenty to suggest that the Levys' attitude to the education of their children was unusually enlightened, and not influenced by considerations of religious orthodoxy. In the prejudiced class-ridden society of Victorian England newly rich Jewish merchants like Lewis and his brothers would have been conscious of the anomalous nature of their position in society. Having not received much formal education themselves, and believing that that this was the key to social advancement, they were determined that their children should receive the best education that money could buy. However, Lewis and Isabelle went against the tradition of their time by ensuring that both their sons and their daughters received an equal standard of tuition. (Unfortunately the money that Lewis spent on his boys' schooling proved a poor investment, as none of them distinguished themselves academically – those honours were left for their sister Amy to claim.) Following the custom of most middle-class Victorian households, Lewis and Nathaniel initially put the instruction of their children into the hands of a governess. Lucy Marks recalled that 'Miss Pateman' was 'sent on to our family from Uncle Lewis's', adding that she 'was supposed to be a very advanced teacher.'[26] By the 1870s Lewis and Isabelle had taken a further step up the social ladder, as by then they had two homes, one in London and a second in Brighton. This meant that they spent a good deal of time parted from their children, and when they were out of town Miss Pateman acted *in loco parentis*.[27] On one occasion she took the children on holiday to Broadstairs – a seaside town on the Kent coast, popular at that time because it had been a favourite haunt of Charles Dickens. Amy wrote to her mother: 'We went to-day to St. Peters, and were much interested by the ancient church which is 800 years old'. In the section of the letter that is addressed to her father she writes: 'You would like to see St. Peter's old church it is so curious and antique.'[28] The impression that the Levys permitted – and possibly encouraged - their governess to take Amy and her brothers and sisters to visit places of Christian worship is reinforced in one of the letters that Amy addressed exclusively to 'Dear Papa', in which she tells him that Miss Pateman 'purposed to take us to St. Paul's Cathedral, but the weather being so unfavourable we shall spend our half holiday at home.'[29]

Although Miss Pateman was clearly held in high esteem by the Levy family, they also took a direct hand in furthering their children's education themselves. Nathaniel's family had to 'earn' their pocket money by once a week writing 'a line of copy-book, a line of Roman letters, a line of Hebrew letters, a line of numerals and for good measure ...to draw something – no matter what.' This work had to be scrutinised by their father, who would 'deduct 1d. or 2d. for bad work.'[30] Lewis and Isabelle's children were similarly encouraged to develop their literary skills, but in a more imaginative way. Like many middle-class Victorian children, the Levy siblings looked to their own resources for entertainment. Among Amy's surviving papers there is an extensive collection of juvenilia, including playbills of productions written by her, listing her brothers and sisters and various family friends as cast members. There are also a number of hand-produced magazines written by Amy, Katie and the younger members of the family. One of these, entitled 'The Poplar Club Journal', was modelled on contemporary periodicals like *Punch*. Each issue contained articles and short stories, some of which were illustrated by a series of sketches executed in imitation of the style of the fashionable illustrators of the day. The contributions were critically 'reviewed' by the family members, with their comments being recorded on the last page of the magazine.[31] 'Citizen Amy', who was the editor of the journal, evidently experienced difficulties in persuading the contributors to submit their copy on time. As a result, following a meeting of the club members, the following warning was given:

> the finement of members failing to produce their contributions was passed the fine amounted to one halfpenny, and some ...might prefer doing so to giving themselves the trouble of writing their papers. I therefore, to prevent this, propose that after having failed to produce his [this?] journal three times the offender must pay the sum of one penny, the sixth three halfpence, and so on. I think such a measure will probably insure the regularity of the Club members, as their pocket money being limited they would be made attentive and particular. [32]

In 1875, when she was thirteen years old, perhaps at the prompting of Miss Pateman, Amy entered an essay for a competition run by the children's journal *Kind Words* and was awarded the Junior Prize.[33] 'Aurora Leigh: A Poem in Blank Verse by Mrs. Browning', began with the earnest declaration: 'As a poet we see woman in her most favourable light; her mind is better constituted for that refinement, that delicacy of touch which is so essential for poetry...' However, despite the conventional sentiments of its opening sentence, the essay contains passages that reveal that, even at the age of thirteen, Amy was beginning to question the values of the society in which she lived, and to develop a commitment to the cause of women's rights. At one point she criticises 'the authoress' for 'introducing too many learned allusions & c.' but concludes that this fault 'is perhaps more excusable in a <u>woman</u> than a <u>man</u>; for it is only natural she would wish to display what public opinion denies her sex – a classical education.'[34] 1875 was also the year in which her first poem appeared in print and, once again, Miss Pateman's guiding hand may have been behind the project, as 'The Ballad of Ida Grey (A Story of a Woman's Sacrifice)' was published in the *Pelican*, a quarterly magazine devoted to the promotion of the social and educational progress of women.[35] 'Ida Grey' is an immature and indifferent composition, with some passages bordering upon doggerel, which is only of interest because it provides further evidence of Amy's early commitment to the feminist cause.

In the ten years between her birth and 1871 (as the census for that year records) the Levy family had moved from the outer suburbs to the centre of the city, to 138 Dorset Square, Regent's Park. However, at some stage in the early to mid-1870s the focus of Lewis' commercial life shifted from London to Brighton. Accordingly, after (presumably) surrendering the lease on the Dorset Square House and resigning his seats at the Berkeley Street Synagogue he moved the family to Brighton on what was intended to be a permanent basis.[36] This move was particularly significant for Amy, as it was to result in her introduction to Edith Creak, her second 'advanced teacher' and the person who was to have the most profound influence upon her development both as a scholar and a feminist. Throughout her life she looked to charismatic individuals for intellectual and emotional support, and Edith Creak was the first of these intellectual mentors.

From the middle of the nineteenth century onwards educational opportunities for girls had expanded rapidly, owing to the simultaneous advancement in the number and quality of girls' secondary schools, and the establishment of the women's colleges at the universities of London, Cambridge and Oxford. Edith Creak had enjoyed the unusual privilege of an excellent education due to the fact that her father, Albert Creak, was the headmaster of a boys' preparatory school in Hove. This bore the somewhat pretentious title of The Wick Gentleman's Boarding School, and here Edith had attended classes alongside the boys. As a result, she had received the classical education denied to the majority of her sex – the fact which had been lamented by Amy in her prize-winning essay. Because of her outstanding abilities as a scholar, Edith Creak had been one of the first five external students admitted to study at Newnham, the college for women established at Cambridge at the instigation of Henry Sidgwick and Millicent Fawcett. The youngest member of the group, she was also the first to benefit from the scholarship 'of forty pounds for four years for a girl coming from outside, who had to reside in Cambridge', which had been inaugurated by Fawcett's long time friend John Stewart Mill and his stepdaughter Helen Taylor. After leaving the university she spent a short time as Assistant Mistress at Plymouth

High School before being appointed Headmistress of the new High School for Girls at Brighton, which opened in June 1876. One of her pupils was later to recall that 'there was not much in her manner which suggested that she had ever had much to do with girls, or at any rate with girls' Schools ... She was a gifted scholar and the greater part of her teaching was in Latin and in Greek.' However, Edith's lack of familiarity with girls' schools had its advantages, for the disciplined teaching that she brought with her was rarely available to young women at that time. [37]

There is no record of when Amy became a pupil at the Brighton High School, but it is likely that she was one of the original intake of seventeen girls, as by 1876 she was already fifteen years old. A definite member of this initial intake was another local girl, Constance Black (later Garnett), who after the death of her mother had spent a miserable period as a boarder at a school in Sussex Square where 'because she was an unbeliever and did not say her prayers, she was not allowed to sleep in the dormitory and corrupt other girls.' 'Conny,' as her friends called her, was just three months younger than Amy and shared her love of intellectual pursuits. Isabelle and Lewis evidently did not regard her as a corrupting influence, and she and Amy became close friends. Conny had been brought up in a household where the children had been encouraged to think for themselves and express their opinions freely, and as a result she was not generally sympathetic to those who did not share her open-minded approach to life. Her grandson Richard Garnett claimed that, by Victorian standards, 'David and Clara Black were not ordinary parents [for] they believed passionately in education for boys and girls alike.' [38] As the Levys likewise made no distinction between their sons and their daughters with regard to their education, this enlightened attitude would undoubtedly have fostered Black's evident affection for them.[39]

While Amy was at the Brighton High School, the family continued to spend regular periods apart. It seems that with her own wealth of experience in the matter, Isabelle was frequently called from home to attend one or other of her sisters or sisters-in-law during their numerous confinements. In these intervals Amy kept up a regular flow of correspondence to her parents and her eldest sister Katie. These letters not only shed light on her state of her mind as she approached adulthood, but also paint a vivid picture of daily life at a progressive girls' school of the era. This, in turn, provides a revealing insight into a significant aspect of the life of the Victorian schoolgirl – the passionate emotional attachments which were frequently established between girls, and sometimes between girl and teacher. Before the twentieth century, when the issue of female sexuality emerged from the closet, casting off the obscure language of medical discourse in which it had previously been shrouded, Sapphic love was generally unrecognised. Indeed Victorian parents, fearful for their daughters' reputations, tended to encourage 'romantic friendships' with other young women, regarding them as a harmless outlet for pent up emotions which might otherwise be directed towards unsuitable young men. Their prime motive for this strategy was to preserve their daughters' value in the marriage market. Within the Jewish community this consideration was paramount. However, parental concern for their daughters' moral welfare was not always the only formative influence upon these intense relationships, for it has been pointed out that the 'control of passionate friendships for familial and social ends was promulgated by virtually every reforming headmistress.'[40]

Edith Creak, the model of the 'reforming headmistress,' was the object of passionate devotion for a number of her pupils, and one of her most steadfast devotees was Amy Levy. While her parents were away from home - and now that Miss Pateman's services had been transferred to the household of Lewis' brother Nathaniel – Amy sometimes went to stay with the Creak family at The Wick, the preparatory school in Hove where Creak had studied alongside her father's pupils, and where her younger brothers William and Alfred were now boarding. In a letter written during one of the intervals when Isabelle was away from home Amy regaled her mother with a lively account of life at The Wick:

> My Dear Mama,
>
> You will find enclosed lists of the things we want, this is the last time we shall trouble you as Mrs. Creak says whatever we want we are to have now. Last night Miss Creak again went out attired in a light and "crinny" silk dress with a "point." Before departing she knelt down and let her "mater" as she calls her, cut her nails, and pin her at the back of her neck: I went in to supper for fun, to see what it was like; only Mrs. Creak, the [mashers?][41] and two or three big boys were there; they had herrings, beer and cheese, of which the two latter I did not partake ... Yesterday being half holiday, Alfred was permitted to take me to and from school in the afternoon; between the times he performed a commission or so for me: I also sent him to Preston St. to refresh his inner man to the amount of 1d as he seemed rather gloomy; that together with a few bullseyes, and Papa's visit had the desired effect of restoring him to cheerfulness. Miss Creak never appears at breakfast; I do not wonder she fattens by the life she leads ...[42]

This unkind remark about her headmistress' expanding waistline does not accord with the comment she made in a letter to Katie that 'I obtained the matrimonial consent to visit my heart's love, and accordingly at about 3.45, with a clean face, a beating heart and Ella for a protector, set out (in my green!) for the Temple (i.e. The Wick).' Recounting how someone she enigmatically describes as 'The trim hind' opened the door and informed her that 'Miss Creak [had] gone out for <u>a holiday</u>! (I suppose she meant a jaunt),' she adds, 'Tomorrow I intend to repeat the experiment, with more success I hope.'[43] Amy's passion for her headmistress appears to have caused her some anxiety. She gave voice to her fears in a strangely prophetic outburst to Katie:

> Frankly I'm more in love with her than ever – isn't it grim? I don't believe it will go for ages, and I can never care for anyone or anything else while it lasts. Don't you despise these egoistic outpourings? Of course this is quite confidential. I make such different future pictures to what I used to – you married, maternal, prudent and [word illegible] – with a tendency to laugh at the plain High Minded Sch. mistress sister, who grinds and lodges with chums and adores 'without return.'[44]

She spoke with prescience, for to adore 'without return' was to be her destiny throughout her adult life.

Amy's request that her confession should be regarded as confidential suggests that her acknowledged difference from her sister was beginning to create problems in her relationship with their mother. This would explain the discrepancy between the sarcastic comment about her headmistress's figure in her letter to Isabelle and the 'egoistic outpourings' in her letter to Katie. A further indication that all was not well between mother and daughter is a throwaway remark made in one of Amy's later letters to Katie: 'perhaps it sounds bad but I'm awfully sorry the fam.'s coming down – it's so luxurious living away from everyone and not being rubbed the wrong way.'[45] But problems at home were not the only aspect of her life to be causing her anxiety at this time, as she was developing doubts about her ethnicity. Once gain, she gave voice to her fears in a letter to her sister:

> Yesterday Conny called for me as I had expected; she happened to mention that my spouse[46] was pining for me, when I said I wondered she had not called as such was the case, and learnt that the pious Mary and fam. 'did not like to visit Jews, no orthodox persons <u>did</u>!' Rich? Of course I do not mind the verdant notions of the Haycrofts, but what if she shared them? The thought has quite haunted me.[47]

Any ambivalence in Conny Black's attitude to Amy seems far more likely to have been inspired by jealousy rather than anti-Semitism. David Black had been forced into premature retirement by ill health and, as a result, the family was very short of money. In contrast the Levys were obviously prospering at this time, and Conny would surely have envied the freedom that financial security bestowed upon her friend. In 1878, both Amy and Conny sat the Cambridge Senior Local examinations. Amy passed with second-class honours, which was a very creditable result, but Conny passed with first-class honours in all subjects and, because 'her marks overall were higher than those of any of the other three thousand girls who had sat the examination in England',[48] she was awarded a scholarship for Newnham College. Nevertheless, despite the scholarship, which was for £35 for three years, she feared that her father would not be able to afford the balance of the fees, which were £60 per annum. In the event, David Black agreed to pay the outstanding sum and, as Lewis Levy evidently had no difficulty in meeting the full cost of the fees for Amy, she and Conny went up to Cambridge together in October 1879.

A few months before she went up to Newnham, in February of that year, Amy contributed to a fierce epistolary debate which raged for several weeks in the correspondence pages of the *Jewish Chronicle*. The exchange had been instigated by a correspondent who chose to identify himself only by the Hebrew letter 'C'. 'C' had first written to register his disapproval of the fact that Jewish women, like their gentile sisters, were exhibiting an increasing tendency to demand their 'rights' and neglect their 'duties'. In her reply, which was printed under the heading 'Jewish Women and Women's Rights', Amy sought to set the record straight. She began by setting out her definition of the rights claimed, maintaining:

> They are but three: the right of spinster and widow householders to the franchise; the right to the same educational advantages as men; the right to exercise the professions and certain classes of business, *i.e.*, book-keeping and secretaryships ... This, I think is a distinct definition and is all I have ever heard claimed by any speaker (and I have heard many) on the subject of Women's Rights...[49]

Amongst Amy's collection of juvenilia there is an autographed sketch depicting a woman in 'bloomer' costume addressing an audience.[50] This bears out her claim that she had heard 'many' speak upon the issue of 'Women's Rights', and is further testimony both to the influence of Miss Pateman, and to the fact that Lewis and Isabelle were unusually open-minded and indulgent to their children's wishes; for it is hard to imagine that many parents of their social standing would allow their daughters such a degree of personal freedom, and yet it is inconceivable that Amy could have attended meetings of this nature without her parents' knowledge or consent.

'C's' response to Amy's letter appeared in the next issue of the *Jewish Chronicle*. After requesting permission 'to grant me sufficient space for a few remarks on Mrs. (or Miss?) Levy's letter' he let loose a tirade of abuse that began with a snide comment about her 'references to "the melancholy crowd of femmes incomprises, so characteristic of the age"', continued with insulting remarks about her supposed reading habits, and concluded by identifying her by association with those ' "restless ambitious women" ... to whom it is the highest possible pleasure to pose as martyrs', adding: 'not content with ordinary women's work ... if they find themselves incapable of anything beyond the ordinary routine of every day life, they put it all down to the heartless want of appreciation of a cold world.' After claiming that 'as a matter of fact, it is, and always has been open to women to make the world happier and wiser by some great discovery or invention', he went on to enquire:

> Why did not a woman discover electricity, or the manifold uses of steam, and why does she not even improve upon previously existing developments of science? Why has not female composer ever made the people the richer by some sweet strains? Beyond Mrs. Browning, what great poetess has the sex given to us? Lady-novelists we have plenty, but only one has been in the first rank, and even she has been largely assisted by her constant association with two of the greatest thinkers of the age, Herbert Spencer and G. H. Lewes.

Having unwittingly alighted on the very subject that was most likely to provoke his opponent, 'C' then proceeded to rub salt in the wound by declaring: 'Everything in this world finds its own level and, were women mentally stronger than men, they would long ago have made this fact evident and have obtained the ascendancy'. At this point he called upon an authority even greater than Herbert Spencer to support his argument, claiming confidently: 'Revealed religion clearly defines the position of Woman. It is entirely different from that of man, but ... equal to, and even surpassing, his usefulness in the scheme of creation.' Woman's divinely decreed mission, as defined by 'C', although noble in conception, was somewhat limited in performance, requiring merely that they be 'delightful companions to man and charming members of society by reason of their admirable intelligence and culture, and the well-directed manner in which they use these valuable qualities.'[51] Amy did not condescend to reply to this diatribe, as the cudgels had already been taken up by another correspondent who skilfully demolished 'C's' argument by inviting him to consider the example of 'our gracious Sovereign the Queen, who occupies the highest political position in the kingdom.' 'Yet', she artlessly added, 'who can say that public business has hardened her heart or prevented her from fulfilling her duties as wife and mother?'[52] Although Amy left no record of her reaction to her epistolary exchange with 'C', her disenchantment with a social structure founded upon the belief that 'divine law' decreed that one half of the human population should sacrifice itself for the convenience of the other undoubtedly played a part in her eventual decision to part company with her religion.

Amy also left no record of her first impression of Cambridge, but to judge by the fulsome tribute she later paid to its aesthetic qualities in her poetry, her reaction must have been similar to that of Constance Black who, from the outset, was entirely overcome by its beauty, writing in later life that 'it made me feel too much moved, I was always wanting to cry. I had never imagined such a lovely place.'[53] In contrast, Amy's early letters home were concerned with more prosaic matters, as in her first few weeks at college she experienced problems that became familiar to succeeding generations of female undergraduates. One of her first letters to Isabelle is an obvious attempt to allay maternal anxiety. It begins with an apology: 'I am very sorry that you were vexed at not receiving another letter from me', and goes on to explain the omission by providing her mother with an outline of her hectic life as a new student:

> I am really so much occupied that it is difficult for me to write more than once a week … [w]hen I am not actually grinding there is always plenty of walking to do [and] going to lecture seems to waste a lot of time. To-day, for instance, I ground for ½ hr. after a hurried breakfast, then went to lecture; after that I came back, ground again, lunched and went to another lecture. Then I went with Conny to Newnham, where we had tea, & we afterwards went for a walk with Maggie (on the way I bought some tennis shoes (3/3)[54]. We rested a little at Norwich House, then went to King's Chapel to hear the organ, & I did not get home till time to dress for dinner. This evening I have been grinding for a few hours, but not as hard as usual, as tomorrow is an easy day. We have a great deal of work, but of course it varies every day; I rather wish I had not so many subjects.

She ends the letter by describing how 'at Newnham the girls give tea-parties at night', adding wistfully 'but here they only ask one or 2 to spend a little time in their rooms.' The letter ends with the poignant comment 'I shall be by no means sorry to come home'. But perhaps fearing that this might be seized upon as an opportunity to keep her at home for good, she adds hastily 'tho' it is very nice being here.'[55]

Amy's difficulty in adjusting to life at Cambridge was principally due to the fact that she had not been allocated a room within the college precincts. Whereas Conny had been accommodated at Newnham Hall, she had been assigned a room in Norwich House, one of the lodging houses within the town taken to accommodate the increasing overspill of female students. However, despite her complaint about the limited opportunities for socialising at Norwich House, she was not entirely bereft of familiar company, as a contemporary house photograph pictures her standing (rather self-consciously) amongst her fellow students – two of whom were her Brighton High School friends Nelly Huggett and Bessy May.[56] Moreover, during her time at Norwich house her former headmistress paid a visit to her alma mater to oversee the progress of her protégées.[57] Amy told her mother: 'Miss Creak and Miss Sullivan come down on Friday; they have taken lodgings near here, and of course we are looking forward to their arrival with great pleasure.' Nevertheless, the letters that record Amy's years at Newnham convey the overall impression that she felt excluded from mainstream college life. The fact that she was lodged in the town may have been the main reason for her sense of isolation, but her acknowledged shyness and lack of confidence undoubtedly exacerbated the problem. She gave voice to her anxieties in her letters home. To her mother she confessed 'to-morrow I am going to the gymnasium as a performer for the first time, & rather funk.' To Katie she confided: 'Tonight we have our Debate, *subject* Browning and Tennyson; I was to have led the opposition (in favour of R.B.) but backed out of it …'[58]

Amy's social anxiety was rooted in her poor self-image. To judge by various disparaging comments that she made about herself in her correspondence, it seems that she disliked her appearance and believed that her character was flawed. Isabelle patently regarded her as a problem child and made little effort to conceal the fact. Katie, on the other hand, was in every way the golden girl of the family. Unlike Amy she had fair hair, a light complexion and features that would have been regarded at the time as more conventionally pretty. She also had a gentler and more biddable personality. Amy's sense of inferiority to her sister may have triggered the depression that haunted her throughout her life. One of her early letters to Isabelle contains the comment: 'I have quite recovered from the "blues" which it was horrid of me to mention.' Her low level of self-esteem is certainly reflected in her choice of the *noms de plume* 'the dog with the bad name' and 'U.G.L.Y.' with which she signed a number of her unpublished manuscripts.'[59] Unfortunately, at Cambridge her problems became compounded by the recognition of her 'difference' from her fellow students.

Although there is nothing to indicate that Amy was the victim of any overt racial or religious discrimination while she was at Newnham, the fact that she was the first Jewish woman to study there at a time when the typical profile of a Cambridge undergraduate was an upper or middle class Anglican, Anglo-Saxon male, must have added to her feelings of alienation and self-doubt. It is clear from contemporary accounts that the young women who had the good fortune to be admitted to the college were inclined to be unruly (hardly surprising under the circumstances, as for many it was their first taste of freedom) and sometimes unkind. On one occasion the Principal, the kindly Miss Clough, took a girl to task for ridiculing the 'extravagant aestheticism both in dress and speech' of one of her fellows.[60] It is therefore probable that Amy's obviously Semitic features caused adverse comment when she first arrived. In her Cambridge notebook there is a draft of a poem entitled 'The Sleepy Poet to his Frame' which includes the lines:

> Little body, all misshapen …

You have brought enough of sorrow,
On the one which groans within …

Her religion would have created an additional difficulty. One of the rules that the young ladies were meant to rigidly obey governed their religious observance. Just before she left Cambridge in 1881, Amy wrote a description of daily life at Newnham College, which was published in the *Cambridge Review*. By this time she had been given a room within the college in the newly erected North Hall, which had been opened in October 1880. After a general description of the buildings and the weekday life of the students she continues:

> So much for six days of the week; Sunday has a distinct character of its own. Each 'woman' wakes with a dim sense of 'something going to happen,' till a certain subtle aroma wafted in through the ventilator above the door dispels the pleasant 'dimness,' and reminds her that it is Sunday and that there are sausages for breakfast. The morning is taken up with church and chapel; each student is expected to have a regular place of worship and to inform the principal of her hall respecting it.[61]

Although, like the majority of acculturated British Jews, the Levys may not have rigidly adhered to the dietary laws of their faith, when away from home, they would probably have avoided eating 'meat, pork and shellfish'.[62] If this was the case, then the Sunday breakfast of sausages would have posed a problem for Amy. Presumably she was granted a dispensation from attending church or chapel as well, but again, such a distinction would have further set her apart from her fellows. One of her contemporaries, Frances Grey, recalled how 'Many of us were confronted for the first time with difficulties in regard to the religious beliefs in which we had been brought up... At such a crisis in a student's mental and spiritual growth a friend who stood on firmer ground could often hold out a hand to another whose footing was not sure.[63]At Cambridge Amy had no friend familiar with the religious beliefs with which she had been brought up, and any doubts she had begun to harbour about her religion or her ethnicity had to be faced alone. It seems that her discomfort with her appearance combined with her natural shyness to make her appear withdrawn and aloof. Amy's contemporary, Frances Grey, who shared a room in North Hall with fellow student Laura Colman, included a brief reminiscence of Amy in her biography: according to Grey she was regarded, although sympathetically, as something of an outsider. She recalled: 'One of the friends whose gifts caused us a good deal of pleasure and some pride was Amy Levy …She was drawn to Laura Colman and to me and would occasionally invite herself to our rooms, alleging that she found the atmosphere favourable for work; and we were drawn to her wistful, wayward, critical nature.'[64] Despite Frances

Grey's recollection of their pride and pleasure in Amy's company, the phrase 'would occasionally invite herself to our rooms' smacks somewhat of desperation on Amy's part, and does not suggest a great degree of intimacy between the three. This impression is strengthened by the use of the words 'wistful', 'wayward' and 'critical' to describe Amy's personality, which conjures up an image of one who longed for friendship but was too proud to acknowledge it. Amy was later to draw upon her experience of College life in her short story 'Cohen of Trinity,' which was written ten years after she left Newnham, and published just three months before her suicide. The following extract sounds an uncanny echo of Frances Grey's account:

> I cannot quite explain my interest [in Cohen] on so slight a knowledge; his manners were a distressing mixture of the bourgeois and the canaille, and a most unattractive lack of simplicity marked his whole personality … I have sometimes reproached myself that I never grew fond of him; but a little reciprocity is necessary in these matters, and poor Cohen had not the art of being fond of people. I soon discovered that he was desperately lonely and desperately unapproachable

In May 1879, a few months before she went up to Cambridge, Amy had a poem accepted for publication in the *Dublin University Magazine*.[65] A narrative verse entitled 'Run to Death', and subtitled 'A True Incident of Pre-Revolutionary French History', it provides a gruesome account of the progress of an aristocratic hunting party who, failing to find a conventional quarry to pursue and reluctant to abandon their sport, unleash their hounds upon a gypsy woman and her baby whom they encounter by chance wandering in the forest. In the verse Amy employs terminology that reflects (but reverses) Tennyson's vision of nature – 'red in tooth and claw' – for it is the 'civilised' huntsmen who, 'careless of the single life', cast the hapless mother and child 'as rubbish to the void.' Her swarthy gypsy (like Elizabeth Barrett Browning's 'Runaway Slave') is portrayed as the innocent victim of a corrupt and decadent culture that, 'careful' of its own 'type', views those of different racial origin as alien, and sometimes scarcely human, beings. Within her later fiction, Amy constructed a consistent tension between the 'fair' and the 'dark'. In general, the 'fair' represent the Anglo-Saxon ideal of physical beauty and, for want of a better expression, 'cultural purity'; the representatives of 'darkness', like the gypsy in 'Run to Death', are presented as either the victims or the icons of the 'forces of darkness'. These 'dark' characters are invariably depicted as being of Semitic or Irish origin. Throughout her adult life, Amy empathised with those who inhabited the margins of society, and was instinctively drawn to dark and wayward women like herself. A fellow student whom she particularly admired was an Irish woman, Alice Lloyd. She wrote enthusiastically to her mother:

> There is a dear little creature here by name Miss Lloyd, who strikes me as particularly pretty. She is slight & dark with a half solemn, half humorous face, & a lot of rough black hair always falling over her face. [66]

Despite or perhaps because of the fact that she was the granddaughter of a former Provost of Trinity College, Dublin, Alice Lloyd was something of a rebel. At Newnham she struck up a friendship with one of the lecturers, Ellen Crofts. Crofts eventually married Francis, the third son of Charles Darwin, and Lloyd married Albert Dew Smith, assistant to Francis' brother Horace. In her reminiscence of her childhood in Cambridge in the 1880s, Ellen Crofts' niece Gwen Raverat recalled that 'Aunt Ellen and her friends [were] 'wonderfully up to date and literary.' She then went on to describe how impressed she had been with the fact that they smoked cigarettes whilst 'sitting in wicker chairs in the delightful untidy veranda' playing word games – 'making rhymes about their friends' – and adding: 'The veranda was full of pretty things ... Persian rugs and gay cushions, and even the dogs' drinking bowls were made of queer Italian pottery.'[67] This description implies that Alice Lloyd's 'aestheticism' was a consciously adopted pose (inviting the supposition that perhaps she had been the target of the ridicule so firmly stamped on by Jemima Clough). Amy, who may have been aware of this, paid tribute to Alice's unconventional persona in her mockingly satirical verse 'To Lallie (Outside the British Museum)':

> There was a friend, my friend, with you;
> A meagre dame, in peacock blue,
> Apparelled quaintly, ...
>
> Your gown was grey, I recollect,
> I think you patronized the sect
> They call "aesthetic."

Another Cambridge woman, who, like Alice Lloyd, was immortalised by Amy in verse, was the wife of Charles Villiers Stanford, the conductor of the Cambridge University Musical Society.[68] A press cutting of Amy's poem 'To Sylvia' which she pasted into her scrapbook is inscribed 'Mrs. Stanford'. Like Alice Lloyd, Jennie Stanford – the former Jennie Wetton – had a pioneering streak in her nature. It has been said of her that, if she had been a man 'she would have climbed Everest or explored the Grand Canyon.'[69] However, although these particular avenues were closed to her, in general she did not allow the limitations imposed upon her by her sex to cramp her style.

Apart from the difference in their religion, Amy Levy and Jennie Wetton came from remarkably similar backgrounds. Like Lewis Levy, Jennie's father 'Champion' Wetton had been something of a maverick, dragging his unfortunate wife and children along in his wake as he 'indulged in a series of risky enterprises around the world.' The last of these was a speculative trip to Australia, where, again like Lewis, he had hoped to make his fortune in the Gold Rush. Sadly, unlike Amy's father, he returned home having failed in his enterprise, a broken man, dying 'at 49 probably from exhaustion'.[70] After her husband's death Jennie's mother took up the reins of the household, disposing of the large Elizabethan farmhouse that was the family home, and moving to more modest accommodation nearby. As a result, the only legacy that Champion left to his daughter was a will to do as she pleased. However, she was not entirely bereft of assets, as she had a remarkable singing voice, and on the advice of George Grove, who was a family friend, she was dispatched to Leipzig 'to study under the famous Goetz'.[71] There, one evening at a party, she was accompanied on the piano by Charles Villiers Stanford, who, unbeknown to her, had been asked to keep a discreet eye on her, as her family feared that her headstrong temperament would lead her astray – as indeed it nearly did (and of which more later). Unaware of Stanford's reputation, she berated him for playing 'much too fast'. Although he meekly obeyed her command, slowing the tempo of his accompaniment, in private he branded her 'an impertinent minx'. But his bruised ego was soon soothed by her winning ways and pretty face, and after a protracted engagement due to his parents' opposition to the match they were finally married in April 1878. After the wedding he bore his bride home in triumph to Cambridge where they were 'received with open arms'. Once installed in her new home Jennie Stanford resumed her musical career, performing her husband's arrangements of traditional Irish melodies at Cambridge Musical Society concerts, and delighting the audience with her beautiful voice, which was enhanced by her classic English rose looks. Amy, who was reputed to have 'had an almost pathetic admiration for physical beauty' also loved music, and after seeing Mrs. Stanford perform she too fell under her spell.[72]

Jennie Stanford inspired two of Amy Levy's finest poems: 'To Sylvia' and 'Sinfonia Eroica' (also dedicated 'To Sylvia'). Both were written after she left Cambridge, in the winter of 1881 or the spring of 1882.[73] Much has been made of the apparent expression of lesbian desire in 'Sinfonia Eroica'. Indeed, the majority of those who have written about Amy Levy in recent years have placed great emphasis upon this supposed aspect of her literary oeuvre, hailing her as a pioneer of lesbian writing. To justify this claim her friendships with women have been seized upon, and the supposed homoerotic message of a number of her poems, including 'Sinfonia Eroica', has been cited. [74] But the only concrete evidence that she harboured romantic feeling towards her own sex is her openly acknowledged schoolgirl crush on Edith Creak which, taken by itself, means nothing. In fact the issue of her sexuality is not at all clear-cut because, viewed from the perspective of the twenty-first century, it is difficult for us to understand just how innocent young Victorian women were. 'Girlhood' lasted more or less until the moment that they set off down the aisle, or, in the case of those who had not succeeded in snaring a husband, they had reached an age when they were deemed to be 'on the shelf', at which point they took on the unenviable status of maiden aunt. Throughout this time any contact that they had with the opposite sex was supervised with extreme vigilance. Strong-minded young women like Jennie Wetton and Amy Levy heartily resented this curtailment of their personal freedom. Wetton caused an outrage in her family when, during a journey back to Leipzig via Berlin, she gave her two elderly chaperones the slip and allowed a dashing officer in the German army to give her a guided tour of the city before escorting her to the station to catch her connecting train. Although, as we have seen, her family were fairly unconventional in Victorian terms, nonetheless they would not sanction any behaviour that might tarnish their daughter's reputation. The Jewish community guarded their daughters with even greater zeal – as Amy was later to highlight with bitter irony in her essay 'Middle-Class Jewish Women of To-Day':

> What, in fact is the ordinary life of a Jewish middle-class woman? Carefully excluded, with almost Eastern jealousy, from every-day intercourse with men and youths of her own age, she is plunged all at once – a half-fledged often half-chaperoned creature – into the "vortex" of a middle-class ball-room, and is there expected to find her own level ...Her parents are jealous of her healthy, objective activities, of the natural employment of her young faculties, of anything in short which diverts her attention from what should be the one aim and end of her existence! If, in spite of all the parental efforts she fail, from want of money or want of attractions, in obtaining a husband, her lot is a desperately unenviable one. Following out the old traditions, the parental authority is strained to the utmost verge, and our community affords us many a half-ludicrous, half-pathetic spectacle of a hale woman of thirty making her way about the world in the very shortest and tightest of leading strings.[75]

Like everyone else, Amy would have had sexual urges, but as a young unmarried woman living in an era when even the most 'advanced' members of society balked at owning up to their 'animal instincts' (as the sex drive was coyly termed), it would have been impossible for her to openly acknowledge this. However, just as 'romantic friendships' between young women were then accepted without question, so effusive expressions of woman-to-woman affection in letters and literature were commonplace, and not necessarily associated with sexual feeling. Lucy Bland has emphasised how important it is 'to stress the *normality* of same-sex loving relationships in many women's lives' at that time.[76] At that date it would certainly have been more readily acceptable for a young girl like Amy to write passionate verse addressed to another woman than to a man. Of course, there may well have been an element of physical attraction in her admiration for Mrs. Stanford, but emotions, particularly in the young, are complex, and their nuances are not always easily expressed. Moreover, nineteenth-century society was not as obsessed with sex as we are nowadays. Before the theories of the sexologists took a hold on the public mind toward the end of the nineteenth century, the idea that people could be categorised according to their sexual orientation in the way that we do today would not be understood. Lillian Faderman, who has made an in-depth study of the history of woman-to-woman relationships highlights the difficulty that the twentieth (and now twenty-first) century reader has in understanding the mindset of the nineteenth-century writer. She explains: 'The twentieth century has rejected … subtleties by insisting that a woman is either a lesbian or she isn't; and if she is, she is abnormal; therefore a woman who loves another woman passionately is abnormal … [nineteenth-century] writers could present the most passionate love scenes between women and not be concerned that they were dealing with "abnormality"'. [77] Indeed, as Janet Oppenheim has pointed out, 'a general sense that close female attachments were abnormal … only began to emerge during the war years'.[78] Within the context of her time Amy Levy would therefore not have considered herself to be 'abnormal', and would consequently have seen nothing amiss in her emotional outpouring 'to Sylvia' in 'Sinfonia Eroica'. She would also no doubt have been appalled at the idea that one of her finest poems might in the future be construed as a work of semi-pornography.

In fact, there is good reason to believe that Amy's feelings for Jennie Stanford were based upon envy as much as anything else. Support for this theory can be found in two of the unpublished manuscripts that are amongst her surviving papers. The first of these, a novelette entitled 'Lallie: A Cambridge Sketch', is a Darwinian narrative of a love triangle in which the conventional 'nineteenth-century maiden' is worsted by the eugenically 'fit' New Woman. Amy's New Woman, Rhoda Cholmoneley, is an amalgam of her two real-life heroines, Edith Creak and Jennie Stanford. The eponymous 'nineteenth-century maiden', Lallie Garvagh (who was modelled on her Irish classmate, Alice Lloyd), is one of the ill-starred 'dark characters' with whom Amy so readily identified. Lallie has, we are told, 'brown hands', a 'brown face', 'dark Irish eyes', and 'curly, Irish hair, which was rather a grief to its owner, because of an uncontrollable tendency to stand out in great wisps from her head'. This precisely matches Amy's description of Alice Lloyd in her letter to her mother: 'slight & dark with a half solemn, half humorous face, & a lot of rough black hair always falling over her face'. Lallie is the only daughter of an elderly don. Ill-educated and underemployed, she passes her time wandering listlessly around the garden or lounging in her father's study listening to the 'half-understood' conversation of the 'learned men' who are his only visitors. The sole focus to her aimless existence is the informal tuition in the classics, given out of pity for her situation by Francis Duchesne, one of her father's younger colleagues. Duchesne is also coaching Rhoda, who is a student at 'Newton College', for the Tripos. It is made clear that in this and every other respect Rhoda is Lallie's superior. Where Lallie is ignorant and untidy, Rhoda is erudite and well-groomed. A veritable English Rose, she has 'well cut delicately united features', a 'broad forehead' (which signals her superior intellect), and 'light-brown hair [that falls in] full free curves'. And whereas Lallie is the archetypical Victorian dutiful daughter, home-bound and at her elderly father's beck and call, Rhoda is a free spirit, a woman who, according to Duchesne is 'without precedent … an entirely modern production, not to be measured according to the old standards.' Duchesne himself is a similarly flawless specimen of well-bred English manhood: 'tall, slight [and] fair' with a face that 'owed its wonderful charm rather to refinement and beauty of expression … than to any striking perfection of form or colour'. Confronted with two such paragons Lallie can have no illusion about her own inferiority. Comparing herself to the soulless Undine,[79] she tells Duchesne that she is a 'horrid little drone who's managed to live … without ever having done anything worth doing'[80]. However, Lallie is not quite as 'soulless' as she believes herself to be, for like her creator, Amy Levy, she loves music. And like Charles Villiers Stanford, Duchesne is an accomplished pianist. While listening to him play, for 'one golden hour,[81]' Lallie is released from the bondage of her humdrum existence and transported into a realm where she is

> conscious of nothing but those enchanting sounds filling the dusty room, and the beautiful pale face bending over the keys; if indeed it could be called consciousness where music and musician were merely the subtly blent elements of a glorious dream

This passage is an echo of the closing lines of 'Sinfonia Eroica':

> Then back you leaned your head, and I could note
> The upward outline of your perfect throat;

And ever, as the music smote the air,
Mine eyes from far held fast your body fair.
And in that wondrous moment seem'd to fade
My life's great woe, and grow an empty shade
Which had not been, nor was not.
I knew
Not which was sound, and which, O Love, was you.

Amy Levy's 'great woe', like that of her imaginary heroine, Lallie Garvagh, was her unshakable belief in her own 'unfitness'. And her encounter with Mrs. Stanford at Cambridge can only have served to reinforce her sense of inferiority. A testament to her poor opinion of herself at this time is the pencil drawing of 'Rhoda Cholmoneley' that accompanies the manuscript of 'Lallie: A Cambridge Sketch'. This, like the text, is signed with the self-deprecating pseudonym 'the dog with the bad name'.

In Rhoda Cholmoneley Amy had created her ideal, a woman with the intellectual power of Edith Creak and the personal charms of Jennie Stanford. But whereas Edith Creak provided her with a model of a level of academic achievement that she could aspire to match herself, Jennie Stanford embodied everything that she knew in her heart that she would never be or have. The second manuscript that gives an insight into her feelings for Mrs Stanford is a draft of a blank verse bearing the title: 'Poeta Esuriens' – The Hungry Poet. It ends with the lines

And shall we not in hatred curse the pow'r
That gave us such a stomach for the fare
We are doomed not to taste of …

An addendum to the manuscript is a sheet of rhyming verse entitled 'A Prayer', which is inscribed at the bottom right hand corner of the page: 'Dec/80 (op.'Poeta Esuriens)'. The paper is adorned in the margin with a number of sketches of the head of a woman that are not only remarkably similar to the sketch of Rhoda Cholmoneley that accompanies Amy's short story, but also bear a striking resemblance to contemporary photographs of Jennie Wetton/Stanford.[82] Aware of the gulf (as she perceived it) between herself - a forlorn, dark-skinned outsider with a limited talent for versifying and storytelling - and the glamorous Jennie Stanford - a self-confident and gifted musician with an established career, classical beauty and an adoring husband – Amy gave vent to her grief and frustration in a poetic outpouring of self-pity and defiance:

> Since that I may not have
> Love on this side of the grave
> Let me imagine love;
> Since not mine is the bliss
> Of clasped hands and lips that kiss,
> Let me in dreams it prove.
> What tho' as the years roll,
> No soul shall melt to my soul
> Let me conceive such thing;
> Tho' never shall entwine
> Loving arms around mine,
> Let dreams caresses bring
> To live, it is my doom,
> Lonely as in a tomb,
> This cross on me was laid:
> My God, I know not why;
> Here in the dark I lie
> Lonely, yet not afraid…
> Yet grant me thus, to find,
> The sweetness in my mind,
> My body must forego;
> Great God wh. Art above,
> Grant me to image love,
> The bliss, without the woe.[83]

In such a frame of mind, Amy was susceptible to any act of kindness. She reported to her mother that 'Madge Nelly, Alice and I went to King's; Conny and Miss Bond were there also; the latter had been to see me and asked me to call on her, I think it was very kind, as I know her very little.' 'Miss Bond' was evidently a former pupil of the Brighton High School, for in an earlier letter Amy had reported: 'Saturday afternoon all the Brighton High sch. people including Miss Bond came to my room and we had gt. fun.' The Bonds were a prominent Cambridge family, and Mr. Bond kept open house for the young friends of his sons and daughters. One of these was Amy's contemporary at Newnham, Ada Brown (later Keynes). She recalled:

> Mr. Bond's hospitable house in Brookside was open to many young people, schoolfellows and friends of his daughters, including several Newnham students, Members of the University who were contemporaries and colleagues of his son, Henry Bond, af-

> terwards Master of Trinity Hall. It was a delightful circle of young people. The elder daughter, Miss Ann Bond, some years older than the rest of us, was one of the kindest and most unselfish people I have ever known …[84]

One of Harry Bond's closest friends was Karl Pearson, a former student at King's, who at that time was lecturing for the Cambridge Extension Movement. It is not now possible to determine precisely when and where Amy Levy and Karl Pearson's paths first crossed, but it is likely that it was at the Bonds' house, as a number of his close friends attended the gatherings there. If this is the case, then just at the moment that Amy was struggling to come to terms with her own feelings about her religion and her sexuality she encountered Pearson, who was engaged in the same quest.

Like the fictional Frank Duchesne, Pearson was a paradigmatic representative of the intellectual exclusivity and glamorous lifestyle that was so attractive to the first female students at Cambridge.[85] At that time he was also something of a 'star' at the university, as in 1879, the same year that Amy entered Newnham, he had been ranked third wrangler in the Tripos examinations. From this distance in time it is difficult to convey the significance of this achievement, but it has been claimed that 'in the late nineteenth century [the Tripos] had something like the status of the Oxford-Cambridge boat race … It would probably have been televised had the technology been available …A great tumult surrounded the announcement of the winners at Senate House [and] the top wranglers … had their pictures the next day in the newspapers' – as Pearson did.[86] However, the intense level of study necessary to shine in the Tripos did not prevent him from pursuing other interests. A keen tennis player, he also dabbled – with varying degrees of accomplishment - in a wide range of subjects. And although he is now remembered as the founding father of statistical methodology, in his youth he aspired to be a poet.

As far as his personal attributes were concerned, he possessed a charismatic personality and, as befitted a follower of Charles Darwin who was destined to become a Professor of Eugenics, he was a model of eugenically desirable physical perfection. But his character, although superficially charming, had a darker and more sinister aspect. Even his friends described him as a cold fish - 'remote', 'intolerant', 'a lump of ice' and 'impersonal' - were just a few of the epithets applied to him by those who knew him well. As a result, he experienced problems in relating to women for although he undoubtedly had the knack of attracting them he was apparently unable to handle the consequences. His curious, somewhat sadistic approach to courtship is best demonstrated in remarks he was to make some years later in a letter to his then fiancée, Maria Sharpe:

> Younger women have had their attractions for me, but it has usually been with a sort

> of half cynical intent of waking them by saying bitter things out of their zest[?] and self-content… the one or two younger women, whom I have half-unconsciously raised feeling in, have been roused because I simply scourged them with hard sayings as they were not wont to be treated.[87]

Nevertheless, despite his poor opinion of young women in general, at the time that Amy first met him they would have had much in common. Like her, he was subject to fits of melancholy, and being by nature aloof and judgemental he had experienced similar difficulty in adjusting to life at the university, where he too was evidently regarded as something of a curiosity. The tutor who had coached him for his unsuccessful attempt to win a scholarship for Trinity described him as 'a little peculiar' – comparing him to 'the character of Kenelm Chillingly in Bulwar's novel.'[88] When he finally went up to King's in 1875 his parents, concerned by his obvious unhappiness, constantly urged him 'to be more sociable so that he might make friends'. While he was at King's he underwent a religious crisis, and refused to attend the compulsory divinity lectures and services in the chapel. This act of defiance generated a heated exchange of letters between him, his father and the college authorities. He explained his actions thus: 'I have conscientious objections to any form of compulsion in Religious matters, believing that freedom is the very essence of Religion, and considering that compulsory attendance at services … tends to destroy entirely all religious feeling.' Of course, Amy was not required to attend services at church or chapel either, and, as we have seen, this probably reinforced her feelings of alienation from her fellow students. And there is also good reason to believe that by this time she too was beginning to question the validity of her own religious beliefs.

A couple of years after he went up to Cambridge, Pearson began to record his thoughts in a commonplace book. This performed the dual function of workbook and confessional - a private space where he could give free expression to his doubts about Christianity and his concerns about the injustices of Victorian society. He also recorded some characteristically caustic comments about the shortcomings of the female sex, and acknowledged his ambition to become 'a mighty poet'. Unfortunately, in this instance, hope triumphed over reason, as the following lines demonstrate:

> A Byron Keats or Shelley would I be.
> (I thought in truth I could be all three)
> The world forsooth I'd revolutionize.
> Abolish kings, priests, customs, mockeries.[89]

While Amy was at Cambridge she was also busy plying her pen, gathering together a collection of verses, which were published by private subscription under the title *Xantippe and Other Verse* by E. Johnson of Cambridge in 1881.[90] The same firm issued Pearson's *The Trinity: A Nineteenth Century Passion Play* in the following year. No record relating to the publication of Amy's work now exists,[91] but Pearson paid 'about thirty pounds for the printing of three hundred copies of his "passion play"'. Messrs. Johnson had agreed to take their own fees from the sales of the book, and this proved to be a costly mistake, as Pearson's work sank virtually without trace. This was not only because of the contentious nature of its subject matter – he represented Mary Magdalene as a sensual seductress who was determined to lead Jesus astray – but also because of the fact that, as his former publisher Charles Kegan Paul unkindly pointed out, he lacked sufficient ability as a poet.[92] In contrast *Xantippe* received considerable notice, and although some critics regretted the author's tendency to dwell upon 'loneliness' and 'melancholy', their opinion of the work was generally favourable. And despite the fact that it was not advertised, the first edition sold out entirely.[93]

In August 1881 the *Literary World* published an article under the heading 'A Newnham Student's Poems'. The unnamed correspondent evidently shared Pearson's poor opinion of women in general, but in this instance he was prepared to be generous. After some introductory comments about the passing of the Three Graces[94] he continued:

> But we have been carried far out of our course in the reflections; our original purpose was to briefly notice the first volume of verse, so far as we know, which has been published by a student at one of these colleges for Miss Levy is, we believe, in residence at Newnham ... We have read her volume with genuine satisfaction, for though there is one poem which wisdom would, perhaps, have omitted,[95] from the first page to the last the workmanship is firm and sound. Slovenliness in literary finish has always been a fault attributed to women, and with more or less of truth; but Miss Levy has so far profited by her training and opportunities and there is hardly a line which will not past muster in the most rigorously critical examination. The literary prizes of the University are not accessible to the women students, but in poetical competition, with an open field, so conscientious a writer would have nothing to fear on that score.

Even today, the strength of the feminist message in 'Xantippe' (the poem from which the volume took its title) is striking. It had been written before Amy went up to Newnham, but her experiences there can only have served to strengthen her belief in the importance of female emancipation. Like 'Run to Death' (which is also included in the collection), 'Xantippe' is a critique of the treatment meted out to 'un-fair' women in an unfair society. The verse takes the form of a soliloquy spoken by Socrates' shrewish wife to her maids on her deathbed. As her life gradually fades away, Xantippe describes the lingering death of her own dreams. An idealist in youth, like George Eliot's Dorothea Brooke, she had anticipated that marriage to an older and wiser man would enable her to realise her own 'high thoughts and …golden dreams', and that under his kindly guidance her mind would blossom. However, she soon discovered that her opinions were not required, and she had to accept the unpalatable fact that all her husband expected in a wife was a 'household vessel'. Socrates the 'high philosopher', like Pearson 'Deigned not to stoop to touch so slight a thing/As the fine fabric of a woman's brain', preferring instead to spend his time in the company of a 'gay group' of male companions. Amy intended no irony here, as the word 'gay' had not at that time acquired the connotation that it has today. That said, her description of 'Alkibiades the beautiful' lying prostrate at the feet of his master does introduce a homosexual *frisson* into the narrative. As a well-brought-up young Victorian, it is highly unlikely that she knew anything about physical relationships between men – or women for that matter - but during her periods of residence at The Wick she would have had a unique opportunity to observe at first hand the intense male bonding that was an accepted aspect of life at a boys school in the nineteenth century. In Amy's poem, the only woman that Socrates deems worthy of regard is 'the fair Aspasia' who, according to his judgement, 'hath a mind … of a strength beyond her race'. Amy is here using the term 'race' to stand for 'sex' and in so doing is signalling her familiarity with Darwinian theory. In *The Descent of Man* Darwin had argued that woman had retained many of the faculties of 'lower races' and that 'the chief distinction in the intellectual powers of the two sexes is shown by man's attaining to a higher eminence in whatever he takes up, than can woman'.[96] She also suggests that Socrates' high opinion of Aspasia's intellect is influenced by the fact that she is 'fair' whereas, like the poem's author, Xantippe is 'black-browed'. Of course, the fact that Socrates is less than 'fair' himself is of no account, for it is only women who are judged by their appearance. And just as Amy Levy could never be a Rhoda Cholmoneley or Jennie Stanford, so swarthy Xantippe is not 'the fair Aspasia'. The bleak description of the dreary demise of her youthful ambition is a remarkable piece of psychological observation – all the more remarkable when account is taken of the fact that when she wrote the verse the author was just sixteen years old:

> A huge despair was stealing on my soul,
> A sort of fierce acceptance of my fate, –
> He wished a household vessel – well 'twas good,
> For he should have it! ……

I called my maidens, ordered out the loom,
And spun unceasing from the morn till eve…
I spun until, methinks, I spun away
The soul from out my body,
the high thoughts
From out my spirit; till at last I grew
As ye have known me, – eye exact to mark
The texture of the spinning; ear all keen
For aimless talking when the moon is up…
… I have wrought
My weary duties, patient to the last

With her fictional creation in her mind, and the example of her mother before her eyes - the living proof of August Webster's dictum that a woman's time is 'needless to the owner and free to whoever takes it, like blackberries in a hedge'[97] – Amy had set out for Newnham with the determination (perhaps not consciously formed) to avoid the fate of women such as her mother and Xantippe. Like many of her fellow students, she left Cambridge without sitting for the Tripos. But as she took her first steps across 'life's great threshold' she could, with justification, hold her head high. The reception of *Xantippe and Other Verse* had been a remarkable achievement for one so young, and its author found herself, at not quite twenty years old, the first Jewish woman to have studied at Newnham College, Cambridge, and a published poet with a burgeoning literary reputation

The Mountains in Fantastic Lines': Dresden and Switzerland, 1881-1883

The mountains in fantastic lines
Sweep, blue-white, to the sky, which shines
Blue as blue gems; athwart the pines
The lake gleams blue.

We three were here, three years gone by;
Our Poet, with fine frenzied eye,
You, steeped in learned lore, and I
A poet too …

Amy Levy, 1861–1889: 'To E'

Shortly after she left Cambridge, in the autumn of 1881, Amy set out upon the first of the extended visits to the continent that were to become a regular feature of her adult life. These journeys were a source of simultaneous anxiety and delight to her, because although her natural shyness made her shrink from the close contact with strangers that travel entailed, she never allowed it to overcome her enjoyment of new sights and sensations. Travel also offered her a welcome means of escape from the family home where, after her return from Cambridge, she was coming under increasing pressure to conform to her parents' expectations. At Newnham she had enjoyed her first taste of independence and did not intend to relinquish this newfound freedom lightly. In order to escape from the demands of her family she needed an income, and during her journeys, the people and the places that she encountered provided her with the inspiration for a series of short stories which she submitted to contemporary journals. The fees that she received from the publication of these lightweight tales were of particular benefit to her at this time, as the uncertain state of her father's financial affairs created problems that were felt particularly keenly by his two eldest, and as yet unmarried, daughters.

Amy's first continental foray took her to Germany, where she spent the winter of 1881 and the early part of 1882 in the city of Dresden. During her stay she kept in touch with her family through a flow of correspondence, much of which has now been lost. But of the six letters that do remain four are addressed to her mother, and these cast a revealing light upon the difficulties that she was beginning to experience in her adult relationship with her parents. However, at the time that the first of the letters was written these problems had not yet surfaced, and she was full of enthusiasm for the places that she visited and the people that she met. This first letter, dated 4th October, was addressed to Katie, and was evidently written shortly after her arrival in Dresden, as it begins with the information that she is awaiting the arrival of her 'first (and at present, only pupil)'. This was the first hint of the troubles that were to come. After commenting 'we are going on with the same humour as before and we continue to marvel at all we see and hear' she regales her sister with a lively and amusing account of the idiosyncrasies of the guests at the pension where she and her travelling companion (referred to in this instance as 'Maggie', but elsewhere as 'Madge') had set up home for the winter.[98] The letter continues with some comments on the recent Jewish festival of Yom Kippur (the Day of Atonement, when observant Jews fast in order to expiate their sins, and which takes place in late September or early October). 'How did everybody fast?' Amy enquired, 'and did you miss your stalwart cohort of last year?' The letter closes with some sisterly advice on the best course to take in order to secure a scholarship, indicating that Katie was hoping to follow in her footsteps, and was preparing herself for entry to Newnham.[99]

The second letter, dated 5th November and addressed to her mother, is far less animated and more perfunctory in tone. After thanking her for forwarding correspondence, she complains 'nothing has happened this week', but on a more optimistic note adds 'next week I am going to an atelier (or sort of drawing school for girls) to sit for my portrait'. This is followed by the wry comment 'I am considered rather beautiful here than otherwise!'[100]

The third letter, dated 10th November (which was her birthday) begins on a more light-hearted note. Thanking her mother for her gift, which was evidently photographs of the younger members of the family, Amy comments: 'We both roared over Ned; I rather think he admires himself in his new clothes'. Going on to describe recent events, one of which was 'a meeting in connection with some tableaux vivants in which I am to take part' she slips in the revelation that 'there is to be a dance [afterwards] given by a literary club where I have been several times.' The letter ends with the aside 'I don't like being twenty at all; I think my arrival in the world was rather an unfortunate occurrence for everyone concerned.'[101]

By 27th November, the date of the fourth letter, her mood has undergone a further decline, and the handwriting (always a good guide to Amy's mental state) shows a marked deterioration. It seems that Isabelle had attributed her daughter's gloomy state of mind to homesickness, but Amy hastily reassured her mother: 'You are mistaken — I have no particular desire to return home, and should be very sorry to cause such an unnecessary expense as Alfred's journey. Some friends of mine are coming out fr. Cambridge very probably, at Easter, & I might perhaps return with them. Meantime, please don't imagine I am miserable here.' It appears that the real reason for her despondent mood was Isabelle's reaction to the news of the tableaux vivants and the dance as, turning to this subject, Amy observes bitterly: 'The dance (most completely decent, I assure you – rather too much so!) I found very amusing as a spectacle, tho' knowing no one I didn't take much part in it. We had 3 old ladies with us … so were well chaperoned.' She was also worrying about money, resentful of the fact that she had to rely upon her father for financial support. After asking her mother to thank 'Papa for his letter' she comments: 'I am delighted to hear from the magnificent way in wh. he talks that he has at last "struck oil"! But you know that I can't feel very happy about myself & the money I spend in spite of all his kindness.' Determined to change the situation, she took a course of action which, in view of her mother's reaction to the dance, she must have known would cause consternation, but went ahead anyway, telling her mother defiantly:

> I have some new pupils 2 boys (11 & 16) for English, but I don't begin with them till after next week. They will bring in 3/- a week so I shall be earning 5/- a week. I am also reading Greek with a Cambridge man here, to whom Mr. Gilderdale (the English clergyman) recommended me. I don't know how much it will be – he wanted to do it for nothing, but of course I did not want that, and he said we wd. settle it afterwards. I will ask him about it next time, & only hope it isn't much; if it is I won't go on long. I am going to-morrow to a Shakespeare reading at his house …[102]

These provoking revelations produced an immediate and predictable response from Isabelle, for, as we have seen, despite her tolerance of her daughters' intellectual aspirations, when the question of their spiritual guidance or the guardianship of their morals was at stake she fulfilled her role as Victorian matriarch to the letter. Fearful for Amy's reputation, she took immediate action to put an end to what she plainly regarded as a compromising situation. The result was the following petulant response from her daughter on 2nd December:

> Thanks for the letter and papers. You will see from my letter to Papa that I have given up the idea of teaching those boys tho' I can't see the matter from your point of view. As to my coach – he has a wife & baby, both of them very nice of their kind; the former called on me yesterday … But seriously, you needn't have any fears on my account; I regret to say that I am as safe as Grandmama cd. be; There wdn't be any impropriety (excepting fr. an outside point of view) in my teaching any number of young men. I have never excited in anyone a desire to 'forget themselves' in any way wh. has its advantages, especially in my present circumstances.[103]

As Amy was well aware, it was the 'outside point of view' that most concerned her mother. But it is clear that, having reached the age of twenty, she was beginning to heartily resent the authority that her parents exerted over her. Aware that the key to her freedom was financial independence, she found her plan to capitalise upon her newly acquired educational skills had been thwarted by what she patently regarded as bourgeois notions of propriety. Unable to defy her mother because of her financial dependence upon her father, her suppressed rage and frustration manifested itself in physical and psychological illness. On 8th December she wrote despairingly to Katie:

> out of the very depths of affliction brought on by a diseased body. God must love me awfully for he chasteneth me without cease; now alas! to the many woes of the spirit and flesh he has added a ceaseless neuralgia, not to speak of a stye-eye & an abscess beneath the arm, which has had to be cut (ugh!) ... I feel so bad that I think if all my Pecks wrote & 'popped' that it wd. afford me but small consolation.

Pecks may be a shorthand reference to the character Pecksniff in Dickens' *Martin Chuzzlewit*. In the slang of the time a 'Pecksniff' was a canting hypocrite. 'Popped' is undoubtedly an abbreviation of 'to pop the question'. The bitter allusion to her 'present circumstances' in the previous letter, together with this ironic comment, is a further indication that, as she had earlier confessed, she did not regard herself as a likely candidate for the only certain means of escape from the family clutches – matrimony. She complained:

> I did secure those boys as pupils but was not allowed to teach them. Don't you call that simply absurd? But what can I do? So I go on from. day to day consuming the paternal substance. I don't see why you shdn't. fling yr. little pennies away at Polish Bank or any other game because you have not succeeded in finding a husband. I feel really sorry for you, for I don't see who there is to rescue you from old maidism ...But never mind, my child, 'thank with brief thanksgiving whatever gods there be that no life lives for ever etc.' & and go yr. little journey gravewards as cheerfully as you can. As for me my soul is dead my heart [drawn as heart shaped symbol] is broken – sour and Sara-like old age has come upon me ere my time Madge and I sit like two aged crones & talk about the past – by mutual consent avoiding any reference to the future.

The letter ends on a sinister note:

> really if this confounded neuralgia don't stop I shall have to hie me to a chemist – no not a chemist – the river; for the German chemist is alas! not permitted to retail one death-fraught drug to the chance customer. Write soon to the profoundly miserable AL.[104]

The facetious reference to the chemist and the river, with its underlying threat, is the first hint that her anger and resentment were turning inwards and becoming self-destructive.

From this time onwards Amy's dissatisfaction with her life was increasingly translated into dissatisfaction with her body. Having no doubt been adjured, as were most Victorian children, to 'honour thy father and thy mother,' she found herself unable to acknowledge the animosity that she felt towards her parents. Tormented by guilt and self-loathing, she redirected her anger towards the community of which they, and she, were a part. In her first letter, written just after Yom Kippur, she had asked Katie:

> Please tell Mama that I went to synagogue yesterday – & a beastly place it was, Zion, unventilated and unrefreshed, sent forth an odour which made me feel Lindery [sic] for the rest of the day. The place was crammed with evil looking Hebrews. Lots of the shops were shut yesterday. ... The German Hebrews make me feel, as a rule, that the Anti-Semitic movement is a most just and virtuous one. [105]

This savage commentary reflects a growing hostility to her co-religionists, which, as time went by, manifested itself in increasingly harsh ridicule of their perceived physical shortcomings. Her own childhood encounter with anti-Semitism, reinforced by her real or imagined social isolation at Cambridge, had made her aware that to the majority of her fellows she would always be regarded as an alien. And although her education had raised her expectations beyond the narrow confines of the drawing rooms of Bayswater, it had also effectively severed her from her tribal roots, leaving her in limbo. Resentment festered in her mind, creating bitterness. But in this instance her bitterness had a positive aspect, for it fired her imagination, enabling her to turn her unhappy experience of life after Newnham into a money-spinning work of fiction. This was her short story 'Between Two Stools', which was published in the journal *Temple Bar* in 1883.[106] The narrative takes the form of letters addressed from 'Miss Nora Wycherley, Pembridge Square, W., to Miss Agnes Crewe, Newnham College, Cambridge'. Essentially a comedy of manners, the plot owes much to the influence of one of Amy's literary idols, Jane Austen. It is constructed upon Nora's attempt to reconcile her life within two opposing cultures, 'professional and commercial' London and 'academic' Cambridge. These are represented in the narrative by the characters of the 'philistine' Stephen Broke and 'scholarly' Reginald Talbot. For young women like Amy and her fictional alter ego, Nora, one of the main attractions of university life was the prospect it offered of an escape from the traditional role assigned to women within middle-class society. However, upon her return to the family home, Nora finds herself irresistibly drawn back into the frivolous world that her experience at Cambridge had taught her to despise. Eventually, despite her presumed intellectual superiority, she falls victim to her own emotions – an aspect of life against which her advanced education proves small defence.

As the tale unfolds, Amy interjects a commentary that may reflect her own experience of her return to the family home:

> I am in the very heart and centre of Philistia .... Everybody is quite respectable, rather dull, and just a little vulgar. We do not go in for noble ideals and high notions; but on the other hand we eschew large vices. ... We are not wicked; we are only on a rather low level of moral and intellectual culture, and present, perhaps, to the thoughtful observer a more depressing spectacle than a den of thieves ... Observe the fine satire of the 'we'; I am, as you see developing a pretty turn for cynicism. Who would not under the circumstances?
>
> Personally I find myself rather desolate, I am willing enough to smoke the pipe of peace with the Philistines, but the Philistines will have none of me. They distrust me: the girls think I want to 'come it' over them; and the young men are continually on the look-out for covert snubbing. One is afraid to call a thing by its right name for fear of being thought pedantic; it is not young-ladylike to have one's facts right or one's sentences logical. A pretty haziness, a charming inconsequence – these are the qualities the Philistine male would fain see in his womankind.

In fact, Stephen Broke is attracted by Nora's independent spirit, and it is only after her overt snubbing that he turns for consolation to the archetypically 'young-ladylike' Sybil Juniper. With a twist of irony characteristic of Amy Levy's later 'romantic' fiction, Reginald Talbot only begins to appreciate Nora's charms when, in a moment of despair, she drops her 'academic' guard and starts a desperate flirtation with the astonished don.

Levy's description of Sybil Juniper anticipates a number of her fictional anti-heroines. We are told that she

> is a most exasperating little person, very pretty in a heterodox manner, with fluffy fair hair, pink and white skin, and quite abnormally small waist and feet, at which last mentioned members my whole family is pleased to sit adoringly. I cannot join in the general worship, and am in consequence considered sinister and a little spiteful. But what rational person could bring themselves to accept this charming, empty headed, rattling creature as 'legal tender for a human being' – to quote George Eliot.

However, despite her low opinion of her rival, Nora - the supposedly 'strong minded woman'- is revealed as being incapable of mental consistency. In contrast, the air-headed Sybil Juniper pursues her quarry with single-minded determination. Nora ultimately falls between the two stools of Broke and Talbot, leaving Juniper the victor in the Darwinian 'struggle for survival' of the late Victorian marriage market. At the dénouement of her tale Amy provides her readers with an amusing alternative interpretation of the nineteenth-century cultural icon 'the fallen woman' for, as others have observed, for the Victorian woman to 'fall' was often simply 'to fall short'.[107] Amy's heroine falls short on two counts: by failing to live up to her own ideals, and by failing to fulfil the expectations of her family by her inability to secure a husband. She tells Agnes:

> In plain English I have played the fool and am suffering for it. Between my two stools I have fallen most woefully to the ground. I dare say I shall get up again one day, and that even all trace of the bruises will have vanished, but that sort of reflection does not console one very much at the time. Meanwhile I am left stranded. Every one is talking of the approaching engagement of Mr. Broke to Sybil Juniper; and Mr. Talbot has started for Rome.

Amy's mockery of her heroine reflects her own unease at her inability to escape from her bourgeois roots at a time when she was also struggling to come to terms with emotional turmoil. Nora relates how, when confronted with the reality of her situation:

> I was very miserable ... I used to read 'Felise' almost every night, and cry over it about as often, especially over one verse;
>
> Let this be said between us here:
> One love grows green when one turns grey;
> This year knows nothing of last year;
>   To-morrow has no more to say
>   To yesterday.
>
> Is it not a terrible poem? and yet I think it is the story of many women's lives.[108]

After her not altogether happy stay in Dresden, and the problems that she had encountered upon her return to the family home, Amy was fired with resolve to look forward to tomorrow, rather than backwards to yesterday. By this time the Levys had re-established their home in the capital (although they still retained the house in Brighton), and Amy was therefore able to take full advantage of the opportunities that London life offered. It was at this time she acquired a ticket for the Reading Room at the British Museum and began to attend meetings of a discussion group which bore the formal title 'A Men and Women's Club', but was known to its members merely as 'the club'.[109] As its formal name implies, the club was essentially a forum where men and women could meet on equal terms in order to discuss a range of issues that were of contemporary interest. Its commitment to social and sexual equality is demonstrated in its rules, which specifically stated that 'Members shall be officially known by their Christian and Surname without the conventional prefix.' This was a revolutionary form of address at that time, as men and women who were quite well acquainted still continued to address one another formally, as Mr,

Mrs. or Miss So-and-so. Throughout the 1880s many similar radical clubs sprang up all over the capital, as this was a decade of social and intellectual ferment. After the slump in trade and the decline in agriculture that had occurred during the 1870s, vast numbers of the rural poor had been driven into the great cities to seek employment. This led to an unprecedented increase in the urban population, with the result that by the mid-1880s a third of the inhabitants of London were living in conditions of dire poverty. The middle classes were particularly concerned by this development, as the uprising of the Paris commune in 1871 was still fresh in the public mind and there were widespread fears that the spirit of rebellion would spread to England. And the slums of the capital were regarded as a rich breeding ground for sedition. To add to the general climate of unease, the religious beliefs that underpinned the rigid Victorian social order were also under attack. After the publication of Charles Darwin's *The Origin of Species* in 1859 and *The Descent of Man* in 1871, many had found themselves adrift on a sea of uncertainty, pondering the question that Benjamin Disraeli had succinctly posed: 'is man an ape or an angel?' The effect of this potent combination of human misery and ideological uncertainty had galvanised the late Victorian chattering classes into action, prompting them to search for new systems of belief that would not only provide an alternative to the faith of their fathers but which, when applied within society, would ensure that a more enlightened social order would arise from the ashes of the old. The newly formed discussion clubs played a key role in this process. Women gained particular benefit from membership of these organisations, as they offered them an unprecedented opportunity to network with other like-minded souls without the constraints imposed upon them in drawing room society. This was to make a significant contribution to the success of campaigns like Josephine Butler's crusade to repeal the Contagious Diseases Act, which cast a harsh public spotlight upon the unsavoury aspects of the Victorian 'double standard' of sexual morality. The Act rendered women in seaports and military towns liable to compulsory examination for venereal disease without any similar requirement being imposed upon the men with whom they had consorted, and from whom they had contracted the diseases in the first place. Fear of venereal disease also fuelled the market for virgins, who were invariably very young girls. These fetched a premium price. In 1885 W.T. Stead's scandalous revelations about child prostitution published in *The Pall Mall Gazette* under the title 'The Maiden Tribute of Modern Babylon' created a storm of public protest that resulted in the passing of the Criminal Law Amendment Act, which raised the age of consent from 13 to 16. The public outcry that was aroused by these two congruent campaigns led Karl Pearson to found his own, better remembered, *The*

Men and Women's Club. Pearson thereby placed himself at the centre of contemporary discourse on 'the woman question', and his club – although short-lived – has since been widely acknowledged as a pioneering force in the late nineteenth-century debate on sex and the role of women in society.

But this was in the future. At the time that Amy became a member of A Men and Women's Club the discussions covered issues that, although forward thinking, were essentially uncontroversial in nature. This is reflected in the fact that her brothers Alfred, Edmund and William attended the club from time to time, and at least three of the meetings were held in the Levy family home. Unlike his sister, Alfred had no academic bent, and had followed his father on to the floor of the Stock Exchange. But despite his professional dedication to commerce he evidently had a social conscience, and appears to have devoted a proportion of his spare time to worthwhile causes. In February 1883 he took part in a short play, 'First Love', which was part of the programme of 'An Entertainment in Aid of St. John's Schools'. The 'Entertainment' was staged in the school rooms in Tottenham Court Road, and the cast also included Conny Black's sister, Grace and two other club members, Ernest Radford and Caroline Maitland.[110] At that time Caroline (who from childhood was always known as 'Dollie' because of her petite stature) was lodging with Grace and her sister Clementina in Albany Street, just around the corner from Tottenham Court Road. Clementina Black had introduced Amy to the club. Like Dollie Maitland Clementina was on intimate terms with the entire Marx family, although she was particularly close to Karl Marx's youngest daughter Eleanor, or 'Tussy' as her fond father called her.[111] Like Dollie, Eleanor was an enthusiastic amateur actress, but there the similarity between them ended, because whereas Eleanor's commitment to socialism kept her feet planted firmly on the ground, Dollie was an altogether more flighty character. A budding poet with mystical leanings, it was said of her that 'her gay silliness was one of her chief charms.[112] Nevertheless, in their different ways, Dollie and Tussy were both to become staunch friends of Amy's.

When the 'Entertainment' was staged in February 1883, Dollie was involved with her own 'first love', as Ernest Radford had fallen for her will-o'-the-wisp charms. They had first met in the Reading Room of the British Museum, which at that time was one of the few public places where young men and women could mix freely together without attracting the censure of Mrs. Grundy, the mythical guardian of the Nation's morals. During the early 1880s Eleanor was a regular visitor to the Reading Room and Dollie often joined her there. On one occasion they had noticed a handsome young man sitting at one of the desks, and while he was out of the room seized the opportunity to leave their cards upon it.[113] Radford, the object of their admiration, evidently lost no time in presenting himself at the door of the Marx household, and Dr. Marx observed with amusement that thereafter Dollie paid 'fearful court' to him during his subsequent visits to the family home.[114] Perhaps this account of Dollie's determined wooing reached Amy's ears and was translated into fiction in Sybil Juniper's single-minded pursuit of Stephen Broke in 'Between Two Stools'. She would definitely have known something of Radford's personal history, as his cousin Lydia and his sister Ada had been her contemporaries at Newnham. After Ada's arrival at the college she had struck up a close friendship with Conny Black, and seems thereafter to have superseded Amy in Conny's affections. According to a contemporary account, Ada was 'an attractive figure, with yellow hair, a pink and white complexion, very blue eyes behind steel-rimmed spectacles and hands and arms as shapely as any sculptor could wish'.[115] This description bears an uncanny resemblance to Amy's verbal portrait of Sybil Juniper in 'Between Two Stools'. However, unlike Sybil Juniper, Ada Radford possessed a powerful intellect, an attribute of which she seems to have been well aware, and in this respect Dollie Maitland's 'gay silliness' seems to better accord with Amy's depiction of Juniper. To judge by later comments that she made in her correspondence, Amy seems to have had an aversion to Ada Radford. Her antipathy may have stemmed from the fact that Ada had commandeered her friend, and perhaps Amy took her revenge for this betrayal with a literary version of the popular Victorian parlour game Picture Consequences. In this game one participant draws a head on a thin strip of paper, folds over the paper to conceal the head and passes it to the next person to draw the body, when the same process is repeated, with the next participant drawing the legs, after which the paper is unfolded to reveal a humorous composite image of a man or woman – or more often, a mixture of the two. Amy seems to have used this formula in 'Between Two Stools' in order to create a fictional but readily identifiable portrait of the body of her rival, Ada Radford, grafted to the head of her feather-brained but romantically determined future sister-in-law, Dollie Maitland.

Within a year or so of meeting, Dollie and Amy were paying frequent calls on one another. Dollie noted the details of these visits in her diary. On several occasions she attended tennis parties at the Levys', once recording with exasperation: 'Amy's aunt is the worst mannered person that I ever met!' Perhaps this was Aunt Bessie with the ten children, whose temper and patience would surely have been sorely tried by her maternal responsibilities. By May 1883 Amy's friendship with Dollie was on a sufficiently firm footing for her to accompany her and her sister Clara on a spring holiday to Hastings. By this time Dollie and Ernest Radford were engaged to be married, and the letters they exchanged during the visit offer an insight into the further decline in Amy's mental and physical health after her return from Dresden. On 1st May Dollie reported:

> We have been to Battle & Normanshurst with the Campbells.[116] Amy had a headache, & did not come. She is rather sad, I wish I could persuade her how much happiness there is in the world. She is morbid and unhappy, & seems to have no spring time in her heart, & no elasticity of spirits – I like her very much now I know her. ... [The Campbells] asked us to go with them to Winchelsea to-morrow, but Amy feels she would like to be quiet; so I've asked them to come here when they get back.[117]

The comment 'I like her very much now I know her' suggests that the friendship did not get off to an easy start. Amy did not suffer fools gladly, and despite (or perhaps because of) her feminist principles, had little sympathy for intellectual frailty in her female acquaintance. Dollie's 'gay silliness' would undoubtedly have grated upon her at first, and it is likely that there was initial constraint between the two. But for all Dollie's superficial air of frivolity, she had a genuinely kind heart, and was a steadfast friend to those she cared for. And Amy, who was always susceptible to kindness, seems to have aroused her ready sympathy. In an effort to divert her new friend's mind from her misery Dollie looked for ways to entertain her that did not involve outings with comparative strangers. She was looking forward to an imminent visit from her fiancée, and enquired, 'I hope you will bring the Heine book?' This was Ernest's *Translations from Heine* which had been published in 1882. It is highly unlikely that Dollie would not have already seen the book herself, but as Heinrich Heine was one of Amy's favourite poets it is reasonable to assume that the request was made on her behalf. As we have seen, Amy was not a person with whom others readily empathised. Her new friends were obviously conscious of her lack of social finesse, as in Radford's reply he enquired 'I hope you have had a good day and that the Campbells have not bored Amy Levy, or vicé versa [sic]'.

Soon after their trip to Hastings, Amy accompanied Dollie on another short holiday, but this time their destination was Cambridge, where they were to join in the May Week celebrations. Dollie wanted to get to know her future sister-in-law, Ada Radford, and also wanted to see Conny Black and 'all the old Harley Street girls' – her former schoolmates at Queen's College Harley Street[118]. She travelled on ahead of Amy and Conny met her at the station. Amy's travelling companion on this occasion was Dollie's close friend and fellow club member, Louis Jeeves. Louis was a talented young artist who, like Amy, was destined to die young.[119] Shortly after their arrival Dollie reported to Ernest: 'Conny has finished her tripos, and seems very well: But there are several drooping people around.'[120] Perhaps she counted Amy amongst the 'drooping people'. Ernest joined the party a day or so later, and Dollie left an account of the happy and activity-packed four-day visit in her diary. There were boating trips on the river, a tennis match at Girton and various gatherings at the Bond household. After returning to London, the group of friends reassembled to hear their fellow club member, Robert Parker, deliver a paper on 'Suicide'.[121] Parker was a particularly close friend of Karl Pearson, who had been his 'philosophical' tennis partner while they were undergraduates at King's College.[122]

A couple of months after her visit to Cambridge, in July 1883, Amy set off for her second Continental holiday, but this time she headed south towards Switzerland. In Switzerland the direct paper trail of her correspondence resumes once more, with three letters bearing the heading: 'Hotel Pension Sonnenberg, Seelisberg, Lucerne'. [123] The first of the letters, which is addressed to Isabelle, was written shortly after her arrival at the hotel. It reveals that despite Amy's admission to 'feeling awfully jolly at present' her anxiety about the strain imposed upon the family budget by her travels was still uppermost in her mind. The letter begins with an apology: 'We are now fairly settled in Seelisberg, having made all arrangements as to rooms etc., The prices I am afraid are rather bad 7 ½ & later 8 fr. a day for a quiet little room at the back of the house au troisieme [on the third floor].' Then, adopting a more enthusiastic tone, perhaps to justify the expense, she gives Isabelle a description of her idyllic surroundings:

> Seelisberg – which consists of two pensions[124] & some scattered châlets seems a simply perfect place as regards scenery & climate. It is very high up; & commands a view over Lake Lucerne (whose water is of a deep aesthetic blue-green) & the surrounding mountains whose size it is difficult to realise until one sees how small the houses at the bottom of them look.[125]

Even today, Seelisberg is much as Amy described it in her letter to her mother. The building that was the Hotel Sonnenberg still stands, and although now somewhat faded in glory, it must have been a magnificent sight in its heyday. In the 1880s the hotel – which had over 300 rooms – was known worldwide, and offered its guests a high degree of comfort and luxury. The impressive range of facilities included a ballroom accommodating five hundred people in which balls were held twice a week, and an indoor spa with a carbonated well. A second outdoor spring ran from a fountain on the vast terrace, which was lit at night by giant candelabra. Guests could amuse themselves with a variety of activities, including billiards, lawn tennis and croquet; and within the extensive grounds there was a small lake, which the guests used as a swimming pool.[126] We can see therefore, that despite her complaint about the expense and the inadequacy of her accommodation, the fact that Amy was able to afford to stay in the hotel at all indicates that the family finances cannot have been in an unduly parlous state at that time. However, there was evidently a collapse in prospect as in her second letter, which is addressed to Katie, she enquired:

> Are we going to be in a very bad way financially all this winter? O why doesn't Mary Robinson[127] or Algernon Charles [Swinburne] want a secretary! I have sent my tale 'perisonally'[128] to the aged Clementina & asked her if she thinks it is any good fr. a magazine point of view. I believe being educated has taken away all chance of my producing 'potboilers' – wh. is a grim reflection.[129]

The 'tale' was undoubtedly one of the series of short stories that she produced at regular intervals throughout the next few years. Manifestly written with an eye on the market, these lightweight productions, which she slightingly dismissed as 'potboilers', were published along with some of her verses in the popular journal London Society in the years 1883 to 1886. The first of the stories, a conventional 'romance' entitled 'The Diary of a Plain Girl',[130] appeared in September 1883, shortly after her return from Switzerland.

Amy's last surviving letter from the Hotel Sonnenberg was addressed to Clementina Black, and was evidently a response to a reply to an earlier request for help in finding a publisher for an unspecified literary work. From Amy's comments, one can deduce that this was not the 'tale' mentioned in the letter to Katie, as she asked 'Clemmy' to approach publishing houses rather than journals: 'I knew Cassell was no good – if you don't mind … Wd. you try Warne, Routledge, Dean & Shaw (48 Paternoster Row).' This last named publisher was John Farquar Shaw, whose offices were at 48 Paternoster Row. Although Shaw was primarily a publisher of religious tracts, he had also issued a number of works relating to poetry. These included Henry Hope Reed's *English History and Tragic Poetry* and *Lectures on British Poets*.[131] After some dismissive remarks about a mutual acquaintance, to which Amy added the plea 'of course Clemmy any feeble twaddle I write is only for your benevolent eye', she then turned once more to the subject of her work, saying that she had 'finished "Medea" after a fashion', adding: 'and I suppose I shall begin upon "Eustace" tomorrow.' [132] From this last comment it appears that Amy was writing and revising poems for publication. This impression is strengthened by her request 'If E. Radford's book is not of great price I wish you wd. Send me a copy.' The book in question would have been Radford's *Translations from Heine*, which Dollie had asked him to bring with him to Hastings. Over the years Amy made a number of her own translations from Heine, and one of the verses in her second collection of poetry, *A Minor Poet*, is subtitled 'After Heine'. It seems therefore that the work she had deputed Clemmy to market on her behalf was *A Minor Poet*. And if this was the case, then it would certainly have been a logical step for her to enlist Clemmy's help at this stage, as she had been instrumental in getting *Xantippe* into print.[133]

Like 'Xantippe', 'Medea', which is subtitled 'a fragment in drama form after Euripides', is an episode in classical mythology retold from a feminist perspective. But unlike Xantippe, Medea is disadvantaged by her race as well as her sex. Amy had written the first draft of the poem during the winter in Dresden, at the time when her anger at the perceived injustice of her lot was beginning to be directed towards her own community. Viewed in the light of her experience at Newnham, a personal appeal can be discerned in Medea's longing for acceptance by the 'strong, fair people, marble-cold and smooth', who despise her 'swart skin and purple hair'. And it is surely 'the hungry poet' Amy, disguised as Medea, who pleads:

> If they would only teach the subtle trick
> By which their hearts are melted into love,
> I'd strive to learn it. I am very meek.
> They think me proud, but I am very meek,
> Ready to do their bidding. Hear me friends!
> Friends, I am very hungry give me love!
> Tis all I ask! Is it so hard to give?

No trace now remains of a work entitled 'Eustace', but the tentative manner in which it is mentioned in the letter suggests that it was at an embryonic stage of development. When writing for the commercial market it was Amy's custom, by and large, to model her own works on those of established literary icons. The reference to 'Eustace' may therefore have been a shorthand reference to the fact that the poem was inspired by a work that would be familiar to the late Victorian reader - Anthony Trollope's *The Eustace Diamonds*. A year after her return from Switzerland, in August 1884, the 'Holiday Issue' of *London Society* included a verse by Amy Levy entitled 'Mariana in the Ballroom'. Although this is essentially a pastiche of Alfred Tennyson's 'Mariana in the Moated Grange' (the verse is headed with the quotation 'He cometh not'), it can also be read as a parody of the episode in chapter 8 of *The Eustace Diamonds* when Lizzie Eustace accepts the hand of Frederic Fawn in a fit of pique after a promised visit from Frank Greystock fails to occur. In Amy's verse the female narrator flirts with 'Freddy' in order to punish 'Frank' for his non-arrival at a dance. The poem is set beneath the 'big chandelier' suspended above the ballroom – an image that brings to mind the twice-weekly dances at the Hotel Sonnenberg.

One o'clock! Neither hasting nor staying,
The dowagers all disappear;
The band the 'third extra' is playing;
O Frank, and you said you'd be here! …

And I try to think Freddy beguiling,
And persuade myself not to look glum;
I am talking and turning and smiling:
O Frank, and you promised to come …

Has the music grown suddenly brighter?
Have they turned on the big chandelier,
That the room's so remarkably lighter?
And I – am I looking severe?

Am I frigid as snowdrifts in Norway?
Am I colder than ice at the Pole?
For Someone stands there in the doorway,
And Someone shall smart in his soul!

I fancied he saw too when I did
(This dancing is bad for the nerves;
I'm glad it is done) I've decided
To treat him the way he deserves

Levy pasted a cutting of this verse into her scrap album for 1884, inscribing it: 'London Society: (holiday number) 1884. Mers-les-Bains: Picardie, 1883 (written)'. Mers-les-Bains is a small seaside resort not far from the port of Dieppe in Picardy. Because of its popularity as a holiday destination for Parisians, regular rail services ran between Paris and Mer-les-Bains' disproportionately grand railway terminus. And since 1825 a ferry service had run between Dieppe and Newhaven – the port closest to the Levys' home town, Brighton. It seems therefore, that by the time she reached Mer-les-Bains the germ of the idea for 'Eustace' had come to fruition in the form of 'Mariana in the Ballroom', and that the poem was written there in the last days of her holiday before her return to England from Dieppe at the close of the summer of 1883.

The August 1884 'Holiday Issue' of *London Society* featured a second work by Amy Levy - a short story entitled 'In Holiday Humour.' This is set in the 'Pension Sonnenthal' on Lake Lucerne, and like 'Mariana' the text is headed with a quotation, but in this case lines taken from Shakespeare's *As You Like It*: 'Come woo me, woo me, for now I am in a holiday humour and like enough to consent'.[134] 'In Holiday Humour' is not one of Amy's best efforts. The plot is constructed around an implausible incident, heavily reminiscent of Maggie Tulliver's fateful river outing in George Eliot's *The Mill on the Floss,* in which the heroine, Olivia Longcroft, is literally and figuratively swept away on a tide of emotion. Like Nora, the narrator of 'Between Two Stools', Olivia (whose nickname 'Livy' suggests a pun on the author's surname) has much in common with her creator. We are told that Livy, 'A modern young lady who has been to Girton', is 'a little too strong minded'. Whilst Livy is chatting to her travelling companion, Marion, as they prepare for an excursion to the other side of the lake, Marion takes Livy to task for having forgotten 'the young man in Paper Buildings who cannot afford to take holidays in Switzerland.' Livy replies, 'the – the person in Paper Buildings has given up caring – if he ever cared … and so have I.' At that time both Karl Pearson and Ernest Radford were pursuing careers at the Bar and occupied rooms in 'Buildings' within the Inns of Court.[135] Fortunately for the fictional Livy, compensation is at hand in the form of Sidney Tressider, a handsome but emotionally volatile young man of independent means. Tressider joins Livy and Marion on their trip to Lucerne where, having installed Livy's chaperone in a comfortable seat in the sunshine (thereby ensuring that she will promptly fall asleep), she and Tressider stroll away from the party. During their walk he tells her that he is about to leave for a climbing trip to the Bernese Oberland with a party of male friends. On an impulse he then proposes to Livy and she accepts, whereupon he decides to abandon his trip. In the wake of this unlikely sequence of events, the pair spend some time wandering around in a daze of happiness before returning to the pier to discover that the steamer has departed without them. Undeterred, Tressider persuades Livy and her negligent chaperone, against their better judgement, to return with him in a hired rowing boat. Half way across the lake the weather suddenly changes (in reflection of Tressider's mercurial temperament) and the party in the boat are nearly drowned. For Livy, the onset of the tempest is a turning point. When the storm passes, after her safe return to dry land, she tells Tressider that she cannot marry him. Like Nora Livy is portrayed as the victim of emotional inconsistency, but in this case it is Tressider's volatility and not her own indecisiveness which is nearly her undoing. Unlike Nora, Livy is able to regain her self-respect by deciding to reject her impulsive suitor and return to London alone.

Both from a professional and a personal point of view, Amy's stay at the Hotel Sonnenberg was a fruitful interlude, and the mild Swiss climate and the stimulating company of her fellow guests played a role in this. For once, despite her habitual unease in the company of strangers – what she described in her letter to her sister as her 'accursed shyness' - she seems not to have been overawed by the fact that the Grand Hotel Sonnenberg had provided, and continued to provide, a roof over some very distinguished heads. She reported to Katie that she regularly shared a table at dinner with 'Miss and Mr. Cross (George Eliot's husband), Miss Crofts and the Fords', adding 'Miss Crofts and the Fords knew them [the Crosses] a little to start with and the friendship is on the ripen.' The Fords in question, John Rawlinson Ford and his wife Helen, were members of a dynasty of Quaker entrepreneurs and philanthropists. Earlier in the letter Amy had mentioned that 'the Ford party has departed in full Alpine rig to climb a mountain', adding 'but Mrs. Ford is still here, she seems very nice. She edits a WS [women's suffrage] magazine to which I am going to contribute'. Helen Ford was a staunch supporter of the women's suffrage campaign, an interest that was shared by her sisters-in-law, Emily and Isabella, the latter of whom was also a childhood friend of Ellen Crofts.[136] In 1865 the Fords had moved into Adel Grange, the main house in the Yorkshire village where the Crofts family lived. Isabella had discovered a soul mate in Ellen Crofts, and they had jointly made a vow to dedicate their lives to 'the improving of the state of the world'. Each kept their promise, as Isabella became a veteran of the women's suffrage campaign and, like Clementina Black, a pioneer of the women's trades union movement, and Ellen became resident lecturer in English at Newnham College.[137]

In May 1883 Ellen Crofts had agreed to marry Francis (Frank), the widowed younger son of Charles Darwin. The Darwin family were already known at the Hotel Sonnenberg, as Frank's sister Henrietta (Etty) had stayed there during her honeymoon after her marriage to Richard Lichfield in 1871. Ellen's decision to marry Darwin cannot have been an easy one to make, as he had suffered from severe fits of depression since the death of his first wife in childbirth. In addition, marriage entailed relinquishing her prized Fellowship at Newnham. Ellen was a determinedly free spirit, and her holiday with the Fords may have been a final taste of liberty before she took on the burdensome role of wife and stepmother.[138] As a Newnham lecturer and a friend of Amy's former classmate Alice Lloyd, she had probably already met Amy. But whether previously acquainted or not, whilst staying at the hotel they became close friends. However, at the beginning at least, Amy's feelings about Ellen Crofts were somewhat ambivalent as, once again, her own lack of self-esteem led her to compare herself unfavourably with her newfound friend. In her letter to Clementina Black she had made the mildly sarcastic comment that 'Miss Crofts is simply delightful; she makes one feel utterly mean and dirty, she is so simple & clean & strong & very charming withal.' This suggests that, at first, she was intimidated by Ellen's air of calm self-assurance. Amy was not the only one of her acquaintances to feel this way, for as her lifelong friend and colleague Jane Harrison noted: 'There was a sort of sureness that made her a real refuge. [But] She was not popular here [at Newnham] … she was very intolerant of any ordinary human worldliness [and] her utter lack of spiritual conventions made many people here uncomfortable with her'.[139] Of course, Ellen's 'utter lack of spiritual conventions' would not have prejudiced Amy against her, and any initial constraint between them was rapidly dispelled.

Three years after her return from Lucerne, in May 1886, *London Society* featured yet another of Amy's verses which, like 'Mariana in the Ballroom', was obviously inspired by her Swiss holiday. 'To E' is a sombre and, in the light of later events, an ominously prophetic poem. Amy later selected it as the concluding verse for her third and (as it turned out) posthumously published collection of poetry, *A London Plane Tree*. She was correcting the proofs of this volume in the days that led up to her suicide, and in view of the poem's later significance I will quote it in full here:

The mountains in fantastic lines
Sweep, blue-white, to the sky, which shines
Blue as blue gems; athwart the pines
The lake gleams blue.

We three were here, three years gone by;
Our Poet, with fine frenzied eye,
You, steeped in learned lore, and I
A poet too.

Our Poet brought us books and flowers,
He read us Faust; he talked for hours
Philosophy (sad Schopenhauer's),
Beneath the trees:

And do you mind that sunny day,

When he, as on the sward he lay,
Told of Lassalle who bore away
The false Louise.

Thrice favoured bard! To him alone,
That green and snug retreat was shown,
Where to the vulgar herd unknown,
Our pens we plied.

(For in those distant days it seems,
We cherished sundry idle dreams,
And with our flowing, foolscap reams
The fates defied)

And after, when the day was gone,
And the hushed, silver night came on,
He showed us where the glow-worm shone; -
We stooped to see.

There, too, by yonder moon we swore
Platonic friendship o'er and o'er;
No folk, we deemed, had been before
So wise and free.

* * * * * * * *

And do I smile or sigh today?
Dead love, or dead ambition, say,
What mourn we most? Not much we weigh
Platonic friends.

On you the sun is shining free;
Our Poet sleeps in Italy,
Beneath an alien sod; on me
The cloud descends.

The pessimistic note on which 'To E' ends reveals that in the three years that had passed since 'we three were here' Amy's mood had undergone a fundamental change. For the letter which she wrote to her mother after her arrival in Lucerne displayed an uncharacteristic *joie de vivre*:

> Today the weather has been all that could be wished; a cloudless blue sky, lots of sun and a gentle breeze. This morning we started on an exploring party – to find out a good place for working. We lighted upon a small rocky pine-grown peninsula jutting over a small secluded blue lake, lying in the midst of the mountains. It is to be our permanent camping out place, indeed I am at present writing this letter stretched out on a rug over a moss grown rock with a wonderful view of blue lake & green hills & blue sky stretching before me. So please excuse any indistinctness of handwriting…Would it be a great trouble to send me my bathing gown … we are going to bathe early in the morning in the small lake … This afternoon we had a most exciting time making tea in Miss Croft's 'Aetna' [a small portable stove] wh. we drank out of a tooth glass, & 'milked' with Swiss milk out of a tin wh. we had to break open on a stone…Excuse more as I am beginning to get rather dreamy …The sheep bells are sounding as I write but I can't see any sheep – the sky is blue as it can be and there is sun all over the place; and the best of all we are the only human feature of the landscape …

The 'small secluded blue lake, lying in the midst of the mountains' described so vividly by Amy in her letter is the Seelisberger Seeli, which at that time was within the grounds of the Hotel Sonnenberg, and was used by the guests as a bathing pool. Even today it is possible to identify the precise spot, the same 'small rocky pine-grown peninsula' jutting out into the strikingly blue water of the lake where she and Ellen Crofts retired to write – the 'green and snug retreat' - which is the setting of 'To E'. But it is not Ellen Crofts, to whom the poem was dedicated, but the third person, 'Our Poet', whose presence is felt most strongly within the verse. The phrase 'fine-frenzied eye' links this individual with Theseus' opening speech in Act V of Shakespeare's *A Midsummer Night's Dream*:

> Lovers and madmen have such seething brains,
> Such shaping fantasies, that apprehend
> More than cool reason ever comprehends.
> The lunatic, the lover and the poet
> Are of imagination all compact,
> One sees more devils than vast hell can hold,
> That is the madman. The lover, all as frantic,
> Sees Helen's beauty in a brow of Egypt.
> The poet's eye in a fine frenzy rolling
> Doth glance from heaven to earth, from earth to heaven;
> And as imagination bodies forth
> The forms of things unknown, the poet's pen
> Turns them into shapes, and give to airy nothing,
> A local habitation and a name.[140]

When penning 'To E' Amy drew upon her memories of 'a local habitation' - the idyllic little lake, where the reflection of the sky and the mountains on the still, blue water conflate 'earth' and 'heaven' – to create a suitably ethereal backdrop for her own meditation upon the seductive power of the imagination and its ability to overcome reason and blind us to the fallibility of human feeling. But the trio of lakeside friends - 'the lunatic', Amy herself, 'the lover', the newly engaged Ellen Crofts, and the unidentified man, 'Our Poet' - also call to mind a second literary allusion: the elopement of Percy Bysshe Shelly with his lover Mary Godwin and her half-mad half-sister Jane Clairmont in the summer of 1814. After an arduous trek through war-torn France, Shelley and his two female companions had settled (briefly) at Brunnen, which is sited on the northern shore of Lake Lucerne directly opposite Seelisberg. Here the fugitive trio planned to establish a 'community of like spirits'.[141] Amy's trio of Platonic friends harbour similar aspirations – or delusions: 'No folk, we deemed, before had been/So wise and free.' And just like Mary Godwin and Jane Clairmont the two females in Amy's verse are depicted as being in thrall to the male member of their party. But although these women are readily recognizable as Ellen Crofts and Amy Levy, the identity of 'Our Poet' is less easy to determine. For although the final stanza seemingly identifies him with the dead Shelley - 'Our Poet sleeps in Italy/Beneath an alien sod' - the catalogue of his personal attributes given in stanzas three and four depict a man very much alive and in touch with the modern world. However, there is an ambiguity in the phrase 'thrice favoured bard', which suggests that 'Our Poet' may have been an ironic nickname bestowed upon him in order both to put emphasis upon the perceived superiority of his male status (Amy pointedly defines herself in lower case: 'I a poet too'), and as an acknowledgement of the trio's shared admiration for one particular literary icon. Shelley was a likely candidate for this role, being at that time 'the hero of the freethinkers' whose rejection of the status quo had been an inspiration to both Marx and Engels. However, by the time that Amy wrote 'To E' (probably in early 1886), like Marx's daughter Eleanor she had discovered to her cost that Shelleyan ideals were all very well in theory but that, for a young woman at least, any attempt to put them into practice carried considerable risk. The person who was responsible for teaching her this salutary lesson was 'Our Poet' – Amy and Ellen's Cambridge friend and colleague Karl Pearson, whose unique persona is encapsulated in the third and fourth stanzas of 'To E'.

Pearson's first visit to Switzerland was with his Cambridge tutor Oscar Browning in the summer of 1877. Whilst *en route* for Lucerne, the pair read Goethe's Faust together.[142] Shortly after his return from the continent he recorded in his commonplace book 'that Goethe's Faust & …Shelley Poems have been the greatest revelations to me of anything I have read'.[143] The crisis of faith that Pearson had experienced at Cambridge had resulted in his rejection of Christianity in favour of German idealism, which finds expression in the works of both Johann Wolfgang von Goethe and Arthur Schopenhauer. The phrase 'he talked for hours' calls to mind Pearson's readiness to hold forth at length on any given subject – as the minute book of the second Men and Women's Club attests. Egon Pearson highlighted this aspect of his father's personality in his memoir, recalling that although in the early to mid-1880s he was still nominally pursuing a career at the bar his interests lay elsewhere, and that he sought relief from the monotony of legal work by writing and lecturing on a wide range of subjects: 'on heat at Barnes, on Martin Luther at Hampstead and on Lassalle and Marx on Sundays at revolutionary clubs round Soho'.[144] Although, like Ellen Crofts, Pearson took himself rather too seriously, he also had a strong romantic streak in his nature. For him emotional experience was allied with a deep-seated love of the natural world. The line 'Our poet brought us books and flowers' replicates his words in a letter quoted by his son: 'Bradshaw once said to me that he held gifts between real friends should only be flowers – and I add wild flowers.'[145]

In August 1883 Pearson and his friend Ralph Thicknesse were lodging at Pearson's customary summertime retreat, which was the village inn at the tiny hamlet of Saig in the Black Forest. During their stay the pair jointly wrote a letter to their friend Robert Parker, who had given the paper on 'suicide' at the post-May Week club meeting. At the time of writing Pearson was manifestly 'in holiday humour', as the eccentric manner in which his contribution to the letter is composed suggests that he was under the influence of drink when it was written.[146] The letter tells of their imminent departure for a walking trip on the Swiss–Austrian border. This bears an uncanny resemblance to the episode in Amy's 'In Holiday Humour' when Livy's impetuous suitor, Sidney Tressider, tells her that he has received an invitation to join a party of male friends on a walking holiday in the Bernese Oberland.[147] But Pearson could not be in two places at once, so how could he have been the third member of Amy's lakeside trio if he was holidaying in Germany as usual? The answer is that by the 1880s Switzerland had one of the most comprehensive railway networks in Europe, and even the smallest towns were easily accessible by train. Todnau, the neighbouring village to Saig, had a direct rail link to Basle, which was just a couple of hours by rail from Lucerne. It would therefore have been relatively easy for him to either break his outward journey or make a separate excursion to Saig in order to spend a few days with the party of his Cambridge friends that gathered at the Hotel Sonnenberg in mid-July. In her first letter from the hotel Amy told her mother: 'to-morrow we propose spending in Lucerne & after that we are going to regularly set to work before the arrival of a whole lot of people on the 19th'. On 8th July Pearson's friend and fellow club member

Hume Pinsent had written to Ada Radford: 'I hope I shall have some time to do some reading before I go to Switzerland.'[148] It is quite possible that, like Pinsent, Pearson was one of the 'whole lot of people' that congregated on the shore of Lake Lucerne in late July 1883. A number of the verses in the collection of poetry that Amy was compiling during her stay at Seelisberg certainly bear the hallmark of their influence, as after her return from Switzerland, for a short time at least, her poetry acquired a more overtly political tone. In *A Minor Poet* (which is essentially an expanded edition of *Xantippe*) the earlier lyrics which were the legacy of her Cambridge years like 'To Sylvia' and 'A Farewell', appear alongside new compositions such as 'Magdalen' and 'Christopher Found'. These new verses carry a distinctly socialist message and address issues that, without doubt, would have been discussed by the trio of Shelleyan 'Platonic friends' during the long, lazy afternoons beside the little lake and later around the dinner table beneath the ornate plasterwork and glittering chandeliers of the grand dining room in the Hotel Sonnenberg.

However, for Amy, the hope of a socialist and feminist new dawn quickly faded. Like her friend Ellen Crofts, who sacrificed her career for love, and ultimately died literally and figuratively of a broken heart, she was soon confronted with the unhappy realisation that those like Karl Pearson, who publicly proclaimed allegiance to the causes of social and sexual equality, did not necessarily adhere to these principles in the conduct of their own lives. This was the message conveyed in the penultimate stanza of 'To E' - the poem written to commemorate Amy Levy's by then faded 'Midsummer Night's Dream':

> Dead love, or dead ambition, say,
> What mourn we most? Not much we weigh
> Platonic friends.

The publication of *A Minor Poet* in 1884 marked a watershed in Amy's personal and professional life. For reasons which will soon be revealed, shortly after this her poetry lost its polemical thrust and became essentially a vehicle for the expression of her own 'moods and thoughts'.[149] Her social life also took a new direction, as she distanced herself from the Cambridge set and sought friendship within a less academically exclusive milieu. But at the end of the summer of 1883 her life seemed full of promise, and she returned to London to resume her studies in the Reading Room, renew her membership of A Men and Women's Club, and to look forward with anticipation to the publication of her second collection of poetry.

From The Début of 'A Minor Poet' to the Debacle of the Men and Women's Club 1884–1885

These deeds, O man, which thou committest,
Prove the survival of the fittest.

Charlotte Perkins Stetson (later Gilman), 1860–1935: 'The Survival of the Fittest'

Upon her return from Switzerland Amy took up the threads of her London life once more. Although they retained their home in Brighton, for some time now the family had also occupied a house in one of the most desirable locations in the capital, at 11 Sussex Place, Regents Park. Sussex Place is the most flamboyant of the terraces that were designed for the Prince Regent by the architect John Nash, and is located on the western side of the park overlooking the boating lake and close to Baker Street. Amy must have been delighted to be living so near to the centre of her beloved city, and would also, no doubt, have been pleased with the fact that Sussex Place had strong literary associations. In 1826 Walter Scott's biographer and son-in-law John Lockhart had taken up residence at number 24 shortly after his appointment as editor of the *Quarterly Review*. Sophia Lockhart was a close friend of the dramatist and poet Joanna Baillie, who was a regular visitor to Sussex Place. When Sir Walter was staying with the Lockharts during his final illness Baillie wrote affectionately to Sophia: 'I will come from Hampstead to sit by him even for a few minutes any morning you please to name'.[150] In more recent years the Poet Laureate's son Lionel Tennyson had moved in to number 4, just a few doors away from the Levy household. Lionel's wife Eleanor was also the daughter of a poet, Frederick Locker-Lampson, whose *London Lyrics* inspired Amy's own 'London' verses. Although there does not appear to have been any contact between the Tennyson and Levy families during the period of their mutual residence in Sussex Place, Amy would undoubtedly have been aware of the comings and goings at the home of her illustrious neighbours. Lionel Tennyson was a close friend of Charles Villiers Stanford, whom he had known since they were at Cambridge together in the early 1870s. Lionel and Eleanor Tennyson were a hospitable couple, and Amy would probably have caught passing glimpses of her former idol, Mrs. Stanford, amongst the constant stream of guests that crossed their threshold. At that time Lionel Tennyson worked as a clerk in the India Office alongside his childhood friend Richmond Ritchie. Ritchie was married to William Makepeace Thackeray's daughter, Anne (Anny). Anny was some twenty years older than her husband, and set in her ways. Lionel and Eleanor could not have been a more different couple. Unconventional, lively and gregarious, they gave the Ritchies the opportunity to mix in a more up-to-date, outgoing circle - something that was particularly welcomed by Richmond. Both Tennysons had a passion for acting and the Ritchies were often guests at their 'theatrical evenings' in which Eleanor, 'dashing and captivating in the latest fashions', played a leading role.[151] Amateur dramatics were evidently all the rage in Sussex Place at that time, as the Levy siblings also staged a number of theatrical performances whilst living at number 11. One of their productions, 'The Unhappy Princess', written by Amy, featured a governess named Girtonia who was probably modelled on Miss Pateman. The Levys left Sussex Place some time before Lionel Tennyson's premature death in 1886, but would no doubt have heard the rumours of the subsequent romantic entanglement between Eleanor and Richmond Ritchie, for despite Anny's best attempts to keep the affair under wraps, as Henrietta Garnett notes: 'people knew. They talked'.[152] Faced with choice between Eleanor and his wife, Ritchie chose his wife. And in 1888 Eleanor, who desperately needed a replacement father for her three orphaned little boys, married one of Amy's Men and Women's Club acquaintances, Augustine Birrell.

Like Eleanor, Birrell had suffered the early loss of his partner when, after only eighteen months of marriage, his wife had died in childbirth, taking their infant daughter with her to the grave. After this tragedy he had retired to Kensington, where he set up home with his unmarried sister and immersed himself in his career at the Bar. But he was a sociable man at heart, and despite his grief he soon resumed his active role in the intellectual life of the city, pursuing his joint interests in literature and radical politics through his membership of a number of the capital's myriad literary and political coteries, one of which was A Men and Women's Club.

The club had its roots in the Shakespeare reading group that met at the home of Karl Marx in Maitland Park Road during the early 1880s. Like her namesake, Eleanor Tennyson, Eleanor Marx had a passion for the theatre. But in accordance with her principles, she employed her talents for the benefit of worthy causes rather than the amusement of her friends. One worthwhile enterprise, to which she applied the skills she had learnt at her father's knee, was the research that she undertook for F.J. Furnivall at the British Museum. Furnivall, a Christian Socialist and a former teacher at the Working Men's College, had an unshakeable faith in the ennobling power of the English language. Determined to make its rich heritage more widely accessible to the average man and woman, to this end he became an indefatigable founder of literary societies. And from the 1870s onwards Eleanor undertook 'endless hackwork' for these societies on his behalf. The project of his that was closest to her heart was his New Shakespeare Society, which met in the Reading Rooms of University College in Gower Street.[153] Indeed, her zeal for this particular organisation was so great that one of her friends complained of being forcibly 'dragged' to the meetings.[154] In due course, Eleanor's passion for the Bard led her to establish her own literary society devoted to his works. Named after the character of the bumbling night watchman in *Much Ado About Nothing*, the Dogberry Club not only gave its founder a further opportunity to study the works of her favourite playwright, but also to indulge her passion for acting. Apart from Eleanor herself, its core members were Dollie Maitland and her sister Clara, Ernest Radford and the playwright Edward Rose.[155] Although in theory the members were meant to take it in turns to host the fortnightly meetings, in practice they were generally held at the Marx family home, where the proceedings were conducted under the benevolent eye of Eleanor's father. It is not clear whether Furnivall attended any of the Dogberry meetings, but someone who definitely did was Eleanor's close friend Marion Skinner. She recalled how 'once the "serious business" of play reading was over' the evening would conclude 'with games and such pastimes as charades and dumb-crambo, chiefly – as it would seem from his extreme enjoyment of them – for the delectation of Dr. Marx.'[156]

A Men and Women's Club appears to have been structured on the lines of the Dogberry, meeting fortnightly at the home of one or other of its members. The meetings of 'the club', as the members called it, were alternately devoted to 'discussion and social intercourse'. The discussion evenings generally began with a paper read by one of the members. Conny Black's future husband, Edward Garnett, left a satirical account of these debates to posterity in his delightful novella *The Paradox Club*. The social or 'casual' evenings, as Dollie referred to them in her diary, often included a musical interlude. In a letter to Dollie, Amy reported: 'I have captured a person with a lovely voice for Tuesday. She will sing "Das Meer hat Seine Perlen" (M.V. White) & "O Per Pieta" (Mozart). Her name is Mrs. Solomon.'[157]

Although A Men and Women's Club was broadly structured on the Dogberry, its *raison d'être* was entirely different. A few of the papers presented at the discussion evenings had literary themes, but others were oriented towards the newly evolving social sciences.

For example, one bore the title 'Consideration of the Functions of the Government', and another 'The Influence of Science on Modern Thought'. This forward-thinking agenda was formulated at the inaugural meeting of the club, which took place on the evening of 4th November 1879. On this occasion Ernest Radford was the sole representative of the 'Dogberries', but in due course Dollie Maitland, Eleanor Marx and Marion Skinner were all signing their names on the club's register. The record of the first meeting states that it took place at 17 Fitzroy Street. At that time the Black sisters were living in Fitzroy Street, although none of them were present at the meeting, which was mainly attended by people who were connected in some way or another with University College. Indeed, the transition from 'Dogberry' to 'Bloomsbury' seems to have been driven by the influence of University College, which had been the first academic institution to open its door to both women and those who were not of the Anglican faith. The University's 'association ... with prominent dissenters and with men of advanced philosophic and religious opinions' was certainly reflected within the eclectic group of men and women who gathered in Fitzroy Street on the chilly November evening to discuss 'the object of the club'.[158] The assembled party included a contingent of medical staff and students from University College Hospital, amongst which were Victor Horsley, a former student at the University who was at that time House Surgeon at the hospital, and his colleague and future brother-in-law Francis Gotch. Both Horsley and Gotch were later knighted for their contribution to the field of neurophysiology, but during the course of their distinguished careers both also found time to support worthy causes. Gotch became a member of the Board of Somerville College and Horsley, who claimed that 'race, sex or social status were unimportant' to him, became an ardent supporter of the Women's Suffrage movement and also promoted the idea of free healthcare for the working classes.[159] Two young medical students accompanied Horsley and Gotch to the meeting. They were Francis De Courcy Skeete, a Barbadian by birth, and [Charles] Ernest Wedmore, brother of the art critic and journalist Frederick Wedmore.[160] The Wedmore brothers were Quakers, and another member of a distinguished Quaker family was also present at the meeting. This was Isabella Ford's sister Emily, who at that time was a student at the Slade School of Art, which was also affiliated with University College. Like Victor Horsley, Emily Ford was a social activist and a staunch supporter of the Women's Suffrage Campaign. Her studio in Chelsea was to become known as 'a meeting ground for people who did things'. One of her circle who indisputably 'did things' was her cousin Edward Pease, who went on to become a founding member of the Fabian Society. Although Pease did not attend the early meetings of the club, he later enrolled as a member.

However, medical men and social activists were not the sole arbiters of the club's agenda, as the wider world of the arts was also represented at the inaugural meeting by the opera singer Charles Santley, who was accompanied by his musician daughter Edith and her friend Esther Yates, a student at the Royal Academy of Music. Another gifted amateur musician was at the meeting: Louis T Rowe. Rowe was also a keen bibliophile, and is now remembered for the collection of rare musical manuscripts that he bequeathed to King's College, Cambridge, where it formed the foundation of the Rowe Music Library. This group may well have been responsible for introducing the musical element into the social evenings.

Although the club was initially dominated by University College men and women, as time went by their influence was superseded by a clique of Cambridge alumni. Ernest Radford was apparently responsible for introducing the Cambridge faction into the club. In December 1880 his college friend Hume Pinsent wrote to Ada Radford: 'I have just been elected a member of a social club of men and women meeting once a fortnight. You will probably have heard of it. I go to my first meeting, a musical one, next Tuesday'.[161] In time, like Hume Pinsent, others that had congregated in the Bond household in Cambridge enrolled as guests and members of the club. These included Harry Bond and his sisters, Amy's friends Annie and Minnie Bond, Karl Pearson, who seems to have been recruited by his friend and tennis partner, Robert Parker, and their mutual friend Ralph Thicknesse. Amy Levy first signed her name on the attendance register as a guest on 17th May 1882. Others who signed in that evening were Ernest Radford, Dollie Maitland, Clementina Black, Marian Skinner and Robert Parker. In the following month, a meeting was held at Goldsmiths Building, Temple at which Pearson signed his name as a guest for the first time. Amy also registered as a guest at this meeting. She first signed in as a member of the club on 19th December 1882, and by the following year Pearson was likewise signing his name as a member.[162] Not long after her return from Lucerne, in October 1883 two club meetings were held at the Levy family home at '11 Sussex Place, Regent's Park'. At the second of these meetings Amy's guests included Pearson, Parker and Ralph Thicknesse.[163] Two months after this, on 4th December, the club meeting was held at Pearson's rooms - 2 Harcourt Buildings, Temple. On that evening Amy's signature appears alongside his in the register – an indication, perhaps, that they were sitting together. One of the guests at this meeting was Amy's younger brother, Edmund. The next meeting on 18th December was again held at 11 Sussex Place. Amy's father and a contingent of the Garnett family, including the head of the household, Richard Garnett (who was at that time Superintendent of the Reading Room at the British Museum), signed in as guests alongside William Archer and Sidney Lee - who later introduced Archer's friend George Bernard Shaw to the club.[164] Amy's other brothers Alfred and William also attended the club as guests on separate occasions during the course of 1883.[165] It is therefore certain that by this time Amy and Pearson knew one another very well, as through their membership of the club he had become acquainted with the closest members of her family and in turn, she had become familiar with the innermost circle of his Cambridge friends.

But club meetings only occupied a limited amount of her time at this stage in her life, as her main aim was to advance her literary career. By 1884 her 'potboilers' were providing her with a small but regular income, but her ambition extended beyond that of a hack writer, and the publication of *A Minor Poet* by T. Fisher Unwin was an important step on the road towards achieving this goal. Her acknowledgement of the significance of this event is the array of cuttings taken from the wide range of publications in which the volume was reviewed, which she pasted into the same scrap album that contains the cutting of 'Mariana in the Ballroom'. On the last page of the album she also made a careful record of monies received during the year – further evidence of her determination to make a financial success of her writing. But there was a downside to the critical attention that she attracted. For despite the fact that the majority of the reviews paid tribute to her talent as a poet, the language in which many of them were couched reflects the endemic sexual bias of the literary criticism of the period. Amy was always sensitive to critical censure, and the patronising tone of many of the notices, and the sneering comments elicited as a consequence of her sex, must have affected her deeply.[166] Commenting on what he described as the 'failure in art in ... the poems dealing with Greek subjects', the critic of the *Oxford Magazine* speculated: 'The author has probably read little Greek, for there are three misprints in a line of Greek she ventures to quote; at all events she thoroughly misses the Greek spirit and tone.' Amy had studied Greek both at the Brighton High School and at Newnham College. Arthur Reed Ropes, writing in the Cambridge Review, adopted a less directly insulting tone, but was equally patronising in his judgement, claiming:

> It is in the shorter poems that Miss Levy's verse is best, when it is subject to the strengthening restraint of rhyme and has only to express a single emotion in direct words ...[167]

A. W. Dole, writing in *The Literary World*, offered a more considered and less disdainful analysis but shared the opinion of other critics that 'Miss Levy's' poems were marred by their excessive pessimism:

> It is deeply to be deplored that one possessing such a high intelligence, fine fancy and extraordinary command of exquisite poetic style, would almost invariably pitch her strains in such a mournful key. If life be as unsatisfactory, illusory and vain as it is here represented as being, one can hardly see why it is worth publishing poetry, or indeed anything which is not issued for purely financial reasons bearing upon a living.[168]

In making this last point, Dole indirectly alighted upon an issue that was of direct consequence not only to Amy, but to other forward-thinking women writers of the era - the conflict between their desire to preserve their artistic integrity, and the need to conform to the accepted standards of the literary market. All women who pursued a literary career had necessarily to be mindful of the demands of the marketplace, but those who sought to employ their talents as a vehicle for social reform found themselves in a particular predicament as, by adopting a political standpoint, they inevitably set themselves at odds with the literary establishment. Many of the women Amy encountered in the Reading Room of the British Museum at this time were battling with this dilemma, engaging in a relentless, wearying struggle to make a living from literature without compromising their cherished beliefs. This aspect of literary life was touched upon by George Gissing, in his novel *New Grub Street*. Gissing, who was an habitué of the Reading Room, had ample opportunity to observe at first hand the hardships endured by the impoverished young women who struggled to earn a meagre living by undertaking hackwork in what he termed the 'valley of the shadow of books'. One such woman was Amy's fellow club member, Helen Zimmern. At around this time the writer Vernon Lee was introduced to Helen Zimmern at an 'at home' held by her friend, Mary Robinson. In a letter to her mother Lee described Helen Zimmern as 'a pleasant intelligent little black woman quite capable of doing good work but who has to do hack reviewing to support her people.'[169] Like Amy, Helen was Jewish and had a dark complexion, hair and eyes – hence Lee's description. She also evidently possessed a shrewd head for business, and regularly farmed out her surplus hackwork to Eleanor Marx who, although no doubt grateful for the work, commented acidly on the arrangement: 'necessity knows no laws, 25/- is 5/-', meaning that Miss Zimmern paid her five out of her earnings of 25 shillings'.[170] Eleanor was not alone in her resentment at the exigencies of literary life. The novelist Margaret Harkness, who was another of Amy's British Museum acquaintances, made a similar complaint in a letter to her cousin, Beatrice Potter:

> I have tried literature now for nearly three years and have worked very hard. I have

> written in many magazines and papers including the Nineteenth Century and National. Also two books of which I was forced to sell the copyright to an inferior publisher; and am preparing a book for Macmillan. I have also written an M.S. which Bentley refused because it was directed against Capital Punishment, and which has been read by a good novelist and pronounced full of promise ... My income last year was £150. I made it by working almost night and day; and wrote the M.S. on Capital Punishment in three months doing other work all the while.[171]

Margaret Harkness' account of her struggle for survival bears a marked resemblance to that of the fictional 'Adelaide' in Amy's poem 'Christopher Found'. Like Amy herself, Adelaide is a 'minor poet'. But like Margaret Harkness she is also angry, embittered, and, having no willing father to support her, financially dependent upon her own literary efforts. The poem takes the form of two contrasting monologues, the first of which is written in octosyllabic rhyming verse - the archaic metre of 'courtly love' and the traditional verse form of the medieval romance. In it Adelaide tells of her quest for her lost lover, Christopher who, it is implied, abandoned her after seducing her some years ago. Unlike the conventional Victorian maiden, rather than sit patiently at home awaiting the return of her errant suitor, Adelaide has set out to travel the world to find him herself. But when she finally tracks him down it is too late, she is no longer young, and the undisguised urgency of her physical need repels him, although she fails to recognise this - blithely assuming that his love for her is undiminished and that their future life together will be an idyll:

> Till the world is dead you shall love but me,
> Till the stars have ceased I shall love but you.

At this point the narrative shifts, and the final stanza of the poem, the epilogue, is spoken by Adelaide's landlady. Unlike the preceding five stanzas, this section of the poem is written in blank verse that is distinguished by coarse, colloquial diction and disjointed phraseology. It is an account of the lonely, miserable end to Adelaide's life, which clearly reflects Amy's own anxiety about her likely destiny (and that of women like Margaret Harkness) in the face of advancing age.

> 'Young, Sir? No.
> Must have seen forty if she'd seen a day!
> A lonesome woman; hadn't many friends;
> Wrote books, I think, and things for newspapers.
> Short in her temper –eyes would flash and flame
> At times till I was frightened. Paid her rent
> Most regular, like a lady.

Ten years back,
They say (at least Ann Brown says), ten years
back
The lady had a lover. Even then
She must have been no chicken
Three months since
She died ... well, well the Lord is kind and just.
I did my best to tend her, yet indeed
It's bad for trade to have a lodger die.
Her brother came a week before she died:
Buried her, took her things, threw in the fire
The littered heaps of paper ...

I never knew her name was Adelaide.[172]

Arthur Reed Ropes found this section of the poem particularly offensive, describing the blank verse as 'bed-makerly'.[173] But Reed Ropes missed the point, as the vocal transition from Adelaide's cultured diction to the landlady's uncouth rambling not only creates a temporal shift, moving the narrative forward from past to present, but also establishes that Adelaide ended her days in a rented room, signalling her diminished social status.[174] The phrase 'It's bad for trade to have a lodger die', which, together with the disclosure that the landlady had never known Adelaide's first name, emphasises the cold, commercial nature of their relationship. But as the landlady obliquely suggests, Adelaide's 'gentility' - the fact that she has had access to a level of education that has enabled her to earn her living through literature - has saved her from the common fate of lower class women in her position who, having been seduced and then cast aside, ended up on the streets. Nevertheless, like many of the women Amy witnessed slaving away at hackwork for a pittance in the Reading Room of the British Museum, Adelaide has been obliged to prostitute her literary skills if not her body in order to make ends meet.

Amy returned to the same theme, but from a different perspective, in another of the verses in *A Minor Poet*. But where 'Christopher Found' tells the story of a gentlewoman fallen upon hard times, 'Magdalen' paints a real-life picture of the misery and degradation of the 'fallen woman.', the social outcast who had no safety net of education or influence to catch her as she fell. The fallen woman was one of Victorian society's most potent female icons. Viewed with a mixture of fear and fascination, she was generally regarded as a victim of her own moral weakness, and deemed unworthy of sympathy unless she expressed fulsome remorse for her 'sins'. One only has to compare Amy's defiant, institutionalised

'Magdalen' with Christina Rossetti's vision of repentant Pre-Raphaelite loveliness, 'Mary Magdalene', to understand the ideological advance that Amy's poem represents. For although Christina Rossetti acknowledged the culpability of the male partner in her poem 'Under the Rose' (later retitled 'The Iniquity of the Fathers Upon the Children'), she offered the conventional consolatory prospect of heavenly salvation for the repentant sinner. What is particularly revolutionary in Amy Levy's portrayal of the Magdalen, from the Victorian point of view, is the fact that she not only makes no apology for the so-called crime, apportioning the blame where it rightly belongs - with the seducer - but also, in Magdalen's stark confession 'I have no faith in God or Devil, Life or Death', holds out no hope of redemption for either transgressor or transgressed.

Critics of *A Minor Poet* appear to have deliberately chosen to ignore these revolutionary aspects of the poem. In the few notices in which it received a mention, emphasis was placed upon Magdalen's 'simplicity' and innocence. Her anger and spirit of rebellion – so clearly demonstrated in the blasphemous enquiry which ends the first stanza – were studiously ignored.

> Pale grew your cheek; you stoopt and bound
> Your handkerchief about the wound;
> Your voice came with a broken sound;
> With the deep breath your breast was riven;
> I wonder, did God laugh in Heaven?

The critic of the 'Court Circular' noted with approval that '"Magdalen" … is an entirely original way of treating the old, sad story. There is no complaint, no reproach even, only a great wide eyed wonder.'[175] This breathtaking misrepresentation of the verse indicates the degree to which Amy Levy's New Womanly 'Magdalen' offended the sensitivities of the 'Old Mannish' late nineteenth-century literati, who would not or could not accept that a woman (and a young one at that) could construe 'the old, sad story' in this way. Christina Rossetti, when warned by her brother Gabriel that the subject of 'Under the Rose' was not suitable for a female poet, replied warmly:

> And whilst it may truly be urged that unless white could be black and Heaven Hell my experience (thank God) precludes me from hers, yet I don't see why the 'Poet mind' should be less able to construct her from its own inner consciousness than a hundred other unknown quantities[176]

The refrain of reversal and negation which resonates throughout Amy's 'Magdalen' carries an uncanny echo of Christina's outburst in her letter:

> Death do I trust no more than life.
> For one thing is like one arrayed,
> And there is neither false nor true
> But in a hideous masquerade
> All things dance on the ages through
> Nothing is known or understood
> Save only pain....

Amy's British Museum notebook provides testimony to her abiding engagement with Christina Rossetti's verse.[177] In her essay, 'The poetry of Christina Rossetti', which appeared in Oscar Wilde's *Woman's World* in 1888, she noted – perhaps with a touch of retrospective bitterness - that: 'With unusual opportunities of culture, breathing from the first an atmosphere almost uniquely favourable to artistic production, she had never had to contend with those difficulties which are apt to confront her sex at the outset of a literary career'.[178] However, despite her impeccable literary credentials, Christina had not lived her life in an ivory tower, entirely immured from the problems of those less fortunate than herself.

In the early 1860s, she had volunteered as an associate Sister at the Highgate Penitentiary.[179] The Penitentiary, which was originally known as the St. Mary Magdalene Home, was a refuge for fallen women. During the nineteenth century Homes like the Highgate Penitentiary proliferated throughout the country. The first Magdalen Home had been founded at Blackfriars in London in 1758 with the objective of saving young women who had strayed from the path of virtue from descending further into a life of prostitution. Working on the principle that 'suffering is good for the soul', those unfortunate enough to be confined within the Homes were subjected to a harsh regime of forced labour in order teach them 'habits of obedience sobriety and industry'. It is obvious, both from the context in which it is set and the spelling of its title, that Amy Levy's 'Magdalen' is a commentary upon the Magdalen system, and there are a number of elements within the poem that suggest she was familiar with the details of Christina Rossetti's 'good works' at the Highgate Penitentiary. But how did Amy, who, although she was an admirer of her verse, was not a close friend of the poet, know so much about this aspect of her life? The answer is through A Men and Women's Club.

One of Christina Rossetti's closest friends was the literary critic and biographer

Anne Gilchrist. Gilchrist was also a close friend of Amy's British Museum acquaintance and fellow club member, Helen Zimmern. Although never a formal member of the club herself, Ann Gilchrist and two of her children, Herbert and Grace, had attended several club meetings at which Amy was present.[180] The Gilchrists had probably been introduced to the club by either Helen Zimmern or one of the Garnett family, as Richard Garnett was a regular visitor to Keats Corner, the Gilchrists' Hampstead home. His daughters May and Olive (who were also members of the club) were close friends of Christina Rossetti's brother William's daughters Helen and Olive. Like their father, Helen and Olive Rossetti were confirmed agnostics, and were therefore unlikely to have given favourable accounts of their aunt's charitable works, which were carried out under the auspices of the Anglican Church. As future followers of the anarchist Prince Kropotkin they were also ardent supporters of society's 'underdogs' and would therefore, in all likelihood, have heartily disapproved of the treatment meted out to the young women that their aunt was endeavouring to 'save.' Those who objected to the Penitentiary system were generally opposed to the unnecessary cruelty inflicted through the dismal regime that the inmates were forced to endure. Amy brings this regimen vividly to life in the opening stanza of her poem:

> The bare, blank room where is no sun;
> The parcelled hours; the pallet hard;
> The dreary faces here within;
> The outer women's cold regard;
> The Pastor's iterated "sin"; –

The Highgate Penitentiary was unusual in the fact that a number of its inmates were middle class. A note in its annual report states that 'of the inmates admitted to St. Mary Magdalene Penitentiary, several have been of the higher class as regards birth and education.' The first Magdalen Homes had segregated the inmates, categorising them according to their 'education or behaviour'. This separation of the 'wheat' from the 'chaff' enabled the Penitentiary workers to identify and try to rehabilitate the less hardened offenders, who they defined as a 'numerous class of women, who are much to be pitied … young women who have been seduced from their friends under promise of marriage and have been deserted by their seducers. Their relations, in the first moments of their resentment, refuse to receive, protect or acknowledge them; they are abandoned by the world …and wretched indeed is their situation!'[181] The age range of the Highgate penitents – from early teens to mid-twenties – suggests that these were similarly vulnerable young women who had either been 'taken in' by an unscrupulous man or thrown out by an uncaring family. For although the Magdalen Homes were founded with the ostensibly high-minded motive of saving 'fallen women', in practice, they were often used by the public as a convenient means of disposing of a troublesome female relative – 'fallen' or not. Moreover, the religious houses to which they were attached regarded the Homes as a handy source of income, as the Penitents were forced to 'wash away their sins' by labouring in the public laundry, which was an integral part of every Home – a satisfactory situation for everyone – except for poor unfortunates who were incarcerated within them. These unfortunate young women often died as a result of the unkind treatment meted out to them by their self-proclaimed 'saviours' – an unpleasant fact alluded to in Amy's poem. But although, as a devout Christian, Christina Rossetti would not have been able to condone 'sin', she was essentially a fair-minded and kindly woman, who would have realised that there was more than one side to the story. Through her work at the Penitentiary she became involved in the campaign for the 'Protection of Minors' – the attempt to shield young girls from sexual exploitation by raising the age of consent to sexual intercourse from thirteen years old, which was the legal limit at that time. In June 1882 Ellice Hopkins (who was, like Christina Rossetti, a High Church Anglican, a - less talented - poet and an indefatigable do-gooder who devoted much of her spare time to saving women from the streets) brought 'new evidence from rescue workers in the East End and refuges like the Highgate Penitentiary' before a Committee of the House of Lords.[182] A petition to raise the age of consent from thirteen to sixteen was circulated, and by the early months of 1883 Christina was writing round to her friends, urging their support for the petition. Although the precise date at which Amy wrote 'Magdalen' is unknown, as *A Minor Poet* was published in 1884, the poem must have been written after the publication of *Xantippe* in 1881. This would place the date of writing at 1882 or 1883, the years when the debate concerning raising the age of consent was at its height. Because of the scale of publicity that the campaign attracted, it is inconceivable that the subject would have escaped the notice of A Men and Women's Club. And given Christina Rossetti's close links with the Gilchrists and the Garnetts, it seems reasonable to assume that her experiences would have been cited during any discussion of the issue at the club meetings.

In fact Amy's Magdalen exactly matches the profile of a typical Highgate penitent because it is clear that she is no 'hardened whore', but a gullible girl who has been deceived by an unprincipled man. Her Magdalen is therefore not represented as the biblical prostitute, but a wholly innocent young woman who is identified with another 'holy innocent' - the virgin mother of Christ. For whereas Mary Magdalene is traditionally depicted draped in a scarlet cloak, Amy's Magdalen – no 'scarlet woman' she – is portrayed wearing a 'half-slipt shawl of dusky blue', the garment that is conventionally associated with the Holy Virgin. A further element that links the poem with Christina Rossetti's experiences at the Penitentiary is the description of Magdalen's fall from innocence, which is symbolically represented by the 'deflowering' of a rose bush:

> And once my hand, on a summer's morn,
> I stretched to pluck a rose; a thorn
> Struck through the flesh and made it bleed
> (A little drop of blood indeed!)

The first two lines of this passage reproduce in truncated form, and in reverse order, the opening lines of Christina Rossetti's 'Under the Rose' which, by 1883, had been retitled 'The Iniquity of the Fathers Upon the Children'.

> Oh the rose of keenest thorn
> One hidden summer morn
> Under the rose I was born

But there is a further aspect of Amy's poem that is as unconventional as its portrayal of Magdalen as a blameless victim, and which, from the Victorian perspective, would have been deeply disturbing. Like 'Xantippe' the poem takes the form of a soliloquy spoken by a woman on her deathbed. Although it has previously been assumed that Magdalen is dying from venereal disease, the link between Amy's poem and Christina Rossetti's work at the Highgate Penitentiary invites an extremely radical interpretation of this aspect of the verse - namely that Magdalen has resorted to abortion in order to avoid a fate that she regarded as 'worse than death'. Like other institutions of its kind, the Highgate Penitentiary was selective in its requirements, admitting 'neither pregnant girls, nor those with illegitimate children, for whom the workhouse and the Foundling Hospital were seen as appropriate alternatives.' If therefore, should her pregnancy be discovered, Magdalen (or her real-life counterpart) faced the prospect of a choice between removal to the workhouse or admission to the Penitentiary then she would have had a great incentive to dispose of the unwanted foetus, for, incredible though it sounds, the Magdalen Homes were regarded as a soft option: 'a more humane alternative [than] the workhouse.'[183] Magdalen's ironic exclamation 'A little drop of blood indeed!' instils the idea in the reader's mind that she has since experienced greater blood loss than this, perhaps suffered a haemorrhage, which was often the outcome of a botched abortion. The penultimate stanza of the verse reinforces this idea:

> The doctor says that I shall die.
> You, that I knew in days gone by,
> I fain would see your face once more,
> Con well its features o'er and o'er;
> And touch your hand and feel your kiss,
> Look in your eyes and tell you this:
> That all is done, that I am free;
> That you, through all eternity,
> Have neither part nor lot in me.

The lines 'That all is done, that I am free;/That you through all eternity/Have neither part nor lot in me' signify a deliberate act, one which has been 'done' to 'free' the woman from the 'part' of her former lover (the unwanted foetus) that threatened her future wellbeing, rather than a chance event like a miscarriage or a stillbirth. Similarly, the last two lines of Magdalen's pitiful musing:

> It is so strange to think on still –
> That you, that you should do me ill!
> Not as one ignorant or blind,
> But seeing clearly in your mind
> How this must be which now has been,
> Nothing aghast at what was seen …

simply a specific and ghastly event, which has occurred in the recent past and is now over – 'which now *has been*' – rather than an ongoing plight.

Throughout the 1880s discussion of 'Malthusian' issues – 'preventive checks', as contraception was coyly termed – were commonplace in advanced circles. In her comprehensive study of late nineteenth-century sexual morality, Lucy Bland notes that at that time most readily available forms of contraception 'required male co-operation'. As a result, 'despite being illegal since 1803, [abortion] was the main form of female birth restriction, widely resorted to by women of all classes.' She cites (somewhat ironically) a study undertaken in the 1890s by Karl Pearson's at that time Research Assistant, Ethel Elderton, in which Elderton 'claimed that 70–80 per cent of all women took abortion drugs.' She concludes: 'All such potions were unreliable and many were poisonous, frequently resulting in ill-health, even death. More dangerous still were abortions performed by instruments by an abortionist, usually a midwife, or sometimes a doctor.' [184] Read in the light of this information, the final stanza of Amy's poem clearly invites the reading that Magdalen has resorted to abortion in order to free herself of her unwanted child. And if this is the case then 'Magdalen' was the only poem written by a woman to address the issue of abortion before Charlotte Mew's 'Saturday Market', which was published more than thirty years later, in 1916.[185]

As the critic of the *Glasgow Herald* pointed out, 'the majority of [Amy Levy's] themes are not such as very young poets most affect.'[186] It is undoubtedly the case that through her membership of A Men and Women's club, Amy gained an insight into the more profound implications of the inequalities between men and women in Victorian society; and this made her ever more determined to challenge the unwritten rules that decreed that women like Adelaide and Magdalen should pay for their 'sins', whilst the men who had 'ruined' them walked away scot-free.

Some time in late May or early June 1884 *A Minor Poet* finally arrived on the shelves of the London bookshops. Like Amy, Ernest Radford had been anxiously awaiting the publication of his own second collection of verse, *Measured Steps*. On 11th June Dollie recorded in her diary: ' "Measured Steps" advertised in the spectator… Ernest went to tennis at the Levys. Brought Amy Levy's book of verses back.' Dollie was unable to accompany Ernest to the Levys' tennis party due to the fact that, she too, was anticipating a significant event – the birth of their first child. But although she did not meet up with Amy on this occasion, during May and June 1884 they saw one another often. On 8th May she had noted: 'Mrs. Rowe, Amy Levy & George [Radford] called. Gracie came & went with us to the Bedford Debating Society discussion on "Spiritualism".' Two days later, on 10th May, she 'Went to see Amy Levy. Walked along by the park.' On 29th May: 'Amy Levy called and stayed to dinner. Mr Shaw came to go with Ernest to the 'Casual' – Ernest read a paper to that society on 'modern poets'.' And again, on 4th June: 'Ernest went to the Levys to tennis.' On 17th June, six days after he had returned from the Levys' tennis party bearing a copy of *A Minor Poet*, Dollie recorded that 'Ernest went to dine with Karl Pearson at the Saville.'[187] A week later, on 23rd June she noted that 'Amy Levy came to dinner.' And two days later, on 25th June, she reported: To the Levys with Ernest in the afternoon to tennis.' Evidently this time her pregnancy had not prevented her from joining the party. Three days after this, there was the final gathering of the club before the members dispersed for the summer. On 28th June Dollie recorded: 'The Club pic nic [sic]. Ernest went off to it about ten; and supported the care(?) and labour of the party.' The club minutes reveal that, as well as Amy, the picnic party included Ernest's brother George and sister Ada, Clementina and Grace Black, May Garnett, the two Rowe brothers Louis and Francis, the Zimmern sisters Helen and Alice, Frederick Wedmore's daughter Millicent, Eleanor Marx's friend Marion Skinner and three of Karl Pearson's Cambridge cohorts, Hume Pinsent, Robert Parker and Ralph Thicknesse. Pearson himself was evidently otherwise engaged - somehow one cannot imagine him casting off his habitual reserve and entering into the spirit of this 'end of term' jamboree. Or perhaps he may have already set off for his summer holiday in the Black Forest.

On 7th July, nine days after the club picnic, Dollie noted: 'Miss Blanche Smith [and] Amy Levy called.' Blanche Smith, an ex-Newnhamite and an occasional visitor to the club, was a friend of Amy's former classmate, Alice Lloyd. Cantankerous and with a tendency to hypochondria, Blanche was evidently not a sympathetic character. Alice was later to describe her as bearing a 'grudge against the world.' However, her disagreeable disposition seems not to have deterred Amy from choosing her as a travelling companion, as on 16th July she paid yet another visit to the Radford household in Brunswick Square.[188] Dollie's diary for that day reads: 'Amy Levy called, & Clemmie came in the morning. Amy starts to-morrow for the Vosges.' Amy was accompanied on her journey by Blanche Smith. Once again, she turned the adventures that they shared together to good account, using them as a basis for two short stories that were published in *London Society* in the autumn of 1884. The first of these, 'In Retreat' (which is sub-titled 'A Long Vacation Experience'), is headed with the month (July) and the address: 'Convent of St. Odile, Odilienberg, Vosges'. This is the place where Amy and Blanche Smith set up home for a fortnight whilst *en route* to their ultimate destination, which was the lakeside resort of Titisee in the Black Forest. Like 'Between Two Stools', 'In Retreat' takes the form of a letter written from one female student to another during the long vacation, but this time the student in question, Melissa, is not studying at 'Newton College' but 'Princess Ida's university' – the name of Alfred Tennyson's imaginary 'University of Women' in his poem 'The Princess'. It can be deduced from the narrative that the real-life Melissa - Amy Levy - and her holiday companion Psyche – alias Blanche Smith – did not initially find life 'in retreat' particularly congenial. Bad food, bed bugs and an argument about a lack of hot water all combined to make their first night at the convent extremely uncomfortable. But in the morning, after settling down in the garden with their books, they were confronted with a scene straight out of a painting by Pieter Breughel. Flinging down her book Melissa cries: "Who cares for ancient Greece? We are in the Middle Ages!" She continues:

> After that we gave ourselves up to the spirit of the hour, and thoroughly explored the convent. There is a great kitchen presided over by a tall Sister, a wilderness of provisions and pots and pans; but much of the food preparation is carried out on deal tables in the corridor, where the pounding of roots, scraping of herbs, and washing of plates seem never to cease. There is an infinity of cooks spoiling any quantity of broth. A door at the end of the corridor leads into a little dim stone passage looking down on a small inner chapel, and containing a ghastly effigy of St. Odile enclosed in a glass sarcophagus ...There are all sorts of stone passages, where clothes are hung to dry, linen is stored &c., and where rats occasionally emerge at night ...

This scene of organised chaos is presided over by a tyrannical Mother Superior who, in the tradition of the Magdalen Homes, rules her flock with a rod of iron – 'an undoubted despot with all the faults of her qualities.'[189]

In the course of the narrative Amy took the opportunity to poke fun at her travelling companion by investing her fictional counterpart, Psyche, with a decidedly frivolous streak: 'Psyche got quite excited at finding herself in the 'Blue Alsatian Mountains' hummed that everlasting tune from beginning to end, and made sentimental allusions to "that lovely waltz with Frank!"' 'The Blue Alsatian Mountains' was the equivalent of a top ten hit of the 1880s, and Amy's reference to 'that lovely waltz with Frank!' suggests that perhaps she had the twice weekly dances at the Hotel Sonnenberg in mind when she wrote this passage. She must have had her tongue firmly in her cheek when she did so, as it is difficult to envisage Blanche Smith casting off her characteristic despondency and permitting herself to be propelled round a ballroom to the strains of a popular dance tune by a dashing young 'masher' – Victorian slang for a flirtatious young man about town.

After saying goodbye to the sisters at St. Odilienberg, Amy and Blanche Smith set off by train for Freiberg im Breisgau - a small town on the edge of the Black Forest. In the second of the short stories that record her 1884 summer holiday, which is entitled: 'In the Black Forest', Amy described Freiburg as 'a bright sunny little place, with gardens and villas, and wide rambling streets.' From here, early the next morning, Melissa and Psyche 'set out for Titisee on the top of a tall diligence [stagecoach], driven by a light-hearted coachman in [a] wonderful shiny black hat.'[190] After a six hour drive (for a journey of just under twenty miles) they arrived at their destination, the 'Gathaus Zum Titisee, Altenweg, Baden'. This is the address that, once again, not only heads the letters that Amy wrote to her family and friends whilst staying at Titisee, but also heads her story 'In the Black Forest'. The first of the letters to bear this heading was directed to Katie, and in it Amy gave an account of her progress that suggests that she was in a state of unusually high spirits.: 'This is a most satisfactory place. I wish we had come here fr. the first' she enthused. Obviously the discomforts of the convent were still fresh in her mind. However, with characteristic pessimism she could not resist adding: 'But I daresay the first raptures will wear off & that I shall have had enough of it before we leave.' One aspect of the holiday that she had patently 'had enough of' was her travelling companion, who was casting a pall of gloom over the proceedings, she grumbled:

> Blanche Smith is regularly seedy – she talks of sending for her sister & staying here all the summer, in wh. case I shall have to return on my own fair hook, wh. I funk, as its [sic] such a long journey.

And she later complained:

> To-day we make an excursion to a little town, going there by post-wagon and returning on our pins [on foot]. I wish I had a more lively companion, but I suppose its seediness makes Blanche so dismal.

The strain of her holiday companion's constant low spirits was evidently beginning to take its toll on her ever fragile psychological balance, because she confided ominously to Katie:

> I console myself with the abnormal wholesomeness of my body … trying to ignore the great she-devil who lyeth ever in wait in the recesses of my heart.[191]

Fortunately the lakeside party offered ample distraction from Blanche Smith's bouts of 'seediness' and her fears about her own mental health. One of her fellow guests at the Gasthaus zum Titisee was a fellow club member and brother of her Cambridge friends Annie and Minnie Bond. She told Katie: 'Harry Bond is sort of head-nurse at this place; goes round with a gang of little German girls whom he teaches rowing'. Having complained that they found Bond 'dull and boring' she added: 'he affords us little satisfaction, the only point in his favour being his sex.' However, more congenial male company was evidently at hand in the elegant and erudite form of Karl Pearson. She continued:

> Carl Pearson[192] came over yesterday afternoon to fetch us for a walk. We went to his village, had coffee & were introduced to his villagers, with whom he chums & who regard him as a sort of King. We went into one little house where a horrible old woman ex-

> claimed: 'Ach Herr Professor! und du hast gesagt dass du dich nie Heirathest! ['Really Professor! and you have told us that you will never marry!']…. no wonder you are so fond of Titisee when there are such beautiful ladies there! etc., etc.,' (at great length.) I suppose one oughtn't to feel uncomfortable on such occasions but I think I did. He hawked us all round the place introducing us as the first English ladies who had ever been to Saig.

She added:

> We are going to give a return coffee party to wh. messrs. Pearson & Bond are to be coyly bidden.

Amy's account of her walk to Pearson's village matches her description of the excursion taken by Psyche and Melissa in 'In the Black Forest':

> Hilarion[193] is living at a village on the top of the hill, a mile or two off. He fetched us for coffee at his inn the other day; it was such a beautiful walk through shady pine-woods, and such a sweet little straggling village, lying amid the hills. These Black Forest folk are charming, very frank and homely, and quite ignoring differences of rank.

At around the time that Amy sent her letter to Katie she also wrote to Dollie Radford, who had just given birth to a son, Maitland, a week after Amy and Blanche had set off for the Vosges. After asking her to thank Ernest for conveying this news, and making a polite enquiry about the new addition to the family - 'is it not exciting to have a baby of one's own. I am sure it is a nice one if there is anything in heredity' - she went on to give Dollie an account of her recent activities:

> Harry Bond is here – very much in his element, the centre of a crowd of admiring little German girls. We have dubbed him 'The Head Nurse' but do not betray us. Carl Pearson has been staying in a village a little way off; we went to coffee at his inn the other day and were introduced to his peasants. He is a sort of little god among them – wh. he rather enjoys I fancy in spite of much philosophy and mathematics. He has gone to Freyburg [sic] to-day to meet Mr. Parker whose marriage has been put off till next month. [194]

Amy's several references to her afternoon walk with Pearson to see 'his village', her confession of her discomfort when praised in his presence by 'the horrible old woman', and the amused but admiring affection for him that she displayed when recounting the details of the visit in her letters (which contrasts with the detached, mocking tone of her remarks about Harry Bond) create the impression that Pearson was an important person in her life at that time. He likewise seems to have singled her out for particular attention, as her comment in her letter to Katie that she and Blanch Smith had been introduced to 'his peasants' as 'the first English ladies who had ever been to Saig' reveals that they were the first women in his circle to be granted the privilege of being shown around his 'village retreat'.

Pearson had been a regular summertime visitor to Saig since the early 1880s. In the spring of 1879 he had studied for a while in Heidelberg, and during this time had developed an interest in German folklore and the history of the Reformation. On completing his studies, before returning home, he took a walking tour through the Black Forest with his brother Arthur. It was then that he discovered Saig, which he instantly realised was the ideal spot to undertake a study of local folklore. Even today, Saig is little more than a tiny hamlet situated in the hills that surround Titisee. There is a painting of the village dating from the early 1880s which reveals that when Pearson first discovered it, it was probably still as it had been in the Middle Ages, consisting of little more than a few modest dwellings, a church and the inn.[195] And as Amy's letter attests, at that time its inhabitants were at a decidedly less advanced stage of social evolution than the recently appointed professor of mathematics and future professor of eugenics who came amongst them to observe them in their habitat – no wonder they looked upon him as a 'sort of King'! [196]

Amy's last letter dating from her visit to Titisee is written on the same distinctive pink writing paper as the two addressed to Katie and Dollie Radford. But this letter differs from the others inasmuch as it has no addressee and bears a different heading: 'Zum Ochsen, Saig Bei Lenzkirch'. Below the address is a rough sketch of a building with a steep roof and many windows, set amongst hills. This was the Gasthof Ochsen – Pearson's erstwhile holiday home. The Gasthof Ochsen still exists, although it is now named the Hotel Ochsen, a reflection of the fact that Saig is now no longer an isolated hamlet but a popular tourist destination; but the building, with its steeply pitched roof and numerous small windows, is still recognisable as the building in Amy's sketch.

At the end of her letter to Dollie, she had made a cryptic comment: 'There is a rumour of the invasion of a gang of Newnhamites, Ada Radfords & things – I pray to the Gods they won't come.'[197] Sadly her prayers were destined to be unanswered, as just over a month later, on 13th September, Ernest Radford recorded in Dollie's diary: 'Ada & Charles turned up from Titisee via the Rhine & Paris last Wednesday.' Amy's instinctive aversion to Ada Radford may, in part, have been due to her forbidding personality. Rigid in her opinions and intolerant of others' faults, her watchword was 'principle'. Beatrice Potter was later to describe her as 'a woman who carries principles into the smallest concerns in life.' If this was the case, although at first one can see no obvious reason for Amy's apprehension at her imminent arrival, all becomes clear when one reads her letter:

> Behold me in my village retreat! I am living in a state of naked impropriety, altogether unchaperoned. My first night of exile was a failure. I didn't get rooms at the Ochs, [the Gasthof Ochsen] so had one found at the Pfarrer – house, [the priest's house] with the

arrangement that I was to board at the inn. [198] The word Pfarrer suggested a homely domestic soul to myself & Miss Corfe who led me up.[199] Not till I was fairly established did I identify it with the grim individual in a cassock who is to be seen curtseying about the churchyard at all hours of the day. When I came back from supper at the Ochs a sort of funk seized me, I bolted my room & put chairs against an inner door. The nasty old woman who brought my bath saw the chairs and scoffed at my fears, & I tried to settle down with my books. Presently a knock came. I opened the door & beheld a tall figure in a cassock, candle in hand, grinning & chuckling in a way which when taken with his normal solemnity, was grim in the extreme. He came to soothe my fears (o irony) assured me that I was 'bei ihm' [by him] & that the hostess at the inn had been wrong, & that my room was not besetzl [occupied] for the next night. He kept on repeating 'ich behalte sie so lange als sie wolle' [You can stay as long as you like], so often & with such fervour, & coming so close, that had it not been for his profession I might have considered myself entitled to hang up my 'at in the 'all. I kept the door very narrowly open, tho' he was evidently anxious to pay me a pastorly visit, & waxed pale & funky, wh. was silly, for of course he meant well – but he was a hale man in the 30s & I was quite at his mercy. I had a grim night; kept on remembering that all the villains [sic] in German tales are priests.

I am now at the Ochs & like my new quarters immensely. It is a most exotic building but everything is awfully good. I have to go in to table d'hôte alone & created much surprise at first. All the people are Germans, so it doesn't matter. I am now on the track of the German owl (cocks only examined).[200]

There is a little group of simple-hearted studenten with whom I rather chum …. Your hair would have stood on end to have seen me last night, after dinner, sitting at the table with no less than three German mashers engaged in animated converse. I think the matrons believe me to be no better than I shd. be, but my men are awfully nice & polite. I have had £2.10 [two pounds ten shillings] from L.S. [*London Society*] & the proof of one of my pot-boilers [this was likely to have been 'In Holiday Humour' which, as we have seen, was published in the holiday edition in August 1884] …. I shall probably stay till Wednesday week & return home with Miss Corfe, as Blanche stays on. The latter joins me at Saig on Friday. I have been working but O the novel is so bad it's no go. I have been wasting my substance in riotous living – had a coffee party & breakfast party the same day: guests Radfords, etc.

As a matter of fact I am writing this at Titisee; I came over for letters & stayed to dinner because of the rain. I must go soon & summon Miss Gardner who is going to walk up with me. She has asked me to call on her in London.

I am sorry you are so sad. From my point of view you are such a lucky beggar! Fixed income, good ears, loving friends, & a credit account with the Heavenly Powers!

My own melancholy is too large for words – O if I needn't go home and start the old struggle for existence .. .

This heartfelt exclamation highlights the way in which Darwinist terminology was pervading her writing, both personal and professional - a development that was undoubtedly attributable to Pearson's influence. The final part of the letter is missing, but the last surviving page ends abruptly: 'A clever German lady here, has asked me to go to dinner and have some music with her at Freybourg [sic] on my way through. She is very witty, a sort of good-looking Magna; she and ….' The profile of the 'clever German lady' given by Amy fits that of Pearson's old friend Emma Debattis. Frau Debattis paid many visits to the Gasthof Ochsen during the 1880s.[201]

The intimate tone of the letter invites the assumption that Amy was writing to Katie. But the line 'Fixed income, good ears, loving friends, & a credit account with the Heavenly Powers!' suggests otherwise, because at that time Katie was a student, still living at home and, like Amy, dependent upon their father for financial support. Could Amy have been writing to one of her brothers instead - perhaps Alfred? Like her, he appears to have had a tendency to depression. And at that time he had regular employment at the Stock Exchange, and was also on intimate terms with her circle of friends. The fact that Amy termed her correspondent a 'lucky beggar' adds weight to this hypothesis, for 'beggar' was a euphemism for 'fellow' - an odd choice of epithet to apply to her sister. [202] However, regardless of to whomsoever the letter was addressed, if he or she bore Amy's interests at heart its recipient must have read its contents with alarm.

From the perspective of our own liberated age, it is difficult to convey the momentous implication of Amy's behaviour which, when considered within the context of her era, can only be regarded as a breathtaking act of defiance against the social code. In the late nineteenth century, when a young woman's reputation could be jeopardised by even the slightest hint of impropriety, her mere presence in Saig without a suitable chaperone would inevitably have damned her in the eyes of the world - regardless of how she conducted herself once there. On her first visit to the village with Pearson she had been accompanied by Blanche Smith because, as a young single man, Pearson by himself would not have been considered a suitable escort for a young unmarried woman. But as her letter makes clear, on this occasion Miss Corfe merely 'led her up' and left her at the mercy of 'the pfarrer'. Amy's former idol Jennie Wetton had incurred the wrath of her family by permitting a young man to escort her from one side of Berlin to the other - a trivial misdemeanour compared to an 'entirely unchaperoned' stay in a remote village inn. Amy's comments that 'I have to go in to table d'hôte alone & created much surprise at first', and 'your hair would have stood on end to have seen me last night sitting at the table with no less than three German mashers engaged in animated converse', followed by the comment 'the German matrons believe me to be no better than I should be' confirms that she was only too aware that she was putting her reputation on the line. No wonder she had taken the precaution of ensuring that the family correspondence was still sent to Titisee - one can imagine Isabelle's reaction if she had discovered what her daughter was up to. But what - or who – could have persuaded her to embark upon such a reckless course of action? The answer to this question is probably Karl Pearson. Indeed, it is difficult to imagine any explanation for Amy's decision to abandon her party of friends at Titisee and take off to stay by herself in such an isolated location other than Pearson's presence in the village. It could be argued that the fact that he is not mentioned in the surviving pages of her letter indicates that he was not there at the time, but it is also possible that the final page or pages of the letter are missing just because his name did appear upon them, and that the recipient destroyed it/them in order ensure that it/they would not fall into less sympathetic hands. When considering this question it is interesting to note that when Amy referred to her recent coffee party she described her guests as 'Radfords, etc.' No mention was made of 'Messrs Pearson and Bond' who, according to her earlier letter to Katie, were to be 'coyly bidden' to join the guests.

But the question remains: why did Amy leave the comfort of the lakeside guest house to take up residence in such a primitive place? The fact that Pearson had introduced Amy and Blanche Smith as 'the first English ladies who had been to Saig', and her comment in her letter that 'all the people [here] are Germans so it doesn't matter', confirms that she was the only English woman in the village at that time. Indeed, any English visitor of either sex was a rarity in Saig. When Pearson had first set foot there a couple of years beforehand the landlady of the inn had told him that 'she had never before had an English guest'.[203] And apart from Amy's reference to her fellow traveller 'the 'clever German lady,' who was plainly a new acquaintance, there is nothing to suggest that she had any other German friends in the vicinity. The only conclusion to be drawn therefore is that while Amy was staying at the Gasthof Ochsen, Pearson was also in the village – although not necessarily staying at the inn, because he also sometimes lodged elsewhere. But if this is the case, then why did he not try to dissuade Amy from joining him there? His interest in the 'woman question', with its focus upon the injustices of the Victorian 'double standard' of sexual morality, would have ensured that he was only too aware of the consequences that followed when a young woman transgressed the rigid rules of behaviour that, at that date, governed every aspect of her life. But Pearson may have had his own interests in mind rather than Amy's when he apparently did nothing to prevent, and maybe even encouraged her to commit what was, on the face of it, an act of sheer folly.

After the postponement of his engagement, Robert Parker had made a spur-of-the-moment decision to join Pearson at Saig. From there the pair planned to embark upon a short walking holiday in the Tyrol. Parker told Pearson that this change in his plans had been roundly condemned by Pearson's mother, with whom he had dined a few days beforehand. She had told him that she was 'very shocked at the idea of my joining you and not going to Scotland with Constance [Parker's fiancée] and Ellen [his sister]' he told Pearson. He seemed to be mildly amused at the consternation that he had caused. Although he would not have been able to say so either to Pearson or his mother, the reason for his impromptu visit to Saig was probably to make an attempt to reconcile his friend to the idea of his forthcoming marriage. At that time they shared lodgings in Harcourt Buildings in the Temple, and one can gather from Parker's earlier letters that Pearson was profoundly unhappy at the prospect of parting from his housemate.

At this stage in his life Pearson seems to have had an almost pathological fear of commitment, and a dread of losing his friends to matrimony. Theodore Porter writes that: 'From about 1878 to 1884 [Pearson] was resolved to remain single, and he repeatedly emphasised to his contemporaries ... the tragic loss they would incur by entering marriage and starting a family.' He cites as an example 'Ralph Thicknesse, who recalled years later to Helga Pearson [Pearson's daughter] the night in August 1883, "when your Father took me out into the most exquisite valley in the Tyrol in the moonlight and said that all I wanted to make me perfect was for me to give up my belief in God & throw over the girl I was engaged to be married to." '[204] Saig was a place where Pearson and his male friends could 'bond' and safely let their hair down - as witnessed in the letter that he and Thicknesse jointly wrote just before they set off for their walking trip in the Tyrol, during the course of which he made his moonlight 'proposal' to his friend. Pearson's correspondence with Parker at this time suggests that he was on a similar mission to persuade him to break his engagement to Constance. [205] It is therefore likely that he had a hidden agenda when he invited Parker to join him at Saig in August 1884. And just as he had done with Ralph Thicknesse in the preceding summer, he was planning to use the time that they spent together to dissuade his friend from taking the final plunge into matrimony.

Parker informed Pearson that he would 'start on 8th and be back by Sunday 24th', asking, 'will that suit your arrangements?'[206] Although the proposed date of their departure for the walking tour is not clear, Amy's letter confirms that he did indeed join Pearson at Saig on 10th August, as they had planned. In the summer of 1884 there was a major outbreak of cholera in continental Europe, and in an earlier letter to Pearson he had expressed concern about the possibility of 'quarantine between Austria and Germany'.[207] At the end of Amy's letter to Dollie she had commented: 'This is a lovely place, much better than the Vosges, where, bye the bye there are no "springs where Truth or cholera may lurk". ' However, as we now know, Dollie's sister-in-law Ada was planning to join the party at Titisee, and it seems that Dollie and Ernest, alarmed at the possible risk, asked Amy for information about the progress of the cholera outbreak. Similar concerns may well have caused a delay in Pearson and Parker's planned departure for the Tyrol. And this might have suited Pearson's purpose very well.

The change in their planned schedule would have meant that Parker was probably in Saig when Amy set out with Miss Corfe to walk up to the village. Indeed it was likely to have been Parker's presence that emboldened Pearson to suggest that Amy join him there, because he was to make a similar attempt to inveigle his future fiancée, Maria Sharpe, to establish a 'unitary home' with him and Ralph Thicknesse at the 'little inn' in the summer of 1888. But what could his motive have been for attempting to lure Amy to the place that up to now he had regarded as a sanctuary where no woman had been permitted to intrude upon his freedom? It is possible that he was genuinely concerned for her welfare, as her already troubled state of mind cannot been improved by the turn that her holiday had taken when, to add to her problems with Blanche Smith, the priggish Ada Radford had joined the lakeside party. It is also evident from her letter that Amy was working on a novel, but was unhappy with its progress, considering it 'no go'. Another reason for her downbeat mood was the reviews of *A Minor Poet* that were evidently still preying on her mind. Her letter to Dollie included a response to Ernest Radford's remarks on the same subject: 'I sympathise with Mr Radford on the subject of reviews. It's a good thing we are not of Keats-like sensibility, otherwise we should have been "snuffed out" by the various "articles" of kind critics.' No doubt Pearson would have also sympathised with this opinion of literary reviews because of the critical drubbing that his own 'Passion Play' had received. But there is another possibility, and that is that he persuaded Amy that by taking a stand against the convention that demanded that an unmarried woman should not been seen in public in the company of a single man (however well she knew him) without being accompanied by a chaperone, she would be striking a blow for female emancipation. If this was indeed the case then his suggestion would have fallen upon fertile ground. In 'In the Black Forest' Amy gives an account of Psyche and Melissa's fellow travellers on the road to Titisee which, like other incidents in the story, has the ring of authenticity:

> There were only two other passengers besides ourselves outside [on top of] the diligence – a married couple, not long past the honeymoon stage, I should say; the woman shrill, sharp-featured; with light hair and eyelashes … very vigilant over the husband, a meek and cheerful little person, evidently much in awe of his wife. I was determined to talk to the man, in spite of the she-dragon, and assailed him with questions in my fluent German – Psyche says it was a positive case of assault.

> The woman expressed much surprise at the fact of our travelling alone. 'And you always go *ganz allein*? [all alone] without a gentleman?' And she clutched at her miserable specimen of manhood with complacent triumph.
>
> You can imagine our scorn. I wonder when the German Haus-frau [housewife] will consider the question of casting off the yoke!'[208]

Pearson may have hoped that the presence in Saig of a fellow club member who had such forthright views on the merits of feminine autonomy - and was not afraid to put them into practice – would be a useful tool in his armoury when trying to persuade Parker to have second thoughts about shackling himself for a lifetime to a woman that he deemed an unsuitable mate for a man of intellect.

Although Pearson favoured the company of his male friends, in other respects he was ahead of his time in his attitude to the relationship between the sexes. In a future essay he was to express profound regret at the way that Victorian society was ordered. This, he claimed, made 'close friendship between single men and women ... almost impossible'.[209] He believed that this unfortunate state of affairs frequently led both sexes to make a catastrophic mistake in their choice of a life partner 'because they ...had not the inclination, nor the knowledge, nor the opportunity to study [their] character before marriage'.[210] He certainly had no intention of making this mistake himself. At this time his ideal of relationship with both men and women could be defined as ascetic - a cerebral partnership of 'intellectual love' - the 'Platonic friendship' sworn 'o'er and o'er' by the trio of friends beside the little lake at Seelisberg in the summer of 1883. Pearson's fear of emotional commitment seems to have stemmed from the problems in his parents' relationship that he had witnessed in his childhood. His father, William Pearson, was a barrister and a Q.C. Something of an autocrat, he dominated his wife, who in consequence transferred her affections on to her children. And delicate little Carl was her particular pet. Carl, on the other hand, seems to have simultaneously loved and despised his mother – a state of mind that was to characterise his relationship with women throughout his life. He described her as 'not a highly-educated woman, nor a clear-sighted woman of strong common sense', and freely acknowledged that what he had observed at home left him with a 'dread of the misery produced by [women's] dependence, [and] by the strength of their transient emotions influencing their whole life.'[211] His opposition to the idea of marriage was also founded on his doubt that it was a suitable state for what he termed a 'progressive soul'.[212] Certainly he did not approve of middle-class women who were slaves to conformity, whom he castigated as 'shopping and society doll[s].'[213] He believed wholeheartedly that all women should find a worthwhile occupation that gave them a purpose in life, and that as men's mastery over their wives was principally due to 'the power of the purse' their interests were best served if they achieved a level of financial independence for themselves. A month after his return from his Black Forest holiday, he gave Parker a tongue-in-cheek verbal sketch of his ideal female companion, whom, he claimed: 'must have some education ... also her own pursuits and conviction that marriage does not destroy individual independence in thought or action. She must have, of course, no superstition as to the superior merits of Jesus or any other emotional prophet ...'[214] Parker obviously chose to ignore his friend's counsel, as his fiancée who later became his bride - although not necessarily addicted to shopping - was by all accounts a 'shallow' and conventional woman.[215] No one could have described Amy Levy in these terms.

But however ardently Amy supported the cause of women's rights, it was one thing for her to nail her colours to the mast on paper, so to speak, but quite another to embark upon a course of action that would imperil her reputation, thereby putting her entire future at risk. The question is why did she do so? It seems likely that by this time she was in love with Pearson. His combination of good looks, charm, and first-class intellect made him particularly attractive to educated, free-thinking women like Amy. Lucy Clifford told Olive Schreiner that she couldn't 'understand any woman seeing him without loving him, and wanting to fall down at his feet'.[216] Certainly, within the limited circle of her Jewish acquaintance, Amy would be unlikely to have encountered a man with his awesome array of physical and intellectual attributes. And although (naturally enough in the circumstances) apart from the two bashful, self-conscious references to him in her letters no direct record of her feelings for him remains, there seems no other explanation for her aberrant behaviour than that she felt as Mrs. Clifford did. Her membership of A Men and Women's club had introduced her into a circle where the unwritten rules that prescribed rigid standards of conduct for women whilst absolving men from any such responsibility for their behaviour were not taken for granted. Gaining admission to this brave new world must have been a particularly heady experience for someone brought up to conform to the rigid, retrogressive customs of the Jewish community. And finally, although it is unwise to make judgements about someone's mental state from a distance in time and without being party to the details of the individual in question's medical history, it seems quite possible that Amy suffered from some degree of bipolar disorder – the symptoms of which are periods of depression followed by intervals of 'mania' when the sufferer is liable, amongst other things, to engage in ill-judged, impulsive behaviour. Janet Oppenheim pointed out that 'late Victorian psychiatry had no idea how to respond to ... manic-depression', and therefore Amy's intense mood swings would not necessarily have aroused the concern of an outside observer.[217] But if this was the case, then when all these factors are considered in combination, it would explain why she so readily fell in with Pearson's suggestion that she join him and Parker at the Gasthof Ochsen.

In the months after Amy's return from her holiday in the Black Forest rifts began to open up between the various factions in the club. After hosting one more meeting in his rooms at Harcourt Buildings on 21st October (which both Amy and her brother Edmund attended), Pearson gradually began to distance himself from the club's proceedings. The ostensible reason for this move was his dissatisfaction with its 'unscientific' agenda – a concern that was broadly shared by his Darwinist oriented clique of Cambridge friends. But his growing distaste for the club was undoubtedly driven by personal considerations. His mood of discontent would have certainly been exacerbated by irritation that Robert Parker had ignored his advice and gone ahead with his postponed wedding. Whilst on his honeymoon he had written to recommend married life to his friend, telling him 'your prophecy of dullness has not been exactly realised', adding 'intellectual pursuits [are] not entirely [unplucked?] for we have read together a good deal and not all poetry and novels but something quite matter of fact in the shape of a volume of Huxley.'[218] Evidently Pearson had expressed fears that his friend's wife would not be sufficiently stimulating company for a man of his level of intellect – an anxiety that seems to have been not entirely without foundation. On 19th November Dollie recorded: 'We went to the club. It was at the Rowe's – a musical evening. I enjoyed it much. <u>Mrs</u>. Parker there (original emphasis): she seems elderly but extremely nice. She has bidden me to theirs to tea. It was a largish meeting. Maggie Johnson came and sang.'[219] Maggie Johnson was probably 'Madge' who had been Amy's wintertime companion during her stay in Dresden. On 2nd December there was yet another club meeting at the Levy family home, before which Dollie and Ernest 'dined with the Levys.' It is obvious that by now the Levy family were in financial difficulty, for they had recently moved from the grand house in Sussex Place to a more modest home around the corner at 26 Ulster Place. Dollie did not mention Pearson in her diary entry, but the record book of the club reveals that he did attend the meeting. The manner in which he signed the register – a barely legible scrawl – suggests that he was in an agitated state at the time, and may have arrived late. It seems unlikely that given his current frame of mind, the paper presented that evening, 'The comparative reliability of Biography & Autobiography', was a subject that would have appealed to him. And in any case, by that time he was actively taking steps to withdraw from the club. On 16th December

Dollie reported: 'To the club with Louie [Jeeves] – Miss Dean & Miss Walker. Tea at Karl Pearson's.' Although Dollie made no comment about their tea-time conversation, five days later, on 21st December, she reported: 'William Thompson & Miss Garnett came to breakfast & Louis glanced in. We discussed the state of the club.' Pearson's last recorded attendance at the club was 10th February 1885. Dollie's granddaughter, Ann MacEwan, gave me an account of the contents of the letter that Dollie subsequently wrote detailing the stormy meeting when Pearson, Parker and Thicknesse staged a dramatic joint exit from the club. After this Pearson was free to pursue his own interests.

Since 1881 he had been corresponding with a woman called Elizabeth Cobb. Mrs Cobb was the wife of a wealthy stockbroker and lived just outside London in what was then the village of Stanmore in Middlesex. Dissatisfied with her own 'limited agenda' – the role of wife and mother – she had sought around for a worthwhile cause to latch on to, and had found that cause in Karl Pearson. Like the unfortunate Mrs. Parker, Elizabeth Cobb would have been judged to be 'elderly' by the standards of her day - she was in her thirties when she and Pearson first met. Whether she could likewise be deemed to be 'nice' is another question. But in her letters to Pearson she was at pains to present her best side, and was soon, metaphorically speaking, throwing herself at his feet. How Elizabeth Cobb and Pearson first met is not entirely clear. It has been suggested that it may have been at one of Pearson's lectures at the South Place Institute in Finsbury.[220] This is quite likely, as Elizabeth's family home before marriage - and where her unmarried sisters Letitia and Maria still lived - was in the neighbouring district of Highbury. The South Place Institute was the spiritual home of non-conformism and, like the Pearsons, the Sharpe family had impeccable non-conformist credentials, being staunch Unitarians. The head of the household, William Sharpe, was, like his future son-in-law Karl Pearson, a lawyer cum polymath. Well-travelled and well connected in the literary and artistic world, according to his grandson, he also had a particular interest in the 'scientific renaissance which followed the publication of *The Origin of Species*.'[221] In November 1881 Pearson had evidently been making enquiries about the family, as Robert Parker had written to him: 'I never heard of Mrs. Cobb but will ask OB [Oscar Browning] about her, he is sure to know.'[222] Evidently Pearson was favourably impressed by what he heard, as he and Elizabeth Cobb were soon on intimate epistolary terms. In 1884, either shortly before or just after his holiday in the Black Forest, Elizabeth Cobb approached Pearson with a view to persuading him to 'number and catalogue the … family's rather valuable collection of German prints.' It was during this process that he was first introduced to her sister Maria.[223] Like Amy's fictional creation, Rhoda Cholmoneley, Maria Sharpe was a paradigm of 'English rose' good looks, with fair hair, blue eyes and fine-boned, regular features. She had an altogether more retiring personality than her sister Elizabeth, but like her, her conventional exterior concealed a forward-thinking and enquiring mind. Outwardly quiet and reserved, her main occupation at that time was tending to their elderly mother. What spare time she had was evidently devoted to genteel pursuits. Her son Egon recollected that in her youth she was 'gifted at watercolour and well read in the literature of her day.'[224] She was therefore possibly an unlikely candidate for a member of what was to become, for a short while, the most daring and revolutionary club of its day.

Three months after his dramatic exit from A Men and Women's Club, Pearson joined forces with Elizabeth Cobb and Maria Sharpe to establish the second Men and Women's Cub in order, as Judith Walkowitz has succinctly put it, 'to talk about sex'.[225] This project had evidently been on their minds for some time. Maria Sharpe later recalled that it was in the autumn of 1884 that 'Bessie [Elizabeth] first mentioned to me Mr. Pearson's proposal [for the club].'[226] The idea was to gather together a group of equal numbers of men and women to undertake an analysis of all aspects, physical and metaphysical, of the relation between the sexes. Once the details of the project were finalised it was agreed that Maria Sharpe would be the club secretary, and the hunt for suitable recruits got underway. Whilst Pearson sought round amongst his Cambridge friends for male candidates, Elizabeth Cobb and Maria Sharpe set about the task of finding female members – a task for which, given the club's intended radical agenda, a level of discretion was required. Elizabeth Cobb seemed particularly anxious to hand-pick women who would match Pearson's somewhat eccentric requirements. After dismissing two potential candidates as being respectively 'shallow' and 'unrefined' (the first of these unlucky applicants was Constance Parker, Robert Parker's wife), Elizabeth recommended to him a Miss Shedlock, whom she predicted he would like because he seemed to respect those women most 'who hate men' and regard 'sympathy a mark of woman's slavish nature.'[227] She evidently waived this consideration with her own first female recruit, who was anything but a 'man hater.' This was Olive Schreiner. To enlist Olive Schreiner as a member was a considerable triumph as far as the club was concerned. A celebrity because of her authorship of the best selling novel, *The Story of an African Farm*, she was also at the heart of the most progressive social and political circle of the day. Eleanor Marx was her intimate friend, and they often met up at the British Museum, as by then Eleanor had entered into a common-law 'marriage' with Edward Aveling and was living in Great Russell Street – immediately opposite the gates of the Museum.[228] Like Eleanor Marx (and another of her close friends, Amy Levy), Olive Schreiner had little time for bourgeois values. She cut a distinctly unconventional figure, even by the unorthodox standards of the British Museum set, walking the streets without either gloves or a veil over her face (both items that were *de rigueur* for respectable women at that time), chatting openly to her male friends and gesticulating freely with her ungloved hands all the while. But although Olive publicly supported the cause of women's rights, in private she made comments which indicate that the company of her own sex was not particularly congenial to her.[229] Nevertheless, despite her ambivalent view of women in general, she obviously had no difficulty in attracting their friendship, and was soon corresponding on the most intimate terms with Elizabeth Cobb. Elizabeth and Olive first met in the autumn of 1884, when they had been introduced by a mutual acquaintance while Olive was on holiday at St. Leonards, a seaside resort on the Sussex Coast. Their shared interest in 'the woman question' had immediately drawn them together and, after some prevarication on Elizabeth's part, Olive had been invited to join the club.[230] Elizabeth's initial hesitation about extending the invitation had been due to the fact that when she first mentioned the idea to Pearson he had exhibited a rather suspicious eagerness to meet the 'interesting Miss Schreiner.' Elizabeth assured him 'of course you are to meet Miss Schreiner some day …' the implication being that she intended to make sure that their introduction was put off for as long as possible. She managed to accomplish this by engineering a variety of excuses that ensured that Olive and Pearson did not finally come face to face until June 1885.[231]

Although Pearson paid lip service to the idea of equality between the sexes, in reality he found it difficult to cope with women who challenged his intellectual supremacy. Whereas a significant number of the female members of A Men and Women's Club had been educated at the newly founded women's colleges, in contrast, only one of the women who became members of the second club had been educated at a university.[232] Olive described them acidly as a collection of 'old maids and man haters' – although her scorn did not prevent her from accepting Elizabeth Cobb's invitation to join the club.[233] The conformist mindset of the club's female contingent was reflected in its timidity when it came to the question of a name for the new club. Pearson initially favoured calling it 'The Wollstonecraft' but a number of the lady members demurred, not wishing to be associated with such a controversial figure. In the end the name of the first Men and Women's Club, was commandeered, but with a change in the definite article from 'A' to 'The'. Thus it became 'The Men and Women's Club'. The issue of the club's name having been settled, Pearson turned his attention to the task of putting forward his own ideas for suitable female candidates to Maria Sharpe. In doing so he exhibited an uncharacteristic deference to her opinion. He suggested that 'Mrs. Aveling would be a very desirable member if it were profitable to obtain her on the condition that her husband was neither a member, nor to be brought as a guest.'[234] Maria made her view of the proposal quite clear, replying politely but firmly: 'I do not consider that Mrs. Aveling would be the right person for a member of our club.'[235] But in any case Eleanor, anticipating this reaction, had already disdainfully dismissed the idea, commenting that it was 'a very different matter to advocate certain things in theory, and to have the courage to put one's theories into practice ... Probably many of the good ladies of the Club would be much shocked at the idea of my becoming a member of it.'[236] Her use of the term 'good ladies' carried the distinct message that she regarded the club as nothing more than a talking shop for middle-class dilettantists. Undeterred, Pearson continued to give 'Miss Sharpe' the benefit of his advice about the prospective female members. On 30th March 1885 he wrote to her from Cambridge:

> I was very pleased to hear your interview with Miss Mills[237] and Miss Eastty[238] had been satisfactory. I should very much like to see the former on my return to town.
>
> What a misfortune with regard to her deafness! It is the very reason which has withheld my mentioning the matter to a Miss Levy, who it seems to me would otherwise have made a useful member.[239]

It is obvious that Pearson was being less than straightforward in his account of his reluctance to mention the club to Amy. The fact that in the letter he referred to her as 'a Miss Levy' confirms that she and Maria Sharpe were not acquainted. Why then, should Pearson feel obliged to excuse himself to Maria for not inviting Amy to join the club? The most likely explanation is that he harboured a guilty conscience about the matter himself. Just as Elizabeth Cobb had employed a variety of ingenious excuses in order to delay introducing him to Olive Schreiner, so he seems to have deliberately exaggerated the extent of Amy's deafness in order to keep her and Maria Sharpe at a distance from one another. After Amy's death, Clementina Black forcefully (and perhaps significantly) publicly went on record to emphasise that her deafness was 'slight'.[240] And despite her greater degree of handicap, although she never became a formal member, Kate Mills maintained a close contact with the club, presenting at least one club paper and corresponding with Maria Sharpe and other members about various aspects of its proceedings. Whatever the true reason for Pearson's reluctance to involve Amy in his new venture, she would have undoubtedly heard about it through her friendship with Olive Schreiner and Eleanor Marx. Realising that she had been passed over as a prospective member, she would have known that he would have played a determining role in that decision. The pain and humiliation that she must have suffered in consequence can only be guessed at.

Having dismissed 'Miss Levy' as a potential member, Pearson turned his attention to Maria Sharpe's own suggestions: ' With regard to Dr. Blackwell[241] I think we should all be interested to hear her, but like Mrs. Butler[242] she would I think be very unsuited for membership …A woman who can call herself a Christian physiologist, prostitutes the name of science, for science is true in itself and can in noway [sic] vary its position with the religious dogma of the student …'[243] Elizabeth Blackwell and Josephine Butler were both formidable adversaries and would most definitely have mounted a challenge to Pearson, who was adamant that club discussion be conducted from a strictly scientific (i.e. Darwinist) standpoint. This left the lady members at a distinct disadvantage. From the outset they were overawed by the men, the majority of whom were lawyers, and had consequently been trained to present an argument cogently and succinctly. They meanwhile were left floundering, forced to fall back upon vague terms like 'feelings' – a word that was anathema to Pearson. This division between the sexes in the club was thrown clearly into focus at the inaugural meeting at which he presented a paper on 'The Woman's Question'. According to Maria Sharpe, this 'set the tone' of the club's future proceedings. Pearson's paper commenced with a wide-ranging outline of the issue, which led him to the conclusion that: 'Not until the historical researches of Bachofen, Girard Teulon, and McLennan, together with the anthropological studies of Tyler and Ploss, have been supplemented by careful investigation of the sanitary and social effects of the past stages of sex-development … will it be possible to lay the foundations of a real science of sexualogy.'ccxliv It is extremely unlikely that any of the ladies present (including the redoubtable Miss Schreiner) had ever heard of any of the eminent gentlemen mentioned by Pearson, and as a result they were at a loss to know how to respond. But by the time he resumed his seat to await his listeners' verdict one thing was perfectly clear, as Olive Schreiner pointed out: by focusing solely on 'the woman's question' his paper had entirely neglected to consider the other side of the problem – man.

The manner in which Pearson and his Cambridge cohorts dominated the club's proceedings exposes the dichotomy at the heart of the late nineteenth-century approach to the 'woman question'. The 'battle of the sexes', which raged in tandem with the proceedings of the club, encapsulated the wider Darwinian 'struggle for survival' experienced by female Victorian intellectuals - or those who aspired to be so - who did not fit within the accepted cultural and tribal parameters of the Anglo-Saxon male-dominated world of the freethinking Victorian intelligentsia. Their attempts to integrate themselves within this select group of social and theoretical pioneers exposed them to the risk – as Amy had discovered to her cost– of falling 'between two stools'.[245] By going against convention they left themselves open to exploitation and, all too often, it was the very men to whom they looked for support and intellectual guidance who took advantage of their vulnerability. Nevertheless, despite the difficulties that they faced, the majority of the female members of the club clung tenaciously to the belief that progress depended upon the spiritual as well as the material advancement of mankind – and that the feminist movement had a crucial role to play in this process.

As for Amy, Pearson's cruel betrayal of their friendship proved a turning point. The unhappy revelation that her idol not only had feet of clay, but was prepared to use them to trample on those who got in his way, was the defining moment that finally confronted her with the realisation that her youthful idealism had been founded upon an illusion. Thereafter she had to face the fact that those who, like Pearson, publicly proclaimed doctrines of egalitarianism and liberation did not necessarily adhere to these principles in the conduct of their own lives. This forced her to acknowledge that by setting out to change a social system that had proved unchangeable all she had succeeded in doing was to change the course of her own destiny – and that henceforward her life would never be the same.

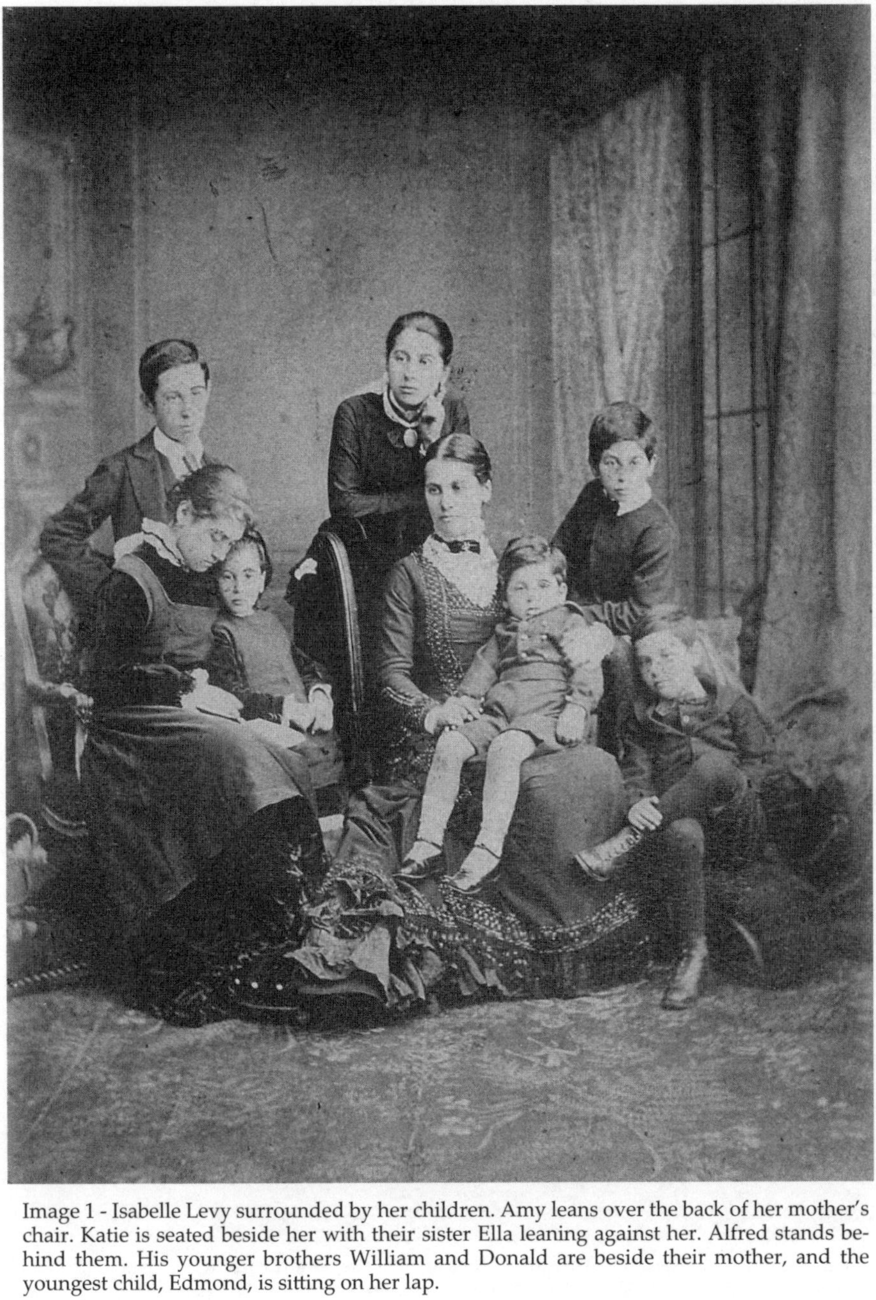

Image 1 - Isabelle Levy surrounded by her children. Amy leans over the back of her mother's chair. Katie is seated beside her with their sister Ella leaning against her. Alfred stands behind them. His younger brothers William and Donald are beside their mother, and the youngest child, Edmond, is sitting on her lap.

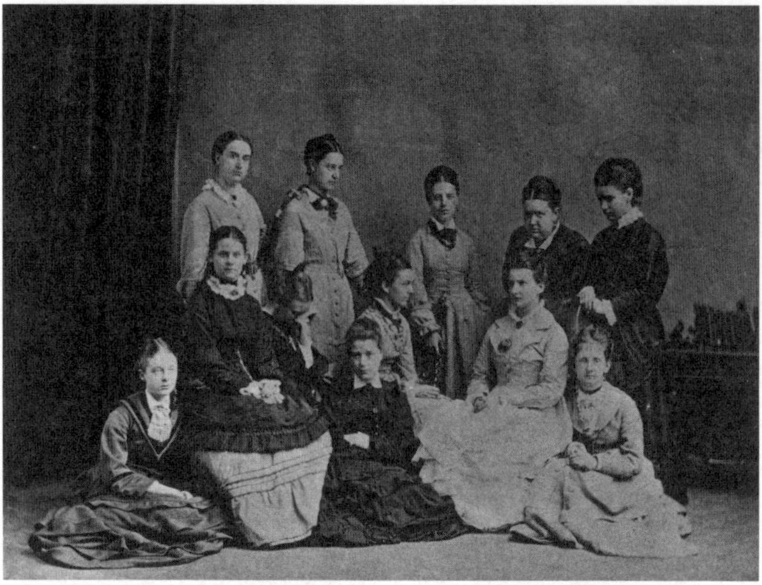

Image 2 - A group of some of the first Newnham students. Edith Creak is standing second from the right back row. Charlotte Martin (later Wilson) is seated second from the left front row.

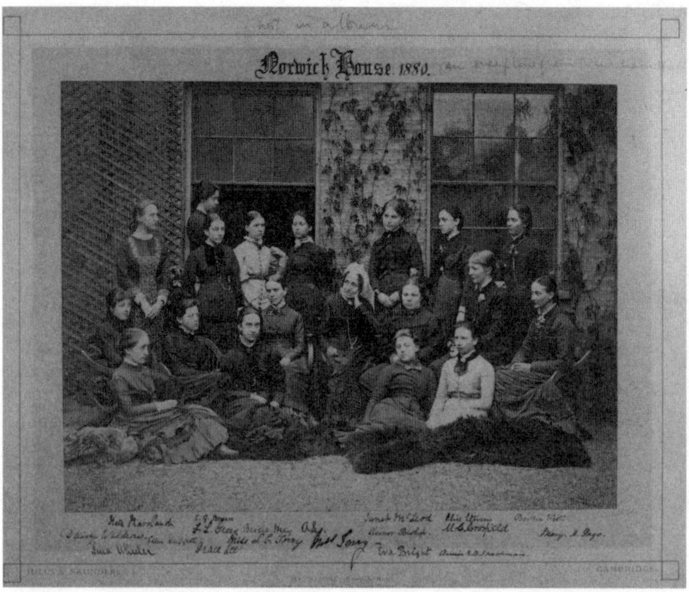

Image 3 - Norwich House 1880. Amy Levy leans against the window frame, back row fifth from the left. All students signed the photograph with their full names except Amy Levy, who just signed her initials.

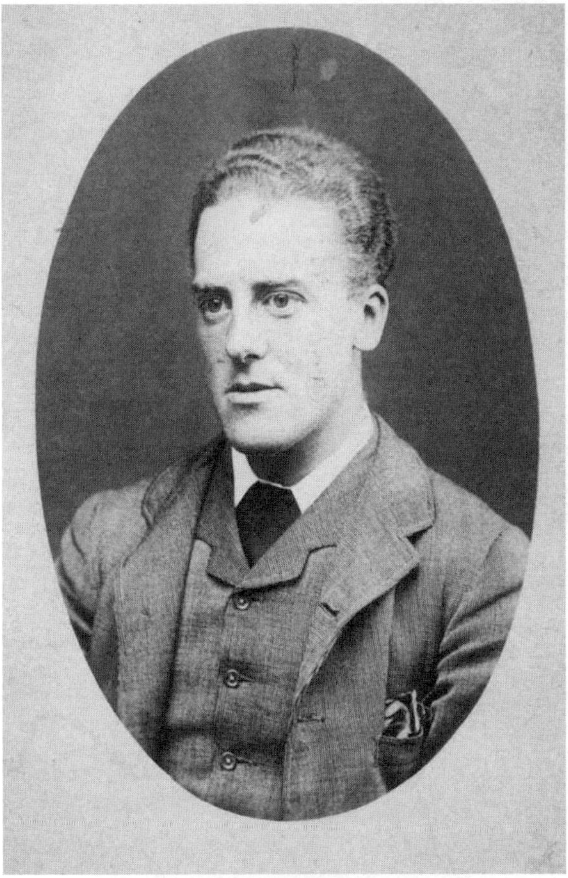

Image 4 - Karl Pearson 1880

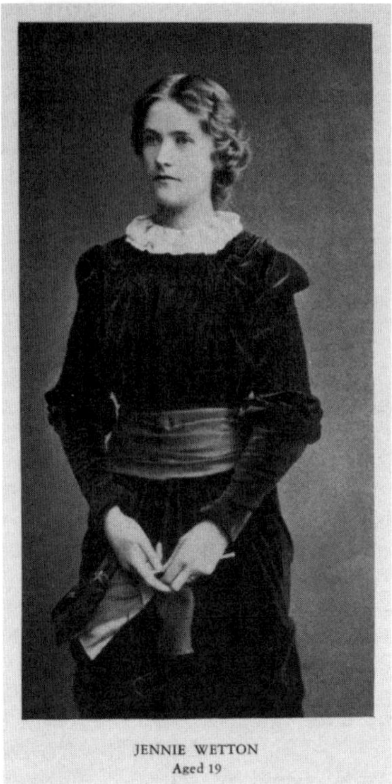

Image 5 - Jennie Wetton Aged 19

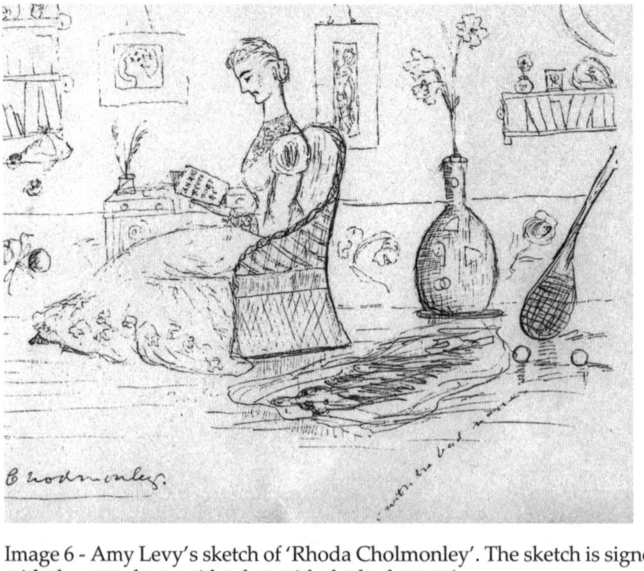

Image 6 - Amy Levy's sketch of 'Rhoda Cholmonley'. The sketch is signed with the pseudonym 'the dog with the bad name'.

Image 7 - Dolly Maitland (Radford)

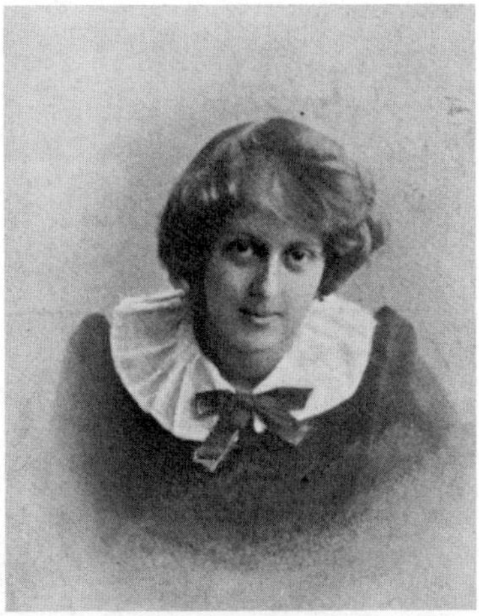

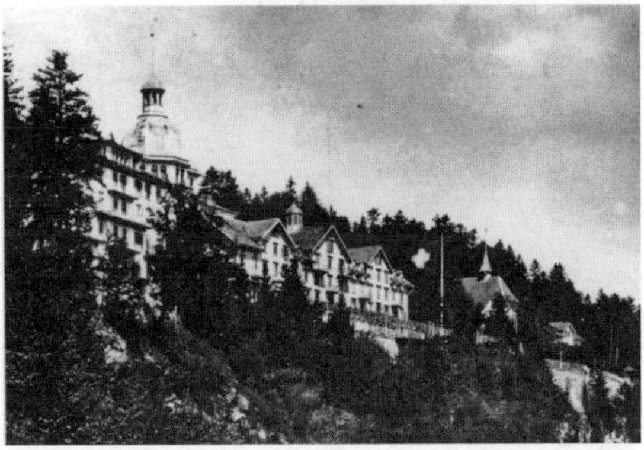

Image 8 - Hotel Sonnenberg, Seelisberg in 1875.

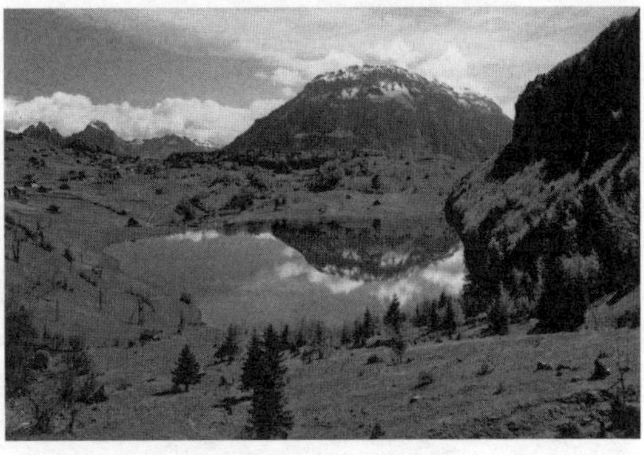

Image 9 - The Seelisberger-Seeli - the former bathing lake of the Hotel Sonnenberg, which is the setting of Amy Levy's poem 'To E'

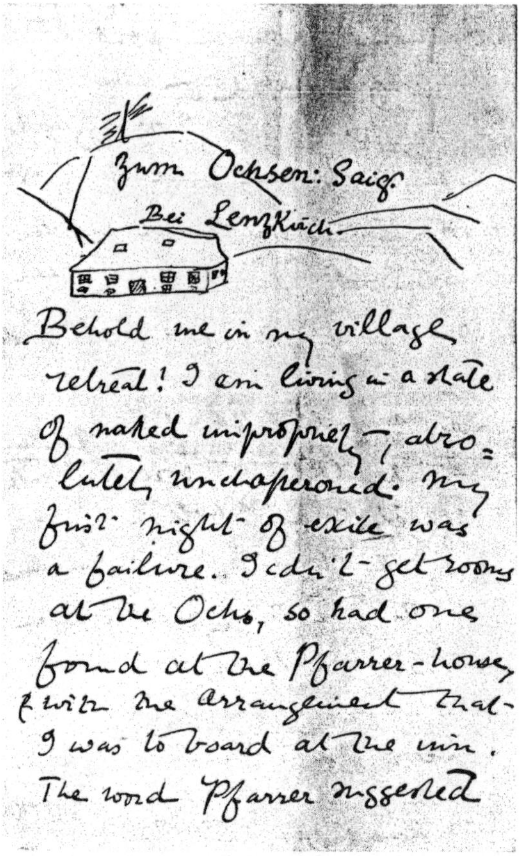

Zum Ochsen: Saig.
Bei Lenzkirch.

Behold me in my village retreat! I am living in a state of naked impropriety, abso=lutely unchaperoned. My first night of exile was a failure. I couldn't get rooms at the Ochs, so had one found at the Pfarrer-house, & with the arrangement that I was to board at the inn. The word Pfarrer suggested

Image 10 - Amy Levy's letter to an unnamed correspondent sent from the Gasthof Ochsen, Saig.

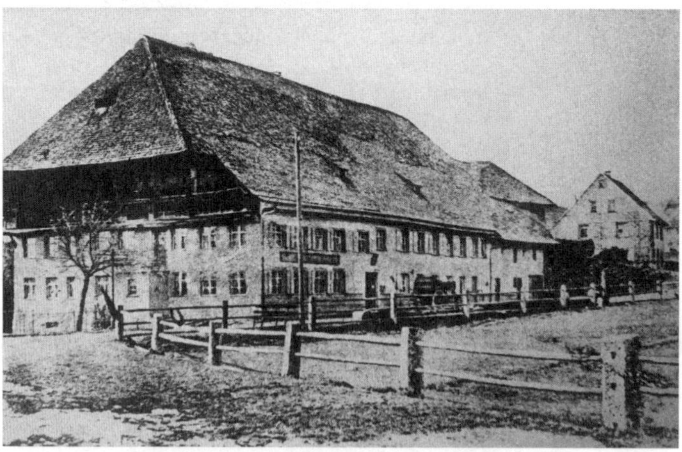

Image 11 - The Gasthof Ochsen c.1905

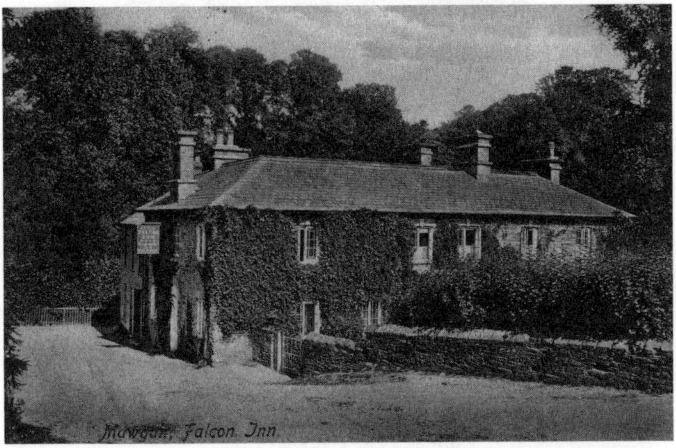

Image 12 - The Falcon Inn Mawgan in Pydar Late 1890s

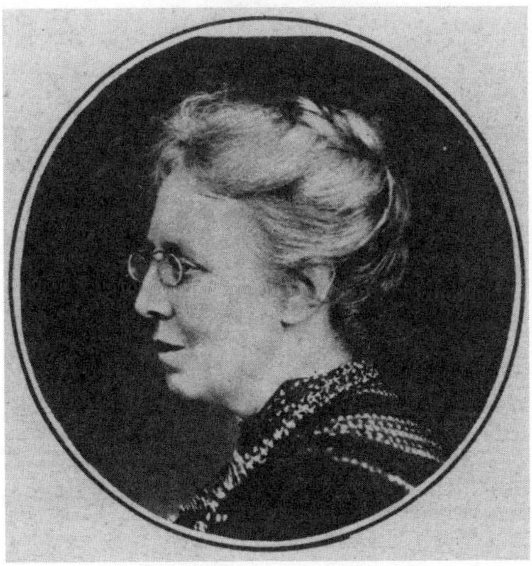

Image 13 - Clementina Black

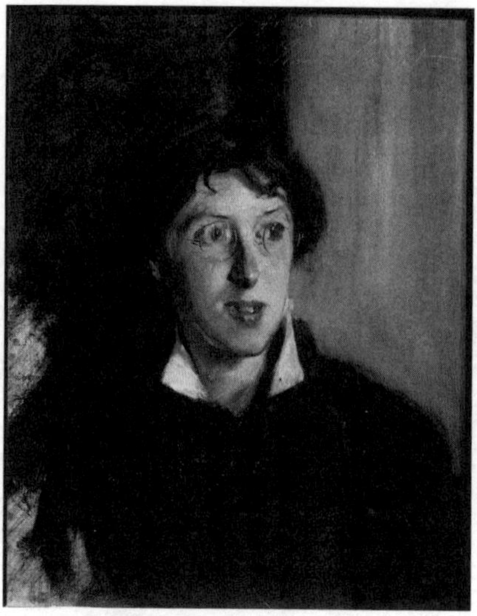

Image 14 - Vernon Lee 1881

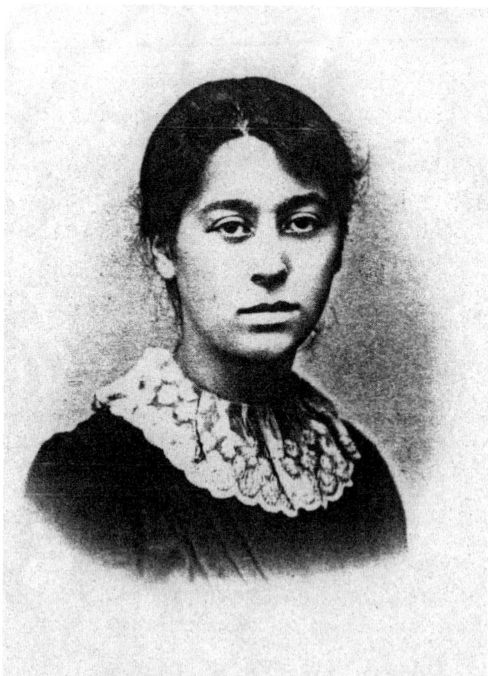

Image 15 - Amy Levy. Studio portrait: 'Montabone - Via de Bianchi' Florence

The Return of the Prodigal Daughter: 1885–1888

There shall be sunlight, scent of rose,
Warm mist and summer rain;
Only this change – I shall not look
Upon your face again.

Amy Levy, 1861 – 1889: 'June'

Not long after the inaugural meeting of the second Men and Women's club, in August 1885, Amy suffered a further blow when her elder sister Katie was married after a short engagement. The brevity of the engagement seems to have been due to the fact that there was parental opposition to the match. Her fiancé, Joseph Solomon, a barrister, was a widower some years older than herself, and already had a family of two young sons. In a letter written to Katie just after the wedding Amy remarked: 'There is an impression in this family that Joe has been rather minus in not writing to Mama or Papa, but certainly he was not well-treated.' [246]

By that time Katie was twenty-five years old, and likely to have been desperate to escape from the family home. She seems, after all, not to have followed Amy to Newnham, and with little chance of earning her own living, faced the prospect of becoming an 'old maid' at the mercy of her parents' every whim. The two surviving letters that Amy wrote to Katie while she was on honeymoon give an amusing account of the wedding and its aftermath. But in one of them she refers to the intensity of the parting kisses she bestowed upon her sister, reflecting her distress at the prospect of losing her lifetime friend and confidante. 'Did you survive my two kisses?' she asked. 'I felt rather bad afterwards.' Others were evidently concerned about her welfare too. She told Katie: 'Jenny … has only just left. Both she and Paul urged me to stay with them.' Jenny de Pass and Paulina Meyerstein were her closest Jewish female friends.[247] The letter ends with the reassurance, 'Mama is alright. I am very happy & my head is very clean.' Clearly, once more, the state of Amy's mental health was worrying her family and close friends. But she was not the only family member whose health was a cause for concern at that time. Her second letter, which is dated 22nd August and sent just two days after the first, begins: 'There is positively nothing to tell you. Willie is at Folkestone, Papa at Ben Rhydding & reports that the heir apparent is considerably better.' Ben Rhydding was a fashionable hydropathic establishment (spa) on the Yorkshire moors. It appears that, like his sister, Alfred was suffering from some form of mental illness, as at that time hydropathy was one of the favoured cures for nervous breakdown - neurasthenia as it was then called. As Janet Oppenheim perceptively noted, the expectations of middle-class parents often created conflict not only with their daughters but also their sons. She claimed that the eldest sons bore a particularly heavy burden within the family because of the 'enormous ... aspirations' that rested on their shoulders. She maintains that the ambivalent feelings that were aroused by their 'desire to rebel against familial restraints,' sometimes led them to retreat into illness: 'Nervous breakdown allowed them to opt out of the conflict, enabling them to express dissent from parental goals without overt confrontation.' This strategy was of double benefit to the afflicted, for: 'By withdrawing from the field of competition the young invalid gained a kind of power over his father.'[248] This seems a particularly likely scenario in Alfred's case, because as 'nouveau riche' members of the aspiring middle class Lewis and Isabelle would have looked to him to establish the family position firmly within the ranks of the gentry. However, all evidence points to the fact that Alfred was a sensitive soul, unfit for the cut and thrust of commerce, and lacking the intellect to enter one of the professions.

Whatever kind of power game may have been being played out between Lewis and his eldest son, it was conducted against a background of increasing concern about his sister Amy's state of mind. Her second letter to Katie started on a friendly enough note: 'I'm glad you're having such a good time.' But her jealousy and low self-esteem soon surfaced, as she told her sister with just a hint of malice:

> The latest thing is your own great beauty – started by 'the aunts' to while away the August hours in London, I suppose. Such terms as 'very beautiful(!)' 'sweetly pretty', 'her great big eyes', float about freely & goad me into paroxysms of envious madness.[249]

The Pearson debacle would have finally confirmed her suspicion that even within the most enlightened circles, she would always be regarded as an outsider, and this would have forced her to accept that it would be futile to seek a life partner beyond the limited confines of her own community. At the same time she would have had to face the fact that her unconventional lifestyle had placed her beyond the pale of respectable Jewish society, rendering her ineligible as a prospective marriage partner within their ranks. This meant that as far as her matrimonial prospects were concerned, like her fictional creation Norah Wycherley, she had effectively 'fallen between two stools' and was now regarded as a pariah both beyond and within her own community. Although she was an idealist, she was no fool, and would have known that this meant she was unlikely to marry, and that in order to avoid the fate that her sister had feared - perpetual dependence upon their father - she would have to look to her own resources to support herself financially for the rest of her life. The limited income that she received through the publication of her poems and short stories and a small contingent of pupils offered no prospect of providing her with sufficient means to maintain the standard of living in which she had been brought up. And notwithstanding her socialist sympathies, she was unwilling to accept for herself the bohemian lifestyle adopted by many of her socialist friends. As she later confided to Vernon Lee:

> Miss Black and her sister are living on the top floor of a house in Fitzroy St; they do their own housework, & are quite & completely domestic, unless when they are attending Socialist or Anarchist meetings .... I confess that my own Philistine, middle class notions of comfort wd. not be met by their ménage.[250]

For women of Amy's social standing, the prospect of passing through adult life without the financial support of husband was an unenviable one. Her British Museum acquaintance Margaret Harkness had faced this same dilemma. In 1876, while she was still living at home in the Dorset village where her father, Robert Harkness, was rector, she had complained to her cousin Beatrice Potter: 'I would marry a fool and be independent only it would kill me .... I am at home in my father's house, I hate the idea of marriage and I have no money.'[251] In similar vein, Amy's last letter written during her stay in Pearson's 'village retreat' had contained the heartfelt plea: 'O if I needn't go home again & begin the old struggle for existence.'[252] Like Margaret Harkness, she was fighting a battle on two fronts – struggling against family tradition as well as social convention in order to gain the financial and intellectual independence that she believed to be essential for her personal and emotional survival.

After the unsettling events of the summer, in October Amy left London and set off by herself for an extended holiday in Cornwall. It appears that in the weeks after Katie's wedding, like Alfred, she too had suffered some form of nervous breakdown. This is revealed in two corresponding accounts – one written by Amy herself, the other in a memoir that was published shortly after her death. Her own version of this episode can be found in her short story 'Out of the World', which appeared in London Society in January 1886.[253] Just like the tales that chronicled her travels in Switzerland and the Black Forest, the narrative takes the form of a letter from Melissa to Psyche, with a heading that matches that of her real-life holiday address:

The Falcon Inn,
St. Mawgan-in-Pydar,
Vale of Lanherne,
Cornwall.

The second reference to her mysterious stay in Cornwall is in Harry Quilter's valedictory essay 'Amy Levy: A Reminiscence and a Criticism', which was published in his *Universal Review* not long after her suicide, in 1890.[254] This corresponds with Amy's own description of her Cornish holiday in 'Out of the World'.

Quilter's reminiscence begins with an account of how 'some years ago' towards the end of a 'long summer's painting on the Cornish coast,' after a journey across country in search of fresh supplies of artists' materials, he had come by chance upon a remote village at the foot of 'a secluded valley whose surrounding hills [were] fledged with fern and slim small-leaved elm.' Needing somewhere to stay for the night, he made enquiries at the local tavern. This was the Falcon Inn. Like the Gasthof Ochsen, the Falcon Inn still exists, but thanks to the modern transport system it is no longer the isolated establishment that it was when Quilter stumbled upon it by chance almost a hundred and thirty years ago. His description of his arrival at the inn, where the landlady greeted him 'in a manner in which dignity and kindliness were subtly blended', after which she showed him into a small sitting room where 'The walls were covered in pictures ...The bookcase was ...crammed with books [and] The mantelpiece too was crowded with photographs, and some big white lilies stood in pots in front of the lattice windows', almost precisely matches the fictional Melissa's experience when:

> Speeding westward across the October country ... on the afternoon of the morrow (for I had spent the night with kind friends at Plymouth) I alighted at a little wayside station, where a wagonette from the Falcon Inn awaited me. A long drive across beautiful autumnal country, a cautious descent into a little green and placid valley, and the carriage drew up before a little oblong stone house, with an unobtrusive sign-board above the door. A kind hostess came out to meet me and led me into a charming room with books, and flowers, and pictures, and a log fire blazing merrily in the grate...

According to Quilter, the female innkeeper of the Falcon was unusually well-informed for a woman of her station in life. Interested in books and music, she had also seen something of the world beyond her isolated Cornish home. Pleased to find a cultured and sympathetic companion to talk to (the only other permanent resident of the inn was 'a father of nearly fourscore') he recounts how, during his stay, she lingered at the doorway of the sitting room each evening while he sat by the fire drinking his whiskey and water, telling him of 'her brief visits to London, of her intense love of music, of the books in the little bookcase ... and how most of them had been given her at various times by friends who had "stayed with us at the Falcon".' One of the photographs on the mantelpiece above the fire was one such friend, 'a small, dark girl, of unmistakably Jewish type, with eyes that seemed too large for the delicate features, and far too sad for their youthfulness of line and contour.' Quilter comments: 'In its way I had rarely seen a face which was at once so interesting, so intellectual, so beautiful, and, alas! so unhappy.' Having learned from his landlady that the woman in the photograph was Amy Levy, Quilter recalls 'after the first subjects of talk had been well exhausted ... my hostess would tell me about [her]', adding in a footnote: 'Let me be accurate, for although my hostess would tell me much of Miss Levy's charm, gentleness and intelligence, she would never tell me any details of her life.'

But how – and why - did Amy end up in such an isolated location surrounded, apparently, by total strangers? In her family memoir Amy's cousin, Lucy Marks, claimed that after Amy's suicide 'There was a rumour that she had an unhappy love affair, but none of the family can give any details.'[255] It is certainly the case that after Amy took her life rumours were circulating that this had not been her first attempt to do so. Shortly after her untimely death Connie Black (by that time Garnett) wrote in a letter to her father-in-law: 'What a sad end ...I can feel no grief for her, poor girl, for I know she had twice made the attempt before, and one cannot wish to prolong an existence as joyless as hers was.'[256] It seems that the shock of Pearson's betrayal in the summer of 1885, which was followed almost immediately by the ordeal of parting with her sister, led to a breakdown which culminated in a suicide bid, and that Amy's solitary Cornish holiday was – like her brother's stay at Ben Rhydding – a period of supervised convalescence in a secluded environment where she could recover her mental balance without attracting unwanted attention. Her description of Melissa's reaction to the marriage of her sister Josephine in 'Out of the World' has a note of authenticity that suggests it was written from personal experience: 'when the excitement of the wedding preparations was over ... and a company of sparrows discussing the rice on the pavement outside was the only reminder of what had occurred, a great blankness fell on my soul'. Harry Quilter claimed that the landlady of the Falcon had told him that Amy 'had come down [to Cornwall] ill ... some two years before, and she had "nursed" her back to health.' But evidently her 'nursing' did not involve the standard treatment of a Victorian invalid – resting quietly on a sofa, or confined to bed in a darkened room. Quite the contrary, for as Quilter records, his landlady told him that 'in her capacity of nurse' she had taken Amy 'into the woods and fields down amongst the caves of the Porth and taught her all those strange, hidden trifles of earth, sea and air, which only the dwellers in, and lovers of, the country know.' Melissa's 'kind hostess' keeps her similarly occupied – and away from the 'brain work' that was at that time considered by some to be so injurious to the female mind. 'I have given up all attempts at work, though I occasionally *improve my French*!' Melissa tells Psyche. 'Do you remember our paper-backed library in the Black Forest last year?' But like Quilter's landlady, Melissa's 'kind hostess' is wise enough to realise that her charge needs mental as well as physical distraction, and whilst instructing her 'in bread-making and cream-scalding' they 'mix Matthew Arnold with [the] pastry' and 'wage war on questions of "the infinite" as [they] chop meat for pies.' This image of incessant chatter and robust activity– clambering down cliff paths, pounding dough and chopping meat whilst discussing the meaning of life is a further indication that Amy's illness was of psychological rather than physical origin.

From the first paragraph, 'Out of the World' is littered with clues that provide a hint of the unbalanced state of its author's mind. The story begins:

> Your most meagre little note announcing your arrival in town was forwarded to me here. Alas my friend! We seem fated never to meet, like the pathetic little man and woman in the weather-prophet toy of one's youth; I used to feel so sorry for the poor woman as she emerged from her gay house, prophesying sunshine, only to find her mate, in obedience to some cruel and inscrutable law of his being, had withdrawn at her approach!

The reference to the 'pathetic little man' and the 'cruel and inscrutable law of his being', which dictated that he withdraw at the approach of his unsuspecting mate, immediately brings to mind Pearson's unkind treatment of Amy earlier in the year. The theme of heartless rejection recurs later in the story when Melissa describes her first sight of the Atlantic ocean, citing lines from Algernon Swinburne's 'The Triumph of Time' - his *cri de cœur* on the theme of a lost 'soulmate':

> I have had one really importance experience – I have seen the Sea .... This was no bathing pond for Cockneys, but the 'great sweet mother, mother and lover of men, the sea' whose 'sweet hard kisses are strong like wine,' whose 'large embraces are keen like pain.' I had quite a little rapture all by myself, for which, alas! I paid with a bad headache next day.

The lines quoted are from stanzas of the poem that specifically image a self-determined death:

I will go back to the great sweet mother,
Mother and lover of men, the sea.
I will go down to her, I and none other,
Close with her, kiss her and mix her with me ….
O fair green-girdled mother of mine
Sea, that art clothed with the sun and the rain,
Thy sweet hard kisses are strong like wine,
Thy large embraces are keen like pain.
Save me and hide me with all thy waves,
Find me one grave of thy thousand graves,
Those pure cold populous graves of thine...[257]

Amongst Amy's unpublished papers is an undated manuscript verse entitled 'Felise to her Lover'. This is a response to Swinburne's 'Felise', which, like 'Xantippe' and 'Medea' retells the story from the woman's perspective. The verse is written in an accomplished parody of Swinburne's distinctive style.[258] Isobel Armstrong has highlighted how 'Swinburne's habit of doubling a word with an alliterative synonym, and doubling that synonymous double with an alliterative phrase … produces an endless chain of substitution in which doubled words and phrases blur and exchange semantic and aural attributes with libidinal energy.'[259] It is certainly the raw 'libidinal energy' of Amy's poem that is its most striking feature. In an era when even the most 'advanced' women poets skirted discreetly around the issue of female sexual desire, she grasps the nettle and, having grasped it, thrusts it into the reader's face. Stanzas thirteen and fourteen are particularly explicit, and are written with such forceful veracity that one cannot but wonder what experience could have inspired them:

Kisses last year you deemed so rare
Serve me today for wine and meat;
That kiss between the breasts; the sweet
Short kisses that you loved to snare
here in my hair.

The hard strong kisses in the night,
Kisses that brought the poppy stain
To my cold cheek, and left it white
With purple fleck; such perfect pain
I feel again.

This last stanza beginning 'The hard strong kisses in the night/Kisses that brought the poppy stain' and concluding with the words 'such perfect pain I feel again' conjures up an explicit image of the loss of virginity. It is small surprise therefore, that the manuscript originally had a scrap of paper attached to it by a paper clip, which bore the brief but telling inscription 'unpublished' – followed by an exclamation mark![260]

'Out of the World' concludes with a seemingly inconsequential episode. Whilst wandering in the churchyard Melissa catches sight of the village 'idiot boy … craning his long thin neck over the churchyard wall.' Her encounter with this unfortunate lad triggers an image that recurs time and again Amy Levy's literary works:

> … the sun was setting behind the tall elms; the children were playing by a gold-tinted brook; a company of geese was promenading the road, engaged in animated conversation …. Nothing could have been more peaceful or rustic, but do you know what happened to me? I thought I heard a distant newsboy calling out Special Editions and terrible catastrophes! My case strikes me as more pathetic than that of poor Susan who imagined a river flowing through Cheapside![261]

Melissa's reaction to the chance encounter with the 'village idiot' calls to mind the aural hallucinations that are sometimes experienced by sufferers of schizophrenia or manic depression. This raises the question, was this a phenomenon that Amy herself had experienced? The cry of the newsboy is a recurring refrain throughout her fiction. In her short story, 'Sokratics in the Strand', in two out of her three novels, and in her poem 'Ballade of a Special Edition', this at that time familiar figure on the streets of London is portrayed as a harbinger of doom. [262] In all these works the resonance of his harsh and persistent voice performs a function akin to that of the Greek chorus or the Shakespearean fool, highlighting or indirectly commenting upon aspects of the narrative at strategic moments. In 'Out of the World', the sound of the newsboy's imagined cry signals a thematic shift in the narrative, shattering Melissa's reverie and bringing her abruptly back to earth into the harsh reality of the everyday world. Amy was patently interested in photography, and her scrap-album contains a number of quirky little images cut out from greetings cards which evidently appealed to her whimsical sense of humour.[263] To similar effect, the juxtaposition of the 'idiot boy,' the spectral newsboy and 'poor Susan' who imagined 'a river flowing through Cheapside' creates an effective visual montage of an unholy churchyard trinity which, in an instant, breaks the spell of Melissa's rural idyll and directs the focus of the narrative away from the nurturing bosom of the countryside back to the Darwinian chaos of London, where the weak and freakish – like 'poor Susan' or mad Melissa and her alter ego Amy Levy – go to the wall.

However, the question remains, how did Amy come to be in St Mawgan in the first place? And who recommended the Falcon Inn to her or – more likely - to her anxious family as a potential refuge? In 'Out of the World' Melissa tells Psyche that 'some one suggested this place as likely to meet the wants of a seedy and penurious spinster desirous of rest and change.' In real-life who could that 'some one' have been? Part of the answer to this question can be found in Harry Quilter's description of the residents of the Falcon Inn, which corresponds with the census record for 1881. On the night of the census the listed occupants of the inn included Samuel Gilbert, aged 70 ('the father, who was nearly fourscore'), his unmarried daughter, Mary Gilbert, described as the 'housekeeper' and a guest, Louisa Jebb, aged 40, recorded as having been born in Ellesmere and described as an 'annuitant'.[264] In fact Louisa Jebb's full time occupation was that of maiden aunt to the family of her brother Arthur who, after his marriage to 'a distant cousin from an Anglo-Irish branch of the family' (confusingly named Eglantyne Louisa Jebb), had become the brother-in-law of Richard Jebb, the Greek scholar, who had been one of the first dons to offer his services as a lecturer at the newly founded Newnham College.[265] Like the Bonds, the Jebbs were a distinguished Cambridge family, and were connected to the Darwins by marriage. In the early 1880s Richard Jebb's American wife, Caroline (Carrie), who was an enthusiastic amateur matchmaker, had earmarked her niece Maud as a prospective wife for the recently widowed Francis Darwin. However, her plans went awry when Francis became engaged to Amy's friend Ellen Crofts in May 1883. Undeterred, the redoubtable Carrie transferred her hopes to Francis' brother, George, this time with success.[266] Richard and Carrie Jebb's own wedding had taken place at his brother Arthur's family home, The Lyth in Ellesmere. After the wedding the Richard Jebbs were frequent visitors to The Lyth, where Aunt Louisa (known to the family as 'Aunt Bun') was the hub of the household. [267] Aunt Bun – 'Man Bun' as she was known locally - was what is known as a 'character.' Unconventional and, indeed, positively anarchic, she encouraged her nieces and nephews to 'make things like boomerangs, kites, popguns, bows and arrows, toboggans' and, best of all, 'over her bedroom fire to melt lead and cast bullets'.[268] But Bun also 'esteemed the mind' and in her youth had reputedly 'taken a course at Newnham' where she had attracted the attention of Jemima Clough, who thought highly of her.[269] A devotee of the theories of Charles Darwin and an advocate of Votes for Women, Bun would also have had much in common with her sister-in-law's unconventional sister-in-law, Ellen Crofts/Darwin. And it may well have been Ellen who, having had heard good accounts of the inn and its kind and sympathetic landlady from Bun Jebb, recommended it as a suitable rest home for Amy to the Levy family.

At first sight, this scenario seems to be founded upon a rather tenuous premise. But there was a further link between the Falcon Inn and Newnham College, which adds more weight to this theory. St Mawgan-in-Pydar adjoins the Prideaux estate, and Prideaux Place was the ancestral home of Sarah Treverbian Prideaux, another of Amy's former Newnham colleagues. In fact, Sarah Prideaux and Ellen Crofts/Darwin proved to be amongst the most steadfast and loyal of Amy's friends from her Cambridge years. In the diary which records the daily activities of the last months of her life, she documented a number of visits to and from 'S.T. Prideaux'. After leaving Newnham Sarah Prideaux had returned to her home in London to teach English alongside Octavia Hill at Miranda Hill's school in Marylebone; but having been advised to take up less sedentary work, she joined forces with her friend Olive Macmillan (another of Amy's Newnham contemporaries and fellow Men and Women's Club member) to set up as a bookbinder.[270] Not long after Amy's suicide Sarah Prideaux bound a commemorative copy of *A London Plane Tree* in her honour, and Ellen Darwin wrote one of the most heartfelt and touching tributes that she received. However, Ellen Darwin and Sarah Prideaux were not Amy's only close friends with West Country connections, because Ernest Radford's family lived in Plymouth, and it is certain that they were the model for the 'kind friends in Plymouth' where Melissa broke her journey *en route* to the Falcon Inn.

But why the Falcon Inn when Amy could presumably have joined her brother at Ben Rydding or a similar hydropathic establishment, of which at that time there were many? Until well into the twentieth century, suicide was a crime. Because of this, and despite the generally high mortality rate, the Victorians had a particular horror of self-inflicted death and went to great lengths to conceal it. [271] After the publication of *A Minor Poet* Amy had become something of a minor celebrity, and if, she had made a suicide attempt in the late summer of 1885 her family would have been desperate to avoid any public disclosure of this information. During the period of her recovery they would therefore have been anxious to ensure that she was placed under the supervision of a discreet, sympathetic and vigilant companion. This would have been difficult to arrange in London as, if Amy were determined enough, the opportunities for escape to make a further attempt upon her life would have been numerous. However, in a remote and isolated village where she was a stranger, the chances of giving her companion the slip would be very much diminished. In the light of this, one can see why she (or more likely her family) alighted upon the Falcon Inn, St. Mawgan-in-Pydar as a safe haven 'Out of the World' where she could regain her mental equilibrium

Whilst Amy was struggling to come to terms with the consequences of Pearson's rejection and her sister's marriage, Clementina Black was also battling ill-health, although the cause of her illness was unquestionably physical rather than psychological. After her mother had died, like Bun Jebb Clementina had become the pivotal figure in the Black household. But years of tending to the welfare of her brothers and sisters and their invalid father whilst at the same time struggling to earn a modest living through her writing had taken its toll, and in the summer of 1885 she was instructed by her doctor to 'strike work for a time.' After spending the autumn with a friend in Switzerland, she went on to Florence where 'she was joined by Miss Amy Levy, and the friends spent a delightful winter there.'[272] It is obvious from comments that she made in her later letters that Amy fell in love at first sight with the city that was the home of her poetic mentor, Mrs. Browning. Unfortunately the only direct remaining record of this pleasant interval is a fragment of a note which provides a vignette of one cosy domestic evening:

> Clemmy is now writing a novel by the fire. Soon it will be seven o'clock & dinner time – a frugal meal to-night: cold veal, cocoa, & half a pound of dried plums wh. I have just bought for 3½d.[273]

One thing that is certain about Amy's stay in Florence is that whilst there she renewed an acquaintanceship with a woman that she had first met some time during the early 1880s in London - either in the Reading Room of the British Museum or at the home of one of their mutual friends, perhaps at the Black sisters' 'anti-servitoresses' lodging in Bloomsbury.[274] This was the writer Violet Paget, more widely known by her *nom de plume*, Vernon Lee.

It has been assumed by some that during this first visit to Italy, Amy Levy not only fell in love with the city of Florence, but also with Vernon Lee. Their friendship certainly inspired her poetic muse, as the lyric verses that date from this not entirely happy period of her life are, paradoxically, some of the finest of her entire poetic oeuvre. However, her letters suggest that although she loved Vernon Lee as a friend, she was not 'in love' with her, and that the strength of her feeling was grounded in psychological dependency rather than physical attraction. In Amy's eyes, like Mrs. Stanford and Karl Pearson, Vernon Lee possessed all the intellectual and physical attributes she believed that she lacked herself. In consequence, as she did with Pearson, she invested the friendship with a degree of emotional significance that inevitably doomed it to fall short of her expectations. The letters that she wrote to Lee after her return from Florence provide a crystal clear account of her feelings. Unlike those that she wrote to 'Clemmy' (with whom no-one has suggested that she was 'in love') they are uniformly formally addressed to 'Miss Paget' or 'My dear Miss Paget'. And the frank and open effusions contained within them stand in marked contrast to the coy and self-conscious references to Pearson in the letters that she wrote during her stay in the Black Forest. Taken overall, they convey the impression of someone ill at ease with her correspondent , an 'outsider' at pains to fit in, in awe of Lee's superior intellect, and ever conscious of the impression that she was making upon her.[275] Unfortunately none of the letters are dated, but their contents indicate the sequence in which they were written. The first evidently dates from the late autumn of 1886, when Vernon Lee had returned to Florence after her customary summertime visit to London. During her visits to the capital Lee wrote to her mother on an almost daily basis. And in one letter, which is dated 3rd June 1886, she made an intriguing reference to Amy: 'I got Eugene's note enclosing Amy Levy's. I feel so sorry no one came on Monday. Brutes and Hogs!'[276] Eugene Lee Hamilton was Lee's invalid half-brother, a fellow poet whom Amy had visited while she was staying in Florence. Two days later Lee reported: 'I had a long Bloomsbury day, I sat with Miss Levy in the morning.' The phrase 'sat with' carries the clear message that this was not a normal social visit, the implication being that Amy was not in the best of spirits, and its purpose was to provide company rather than conversation. It appears from Lee's remark in her earlier letter that after her return from London Amy was being ostracised by some of her former friends. One wonders why. Did it have any connection with the Pearson debacle? What we do know from Amy's own letters to Lee is that by the autumn of 1886 she had turned against her alma mater, writing with bitter sarcasm:

> I was in Cambridge last week for some days, and found people rather depressing and depressed as usual. Stimulating themselves with tea and steadying themselves with potassium of bromide, and taking no pleasure in anything apparently. A big price for intellectual exclusiveness.'[277]

In late December of the same year, she voiced similar sentiments, writing of Lee's friend Dorothy Blomfield (a member of a distinguished clerical family who was, like Amy, a 'minor poet', although a more conventional and less accomplished one): 'there is something so generous about her, generous in an extended sense; her sort of mind is so refreshing, after the academic mind which, within a comparatively short time, represented culture to me as distinguished from Philistinism'.[278] In the early months of 1887 Amy was still in the grip of depression. Excusing herself for her delay in replying to a letter from Lee she confessed: 'I …have been in the depths rather, not so much from abstract pessimism, as fr. various tangible causes.'[279] Although Amy was non-specific about the 'tangible causes' of her low spirits, a hint that her rejection by Pearson was one of them can be inferred from the passage that immediately follows:

> Mr. Thicknesse's address is, I believe, 1 Stone Buildings, Lincoln's Inn. Poor man, I hear he does not get on at the Bar & wants badly to be married to a person he has been engaged to for years.[280]

Her tentative recall of Thicknesse's address and her obviously second-hand account of his current domestic problems reveal that by this date Amy was no longer in touch with core contingent of Pearson's Men and Women's Club.[281]

If Lee did indeed have an inkling of the underlying cause of Amy's melancholy mood she would have understood perfectly well how she felt. In the 'Autobiographical Notes' that she kept from this period, she recalled the pain of her unrequited love for her friend Annie Meyer.[282] After Annie's death in 1884 her niece, Alice Callendar, had told Lee cruelly that her aunt had never returned her love. In her 'notes' Lee commented:

> We can never love one friend so much as when we have been given the cold shoulder by another. The not meeting what one wants arouses our creative powers, makes us create that person of some semi-imagined reality…[283]

By the time that she wrote these words Lee had transferred her affections to Mary Robinson, and it is clear that by this time Amy had likewise switched her emotional dependency from Karl Pearson to Vernon Lee. However, the reality of Amy's feelings for her new friend is made quite plain in her letters, as the following quotations illustrate: 'I am so tremendously glad that there is some sort of chance of seeing you. You are something of an electric battery to me … & I am getting faint fr. want of contact!', and: 'I can't tell you what a difference it has made to me to have known you. I thought I was beyond the reach of human aid as it were … & if you have not converted me to optimism …you have made things look & feel a great deal better.'[284] Interestingly enough, Arthur Symons described Lee in similar terms, writing to Mary Robinson: 'I do not wonder you miss Vernon, she must be a most electrical companion with her strong, swift spirit and illimitable vigour'.[285] Lee's 'strong, swift spirit' and 'illimitable vigour' obviously had a similarly tonic effect on Amy's dejected spirits.

The letter in which Amy confessed that Lee had 'made things look and feel a great deal better' was written to thank her for one of the two boxes of violets that Lee had sent from Florence to Amy and her friend Dorothy Blomfield. 'The flowers were like a breath of Florence wafted into one's room' Amy enthused: 'I had a distinct vision, when they came, of Parma violets heaped against the Strozzi stones, & those fields on Bellosguardo with the anemones.'[286] This last vision was to inspire one of Amy's most poignant verses, which she dedicated 'To Vernon Lee'. She closed her letter with a description of a dinner that she had recently attended. This passage has been interpreted by some as a 'flirtatious' address:

> I wore some of your flowers last night at a dinner party – they are still fresh and sweet. I wore a black dress open in the front and sticking out behind as much as you could desire; and went in with a person of the masher species.

This obviously tongue-in-cheek account provides an accurate description of the fashionable female evening dress of the mid-1880s, which featured a low décolleté and an exaggerated bustle that created a shelf-like effect. Like many of their serious-minded contemporaries, both Vernon Lee and Amy Levy eschewed the latest fashions, preferring the 'rational dress' that was the hallmark of the late Victorian intellectual. In the early 1880s John Singer Sergeant painted a portrait of Vernon Lee wearing the tailored, masculine style of clothing made popular by the rational dress movement. A provincial newspaper reported that 'while at Cambridge [Amy Levy] distinguished herself by wearing wondrous aesthetic dresses'.[287] This style of clothing featured loose, unstructured garments that allowed the wearer to dispense with the constraints of a corset. One of Amy's Newnham contemporaries, Ada Radford, was also an aficionado of rational dress, but in her case her dedication to the cause of comfort seems to have bordered on fanaticism. Described as 'a determined Bohemian whose dress and manner expressed her progressive convictions', her sartorial taste inspired this unkind comment from Beatrice Potter: 'my distaste is [for] her clothes, I could forgive them if they were not worn on *principle*' .[288] Viewed in this light, Amy's sarcastic comments about her own evening attire and her contemptuous dismissal of the man who escorted her in to dinner as 'a person of the masher species' can be read as nothing more than a sarcastic avowal of her disdain for bourgeois values. It also indicates that like her fictional creation Nora Wycherley, whose 'absence of stays and crinolette almost wrung tears from the various members of [her] family', after her return from Florence she was likewise being unwillingly drawn back into 'the very heart and centre of Philistia' by her anxious relatives.[289]

Like Clementina Black and, to a lesser extent, Amy Levy, Violet Paget had been brought up in a household where she and her half-brother had been encouraged to think for themselves. But unlike Amy, her unconventional education had given her a psychological balance that had enabled her to accept the limitations of life and focus her considerable intellectual power towards an understanding of what was to her the most spiritually sustaining human activity – the creation and appreciation of art. This aspect of her character was particularly appealing to Amy, who admired Lee's enthusiasm for the aesthetic and her conviction that the gospel of beauty should be spread throughout every stratum of society. 'Dorothy and I agreed that you made life interesting & vivid in quite a wonderful way' she told Lee, 'that time in Florence has made all the difference to me, & has made it more possible to carry on the – to me – burdensome business of living.'[290]

Lee's ideas about the role of the arts in society have been compared to those of Leo Tolstoy. Like him, she believed that 'such consoling things' should not be the sole preserve of the privileged classes, but should 'bring pleasure to those who need [it] most, the disinherited poor.' 'Art, music, beautiful nature, poetry .... All this has in reality but one fault: that it is unequally distributed' she wrote.[291] Her generosity of spirit stood in stark contrast to the sterile view of the matter held by Pearson. This was reflected in his later adherence to the theory of eugenics, which was intended to limit the numbers of the 'disinherited poor' thereby improving the physical stock of the intellectual élite. In contrast, Lee aspired to elevate the minds of the dispossessed mass of the people, and, in so doing, increase the general stock of what she later described as 'that despised thing *happiness*'. [292] In one of her letters to Lee, Amy enquired: 'I saw a notice about Juvenilia that is coming out in the Athenaeum; is it political-economical?' Although the collection of essays that were published under the title *Juvenilia* were not, strictly speaking, 'political-economical', as Lee's biographer Peter Gunn notes, they do reveal 'a significant change in the orientation of her interests [in her] attitude to society and to the place of art in social life.'[293] This change came about through her visit to the Ford family home at Adel near Leeds in 1884. Whilst there she witnessed at first hand the appalling conditions endured by the slum dwellers and the agricultural labourers in the industrial towns and the bleak countryside of the North of England. Her newfound sympathy for the, as she termed it, 'great living mass, travelling and suffering on its onward path' was, presumably, the motive for her request to Amy for details of Ralph Thicknesse's current whereabouts. During the course of 1887 the second Men and Women's Club discussed a number of papers on socioeconomic themes, and in March of that year Pearson presented his own contribution, entitled 'Sex and Socialism'. In the teeth of fierce opposition from the female members of the club, Thicknesse supported Pearson in the heated discussion that followed the delivery of his paper.[294] Like the women of The Men and Women's Club, Lee was obviously unimpressed with Pearson's argument, because in 1888, following the publication of *The Ethic of*

Freethought (which included the aforementioned paper on 'Sex and Socialism'), she wrote him a letter in which, in the most deferential manner, she ruthlessly exposed the arrogance, inconsistency and hypocrisy at the heart of his approach to the tripartite issue of religion, the woman question and socialism.[295]

However, try as Amy might to distance herself from the 'academic exclusiveness' of the Cambridge circle, and however preoccupied she became with her own inner voyage of discovery, she could never entirely turn her back upon her commitment to the feminist cause. This dilemma manifested itself in the tension between idealism and reality – art and life – which is the distinguishing characteristic of her later writing. This dichotomy is overtly expressed in the concluding stanza of her sublimely poignant tribute 'To Vernon Lee' which was written to commemorate one of the springtime walks they had taken together on Bellosguardo:[296]

> Thereby ran on of Art and Life our speech;
> And of the gifts the gods had given to each –
> Hope unto you, and unto me Despair

Lee left a similar record of their springtime ramble to posterity in her essay 'Beauty and Sanity', which was included in her collection *Laurus Nobilis*, published in 1909. She recalled:

> I used at one time to have frequent discussions on art and life with a certain poor friend of mine, who should have found sweetness in both, giving both sweetness in return, but, alas, did neither. We were sitting in the fields where the frost-bitten green was just beginning to soften into minute starlike buds and mosses, and the birds were learning to sing in the leafless lilac hedgerows, the sunshine, as it does in spring, seemed to hold the world rather than merely to pour on to it. 'You see,' said my friend, 'you see, there is a fundamental difference between us. You are satisfied with what you call *happiness*; but I want *rapture and excess*.' … those words 'rapture and excess' spoken in such a childlike simplicity of spirit, have always remained in my mind.[297]

Amy was planning to return to Florence in 'the second week of February' 1887, but before her plans could come to fruition, fate intervened. She informed Lee regretfully:

> Here is bad news fr. my own point of view, at least, very bad news indeed. I am not coming to Florence after all. I can't exactly give the reasons as they concern other people besides myself. But I am horribly disappointed … I felt all along, that Florence was too good to come over again. [298]

The likely reason for Amy's abandonment of her planned trip was the current state of her father's financial affairs. In a newspaper article written during Amy's second visit to Italy in 1888, it was claimed that 'soon after leaving college her father [had] suffered some serious money losses',[299] and in her family memoir, Amy's cousin, Lucy Marks, recalled: '[My father] & Lewis went on the Stock Exchange and in due course lost every penny they possessed – But this did not happen till I (born 1872) was about fifteen.'[300] This would date the year of the loss of Lewis' fortune as around 1887 - just the time when Amy was planning her return visit to Italy. But financial difficulties were the least of the problems confronting the Levy family at that time, as Alfred's health was once again giving cause for concern. This time the efforts of his physicians did not have a happy outcome. On 3rd June a brief notice appeared in the *Jewish World*: 'Alfred Lewis, eldest son of Lewis and Isabelle Levy died 27 May at the age of 25.'[301]

Alfred's death certificate records that he had 'no occupation' and that he died at Gorleston in the County of Suffolk. Gorleston-on-Sea was a satellite of Great Yarmouth, which, like Ben Rhydding, was a favoured Victorian health resort. Unfortunately, in Alfred's case it failed to live up to its reputation. The cause of death given on the certificate is 'paralysis and exhaustion'. This indicates that Alfred's death was a prolonged one, 'exhaustion' being the late Victorian shorthand term for a lingering death. This is confirmed by the fact that Alfred died in the house of a local doctor. At that time it was common practice for patients suffering from 'grave cases of neurasthenia' who needed round the clock supervision to be dispatched 'to the home of a medical practitioner who took lodgers'.[302] It has been suggested by Linda Hunt Beckman that Alfred might have died from tertiary syphilis, or General Paralysis of the Insane, as it was historically known.[303] This is an unsatisfactory explanation on several counts. Hunt Beckman bases her claim on the contents of a letter which Vernon Lee wrote to her friend Bella Duffy not long after Amy's death. In this curious missive, Lee gloatingly claimed that Amy feared that 'she was on the verge of a horrible and loathsome form of madness apparently running in the family and of which she had seen a brother of hers die.' But there is nothing else to suggest that syphilitic illness was rife within the Levy family. And to judge by the regular arrival of Isabelle's healthy children, she certainly did not experience the string of miscarriages and stillbirths that mothers infected with the disease usually endured.[304] Of course, as Hunt Beckman points out, Alfred could have contracted syphilis 'on his own', but in that case, on what grounds did Amy fear that the infection had been passed to her? It should be borne in mind, however, that at this time Lee herself was ill, still suffering from the nervous breakdown that had followed Mary Robinson's announcement that she was to marry James Darmesteter. She may therefore have been experiencing delusions herself. Her friend

Henry James alluded to the inconsistencies in her personality when he claimed that 'in her books "there is a great second-rate element in her first-rateness"' adding 'Where friendship is concerned "she is a tiger-cat"'.[305] It is definitely the case that Lee adopted a 'cat and mouse' approach to her friendship with Amy, blowing hot and cold by turns, describing her to her mother as a 'poor little person' whom she did 'not love' and yet writing with apparent affection about her 'sweetness' and 'childlike simplicity of spirit' in her essay in *Laurus Nobilis*.

Returning to the issue of Alfred's death, the Victorians believed that nervous disorders 'were either inherited or self-induced through harmful habits.' However, in the late Victorian era diagnostic techniques, particularly when applied to the mentally ill, were inaccurate to say the least. Janet Oppenheimer suggested that some patients suffering from 'severe depression' may have been misdiagnosed, and that a 'transient ischemic cerebrovascular attack' (a minor stroke) could also account for their symptoms.[306] This is in accordance with the opinion of a medical practitioner who was shown a copy of Alfred Levy's Death Certificate at my request. He felt that 'a sub-arachnoid haemorrhage [which] is caused by congenital weakness and is found in the young' (in effect, a major stroke) is a likely explanation for the given cause of death.[307] But if Alfred had suffered a minor stroke before the final cataclysmic episode that ended his life, it may have left him with some level of mental impairment. This would not only explain why he needed constant medical supervision, but might also account for Amy's fear that she was on the brink of insanity herself.

After Katie, Alfred was Amy's closest sibling, both in age and in outlook. There is a hint in Amy's correspondence that he was a regular visitor to Cambridge during her residence at Newnham. In a postscript to a letter to her mother dating from this time, she had asked: 'I am going to a little dance Thursday; if you do not object to my getting some shoes .... Please write soon or ask Alfred to say if you mind.'[308] After Amy left Cambridge and travelled to Dresden, when her mother feared that she was unhappy there, she had offered to send Alfred to collect her if she wanted to come home. It is also possible that Alfred had escorted Amy to Italy when she joined Clementina Black there in the winter of 1885. At that time, like Amy, he was convalescing from an illness, and her trip to Florence to join Clemmy may have provided him with the opportunity to accompany her in the role of chaperone on her outward journey. His death certainly seems to be commemorated in two verses that were inspired by Amy's stay in the city. These are 'A Reminiscence' and its sister poem 'Sequel to a Reminiscence', both of which appear sequentially in *A London*

Plane Tree. Unlike many of the other poems in the collection, both verses are written in Amy's own, undisguised voice. The first, 'A Reminiscence', was evidently inspired by an evening visit that she made whilst staying in Florence. In a postscript to a letter that she wrote to Lee shortly after the abandonment of her planned return to Italy she recalled wistfully: 'I hear that Mr James has the Crosses' old rooms. I remember seeing you there, so well, one evening last year; with Mr. Cross, Mr. Benson and some American cigarettes'.[309] The first two stanzas of the poem appear to replicate this scene:

> It is so long gone by, and yet
> How clearly now I see it all!
> The glimmer of your cigarette,
> The little chamber, narrow and tall.
>
> Perseus; your picture in its frame;
> (How near they seem and yet how far!)
> The blaze of kindled logs; the flame
> Of tulips in a mighty jar.

But the third, final stanza contains an enigmatic reference to death:

> Florence and Springtime: surely each
> Glad things unto the spirit saith.
> Why did you lead me in your speech
> To these dark mysteries of death?

And the poem that follows, 'Sequel to a Reminiscence', depicts the bewilderment that follows sudden bereavement:

> Not in the street and not in the square,
> The street and square where you went and came;
> With shuttered casement your house stands bare,
> Men hush their voice when they speak your name ….
>
> Not here but somewhere where I can reach!
> Can a man with motion hearing and sight,
> And a thought which answered my thought and speech,
> Be utterly lost and vanquished quite?

Amy also seems to have commemorated Alfred's death in another of her poems. It was her habit to include manuscript copies of her verses in her letters to her friends. One that she sent to Lee was 'Lohengrin'. This first appeared in print in *The Academy* in March 1886. 'Lohengrin' is a variation on the leitmotiv of life after the death of God, which features in a number of the verses in *A London Plane Tree*. The fact that Amy made a gift of the manuscript to Lee suggests that the poem was of particular significance to her. As its title indicates, 'Lohengrin' is based upon the libretto of Wagner's opera of the same name. At the close of the final scene, Lohengrin's true identity as the son of Parsifal, King of the Grail, has been revealed, and he must therefore return to the mythical Kingdom, leaving behind his newly married bride, Elsa. But before he is borne away in the magic boat, Lohengrin returns Elsa's brother (who has been turned into a swan by the villain Ortrud) into human form once more. As the boat recedes into the distance, Elsa dies of grief in her brother's arms. The first stanza of Amy's verse is a précis of this final scene, but in the second stanza the impersonal narrative voice changes to that of a personal lament:

> God, we have lost Thee with much questioning.
> In vain we seek Thy trace by sea and land,
> And in Thine empty fanes where no men sing.
> What shall we do through all the weary days?
> Thus wail we and lament. Our eyes we raise,
> And, lo, our Brother with an outstretched hand.

Amy's deliberate use of the capital letter in the word 'Brother' in the last line of the stanza specifically identifies Elsa's newly returned sibling with Christ the 'beloved Son of God', redeemer of mankind. She was to replicate this device at the beginning of her novel, *Reuben Sachs*, when she headed the first chapter with a quotation from the New Testament Gospel of St. Matthew: 'This is my beloved Son'. This line appears directly above the stark declaration that introduces the narrative: 'Reuben Sachs was the pride of his family.' [310] The parallels between Reuben Sachs and Alfred Levy are obvious. Reuben is first depicted returning, like the prodigal son, from a sea voyage 'to the antipodes' taken in the wake of a 'nervous break-down.' And similarly to Alfred (the first 'beloved son' born to Lewis and Isabelle after two successive daughters) at the end of the novel he is killed off with a massive heart attack. His supposed nervous breakdown is thereby revealed as a symptom of an underlying medical condition that ultimately proves fatal. Unlike *Reuben Sachs*, 'Lohengrin' was written before Alfred's untimely death, and it may be that it was intended as an expression of Amy's gratitude for his filial loyalty. After turning her back upon her own community, she had joined Pearson and his friends in their crusade for the 'new Jerusalem', but had fallen by the wayside. Having, metaphorically speaking, watched her 'knight errant' recede into the mist, what could have been more natural than for her to turn for support and solace to the younger brother, the 'saviour' who had so willingly held out his hand to help her in the past.

Not unnaturally, at this difficult time in her life Amy began to reconsider her attitude to her 'own people'. This was partly due to the fact that by this time the Levy family were no longer living in Regent's Park, and were now living in Bloomsbury, which was a less prestigious area of the capital with a more cosmopolitan population. Their new address (which headed the majority of the letters that Amy wrote to Vernon Lee) was 7 Endsleigh Gardens. Although the move had probably been forced upon the family by financial exigency, it was a not wholly unfortunate turn of events for Amy, as many of her oldest and closest friends, like the Black sisters, the Radfords and Eleanor Marx, lived nearby. From her point of view, Endsleigh Gardens also had the advantage of being at the capital's intellectual heart, just around the corner from University College in Gower Street and a short walk from the British Museum. But it was also close to another eminent seat of learning. This was Jew's College in Tavistock Square, where Jewish scholars were prepared for entry into the ministry. The College had moved to Tavistock Square from its original site in Finsbury in 1881. The Levy family's move to Endsleigh Gardens therefore located Amy, both literally and figurative, between the two ideological traditions that had had the most profound influence upon her life, for whilst the Talmudic scholars promulgated the doctrine of the Old Testament at Jew's College, Pearson and his like-minded colleagues were spreading the new creed of Social Darwinism at University College.

After her return to London, in the late spring of 1886, revitalised by her Italian holiday, Amy had embarked upon an ambitious programme of work, study and socialising with the new circle of acquaintance that she had acquired through her friendship with Vernon Lee. However, despite her renewed enthusiasm for life and literature, in characteristic fashion she felt obliged to deprecate her own particular efforts, telling Lee:

> Miss Blomfield came yesterday afternoon & we have agreed to read some Italian together, beginning on a modern novel .... I went some time ago to see Miss Robinson[311]; she is very charming, but hasn't the same personal attraction for me that Miss Blomfield has ...I have finished Villari, and contemplate attacking Machiavelli's History of Florence; & my story is finished & in the act (or rather state) of being copied out. But please don't have an idea that I am very industrious! It makes me blush to think of people like you and the Robinsons.[312]

Amy's instinctive personal antipathy to Mary Robinson – whose poetry she fervently admired – was likely to have been aroused by her sensing a reciprocal, but concealed, aversion on Mary's side. After her engagement to James Darmesteter in late August 1887, she confessed to her fiancé: 'I am so glad you are a Jew! I used to dislike Jews so much I could not bear to know them; I was always honestly ashamed of this prejudice which, however, I could not conquer'.[313] Dorothy Blomfield patently did not share Mary Robinson's prejudice against Jews, and she and Amy became close friends. In the light of their friendship it is interesting to observe that her grandfather, Charles James Blomfield, the late Bishop of London, had made sympathetic comments about the Jewish community in a debate in the House of Lords in February 1851.[314] Like Mary Robinson, Dorothy Blomfield had been introduced to Amy by Vernon Lee. And like Amy, Dorothy was a published author, although in her case her published works mainly consisted of liturgical compositions. The family history records that she was the 'author of the well known hymn "O Perfect Love" and also of the poem "God's Garden"'.[315] As this indicates, Dorothy was a Christian – although evidently not a very convinced one. In one of her letters to Lee, Amy commented disapprovingly:

> Miss Blomfield & I took to talking about the infinities the other day; we do not agree on that rather wearisome subject, as no doubt you know. The vaguely pious person, disbelieving & believing in Christ, is an anomaly beyond my comprehension. If you go in for vague belief, fling away the Bible you ought to & must.[316]

Perhaps this conversation prompted Amy to question the validity of her own attitude to her religion.

Amy's quarrel with Judaism was rooted in her opposition to the role of women within Jewish society. She regarded Jewish men as 'Orientals at heart', whose womenfolk were, for the most part, consigned to a life of cloistered, pampered idleness. The minority of Jewish women with ambitions beyond this futile existence were condemned to a wearisome struggle, which left them 'beating themselves in vain against the solid masonry of our ancient fortifications'.[317] In order to achieve her own ambition to establish herself as a writer within the mainstream of English literature Amy had had to overcome the obstacles of both her sex and her ethnicity. Accordingly, up until this time, at least in her prose works, she had sought to transcend what she termed 'the tribal limits'. Her move to Bloomsbury, which placed her both geographically and spiritually at the heart of the London Jewish community, seems to have finally confronted her with both the inconsistency and the injustice of her approach to her religion and her cultural heritage. Henceforward she looked upon her community and their customs with more sympathetic eyes. This change of heart first manifested itself in a series of essays that appeared in the Jewish Chronicle throughout the spring, summer and late autumn of 1886. Her father is said to have had a hand in their publication. At that time one of his close friends was Asher Myers, the editor of the *Jewish Chronicle*. Myers was regarded as something of a maverick within the Jewish community. He was a member of a group of Jewish intellectuals who lived in what was then known as the 'Jewish Bohemia of Kilburn'. This group, who styled themselves 'The Wanderers', held forward-thinking views. Like his fellow 'Wanderer', the journalist and future novelist and playwright Israel Zangwill, Myers was an advocate of female emancipation, and under his editorship the *Jewish Chronicle* proved 'an unstinting ally in women's progress towards autonomy in the public sphere'.[318] Perhaps because of his sympathy for the cause of women's rights, he took an interest in his friend Lewis' daughter's literary career, and agreed publish a series of articles written by her on Jewish themes.[319]

The first of this series, entitled 'The Ghetto at Florence', was obviously inspired by Amy's visit to the city with Clementina Black. The fragment of the (previously quoted) letter describing the fireside evening that they spent there together ends with the words::

> I have often thought of Papa in my walks – & of how he wd. enjoy the narrow, picturesque streets & clear air. Yesterday we walked through the Jewish quarter on our way to S. Lorenzo, but the old ghetto is deserted & shown for 6d.[320]

In 'The Ghetto at Florence', for the first time Amy gave public voice to her feelings of tribal guilt. The essay anticipated her novel *Reuben Sachs*, inasmuch as it was a homily upon the contrast between the 'struggling, choked existence' of the unworldly inhabitants of the ghetto and the thrusting commercially centred life of the Jewish community in the modern city. Her description of the deserted back streets of the old ghetto possesses a haunting poignancy which stands in sharp contrast to the acerbic irony of the Darwinian analysis of contemporary Florentine Jewry that immediately follows it.

> How dreary, how inexpressibly gloomy [the ghetto] is!' she wrote.

> Even the moonlight, that wonderful moonlight of an Italian spring, cannot penetrate into these courts and alleys, around which the tall houses crowd so closely. The air strikes chill and damp; are those human faces, or the faces of ghosts, that peer so wistfully through the grated lower windows? Is it the sound of human footsteps, or the sound heard in a dream, that echoes on the close, irregular pavement, that startles one from the gloom of unexpected angles and archways? It is only sentimentalists, like ourselves, that trouble themselves in this unnecessary fashion. There are a great many Jews here to-night, evidently quite undisturbed by 'inherited memory'. A sprightly, if un-

> handsome, son of Shem urges us, in correct cockney, to take shares in a lottery; another, with his wife on his arm, trips gaily from booth to booth; the repressed energy, the stored exuberance of centuries is venting itself with its wonted force.[321]

The tension created between past and present, pathos and pragmatism in this passage reflects Amy's increasing awareness of the dichotomy between the two determining ideological influences of her life – the fundamental asceticism of rabbinical tradition, and the relentless determinism of Darwinian theory. The paragraph draws towards its conclusion with the sombre reflection: 'We ourselves, ourselves, it is to be feared, are not very good Jews; is it by way of "judgement" that the throng of ghosts haunts us so persistently tonight?'

This same motif of memory, remorse and judgement re-emerged in her poem 'The Last Judgement', which detailed the final reckoning of a life wasted in futile dreams. She chose 'The Last Judgement' for inclusion in *A London Plane Tree*, the collection of poetry that she was preparing for publication in the weeks before her suicide. The verse, perhaps, encapsulated her own 'last judgement' on her life, that in pursuing her idealistic vision, she had betrayed the principles of her religion and cut herself irrevocably adrift from her own community. However, although the sentiments expressed in the poem are intensely personal ones, they are not voiced by the author herself but, as the last line reveals, by a man, the 'Minor Poet' James Thomson, who had inspired the title of her second collection of verse. Deborah Epstein Nord, who was one of the first to identify Amy with the radical socialist/feminist circle in which she moved, also drew attention to her tendency to speak in her poetry from behind the mask of an assumed persona. Noting the number of her more intimate lyrics that are addressed to another woman, she concludes that the underlying reason for her adoption of this device was not necessarily 'because she was a lesbian', adding that the lyrics 'do not at all give that impression', but rather to enable her to achieve the 'impersonality' which allowed her 'to speak freely as a woman [in order] to express private feeling in a veiled way.'[322] In 'The Last Judgement' it is likely that Amy chose to assume the mask of James Thomson not only 'to express private feeling in a veiled way', but also because she saw her own destiny reflected in his life. In her essay, 'James Thomson: A Minor Poet', which appeared in *The Cambridge Review* in February 1883, she described his works as resounding with 'the coarse cry of the imperfect human being crushed beneath a load which he is not formed to bear.'[323] In similar vein Amy's fictive 'Minor Poet' defines himself as 'A creature maimed and marred from very birth. A blot, a blur, a note/ All out of tune with this world's instrument.' Thomson himself described his existence as 'a long defeat.' Although, like Amy, he had achieved a measure of fame as a 'minor poet', after the death of his childhood sweetheart, Matilda Weller, his personal life had taken a downward path, culminating in a miserable, self-inflicted death. Having taken to the bottle after the loss of his love he relentlessly drank himself into oblivion, finally expiring in University College Hospital, where, according to Bertram Dobell, he had been taken from the lodgings of his close friend, the blind poet Philip Bourke Marston.'[324] Marston (who had been engaged to the late sister of one of Amy's British Museum acquaintances, the poet and children's novelist, Edith Nesbit) was undoubtedly the inspiration for Tom Leigh, the narrator of the epilogue of 'A Minor Poet'.[325]

But above all, it was Thomson's epic poem 'The City of Dreadful Night' that struck a particular chord with Amy. She maintained that the verse was 'his masterpiece', 'the almost perfect expression of a form of mental suffering which I can convey by no other means than the use of a very awkward figure – by calling it "grey pain", "the insufferable inane" which makes a man long for the "positive pain".' She added: 'Most of us at some time in our lives have wandered in the City of Dreadful Night; the shadowy forms, the dim streets, the monotonous tones are familiar to us'.[326] In fact, Amy's depiction of Thomson's 'lost city' corresponds to a remarkable degree with her description of the old ghetto at Florence:

> … The city, with …. it's vast unruined streets where the lamps always burn 'tho there is no light in the houses', rises before us, a picture distinct, real in itself, real in the force of its symbolic meaning. The wanderer goes down into the city; all is dim and shadowy; the dismal inhabitants, whose faces are 'like to tragic masks of stone' are few and far between, holding little intercourse with one another, communing each man with himself …

Anticipating her evolutionary analysis of the contrast between the imaginary occupants of the old ghetto and real-life Florentine Jewry, she highlights, with bitter irony, the Darwinian philosophy underlying Thomson's vision:

> Hell itself is eagerly sought, a much-desired goal, as a refuge from the void agony of the city …. Yes, here in the City of Dreadful Night these are good-tidings …. there is no God; no 'fiend with names Divine' made and tortured us; 'we bow down to the universal laws' there is no life beyond the grave, and each man is free to end his life at will.[327]

Like the ghostly occupants of the old ghetto, peering wistfully from the grated windows, and the dismal wraithlike inhabitants of 'The City of Dreadful Night', wandering in aimless despair, Amy clearly regarded herself and Thomson as spirits condemned to relentless torment. 'A Last Judgement' concludes with the rhymed couplet:

This is the tale I have to tell
Show the fellow the way to hell.

By the mid-1880s Amy's own 'dreadful night' had begun to descend. Her sister's marriage and Pearson's betrayal were the main, but by no means the only, reasons for her psychological decline. It has been pointed out that Amy's 'particular position as an Anglo-Jewish outsider' gave her a unique insight into the obstacles in the path of non-Christian writers who aspired to establish themselves within the canon of English literature.[328]This consideration may have prompted her to attempt to make a life in literature 'beyond the tribal limits'. And this, in turn, resulted in her flirtation with Social Darwinism, as personified in the desirable form of its paradigmatic representative, Karl Pearson. But Social Darwinism presented her with a further difficulty. One scholar who has made an extensive study of British-Jewish literature has highlighted the 'structural ambivalence' towards the Jew expressed in 'a wide variety of texts by socialist [Darwinist] authors.' He cites George Bernard Shaw as being one of the first of these authors to engage in the Semitic discourse which eventually became known as 'the socialism of fools.' [329] A one-time aspirant suitor of Eleanor Marx, Shaw was personally acquainted with Amy through their joint attendance at the Reading Room of the British Museum and meetings of the first Men and Women's Club. Shaw's novel *An Unsocial Socialist* (which was written in the Reading Room of the British Museum in 1884)[330] has been identified as one of the earliest texts to conflate 'anti-capitalism' with anti-Semitism.[331] In the opening scenes of the novel, the male protagonist, the heartless Sidney Trefusis (who was reputedly modelled on Eleanor Marx's common-law husband, Edward Aveling), elopes with the daughter of a Jewish banker, John Jansenius. Shaw describes Jansenius in terms that illustrate the way in which casual, unconsidered anti-Semitism permeated the discourse of even the most supposedly enlightened elements of Victorian society. Jansenius, Shaw writes, was

> a man of imposing presence … His aquiline nose and keen dark eyes proclaimed his Jewish origin, of which he was ashamed. Those who did not know this naturally believed that he was proud of it … Well instructed in business, and subject to no emotion outside the love of family, respectability, comfort, and money he had maintained the capital inherited from his father and made it breed new capital in the usual way …'[332]

Shaw's unflattering portrayal of John Jansenius as a cold-hearted, money-grabbing capitalist was far from unique. The identification of Judaism with capitalism was commonplace in socialist circles at that time. British Museum acquaintances Beatrice Potter and Margaret Harkness, whilst supportive of the oppressed Jewish factory workers of the East

End, had little sympathy with their well-to-do West End counterparts. But even when they portrayed less fortunate Jews in a sympathetic light they resorted to stereotype. In her novel *In Darkest London* Margaret Harkness wrote:

> The down-trodden Gentiles seem to have lost their faith: they speak of death as "the great secret," while the Jew calls death "God's kiss," even when it comes to him in the crowded dens of sweaters or the filthy rooms which he shares with new-comers from the Continent. Moreover, he knows how to grow rich. He leaves the East End to settle in Bayswater; he does not content himself with husks, like our Gentile swine who fill the public houses ...[333]

And whilst posing as a 'sweater' in the East End Beatrice Potter recorded in her diary:

> The "missus" [whom she had earlier described as 'a stout clever-looking Jewess'] bustles into the room. She is a big woman ...with strongly Jewish features and only one eye. Her hair is crisp and has been jet black ...Her dress is stamped velvet of a large flowery pattern; she has a heavy watch chain [and] plentiful rings ...[334]

These quotations demonstrate that the egalitarian, scientific and 'rational' society predicted and promoted in the writing of many of Amy's circle of acquaintance offered little welcome to those of her ethnic origin and social background. On the contrary, they were regarded as vulgar materialists who were an undesirable impediment to social progress. As a Jew, Amy had been brought up in a tradition that demanded strict adherence to the Law of Moses. Having turned her back on the uncompromising creed of her childhood she had embraced what turned out to be the equally uncongenial 'new creed' of Social Darwinism. And just as she had rejected the faith of her fathers, so the founding fathers of the 'new faith' had rejected her. Having eagerly anticipated the prospect of the new Eden proffered by scientifically oriented socialists like Karl Pearson and his Cambridge friends, like Lewis Carroll's Alice she found her entry into their magic garden blocked because, metaphorically speaking, her face did not fit. Both Judith Quixano's cry of anguish in the concluding pages of *Reuben Sachs* and 'The Last Judgement' (which is replete with Old Testament biblical allusion) are testimony to her recognition that her attempt to seek a life 'beyond the tribal limits' had proved a chimera.

In the last of her series of essays for the *Jewish Chronicle* Amy gave vent to her bitterness and frustration at the situation that she found herself in, lamenting the fact that:

> Jewish men and women of any width of culture are driven to finding their friends of the other sex in the Gentile camp. ...this state of things falls most hardly on the women. As a matter of fact, so many of our men are absorbed in money making, and are moreover such genuine Orientals at heart, that they scarcely feel the need of feminine society in its higher forms. Whereas the women, such of them as are beginning to be conscious of the yoke, are more readily adaptable, more eager to ab-

> sorb the atmosphere around them; and by reason of their extra leisure have in many cases outstripped their brothers in culture. Thus with greater social capabilities they have far less social opportunity.

The essay ends with an embittered summary of the current state of affairs:

> But when all is said, to a thoughtful person, thoughtfully surveying the feminine half of our society, the picture is depressing enough. On the one hand, he sees an ever increasing minority of single women beating themselves in vain against the solid masonry of our ancient fortifications ... sometimes succeeding in scaling the wall and departing, never to return, to the world beyond. On the other a crowd of half-educated, idealess, pampered creatures, absorbed in material enjoyments ... whose highest desire in life is the possession (after a husband) of a sable cloak and at least one pair of diamond earrings. Looking at them it is perhaps hard to realise the extent of our undeveloped social resources; of the wickedness of our wilful neglect of some of the most delicately-flavoured fruits that the gods can make to grow...

In 'Jewish Humour', the essay that preceded 'Jewish Women of To-Day', Amy considered the reasons for her community's insularity and self-interest. She identified this unpleasant trait, in part, as 'the result ... of prolonged life in cities', enquiring rhetorically, 'How long is it since [the Jew] gave up pasturing his flocks and took (perforce) to trade?' and adding:

> he hardly has left, when all is said, a bucolic drop of blood left in his veins. He has been huddled in crowded quarters of towns, forced into close and continual contact with his fellow-creatures; he has learned to watch men's faces; to read men's thoughts; to be always ready for his opportunity. If he could raise a laugh at his neighbour's expense when his neighbour's demeanour was such a matter of importance to him, who will grudge him the solace and the vengeance?

She then turned her fire on her community's detractors, sneering: 'To make the comic character of a play or a novel a Jew is a sufficiently common device; as unsuccessful, it must be added as it is common. Perhaps these Merry-Andrews[335] of fiction have their uses, and serve to rouse the laughter of the Gentile public; perhaps we have a comic side which we ourselves are incapable of perceiving, and yet we are by no means sparing of one another in this respect'.

Amy's final contribution to the *Jewish Chronicle* was entitled 'Jewish Children'. Once again the essay dwells upon the effect of urban life on the Jewish psyche. In the light of her own fragile mental condition, the following passage is most telling:

> It must not be forgotten that the very things which go to make up the peculiar and irresistible charm of young Israel constitute at the same time his danger. Such vivacity, such sense of fun, such sensibility and intelligence at so early an age, could only be the product of a very delicate and elaborate organism; a bit of mechanism that will not bear to be tampered with rashly. We scarcely need Mr. Sully and his psychology to tell us that mental precocity is by no means necessarily the forerunner of mental mediocrity,

> but it may always be accepted as the sign of a highly developed nervous organisation. And the Jewish child, descendant of many city-bred ancestors as he is, is apt to be a very complicated little bundle of nerves indeed..

Amy was obviously familiar with the theories of James Sully, whose interest was in 'genetic' (i.e. evolutionary) psychology.[336] Welcoming the fact that 'English society is beginning at last to give ear to the teachings of psychology and physiology and to recognise the careful training in youth of human beings', she regretted that 'The Jewish community, conservative as ever, absorbs very slowly the modern educational doctrine. Both parents and children suffer, as I pointed out, from the defects of their qualities'. Concluding that the entire community had a duty to 'direct the manifold energies of our little ones into the proper channels', she concluded: 'the scientific teachings of the day are bound eventually to permeate even the close-grained stratum of Jewish conservatism … But the process is a slow one … The rate of mental and nervous diseases amongst Jews is deplorably high; we are suffering no doubt for the conditions of our past existence … the comparative smallness of our numbers, our centuries of city life'. This observation is in direct opposition to the positive portrait of urban life given in poems such as 'Ballade of an Omnibus' and 'A Village Garden' and her novel *The Romance of a Shop*. Rather it reflects the jaded view of the metropolis voiced in the closing passage of her last, posthumously published short story 'Wise in her Generation'. By that time the city was, for Amy, no longer symbol of freedom - a space where she could wander at will and let her imagination roam freely. Instead, in her mind it had become the sinister embodiment of Darwinian Theory, the 'huge, hideous struggle for struggle for existence' that is the essence of the human condition.

'Jewish Children' appeared in the *Jewish Chronicle* in November 1886. In the year that followed Amy needed all the reserves of 'Jewish humour' that she could muster, as the period 1887 8 was a challenging time for her. As well as the loss of her beloved brother, the family finances were in turmoil, and her father's financial problems made it all the more imperative that she increase her own earnings. Up to now she had relied on the fees that she received from the publication of her short stories and journalistic pieces like the series of *Jewish Chronicle* essays as the mainstay of her income. But these sources alone would not provide her with the financial security that would enable her to live an independent life. She therefore decided to turn her hand to a novel. She had made sporadic attempts at novel writing before – in her letter from Saig she had complained: 'O the novel is so bad – its no go' - but this time she played safe, taking the formula that had worked so well in her short fiction, drawing on her own recent experience in the construction of her plot.

The Romance of a Shop is the story of three sisters, Gertrude, Lucy and Phyllis Lorrimer and their half-sister Fanny. Forced to 'consider their future' after the unexpected death of their father leaves them in penury, the girls reject the offer of help from their mother's overbearing sister, who proposes that one live with her and others try their luck in India. Loathing the idea of, as one critic put it, a life of 'genteel dependence and servitude', the sisters decide to go into business, turning what had previously been a pastime into a means of earning a living, by setting themselves up as photographers in a shop in London's Baker Street.[337] This move leads to romance – at least for Gertrude and Lucy, in the respective forms of Lord Norwood who, like Karl Pearson, is a modern man of science, and Frank Jermyn, a dashing young painter and illustrator for *The Woodcut*, a popular journal modelled on *The Illustrated London News*. But it is the youngest Lorrimer sister, Phyllis, who provides the dramatic climax to the narrative when she goes off the rails in spectacular style under the influence of the villain of the piece, the artist Sidney Darrell. Phyllis' downfall leads to a conventional Victorian ending, as the three older Lorrimer sisters marry and live happily ever after, and Phyllis pays for her sins by dying of consumption.

Notwithstanding its conventional ending, *The Romance of a Shop* is in other respects a highly unconventional Victorian novel. It would be interesting to know if Amy had read Emile Zola's *Au Bonheur des Dames* (The Ladies' Delight), which had been translated into English by F. Belmont in 1883. Although *The Romance of a Shop* bears little direct resemblance to Zola's novel, it does exhibit the strong influence of the French Naturalist movement of which he was the founder. But above all, like Zola's book, it is a celebration of city living that is consciously modern in both subject and substance. Like its author, Amy Levy, the Lorrimer sisters eagerly grasp all the opportunities that modern London has to offer, and Amy's intimate knowledge of and affection for the city is manifest throughout the text. In fact her life history is reflected on almost every page. For instance, Lord Norwood lives in Sussex Place, and Gertrude's description of the house, which is 'situated about midway in the terrace', and its large dinging-room 'decorated in each gloomy corner by greenish figures of a pseudo-classical nature, which served the purpose of supports for the gas-globes' is obviously a portrait of the Levys' former residence. The character of Lucy Lorrimer may similarly have been a sketch drawn from life, in this case Alice Hughes, daughter of the portrait painter Edward Hughes. In around 1886 Alice Hughes opened a photographic portrait studio next to her father's house in Gower Street, not far from the by then Levy family home in Endsleigh Gardens. There she made photographic studies for her father's paintings – just as Lucy Lorrimer does for Frank Jermyn. But it is the heroine of the story, Gertrude Lorrimer, who bears the most obvious resemblance to the author in person. Like Amy Levy, Gertrude is a free spirit who refuses to abide by convention. In 1925, many years after Amy's death, Katie Solomon (née Levy) wrote the following letter to *The Observer*: [338]

> In connection with your article about the omnibus, your readers might be interested in the following verses. The writer was among the first women in London to show herself on the top of omnibuses. She excused herself to her shocked family circle by saying that she had committed the outrage in company with the daughter of a dean who was the granddaughter of an Archbishop of Canterbury.

There followed a transcript of Amy Levy's 'Ballade of an Omnibus'.[339]

In the 1880s respectable women were not supposed to travel on the open top of omnibuses, thereby exposing themselves to the gaze of any random passer by in the street. Katie's letter is a touching testament to her sister's free spirit and appetite for adventure. The heroine of her novel, Gertrude Lorrimer, enters into the life of the city with similar gusto:

> At Baker Street Station they parted; Phyllis disappearing to the underground railway; Gertrude mounting boldly to the top of an Atlas omnibus.
>
> "Because one cannot afford a carriage or even a hansom cab, she argued to herself, "is one to be shut away from the sunlight and the streets?"
>
> Indeed, for Gertrude, the humours of the town had always possessed a curious fascination. She contemplated the familiar London pageant with an interest that had something of passion in it; and for her part was never inclined to quarrel with the fate that had transported her from the comparative tameness of Campden Hill to regions where the pulses of the great city could be felt distinctly as they beat and throbbed ...[340]

The first line of this passage is an echo of a remark made by Amy in a letter written to Vernon Lee at the beginning of 1887. After telling Lee that she was 'in the 17th Chapter of my novel' (this would have been *The Romance of a Shop*), toward the end of the letter she enquired: 'When are you coming here? ... I wonder if I shall see anything of you? It seems simply ages since I said goodbye to you in the Underground Railway of all places, do you remember?'

In fact Amy Levy and Vernon Lee were destined not to meet that year. As was her custom in the mid-1880s, Lee spent the early months of the summer in London, but she was suffering from periodic bouts of neuralgia and nervous depression, and this seems to have prevented her from meeting up with Amy. At a time when she was still struggling to come to terms with Alfred's death, the apparent collapse of the 'rock' on which she depended evidently alarmed Amy. She wrote a pleading letter to her friend:

> My dear Miss Paget,
>
> This is indeed bad news – that you are here & too smashed to see people. Do you think there is no chance of yr. being visible in London either on yr. way to or fr. Scotland. You really mustn't be one of the people to get nervy and smashed – it takes away the ground fr. one's feet; you are such a rock – morally & mentally speaking – that one cannot reconcile oneself to the idea of yr. being physically out of sorts.[341]

In early August, Lee set off for the trip to the north of England and Scotland that Amy had mentioned in her letter. During her stay at Charleton, the Fifeshire home of the Anstruther Thomson family, she received devastating news. Her long-time 'romantic' friend Mary Robinson announced, without warning, that she was engaged to be married. On 30th August Lee wrote to her mother:

> Last week I received half a sheet of notepaper from Mary telling me that she has engaged herself to marry James Darmesteter, a Jewish professor at the Collège de France, whom I have seen once .... And she had seen *thrice,* including the occasion upon which she asked him (for she says she asked him rather than he her) to marry. ... I don't know how I should have felt if good luck had not put me into the house of one of the most wonderfully good and gentle, and strong and simple of all created things .... Kit Thomson.[342]

The sudden news of Mary Robinson's engagement resulted in a catastrophic breakdown in Lee's health which entirely put an end to the possibility of her giving Amy the support she needed at this difficult time. Lee patched up her quarrel with Robinson, after a fashion, and they spent some time in Italy together in the late autumn and winter, but her mental and physical wellbeing had been dealt a blow from which it never fully recovered. In the midst of her personal crisis, in November 1887, Lee received another letter from Amy, who was once more considering a visit to Florence:

> It is beginning to be very foggy in London & my thoughts turn often to Florence. I don't think, however, that I shall come out before February if I am able to come at all. Miss Blomfield seems doubtful about her plans, so I wrote to Miss Wimbush who, as you know, has a flat in the Via Romana, but she doesn't expect to have room for me in the spring.[343]

The letter ended with a poem, 'The Birch Tree at Loeschwitz'.[344]

In the end Amy's planned trip was put off yet again. There are only a few remaining brief glimpses into her daily life during the early and middle months of 1888. The first is when she appeared on the guest list of the 'Boat Race' party that Dollie and Ernest Radford held at their home in Hammersmith on 24th March (her fellow guests included 'Miss [Grace] Gilchrist', 'G.B. Shaw', 'May Morris'[345]and 'Dr. Furnivall'), the second on Sunday 3rd June when she once again visited the Radfords, and the third when she went to 'the Academy' with Dollie on 14th June.[346] But Amy's health was in obviously in decline yet again, and by the autumn, like Lee, she was in need of help. By this time, Lee was once more being nursed by Kit Anstruther-Thomson at Charleton. However, despite her own suffering, she did not forget her ailing and melancholy friend in London. On 2nd October 1888, she wrote to her mother:

> Poor Miss Levy is ordered abroad for her health and writes to me for addresses of pensions.... She is very forlorn, poor little body, for her deafness has not diminished. I suppose she would not do as Eugene's reader? She knows French and German, is as quiet as a mouse & would, I imagine, be only too grateful for a little kindness ... at all events Miss Levy might be tried, if you asked her for a few days until she had found her pension. If suitable she might stay on. Of course she has never hinted anything of the kind, nor have I to her.[347]

Amy did not seem to welcome the idea that she was regarded as an object of pity and a candidate for charity. In the end, she made her way to Florence under her own auspices, from where she wrote to Katie:

> I have now been here a week & am, so far, not particularly spry. Its a bit lonely. If it weren't for kind little Bertha[348] & La Guerre et la Paix I don't know where I shd. be.

The letter also sheds further light on her reasons for rejecting Lee's offer. She remarked unenthusiastically:

> Lee-Hamilton has sent me his poems with a well-turned compliment scrawled on the fly-leaf. I called the other day, but thank God, he was out. However I have had a special request to go again. The poems are dreadful; I must look through them, I suppose, before I go.[349]

Lee's letters to her mother reveal that they were in a constant state of anxiety about Eugene, whose illness was without doubt psychosomatic in origin. (After lying semi-paralysed for twenty years, shortly after his mother's death he unexpectedly regained the use of his limbs, and soon afterwards married the feminist novelist Annie Holdsworth. They had a child, a little girl, who died in infancy – much to Lee's grief.) Because of Lee's obvious concern about her half-brother's welfare, Amy may have falsely suspected that she was being 'set up' as his prospective bride. He certainly did not regard her with the same lack of enthusiasm that she had for him, as after her suicide he wrote a maudlin poetic tribute, entitled 'Fumes of Charcoal September 1889', in which he pleaded:

> … Oh Amy, in the land
> Of the sweet light and of the sweet live air,
> Did you ne'er sit beside a friend's wheeled bed,
>
> That you could thus destroy, at Hell's command,
> All that he envied you, and choke the fair
> Young flame of life, to dwell with the wan dead?[350]

Despite Amy's complaint of loneliness, and her forlorn comment, 'I am going through all the sights again as a matter of duty', her first bulletin to Katie from Florence was reasonably cheerful. However, her second letter reveals a marked deterioration in her mood. It is addressed 'Dear Saint' and, after solicitous enquiries about her little nephew's health and an account of her progress with *La Guerre et la Paix* [*War and Peace*], she confesses:

> Things are looking up as regards people, but I'm not well and horribly sad. I don't think so much time for thinking over one's sunken ships is exactly good for one. Vernon has been most kind in sending people to see me, & I have 5 tea-parties booked for this week. Her great friend Miss Bella Duffy is the most hopeful. She has simply urged me to go there at all hours and days. She is a very handsome woman, but terribly lame; & awfully witty & amusing.[351]

After a description of her social activities and the progress of her new novel, *Reuben Sachs* – 'The proofs are now dispatched to Macmillan. The title page has 1888 on it, so any day you may wake up to find yourself once more an aunt' – Amy concludes:

> I am so sick – its almost impossible to get exercise enough. One can't walk forever about a little town, & I daren't go Italian country walks alone …. I'm rather preying on myself just now, & examine the Arno critically a good deal with a view to its depth.
>
> Perhaps some of the new people who have called will walk, but Miss Duffy is so lame. We had a little walk the other day, & the pace at wh. we went nearly froze me to death.
>
> I feel in coming to Florence to get well that I've played my last card & lost. (Don't mention these [word illegible] at home, or to anyone else will you?) I have such a ghastly headache that I must leave off. Do write. Everyone seems to have forgotten ones existence – not a line fr. Clemmy.[352]

Although she was (somewhat unreasonably) irritated by Duffy's lameness, Amy generally regarded her as an agreeable companion. She told Katie: 'Miss Duffy is the chief social feature of Florence for me, & I see her nearly every day.' It seems that by this time Lewis may have recovered some of his money, as towards the end of her letter, Amy informed her sister: 'It is on the cards that I may go to Rome after Christmas, at least if the periodical financial smash hasn't come off.' Perhaps the anticipated 'smash' did occur, as on 7th January she noted in her diary: 'Called on E. L. H. dined with B. D. left Florence 8.45 p.m.'. From this point onwards a more comprehensive record of Amy's daily activities exists thanks to the 'Calendrier 1889', which is the sole surviving direct record of her last months of life. This document is inscribed 'Amy Levy: In Memory of November 1888: from Bella Duffy: Florence.'

The Final Scene and The Last Act: 1889

I have no more to give, all that was mine
Is laid, a wrested tribute, at thy shrine;
Let me depart, for my whole soul is wrung,
And all my cheerless orisons are sung;
Let me depart, with faint limbs let me creep
To some dim shade and sink me down to sleep.

Sarojini Naidu (1879–1949): 'To the God of Pain'

Amy left Florence for the last time at 8.45 pm on 7th January 1889. She recorded the details of her departure in the 'Calendrier 1889' which had been the parting gift from Bella Duffy. This is the only one of Amy's diaries to survive the cull of her papers that took place after her death, and as such it provides a unique insight into her daily life at this significant juncture. In particular, the detailed record that it contains of the hectic round of social calls and literary work that occupied her last months belies the rumour that circulated after her death that by this time she was a melancholy, reclusive semi-invalid. This false image was to have a major impact on the later critical approaches to her writing. But the diary is also important because of the indirect evidence that it provides of the mental decline that heralded her death. It appears that the determining influence that finally pushed her over the brink to suicide was Olive Schreiner's revelation of Karl Pearson's engagement to Maria Sharpe in August 1889. The unhappy outcome of Olive's own emotional entanglement with Pearson is well documented. After Amy took her life it was reported in the press that they had entered into a 'suicide pact' together. Amy's handwriting was a consistent monitor of the state of her mind, and the marked deterioration in the handwriting in the diary precisely corresponds with the period in early June when Olive had returned to London, and Pearson's attachment to Maria Sharpe became public knowledge. After this the handwriting of the entries becomes increasingly irregular, reflecting Amy's physical restlessness as she roamed from place to place in the company of sympathetic female friends or made excursions to various parks and gardens where she spent the day sitting in silent contemplation. But in the early months of 1889 after her return from Florence, despite the pessimistic letters that she had sent to Katie during the last weeks of her stay, no hint of melancholy can be discerned in the entries in the diary. In fact, quite the contrary, for at that time it appears that her life was filled with activity and purpose.

In the 1880s the journey from Florence to London was an arduous affair, and Amy decided to break her journey in Paris. Her decision seems to have been influenced by the fact that a number of her friends were staying in the city at the time. She reached Paris at 7am on 9th January after what must have been a gruelling night on the train from Turin, and upon arrival promptly retired to bed until 5.30 in the afternoon. In the evening she paid a call on Jenny de Pass who was staying at the St. James Hotel in the Rue de Rivoli. On the following day she set out to explore the city in company with Vernon Lee's friend and general factotum Kit Anstruther-Thomson. At this time, like Amy, Lee was homeward bound, travelling back to Florence from Tangiers where she had spent the winter recovering from the physical and mental collapse that followed after she received the news of Mary Robinson's engagement. During her absence Kit Anstruther-Thomson had taken the opportunity to return to Paris to complete her studies at the studio of the painter Carolus Duran, and after a morning spent in the Louvre she took Amy to Duran's studio in Montparnasse.[353] The pair then went on to the nearby Musée du Luxembourg where the much-admired portrait of his wife, 'Lady with a Glove', was on display. In the 1880s Paris was a Mecca for young female artists, many of whom, like Anstruther Thomson, had come from abroad to study at the progressive ateliers (studios) where women were allowed to work alongside men. This gave them access to an advanced level of tuition that was denied them at the traditional academic institutions. One of these pioneering young women was the Polish artist Anna Bilinska.[354] A couple of days after her visit to Duran's atelier Amy recorded that she had 'tea at Bilinska's studio.' Anna Bilinska was a woman with whom she would have felt an immediate bond. Like Amy, she had cast aside the constraints of a middle-class upbringing to forge her own path in life. A dedicated feminist and a determined bohemian, she had studied at the prestigious Academie Julian at the same time as Marie Bashkirtseff.[355] At the Academie women were positively encouraged to break the boundaries of artistic convention, and Bilinska demonstrated her independence by undertaking several semi-nude studies of men. However, like Amy, her apparent strength of mind masked a deep-seated emotional vulnerability. In 1884, after the loss in quick succession of her father and fiancée, she suffered a severe nervous breakdown and - just as Amy had fled to Cornwall in the wake of Pearson's rejection and her sister's marriage – Bilinska had retired to Brittany in order to recover her health. By 1886 she was well enough to return to Paris where, in recognition of her talent, Julian appointed her head of her own studio. And it was there that she entertained Amy to tea.

The evening before her meeting with Anna Bilinska, Amy had enjoyed her own taste of *la vie boheme*, for she recorded in her diary that she had 'dined at the Chat Noir'. The cabaret restaurant Le Chat Noir was situated in the heart of Montmartre, which was the haunt of the Parisian avant-garde. The art critic and journalist Theodore Child described Montmartre in 1889 as 'a [place] where all that is conventional is held in abomination.'[356] But the artistic fraternity of Montmartre did not welcome women within their ranks, and as a result Le Chat Noir was a decidedly male oriented establishment. Cliquey and 'academic', the 'celebrated poets, painters and sculptors' who were its regular clientele were customarily to be found in impassioned debate about the quality of 'a sonnet ... the merits of a new comedy or the charms of a new picture'. [357] Unfortunately these exchanges, which were conducted under 'a canopy of smoke', and during which quantities of alcohol were routinely consumed, tended to degenerate from high-minded discussion into drunken brawling. As a result, as Child pointed out, respectable women approached Le Chat Noir with caution. It was a place, he claimed, where 'you do not expect to find Parisian matrons and their daughters'. According to her diary, Amy's dining companion on that evening was another member of Vernon Lee's Florentine circle. This was Eleanor, one of the unmarried sisters of George Eliot's widower John Cross. In an earlier letter to Lee, Amy had described Eleanor Cross as a model of 'respectable spinsterhood'.[358] The fact that Amy was prepared to venture into such a place without a suitable male escort is yet another instance of her reckless disregard for social convention, but the upright Miss Cross was not the obvious choice of partner for such an enterprise, and why she agreed to accompany her is a mystery.

The Rabelaisian ethos of the restaurant was reflected in its décor. Dominating the scene, above an array of exotic bric-a-brac, was a large 'strange coloured' six-panel stained glass window. This remarkable piece, which was entitled *veaux d'or* [golden calf], was intended to symbolise the loss of innocence of 'the cabaret itself, and the society in general, to a succumbing avarice'. It was the work of the illustrator and caricaturist Adolphe Willette. Willette was an anti-Semite, and his window featured a number of stereotypically negative representations of the Jew, culminating in a portrait of 'the king of wealth, and thus, power ... represented by the ... image of a Jew who holds the hand of a no-longer virtuous dancer'.[359] One can only wonder what Amy made of this creation. Because of a lack of documentary evidence it is impossible to determine whether this was her first visit to Le Chat Noir, but if it was, it is an irony that it took place a couple of days after the announcement of the publication of her novel *Reuben Sachs*, in which she had painted her own portrait of the 'succumbing avarice' of bourgeois Anglo-Jewry, which led to charges of anti-Semitism being levelled against *her*. Although she may not have anticipated the level of hostility that the publication of her novel would arouse, she must surely have been struck by the similarity between the image of the Jew and the 'no-longer virtuous dancer' in Willette's stained glass panel and the final glimpse of Reuben Sachs and the 'Gaiety Girl' that she had given to her readers in the concluding pages of the novel:

> But rumours of [Reuben] had reached her. He had addressed his constituents with great *éclat* in the recess, and was already beginning to attract attention from the leader of his party.
>
> As for more intimate matters, there were reports connecting his name with Miss Cordozo, Miss Lee-Harrison and a chorus girl at the Gaiety.
>
> Some people said he was only waiting for old Solomon's death to marry the chorus girl.

The diversity of Amy's itinerary during her brief visit to Paris is an illustration of the almost schizophrenic dichotomy within her personality between an urge to rebel and a yearning to conform. Her brief stay in the city had taken her from the bourgeois luxury of the St. James Hotel via the artistic fraternity of Montparnasse to an evening spent rubbing shoulders with the Parisian demi-monde in Montmartre. That evening proved to be Amy's final act of revolt, as her freedom to do as she pleased ended at the conclusion of what proved to be her last continental journey, when she arrived at her parent's home in Endsleigh Gardens on the evening of 17th January.

The days that followed her return home were filled with a round of reunion visits to family and friends. On 19th January she recorded that 'Jenny [came] to lunch' and on 20 that 'Pauline called.' Jenny de Pass and Pauline (or Paulina) Meyerstein had been the first to rally round to offer support after the trauma of Katie's wedding in 1885. The ready welcome that they extended to Amy upon her return home suggests that they, at least, bore no grudge against her for the unflattering portrait of her co-religionists that she had painted in *Reuben Sachs*.

After her return to Bloomsbury, as well as taking up the reins of her London social life once more, she resumed her literary work at the 'BM' – her shorthand term for the Reading Room at the British Museum. In her final letter from Florence she had revealed that Lewis Levy's finances were in one of their periodic states of crisis, and this would undoubtedly have given the spur to her literary career. The careful month-by-month record that she kept of 'money received 1889' on the back page of the Calendrier is an indication of the importance that she attached to her income at that time. The first hint of a new literary project came on 22nd January, when she noted that she had 'called on Mr. Nicholl of the BW'. This was William Robertson Nicholl, editor of the *British Weekly*. Two days after her meeting with Nicholl she recorded: 'began MM' - her third novel, *Miss Meredith*. According to the diary Levy 'finished MM' on 8th March, and it made its first appearance in print soon afterwards, running in serialised form in the *British Weekly* during the period April to June 1889. *Miss Meredith* is the least innovative of Amy's three novels, being essentially a reworking of her earlier Brontë-inspired novelette *Griselda*. As such, it is little more than a pale imitation of *Jane Eyre* but this time in an Italian setting. Critics, past and present, have pondered the question why, after producing two groundbreaking works of fiction, Amy should have decided to revert to a literary genre – that of the Victorian governess – that by the mid-1880s was becoming distinctly passé. However, the timescale in which the work was written and published suggests that it was a commissioned piece, and if, as seems to be the case, it was Nicholl who commissioned it, then this would account for its pedestrian qualities. Magazine editors in general were more exacting in their requirements than publishers. Some of them included clauses in their contracts which 'required that nothing was to be included that could not be read out in a family circle'.[360]But in any case, Nicholl was a devout Christian, whose own literary preference was for sentimental, moralistic Scottish tales, and the readers of the *British Weekly* would therefore not have expected to find 'advanced' works of fiction within its pages. Amy would have known this and tailored her narrative accordingly. And if she had been required to write an uncontroversial novel at short notice, what could be easier than to adopt a strategy that she had used on a number of previous occasions, taking a tried and tested storyline and embellishing it with details gleaned from her own experience – in this instance her recent travels in Italy.

On the same day that she submitted the manuscript of *Miss Meredith* to the *British Weekly*, Amy recorded that she had sent off the 'proofs of Cohen'. 'Cohen of Trinity' appeared in *The Gentleman's Magazine* in May 1889. Although she must have been working on the two pieces simultaneously, the contrast between them could not be greater. Whereas *Miss Meredith* was conceived as a purely commercial enterprise, 'Cohen of Trinity', although partly a response to the critical reception of *Reuben Sachs*, was essentially born out of Amy's by now heartfelt contempt for the Cambridge set and the values that they represented. As she herself had done, Cohen gains an entrée into the exclusive, academic world of the University only to discover that he is viewed by his peers as a curiosity rather than a colleague. The narrator of the story, who is a gentile and either a fellow student or a don, gives the readers a first sight of Cohen as he approaches 'across the meadows towards the sunset, his upturned face pushed forwards catching the light, and glowing also with another radiance than the rich, reflected glory of the heavens'. This passage, which signals that at heart Cohen is a visionary and an idealist, stands in sharp contrast to the subsequent description of his appearance as he emerges from the marshland:

> A curious figure: slight, ungainly; shoulders in the ears; an awkward rapid gait, half slouch, half hobble. ... his dusty trencher cap pushed to the back of his head revealed clearly the oval contour of the face, the full prominent lips and full prominent eyes and the curved beak of a nose with its restless nostrils

Amy's portrayal of Cohen as a species of 'pond life', a grotesque, primitive creature, a cross between an amphibian and a bird of prey, establishes the disjunction between his inner qualities and his outer appearance. Indeed, throughout the narrative he is portrayed as an anomaly – a laboratory specimen rather than a human being. The image of Cohen as a lower form of life is reinforced when he quotes 'with reference to himself' lines from Browning's 'Caliban Upon Setebos':

> ...hath spied an icy fish
> That longed to 'scape the rock stream where she lived.
> And thaw herself within the lukewarm waves,
> O' the lazy sea ...
> Only she ever sickened, found repulse
> At the other kind of water not her life,
> Flounced back from bliss she was not born to breathe
> And in her old bonds buried her despair,
> Hating and loving warmth alike.[361]

Aware of his own deficiencies Cohen has conceived a hopeless admiration for 'Norwood and his set'. But, asks the narrator, 'what connection could there be between those young puritans, aristocrats and scholars, the flower of the University ... and a man of Cohen's way of life'. The answer, as Amy makes clear, is that Cohen, with his robust individuality, the creator of an artistic *tour de force*, is spiritually and intellectually more than the equal of the eugenically 'fit' but narrow-minded and priggish Lord Norwood. In this respect 'Cohen of Trinity' opposes Amy's 'sketch' of Jewish life in *Reuben Sachs*, where physical deformity signals moral and intellectual degeneracy. In 'Cohen of Trinity' it is Norwood and the narrator, the embodiment of the exclusive world of academia, who represent moral decay. They wrongly assume that Cohen's newly acquired 'widespread popularity' and recently inherited wealth will 'surely have satisfied, for the time being at least, even his enormous claims'. But fame and fortune mean nothing to Cohen – 'desperately lonely and desperately unapproachable', he wants merely to be accepted and valued for what he is:

> Nothing, he said …can alter the relation of things – their permanent essential relations … 'They *shall* know, they *shall* understand, they *shall* feel what I am'. That is what I used to say to myself in the old days. I suppose, now, 'they' do know, more or less, and what of that?

Shortly after making this revelation Cohen 'sent a bullet through his brain'. 'In his hour of victory the sense of defeat had been the strongest'. As Amy herself had no doubt discovered, public acclaim can throw private misery all the more clearly into focus. And for Cohen, as for his creator, no amount of worldly success could compensate for personal rejection.

The last days of March were relatively quite ones for Amy, but this was soon to change, as April and May were particularly busy months. According to her diary every waking moment was taken up with a hectic round of social calls or literary work. On 1st April she 'sent "Addenbroke" to Macmillans.' On the 3rd she gave a tea party and (unfortunately for her future biographers) 'Refused application fr. "Star" for interview'. On the 5th, she 'sat to E+' and afterwards 'wrote a sonnet "London Poets"'. E+ was a shorthand reference to Eleanor Cross, who had been her dining partner at Le Chat Noir. Was she painting Amy's portrait? Intriguingly, on 15th January 1890, the 'London Correspondent' of the *Glasgow Herald* reported that 'a portrait of the late Miss Amy Levy by a young Jewish artist will probably be seen at the Grosvenor [Gallery]'. Miss Cross was not Jewish, and there seems to be no trace of this portrait. But to return to Amy's diary, on 7th March she paid a visit 'to Berthas' and 'met Stepniak at the Fords.'[362] In the evening she dined with her friend Effie Stevens, but before retiring to bed read 'Salt's Life of James Thomson'. Despite this session of late-night reading, next morning she was up and out - off 'To Macmillans with poems'. These were the verses she had been collecting since her return from Italy, which were to be published under the title *A London Plane Tree*. On 9th April, after calling on a friend with Katie, she attended a lecture at the Somerville Club and then set to work correcting the proofs of *Miss Meredith*. Next day, after a further session of proofreading, she entertained Robert Garnett to tea and afterwards: 'M[argaret] Bateson dined and we went to [the] theatre'. On the 11th she once more spent the day correcting proofs, and in the evening attended a concert given by the Philharmonic with her friend Bertha Thomas.

After this she sat up late into the night 'read[ing] Swinburne's new poems'. On the day afterwards she again 'sat to E. Cross', 'dined at the Holborn with Tom S'[363] and then went on 'to [an] at home of [the] Fabian Society.' The following day's activities included another session of proof reading, a visit to the 'club' (the University Club for Ladies in Bond Street) and a further trip to the theatre to see 'Richard III with papa'. Clearly the pace of her social life was beginning to take its toll, for on the day after this she 'stayed in bed till 4', but rose in time to entertain 'Stepniak to tea' and 'Jenny [de Pass] to dinner'. The brief respite from her punishing daily schedule evidently failed to revive her flagging spirits, as on the day afterwards she was 'In bed all day'. Nevertheless, she still managed to summon up the energy to receive a bedside visitor – 'Jenny' - and to write a verse, 'The Old House'. Perhaps this was another commissioned piece, as on 19th April she recorded 'Called on Mrs. Joseph with Effie … ' "Old House" in "Spectator".' On the same day her family departed for Brighton and she went to stay at the Stevens' flat in Cromwell Road. Euphemia [Effie] Maulden Stevens (née Scott) had been Amy's schoolmate at the Brighton High School.

Her visit to the Stevens' set the pattern of her life for the next few weeks, as during this period her busy London agenda was punctuated by trips into the countryside to visit various friends. On 26th April she set off 'To Cambridge, to stay with the Francis Darwins.'[364] Three days later she returned briefly to town, but on 2nd May was off again, this time to 'Dorking with Jenny'. Here she renewed another old acquaintanceship; for on the day after her arrival she recorded that she had 'called on the Grant Allens & walked with them.' According to his friend Frank Harris, Allen was a delightful walking companion, as his interest 'in every human interest' made him a lively, if unremitting conversationalist.[365] Amy was always happy to listen and observe rather than to talk herself, and her pleasure in his company is evident from the fact that on each of the next seven days she met up with him at some stage. Like Pearson, Allen was a follower of Charles Darwin, and had a similar interest in the application of eugenic theory to the 'woman question'. But unlike Pearson, he chose to disseminate his ideas through lurid works of fiction rather than dry scientific treatises. Sadly, his abilities as a novelist did not match his skills as a conversationalist, for he was unable to create either a convincing character or a plausible plot. He had a particular penchant for peopling his narratives with intrepid 'Girton girls' whose advanced ideas ensured that they came to a sticky end; and his most daring creation of this genus was Herminia Barton, the New Woman heroine of *The Woman Who Did*. What Herminia 'did' caused a public outcry (thereby making Allen's fortune), for she chose – as a matter of principle – to cohabit with a man and bear his child outside wedlock. Although

The Woman Who Did did not appear in print until 1895, long after Amy's visit to Dorking, the issue of the morality of marriage was clearly uppermost in Allen's mind during her stay, as he took the opportunity to sound out her opinion on this and other related issues. On 12th May she recorded: 'Lunched with the Grant Allens .... Discussed the woman question in the evening. G. A. thinks marriage not a permanent inst.' In fact Allen may have gained more from the conversation than just Amy's opinion of the woman question, for in a striking number of aspects his heroine bears a marked resemblance to her. Like Amy, Herminia supports herself by journalism, writes poetry, socialises with Socialists and publishes a 'deeply pessimistic' novel. Allen's fictional title for this work, *A Woman's World*, echoes that of Oscar Wilde's *The Woman's World* – a journal to which at that time Amy was a regular contributor. At the dramatic dénouement of the tale Herminia takes her life – an outcome that Allen specifically links to the corrupting influence of her 'advanced' education. Shortly after Amy's own real-life suicide, he publicly singled her out as an example of the deleterious effects of what he termed the 'great movement ... for the Higher Instruction of Women'.[366] In view of the remarkable number of similarities between Allen's fictional heroine and Amy Levy, one cannot but wonder whether she provided him with the model of 'the woman who did'. Certainly Amy left her own literary tribute to her conversation with Allen. A manuscript copy of 'A Ballad of Religion and Marriage', her bitterly satirical riposte to his view of the woman question, has recently come to light amongst his papers, and the question of its significance will be discussed later.

A few days before setting off for her visit to the Darwins at Cambridge, Amy had noted laconically in her diary 'Macmillan chucks poems.' Undeterred by this setback she had set out the next morning for the offices of T. Fisher Unwin in Paternoster Row. Fisher Unwin had published her earlier collection of verse *A Minor Poet* in 1884, and upon her return from Dorking good news awaited her. On 13th May, she recorded: 'Fisher takes poems'. On 15th May she reported feeling 'seedy all day', but despite her indisposition she still managed to 'read a novel of Ouida's,' and on the day after was back in action once more: 'To Effie's and K's.' A few days after this she paid a visit to her dressmaker, presumably to prepare her wardrobe for the round of social events that followed. On 22nd May she held 'a party in my rooms (about 40).' On the 25th: 'Dined at the George Macmillans. Took in H.F. Wilson'[367] and on the 30th attended the 'Ladies Literary Dinner at Criterion' – to which she added the comment 'Mona Caird in the chair. I returned thanks for fiction'.

On 1st June the social correspondent of the *Star* reported:

> The ladies first dinner may be described as a success … Certainly the most interesting personage was the youthful and brilliant author of 'Reuben Sachs', the Jewess Miss Amy Levy. She has a charming animated face, and responded briefly to the toast to Fiction.

On 3rd June, three days after her triumphant appearance at the Ladies Literary Dinner, her diary entry for the day contained a rare personal comment: 'Began E (will it ever be finished?)'. This was followed by the information that she had 'Dined at the Stevens where I met Mr. Thicknesse.' 'To E' is the ominously prophetic swan song that brings *A London Plane Tree* to a close.[368] Although the poem is dedicated to Ellen Darwin (formerly Crofts), as we have seen, there are a number of clues within the text of the poem that identify Pearson as the leading member of the trio of 'Platonic friends' with whom Amy had shared pleasant afternoons basking in the sunshine on the shore of the little bathing lake of the Hotel Sonnenberg. This being the case, her encounter with his friend and travelling companion, Ralph Thicknesse, at the Stevens' flat would certainly have revived poignant memories of that happy interlude. Amy's enigmatic comment in her diary can therefore be read as an anguished cry of recognition that whilst Pearson's friends remained within her orbit she was unlikely to be able to put the past behind her

Like Tom Stevens, Ralph Thicknesse was a member of the second Men and Women's Club, which by that time was in its death throes. By the early summer of 1889 Pearson had followed Maria Sharpe to her holiday destination at Bergen in Norway and from that time onwards they were secretly engaged[369]. This was an unexpected development, as before this he had always emphatically declared that he would 'never marry'. His pursuit of Maria to Norway was also a reversal of the strategy that he had employed in the previous year, when he had attempted to inveigle her to join *him* on his annual holiday at Saig - just as he had persuaded Amy to join him there in 1884. On this occasion his proposal had been gently but firmly rebuffed by Maria in a letter which she addressed to 'Messrs Pearson and Thicknesse' at their Black Forest 'village retreat':.

> I was very pleased and touched to be remembered by you on your holiday, & very glad that you could send such good accounts of your enjoyment & welfare. … The idea of the 'unitary home' in the little inn sounds most delightful, too delightful to me to come true I think, as I am in rather a stern mood just now, trying to act in the 'living present'[370] with moderate good sense & 'trusting no future however pleasant!' From these sombre remarks it would not appear that I have quite got into a holiday humour.[371]

This last comment seems to be a sly allusion to Amy's short story 'In Holiday Humour', which she based upon her stay in Seelisberg, and which is headed with a quotation from *As You Like It:* 'Come woo me, woo me, for now I am in a holiday humour and like enough to consent.' As Judith Walkowitz pointed out, in her relationship with Pearson Maria Sharpe 'played her hand shrewdly.' Her behaviour was never anything less than correct. The comment in her letter suggests that she was aware of the details of Pearson's former friendship with Amy and that she was sending him an oblique message that she was not going to compromise her reputation by accepting his invitation to join 'the unitary home' at the inn at Saig – whatever her feelings for him might be.

Maria's introduction to Pearson and the Men and Women's Club had revolutionised her life, converting her to socialism and giving her the confidence to pursue her own research, and to lay claim to a room in the family home in which to work. Her membership of the club had also given her a theoretical insight into various aspects of the woman question, and this had inspired her to undertake a study of the work of the pioneering Norwegian dramatist Henrik Ibsen. She applied herself assiduously to this task both in the newly acquired room of her own and in the Reading Room of the British Museum. Amy's diary reveals that she made visits to the Reading Room in February, March, late June and July 1889 (by which time Maria was in Bergen) but none in April and May. Maria would have been working in the Museum during these two months, which might explain Amy's absence from the Reading Room at this time. In early June Maria's efforts were rewarded when her club paper, 'Henrik Ibsen: His Men and Women', was published in the *Westminster Review*. The publication of the article coincided with the opening of London's first unbowdlerised production of Ibsen's A Doll's House, which was privately staged at the Novelty Theatre. On the opening night, on Friday 7th June, Pearson booked a dozen tickets in the dress circle. As well as Maria and other former members of the Men and Women's Club, his party included three of Amy's closest friends, Olive Schreiner, Dollie Radford and Eleanor Marx. The latter was a surprising addition to the group, given Maria's earlier opposition to the suggestion that she should be invited to join the club. Amy was not included in the party, although she was in London on that day. According to her diary, on the afternoon of Pearson's theatre outing she visited her neighbours, the Rossettis, where there was 'good singing'. Arthur Symons, who was also at the Rossettis' musical 'at home', noted Amy's presence there.[372] He had come to London with the express purpose of seeing Ibsen's play and, like Pearson, had tickets for the first night. While in town he also met up with Olive Schreiner, and later noted that on the following Monday they spent the afternoon discussing, amongst other things, 'the play we had both seen on Friday'.[373]Because of the controversial nature of the play, it is likely that Symons discussed the forthcoming evening at the Rossettis' afternoon gathering.

On the day after her encounter with Symons at the Rossettis' house Amy spent some time sitting with her old friend Jenny de Pass 'in Kensington Gardens.' After this the entries in her diary become increasingly scrawled and perfunctory. From mid-June she seemed unable to settle anywhere for any length of time. After paying a further visit to the Grant Allens at Dorking, she made an excursion 'To Cassiobury Park by myself for the day.' On the day after her solitary vigil in Cassiobury Park she went 'To Pangbourne with Bertha [Thomas]' where she recorded that the pair 'rowed to Goring & back (9 miles).' Throughout the next month, Bertha evidently made valiant – and strenuous – efforts to distract her friend from her misery. On 29th July they once again: 'Rowed from Pangbourne to Goring' – but on this occasion making the return trip on the following day. After this Amy noted that the gallant Bertha returned (no doubt thankfully) 'to London.' Bertha Thomas' kindness to Levy is commemorated in her poem 'The End of the Day', which is dedicated 'to B. T.' The verse describes the pleasure of physical exhaustion, which induces 'divine indifference':

> Where grief a shadow grows to be,
> And peace a possibility.[374]

On the day after her first river outing with Bertha Thomas, Amy recorded that she had been 'To Olive Schreiner's with Effie.' Pearson's invitation to Olive to join his theatre party had evidently healed the rift between them. Although she strenuously denied it, all those who knew them both well were in no doubt that she was in love with him; but in 1886 they had fallen out in a dispute that involved Maria Sharpe's sister, Elizabeth Cobb. Pearson's vindictive behaviour in the aftermath of their quarrel had driven Olive into a period of self-imposed exile on the continent. By 1889 she had decided to return to her native South Africa, and came back to London in early April to prepare for her departure for the Cape. The rift between Olive Schreiner and Pearson had been caused by what Olive's biographer Phyllis Grosskirth has labelled 'The Hinton Imbroglio'. James Hinton's *Life and Nature* was a highly influential text for nineteenth-century freethinkers. He advocated a philosophy of free love, a return to nature to counter the pernicious influence of Victorian morality, which he defined as 'those vile laws that make man a beast and crush woman to hell.' The early meetings of the Men and Women's Club had been beset by disputes about 'Hintonism'. On the one hand the members were attracted by his repudiation of 'Victorian values', but on the other were alarmed by his supposed advocacy of nudism and polygamy. Pearson took it upon himself to discover the truth about Hinton's view of these matters, and to this end applied for information to a club associate and his former pupil, the novelist Emma Brooke. She had known Hinton when she was a girl, and in reply to Pearson's enquiries regaled him with a lurid account of Hinton's behaviour on an occasion when she had found herself alone in his company. Acting upon his own dictum that 'there are no things you may not do if love and the service of your fellows command them', he had tried to force himself upon her, justifying his behaviour on the grounds that it would be 'ennobling' for her, and of service to him, were she to 'sacrifice' herself in order to satisfy his 'needs'. She told Pearson:

> It does not take so much to confuse the ideas of right and wrong in a girl's head and to set her out in life with the persuasion that to "Sacrifice" herself for a man she loves is both ennobling and necessary. But this was Hinton's method with girls and while seducing their minds ... he helped himself liberally to such favours as he could get by the way.[375]

Pearson seized upon this juicy nugget with delight, as it confirmed his suspicions about the dubious doctor.

Unfortunately for all parties concerned, Olive had struck up a friendship with Hinton's sister-in-law, Caroline Haddon. Miss Haddon had been invited to attend a meeting of the club and had been so delighted with it that she had described it enthusiastically as 'Hintonian'. Pearson was outraged. Although by this time Olive harboured doubts about Hinton herself, she took Caroline Haddon's side in the dispute, writing to Havelock Ellis: 'I'm going to stick up for Miss Haddon like old boots. Compared to those white-washed sepulchres, the Hintonians are simply saints.' Just who the 'white-washed sepulchres' were she did not say, but a hint of the identity of one of them is contained in the series of letters that she exchanged with Pearson after Hinton's son was arrested for bigamy. When Pearson heard news of the arrest he was triumphant – his mistrust of Hinton had been vindicated. Schreiner wrote pleadingly to him

> There is something I want to say to you. I've wanted to say it to you for a long time. You of all people would be the best to combat the Hinton-theory. Your head is clear and true, but the fear comes to me 'What if in doing it he were fighting for himself?' Long ago when I read that sentence in your club paper it put me in such a rage ... I couldn't speak to you about that sentence ...because I felt I hadn't a right to. It was a kind of personal matter, and didn't bear on the general subject. Afterwards I heard it implied that you were an Hintonian. It made me very bitter. Now have you not perhaps heard this; have you not thought bitterly of that sentence and wished it unwritten?[376]

The sentence in question is in the section of Pearson's paper 'The Woman's Question,' in which he speaks of the position of 'single women in the community':

> The writer of a recent pamphlet has spoken of the stifled cry of the un-married woman .... 'Give me Children or I die'. It is an open question how far there is a physiological basis to this cry. It has, however, led certain disciples of James Hinton to replace his chief argument for polygamy, namely, the evil of unsatisfied sexual desire, by an appeal to the insatiable and passionate wish of women to give society what they alone can give.[377]

Olive evidently had in mind Pearson's reference to Hinton's belief in 'the evil of unsatisfied sexual desire,' which he indirectly appeared to endorse. She continued:

> Is there no little element of self, the desire to right yourself in your bitterness against Hinton? Look deep into your heart and see. It would be such a terrible thing if while you seemed to be fighting only for abstract truth and right there was an element of self in it! I can't bear to think of this. You must be so absolutely pure and fleckless. ... You *must* look into your own heart, and see if all your hatred against Hinton is abstract. Is there no element of selfishness, is there nothing that Karl Pearson has suffered that influences you .... The great danger which we who would fight for or lead humanity have to guard against is the mixing up of our personal interest with the things we fight for ....

Had Olive heard rumours of the Amy Levy debacle, and was she alluding to this in her letter? Although Pearson took rapid steps to reassure her about his impartiality on 'the Hinton question', shortly afterwards he seized upon her objection to his having discussed her attitude to the Hinton affair with Elizabeth Cobb as an excuse to sever their relationship. The brutal manner in which he abruptly broke off all communication with her recalls his earlier callous treatment of Amy. At this point Schreiner's fragile *sang froid* gave way. She collapsed, both physically and mentally. Her friend Brian Donkin (Eleanor Marx's physician) was so concerned about her state of mind and the possible consequences that might ensue that he wrote a stern letter to Pearson, reminding him of his responsibility in the matter. When Olive discovered what Donkin had done she was utterly dismayed, and sent the following contrite message to Pearson:

> I am afraid Dr. Donkin in the kindness must have written to you telling you I was very bad. I'm much better than last week .... Don't trouble to come if busy. And please, we won't mention Mrs. Cobb and you'll just have talk about our work, like we used to have last year when you came to see me .... Don't come unless you want to please .... Thank you for speaking so truthfully to me.[378]

Pearson ignored this pathetic plea, and Olive left for Switzerland without seeing him again. On 8th January 1887, she wrote to Edward Carpenter:

> I made a great mistake in not seeing Mr. Pearson even in the distance before I left. I spent all the last days waiting in the rain before University College hoping to catch a glimpse of him as he passed, but I didn't. I felt so when my father died.[379]

For the next two years she wandered from place to place, trying, without success, to cast Pearson from her mind. On 10th January 1889, she wrote to Carpenter from Mentone:

> Thank you, dear old Edward, for your letter. Thank you for telling me you had seen my friend Karl Pearson. I knew you would love him if you ever met him...I wish sometimes I could just take his hand for a moment and sit and talk over those matters that interest us, or better still sit and say nothing at all...'.[380]

In April 1889, Olive returned to England. By this time she was clearly on the brink of a breakdown. In March she had been suffering from paranoid delusions, and on 18th April had written in despair to her friend and former lover Havelock Ellis: 'Harry, the world isn't fair, I haven't sinned so much more than other people to be hunted down so. If it goes on a little more I will kill myself ... I will try to finish my book and then I will kill myself.'[381] By the beginning of April she was back in London, but was soon off again to Eastbourne. She confessed to Ellis: 'I don't mind if I keep out of London. Isn't it funny I can't feel any more.'[382] By 23rd June, she was in a more positive frame of mind, reporting to Ellis: Yes, I am better than I have ever been in England .... That Friday night when I went to see *Nora* [383] ... did me good.' It appears that the olive branch that Pearson had offered in the form of the theatre invitation had restored her faith in him. But by early July she had suffered a reverse. She confided to Ellis:

> I was very well and strong till — and — came; I now feel like a little child hardly able to creep from one room to another. You can't understand that to feel any human creature hopelessly false is more terrible to me than all poverty, all loneliness, all death. The fact of a nature such as Edward Aveling's, for instance, is more terrible to me ... than all the close sorrows of my personal life. The thing which ... alone touches me quite close, is anything bearing on my conception of human nature. ... I care nothing for fame or success and still less for love, —'s or any one else. I want — to be noble, and want myself to be so.[384]

Although the identity of the 'hopelessly false' 'human creature' that betrayed Olive's faith in human nature has been expunged from the letter there is every reason to believe that she was referring to Pearson. The letter is dated 6th July. During the last week of June and the first week of July, Amy visited Schreiner three times, on one occasion accompanied by Effie Stevens. It seems that they may have been the visitors who finally confirmed Olive's suspicions about Pearson's ostensibly disinterested pursuit of James Hinton.

Just after her fateful visit to Olive Schreiner, Amy was reunited with her old Florentine friends Bella Duffy and Vernon Lee. On 19th July, she reported that after visiting 'Mrs. Rossetti's' she had tea with 'Bella' at the 'club'. Next day she 'called on Vernon Lee who was in town for a few days.' At this point there is a discernible improvement in the handwriting in her diary. On the following day she 'Had tea at Bella Duffy's … we talked of the Soul', a subject which seems to have been uppermost in her mind at this period. On 24th July she 'Lunched with Effie. With her to Bella Duffy's.' But on 27th July she met up with Olive Schreiner once again. Amy had not seen her for over three weeks, since which time Olive had written the letter to Ellis. After this date, Amy's handwriting deteriorates once more. On the last days of July she spent yet more time rowing up and down the Thames between Pangbourne and Goring, with Bertha Thomas.

August saw a further marked decline in the handwriting of the entries in the diary. On 6th August she set off on a picnic, followed by another aquatic trip, 'on the canal' to visit 'J' (probably Jenny de Pass) with 'Alfred Goodman [Levy]' – her cousin. The spaces in the diary between 7th and 29th August are scrawled across with the words: 'ill at Endsleigh Gardens, corrected proofs of *A London Plane Tree* etc.' At some time during this interval Amy received an invitation to stay with Vernon Lee, Kit Anstruther-Thomson and Evelyn Wimbush at the holiday cottage they had rented at Ben Rhydding, near Ilkeley. Perhaps because of the unhappy associations of the place where her now-dead brother had spent a period of convalescence in 1885 Amy sent an uncharacteristically stilted reply to this kind offer:

> My dear Miss Paget,
>
> I have put off answering yr. most kind note, as I wished to think it over. I can't tell you how good I think it of you to have asked me to stay with you, &, had circumstances been otherwise I shd. have been delighted to come. But I'm not well – either in soul or body – & I have refused all invitations to stay with my friends. And I must refuse yrs. too, one of the most attractive ….[385]

Amy was clearly being economical with the truth when she told Lee that she had 'refused all invitations', as on 28th August Olive wrote to Ellis: 'This letter of Amy's may interest you. … I am going to St. Leonards with Amy Levy from Saturday to Tuesday as my chest is getting worse.'[386] Amy's entry in her diary for 31st August reads: 'to St. Leonards and Folkestone with Olive Schreiner.' Their stay at St. Leonards was very brief, as on the same day, 31st August, Olive wrote to Ellis from Folkestone: 'We had to come on here because Amy Levy didn't like St. Leonards.' The town had unhappy associations for Olive, as she had first met Elizabeth Cobb there. She may have mentioned this fact to Amy – thus reviving unhappy memories for her also. On 1st September the pair were off again – as Amy recorded – 'To Margaret's Bay with O.S.' On 2nd September – in accordance with the timetable given by Olive to Ellis – they returned 'Back to London.' On 3rd September Amy set off again, this time by herself, to St. Albans.

On 10th August, Pearson had made a request to Maria Sharpe: 'There is just one thing I wish to do, when you will allow me to think of the matter [of our marriage] as settled – to let Mrs. Wilsonccclxxxvii tell Olive Schreiner. It is just possible that it might be helpful, and if one has only had an idle fancy it can do no harm.' It appears from later letters that Charlotte Wilson exchanged with Pearson that she had indeed broken the news of his engagement to Olive, as he had asked Maria to allow her to do. As Pearson had consistently maintained that he 'would never marry' it is inconceivable that Olive (who was not noted for either taciturnity or discretion) would have been able to resist discussing the matter with Amy.

Amy made the final scrawled brief entry in her diary, 'alone at home all day,' on 8th September. On the following evening she sealed herself into the small room in her parents' house at Endsleigh Gardens, lit the charcoal fire in the grate, went to sleep, and died some time during the night. According to her wish, her body was cremated, on Friday 13th September. The sole attendants at this last sad rite were the Rabbi of the West London Synagogue and Tom Stevens, the husband of her faithful friend Effie. In life, Amy had achieved the distinction of becoming the first Jewish woman to study at Cambridge. In death, she achieved a second, less happy, distinction, by becoming the first Jewish woman to be cremated in this country.

The Aftermath: 1889 and Beyond

She chose to die.
Grave here, beneath our helpless flowers,
'She chose to die' –

Ernest Radford 1857-1919: Tribute to Amy Levy: *The Pall Mall Gazette*

On Sunday 15th September the small oak coffer containing Amy Levy's ashes was interred at the Jewish Cemetery in the Balls Pond Road. The *Globe* reported:

> The custom of ladies attending Jewish funerals is being slowly adopted, and there was quite a number of them at the cemetery. The service is simple and touching .... The coffin or chest, covered with floral offerings ... is placed upon a bier ... and the minister standing in front reads the burial service. .... When the grave is reached a few appropriate sentences from the Scripture are recited, comparing man to the transient blossom of the field ... [388]

No sooner had Amy been laid to rest, than rumours began to circulate about the reason for her suicide. Ten days later, on 24th September, Ernest Radford's poetic tribute to Amy, 'An Inscription for an Urn', was published in the *Pall Mall Gazette*. The verse expresses his bewilderment at the unnecessary waste of life displayed in the manner of her death. And his reference to the funeral flowers is followed by lines that could be interpreted as a cryptic reference to his friend Karl Pearson:

She chose to die.
Grave here, beneath our helpless flowers,
'She chose to die' –
Alas! the sun forsook her sky
Whatwhile he gladdened other bowers.
She tasted life – a few sad hours –
Then chose to die.[389]

Two days after this, the paper published Grant Allen's poetic tribute to the friend with whom he had so recently tramped the Surrey hills discussing 'the woman question'. His verse includes a similar reference to Amy's 'sunless' existence, which he attributes to the pressure of the age in which she lived:

This bitter age that pits our maids with men
Wore out her woman's heart before its time.

Too wan and pale
She strove to scale
The icy peaks of unimagined rhyme.
There worlds broke sunless on her frightened ken;
The mountain air struck chill on her frail breath.
Fainting she fell, all weary with her climb,
And kissed the soft sweet lips of pitying death.[390]

Clementina Black's sister Grace had taken upon herself the sad task of breaking the news of Amy's death to Ernest and Dollie Radford. On 16 September, a week before Ernest's verse appeared in the *Pall Mall Gazette*, she sent them the following letter:

> Clemmie wrote to me on Friday this:– 'When I arrived here on Tuesday morning I found the woman who was in charge of the house at Endsleigh Gardens had been to say Amy was ill and would I come round. I went as soon as I had had some breakfast expecting to find her slightly unwell and found Mrs. Levy and Katie in the most terrible grief. She had got charcoal, shut herself into a little room and so painlessly killed herself during the night.'
>
> That is all I know.
>
> I had thought she had been so much more hopeful and happy lately. She certainly seemed so. If she had only had more patience!
>
> I cannot bear that this should grieve Dollie: as I know it must.[391]

The Radfords were still mourning the death of their friend and fellow club member Louis Jeeves, who had died unexpectedly from diphtheria in 1888. However, although there are several references to Louis' death in their diary and correspondence, they made no mention of Amy's suicide save for the brief, retrospective reference to 'Amy Levy's death' made by Ernest in Dollie's diary in mid-November 1889.[392] Grace Black does not say when she last saw Amy, but the fact that Clementina had taken the time to eat breakfast before leaving for Endsleigh Gardens, and her comment that she had expected to find Amy 'slightly unwell', implies that similar requests had been made before, and were not to be taken too seriously. Amy had certainly been unwell in the last weeks of her life, and had looked to her friends for emotional support. She did not attend Conny Black's wedding in Brighton on 31st August, because this was the day that she set off 'to St. Leonards and Folkestone with Olive Schreiner.' Evidently she was still in the same restless frame of mind that she had been in in July, when she and Bertha Thomas had repeatedly rowed up and down the river to Pangbourne. On the day that they left London Olive wrote to Havelock Ellis: 'We had to come on here [to Folkestone] because Amy Levy didn't like St. Leonards'.[393]

Like Grace Black, Olive had been one of the first to hear the news of Amy's suicide. On 11th September she had written to Edward Carpenter:

> I should have written yesterday but I had had a blow that somewhat unfitted me. My dear friend Amy Levy had died the night before. She killed herself by shutting herself up in a room with charcoal. We were away together for three days last week. But it did not seem to help her; her agony had gone past human help.
>
> The last thing I sent her was the 'Have Faith' page of *Towards Democracy*.[394] She wrote me back a little note, 'Thank you, it is very beautiful, but philosophy can't help me. I am much too shut in with the personal.' You need not refer to this when you write I only tell you that you may know why I didn't write sooner.[395]

Olive does not divulge who told her the news of Amy's death, but her request to Carpenter that 'You need not refer to this when you write, I only tell you that you may know why I didn't write sooner' is the first sign that those who had been closest to Amy were attempting to prevent the news from spreading. In a letter that he wrote to James Dykes Campbell[396] in mid-September Arthur Symons made a similar request. The erratic way in which the letter is phrased suggests that at the time of writing it he was apparently in a state of nervous fluster:

> My dear Campbell,
>
> Have your heard? – Amy Levy killed herself – with charcoal fumes. I have only heard that, and that she 'wanted to be happy.' ... I cannot tell you how sorry I am. I never knew her – only once saw her [at the Rossettis] – but Miss Schreiner was very anxious for us to meet, as she thought we should like each other. It will be a great blow to O.S. ... I know how sorry you will be. Don't mention anything of this to anyone, unless it becomes generally known.[397]

Symonds' claim 'I have only heard that' matches Grace Black's emphatic statement in her letter to the Radfords: 'That is all I know'. Likewise, Olive's insistence to Carpenter that 'You need not refer to this when you write' and Symons' request to Dykes Campbell that the matter not be mentioned to anyone 'unless it becomes generally known' suggest that they were aware that rumours were beginning to circulate, and that they were attempting to stem the flow of gossip. But because of Amy's public profile, and the sensational way in which she met her end, their efforts were destined to be in vain.

On 17th September the *Star* recorded:

> Everyone is regretting the death of Miss Amy Levy .... Only last week Miss Levy was at Hastings with Olive Schreiner. One's regrets for the loss of so promising a young writer are deepened by the knowledge that her life was not a very happy one. But of that nothing further should be said; it is enough to say that in self-denial, honest work and devotion to duty Miss Amy Levy won a place even higher than that to which, in her literature, her genius entitled her.[398]

This enigmatic notice by an unnamed correspondent gives the first hint that Amy's death was being linked with Olive Schreiner. It was later claimed that Amy's suicide 'caused a sensation in literary London. Rumours were afloat – rumours which persisted for years.'[399] These rumours were linked with the following paragraph, which appeared in the 'Occasional Notes' column of the *Pall Mall Gazette* on 1st April 1892:

> Agreements to commit suicide are all very well, but how can one party to such an agreement be sure that the other will keep it? There was a case in point yesterday at the Marylebone police court .... The story recalls a similar, but more tragic, occurrence not many years ago in which two literary ladies were the actors. These authors – one of whom is widely famous – were spending a holiday at the seaside together, and both were indulging in very gloomy views of life. After discussing the question, they both agreed to commit suicide, and the younger hurried home and but too effectively carried out her purpose. The other happily thought better of the matter, and refused to fulfil her terms of the contract. The only pity is that she did not let the other party to the agreement know in time. But that is the standing difficulty in the way of compact to commit suicide.[400]

Of course, given the date of its publication, the paragraph was probably intended to be read as an April fool's joke. But Olive Schreiner took it seriously. On 23rd April she wrote to her former lover Havelock Ellis, enclosing a copy of the cutting:

> A funny idea has struck me about the enclosed cutting, that perhaps I am meant! So many lies have been told about me already that I now wonder nothing .... What makes it likely that I am meant is that it is exactly the *opposite* of the truth; I was always trying to cheer up Amy Levy (if it be intended for her) and professing that I found life so delightful and worth living .... In her last note to me she said 'You care for science and art and helping your fellow-men, therefore life is worth living for you: to me it is worth nothing', and the last thing that I sent her was Edward Carpenter's 'Do not hurry, have faith', which she sent back to me the night before her death with the words. 'It might have helped me once; it is too late now; philosophy cannot help me.' [401]

Olive was clearly being economical with the truth in her protestation to Ellis, as she must have known perfectly well that she and Amy were the literary ladies in question. The tone of the letter suggests that she sent Ellis the cutting in order to gauge his reaction, as she seems to have suspected, with some justification, that he was the perpetrator of the rumour. During her period of self-imposed exile on the Continent, after Pearson had so abruptly and callously broken off their relationship, she had written to Ellis from Mentone. At that time she was obviously on the brink of a breakdown, suffering from delusions. In her letter she poured her heart out to him, declaring: 'If it goes on a little more I will kill myself … I will try to finish my book and then I will kill myself'. In a postscript she had pleaded: 'Harry you mustn't talk about this to anyone.'[402] But perhaps Harry had talked. On 18th September 1889, the day after the obituary containing the information that Amy had been on holiday with Olive just days before she took her life appeared in the *Star*, Ellis set off with Arthur Symonds to spend a week in Paris exploring the Exposition Universelle.[403] Given the fact that both men knew both Olive and Amy, it is inconceivable that they did not discuss the sensational news of Amy's suicide at some point during their trip.

By the time that Amy died, Ellis and Pearson were not on the best of terms. Before Olive met Pearson she and Ellis had been lovers, but (on her side at least) the relationship had begun to cool, and after she had been introduced to the fascinating young Professor she promptly transferred her affections to him, although she still managed to retain Ellis' friendship, straining it to the limit by constantly regaling him with details of her problems with Pearson. At that time Ellis was a devoted follower of James Hinton. When others of his circle, in particular Pearson, began to question Hinton's motives, he remained doggedly loyal to the dubious doctor, largely because Hinton's sister-in-law Caroline Haddon had financed his medical studies, thus enabling him to become a doctor himself. During the 'Hinton Imbroglio' Miss Haddon had broken down under Pearson's relentless pressure, and Ellis wrote him a strong letter of protest.[404] Pearson had never warmed to Ellis, and never forgave him for supporting Hinton.[405] In the end the uneasy truce between the two men collapsed. In the 1930s Ellis wrote to a friend: 'I have always admired Pearson's work. Personally I have experienced both his pleasant and unpleasant sides … he withdrew his *Grammar of Science* from my [Contemporary Science Series], without a word to me. I know other cases in which he had behaved the same way, only much more brutally. There must be an element of morbidity in it …'[406] Ellis was undoubtedly thinking of Pearson's treatment of Olive when he wrote these words but his use of the plural suggests that hers was not the only case that was in his mind at the time.

By early October 1889, Amy's family and close friends were becoming increasingly concerned about the rumours that were circulating in the press. Their anxiety is revealed in a letter that Clementina Black wrote to the editor of the *Athenaeum* with the objective, she said, of doing 'justice to both the dead and the living'. The letter began with the emphatic declaration: 'I was a close friend of Miss Levy for many years, and my testimony is that of personal knowledge'. It continued:

> It is not true that she ever left her father's house otherwise than on visits to friends or holiday journeys; nor that she suffered from failing eyesight, nor from the loss of her sense of humour .... She did suffer for several years from slight deafness and from fits of extreme depression, not the result of unhappy circumstances or of unkind treatment, but, as those believe who knew her best, of her lack of physical robustness and of the exhaustion of strenuous brain work. Most emphatically, it is not true that her family and her personal friends among the Jewish community treated her coldly on account of the publication of 'Reuben Sachs'.... Her parents were justly proud of her; it was impossible to be more uniformly indulgent, more anxious to anticipate her every wish than they were. At the time of her death they were out of town; but she had been with them a only few days before, had parted with them on the best of terms and was expected to rejoin them the next week. Her sister was with her on the afternoon before her death, and from her also parted affectionately....[407]

This letter was mentioned in notices which appeared in both the *Star* and the *St. James' Gazette*.[408] The latter appeared the day *before* Clementina's letter appeared in the *Athenaeum*, suggesting that either the letter was syndicated, or that the editor of the *Athenaeum* had released details of the contents to other colleagues in the press. This in itself is an indication of the growing level of public interest in the enigma of Amy's death.

Clementina Black's ire had been specifically aroused by an obituary notice that appeared in *The Ladies Pictorial* in October 1889. The unattributed author of the piece recited an extravagant litany of distorted facts, including the claim that Amy had ranked herself 'with passionate feeling amongst the poor of the East [End]', and continuing:

> With mental power to attack the problems of the age, she lacked in a pitiable degree the bodily vigour to sustain her in fight .... Sharing to a large extent the views upon religious belief of which her friend Olive Schreiner has made brilliant confession in her famous book [*The Story of an African Farm*], Miss Levy, by instinct simple and trustful as a child, once more found her nature at deadly feud with her intellectual conclusions.
>
> Denied the cravings of her heart, full of doubt as to the empty negation she professed, a terrible unrest settled on her, and all that was clear to her few friends was that her health was rapidly growing worse. So weak had she become that during the last year her literary work was practically nil, and this tightened the grip of hopelessness in which she lay. With failing sight and growing deafness, Miss Levy suffered so intensely that she thought a day passed painlessly was worth a special line in her diary. The sparkling humour died out; all satisfaction from the fame she had won faded from memory, and in absolute loneliness, friends and family far away from her, the sad end came. Within a day the proof sheet arrived of her last story, just accepted for *The Woman's World*, in the pages of which her pathetic death will be found foreshadowed.

The phrase 'Denied the cravings of her heart' appears to hint at a romantic disappointment. And, once again, this enigmatic statement was preceded by a reference to Olive Schreiner. But most significantly, whomsoever the author was, he or she was evidently familiar with Amy's (at that date) unpublished short story, 'Wise in her Generation', in which she gave full and frank expression to her disillusionment with life. This story, one of her most powerful pieces of prose writing, was eventually published in Oscar Wilde's *The Woman's World* in 1890. The extraordinary mélange of distorted fact, hyperbolic language but also penetrating insight which marks the obituary suggests that Wilde himself was the author, as a less overstated version of the claims made about Amy's health in the *Lady's Pictorial* is repeated at the end of his own later tribute to Amy in *The Woman's World*:[409]

> The loss is the world's, but perhaps not hers. She was never robust; not often actually ill, but seldom well enough to feel life a joy instead of a burden; and her work was not poured out lightly, but drawn drop by drop from the very depths of her own feeling. We may say of it that it was in truth her life's blood.[410]

The impression that Wilde was the author of the article in the *Lady's Pictorial* is reinforced by Louise Chandler Moulton's report of his comments on Amy, which she included in her regular column in the *Boston Herald* on 17th March 1889. 'I first heard of Amy Levy in the autumn of 1887', she wrote:

> Oscar Wilde had assumed editorship of 'The Woman's World', and was telling me his plans for the new number, which was to be issued in December of '87. 'The most wonderful thing in the number,' he said, 'will be a story, one page long, by Amy Levy, the daughter of Levy of the Daily Telegraph - a mere girl, but a girl of genius.'[411]

The then Editor of the *Daily Telegraph* Joseph Moses Levy was not related to Amy, so it seems that whatever Wilde knew or thought he knew about her at that time, he did not know much about her family.[412] The story that he had eulogised to Louise Chandler Moulton was 'A Recent Telepathic Occurrence at the British Museum'.[413] In October 1887 he had written to Amy: 'I hope you will send me another short story. I think your method as admirable as it is unique. I am having your article on clubs illustrated.'[414] Amy's essay 'Women and Club Life' appeared in *The Woman's World* in June 1888.[415]

'A Recent Telepathic Occurrence at the British Museum' is, as Wilde said, a very short story indeed. It drew upon Amy's knowledge of the activities of the Society for Psychical Research. Whilst staying with 'the Francis Darwins' in April 1889, she had noted in her diary that she had visited 'Frank Myers' and 'talked of the immortality of the soul'.[416] Frederic Myers, who was one of the Society's founders, was a close friend of Francis Darwin. He first coined the term 'telepathy', which he described as 'a mutual gravitation or kinship of spirits'. Amy's story describes a telepathic incident of this kind, a 'crisis apparition', which is an occurrence in which the image of a person in a state of extreme stress (for instance, on the point of death) appears before an absent friend or relative.

The narrative commences with a typical Victorian deathbed scene. A young girl lies dying surrounded by grieving relatives and friends. She does not fear death, indeed, she seems to welcome it. Her only regret on parting from life is that her secret will die with her. This secret, which is 'sapping [her] young life at the very spring', is her undeclared, unrequited love for a young Professor. The scene then shifts to the Reading Room of the British Museum, where the Professor sits poring over his books. Grumbling to himself about the disruptive presence of women in the Reading Room – 'They've no business to have women here at all' (at that time the male Readers tended to resent the incursion of women into what they regarded as their exclusive territory)[417] his attention is suddenly caught by a young woman standing nearby. '*She* here! She of all people; here of all places in the world' he thinks to himself. 'What had brought her? What accursed feminine impulse had prompted her to disturb him, to come between him and his work'. Mentally cursing, 'Get thee behind me Satan!' he returns to his books. But at that moment 'the great dim globes' in the vast glass dome of the Reading Room are illuminated, the Professor raises his head, and involuntarily glances towards where the young woman had been standing, only to discover that she has disappeared without a sound, not even the 'oft-vituperated rustle of feminine skirts'. Angrily leaping to his feet he vows: 'She should not escape him thus; for once, from his own lips she should hear what he thought of her'. But to no avail, the woman has apparently vanished into thin air. A few hours later, on his way home, someone stops him in the street and tells him that the young woman is dead. Reeling from shock, the Professor stumbles up the staircase of his lodging house to his room where:

> Crouched there by the table, his head bowed over the papers and manuscripts, he saw it all as by a flash – saw it and understood.
>
> She had thought that it would die with her, the poor secret, so jealously guarded. Love, stronger than death, and for once more merciful had betrayed her. For two people knew it now - her secret, which was also his.

Amy's description of the Professor bears some resemblance to her now absent friend, Karl Pearson: 'The Professor was young (as Professors go), but already he was growing bald at the temples, and much poring over manuscripts had made eye glasses a necessity for eyes that had once been as keen as a hawk's'. In 1884 Robert Parker had written to Pearson: 'You know you really must take care of your eyes! You ought to have seen about them long ago'[418]. And in a letter to Maria Sharpe written during their secret engagement, Pearson had complained that his hair was 'disappearing with alarming rapidity'.[419] A picture taken in 1896 reveals that by then his hair had entirely receded at the temples, leaving just a small peak at the centre of the crown. The professor's petulant complaint about the unexpected arrival of the young woman beside his desk, also apparently mimics Pearson's habitual grumbling that Olive Schreiner satirised in her letters: '(*Professor K. Pearson to himself*) "This benighted individual wants one to go running about after every fourth woman in London; and at the same time expects one to produce work that shall stand the test of the ages! Humph!" ...'[420] Whether any of Amy's friends would have recognised the resemblance between her fictional professor and her former friend is a matter for conjecture. What is certain is that two years after Wilde's request to Amy for 'another story' like 'A Telegraphic Occurrence', her own 'secret' had died with her.

But who might have known Amy's secret, and what were its consequences for those she left behind? If Lucy Marks' memory served her correctly, Amy's distraught family believed that her suicide was caused by 'an unhappy love affair.'[421] This directly contradicts Clementina Black's statement in her letter to the *Athenaeum* that 'those who knew her best' believed her depression was 'not the result of unhappy circumstances or of unkind treatment, but ... her lack of physical robustness and of the exhaustion of strenuous brain work.' This assertion is also at odds with Amy's own account of her state of mind on the evening before her death, when she wrote to Olive Schreiner that she was 'too shut in with the personal'. This implies that rather than her being in a state of general malaise, there was a specific issue preying on her mind. Although she would have been unable to admit it to anyone else, Olive probably knew what that issue was, as she had been the one to break the news of Pearson's engagement to Amy, and would therefore have witnessed at first hand her reaction to this unexpected blow. Olive's request to Edward Carpenter that he should not mention Amy's death in his reply to her note suggests that she wished to put an end to any further discussion of the matter. She may have hoped by that by refusing to talk about it, her connection with the unhappy event would soon be forgotten. But her hope was in vain, as an even more dramatic development was about to occur.

Pearson evidently harboured some guilt about his past behaviour, for in a letter written from Saig, dated 8th September 1889 (just two days before Amy committed suicide), he had unburdened his conscience to Maria Sharpe, confessing that: 'In the friendship of men and women it is very very hard to draw the line of what is kind and what is unkind'. He continued:

> To simply say such friendship is impossible; here are my thoughts ...There is too much that men and women want from each other, and yet it is so difficult to give and take freely. Believe me, I have found it, especially in the years gone by, so hard to do without woman's friendship and yet seen that, however cautious and self-controlled one might be oneself, there was always danger, perhaps evil produced which one would

> have done anything to avoid. *It was just such experience* [my emphasis – was this a reference to Amy?] that led me to tell Olive Schreiner at the beginning of our friendship that it should and could only be the free open friendship of man to man. Anything I have written to her you could and might read.[422]

Pearson returned to London on 12th September, two days after Amy's death. Immediately upon his return he paid a visit to his mother at Pinner, and does not seem to have had any contact with his Cambridge or British Museum friends until later in the month. When Maria returned to England four days later, on 16th September, she likewise went directly to her family home in Highbury. As the first obituary notices on Amy did not appear in the press until around 18th September, it is quite possible that neither Maria nor Pearson were aware of her death until after this date. On 21st September Pearson told Maria that he was 'just off to the [British] Museum.' He may have first heard the news there. On the same day, Parker wrote to congratulate Pearson on his engagement.[423]

Not long after this, Maria Sharpe underwent a severe emotional crisis, broke off her engagement and refused to see Pearson for several months. The letters that she wrote to him during the period from mid-August to early October 1889 were later destroyed, at her request.[424] According to Elizabeth Cobb, Maria had become 'utterly unlike herself.'[425] The explanation given by her and by members of Pearson's family for this precipitate change of heart was that Maria (who was by this time in her late-thirties) had taken fright at the realisation that she was several years older than her fiancé.[426] But in a letter to Robert Parker, dated 30th September 1889, Pearson explicitly contradicted this unsatisfactory explanation. He wrote: 'Mrs. Cobb & the others want to believe she is ill but it is not so. They think it is only a pause but it is really all over.'[427] During the next two weeks, Maria came under relentless pressure from Pearson. Her replies to him reveal a scenario of fear, lack of self-respect and emotional paralysis. On 11th October, she wrote: 'I cannot trust myself in letters and if I cannot speak to you fully I will not write.'[428] On 19th October she told him: 'I am sending back your letters I can do nothing else & knew I must before yesterday I cannot help you because I cannot give you understanding love...'[429] Pearson evidently believed that Maria was not revealing the real reason for her change of heart. Nevertheless, her comment that she 'could not give [him] understanding love' carries the implication that there was something for her to be understanding about. Her resistance was clearly driving him to distraction. His anxiety drove him to express himself with increasing ferocity. On 22nd October he urged her: 'till you tell me very solemnly that you can feel no love, understanding or blind, towards me. Then I leave you not because leaving you will help my life, but because I will not bring something which you must loathe near you.'[430]

The phrase 'understanding or blind' matches Maria's own admission that she could not offer him 'understanding love.'

Right from the outset, Maria had reservations about accepting Pearson's proposal. When he followed her to Bergen in order to ask for her hand in marriage, she had fended him off, asking him for time to consider her answer. After leaving her with her sister Letitia and her inseparable companion Lina Eckenstein, Pearson duly departed for Saig. But no sooner had he left, than he began to bombard her with letters, most of which presented him in the worst possible light. A rationalist to his fingertips, he was determined to leave no stone unturned in an effort to give her all the information he could about himself in order to provide her with the basis on which to make a rational decision to accept him as a husband. It never seems to have occurred to him that her eventual acquiescence to his proposal was in doubt. He told her of his father's 'strong and passionate and almost ruthless selfishness', which he informed her he had inherited. He then went on to say that the effort of repressing these characteristics had left him with an 'almost equally vicious tendency to periods of depression and moroseness'. He also described his strenuous attempts to master his emotions by 'crushing' them at will.[431] Although to anyone who knew Pearson well, these revelations can hardly have come as a bolt from the blue, they would not have served to reassure a nervous prospective bride. Maria had been a first-hand witness of his self-righteous condemnation of Caroline Haddon and his subsequent vendetta against her brother-in-law, James Hinton. The ruthless way in which he pursued this war of attrition could not have exactly endeared him to her, and his letters can have done nothing to alleviate her qualms.

Pearson also discreetly questioned *her* about her past life, writing: 'Someday, perhaps, if you should wish it, you shall tell me about your earlier friendships. It may mean something gone, which you cannot give again and which I have no right to expect – it may mean just a little corner of the past to be quietly known and left in quiet seclusion.'[432] He then gave her a glimpse into a secluded little corner of his own past, giving her his thoughts on friendship between men and women (previously quoted), telling her that in the past he had found it 'so hard to do without woman's friendship' but that 'however cautious and self-controlled one might be oneself', there was a risk of misunderstanding, which resulted in 'danger, perhaps evil' being produced; adding that 'it was just such [an] experience' that had led him to tell Olive Schreiner that their friendship must be on a 'man to man' basis. If, as seems likely, Maria had heard about Amy's venture in Saig (and the way she declined Pearson's invitation to her to join him there in the summer of 1888 certainly hints at this), and considering that Pearson wrote these words only a couple of days before Amy took her life, on hearing the news of Amy's suicide Maria may well have feared that he had Amy in mind when making this confession. She may also have realised that his decision to exclude Amy from the club (which he gone out of his way to mention to her) may have played a role in her death. If this is the case, then Pearson was surely right to fear that Maria 'must loathe' him. He would also have been painfully aware that her rejection of *him* would serve to confirm the rumours in the eyes of the world. Pearson ended the letter in which he had asked her to swear that she felt 'no love, understanding or blind' for him by telling her that he would wait for her, and asking her to return all his letters 'except this one.' For whatever reason, he seems to have gone to considerable lengths to conceal their parting from all but his closest friends.

On 5th October, a few days before Olive's departure for South Africa, Charlotte Wilson had written Pearson an anguished letter. Mrs. Wilson was one of his most trusted friends, and she was also a close friend of Olive's. She was the person that he had sought Maria's permission to approach to break the news of their engagement to Olive. At that time Mrs. Wilson lived not far from Pearson in Hampstead, but it is likely that she first got to know him at Cambridge.[433] Charlotte Martin, as she was then, had studied at Newnham between 1872 and 1875.[434] Her fellow students had included Amy's future headmistress, Edith Creak, Blanche Smith's sister Jane, and Emma Brooke – to whom Pearson had applied for information about James Hinton during the 'Hinton imbroglio'. Shortly after leaving Newnham, Charlotte had married a stockbroker, Arthur Wilson. When they were first married, the Wilsons set up home in a large and rather grand house in Elm Row, Hampstead. But in due course Mrs. Wilson fell under the spell of the Russian anarchist Peter Kropotkin, and became converted to anarchist-communism. She was what was termed at the time a 'strong-minded woman', and having decided that she could no longer live on what she described as her husband's 'wages of iniquity', she rented a small farmhouse on the border of Hampstead Heath, where, with the long-suffering Arthur, she proposed to go into chicken farming - or as her friend Edith Nesbit put it, 'to keep herself by keeping fowls!' Whilst living at Elm Lodge Charlotte had gathered together a group of socialistically minded men and women to study Karl Marx's *Capital*. Pearson had been one of the first that she had approached to join the group. Originally called The Hampstead Marx Circle, under the Secretaryship of her Newnham friend, Emma Brooke, it became known as the Hampstead Historical Society. Charlotte continued to host Hampstead Historical Society meetings when she moved to her smallholding on the edge of the heath, but by this time she had also joined the Fabian Society, and at Fabian meetings had got to know Sidney Webb (who later married Beatrice Potter), George Bernard Shaw, and Graham Wallas (who was to marry Ada Radford). Through the Fabian Society, she had also become acquainted with Emily Ford and her cousin Edward Pease. Charlotte Wilson later wrote a history of Wyldes (as the farmhouse was known) and amongst the visitors to the house that are listed on the final page of her little book are a number of people that Amy knew well. Apart from Karl Pearson and Olive Schreiner, they include Havelock Ellis, Ann Clough (Principle of Newnham), Amy's fellow Men and Women's Club member Anne Gilchrist and 'Stepniak'. Amy recorded in her diary that she had tea with Sergey Stepniak on two occasions in April 1889.[435] She also noted that she attended one Fabian Society 'At Home'. It is therefore quite possible that she knew Mrs. Wilson herself, although there is no record of their having met in either her letters or her diary. But whether she was personally acquainted with Charlotte Wilson or not, Mrs. Wilson was frequently to be found in the Reading Room at the British Museum, which was a hotbed of literary gossip. It is therefore certain that she would have known all about Amy Levy.

It has previously been assumed that Charlotte Wilson's letter refers to the break up of Pearson's engagement.[436] But when read in the light of her familiarity with Amy's circle of friends, his callous treatment of Amy, and the rumours that were circulating linking her suicide with Olive, an entirely different interpretation can be put upon her words:

> You may want me to be silent. But Olive Schreiner? I sent her at once your previous letter; is it right that she should leave England under a misconception with regard to what vitally concerns you? I think that no human being ever had a truer *friend*, in the best and highest sense of that word than she is towards you in her deepest and most fundamental feelings. I will do exactly as you wish, but I believe it would be best to send on to her your note of last night. She sails next Wednesday.

> Is not the real remedy for existing miseries to raise the emotions to a higher level, to aim at bringing them into harmony with reason & the intellectual life, rather than at crushing them out? Never mind the individual pain of the first who try; it is part of the growing pain of humanity. The best possibilities of the future must be built up of our broken lives, the broken lives of very many of those who first consciously attempt, not merely to theorise about the new ideal of the relations of men & women, but to live it out. Every Revolution has drowned its own children; do you think that we who are in the forefront of this great period of transition can or ought to escape? We have talked and written about this tremendous problem; we have urged others to boldly meet & grapple with it. Now the practical difficulties are entering like swords into our own lives. Can we slink like cowards into the crowd cursing the human emotions? Have we not to meet and grapple with our own suffering until we can so conquer it as to see its relation to the suffering of the world & use it for the common good? – use it to decrease the frequency of such pain for those who come after, as it can only be decreased when the common experience is enlarged on this matter.

> Forgive me if I intrude on your trouble by too many words. I should not dare to do so if they were cheaply spoken – but if one is oneself lost in the depths one longs to point another wandering there towards any ray of light one sees – however feeling.[437]

This last comment - 'however feeling' – carries the implication that Charlotte was not particularly happy herself with Pearson at this time. She evidently received a positive response to her request, as on 11th October she informed him: 'I sent your two notes to Miss Schreiner, she sails on Wednesday.'[438]

The emphatic tone and the strength of feeling displayed in Charlotte Wilson's letter do not at all convey the impression of a conventional expression of condolence on a broken engagement. Why, for example, should she say that 'the best possibilities of the future must be built up of … the broken lives of … those who first consciously attempt, not merely to theorise about the new ideal of the relations of men & women, but to live it out'? After all, Pearson had asked Maria to marry him, and there was nothing new or revolutionary about that. Certainly the claim that 'every Revolution has drowned its own children', followed by the statement 'We have talked and written about this tremendous problem; we have *urged others* [my emphasis] to boldly meet & grapple with it. Now the practical difficulties are entering like swords into our own lives', suggests a far more serious problem than Maria's ostensible qualms about her age. These words also call to mind to Olive's earlier comment to Pearson: 'The great danger which we who would fight for or lead humanity have to guard against is the mixing up of our personal interest with the things we fight for.' This remark was made in the letter in which she indirectly accused him of hypocrisy in his crusade against 'Hintonism'.[439] What Charlotte Wilson's letter does confirm beyond doubt, is that there was a direct connection between Olive Schreiner and Maria Sharpe's decision to terminate her engagement. Why, otherwise, would the letter have been written at all? But as Pearson's letters to Maria make abundantly clear, he had never attempted to conceal the details of his relationship with Olive from her, and was always adamant that he regarded Olive purely as a colleague and a friend. Nevertheless, just as he had expressed anxiety about Olive's response to the news of his engagement, so it appears he was uncertain of how she might react when she heard that it was at an end.

Charlotte Wilson's subsequent letters to Pearson bear witness to the depth of his 'trouble' at this time, as they reveal that he was taking active steps to dispose of his house, and planning to resign his Professorship in order leave London and make his life elsewhere, possibly in another country.[440] This dramatic gesture seems entirely at odds with the pragmatic and decidedly unromantic approach he had adopted in his previous relationships with women. On 11th October, a week after Olive's departure for the

Cape,[441]Charlotte informed him:

> We have named your house to several people, but unfortunately as yet without success ... I mentioned to Mr. Wilson the sum spent on repairs, premiums etc., & the rent & he thinks you might well ask from £75 to £80 & that you were more likely to get that than to get the premium back & £50 yearly.[442]

It is obvious from these comments that Pearson's departure was envisaged as a long-term arrangement. On 1st January 1890, Mrs. Wilson wrote a further letter to Pearson, on the same subject. He had evidently made enquiries about Olive's whereabouts, as the letter begins with an account of her movements, and continues:

> I hope you will shortly find a desirable tenant for your house. Of course we mention it to every likely person. I did not tell Miss Brooke or anyone that you wished to let it furnished.
>
> I shall be so glad to hear that you have found work in a new place. Nothing refreshes one's dormant energy like a change of interests in a new scene...[443]

On 13th November, Frau Debattis, Pearson's long-time holiday companion at Saig, sent him a cryptic letter of condolence, which confirms the scenario described by Charlotte Wilson. Frau Debattis told Pearson:

> it has gladdened me to know that you had sufficient trust at least to tell me of your troubles .... It would be best if you could go away for a while ... but not on your own. Solitude over excites the spirit and, since you are already an eccentric man, you must be sensible and do everything you can to restore the equilibrium of your physical and mental faculties!

She then urged him:

> In your place I would not by any means give up your career. Do this only in a case of extreme emergency! Because everywhere there is a throng of superfluous applicants for all areas of employment. So keep what you have and what is commensurate with your abilities. [Frau Debattis had included a newspaper cutting about the number of applicants for a post in Germany, which suggests that Pearson had asked her about employment prospects there] But perhaps two or three weeks' leave – that would do you good.

She then made a rather curious remark: 'What may have caused your fiancée to break off the engagement was your demand of an ideal state of living together. She feared the danger of weakening in such close proximity and of experiencing conflict'. This implies that Pearson had told her that he had proposed that he and Maria live together platonically. But in his letters to Maria there is no hint of this suggestion. All references to their future life together make it quite clear that he had a conventional marital relationship in mind. Frau Debattis also seems to have doubted the veracity of this explanation, suggesting: 'you might become reconciled with your fiancée and you could ask about the actual reasons for her breaking of the engagement. Of course, it will be difficult – almost impossible – for her to express it …' The letter ended with the assurance: 'Adieu dear young friend. Do not despair. Life still has much that is beautiful to offer.'[444]

Despite Emma Debattis' optimism, Pearson's 'trouble' evidently did not diminish. By April 1890 he still believed himself to be hunted and haunted, imagining ghosts of the past pursuing him at every turn. On 4th April, Robert Parker wrote a reassuring reply to his anxious enquiry:

> Your letter arrived the morning after my last was written …. I quite understand your feelings on reading the Egoist, for I felt something the same. I imagine most men would detect something of themselves in Sir Willoughby. You must not imagine that the book was lent to you as having any particular bearing on your personal experience or indeed that it has any such bearing …. What you say of caricature is I think only partially true: egoism as a rule passes as good current coin of the realm. It is only when you are in the secret that you take it for something else and once in the secret you can hardly imagine how others can be deceived, it seems so gross & ridiculous …. and after all Sir W came out of it exceedingly well from the standpoint of a man spectator …. But it won't do to let your tendency to self dissection run riot or become morbid: you ought to be here or I with you that we might laugh our foibles to the East wind and enjoy the sun upon the downs and realise our own nothingness as an incentive to achieve some better good.[445]

Although Parker, who was evidently *au fait* with the details of Pearson 'secret', assured his friend that he 'must not imagine that the book was lent to you as having any particular bearing on your personal experience or indeed that it has any such bearing', under the circumstances it is quite understandable that Pearson might detect an ulterior motive in being presented with a book which recounts the tale of a man who fell between two stools by abandoning a 'seedy and penurious spinster',[446] a 'paragon of cleverness'[447] but a 'portionless … poetess'[448] who 'almost proposed to her hero in her rhymes',[449]for a more conventionally favoured woman, who had 'money … health and beauty',[450] 'did not court to win him,'[451] and ultimately jilted him!

Despite Pearson's fears – 'from the standpoint of a man' – like Sir Willoughby Patterne, there was a happy ending to his story. After holding out for seven months, in April 1890 (the same month in which Parker wrote to Pearson to reassure him about his reading of *The Egoist*) Maria agreed to meet Pearson again. It is unclear why she changed her mind, but a few days before doing she wrote him a letter in which she claimed that: 'Self doubts *alone* [my emphasis] trouble me now, and only being with you and feeling it is right for you can quiet me.'[452] Thirty seven years later, just before Maria's death, Pearson wrote a letter to his sister-in-law Elizabeth Cobb (whom he addressed as 'My dear Bessie') in which he gave a heartfelt - and heartrending - summing up of his marriage:

> As I look back on it now, I think life has been largely a failure. I have sacrificed everything – Maria would say wife and children included – to the idea of establishing a new tool in science .... Thirty years hence a curve or symbol will be called 'Pearson's' and nothing more remembered of that toil of the years. It is not so much the waste of mine but of others' lives, in particular Mia's. She has been a splendid wife, if you mean by that, that she has ever worked for her husband's purposes. But she has done it from her inbred sense of duty, and not for something else ..... *Marrying as we did after what had happened previously* [my emphasis] I ought to have realised that I had still to win her, but I spent my life over my work and she sacrificed her life in looking with slender means after home and children. What she has been feeling all these years comes out now, when she is less clear in mind and has less control of herself. That very night after you came she said to me: 'You must not let other people say *that you have killed me*' [my emphasis]. I don't suppose 'other' people would say so, but I know what she meant that I was to say so myself .... I do not blame Mia for this want of trust. I blame myself for never really having won her confidence. Only I cannot let you of all people believe that our marriage has been an ideal one. It wanted delicacy of handling to make it so, and I have given too little time and thought to it .... Now that the end is drawing nigh she discloses against her will, what has been the undercurrent all these long years, and I can do nothing.[453]

Pearson requested that Elizabeth destroy the letter but, in the event, it was never sent.

In 1896, Olive Schreiner made a damning indictment of Pearson's character in a letter to Lady Constance Lytton, with whom she had become acquainted during the suffrage campaign. Referring to the photograph of herself, which Constance Lytton had enclosed, Olive comments:

> I think it is beautiful but it makes me too sad. There is a great tragedy in the lives of modern women that women of the old style perhaps know nothing. It is the tragedy which arises when a man cannot love a woman *because she is too much his superior* [original emphasis] intellectually and emotionally she moves in a higher world than that in which he can move .... When once a good woman has seen into the depths of a man's soul and seen nothing there, then his power to touch her is gone forever. He might have been dead and buried for a thousand years for anything he is to her. One would like to take him and plant little flowers all over him, like a grave .... I wasted the best years of my girlhood over one man. I didn't want to marry him, he was supposed to be dying, to have only a few months to live when I met him, and I worshipped him. This went on year after year. I never met him ...

At first sight, this last remark – 'I never met him' – makes no sense, as it contradicts the previous sentence in which she had told Constance Lytton: 'he was supposed to have only a few months to live when I met him'. However, throughout her correspondence, when

Olive was writing about subjects that aroused her emotions, she had a tendency to muddle the meaning of her sentences. The remark is therefore more likely to be a reference to the delay in her meeting with Pearson that had been engineered by Elizabeth Cobb. In a letter written to Ellis, in July 1907, Olive mentioned that when she first knew Pearson he had told her that he was dying of 'a terrible incurable disease'.[454] The letter continues:

> I believed nothing anyone told me of his nature. He is a most remarkable man with real genius and almost European reputation. Everyone said he was selfish and mean, but I never believed it, *because I didn't know him*! One day a letter was shown me, at his request, in which he talked slightingly of a woman he was bound to be loyal to [Perhaps this was one of the 'two notes' shown to Olive by Mrs. Wilson at Pearson's request just before Olive's departure for the Cape] … from the moment I read it he was dead and buried as though he had never existed for me AND I WAS FREE.[455]

The phrase 'he was dead and buried' recalls a phrase in a letter that Olive wrote to Edward Carpenter from Mentone in January 1889 in the aftermath of her break up with Pearson. In the letter she had asked Carpenter:

> If you ever should go to Mr. Pearson's again, would you send me something out of his garden; pick it for yourself. You know my heart lives always in that little study in Hampstead …. Now I know that he never wanted my friendship I can rest. It's to me as if he was buried personally but so beautiful to know he's alive and working impersonally.[456]

In 1895, the year before Olive wrote her letter to Constance Lytton, Amy's friend and erstwhile walking companion Grant Allen had published a novel entitled *Under Sealed Orders*.[457] *Under Sealed Orders* is, for Allen, a characteristically implausible tale of espionage and intrigue, interwoven with a subplot that involves three young New Women. These are Sacha Cazalet (the heroine of the story), Ionê Dracopoli, a former 'Girton Girl' turned intrepid adventuress, who has made a solo expedition on horseback across Morocco dressed in 'Turkish trousers' (she is obviously based on the New Woman novelist Ménie Muriel Dowie), and Hope Braithwaite, otherwise known as 'Blackbird'. Blackbird is an Oxford-educated, sad and sickly composer of romantic songs. Halfway through the story she commits suicide.

Blackbird is obviously the alter-ego of Amy Levy. Indeed, the number of clues to her real-life counterpart that Allen scatters throughout the text is breathtaking. Anyone who knew Amy during her lifetime, having read the novel, would have been left in no doubt that she inspired this character.[458] The first clue to Blackbird's identity comes when Sacha tells her shocked brother that she is setting up home with Ionê and Blackbird. 'Well, let me see; this is how it happened', Sacha tells Owen, 'After I ... came up to town to these lodgings ...I proposed to Blackbird, who is miserable at home – all her people are Philistines – that she should come and take rooms with me as a social experiment'. The 'social experiment' – the girls 'mean to do [their] own work and keep no servants' - is a replica of the Black sisters' 'anti-servitoresses' lodging in Albany Street that was so disparagingly commented upon by Amy in her letter to Vernon Lee. When Blackbird finally makes an appearance in person, her physical resemblance to Amy Levy is apparent. Aged twenty-seven (the age that Amy was when she took her life), she is described as being 'tiny, like a doll ... too fragile for this earth'. Her most striking feature is her eyes: 'Such eyes Owen had never seen in his life before. They were black and lustrous, and liquid like a gazelle's; and they turned upon him and flooded him with sad light every time she spoke to him...' This description not only corresponds with Harry Quilter's account of Amy's photograph on the mantelpiece at the Falcon Inn, 'a small, dark girl, of unmistakably Jewish type, with eyes too large for the delicate features, and far too sad for their youthfulness of line and contour', but also matches Amy's fellow poet Graham R. Thomson's comments in her review of the posthumous re-print of Amy's *A Minor Poet*. Commenting on the portrait that appeared on the frontispiece of the book, Graham Thomson writes: '[It] is an excellent reproduction from a photograph, ...as satisfactory as such a portrait can be [although] it hardly does justice to the deep beautiful eyes and the firm fine lines of the mobile mouth'.[459] These two descriptions of Amy's real-life features correspond with a contemporary fictional portrait. This is Israel Zangwill's description of the writer Esther Ansell in *The Grandchildren of the Ghetto*. Zangwill may have met Amy through his association with the Kilburn Wanderers, as his fellow 'Wanderer', Asher Myers, knew Amy's father well. In Zangwill's book, Esther, who has written a highly controversial novel, as Amy did, is described as having 'a face that would have been almost plain but for the soul behind. It was dark, with great earnest eyes... Seen from the front the face fascinated again, in the Eastern glow from its colouring, in the flash of the white teeth, in the depths of the brooding eyes...'[460]

But the most compelling piece of evidence that Blackbird is Amy Levy is the fact that on several occasions throughout the narrative Allen almost literally takes the words out of her mouth. For instance, when Blackbird confides to Henley Stokes, 'When wasn't I tired I should like to know ... I've been tired uninterruptedly, dead tired, dog tired! It's the epitome of my existence', Allen replicates the opening words of Amy's 'The End of the Day': 'Dead tired, dog tired, as the vivid day/Fails and slackens and fades away...' Or again, when Blackbird declares 'Perhaps the reason I love sleep so well is because he seems to promise Death, too, will be gentle', the passage echoes the closing lines of the final stanza of Amy's 'The Promise of Sleep':

> And now I think of only this,
> How gently I may woo
> The gentle sleep who promises,
> That death is gentle too.

But most telling of all is the following extract:

> Mr. Hayward left that evening by the night mail for Paris. As soon as he was gone, a blank fell upon the party. After the cumulative excitement of the last few weeks, it seemed almost impossible for them to settle down once more to the humdrum routine of every-day life – the 'domestic round of roast and boiled' as Blackbird loved to call it.

This not only resembles Amy's description of the aftermath of Melissa's wedding in 'Out of the World': 'when the excitement of the wedding preparations was over ... and a company of sparrows discussing the rice on the pavement outside was the only reminder of what had occurred, a great blankness fell on my soul', but also, more significantly, includes a quotation of a line (albeit with two words transposed) from Amy's 'A Ballad of Religion and Marriage', the second stanza of which begins:

> Monogamous, still at our post,
> Reluctantly we undergo
> Domestic round of boiled and roast,
> Yet deem the whole proceeding slow.

At the time that Allen wrote *Under Sealed Orders* 'A Ballad of Religion and Marriage' had not appeared in print, but shortly before she died Amy had given him a manuscript copy of the verse. This poem and its significance will be discussed in the next chapter.

The event that causes Blackbird to commit suicide is her friend Henley Stokes' proposal of marriage. Like Herminia Barton in *A Woman Who Did*, Blackbird is appalled at the suggestion:

> 'Married!' she cried, flashing fire at him from both those glowing eyes. 'Married! Married! Married! Oh, Henley! I wonder *you* who love me so well – for I'm *sure* you love me – I wonder you don't see for yourself the reason *why* I can't be married!'

The reason that Blackbird gives for her refusal of Henley's proposal is, in Allen's eyes at least, a logical one:

> I will tell you the reason [Blackbird said] with a terrible forced calm … Henley, you're a man, and you love me as a woman. But will you have the truth? I'm not a woman at all – not in the sense you mean … All of the woman that was ever in me, or ought to have been in me has been educated out, crushed and killed by teaching. It's all gone off in music, or mathematics, or chemistry, or Greek. The rest of you are creatures of flesh and blood. I'm not even as you are. I'm all brain and nerves. The flesh and blood are bred out of me. I've nothing left to love you with.

At an earlier point in the narrative, Allen had made it quite clear who should carry the blame for Blackbird's sad life. 'My own people are strong, you know … and they always bully me', Blackbird tells Henley. 'They're Philistines, of course; but, do you know I think Philistines are really the very worst on education. From the day I was born, almost, they kept me constantly at it. Papa's a colonial broker …he decided from the time I was a baby in arms I was to be thoroughly well educated. And educated I was … And then at seventeen I was sent to Lady Margaret.'[461] One can only imagine the pain felt by Amy's parents should they have read these words. Clementina Back's letter to the *Athenaeum* was intended to scotch notions like this, but here was Allen voicing them in public yet again when Amy was no longer there to defend either herself or her family – with a friend like him who would need an enemy?

But maybe someone did spring to their defence. In 1898, the year of Eleanor Marx's suicide, Dollie Radford published her only novel, *One Way of Love: An Idyll*.[462] It has been assumed that the story, which ends with an implied suicide, was inspired by Eleanor Marx's self-inflicted death following Edward Aveling's betrayal when, after living 'in sin' with Eleanor for thirteen years, he secretly married an actress in June 1897.[463] But Dollie Radford's late granddaughter, Ann MacEwen, stated most emphatically that this was incorrect, and that she had documentary proof that Dollie began writing the novel in 1896, a full year before Eleanor's self-inflicted death.[464] However, 1896 was the year after *Under Sealed Orders* first appeared in print.

One Way of Love is the tale of a young woman deceived by a 'cold and selfish' man. The heroine Sacha, who shares the name of the main female protagonist of Allen's novel, is, like her, an orphan. Brought up by an uncaring aunt and uncle, she spends much of her time daydreaming of the 'soulmate' who will one day rescue her from her lonely, loveless existence. She gives voice to her unhappiness in poems, which she copies into a secret notebook. Her dream seems about to come true when she meets the summertime visitor of her aunt's neighbours – the handsome young barrister Arthur West. (When Amy first met Pearson he was nominally pursuing a career at the Bar.) Flattered by Sacha's undisguised admiration, Arthur amuses himself by indulging in a holiday dalliance with her. During an idyllic summer's afternoon walk, he questions Sacha about her feelings for him, implying that he shares them. Kissing her passionately, he leaves her with a promise to visit her the next day. But the next morning he fails to arrive. After waiting for him forlornly for most of the afternoon, Sacha learns from her aunt's tea-time visitors that he has returned to London apparently without sending her a word. She later receives a cruel little letter from him, in which he addresses her as an old and distant acquaintance. Sacha refuses to believe that Arthur does not care for her, and (like Amy's Adelaide) sets off in pursuit of her errant lover.

Once in the city, she searches out her old governess, who now runs a junk shop cum lodging house. Like the heroine of Allen's novel, Sacha finds herself living in a 'ménage a trois' with Madame's two other lodgers, Janet and Katherine, who is known as The Sphinx. The Sphinx has a mysterious young male friend known only as Oedipus, whom she has not seen for some time. [465] One evening the Sphinx returns in high spirits, telling Janet and Sacha that she has been reunited with Oedipus, and that he has asked her to marry him. The girls arrange a party in honour of the pair, but when the appointed evening arrives and Oedipus enters the room, Sacha discovers to her horror that her friend's fiancé is her betrayer, Arthur West.

Sacha has told her friends of her quest to find her lost love without revealing his name. But after her unexpected encounter with West, she is unable to conceal her distress, and everyone – including the Sphinx – guesses her secret. At the end of the evening, Madame advises the distraught Sphinx to throw away her engagement ring, but the Sphinx realises that by ending her relationship with her faithless fiancé she will expose Sacha's naïve folly. She replies:

> That is the thing I cannot do. I shall keep my promise. This is the only way; this way which is best for all of us. O Madame, Madame, I shall keep his ring; that is my tragedy.[466]

Like Maria Sharpe, the Sphinx's 'inbred sense of duty' condemns her to spend a lifetime with a man she can no longer trust.

The next day Sacha disappears. Her friends and family search in vain for a trace of her, but all that remains is her poem:

In that new land to which I sail
I shall endure in hope alway
For in my quest I cannot fail
Where love does stay.[467]

These lines recall an earlier passage in the narrative, when, during a late-night Thames-side walk with Sacha, Janet comments that the river is 'full of mystery and promise at night; it makes me want to float down to the sea, as the daffodils and wall-flowers do when they bubble over their great baskets in our street in the spring-time.' Sacha replies: 'Yes … but the sea does not give anything more; it only promises – like the river.' This passage, which recalls both Blackbird's declaration 'Perhaps the reason I love sleep so well is because he seems to promise Death, too, will be gentle,' and Amy Levy's 'gentle sleep – who promises/That death is gentle too', invites the reader to conclude that Sacha has thrown herself into the river in order to reach her 'promised land'.

All evidence points to the conclusion that *One Way of Love* is the story of the failed relationship of Amy Levy and Karl Pearson, rather than that of Eleanor Marx and Edward Aveling. Like Clementina Black, Dollie Radford was a close friend of the entire Levy family, and like Clementina, she too, would have burned with indignation at the thought that they had been publicly maligned. But unlike Clementina, she could not openly censure Allen without drawing attention to the fact that he had created a caricature of Amy Levy in his novel – thus causing further distress to her family. Neither could she openly disclose the real reason for Amy's suicide without betraying her 'secret'. But she could write her 'Idyll' as a riposte to *Under Sealed Orders*, in order to send an oblique message to those who had known and loved Amy Levy that it was not her parents but Karl Pearson, alias Arthur West, who should be held responsible for the fact that she 'chose to die'.

'A Ballad of Religion and Marriage': Amy Levy's Doctrine of Dissent

> Grant, in a million years at most,
> Folks shall be neither pairs nor odd –
> Alas! we shan't be here to boast
> 'Marriage has gone the way of God!'
>
> Amy Levy, 1861–1889: 'A Ballad of Religion and Marriage'

In around 1915, approximately twenty six years after Amy committed suicide, Clement King Shorter issued a small pamphlet entitled: 'A Ballad of Religion and Marriage' by Amy Levy. It was inscribed: 'Of this pamphlet 12 copies only have been printed for private circulation'. This was the first time that the poem had appeared in print. A manuscript copy of 'A Ballad of Religion and Marriage' has recently come to light amongst Grant Allen's papers. Amy frequently made gifts of copies of her verses to her friends, and in all probability she gave the manuscript to Allen either during or shortly after her visit to Dorking with Jenny de Pass in May 1889. In other words, not long before she took her life. 'A Ballad of Religion and Marriage' is essentially a rebuttal of the analysis of the woman question outlined in a corresponding pair of essays written by Grant Allen and her former friend Karl Pearson. In this bitter, satirical verse, Amy gave a summing up of her (by then) jaded view of 'the woman question'. I believe that this was, in effect, her literary suicide note, and as such it is a very important document, as it gives an insight into the thoughts that were going through her mind during the last months of her life.

In literary convention, the envoi of a ballad is addressed to the 'Prince' – thought by some to represent the prince of darkness - Satan. The first line of the envoi of 'A Ballad of Religion and Marriage', 'Grant, in a million years at most', confirms that in this instance 'the prince of darkness' addressed is Grant Allen. Amy's chosen poetic form also replicates his 'A Ballade of Evolution' in *The Evolutionist at Large*, a book that she recorded in her diary as having read in February 1889. But despite its obvious association with Allen, there is an undercurrent flowing beneath the surface of the verse that reveals a second, shadowy 'prince' whose views on 'the woman question' were even more uncompromising than his. This was Karl Pearson. At the inaugural meeting of the second Men and Women's Club in July 1885, Pearson had launched the club's proceedings by presenting a paper entitled 'The Woman's Question'. Like 'A Ballad of Religion and Marriage', the paper was subsequently issued as a pamphlet 'for private circulation'. It was also included in the collection of essays that was issued under the title of *The Ethic of Freethought* in 1887.[468] Two years after this, in October 1889, Grant Allen's essay 'Plain Words on the Woman Question' was published in the *Fortnightly Review*.[469] Although this did not appear in print until after Amy's death, it is likely to have been written at an earlier date. Amy recorded in her diary that she had 'discussed the woman question' with Grant Allen during her visit to the Allen household in May of that year. And as Pearson's essay had caused something of a stir in feminist circles, it would almost certainly have figured in their conversation.

Given the fact that 'A Ballad of Religion and Marriage' was addressed to Allen, it is likely that he was the sole recipient of a manuscript copy of the verse. If this is the case, then he must have passed it on to Clement Shorter. But why choose Shorter? Although by the time that the ballad was issued in 1915 Shorter was a successful and distinguished journalist, having for some years edited the *Illustrated London News* and founded and edited two other national newspapers, the *Sketch* and *The Sphere*, at time that Amy wrote it he had just given up his job as a clerk in Somerset House and was embarking on his journalistic career, writing weekly articles on books and their authors for the 'All About Books' column of *The Star*.[470] And the Obituary notice in *The Star* was the first to link Amy's death with Olive Schreiner. A number of Shorter's friends at that time had also known Amy. These included William Robertson Nicholl, who had serialised *Miss Meredith* in his *British Weekly* in March 1889, James Dykes Campbell, who had first made Amy's acquaintance at Hastings in 1883, and Dr Garnett, whom Shorter often visited at 'his home in the British Museum'. (Richard Garnett wrote the entry on Amy Levy for Sidney Lee's *Dictionary of National Biography*.) But in the context of the publication of 'A Ballad and Religion and Marriage' Shorter's most significant friend who had also been a close friend of Amy's was Grant Allen.[471] During the late 1880s Allen had become the target of Karl Pearson's caustic pen. With the same callous disregard for the effect of his words or deeds on others that he exhibited when withdrawing his *Grammar of Science* from Havelock Ellis' 'Contemporary Science Series', he ridiculed Allen's attempts to make science accessible to the working man. In an article written after the publication of Allen's *Force and Energy* in 1888, he sarcastically advised him to 'do penance at once by writing us a blood-curdling Christmas ghost story and promising to entertain no more heresies', later expressing regret for the fact that the days were gone when 'misinformed heretics such as Allen were burned'.[472] Allen's motivation in passing the manuscript of Amy's ballad on to Shorter may have been to take revenge for these slights. Pearson took himself very seriously indeed. His reaction to reading Meredith's *The Egoist* revealed his horror at the prospect of becoming the butt of others' jokes. Allen's unkind and very obvious portrait of Amy Levy in *Under Sealed Orders* is testimony to the fact that he had no scruple in publicly poking fun at one who had considered him a friend. How then might he behave towards one whom he regarded as a foe?

If Allen wished to get his own back on Pearson, what better way of doing it than by linking his name, yet again, to Amy Levy, thereby swelling the tide of gossip and innuendo that was threatening to engulf him at that time? When passing the Ballad on to Shorter, Allen could easily have slipped in the information that it was not only directly addressed to him, but also, indirectly, to Karl Pearson. Those who were *au fait* with the rumours that were circulating in the wake of Amy's death might then connect the ballad's message with him. The 'nudge and wink' references linking Olive Schreiner and Amy Levy that appeared in the press in the weeks after her suicide suggest these rumours were already widespread within in literary circles. Those in the know thereafter had no problem in identifying the *Pall Mall Gazette*'s suicidal 'literary ladies' as Amy and Olive (it was Ellis' animosity towards Pearson that made Olive suspect that he was responsible for circulating this particular item of gossip). If then, amongst the London literati, the Ballad had become associated with Pearson, it could explain the chronological gap between the poem's composition and its eventual publication in 1915. By that time Amy had been dead for twenty six years and Allen had been dead for almost sixteen, although Pearson was still very much alive. But Shorter may have felt that sufficient time had elapsed for enough dust to have settled on the unhappy circumstances of Amy's death to permit the ballad, which is a very fine piece of work indeed, to appear in print for the first time. But the fact that when the ballad was issued '12 copies only … for private circulation' were printed, indicates that it was still considered unsuitable for widespread distribution. This is apparently confirmed by the fact that for some years after its publication 'A Ballad of Religion and Marriage' was housed on the 'Suppressed Safe' shelf of the British Museum Reading Room.[473] The Suppressed Safe shelf contained works that were separated from those in the general catalogue because they were considered to be controversial in one way or another. In 1913 (around the time that the pamphlet of Amy's Ballad was issued by Shorter), an article entitled 'The Taboos of the British Museum Library' appeared in *The English Review*. [474] This details some of the criteria for the exclusion of books from the general catalogue, which included that the item was either considered to be 'subversive of the throne …subversive of religion' or that it was of 'an improper or obscene character'. 'A Ballad of Religion and Marriage' obviously did not fall into the first category, although it may have been deemed to have been 'subversive of religion'. And some of the ideas expressed within it would certainly have been considered improper at the time that it was written. But the outbreak of the First World War had finally brought an end to the Victorian order, destroying, for many, faith in a beneficent Almighty, and banishing the spectre of Mrs Grundy. So it is also possible that lingering concerns about the rumours that had circulated in the aftermath of Amy's death influenced the decision to exclude it from access to the general public. In view of this possibility it is worthwhile to take a detailed look at the ballad in order to ascertain the extent to which the views of the woman question held by Grant Allen, Karl Pearson and Amy Levy are interwoven within the text.

In their respective essays on the woman question both Allen and Pearson set out their agenda for the preservation and advancement of the human race, giving voice, in no uncertain terms, to their anxiety about the implication which the campaign for female emancipation might hold for the future of the human species. The contrasting styles in which the two essays are written reflect the authors' divergent personalities. Pearson's paper is presented with dry and scholarly precision, Allen's with impassioned hyperbole. Like Pearson, Allen was what his friend Edward Clodd termed a 'consistent evolutionist', and consequently he founded his argument on sound Darwinian principles.[475] Although he expressed 'sympathy with the modern woman's demand for emancipation' – declaring boldly 'I am an enthusiast on the Woman Question' – his empathy with modern woman's desire for social and professional autonomy did not prevent him from mounting a scathing attack upon what he termed the 'so-called Women's Rights movements'. He squarely placed the blame for the current unhappy state of affairs on the 'movement for the Higher Education of Women', which, he maintained in characteristically histrionic style, was 'sacrificing the race to a handful of barren experimenters'. He reiterated this claim in a later essay, entitled 'The Girl of the Future,' in which he held up as a warning to womanhood the sad example of the 'few hundred pallid little Amy Levys sacrificed … before the face of our fashionable Juggernaut' - the 'fashionable Juggernaut' being the 'great movement in England and America for the Higher Instruction of Women'.[476] In 'Plain Words on the Woman Question', looking to the future, he reassured his readership that the situation was 'destined by natural means to cure itself with time … in a hundred years things will have righted themselves' (a phrase which calls to mind the first lines of the envoi of Amy's ballad: 'Grant, in a million years at most/ Folks shall be neither pairs nor odd'). Nevertheless, in the meantime he held out the alarming prospect that 'there is a danger that many of the most cultivated and able families of the English-speaking race will have become extinct, through the prime error of supposing that an education which is good for men must necessarily also be good for women.' His solution to this problem was to abandon 'the scheme of female education now in vogue' in favour of a scheme which should be 'mainly a scheme for the education of wives and mothers'. But if society chose to ignore his advice and woman was deflected from her natural path, 'the main stream of feminine life, which must always consist of the maternal element', then the consequences for the future of society would be dire. Higher education would destroy women's appetite for motherhood, creating an environment where 'you sacrifice the many to the few, the potential wives to the lady-lecturers'.

Like Allen, Pearson plainly balked at the prospect of a future society populated by ladies who would be qualified to lecture him, instead of vice versa. And although he too dressed himself up as a supporter of women's emancipation, he harboured similar reservations about the future role of women as his fellow emancipationist. Like Allen he also defined the distinction between man and woman as being founded 'in the capacity for child-bearing', and expressed corresponding doubts about the desirability of higher education for women. But when considering the wider question, 'Is it or is it not possible for the sexes to mix freely in all relations of life', he made a very revealing statement, insisting that 'whereas friendship between a man and a married woman is possible close friendship between single men and women is almost impossible.' This was, no doubt, a reflection of the fact that his married woman friend Elizabeth Cobb was amongst those present at the club meeting at which the paper was first presented, but he may also have had other more private personal reasons for making this emphatic pronouncement. He went on to explain:

> It may be due to something inherent in human nature, the existence of sexual attraction. … or it may be due to an artificial relation, the outcome of a false social system. It may be needful that existing society should put its veto on such friendships, but we may still question whether this veto be not a real hindrance to human development. So far is this restriction carried in some ranks of life at present that, if a single man and woman are once seen walking alone together, society points its finger; if they are seen twice society pronounces them engaged; if this be denied, on the third occasion it damns, not the man's be it noted, but the woman's reputation.[477]

In view of the disastrous consequences of Amy's 'close friendship' with Pearson, which had damned not his reputation but hers, one cannot help but wonder whether he had this experience in mind when making this claim. His admission to Maria Sharpe that 'I have found it, especially in the years gone by, so hard to do without woman's friendship and yet seen that, however cautious and self-controlled one might be oneself, there was always danger, perhaps evil produced which one would have done anything to avoid' adds weight to this hypothesis. Certainly his words strengthen the impression that Amy's unaccompanied stay at his 'village retreat' was made, at his prompting, in order to make a stand against the prevailing 'false social system'.

Turning to the question of 'marriage itself,' Pearson commented:

> It has been argued that this institution is plastic, and that its present form is not necessarily the fittest, but possibly only a phase in the evolution of sex. ...I must yet confess that there seems to me no prospect that the educated woman of the future will regard marriage and its duties from the same standpoint that man has done; it is difficult to conceive she will sanction the Church-Service view of the institution ....[478]

Unlike Allen, Pearson did not regard these problems as a passing phase, and saw stormy waters ahead:

> There have been periods in the world's history when there was an approach to equality between the two sexes, but these periods have been marked by an equality in freedom, rather than by an equality in restraint. .... If the growing sex-equality connote sex-freedom – a return to general promiscuity – then it connotes a decay of the State, and it will require a second Pauline Christianity and a second subjection of one sex to restore stability. But sex-equality must either be marked by the cessation of prostitution among men, or, if it remains, by the like freedom to women. ... We shall have the choice between equal promiscuity and equal restraint. The misfortune for society is that the former is a much easier course to take than the latter, and one which history shows us has generally been adopted.

Nevertheless, despite his gloomy prognosis he saw light at the end of the tunnel:

> Yet there is one ray of hope, which may after all forecast the dawn of a new social era .... That the past subjection of women has tended largely to expand man's selfish instincts I cannot deny; but may it not be that this very subjection has so chastened woman, so trained her to think rather of others than of herself, that after all it may have acted more as a blessing than a curse to the world? May it not bring her to the problems of the future with a purer aim and a keener insight than is possible for man? She may see more clearly than he the real points at issue, and as she has learnt self-control in the past by subjecting her will to his, so in the future she may be able to submit her liberty to the restraints demanded by social welfare, and to the conditions needed for race-permanence.[479]

On reading this last passage Amy must have given a hollow laugh, because the outcome of her own willingness to submit to Pearson's 'selfish instincts' had certainly proved to be a chastening experience for her, giving her a 'keener insight' into 'the real points at issue', making her view the woman question in an entirely different light. 'A Ballad of Religion and Marriage' was the result.

In 'The Woman's Question' Pearson had posed the question, will 'The disgust generated by the ecclesiastical conception of marriage' necessarily lead to the demise of the institution itself? The first two stanzas of the ballad are a satirical précis of Pearson's enquiry:

> Swept into limbo is the host
> Of heavenly angels, row on row;
> The Father, Son and Holy Ghost,
> Pale and defeated, rise and go.
> The great Jehovah is laid low,
> Vanished his burning bush and rod –
> Say, are we doomed to deeper woe?
> Shall marriage go the way of God?

The second stanza provides the answer, with an ironic affirmation of Allan's assertion that 'educating [women] like men' produces within them a false 'distaste … for the functions which nature intended them to perform'.[480] In his two essays on the woman question, Allen had singled out the opinions of Mona Caird for particular censure. Amy knew Mona Caird well, having met her on several occasions at the 'At Homes' held by her friend and fellow poet Graham R. Tomson.[481] Also, as Amy recorded in her diary, Mona Caird had chaired the Ladies' Literary Dinner at which she herself had 'returned thanks for fiction'[482].

Mona Caird (née Alison) was a radical journalist and a feminist who, after her marriage to the son of a Scottish landowner, went against convention by styling herself 'Mrs. Mona Caird' rather than 'Mrs. James Henryson-Caird'. In the same essay in which he had singled out Amy as the undesirable herald of 'the girl of the future', Allen had also taken Mona Caird to task, commenting sourly: 'thumbscrews will not drive me to violate the genius of our mother tongue by describing this … lady as "Mrs. Mona Caird"'. But the New Woman, 'Mrs Mona Caird', had only just fired the first salvo in her campaign to challenge society's view of wedlock. In August 1888 (the year after Pearson's The Ethic of Freethought was published) she generated a heated debate when her own essay on the 'woman question', entitled simply 'Marriage', was printed in the *Westminster Review.* [483] Her friend and fellow women's rights activist Elizabeth Cady Stanton recorded that during a visit to London earlier that year she 'spent a few days with Mrs. Mona Caird who was reading Karl Pearson's lectures on "Woman" and expounding her views on marriage, which she afterwards gave to the *Westminster Review*'. [484] Unlike the well-intentioned but inadequately educated ladies of The Men and Women's Club, Mona Caird was sufficiently well informed to be able to take Pearson on on his own terms. In one of her later essays on the same subject, she cited an impressive range of sources that included the evolutionary anthropologists J.F.McLennan and J.J. Bahofen, whose research had previously been cited by Pearson in 'The Woman's Question'[485]. Tellingly, perhaps in reflection of the nickname bestowed upon her unfortunate husband, 'No one Caird', in 'Marriage' she made the bold assertion that 'the woman takes unconscious vengeance [on man] item by item. Through her, in great measure, marriage becomes what Milton calls "a drooping and disconsolate household captivity".'[486] An echo of this statement resonates in the second stanza of Amy's ballad:

> Monogamous, still at our post,
> Reluctantly we undergo
> Domestic round of boiled and roast,
> Yet deem the whole proceeding slow.
> Daily the secret murmurs grow;
> We are no more content to plod
> Along the beaten paths – and so
> Marriage must go the way of God.

The line 'Yet deem the whole proceeding slow' contains a *double entendre,* as in the slang of the day, the word 'slow' carried a distinct sexual connotation, meaning not only 'hum-drum,' 'dull,' and 'spiritless' but also 'sexually timid'. [487] Perhaps this was an allusion to Pearson's views on the desirability of 'free unions'. Certainly the line that follows it, 'Daily the secret murmurs grow', is a variation on the theme of his claim 'Taking marriage as it is, we may ask how far it necessarily cramps a woman's growth .... There are many women who distinctly affirm that it does.'

The third stanza gives an ironical outline of his analysis of 'historical precedent', in which he maintained:

> The right and wrong of the sex-relations ... is synonymous with the stability and instability of society. If the growing sex-equality connote sex-freedom – a return to general promiscuity – then it connotes a decay of the state ...

The stanza begins:

> Soon, before all men, each shall toast
> The seven strings unto his bow,
> Like beacon fires along the coast,

The flames of love shall glance and glow

The scene of rumbustious licentiousness depicted in these lines is described in deliberately masculine terms: 'The seven strings unto *his* bow'. And line three, 'Like beacon fires along the coast,' specifically identifies this free-for-all with societal instability, as the phrase 'beacon fires' is an allusion to the beacons that were set up along the coast of England to give advance warning of the anticipated French invasion during the Napoleonic wars that followed the French Revolution:[488] However, a subtle shift occurs in line five, when the referent 'men' becomes 'man,' thus widening the scope of the scene of unfettered debauchery to include all mankind. This echoes Pearson's comment, 'Sex-equality must be marked by the cessation of prostitution among men, or, if it remains, by the like freedom to women.' This, in turn, mirrors his outline of historical precedent, when an era of 'sex-equality' is inevitably followed by 'a return to general promiscuity.' Likewise, in the riotous Bacchanalia of Amy's imagined new society, both men *and* liberated women are free to behave as they please.

Nor let nor hindrance man shall know,
From natal bath to funeral sod;
Perennial shall his pleasure flow
When marriage goes the way of God.

The consequences of this wholesale destruction of the social order are outlined in the envoi:

Grant, in a million years at most,
Folks shall be neither pairs nor odd –
Alas! we shan't be here to boast
'Marriage has gone the way of God!'

Although the envoi is addressed to Grant Allen, the lines could also be read as a response to Pearson's enquiry: 'Granted that there is a large and increasing number of single women, we shall have to consider whether they are hopelessly handicapped by the present competitive constitution of society'.[489] Amy provides the answer to this question in her envoi. Allen had suggested that 'in a hundred years things will have righted themselves', but she had no such illusions. Even if women were to gain an equal degree of freedom to men, and 'Folks [are] neither pairs nor odd', in a million years nothing will have changed, as, in the Darwinian universe, all human beings must be aggressively competitive with one another in order to survive. Pearson's 'ray of hope', his patronising assertion that

> [woman] may see more clearly than [man] the real points at issue, and as she has learnt self-control in the past by subjecting her will to his, so in the future she may be able to submit her liberty to the restraints demanded by social welfare, and to the conditions needed for race-permanence[490]

is specifically denied by Amy in the envoi of her ballad. She harboured no such sanguine hopes for the future: 'Alas! We shan't be there to boast "Marriage has gone the way of God!"' This line is her reluctant acknowledgement that although the institutions of religion and marriage are undesirable in themselves, they provide a necessary defence against the destructive chaos of anarchy, which will be the inevitable consequence if the chains that hold the competitive human instinct in check are finally broken. Once the restraining bonds of religion and matrimony are removed, in the ensuing maelstrom even the fittest will not survive. For woman there is no way out of the dilemma – without religion and marriage the human race is doomed – within them woman is enslaved. This gloomy analysis, encapsulated within the final four lines of her verse, was Amy's last word on the subject which had been of such direct concern to her, and which had indirectly brought her so much sorrow. 'A Ballad of Religion and Marriage' was her final poetic admission of defeat.

Amy had expressed similar views in two of her last prose works. These were her second novel *Reuben Sachs* and her posthumously published short story 'Wise in her Generation'. The unnamed author of the obituary notice in the *Lady's Pictorial* claimed that in 'Wise in her Generation' Amy foretold her own death. Not long after Amy died, in October 1889, Beatrice Potter, a woman not renowned for effusive expressions of sympathy, made the following comments in her diary:

> The very demon of melancholy gripping me, my imagination fastening on Amy Levy's story, a brilliant young authoress of seven-and-twenty, in the hey-day of success, who has chosen to die rather than stand up longer to live. We talk of courage to meet death; alas, in these terrible days of mental pressure it is courage to *live* that we most lack, not courage to die. It is the supreme courage of fighting for an unknown cause, that fails us now and then. Poor Amy Levy! If there be no other faith for humanity than to eat, drink and be merry, for tomorrow we die, she has done well and wisely in choosing death for to our natures such contentment, such merriment is not possible; we are the 'unfit' and the sooner we leave our room to others the better.[491]

As these remarks indicate, Potter herself was no stranger to emotional suffering. In the early 1880s she had fallen deeply in love with Joseph Chamberlain but, having endured his cruel game of emotional cat and mouse for a number of years, had finally acknowledged that his view of a life partnership did not correspond with hers, and severed their relationship. Upon being jilted by Potter, the fifty-five year old Chamberlain promptly turned for solace to the pretty twenty-three year old daughter of a member of the American government. They were married in 1888. Despite her recognition that she could never have been happy as Chamberlain's wife, the news was a devastating blow to Beatrice. She described her reaction to the news of Chamberlain's engagement in her diary: '"Chamberlain's marriage" placarded all over the city… I had heard of the rumours for some time, but hardly believed it. … A gasp, as if one had been stabbed, and then it is over…[492] This bears a striking resemblance to Amy's description of Judith Quixano's response when she hears the newsboy's cry heralding the death of her romance in Reuben Sachs:

> Judith shivered …The noise in the street was very loud, and words could be distinguished.
>
> "What is it they are saying?" [Reuben] cried …
>
> Outside the house stood a dark figure, a narrow crackling sheet flung across one shoulder. A voice mounted up, clear in discordance through the mist:
>
> "Death of a Conservative M.P.! Death of the member for St. Baldwin's" …
>
> Cold, white trembling she heard the words and knew they were her sentence …"[493]

In April 1888, at the time when Beatrice Potter recorded her reaction to the news of Chamberlain's engagement in her diary, Amy was planning the plot of *Reuben Sachs*. One therefore cannot but wonder if the similarity between Beatrice Potter's real-life experience and Judith Quixano's fictional one was entirely coincidental. At that time Beatrice was researching into the conditions in the sweatshops of the East End for her cousin, Charles Booth. This not only entailed long hours studying in the Reading Room of the British Museum, where she probably encountered Amy working on her novel, but also involved extensive contact with the Jewish community. In the same entry she noted: 'Large dinner at the Adlers (Chief Rabbi) to meet me. The Jews have opened their arms to the dark-eyed Christian who is studying their East End life.'

While the Jewish community were opening their arms to Beatrice Potter, Amy Levy was hard at work in the Reading Room and elsewhere, preparing to deliver a bombshell that would result in some of them closing their doors to her. By the late spring of 1888, having completed the manuscript of *The Romance of a Shop* for T. Fisher Unwin, she set to work in earnest on *Reuben Sachs: A Sketch*. This was published by the father of her Newnham contemporary Olive Macmillan later in the same year.[494] *Reuben Sachs* anticipates 'A Ballad of Religion and Marriage' inasmuch as the destiny of its heroine, Judith Quixano, replicates the bleak analysis of the future for womankind that Amy outlined in the envoi of her ballad. Taken together, these two novels trace the course of Amy Levy's own life trajectory: *The Romance of a Shop* documenting her 'voyage out' when she made her bid for freedom after return from Cambridge *Reuben Sachs* chronicling her 'return to the fold' in the aftermath of her unhappy foray 'beyond the tribal limits'. But while the drama of *The Romance of a Shop* unfolds within the familiar setting of the London cityscape, in Reuben Sachs Amy Levy introduced her readership to an environment that, for the majority of them, would have been totally unfamiliar territory. This was the closed, conservative heart of the London Jewish community. In one of the essays that she had written for the *Jewish Chronicle*, Amy had expressed regret that there had been 'no serious attempt at serious treatment of ... the complex problem of Jewish life and Jewish character. The Jew... as we know him today... living, moving and having his being both within and without the tribal limits'.[495] *Reuben Sachs* was her attempt to rectify this omission. But in attempting to paint an authentic picture of contemporary Jewish life she gave grave offence to many within her community. The aspect of the novel that caused the most distress was the unflattering portrait she painted of what she regarded as their physical and moral shortcomings. But the timing of the novel was also spectacularly ill-judged. The last decades of the nineteenth century witnessed the rise to social prominence of two powerful Jewish dynasties – the Rothschilds and the Sassoons. Both families enjoyed the patronage of the Prince of Wales. The Prince, who was a notorious *bon viveur*, preferred the company of 'cosmopolitan, quick-witted Jews' because with them 'he could shoot, hunt, sail, guzzle and gamble in the grandest style without the gloomy protocol of Royal castles or some of the draughtier stately homes.'[496] The Sassoons' rise to Royal favour had been due, in part, to the sustained efforts of one of the more flamboyant members of their clan. This was Reuben Sassoon, great-uncle of the future poet Siegfried Sassoon.[497] Reuben, who, according to contemporary accounts, 'seemed to sparkle perpetually, from his gold teeth to the flashing diamond on his finger', had become a particular favourite with the Prince. However, while the wealthy Sassoons were reaping the benefits of their royal patronage, vast numbers of their dispossessed co-religionists were fleeing the pogroms in Eastern Europe. The established Anglo-Jewish community resented the influx of these impoverished aliens, believing that their presence would generate anti-Semitism within the wider population, thus threatening their own position in society. And those members of the community, like the Sassoons, who had the most to lose, also had the most to fear from any increase in anti-Semitic feeling. Set against this background it is unsurprising that Amy's novel, written at a time when Jewish sensitivities were running high, and with a title that either by accident or design called to mind one of the most prominent Jewish members of the Prince of Wales' notorious circle, should have stirred up resentment within Anglo-Jewry.

In the introduction to the recent reprint of *The Romance of a Shop*, Susan Bernstein states that the novel reflects 'a shifting consciousness, a mode of representation hovering between romance and realism'.[498] In *Reuben Sachs*, romance flies out of the window and realism comes to the fore, with an account of the unhappy fate of a Jewish woman who gives her heart in a relationship that is unsanctioned by her family. Whereas the Lorrimer sisters are independent-minded New Women, lively, adventurous and untrammelled by convention, Judith Quixano, the heroine of *Reuben Sachs*, is a traditional old-fashioned girl. Home-bound, dutiful, and devoid of ambition, she sees herself merely as 'one of a vast crowd of girls awaiting their promotion by marriage'. Judith is the daughter of an unworldly and impoverished Jewish scholar. Adopted at the age of fifteen by her rich uncle, Israel Leuniger, throughout her childhood and adolescence she has been treated as his own child. But when she reaches adulthood, which brings with it the question of her marriage, she is at a distinct disadvantage to her cousin Rose with whom, up to now, she has shared everything on equal terms. A pragmatist to her finger tips, Judith knows that because only a modest sum has been settled on her by her uncle as an inducement to a prospective bridegroom, her value in the marriage market is limited. Since childhood she has worshipped her cousin - or not quite cousin - Reuben Sachs. And Reuben also admires Judith. Amy tellingly emphasises that the 'fiction of cousinship ...had made possible [between Reuben and Judith] what is rare all the world over, but rarer than ever in the Jewish community – an intimacy between young people of opposite sexes'. She had made this point in print before, in her essay 'Middle Class Jewish Women of To-Day' in which she had lamented the 'oriental' attitude of Jewish men towards their womenfolk, complaining bitterly: 'Within [the Jewish community] frank and healthy intercourse between both sexes is almost impossible ... Once the all-important business of marriage and settlement is over and done with, they find that they have nothing to say to one another ...' Reuben and Judith have plenty to say to one another, a fact that is observed with disquiet by the Leunigers and Reuben's mother. However, they comfort themselves with the belief that 'Reuben will do nothing rash' – a belief which turns out to be fully justified. Some months later, at the Leunigers' ball, Reuben spies Judith *tête-à-tête* with his friend Bertie Lee-Harrison, a young aristocrat who has converted to Judaism. After tearing Judith's dance card to shreds in a fit of jealously, he is on the point of declaring his love for her, when his declaration is brought to an abrupt halt by the cry of the newsboy floating up from the street announcing the death of the MP whose seat he hopes to win. With the relieved look of a man 'who has escaped great danger', he promptly turns on his heels, allowing the flowers that he has just taken from Judith's corsage to fall to the floor, crushing them under his feet as he passes from the room. Judith, realising that her fate is sealed, returns home, cries herself to sleep and shortly afterwards accepts the hand of Bertie Lee-Harrison - to the delight and relief of her adoptive family. But Reuben proves to be not as mentally and physically resilient as he seems, and shortly after his election to the House of Commons he dies, both literally and figuratively, of a broken heart.

Intriguingly, Reuben Sachs had previously made a brief appearance in an unpublished short story that Amy wrote not long after she left Cambridge. 'St. Anthony's Vicarage' is yet another of her prose works in which culture and commerce are represented as opposing forces. In the closing stages of the narrative, during a discussion that takes place at a dinner party, one of the characters interjects the following commentary: 'I will make a very cynical remark, said Reuben Sachs, the Jew, who chanced to be one of the party. I never had the slightest faith in your mute inglorious Miltons.[499] The fit survive – they must – it's a law of nature'. Viewed in retrospect, this is a deeply ironical statement, as in the later novel that bears his name Reuben Sachs is destined not to survive. From the first paragraph onwards, it is made clear that the 'unfitness', which ultimately brings about his death, is caused by his struggle to transcend the limits of the community into which he had been born:

> After a highly successful career at one of the great London day-schools[500], he had gone up on a scholarship to the University ...the fact that he was a Jew had proved no bar to his popularity; he had gained many desirable friends and had, to some extent, shaken off the provincialism inevitable to one born and bred in the Jewish community.

But:

> In the midst of so much that was highly promising his health had broken down suddenly ... it was a case of over-work, of over-strain, of nervous break-down ... "More than half my patients are recruited from the ranks of the Jews," said the great physician whom Reuben consulted.

Despite the strain that it puts upon his constitution, Reuben revels in his double life which, we are told, 'owes something of its piquancy to the fact that it was led partly in the democratic atmosphere of modern London, partly in the conservative precinct of the Jewish community'. Amy emphasises that it is Reuben's involvement with the wider world that makes him so fascinating to Judith, although she does not share his passion for the city. Like the other women in her family circle, she has hardly any experience of life outside what Amy terms 'the tribal duckpond'. Her only direct contact with the population at large is either when she takes the omnibus to visit her parents and younger brothers (and unlike Gertrude Lorrimer she regards the omnibus as a means to an end rather than a 'transport of delight'), or when she is roped in to accompany her cousins Rose and Adelaide on their shopping expeditions to Whiteley's in Bayswater. In the 1880s, like its fictional Parisian counterpart *Au Bonheur des Dames*, Whiteley's department store was an attraction that drew shoppers from all over London and the suburbs.[501] Amy highlights the store's bustling, cosmopolitan ambiance in her account of the girls' shopping expedition: '"What a crowd!" ejaculated Adelaide … as she turned from the contemplation of some cheap ribbons in a basket. She had to the full the gregarious instincts of her race, and Whiteley's was her happy hunting ground'. This passage echoes Pearson's disparaging comments on the 'Hundreds of women - mere dolls – gazing intently into shop windows at various bits of coloured ribbon' in 'The Woman's Question'.[502] It also reflects the widely held opinion within Victorian society that Jews were both penny-pinching and vulgar. But although in *Reuben Sachs* Amy cast a harsh spotlight upon the shortcomings of her people, she also paid tribute to their virtues of tribal loyalty and love of tradition. Her true feelings for her ethnic family are revealed most clearly in the closing passages of the novel.

If Reuben's life 'beyond the tribal limits' has weakened his heart, his treatment of Judith has turned hers to stone. When told of Reuben's death by her husband, she does not faint as other women might, but instead turns her 'stony face' towards him and calmly veers the conversation in another direction. But as soon as Bertie has left to attend Lady Kemy's party, she moves over to the window, where she sits still as a statue, looking out across Kensington Gore towards the Albert Memorial surmounted by its gilded cross. The sight of this brash, glittering symbol of the British establishment, the nirvana that Reuben had sacrificed his life (and hers) to enter, finally confronts her with the enormity of her loss. And Judith Quixano's unspoken *cri de coeur* at her realisation that she has been cast her adrift from her own people for ever, is surely also the author's:

> A sudden longing for the old faces, the old ties and associations came over her … a strange fit of home-sickness, an inrushing sense of exile.

> Her people – oh, her people! To be back once more among them! When all was said, she had been so happy there.

Amy's last, posthumously published short story 'Wise in her Generation' gives a similar account of the wisdom that is gained through a disappointment in love. In many respects the story is a retelling of *Reuben Sachs*, because like Judith Quixano, Virginia Warwick, the heroine of the tale, is the victim of a highly competitive 'false social system' in which young girls are sacrificed on the altar of matrimony in the cause of financial gain or social advancement. During her first London season Virginia falls in love with a handsome young barrister, Philip Shand. Although Philip does not directly declare his love for her, like Arthur West in Dollie Radford's *One Way of Love* 'with every look, with every tone, he says *"I love you"*'. But Virginia is in for a shock: 'One day a bolt falls from the sky; [Philip] is going to be married to a woman of fortune, of good connections'. Like Reuben Sachs, Philip believes in the Darwinist doctrine of the survival of the fittest and, accordingly, has ensured his own survival by paying court to an heiress, although he still maintains an interest in Virginia. Philip's duplicity has been a salutary experience for Virginia, hardening her heart (like Judith Quixano's) and making her cynical. Pondering on her newly acquired cynicism, Virginia – the now wise virgin – reflects:

> Without knowledge of life there can be no true enjoyment of life. Life, I maintain, in the face of the sentimentalists, to be an acquired taste. For the educated palate there are all sorts of gustatory surprises … far more delicious than, if not quite so wholesome as, the roast meat and boiled pudding of domesticity. You were right Philip; and I, who once believed myself your victim, crushed beneath the Juggernaut-car of your ambition – I was wrong. [503]

This passage sounds a striking echo of the second stanza of 'A Ballad of Religion and Marriage', in which the 'domestic round of boiled and roast' is deemed 'slow'. The word Juggernaut also, ironically, anticipates Grant Allen's comment that Amy Levy had been 'sacrificed … before the face of our fashionable Juggernaut.'

In order to avenge her betrayal, like Judith, Virginia attempts to reassert her hold on her faithless lover by encouraging the attentions of a wealthy baronet, Sir Guy Ormond. At this point the author makes a cameo appearance in the narrative in the guise of 'Medora Grey, the poetess', who has designs on Sir Guy herself. Contemplating the dowdy and desperate Medora with a pitying gaze Virginia thinks: 'Heaven save me from the laurels of female third-rate celebrity! Unless one happens to be a Patti or Lady Burdett-Coutts, or Queen Elizabeth there is only one way of success open to a woman: the way of marriage'.[504] Virginia subsequently has no difficulty in luring Sir Guy away from her ill-favoured rival, but just as her plan comes to fruition, with the baronet's proposal of marriage, her determination fails her. She has not yet developed the necessary Darwinian tools of survival to enable her to go for the kill. This revelation causes the scales to fall from her eyes, as realisation dawns that in the 'huge, hideous struggle' of human existence, integrity is an impediment to survival. As with Judith Quixano, the last time we catch sight of Virginia she is gazing out of her window across the city:

> The wind is soft and very sweet; there is no sound save the distant murmur of the Great City.
>
> Black, black in its heart is the City; the blackness of man's heart is revealed in its huge, hideous struggle for existence.
>
> Better to be unfit and perish, than survive at such a cost.

At this point Virginia sends away her maid, and we are left to assume that shortly afterwards she throws herself from the window.

Emily Brontë's lament

> Twas grief enough to think mankind
> All hollow, servile, insincere;
> But worse to trust to my own mind
> And find the same corruption there[505]

is echoed in Amy Levy's final forlorn acknowledgement that 'the blackness of man's heart' is universal and inescapable. And just as Judith Quixano's impassioned lament for the loss of her people and Virginia Warwick's *cri de cœur* 'better to be unfit and perish' was their cry of protest against 'the pitiless order of things',[506] so 'A Ballad of Religion and Marriage' was Amy Levy's ultimate admission of defeat. Like her fictional heroines she was confronted with a painful choice. In order to survive in society as it is presently ordered she must, like Judith Quixano, bow to 'Inevitable Law',[507] which meant compromising her principles, as Pearson had done by proposing marriage to Maria Sharpe. Alternatively, if she could not face either a life lived alone in penury or with a man in a state of loveless, legalised prostitution, like Virginia Warwick, she must 'Slay my body utterly'.[508] She chose the second honest and honourable option.

In January 1890, Ellen (Crofts) Darwin's tribute to 'The Poems of Amy Levy' was published in the *Cambridge Review*. She claimed that although Amy's verse

> is indeed only poetry by starts and flashes ... in spite of all, it is stamped with the mark of genius – it possesses the power of strong feeling. Such is the poetry of Emily Brontë and Amy Levy. I do not wish to compare the poetry of these two women. It is as different as their natures were different, but it has this one thing in common – it was written with their heart's blood.

This last line almost precisely replicates Oscar Wilde's words in his obituary of Amy Levy, when he described her work as 'her life's blood'.[509] Ellen Darwin continued:

> I do not think that anyone could confuse her poetry with the conventional poetry of cultivated weariness and despair .... It is the pathos of one who realises intensely and exclusively what life can offer to the young and eager – the joy of loving and of being loved and understood; but of one who has herself never attained it – who has only passionately felt the other side – of failure, of disappointment, of disillusion, and despair .... It is this personal struggle for life and joy continually beaten back that gives the tone to Amy Levy's poems. In them it takes different forms, but it is almost invariably the tragedy of the waste and wreck of feeling either against *hard human hearts* [my emphasis] or through circumstances.

Ellen's tribute to the friend who had paid tribute to *her* in 'To E' - the poem that commemorated the idyllic, sunny afternoons that the trio of 'Platonic friends' had spent together beside the little lake in the grounds of the Hotel Sonnenberg in 1883 - concluded with a heartfelt plea:

> Death as she found it brings with it no solemnity or silence to cover her memory, but leaves it the prey of curiosity and wonder. From this no friend can shield her. But perhaps those who have suffered and endured will be tender to the memory of one who has suffered and despaired.[510]

Through the scientific methods she chose for the execution of her death and the disposal of her body, Amy Levy proclaimed herself a veritable 'girl of the future'. In her life, in the method of her death, and in her writing she exhibited a level of insight, knowledge and accomplishment that distinguished her from the majority of her peers. As Ellen Darwin and Oscar Wilde both indirectly acknowledged, Amy Levy was no mere pedlar of potboilers, no superficial 'poetess'. Her literary work – her 'life's blood' – was wrung from bitter experience. In all these aspects, she can truly be judged to have been 'Wise in her Generation', but her wisdom was gained at a terrible cost.

Conclusion

> Shall I wander in vain for my country?
>   Shall I seek and not find?
> Shall I cry for the bars that encage me,
>   The fetters that bind?

Amy Levy, 1861–1889: 'Captivity'

Almost forty years after Amy Levy's death, Virginia Woolf wrote: 'No age can have been as stridently sex-conscious as our own; those innumerable books by men about women in the British Museum are a proof of it.' The story of Amy Levy's life is testimony to the fact that 'sex-consciousness' was as rife in the eighteen eighties as it was in the nineteen twenties, and that Virginia Woolf's claim that the campaign for female emancipation was the cause of men's 'extraordinary desire for self assertion' was as relevant then as it was when she was writing *A Room of One's Own* in 1928.[511]

What Virginia Woolf termed 'sex consciousness' was a by-product of the social segregation of men and women that had been established within middle-class Victorian society. This had created the 'false social system' deplored by Karl Pearson in 'The Woman's Question'. One of the most pervasive images that this system produced was 'the angel in the house' - the fictional domestic Goddess who was the bane of the progressive Victorian woman's life. The role assigned to this paragon of virtue was the creation of an ordered, peaceful haven for her bread-winning husband to return to, and her brood of children to grow up in. In reality, as Grant Allen and Karl Pearson both pointed out in their essays on the woman question, demographic changes in the population meant that by the last decades of the nineteenth century there was a growing band of women who were destined to remain single throughout their lives. These women were all too often condemned to a solitary, servile existence, toiling as governesses or acting as ladies' companions, subjugating their own needs and desires to the whims and fancies of strangers. The alternative, which was to remain within the family home (if they had one), entailed reliance upon the charity of sometimes reluctant parents or siblings in order to keep a roof over their head and food on their plate. The 'Angel' at least had the consolation of her children which, as Amy observed in the closing sentence of *Reuben Sachs*, gave life a 'quickening of purpose'. But married or single, all women were subject to the stringent rules of behaviour that denied them the social and sexual freedom taken for granted by men. This double standard of sexual morality created the second category of iconic Victorian womanhood, the fallen woman. But towards the end of the nineteenth century, from the survival struggle of the 'odd woman', a new species began to evolve. This was the New Woman. The emergence of the New Woman signalled a radical change in late Victorian society, as she set about the task of slaying the angel in the house and raising the fallen woman from the gutter.

Unfortunately, her efforts were consistently undermined by her self-proclaimed male supporters, like Grant Allen and Karl Pearson, who, whilst paying lip service to the concept of female emancipation, were busily engaged in a vigorous rearguard action in order to ensure that woman's advancement did not threaten the supremacy of their own sex. Their innumerable 'books … about women in the British Museum' are an enduring testimony to the anxiety which the emerging New Woman aroused in the breast of late nineteenth-century man. By defining and categorising the 'natural' female attributes, these Darwinist male analysts of the female of the species set out to substitute one set of absolute rules for another. In their discourse on the woman question divine decree – the Biblical 'word' – was replaced by natural law – Darwinist theory. But as far as women were concerned, the end result was the same. Instead of being confined to the drawing room by considerations of propriety, they were to be shackled to the nursery in the interests of the future of the race.

The quest for a wider role in the world inevitably drew the New Woman into the perilous uncharted waters of sex. Conventional wisdom decreed that the independent-minded single woman was a menace to society. In reality, the reverse was the case, and the established social order posed a real and significant threat to her, not only by limiting her capacity to support herself financially, but also by exposing her to the risk of becoming a social pariah. Those women, who took a principled stand against convention, as Amy Levy did, frequently discovered that doors that had previously been open to them were closed in their face thereafter. Amy's friend Eleanor Marx understood this quite well. She freely acknowledged that her decision to live openly with Edward Aveling would be likely to alienate many of her acquaintance, even though they were supposedly 'free-thinkers'. Her concern proved to be fully justified. Pearson's reaction when confronted with Maria Sharpe's admission that she had changed her mind about free unions is an example of the kind of *volte face* that Eleanor experienced. Despite his contempt for the institution of matrimony, when faced with Maria's change of heart, which occurred just at the time when he had begun to consider her as a future bride, his latent conservatism came to the fore. His reply to her revealed his alarm at the idea that the woman he might marry would sanction the notion (previously held by him) that it was acceptable for a woman to give herself to a man outside wedlock. He wrote angrily:

> Should [a woman who believed in free unions] ... put her views into practice, or to venture to teach them, she will be a social outcast ... Believe me, no woman ought at the present day to disbelieve in marriage, unless they had £10,000 a year, or a saleable beauty, or the power to write *Adam Bede* .[512]

Eleanor's apprehension about the social ostracism she was likely to face after setting up home with Aveling, together with Pearson's response to Maria's revelation of her altered view of free unions, demonstrate that in reality the advanced woman's supposed immorality, and the threat that this was deemed to pose to society, was largely illusory. For women like Amy Levy and Eleanor Marx, whose unconventional lifestyle had denied them the option of a conventional marriage, their challenge to the moral code was undertaken in a spirit of pioneering determination rather than wanton licentiousness. They were perfectly well aware that by throwing down the gauntlet to 'Mrs. Grundy', they were exposing themselves to considerable personal risk. Once again, the men (like Aveling and Pearson) who were the first to rush to help them in their noble enterprise were also the first to desert the ship once storm clouds gathered overhead. Small wonder that Amy came to question whether the effort was worthwhile. In her poem 'Captivity' she gave anguished voice to her recognition that the price of freedom was probably too high:

> The lion remembers the forest,
> The lion in chains;
> To the bird that is captive a vision
> Of woodland remains
>
> One strains with his strength at the fetter,
> In impotent rage;
> One flutters in flights of a moment,
> And beats at the cage ...
>
> When the chain shall at last be broken,
> The window set wide;
> And I step in the largeness and freedom;
> Of sunlight outside;

Shall I wander in vain for my country?
    Shall I seek and not find?
Shall I cry for the bars that encage me,
    The fetters that bind?

Like Emily Dickinson's 'The Duel' (the poem that heads the Preface to this biography), Amy Levy's 'Captivity' encapsulates the conflict between 'feminist' hope and 'feminine' despair, which was the hallmark of the poetry of the New Woman. Both poems are a clarion call to freedom, which is immediately tempered by doubt. And both characterise the almost schizophrenic mindset of the forward-thinking late nineteenth-century women writer, for whom the power of the pen was a double-edged sword. By taking power into her own hands, becoming an author in order to challenge authority, she transgressed her assigned feminine role which, in the Victorian era, was predicated on powerlessness and reticence. In so doing she effectively 'unsexed' herself. Falling between the two stools of conviction and convention, she became yet another variant of the fallen woman – a victim this time, not of her own immorality, but of her own audacity.

I aimed my pebble, but myself
Was all the one that fell.
Was it Goliath was too large,
Or was myself too small?

Emily Dickinson answered her own question by voluntarily withdrawing from the world, but as she was aware, there was an alternative way out of the dilemma – the one chosen by Eleanor Marx and Amy Levy – through death.

The labels (Jew, lesbian, depressive), which have been pinned on Amy Levy by scholarly researchers and literary analysts in recent years have tended to categorise her as a marginal, marginalised individual, who played a minor role in the literary life of her time. But in reality, as her life story reveals, far from being an isolated and anomalous figure within late Victorian literary society, she was a central member of the circle of writers, intellectuals and political activists who were at the cutting edge of modern thought. Within ten years of her death, novels written by women like Emma Frances Brooke, Ménie Muriel Dowie and 'George Egerton' had drawn the New Woman out of the shadows and placed her firmly centre stage within the public spotlight. Their mainstream male contemporaries like George Gissing, Thomas Hardy and H.G. Wells were quick to jump on this revolutionary new bandwagon. And if, as Grace Black had lamented, Amy had only had 'more patience',[513] her name would undoubtedly have endured alongside theirs.

The story of Amy Levy's life is the story of modern woman's first faltering steps on the road to freedom. Unfortunately, Amy herself was ill-equipped to undertake the journey. Despite her passionate desire to 'conquer and attain',[514] her ethnicity, her gender, and the power of her intellect were factors that individually would have presented her with problems. In combination, they proved fatal. As her realisation of the hopelessness of her situation dawned, her constitution, which was never robust, was further weakened by the knowledge that her yearning (like Beatrice Potter's) for 'love and support'[515] was unlikely to be realised. Her psychological collapse was not, as Grant Allen claimed, due to the pressure of 'Higher Instruction' on the brain, but was the result of her realisation that she was beating her head against the brick wall of convention. As Beatrice Potter herself observed, Amy's misery was the by-product of the era in which she lived: 'in these terrible days of mental pressure it is courage to live that we most lack, not courage to die.'[516]

Amy Levy failed in her mission of survival because, in the final analysis, she was unable to reconcile the reality of her life with the 'cravings of her heart'.[517] However, as Ellen Darwin perceptively noted, this dichotomy was the driving force behind her poetic vision. It also inspired some of her finest prose writing.[518] This biography has shown that it was her relationship with Karl Pearson and his Cambridge educated 'men of the future' that was responsible for the marked shift of focus that occurred in both her life and her writing during the mid-1880s. And just as her friend Eleanor Marx took her life after her discovery of Edward Aveling's secret marriage, so Amy Levy's suicide was the result of Olive Schreiner's revelation of Karl Pearson's secret engagement to Maria Sharpe. Amy's early poetry had been fired with passionate feminist commitment. By the time that she began correcting the proofs of *A London Plane Tree* shortly before she took her life, in August 1889, this conviction had diminished into weary fatalism. This change was due to her final acknowledgment that, like her fictional anti-heroine Xantippe, her 'woman mind had gone astray'.[519] Man's character would never change, and, in consequence, her 'high thoughts and golden dreams'[520] amounted to nothing.

I will leave the last judgement on Amy Levy's life to her friend Vernon Lee, who provided a summing up of her tragedy in her essay 'Beauty and Sanity':

> I used at one time to have frequent discussions on art and life with a certain poor friend of mine, who should have found sweetness in both, giving both sweetness in return, but, alas, did neither. We were sitting in the fields where the frost-bitten green was just beginning to soften into starlike buds and mosses, and the birds were learning to sing in the leafless lilac hedgerows, the sunshine, as it does in spring, seemed to hold the world rather than merely to pour on to it. 'You see,' said my friend, you see, there is a fundamental difference between us. You are satisfied with what you call *happiness*; but I want *rapture and excess.*'

> Alas, a few years later, the chance of happiness had gone. The door was opened, of which Epictetus wrote that we might always pass through it; in this case not because 'the room was too full of smoke,' but, what is sadder by far, because the room was merely whitewashed and cleanly swept.
>
> But those words 'rapture and excess,' spoken in such childlike simplicity of spirit have always remained in my mind. Should we not teach our children, among whom there may be such a one as that one was, that the best thing life can give is just that despised thing happiness?dxxi

For women like Amy Levy, whose life circumstances conspired to render her unfit to fulfil her designated role in the society into which she was born, happiness was a rare commodity. Her life became an unceasing and bitter struggle for survival. It was to her cost that the effort finally defeated her, but to our gain that she was not vanquished before she had immortalised her life in her writing.

Notes

[1] Chandler Moulton, Louise. 'A Young English Genius'. *Boston Herald*. 17th March 1889.

[2] Although the few photographs of Amy Levy portray her with her hair tied back, a diary entry that she made towards the end of her life she refers to having her 'hair cut'. A number of Amy's close friends including Dollie Radford and Edith Nesbitt had cut their hair short.

[3] Information given to me by Katherine Solomon, granddaughter of Katie Solomon and grandniece of Amy Levy.

[4] The present owners of the archive are Camellia PLC, to whom I am indebted for permission to examine the Levy papers. Citations from material in the archive will henceforth be attributed: 'Camellia PLC'

[5] I am indebted to Dr. Joseph, who is an eminent Jewish genealogist, for providing me with a photocopy of this document. Dr. Joseph is a descendant of Amy Levy.

[6] Levy, Sharona Anne. *Amy Levy: The Woman and Her Writings*. Unpublished thesis. Oxford University, 1989. Sharona Levy cites no source for this information, but she did speak at length to Beth Zion Abrahams. As far as I am aware, Sharona Levy is not related in any way to Amy Levy.

[7] Last Will and Testament of Amy Levy, granted probate in 1890. Public Records Office.

[8] Glage, Liselotte. *Clementina Black: A Study in Social History and Literature*. Heidelberg: Carl Winter, Universitatsverlag, 1981. 22.

[9] MacEwen: Grace Black to Ernest Radford, 16th September 1889.

[10] 'Mainly About People'. *Star*. 23rd September 1889: 1.

[11] For instance, a large part of Ada Radford's correspondence was left to Newnham College on the condition that it was not to be made available for public scrutiny before the year 2000. In the summer of 1999, with the millennium almost at hand, Ann Thomson, Clerk to the Newnham College Archive, arranged for me to gain access to the restricted Radford papers. I understand that I was the first scholar to be given permission to examine the documents. Although there is no reference to Amy Levy in the correspondence, I gained some useful background information about Hume Pinsent and other members of her circle. There may be direct references to Amy Levy in Radford's two locked diaries, for which – unfortunately – the keys have been lost.

[12] The London Met Office records that on 9th September, the date of Amy's suicide, there was 'an anticyclone (area of high pressure) over Northern France resulting in a fine, warm day'. The evening temperature was recorded as 67 deg. F (19.4 deg. C) with light West to South Westerly winds. This is significant, because Amy was generally at her happiest during fine, warm weather. I am indebted to Mark Beswick, Archive Information Officer at the National Meteorological Archive for this informa-

tion.

[13] See Introduction note 1.

[14] See letter from Clementina Black. 'Literary Gossip' *The Athenaeum* 5th October 1889.

[15] Booth, Charles. *Descriptive Map of London Poverty.* Online Archive.

[16] This quotation is taken from Lucy Marks' hand-written account of the Levy family history. Lucy Marks was Amy Levy's cousin.. Further citations from this account will be attributed: Marks.

[17] Surviving photographs of Amy Levy indicate that she was of below average height.

[18] Marks.

[19] Marks.

[20] Joseph, Anthony. 'The Jewry of South West England and its Australian Connections.' *Transactions of the Jewish Historical Society*, XXIV (1974).

[21] See Hunt Beckman, Linda. *Amy Levy: Her Life and Letters.* Athens, Ohio: Ohio University Press, 2000. 18.

[22] Camellia PLC.

[23] Camellia PLC.

[24] The record of Lewis Levy's rental of three seats at the West London Synagogue and related correspondence forms part of the Archive of the West London Synagogue, Special Collections, Parkes Centre, University of Southampton.

[25] During the morning service the male members of the congregation repeat the invocation: 'Blessed art thou, O Lord our God, King of the universe, who has not made me a woman,' which is followed by the response of the female members: 'Blessed art thou, O Lord our God, King of the universe, who has made me according to thy will.' *The Authorised Daily Prayer Book of the United Hebrew Congregations of the British Empire.* London: Eyre and Spottiswoode Ltd., 1935 (5965). 6

[26] Marks.

[27] In Levy's 'Calendrier 1889', a number of entries refer to the family going to or returning from Brighton. Camellia PLC.

[28] Camellia PLC.

[29] Camellia PLC.

[30] Marks.

[31] Camellia PLC.

[32] Camellia PLC.

[33] *Kind Words Magazine for Boys and Girls* was published by The Sunday School Union, 56 Old Bailey, London EC1. Although the journal had had a predominantly Christian ethos, it also covered subjects of general interest, including new discoveries in science and the natural world. At the time of the pub-

lication of Amy's essay, the journal was running a series of articles on 'Modern British Poets'.

[34] Camellia PLC. Quoted from a press cutting of the essay.

[35] The *Pelican* was edited by Richard King Jnr. and published by Simkin Marshall. In her article on Amy Levy Beth Zion Lask (née Abrahams) asserts that the second half of the poem was never published, as the issue in which it was due to appear 'never saw the light of day.' This claim appears to be erroneous, as a press cutting of the second half of the poem is included amongst Amy's papers. Camellia PLC.

[36] In November 1878 Lewis Levy wrote to the West London Synagogue to resign the three seats that he held there because 'we are living altogether in Brighton'. Archive of the West London Synagogue of British Jews. Special Collections, Parkes Centre. University of Southampton.

[37] For an account of Edith Creak's education see Mrs. M. G. Mills. *Brighton and Hove High School 1876–1952*. Brighton: Brighton Herald Ltd., 1953, and Hamilton, Mary Agnes. *Newnham: An Informal Biography*: London: Faber & Faber, 1936.

[38] Garnett, Richard. *Constance Garnett: A Heroic Life*. London: Sinclair-Stevenson, 1991. 25.

[39] Shortly after Amy's suicide Connie Black (by then Garnett) commented in a letter to her sister: 'What a sad end to a sad life. I can feel no grief for her ... But her poor mother –I cannot bear to think of her.' Garnett 68.

[40] Vicinus, Martha. *Independent Women: Work and Community for Single Women 1850–1920*. London: Virago, 1985. 188–189.

[41] The word is difficult to read but appears to be 'mashers' – at that time a commonly used slang term for a dandy or a fop.

[42] A former pupil of Edith Creak's described her as 'big and very, very fat with a hearty laugh'. See Mills, M.G., 16.

[43] Camellia PLC.

[44] Camellia PLC.

[45] Camellia PLC.

[46] This ironic reference to Levy's 'spouse' reinforces the widespread acceptance of 'passionate friendships' between girls.

[47] Camellia PLC.

[48] Garnett. 29

[49] Levy, Amy. 'Jewish Women and "Women's Rights".' *The Jewish Chronicle*. 7 Feb. 1879: 5.

[50] The term 'juvenile' should not be taken as an indication that Amy was a child when this sketch was made. Many of the drawings in the same album are records of identifiable events that took place when she was in her mid-to-late teens.

[51] 'C'. 'Jewish Women and "Women's Rights".' *The Jewish Chronicle*. 21st February 1879: 5.

[52] 'A Jewess and a Lover of Fair Play': 'Jewish Women and "Women's Rights".' *The Jewish Chronicle*. 14th February 1879: 5.

[53] Garnett. 30

[54] Three shillings and three pence in old English money. That Amy felt it necessary to tell her mother the price that she paid for the shoes reveals that, like most students today, her budget was limited.

[55] Camellia PLC.

[56] Newnham College archive.

[57] Amy's letter is headed '1880 Norwich House'. Camellia PLC

[58] Camellia PLC.

[59] Amy's choice of the pseudonym U.G.L.Y. may have been inspired by Eliza Cook's 'Song of the Ugly Maiden'

[60] Clough, Blanche Athena. *Memoir of Anne Jemima Clough*. London: Edward Arnold, 1897. 218. Anne Jemima Cough, the Principal of Newnham College, was the sister of the poet Arthur Hugh Clough. Formerly the secretary of the North of England Council for Promoting the Higher Education of Women, in 1871 she was persuaded by Henry Sidgwick to take charge of the first residence for women students at Newnham in Regent Street, Cambridge.

[61] Levy, Amy. 'Newnham College – "II The Students".' *Cambridge Review*. The article appears under the pseudonym '-x.' The passage quoted is from a press cuttings pasted into Amy's scrap book. The cuttings provide no further edition details. Camellia PLC.

[62] See Endelmann, Todd M. *The Jews of Britain 1656 to 2000*. Berkeley, Los Angeles and London: University of California Press. 2002. 115

[63] Gray, Frances R. *And Gladly Wolde He Lerne and Gladly Teche – A Book About Learning and Teaching*. London: Sampson Low, Marston & Co. Ltd., n.d. 28. Grey later became headmistress of St. Paul's School.

[64] Gray. 28–29.

[65] 'Run to Death: A True Incident of Pre-Revolutionary France' was written in 1876 when Levy was 15. The poem was first published in the *Dublin University Magazine* in May 1879. Amy later included the poem in *Xantippe*, her first collection of verse.

[66] Alice Lloyd (later Dew Smith) was the Granddaughter of Bartholomew Lloyd, Provost of Trinity College Dublin.

[67] Raverat, Gwen. *Period Piece: a Cambridge Childhood*. London: Faber & Faber, 1932. 193.

[68] (Sir) Charles Villiers Stanford 1852-1924. Composer. Stanford was appointed Professor of Composition at the Royal College of Music in 1883 and Professor of Music at Cambridge in 1887.

[69] See Plunket Greene, Harry. *Charles Villiers Stanford.* London: E. Arnold & Co., 1935. 62.

[70] Dibble, Jeremy. *Charles Villiers Stanford: Man and Musician.* Oxford: Oxford University Press, 2002. 84-5.

[71] (Sir)George Grove 1820-1900. Musicographer. While editor of Macmillan's Magazine he instigated the publication of the *Dictionary of Music and* Musicians. He was appointed the first director of the Royal College of Music in 1882. Herman Goetz 1840-1876. Pianist, organist and composer.

[72] The report of Amy's admiration for physical beauty was made in 'The Tragedy of Amy Levy' *Pall Mall Gazette* September 25 1891. 4.

[73] 'To Sylvia' and 'Sinfonia Eroica' were first published in the *Cambridge Review* in March 1882 and later reprinted in *A Minor Poet.* Amy's dedication 'to Sylvia' was probably a reference to William Shakespeare's song 'Who is Sylvia'.

[74] See, for example: Hunt Beckman, Linda. *Amy Levy: Her Life and Letters.* Ohio: University of Ohio Press, 2000. 87.

[75] Levy, Amy 'Middle-Class Jewish Women of To-Day.' *The Jewish Chronicle.* 17th September 1886: 7.

[76] Bland, Lucy *Banishing the Beast: English Feminism and Sexual Morality 1885-1914.* London: Penguin Books. 1995. 170

[77] Faderman, Lillian. *Surpassing the Love of Men: Romantic Friendship and Love Between Women from the Renaissance to the Present.* London: The Women's Press, 1991. 172

[78] Oppenheim, Janet. *Shattered Nerves: Doctors, Patients and Depression in Victorian England.* New York and Oxford: Oxford University Press, 1991. 204.

[79] Amy is referring to Friedrich de la Motte Fouquet's *Undine* in which the water nymph Undine marries a knight in order to gain a soul.

[80] Charles Darwin makes specific reference to 'the service rendered to the community' by 'the worker-bees which kill their brother drones' in *The Descent of Man*

[81] The last line of 'To Sylvia'

[82] See Plunkett Greene, photograph of Jennie Wetton and Dibble, Jeremy. *Charles Villiers Stanford: Man and Musician.* Oxford: Oxford University Press. 2002 photograph of Jennie Stanford by Hubert von Herkomer, 1883.

[73] Amy included a slightly amended version of this poem in *Xantippe and Other Verse.* Cambridge. E. Johnson & Co., 1881.

[74] Keynes, F.A. *Gathering up the Threads.* Cambridge: W. Heffer & Sons Ltd., 1950. 39. In view of Keynes' reference to Ann Bond being 'some years older than the rest of us' it is likely that the 'Miss Bond' mentioned by Amy in her letters was her younger sister, Minnie Bond.

[85] One of the early students described her sister's experience of being admitted to lectures at King's

for the first time: 'They were met on King's bridge … by an undergrad – he directed them where to go (they were taken) into the hall where they were put into lovely leather chairs – with pens and ink & there they were 4 of them and Miss C. – surrounded by about 50 men.' See Phillips, Ann (ed). *A Newnham Anthology*. Cambridge: Cambridge University Press, 1979. 9.

[86] See: Porter, Theodore M. *Karl Pearson: The Scientific Like in a Statistical Age*. Princeton and Oxford: Princeton University Press, 2004. 40. The Tripos results were reported in *The Times* on 24th January, 1879, and Pearson's picture (a line drawing) appeared in *The Graphic* on 4th February. Pearson Papers.

[87] Pearson to Sharpe, 8th September 1889. Pearson Papers. This confessional letter, which was written after his engagement to Maria Sharpe, just two days before Amy committed suicide, provides a revealing insight into Pearson's ambivalent attitude to women.

[88] E.G.E.L. Bulwer-Lytton. *Kenelm Chillingly*. Edinburgh: William Blackwood & Sons, 1873. Kenelm, the only child of elderly parents, is described as 'solemn, precocious and sceptical'.

[89] Porter. 28

[90] Levy, Amy. *Xantippe and Other Verse*. Cambridge: E. Johnson & Co., 1881. The volume took its title from the poem that had appeared in the *Dublin University Magazine* in 1878.

[91] Apart from the report that Constance Black's sister Clementina is reputed to have played a role in getting the work into print. See Glage, Liselotte. *Clementina Black: A study in social history and literature*. Heidelberg: Carl Winter, 1981. 21.

[92] Porter. 87

[93] Obituary notice: 'Amy Levy'. *The Woman's World*. London: Cassell & Co. Ltd., 1890. 51.

[94] The passing of the 'Three Graces' by the Senate gave female students admission to 'the Previous Examination and Tripos Examinations of the University' and entitled the successful candidates to a certificate. The second Grace decreed that 'In each class of female students in which the names are arranged in order of merit, the place which each of the students would have occupied in the corresponding Class of Members of the University shall be indicated.'

[95] Possibly 'Run to Death'?

[96] See Hawkins, Mike. *Social Darwinism in European and American Thought 1860-1845*. Cambridge: Cambridge University Press, 1997. 251. Hawkins writes: 'Darwin, like Huxley, was in favour of the extension and the improvement of the education of females, but both men were convinced that because of their biologically determined disadvantages women could not compete with men on equal terms in the same spheres.' Pearson was to express similar views in his essay 'The Woman's Question'.

[97] Webster, August. *A Housewife's Opinions*. London: Macmillan, 1879.

[98] Linda Hunt Beckman claims that Madge/Maggie's full name was Margaret Johnson. Amy refers to

'Madge' in one of her letters from Newnham. There is no record of a Margaret Johnson on the Newnham College Register during the period of Amy Levy's residence there. There is however, an entry for a Gertrude Mary Johnson for the year 1880.

[99] At that time Katie was studying at the London Academy. By this date the family were living at 11 Sussex Place, Regents Park, which was a very prestigious address. When taken in combination with Amy's subsequent comments in the letter, this indicates that at this time the Levys may have been living somewhat beyond their means.

[100] A photograph of Amy taken at 'R. Eiche's Atelier, Dresden, 38 Pragerstrasse'. The photograph is signed 'Amy Levy, 1882'. Camellia PLC

[101] Camellia PLC

[102] Camellia PLC.

[103] Camellia PLC

[104] Camellia PLC.

[105] The reference to the congregation being 'unventilated and unrefreshed' is an allusion to the fact that the congregation had been fasting. This, together with Amy's reference to the shops having been closed, establishes that her attendance at synagogue was to mark Yom Kippur - the Day of Atonement. This is the most sacred festival in the Jewish calendar.

[106] Levy, Amy. 'Between Two Stools'. *Temple Bar*, 69: 337–350.

[107] Leighton, Angela (ed). *Victorian Women Poets: A Critical Reader*. Oxford: Blackwell, 1996. 217.

[108] The poem quoted is Swinburne's 'Felise', which appeared in his first series of 'Poems and Ballads', published in 1866.

[109] This issue has caused some confusion, largely because Karl Pearson (who was a member of the first Men and Women's Club) later commandeered the name for his own, more radical *The* Men and Women's Club. The first club's record book, which is housed in the Pearson Papers, UCL, is clearly labelled: 'A Men and Women's Club'. Confusion about the name has arisen primarily because Dollie Radford refers to it merely as 'the club' in her diary. This is the main source of information about the first Men and Women's Club's proceedings. But Dollie Radford's granddaughter, Ann MacEwen, confirmed that the club's full name was definitely 'A Men and Women's Club'.

[110] Alfred Levy is listed as a cast member of 'First Love'. MacEwan.

[111] Eleanor's nickname was pronounced 'Toosy'.

[112] Garnett. 40

[113] The practice of leaving a *carte de visite*, or calling card, was an established custom within the middle and upper classes. In this instance by leaving their cards on Ernest Radford's desk, Eleanor and Dollie would have conveyed the message that he was invited to pay a call at the Marx family home.

[114] According to Yvonne Kapp 'Marx wrote to Jenny [his daughter] in April 1881: "Tussy has discovered a new *Wunderkind* among the Dogberries [the Marx Shakespeare reading club members], a certain Radford; this youth is already a barrister-at-law .... He looks well, a cross between Irving and Lassalle .... An intelligent and somewhat promising boy .... Dolly Maitland pays fearful court to him."' Kapp. Vol. I 194n.

[115] *Newnham College Roll* 'Letter'. January 1935. 37–39.

[116] James Dykes Campbell and his wife. Dykes Campbell was an author, and Honorary Secretary of the Browning Society. He had a wide circle of literary acquaintance, including Walter Pater and Arthur Symons.

[117] MacEwan.

[118] Dollie Radford diary entry, 6th June1883.

[119] Louis Jeeves died of diphtheria a year before Amy, in 1888.

[120] Garnett. 34.

[121] MacEwan.

[122] Porter. 32-33

[123] There has been some confusion about precise timing of Amy's visit to Switzerland. Beth Zion Abrahams, who was the original custodian of the Levy papers, believed that she travelled there in 1884, but more recently, Linda Hunt Beckman has claimed that Amy journeyed on to Lucerne after leaving Dresden in 1882. The evidence she cites for this claim is an annotation made by Amy in her own copy of *A Minor Poet*, which records that 'Medea' (one of the verses included in the volume) was written in 'Dresden and Lucerne in 1882'. But in the letter that Amy wrote to Clementina Black from the Hotel Sonnenberg she asks her to help her find a publisher for a work that is obviously her second collection of verse, *A Minor Poet*. At that date a number of the poems in the collection had yet to be written – a fact that Hunt Beckman acknowledges with a degree of puzzlement, writing: 'It is surprising that [Amy Levy] is already asking Clementina Black to help her find a publisher, for *A Minor Poet* was not to appear until 1884; indeed some of the poems had not been composed at the time that this letter was penned'. Of course it would not be surprising that Amy was seeking a publisher for her collection of verses if her letter had been written in 1883, as I am certain that it was. It is now probably impossible to determine precisely when Amy made the note about 'Medea' in her copy of *A Minor Poet*, but it may well have been some time after its publication. If so, the precise chronology of the composition of the verse could have become confused in her mind. It seems to me a far more likely scenario that she wrote the first draft of 'Medea' in Dresden in early 1882 and revised it for publication at Lucerne in July 1883.

[124] The Hotel Sonnenberg had a sister hotel at Emmetten, a short distance away.

[125] Camellia PLC.

[126] Information given on the facilities offered by the hotel is taken from the Swiss Tourist Authority guide to Emmetten and Seelisberg.

[127] Agnes Mary Frances Robinson, 1857–1944. Poet, biographer and critic. Mary Robinson was married twice, the first time to James Darmesteter, professor at the Collège de France. Darmesteter wrote an enthusiastic review of Amy Levy's *Xantippe*. A cutting of this review, inscribed by Amy: 'Reone (sic) Politique et Literaire' (no further edition details given) is pasted into Amy's scrap book. Camellia PLC. Mary Robinson attended a meeting of the Men and Women's Club on 21st November 1882. Pearson Papers.

[128] This comment may be as an allusion to the mythical figure of the Peri. An alternative explanation is that Amy is poking fun at the accent of one of her friends. Ann MacEwen, who was Ernest Radford's daughter, suggested that Ernest (whose family were drapers from Plymouth) may have spoken with a slight Devonshire accent.

[129] Camellia PLC.

[130] Levy, Amy. 'The Diary of a Plain Girl.' *London Society*. September 1883. 295–304.

[131] *A Minor Poet* was published by T. Fisher Unwin, in the following year, 1884. Fisher Unwin had offices near John Farquar Shaw's premises in Paternoster Square.

[132] A reference to the 'fragment in drama form after Euripides', which she had begun shortly after leaving Cambridge

[133] See 'Clementina Black: A Character Sketch'. *The Young Woman* Volume I October 1892 – September 1893. 315.

[134] Levy, Amy. 'In Holiday Humour'. *London Society*. August 1884. 177–184.

[135] The 'Buildings' within the Inns of Court were where barristers traditionally lived and worked. Paper Buildings is within the Inner Temple. Karl Pearson's address at this date was 2 Harcourt Buildings, Temple

[136] Emily Ford was one of the founder members of A Men and Women's Club. She was close to her cousin, Edward Pease, one of the founding members of the Fabian Society. On 25th June 1881 Pease attended a meeting of the club, probably at Emily's instigation. His fellow guest at the meeting was Eleanor Marx.

[137] Hannan, June. *Isabella Ford.* Oxford: Basil Blackwell, 1989. 16.

[138] Ellen Crofts had to resign her post of Lecturer at Newnham after her marriage

[139] Robinson, Annabel. *The Life and Work of Jane Ellen Harrison.* Oxford: Oxford University Press, 2002. 161.

[140] Lines from Act V Scene I of William Shakespeare's *A Midsummer Night's Dream*

[141] See Holmes, Richard. *Shelley The Pursuit*. London: Quartet Books, 1976. 236. Shelley's party set up home for a short while in Brunnen, which is directly opposite Seelisberg on the other side of Lake Lucerne

[142] Porter. 32

[143] Porter. 30.

[144] Pearson's own words quoted in his obituary in *The Times*, April 1936.

[145] E Pearson. 120

[146] Pearson to Parker, 18th August 1883. Pearson Papers.

[147] Levy. 'In Holiday Humour'.

[148] Hume Pinsent to Ada Radford, 8th July 1883. Newnham College Archive.

[149] Title of one of the sub-sections of Levy's *A London Plane Tree.*

[150] *The Collected Letters of Joanna Baillie*. Ed Judith Bailey Slagle. Madison, New Jersey: Fairleigh Dickinson University Press, 1999. 155

[151] Garnett, Henrietta. *Anny: A Life of Anne Thackeray Ritchie*. London: Chatto & Windus, 2004. 232.

[152] Garnett. 253

[153] See Kapp. Vol. I. 192-3.

[154] Benzie, William. *Dr. F. J .Furnivall: A Victorian Scholar Adventurer*. Norman, Oklahoma: Pilgrim Books Inc., 1983. 23, 27. Benzie quotes Kapp, Yvonne. *Eleanor Marx: Family Life*. London: Virago, 1979. 172, 187.

[155] *The Daughters of Karl Marx: Family Correspondence 1866–1898*. Commentary and notes by Olga Meier. London: Andre Deutsch, 1982. 133.

[156] Comyn, Marian. 'My Recollections of Karl Marx.' *The Nineteenth Century and After*, XCI (January 1922). 161–169.

[157] MacEwan. 'Das Meer hat Seine Perlen' was by Maud Valerie White. Anglo-French composer. She was the first woman to be awarded the prestigious Mendelssohn scholarship. On 11th May 1880 Maud Valerie White registered as a guest at one of the club meetings. This was before Amy became a member.

[158] Setton, Dr. Walter. 'University of London. The First Step'. *The Times*, 9th February 1925. 13.

[159] Horsely was an archetypical 'dissenter', it having been said of him that 'if he could see no reason for a convention he would reject it completely.' See Powell, Michael. Sir Victor Horsely: An Inspiration. *British Medical Journal* , 333 (2006). 1317-1319.

[160] Although, like Augustine Birrell, Frederick Wedmore did not attend this first meeting of the club,

like Birrell, his name appears on the visitors list of later meetings

[161] Hume Pinsent to Ada Radford. 8th December 1880. Newnham College Archive.

[162] Pearson first signed his name as a member on 12th November 1883.

[163] Ralph Thicknesse, a barrister, was appointed Secretary of the Minors' Protection Committee in 1885. See Bland, 8–9.

[164] William Archer, dramatic critic for *The World*. Sidney Lee was appointed assistant editor of the *Dictionary of National Biography* in 1883. Shaw attended the club as a guest on 19th May 1885, just before the club's demise. Levy attended this meeting.

[165] W. J. Levy registered as a guest on 20th March 1883. A. L. Levy registered as a guest on 20th November of the same year. A Men and Women's Club minute book. Pearson Papers.

[166] In a letter that followed the publication of her own *Minor Poet* and Radford's *Measured Steps* she comments: 'ask Mr. Radford if he thinks it worse to be accused of "drivelling idiocy" or "wild insensate folly."' MacEwan.

[167] Scrapbook. Camellia PLC. The cutting is inscribed in Levy's hand: 'Cambridge Review (Arthur Reed Ropes).'

[168] Scrapbook. Camellia PLC. Cutting headed 'The Literary World' and inscribed in Amy's hand: 'A.W. Dole.'

[169] Cooper Willis, Irene (ed). *Vernon Lee's Letters*. Privately printed, 1937. 65.

[170] Tsuzuki, Chushichi. *The Life of Eleanor Marx 1855–1898: A Socialist Tragedy*. Oxford: Clarendon Press, 1967. 169; and Kapp, 32 and 248. Kapp records the name incorrectly as 'Zimmerman'.

[171] 'Margaret Harkness'. *Dictionary of Labour Biography*, VIII: 103–113.

[172] The poem is reproduced here exactly as it appears in *A Minor Poet*.

[173] Arthur Reed Ropes 1859 - 1933. Poet and lyricist. Fellow of King's College, Cambridge.

[174] Martha Vicinus claims 'Few women who worked could afford a flat or a house and communal living was cheaper and pleasanter than a boarding house .... Furnished lodgings might lead to a loss of status.' Vicinus, Martha. *Independent Women: Work and Community for Single Women 1850–1920*. London: Virago Press, 1985. 36–37.

[175] Cutting from Amy's scrapbook headed *The Court Circular*. 509. Cutting inscribed 'June, 1884'. Camellia PLC.

[176] See Leighton, Angela and Reynolds, Margaret (eds). *Victorian Women Poets: An Anthology*. Oxford UK and Cambridge USA: Blackwell, 1991. 221.

[177] The notebook contains extracts from Rossetti's verse, including 'Monna Innominata.' Camellia PLC.

[178] Levy, Amy. 'The Poetry of Christina Rossetti'. *The Woman's World*, I (1888): 178–180.

[179] Thomas, Frances. *Christina Rossetti*. London: Virago, 1994. 188.

[180] On 6th February 1883 Anne and Herbert Gilchrist registered as guests. On 15th May Grace Gilchrist likewise registered. A Men and Women's Club minute book. Pearson Papers.

[181] Allen, Thomas. *A History of the County of Surrey Comprising every Object of Topographical, Geological or Historic Interest.* Vol VI. London, Isaac Taylor Hinton. 1831.

[182] Marsh, Jan. *Christina Rossetti: A Literary Biography*. London: Jonathan Cape, 1994. 225. I am indebted to Jan Marsh for her extensive account of the regime of the Highgate Penitentiary in the above work.

[183] Allen.

[184] Bland, Lucy. *Banishing the Beast: English Feminism & Sexual Morality 1885–1914*. London: Penguin Books, 1995. 190.

[185] Mew's 'Saturday Market' included in *The Farmer's Bride* (London: Westminster Press, 1916) describes the sorrow and suffering of the aftermath of an abortion.

[186] Quote from a cutting in Levy's scrapbook. No further edition details given. Camellia PLC.

[187] The Savile Club, which took its name from its second home in Savile Row, attracted members from the literary, musical and scientific professions. A number of Savilians either met or knew Amy Levy. These included Thomas Hardy, W.B Yeats, Sir Charles Villiers Stanford, Grant Allen and Karl Pearson.

[188] See Dew Smith, Alice (née Lloyd). Newnham College Roll letter, 1927. 73.

[189] Levy, Amy 'In Retreat: A Long Vacation Experience'. *London Society*. September 1884: 332-335

[190] Levy, Amy. 'In the Black Forest'

[191] Amy's reference to the 'she-devil' is a reflection of the traditional myth that those suffering from depression were possessed by the devil.

[192] Note that Amy spells Pearson's first name with a 'C' instead of a 'K'. This confirms that their friendship began at Cambridge. See Chapter 1, also Porter. 15

[193] In Tennyson's epic poem Hilarion is the rejected suitor of Princess Ida, who has forsworn the company of men.

[194] MacEwen. During the summer Parker and Pearson planned to make a short trip to the Tyrol. On 26th July 1884, Pearson wrote to Parker from Saig: 'I shall very likely come down to Freiburg to meet you, if I feel sure of your time of arrival, as I can show you a thing or two on the way up.' Pearson Papers.

[195] During the course of my research for this book I visited Saig on several occasions, and am indebted to Frau Stehl, the present proprietor of the Gasthof Ochsen, for pointing out this painting to me. Drawings of local personalities by the same artist who painted the picture that I was shown are amongst Pearson's Saig memorabilia in the Pearson Papers. During my stay at the Gasthof Ochsen, Frau Stehl

allowed me to examine the few surviving pages of the hotel register, which date from the 1880s. Karl Pearson and Robert Parker's signatures appear on the register to record a stay of three days between 26th and 28th April 1886.

[196] Pearson was appointed to the chair of Applied Mathematics and Mechanics at University College, London in June 1884. See Pearson, Egon. 14.

[197] 'In Retreat'. *London Society*. October 1884: 392-394. Camellia PLC.

[198] On 4th July 1884, Pearson wrote to Parker: 'I have made the acquaintance of the priest and the schoolmaster who are both new, and find very interesting points in both.' A sketch of the 'pfarrer' (dated 1890), which accords with Amy's description, is included amongst Pearson's 'Saig' papers. Pearson Papers.

[199] Catherine Corfe. b. 14th September 1856 in London. Newnham 1874 until Michaelmas term 1879 (thus overlapping with Amy). Catherine Corfe went up to Newnham at the same time as Ellen Crofts and Blanche Smith. In 1890 she was appointed music mistress at Amy's former alma mater, the Brighton High School.

[200] According to *The Routledge Dictionary of Historical Slang* (London: Routledge & Kegan Paul, 1973), one definition of an 'owl' is 'a member of Sidney Sussex College, Cambridge'. According to the same source, 'cock' has a number of definitions, one of which is 'a leader'. In a letter written from Newnham, Amy described Helen Gladstone, a staff member and daughter of the Liberal statesman, as 'a sort of cock', which suggests that this was the meaning of the word that Amy had in mind.

[201] Pearson described Debattis as 'of French Huguenot descent … an enthusiastic for Ibsen … her mission in life seems to be to get hold of all the light-haired German Fraulein of 18 to 20 years & tell them that they are immoral if they do not earn their own livelihood. She comes like a firebrand into these peaceful German domestic groups and it is only her wit and real good-heartedness which enables her to survive the friction which she occasionally produces.' Karl Pearson to Maria Sharpe, 10th August 1889. Pearson Papers. Three of Debattis' letters to Pearson are included in the Pearson Papers.

[202] See Partridge, Eric. *The Routledge Dictionary of Historical Slang*. London: Routledge and Kegan Paul, 1973. 60

[203] Porter. 98.

[204] Porter. 57

[205] This is evident from the correspondence he exchanged with Parker around this time.

[206] Robert Parker to Pearson, 21st July 1884. Pearson Papers.

[207] Parker to Pearson, 1st August 1884. Pearson Papers. Vernon Lee also mentioned the cholera outbreak in her correspondence with her mother. See Cooper Willis, 155.

[208] Levy, Amy. 'In the Black Forest'.

[209] Pearson, Karl. *The Ethic of Freethought*. London: Adam & Charles Black, 1901. 362

[210] Ibid.

[211] Karl Pearson to Maria Sharpe, 10th August 1889. Pearson Papers.

[212] Karl Pearson to William Conway, 7th July 1884. Also cited by Porter. 57.

[213] See Karl Pearson to Maria Sharpe, 6th January 1888. Pearson Papers.

[214] Pearson to Parker, 19th September 1884. Pearson Papers.

[215] See Walkovitz, Judith R. *City of Dreadful Delight: Narratives of Sexual Danger in Late-Victorian London*. London: Virago Press, 1994. 139

[216] Porter. 145

[217] Oppenheim. 73.

[218] Parker to Pearson. 17th September 1884. Pearson Papers

[219] The club minutes record the presence of both Constance Parker and Margaret Johnson. Pearson Papers.

[220] See First, Ruth and Ann Scott. *Olive Schreiner*. London: Andre Deutsch Ltd., 1980. 146.

[221] See Pearson, Egon. 115.

[222] Parker to Pearson. 13th November 1881. Pearson Papers.

[223] First and Scott. 170.

[224] Ibid.

[225] Walkowitz. 135.

[226] Sharpe, Maria. 'Autobiographical Notes of the Men and Women's Club 1885–9'. Pearson Papers.

[227] Walkowitz. 139.

[228] Kapp. Vol II. 19

[229] Schreiner described middle-class women as 'wicked mean and jealous.' See Brandon, 47. Schreiner's friend, Mrs. Brown, also recorded Schreiner's unflattering description of what she termed 'one of those infernal gatherings of women.' See S. C. Cronwright Schreiner. *The Life of Olive Schreiner*. London: T. Fisher Unwin, 1924. 183–184.

[230] Ibid.

[231] See Brandon, Ruth. *The New Women and the Old Men: Love, Sex and the Woman Question*: London: Flamingo, 1991. 47–48.

[232] See Walkowitz. 141.

[233] Schreiner to Pearson, 15th October 1885. Pearson Papers.

[234] Pearson to Sharpe, 10th February 1886. Pearson Papers.

[235] Sharpe to Pearson, 11th February 1886.

[236] See First and Scott. 147.

[237] Kate Mills (dates unknown) was 'a social worker who had made a detailed study of 'the relations of the sexes on many sides.' See Bland, 166.

[238] Annie Eastty (dates unknown) was 'an unmarried free-thinking school mistress from Bermondsey.' According to Bland, Pearson made free use of Eastty's ideas, without acknowledgement, in his opening paper for 'The Men and Women's Club'. See Bland, 22 and 6 respectively. Annie Eastty may have been the sister of Minnie Eastty, who married Ernest Black (brother of Constance and Clementina) in 1894. See Garnett, *Constance Garnett*, 132 and 157 respectively. Annie Eastty was a member of the first 'Men and Women's Club'.

[239] Sharpe had written to Pearson: 'we saw Miss Mills and Miss Eastty today. Miss Mills is, as you know, deaf and her deafness is such that you must sit near her and speak loud and distinctly, not shouting, to make yourself heard. This is often a very great drawback to anything like general discussion.' Sharpe to Pearson, 26th March 1885.

[240] See Black. *Athenaeum*, 5th October 1889: 457.

[241] Elizabeth Blackwell (1821–1910), having graduated from medical school in New York State in 1849, subsequently became the first British woman to have her name entered on the Medical Register of the United Kingdom. In 1868 she founded the London School of Medicine for Women. See Parry, Melanie (ed). *Chambers Biographical Dictionary of Women*. Edinburgh: Chambers, 1996. 81.

[242] Josephine Butler (1828-1906), the daughter of a radical agricultural reformer, married George Butler in 1852. After their move to Liverpool, Butler began her work with destitute women and prostitutes. She is now best remembered for her participation in the 'Great Crusade' to repeal the Contagious Diseases Act. Her account of the campaign, *Personal Reminiscences of a Great Crusade*, was published in 1896. She wrote several biographies, as well as many articles on social reform. See Blain, Virginia, Patricia Clements and Isobel Grundy (eds). *The Feminist Companion to Literature in English*. London: Batsford, 1990. 163–164.

[243] Sharpe to Pearson, 26th March 1885.

[244] Pearson, Karl. 'The Woman's Question'. *The Ethic of Freethought*. London: Adam and Charles Black, 1901. 355

[245] Levy, Amy. 'Between Two Stools'. *Temple Bar*, 69 (1883): 337–350.

[246] Both letters dated, and both are unexpurgated. The first letter is headed 'Aug. 19 '85' and the second 'Aug. 22nd'. Camellia PLC.

[247] Amy commemorated her friendship with de Pass and Myerstein in her poem 'A Game of Lawn Tennis'.

[248] Oppenheim. 167-168.

[249] Camellia PLC

[250] Colby College Special Collections, Waterville, Maine. All further references attributed: Colby College.

[251] Margaret Harkness to Beatrice Potter, September 1876. Passfield Papers. BLPES, LSE.

[252] Camellia PLC.

[253] Levy, Amy. 'Out of the World'. *London Society*. Jan. 1886: 53–56.

[254] Quilter, Harry. 'Amy Levy: A Reminiscence and a Criticism'. *The Universal Review*, 24 (1890): 492–507.

[255] Marks.

[256] Garnett 68. Letter quoted: Constance Garnett to Richard Garnett, 13th September 1889. Estate of the late David Garnett, Hilton Hall.

[257] Swinburne, Algernon Charles. 'The Triumph of Time'. *Poems and Ballads*. First Series (1866).

[258] Camellia PLC

[259] Armstrong, Isabel, 'Swinburne: Agnostic Republican'. *Victorian Poetry: Poetry, Poetics and Politics*. London: Routledge, 1993. 402.

[260] This item, written in the hand of Beth Zion Abrahams, who was the original custodian of Amy Levy's papers, was attached to the manuscript when I originally examined it, but was missing after the renovation of the documents.

[261] Levy, Amy. 'Out of the World'.

[262] *The Romance of a Shop* (London: T. Fisher Unwin, 1888) and *Reuben Sachs* (London: Macmillan, 1888). 'Sokratics in the Strand', *Cambridge Review*. 6th February 1884: 163–164. 'The Ballad of a Special Edition'. *A London Plane Tree*. London: T. Fisher Unwin, 1889.

[263] In Amy's first novel, *The Romance of a Shop*, the Lorrimer sisters open a photographic studio. There is a photograph of Amy in Great Cumberland Place (near Marble Arch in the West end of London) taken by her cousin Alfred Goodman, who was evidently a keen amateur photographer. Photograph and scrap-album: Camellia PLC.

[264] Information provided by North Cornwall Record Office.

[265] Mulley, Clare. *The Woman Who Saved the Children: A Biography of Eglantyne Jebb Founder of Save the Children*. Oxford: Oneworld Publications, 2009. 11 See also Hamilton, Mary Agnes. *Newnham: An Informal Biography*. London: Oxford University Press, 1964. 208–209.

[266] See Chapter 1. Reverat.

[267] Wilson, Francesca M. *Rebel Daughter of a Country House: The life of Eglantyne Jebb*. London: George Allen and Unwin, 1967. 32

[268] Mulley. 20.

[269] See Wilson 36. Ann Thomson, Clerk to the Newnham College Archive can find no trace of the first

Louisa (Bun) Jebb, but her niece (also Louisa Jebb) enrolled at Newnham in 1892. Nevertheless, 'Bun' would have known Jemima Clough well through her brother's connection with the college.

[270] See: Tidcombe, Marianne. *Woman Bookbinders 1880-1920*. London: OAK Knoll Press at the British Library) 1996. 104.

[271] Gates, Barbara T. *Victorian Suicide: Mad Crimes and Sad Histories*. Princeton, New Jersey: Princeton University Press, 1988. xiii.

[272] Cameron, Mary. *The Young Woman* Vol I October 1892 – September 1893. 315.

[273] Camellia PLC.

[274] Lee wrote to her mother: 'Saturday afternoon after seeing Miss Levy, I went to Miss Black's anti-servitoresses lodging.' At that time the Black sisters were living in Fitzroy Street, Bloomsbury. See Gunn, Peter, *Vernon Lee: Violet Paget 1856-1935*. London: Oxford University Press, 1964. 116.

[275] These letters are housed in the Special Collections, Miller Library, Colby College, Maine.

[276] Letter dated 3rd June 1886. Cooper Willis, Irene (ed). *Vernon Lee's Letters*. Privately Printed, 1937.

[277] Amy Levy to Violet Paget. Letter dated 26th November. Amy mentions in the letter that she has sent 'A Phantom Lover' to her brother in America'. This was Vernon Lee's novella that was published in 1886, this confirms the year in which Amy's letter was written

[278] The letter includes the enquiry 'have you been doing anything pleasant for Christmas?' and ends 'with every good wish for 1887'. This means that it must have been written towards the end of December 1886.

[279] This letter can be identified as having been written in February 1887 because Amy mentions that 'Miss Black has just been made secretary of the Women's Protective League …' This event occurred in February 1887.

[280] Colby College.

[281] The information given to Lee by Amy was probably obtained from Thomas Stevens, husband of one of Amy's closest female friends Euphemia Maulden (Effie) Stevens. Like Pearson, Parker and Thicknesse, Stevens was a barrister and a member of the second Men and Women's Club.

[282] According to Peter Gunn, Annie Meyer was 'a shadowy figure'. Vernon Lee may have met Annie Meyer in Florence, as Mme Meyer's husband was a friend of William Stillman, who was at that time Italian correspondent of *The Times*. Gunn 96.

[283] Lee, Vernon. 'Autobiographical Notes'. Unpublished. Vineta Colby cites this quotation from the letter in *Vernon Lee: A Literary Biography*. Charlottesville and London: University of Virginia Press, 2003. 53

[284] Colby College. The letter is headed in Amy's hand: 'Nov.' Cooper Willis identifies it as having been written in 1887.

[285] Arthur Symons to Mary Robinson February 1883. Colby. 51.

[286] Camellia PLC.

[287] 'In Celebrity's Wake: Literary Lions in Undress' *Hampshire Telegraph and Sussex Chronicle*. 22nd February 1889.

[288] MacKenzie, Norman and Jeanne. *The First Fabians*. London: Quartet Books, 1979. 247-248.

[289] Levy, Amy. *Between Two Stools*

[290] Colby College.

[291] See Gunn, Peter *Vernon Lee: Violet Paget, 1856-1935*. London; Oxford University Press, 1964. 111.

[292] Lee, Vernon. 'Beauty and Sanity.' *Laurus Nobilis: Chapters on Art and Life*. London: John Lane, 1909. 155–156.

[293] Gunn. 111

[294] See Walkowitz. 157.

[295] Pearson Papers.

[296] Bellosguardo is sited on the hillside just beyond the boundary of the city of Florence. It was popular with the literati. The American writers James Fennimore Cooper and Nathaniel Hawthorn had lived there, as did Fenimore Cooper's great-niece, Constance Fenimore Woolson. When she was lodging in the Villa Castetellani in 1886, her friend Henry James took lodgings in the nearby Villa Brichieri-Colombi. While he was in Florence he paid regular calls on Vernon Lee. See: Edel, Leon. *Henry James: A Life*. New York, Cambridge, Philadelphia, San Francisco, London, Mexico City, Sao Paulo, Singapore, Sydney: Harper & Row, 1985. 331-332, 335. Amy mentions 'Mr. James' rooms' in a letter to Lee. Colby College. See note 63.

[297] Lee. *Laurus Nobilis*. 156. See also Levy, Sharona. Unpublished thesis: *Amy Levy*. Chapter 1.

[298] Although undated, the letter can be identified as having been written in 1887, as Amy mentions in passing that '[e]veryone is talking about Mr. Haggard's She,' which was published in that year. Colby Collection.

[299] 'In Celebrities Wake' *Hampshire Telegraph and Sussex Chronicle*. 2nd February, 1889.

[300] Marks.

[301] *The Jewish World*. 3rd June 1887: 1. Alfred was, in fact, 24 when he died.

[302] Oppenheim. 125.

[303] Hunt Beckman, Linda. *Amy Levy: Her Life and Letters*. Athens Ohio: Ohio University Press, 2000. 209

[304] I am indebted to Dr. E. Macdonald for her advice on this issue. She advised me that, apart from the fact that no other family member appears to have been affected by the disease, Alfred's age would seem to rule this theory out. There is normally a time gap of fifteen to twenty years before symptoms appear, and severe symptoms would not generally appear until some years after this.

[305] Mannocchi, Phyllis F. 'Vernon Lee: A Re-Introduction and Primary Bibliography.' Colby College. Lee dedicated her novel *Miss Brown* to James. James disliked the book, and told Lee so in no uncertain terms. When they next met in London, Lee wrote to her mother: 'James is very friendly with that curious mixture of ... absolute social and personal insincerity and extreme intellectual justice and plain spokenness'. Gunn 106.

[306] Oppenheim. 103, 169.

[307] Information given by Shirley Harris, General Secretary, Great Yarmouth and District Archaeological Society. I had specifically enquired whether the cause of death given could be a disguised suicide, but was told that the fact that the certificate was issued the day after the death excludes this possibility.

[308] Camellia PLC.

[309] Colby College. 'Mr James' was Henry James and 'Mr Cross' was his friend John Cross, George Eliot's widower (see Chapter 2). Mr Benson was probably Henry James' friend the American artist Eugene Benson. Benson's 'numerous articles' were published under the title *Art and Nature in Italy*.

[310] Matthew 3: 17.

[311] Agnes Mary Frances Robinson (later Darmesteter then Duclaux) 1857–1944. Poet, biographer and critic. Daughter of a wealthy London banker, her education included periods of study in Brussels, Italy and University College, London. When in London, Robinson's parents entertained many leading literary figures, including Henry James, Robert Browning, Oscar Wilde, George Moore and Thomas Hardy. It is possible that Amy was introduced to Oscar Wilde by the Robinsons, as she mentions going 'to the Robinson's party' in her 'Calendrier 1889'. See *The Feminist Companion to Literature*. Blain, Clements and Grundy (eds), and Gunn. Calendrier. Camellia PLC.

[312] Colby College.

[313] Quoted by Sharona Levy. 201. the reference is cited: 'M. Robinson, letter to J. Darmesteter, 16 Sept. 1888. Robinson family correspondence.'

[314] See Feinstein, Israel. *Jewish Society in Victorian England*. London: Valentine Mitchell, 1993. 67.

[315] Blomfield, E. V. *An Account of the Blomfield Families with Eleven Pedigrees*. Privately printed, 1950, Chapter II, 28. (Only 30 copies were issued.)

[316] Miller Library, Colby College.

[317] Levy, Amy. 'Middle Class Jewish Women of To-Day'. *Jewish Chronicle*. 17th September 1886: 7.

[318] Cesarani, David. *The Jewish Chronicle and Anglo-Jewry 1841-1991*. Cambridge: Cambridge University Press, 1994. 92-93.

[319] Zion Lask, Beth. 'Amy Levy and the J. C.' *Jewish Chronicle*. 17th November 1963: 13.

[320] Camellia PLC.

[231] Levy, Amy. 'The Ghetto at Florence'. *Jewish Chronicle*. 26th March 1886: 9.

[322] Epstein Nord, Deborah. 'Neither Pairs Nor Odd: Female Community in Late Nineteenth-Century London.' *Signs*, 15 (Summer 1990): 733–754.

[323] Levy, Amy. 'James Thomson: A Minor Poet'. *Cambridge Review*. 21st February 1883: 240–241. 28th February 1883: 257–258.

[324] Dobell, Bertram. '*James Thomson: The City of Dreadful Night and Other Poems*'. London: Bertram Dobell, 1910. v-xxiv.

[325] See Briggs, Julia. *A Woman of Passion: The Life of E. Nesbit 1858–1924*. London: Hutchinson, 1987. 30–31. Mary Nesbit died in 1831. Julia Briggs writes: 'Her lover [Marston] never really recovered from her loss.'

[326] Levy, Amy. 'James Thomson: A Minor Poet'.

[327] Ibid.

[328] See: Cynthia Scheinberg. 'Canonizing the Jew: Amy Levy's Challenge to Victorian Poetic Identity'. *Victorian Studies*, 39 No. 2 (Winter, 1996): 173–200.

[329] Cheyette. 94.

[330] See Michael Holroyd's Introduction to G. Bernard Shaw. *An Unsocial Socialist*. London: Virago, 1980.

[331] Cheyette. 95.

[332] Ibid. 12–13.

[333] Harkness, Margaret. *In Darkest London*. London: Black Apollo Press, 2003. 167.

[334] *The Diary of Beatrice Webb: Volume One 1873-1892* Ed. Norman and Jeanne MacKenzie, .London: Virago Press Ltd., 1982. 243.

[335] A Merry-Andrew is a clown or buffoon.

[336] See Valentine, E.R. 'James Sully'. *The Psychologist*, 14. 2001 405

[337] Review: 'The Romance of a Shop' by Amy Levy. *Birmingham Daily Post*. 28th December 1888

[338] 1925 was the centenary of the first omnibus service in the capital.

[339] Levy, Amy. 'The Ballade of an Omnibus'. *The Star*. 18th February 1888.

[340] Levy, Amy. *The Romance of a Shop*. Ed. Susan David Bernstein. Ontario, Canada: Broadview Press, 2006. 80

[341] Colby Collection.

[342] Gunn. 118.

[343] Colby Collection.

[344] Colby Collection.

[345] Daughter of William Morris

[346] MacEwen.

[347] Cooper Willis. 291–292.

[348] Bertha Thomas, the novelist and a friend of Lee's.

[349] Camellia PLC.

[350] Lee-Hamilton, Eugene. 'Fumes of Charcoal September 1889'. See New, 554–555.

[351] Camellia PLC. Bella Duffy was described by Mary Robinson as 'the Irish doctor's daughter, so witty, with her beautiful melancholy brows and eyes.' See Gunn, 77.

[352] Camellia PLC.

[353] Carolus Duran. Charles Auguste Emile Durand, 1838-1917. Studied at the Lille Academy. Head of one of the foremost ateliers in Paris, he was best known as a portrait painter. Vernon Lee's childhood companion John Singer Sargent was his protégé. In 1889 Durand was made a commissioner of the Légion d'honneur.

[354] Anna Bilinska Bohdanowicz, 1857-1893. Born in the Ukraine, Bilinska studied in Russia Warsaw and Paris. In 1889 she was awarded a gold medal at the Paris Exposition Universelle.

[355] Like Duran, Julian founded his Academie in order to provide women with the same disciplined training in fine arts that was offered exclusively to men at the Ecole des Beaux-Arts. Lee's friend, Flora Priestly, with whom Amy had dined just before she left Florence, was also a protégée of Julian's.

[356] See Child, Theodore: 'Characteristic Parisian Cafés'. Harper's *New Monthly Magazine* No: CCCLXVII, Vol LXVIII (April 1889): 687-703. Patrons of Le Chat Noir included the poets Paul Verlaine and Stéphane Mallarmé and the artists Pierre August Renoir, Edgar Degas and, of course, Henri de Toulouse-Lautrec.

[357] The waiters were dressed in the costume of the Academie Française. The intention was to facetiously demonstrate 'what one may come to in literature by dint of industry and good conduct'. Child 702. But the fact that there were no female members of the Academie also signalled the predominantly masculine culture of the restaurant.

[358] Amy first mentioned having met 'Miss and Mr. Cross George Eliot's husband' in a letter written from the Hotel Sonnenberg in 1883.

[359] See Cate, Phillip Dennis: 'The Spirit of Montmartre'. Phillip Dennis Cate and Mary Shaw (eds.). *The Spirit of Montmartre: Cabarets, Humour and the Avant-Garde, 1875-1905* New Brunswick, New Jersey Rutgers, The State University, 1996. 38.

[360] Morton, Peter. *Grant Allen 1848-1899: A Bibliography.* 'Victorian Fiction Research Guide 31. Queensland: Victorian Fiction Research Unit, School of English, Media Studies and Art History, 2002. 6

[361] Amy quoted this same passage at the end of 'Out of the World' – the story which she based upon the visit to Cornwall that followed her suicide attempt in 1885.

[362] Stepniak – See note 43 Chapter 5.

[363] Tom Stevens, husband of her close friend Euphemia Maulden Stevens.

[364] Francis Darwin was the third son of Charles Darwin, and his wife, the former Ellen Crofts, had been Amy's holiday companion at the Hotel Sonnenberg

[365] Harris, Frank. *Contemporary Portraits: Fourth Series*. London: Grant Richards, 1924. 93-98.

[366] Allen, Grant. 'The Girl of the Future.' *Universal Review*, VII No. 25: 49–64. Commenting upon the recent 'great movement … for the Higher Instruction of Women', Allen claimed: 'A few hundred pallid little Amy Levys sacrificed on the way are as nothing before the face of our fashionable Juggernaut.'

[367] George Macmillan, a university friend of Oscar Wilde, was a partner in the family publishing firm which had recently issued Amy's *Reuben Sachs*. H.F. Wilson, Fellow of Trinity College Cambridge. Wilson later became Secretary to Joseph Chamberlain at the Colonial Office.

[368] The poem first appeared in the May issue of *London Society* in 1886. Amy's comment suggests that she was revising the verse for inclusion in *A London Plane Tree*.

[369] The engagement was not made public until August 1889

[370] Words from 'A Psalm of Life' by Henry Wadsworth Longfellow: 'Trust no future however pleasant/ Let the dead past bury its dead/Act, - act in the living present/ Heart within and God o'erhead.'

[371] Maria Sharpe to Pearson, 3rd August 1888. Pearson Papers.

[372] Beckson, Karl, and John M. Munro. (eds) *Arthur Symons Selected Letters, 1880–1935*. Iowa City: University of Iowa Press, 1989. 49.

[373] *Arthur Symons Selected Letters* Ed. Beckson and Munro. 50, and Cronwright Schreiner, S. C. (ed). *The Letters of Olive Schreiner 1876–1920*. London: T. Fisher Unwin, 1924. 185

[374] Levy, Amy. 'The End of the Day'. *A London Plane Tree*.

[375] Brooke to Pearson, 4th December 1885. Pearson Papers.

[376] *Olive Schreiner Letters*. Ed. Rive. 112.

[377] Pearson, Karl. 'The Woman's Question'. *The Ethic of Freethought*. London: Adam and Charles Black, 1901,.359. (1st ed. 1888.)

[378] *Olive Schreiner Letters*. Ed. Rive. 118.

[379] Ibid. 146.

[380] *Olive Schreiner Letters*. Ed. Rive. 146.

[381] Ibid. 151.

[382] *The Letters of Olive Schreiner* Ed. Cronwright Schreiner. 163.

[383] Schreiner mistakenly refers to Ibsen's *A Doll's House* as *'Nora'*

[384] *The Letters of Olive Schreiner*. 165.

[385] The date of this letter can be identified because it includes a reference to the fact that 'Mr. Sargent'

had recently painted Kit Anstruther-Thomson's portrait. Lee referred to this same event in a letter to her mother, dated 30th August 1889. Cooper Willis. 311.

[386] *The Letters of Olive Schreiner*. 167. The passage following the reference to Levy's letter has been omitted, probably because it contained information of a personal nature.

[387] Charlotte Mary Wilson (1854–1944). Newnham contemporary of Ellen Crofts and Emma Frances Brooke. A Fabian and an Anarchist, Wilson met Pearson through her Hampstead-based Karl Marx Club.

[388] 'Cremation of a Jewish Poetess'. *Globe*. 16th September 1889: 2. The passage mentioned begins: 'As for man, his days are like grass; he flourishes like a flower of the field; for a wind passes over it and it is gone …' See 'Home Service Prior to a Funeral'. *The Authorised Daily Prayer Book of the United Hebrew Congregations of the Commonwealth.*

[389] Radford, Ernest. 'An Inscription for an Urn'. *Pall Mall Gazette*. 24th September 1889: 2.

[390] 'G. A.' 'For the Same Urn: Another Inscription.' *Pall Mall Gazette*. 26th September 1889: 2.

[391] MacEwan.

[392] 12th November 1889. Radford writes: 'much has happened in this year. Amy Levy's death.' He then goes on to list other events that happened during the year. MacEwan.

[393] Cronwright-Schreiner, S.C. *The Letters of Olive Schreiner*. London: T. Fisher Unwin, 1924. 167.

[394] Carpenter, Edward. 'Have Faith'. *Towards Democracy*. London: T. Fisher Unwin, 1892. 172–179. The message in the verse is one of reassurance in the face of adversity.

[395] *Olive Schreiner Letters*. Ed Rive. 157.

[396] Amy first met the Dykes Campbells during her holiday at Hastings with Dollie Radford in 1883.

[397] Symons. *Selected Letters*. 52.

[398] 'Mainly About People.' *Star*. 17th September 1889: 1.

[399] The extract quoted is from a newspaper cutting of an article entitled 'Jewish Associations of Olive Schreiner'. Rachel Beth Zion Abrahams was the author of the article. Miss Abrahams (later Mrs. Lask) knew Amy's youngest sister Ella. The newspaper cutting does not have any edition details other than *Jewish Herald* and the year 1955. Camellia PLC.

[400] 'Occasional Notes'. *Pall Mall Gazette*. 1st April 1892: 2.

[401] Kapp. Vol. II. 259.

[402] *Olive Schreiner Letters*. Ed. Rive. 152.

[403] See Symons. *Selected Letters*. 52. Also Cronwright-Screiner. 167.

[404] Ibid. 99.

[405] Ibid. 170.

[406] Ibid. 172.

[407] Black, Clementina. 'Literary Gossip'. *Athenaeum*. 8232. 5th October 1889: 457.

[408] See *Star*. 11th October 1889: 1; and *St. James's Gazette*. 4th October 1889: 12.

[409] Although the article is not attributed to Wilde, Beth Zion Lask was quite certain that he was the author.

[410] Wilde, Oscar. 'Amy Levy'. *The Woman's World*, 3 (1890): 51–52.

[411] Chandler Moulton, Louise. 'A Young English Genius: Graceful Prose and Poetry of Amy Levy'. *Boston Herald*. 17th March 1889: no page details given on press cutting. Camellia PLC.

[412] Wilde had evidently not met Amy at that date, although they did eventually get to know one another. On 27th June 1889 Amy recoded in her diary that she 'met Oscar Wilde' at Graham Tomson's party.

[413] *The Woman's World* London, Paris & Melbourne, 1888. 31

[414] *The Complete Letters of Oscar Wilde*. Ed. Merlin Holland and Rupert Hart-Davis. London: Fourth Estate, 20009. 326.

[415] Ibid. 364.

[416] Entry dated 27th April. Camellia PLC.

[417] Ernest Radford, had complained that 'the feminine element [in the Reading Room] was a distracting one'. MacEwan.

[418] Robert Parker to Karl Pearson. 23rd December 1884. Pearson Papers.

[419] Karl Pearson to Maria Sharpe. 8th September 1889. Pearson Papers.

[420] Rive. 85.

[421] Marks.

[422] Karl Pearson to Maria Sharpe, 8th September 1889. This letter contains Pearson's curious comments on his attitude to women (previously quoted).

[423] Pearson Papers.

[424] See Bland, 176. Sharpe finally terminated her engagement to Pearson on 26th September.

[425] Ibid.

[426] See the letter written by Fanny Pearson, 22nd April 1890. Pearson Papers.

[427] Pearson Papers.

[428] Pearson Papers.

[429] Maria Sharpe to Karl Pearson, 19th October 1889. Pearson Papers.

[430] Pearson to Maria Sharpe, 22nd October 1889. Pearson Papers.

[431] Pearson to Maria Sharpe, 30th July 1889. Pearson Papers.

[432] Pearson to Maria Sharpe. 8th September 1889. Pearson Papers

[433] See Venning, Philip. *Wyldes: A New History*. London: Wyldes, North End, NW3.

[434] Olivier, Hermia. *The International Anarchist Movement in Late Victorian London.* London, Canberra and New York. St Martin's Press, 1983. 27. Although Hermia Olivier claims that Charlotte Wilson entered Newnham in 1873, the *Newnham College Roll* registers her entry as 1872.

[435] Sergey Mikhailovitch Kravchinsky, 1851-1895. Commonly known by his *nom de guerre* 'Stepniak', he fled to England after assassinating a Russian General in St. Petersburg. In 1890 he founded the 'Society of Friends of Russian Freedom' and edited the Society's journal *Free Russia.* A cultured man, a devotee of music and literature, and a spellbinding conversationalist, he was reputedly 'the only man who ever succeeded in reducing Bernard Shaw to silence'. At the age of 44 he was killed by a train at a railway crossing near his home in the London Suburb of Bedford Park. Like Amy Levy, he was cremated at Woking

[436] The letter is inscribed in pencil (presumably by the archivist at University College): 'Maria Sharpe had told Karl that she felt she could not marry him – should not Olive about to sail for South Africa be told?'

[437] Pearson Papers.

[438] Wilson to Pearson. Pearson Papers.

[439] *Olive Schreiner Letters.* Ed. Rive. 112.

[440] See Wilson to Pearson, 11th October 1889 and 9th January 1890, in which she writes: 'I shall be so glad to hear that you have found work in a new place. Nothing refreshes ones dormant energy like a change of interests in a new scene. I found that in Rome.'

[441] On 4 October it was reported: 'Miss Olive Schreiner sailed for the Cape the day before yesterday': *Pall Mall Gazette.* 4th October 1889: 6.

[442] Pearson Papers.

[443] Pearson Papers.

[444] Pearson Papers. I am indebted to Claire Burke for the translation from the original German.

[445] Pearson Papers. The letter was addressed from Parker's Haselmere cottage – hence the last sentence.

[446] Levy. 'Out of the World'.

[447] Meredith, George. *The Egoist.* London: Penguin, 1968. 51.

[448] Ibid. 48

[449] Ibid.

[450] Ibid.

[451] Ibid. 51.

[452] See Bland. 180.

[453] Pearson Papers.

[454] First and Scott. n162.

[455] *Olive Schreiner Letters*. Ed. Rive. 296–297.

[456] Ibid. 147.

[457] Allen, Grant. *Under Sealed Orders* (in three volumes). London: Chatto and Windus, 1895.

[458] Morton, Peter. *The Busiest Man in England: Grant Allen and the Writing Trade, 1875-1900*. New York and Basingstoke: Palgrave Macmillan, 2005. 120. Also, Grant Allen Annotated Bibliography. http://petermortonhomepage.blogspot.com

[459] Thomson, Graham R. 'A Minor Poet'. *The Illustrated London News*. 21st November 1891. 667

[460] Zangwill, Israel. *The Grandchildren of the Ghetto*. 'The Wayfarer's Library'. London: J.M. Dent & Sons Ltd, (n.d.). 24. Joseph H. Udelson specifically identifies Esther Ansell as Amy Levy. See: Udelson, Joseph H. *Dreamer of the Ghetto: The Life and Works of Israel Zangwill*. Tuscaloosa and London, The University of Alabama Press. 1990. Udelson writes; In "Grandchildren of the Ghetto" the stories are told of Israel Zangwill and Amy Levy.' 101.

[461] 'Lady Margaret' is Lady Margaret Hall, the first women's college at Oxford. The college was founded in 1878, seven years after the foundation of Newnham.

[462] Radford, Dollie. *One Way Of Love: An Idyll*. London: T. Fisher Unwin, 1898.

[463] See Tsuzuki. 330. When Aveling married Eva Frye his first wife, Isabelle Campbell Aveling, had been dead for nearly five years. Ibid 299.

[464] MacEwen. The source of this information is Dollie Radford's correspondence with her son Maitland, who was the late Ann MacEwen's father.

[465] Oedipus delivered Thebes from the Sphinx by solving her riddle.

[466] Radford. 175.

[467] Ibid. 183.

[468] Pearson, Karl. 'The Woman's Question'. *The Ethic of Freethought*. London: Adam and Chares Black, 1901. A note on the frontispiece records: 'First Edition issued 1887 dated 1888'.

[469] Allen, Grant. 'Plain Words on the Woman Question'. *The Fortnightly Review*, 46 (1889): 448–458. This article received notices in October 1889.

[470] Pope, Wilson. *The Story of The Star: 1888-1930*. London: The Star, 1938. 5.

[471] Shorter, Clement. C.K.S. *An Autobiography. A fragment by himself*. Ed. J.M. Bulloch. Privately Printed, 1927. xiii, 77, 88.

[472] Morton, Peter. *The Busiest Man in England: Grant Allen and the Writing Trade, 1875-1900*. New York and Basingstoke: Palgrave Macmillan, 2005. 103

[473] See Kearney, Patrick J. Website: *Scissors and Paste Bibliographies*. 'British Museum 'SS' Catalogue, 1945.

[474] See: Fryer, Peter. *Private Case, Public Scandal*. London: Secker & Warburg, 1966.

[475] Clodd, Edward. *Grant Allen: A Memoir*. London: Grant Richards, 1900. 195.

[476] Allen. 'The Girl of the Future'.

[477] Ibid. 362.

[478] Pearson. 367.

[479] Pearson. 'The Woman's Question'. 378.

[480] Allen. 'Plain Words on the Woman Question'. 453.

[481] Graham R. Tomson, formerly Rosamund Armytage, had caused a sensation when, following a legal separation from her first husband, shortly afterwards she set up home with the painter Arthur Tomson. In one of Amy's diary entries she recorded: recorded that Graham Tomson had 'told [her] her history'. Camellia PLC

[482] Camellia PLC

[483] Caird, Mona. 'Marriage'. *The Westminster Review.* August 1888.

[484] Stanton, Elizabeth Cady. *Eighty Years and More: Reminiscences of E.C. Stanton*. London: T. Fisher Unwin, 1898.

[485] Caird, Mona. 'The Emancipation of the Family'.

[486] Caird, Mona. '*The Morality of Marriage*'. London: George Redway, 1897. 64–65.

[487] See *The Routledge Dictionary of Historical Slang*.

[488] French forces made an attempt to invade Ireland as a stepping stone to England in 1796. The first French 'Army of England' assembled on the French coast in 1798, but the invasion was postponed and finally called off. 1889, the year in which Amy wrote 'A Ballad of Religion and Marriage', was the centenary of the French Revolution.

[489] Pearson. 359.

[490] Pearson. 378.

[491] Webb, Beatrice. *My Apprenticeship.* London: Longmans, Green and Co., 1926. 399.

[492] Webb, Beatrice. Diary entry for 20th April, 1888. *The Diary of Beatrice Webb: Volume One 1873-1892. Glitter Around and Darkness Within*. Ed. Norman and Jeanne MacKenzie. London: Virago Press Ltd., 1982. 250.

[493] Levy, Amy. *Reuben Sachs: A Sketch*. London: London and New York, Macmillan & Co.,1889. 173.

[494] Olive's MacMillan's father, Alexander and his brother Daniel had founded the publishing firm of MacMillan & Co in 1843.

[495] Amy, Levy 'The Jew in Fiction'. *The Jewish Chronicle*. 4th June 1886. 13.

[496] Jackson, Stanley. *The Sassoons.* London: Heinemann, 1968. 68.

[497] Jackson. 67, 68.

[498] Bernstein (ed). 11.

[499] 'Mute inglorious Miltons' is a phrase taken from a line in 'Elegy written in a Country Churchyard' by Thomas Gray (1716-1771).

[500] This was possibly meant to be University College School. Founded in 1830, University College accepted pupils from all religious faiths. Karl Pearson (whose family were Quakers) attended the school from the age of nine to sixteen years old.

[501] *Au Bonheur des Dames* by Emile Zola was first translated into English in 1883. It has been suggested that this novel may have influenced *The Romance of a Shop*.

[502] See note 7.

[503] Amy Levy. 'Wise in her Generation'. *The Woman's World*, 3 (1889): 20.

[504] 'Patti' was Adelina Patti, the acclaimed nineteenth-century opera singer. Baroness Angela Burdett-Coutts was the philanthropist founder of the NSPCC. Upon inheriting her grandfather's fortune in 1837 Lady Burdett-Coutts became the wealthiest woman in England.

[505] Brontë, Emily. 'I am the only being whose doom'. *The Complete Poems of Emily Jane Brontë*. Ed. C. W. Hatfield. New York: Columbia University Press, 1941. 36.

[506] Levy, Amy. 'Impotens'. *A London Plane Tree*.

[507] Levy, Amy. 'Sonnet'. *Xantippe*: This 'Sonnet' was reprinted in *A Minor Poet* in 1884.

[508] Levy, Amy. 'To Death'. *A Minor Poet*.

[509] Wilde, Oscar. 'Amy Levy'. *The Woman's World*, 3 (1890): 51–52.

[510] Darwin, Ellen (née Crofts). 'The Poems of Amy Levy'. *Cambridge Review*. 23rd January 1890: 158.

[511] Woolf, Virginia. *A Room of One's Own*. London: Granada, 1977. 94.

[512] Letter dated 24th March 1889. Pearson Papers.

[513] Black to Radford, 16th September 1889. MacEwan.

[514] Levy, Amy. 'Xantippe'. *A Minor Poet*.

[515] MacKenzie, Norman and Jeanne (eds). *The Diary of Beatrice Webb*. Vol. 1 1873–1892. London: Virago, 1982. 116.

[516] Webb. 447.

[517] See Obituary. *The Lady's Pictorial*. 21st September 1889: 358.

[518] See Chapter 7 note 42.

[519] Levy, Amy. 'Xantippe'.

[520] Ibid.

[521] Lee. *Laurus Nobilis*. 155–6.

Index